COST AND
MANAGE
ACCOU

COST AND MANAGERIAL
ACCOUNTING

J. OWEN CHERRINGTON
BRIGHAM YOUNG UNIVERSITY

E. DEE HUBBARD
BRIGHAM YOUNG UNIVERSITY

DAVID H. LUTHY
UTAH STATE UNIVERSITY

The authors gratefully acknowledge the timely reviews and inciteful comments provided by John W. Hardy, Brigham Young University, as we developed this textbook.

wcb

WM. C. BROWN PUBLISHERS
DUBUQUE, IOWA

wcb group

Wm. C. Brown
Chairman of the Board
Mark C. Falb
President and
Chief Executive Officer

wcb
Wm. C. Brown Publishers, College Division

Lawrence E. Cremer
President
James L. Romig
Vice-President,
Product Development
David A. Corona
Vice-President,
Production and Design
E. F. Jogerst
Vice-President, Cost Analyst
Marcia H. Stout
Marketing Manager
Linda M. Galarowicz
Director of Marketing Research
Marilyn A. Phelps
Manager of Design
William A. Moss
Production Editorial Manager
Mary M. Heller
Visual Research Manager

Book Team
Kathleen L. Loy
Editor
Rhonda M. Kronfeldt
Assistant Developmental Editor
Mark Elliot Christianson
Designer
Julie Avery Kennedy
Senior Production Editor
Mavis M. Oeth
Permissions Editor

Cover:
Merrill Wood/The Image Bank, Chicago

Printed in the United States of America
10 9 8 7 6 5 4 3 2 1

To our parents who taught us how to work and to our families who support us in our work.

CONTENTS

Chapter 3
COST BEHAVIOR 51

Chapter 4
CONTRIBUTION REPORTING: A FORMAT FOR COST ANALYSIS AND ALTERNATIVE COST GROUPINGS   89

PART II

PLANNING BUSINESS ACTIVITIES

Chapter 5
BUDGETING   121

Chapter 6
FLEXIBLE BUDGETING AND RESPONSIBILITY REPORTING   161

Chapter 7
COST-VOLUME-PROFIT ANALYSIS   199

PART III

COST DETERMINATION

PART IV

COST CONTROL

Chapter 16
STANDARD COSTS FOR FACTORY OVERHEAD   533

Chapter 17
ACCOUNTING SYSTEMS FOR MANAGEMENT PLANNING AND CONTROL   569

Chapter 18
VARIABLE COSTING AND GROSS MARGIN ANALYSIS   623

Chapter 19
SEGMENT PERFORMANCE   661

PART V

DECISION ANALYSIS

Chapter 23
CAPITAL BUDGETING: PART II   819

Chapter 24
PROFESSIONAL EXAMINATIONS   859

PREFACE

C ost and managerial accounting is a specialized area of accounting that attempts to satisfy the information needs of management. Management at all levels within an organization has the responsibility of planning, coordinating, executing, and controlling business operations. A large part of the information required to do these jobs effectively is accounting oriented, and it is the job of the cost accountant to accumulate, prepare, and interpret this information.

Cost accounting is the process of accumulating the costs of a manufacturing process and identifying them with the units produced. It is a unique subfield of management accounting that interfaces with both managerial and financial accounting. Data prepared by the cost accountant is used in financial reporting to value ending inventories and the cost of goods sold. The same data is broken down by manufacturing component, by department, or by individual worker within a department in management reports to assist management in operating the business.

The study of cost and managerial accounting usually takes one of three focuses:

1. Managerial focus. Heavy emphasis is placed on how management interprets, applies, and implements cost accounting information in the decision process of the organization.
2. Cost finding or cost determination focus. The primary emphasis is on determining the cost per unit to manufacture a finished product. A considerable amount of time is spent in learning the procedures to be followed and the journal entries to be made to allocate and accumulate manufacturing costs.
3. Quantitative orientation. Heavy emphasis is placed on the many quantitative tools and operations research methods that are useful in analyzing and interpreting cost data.

In writing this textbook we have tried to balance the emphasis on each of these three areas. As each topic is discussed we cover the relevant cost finding techniques and provide examples of the journal entries required to record the data. We also identify the relevant quantitative techniques that can be used to analyze the data, to identify what the data means, and how management should use it in the decision-making processes. We believe that the balance provided in this textbook is the most efficient way to study cost and managerial accounting.

Organization and Features of the Text

Cost and Managerial Accounting covers the cost accounting topics generally required of a cost accountant at an entry level position. It is specifically designed for a cost or managerial accounting class in the curriculum of an accounting major. However, it may also be used as the textbook for a cost or managerial accounting course in an MBA program. The 24 chapters contained in this book provide an abundance of material for a two-semester or three-quarter cost or managerial series. Financial accounting is the only prerequisite for use of this textbook.

The presentation of topics throughout the text is conceptually sound. The overview in part I provides the general framework of cost and managerial accounting used throughout this text. This provides a basis for planning business activities, which is the topic of part II. Implementation of these activities requires the cost accountant to record, classify, and summarize the costs. These activities are part of cost determination, which is the subject of part III. Finally, this cost data is used to control business activities and to assist in management decisions, which are the topics discussed in parts IV and V respectively.

Each chapter includes the following:

1. Chapter outline: A list of all headings and major subheadings provides students with an overview of the chapter's content.
2. Learning objectives: Learning objectives help students to identify what the chapter contains and what they should be able to do upon completing the chapter.
3. Chapter content: Each chapter proceeds from basic concepts to complex topics in a logical manner. Current terminology and up-to-date accounting procedures are used throughout. Numerous examples and illustrations appear as they would in an actual business setting.
4. Key terms: Throughout the chapter important terms are set in bold type. Each term is defined in the glossary.
5. Summary: A brief synopsis of the chapter helps students to organize and review the key concepts.
6. Self-study problem: A sample problem with a suggested solution allows students to test their knowledge of the chapter material and to obtain immediate feedback.
7. Suggested readings: A list of four to six references provide additional reading on chapter related material.
8. Problem material: The problem material includes discussion questions, exercises, and problems. Discussion questions provide a quick check on the students' understanding of basic concepts covered in the chapter. Exercises generally require some computations and require less time than problems. Problems cover more than one concept and are designed to help students to integrate the various concepts within a chapter and between chapters.
9. All key terms are integrated at the end of the book in a comprehensive glossary that serves as a valuable reference tool.
10. Several topics are covered in appendices to chapters. These include review topics such as the time value of money, that are taught in other courses but are integral to the chapter material, and advanced topics, such as matrix algebra, that build upon the chapter material.

Support Materials

The support materials include the following:

1. Instructor's Manual. The Instructor's Manual assists the instructor in preparing lectures, answering student questions, and preparing examinations. It contains (*a*) lecture outlines for each chapter that highlight important concepts and give examples for class discussion and (*b*) test material with solutions. The test material has objective questions and short problems with answers provided for both. The quantity of questions and problems allows the instructor to be selective and vary the content of examinations each term.
2. Solutions Manual. The Solutions Manual provides the solutions to all discussion questions, exercises, and problems contained in the text.
3. Student Study Guide. The Student Study Guide will assist students in reviewing the chapter content, checking progress in understanding the concepts, and preparing for the examinations. Each chapter contains (*a*) suggestions for chapter study, (*b*) a summary of key concepts and study guide, (*c*) a glossary, and (*d*) self-study questions, exercises, and problems with solutions.

Contribution of Others

We wish to express many thanks to the staff of Wm. C. Brown Publishers who have contributed so much to the development and production of this text. Particularly we wish to acknowledge the efforts and encouragement of the editorial staff in both starting and completing the project. Others, who erroneously think their work is thankless, include Lynne Niznik as development editor, and Julie Kennedy as senior production editor. Their efforts have been critical to the success of the text.

We wish to acknowledge the helpful criticisms and valuable suggestions of those who reviewed all of the manuscript or a portion of it. They include the following:

James R. Bentley
Portland State University

William F. Crum (Emeritus Professor)
University of Southern California

Troy Daniel
Mississippi State University

Richard A. Grimland (participated in focus group)
University of Iowa

H. Peter Holzer
University of Illinois at Urbana-Champaign

Steve Kaplan
Arizona State University

Bruce Johnson
Northwestern University

John C. Lere
St. Cloud State University

Corine Norgaard
University of Connecticut

Kevin D. Stocks
Brigham Young University

Gary E. White
Texas Tech University

Finally, we wish to express gratitude to our families for their endless patience and timely encouragement. We dedicate this book to them for their support.

COST AND MANAGERIAL ACCOUNTING

OVERVIEW OF COST AND MANAGERIAL ACCOUNTING

PART

I

Chapters 1 through 4 provide an overview of cost and managerial accounting. We will first consider the relationship between cost and managerial accounting and how they differ from financial accounting and other more specialized areas of accounting.

Basic to the study of cost accounting is a clear understanding of (*a*) terminology used to describe various cost classifications, (*b*) behavioral patterns most commonly exhibited by each cost, and (*c*) procedures used to quantify cost behavior. Costs may also be grouped in a variety of ways to provide meaningful information for statement users. The traditional statement presentation will be reviewed and alternative reporting formats will be introduced.

INTRODUCTION TO MANAGERIAL AND COST ACCOUNTING

1

OUTLINE

Managerial accounting is an internal accounting process designed to provide management with the necessary information to operate the business successfully. Cost accounting is the specialized area involved with accumulating the costs of a manufacturing process and identifying them with the units produced. This information is used for both financial and managerial reporting. This chapter introduces the concept of cost accounting and its relationship to financial and managerial accounting. After completing this chapter you should be able to:

1. identify what cost accounting is and explain how it relates to financial and managerial accounting.
2. identify professional organizations that have a role in the development of cost accounting procedures and practices.
3. describe and compare the functions of a controller within an organization with the functions performed by a treasurer.

SPECIALIZED AREAS OF ACCOUNTING

Accounting is the process of recording, classifying, summarizing, and reporting the economic activities of an organization. Accounting is a service activity intended to provide useful information to statement users to assist in their decision-making process. Therefore, the users and uses of accounting reports have a significant impact on the accounting process and the type of information that is reported.

Users of accounting information can be broadly classified into two types—external users and internal users. Each group has a different set of problems with different informational needs. Accounting has responded by developing subfields or areas of specialization. These include financial accounting and managerial/cost accounting.

Financial Accounting

Financial accounting specializes in satisfying the information needs of external users, such as stockholders, potential investors, creditors, and agencies of the federal, state, and local governments. Financial accounting can be subdivided further into financial reporting, auditing, income taxes, and SEC reporting to meet the needs of each of these users.

Stockholders and potential investors make decisions concerning the buying, holding, or selling of an ownership interest in a business organization. Creditors make decisions concerning the lending of money and the amount of interest to charge. Information on the profitability of the company as a whole and its current financial position are relevant to these kinds of decisions. Status and progress reports are essential because financial resources are scarce and the various parties who have their resources "at risk" can legitimately expect them to be used productively. *Financial reporting* provides this information in the traditional balance sheet, income statement, statement of changes in financial position, and statement of changes in owners' equity.

Auditing is an area within financial accounting that deals with the concepts and procedures of attesting to the fairness of external reports. The financial reports outlined above are prepared by management and their staff of internal accountants. Stockholders, potential investors, and creditors typically do not have access to the accounting records of the company to verify their accuracy. Auditors, therefore, are employed as a third party to provide an independent review. They review the accounting system, sample transactions to see if they have been accounted for properly, and render an opinion concerning the accuracy and adequacy of the financial statements. This does not, however, guarantee that the accounting and reporting process is perfect and that no errors have been made during the period.

Governmental agencies associated with accounting are concerned primarily with raising money to finance government operations and with insuring that adequate disclosures are made by companies selling securities to the general public. Government revenue is obtained through taxation. *Income tax accounting* is a specialized field of financial accounting that deals with tax planning and compliance with federal, state, and local tax laws.

Securities and exchange commissions have been established on the federal and state level to identify minimum disclosure requirements and to monitor the activities of companies selling their stock to the general public. *SEC reporting* is a specialized field of financial accounting that deals with meeting the reporting requirements of the securities and exchange commissions.

Managerial/Cost Accounting

Managerial accounting specializes in satisfying the information needs of internal users. Internal users include both line and staff personnel at top, middle, and lower levels of management. Since management has the responsibility to prepare financial statements for external reporting, management accounting also includes the preparation of external reports as illustrated in the following definition of management accounting.

> Management accounting is the process of identification, measurement, accumulation, analysis, preparation, interpretation, and communication of financial information used by management to plan, evaluate, and control within an organization and to assure appropriate use of and accountability for its resources. Management accounting also comprises the preparation of financial reports for non-management groups such as shareholders, creditors, regulatory agencies, and tax authorities.[1]

Management in business organizations has the responsibility to use available resources as effectively and as efficiently as possible to accomplish organizational objectives. To fulfill these responsibilities, management must make decisions concerning desirable organizational objectives, resource utilization, and personnel effectiveness. The type of information that is useful for making these decisions is entirely different than most information provided to external users. Managerial accounting has been developed to provide information to management to assist them in operating the business successfully.

Cost accounting is the process of accumulating the costs of a manufacturing process and identifying them with the units produced. It is a unique subfield of managerial accounting that interfaces with both managerial and financial accounting. Cost accounting is primarily applied to manufacturing organizations that combine and process raw materials into a finished product. Financial reporting must have a cost per unit for the finished product to use in valuing ending inventory and in valuing the cost of goods sold. Management of the organization needs similar cost data to control the manufacturing process. However, they need this data broken down for each manufacturing operation and for each component that makes the finished product. Cost data must be broken down by product, by department, and even by individual worker within the department. For example, it is not good enough to know that the cost to produce a finished product is too high. Management must be able to identify where it is costing too much and what they can do to reduce costs.

Information systems specialize in the analysis and design of accounting and management information systems. Some companies include the information systems area as a subfield within managerial accounting. However, most larger organizations have a separate information systems division that designs and operates the computer-based information processing system. Regardless of where the function is located, they rely heavily

---

1. Management Accounting Practices Statement Promulgation Subcommittee, "Statements on Management Accounting," (New York: National Association of Accountants, 1981), p. 4.

on personnel in managerial accounting to identify the type of system that should be developed and the content of the reports.

This text is primarily concerned with the fields of managerial and cost accounting. Where it is appropriate, we discuss the relationship of managerial/cost accounting to the areas of financial reporting, including income taxes, and to systems analysis and design.

AUTHORITATIVE SUPPORT FOR ACCOUNTING CONCEPTS AND PROCEDURES

All fields of accounting have identified a group of acceptable concepts, procedures, and practices. The extent to which these concepts and procedures have been codified and systematized into a standard set of rules and procedures, however, varies between the various subfields. We will identify the authoritative groups in each area of accounting and discuss the reason for a lack of more extensive codification in the managerial/cost accounting area.

Generally Accepted Accounting Principles

Financial accounting is most advanced in codifying generally accepted principles and practices. The nature of the work being performed and the uses of the financial reports have caused this extensive codification. Users of financial accounting data are generally outside the organization, have no access to organizational records, and make decisions that involve the comparison of one company against another. Companies appearing to be the strongest and having the greatest earning potential are those in which investors buy stock and to which creditors lend money. They are also the companies from which the government tries to collect the most income taxes. So there can be accurate comparisons and fair taxation, all companies must use the same set of accounting principles.

Various professional organizations, governmental agencies, and special interest groups that were created through the efforts of concerned professionals have developed extensive codification in financial accounting. The Congress and Internal Revenue Service have created a very large tax code to be followed in filing income taxes. The Financial Accounting Standards Board (FASB) and the American Institute of Certified Public Accountants (AICPA) have developed a large set of Generally Accepted Accounting Principles (GAAP) to be followed in financial reporting. The Securities and Exchange Commission (SEC) has also had a significant influence on the development of GAAP. In addition, they have identified a set of minimum disclosure requirements that must be satisfied in filings with them.

Cost Accounting Standards

Managerial/cost accounting is not codified as well as financial accounting, but then the nature and objectives of the work are also very different. The primary objective of managerial/cost accounting is to help management operate the business successfully. Every business is different, with different products, different objectives, and different management styles. What is relevant to one organization may not be relevant to another. A procedure that works well with one style of management may not work well with another style. Therefore, managerial/cost accounting must be flexible to meet the differing needs of each organization.

There are some rules that must be followed in developing the data to be used as part of the external reports. These rules govern the valuation of raw materials, goods that are still in the manufacturing process, and ending inventories. The other concepts and procedures that are included in cost accounting have been found to be useful in a variety of organizations and to a variety of decisions. You need to be able to identify the practices that are dictated by GAAP from those that are not. Always make sure you understand the concept so adjustments can be made for the differing needs of an organization.

Managerial accounting draws relevant concepts and procedures from a broad spectrum of disciplines. Various concepts come from fields such as economics, banking, finance, engineering, operations research, quantitative analysis, statistics, and several of the behavioral sciences.

The major organization responsible for the development of cost accounting procedures is the National Association of Accountants (NAA). Another organization that has had some input is the Financial Executives Institute (FEI). The NAA has a Management Accounting Practices Committee, which is charged to develop guidelines on managerial accounting concepts, policies, and practices. A separate subcommittee on statement promulgation identifies the subject areas to be explored and oversees progress on each project from initiation to completion. The results of these committees are published in "Statements on Management Accounting."[2]

Another organization that had some influence in the development of cost accounting procedures is the Cost Accounting Standards Board (CASB). This unique organization was created by Congress through legislation (PL 91–379), passed August 15, 1970. The CASB was charged with the responsibility of formulating standards to be used in obtaining systematic and uniform treatment of various costs incurred by firms contracting with the federal government on defense contracts. Having completed this charge, the CASB is no longer an active institution like the SEC or the FASB.

The standards promulgated by the CASB are required only in costing defense contracts, but other departments of the federal government may choose to do their procurement under these same standards. A number of standards have been issued, and some have had an impact on cost accounting procedures that are applied to nongovernment operations. These standards will be referred to as appropriate in the subsequent chapters of the text.

THE MANAGEMENT PROCESS

The management process summarizes the major activities performed by management in leading an organization. A brief review of the management process and the contribution of managerial/cost accounting to each activity will help clarify the subject matter you are studying.

A manager's work generally involves a cycle: (a) setting organizational objectives, (b) formulating an operating plan, (c) implementing the plan and monitoring the activities on a day-to-day basis, (d) measuring results, and (e) evaluating the results to see if the plan was properly implemented and the objectives of the organization are being accomplished. Figure 1.1 illustrates the management cycle.

Organizational objectives are rather broad and general but they provide direction to all other activities. For example, a shoe manufacturer may have the following organizational objectives:

1. Manufacture a top-of-the-line variety of women's shoes.
2. Have an annual growth rate of 10% and increase market share from 15% to 25% over the next five years.
3. Maintain a 20% rate of return on owners' equity.

Organizational objectives are not changed frequently, although slight modifications may be made on an annual basis to keep them current and at a realistic level of aspiration.

2. Ibid.

Figure 1.1   The management cycle

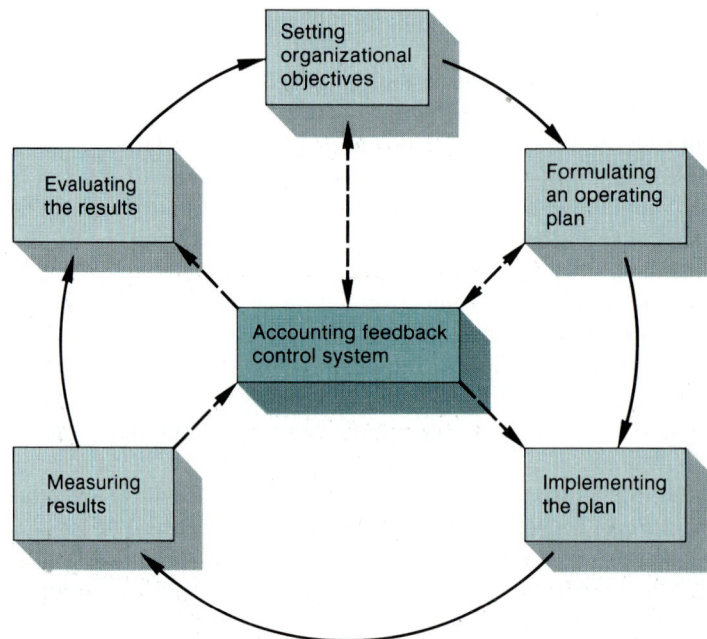

The *operating plan* is for a specified time period, such as one year, and is prepared in detail. This plan is essential in directing the organization toward achieving its long-term objectives. Without a detailed plan the organization may drift and not be successful.

Central to each of these planning activities is the accounting system. Financial resources available to the business, as indicated in accounting reports, are frequently a limiting factor in the development of organizational objectives. Results of operations in the prior year are generally the starting point in developing a plan for the current year. Accountants may also have other responsibilities with various aspects of the planning process, including market studies, analysis of product potential, analysis of major equipment purchases, and development of manufacturing cost estimates for individual products.

The result of the planning process is a budget representing the formal plan of operations for the coming year. Individual budgets may be prepared for personnel, plant and equipment, production, finance, and marketing. The budget not only provides direction to organizational activities but it also provides a base to which actual results can be compared.

The lines and the direction of the arrows to and from the accounting feedback control system in the center of the management cycle (see fig. 1.1) indicate the flow of information. For example, the line and arrow from the accounting feedback control system box to the formulating an operating plan box indicates the flow of information on prior results, organizational objectives, constraints, and other information outlined above. The arrow back to the accounting feedback control system box indicates the flow of budget information into the accounting system to be used as a basis to evaluate efforts to implement the plan.

Implementing the plan involves the day-to-day activities of operating the business. Decisions regarding personnel, production, products, markets, equipment, and financing must be made frequently through a day, month, and year. Each decision must be made so the organization can move toward achievement of its annual operating plan and long-term objectives.

The accounting function *measures* the *results* of operations and compares them with the planned level of operations. Differences between the actual results and planned results help management to evaluate each area of the business and to identify areas of the business in which corrective action is required. This is the function of the accounting feedback control system at the center of the management cycle (see fig. 1.1). This feedback control process helps management to answer such questions as: (*a*) Is the firm on "target" in achieving its objectives? (*b*) Which areas of the business are doing well and which are doing poorly? and (*c*) What type of minor or major adjustments are required in order to reach the goals set previously?

The process of operating the business on a day-to-day basis to implement the plan or budget, measuring the results of operations, evaluating the results, and taking corrective action in subsequent operations occurs over and over again throughout the weeks and months of the year. At the end of the year the financial results are tabulated and compared to the annual budget to *evaluate* the success of the organization. These results and the evaluation are then input into the planning process for the next period.

Notice from the above discussion that accounting information is the basis for each management activity. It is the basis for identifying organizational objectives and developing an annual budget. The accounting process measures the results of operations and compares them to the budget. The differences between the two help management to identify areas of the business where corrective action is required. The final results for the year are similarly developed and used as a basis for planning the next period.

THE CONTROLLER'S ROLE

Functions of the Finance Division

Responsibility for financial planning, financial management, and reporting belong to a chief financial officer. The title given to that officer may vary from company to company, but we will call that person the *financial vice-president*. In larger organizations the financial vice-president is assisted by two other individuals called the treasurer and the controller. Organization charts differ from organization to organization because of their sizes, types of products or services, and management style. However, the organization chart shown in figure 1.2 illustrates the position of the controller and the treasurer, both to each other and with other officers of the company.

Regardless of the size or type of business, accounting and finance are basic to all business activities. Engineering design, product manufacturing, sales, and all other business activities have an economic impact. Money must be made available to carry out these activities; the results of these activities have an impact on the profits of the company.

Major activities that are assigned to the accounting and finance department of the organization include setting financial goals, evaluating alternatives, acquiring capital, and establishing financial controls.

Setting Financial Goals   The financial goals of a company are part of the organizational objectives. Financial goals are generally a function of past performance, in light of current operating conditions and future expectations. The financial officers analyze sales trends, production costs, earnings, and capital outlays and interpret these trends in light of their probable effect on company operations. Part of this analysis includes forecasting the general economy, industry trends, and governmental policies and programs.

Figure 1.2   Typical organization chart

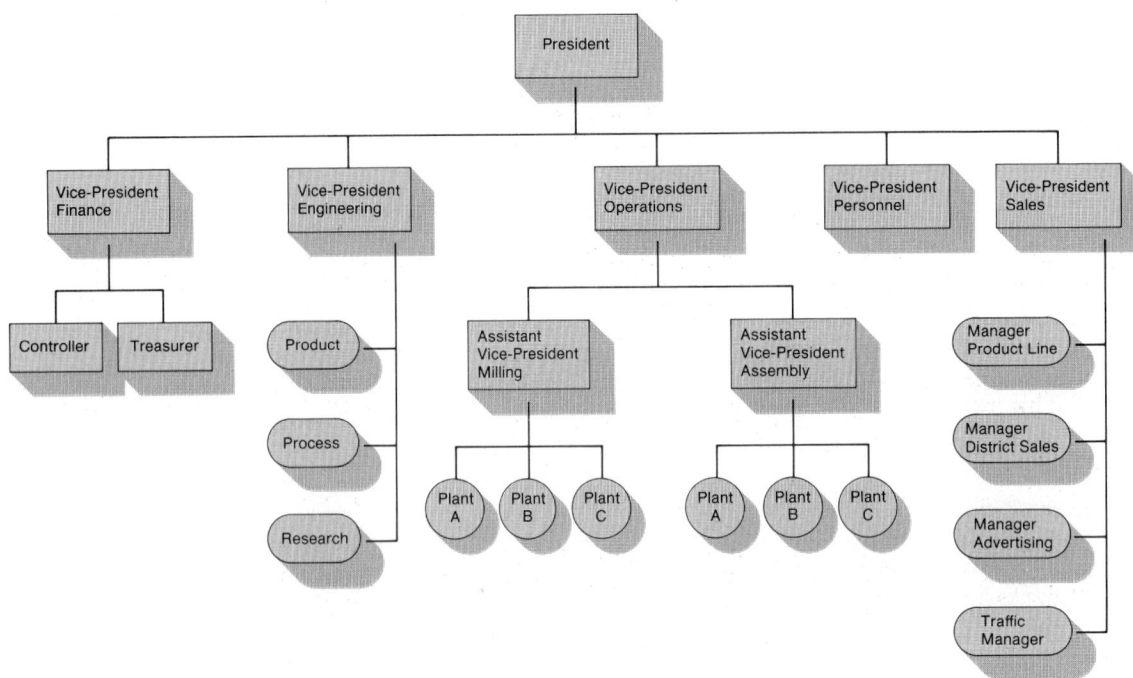

Other factors also considered include labor conditions, material costs, competitive forces, and technological advances. The result of these analyses is a recommendation made to top management that eventually becomes part of long-term objectives and the annual operating budget.

Evaluating Alternatives   Many investment proposals come from throughout the organization. These may include proposals to buy new equipment, construct a new warehouse, or manufacture a part rather than acquire it externally. The organization wants to invest in the alternatives that offer the greatest return on their investment. It is the responsibility of the accounting and finance division to translate the proposals into dollars, which can be used as a common basis for the evaluation.

Acquiring Capital   Before any proposal can be implemented, management must make sure they have the necessary capital. Once again, the accounting and finance division provides the answer. If there is not sufficient capital available, the accounting and finance division assists in obtaining the required amounts. They assist in deciding whether capital can be generated internally through normal operations, savings in operating expenses, and liquidating company held assets, or whether it must be acquired from an outside source. Alternative outside sources include short- or long-term borrowing or increased equity capital by the sale of common or preferred stock.

Establishing Financial Controls   Once the firm invests in the proposal, the accounting and finance division monitors its activities to see if they are in line with expectations. The accounting and finance division provides control when it questions waste or inefficiency or when it suggests an improved production method. The main purpose of the control is to increase rate of return on the existing investment.

Controller Responsibility versus Treasurer Responsibility

In smaller organizations the entire accounting and finance division will be under one individual. As the organization grows, the functions of the controller and treasurer are separated and each may have an assistant or many people working under them. Let's assume we are working with a larger organization; we will identify the responsibilities and major duties included within each of these areas.

Treasurer   The **treasurer** is the financial executive responsible for all functions classified under money management. This individual has the following major areas of responsibility:

1. Providing capital. Identify the capital needs of the organization and organize a plan to provide the money required. This includes:
   a. Preparing statements on the company's financial condition.
   b. Advising the company on financial matters.
2. Investor relations. Establish and maintain a market for company securities. This includes:
   a. Reporting at the annual stockholders' meeting.
   b. Signing stock certificates.
   c. Negotiating the sale of securities.
   d. Maintaining the stock book and preparing dividend payments.
3. Short-term financing. Maintain adequate sources of short-term loans from banks and other lending institutions.
4. Investments. Invest excess funds on either a short- or long-term basis that is consistent with cash needs.
5. Banking. Maintain banking arrangements for receiving, holding, and disbursing company monies. This includes:
   a. Receipting money into the company.
   b. Signing all checks.
   c. Maintaining records to account for money received and paid by the company.
6. Credit and collection. Establish procedures for granting credit and follow up on the collection of accounts.

Controller   The title of controller is somewhat misleading. Strictly speaking, only line managers control. The controller is a staff person and, except in the role of manager of the controller's office, provides no direct control on the operation of the organization. The term controller has evolved from "comptroller," which is based on the French noun "compte," which means to account. Thus the title controller historically relates to accounting, not to controlling. Generally, the **controller** is responsible for all accounting activities within the organization.

The responsibilities of the controller combine several areas of accounting:

1. General accounting. Maintain the company's accounting books, accounting records, and forms. This includes:
   a. Preparing balance sheets, income statements, and other statements and reports.
   b. Giving the president interim reports on operations for the recent quarter and fiscal year to date.
   c. Supervising the preparation and filing of reports to the SEC.
2. Budgeting. Prepare a budget outlining the company's future operations and cash requirements.

3. Cost accounting. Determine the cost to manufacture a product and prepare internal reports to management of the processing divisions. This includes:
   a. Developing standard costs.
   b. Accumulating actual cost data.
   c. Preparing reports that compare standard costs to actual costs and highlight unfavorable differences.
4. Performance reporting. Identify individuals in the organization who control activities and prepare reports to show how well or how poorly they perform.
5. Data processing. Assist in the analysis and design of a computer-based information system. Frequently the data processing department is under the controller and the controller is involved in management of that department as well as other communications equipment.
6. Other duties. Other duties may be assigned to the controller by the president or by corporate by-laws. Some of these include:
   a. Tax planning and reporting.
   b. Service departments such as mailing, telephone, janitors, and filing.
   c. Forecasting.
   d. Corporate social relations and obligations.

As you can see from this list, the controller has a wide variety of areas to control. The controller must be familiar with details in all facets of the business. The controller is a special individual in the company who probably has, other than the chief executive officer, the best knowledge of products, manufacturing facilities, pricing, and competitive conditions. The controller has a unique position within the company and can observe and influence both the magnitude and direction of profits.

Summary

Managerial accounting is an internal accounting function designed to provide management with the necessary information to operate the business successfully. Cost accounting is the process of accumulating the costs of a manufacturing process and identifying them with the units produced. The unit cost data is used in financial reporting to value ending inventories and cost of goods sold. It is also used by management to evaluate the manufacturing process and identify the areas that need attention.

There are several professional organizations with an interest in the development of managerial/cost accounting standards, concepts, and practices. These include the Financial Executives Institute (FEI), Cost Accounting Standards Board (CASB), and the National Association of Accountants (NAA). The NAA has been the most active and has formed a Management Accounting Practices Committee who publishes "Statements on Management Accounting."

The controller is the financial executive who is responsible for accounting, budgeting, cost accounting, performance reporting, data processing, and a variety of other activities. The controller assists management by accounting for the company's activities, comparing them to the plan or budget, and identifying areas of the organization that need management's attention. Both the controller and the treasurer are within the accounting and finance division of the company, but the treasurer is primarily responsible for money management, which includes identifying capital needs, short-term financing, investments, investor relations, banking, and credit and collections.

Suggested Readings

Cost Accounting Standards Board. *Standards, Rules and Regulations As of June 30, 1975.* Washington, D.C.: Cost Accounting Standards Board, 1975.

Curtis, Edward T. *Company Organization of the Finance Function.* AMA Research Study #55. New York: American Management Association, 1962.

Goodman, Sam R. *Organizing the Treasurer-Controller Function for Effective Financial Management.* Englewood Cliffs, N.J.: Prentice-Hall, 1971.

Goodman, Sam R., and Reece, James S. *Controller's Handbook.* Homewood, Ill.: Dow-Jones Irwin, 1978.

National Association of Accountants. *Definition of Management Accounting.* Statements on Management Accounting #1A. New York: National Association of Accountants, 1981.

Discussion Questions

1. What is accounting?
2. What is financial accounting?
3. Identify and briefly describe the subdivisions of financial accounting.
4. What is managerial accounting? How does it differ from financial accounting?
5. What is cost accounting? How does cost accounting relate to both financial and managerial accounting?
6. Define and briefly describe Generally Accepted Accounting Principles (GAAP).
7. How are Generally Accepted Accounting Principles formulated?
8. Identify the primary aspects of cost accounting that come under the provisions of GAAP.
9. Identify and briefly describe the organizations that formulate policies and practices covering financial and managerial/cost accounting.
10. Describe and briefly discuss the purpose of the Cost Accounting Standards Board.
11. Identify and briefly discuss the steps in the management process.
12. What is the role of managerial/cost accounting in (*a*) the planning process, and in (*b*) the control (feedback) process?
13. Describe the controller's function. What does the controller control? Is the controller a part of the management team? Explain.
14. How do the roles of the treasurer and controller differ?

BASIC COST CONCEPTS

2

OUTLINE

I n chapter 1 we described cost accounting as the process of collecting costs for use in financial statements for external users and for management. People are often confused by the variety of terminology used to describe a cost. In order to prepare the cost data so it can be used effectively, you must understand what a cost is, what is meant by cost objects, the many ways that costs can be classified, how a cost differs from an expense, and the typical financial statements used by manufacturing organizations.

This chapter describes basic cost concepts and terminology. The concepts and terminology presented here will be used repeatedly throughout the text. After completing this chapter you should be able to:

1. define cost and explain a cost object.
2. distinguish between a cost and an expense.
3. explain each of the following cost classifications:
   a. time period for which the cost is computed.
   b. management function.
   c. generally accepted accounting treatment.
   d. traceability to products.
   e. cost behavior.
   f. decision significance.
   g. managerial influence.
   h. commitment to cost expenditure.
4. prepare basic financial statements used by a manufacturing company including a cost-of-goods-manufactured statement and a cost-of-goods-sold statement.

BASIC COST CONCEPTS

Definition of Cost

Cost, as used in accounting, refers to an outlay or expenditure of money to acquire goods and services that assist in performing business operations. Occasionally an item will be acquired by giving up an asset other than cash, such as trading marketable securities for inventory. In these cases, cost is a measurement, in monetary terms, of the amount of resources (market securities) used to acquire the goods (inventory) or services.

Goods and services that are acquired by manufacturing organizations include raw materials, production labor, production supplies, land, buildings, and equipment. These and similar costs are incurred in an effort to combine raw materials and process them into a finished product.

Cost Objectives

A **cost objective** is defined as the purpose for which a cost is measured, assigned, or classified. Cost objectives fall into two major areas—financial statement preparation for external users and special report preparation to assist internal management in operating the business successfully. Terminology frequently used to describe these two activities are *cost finding* and *cost analysis* respectively. Cost analysis includes activities such as preparation of the budget, performance analysis, and pricing decisions.

Within these two major areas, cost has many objectives. This can be illustrated by comparing the word cost to a word like clothing. Clothing describes a variety of articles that may be used to cover the body. There are many different types of clothing, and clothing can be worn for several different purposes or to accomplish different ends. Also the same clothing can be worn for a variety of purposes. For example, the same pair of jeans may be worn to church, to a disco, to the beach, or perhaps even to your wedding. The only difference in the jeans is in the way they are prepared through washing and pressing.

The expenditure of money, as with clothing, can be for a variety of purposes and can be used to accomplish different objectives. Some of the common cost classifications are based on (a) time, historical as opposed to future; (b) benefit, an asset as opposed to an expense; and (c) function within an organization, production as opposed to selling and administration.

The same cost can be included in several objects and can be used as a basis for making a variety of decisions. For example, take the actual cost of producing a product that has been sold. It would be classified as a historical production cost, whose benefit has expired, and would be reported in the income statement as cost of goods sold. Management can use that cost data to (a) evaluate a product's profitability, (b) evaluate management's effectiveness in producing the product, or (c) determine how to adjust the product or process to improve future profitability. The same cost data are used, but the data might need to be organized and presented differently in each case so the data can be most useful.

Therefore, when we talk about cost objectives, we are talking about the different ways that costs can be classified or grouped. The type of classification or grouping is contingent on the decision at hand and the type of information that is most useful in making the decision.

Cost Objectives and Cost Objects
The terms cost objective and cost object are sometimes used interchangeably. There is, however, a difference and care should be taken to use the terms correctly.

As stated previously, a *cost objective* is the purpose for which a cost is measured, assigned, or classified. The usefulness of cost information is in the assistance it provides in making a decision. Knowing that a decision needs to be made, the cost information is identified that will assist in the decision-making process. This provides the objective to be used in measuring, classifying, and assigning various costs.

A *cost object* is generally some visible or tangible product or substance. A computer manufactured by IBM or an automobile manufactured by General Motors are examples of cost objects. The objective is to determine the cost to manufacture a finished product. The object is the finished product itself.

Expired versus Unexpired Costs
A cost is incurred when goods and services are acquired. Goods and services are generally acquired on account or by paying cash immediately. The journal entry to record the purchase is a debit to the resource acquired and a credit to cash or accounts payable. It is important that the resource debited be properly classified and correctly identified as an asset or as an expense. If the acquired resource will provide future benefits, the debit should be recorded as an asset. This asset is referred to as a **capitalized cost** or an **unexpired cost.** On the other hand, if the usefulness or benefit of the asset is received immediately, the debit should be recorded as an expense or an **expired cost.** The following are examples of both expired and unexpired costs.

Unexpired Costs	*Expired Costs*
Cost of unsold inventory	Cost of inventory sold
Prepaid rent	Rent for the current period
Unused supplies	Salesmen's salaries
Buildings	Depreciation on buildings

Assets are carried forward on the balance sheet as *unexpired costs* to be written off or expensed in a future period. When they are written off, they become an expired cost. The name we use for this process differs among assets—for tangible fixed assets it is called "depreciation," for intangible assets it is called "amortization," and for natural resources it is called "depletion." Manufacturing deals primarily with the manufacture of a finished product. The manufactured product and all costs associated with it are classified as unexpired costs because of the future benefit expected when it is sold. At the time of sale the product's cost becomes an expired cost and is written off as part of cost of goods sold.

The **matching concept** is the criterion used to determine when a cost (asset) becomes an expense. Income determination is based on the concepts of *revenue recognition* and *matching of expenses*. The revenue recognition concept identifies a point in the earning process when revenue is considered earned. For most merchandising and manufacturing firms, the point of sale is considered to be the most critical event, the point at which the earning process is essentially complete and the point at which revenue should be recognized in the income statement.

The matching concept requires costs incurred in operating the enterprise to be associated with the revenues they generate on the income statement. The revenues that have been earned during the period are first identified and the expenditures or costs incurred in generating those revenues are matched with them in the same fiscal time period.

The timing of the receipt of benefit from an acquired resource determines whether it is classified as an asset or an expense. If the benefit is received immediately, it is called an expired cost and is expensed immediately. If the resource contains benefits to be received in the future, it is called an unexpired cost and is capitalized on the accounting records as an asset.

COST CLASSIFICATIONS

Cost objectives were defined earlier as the different ways costs may be classified and grouped, or the different purposes for which costs are measured. There are several standard cost classifications and each classification has its own unique terminology. We will provide a rather comprehensive list of the different ways costs may be grouped, the concepts underlying each, and the terminology commonly used. Remember that the same cost may be included in several or in all of the following classifications.

Time Period for Which the Cost Is Computed
Time can be broadly classified into *past* and *future*. Costs can also be classified according to these same time periods (see fig. 2.1). **Historical costs** are those that were incurred in a past period. Future costs are generally called **budgeted costs** and are those that are expected to be incurred in a future period.

Example: The $10,000 cost of a delivery truck acquired in 19X3 is a historical cost in the financial statements of 19X4. The $15,000 cost to acquire a new delivery truck in 19X5 to replace the existing truck is a budgeted cost. Notice that the budgeted cost is an estimate. The actual invoice price on the new truck may be higher or lower than the budgeted amount.

Generally in accounting no adjustment is made for the change in the purchasing power of the dollar when comparing historical costs with budgeted costs. High rates of inflation in recent years have created some problems in the comparability of these numbers, but as yet there has not been any comprehensive adjustment. Several methods to adjust for inflation are currently being considered but the accepted method simply hasn't been decided upon.

Management Function
An organization may be separated into functional areas. A manufacturing company's functional areas generally include *manufacturing, marketing,* and *general administra-*

Figure 2.1   Time period classifications

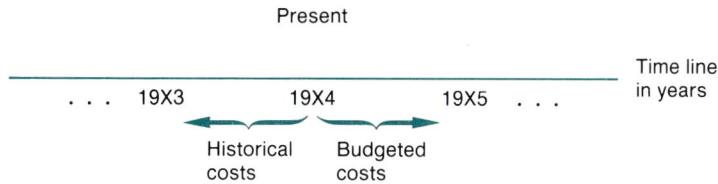

Present

```
                                                              Time line
    . . .   19X3          19X4          19X5   . . .          in years
                     ⟵‿‿‿⟶ ‿‿‿⟶
                     Historical   Budgeted
                     costs        costs
```

tion. One individual, such as a vice-president of manufacturing or a vice-president of marketing, has primary responsibility for that functional area. In order to evaluate the effectiveness of the functional area and the individual in charge of it, costs must be grouped by functional area.

Manufacturing costs include all costs from the acquisition of raw materials, through production, until the product can be turned over to the marketing division to be sold. Manufacturing costs include the cost of the raw materials, payroll costs for people working on the product, and incidental costs such as taxes, power, depreciation, and repairs associated with the manufacturing equipment.

Selling costs are all costs associated with marketing and selling a product. They include all costs incurred by the marketing division from the time the manufacturing process is complete until the product is delivered to the customer. These costs include advertising, promotional offers, freight to deliver the product, and warehouse costs while the product is waiting to be sold.

Administrative costs are all costs associated with the management of the company and include accounting, legal, and administrative personnel. Interest costs are also included among administrative costs.

Generally Accepted Accounting Treatment

The alternatives in accounting for a cost are to expense it or capitalize it. Figure 2.2 illustrates the thought process used in determining how to account for a given cost. Costs that are expensed in the period in which they are incurred are called **period costs.** Period costs possess no future benefits and are generally associated with a nonmanufacturing area of the business. Examples of period costs include advertising, interest, president's salary, and sales commissions.

Product costs consist of all costs associated with the manufacturing function of the business. They include material, labor, and other factory costs associated with assembling and processing the units. Since the company still holds the product and its usefulness has not yet expired, it is not appropriate to expense these costs. They are capitalized as inventory and held as unexpired costs until they are sold.

A **capital cost** is similar to a product cost in that it is also capitalized as an asset. However, capital cost is the term used to describe the acquisition of plant and equipment. These items are capitalized as tangible fixed assets and are depreciated over their useful life. Product costs are reserved for inventoriable costs associated with the manufacturing process.

Traceability to Products

A **direct cost** is one that can be economically traced to a single cost object. In manufacturing, the cost object is a unit of finished product. An **indirect cost** is one that is not directly traceable to the manufactured product, is associated with the manufacture of

Figure 2.2   Accounting treatment classification

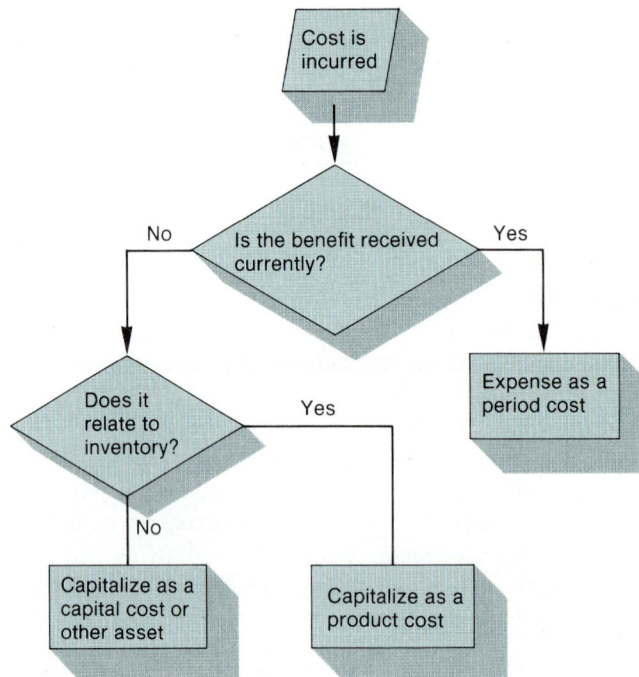

two or more units of finished product, or is an immaterial cost that cannot be economically traced to a single unit of finished product.

A comparison of the labor cost of an assemblyman and a repairman in a cabinet shop will illustrate the difference between direct and indirect costs. The assemblyman's salary is typically classified as a direct cost because it is a significant portion of the cabinet's total cost and because it is easy to trace the assemblyman's efforts to a particular set of cabinets. The assemblyman works for an extended period of time on one set of cabinets, so it would be fairly easy to set up a time clock system to have him punch in and out as cabinets are completed.

The machine repairman's salary would probably be classified as an indirect cost. It is difficult, or impossible, to trace the repairman's efforts to a unit of output. The repairman is responsible for keeping all machines running properly. Since the repairman works on several machines and the machines work on several different cabinets each day, we cannot trace his salary to a particular cabinet. Also, the repairman's salary is generally immaterial in relation to the total cost of the product. However, even if it were material, the lack of traceability would require that it be classified as an indirect cost.

The economics of tracing a cost to a particular unit of finished product is an important distinction between direct costs and indirect costs. Take a consumer product that requires a few screws and a little glue to complete the assembly. Both of these items can be traced to a particular unit of finished product and would, therefore, qualify as a direct cost. However, these items are usually classified as indirect costs because their dollar amounts are immaterial when compared to the other materials going into the product. Also, the cost involved in tracing and recording the items as a direct cost would be much greater than the benefit of having that information.

Cost Behavior

Cost behavior describes how a cost changes with time or with changes in volume. **Variable costs** are costs that vary in total as the volume of production or sales changes. For example, if it takes $10 of lumber to make one unit of finished product and five units are produced, the total cost of the lumber is $50. The total variable cost increases proportionately with the number of units produced, but the cost of each unit remains the same.

Fixed costs remain constant in dollar amount as volume of production or sales changes. Straight-line depreciation on a piece of equipment is an example of a fixed cost. The amount of depreciation is the same regardless of the number of units it produces.

Decision Significance

A decision involves making choices among alternative courses of action. The decision maker generally collects cost information to assist in making the decision. **Relevant costs,** also called **differential costs,** are future costs that are different under one decision alternative than under another decision alternative. They are costs that make a difference in a decision-making process. **Irrelevant costs** either do not relate to any of the decision alternatives, are historical in nature, or are the same under all decision alternatives. Irrelevant costs are generally excluded from the cost analysis.

Example: Suppose it is Friday night and your best friend wants you to go out on the town. As you discuss the situation you decide that you will have to take a taxi into town at a cost of $10 and that the alternatives for the evening are a dinner at $40 or a show for $50. You also notice in the paper that the price of a haircut has just gone to $12. The cost of a show the last time you went to town was only $30. You are very cost conscious and want to select the alternative that minimizes your cost. What are the relevant costs?

There are only two relevant costs—the dinner at $40 and the show at $50. The cost of the taxi is the same for both alternatives and the price of a haircut does not relate to either alternative. The $30 cost to go to the show on your last trip to town is historical and also irrelevant to the current decision.

Managerial Influence

Managerial influence refers to the ability of a manager to control a particular cost. Remember that all costs are controlled by someone at some level in the organization if the time period is long enough. However, when we focus in on a particular manager, at a particular level in the organization, and for a short period of time, there are some costs that can be influenced and some that cannot.

A **controllable cost** is one that is subject to significant influence by a particular manager within the time period under consideration. **Uncontrollable costs** are those costs over which a given manager does not have a significant influence.

Example: Suppose we are evaluating the performance of Sandra who is the manager of Department D in a pajama factory. Department D has twenty employees. They lay out how the pajama pieces are to be cut from the bolts of cloth and cut out the pieces. The amount of cloth used and the amount wasted are items that Sandra can influence. The costs associated with these are controllable costs.

Department D was recently moved from the old section of the factory into the new wing. The depreciation on the section they occupy has more than doubled with the move. Depreciation expense to Sandra is an uncontrollable cost. It results from a decision to build a new wing on the factory and to move Department D into it. Sandra had no input into these decisions. The cost of the building and depreciation on it is controlled by someone at a higher level of management.

Commitment to Cost Expenditure

Commitment to a cost expenditure focuses on fixed costs as opposed to variable costs, and on budgeted costs as opposed to historical costs. Budgeted fixed costs can be broadly classified into committed costs and discretionary costs. A **committed cost** is one that is an inevitable consequence of a previous commitment. Property tax budgeted for the coming year is an example of a committed cost. Suppose top management made the decision two years ago to construct a new warehouse. After it was completed, the tax commission placed an assessed value on it and a property tax notice is now received annually according to the tax laws. The property taxes must be paid or the warehouse will be seized by the tax authority and sold to cover the unpaid taxes. Property tax is a committed cost that resulted from the decision to construct the warehouse.

A **discretionary cost,** also called a **programmed cost** or a **managed cost,** is one for which the size or the time of incurrence is a matter of choice. There are some nonrecurring costs for which a final commitment has not yet been made and that can be postponed until a future period or cancelled entirely. Replacing the carpet in the administrative offices and repainting the walls of the factory are examples of a discretionary cost where the right *timing* is a matter of judgment. Even though the carpet is beginning to show some wear, it could continue to be used for several months without any interruption to normal operations.

Another type of discretionary cost is one that is part of normal recurring operations and fills a function that is necessary for the operation and maintenance of facilities, but can be changed in amount by management decision. Advertising, employee training, or outside consulting services are examples of discretionary costs where the right *amount* is a matter of judgment. Employee training is both normal and necessary for efficient operations. However, the amount of training and the related cost of the training programs is largely up to management's discretion.

Other Cost Classifications

Several other cost classifications are frequently used in discussing cost accounting and management decisions, but generally are excluded from the record-keeping process. Their primary usefulness is in helping to place a correct perspective regarding the potential benefit of a possible course of action. These classifications include marginal costs, out-of-pocket costs, sunk costs, and opportunity costs.

Marginal costs, also called **incremental costs,** are the costs associated with the next unit or the next project. The term marginal cost is widely used in economics to refer to the added cost associated with the production of an additional unit of output. The accounting use is an adaptation of the economic concept. Generally it refers to the incremental cost associated with an additional project as opposed to the next discrete unit.

Out-of-pocket costs are defined as costs that must be met with a current expenditure. Generally, an out-of-pocket cost is a cash expenditure associated with a particular decision alternative. For example, if you decide to drive your boss to lunch and pick up the tab for $15, your out-of-pocket cost for the luncheon decision is $15. The total cost associated with your decision would have to include gas, oil, and wear and tear on your automobile. However, these costs are either historical or have not yet been incurred and are not considered as out-of-pocket costs of the luncheon.

Sunk costs are defined as past costs that have already been incurred. Because sunk costs are historical costs, they are generally irrelevant to decisions affecting the current or future use of the asset. Let's continue with the example above. Let's suppose that your automobile was purchased two years ago for $7,000. The $7,000 cost is referred to as a sunk cost and is not relevant to decisions relating to the automobile's current and future use. The fact that you paid $7,000 as opposed to $5,000 does not affect your decision to use it to drive to lunch. It will continue to depreciate in the parking lot the same as while driving it to the restaurant.

Opportunity cost is defined as the cost or value of an opportunity foregone when one course of action is chosen over another. Opportunity cost is not an out-of-pocket cost, or even a future cost associated with the selected alternative, but is the lost opportunity associated with each of the alternatives that are rejected.

Example: Suppose you work in a warehouse and your employer comes to you at lunch and indicates that a large shipment of merchandise is scheduled to arrive at 5:00 P.M. He inquires about the possibility of working two overtime hours at $15 per hour ($15 × 2 = $30) to assist in unloading and storing the merchandise. You are to tell him whether or not you will be able to do it by 3:00 P.M.

During lunch you remember the community league baseball game is scheduled for 6:00 P.M., and you decide to support the team and play the game rather than work the overtime. The opportunity cost associated with your decision is $30. This amount ($30) is the cost (value) of the opportunity foregone (unload the merchandise) by choosing to play the ball game.

Illustration of Cost Classifications

There are many interrelationships and overlaps in the object classifications outlined above. A given cost may appear in several different classifications. The key is to identify the cost object and then classify the cost according to the cost objective. A short example will illustrate the interrelation and the classification process.

Example: Julie Bean is the production manager for a garment manufacturer. A decision needs to be made about the type of fabric to be used to make a shirt. The fabric that has been used in the past cost $4.00 per yard but it is currently unavailable. Similar fabric from another supplier will cost $5.00 per yard. The fabric cost can be classified as follows:

1. Time period: The $4.00 cost is an *historical cost,* while the $5.00 cost is a *budgeted cost.*
2. Management function: The fabric cost is a *manufacturing cost.*
3. Accounting treatment: Whatever is paid for the fabric will be capitalized as a *product cost* and carried in inventory until it is sold.
4. Traceability to product: The fabric is a *direct cost* because it represents a significant portion of the cost of the product and can be traced to a specific unit of finished product.
5. Cost behavior: Both the $4.00 and $5.00 cost per yard are *variable costs.* The total fabric cost increases proportionately with the number of yards purchased.
6. Decision significance: In making a purchase decision, the $4.00 cost is *irrelevant.* The $5.00 cost is *relevant* because it can be compared with the price of other fabrics of similar quality to select the best alternative.
7. Managerial influence: For Julie Bean this is a *controllable cost* since she is in charge of production and can control the amount produced and the quality of the fabric.
8. Other: The fabric is an *out-of-pocket cost* associated with producing additional shirts.

As can be seen from the list and discussion above, there are a variety of objectives for which costs can be measured. Figure 2.3 illustrates the cost objectives and classifications commonly used. Each of these will be used in more detail throughout the text as we apply them to cost accounting procedures and management decisions.

Figure 2.3   Cost classifications and terminology

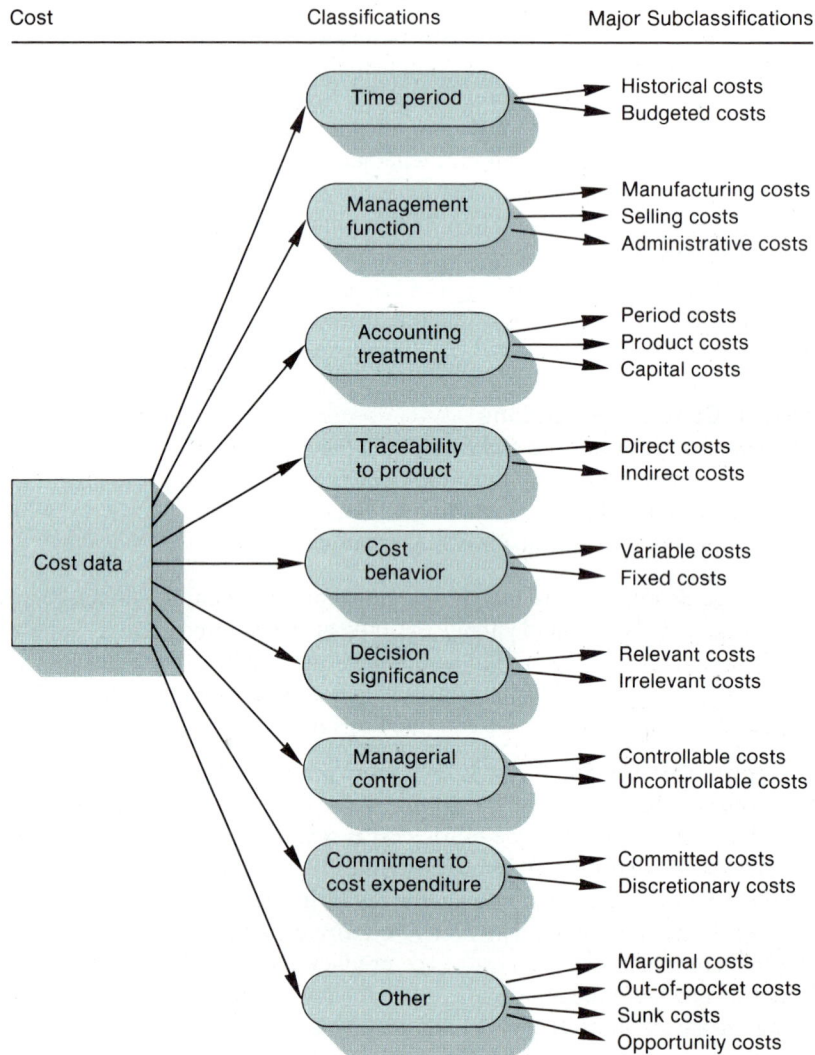

Cost	Classifications	Major Subclassifications

Cost data

Time period
- Historical costs
- Budgeted costs

Management function
- Manufacturing costs
- Selling costs
- Administrative costs

Accounting treatment
- Period costs
- Product costs
- Capital costs

Traceability to product
- Direct costs
- Indirect costs

Cost behavior
- Variable costs
- Fixed costs

Decision significance
- Relevant costs
- Irrelevant costs

Managerial control
- Controllable costs
- Uncontrollable costs

Commitment to cost expenditure
- Committed costs
- Discretionary costs

Other
- Marginal costs
- Out-of-pocket costs
- Sunk costs
- Opportunity costs

BASIC FINANCIAL STATEMENTS FOR A MANUFACTURING COMPANY

Financial statements for a manufacturing company are slightly different than financial statements for a merchandising or service organization. The basic difference is the presence of several inventories and a manufacturing process. Service organizations have no inventory and do no manufacturing. For example, law firms provide legal services and accounting firms provide accounting services. Costs for a service organization are for operating and administrative activities.

Merchandising organizations such as wholesalers and retailers purchase products in a saleable form. They provide the products to others in convenient and attractive locations. During the holding period, the product cost is recorded as finished goods in-

Figure 2.4 Cost-of-goods-sold statement for merchandising and manufacturing firms

Merchandising		Manufacturing	
Beginning inventory	$125,000	Beginning finished-goods inventory	$ 75,000
Plus: Purchases (net)	675,000	Plus: Cost of goods manufactured	900,000
Goods available for sale	$800,000	Goods available for sale	$975,000
Less: Ending inventory	150,000	Less: Ending finished-goods inventory	100,000
Cost of goods sold	$650,000	Cost of goods sold	$875,000

ventory. Costs incurred by retailers are selling, administration, and the cost of merchandise purchased for resale.

Manufacturing organizations perform selling and administrative functions similar to retail firms. In addition, **manufacturers** perform a manufacturing function, which converts raw materials into units of finished product. Rather than purchasing goods that are ready for resale, a manufacturing firm buys raw materials, labor, and other manufacturing components needed to convert the raw materials into finished products. This difference shows up in the cost-of-goods-sold statements illustrated in figure 2.4. In addition, the balance sheet at the end of the period will show ending inventories for raw materials, work in process, and finished goods. Our objective here is to explain the computation of cost of goods manufactured and to illustrate the development of external financial statements for a manufacturing organization.

Accounting for the manufacturing process has the *finished product* as the primary *cost object*. The cost accounting system is designed to accumulate the manufacturing costs and assign them to the units produced. We will first identify the terminology used for the different types of manufacturing costs and then illustrate how they are combined into a statement of cost of goods manufactured.

Product Costs

Product costs are classified for accounting purposes into direct material, direct labor, and indirect manufacturing costs. The criteria used in the classification are the type of cost, traceability to a particular unit of finished product, and materiality.

Direct Material Product costs that relate to the use of raw materials and supplies must be identified as direct material or indirect material. **Direct material** includes the raw material components that can be physically identified with or traced to the finished product. They are distinguished from indirect materials by the ability to identify them economically with a finished product. Indirect materials lack traceability to the finished product and are included as an element of indirect manufacturing costs.

The type of manufacturing process and the products being produced must be identified in order to evaluate whether a raw material input is direct or indirect. For example, paper used in a printing shop would be classified as direct material. The paper is a significant part of each printing job and can be easily identified with the finished product. However, paper used in a glass factory to pack around the finished products for shipping would probably be classified as indirect material. Here the paper is an insignificant part of the finished product and it is not economically feasible to identify the quantity and cost of the paper used with each product. Other examples of direct materials include

Figure 2.5   Relationship of manufacturing costs

Production Costs	Other Classifications	
	Prime Cost	Conversion Cost
Direct material	*	
Direct labor	*	*
Factory overhead		*

wheat in a flour mill, seats to be installed in manufacturing an airplane, and lumber in manufacturing wooden tables.

Direct Labor   Salaries and wages properly classified as a product cost must be separated into direct labor or indirect labor for accounting purposes. **Direct labor** includes the cost of employees who work directly on the product and whose efforts can be economically traced to a particular unit of finished product. Examples of direct labor include the salary of a lathe operator in a machine shop, a mechanic's wage in an auto repair shop, and the staff accountant's salary on an audit with a CPA firm.

Indirect labor lacks traceability and is included as an element of indirect manufacturing costs.

Indirect Manufacturing Costs   **Indirect manufacturing costs** include all manufacturing costs other than direct materials and direct labor. There are several other titles commonly used to describe this group of manufacturing costs, including *factory overhead, manufacturing overhead,* and *factory burden.* Although *indirect manufacturing cost* is more descriptive of the type of costs it includes, **factory overhead** is used more frequently in practice. Become familiar with each of these terms and recognize that they all refer to the same class of manufacturing costs.

Any product costs that cannot be classified as direct material or as direct labor are included in factory overhead. Examples of factory overhead include:

1. indirect materials such as glue, nails, screws, and sandpaper.
2. indirect labor such as a supervisor's salary and janitorial services.
3. taxes on manufacturing facilities.
4. utilities for the manufacturing process.
5. depreciation on manufacturing facilities.

Factory overhead arises from a variety of sources, which can be grouped into three main categories: (*a*) current period disbursements for items such as utility and telephone bills of the factory, (*b*) reassignments or regroupings from current asset or current liability accounts for indirect materials and indirect labor, and (*c*) end of period adjusting entries for depreciation, expired insurance, and other amortizations of previously incurred costs.

Prime costs and conversion costs are two other terms used to describe production costs. **Prime costs** are the most important or significant costs traceable to units of finished product. They include direct material and direct labor. **Conversion costs** are those required to convert raw materials into a finished product and consist of direct labor and factory overhead. As noted earlier, the same cost may be given different titles and used for different purposes. Paper in a copy center, for example, would be classified as direct material for accounting purposes, but it would also be called a prime cost. These relationships are illustrated in figure 2.5.

Figure 2.6   Flow of costs through manufacturing accounts

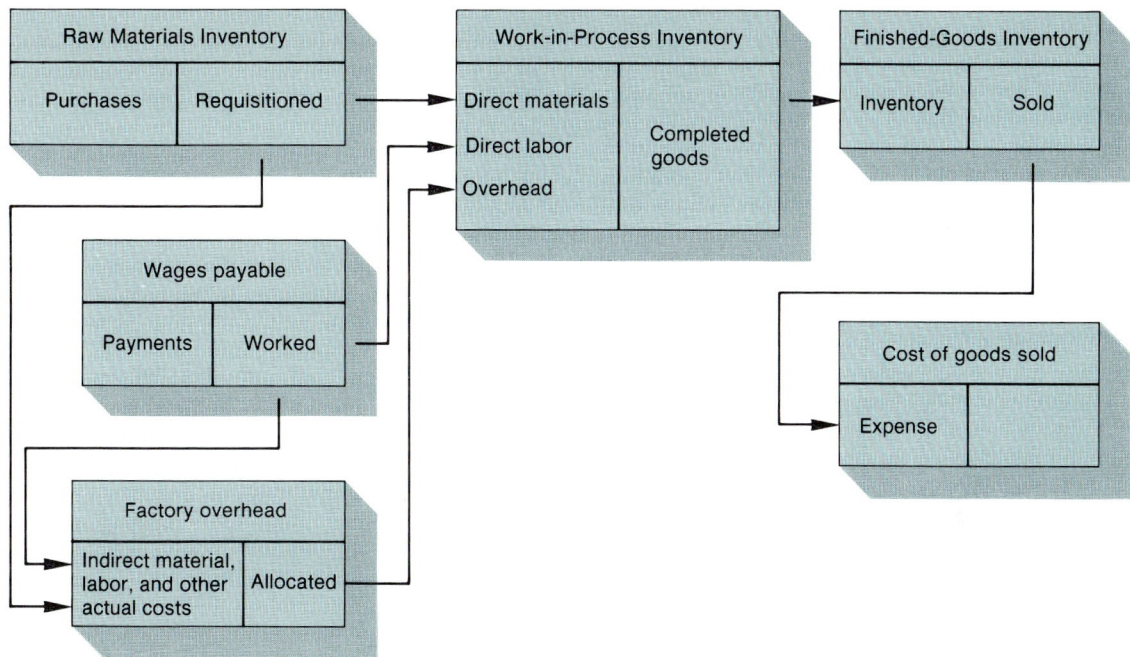

Flow of Product Costs

Manufacturing enterprises typically have three inventory accounts to support the flow of costs through the production process—raw materials inventory, work-in-process inventory, and finished-goods inventory. The flow of costs through these manufacturing accounts is illustrated in a T-account form shown in figure 2.6.

Direct Material and Direct Labor   Purchased raw materials are recorded in the raw materials inventory account and held there until they are requisitioned by a production supervisor. Direct materials are transferred into the work-in-process inventory while indirect materials are transferred to a clearing account called factory overhead.

Payroll obligations to production workers are paid through normal payroll channels. Direct labor is transferred into work in process but indirect labor is transferred to factory overhead. The factory overhead account accumulates the actual indirect manufacturing costs as debit entries. Periodically, overhead is allocated to work in process.

Factory Overhead   Most firms find it necessary to make advance estimates of factory overhead and to use "predetermined" factory overhead rates to charge overhead into production. We will explain why this is done and illustrate how it is accomplished.

The input relationship of direct materials and direct labor costs to the product is generally one-to-one. As units of product are produced, the materials and labor costs must be incurred. Therefore, it is possible and logical to make a direct charge to the units for these costs as they are incurred. However, the situation is quite different for factory overhead. These costs are indirect to the product and the one-to-one relationship does not exist for most overhead items. For example, facilities costs (depreciation and taxes on equipment and buildings) are related to time periods, not to the units produced. Therefore, special procedures are required to assign these costs to the units produced during that period of time. Also, many items of overhead that vary with the number of units produced are not found in a one-to-one variable relationship with the product. For example, annual repair and maintenance may vary according to the number of units produced. However, the pattern of weekly or monthly expenditures for repair and maintenance may not relate to the flow of units. Some firms, in fact, do only minimal maintenance when production is high, but they do large amounts of maintenance when production is low or down completely. This type of situation also creates a need for special handling of overhead.

Many firms use a *predetermined factory overhead rate* in an attempt to effectively manage overhead and to charge it to the units produced on an equitable and timely basis. The results of using a predetermined rate will be to charge overhead to the units produced on an *estimated* one-to-one basis; that is, the overhead is treated *as if* its relationship to the units is the same as material and labor costs.

Example: Suppose direct material costs are $10.00 per unit and direct labor costs are $8.00 per unit to produce a chrome-legged, vinyl-seat chair. Suppose, also, that factory overhead is estimated at $150,000 for the year and it is estimated that 10,000 chairs will be produced. An estimate of the factory overhead required to produce each unit is computed by dividing the total estimated overhead by the estimated volume of production as follows:

$$\text{Estimated overhead rate per unit of volume} = \frac{\text{Estimated total overhead}}{\text{Estimated volume of production}}$$

$$= \frac{\$150,000}{10,000 \ \text{units}}$$

$$= \underline{\$15 \ \text{per chair}}$$

Each chair will be charged with the following costs:

Materials:	1 × $10 = $10
Labor:	1 × $ 8 = 8
Factory overhead:	1 × $15 = 15
Total cost:	$33

Note that the estimate of overhead to be incurred and the number of units to be produced are made before the production period begins. Actual overhead or actual units produced may turn out to be different from the estimates. This gives rise to *over-* or *underapplication* of overhead, which is a problem we will address later in the text. Let us emphasize here that the use of the predetermined rate enables the firm to do timely and equitable costing, which is not possible if such rates are not used.

Several decisions must be made and several steps taken in deriving predetermined overhead rates. The process includes the following:

1. Estimating factory overhead costs for the period.
2. Identifying an appropriate measure of volume. This is sometimes called an activity base or capacity base. Alternative measures include units produced and direct-labor hours worked. Units produced were used in the example above.
3. Selecting a volume of output applicable for the production period.

Once the firm has established the overhead rate, they are in a position to charge overhead into work in process and to the product as production occurs.

Example: ABC Company has developed the following information during their planning process for the coming year.

1. The estimate or budget of factory overhead is:

Fixed costs   = $100,000
Variable costs = $ 75,000 at 10,000 direct-labor hours

2. The most appropriate capacity base for overhead application is direct-labor hours.
3. The estimate of a reasonable level of activity is 10,000 direct-labor hours.

The overhead rate would be:

$$\frac{\$175,000}{10,000 \;\; \text{hours}} = \$17.50 \text{ per direct-labor hour}$$

During June, if 1,500 direct-labor hours were worked, overhead applied or charged to production would be:

1,500 × $17.50 = $26,250

During June, overhead incurred would be accumulated on the debit side of the factory overhead account. The amount allocated to work in process would be recorded as a credit to the factory overhead account. Suppose the total overhead incurred was $26,750.

At the end of June, the factory overhead position is:

Factory overhead incurred $26,750 (debits)
Factory overhead applied   26,250 (credits)
Factory overhead underapplied $500 (debit balance)

The accounting, reporting, and analytical treatments of the over- or underapplied factory overhead will be presented in chapter 13

Work in Process and Finished Goods   The work-in-process inventory contains the costs associated with the units under construction. A "cost attach" concept is frequently used to describe the cost accumulation process while in the work-in-process inventory. Raw materials are changed into finished products as a result of the conversion costs. We account for these costs as if they "attach" to the raw materials. When the units are complete, a manufacturing cost per unit is computed by dividing total product costs by the units produced. The cost associated with the finished units is transferred to the finished-goods inventory account and held there until the units are sold. The cost associated with the units sold is then expensed as part of cost of goods sold.

Illustration of Financial Statements

Manufacturing companies have the same basic financial statements as other profit-oriented businesses—a balance sheet, an income statement, a statement of changes in owners' equity, and a statement of changes in financial resources. The balance sheet and the income statement, however, must be modified slightly to include the additional inventories and the results of the manufacturing process.

The balance sheet of a manufacturing firm shows three inventory balances—raw materials, work in process, and finished goods. The income statement shows cost of goods manufactured in the cost-of-goods-sold sections and has a schedule to summarize the work-in-process activities for the period. It shows the beginning balance in work in process, plus direct material, direct labor, and factory overhead transferred into work in process during the period, and subtracts the ending balance of work in process to give the cost of goods manufactured.

A hypothetical company known as Basic Company will be used to illustrate the manufacturing statements. The Basic Company manufactures a single product called Basic. They are located in Basicville, just south of Chicago. They have a single manufacturing plant and a small company headquarters adjacent to the factory where selling and administrative activities occur. Basic is sold directly to selected retailers throughout the United States by Basic Company's own sales staff. There are two sales territories—an eastern division and a western division.

Results of operations for 19X1, the first year of operations, are summarized as follows:

1. Production data. There was no work in process at the beginning of the year. During the year they began the production of 12,000 units of Basic and incurred the following costs:

Direct material	$ 54,500
Direct labor	68,000
Factory overhead	136,000

At the end of the year, there were 2,000 incomplete units still in work in process. These units are incomplete as to material, labor, and overhead. The following costs have been incurred on these unfinished units:

Direct material	$ 4,500
Direct labor	5,000
Factory overhead	10,000
Total	$19,500

2. Administrative costs. The total administrative costs for the year were $75,000. Basic Company has several accounts to accumulate and control these costs but we have lumped them together to simplify the example.

3. Marketing activity and marketing cost data. During the year 9,500 units of Basic were sold at $35.00 per unit, leaving 500 units in ending finished-goods inventory. Marketing costs totaled $30,000 for the year.

Figure 2.7 illustrates a schedule of cost of goods manufactured. Notice that this schedule summarizes the work-in-process account for the year. "Direct material," "direct labor," and "factory overhead" are combined into "total manufacturing costs." This number is added to "beginning work in process" to give "total work in process," and "ending work in process" is subtracted to give "cost of goods manufactured." Notice that the cost of goods manufactured is divided by the units completed for a cost per unit.

The cost of goods manufactured is carried to the "cost of goods sold" section of the income statement as illustrated in figure 2.8. "Cost of goods manufactured" is combined with "beginning finished-goods inventory" to give "goods available for sale." "Ending finished-goods inventory" is subtracted to give "cost of goods sold." Notice that the inventory is identified as finished goods to distinguish it from the inventories of raw materials and work in process. Some companies integrate the schedule of cost of goods manufactured into the cost-of-goods-sold section of the income statement. The **gross margin** is computed on the income statement by subtracting cost of goods sold from sales revenue.

Figure 2.7

Basic Company
Schedule of Cost of Goods Manufactured
Year Ending December 31, 19X1

Beginning work-in-process inventory		$ –0–
Plus: Direct material	$ 54,500	
Direct labor	68,000	
Factory overhead	136,000	
Total manufacturing costs		258,500
Total work in process		258,500
Less: Ending work in process		19,500
Cost of goods manufactured		$239,000

Cost per unit ($239,000 ÷ 10,000 units) = $23.90

Figure 2.8

Basic Company
Income Statement
Year Ending December 31, 19X1

Sales (9,500 units @ $35)		$332,500
Less: Cost of goods sold		
Beginning finished-goods inventory	$ –0–	
Plus: Cost of goods manufactured	239,000	
Goods available for sale	239,000	
Less: Ending finished-goods inventory	11,950[a]	
Cost of goods sold		227,050
Gross margin		105,450
Less: Administrative expenses	75,000	
Selling expenses	30,000	
Total		105,000
Net income		$ 450

[a]500 units at $23.90 each

The balance sheet of Basic Company for December 31, 19X1 is shown in figure 2.9. Notice the inventories of raw materials, work in process, and finished goods are included as current assets.

Accounting for the manufacturing activities of Basic Company as illustrated above is part of the cost finding function of cost accounting. The manufacturing cost per unit was used to value the ending finished-goods inventory and to measure the cost of goods sold.

Figure 2.9

Basic Company
Balance Sheet
December 31, 19X1

Assets

Current:

Cash		$ 8,000
Accounts receivable		28,000
Inventories:		
Raw materials	$ 34,500	
Work in process	19,500	
Finished goods	11,950	65,950
Total current assets		$101,950

Fixed assets:

Property, plant and equipment (net)		570,050
Total assets		$672,000

Liabilities

Current:

Accounts payable		$ 41,000
Wages payable		4,500
Payroll taxes payable		1,200
Total current liabilities		$ 46,700

Long term:

Mortgage	120,000	
Bonds	240,000	360,000
Total liabilities		$406,700

Owners' Equity

Common stock	$264,850	
Retained earnings	450	
Total owners' equity		265,300
Total liabilities and owners' equity		$672,000

Summary

This chapter has described the basic cost concepts and terminology. Cost is defined as a monetary measurement of the amount of resources used for some purpose. The many different ways that costs may be classified and grouped, or the different purposes for which costs are measured are called cost objectives.

In analyzing costs for accounting purposes, it is important to distinguish properly between assets and expenses. A cost should be classified as an asset when it has the potential to provide future benefits. These unexpired costs are capitalized as assets and reported on the balance sheet. A cost should be recorded as an expense when its benefits are used up. These are called expired costs and are reported on the income statement.

Costs may be classified by many different objectives—by time period, by management function, by accounting treatment, by traceability to product, by cost behavior, by decision significance, by managerial control, and by commitment to expenditure. It is important for you to understand the criteria and terminology used in each of these classifications.

The basic financial statements used for a manufacturing company are the same as those used for merchandising and service organizations. However, minor modifications must be made to report additional inventories on the balance sheet and the results of operations in the income statement. The current asset section of the balance sheet reports three inventories: raw materials, work in process, and finished goods. The cost-of-goods-sold section of the income statement contains a schedule of cost of goods manufactured.

Self-Study Problem

Review Incorporated manufactures signs for retail outlets. The following information is available for November, 19X2.

	Inventories	
	November 1	*November 30*
Raw materials	$ 12,500	$15,000
Work in process	47,700	38,300
Finished goods	116,400	81,200

Raw materials purchased	$ 35,400
Direct-labor cost (5,440 hours @ $5)	27,200
Sales revenue	251,000
Marketing expenses	45,220
Administrative expenses	31,900
Factory overhead costs incurred	52,790

Factory overhead rate is $10 per direct-labor hour worked.

Required

1. Prepare a statement of cost of goods manufactured.
2. Prepare an income statement. Show the computation of cost of goods sold in detail.
3. Separate costs into period and product cost classifications. Compute total period costs and total product costs for November.
4. Was overhead over- or underapplied for November and by what amount?

Solution to the Self-Study Problem

Requirement 1

Review Incorporated
Statement of Cost of Goods Manufactured
November, 19X2

Manufacturing costs:			
Raw materials—Beginning inventory	$12,500		
Plus: Purchases	35,400		
Raw materials available	47,900		
Less: Ending inventory	15,000		
Raw materials used	$32,900		
Direct-labor cost	27,200		
Factory overhead (5,440 hours @ $10)	54,400		
Total manufacturing costs		$114,500	
Beginning work-in-process inventory		47,700	
Total work in process		162,200	
Less: Ending work in process		38,300	
Cost of goods manufactured		$123,900	

Requirement 2

Review Incorporated
Income Statement
November, 19X2

Sales revenue		$251,000
Beginning finished-goods inventory	$116,400	
Plus: Cost of goods manufactured	123,900	
Goods available for sale	240,300	
Less: Ending finished-goods inventory	81,200	
Cost of goods sold		159,100
Gross margin		91,900
Less: Operating expenses		
Selling	45,220	
Administrative	31,900	
Total		77,120
Net income		$ 14,780

Requirement 3

Period costs:	
Marketing expenses	$ 45,220
Administrative expenses	31,900
Total	$ 77,120
Product costs:	
Raw materials used	$ 32,900
Direct-labor cost	27,200
Factory overhead costs incurred	52,790
Total	$112,890

Requirement 4

Factory overhead costs incurred	$ 52,790
Factory overhead costs applied	54,400
Overapplied	$ 1,610

Suggested Readings

American Management Association. *Direct Costing: A Look at Its Strengths and Weaknesses.* New York: American Management Association (Finance Division), 1964.

Beresford, Dennis R., and Neary, Robert D. "Allocation of Direct and Indirect Costs." *Financial Executive* 48 (August 1980):10.

Brummel, R. Lee. *Overhead Costing: The Costing of Manufactured Products.* Ann Arbor, Mich.: Bureau of Business Research, School of Business, University of Michigan, 1957.

Demski, Joel S. *Cost Concepts and Implementation Criteria.* New York: American Institute of Certified Public Accountants, 1969.

Fremgen, James M. *Accounting for Managerial Analysis.* Homewood, Ill.: R. D. Irwin, 1972.

Fultz, Jack F. *Overhead, What It Is and How It Works.* Cambridge, Mass.: Abt Books, 1980.

Goodman, Sam R., and Reece, James S. *Controller's Handbook.* Homewood, Ill.: Dow-Jones Irwin, 1978.

Discussion Questions

1. Define cost.
2. What is meant by cost objectives?
3. How does a cost objective differ from a cost object?
4. What are the basic criteria used to distinguish between expensing and capitalizing an expenditure?
5. Are financial statements prepared according to generally accepted accounting procedures based primarily on historical costs or budgeted costs? Explain.
6. Are management reports prepared to assist managers in making wise decisions based primarily on historical costs or budgeted costs? Explain.
7. What is meant by the functional areas of an organization?
8. Distinguish between product and period costs.
9. What is a direct cost and how is it different from an indirect cost? Give five examples of direct costs, including a description of the product for which it would be considered direct.
10. What is meant by cost behavior?
11. What criteria are used to distinguish between a relevant cost and an irrelevant cost?
12. During a performance evaluation a manager said, "Advertising is an uncontrollable cost!" Is this statement true or false? Explain.

13. When discussing committed as opposed to discretionary costs, are we talking about fixed costs or variable costs? How do budgeted costs and historical costs relate to the same issue?
14. Define an out-of-pocket cost.
15. Define sunk costs.
16. What is an opportunity cost?
17. Describe the differences in the financial statements of a manufacturing and a merchandising organization.

Exercises

Exercise 2.1   Cost Terms

Match the items in column 1 with the best choice in column 2.

1. Total fixed costs	a. Costs incurred during a period
2. "Incurred" costs	b. Total amount remains constant
3. Prime costs	c. What costs are expected to be
4. Cost of goods manufactured	d. Control account for accumulating the costs of production
5. Total manufacturing costs	e. Expired costs
6. Conversion costs	f. Direct materials and direct labor
7. Unit variable costs	g. Cost of completed production after adjustment for work-in-process inventories
8. Costs not assigned to products	
9. Expenses that are matched against revenues	h. Period costs
10. Materials, labor, and factory overhead	i. Direct labor and factory overhead
11. Work-in-process control	j. Added cost of a new product
12. Cost of goods sold	k. Remains constant per unit
	l. Costs of manufacturing (or costs of production)
	m. Direct materials, direct labor, and factory overhead
	n. Cost of goods manufactured adjusted for the finished-goods inventory change

Exercise 2.2   Cost Relationships and the Costs of Production

Presented below is fragmentary information pertaining to the operations of the Something's Missing Company for the year 19X8:

Stores (Materials) Control

1/1 Balance	5,000	
12/31 Balance	2,000	

Work-in-Process Control

1/1 Balance	?	35,000 Cost of goods manufactured
Direct labor	20,000	
Factory overhead	10,000	
12/31 Balance	15,000	

Finished-Goods Control

1/1 Balance	15,000	
12/31 Balance	?	

Sales were $100,000, which produced a gross profit of 55%. Materials are a third of the current total costs of manufacturing.

Required

Bring the T-accounts completely up to date.

Exercise 2.3   Inventory Calculation (CPA)

On January 1 the finished-goods inventory of the Smith Company was $600,000. During the year, Smith's cost of goods manufactured was $3,800,000 and sales were $4,000,000 with gross profit of 10% of sales.

Required

Determine the cost assigned to the December 31 finished-goods inventory.

Exercise 2.4   Income Statement

Johnson Incorporated submits the following data for December 19X2:

Direct-labor cost is $60,000.
Cost of goods sold is $222,000.
Factory overhead is applied at the rate of 150% of direct-labor cost.

Inventory accounts showed these beginning and ending balances:

	December 1	December 31
Finished goods	$30,000	$35,000
Work in process	19,200	26,000
Materials	14,000	14,800

Other data:

Marketing expenses	$ 28,200
General and administrative expenses	45,800
Sales for the month	364,000

Required

Prepare an income statement with a schedule showing cost of goods manufactured and sold.

Exercise 2.5   Income Statement—Profit Percentage

The Hardy Company's ledger shows the following information on August 31, 19X0:

Sales for the month	$157,000
Inventories, August 1:	
Finished goods	2,950
Work in process	2,300
Materials	1,900
Purchases of materials during August	70,000
Direct labor	33,676
Factory overhead is applied at 50% of direct-labor cost	
Inventories, August 31:	
Finished goods	4,635
Work in process	3,100
Materials	2,150
Other expenses incurred during August	
Marketing expenses	11,560
Administrative expenses	8,840

Required

1. Prepare an income statement for the month of August.
2. Determine the percentage of income to sales, before income tax.

Exercise 2.6   Cost-of-Goods-Sold Statement (CGAA)

The following data are provided by the controller of the Megan Corporation:

Cash			$ 240,000
Accounts receivable			348,000

	Inventories		
	January 1	December 31	
Finished goods	$44,200	$66,000	
Work in process	29,800	38,800	
Materials	88,000	64,000	
Materials purchased			$ 366,000
Sales discount			8,000
Factory overhead (excluding depreciation)			468,400
Marketing and administrative expenses (excluding depreciation)			344,200
Depreciation (90% manufacturing, 10% marketing and administrative expenses)			116,000
Sales			1,844,000
Direct labor			523,600
Freight on materials purchased			6,600
Rental income			64,000
Interest on bonds payable			16,000

Required

Prepare a cost-of-goods-sold statement.

Exercise 2.7   Cost-of-Goods-Sold Statement (CPA)

The following data relate to the Barkley Corporation:

	Inventories	
	Ending	Beginning
Finished goods	$95,000	$110,000
Work in process	80,000	70,000
Direct materials	95,000	90,000

Costs incurred during the period:

Cost of goods available for sale	$684,000
Total manufacturing costs	584,000
Factory overhead	167,000
Direct materials used	193,000

Required

Prepare a cost-of-goods-sold statement.

Exercise 2.8 Cost-of-Goods-Sold Statement—Unit Cost Determination

The records of Raydeleh Incorporated show the following information as of May 31, this year (May 31st is the end of the fiscal year):

Materials used	$880,000
Direct labor	580,000
Indirect labor	92,000
Light and power	8,520
Depreciation	9,400
Repairs to machinery	11,600
Miscellaneous factory overhead	58,000
Work-in-process inventory, June 1, last year	82,400
Finished-goods inventory, June 1, last year	68,600
Work-in-process inventory, May 31, this year	85,000
Finished-goods inventory, May 31, this year	63,000

During the year 36,000 units were completed.

Required

Assume actual overhead is considered in 1 and 2 below:

1. Prepare a cost-of-goods-sold statement for the year ending May 31, this year.
2. Determine the unit cost of goods manufactured for the year.
3. Determine the amount of over- or underapplied factory overhead if the company had applied factory overhead on the basis of 30% of direct labor.

Exercise 2.9 Cost Concepts (CMA)

1. For a manufacturing company, which of the following is an example of a period rather than a product cost?
   a. depreciation on factory equipment
   b. wages of salespeople
   c. wages of machine operators
   d. insurance on factory equipment
2. Prime cost and conversion cost share what common element of total cost?
   a. variable overhead
   b. fixed overhead
   c. direct materials
   d. direct labor
3. Indirect materials are
   a. a prime cost.
   b. a fixed cost.
   c. an irrelevant cost.
   d. a factory overhead cost.
4. Factory overhead
   a. is a prime cost.
   b. can be a variable cost or a fixed cost.
   c. can only be a fixed cost.
   d. includes all factory labor.
5. Direct materials costs are a

	Conversion	Manufacturing	Prime
a.	Yes	Yes	No
b.	Yes	Yes	Yes
c.	No	Yes	Yes
d.	No	No	No

Exercise 2.10   Cost Concepts—Basic Statement Relationships (CMA)

Selected data concerning the past fiscal year's operations (000's omitted) of the Televans Manufacturing Company are presented below:

	Inventories	
	Beginning	Ending
Raw materials	$75	$ 85
Work in process	80	30
Finished goods	90	110

Other data:

Raw materials used	$326
Total manufacturing costs charged to production during the year (includes raw materials, direct labor, and factory overhead applied at a rate of 60% of direct-labor cost)	686
Cost of goods available for sale	826
Selling and general expenses	25

Required

1. Determine the cost of raw materials purchased during the year.
2. Determine the direct-labor costs charged to production during the year.
3. Determine the cost of goods manufactured during the year.
4. Determine the cost of goods sold during the year.

Problems

Problem 2.1   Inventory Valuation—Cost of Goods Sold and Unit Costs

The cost department of the Randall Corporation prepared the following data and costs for the year 19X2.

	Inventories	
	January 1	December 31
Finished goods	$48,600	To be determined
Work in process	81,500	$ 42,350
Materials	34,200	49,300
Depreciation—factory equipment		21,350
Interest earned		6,300
Finished-goods inventory: January 1: 300 units; December 31: 420 units, all from current year's production		
Sold during 19X2: 3,880 units at $220 per unit		
Materials purchased		$364,000
Direct labor		162,500
Indirect labor		83,400
Freight in		8,600
Miscellaneous factory overhead		47,900
Purchases discount		5,200

Required

Assume Randall charges actual factory overhead to production.

1. Determine the unit cost of the finished-goods inventory, December 31.
2. Determine the total cost of the finished-goods inventory, December 31.
3. Determine the cost of goods sold.
4. Determine the gross profit total and the gross profit per unit.

Problem 2.2   Income Statement

In an accounting conference, discussion turned to the possibility of preparing financial statements from a few key accounts, together with financial or cost ratios.

The assistant controller of a participating firm provided the following data: pre-tax income for the year, $1,200,000; pre-tax income rate on sales, 10%; gross profit rate, 40%; rate of marketing expenses to sales, 15%; 5% bonds payable represent 37.5% of the total liabilities of $2,000,000; and all other expenses not identified previously are administrative expenses.

Required

Prepare an income statement for the year based on the above information.

Problem 2.3   Income Statement—Cost and Profit Ratios

The records of the Yukon Refrigerator Company show the following information for the three months ended March 31, 19X8:

Materials purchased	$1,946,700
Inventories, January 1, 19X8:	
Finished goods (100 refrigerators)	43,000
Materials	268,000
Direct labor	2,125,800
Factory overhead	764,000
Marketing expenses	516,000
General and administrative expenses	461,000
Sales (12,400 refrigerators)	6,634,000
Inventories, March 31, 19X8:	
No unfinished work on hand	
Finished goods (200 refrigerators)	
Materials	167,000

Required

Assume Yukon charges actual factory overhead to production.

1. Prepare an income statement for the period, with a complete backup for cost of goods manufactured and cost of goods sold.
2. Determine the number of units manufactured.
3. Determine the unit cost of refrigerators manufactured.
4. Determine the gross profit per unit sold.
5. Determine the income per unit sold.
6. Determine the ratio of gross profit to sales.
7. Determine the income to sales percentage.

Problem 2.4   Manufacturing Statements—Product Costs and Period Costs

The following data were taken from the records of the Stewart Company at the end of the fiscal year just completed.

Direct material purchased	$102,000
Direct material issued	90,000
Direct-labor costs	60,000
Factory supervision	10,000
Machine maintenance and repairs	8,000
Factory heat, light, and power	7,000
Depreciation of factory machinery and equipment	10,000
Factory rent	15,000
Miscellaneous factory costs	2,000
Sales revenue	295,000
Inventories of work in process:	
Beginning of year	25,000
End of year	35,000
Inventories of finished goods:	
Beginning of year	40,000
End of year	50,000
Marketing and administrative expenses	75,000

Required

Assume actual factory overhead is charged to production.

1. Prepare the following for the year just ended: (*a*) statement of cost of goods manufactured and (*b*) income statement including a cost-of-goods-sold section.
2. Identify the product costs incurred for the year.
3. Identify the amount of product costs that are (*a*) the prime costs and (*b*) the conversion costs.
4. Identify the period costs for the year.

Problem 2.5   Manufacturing Statements

The following data were taken from the records of *The Company* for the year just ended.

Materials issued:		
Direct	$200,000	
Factory supplies	12,000	$212,000
Factory payroll:		
Direct labor	500,000	
Indirect labor	100,000	600,000
Maintenance and repair of factory equipment		20,000
Power for machine operation		8,000
Factory rent, heat, and light		40,000
Depreciation of factory equipment and machinery		20,000
Payroll taxes (factory payroll)		60,000
Inventories, January 1:		
Work in process		60,000
Finished goods		100,000
Inventories, December 31:		
Work in process		80,000
Finished goods		120,000

Required

Assume *The Company* applies factory overhead at the rate of 50% of direct-labor costs.

1. Prepare the following for the year just ended: (*a*) cost-of-goods-manufactured statement, and (*b*) a condensed statement of cost of goods sold.
2. Prepare a schedule of factory overhead incurred showing under- or overapplied overhead.

Problem 2.6   Manufacturing Statements and Predetermined Overhead Rates

Clout & Company applies factory overhead on a direct-labor cost basis. The application rate for the fiscal year 19X3 was obtained from the following budgeted costs:

Direct-labor cost	$2,400,000
Factory overhead	3,600,000

The information given below was collected on July 31, 19X3 (balances in inventories):

	July 1	July 31
Work in process	$80,000	$100,000
Finished goods	50,000	40,000

During July, costs were recorded as follows:

Direct materials issued for production	$600,000
Direct-labor costs	240,000
Factory overhead costs	350,000

Required

1. Using the applied factory overhead costs, prepare: (*a*) a statement of cost of goods manufactured and (*b*) a statement of cost of goods sold.
2. Determine the under- or overapplied factory overhead for the month of July.
3. If the factory overhead account had a credit balance of $3,000 on July 1, determine the balance in the account on July 31.
4. Explain some possible reasons for the under- or overapplication of overhead during the month of July.

Problem 2.7   Cost Terms and Concepts

You have a job that pays $1,500 per month. While playing Pac Man for the hundredth time, you have an idea for a new videogame. You are thinking of resigning from your job and starting a new company to manufacture this new game. Your company, Super Games Inc., will rent a small building for $100 a month. You have already paid $100 to assure the building is available if you decide to go into business making the games. The material cost per unit is estimated to be $5, and the labor cost per unit will be $3. You will need to buy a new piece of equipment that will cost $2,000. A part-time worker will keep the books and make out billings. This worker will be paid $100 a week. A sales commission of $1 per game will also be paid. If you keep your current job, you could sell the rights to the idea to another company and receive a royalty of $1.00 per game.

With respect to your decision about whether you should go into business for yourself or keep your current job and contract with another company to produce the game, classify the costs identified on page 47 by placing checks in the appropriate columns.

Cost	Product Cost	Period Cost	Fixed Cost	Variable Cost	Prime Cost	Factory Overhead Cost	Sunk Cost	Opportunity Cost
1. Your current salary								
2. $100 advance rent								
3. Building rent								
4. Material cost								
5. Labor cost								
6. Deprecia-tion on equipment								
7. Cost of part-time worker								
8. Sales commission								
9. Royalty								

Problem 2.8   Summary Problem on Cost Classifications and Statements Using Predetermined Overhead Rates

The following information relates to the operations of the Jones Company for the year 19X8 (000's omitted).

	Inventory/Balance	
	1 Jan. 19X8	*31 Dec. 19X8*
Raw material	$ 750	$ 650
Work in process	400	450
Finished goods	1,250	1,100

Additional data:

Raw materials purchased	$ 500
Direct labor	?
Factory utilities	250
Factory rent	300
Indirect materials	150
Supplies used in shipping to customers	100
Foreman's salary	50
Finished-goods warehouseman's salary	40
Total manufacturing costs added this period	2,080

Factory overhead is applied at the rate of $1.30 per dollar of direct-material cost used.

Required

Assume the raw materials inventory includes direct materials only.

1. Prepare a statement of cost of goods manufactured and sold using applied overhead, with a separate schedule of factory overhead costs showing under- or overapplied overhead.
2. What were the costs of production for the year? Of the production costs which costs are *prime costs?* Which are *conversion costs?*
3. Identify the period costs. Explain how period costs are treated in preparing a complete set of financial statements.

Problem 2.9   Cost Statements and Inventory Determination—Incomplete Data

A devastating fire swept through the finished-goods warehouse, the factory, and the factory office of Yugotta Bee Kidden & Sons, Inc., on September 28. As an insurance investigator you have been able to piece together the following information by conferring with accounting, engineering, and administrative personnel and by analysis of certain accounting records, which fortunately were kept in the general ledger in the main office:

1. Raw materials having a cost of $388,600 were purchased in September.
2. Raw materials costing $436,200 were requisitioned for use in the factory during September. Raw materials are 40% of the total manufacturing costs.
3. Inventories at the beginning of September were as follows:

Raw materials	$121,300
Work in process	78,700
Finished goods	364,200

4. Of the costs put into production since August 31, 88% are the cost of goods manufactured.
5. Sales during September to the date of the fire totalled $1,299,300.
6. The "recipe" and an analysis of "normal" costs show that factory overhead is 50¢ per $1 of direct labor and further that factory overhead is 20% of current manufacturing cost. It must be assumed that these normal relationships were in effect for costs put into production during September.
7. The payroll records were at the plant and were destroyed by the fire.
8. Gross profit is "normally" 30% of sales, and this relationship must be assumed also for September.
9. The proportion of cost for direct labor, direct material, and factory overhead is the same for work-in-process and finished-goods inventories.

Required

Prepare a clearly documented estimate of the cost of raw materials, work in process, and finished goods at the time of the fire.

Problem 2.10 Manufacturing Statements—Working from Incomplete Data

The following fragments of data have been collected from the records of the Questionable Company for the year just ended.

Raw materials—beginning of year $180,000; end of year $190,000; purchases $410,000.

Work in process—beginning of year $140,000; end of year $160,000. Finished goods—beginning of year $220,000; end of year $190,000.

Factory overhead incurred was $387,000 and there is a debit balance of $7,000 in the overhead account at year end.

The cost of goods sold for the year was $1,170,000 which includes the under-applied factory overhead.

Required

Prepare a statement of cost of goods manufactured and extend it into a cost-of-goods-sold statement. Show support for your determination of all amounts used in the statements that are not given in the facts above.

COST BEHAVIOR

OUTLINE

T he way cost changes with time and with changes in volume is referred to as the *cost's behavior pattern.* Understanding cost behavior patterns is important in classifying and reporting costs and it is essential in using cost data correctly in decision making. This chapter identifies various cost behavior patterns associated with the manufacturing process and the methods used to quantify them. After completing this chapter you should be able to:

1. distinguish between total cost and unit cost.
2. identify the various cost patterns that are used to describe changes in cost when there are changes in the volume of output.
3. compute total manufacturing costs and develop a total manufacturing cost curve.
4. develop an equation from a set of data to mathematically express a linear cost relationship and plot it on a graph.

RELEVANT TERMINOLOGY FOR MANUFACTURING COST BEHAVIOR ANALYSIS

One of the cost objectives discussed in chapter 2 was the generally accepted accounting treatment, which includes product costs, period costs, and capital costs. Costs associated with the manufacturing process are called product costs and are capitalized as part of inventory. Product costs are subdivided further into direct materials, direct labor, and factory overhead.

Direct material includes the raw material components that can be physically identified with or traced to the finished product. Direct labor is the labor time and corresponding dollars spent in converting the raw material into a finished product. The direct material and direct labor combined are the prime costs of a finished product.

Factory overhead includes all manufacturing costs other than direct material and direct labor. Indirect material, indirect labor, employee benefits, supervision, and depreciation on manufacturing equipment are examples of factory overhead. Factory overhead and direct labor are conversion costs associated with translating raw materials into a finished product.

This chapter uses these manufacturing costs to illustrate cost behavior patterns. Other costs such as selling, general, and administrative costs exhibit the same behavior patterns as illustrated for product costs. The procedures shown here for quantifying and graphing product cost patterns are applicable to any category of cost.

Before we begin to discuss behavior patterns and methods of quantifying them, we should explain why they are important and how they are useful to management. Another important item to discuss is the distinction between the total manufacturing cost and the unit manufacturing cost.

Importance of Behavior Patterns to Management Decisions

Cost accounting provides management with relevant cost data to assist them in operating the business effectively. The management process includes developing an operating plan, implementing the plan, and evaluating the results of operations. Cost behavior patterns are particularly relevant in developing an operating plan and in evaluating the results of operations.

In developing an operating plan it is essential to know how each cost will behave with respect to time and the volume of production. Some costs, such as rent on the manufacturing facility, will be fixed and a constant amount must be paid each month. Other costs, such as direct materials, will be variable depending upon the amount of material to be purchased and used for the planned level of production. Other costs, such as heat and electricity in the factory, will be part fixed and part variable. Such costs are called mixed costs or semivariable costs. Some heat and power must be used even though nothing is produced. However, the usage of both will go up sharply as production increases. The behavior patterns exhibited by these and other manufacturing costs must be known in order to prepare an accurate operating plan.

Actual operations seldom go exactly as planned. Perhaps management expected to produce 10,000 units of finished product, but because demand was stronger than anticipated, production was increased to 12,000 units. The actual cost to produce 12,000 units will not be the same as was planned for 10,000 units. In order to get meaningful data to evaluate the results of operations, adjustments need to be made to the budget for costs that vary according to the number of units produced. Cost behavior patterns must be known in order to adjust the variable costs for changes in the volume of production.

Knowledge of cost behavior patterns is also very useful for special management decisions. Suppose management planned on producing 10,000 units of finished product, but because demand is so weak they have decided to cut production back to 6,000 units. A good cost analyst who knows the behavior of each cost will be able to advise management on the costs that can be reduced and by how much. This will help management to concentrate their energies on reducing the right costs.

Total and Unit Manufacturing Costs

A manufacturing process generally produces several units of a product at the same time. Care must be taken in identifying the manufacturing cost as either a total or a unit cost. **Total cost** refers to all costs associated with a particular activity, generally the production of a group of finished products or the cost for a period of time. Total cost can also be limited to a specific category, such as total direct-material cost or total direct-labor cost. For example, total direct-labor cost refers to the total cost of all workers whose efforts are traceable to the finished products.

The **unit cost** is the cost associated with a single unit of product. Unit cost can also be limited to a specific cost category, such as direct material or direct labor. The unit cost of direct material is the cost of materials that are traceable to *one* unit of finished product. Total cost per unit refers to the **total manufacturing costs** (including direct material, direct labor, and factory overhead) required to produce *one* unit of finished product.

The unit cost is computed by dividing total cost by the number of units included in the group. An accurate label should always be associated with a cost, such as "total manufacturing cost" or "direct-labor cost per unit."

Example: Bells Incorporated used $120,000 of direct materials, $84,000 of direct labor, and $42,000 of factory overhead to manufacture 10,000 units of finished product. Total and unit costs are represented as follows:

Total manufacturing cost: ($120,000 + $84,000 + $42,000)	$246,000
Manufacturing cost per unit: ($246,000 ÷ 10,000 units)	$24.60
Direct-labor cost per unit: ($84,000 ÷ 10,000 units)	$8.40

One use of unit cost information is in valuing the units in ending inventory and in determining the amount of cost of goods sold. Generally accepted accounting principles require manufacturing organizations to value their inventory at cost, which includes prime costs plus a proportionate share of factory overhead.

Example: Bells Incorporated, in the previous example above, produced 10,000 units at a cost of $24.60 per unit. If 7,000 units were sold during the period, the manufacturing cost would be reported as:

Finished-goods inventory:	
(3,000 units × $24.60)	$73,800
Cost of goods sold:	
(7,000 units × $24.60)	$172,200

COST PATTERNS

Various costs behave differently with changes in time and in the volume of activity. Changes in volume generally have a different impact on total cost than they do on unit cost. There are a variety of behavior patterns commonly exhibited. These include fixed, variable, semivariable, and step variable. The nonlinearity of costs is also a relevant consideration.

Fixed Cost

A fixed cost is defined as a cost that remains constant in total regardless of the level of volume. The salary of a supervisor in a production department, for example, would be classified as a fixed cost. The salary is fixed, at say $2,500 per month, regardless of the volume of production achieved by the department.

Fixed costs remain constant in total but the cost per unit decreases with an increase in the number of units produced. In other words, fixed cost per unit varies inversely with volume. Suppose the production department above produces 100 units in a given month. The cost per unit for the supervisor's salary is $25.00 ($2,500 ÷ 100 units). If production increased to 1,000 units, the cost per unit decreases to $2.50 ($2,500 ÷ 1,000). At 10,000 units per month, the cost goes down to $.25 per unit ($2,500 ÷ 10,000 units).

Figure 3.1 illustrates the fixed cost pattern for both total cost and cost per unit when volume changes. The vertical axis represents dollars (total cost or cost per unit), and the horizontal axis represents volume (number of units produced).

Figure 3.1   Graphical representation of fixed costs

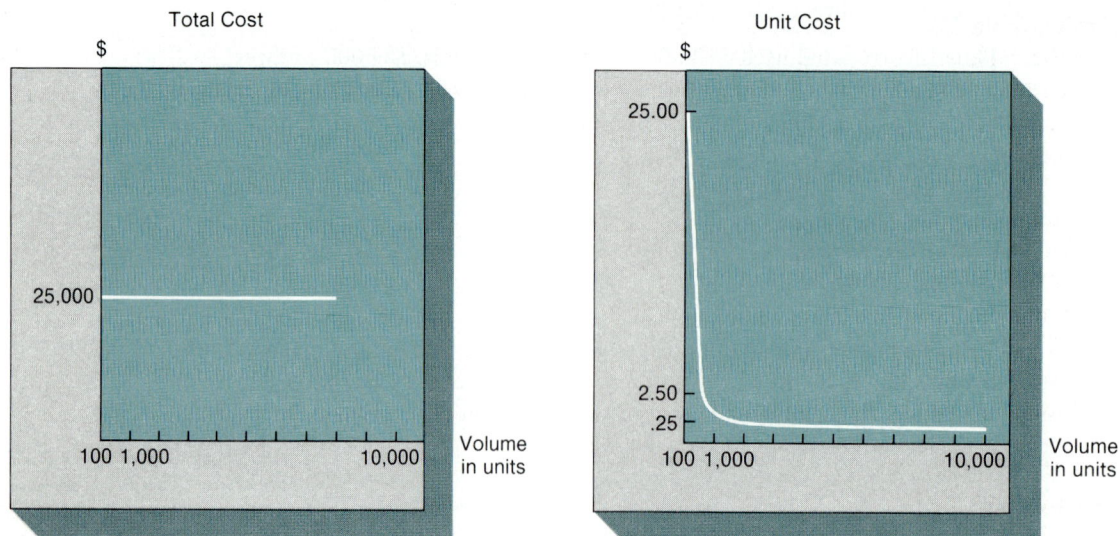

Figure 3.2   Graphical representation of variable costs

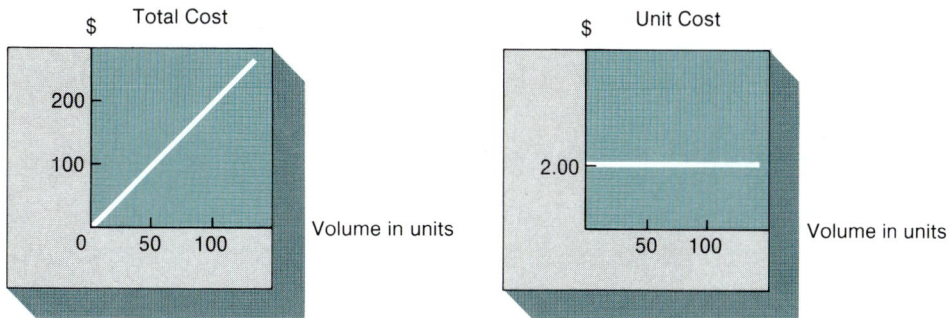

Variable Cost

As defined in chapter 2 a variable cost is a cost that changes in total as the volume changes. Assuming a linear cost function, total variable cost increases proportionately with increases in volume. When volume decreases, there is a proportionate reduction in the total variable cost. The piece-rate of a seamstress in a pajama factory is an example of a variable cost. The seamstress is paid $2.00 for each pair of pajamas that are assembled. If 50 pairs are assembled in one day the total labor cost for the seamstress is $100. If 100 pairs are assembled, the cost is $200.

The cost per unit of a variable cost remains constant regardless of the volume of production. In the example above, the seamstress is paid $2.00 per unit and that amount does not change regardless of the number of pajamas assembled. Figure 3.2 illustrates the cost pattern for both total variable cost and variable cost per unit as volume changes.

Notice that both total fixed cost and total variable cost are shown as a linear or straight-line relationship. Also, each example was descriptive of either a fixed cost or a variable cost but not both costs combined. There are several costs that do not follow the patterns described above either because they contain both a fixed and a variable element or because they do not follow a linear relationship.

Semivariable Cost

A **semivariable cost** is sometimes referred to as a **mixed cost** because it contains both a fixed cost portion and a variable cost portion. The fixed portion is the minimum cost required if no output is produced, but as output increases, cost also increases as with a variable cost.

An example of a semivariable cost is the cost of natural gas that is used to heat a manufacturing facility. The pricing structure of some gas companies includes a flat fee, called a hook-up fee, plus an amount for each cubic foot of gas consumed. The price might be $100 per month plus $.05 per cubic foot of gas. The fixed element is $100 per month, which must be paid even if no gas is used, and the variable element is the $.05 per cubic foot. If 1,000 cubic feet are consumed the total cost is $150 ($100 + (1,000 × $.05)). At 5,000 cubic feet the total cost is $350 ($100 + (5,000 × $.05)). Figure 3.3 shows a graphical representation of a semivariable cost.

Step-Variable Cost

A **step-variable cost** is a variable cost that increases or decreases in "chunks" of cost with small changes in volume. A given amount of cost will sustain some increase in volume without any increase in cost. At some point, however, the cost must be increased by a

Figure 3.3   Graphical representations of other cost patterns

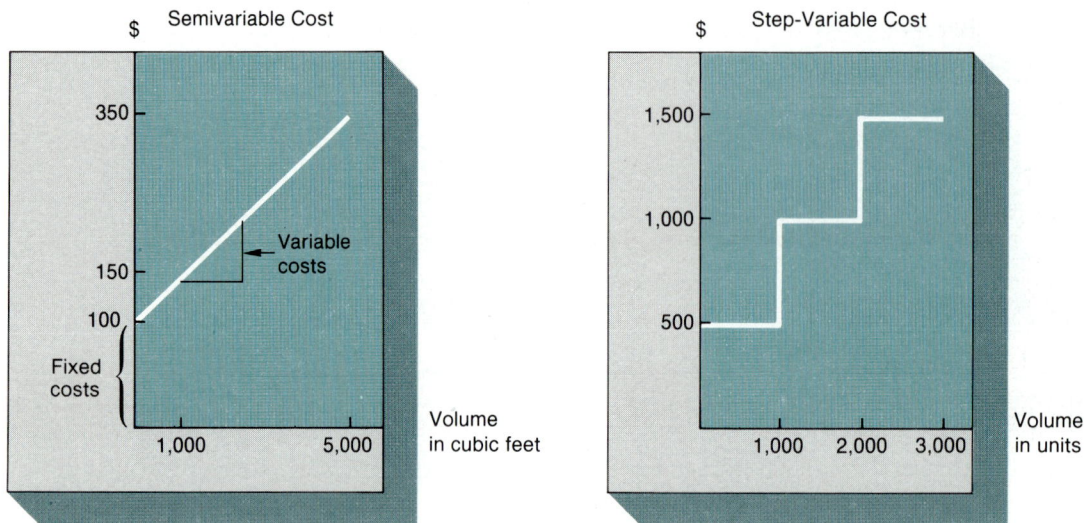

fixed amount in order to continue to increase volume. Cost increases come in indivisible chunks and, therefore, the cost curve has a steplike pattern as illustrated in figure 3.3.

An example of a step-variable cost is a supply clerk who has the responsibility to deliver raw materials to production workers. One clerk with a monthly salary of $500 can keep all production employees adequately stocked as long as production does not exceed 1,000 units per month. When this level is exceeded, an additional supply clerk must be employed at $500 per month, which raises the total cost for supply handling to $1,000. This pattern continues as the volume of production increases.

Nonlinear Costs

A linear cost is one that has a straight-line relationship with total cost remaining unchanged, or if it changes, the change is in equal increments for all levels of volume. Some costs, however, do not follow this linear relationship. They may increase at a faster rate or a slower rate as volume increases. An example of each is described below and is illustrated in figure 3.4.

Increasing Cost   A gasoline refinery has established contracts to supply one billion barrels of crude oil at an agreed price of $22 each. If the company wants to increase production above the levels provided by these contracts, it must acquire the additional crude oil on the spot market, which is consistently higher than the contract price.

Decreasing Cost   A mill manufacturer can receive a quantity discount on motors when the number of motors purchased each month exceeds 1,000. The first 1,000 motors cost $80 each, but additional motors cost only $70 each.

Accountants need to understand the various cost patterns and be able to correctly identify the pattern that any particular cost will follow when volume changes. Care must be taken to differentiate between total cost and cost per unit. This ability will be very valuable in understanding the manufacturing process and in using cost data correctly for all types of business decisions.

Figure 3.4   Graphical representations of nonlinear costs

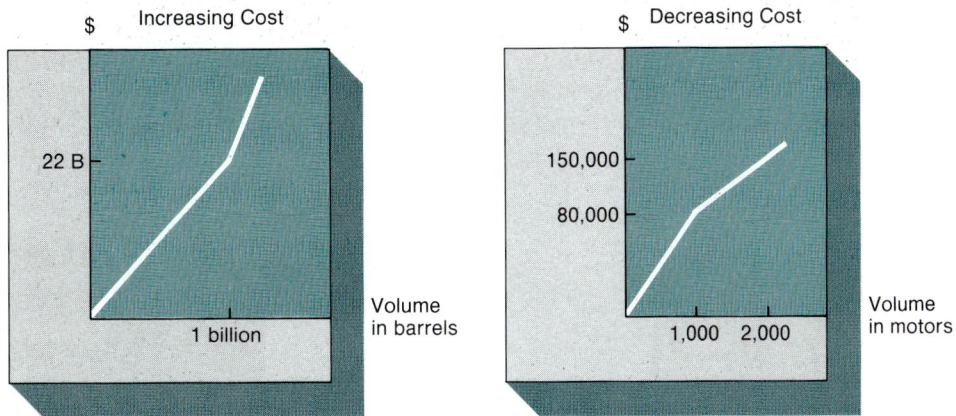

TOTAL MANUFACTURING COSTS

Product costs are categorized into direct material, direct labor, or factory overhead. Each of these costs follow one or more of the patterns described above. Two approaches can be used to analyze and quantify cost behavior: (*a*) industrial-engineering approach and (*b*) historical cost analysis. In reality, some combination of the two approaches is generally followed. Separate analysis is frequently required on each cost and, sometimes with different analytical tools, to predict cost behavior. We will first discuss the behavior patterns commonly exhibited by each product cost and then discuss approaches to quantifying them.

Product Cost Patterns

Direct material is almost always a variable cost. Manufactured products are always made from some type of raw material and there is generally a list of required materials that specifies the quantities of each required to produce a finished product. Except for waste and/or dissipation of some raw materials, there is a one-to-one correspondence between the input of raw materials and the output of finished products.

Direct labor is also a variable cost for most companies. Employees typically perform the same function day after day, and there is high correlation between the amount of time worked and the number of finished products produced. However, some factors complicate the analysis of direct labor and make it more difficult to predict than direct material. In some industries, direct labor is relatively fixed within ranges of productivity. For example, one hundred direct laborers may be required to operate the factory when production is between 1,000 and 1,200 gallons per hour. As production increases, additional laborers are required. In these cases, direct labor is more like a step-variable cost, except the steps come in fairly small increments. Also, union contracts sometimes call for a guaranteed wage, which causes direct labor to exhibit a fixed cost pattern.

The presence of a learning curve is another complicating factor. A new employee generally cannot produce as much as an experienced employee. Over time, the speed with which an employee can produce a product increases and more units of finished product can be produced within any given period of time. When this is measured and graphed it is called the learning curve. At any point in time, a business will have employees at all

Figure 3.5   Total manufacturing cost curve

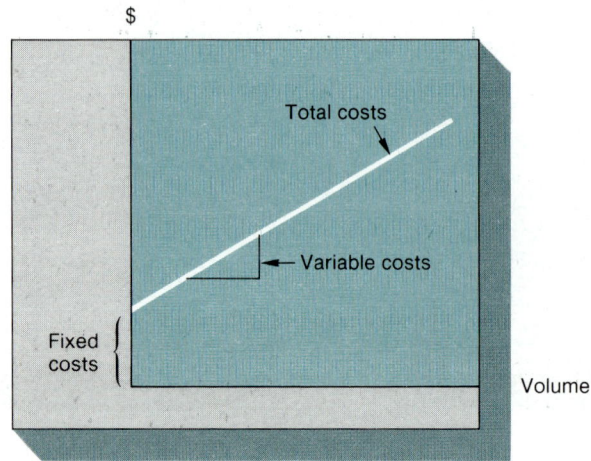

different points on the learning curve. Over time as old employees leave the company, as new employees are hired, and as existing employees move up their learning curve, the average productivity of all employees will probably not change much. This is especially true when there are several employees. Therefore, the effects of the learning curve are generally ignored by companies that produce the same products continually.

Factory overhead is a combination of all cost patterns because it consists of many different kinds of cost. For example, straight-line depreciation on the equipment is a fixed cost. Indirect material is an example of a variable cost. Supervision and custodial work exhibit a step-variable pattern. When all the various costs are combined, the resulting cost curve is a semivariable cost pattern.

The most common pattern associated with each category is summarized as follows:

Manufacturing Cost	Cost Pattern
Direct material	Variable cost
Direct labor	Variable cost
Factory overhead	Semivariable cost

Total manufacturing cost is the combined total of the product cost patterns described above. The resulting total cost curve is illustrated in figure 3.5. Notice that the total manufacturing cost curve is similar to the semivariable cost curve (see fig. 3.3) in that it contains both a fixed and a variable portion. The fixed portion is composed of the factory overhead costs that are not affected by different levels of production. These include such items as property tax and depreciation on the manufacturing facilities. The variable portion is made up of direct materials, direct labor, and variable factory overhead, which are all dependent upon the volume of production.

Total Cost Curve

The total manufacturing cost curve is shown as a straight line. This is considered an average and a good approximation of all the product costs combined. It should be recognized that some individual costs have a step-variable pattern and others have an increasing or

Figure 3.6   Comparison of total cost curves in economics and accounting

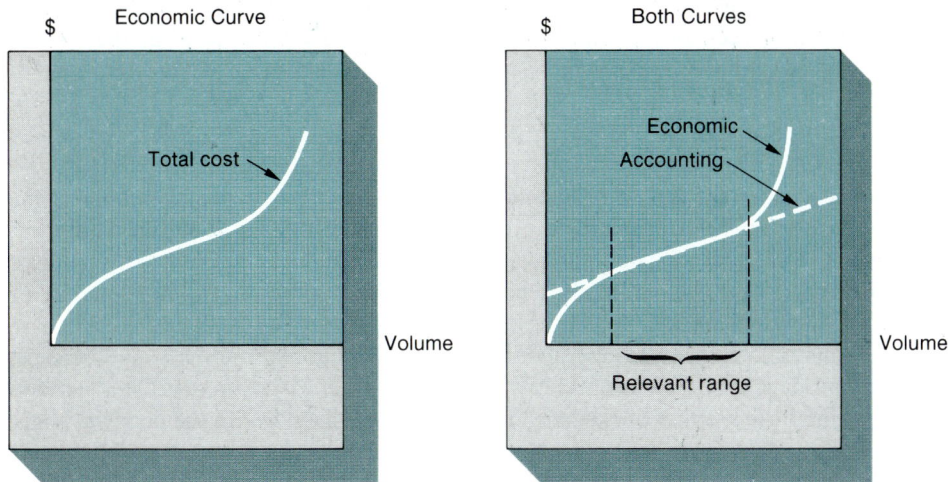

a decreasing variable rate. Nevertheless, the major variable costs—including direct material, direct labor, and a large part of factory overhead—are linear. The deviation of other cost patterns is generally minor and they very often counterbalance each other. Experience has shown that combining them into a straight line is a good representation of total manufacturing costs within the range of production normally achieved by an enterprise.

Relevant Range of Production

The **relevant range of production** is a range of operating volume within which the cost relationships will be reliable. At extremely low levels of production, some fixed costs can be avoided. For example, a supervisor's salary, which is considered part of the fixed factory overhead, could be avoided by laying off the supervisor and by having another supervisor cover both areas. One supervisor can do an adequate job because of fewer employees and lower production. When these types of cost reductions are employed, the total cost curve approaches zero as the volume of production approaches zero.

In an attempt to achieve extremely high levels of volume, some costs will increase at a faster than normal rate. The increase in cost usually results from production problems such as excessive waste of raw materials, labor inefficiencies due to congested work areas, and additional overhead costs due to excessive repair and maintenance on machinery that is overutilized. When these types of factors are considered, the total cost curve turns up as the volume of production approaches the maximum capacity. This type of analysis is normally employed by the economist. The typical total cost curve used in economic analysis is shown in figure 3.6. Figure 3.6 also shows the economist's total cost curve with an accountant's total cost curve superimposed over it. Notice that the total cost curve within the relevant range is almost a straight line for both curves. Cost accountants simplify the analysis by assuming a linear cost curve but qualify it as only being reliable within the relevant range of production.

ANALYSIS OF COST BEHAVIOR

Industrial-engineering analysis and *historical cost analysis* are two approaches to ana-lyze cost behavior. The objective is to develop a mathematical formula to describe each product cost as well as the total cost curve. Both approaches can be used on each product cost, but not with the same amount of ease. Typically, a combination of the two ap-proaches is used in deriving the total cost curve.

Industrial-Engineering Approach

An industrial-engineering approach takes a forward look at the problem and attempts to quantify expected cost behavior. The basic issue is—what *should be* the amount of ma-terials, labor, or overhead required to produce a finished product given the production facilities of the enterprise? The total cost curve is based on the most efficient method of operations and the existing facilities. Therefore, they are limited in the short-run by the existing production facilities.

Industrial engineers utilize such techniques as time-and-motion studies and rely heavily on product specifications and raw material characteristics to develop a standard quantity of inputs to produce one finished unit. They work closely with the financial people in the organization to price the various components of the production process. The price that is expected to be paid during the coming period is generally used.

The process followed by an industrial engineer in developing the individual prod-uct cost curves is different for each cost. Raw materials, direct labor, and factory overhead will be considered individually.

Raw Materials   Product specifications are important in determining the type, quantity, and quality of raw materials. For example, a product that must be able to operate in temperatures of forty degrees below zero will probably require raw materials that are much different than if the minimum operating temperature is sixty degrees above zero.

The form and shape of the raw material at the time of acquisition is also im-portant. For example, if the required raw material is a round piece of aluminum three inches in diameter, there will be a considerable amount of scrap if the aluminum can only be purchased in large rectangular sheets.

The quality and condition of the raw materials must be closely correlated with the production process. Labor and machine time may be required when raw materials must be preprocessed into a usable form for normal production. For example, the labor standard as well as the raw material standard must be adjusted if the supplier of the three-inch aluminum pieces described above goes bankrupt and the company is forced to cut their own circles from large rectangular sheets. Labor and machine time that could have been used elsewhere are tied up in preparing the raw materials.

The result of the engineering study on direct materials will be a list of raw ma-terials of a specific type, quality, and quantity required to produce each unit. The pur-chasing department then prices them at expected prices for the coming period and totals them. This is the raw material cost per unit and the variable cost of direct materials.

Direct Labor   Time-and-motion studies are one of the more common techniques that identify the amount of direct-labor time required to perform the activities involved in producing a finished product. A complete time-and-motion analysis would include every job in the manufacturing process. The individual movements required by each worker to produce the product are first identified. Each movement is then timed, giving appropriate allowance for fatigue, breakdowns, and rest breaks. The times are accumulated by job classifications and priced at the expected wage rates for the coming period. The total amount is the variable cost of direct labor.

Factory Overhead   Engineering analysis is least effective in making a direct estimate of the amount of factory overhead that should be incurred. Factory overhead is composed of many different types of costs. Individually these costs may be relatively small, but in total they account for a significant part of total production cost.

The various types of overhead costs can generally be identified and some of them can be quantified as discussed above for direct materials or analyzed as discussed above for direct labor. Custodial service is an example. The size of the manufacturing facility can be measured and studies can be performed to determine the number of custodians required, and hence, the amount of indirect labor incurred for custodial service.

Repair and maintenance cannot be analyzed in quite the same way. The amount of repair and maintenance will depend on the number of repair hours that will be worked during the period and the cost of the parts that are used. Studies of existing machines to determine which ones will break down and the amount of time and parts required to repair them will probably not be very accurate. The best information for estimating repair and maintenance for a period, assuming a consistent pattern of equipment replacement, is the amount of repair and maintenance required in prior periods. This utilizes the historical approach discussed in the next section.

A detailed study of each overhead cost would be very time consuming and costly. The resulting formula may be very accurate, yet it would probably be very complex. The added precision is usually not worth the added complexity.

The industrial-engineering approach and the historical approach are generally combined to determine estimated factory overhead. Historical data is used as a starting point for projecting overhead costs and developing an overhead cost curve for the coming period. Engineering studies are then used to analyze the effects of anticipated changes in specific aspects of factory overhead on the cost curve. This makes the overhead cost curve easier to develop, yet applicable to the coming period.

Historical Cost Approach

A historical cost approach develops a total cost curve from cost data of prior operations. The first step is to collect the historical data to be used in the analysis. Operating data for the past year or two are commonly used. Any prior year or group of years could be used, but the period of time selected should be representative of future operating results. The data should include (*a*) the amount of cost incurred for each production cost—direct material, direct labor, and factory overhead—and (*b*) the volume of activity, such as units produced. The data is broken down into short time intervals, such as monthly, weekly, or quarterly, consistent with the reporting cycle of the company.

Direct Costs: Materials and Labor   Direct costs for both material and labor vary according to the number of units produced. Since there are no fixed costs involved, the variable rate for each cost curve can be computed by dividing the total cost incurred by the number of units produced.

Factory Overhead   Factory overhead is somewhat more complicated because it is composed of many different manufacturing costs that exhibit a variety of cost patterns. Individual cost data on each element of factory overhead may not be readily available for analysis. An approach is needed to analyze total factory overhead to develop a mathematical formula for a semivariable cost curve. Three methods commonly used are (*a*) high-low method, (*b*) scattergraph method, and (*c*) least-squares method. Before these methods are discussed and illustrated, we will review the mathematical properties of a straight line.

Figure 3.7   Mathematical properties of a straight line

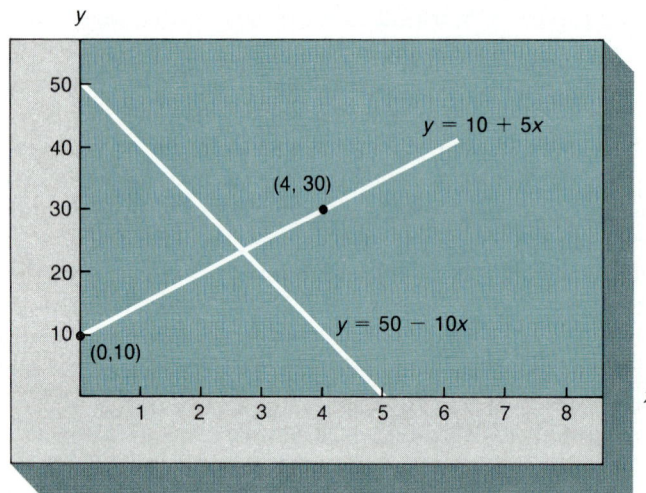

QUANTIFYING COST BEHAVIOR

It is useful when working with the different costs and behavior patterns to be able to quantify them mathematically. Each of the product cost patterns can be represented by a mathematical equation. Since we assume linear relationships for almost all cost analysis in accounting, we will limit our discussion to the mathematical equation of a linear cost function. We will first discuss the mathematical properties of a straight line and then discuss several methods used within historical cost analysis for developing an equation from a given set of data.

Mathematical Properties of a Straight Line

Mathematically, a straight line can be described by the following equation:

$$y = a + bx$$

The symbols y and x represent variables. The symbol y is the **dependent variable,** which is the variable under investigation and is described by another variable. The symbol x is the **independent variable,** which is used to describe the dependent variable. The symbols a and b are constants for a given line; a is called the y-intercept and b is called the slope. The **y-intercept** identifies the amount of y when x is zero. The **slope** is the amount of change in y for each unit of x. For example, the equation $y = 10 + 5x$ describes a straight line with an intercept of 10 and a slope of 5. As shown in figure 3.7, the line intersects the vertical axis at 10 and slopes upward at a rate of 5 units of y for each unit of x.

When plotted on a graph, the vertical axis represents values of the dependent variable y and the horizontal axis represents values of the independent variable x. Any two points on a line can be used to plot the straight line. One of the points often used is the y-intercept. For the example above, the coordinates of this point are (0, 10), representing the values of x and y respectively. Another point may be obtained by selecting a value for x and solving the equation for y. For example, 30 is the value computed for y when 4 is selected as the value for x ($10 + 5(4) = 30$). The point representing the corresponding values of x and y (4, 30) is located on the graph and the two points are connected with a ruler.

A line that slopes downward has a negative value for the slope. For example, the equation $y = 50 - 10x$ results in smaller values of y as x increases. Thus, y decreases by 10 for each unit increase in x. Since we will be working primarily with total costs that increase as volume increases, we will not be working much with negative sloping lines.

The straight line equation can be applied to the various manufacturing costs. The value of a represents the amount of fixed costs and b represents the variable rate per unit of output. The independent variable x is a volume of output, such as units produced. The dependent variable y is the total cost, such as total direct labor, total factory overhead, or total manufacturing cost. This basic equation may be used as a cost formula to represent or predict total costs when volume changes.

$$y = a + bx$$
Total cost = Fixed cost + Variable rate per unit times volume

Fixed Cost Equation   A manufacturing cost such as a supervisor's salary, which consists of fixed cost entirely, would be represented by the following equation:

$$y = a + b(x)$$
Salary = $2,500 + 0(x)

Figure 3.8 shows that the slope of the line is zero. Regardless of the volume of output, the supervisor's salary remains at $2,500. Even when x is zero, the supervisor will continue to be paid $2,500. Therefore, the line is horizontal and intersects the y axis at $2,500.

Variable Cost Equation   A manufacturing cost such as direct material, which is entirely variable, would be represented by the following equation:

$$y = a + b(x)$$
Direct material = 0 + $1.20(x)

Figure 3.8 shows that y will be zero when x is zero, which means that no direct material cost will be incurred if nothing is produced. As x increases, y increases. Direct materials cost $1.20 for each unit of output. Therefore, the cost curve comes out of the origin and slopes upward at a rate of $1.20 per unit.

Semivariable Cost Equation   A semivariable cost has both a fixed and variable cost portion. An example is an equipment lease that specifies a minimum monthly payment plus a variable amount based on usage. This cost would be represented by the following equation:

$$y = a + b(x)$$
Lease cost = $2,000 + $1.00(x)

The fixed cost is $2,000 per month and the variable rate is $1.00 per unit of output. Figure 3.8 shows the y-intercept at $2,000 with an upward slope.

Recall that the total manufacturing cost curve is similar to a semivariable cost curve. An equation for total manufacturing costs can be developed by adding the separate costs.

Example: Milky Incorporated produced milk cans at the following cost:

Direct material	$12.50 per can
Direct labor	7.50 per can
Overhead:	
Variable	5.00 per can
Fixed	$6,000 per month

Figure 3.8   Cost equations

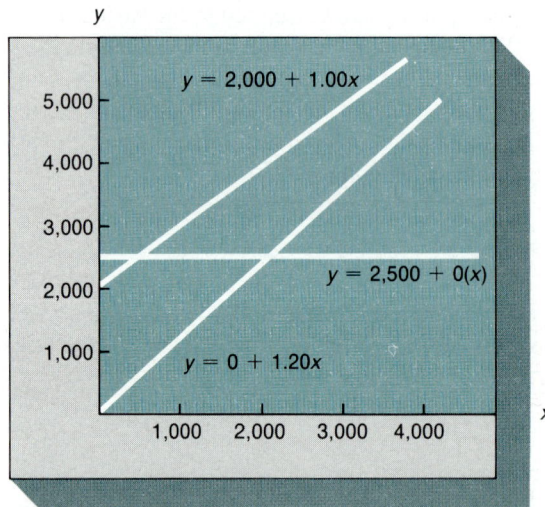

The total manufacturing cost equation is:

Cost = $6,000 + $25(x)
where x = number of cans produced

The projected manufacturing cost to produce 200 milk cans in December is computed as follows:

Cost = $6,000 + $25(200) = $11,000

Methods for Developing an Equation

The cost equations illustrated above are very useful in describing a cost's pattern of behavior and in evaluating the impact that various decisions will have on the cost of production. For any cost in a given situation we may have some idea of its pattern but we may not know the exact equation. This is particularly true with factory overhead, which is composed of several different elements and different cost patterns. Given a set of data that includes the amount of cost incurred at various levels of output, over time, we need a way to quantify the values of the constants a and b for a cost equation. Three common estimation methods are the high-low method, the scattergraph method, and the least-squares method. Each of these methods will be explained and illustrated.

Figure 3.9 shows the amount of factory overhead incurred during the last six months of 19X1 for Hart Assembly Company. Also shown is the number of units manufactured each month. A factory overhead cost equation is desired to compute the amount of factory overhead that should be incurred at various levels of output. Factory overhead is the dependent variable y, and units produced is the independent variable x.

High-Low Method   The **high-low method** selects a high level of volume and a low level of volume for use in developing the cost equation. The variable rate b is determined by analyzing the change in cost that corresponds to the change in volume between the high and low points. Remember that fixed costs do not change in total with changes in volume. Therefore, the change in total cost that results from a change in volume is entirely due

Figure 3.9

Hart Assembly Company
Summary of Factory Overhead
Six Months Ending December 31, 19X1

Month	Factory Overhead	Units Produced
July	$ 4,200	70
August	3,800	60
September	5,400	100
October	5,100	120
November	5,000	120
December	5,900	130
Total	$29,400	600

to variable costs. Variable cost is then subtracted from total cost at a particular volume of activity to compute fixed costs.

Using the data presented in figure 3.9, a cost equation can be developed for factory overhead. The following steps are used:

Step 1 Select the high and low points of activity. The highest level of activity was 130 units in December and the lowest level was 60 units in August. An analysis indicates that the data for December and August are representative of normal operations.

Step 2 The variable rate is computed by dividing the change in cost by the change in volume. The change in cost and the change in volume are first computed:

	Overhead Cost	Units Produced
High point	$ 5,900	130
Low point	3,800	60
Change	$ 2,100	70 units

The change in cost is then divided by the change in volume for the variable rate:

$$\text{Variable rate} = \frac{\text{Cost change}}{\text{Volume change}} = \frac{\$2,100}{70 \text{ units}} = \$30.00 \text{ per unit}$$

Step 3 Compute fixed cost by multiplying the variable rate times the volume at either the high or low point and subtract that amount from total factory overhead at that point. Supposing the *high point* is selected, the fixed cost of $2,000 per month is computed as follows:

Factory overhead	$5,900
Variable cost ($30 × 130 units)	3,900
Fixed cost	$2,000 per month

Notice that the same answer is obtained if the *low point* is selected:

Factory overhead	$3,800
Variable cost ($30 × 60 units)	1,800
Fixed cost	$2,000 per month

Figure 3.10   Scattergraph

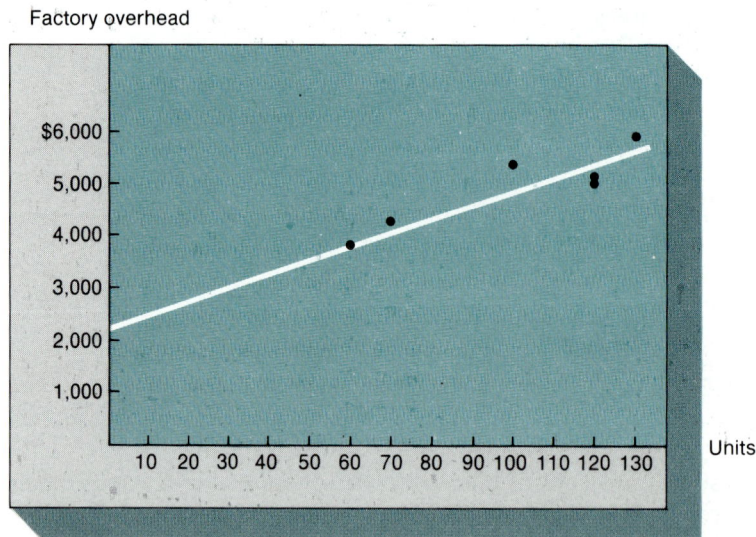

Step 4   Develop the mathematical equation. Factory overhead is equal to fixed costs plus the variable rate multiplied by volume:

Factory overhead = $2,000 + $30.00(x)

The main advantage of the high-low method is that it is easy to apply. A potential problem, however, is its accuracy. Most of the collected data are not used. The formula is based only on two points, and it will be biased if the points selected are not representative of the entire data set. Care must be taken to select high and low points of activity that are representative of normal operations and within the relevant range of activity. This can be seen by referring back to figure 3.6, which compares the accounting and economic cost curves. The economic cost curve is more accurate than the accounting cost curve outside the relevant range of production. If the high point and low point follow the economic cost curve and are both outside the relevant range, the cost curve developed by this method will have a steeper slope than is representative of normal operations within the relevant range.

Scattergraph Method   The **scattergraph method** plots the data on a graph, which is called a **scatter diagram** or scattergraph. A straight line, called a regression line, is inserted among the points on the graph by a visual fit. The line is intended to represent an average of the plotted points, so approximately half of the points will be on either side of the line. In drawing the line you should attempt to minimize the vertical distance between the plotted points and the line. The point at which the regression line intersects the vertical axis (y-intercept) determines the estimated amount of fixed costs and the slope of the line determines the variable rate.

The scatter diagram in figure 3.10 shows the data from figure 3.9. The data from the figure have been plotted on the graph. A regression line has been drawn by a visual fit.

The point at which the regression line intersects the vertical axis is the total fixed costs. As shown in figure 3.10, it is at approximately $2,200. The subjectivity involved in identifying the point of intersection indicates one of the weaknesses of this method.

An estimate of the variable rate can then be computed by subtracting the fixed costs from the total factory overhead at some point along the regression line and dividing the difference by the units produced. The July data (70 units at $4,200) is on the line and will be used to compute the variable rate.

Factory overhead	$4,200
Fixed cost	2,200
Variable cost	$2,000
Divided by units produced	÷ 70
Variable rate	$28.57 per unit

Cost equation:

Factory overhead = $2,200 + $28.57(x)
where x = units produced

Advantages of the scattergraph method are that it uses all the data in developing the formula and it is fairly quick and easy to apply. However, once again, care must be taken to make appropriate adjustments for extraneous circumstances that cause abnormal fluctuations in cost behavior. Plotting the data on a graph helps to identify an abnormal bit of cost data. If one of the plotted points is way out of line with the others, it is probably the result of extraneous circumstances and should be ignored in visually fitting the regression line.

The biggest problem in using this method is in fitting a line to the plotted points. An "accurate" visual fit will provide a formula as accurate as if it were measured mathematically. However, a slight misplacement can cause a significant error in the y-intercept (fixed costs), the slope (variable rate), or both. Because the scattergraph method is subjective and imprecise and does not allow for more sophisticated statistical analysis, a least-squares regression analysis is often required.

Least-Squares Method   The **least-squares method** uses a mathematical technique to fit the best line possible to the observed data. It identifies the formula for a regression line that minimizes the sum of the squares of the lengths of the vertical-line segments drawn from the observed data points on the scattergraph to the regression line. Figure 3.11 shows the vertical distance between the observed points and the regression line. The squared sum of these is minimized by this method. The idea is that the smaller the deviations of the observed values from this line (and consequently the smaller the sum of squares of these deviations), the better the fit of the line to the data points.

The following are the least-squares formulas to compute a and b. The point of intercept on the vertical axis and the slope, respectively, are:

$$a = \frac{(\Sigma y)(\Sigma x^2) - (\Sigma x)(\Sigma xy)}{n(\Sigma x^2) - (\Sigma x)^2}$$

$$b = \frac{n(\Sigma xy) - (\Sigma x)(\Sigma y)}{n(\Sigma x^2) - (\Sigma x)^2}$$

where Σx = the total of the observed values of the independent variable
Σy = the total of the observed values of the dependent variable
n = the number of observations
Σx^2 = the summation of the squared values of the independent variable
Σxy = the total of the products of the dependent variable multiplied by the independent variable

The intermediate computations that are required to use the above formulas are illustrated in figure 3.12. The observed values of x (units produced) and y (factory overhead) are totaled for the values of Σx and Σy, respectively. The units produced are multiplied by the factory overhead for each month, and the products are totaled for the value

Figure 3.11   Deviations of observed points from the fitted regression line

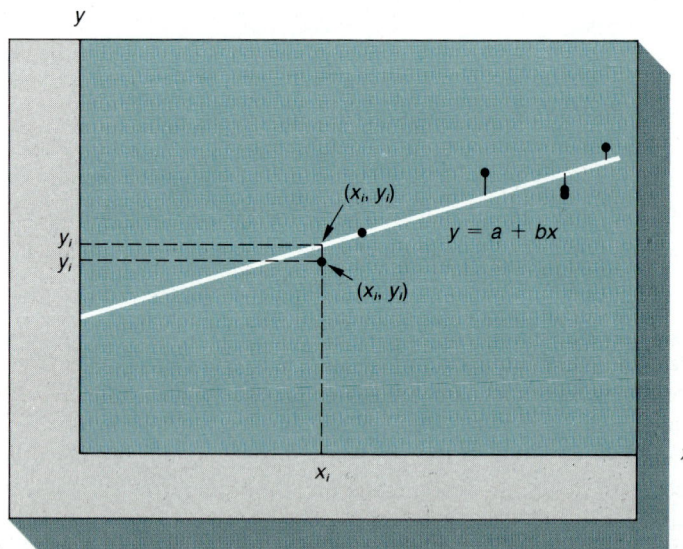

Figure 3.12   Least-squares regression analysis

Month	x Produced	y Overhead	xy	x²
July	70	$ 4,200	294,000	4,900
August	60	3,800	228,000	3,600
September	100	5,400	540,000	10,000
October	120	5,100	612,000	14,400
November	120	5,000	600,000	14,400
December	130	5,900	767,000	16,900
Total	600	$29,400	3,041,000	64,200

of Σxy. The units produced each month is squared, and the results are totaled for the value of Σx^2. These values are substituted into the above equations to compute the values of a and b.

$$a = \frac{(29,400)(64,200) - (600)(3,041,000)}{(6)(64,200) - (600)^2}$$
$$= \underline{\$2,496}$$

$$b = \frac{(6)(3,041,000) - (600)(29,400)}{(6)(64,200) - (600)^2}$$
$$= \underline{\$24.04}$$

The resulting cost equation is:

Factory overhead = $2,496 + $24.04(x)
where x = units produced

An alternative computation for the least-squares regression analysis is explained and illustrated in the appendix on page 70.

Comparison of Methods   The methods described above differ widely in their ease of application and in the precision of the resulting cost formula. Notice the difference in the results:

	Fixed Costs	Variable Rate
High-low method	$2,000	$30.00
Scattergraph method	2,200	28.57
Least-squares method	2,496	24.04

The least-squares method provides a regression line that, mathematically speaking, is the best fit for all the observed data points. The high-low method and the scattergraph method are intended only as approximations of the least-squares method.

However, the precision offered by the least-squares method is not always needed. Perhaps we are trying to estimate what factory overhead will be in the coming year and we are looking at the prior year to give us some idea as to what might be expected. Since economic conditions are never the same from year to year, an approximation of the prior year's cost equation might be good enough. The important thing is to select a method that is adequate for its intended use.

Application of Cost Patterns

A clear understanding of the various cost patterns is essential. A significant part of the accountant's work is involved in identifying cost patterns, grouping them with other costs having similar patterns, and using them properly in making wise business decisions.

Summary

This chapter identified the various cost patterns associated with the manufacturing process and described some of the ways that costs may be classified and quantified. Product costs include all costs associated with the manufacturing process and are broadly classified into (*a*) direct materials, (*b*) direct labor, and (*c*) factory overhead. Materials and labor that are traceable to the finished product are classified as direct or prime costs. Indirect material and labor and all other manufacturing costs are included in factory overhead.

Manufacturing costs exhibit different patterns as volume changes. The most common patterns are called (*a*) fixed, (*b*) variable, and (*c*) semivariable. Care must be taken to distinguish between total cost and cost per unit when working with the various cost patterns. Fixed costs remain constant in total, but the cost per unit decreases as volume increases. Variable costs increase in total as volume increases, but the cost per unit remains constant. Semivariable costs have both a fixed and a variable cost element.

Total manufacturing costs combine the cost of direct labor, direct material, and factory overhead. The total manufacturing cost curve exhibits a semivariable cost pattern that can be represented by the following straight line equation:

$$y = a + bx$$

where y = dependent variable or total cost
x = independent variable or volume
a = y-intercept or fixed cost
b = slope or variable rate

Three common methods of developing a cost equation from a set of data are high-low, scattergraph, and least squares. The amount of precision desired in the equation is important in selecting the method to be used. The least-squares method is the most difficult to apply but provides the best possible line for the observed data.

Appendix   *Alternative Approach to Least-Squares Regression Analysis*

This appendix explains and illustrates an alternate approach to the least-squares regression analysis. Recall that the objective of the least-squares method is to minimize the squared sum of the vertical distance between the observed points and the regression line. This concept is highlighted in the following equations. The least-squares formula to compute *b,* the slope of the line, is:

$$b = \frac{\displaystyle\sum_{i=1}^{n} (x_i - \bar{x})(y_i - \bar{y})}{\displaystyle\sum_{i=1}^{n} (x_i - \bar{x})^2}$$

where $\bar{x}$ = the sample mean of the independent variable
$\bar{y}$ = the sample mean of the dependent variable
x_i = the observed values of the independent variable from 1 to n
y_i = the observed values of the dependent variable from 1 to n

The least-squares formula for computing *a,* the point of intercept on the vertical axis, is:

$$a = \bar{y} - b\bar{x}$$

The steps in performing the calculations are:

Step 1 Compute the sample means ($\bar{x}$ and $\bar{y}$) from the observed set of data. The mean is computed by summing the values of the variable and dividing by the number of observations.

$$\bar{x} = \frac{\displaystyle\sum_{i=1}^{n} x_i}{n}$$

Figure 3.13 shows these computations.

Step 2 Compute *b,* the slope or variable rate, using the equation above. Four intermediate computations are required.

1. Compute the difference between the observed value of each *dependent* variable (x_i) with the sample mean ($\bar{x}$).
2. Compute the difference between the observed value of each *independent* variable (y_i) with the sample mean ($\bar{y}$).
3. Multiply the differences computed in numbers 1 and 2 above for each observation [$(x_i - \bar{x}) (y_i - \bar{y})$] and sum the products.
4. Square the differences computed in number 1 above for each observation and sum the result. These computations are also shown in figure 3.13. The totals of the two columns on the right-hand side of the table are used in the equation.

$$b = \frac{101{,}000}{4{,}200} = \$24.04 \text{ per unit}$$

Figure 3.13 Least-squares regression analysis (alternative computation)

Month	x Units produced	y Factory overhead	$x_i - \bar{x}$	$y_i - \bar{y}$	$(x_i-\bar{x})(y_i-\bar{y})$	$(x_i-\bar{x})^2$
July	70	$ 4,200	−30	−700	21,000	900
August	60	3,800	−40	−1,100	44,000	1,600
September	100	5,400	−0−	500	−0−	−0−
October	120	5,100	20	200	4,000	400
November	120	5,000	20	100	2,000	400
December	130	5,900	30	1,000	30,000	900
Total	600	$29,400			101,000	4,200
Divide by n	÷ 6	÷ 6				
Mean $\bar{x}$	100 units					
Mean $\bar{y}$		$ 4,900				

Step 3 Compute *a,* the vertical intercept or fixed cost, by entering the values computed above into the formula.

$a = \bar{y} - b\bar{x}$
$a = 4,900 - 24.04(100) = \underline{\$2,496}$ per month

Step 4 Develop the cost equation.

Factory overhead = $2,496 + $24.04($x$)
where x = units produced

Self-Study Problem

The following set of data is available from the historical accounting records to develop a mathematical equation for factory overhead.

Month	Units Produced	Factory Overhead
January	15	$4,000
February	11	3,000
March	10	3,400
April	8	2,600
May	20	5,000

Required

Develop an equation in the form of $y = a + bx$ where y is factory overhead, a is the fixed element of factory overhead, and b is the variable element. Use each of the following methods:

1. High-low method
2. Scattergraph method
3. Least-squares regression analysis

Solution to the Self-Study Problem

Requirement 1

The high and low volumes are at 20 and 8 units, respectively. Using these two points, the variable cost is computed as follows:

	Factory Overhead	Units Produced
High point	$5,000	20
Low point	2,600	8
Change	$2,400	12 units

$$\text{Variable rate} = \frac{\$2,400}{12 \text{ units}} = \$200 \text{ per unit}$$

The fixed cost can then be determined by using one of the selected points. High point:

Factory overhead	$5,000
Variable cost ($200 × 20)	4,000
Fixed cost	$1,000

The factory overhead formula is:

Factory overhead = $1,000 + $200($x$)
where x = units produced

Requirement 2

The scattergraph method plots the data as illustrated in figure 3.14 and visually fits a line to the data points.

Figure 3.14   Scattergraph method

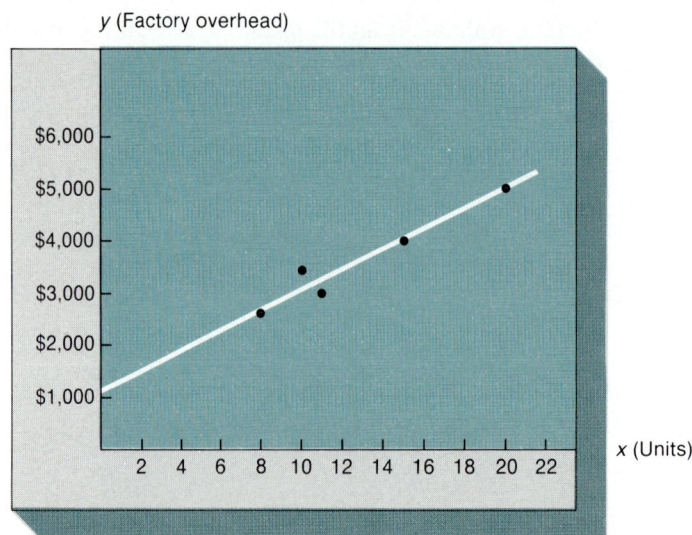

It appears that the factory overhead cost curve intersects the vertical axis at about $1,200 and passes through the April point of 8 units at $2,600 total overhead. Using these two points, the variable rate is computed as:

Factory overhead	$2,600
Fixed cost	1,200
Variable cost	$1,400
Divided by units produced	8
Variable rate	$175 per unit

The factory overhead formula is:

Factory overhead = $1,200 + $175(x)
where x = units produced

Requirement 3

Figure 3.15 is developed to compute the intermediate values required for use in the least-squares equations.

The values computed in the table are substituted into the equations to compute a and b, the fixed cost and variable rate, respectively.

$$a = \frac{(\Sigma y)(\Sigma x^2) - (\Sigma x)(\Sigma xy)}{n(\Sigma x^2) - (\Sigma x)^2}$$

$$= \frac{(18,000)(910) - (64)(247,800)}{(5)(910) - (64)^2}$$

$$= \$1,147 \text{ fixed costs}$$

$$b = \frac{n(\Sigma xy) - (\Sigma x)(\Sigma y)}{n(\Sigma x^2) - (\Sigma x)^2}$$

$$= \frac{(5)(247,800) - (64)(18,000)}{(5)(910) - (64)^2}$$

$$= \$192 \text{ variable cost}$$

The factory overhead formula is:

Factory overhead = $1,147 + $192(x)
where x = units produced

Figure 3.15   Least-squares method

Month	x Units	y Overhead	xy	x²
January	15	$ 4,000	$ 60,000	225
February	11	3,000	33,000	121
March	10	3,400	34,000	100
April	8	2,600	20,800	64
May	20	5,000	100,000	400
Total	64	$18,000	$247,800	910

Suggested Readings

Dean, Joel. *Statistical Cost Estimation*. Bloomington, Ind.: Indiana University Press, 1976.

Goodman, Sam R., and Reese, James S. *Controller's Handbook*. Homewood, Ill.: Dow-Jones Irwin, 1978.

Kleinbaum, David G., and Kupper, Lawrence L. *Applied Regression Analysis and Other Multivariable Methods*. North Scituate, Mass.: Duxbury Press, 1978.

McElroy, Elam E. *Applied Business Statistics*. 2d ed. San Francisco: Holden-Day, 1979.

Mason, Robert D. *Statistical Techniques in Business and Economics*. 4th ed. Homewood, Ill.: Richard D. Irwin, 1978.

National Association of Accountants. Accounting Practice Report #10. *Separating and Using Costs as Fixed and Variable*. New York: National Association of Accountants, 1960.

Discussion Questions

1. What is meant by a cost's behavior pattern?
2. When someone says, "The cost per unit remains constant as volume increases," are they talking about a fixed cost or a variable cost? Explain.
3. When someone says, "The cost per unit decreases as volume increases," are they talking about a fixed cost or a variable cost? Explain.
4. Define a semivariable cost.
5. Define a step-variable cost.
6. How does a step-variable cost differ from a semivariable cost?
7. Describe the relevant range of production. Why is it important when talking about cost behavior from an accountant's perspective?
8. Describe the industrial-engineering approach to quantifying cost behavior for direct labor.
9. Describe the historical cost approach to quantifying cost behavior for direct labor.
10. In the formula $y = a + bx$, which symbol represents the dependent variable? Why is it called a dependent variable?
11. In the formula $y = a + bx$, which symbol represents the independent variable? Why is it called an independent variable?
12. Describe what is meant by y-intercept and slope when dealing with the mathematical properties of a straight line.
13. Why are the two points selected for the high-low method so important? Suppose the low point selected is higher than is representative of the data set. What will be the impact on the resulting cost curve?
14. What is the major benefit of using the least-squares method as opposed to the high-low or scattergraph methods? Under what circumstances can we justify using the high-low or scattergraph methods rather than the least-squares regression analysis?
15. Why is knowledge of a cost's behavior pattern important to a cost accountant?

Exercise 3.1 Cost Concepts (CMA)

1. The term conversion costs refers to
   a. manufacturing costs incurred to produce units of output.
   b. all costs associated with manufacturing other than direct-labor costs and raw material costs.
   c. costs associated with marketing, shipping, warehousing, and billing activities.
   d. the sum of direct-labor costs and all factory overhead costs.
   e. the sum of raw material costs and direct-labor costs.
2. The term prime costs refers to
   a. manufacturing costs incurred to produce units of output.
   b. all costs associated with manufacturing other than direct-labor costs and raw material costs.
   c. costs that are predetermined and should be attained.
   d. the sum of direct-labor costs and all factory overhead costs.
   e. the sum of raw material costs and direct-labor costs.
3. Costs that are inventoriable are
   a. manufacturing costs incurred to produce units of output.
   b. all costs associated with manufacturing other than direct-labor costs and raw material costs.
   c. costs associated with marketing, shipping, warehousing, and billing activities.
   d. the sum of direct-labor costs and all factory overhead costs.
   e. the sum of raw material costs and direct-labor costs.
4. The term variable costs refers to
   a. all costs that are likely to respond to the amount of attention devoted to them by a specified manager.
   b. all costs associated with marketing, shipping, warehousing, and billing activities.
   c. all costs that do not change in total for a given period of time and relevant range but become progressively smaller on a per unit basis as volume increases.
   d. all manufacturing costs incurred to produce units of output.
   e. all costs that fluctuate in total in response to small changes in the rate of utilization of capacity.
5. The term committed costs refers to the
   a. costs that management decides to incur in the current period to enable the company to achieve objectives other than the filling of orders placed by customers.
   b. costs that are likely to respond to the amount of attention devoted to them by a specified manager.
   c. costs that are governed mainly by past decisions, which established the present levels of operating and organizational capacity, and that only change slowly in response to small changes in capacity.
   d. costs that fluctuate in total in response to small changes in the rate of utilization of capacity.
   e. amortization of costs that were capitalized in previous periods.

6. The term discretionary costs refers to the
   a. costs that management decides to incur in the current period to enable the company to achieve objectives other than the filling of orders placed by customers.
   b. costs that are likely to respond to the amount of attention devoted to them by a specified manager.
   c. costs that are governed mainly by past decisions, which established the present levels of operating and organizational capacity, and that only change slowly in response to small changes in capacity.
   d. amortization of costs that were capitalized in previous periods.
   e. costs that will be unaffected by current managerial decisions.
7. Those costs referred to as controllable costs are
   a. costs that management decides to incur in the current period to enable the company to achieve objectives other than the filling of orders placed by customers.
   b. costs that are likely to respond to the amount of attention devoted to them by a specified manager.
   c. costs that are governed mainly by past decisions, which established the present levels of operating and organizational capacity, and that only change slowly in response to small changes in capacity.
   d. costs that fluctuate in total in response to small changes in the rate of utilization of capacity.
   e. costs that will be unaffected by current managerial decisions.

Exercise 3.2   Cost Behavior Concepts (CMA)

The assumptions, concepts, and terminology used by economists and accountants often differ and seem to conflict. For instance, the economist normally assumes that the functions for total revenue, variable (marginal) cost, and total cost have curvilinear characteristics; while the accountant traditionally assumes that these same functions behave in a linear fashion.

Required:

1. Explain the economic concept behind the economist's assumption of curvilinear functions for the following:
   a. total revenue
   b. variable (marginal) cost
   c. total cost
2. Explain why the accountant's assumption of linear functions need not invalidate accounting analyses.

Exercise 3.3 Cost Behavior Concepts

1. Within a relevant range, the amount of variable cost per unit
   a. differs at each production level.
   b. remains constant at each production level.
   c. increases as production increases.
   d. decreases as production increases.
2. Which of the following methods can be used to determine the fixed and variable elements of a semivariable expense?
   a. statistical scattergraph method
   b. linear programming
   c. input-output analysis
   d. program evaluation review technique
3. In order to identify costs that relate to a specific product, an allocation base should be chosen that
   a. does *not* have a cause and effect relationship.
   b. has a cause and effect relationship.
   c. considers variable costs but *not* fixed costs.
   d. considers direct materials and direct labor but *not* factory overhead.

Exercise 3.4 Cost Behavior—High-Low Method

Jackson Incorporated is preparing a flexible budget for 19X1 and requires a breakdown of the cost of steam used in its factory into the fixed and variable elements. The following data on the cost of steam used and direct-labor hours worked are available for the last six months of 19X0:

Month	Cost of Steam	Direct-Labor Hours
July	$ 15,850	3,000
August	13,400	2,050
September	10,370	2,900
October	19,800	3,650
November	17,600	2,670
December	18,500	2,650
Total	$101,520	16,920

Required

1. Assuming that Jackson uses the high-low method of analysis, determine the variable cost of steam per direct-labor hour and the fixed cost total for steam cost.
2. Express your results in requirement 1 in $y = a + bx$ formula form.

Exercise 3.5 Separating Mixed Costs—Comparison of Methods

Maywood Resort Lodge has the following data for their room upkeep costs and number of guest days of occupancy for the second half of the year:

	Room Upkeep Costs	Number of Guest Days of Occupancy
July	$4,585	10,500
August	4,628	10,750
September	4,475	9,850
October	4,780	11,650
November	4,508	10,050
December	4,750	11,450

Required

1. Separate the room upkeep costs into fixed cost per month and variable cost per guest day using the following methods:
   a. High-low
   b. Scattergraph
   c. Least squares
2. Express the results you obtained in requirement lc in equation form.
3. What amount of room upkeep costs would you estimate for 10,000 guest days?
4. Comment on the differences (if any) in the fixed and variable cost results when the different methods were applied in requirement 1. Why do the differences occur?

Exercise 3.6 Separating Mixed Costs By Using Different Alternative Methods

The cost analyst of Mega Manufacturing is engaged in analyzing the power and light costs to determine the fixed element and the variable rate. Several activity bases have been tested. The analyst is about to test the power and light costs using direct-labor hours as the activity base. The following data have been assembled for the past six months:

Month	Power and Light Costs	Direct-Labor Hours
August	$3,096	594
September	2,810	482
October	3,334	700
November	3,068	560
December	3,270	570
January	3,400	710

Required

1. Determine the dollar amount of fixed power and light costs and the variable rate per direct-labor hour using the following methods:
   a. High-low
   b. Least squares
2. Determine your estimate of power and light costs expected at the 600 direct-labor hour level of activity using the results you obtained in requirement 1a.
3. Identify two or three possible alternative activity bases that could be used instead of direct-labor hours and briefly describe the desirable and undesirable aspects of using each as a base for cost estimation.

Exercise 3.7 Cost Behavior Identification

The following cost items are found in the cost ledger of the HLC Company:

1. Factory heat, light, and power
2. Rent on factory raw materials warehouse
3. Repairs to factory equipment
4. FICA taxes on direct-labor payroll
5. Factory supervisor
6. Custodial supplies
7. Direct labor
8. Indirect material
9. Depreciation on factory equipment
10. Fire and comprehensive insurance on the factory production facility

Required

Classify each of the items above according to cost behavior (fixed, variable, or semivariable). Briefly explain the reasons for your classifications.

Exercise 3.8 Cost Relationships to Objects

Refer to the list of cost items in exercise 3.7 for the HLC Company.

Required

Classify each item in the list of costs as being either direct or indirect with respect to units of product being produced.

Exercise 3.9 Cost Identification

The Smallco Industries Company started business about five years ago. Recently the company made a significant shift in product emphasis. A new product has been designed that requires the following costs: direct materials $25 per unit; direct labor $35 per unit; production supervision $1,500 per month; rental on warehouse for raw materials and finished-goods inventory storage $1,000 per month; product advertising $1,200 per month; sales commission $8 per unit sold; monthly depreciation on new factory equipment for production of new product $400.

Required

Make a comprehensive classification of the cost items referred to for the new product of the Smallco Industries Company. Determine whether each item is variable, semivariable, or fixed in behavior pattern; whether it is a product (inventoriable) cost or a period cost; whether the product costs are direct or indirect to the new product; and whether the period costs are marketing or administrative costs.

Exercise 3.10   Product versus Period Cost Classification

A basic classification of costs is product versus period costs. Product costs are known as inventoriable costs and period costs are expenses (i.e., are matched against revenue in the period of incurrence). The Malcoa Company shows the following items among a lengthy list of costs involved with the company's month-by-month operations.

1. Depreciation on the computerized telephone call transfer system
2. Factory heat, light, and power
3. Advertising expenditures
4. Boxes used to package the finished product
5. Lubricating materials for factory machines
6. Depreciation of salespersons' automobiles
7. Payroll of machine operators
8. Payroll of finished-goods warehouse employees
9. Depreciation of the president's jet aircraft
10. Costs incurred for reserving conference rooms at a resort hotel for the annual executives' conference

Required

1. Identify each cost item listed as a product (inventoriable) or period cost.
2. Explain the reasons for your classifications in requirement 1.
3. Explain the reasons why a company would be concerned with product versus period cost classifications.

Problems

Problem 3.1   Cost Estimates from Cost Behavior Equations

The Company's cost department has kept weekly records of production volume in units, electric power used, and direct-labor hours. For the past three months production experience has ranged between 500 and 2,000 units per week. The production for the current period is 1,200 units per week. The following estimation equations have been determined:

For electric power:

$y = 1,000 + .4x$
where y = electric power costs
x = number of units produced

For direct labor:

$y = 100 + 1.2x$
where y = direct-labor hours
x = number of units produced

Required

1. Estimate the electric power costs and direct-labor hours required for the next period in which the number of units produced is expected to run 200 units per week greater than the past weekly period.
2. What assumptions were implicit in your analysis in requirement 1?
3. How reliable are the relationships that exist between the variables used in the equations determined by the cost department? What factors might cause the equations to be unreliable in predicting electric power costs and direct labor costs?

Problem 3.2   Cost Behavior Determination

The Alma Plant manufactures the industrial product line of CJS Industries. Plant management wants to be able to get a good, yet quick, estimate of the manufacturing overhead costs that can be expected each month. The easiest and simplest method to accomplish this task seems to be to develop a cost formula for manufacturing overhead.

The plant's accounting staff suggested that simple linear regression be used to determine the cost behavior pattern of the overhead costs. The regression data can provide the basis for the cost formula. Sufficient evidence is available to conclude that manufacturing overhead costs vary with direct-labor hours. The actual direct-labor hours and the corresponding manufacturing overhead costs for each month of the last three years were used in the linear regression analysis.

The three-year period contained various occurrences not uncommon to many businesses. During the first year, production was severely curtailed for two months due to wildcat strikes. In the second year, production was reduced in one month because of material shortages and then increased (overtime scheduled) during two months to meet the units required for a one-time sale order. At the end of the second year, employee benefits were raised significantly as the result of a labor agreement. Production during the third year was not affected by any special circumstances.

Various members of Alma's accounting staff raised some issues regarding the historical data collected for the regression analysis. These issues were as follows:

1. Some members of the accounting staff believed that the use of data from all 36 months would provide a more accurate portrayal of the cost behavior. While they recognized that any of the monthly data could include efficiencies and inefficiencies, they believed these efficiencies and inefficiencies would tend to balance out over a longer period of time.
2. Other members of the accounting staff suggested that only those months that were considered normal should be used so the regression would not be distorted.
3. Other members felt that only the past 12 months should be used because they were the most current.
4. Some members questioned whether historical data should be used to form the basis for a budget formula.

The accounting department ran two regression analyses of the data—one used the data from all 36 months and the other used only the data from the past 12 months. The information derived from the two linear regressions is shown below.

Least-Squares Regression Analyses

	Data from All 36 Months	Data from Most Recent 12 Months
Coefficients of the regression equation:		
Constant	$123,810	$109,020
Coefficient of independent variable (dollars per direct labor hour)	$ 1.6003	$ 4.1977

Required

1. From the results of Alma Plant's regression analysis, which used the data from all 36 months, do the following:
   a. Formulate the cost equation that can be employed to estimate monthly manufacturing overhead costs.
   b. Calculate the estimate of overhead costs for a month when 25,000 direct-labor hours are worked.

2. Using *only* the results of the two regression analyses, explain which of the two results (12-months versus 36-months) you would use as a basis for the budget formula.
3. How would the four specific issues raised by Alma's accounting staff influence your willingness to use the results of the statistical analyses as the basis for the cost formula? Explain your answer.

Problem 3.3   Cost Behavior Concepts—Least-Squares and High-Low Methods (CMA)

Armer Company is accumulating data to be used in preparing its annual profit plan for the coming year. The cost behavior pattern of the maintenance costs must be determined. The accounting staff has suggested that linear regression and the high-low method of analysis be employed to test cost behavior and to derive an equation in the form of $y = a + bx$ for maintenance costs. Data regarding the maintenance hours and costs for last year are as follows:

	Hours of Activity	Maintenance Costs
January	480	$4,200
February	320	3,000
March	400	3,600
April	300	2,820
May	500	4,350
June	310	2,960
July	320	3,030
August	520	4,470
September	490	4,260
October	470	4,050
November	350	3,300
December	340	3,160

Required

Answer the following questions:

1. In the standard regression equation of $y = a + bx$, the letter b is best described as the
   a. independent variable.
   b. dependent variable.
   c. constant coefficient.
   d. variable coefficient.
   e. coefficient of determination.
2. The letter y in the standard regression equation is best described as the
   a. independent variable.
   b. dependent variable.
   c. constant coefficient.
   d. variable coefficient.
   e. coefficient of determination.
3. The letter x in the standard regression equation is best described as the
   a. independent variable.
   b. dependent variable.
   c. constant coefficient.
   d. variable coefficient.
   e. coefficient of determination.

4. If Armer Company uses the high-low method of analysis, the equation for the relationship between hours of activity and maintenance cost would be
   a. $y = 400 + 9.0x$.
   b. $y = 570 + 7.5x$.
   c. $y = 3,600 + 400x$.
   d. $y = 570 + 9.0x$.
   e. some equation other than those given above.
5. Based on the data derived for question 4, if 420 maintenance hours were budgeted for a given month, the budgeted maintenance cost would be
   a. $4,180.
   b. $7,380.
   c. $4,350.
   d. $3,720.
   e. some amount other than those given above.

Problem 3.4   Least-Squares Analysis

Refer to the data in problem 3.3.

Required

1. Determine the a and b values for the $y = a + bx$ equation by the least-squares method.
2. If 420 maintenance hours were budgeted for a given month, how much should be budgeted for maintenance cost using your answers in requirement 1?

Problem 3.5   Cost Behavior and Cost Formulas—High-Low Method

Davis Company shows total overhead costs and direct-labor hours for a four-month period as follows:

Month	Labor Hours	Total Overhead Costs
July	100,000	$348,000
August	80,000	300,400
September	120,000	395,600
October	140,000	443,200

Suppose that for simplification purposes there are only three items of overhead. These three items have been analyzed for August at the 80,000 direct-labor hour level of volume and the following behavior and amounts have been identified:

Supplies (variable)	$104,000
Depreciation (fixed)	80,000
Equipment repairs (semivariable)	116,400

Required

1. Assume that the cost behavior relationships for the total overhead remain the same in October as in August. Determine the dollar amount of supplies, depreciation, and equipment repairs in the $443,200 of total overhead in October.
2. Determine the variable and fixed portions of equipment repair costs.
3. Express the Davis Company's *total* overhead cost in formula form, $y = a + bx$.
4. Determine the estimate of total overhead costs at the 95,000 direct-labor hour level.

Problem 3.6   Cost Behavior and Cost Statements

The Cove Corporation shows the following selected account balances for the year ending December 31:

Beginning materials inventory (Jan. 1)	$ 50,000
Ending materials inventory (Dec. 31)	60,000
Direct materials used	266,000
Indirect materials used	24,000
Indirect labor	130,000
Property taxes on factory	46,000
Depreciation on factory equipment	72,000
Rent on factory building	120,000
Factory utilities	17,200
Insurance on factory facilities	10,400
Beginning work in process (Jan. 1)	69,000
Beginning finished goods (Jan. 1)	230,600

The total direct-labor portion of the payroll for the year was lost in the computer and needs to be reconstructed. The ending inventories (Dec. 31) of work in process and finished goods need to be computed. Before the direct-labor cost total was lost, some processing totals had been determined that showed the following:

Total manufacturing costs	$ 937,600
Cost of goods available for sale	1,144,800
Cost of goods sold for the year	932,400

Required

1. Set up a detailed schedule of the cost of goods manufactured and extend the schedule to show the cost of goods sold. (Refer back to chapter 2 as needed.) Be sure you find the missing direct-labor cost.
2. Prepare a list classifying each item included in the total manufacturing cost as either variable or fixed. Note: Ignore the semivariable classification and select the cost behavior classification that best reflects the cost item.
3. Assume that during the past year there was no work in process at either the beginning or end of the year and that 40,000 units were produced during the year. Determine the unit costs of materials, labor, and factory overhead applicable for the year.
4. The marketing department has just released an analysis of expected market response for next year. They estimate Cove Corporation unit sales next year of 64,000 units. The production manager has requested that you provide him with an estimate of unit costs for materials, labor, and factory overhead for next year.
5. Explain to the production and marketing managers and Cove Corporation's president the reason(s) for any differences between unit costs in requirements 3 and 4 above.

Problem 3.7   Cost Behavior—Comparison of Various Methods

Community Hospital reports the following operating costs and nursing hours in the emergency room over a five-month period:

Month	Nursing Hours	Operating Costs
March	1,500	$27,000
April	1,700	29,000
May	1,000	25,500
June	1,200	25,000
July	800	23,500

Required

1. Determine the variable operating costs per nursing hour and the fixed operating costs per month using the high-low method.
2. Determine the variable and fixed portions of cost using the least-squares method.
3. Estimate operating costs for 1,300 nursing hours using each of the results you obtained in requirements 1 and 2 above. Comment on your results.

Problem 3.8   Cost Behavior—Alternative Volume Bases and Least-Squares Analysis

The Graybar Concrete Pipe Company is in the process of analyzing cost behavior for planning and decision-making purposes. A significant issue is deciding on the "best" base to use as the volume variable. The cost department suggests direct-labor hours. The production superintendent doesn't think direct-labor hours relates very well to overhead costs because the company produces several different sizes of pipe. Production suggests using tons of pipe produced as a base. The controller suggests that repairs and maintenance, which has been identified as a mixed cost, should be analyzed alternatively using tons and direct-labor hours with the least squares method.

The following information has been gathered for each quarter of the most recent two years:

	Tons of Pipe Produced	Direct-Labor Hours	Repairs and Maintenance Costs
Last year:			
First quarter	36,000	20,000	$200,000
Second quarter	50,000	18,000	210,000
Third quarter	60,000	16,000	170,000
Fourth quarter	56,000	22,000	240,000
Two years ago:			
First quarter	30,000	10,000	100,000
Second quarter	22,000	6,000	90,000
Third quarter	42,000	8,000	120,000
Fourth quarter	24,000	12,000	150,000

Required

1. Determine the variable rate and the fixed amount of repairs and maintenance costs using the least-squares method and direct-labor hours as the volume variable. Express your results in formula form, $y = a + bx$.
2. Repeat requirement 1 using tons of pipe produced as the volume base.

Problem 3.9   Identification of Cost Behavior Patterns (CPA)

Some cost behavior patterns that might be found in a company's cost picture are shown in the graphs below. On each graph the vertical axis represents dollar cost and the horizontal axis represents level of activity (e.g., number of labor hours, number of units, etc.).

Required

For each of the following situations, identify the graph that best depicts the cost behavior pattern described. A particular graph may be applicable to more than one situation.

1. Cost of materials, where the cost decreases 5 cents per unit for each of the first 200 units purchased, after which the unit cost remains constant at $2 per unit.
2. Bill for power costs where there is a flat fixed charge plus a variable cost after a certain number of kilowatt hours are used.
3. Municipal water and sewer bill, computed as follows:

First 100,000 gallons or less	$100 flat charge
Next 1,000 gallons	.003 per gallon
Next 1,000 gallons	.006 per gallon
etc.	

4. Depreciation of equipment; the straight line method is used. When the depreciation rate was established, the firm expected the obsolescence factor would be greater than the wear and tear factor.

5. Rent on a factory facility donated by the city. The agreement calls for a fixed rental payment unless 100,000 or more labor hours are worked, in which case no rental will be paid.
6. Salaries of technicians where the following situations apply:

0 to 1,000 machine hours	one technician
1,001 to 2,000 machine hours	two technicians
etc.	

7. Cost of direct labor.
8. Rent on a building donated by the state in order to entice the firm to do business in the state. The agreement calls for a rental payment of $100,000, reduced by $1 for each direct-labor hour worked in excess of 200,000 hours, but a $20,000 minimum rental must be paid.
9. Lease payments on a machine. The lease agreement calls for a minimum payment of $1,000 up to 400 hours of machine time. An additional charge of $2 per hour is paid after 400 hours of machine time is used, up to a maximum charge of $2,000 per period.

Problem 3.10   Cost Behavior Concepts—Summary of Chapters 2 and 3

Lundy Industries produces and sells chips used in microcomputers. The company purchases basic materials to specification from other suppliers, does a minimum of adaptation, and sells finished chips to computer component distributors. Information regarding Lundy's operations for the month of September is as follows:

1. 20,000 chips were produced at a cost of $1 each for basic materials and $.75 each for out-of-pocket processing costs. Production capacity costs (i.e., depreciation, factory building and equipment, etc.) for September were $10,000. There were no beginning and ending work in process inventories.
2. 1,000 finished chips were on hand on September 1, carried at a cost of $2,250. 1,200 chips were on hand on September 30.
3. Lundy has $2,200 of selling costs each month (for advertising, utilities, depreciation on selling equipment, etc.). Lundy also pays transportation on shipments to distributors, which averages $.30 per chip, and a sales commission of 5% on a fixed sales price of $5 per chip.
4. Lundy's officers' salaries are $2,500 per month, and monthly office staff salaries are $1,000. Other administrative-type activities (i.e., mailing, communication, etc.) average $.20 per chip sold.

Required

1. Determine the variable and fixed costs of production, marketing, and administration. Indicate in each category the totals for the month of September as well as the total variable and total fixed cost portions of the respective overall totals.
2. Prepare an income statement for the month of September with appropriate sections showing the cost of goods manufactured, cost of goods sold, and operating expenses.

CONTRIBUTION REPORTING: A FORMAT FOR COST ANALYSIS AND ALTERNATIVE COST GROUPINGS

4

OUTLINE

The basic objective of cost accounting is to accumulate manufacturing costs and to organize them in a meaningful way for use by management in the operation of the business and for external reporting in traditional financial statements. Chapter 2 identified several ways of classifying costs and illustrated the process by which costs are combined and prepared for external reporting. Chapter 3 focused on two cost objectives—generally accepted accounting treatment and cost behavior. Product costs were used to illustrate the various cost patterns and the methods used to analyze and quantify them.

This chapter focuses on some of the internal uses of cost accounting data. This chapter shows how cost information can be organized, classified, and reported to management in a format that is meaningful for many management decisions. This format is called "contribution reporting" and is based on the cost behavior and cost function classifications described in previous chapters.

After completing this chapter you should be able to:

1. classify costs by both behavior and function.
2. describe the contribution reporting format and arrange costs within that format.
3. compute contribution margin.
4. prepare an income statement in a contribution reporting format.
5. identify relevant costs and make good decisions in situations that require alternative cost groupings.

RELEVANT COST OBJECTIVES AND TERMINOLOGY FOR CONTRIBUTION REPORTING

Cost information that is assembled in the accounts and reported on the traditional cost-of-goods-manufactured statement for external users will generally be inadequate for internal uses. This is particularly so in large and complex manufacturing firms. The format of the external reports is not convenient to enable management to plan, control, and evaluate operations and to make good decisions. The following section introduces a conceptual framework for capturing and recording cost data that can be used in a variety of reports. Cost data is stored in a company's data base and extracted as needed for management reports.

Data Bank Concept

A data bank is a useful concept to bridge the gap from the traditional product-related format to other formats that may be more useful for internal uses. The **data bank** or data base contains all the information that relates to a particular organization. Try to picture a large collection device, like a memory bank in a computer, into which all cost data flow. The data is coded according to several different classifications such as management function, accounting treatment, traceability, and cost behavior. The data bank concept is illustrated in figure 4.1.

The data bank provides the capability of extracting data according to any cost objectives and assembling it into whatever format is most useful to management. One possible format is an income statement with supporting schedules of cost of goods manufactured and cost of goods sold. Another possible format is a contribution report.

There are a variety of reports that can be developed from the data base. This chapter describes the contribution report and illustrates its usefulness to management.

Relevant Cost Objectives

Chapter 2 provided a rather comprehensive review of cost objectives. There are three primary cost classifications that are used in developing a **contribution report**—management function, cost behavior, and decision significance. Each of these cost objectives will be briefly reviewed.

Figure 4.1   The data bank concept

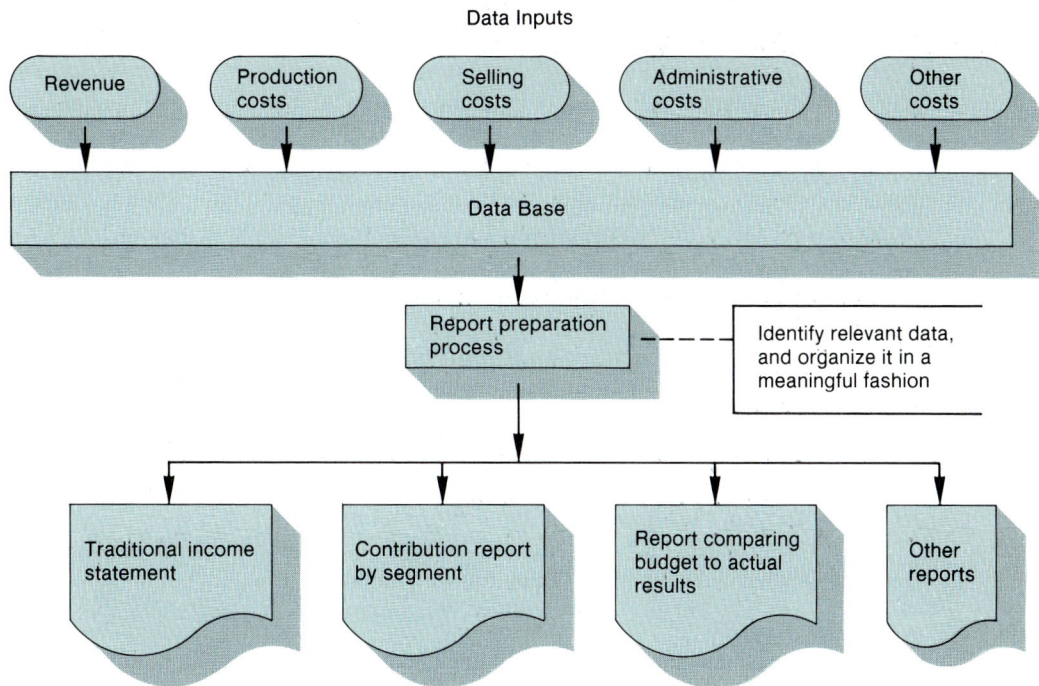

Data Inputs

| Revenue | Production costs | Selling costs | Administrative costs | Other costs |

Data Base

Report preparation process -------- Identify relevant data, and organize it in a meaningful fashion

| Traditional income statement | Contribution report by segment | Report comparing budget to actual results | Other reports |

Management Function   Management function identifies the functional area of the organization responsible for the activity that incurred the cost. The major functional areas for a manufacturing organization are manufacturing, marketing, and general administration. In preparing contribution reports we will combine marketing and general administrative costs into one category called "selling and administrative expenses" or some similar title.

Cost Behavior   Cost behavior describes the way a cost changes as volume changes. The most common cost patterns are fixed, variable, and semivariable. A fixed cost remains constant in total regardless of the level of production. Total variable costs vary proportionately with changes in production. Semivariable costs have both a fixed and variable element. The fixed portion is the amount incurred at a zero production level. The variable portion is the increase that results as production increases. In preparing a contribution report we will split the semivariable cost into its fixed and variable components and combine them with other fixed and variable costs, respectively. As such only fixed and variable costs will be included on the report.

Decision Significance   Decision significance refers to the relevance of a cost in making a particular decision. Relevance is a key concept when drawing costs from the data bank for a special report. Important questions in determining relevance are—which costs are relevant to, make a difference in, or are likely to be influenced by the situation?

For management decision making **relevant costs** are generally those future costs that differ among the alternatives. The typical situation with which managers must deal involves comparing the current situation with one or more alternatives. Only certain costs change when embarking on one of the alternative courses of action. The costs that change are those that will make a difference and are, therefore, relevant costs.

In selecting costs for external reports relevant costs are specified by generally accepted accounting principles (GAAP). Standard setting bodies have tried to anticipate the decisions of external users and have identified the information that is relevant to those decisions. These information requirements are contained in GAAP.

The primary responsibility for identifying relevant costs for internal decisions that require special cost groupings is left to the cost accountant and the decision maker. They are free to draw information from the data base as well as from external sources, such as general economics, statistics, and marketing analysis. The first thing that must be done in selecting relevant costs is to clearly identify the decision for which the cost data will be used. Two questions can then be asked in identifying relevant costs information—(*a*) is the information representative of a *future* expected cost and (*b*) is the cost information *different* from cost information that will exist regardless of the alternative chosen. A positive answer to both questions indicates a relevant cost.

Cost Groupings for Contribution Reporting

In contribution reporting the costs are grouped *first* by *cost behavior* and *then* by *management function*. A relevant cost is analyzed to see if it is a fixed or a variable cost. Within the classification it is then analyzed and grouped according to management function. Costs in each of these categories may be divided into product lines or operating units of a company, but that depends on the decision at hand.

The following variable and fixed categories with the related product and nonproduct subdivisions are used in contribution reporting.

I. Variable costs
   A. Manufacturing costs (product costs)
      1. Direct materials
      2. Direct labor
      3. Variable factory overhead
   B. Other costs (nonproduct costs)
      1. Selling
      2. Administration
II. Fixed costs
   A. Manufacturing costs (product costs)
      1. Fixed factory overhead
   B. Other costs (nonproduct costs)
      1. Selling
      2. Administration

THE CONTRIBUTION MARGIN CONCEPT

Contribution margin is a concept that has been developed for internal reporting to management. The same basic cost and revenue data that are reported externally are used in preparing contribution reports. The cost data are merely grouped differently to compute an intermediate number called contribution margin rather than the traditional gross margin.

Definition of Contribution Margin

Contribution margin is defined as *revenue less variable costs*. Fixed costs are subtracted from the contribution margin to equal the net income. These relationships are illustrated in figure 4.2.

Contribution reporting emphasizes variable and fixed costs. The contribution margin represents the amount available after sales revenue has covered all variable costs. Variable costs here include both product as well as nonproduct costs. The contribution

---

Figure 4.2   Income statement using contribution report format

		%
Sales	$100,000	100
Less: Variable costs	60,000	60
Contribution margin	$ 40,000	40
Less: Fixed costs	25,000	25
Net income	$ 15,000	15

---

margin is the amount available to cover fixed costs, both product and nonproduct, and provide net income.

Contribution reporting focuses on short-run profitability. Revenues and variable costs can generally be influenced by decisions of management within a relatively short time period, such as an operating cycle of the business. Fixed costs generally cannot be changed in a short time period. Therefore, the contribution margin is the number that is most sensitive to management's decisions and can help them plan operations and evaluate results.

Contribution Margin Ratio

The contribution margin ratio is a ratio of the contribution margin to the sales revenue. It can be computed on the contribution margin of the company as a whole, individual divisions or segments of the company, or even on individual products. The formula to compute the contribution margin ratio for an entire company is:

$$\text{Company contribution margin ratio} = \frac{\text{Contribution margin}}{\text{Sales revenue}}$$

When the contribution margin ratio is computed for a single product, the contribution margin (sale price less variable costs) is divided by the sale price of the product.

$$\text{Product contribution margin ratio} = \frac{\text{Sale price—Variable costs}}{\text{Sales price}}$$

In figure 4.2 the contribution margin ratio of the company is shown as 40%. This figure also shows that 60% of the sales revenue goes to cover variable costs and 40% is available to cover fixed costs and provide net income.

Contribution Margin versus Gross Margin

The primary difference between contribution margin and gross margin is the cost objectives used in computing each intermediate result. Remember that revenues less expenses equals net income in both statements. However, for internal contribution reports, the contribution margin is based on a cost behavior classification system. Revenues less variable costs equals the contribution margin, less fixed costs equals the net income. The cost objective here is cost behavior (fixed/variable).

For external income statements an intermediate result called the gross margin is computed. The gross margin is based on the accounting treatment classification by which total product costs, both fixed and variable, are subtracted from sales to give the gross margin. Period costs are then subtracted from the gross margin for the net income. The cost objective here is accounting treatment (product/period).

An Example of Contribution Reporting

The following example will illustrate the data bank concept and show how alternative reports can be developed from the same basic set of data. Cost and revenue data for Hartshorn Incorporated are summarized below as it might be contained in the data base. A traditional income statement will be developed using the product/period cost classification. The contribution report will then be developed using the variable/fixed cost classification.

Hartshorn Incorporated manufactures and sells one style of briefcase. The following production, selling, and administrative data are for the year ending December 31, 19X1:

1. Production for the year was 100,000 briefcases at a cost of:

		Total	Per Unit
Direct material		$ 545,000	$ 5.45
Direct labor		925,000	9.25
Factory overhead:			
Variable	$472,000		4.72
Fixed	318,000		3.18
Total factory overhead		790,000	
Total manufacturing cost		$2,260,000	$22.60

There was no beginning or ending inventory of work in process.

2. Sales for the year totaled 100,000 units at $50 each. There were no beginning or ending finished-goods inventories.
3. Selling expenses were $1,200,000, of which $650,000 were fixed and $550,000 were variable.
4. Administrative expenses totaled $750,000, of which $270,000 were fixed and $480,000 were variable.

Figure 4.3 illustrates the traditional income statement based on the product/period cost classification. Cost of goods sold, which represents product costs, is subtracted from sales for gross margin. This is the amount available to cover period costs and provide a net income.

Figure 4.4 illustrates the contribution report that is based on a variable/fixed cost classification. Variable costs are subtracted from the sales revenue for the contribution margin. This is the amount available to cover fixed costs and provide a net income. Notice that sales and net income are the same on both statements.

Remember that the contribution margin format focuses on the units sold. What was included as part of cost of goods sold under the traditional format is split between variable and fixed costs on the contribution report. This can be illustrated as follows:

Traditional format:		
Cost of goods sold		$2,260,000
Contribution margin format:		
Direct materials	$545,000	
Direct labor	925,000	
Variable factory overhead	472,000	
Fixed factory overhead	318,000	
Total		$2,260,000

Notice also that by totaling the variable and fixed selling expenses on the contribution report you have the same total operating expenses included on the traditional income statement.

This example assumes no beginning or ending inventories of finished goods. Having inventory requires a cost flow assumption and a selection of direct or absorption costing which is covered in detail in Chapter 18.

Figure 4.3

Hartshorn Incorporated
Income Statement—Traditional Format
Year Ending December 31, 19X1

Sales revenue (100,000 units @ $50)		$5,000,000
Less: Cost of goods sold (product costs)		
Beginning finished-goods inventory	$ –0–	
Plus: Cost of goods manufactured	2,260,000	
Goods available for sale	$2,260,000	
Less: Ending finished-goods inventory	–0–	
Total cost of goods sold		2,260,000
Gross margin		$2,740,000
Less: Operating expenses (period costs)		
Selling expenses	$1,200,000	
Administrative expenses	750,000	
Total		$1,950,000
Net income		$ 790,000

Figure 4.4

Hartshorn Incorporated
Income Statement—Contribution Format
Year Ending December 31, 19X1

Sales revenue (100,000 units @ $50)		$5,000,000
Less: Variable costs		
Direct material (100,000 units @ $5.45	$545,000	
Direct labor (100,000 units @ $9.25)	925,000	
Factory overhead (100,000 units @ $4.72)	472,000	
Selling	550,000	
Administrative	480,000	
Total variable costs		2,972,000
Contribution margin		2,028,000
Less: Fixed costs		
Factory overhead (100,000 units @ $3.18)	318,000	
Selling	650,000	
Administrative	270,000	
Total fixed costs		1,238,000
Net income		$ 790,000

      In summary, the same basic data used in preparing a contribution report are used in a traditional income statement. The costs are just grouped differently. Gross margin as presented on the income statement represents the amount of mark-up the company has on the product. The contribution margin represents the results that are most sensitive to management decisions in the short-run.

To illustrate the usefulness of the contribution format, let's assume management is contemplating two changes in the manufacturing process and wants to know the impact of the decisions on the results of operations. The first change is a substitution of cheaper materials that will reduce direct-material cost by $.10 per unit. The second change is to a piece rate incentive system for direct labor associated with the assembly of the brief-cases, which would specify $9.20 per unit. Before reading on, study figures 4.3 and 4.4. See which statement enables you to compute the change in net income as a result of these decisions.

It is easier to see the impact of these decisions on the contribution report than on the traditional income statement. The cost of direct materials will be reduced by $9,000 (90,000 units @ $.10) and direct labor by $4,500 [90,000 units @ ($9.25 − 9.20)]. The combined result increases the contribution margin by $13,500. Since fixed costs remain unchanged, the net income will also increase by $13,500.

OTHER CONTRIBUTION REPORTS

The format of the contribution report facilitates reporting by different segments of business operations, such as product line, territory, or division. This type of analysis is useful in planning, performance evaluations, and decision making.

Total Company Report

Figure 4.5 contains an income statement using a contribution format. It will be used to illustrate reporting by divisional segments and by product lines. To simplify the report, some of the costs have been combined. Direct material, direct labor, and variable factory overhead are combined into one category called variable product costs. Also, fixed costs include fixed factory overhead and fixed selling and administrative expenses.

Segment Reports

Classifying costs by behavior facilitates the analysis, separation, and break-down of costs by segment. A **segment** is a separable part or activity of a company about which cost data may be prepared for analysis. The objective is to identify the results of operations that are directly related to a particular division, product, or area of responsibility. This is important in making decisions concerning a division or product, such as how effective was the division manager in controlling operations or how much does a product contribute to company profitability?

Figure 4.5

Walter Manufacturing Company
Total Company Income Statement Using a Contribution Format
Year Ending December 31, 19X2

Sales		$270,000
Less: Variable costs		
Manufacturing costs	$120,000	
Selling and administrative	30,000	
Total variable		150,000
Contribution margin		120,000
Less: Fixed costs		93,000
Net income		$ 27,000

Figure 4.6

Walter Manufacturing Company
Contribution Report by Division
Year Ending December 31, 19X2

	Total Company	Segment	
		Division #1	Division #2
Sales	$270,000	$150,000	$120,000
Less: Variable costs			
Manufacturing costs	120,000	81,000	39,000
Selling and administration	30,000	21,000	9,000
Total variable costs	$150,000	$102,000	$ 48,000
Contribution margin	120,000	48,000	72,000
Less: Direct fixed costs	45,000	24,000	21,000
Divisional segment margin	75,000	$ 24,000	$ 51,000
Less: Common fixed costs	48,000		
Net income	$ 27,000		

One application of contribution reporting is to separate the total company information into divisions. Figure 4.6 contains a breakdown by division for the Walter Manufacturing Company.

Notice in the segmented report that the fixed costs are divided into (*a*) **direct fixed costs,** which are those that can be identified specifically with each division, and (*b*) **common fixed costs,** which are those that are common to both divisions. In the example, total fixed costs are $93,000. Of this amount, $45,000 can be identified to a division and $48,000 is common. Perhaps Division #1 and Division #2 each have their own manufacturing facility and marketing staff so we can identify $24,000 and $21,000, respectively, as fixed factory overhead and fixed selling expenses. Suppose also that the company headquarters has an administrative staff that includes the president's salary and similar costs that benefit the entire company but cannot be identified to any division. The $48,000 of common fixed costs consists of these kinds of expenditures.

The common fixed costs are not allocated to the segments because any allocation procedure would be arbitrary and the division manager has no control over them. The contribution margin less direct fixed costs equals the divisional **segment margin.** This represents the contribution of the division to cover common fixed costs and provide a net income for the company as a whole. Notice that no attempt is made to compute a bottom-line net income for individual segments. This is computed only for the firm as a whole.

The division reports can be broken down further into separate products as illustrated in figure 4.7 for Division #2. Notice that the titles and structure of the report are very similar to the division segment report except for the bottom portion. The result obtained when subtracting direct fixed costs from the contribution margin is called the product-line segment margin. Again, no attempt is made to allocate common fixed costs of Division #2 that cannot be traced to a particular product. The bottom-line number is the divisional segment margin. This contains the results of the activities that the division manager controls and is responsible for.

Figure 4.7

Walter Manufacturing Company
Contribution Report by Product for Division #2
Year Ending December 31, 19X2

| | Division #2 | Segment | |
		Deluxe Model	Regular Model
Sales	$120,000	$ 45,000	$ 75,000
Less: Variable costs			
Manufacturing costs	39,000	15,000	24,000
Selling and administration	9,000	6,000	3,000
Total variable costs	$ 48,000	$ 21,000	$ 27,000
Contribution margin	72,000	24,000	48,000
Less: Direct fixed costs	9,000	3,000	6,000
Product-line segment margin	63,000	$ 21,000	$ 42,000
Less: Common fixed costs	12,000		
Divisional segment margin	$ 51,000		

SELECTED APPLICATIONS OF CONTRIBUTION REPORTING

Contribution reports help management to plan, operate, and control the business in a variety of ways. From all the possible special analyses and applications, we have selected three to be illustrated here: (a) planning and comparing actual results against the plan, (b) evaluating the option of dropping a product line, and (c) analyzing a special pricing decision. Other applications of contribution reporting will be discussed throughout the text.

Planning and Comparing Actual Results Against the Plan

The planning process involves setting objectives and forecasting expected revenues and costs. The process is usually finalized in financial terms and appears in the form of a budget. The budgeting of revenues and costs occurs for each product, each department, and each division of the company. An overall summary is usually prepared for the total company in the form of a forecasted income statement, balance sheet, and statement of changes in financial position.

The arrangement of revenues and expenses in the contribution format facilitates the budgeting process. By categorizing costs by behavior, the contribution approach places costs in sharper perspective for evaluating the possible effect of anticipated programs and decision alternatives. Figure 4.8 shows a budgeted income statement in a contribution format.

The contribution format expedites and helps to put into proper perspective the comparative report at the end of the period. Figure 4.9 shows a year-end comparative income statement with the actual results compared with the budget. Pay particular attention to the column of variances. The variance represents the difference between budget and actual. The variance is unfavorable when actual sales or income are less than budget or actual expenses are greater than budget. Notice that the net income is "off target" by $4,500. Actual sales were $3,000 less than budgeted sales and, therefore, is labeled as an unfavorable variance. Every category of expenses except for "other variable expenses" also shows unfavorable variances. This type of comparative report highlights the differences between budgeted and actual results that account for the lower than expected net income. This helps management to focus their attention on the problem areas of the business.

Figure 4.8

Amfac Manufacturing
Budgeted Income Statement
Calendar Year 19X4

	Budget
Sales	$100,000
Less: Variable expenses	
Variable cost of sales	$ 45,000
Other variable expenses	15,000
Total variable expenses	$ 60,000
Contribution margin	$ 40,000
Less: Fixed expenses	
Manufacturing	$ 13,000
Selling	13,000
Administrative	4,000
Total fixed expenses	$ 30,000
Net income	$ 10,000

Figure 4.9

Amfac Manufacturing
Contribution Income Statement Comparing Actual with Budget
Year Ending December 31, 19X4

	Budget	Actual	Varience[a]
Sales	$100,000	$97,000	$3,000 U
Less: Variable expenses			
Variable cost of sales	$ 45,000	$46,000	$1,000 U
Other variable expenses	15,000	14,500	500 F
Total variable expenses	$ 60,000	$60,500	$ 500 U
Contribution margin	$ 40,000	$36,500	$3,500 U
Less: Fixed expenses			
Manufacturing	$ 13,000	$13,700	$ 700 U
Selling	13,000	13,000	–0–
Administrative	4,000	4,300	300 U
Total fixed expenses	$ 30,000	$31,000	$1,000 U
Net income	$ 10,000	$ 5,500	$4,500 U

[a]U—Unfavorable variance
F—Favorable variance

Evaluating the Option to Drop a Product Line

Evaluating the option to drop a product line is often confused by the allocation of fixed costs that do not relate directly to the product. The contribution approach helps management to make a correct decision by classifying costs correctly.

Consider the case of the Misguided Company, which produces three products. This rather small company has always reported their results of operations for the total company using the traditional income statement format. However, the president recently

Figure 4.10

Misguided Company
Product-Line Profitability Report
June 19X5

	Total Company	*Product A*	*Product B*	*Product C*
Sales	$25,000	$12,500	$ 7,500	$ 5,000
Less: Cost of goods sold[a]	15,500	7,950	3,750	3,800
Gross margin	$ 9,500	$ 4,550	$ 3,750	$ 1,200
Less: Selling and administrative expense	7,500	2,950	2,550	2,000
Net income	$ 2,000	$ 1,600	$ 1,200	$ (800)

[a]Computed in accordance with generally accepted accounting principles for external financial statements.

requested profit performance information for each product to evaluate their profitability. In response to that request, the report shown in figure 4.10 was prepared by the accountant for the month of June. Notice that it is in the traditional income statement format.

Based on the information contained in the request, the president has questioned whether to discontinue product C. "After all," said the president, "it looks like we are losing about $800 per month by producing that product." What would be your recommendation to the president?

A wise recommendation would be to analyze the costs more closely to see if all the costs assigned to product C would be avoided if its production is discontinued. If all the costs assigned to it could be avoided by discontinuing its production, then discontinuance is a correct decision and profitability will improve by $800 per month. On the other hand, the decision is complicated if some of the costs will continue regardless of the decision to discontinue product C.

A more careful analysis suggests that the report shown in figure 4.10 represents an application of a good tool in an incorrect context. Remember GAAP requires factory overhead to be allocated to each product. Thus, some portion of cost of goods sold for product C includes fixed factory overhead, which may continue even if it is discontinued. Remember also that a major portion of selling and administrative expenses are frequently common costs that cannot be identified with any specific product. Most of the selling and administrative costs allocated to product C may continue even if that product is discontinued. Cost allocation shown in figure 4.10 is proper and necessary for purposes of inventory valuation and conventional income reporting. However, to extend those same procedures into product-line performance analysis represents an improper use of information.

Some arbitrary allocations of both fixed factory overhead and selling and administrative expenses have been made in order to assign all of these costs to individual products. Therefore, the results shown do not give an accurate picture of the contribution being made by each product to cover common fixed costs, which will be incurred regardless of this decision, and to provide net income. A recasting of the statement into a contribution format is shown in figure 4.11.

Notice that no net income figure is computed for individual products because of the presence of common fixed costs. The product-line contribution margin, however, shows the amount by which the firm would be better off or worse off by discontinuing a partic-

Figure 4.11

Misguided Company
Product-Line Profitability Report
June 19X5

	Total Company	Product A	Product B	Product C
		Segments		
Sales	$25,000	$12,500	$ 7,500	$ 5,000
Less: Variable costs	10,500	5,000	2,500	3,000
Contribution margin	$14,500	$ 7,500	$ 5,000	$ 2,000
Less: Direct product-line fixed costs	2,500	1,000	800	700
Product-line margin	$12,000	$ 6,500	$ 4,200	$ 1,300
Less: Common fixed costs	10,000			
Net income	$ 2,000			

ular product. All products are providing a positive contribution margin and unless there are more profitable alternatives, all of them should be continued. Total profits of Misguided Company would be $1,300 lower if product C is discontinued unless the facilities currently devoted to that product could be utilized on another product that will produce a higher product-line contribution margin. This raises the question of alternative uses of facilities, which will be discussed in a later chapter.

Analyzing a Special Pricing Decision

Many firms find themselves with production capacity in excess of their current needs. In this condition it is not unusual for the firm to receive an opportunity to produce additional units of a product, perhaps under a different brand name, for another firm at a reduced price. The decision management must make is whether or not to accept the special offer at the reduced price. As a general rule, *management should accept the offer as long as it provides a positive contribution to company profits and does not interfere with normal sales.* Once again, fixed costs complicate the decision and the contribution format assists in the analysis.

To illustrate, suppose Marshall Manufacturing Company, a United States firm, has the capacity to produce 160,000 electric motors per year. Presently, they are producing and selling only 135,000 motors to regular customers throughout the United States at a price of $40 per motor. They have recently received an offer from a Canadian firm to buy 15,000 motors for $33 each, which they will sell in Canada under their own brand name.

Using GAAP, Marshall Manufacturing Company has determined that selling and administrative expenses are $2 per motor and production costs are $34 per motor. The production cost is based on the following cost per motor at the 135,000 unit level of production.

Materials	$16
Labor	8
Factory overhead	10
Total cost	$34

The manager of Marshall Manufacturing Company wants to reject the offer because, "The company will lose $3 on every motor! On 15,000 motors we will lose $45,000

Figure 4.12

Marshall Manufacturing Company
Contribution Approach to Special Offer Analysis

		Per Motor
Price offered		$33
Less: Variable costs[a]		
Materials	$16	
Labor	8	
Factory overhead	4	
Selling and administrative	2	30
Contribution margin		$ 3 × 15,000 motors = $45,000

[a]These represent the incremental costs that will be incurred if the special order is accepted.

and no one is foolish enough to do that!" The following analysis was being used by the manager:

Price offered		$33
Less costs:		
Production	$34	
Selling and administration	2	
Total		36
Net loss		$(3)

In an attempt to negotiate a more favorable result, the manager suggested a $38 price to the Canadian company. However, the Canadian firm rejected the counter offer and claimed to have a tentative offer from another supplier at a $34 price. Is Marshall Manufacturing Company making a correct decision to reject the $33 price?

More careful analysis of production costs reveal the presence of fixed costs that will not change regardless of this decision. The company has $810,000 of fixed production costs that have been converted to a unit cost by dividing them among the 135,000 units. The $10 factory overhead cost really consists of $6 fixed ($810,000 ÷ 135,000 units) and $4 variable. The fixed costs are irrelevant in this decision, and they confuse the contribution of the special order to company profitability.

The costs can be restructured into a contribution format as illustrated in figure 4.12. The special order will provide a contribution margin of $3 per unit, or a total of $45,000. A $45,000 addition to profits is much different than the $45,000 loss expected by the manager.

Marshall Manufacturing Company may still reject the offer for one or more of a variety of reasons, such as (a) inability to assess the potential impact of accepting the offer on regular customers, (b) alternative uses of the production facility that yield a contribution margin in excess of $45,000, or (c) expected inability of the Canadian firm to pay in a timely fashion. By using the contribution approach, at least management has the correct quantitative information about the offer. The information available under GAAP is often inaccurate and misleading for internal management decisions.

Summary

This chapter focused on some of the internal uses of cost accounting data by showing how cost information needs to be organized, classified, and reported to help management make good decisions.

A contribution report is frequently used for internal reports to management. This report is based primarily on cost behavior and secondarily on management function. Costs must first be categorized as either fixed or variable. Within these categories they can be further subdivided according to management function or, in the case of fixed costs, according to how easily they can be traced to products, departments, or other segments of the business.

Contribution margin is defined as revenue less variable costs. It is the amount that is available to cover fixed costs and generate a profit. The contribution margin ratio is the contribution margin divided by the sales revenue. When preparing segment reports, fixed costs are categorized according to their traceability to the segments. Direct fixed costs are subtracted from the contribution margin to give a segment margin. This represents the contribution of each segment toward covering common fixed costs and providing net income for the company as a whole.

Three examples of management decisions were given to illustrate the application of contribution reporting: (a) planning and comparing actual results against the plan, (b) evaluating the option of dropping a product line, and (c) analyzing a special pricing decision. In each of these cases, the contribution report helped to focus on the relevant costs for the decision.

Self-Study Problem

Pruning Incorporated manufactured and sold 2,500 pruning machines during 19X5 through normal marketing channels. There were no beginning or ending inventories of work in process or finished goods for the year. During the year the following costs were incurred:

Direct materials	$25,000
Direct labor	50,000
Factory overhead	100,000
Selling and administrative costs	60,000

Each pruning machine sold for $100. Analysis of the cost data showed that 50% of the factory overhead and 40% of the selling and administrative costs are fixed.

Required

1. Prepare an income statement using the traditional format.
2. Prepare an income statement using a contribution margin format.
3. Suppose the company is operating at only 60% of capacity and that they have received a special offer from China to buy 1,000 pruning machines at $55 each. The terms of the sale will specify FOB shipping point, and, therefore, Pruning will avoid half of the variable selling and administrative costs. Is this a profitable offer for the company?

Solution to the Self-Study Problem

Requirement 1

Pruning Incorporated
Income Statement—Traditional Format
Year Ending December 31, 19X5

Sales revenue (2,500 units × $100)	$250,000
Less: Cost of goods sold	175,000
Gross margin	75,000
Less: Selling and administrative	60,000
Net income	$ 15,000

Requirement 2

Pruning Incorporated
Income Statement—Contribution Format
Year Ending December 31, 19X5

Sales revenue (2,500 units × $100)		$250,000
Less: Variable costs		
Direct materials	$25,000	
Direct labor	50,000	
Factory overhead (50%)	50,000	
Selling and administrative (60%)	36,000	
Total variable costs		161,000
Contribution margin		$ 89,000
Less: Fixed costs		
Factory overhead (50%)	$50,000	
Selling and administrative (40%)	24,000	
Total fixed costs		74,000
Net income		$ 15,000

Requirement 3

The relevant costs on a unit cost basis are:

Sale price		$55.00
Less: Variable costs		
Direct materials ($25,000 ÷ 2,500 u.)	$10.00	
Direct labor ($50,000 ÷ 2,500 u.)	20.00	
Factory overhead ($50,000 ÷ 2,500 u.)	20.00	
Selling and administrative		
[($36,000 ÷ 2,500 u.) × 50%]	7.20	
Total		57.20
Contribution margin (loss)		($2.20)

This is not a profitable offer for the company. They will lose $2.20 per unit.

Suggested Readings

Goodman, Sam R., and Reece, James S. *Controller's Handbook.* Homewood, Ill.: Dow-Jones Irwin, 1978.

Luoma, Gary A. "Accounting Information in Managerial Decision-Making in Small and Medium Manufacturers." *NAA Research Monograph #3.* New York: National Association of Accountants, 1968.

McCormick, Edmund J. "Sharpening the Competitive Edge for Profits." *Financial Executives* (April 1975):22.

Mullis, Elbert W. "Variable Budgeting for Financial Planning and Control." *Management Accounting* (February 1975):43.

Discussion Questions

1. Explain why the net income is the same on an income statement prepared under the contribution margin format as when prepared under the traditional format.
2. Define contribution margin and explain its computation.
3. What is the contribution margin ratio and how is it computed?
4. Why are common fixed costs not allocated to divisional segments of a company under the contribution reporting format?
5. Describe what is meant by divisional segment margin.
6. What is the benefit of a contribution margin report to managers in managing the business?
7. Is a contribution report based on cost behavior first and management function second, or management function first and cost behavior second? Explain.
8. Identify the general rule that should be used by management in a decision involving the discontinuance of a product line.
9. Identify the general rule that management should follow in a special order decision at a reduced price.
10. On a year-end contribution report comparing actual results with budgeted results when actual sales exceeded budgeted sales, which costs would you expect to have unfavorable variances?
11. What is the benefit of a segmented report by product line?
12. Assuming a positive contribution margin, if sales price and variable costs both increase by the same percentage, will the contribution margin ratio increase, decrease, or remain the same? Explain.
13. Describe the difference between gross margin and contribution margin.
14. Is a contribution report focused more on the short-run or the long-run with respect to management decisions? Explain.
15. Who decides what relevant costs are to be included on internal management reports?

Exercises

Exercise 4.1 Basic Contribution Statement

The Hardy Company has the following data covering the month of August:

Sales (11,000 units)	$160,000	
Inventories of finished		
goods—August 1	3,000[a]	(300 units)
August 31	?[a]	(500 units)
Materials used	62,000	
Direct labor	40,000	
Factory overhead	20,000	(50% fixed costs)
Marketing expenses	12,000	(60% variable)
Administrative expenses	10,000	(30% variable)

[a]Variable production costs only

There were no work-in-process inventories.

Required

Prepare a contribution income statement for the month of August.

Exercise 4.2 Basic Contribution Statement

The following incomplete data relate to the Barkley Corporation for the year:

Direct labor	?
Materials used in production	$193,000
Factory overhead (60% fixed)	160,000
Total variable manufacturing costs incurred this period	482,000
Finished-goods inventory Jan. 1[a]	90,000
Finished-goods inventory Dec. 31[a]	80,000
Sales	800,000
Sales commissions	10% of sales
Other sales expenses (all fixed)	80,000
Administrative expenses (all fixed)	60,000

[a]Variable costs of production only

Required

Prepare in good form a contribution income statement.

Exercise 4.3   Conversion of Information to the Contribution Basis

Raydeleh Incorporated wants to convert its accounts to a contribution basis. Assume that there were no work-in-process inventories at the beginning or end of the year. Assume also that the finished-goods inventories based on variable costs were $56,000 at the beginning of the year and $50,000 at the end of the year.

Additional information indicates that depreciation is determined on a straight-line basis, miscellaneous factory overhead remains relatively constant each period, and all other items of overhead tend to move up and down with changes in production volume. The company does not use predetermined overhead rates.

Required

1. Identify and sort the costs of Raydeleh into variable and fixed categories.
2. Determine the variable costs of goods manufactured and the variable manufacturing cost per unit.
3. Determine the variable cost of goods sold.

Exercise 4.4   Basic Contribution Income Statements

The Lucky Company has capacity to produce 400,000 units each year. The materials, labor, and overhead variable production costs are $24 per unit. Variable selling expenses are $10 per unit. Fixed factory overhead is $1,000,000 per year. Fixed selling expenses are $275,000 per year. All administrative expenses are fixed and amount to $325,000 per year. The firm produces and sells a single product at a current price of $48 per unit.

Required

1. Prepare an income statement on a contribution basis assuming (*a*) there are no inventories at the beginning and end of the year and (*b*) operations are at capacity.
2. Assume that next year operations are expected to drop by 25% from the capacity level because of a worldwide depressed market for the product produced by the Lucky Company. Determine the effect this expected drop-off will have on earnings. Assume cost and price relationships will remain as stated in the original data. Use the contribution approach.

Exercise 4.5 Contribution Income Statements

The Cheery-Hub Company produces novelty wheel covers for the Big Wheel Company. Last year 500,000 units were produced and sold. The following conventional income statement was prepared:

Sales	$1,000,000
Cost of goods sold	500,000
Gross margin	$ 500,000
Operating expenses	300,000
Net operating income	$ 200,000

Additional data:

1. The cost of goods sold includes 30% materials, 40% labor, and the rest is factory overhead. The factory overhead is ⅔ fixed costs.
2. Operating expenses include sales commissions of 5% of sales revenue. The remaining operating expenses tend to be stable in amount from year to year even when volume moves up or down.

Required

Convert the income statement to a contribution statement.

Exercise 4.6 Contribution Reporting and the Effect of Changes in Factors

Refer to the basic data in exercise 4.5. Consider the following possible changes contemplated by the president:

1. A 10% increase in sales price
2. A $25,000 increase in the advertising budget to maintain the same unit sales as last year
3. A 5% wage increase to factory workers based on an incentive to cut average production time by 2%

Required

1. Prepare an estimated income statement for the president of Cheery-Hub Company on a contribution basis for next year. Incorporate the expected changes indicated above.
2. Do you recommend that the president proceed with the contemplated changes? Why?

Exercise 4.7   Contribution Reporting—Product Emphasis

Assume that a division of the CHL Company has sales of two products as follows:

	Product A	Product B
Sales	$40,000	$20,000
Less variable expenses	30,000	10,000
Contribution margin	10,000	10,000
Less direct fixed expenses	2,000	3,000
Product-line margin	$ 8,000	$ 7,000

The CHL Company plans to spend $1,500 on advertising in the division for either product A or product B. If spent on product A, sales will increase by $5,000. If spent on product B, sales will increase by $4,000.

Required

1. On which product line should the company spend the advertising funds? Show your calculations.
2. Assume that the division referred to above has fixed costs of $12,000 that are common to all division operations. This amount has been assigned in the past to the two products on the basis of sales revenue. Do these common fixed costs have any bearing on which product the advertising fund should be spent? Explain.

Exercise 4.8   Contribution Reporting—Product-Line Performance

The Garrity Company experienced a loss for the second quarter as shown by the following income statement.

Sales	$600,000
Less: Cost of goods sold	350,000
Gross margin	$250,000
Less: Operating expenses	$265,000
Net income (loss)	$(15,000)

In order to pinpoint the problem, the manager has asked for an income statement by product line. Accordingly, the accounting department has developed the following cost and revenue data:

	Product X	Product Y	Product Z
Sales	$200,000	$100,000	$300,000
Contribution margin ratio	30%	60%	45%
Direct fixed expenses	$ 65,000	$ 35,000	$ 90,000

Required

1. Prepare an income statement broken down by products, as desired by the manager. Explain to the manager the probable reasons for the net loss.
2. The marketing department feels that sales of product X could be increased by 50% if advertising were increased by $10,000 quarterly. Would you recommend the increased advertising? Show computations.

Exercise 4.9 Limitations of Conventional Costing Methods (AICPA)

One of your clients operates a self-service discount store. Management of the store has consistently encountered difficulty in using traditional accounting data as a basis for decisions such as which departments to operate, which products to promote, and which marketing methods to use.

Required

Identify several overhead costs (or costs not applicable specifically to a particular aspect of operations, such as a department or a product) and explain how the existence of such costs may limit the use of traditional accounting data in making decisions in a discount store.

Exercise 4.10 Contribution Reporting—Product Performance

The Charitable Company's most recent income statement, prepared on a contribution basis, showed the following:

Sales	$120,000
Less: Variable expenses	80,000
Contribution margin	$ 40,000
Less: Fixed expenses	35,000
Net income	$ 5,000

The president isn't happy with operating results of only 4.2% of sales and wants a thorough analysis of what can be done to improve results. As an expert analyst of operating results you have determined the following:

1. The firm has two sales districts—northern and southern. The northern district produces 66% of total sales and incurs 54% of the variable expenses.
2. Of the fixed expenses $20,000 is common to all operations of the company and $6,000 of the remaining $15,000 represents direct advertising and promotional efforts in the southern district with the balance being traceable to the northern sales district.

Required

1. Explain how you might proceed to analyze reasons for the poor operating performance of the company.
2. Prepare a segment report for each sales district tied to the report for the company as a whole.
3. Do the reports prepared in requirement 2 shed any light on where the company's operating problems exist? Explain.

Problem 4.1 Contribution Analysis—Special Offer Decision

The Midland Company is a furniture manufacturer having several product lines. Income data for one of the products for the year just ended follows:

		(in millions)
Sales (400,000 units @ $200 average price)		$80
Variable costs:		
Direct materials @ $70	$28	
Direct labor @ $20	8	
Variable factory overhead @ $10	4	
Sales commissions @ 15% of selling price	12	
Other variable costs @ $10	4	
Total variable costs @ $140		56
Contribution margin		$24
Fixed costs:		
Discretionary @ $30	12	
Committed @ $20	8	
Total fixed costs		$20
Operating income		$ 4

Near year end, the Odessa Company, a customer, offered $160 each for 3,000 units. This offer would be in addition to the 400,000 units already sold (indicated above). The acceptance of this special order by Midland would not affect regular sales. The salesman negotiating the offer indicates that as sales commission, he will accept a flat fee of $12,000 if the order is accepted.

Required

If the offer is accepted, what will be the effect on operating income?

Problem 4.2 Contribution Analysis—Product Emphasis Decisions

Kevin Company manufactures two different products—spades and hoes. The following information is available concerning the products:

	Total Company	Spades	Hoes
Sales	$20,000	$13,000	$7,000
Less: Variable expenses	14,000	9,500	4,500
Contribution margin	$ 6,000	$ 3,500	$2,500
Less: Direct fixed expenses	3,000	1,400	1,600
Product-line segment margin	$ 3,000	$ 2,100	$ 900
Less: Common fixed expenses	1,500		
Net income	$ 1,500		

The vice-president of marketing has just authorized an expenditure of $500 on advertising for *either* the spades or the hoes.

Required

1. Assuming the $500 advertising funds will increase dollar sales of either product by an equal amount, toward which product should the funds be applied? Explain.

2. (Consider this requirement independent of requirement 1.) Assuming spade sales will increase by $3,000 or hoe sales will increase by $2,200 upon alternative application of the advertising funds, toward which product should the funds be applied? Show your calculations.

Problem 4.3   Contribution Reporting—Comparative Operating Results

Dave Randell, president of Randell Incorporated, is frustrated and upset with the latest financial statement results of his company. He has just made the following comment to you and others in the accounting department: "These reports seem unbelievable. Our sales in the fourth quarter were up about 23% over the third quarter, yet this income statement shows a drop in net income for our latest quarter. Your accountants must be having problems getting the correct information through our new computer." The comparative income statements to which Randell is referring are shown below:

Randell Incorporated
Income Statements
for the Last Two Quarters

	Third Quarter		Fourth Quarter	
Sales		$630,000		$774,900
Cost of goods sold				
Beginning finished-goods inventory	$100,000		$131,250	
Cost of goods manufactured	312,500		218,750	
Cost of goods available for sale	$412,500		$350,000	
Ending finished-goods inventory	131,250		4,063	
Cost of goods sold	$281,250		$345,937	
Plus: Underapplied overhead	–0–	281,250	60,000	405,937
Gross margin		$348,750		$368,963
Less: Selling and administrative expenses		258,000		282,840
Net income		$ 90,750		$ 86,123

After studying the statements further, Randell is certain that there must be a mistake somewhere in the fourth quarter figures and has asked you to identify the problem before the preliminary operating results are released to the media.

You review the figures and report back to Randell that the problem is a drop-off in production in the fourth quarter because the manufacturing plant in Niagara experienced some unexpected problems with obtaining raw materials. You explain that this production decline caused the drop-off in earnings.

Randell is mystified by your explanation. He can't understand why an increase in sales should not be accompanied by an increase in net income unless costs went haywire somewhere and he can't see any evidence of a cost problem. He concludes the conversation by saying, "If your statements can't show an earnings increase when sales increase by 23%, we had better call back those computer systems consultants and have them recheck our fancy new computerized information system."

Budgeted unit sales and production for the year along with actual unit sales and production for the last two quarters are as follows:

	First	Second	Third	Fourth
Budgeted sales	12,000	20,000	20,000	20,000
Actual sales	12,000	21,600	18,000	22,140
Budgeted production	20,000	20,000	20,000	20,000
Actual production	20,000	20,000	20,000	14,000

Fixed factory overhead is $200,000 each quarter and variable costs of production are $5.625 per unit. Fixed factory overhead is applied to each unit produced at the rate of $10 per unit. Any under- or overapplied is disposed of directly to cost of goods sold each quarter. The company uses the first-in, first-out inventory costing method. Variable selling and administrative expenses are $6 per unit sold and the balance of selling and administrative expenses is fixed costs.

Required

1. Explain the characteristics of the traditional costing procedures the company used that may have caused the drop in earnings when sales increased.
2. Prepare contribution income statements for each of the last two quarters and explain to Randell what these contribution statements show in comparison to the statements presented originally (if you haven't already included this explanation above).

Problem 4.4   Contribution Analysis—Operating Performance

MacCene Graybar is particularly elated over the Graycene company's latest monthly operating results. The firm finally achieved the goal of leading the industry in the net income percentage of sales. As shown below the company earned 6% on sales revenue, which is well above the industry average of 4.5%.

Graycene manufactures three products that are sold worldwide. The condensed income statement for the latest month follows:

		$	%
Sales		600,000	100.0
Cost of goods sold		403,800	67.3
Gross margin		196,200	32.7
Operating expenses:			
Marketing	90,000		
Administrative	70,200	160,200	
Net income		36,000	6.0

Ms. Graybar has been discussing the above results and plans for the future with the controller. As they concluded their discussion the controller commented: "By the way, James Bright, our new employee in accounting, the recent graduate from the Hampstead Professional School of Accountancy, has a head full of high sounding ideas about things that could be done in reporting operating results. He thinks costs should be broken down into fixed and variable, direct and common, etc., and that we should break our income statement down to show the performance of each of our three products. He has been doing all sorts of figuring. Well, for example, look at this sheet."

Product	Sales	Variable Production Costs	Marketing Expense % of Sales	Fixed Production Expenses	Fixed Marketing Expense Direct to Product
X	$300,000	$165,000	6	$12,000	$18,000
Y	120,000	56,400	6	54,000	10,800
Z	180,000	63,000	6	53,400	6,000

"James proposes to use this kind of data to show how each product is contributing to the operating results of the company."

Ms. Graybar's response was: "We don't need to bother with such costly foolishness. The company is doing well and besides, we know that product Y is the 'Cadillac' of that type of product in the industry. Tell James to get busy spending his time on more meaningful work."

Required

Do you agree with Ms. Graybar's perception of what James Bright proposes to do? What analysis could you do from James Bright's data that you could present to Ms. Graybar to demonstrate that James may know about some tools and methods in his accounting program that give useful insights? Prepare such a presentation. (Assume that all costs not referred to in James' breakdown are fixed and not identified directly with any of the three products.)

Problem 4.5   Contribution Analysis—Product-Line Decisions (CMA)

Bundt Foods Company produces and sells many products in each of its 35 different product lines. From time to time a product or an entire product line is dropped because it ceases to be profitable. The company does not have a formalized program for reviewing its products on a regular basis to identify which products should be eliminated.

At a recent meeting of Bundt Foods' top management, one person stated that there probably were several unprofitable products or possibly an unprofitable product line. After considerable discussion, management decided that Bundt Foods should establish a formalized product evaluation program. This program would review the company's individual products and product lines on a regular and on-going basis to identify problem areas.

The vice-president of finance has proposed that a person be assigned to the program on a full-time basis. This person would work closely with the marketing and accounting departments to determine (a) the factors that indicate when a product's importance is declining and (b) the underlying data that would be required in evaluating whether a product or product line should be discontinued.

Required

1. Identify and explain briefly the benefits (other than the identification of unprofitable products or product lines) Bundt Foods Company can derive from a formalized product discontinuance program.
2. In developing Bundt Food Company's product discontinuance program:
   a. Identify the factors that would indicate whether a product's or product line's importance is diminishing.
   b. Identify the data provided by the accounting department that would be useful in evaluating a product or product line.

Problem 4.6   Reporting Format—Common Expense Allocations

The Orem Company has three divisions. Performance in each division is evaluated on the basis of division net income before taxes. This net income figure includes an assignment of general corporate overhead based on the sales produced in each division. Statements covering operations for the third quarter are as follows (000's omitted):

	Total Company	L	M	N
Sales	$9,600	$4,000	$2,400	$3,200
Cost of goods sold	$4,460	$2,100	$1,080	$1,280
Division operating expense	1,070	500	250	320
Corporate expenses	1,920	800	480	640
Total expenses	$7,450	$3,400	$1,810	$2,240
Net income before taxes	$2,150	$ 600	$ 590	$ 960

The management team in division L is disgruntled with both the operating results and the form of presentation of those results. In that division, they have deliberately retained a line of products that account for 35% of their sales but only 10% of their *division* profits. Division L's management retained this low-margin product, until it could be replaced with a higher margin product, because they felt that the product was still contributing to profit. Now, they think that the product might be an overall loser considering that corporate general expenses are assigned on the basis of sales revenue.

Required

1. Recast the operating statements in a better format to show just what each division's contribution is. Include a breakdown in division L between the low-margin product and the remainder of their business.
2. Comment on the appropriateness of the base used for allocating the corporate general expenses.

Problem 4.7   Contribution Income Statement

The conventional income statement of the Park Company is shown below for the month just ended:

Sales (45,000 units)		$180,000
Cost of goods sold:		
Direct materials	$45,000	
Direct labor	45,000	
Factory overhead	49,000	139,000
Gross margin		$ 41,000
Selling expenses:		
Sales commissions	$ 9,000	
Shipping costs	1,800	
Advertising	10,000	
Executive salaries	10,000	
Administrative expenses	12,450	43,250
Net loss		$ (2,250)

Additional data:

1. Eighty percent of the factory overhead is fixed.
2. Sales commissions and shipping costs are based on sales revenue.
3. Thirty percent of administrative expenses are variable with sales revenue.

Required

Restructure the income statement in contribution format. Show sales, variable costs, and fixed costs. Also show a column indicating unit costs for each category of costs in the statement. Round unit costs to the nearest penny.

Problem 4.8   Analysis of Alternatives to Improve Performance

Refer to the data and the additional facts for problem 4.7. The manager of Park Company is understandably displeased with last month's operating results. The manager, as well as other company executives, expect a profit of 8% of sales.

An analysis of possible options has been made, and the following have been identified:

1. Plant capacity is 75,000 units per month. The sales manager has estimated that a 10% sales price reduction would increase sales to 90% of capacity.
2. Instead of a price reduction, which the manager objects to, the sales manager estimates that an increase in advertising effort may bring sales to 90% of capacity. He is a little uncertain about how much the increase in advertising expenditures could be.

Required

1. Using the contribution format, evaluate the results which the first alternative option would produce. Will this option produce the profit objective of 8% of sales?
2. If the second option is followed and sales reach 90% of capacity, how much could be spent on advertising and still obtain the profit objective of 8% of sales? Use the contribution format.

Problem 4.9   Evaluation of Reporting Formats

Refer to the data in problems 4.7 and 4.8.

Required

Discuss the results shown in your analysis of these problems. In your discussion, contrast the results you show with the results shown by the use of the conventional income statement in problem 4.7.

Problem 4.10   Evaluation of Contribution and Conventional Income Reports

Refer again to the data in problems 4.7 and 4.8. Your colleague from First-Rate U prepared the analysis shown below for option 2 indicated in problem 4.8:

Sales		$270,000
Cost of goods sold:		
Direct materials	$67,500	
Direct labor	67,500	
Factory overhead	73,500	208,500
Gross margin		$ 61,500
Selling expenses:		
Commissions	$13,500	
Shipping costs	2,700	
Advertising	(9,975)[a]	
Executive salaries	15,000	
Administrative salaries	18,675	39,900
Net income (target of 8% of sales)		$ 21,600[a]

[a]Advertising expense backed into from having set net income at 8% of sales. Obviously the profit objective cannot be reached by increasing sales by increased advertising since there is no possibility of increasing advertising.

Required

Make a complete evaluation of the statement prepared by your colleague from First-Rate U. Critique the positive and negative aspects of your colleague's analysis.

PLANNING BUSINESS ACTIVITIES

PART

II

Planning the activities of a business organization is covered in chapters 5 through 7. The budget is the final result of the planning process and provides an estimate of operating results for a future time period. Flexible budgeting is a tool that assists in developing an accurate budget. It adjusts for different cost patterns so that estimated costs are consistent with the expected level of volume. Cost-volume-profit analysis is another planning tool that helps evaluate the relationships between costs and volume and their impact on profits.

BUDGETING

5

OUTLINE

W hen the word "budget" is spoken, most people automatically experience some negative or adverse emotional feelings. To them, a budget is a device that limits their activity, restricts their spending, or requires them to do something they would rather not do. However, individuals who are financially successful and almost all business organizations find that the budgeting process is very useful in planning future activities. The budget itself is a useful document to evaluate the success of those activities. This chapter identifies what a budget is, how it should be developed and utilized to make an organization successful, and how to avoid the undesirable behavioral problems often associated with a budget.

After completing this chapter you should be able to:

1. explain what a budget is and why it is important to an organization.
2. identify the procedures followed in developing a master budget.
3. develop a master budget with supporting schedules.
4. describe the procedures that should be followed in developing and implementing a budget so that behavioral problems are minimized and the budget is successful.

BUDGETING IN GENERAL

A **budget** is an itemized estimate of the operating results of an enterprise for a future time period. The form of the budget varies from organization to organization but it is usually consistent with the form of the normal financial statements. The major difference between the budget and the financial statements is the data used to develop each. Financial statements are based on actual results of past operations, whereas budgets are based on planned operations for a future time period. For this reason, budgets are sometimes referred to as **pro-forma statements.**

The Purpose of a Budget

The purpose of the budget is to provide a blueprint or a *plan of operations* for the enterprise. The budgeting process provides a basis for (*a*) coordinating and implementing the plan, (*b*) motivating organizational members to perform well, and (*c*) controlling and evaluating the activities for the budgeted period.

Coordination and Implementation   In large and diverse organizations the problems of coordination become very important. An important role of budgeting is to improve the coordination among the various units of the organization. Planning or budgeting means establishing objectives in advance and identifying the steps by which the objectives are to be accomplished. The planning process initiates coordination and clarification of sub-goals to achieve major enterprise goals. The coordinated plan or budget provides a blueprint for implementation and control.

Motivation   Motivating organizational members to perform well is generally associated with rewards and punishments rather than with budgeting. The opportunities to participate in developing the budget and in other decision-making areas are highly rewarding and very desirable to many employees. A budget also plays a potential role in motivation because of its goal-setting properties. Goal setting is related to performance. As individuals set higher performance goals, actual performance levels generally increase. If the budget is used properly, it has the potential of serving as a performance goal and, therefore, can be a significant factor in motivation. The motivational impact of the budget is not limited to production workers or supervisors but also extends to top managers as they commit themselves to certain performance levels for their annual financial statements.

Figure 5.1   The budget in the control cycle

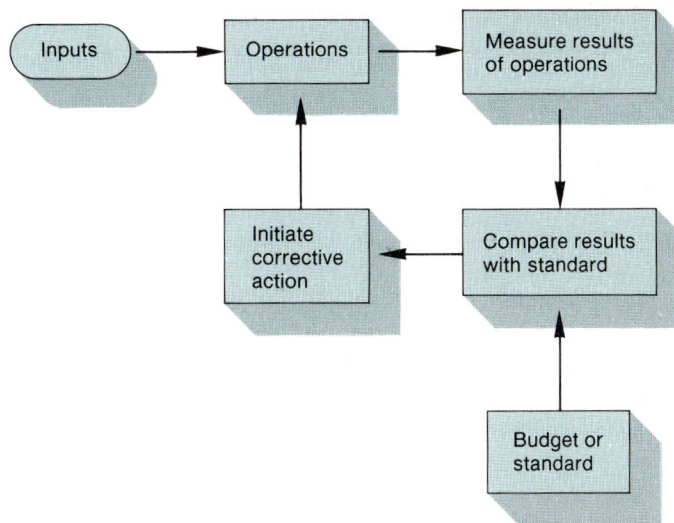

Control and Evaluation   Maintaining control over the activities occurring within an organization is an important responsibility of management. The fundamentals of managerial control consist of (*a*) defining what constitutes a standard of acceptable performance, (*b*) measuring actual performance, (*c*) comparing the standard with the actual performance level, and (*d*) communicating the results to the applicable areas throughout the organization and taking corrective action if needed. Figure 5.1 illustrates the control cycle and the role of the budget as the standard for comparison.

The purpose of a budget in managerial control is to specify the standard of acceptable performance. Without a standard the function of managerial control breaks down. It is impossible to evaluate the acceptability of the actual performance level unless there is a standard for comparison. When an explicit standard has not been established in advance, it is quite likely that the individual examining the reports substitutes his or her own subjective standard. When this happens, those being evaluated are subject to the capricious whims of the evaluator.

In summary, budgeting is a very important organizational process. An understanding of organizational goals comes during the development of the budget as each manager develops a statement of attainable goals for his or her organizational unit. The estimates of the individual subunits may not initially provide a coordinated plan, and revisions are required as they are combined into a total enterprise budget. Nevertheless, these problems are resolved before actual operations. When the plan is implemented, the budget provides a basis for comparing actual results to maintain control over the operations.

Budgeting Relative to Time

Development of an annual budget is only one segment of the on-going planning process of a business. In order for the planning process to be most successful, there must be some (*a*) long-range goals, (*b*) intermediate objectives, and (*c*) a short-term plan of action.

Long-Range, Intermediate, and Short-Term Budgets   The long-range goals identify the direction of the company over a five- to ten-year period. The goals are stated in rather general terms but they deal with specific areas in which the company intends to be successful. Areas often covered in long-range planning include sales, research and development, capital expenditures, personnel policies, and financial position. The following are some examples of long-range goals:

1. Increase our share of the market from 30% to 35%.
2. Construct a new manufacturing facility complete with new equipment.
3. Develop a research and development team with an international reputation.
4. Improve our equity ratio from 40% to 45%.

Intermediate objectives identify the specific steps that will lead to accomplishing the long-term goals. They provide a link between the short-term plan and the long-term objectives. Too often an enterprise will develop grandiose ideas about how great and profitable they will be in the future without critically evaluating the feasibility of accomplishment. Long-range goals need to be broken down into workable steps that will lead to achieving the long-term objective, if accomplished. The long- and short-term plans are merged into an integrated strategic plan by the intermediate objectives. For example, the intermediate objectives required to increase the share of the market from 30% to 35% may include:

1. Introduce one new product each year.
2. Improve advertising coverage by introducing an advertising campaign on the national television media.
3. Improve the quality of our sales force by an annual training seminar.

The short-term plan, called a budget or annual forecast, identifies the activities to be accomplished during the coming year. Most people think of the budgeting process as the development of this annual document. However, the development of the annual budget is heavily dependent on the long-term and intermediate objectives. The remainder of this chapter focuses on the content of the annual budget and the process by which it is developed.

Continuous Budgeting   One of the problems in preparing a budget only once each year is the disruption of normal operations while the budget is being prepared. A large amount of time is required by many people throughout the organization in order to prepare a good budget. Also, unforseeable events may occur during the year to make the budget a poor standard of performance. A technique called continuous budgeting has been developed to avoid these problems.

Continuous budgeting requires that the budget for the next fiscal year (four quarters) be revised and updated at the end of each quarter. Actual operating results are prepared at the end of each quarter and compared to the budget for that quarter. Based on these results and new information and events during the quarter, the budgets for the next three quarters are revised. In addition, a new fourth quarter budget is developed and added to the remaining three quarters to always maintain a budget for the next four quarter period. Continuous budgeting spreads the time required to prepare the budget over the entire year and provides a more meaningful budget throughout the year. Figure 5.2 illustrates continuous budgeting and the time period that it covers.

Relationship of Budgets to Standards

A budget is a formal quantitative expression of planned operations for a future time period. A budget is generally prepared for an entire business organization, however, the term budget is also used to describe the expected operations of major segments of a business.

Figure 5.2   Continuous budgeting

Date	Activity	Contents of the Budget
1/1/X1	Prepare an annual budget consisting of four quarters.	1/1/X1 4/1/X1 7/1/X1 10/1/X1 1/1/X2
4/1/X1	Evaluate first quarter results, revise next three quarters, and add a new fourth quarter to the fiscal year budget.	4/1/X1 7/1/X1 10/1/X1 1/1/X2 4/1/X2 Revise New
7/1/X1	Evaluate second quarter results, revise next three quarters, and add a new fourth quarter to the fiscal year budget.	7/1/X1 10/1/X1 1/1/X2 4/1/X2 7/1/X2 Revise New

Figure 5.3   Master budget

Budgeted Income Statement:

Sales forecast
Production budget
    Direct materials
    Direct labor
    Factory overhead
Cost of goods sold
Selling expense budget
Administrative expense budget

Budgeted Balance Sheet:

Cash budget
    Cash receipts
    Cash disbursements
Capital expenditure budget

Budgeted Statement of Changes in Financial Resources

The term **standard** is used to describe production data relative to *one unit* of product. For example, the production standard identifies the *amount* and *cost* of direct material, direct labor, and factory overhead required to manufacture one unit of finished product.

Budgets and standards are related. When the production budget is broken down on a unit basis it is called a standard. Standard costs are nothing more than budgeted manufacturing costs on a unit basis. However, in developing the budget, the standards are generally developed first and then used as a basis for developing the budget. Standard cost data are also very useful in controlling operations, which will be discussed in detail in chapters 15 and 16.

Master Budgets

The types of budgets and the extent of the budgeting activity vary considerably from organization to organization. In smaller organizations there may only be a sales forecast, a production budget, or a cash budget. Larger organizations generally prepare a master or comprehensive budget.

A **master budget** involves the development of a complete set of financial statements for the budget period with supporting schedules. Figure 5.3 summarizes the budgets and schedules that should be included with a master budget.

Some aspects involved with the development and reporting of a master budget include (*a*) flexible budgeting, (*b*) capital budgeting, and (*c*) performance reporting. These will be discussed in more detail elsewhere in this text.

Flexible Budgeting   Flexible budgeting is used in the development of the overhead portion of the production budget. Overhead is generally composed of both fixed costs, which remain constant when production changes, and variable costs, which increase as production increases. Flexible budgeting is designed to determine the amount of overhead that should be incurred at various levels of production.

Capital Budgeting   Capital budgeting is used to determine the desirability of investing in fixed assets. These projects or decisions are significant in amount and have a relatively long useful life. The time value of money is an important aspect of these decisions and most capital-budgeting decisions models use present value concepts to adjust for the time value of money.

Performance Reporting   Performance reporting is a technique used to report the results of operations. The actual results are compared with budgeted expectations so that the effectiveness of an individual can be evaluated. Critical to performance reporting is identifying who within the organization has the ability to control an item and should, therefore, be held responsible for it.

DEVELOPING A MASTER BUDGET

The primary responsibility for developing a master budget is given to the controller and his or her staff. In larger organizations a special "budget committee" will be formed.

Budget Committee

The budget committee is composed of several key executives from various segments of the organization. People from finance, sales, purchasing, production, engineering, and accounting are usually represented. The procedures followed by this committee in developing the budget are largely determined (*a*) by the authority they have over the final budget and (*b*) by the amount of participation they allow from others within the organization.

The authority of the budget committee is determined by the philosophy of top management. Top management may have a predetermined profit objective in mind and will look to the budget as a means to accomplish it. The profit objective may be stated in a variety of ways, such as a rate of return on net assets, earnings per share, or a specific amount of net income. These profit objectives may be based on operating results of previous years adjusted for expectations about the coming year, or they may be based upon some desired level of profitability. When top management has a predetermined profit objective, the budget committee must recognize it and develop a budget that will produce it.

If top management has no specific profit level in mind, the budget committee must first develop some notion about what is a fair and reasonable expectation for the budget period. Without this, the budget process often turns into a "game" and much of the benefit is lost.

The budget committee may or may not invite other members in the organization to participate in developing the budget. In estimating sales for the coming period, for example, salespeople may be asked to project the number of units of each product they expect to sell in their territory. The sales representative on the budget committee would use these as a basis for developing the sales forecast for the entire company. Participation

Figure 5.4   Flowchart of activities in developing a budget

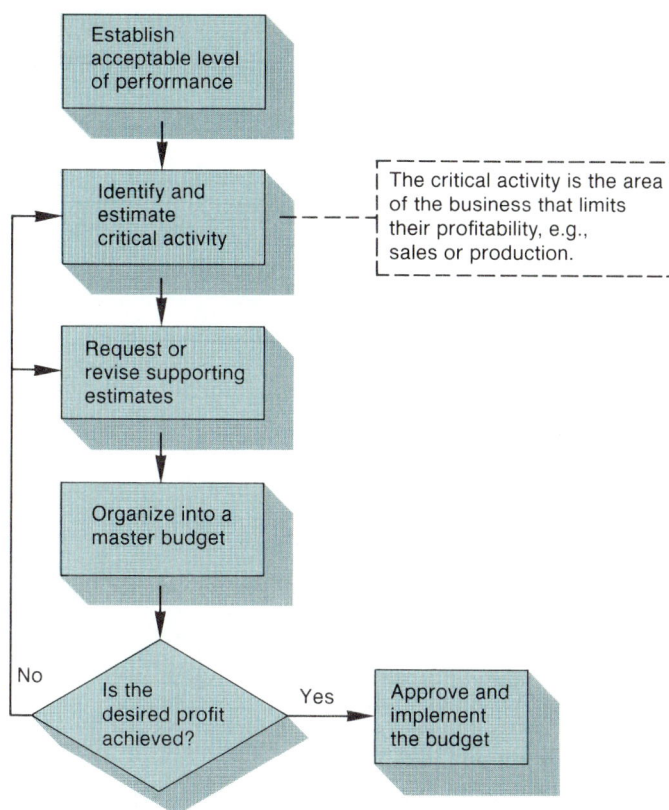

could be carried to the extreme and every person in the organization could be asked to estimate productivity in their individual areas. On the other extreme, the budget committee may allow no participation. They merely develop a budget that will achieve the desired profit and pass it on as the standard of performance for the budget period. More will be said about the behavioral considerations associated with employee participation in developing the budget later in this chapter.

Process of Developing a Budget

The budget is developed in a step-by-step process, but it may take several iterations before the final budget is acceptable. Figure 5.4 illustrates the steps that are followed in developing the budget.

Each enterprise must identify their "critical activity." This is the area of the business or activity that limits their productivity or profitability. The selling process is the critical activity for most manufacturing organizations. These organizations can typically produce all the units they want, but finding someone to buy them at a price that provides a reasonable return on their investment is the limiting or critical factor. In organizations where there is a backlog of orders, production becomes the critical activity.

Emphasis should first be placed on estimating the volume of the critical activity. This estimate is then used by other areas of the business to develop the supporting functions. These estimates are brought together to develop a master budget consisting of a

Figure 5.5   Coordinated budgeting

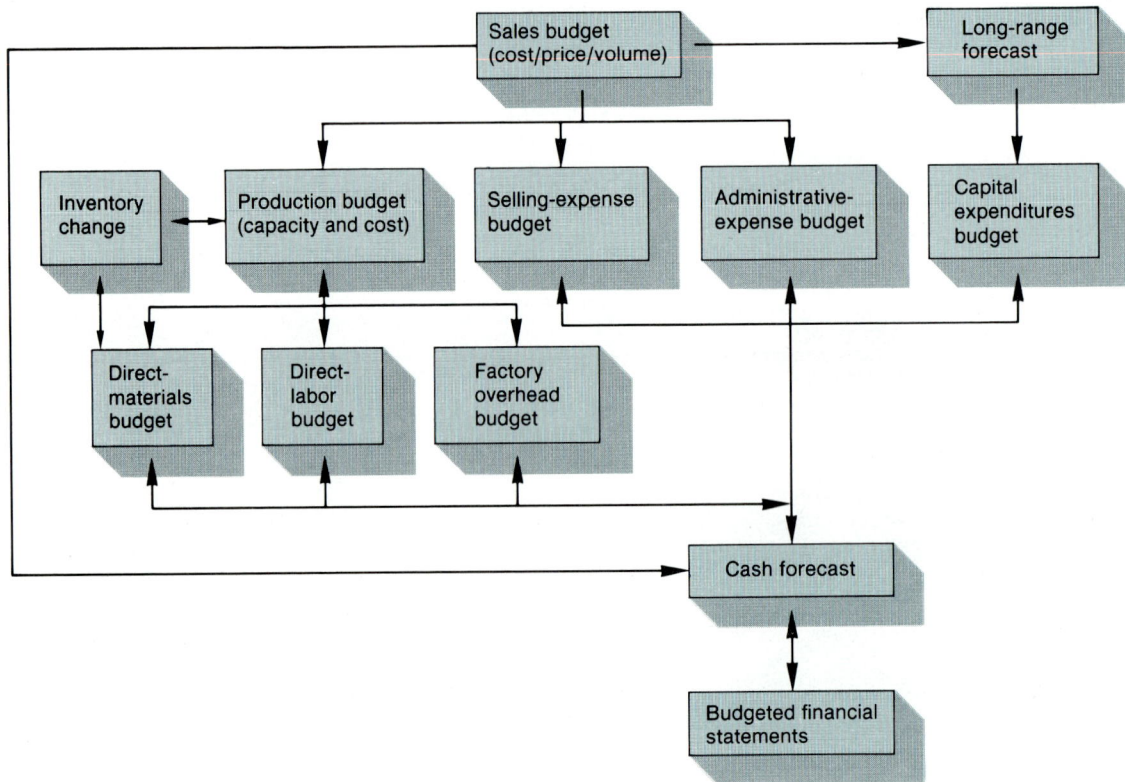

complete set of pro forma statements. The resulting profitability is compared to the desired profitability. If the desired profitability is achieved, the budget is complete. If it is not achieved, estimates are changed and the budget is revised. Several iterations are often required to obtain a satisfactory budget.

MASTER BUDGET EXAMPLE

L & M Incorporated will be used to illustrate the development of a master budget. L & M Incorporated manufactures and sells one product called a Joe-go. They desire an after-tax rate of return of 18% on the average net assets employed during the year. Experience has shown that selling Joe-gos is their critical activity. The budget committee has outlined the following steps for developing their budget. Figure 5.5 illustrates the coordination among these steps.

Step 1   Prepare a sales forecast by quarter showing foreign sales separate from domestic sales.

Step 2   Determine the desired ending inventory levels of raw materials and finished goods for each quarter.

Step 3   Prepare a production budget separately identifying the amount of materials, labor, and overhead.

Step 4   Prepare a direct-materials budget.

Figure 5.6

L & M Incorporated
Balance Sheet
January 1, 19X1

Assets				*Liabilities*	
Current				Accounts payable	$ 7,000
Cash		$ 25,800		Taxes payable	3,000
Accounts receivable				Mortgage payable	42,000
(net)		12,000		Total	$52,000
Raw materials					
inventory		8,000		*Owner's Equity*	
Finished-goods				Common stock (no par)	24,000
inventory		19,200		Retained earnings	79,000
Total current		65,000		Total	$103,000
Fixed				Total liabilities and owner's equity	$155,000
Land		40,000			
Building and					
equipment	$60,000				
Less: Accumulated					
depreciation	10,000	50,000			
Total assets		$155,000			

Notes:

1. Raw materials inventory consists of 20,000 units of material *A* at $.25 per unit and 3,000 units of material *B* at $1.00 per unit.
2. Finished-goods inventory consists of 8,000 units of Joe-gos at $2.40 per unit.
3. Building and equipment consists of $36,000 of building with a useful life of 20 years and $24,000 of equipment with a useful life of 16 years. Straight-line method and zero salvage values are used. The building is used 50% for production and 50% for administration.
4. Taxes payable are due January 15, 19X2.
5. The mortgage is $40,000 with $2,000 of accrued interest. It carries a 10% interest rate. Accrued interest for the prior year and a $10,000 principal payment are due on June 30 of each year.

Step 5   Prepare a cost-of-goods-sold budget.
Step 6   Prepare a selling-expense budget.
Step 7   Prepare an administrative-expense budget.
Step 8   Prepare a cash forecast of receipts and disbursements.
Step 9   Prepare a budgeted income statement.
Step 10 Prepare a budgeted balance sheet.

Figure 5.6 shows the balance sheet of L & M Incorporated at the beginning of the current year. The notes to the balance sheet provide valuable information about the composition of the accounts. This information is essential in developing the budget. The master budget will be developed according to the steps outlined above.

Sales Forecast

An accurate sales forecast for L & M Incorporated is critical because most of the other budgets are at least partially based upon it. Factors to consider when estimating sales volume include general economic conditions, price, and actions of competitors.

The sales forecast for L & M Incorporated must separate domestic sales from foreign sales due to a sale price differential. A price of $4 per unit is charged for domestic sales and $5 per unit is charged for foreign sales. The sales forecast in units is obtained from the sales managers of each territory as shown in figure 5.7. Estimates indicate that

Figure 5.7

L & M Incorporated
Sales Forecast
Year Ending December 31, 19X1
and First Quarter of 19X2

| | Quarters in 19X1 (in units and dollars) | | | | | 1st Quarter |
	1	2	3	4	Total	19X2
Domestic						
–East	10,000	12,000	15,000	15,000	52,000	12,000
–West	6,000	6,000	10,000	7,000	29,000	8,000
Foreign	12,000	18,000	15,000	12,000	57,000	16,000
Total	28,000	36,000	40,000	34,000	138,000	36,000
Sales[a]						
–Domestic	$ 64,000	$ 72,000	$100,000	$ 88,000	$324,000	
–Foreign	60,000	90,000	75,000	60,000	285,000	
Total	$124,000	$162,000	$175,000	$148,000	$609,000	

[a]Domestic sales are projected at $4.00 per unit and foreign sales at $5.00 per unit.

sales will take place uniformly throughout each quarter, and a total of 138,000 units will be sold during the year. Unit sales are priced at the appropriate dollar amounts to show sales in dollar amounts. Total sales for the year are expected to be $609,000.

Ending Inventory Levels

There are two types of raw materials required for the production of a Joe-go—two units of raw material A and one unit of raw material B. Since the supply of both raw materials is expected to be tight throughout the year, the purchasing agents with the approval of top management have decided to maintain an inventory at the end of each quarter that is half the anticipated usage for the following quarter.

The demand for finished Joe-gos is fairly predictable and uniform throughout the year. Therefore, management has decided that the finished-goods inventory at the end of each quarter should be equal to one-fourth the expected sales of the following quarter. Figure 5.8 shows the desired amounts of raw materials and finished-good inventories at the end of each quarter.

The desired ending inventory for raw material A in the first quarter is computed by multiplying the second quarter unit sales of 36,000 units (from fig. 5.7) by one half and then multiplying by two units. Expected sales are multiplied by one half in order to maintain an ending inventory at half the sales volume anticipated for the following quarter. It is then multiplied by two because two units of material A are required for each unit of finished product.

The computations for material B and finished goods follow a similar pattern. The footnote to figure 5.8 shows the first quarter computations.

Production Budget

Enough finished goods must be available for sales and for the desired inventory levels outlined above. Some finished goods are available in beginning inventory, but most of the goods will be manufactured during each quarter. The amount to be produced each quarter is computed as follows:

Expected sales + Desired ending inventory − Beginning inventory = Production

Figure 5.8

L & M Incorporated
Desired Ending Inventories of Raw Materials
and Finished Goods
Year Ending December 31, 19X1

	Quarter			
	1	*2*	*3*	*4*
Raw materials				
A	36,000[a]	40,000	34,000	36,000
B	18,000[b]	20,000	17,000	18,000
Finished goods	9,000[c]	10,000	8,500	9,000

[a]36,000 × 1/2 × 2 units = 36,000
[b]36,000 × 1/2 = 18,000
[c]36,000 × 1/4 = 9,000

Figure 5.9

L & M Incorporated
Production Budget
Year Ending December 31, 19X1

	Quarter				
	1	*2*	*3*	*4*	*Total*
Units for sales	28,000	36,000	40,000	34,000	
Desired ending inventory	9,000	10,000	8,500	9,000	
Total needed	37,000	46,000	48,500	43,000	
Less: Beginning inventory	8,000	9,000	10,000	8,500	
Production (units)	29,000	37,000	38,500	34,500	139,000
Cost of production					
Raw materials					
A ($.50/unit)	$14,500	$18,500	$19,250	$17,250	$ 69,500
B ($1.00/unit)	29,000	37,000	38,500	34,500	139,000
Direct labor ($.60/unit)	17,400	22,200	23,100	20,700	83,400
Overhead ($.40/unit)	11,600	14,800	15,400	13,800	55,600
Total	$72,500	$92,500	$96,250	$86,250	$347,500

The number of units to be manufactured each quarter is shown in figure 5.9. It is expected that a total of 139,000 units will be manufactured during the year. Unit sales each quarter are obtained from figure 5.7 and the desired ending inventory is obtained from figure 5.8. Remember that the ending inventory in one quarter is the beginning inventory of the following quarter. Notice that the 139,000 units to be produced is 1,000 units more than expected sales because of the planned increase in ending finished-goods inventory.

The production costs must be developed for materials, labor, and overhead. The cost of raw materials is developed as part of the raw materials purchases budget discussed below. Based on existing and anticipated market conditions, prices of $.25 per unit and $1.00 per unit are anticipated for raw materials *A* and *B* respectively. Remember that

Figure 5.10

L & M Incorporated
Overhead Production Budget
Calendar Year 19X1 at 139,000 Units of Production

Variable overhead costs		
Indirect materials	$10,000	
Indirect labor	8,800	
Utilities—variable portion	3,000	
Repair—variable portion	6,000	
Total variable cost		$27,800
Fixed overhead cost[a]		
Property tax and insurance	3,000	
Depreciation	2,400	
Supervision	15,000	
Utilities—fixed portion	2,000	
Repair—fixed portion	5,400	
Total fixed cost		27,800
Total overhead cost		$55,600
Overhead cost per unit ($55,600 ÷ 139,000)		$ .40

[a]Notice that the overhead is $27,800 of fixed cost plus $.20 of variable cost for each unit produced
($27,800 ÷ 139,000 units = $.20/unit)

two units of material A ($.25 × 2 = $.50 per Joe-go) and one unit of raw material B are required to make each Joe-go.

The direct-labor cost is developed by estimating the amount of direct labor required to manufacture each unit of Joe-go and by pricing it at the expected direct-labor wage rate. Engineering and time-and-motion studies have shown that it takes five minutes of direct-labor time to produce each unit. The wage rate specified in the union contract is $7.20 per hour. Therefore, the direct-labor cost to produce one Joe-go is expected to be $.60 per unit ($7.20 ÷ 12 units per hours = $.60).

The overhead costs expected to be incurred during the year 19X1 are summarized in figure 5.10. Notice that these are estimated for the entire year at the anticipated production level of 139,000 units. Since some overhead costs are fixed and some are variable, the length of time *and* the level of production are both important variables when projecting overhead. The overhead cost per unit at this level of production is $.40.

Notice the relationship between the production standards and the production budget. The standards for manufacturing one Joe-go are shown in figure 5.11. The production budget is developed by applying the standards by the expected volume. Each manufacturing cost is multiplied by the number of units to be produced to compute the production cost for each quarter. The total production cost by quarter is shown in figure 5.9.

Raw Materials Purchases Budget

There are two important aspects to the raw materials purchases budget: (*a*) the quantity to be purchased and (*b*) the expected price. Enough raw material must be purchased to meet production needs and satisfy the desired level of ending inventory. However, some raw material is already available in the beginning inventory. The amount of raw material to be purchased each quarter is computed by adding the amount used in production to the desired ending inventory and subtracting the beginning inventory as shown in figure 5.12.

Figure 5.11

L & M Incorporated
Production Standards Per Unit of Joe-go
Year Ending December 31, 19X1

Production Component	Quantity of Component	Price of Component	Cost per Finished Unit
Raw material			
A	2 units	$.25/unit	$ .50
B	1 unit	1.00/unit	1.00
Direct labor	1/12 hour	7.20/hour	.60
Overhead	1 unit	.40/unit	.40
Total			$2.50

Figure 5.12

L & M Incorporated
Raw Materials Purchases Budget

	Quarter			
	1	2	3	4
Raw Material A:				
Production needs[a] (units)	58,000	74,000	77,000	69,000
Desired ending inventory[b]	36,000	40,000	34,000	36,000
Total needed	94,000	114,000	111,000	105,000
Less: Beginning inventory	20,000	36,000	40,000	34,000
Quantity to be purchased	74,000	78,000	71,000	71,000
Price	$ .25	$ .25	$ .25	$ .25
Purchases—Material A	$18,500	$19,500	$17,750	$17,750
Raw Material B:				
Production needs (units)	29,000	37,000	38,500	34,500
Desired ending inventory	18,000	20,000	17,000	18,000
Total needed	47,000	57,000	55,500	52,500
Less: Beginning inventory	3,000	18,000	20,000	17,000
Quantity to be purchased	44,000	39,000	35,500	35,500
Price	$1.00	$1.00	$1.00	$1.00
Purchases—Material B	$44,000	$39,000	$35,500	$35,500
Total purchases	$62,500	$58,500	$53,250	$53,250

[a]Two units are required for each unit of finished goods (2 × 29,000 = 58,000 units). See figure 5.9 for production needs.
[b]See figure 5.8 for desired ending inventory.

The amount of raw material needed for production is based on the production budget (fig. 5.9). For example, in the first quarter, 29,000 units of finished product are to be produced. Each unit of finished product requires two units of raw material A, so 58,000 units of raw material A are needed for production. The desired ending inventory of each raw material was computed earlier and is shown in figure 5.8. The beginning inventory of each quarter is the ending inventory of the preceding quarter.

Figure 5.13

L & M Incorporated
Cost-of-Goods-Sold Budget
Year Ending December 31, 19X1

Beginning finished-goods inventory[a]	$ 19,200
Plus: Cost of goods manufactured[b]	347,500
Goods available for sale	366,700
Less: Ending inventory[c]	22,500
Cost of goods sold	$344,200

[a]See figure 5.6.
[b]See figure 5.9.
[c](9,000 units $\times$ $2.50 = $22,500) See figure 5.8 and figure 5.11.

The expected purchase price is developed by the purchasing agent for each element of raw material. Factors that are considered in developing the price are the current price, expected supply and demand, and available quantity discounts. Prices of $.25 per unit and $1.00 per unit are anticipated for raw materials *A* and *B* respectively. The price is multiplied by the quantity needed to obtain total purchases for each quarter.

Cost-of-Goods-Sold Budget

The cost-of-goods-sold budget is similar in form to the normal cost-of-goods-sold statement. Figure 5.13 shows a cost-of-goods-sold statement for the year ending December 31, 19X1.

The beginning inventory of finished goods is taken from the January 1, 19X1 balance sheet shown in figure 5.6. Cost of goods manufactured is the result of the production budget illustrated in figure 5.9. Ending finished-goods inventory is based on the desired ending inventory of finished goods developed in figure 5.8 and the production standard developed in figure 5.11. The 9,000 units of ending inventory are valued at the production cost of $2.50 to give the ending inventory of $22,500.

Selling-Expense Budget

Selling expenses, which include sales commissions and freight-out, are developed by the sales managers and their staff. Selling expenses are entirely variable but the amounts differ for domestic and foreign sales. Domestic selling expenses are expected to be 10% of domestic sales, whereas foreign selling expenses are expected to be 20% of the foreign sales. Figure 5.14 shows the expected selling expenses by quarter for 19X1.

The expected sales in domestic and foreign areas as computed in the sales forecast (see fig. 5.7) are used to develop the dollar amounts of selling expense each quarter. For example, foreign sales in the first quarter of 19X1 are expected to be $60,000. Of this amount 20% is the $12,000 of selling expenses budgeted for foreign sales.

Administrative-Expense Budget

The administrative expenses are also summarized in figure 5.14. The controller is responsible for developing the administrative-expense budget, which includes all expenses involved with the general management of the organization. Financing charges, uncollectable accounts receivable, and tax expenses are handled as separate items because of their interdepartmental relationship.

The controller estimates that salary and depreciation will be constant each quarter at $21,000 and $225 respectively. Other cash expenses will vary from quarter to quarter

Figure 5.14

L & M Incorporated
Selling and Administrative Expense Budget
Year Ending December 31, 19X1

	Quarter				
	1	*2*	*3*	*4*	*Total*
Selling expenses:					
Domestic	$ 6,400	$ 7,200	$10,000	$ 8,800	$32,400
Foreign	12,000	18,000	15,000	12,000	57,000
Total	$18,400	$25,200	$25,000	$20,800	$89,400
Administrative expenses:					
Salary	$21,000	$21,000	$21,000	$21,000	$84,000
Depreciation	225	225	225	225	900
Other cash					
expenses	12,000	12,500	13,000	12,500	50,000
Total	$33,225	$33,725	$34,225	$33,725	$134,900

as shown in the administrative budget, with slightly higher expenses occurring in the summer months.

Cash Forecast of Receipts and Disbursements

The cash budget is vital in forecasting cash needs and in planning short-term investments to effectively utilize surplus cash. A cash budget shows how the cash balance will change during a period of time for budgeted cash receipts and cash disbursements. The forecast starts with the beginning cash balance. Cash receipts are added and cash disbursements are subtracted to compute the ending cash balance. It is important to break the cash budget into small time intervals, such as monthly or quarterly, to identify periods when additional cash will be needed or when excess cash is available for short-term investments. A cash forecast will be prepared on a quarterly basis for L & M Incorporated in order to pinpoint any cash flow problems.

Experience has shown that a minimum cash balance of $10,000 is required to maintain normal business operations. If this amount cannot be maintained during a quarter, the company will draw on their line of credit from the bank. The loan is made at the beginning of the quarter in which the shortage is expected to occur. The money is borrowed in multiples of $1,000 at an interest rate of 12% per year. The loan can be paid back at the end of any quarter in which there is available cash, along with any accrued interest.

The accrual concept is ignored when developing the cash forecast. The criterion used in cash budgeting is receipt or payment of cash. Therefore, such items as interest on the mortgage are included in the cash forecast when they are paid not as they are accrued. Such items as depreciation that do not involve cash are excluded in developing the cash forecast.

The collection and payment policies of a business are very important in developing the cash forecast. The majority of sales are on account and the following schedule summarizes the timing of cash collections by L & M Incorporated:

90% of each quarter's sales are collected in the quarter of sale.
9% are collected in the following quarter.
1% are uncollectible.

Figure 5.15

L & M Incorporated
Cash Forecast
Year Ending December 31, 19X1

	Quarter			
	1	2	3	4
Beginning cash balance	$25,800	$10,450	$10,210	$13,630
Plus: Cash receipts				
Sales[a]	123,600	156,960	172,080	148,950
Total cash	149,400	167,410	182,290	162,580
Less: Cash disbursements				
Material purchases[b]	57,000	59,300	54,300	53,250
Direct labor[c]	17,400	22,200	23,100	20,700
Overhead-variable[d]	5,800	7,400	7,700	6,900
Overhead-fixed[e]	6,350	6,350	6,350	6,350
Selling expenses[f]	18,400	25,200	25,000	20,800
Administrative expenses[g]	33,000	33,500	34,000	33,500
Interest-mortgage		4,000		
Mortgage		10,000		
Taxes payable	3,000	2,250	2,250	2,250
Total payments	140,950	170,200	152,700	143,750
Cash balance (deficiency)	8,450	(2,790)	29,590	18,830
Required loans	2,000	13,000		
Loan repayments			15,960	
Ending cash balance	$10,450	$10,210	$13,630	$18,830

[a]From figure 5.16.
[b]From figure 5.17.
[c]See figure 5.9.
[d]$.20 per unit (fig. 5.10) times the units produced (fig. 5.9).
[e]25% of fixed factory overhead, excluding depreciation (fig. 5.10) each quarter.
[f]See figure 5.14.
[g]Administrative expenses (fig. 5.14) excluding depreciation.

Payment for purchases and other operating costs are as follows. With the exception of raw materials purchases, all production costs, selling, and administrative expenses are paid in the period incurred. Raw materials purchases are paid 80% in the quarter of the purchase and 20% in the subsequent quarter. Figure 5.15 contains the cash forecast for 19X1. The computations followed in developing cash receipts, cash disbursements, and cash balance will be explained individually.

Cash Receipts   Quarterly sales for L & M Incorporated must be separated into (a) the amount collected in the quarter of sale, (b) the amount collected in the following quarter, and (c) uncollectible accounts. Uncollectible accounts are a non-cash expense that does not effect cash flows. They are excluded from the sales forecast. Figure 5.16 illustrates a convenient format for performing these computations.

The $12,000 amount collected in the first quarter is the accounts receivable balance reported in the balance sheet of January 1, 19X1 (see fig. 5.6). Of the first quarter sales of $124,000, $111,600 (90% × $124,000) will be collected in that quarter, $11,160

Figure 5.16

L & M Incorporated
Schedule of Cash Receipts
Year Ending December 31, 19X1

Quarter of Sale	Amount	1	2	3	4	Year-End Accounts Receivable	Uncollectible Accounts
		Quarter of Collection					
Prior year:							
4th Quarter		$ 12,000					
Current year:							
1st Quarter	$124,000	111,600	$ 11,160				$1,240
2d Quarter	162,000		145,800	$ 14,580			1,620
3rd Quarter	175,000			157,500	$ 15,750		1,750
4th Quarter	148,000				133,200	$13,320	1,480
Total		$123,600	$156,960	$172,080	$148,950	$13,320	$6,090

Figure 5.17

L & M Incorporated
Schedule of Cash Disbursements for Material Purchases
Year Ending December 31, 19X1

Quarter of Purchase	Amount	1	2	3	4	Year-End Accounts Payable
		Quarter of Payment				
Prior year:						
4th Quarter		$ 7,000				
Current year:						
1st Quarter	$62,500	$50,000	$12,500			
2d Quarter	58,500		46,800	$11,700		
3rd Quarter	53,250			42,600	$10,650	
4th Quarter	53,250				42,600	$10,650
Total		$57,000	$59,300	$54,300	$53,250	$10,650

(9% × $124,000) will be collected in the second quarter, and $1,240 (1% × $124,000) are expected to be uncollectible. Sales in each subsequent quarter are separated in a similar manner.

Cash Disbursements   Raw materials purchased by L & M Incorporated must be separated into (*a*) the amount paid in the quarter of purchase and (*b*) the amount paid in the following quarter. Figure 5.17 illustrates this computation.

The $7,000 balance in accounts payable on January 1, 19X1 must be paid during the first quarter. Of the $62,500 of raw materials purchased in the first quarter, $50,000 ($62,500 × 80%) will be paid in that quarter and $12,500 ($62,500 × 20%) will be paid in the next quarter. Purchases in each of the other quarters are separated in a similar manner. The total cash payments for raw materials are carried to the cash forecast in figure 5.15.

Cash disbursements for most of the other manufacturing expenses are fairly straightforward. The quarterly amounts for direct labor are obtained from the production budget shown in figure 5.9. Factory overhead must be split into the variable and fixed portion. Variable overhead is $.20 per unit (from fig. 5.10) times the number of units produced (from fig. 5.9). For example, in the first quarter 29,000 units of production will result in $5,800 (29,000 units $\times$ $.20) of variable overhead.

Fixed factory overhead totaling $27,800 (from fig. 5.10) will be incurred uniformly throughout the year. The depreciation of $2,400, however, must be excluded because it is a non-cash expense. The balance of $25,400 ($27,800 − $2,400) will be paid uniformly throughout the year so $6,350 ($25,400 $\times$ 25%) is budgeted for each quarter.

Selling expenses, as developed in figure 5.14, are carried directly to the cash forecast. Depreciation expense must be excluded from the administrative expenses before they are carried to the cash forecast. Also, the mortgage payment plus accrued interest must be paid at the end of the second quarter.

The $3,000 tax payment in the first quarter is the final payment for income tax due on 19X0 net income. This was the amount shown in the January 1, 19X1 balance sheet. The $2,250 tax payments in the second, third, and fourth quarters represent estimated income tax payments for 19X1. The estimated income tax is $8,985 (from fig. 5.18), and tax laws require that at least 90% of this amount be deposited through timely quarterly payments.

Cash Balance   The beginning cash balance of $25,800 is obtained from the balance sheet on January 1, 19X1 (see fig. 5.6). It is increased by cash receipts and reduced by cash disbursements, both of which include any bank loans or repayments to maintain an adequate cash balance. The ending cash balance of one quarter is the beginning cash balance of the next quarter.

Notice that a cash shortage is expected in the first and second quarters, which will require the company to draw upon their line of credit from the bank. A loan of $2,000 will be needed at the beginning of the first quarter and $13,000 will be needed at the start of the second quarter to maintain the $10,000 minimum balance. Both loans will be paid back at the end of the third quarter with interest computed as follows:

$$\$2,000 \times 12\% \times \tfrac{3}{4} = \$180$$
$$13,000 \times 12\% \times \tfrac{1}{2} = \underline{780}$$
$$\text{Total interest} \quad \underline{\$960}$$

Budgeted Income Statement

Most of the information for the income statement shown in figure 5.18 has already been developed. Sales, cost of goods sold, selling expenses, administrative expenses, and uncollectible accounts are all taken from prior schedules. Interest expense is computed on the mortgage and the line of credit from the bank as shown in the footnote for figure 5.18.

The average income tax rate for L & M Incorporated is expected to be 30%. If operations proceed as planned, the income tax expense and tax payable for the year will be $8,985 (30% $\times$ $29,950). Quarterly tax deposits of $2,250 are planned for the second, third, and fourth quarters, so taxes payable at the end of 19X1 will only be $2,235. This amount is shown as a current liability in the year-end balance sheet.

Budgeted Balance Sheet

All of the information for the balance sheet has been developed in the process of preparing the other schedules. However, some of the data must still be manipulated slightly to get it into a usable form. The footnotes to the budgeted balance sheet in figure 5.19 identify the source of the data and any required computations.

Figure 5.18

L & M Incorporated
Budgeted Income Statement
Year Ending December 31, 19X1

Sales		$609,000
Less: Cost of goods sold		344,200
Gross profit		264,800
Less: Other expenses		
Selling expenses	$ 89,400	
Administrative expenses	134,900	
Interest[a]	4,460	
Uncollectible accounts	6,090	
Total		234,850
Net income before taxes		29,950
Tax expense (30%)		8,985
Net income		$ 20,965

[a]Interest expense consists of:
$40,000 \times 10\% \times 1/2 = \$2,000$
$30,000 \times 10\% \times 1/2 = \$1,500$
$\$ 2,000 \times 12\% \times 3/4 = \$ 180$
$\$13,000 \times 12\% \times 1/2 = \$ 780$
$\$4,460$

Figure 5.19

L & M Incorporated
Budgeted Balance Sheet
December 31, 19X1

Assets

Cash[a]		$ 18,830	**Liabilities**		
Accounts receivable			Current		
(Net)[b]		13,320	Accounts payable[a]		$ 10,650
Raw materials			Taxes payable		2,235
inventory[c]		27,000	Mortgage payable[f]		31,500
Finished-goods			Total		$44,385
inventory[c]		22,500			
Total current		$81,650	**Owner's Equity**		
Fixed:			Common stock (no par)		24,000
Land		40,000	Retained Earnings:		
Building and			Beginning	$79,000	
equipment	$60,000		Plus: Net income[g]	20,965	$ 99,965
Less: Accumulated			Total		$123,965
depreciation[d]	13,300	$ 46,700	Total liabilities and		
Total assets		$168,350	owner's equity		$168,350

[a]See figure 5.15 ending balance.
[b]From figure 5.16.
[c]Estimated inventories from figure 5.8, priced at estimated cost.
  $(36,000 \times \$.25 + 18,000 \times \$1.00 = \$27,000)$
  $(9,000 \times \$2.50 = \$22,500)$
[d]Accumulated depreciation from figures 5.10 and 5.14 plus the balance of January 1, 19X1.
[e]From figure 5.17.
[f]Mortgage balance, $30,000, plus accrued interest at 10% for 6 months.
[g]From figure 5.18.

Analysis of the Budget

The budget must be analyzed to see if it is complete and acceptable as a plan of operations for the coming year. The budget committee reviews the budget to make sure no significant items have been omitted and that it is internally consistent. They must also evaluate it to see if it provides a rate of return that is acceptable to top management.

Top management of L & M Incorporated has specified a desired after-tax rate of return of 18% on the average net assets employed during the year. The rate of return provided by this budget is 18.5%.

Average net assets	$113,480
($103,000 + $123,960 ÷ 2)	
Rate of return	18.5%
($20,965 ÷ $113,480)	

The budget satisfies the profit objective for the coming year and will probably be acceptable to top management. If they are able to operate within the guidelines specified by the budget, they will achieve their desired growth and profitability.

If the budget does not meet the desired objectives of top management, the budget committee must work with their people to identify areas in which changes can be made so the objectives will be achieved. This is probably the most difficult aspect of budgeting. It generally requires someone to do something they would rather not do. The process by which the budget is changed is also very important. If the budget committee has had broad participation by others within the organization in developing the budget to this point, and if they now change the budget without involving the same people, those people are likely to believe that they had no real input in the first place. They will probably not be as willing to participate in developing future budgets and their commitment to achieve the revised budget will probably not be as great because of their adverse feelings toward it.

BEHAVIORAL CONSIDERATIONS OF BUDGETING

A tremendous amount of research and material has been written about the behavioral implication of budgeting. Anyone who is closely involved with the budgeting process should study this research in some detail. Several significant propositions or rules regarding the behavioral aspects of budgeting can be gathered from such literature. Several of the more significant conclusions will be summarized as follows:

Proposition No. 1.   Whether budgeting in an organization is constructive or destructive will depend largely on the effectiveness of management in administering it. Budgets that are properly set and administered can be of great assistance in planning, motivating, and controlling the activities of people. When improperly administered they may cause increased tension, resentment, suspicion, fear, and mistrust among employees.

Proposition No. 2.   Planning, in preparation for developing the budget, is one of the most important parts of developing a good budget. Adequate preplanning allows everyone to be working on the same assumptions, targeted goals, and agenda. Everyone must understand the limitations and constraints of their participation and the bounds of their decision making. The level of activity the organization expects to achieve within the coming year should be communicated to those individuals participating in the development of the budget. All individuals involved in developing the budget should understand how their activity will fit into the entire organization and what constraints will be placed upon them by upper-level administrative decisions.

Proposition No. 3.   Participation should be allowed and encouraged at each level within the organization. The activity of developing the budget should be structured so the relevant people are there. The relevant people are those who are responsible for implementing the budget, who have the ability to control the item that is budgeted, and who will be rewarded according to its accomplishments. Emotional problems will be minimized if people are allowed to participate in setting their budgets, if they are consulted when changes are made, and if they have ample opportunity to explain unfavorable variances from budgeted objectives. There are generally three benefits of allowing employees to participate in developing the budget: (a) employees tend to accept the budget as their own plan of action, (b) participation tends to increase morale among employees and toward management, and (c) employee cohesiveness is increased and productivity will also increase if dictated by the group norm.

Proposition No. 4.   Even though budgets are quantitative tools, considerable emotion is connected with both the controller and the controlled. The individual in control often uses the budget as a medium of personality expression. The people being controlled often have feelings of fear and anxiety because their success and promotion are tied directly to the budget. The climate for preparing the budget should be structured so that individuals are "freed-up," rather than anxious and defensive. The structuring of the proper climate requires that each individual has the freedom and authority to influence and accept his or her own performance level and then the responsibility for accomplishing it. This activity should be structured so that it is (a) problem oriented or opportunity oriented and (b) oriented to the problems and opportunities of the participant.

Proposition No. 5.   A major consideration in developing a budget or a standard is the *level of difficulty* that should be associated with successful achievement. The budget could be set so tight (difficult) that it will never be achieved or it could be set very loose (easy) so that it will always be achieved. Since the budget is regarded as a standard of performance that the individual must reach to be successful, a budget that is set too high or too low fails to provide motivation. Optimal levels of motivation occur when the probability of successful achievement are about 50:50, that is when the chance of success and failure are approximately equal. Challenging but attainable goals, once achieved, produce feelings of success, confidence, and satisfaction. This in turn raises aspiration levels and feelings of self worth. The budget can still be difficult and challenging, but it should be attainable.

Proposition No. 6.   The most important principle of learning involved in budgeting is that an individual tends to perform acts that are rewarded and avoids doing those that are penalized. People want to know what is expected of them and what they must do to be rewarded. The budget is one of the most visible and widely used tools for identifying rewards and reward contingencies. Care must be taken when developing the budget to establish rewards and reward contingencies that will lead to achieving organizational goals. Inappropriate reward contingencies will probably result in internal strife among departments and department managers.

Proposition No. 7.   Budgets are most effective when they are used to control costs at an efficient level of operation. A clear distinction should be maintained between the objectives of a budget and the objectives of a cost-cutting industrial engineering study. An industrial engineering study is very useful in developing some aspects of the budget, especially the type and quantity of direct material and direct labor requirement for a manufacturing process. It is also useful identifying areas in which cost reduction is possible through changes in the manufacturing process. This change may be in the way a worker performs a job or a change in the equipment used in the process. A cost reduction study, however, is a separate activity that may not have an immediate impact on the budget.

One major criticism of budgeting is that it is used as a "cost reduction" tool rather than a "cost control" tool. Budgeting may result in cost reductions by making people more aware of the need to control the costs. The mere process of measuring and reporting operating data may cause some people to improve their level of performance. However, if an individual is doing an efficient job under the current production process and is providing a fair day's work for the pay received, it is not reasonable to expect performance to improve and thereby reduce costs merely by tightening the budget. If additional cost reductions are required, engineering studies should be used to identify alternative production processes and techniques. The objective of the budget is to control costs at an efficient level of operation.

Summary

In summary, the critical problem is not in determining when a budget should or should not be used. Every organization has some type of plan that in reality is a budget. Some companies have a more elaborate budget and budgeting process than others, but all of them have some kind of budget. The critical problem is how to structure the budgeting process and how to prepare a budget that will help the organization achieve its goals and be successful.

A budget is an itemized estimate of the operating results of an enterprise for a future time period. It provides a plan for coordinating and implementing activities, motivating people to perform well, and controlling and evaluating their results. The annual budget is part of a long-range planning process, which includes long-range goals and intermediate objectives, in addition to the budget.

In developing the budget, the acceptable level of performance that is required to accomplish the intermediate and long-range goals should be established first. The organization must then identify and estimate the critical activity. Generally, selling is the most critical activity but, for some businesses, production is the limiting factor. Estimates are developed for other areas of the business that are required to support the critical activity. This includes raw materials purchases, production costs, selling and administrative expenses, and cash forecasts. These are developed as supporting schedules for the budgeted financial statements including the income statement and balance sheet.

Behavioral considerations in developing the budget are at least as important as the quantitative estimates. The success of the budget is largely determined by the way it is administered. Therefore, planning the strategy to be used in preparing the budget is very important. Relevant people should be involved and should be allowed to participate in developing the budget. The climate should be problem or opportunity oriented in order to reduce the emotional problems often associated with the budget. The budget should be difficult and challenging, yet it must be attainable. Care must also be taken to include rewards and reward contingencies within the budget that will lead to organizational goals.

Self-Study Problem (AICPA adapted)

The January 31, 19X6, balance sheet of Shelpat Corporation follows:

Cash	$ 8,000
Accounts receivable (net of allowance for uncollectible accounts of $2,000)	38,000
Inventory	16,000
Property, plant, and equipment (net of allowance for accumulated depreciation of $60,000)	40,000
	$102,000
Accounts payable	$ 82,500
Common stock	50,000
Retained earnings (deficit)	(30,500)
	$102,000

Additional information:

1. Sales are budgeted as follows:
   February $110,000
   March $120,000
2. Collections are expected to be 60% in the month of sale, 38% the next month, and 2% uncollectible.
3. The gross margin is 25% of sales. Purchases each month are 75% of the next month's projected sales. The purchases are paid in full the following month.
4. Other expenses for each month, paid in cash, are expected to be $16,500. Depreciation each month is $5,000.

Required

1. Compute budgeted cash collections for February 19X6.
2. Prepare a pro forma income (loss) statement before income taxes for February 19X6.
3. Compute the projected balance in accounts payable on February 29, 19X6.

Solution to the Self-Study Problem

Requirement 1

Cash collections in February will come from February's sales and from accounts receivable collections for January's sales.

Month of Sale	Cash Collected	
January	$ 38,000	(Balance on accounts receivable)
February	66,000	($110,000 × 60%)
Total	$104,000	

Notice that the $38,000 balance in accounts receivable is net of the allowance for uncollectible accounts.

Requirement 2

Shelpat Corporation
Income Statement
February, 19X6

Sales		$110,000
Less: Cost of goods sold (75%)		82,500
Gross margin (25%)		27,500
Less: Other expenses		
Cash expenses	16,500	
Uncollectible accounts		
(2% × $110,000)	2,200	
Depreciation	5,000	
Total		23,700
Net income		$ 3,800

Requirement 3

The January 31 balance of accounts payable of $82,500 will be paid in February. February purchases are 75% of expected sales in March or $90,000 (75% × $120,000). Since purchases are paid in full the following month, the accounts payable balance on February 29, 19X6 will be $90,000.

Suggested Readings

Cherrington, David J., and Cherrington, J. Owen. "Participation, Performance, and Appraisal." *Business Horizons* 17 (December 1974): 35–45.

————. "The Role of Budgeting in Organizational Improvement." *Michigan Business Review* 27 (July 1975): 12–16.

————. "Budget Games for Fun and Frustration." *Management Accounting* (January 1976): 28–33.

Becker, Selwyn, and Green, David, Jr. "Budgeting and Employee Behavior." *The Journal of Business* 37 (April 1964): 292–402.

Schiff, Michael, and Lewin, Arie Y. "The Impact of People on Budgets." *The Accounting Review* (April 1970): 259–68.

Goodman, Sam R., and Reece, James S. *Controller's Handbook*. Homewood, Ill.: Dow-Jones Irwin, 1978.

Discussion Questions

1. Describe a budget.
2. Why is it so important for business organizations to have a budget?
3. How does an annual budget tie in with the long-term goals and intermediate objectives of an organization?
4. How does continuous budgeting differ from annual budgeting?
5. What are the major benefits of continuous budgeting?
6. Describe the relationship of a budget to a standard. What role do standards play in developing a budget?

7. What is a master budget and how does it differ from flexible budgeting and capital budgeting?
8. What is the role of the budget committee in developing a budget?
9. Describe the process by which the budget is developed. Why is it important to identify the critical activity or limiting factor and what part does it play in the development of the budget?
10. What are pro forma statements?
11. Why is planning, in preparation for developing the budget, so important?
12. Should a company allow broad-based participation in developing the budget? Why?
13. What is the meaning behind the following—the budget should be problem oriented or opportunity oriented rather than a finger point device?
14. How difficult should the budget be? In order to achieve the optimal level of motivation, what should be the probability of success?
15. Why are the rewards associated with achieving the budget so important?
16. Is a budget a cost control or a cost reduction tool? Explain.

Exercises

Exercise 5.1 Production Budget

The estimated sales of three products for the third quarter of the year for Nesbit Company are as follows:

Product	Estimates Sales (units)
Zeon	32,000
Neon	36,000
Genon	54,000

Finished-goods inventories estimated at the beginning of the quarter and the target inventories at the end of the quarter are as follows:

Product	July 1	September 30
Zeon	6,000	6,600
Neon	11,000	9,500
Genon	14,000	12,500

Required

Prepare a production budget for the third quarter.

Exercise 5.2 Sales, Production, Direct-Materials and Direct-Labor Budgets

Cranston Company estimates the following unit sales in each of its five sales districts during the fourth quarter of the year:

	District				
Month	1	2	3	4	5
October	850	685	430	1,100	1,115
November	795	610	405	990	850
December	760	730	490	1,280	1,035

The sales price is $85 per unit.

Raw materials ending inventory is desired to be 45% of the following month's production. Raw materials inventory on October 1 is 2,800 units. January production is expected to be 2,600 units. Raw materials purchase price is $53 in October and $55 in November and December. Desired ending finished-goods inventory in units for October, November, and December is 3,000, 3,400, and 3,200 respectively. October 1 finished-goods inventory is 3,000 units.

It takes one unit of raw materials and 2.5 hours of direct labor at a cost of $10 per hour to complete one unit. One unit of direct materials is required for each unit of finished product.

Required

Prepare a sales budget, production budget, direct-materials purchase budget, direct-materials use budget, and direct-labor budget for the fourth quarter for Cranston Company. (Show both quantities and costs on the materials and labor budgets.)

Exercise 5.3   Production and Direct-Materials Budgets

Lamar Incorporated estimates sales for the second quarter as follows:

April	2,550 units
May	2,475 units
June	2,390 units

The target ending inventory of finished products is as follows for each month in the quarter:

April 1	2,000
April 30	2,230
May 31	2,190
June 30	2,310

Two units of material are required for each unit of finished goods. Production for July is estimated at 2,700 units to start building inventory for the fall sales period. Lamar's policy is to have an inventory of raw materials at the end of each month equal to 60% of the following month's production needs in order to accommodate supplier and shipping lead time and to keep production going on schedule.

Raw materials are expected to cost a uniform $4 per unit throughout the purchase period.

Required

1. Prepare a production budget.
2. Prepare a direct-materials purchase budget showing units and costs.
3. Prepare a direct-materials usage budget showing units and costs.

Exercise 5.4   Direct-Labor and Factory Overhead Budgets

Samson Corporation produces a product known as Samco. An acceptable productivity result to produce one Samco is two hours of direct labor. Samco requires moderate technical skill in the production process so the going labor rate is $12 per hour. Scheduled production for the third quarter is as follows:

July	2,200 units
August	2,500 units
September	1,800 units

Fixed factory overhead consists of $4,000 per month of items that come from adjusting entries, $3,500 of indirect materials and labor, and $2,300 of items that are on-going current period disbursement items.

Variable factory overhead includes $1.00 per labor hour of labor-related costs and $.50 per labor hour of items that require current period disbursement.

Required

1. Prepare a direct-labor budget for each month in the third quarter showing required hours and labor costs.
2. Prepare a factory overhead cost budget for each month in the third quarter showing a breakdown of costs into sections covering variable costs and fixed costs, with a further breakdown in the variable and fixed costs sections into the broad categories of overhead indicated in the facts.

Exercise 5.5   Selling Expense and Cost-of-Goods-Sold Budgets

Treewood Company estimates sales for the second quarter as follows:

April	$ 98,500
May	102,750
June	108,350

Selling expenses include fixed items of $6,500 per month, sales commissions of 5% of sales, and other items such as travel and variable advertising of 11% of sales.

The following production costs are estimated for the second quarter as a whole:

Direct materials	$35,000
Direct labor	45,000
Factory overhead	22,500

The monthly breakdown of quarterly production costs is expected to be as follows:

April	30%
May	45%
June	25%

Expected end-of-month finished-goods inventory are:

March	$24,000
April	27,000
May	32,000
June	26,000

Required

1. Prepare selling expense budgets for each month in the second quarter.
2. Prepare monthly cost-of-goods-sold budgets, showing a breakdown of materials, labor and factory overhead costs. Also prepare a monthly budget of pretax net income.

Exercise 5.6   Production Budget

Mather Electric has estimated sales for the first four months of 19X4 as follows:

	Sales in Units
January	5,000
February	7,500
March	9,000
April	8,000

Mather is now preparing a production budget for the first quarter of 19X4. They have determined that ending inventory must equal 20% of the following month's sales. The ending inventory at December 31, 19X3 is 1,000 units.

Required

How many units must be produced in each month of the quarter?

Exercise 5.7   Raw Materials Purchase Budget

Broadway Toys makes and distributes toys to retail outlets. A new product requires *3 pounds* of materials in manufacturing. The materials are all purchased from an outside supplier at *$1.50 per pound*. After studying the sales budget for the upcoming quarter, you have determined budgeted production to be:

	Production in Units
April	10,000
May	11,000
June	9,000
July	12,000

It has been found that a raw materials supply of 25% of the monthly production must be on hand at the beginning of each month. As of April 1, there exists 7,500 pounds of the raw materials.

Required

Compute the budgeted purchases of raw materials for April, May, and June. Show your calculations in dollars and pounds.

Exercise 5.8   Sales Budget

Wisteria Products Company has estimated annual sales by region as follows:

	Annual Sales in Units
North	30,000
Central	18,000
South	40,000
Total	88,000

Wisteria has been growing steadily and has built into the sales projections a quarterly growth factor. The expected quarterly sales for *each region* is broken down as follows:

Quarter	Percentage of Annual Sales
1st	22
2d	24
3rd	26
4th	28
	100

For budgeting purposes the sales price per unit is estimated to be $2.50. This price is the same for each region and will remain constant throughout the year.

Required

Prepare a sales budget for each quarter and for the year broken down on a regional basis. Show quantity and dollar values in the budget.

Exercise 5.9   Production Budget

Refer to your sales budget prepared for the Wisteria Products Company in exercise 5.8. Wisteria has found in previous years that it is necessary to have a quarterly ending inventory equal to 10% of the following quarter's sales. Production for all regions is done at one location and the inventory shown at the beginning of the first quarter is *2,000 units*. Assume that sales expectations for each year are the same as for the current budget year.

Required

Present a production budget for each quarter and for the year to the management of Wisteria Products Company.

Exercise 5.10   Raw Materials Purchases Budget

Refer to the budgets you prepared for the Wisteria Products Company in the exercises 5.8 and 5.9. The product for which these budgets have been prepared is a room fragrance. The liquid raw material used in production is purchased from one supplier and costs $12 per gallon. Each unit produced requires 8 ounces of the fluid. Wisteria Company has discovered that the raw materials ending inventory for each quarter must be *20%* of the following quarter's production needs. Assume 250 gallons of the required liquid raw material are on hand at the beginning of the year.

Required

Prepare a raw materials purchase budget for each quarter and the year totals. Show unit production needs, purchase needs in gallons, and costs. Round dollar amounts to the nearest $1.00.

Problems

Problem 5.1   Budgeting—Basic Concepts and Procedures (CMA)

The Russon Corporation is a retailer whose sales are all made on credit. Sales are billed twice monthly, on the 10th of the month for the last half of the prior month's sales and on the 20th of the month for the first half of the current month's sales. The terms of all sales are 2/10, net 30. Based upon past experience, the collection experience of accounts receivable is as follows:

Within the discount period	80%
On the 30th day	18%
Uncollectible	2%

The sales value of shipments for May 19X0 and the forecast for the next four months are:

May (actual)	$500,000
June	600,000
July	700,000
August	700,000
September	400,000

Russon's average markup on its products is 20% of the sales price.

Russon purchases merchandise for resale to meet the current month's sales demand and to maintain a desired monthly ending inventory of 25% of the next month's sales. All purchases are on credit with terms of net 30. Russon pays for one-half of a month's purchases in the month of purchase and the other half in the month following the purchase.

All sales and purchases occur uniformly throughout the month.

1. How much cash can Russon Corporation plan to collect from accounts receivable collections during July 19X0?
   a. $574,000
   b. $662,600
   c. $619,000
   d. $608,600
   e. None of the above answers is correct.
2. How much cash can Russon plan to collect in September from sales made in August 19X0?
   a. $337,400
   b. $343,000
   c. $400,400
   d. $280,000
   e. None of the above answers is correct.
3. The budgeted dollar value of Russon's inventory on August 31, 19X0 will be
   a. $110,000
   b. $80,000
   c. $112,000
   d. $100,000
   e. some amount other than those given above.

4. How much merchandise should Russon plan to purchase during June 19X0?
   a. $520,000
   b. $460,000
   c. $500,000
   d. $580,000
   e. None of the above answers is correct.
5. The amount Russon should budget in August 19X0 for the payment of merchandise is
   a. $560,000
   b. $500,000
   c. $667,000
   d. $600,000
   e. some amount other than those given above.

Problem 5.2   Cash Budgeting—Cash Receipts

Reid Company is developing a forecast of March cash receipts from credit sales. Credit sales for March are estimated to be $320,000. The accounts receivable balance at February 28 is $300,000; one-quarter of the balance represents January credit sales and the remainder is from February sales. All accounts receivable from months prior to January have been collected or written off. Reid's history of accounts receivable collections is as follows:

In the month of sale	20%
In the first month after month of sale	50%
In the second month after month of sale	25%
Written off as uncollectible at the end of	
the second month after month of sale	5%

Required

Based on the information above, determine the cash receipts Reid Company is expecting from credit sales during March.

Problem 5.3   Cash Budgeting—Cash Balance

Fields Corporation projects the following transactions for its first year of operations:

Proceeds from issuance of common	
stock	$1,000,000
Sales on account	2,200,000
Collections of accounts receivable	1,800,000
Cost of goods sold	1,400,000
Disbursements for purchases of	
merchandise and expenses	1,200,000
Disbursements for income taxes	250,000
Disbursements for purchase of fixed	
assets	800,000
Depreciation on fixed assets	150,000
Proceeds from borrowings	700,000
Payments on borrowings	80,000

Required

Determine the projected cash balance for December 31.

Problem 5.4   Cash Budgeting—Cash Disbursement

Mapes Corporation has estimated its activity for January. Selected data from these estimated amounts are as follows:

Sales	$1,400,000
Gross profit (based on sales)	30%
Increase in trade accounts receivable during month	$ 40,000
Change in accounts payable during month	$ 0
Increase in inventory during month	$ 20,000

Variable selling, general, and administrative expenses include a charge for uncollectible accounts of 1% of sales.

Total selling, general, and administrative expenses are $142,000 per month plus 15% of sales.

Depreciation expense of $80,000 per month is included in fixed selling, general, and administrative expenses.

Required

What are the estimated cash disbursements for January?

Problem 5.5   Determining Change in Cash Balance

Sussex Company has budgeted its operations for February. No change in inventory level during the month is planned. Selected data from estimated amounts are as follows:

Net loss	$100,000
Increase in accounts payable	40,000
Depreciation expense	35,000
Decrease in gross amount of trade accounts receivable	60,000
Purchase of office equipment on 45-day credit terms	15,000
Provision for estimated warranty liability	10,000

Required

How much change in cash position is expected for February?

Problem 5.6   Cash Budgeting (CMA)

United Business Education, Inc. (UBE), is a nonprofit organization that sponsors a wide variety of management seminars throughout the United States. In addition, it is heavily involved in research into improved methods of educating and motivating business executives. The seminar activity is largely supported by fees and the research program from member dues.

UBE operates on a calendar year basis and is in the process of finalizing the budget for 19X1. The following information has been taken from approved plans, which are still tentative at this time.

Seminar Program

Revenue. The scheduled number of programs should produce $12,000,000 of revenue for the year. Each program is budgeted to produce the same amount of revenue. The revenue is collected during the month the program is offered. The programs are scheduled so that 12% of the revenue is collected in each of the first five months of the year. The remaining programs, accounting for the remaining 40% of the revenue, are distributed evenly through the months of September, October, and November. No programs are offered in the other four months of the year.

Direct Expenses. The seminar expenses are made up of three segments:

1. Instructors' fees are paid at the rate of 70% of the seminar revenue in the month following the seminar. The instructors are considered independent contractors and are not eligible for UBE employee benefits.
2. Facilities fees total $5,600,000 for the year. They are the same for each program and are paid in the month the program is given.
3. Annual promotional costs of $1,000,000 are spent equally in all months, except June and July when there is no promotional effort.

Research Program

Research Grants. Many projects in the research program are nearing completion. The other main research activity this year includes the feasibility studies for projects to be started in 19X2. As a result, the total grant expense of $3,000,000 for 19X1 is expected to be paid out at the rate of $500,000 per month during the first six months of the year.

Salaries and Other UBE Expenses

Office Lease. Annual amount of $240,000 paid monthly at the beginning of each month.

General Administrative Expenses. $1,500,000 annually or $125,000 a month for telephone, supplies, postage, etc.

Depreciation Expense. $240,000 a year

General UBE Promotion. Annual cost of $600,000, paid monthly

Salaries and Benefits.

Number of Employees	Annual Salary Paid Monthly	Total Annual Salaries
1	$50,000	$ 50,000
3	40,000	120,000
4	30,000	120,000
15	25,000	375,000
5	15,000	75,000
22	10,000	220,000
50		$960,000

Employee benefits amount to $240,000 or 25% of annual salaries. Except for the pension contribution, the benefits are paid as salaries are paid. The annual pension payment of $24,000, based on 2.5% of salaries (included in the total benefits and the 25% rate), is due April 15, 19X1.

Other Information

Membership Income. UBE has 100,000 members, each of whom pays an annual fee of $100. The fee for the calendar year is invoiced in late June. The collection schedule is as follows:

July	60%
August	30%
September	5%
October	5%
	100%

Capital Expenditures. The capital expenditures program calls for a total of $510,000 in cash payments to be spread evenly over the first five months of 19X1.

Cash. Cash and temporary investments at January 1, 19X1 are estimated at $750,000.

Required

1. Prepare a budget of the annual cash receipts and disbursements for UBE for 19X1. Include data for each month.
2. Prepare a cash budget for UBE for January 19X1.
3. Using the information you developed in requirement 1 and 2, identify two important operating problems of UBE.

Problem 5.7   Budgeted Income Statement (CMA)

Rein Company, a compressor manufacturer, is developing a budgeted income statement for the calendar year 19X2. The president is generally satisfied with the projected net income of $700,000 for 19X1, resulting in an earnings per share figure of $2.80. However, next year the president would like the earnings per share to increase to at least $3.

Rein Company employs a standard absorption cost system. Inflation necessitates an annual revision in the standards as evidenced by an increase in production costs expected in 19X2. The total standard manufacturing cost for 19X1 is $72 per unit produced.

Rein expects to sell 100,000 compressors at $110 each in the current year (19X1). Forecasts from the sales department are favorable and Rein Company is projecting an annual increase of 10% in unit sales in 19X2 and 19X3. This increase in sales will occur even though a $15 increase in unit selling price will be implemented in 19X2. The selling price increase was absolutely essential to compensate for the increased production costs and operating expenses. However, management is concerned that any additional sales price increase would curtail the desired growth in volume.

Standard production costs are developed for the two primary metals used in the compressor (brass and a steel alloy), the direct labor, and manufacturing overhead. The following schedule represents the 19X2 standard quantities and rates for material and labor to produce one compressor.

Brass	4 pounds @ $5.35/pound	$21.40
Steel alloy	5 pounds @ $3.16/pound	15.80
Direct labor	4 hours @ $7.00/hour	28.00
Total prime costs		$65.20

The material content of the compressor has been reduced slightly, hopefully without a noticeable decrease in the quality of the finished product. Improved labor productivity and some increase in automation have resulted in a decrease in labor hours per unit from 4.4 to 4.0. However, the significant increases in material prices and hourly labor rates more than offset any savings from reduced input quantities.

The manufacturing overhead cost per unit schedule has yet to be completed. Preliminary data is as follows:

Overhead Items	Activity Level (units)		
	100,000	110,000	120,000
Supplies	$ 475,000	$ 522,500	$ 570,000
Indirect labor	530,000	583,000	636,000
Utilities	170,000	187,000	204,000
Maintenance	363,000	377,500	392,000
Taxes and insurance	87,000	87,000	87,000
Depreciation	421,000	421,000	421,000
Total overhead	$2,046,000	$2,178,000	$2,310,000

The standard overhead rate is based upon direct-labor hours and is developed by using the total overhead costs from the above schedule for the activity level closest to planned production. In developing the standards for the manufacturing costs, the following two assumptions were made.

1. Brass is currently selling at $5.65 per pound. However, this price is historically high and the purchasing manager expects the price to drop to the predetermined standard early in 19X2.
2. Several new employees will be hired for the production line in 19X2. The employees will be generally unskilled. If basic training programs are not effective and improved labor productivity is not experienced, then the production time per unit of product will increase by 15 minutes over the 19X2 standards.

Rein employs a LIFO inventory system for its finished goods. Rein's inventory policy for finished goods is to have 15% of the expected annual unit sales for the coming year in finished-goods inventory at the end of the prior year. The finished-goods inventory at December 31, 19X1, is expected to consist of 16,500 units at a total carrying cost of $1,006,500.

Operating expenses are classified as selling, which are variable, and administrative, which are all fixed. The budgeted selling expenses are expected to average 12% of sales revenue in 19X2, which is consistent with the performance in 19X1. The administrative expenses in 19X2 are expected to be 20% higher than the predicted 19X1 amount of $907,850.

Management accepts the cost standards developed by the production and accounting department. However, they are concerned about the possible effect on net income if the price of brass does not decrease and/or the labor efficiency does not improve as expected. Therefore, management wants the budgeted income statement to be prepared using the standards as developed but considering the worst possible situation for 19X2. Each resulting manufacturing variance should be separately identified and added to or subtracted from budgeted cost of goods sold at standard. Rein is subject to a 45% income tax rate.

Required

1. Prepare the budgeted income statement for 19X2 for Rein Company as specified by management. Round all calculations to the nearest dollar.
2. Review the 19X2 budgeted income statement prepared for Rein Company and discuss whether the president's objectives can be achieved.

Problem 5.8 Budgets and Human Behavioral Considerations (CMA)

RV Industries manufactures and sells recreation vehicles. The company has eight divisions strategically located near major markets. Each division has a sales force and two to four manufacturing plants. These divisions operate as autonomous profit centers responsible for purchasing, operations, and sales.

John Collins, the Corporate Controller, described the divisional performance measurement system as follows: "We allow the divisions to control the entire operation from the purchase of raw materials to the sale of the product. We, at corporate headquarters, only get involved in strategic decisions, such as developing new product lines. Each division is responsible for meeting its market needs by providing the right products at a low cost on a timely basis. Frankly, the divisions need to focus on cost control, delivery, and services to customers in order to become more profitable.

"While we give the divisions considerable autonomy, we watch their monthly income statements very closely. Each month's actual performance is compared with the budget in considerable detail. If the actual sales or contribution margin is more than 4 or 5% below the budget, we jump on the division people immediately. I might add that we don't have much trouble getting their attention. All of the management people at the plant and division level can add appreciably to their annual salaries with bonuses if actual net income is considerably greater than budget."

The budgeting process begins in August when division sales managers, after consulting with their sales personnel, estimate sales for the next calendar year. These estimates are sent to plant managers who use the sales forecasts to prepare production estimates. At the plants, production statistics, including raw material quantities, labor hours, production schedules, and output quantities, are developed by operating personnel. Using the statistics prepared by the operating personnel, the plant accounting staff determines costs and prepares the plant's budgeted variable cost of goods sold and other plant expenses for each month of the coming calendar year.

In October, each division's accounting staff combines plant budgets with sales estimates and adds additional division expenses. "After the divisional management is satisfied with the budget," said Collins, "I visit each division to go over their budget and make sure it is in line with corporate strategy and projections. I really emphasize the sales forecasts because of the volatility in the demand for our product. For many years, we lost sales to our competitors because we didn't project high enough production and sales, and couldn't meet the market demand. More recently, we were caught with large excess inventory when the bottom dropped out of the market for recreational vehicles.

"I generally visit all eight divisions during the first two weeks in November. After that the division budgets are combined and reconciled by my staff, and they are ready for approval by the board of directors in early December. The board seldom questions the budget.

"One complaint we've had from plant and division management is that they are penalized for circumstances beyond their control. For example, they failed to predict the recent sales decline. As a result, they didn't make their budget and, of course, they received no bonuses. However, I should point out that they are well rewarded when they exceed their budget. Furthermore, they provide most of the information for the budget, so it's their own fault if the budget is too optimistic."

Required

1. Identify and explain the biases that corporate management of RV Industries should expect in the communication of budget estimates by its division and plant personnel.
2. What sources of information can the top management of RV Industries use to monitor the budget estimates prepared by its divisions and plants?

3. What services could top management of RV Industries offer the divisions to help them in their budget development, without appearing to interfere with the division budget decisions?

4. The top management of RV Industries is attempting to decide whether it should get more involved in the budget process. Identify and explain the variables management needs to consider in reaching its decision.

Problem 5.9   Cash Budgeting—Summary Problem (CMA)

Requirements 1 through 4 relate to data to be reported in the statement of changes in financial position of Debbie Dress Shops Incorporated, based on the following information:

Debbie Dress Shops, Inc.
Balance Sheet

	December 31	
	19X1	*19X0*
Assets		
Current		
Cash	$ 300,000	$ 200,000
Accounts receivable (net)	840,000	580,000
Merchandise inventory	660,000	420,000
Prepaid expenses	100,000	50,000
Total current assets	1,900,000	1,250,000
Long-term investments	80,000	—
Land, buildings, and fixtures	1,130,000	600,000
Less: Accumulated depreciation	110,000	50,000
	1,020,000	550,000
Total assets	$3,000,000	$1,800,000
Equities		
Current liabilities:		
Accounts payable	$ 530,000	$ 440,000
Accrued expenses	140,000	130,000
Dividends payable	70,000	—
Total current liabilities	740,000	570,000
Note payable (due 19X4)	500,000	—
Stockholder's equity:		
Common stock	1,200,000	900,000
Retained earnings	560,000	330,000
	1,760,000	1,230,000
Total liabilities and stockholder's equity	$3,000,000	$1,800,000

Debbie Dress Shops, Inc.
Income Statement

	Year Ending December 31	
	19X1	*19X0*
Net credit sales	$6,400,000	$4,000,000
Cost of goods sold	5,000,000	3,200,000
Gross profit	1,400,000	800,000
Expenses (including income taxes)	1,000,000	520,000
Net income	$ 400,000	$ 280,000

Although the corporation will report all changes in financial position, management has adopted a format emphasizing the flow of cash.

All accounts receivable and accounts payable relate to trade merchandise. Accounts payable are recorded net and always are paid to take all of the discount allowed. The allowance for doubtful accounts at the end of 19X1 was the same as at the end of 19X0; no receivables were charged against the allowance during 19X1.

The proceeds from the note payable were used to finance a new store. Capital stock was sold to provide additional working capital.

1. Cash collected during 19X1 from accounts receivable amounted to
   a. $5,560,000.
   b. $5,840,000.
   c. $6,140,000.
   d. $6,400,000.
2. Cash payments during 19X1 on accounts payable to suppliers amounted to
   a. $4,670,000.
   b. $4,910,000.
   c. $5,000,000.
   d. $5,150,000.
3. Cash receipts during 19X1 that were not provided by operations totaled
   a. $140,000.
   b. $300,000.
   c. $500,000.
   d. $800,000.
4. Cash payments for noncurrent assets purchased during 19X1 were
   a. $80,000.
   b. $530,000.
   c. $610,000.
   d. $660,000.

Problem 5.10   Budgeting and Implementation Considerations (CMA)

Springfield Corporation operates on a calendar year basis. It begins the annual budgeting process in late August when the president establishes targets for the total dollar sales and net income before taxes for the next year.

The sales target is given to the marketing department where the marketing manager formulates a sales budget by product line in both units and dollars. From this budget, sales quotas by product line in units and dollars are established for each of the corporation's sales districts.

The marketing manager also estimates the cost of the marketing activities required to support the target sales volume and prepares a tentative marketing expense budget.

The executive vice-president uses the sales and profit targets, the sales budget by product line, and the tentative marketing expense budget to determine the dollar amounts that can be devoted to manufacturing and corporate office expense. The executive vice-president prepares the budget for corporate expenses and then forwards to the production department the product-line sales budget in units and the total dollar amount that can be devoted to manufacturing.

The production manager meets with the factory managers to develop a manufacturing plan within the cost constraints set by the executive vice-president. The budgeting process usually comes to a halt at this point because the production department does not consider the financial resources allocated to be adequate.

When this standstill occurs, the vice-president of finance, the executive vice-president, the marketing manager, and the production manager meet together to determine the final budgets for each of the areas. This normally results in a modest increase in the total amount available for manufacturing costs, while the marketing expense and corporate office expense budgets are cut. The total sales and net income figures proposed by the president are seldom changed. Although the participants are seldom pleased with the compromise, these budgets are final. Each executive then develops a new detailed budget for the operations in his or her area.

None of the areas has achieved its budget in recent years. Sales often run below the target. When budgeted sales are not achieved, each area is expected to cut costs so the president's profit target can still be met. However, the profit target is seldom met because costs are not cut enough. In fact, costs often run above the original budget in all functional areas. The president is disturbed that Springfield has not been able to meet the sales and profit targets and has hired a consultant who has had considerable experience with companies in Springfield's industry. The consultant reviewed the budgets for the past four years. The consultant concluded that the product-line sales budgets were reasonable and that the cost and expense budgets were adequate for the budgeted sales and production levels.

Required

1. Discuss how the budgeting process as employed by Springfield Corporation contributes to the failure to achieve the president's sales and profit targets.
2. Suggest how Springfield Corporation's budgeting process could be revised to correct the problems.
3. Should the functional areas be expected to cut their costs when sales volume falls below budget? Explain your answer.

FLEXIBLE BUDGETING AND RESPONSIBILITY REPORTING

6

OUTLINE

In chapter 5 we discussed the importance of a budget, procedures followed in developing a budget, and some of the behavioral problems associated with the development process. The budget developed there may be referred to as a "static budget" in that no allowance was made to adjust budgeted expenditures for unexpected changes in the level of sales and/or the level of production. This creates a problem in evaluating the effectiveness of the organization in meeting the budgeted objectives whenever the level of sales or the level of production is not the same as outlined in the budget. A technique called "flexible budgeting" has been developed to assist in preparing the budget and in evaluating the operating results.

An important part of flexible budgeting is quantifying the various cost relationships and selecting a measure of volume that is a good predictor of the amount of cost that should be incurred. Chapter 3 discussed the high-low method, scattergraph method, and least-squares method for developing a cost equation. This chapter uses these methods to select from among alternative measures of volume the one that is the best predictor of cost.

The usefulness of both the budget and the results of operations are enhanced when they are presented together with any significant deviations between them highlighted to attract management's attention. Reports for internal use should be broken down by segment, consistent with an individual's area of responsibility, and contain only those items that the individual can control. These reports have an important impact on behavior because of the feedback they provide and because they are often used to evaluate performance.

This chapter introduces flexible budgeting and responsibility accounting and discusses some of the behavioral aspects of reporting. After completing this chapter you should be able to:

1. describe what a flexible budget is and why it is useful.
2. prepare a flexible budget.
3. select the activity base or measure of volume that has the highest correlation with cost.
4. prepare meaningful performance reports.
5. discuss some of the significant behavioral aspects of performance reporting.

FLEXIBLE BUDGETING

The annual or quarterly budget as developed by the procedures outlined in chapter 5 is referred to as a **static budget.** Generally it is prepared at the beginning of an accounting period and serves as an operating plan for the accounting period. This budget is static in that it is relevant to only *one level of business activity*. For most manufacturing enterprises, selling is the critical activity and the level of production is closely tied to expected sales. The most likely level of sales is projected, the production level is determined, and the production and sales budgets are developed for *that* level of business activity. If, however, the actual level of production or sales is not as planned, a comparison of the static budget with actual performance is not meaningful in evaluating the efficiency of the enterprise. There are two common factors that could account for the difference between budgeted data and actual operating data:

1. The change in the level of business activity. A higher (lower) level of production should result in higher (lower) production costs than budgeted merely because of the number of units involved. Likewise, selling more (less) units than expected will cause higher (lower) selling expenses than planned for in the budget.

Figure 6.1

Planning Schedule for Production Budget
Year Ending December 31, 19X1

Manufacturing Costs	Unit Cost	Volume of Production			
		9,000	9,500	10,000	10,500
Direct material	$ 3.60	$ 32,400	$ 34,200	$ 36,000	$ 37,800
Direct labor	5.70	51,300	54,150	57,000	59,850
Variable overhead	2.00	18,000	19,000	20,000	21,000
Variable costs	$11.30	$101,700	$107,350	$113,000	$118,650
Fixed costs		7,000	7,000	7,000	7,000
Total cost		$108,700	$114,350	$120,000	$125,650

2. The efficiency of the employees. The efficiency with which workers perform their tasks can cause actual operating results to be different than the budget. For example, production costs will be higher when production workers perform sloppy work or waste time in moving from one activity to the next.

A budget that eliminates the effects of a change in the level of business activity provides a meaningful evaluation of the efficiency of the people. This kind of budget is called a **flexible budget.**

Flexible Budgeting Defined

Flexible budgeting is a technique that is used to adjust the budget for *various levels of business activity.* Volume of business activity may be specified in a variety of ways, but one common measure is the number of units manufactured or the number of units sold. In developing the flexible budget, expected or budgeted cost relationships are quantified so the budget can be easily adjusted to any level of business activity. In essence, the flexible budget says, "You tell me your level of business activity for the period and I'll tell you what your costs should have been."

Flexible Budget Example

An example will illustrate how a flexible budget is used and why it is important for performance evaluations. Suppose that the expected cost of producing one unit of finished product consists of the following:

Manufacturing Costs	Standard	Cost per Unit
Direct material	(3 lbs. @ $1.20 per lb.)	$3.60
Direct labor	(1 hour @ $5.70 per hour)	5.70
Variable overhead	($2.00 per direct-labor hour)	2.00
Fixed overhead	($7,000 ÷ 10,000 units)	.70
Total cost per unit		$12.00

Notice that the variable overhead is expected to vary in proportion to the number of direct-labor hours worked. Also, notice that the fixed overhead is expected to be $7,000 for the year. At a planned production level of 10,000 units, the cost per unit is $.70. Remember that fixed costs do not change when production changes, so $7,000 is expected to be spent on fixed overhead regardless of the actual level of production.

Figure 6.1 shows the budgeted cost data used in preparing the budget for 19X1. It shows the amount of cost that should be incurred at 9,000, 9,500, 10,000, and 10,500

Figure 6.2

Production Report
Year Ending December 31, 19X1

Manufacturing Costs	Budgeted Costs[a]	Actual Costs[b]	Variance Favorable (Unfavorable)
Direct material	$ 36,000	$ 41,500	($ 5,500)
Direct labor	57,000	61,900	(4,900)
Variable overhead	20,000	21,800	(1,800)
Fixed overhead	7,000	7,200	(200)
Total	$120,000	$132,400	($12,400)

[a]Budgeted costs are for 10,000 units of production.
[b]Actual production level was 11,000 units.

Figure 6.3

Revised Production Report
Year Ending December 31, 19X1

Manufacturing Costs	Budgeted Cost @ 10,000 Units	Budgeted Cost@ 11,000 Units	Actual Cost@ 11,000 Units	Variances[a] Production Level	Variances[a] Efficiency	Variances[a] Total
Direct material	$ 36,000	$ 39,600	$ 41,500	($ 3,600)	($1,900)	($ 5,500)
Direct labor	57,000	62,700	61,900	(5,700)	800	(4,900)
Variable overhead	20,000	22,000	21,800	(2,000)	200	(1,800)
Fixed overhead	7,000	7,000	7,200	–0–	(200)	(200)
Total	$120,000	$131,300	$132,400	($11,300)	($1,100)	($12,400)

[a]Variances are identified as favorable or unfavorable by the parenthesis—favorable, (unfavorable).

units of production. Since 10,000 units was considered the most likely level of production for 19X1, the data shown in that column were adopted and included in the master budget.

However, actual production during 19X1 was 11,000 units. Figure 6.2 shows the budgeted production cost data for 19X1 at the projected production level of 10,000 units. Also shown are the actual production costs incurred during the year at the 11,000 unit production level. The difference between actual and budgeted costs are shown as variances. When actual cost exceeds budgeted cost it is considered an unfavorable variance and is enclosed within parentheses.

An initial review of the production report illustrated in figure 6.2 would lead a person to believe the production process was very inefficient. However, a significant part of the unfavorable variance resulted from the production level being higher than budgeted. Actual production was 11,000 units rather than 10,000 units as planned.

Figure 6.3 shows a revised production report. A column showing a revised budget for the actual production level is developed from the standard cost data shown earlier. The variance is also split between (a) the portion attributable to the effectiveness of the organization in increasing the production level and (b) the portion attributable to production efficiencies or inefficiencies.

Of the $12,400 ($132,400–$120,000) unfavorable variance between actual and budgeted production costs, $11,300 of it is attributable to the change in production level. The other $1,100 relates to the efficiency of the production process. This is further divided into the various production components. Direct materials and fixed overhead show unfavorable variances, while direct labor and variable overhead show favorable variances. Variance analysis (discussed in chaps. 15 and 16) further divides the variances for individual components of production into a price variance and a usage (or efficiency) variance. For example, the $1,900 unfavorable direct-material variance may have resulted from (*a*) using more (less) than three pounds of raw material per unit, (*b*) paying more (less) than $1.20 per pound, or (*c*) some combination of (*a*) and (*b*).

Flexible Budget Formula

The cost behavior exhibited by the various components of production was discussed in detail in chapter 3. Direct material and direct labor are both variable costs that increase proportionately with increases in the level of production. Factory overhead is a semivariable or mixed cost because it includes both a fixed and a variable cost element. Assuming linear cost relationships, the total expected production cost can be represented by the following equations:

Mathematical formula for a straight line:

$y = a + b\,(x)$

Flexible budget formula:

Total cost = Fixed costs + Variable cost per unit of volume × Volume level
where y = dependent variable or total production cost
$\quad x$ = independent variable, representing a measure of volume or an activity base
$\quad a$ = point of intersection with the vertical axis or an estimate of the fixed costs
$\quad b$ = slope of the cost line or an estimate of the variable costs per unit including direct materials, direct labor, and variable overhead

The total production cost formula in the example above is:

Total production cost = $7,000 + $11.30 (units)

At 10,000 units of production, the expected cost is $120,000.

$7,000 + $11.30 (10,000) = $120,000

At 11,000 units of production, the expected cost is $131,300.

$7,000 + $11.30 (11,000) = $131,300

Once it has been developed, the flexible budget formula is very useful in developing the budget and in evaluating the results of operations. A budget may be developed and revised several times before it is acceptable to top management. The flexible budget formula can assist in developing budget data for various levels of business activity. At the end of the accounting period, the flexible budget is useful in adjusting the budgeted data to the actual level of business activity achieved during the period. This is essential in correctly evaluating the efficiency or inefficiency of the enterprise during the period.

DEVELOPING THE FLEXIBLE BUDGET FORMULA

Flexible budgeting can be used in a variety of businesses to estimate and control costs. It is particularly useful in manufacturing enterprises for estimating both production costs and selling expenses. However, any enterprise with both fixed and variable costs can effectively use flexible budgeting. First we will focus on developing the flexible budget for the production process of a manufacturing firm. Then we will show how flexible budgets are used to estimate and control selling and administrative expenses.

Analyzing Cost Behavior in a Production Process

An industrial engineering analysis and historical cost analysis are two approaches to analyzing costs and developing a flexible budget formula. The industrial engineering approach looks forward and attempts to identify what the costs should be for the coming period using the most efficient method of operation in the existing facility. The historical cost approach uses prior operating cost data to predict future costs. In reality, some combination of the two approaches is generally used.

Chapter 3 discussed the high-low, scattergraph, and least-squares methods for identifying and analyzing cost patterns. We will focus on the historical cost analysis and show how these methods are used to develop the flexible budget formula and to select an activity base that is the best predictor of the amount of cost that should be incurred.

You will recall that the first step in using an historical cost analysis is to collect the historical data to be used. Any prior year or group of years could be used, but the period of time selected should be representative of future operating results. The data should include (*a*) the amount of cost incurred for each element of production—direct material, direct labor, and factory overhead—and (*b*) the volume of activity achieved for several alternative measures—such as units produced, machine hours worked, and direct-labor hours worked. The data are broken down into short time intervals, such as monthly, weekly, or quarterly, consistent with the reporting cycle of the company.

Remember that direct materials and direct labor are traceable to the product and vary according to the number of units produced. However, factory overhead is a mixed cost, the variable portion of which may vary according to a variety of things. These are called **activity bases** or *volume measures* and include such things as units produced, hours worked, and orders processed. It is important to identify the activity base that is the best predictor of factory overhead. Therefore, several measures of volume are usually identified and data is collected on each of them.

Thompson Manufacturing Company will be used to illustrate (*a*) the development of a flexible budget formula for material, labor, and overhead and (*b*) the selection of the activity base that is the best predictor of factory overhead.

Figure 6.4 shows the cost data that was collected for Thompson Manufacturing Company during the last eight months of 19X4. The operations for 19X5 are expected to be similar to 19X4 with the exception of December. A bad winter storm caused power shortages and disrupted operations for almost two weeks. Overhead costs remained high, but productive output was almost zero. Therefore, the data from December is excluded from the analysis. The other seven months are considered useful in projecting and quantifying cost behavior patterns. The data show by month the number of sprinkler heads produced, the number of direct-labor hours worked, and the manufacturing costs incurred. Units produced and direct-labor hours worked are the activity bases to be studied.

Direct Costs: Materials and Labor

Direct costs for both material and labor vary according to the number of units produced. Since there are no fixed costs involved, the variable rate for the flexible budget formula can be computed by dividing the total cost incurred by the number of units produced.

The cost per unit of $1.20 for direct material is computed by dividing total material cost by the units produced as follows:

$$\frac{\text{Total cost}}{\text{Units produced}} = \frac{\$9,660}{8,050} = \underline{\$1.20}$$

The direct-material portion of the flexible budget formula is represented by the following equation:

$$\text{Direct-material cost} = 0 + \$1.20(x)$$

where x = units produced

Figure 6.4

Thompson Manufacturing Company
Manufacturing Cost Summary
Eight Months Ending December 31, 19X4

	Manufacturing Costs			Volume	
Month	Direct Material	Direct Labor	Factory Overhead	Units Produced	Direct-Labor Hours Worked
May	$1,920	$ 2,300	$ 4,200	1,600	840
June	1,440	1,740	3,500	1,200	670
July	1,080	1,310	3,100	900	460
August	720	880	2,200	600	320
September	960	1,170	2,600	800	390
October	1,680	1,740	3,900	1,400	620
November	1,860	2,140	3,600	1,550	860
December	—[a]	—[a]	—[a]	—[a]	—[a]
Total	$9,660[a]	$11,280[a]	$23,100[a]	8,050[a]	4,160[a]

[a]December data is not considered representative of normal operations and is excluded from the total and from any further analysis.

Figure 6.5   Direct costs

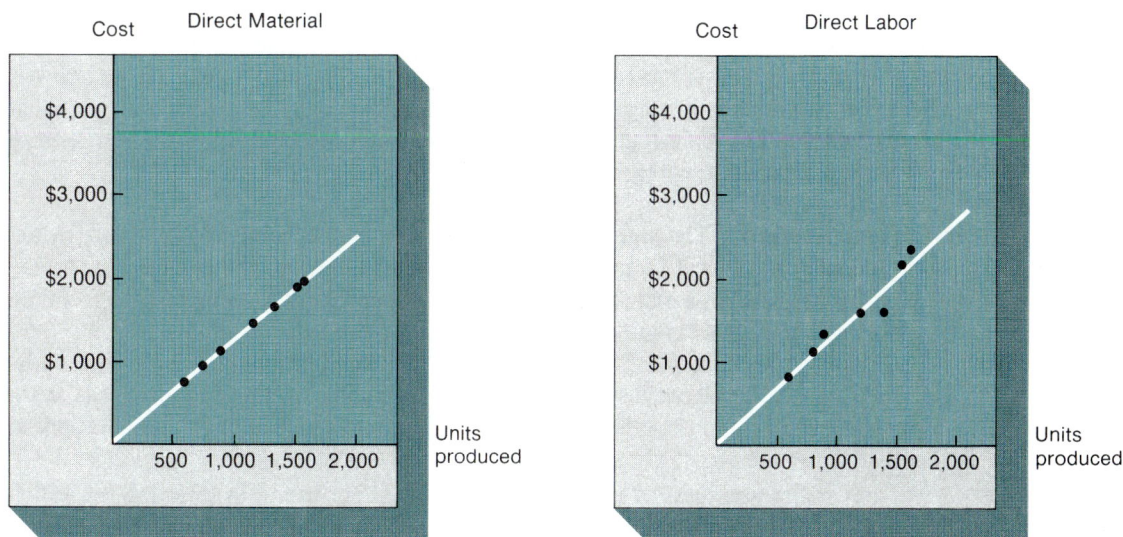

Figure 6.5 illustrates in graphical form the observed data and the line representing the equation above. Notice that the direct-material cost in each month is equal to $1.20 times the number of units manufactured. Thus, each data point is on the line and the cost per unit could have been computed by selecting any month and dividing the output into the cost incurred.

The direct-labor cost per unit is computed in the same manner and the direct-labor portion of the flexible budget formula looks as follows:

$$\frac{\text{Total cost}}{\text{Units produced}} = \frac{\$11,280}{8,050} = \$1.40 \text{ per unit}$$

Direct-labor cost $= 0 + \$1.40(x)$

where $x =$ units produced

Figure 6.5 also shows in graphical form the observed direct-labor cost data and the line representing the equation above. Notice that there is some variability of the points around the line. Thompson Manufacturing Company employs a lot of part-time help and the wage rate of each employee is determined by the length of employment with the company. Since the composition of the work force changes each week, the direct-labor cost relative to the number of units produced also changes. The $1.40 per unit is an average cost for the entire year and is probably the best predictor available for the coming year.

Factory Overhead

Factory overhead is somewhat more complicated because it is composed of many different manufacturing costs exhibiting a variety of cost patterns. Each element of overhead could be studied and a separate formula developed for each. Some companies with a significant portion of their manufacturing costs tied up in overhead find it useful to study each major element of overhead and prepare a separate formula for each. However, for most companies, the increased development cost and added complexity are not worth the added precision. Therefore, two assumptions are made:

1. The variable cost portion of factory overhead is linear in relation to the activity base of the firm.
2. One activity base can be identified that will adequately predict variable overhead.

Our objective is to develop the overhead portion of the flexible budget formula, which identifies the fixed cost in total and the variable rate for the activity base selected. Several activity bases are usually studied to select the one that is the best predictor of changes in variable overhead. The high-low method is not as useful as either the scattergraph method or a least-squares regression analysis in selecting the activity base.

High-Low Method   The high-low method determines a variable overhead rate by analyzing the change in total factory overhead that corresponds to the change in *volume* of activity between the *high* and *low points*. Variable overhead is then subtracted from total overhead at a particular volume of activity to compute fixed overhead.

Using the data for Thompson Manufacturing Company, two flexible budget equations can be developed for factory overhead—one using units produced as the independent variable and the other using direct-labor hours worked. The computations are shown in figure 6.6.

A major weakness of this method is that it is not useful in selecting the activity base that is the best predictor of variable overhead. It is difficult to select between the flexible budget formula based on units produced as opposed to direct-labor hours worked in the Thompson Manufacturing Company example.

Scattergraph Method   The scattergraph method plots the data on a scatter diagram with the overhead cost on the vertical axis and the activity base on the horizontal axis as illustrated in figure 6.7. A regression line is inserted by a *visual fit* and the *y*-intercept and slope of the line are used to determine the fixed cost and the variable rate, respectively, in the flexible budget equation. A major problem in using the scattergraph method

Figure 6.6   High-low point analysis

	Factory Overhead	Units Produced	Direct-Labor Hours Worked
High point	$4,200	1,600	840
Low point	2,200	600	320
Change	$2,000	1,000	520

Variable rate:

$$\frac{\$2,000}{1,000} = \$2.00 \text{ per unit}$$

$$\frac{\$2,000}{520 \text{ hrs}} = \$3.85 \text{ per hour}$$

Fixed cost:

	Units	Hours
Factory overhead	$4,200	$4,200
Variable cost:		
(1,600 units @ $2.00)	3,200	
(840 hours @ $3.85)		3,234
	$1,000	$ 966

Flexible budget equation for factory overhead:

Units:

Factory overhead $= \$1,000 + \$2.00(x)$
where $x =$ units produced

Direct labor:

Factory overhead $= \$966 + \$3.85(x)$
where $x =$ number of direct-labor hours worked

Figure 6.7   Scattergraph method

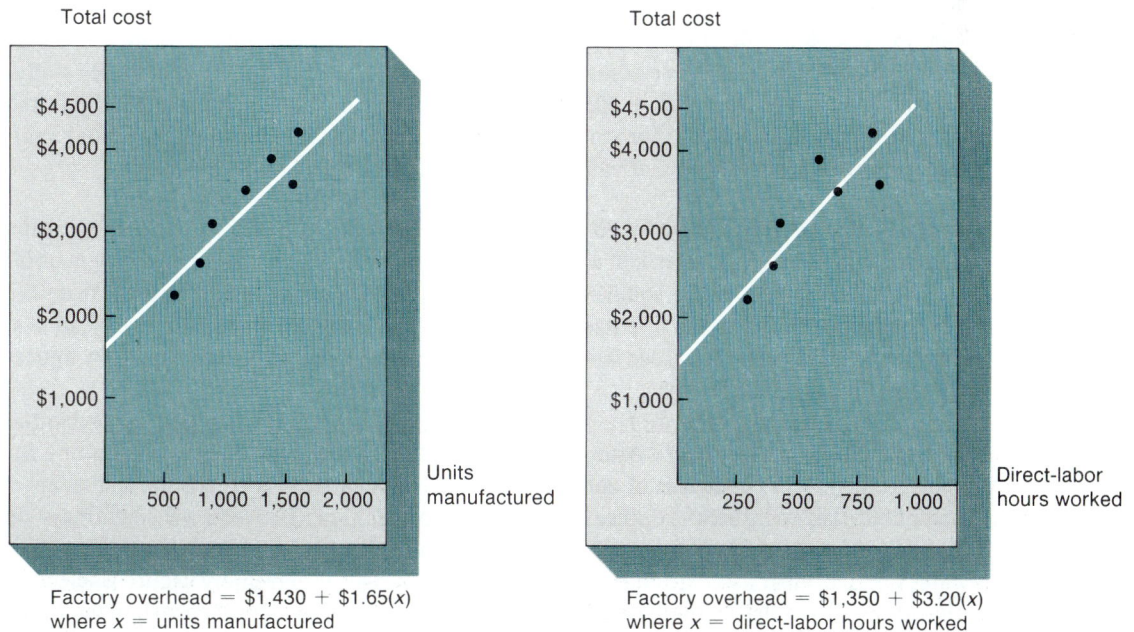

Factory overhead $= \$1,430 + \$1.65(x)$
where $x =$ units manufactured

Factory overhead $= \$1,350 + \$3.20(x)$
where $x =$ direct-labor hours worked

Figure 6.8

Thompson Manufacturing Company
Least-Squares Regression Analysis
Units Produced as Activity Base

Month	*x* Units Produced	*y* Factory Overhead	*xy*	*x²*	*y²*
May	1,600	$ 4,200	$ 6,720,000	2,560,000	$17,640,000
June	1,200	3,500	4,200,000	1,440,000	12,250,000
July	900	3,100	2,790,000	810,000	9,610,000
August	600	2,200	1,320,000	360,000	4,840,000
September	800	2,600	2,080,000	640,000	6,760,000
October	1,400	3,900	5,460,000	1,960,000	15,210,000
November	1,550	3,600	5,580,000	2,402,500	12,960,000
Total	8,050	$23,100	$28,150,000	10,172,500	$79,270,000

$$a = \frac{(\Sigma y)(\Sigma x^2) - (\Sigma x)(\Sigma xy)}{n(\Sigma x^2) - (\Sigma x)^2}$$

$$= \frac{(23,100)(10,172,500) - (8,050)(28,150,000)}{(7)(10,172,500) - (8,050)^2}$$

$$= \$1,308$$

$$b = \frac{n(\Sigma xy) - (\Sigma x)(\Sigma y)}{n(\Sigma x^2) - (\Sigma x)^2}$$

$$= \frac{(7)(28,150,000) - (8,050)(23,100)}{(7)(10,172,500) - (8,050)^2}$$

$$= 1.73$$

Flexible budget formula:
overhead = $1,308 + 1.73($x$)
where x = units produced

is the difficulty and subjectivity associated with developing the mathematical equation for the budget line drawn on the graph. Reading the y-intercept and any other point along the regression line is a subjective estimate at best.

The scattergraph method assists in selecting between alternative activity bases. The activity base that provides the best fit to the regression line should be selected. This can often be determined by a visual analysis of the scatter diagrams. The measure that has the plotted points clustered closest to the regression line provides the best fit. By studying the graphs in figure 6.7 it appears that the graph for units manufactured has the plotted points closer to the regression line and thus provides the best fit. The visual analysis, however, is subjective and cannot be quantitatively measured.

Least-Squares Regression and Correlation Analysis   The least-squares regression analysis computes the y-intercept and slope of the regression line *mathematically* in order to minimize the sum of the squares of the lengths of the vertical-line segments from the observed data points to the line itself. The computations for developing an overhead cost curve using the units produced and the direct-labor hours worked are shown in figures 6.8 and 6.9 respectively.

A desirable feature of a least-squares regression analysis is that a correlation analysis can be performed to determine, quantitatively, how good the regression line fits the data points. **A coefficient of correlation** (sometimes called a correlation coefficient) is computed that measures the linear association (correlation) between two variables—in our example, the manufacturing overhead and an activity base. A high coefficient indicates greater linear association between the variables. This is extremely useful in selecting the activity base that is the best predictor of the amount of overhead cost that should be incurred.

Figure 6.9

Thompson Manufacturing Company
Least-Squares Regression Analysis
Direct-Labor Hours Worked as Activity Base

Month	*x* Direct-Labor Hours Worked	*y* Factory Overhead	*xy*	*x²*	*y²*
May	840	$ 4,200	$ 3,528,000	705,600	$17,640,000
June	670	3,500	2,345,000	448,900	12,250,000
July	460	3,100	1,426,000	211,600	9,610,000
August	320	2,200	704,000	102,400	4,840,000
September	390	2,600	1,014,000	152,100	6,760,000
October	620	3,900	2,418,000	384,400	15,210,000
November	900	3,600	3,240,000	810,000	12,960,000
Total	4,200	$23,100	$14,675,000	2,815,000	$79,270,000

$$a = \frac{(\Sigma y)(\Sigma x^2) - (\Sigma x)(\Sigma xy)}{n(\Sigma x^2) - (\Sigma x)^2}$$

$$= \frac{(23,100)(2,815,000) - (4,200)(14,675,000)}{(7)(2,815,000) - (4,200)^2}$$

$$= \$1,642$$

$$b = \frac{n(\Sigma xy) - (\Sigma x)(\Sigma y)}{n(\Sigma x^2) - (\Sigma x)^2}$$

$$= \frac{(7)(14,675,000) - (4,200)(23,100)}{(7)(2,815,000) - (4,200)^2}$$

$$= 2.76$$

Flexible budget formula:
overhead = $1,642 + 2.76(x)$
where x = direct-labor hours worked

A formula for computing r, the coefficient of correlation, is:

$$r = \frac{n(\Sigma xy) - (\Sigma x)(\Sigma y)}{\sqrt{[n\Sigma x^2 - (\Sigma x)^2][n\Sigma y^2 - (\Sigma y)^2]}}$$

An alternative computation is illustrated in appendix A. The intermediate values developed for computing the values of a and b for the regression line can be substituted into the above equation to compute the value of r. The value of r using (a) units produced as the activity base and (b) direct-labor hours worked as the activity base is computed below.

Units produced as the activity base (numbers are obtained from fig. 6.8):

$$r = \frac{(7)(28,150,000) - (8,050)(23,100)}{\sqrt{[(7)(10,172,500) - (8,050)^2][(7)(79,270,000) - (23,100)^2]}}$$

$$= .95$$

Direct-labor hours worked as activity base (numbers are obtained from fig. 6.9):

$$r = \frac{(7)(14,675,000) - (4,200)(23,100)}{\sqrt{[(7)(2,815,000) - (4,200)^2][(7)(79,270,000) - (23,100)^2]}}$$

$$= .86$$

The range of possible values for r is from -1 to $+1$. It is a dimensionless quantity in that it is independent of the units of measurement of both x and y. Whether r is positive or negative depends on the slope of the regression line. Since the regression line for factory overhead generally slopes upward, the r value will be positive for this type of analysis.

The association between x and y increases as the absolute value of r increases. When applied to the factory overhead problem, a high absolute value of r indicates high correlation between factory overhead and the activity base being evaluated. When r is close to 1, for example, high factory overhead should be incurred during months of high production. Likewise, months in which a low number of units are produced should have low factory overhead. If r is close to zero, there is little, if any, linear association between the activity base being studied and factory overhead.

The value of r, the coefficient of correlation, is often squared to compute a **coefficient of determination.** The coefficient of determination represents the amount of variation in y that is explained by x. For most people r^2 is easier to interpret than r because it represents the *percentage* of variation in y that is explained by x.

The coefficient of determination (r^2) is computed below for each activity base being studied for Thompson Manufacturing Company.

Activity Base	r Coefficient of Correlation	r^2 Coefficient of Determination
Units produced	.95	.90
Direct-labor hours worked	.86	.74

A coefficient of determination of .90 for units manufactured as the activity base means that 90% of the variation in factory overhead can be explained by the number of units manufactured. An r^2 of .74 for direct-labor hours worked as the activity base means that 74% of the variation in factory overhead can be explained by the number of direct-labor hours worked.

The values of r and r^2 can be used to select the activity base that is the best predictor of factory overhead. The higher r value for units manufactured means that it is more highly correlated with the factory overhead than direct-labor hours worked. The difference between the values of r^2 identifies how much better it is as a predictor. Units manufactured accounts for 16% (.90 − .74) more of the variability in manufacturing overhead than direct-labor hours worked.

In summary, the methods for analyzing cost behavior are not equally applicable in selecting the activity base that is the best predictor of the cost that should be incurred. The scattergraph and least-squares regression methods provide useful information for this decision. However, a least-squares regression and correlation analysis is most useful because it quantifies the relationship between the variables and measures the variability in the dependent variable that is accounted for by changes in the independent variable.

Flexible Budgeting for Selling and Administrative Costs

Flexible budgeting is useful in estimating and controlling selling and administrative costs. In fact, flexible budgeting is useful for estimating any cost with both a fixed and variable element. A flexible budget formula is developed that identifies the fixed cost and the variable rate. The procedures for developing the flexible budget formula for selling and administrative costs are the same as illustrated for the production costs. Several activity bases are generally studied to determine the one that has the highest correlation with total cost.

Once the flexible budget formula is developed, it can be used to estimate cost at a predicted level of operations as well as to identify the amount of cost that should have been incurred at the actual level of operations. This facilitates cost control and performance evaluations.

Thompson Manufacturing Company followed standard procedures to compute a flexible budget formula for selling and administrative expenses. Individual cost elements were identified, data were collected and analyzed, and the following results were obtained:

Cost Element	Fixed per Month	Variable per Unit
Salary and wages	$1,250	$ .80
Office building	1,000	.50
Freight out	-0-	.20
Total	$2,250	$1.50

Formula:

Total cost $= \$2,250 + \$1.50(x)$

where x = units sold

During January 19X5, Thompson Manufacturing Company expected to sell 700 units. Total selling and administrative costs were expected to be $3,300.

Total cost $= \$2,250 + \$1.50(700)$

$= \$3,300$

However, the actual cost in January was $3,200 and only 650 units were sold. Figure 6.10 shows an analysis of the difference between the actual costs incurred and the amounts that should have been incurred at 650 units of sales. Notice that salary and wages costs were more than expected but the costs of the office building and freight out were less than expected. The net effect was a $25 favorable variance between actual and estimated costs.

RESPONSIBILITY ACCOUNTING

An accounting system is useful if it helps to predict the costs that should be incurred, to accumulate the costs actually incurred, and to provide reports that summarize both budgeted and actual costs in a meaningful way. Accounting reports are a significant part of performance evaluations. Therefore, care must be taken to identify responsibility for an item and the reports should be consistent with that responsibility.

Responsibility Accounting Defined

Sound management practices and good internal controls require that someone be assigned to manage every activity that provides a revenue or incurs a cost. Responsibility should rest on only one individual for each activity or cost. Each individual should understand his or her stewardship and should be held accountable for it. **Responsibility accounting** is

---

Figure 6.10

Thompson Manufacturing Company
Selling and Administrative Expense Analysis
January 19X5

Cost Element	Estimated Costs			Actual Cost	Variance Favorable (Unfavorable)
	Fixed	Variable[a]	Total		
Salary and wages	$1,250	$520	$1,770	$1,950	($180)
Buildings	1,000	325	1,325	1,130	195
Freight	-0-	130	130	120	10
Total	$2,250	$975	$3,225	$3,200	$ 25

[a]The variable costs are based on the budgeted rate at 650 units sold.

Figure 6.11   Latham, Inc., organization chart

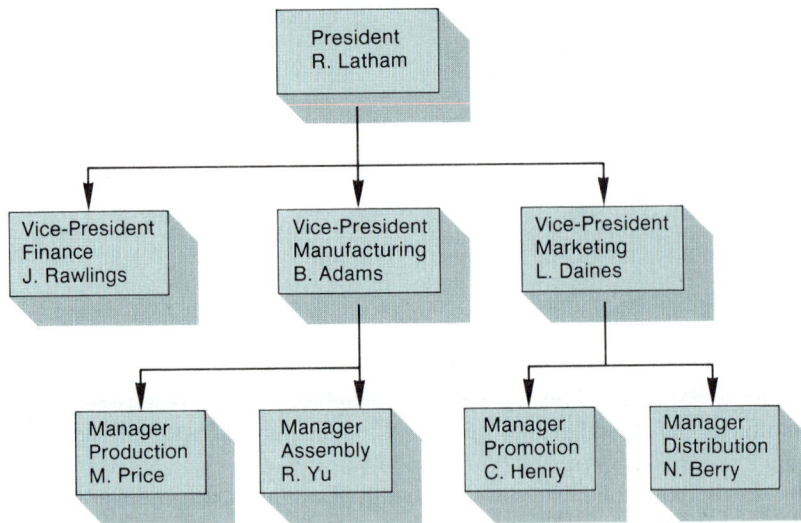

a form of internal reporting that is based on the ability to control. Each individual's report contains the items they have the ability to control.

Relationship to Segmented Reporting

Segment reporting is the process of breaking up an enterprise into reportable segments and preparing financial information by segments. Segmented reports discussed here are used primarily for internal management use. However, they may also be useful in developing segmented reports that are required for external reporting.[1] Chapter 19 identifies various types of responsibility centers, discusses cost allocation as it relates to segmented reporting, and evaluates its usefulness in various decisions concerning the segment. Our objective here is to identify what segment reporting is, how it relates to responsibility accounting, and its impact on performance evaluations.

Form and Content of Reports

The accounting system and the reports should be consistent with the assignment of responsibility. Figure 6.11 shows an organization chart for Latham Products, Incorporated. This chart shows the key people who have responsibility for the operations and financial policies of the company. If the company does well, they will receive the credit. When problems arise, it is their responsibility to identify and correct them.

A **pyramid reporting** structure is used to report on each individual's area of responsibility. Individuals at the bottom of the organization chart receive reports on individual items within their area of control. Individuals at middle and upper levels of management receive reports with summary information on the results of operations controlled by people under them, as well as detailed information on individual items over which they have control.

The Latham Products example can be used to illustrate the pyramid reporting structure. Mr. Price, the production manager, should receive only production information

[1]The basic rules and procedures for external segmented reporting are specified by the Financial Accounting Standards Board in Statement No. 14. External Segment reporting is covered in most financial accounting textbooks.

Figure 6.12

Latham Products, Inc.
Segment Reports

Company Cost Summary Report—President
September 19X3

	Budget		Actual		Variance	
Item	Month	Year to Date	Month	Year to Date	Month	Year to Date
Finance	$ 21,600	$ 194,400	$ 20,200	$ 190,000	$1,400	$ 4,400
Manufacturing	69,700	623,000	72,800	637,700	(3,100)	(14,700)
Marketing	37,200	334,800	46,300	338,900	(9,100)*	(4,100)
Political contributions	1,000	9,000	-0-	-0-	1,000*	9,000*
Interest	4,000	36,000	3,600	32,100	400	3,900
Depreciation	12,000	108,000	12,000	108,000	-0-	-0-
Total	$145,500	$1,305,200	$154,900	$1,306,700	($9,400)	($ 1,500)

Manufacturing Cost Summary—Vice-President Manufacturing
September 19X3

	Budget		Actual		Variance	
Item	Month	Year to Date	Month	Year to Date	Month	Year to Date
Production	$32,100	$288,900	$34,700	$295,000	($2,600)	($6,100)
Assembly	29,500	261,100	28,900	262,300	600	(1,200)
Indirect labor	6,000	54,000	5,800	53,400	200	600
Other	2,100	19,000	3,400	27,000	(1,300)*	(8,000)*
Total	$69,700	$623,000	$72,800	$637,700	($3,100)	($14,700)

Production Cost Summary—Production Manager
September 19X3

	Budget		Actual		Variance	
Item	Month	Year to Date	Month	Year to Date	Month	Year to Date
Material A	$ 9,000	$ 81,000	$ 9,400	$ 80,900	($ 400)	$ 100
Material B	6,000	54,000	5,700	55,000	300	(1,000)
Direct labor	15,000	135,000	15,500	138,000	(500)	(3,000)
Set up	2,100	18,900	4,100	21,100	(2,000)*	(2,200)*
Total	$32,100	$288,900	$34,700	$295,000	($2,600)	($6,100)

( ) Parentheses indicate unfavorable variances.
*Asterisk indicates significant deviations from the budget.

on his report and it should be in enough detail to evaluate the production activities and to take corrective action as needed. Ms. Adams, the vice-president of manufacturing and assembly, should receive summary information on both production and assembly as well as other manufacturing information that cannot be identified specifically with either production or assembly.

Figure 6.12 shows the reports that have been prepared for part of Latham Products. Notice the form of the reports and their relationship to each other. Summary information from lower levels are included on the president's and vice-presidents' reports. If for some reason they need additional detail on a lower level, they merely request a copy of that report.

The form and content of the reports are important. Some basic rules include the following:

1. The title should clearly identify the area of responsibility and the time period covered.
2. The level of detail within the report should be appropriate for the level of the report within the organization. For example, a report for the production manager should detail each type of raw material and each class of direct labor required for production. The vice-president of manufacturing, however, will only have summary data for each production area.
3. Actual operating data as well as budgeted operating data should be shown on the report. The budget identifies a level of business activity that will result in organizational success, if that level is achieved. Therefore, it is an appropriate standard to which actual results can be compared to identify areas of the operation in which management attention is needed.
4. Any significant deviations from the budget should be highlighted. Deviations from the budget can be shown as actual amounts (dollars or units) or in percentage amounts. Sound management practices suggest that managers should spend their time working in areas of the organization that are out of control or where the greatest benefit can be achieved. Accounting reports can help management use their time effectively by identifying what is considered a material or significant deviation and then highlighting it on the report. The report generally shows the variance between actual data and budgeted data with a star or asterisk, which indicates those in need of management's attention.
5. Noncontrollable items should be distinguished from controllable items. Noncontrollable items should be excluded from the report. If for some reason they are included, they should be separated from the controllable items and clearly labeled. This is necessary so the reports can be used for performance evaluations. An individual should not be held responsible for something over which there is little or no control.

Analysis of Budget Variances: Management by Exception

Management by exception suggests that managers should concentrate their time on areas with significant deviations from the budget or from normal operations. Identifying significant deviations is not always easy. Two approaches commonly used are (a) a fixed percentage of the budget and (b) a statistical analysis of current operations relative to prior operations.

Fixed Percentage of the Budget　A fixed percentage of the budget is based on the concept of materiality. The materiality of an item is generally based on its amount relative to another quantity. The budget is often used as the standard, and a fixed percentage between 5% and 10% is common.

Example:　Triple A Productions uses 10% as the criterion for determining significant deviations from the budget. One of the following variances would be identified as material.

September 19X3

Cost	Budget	Actual	Variance[a] ( ) Unfavorable
Indirect labor	$30,000	$32,500	($2,500)
Supervision	21,000	20,000	1,000
Heat, light, and power	16,500	19,400	(2,900)[a]

[a]Indicates a material deviation from the budget.

Figure 6.13   Triple A Productions

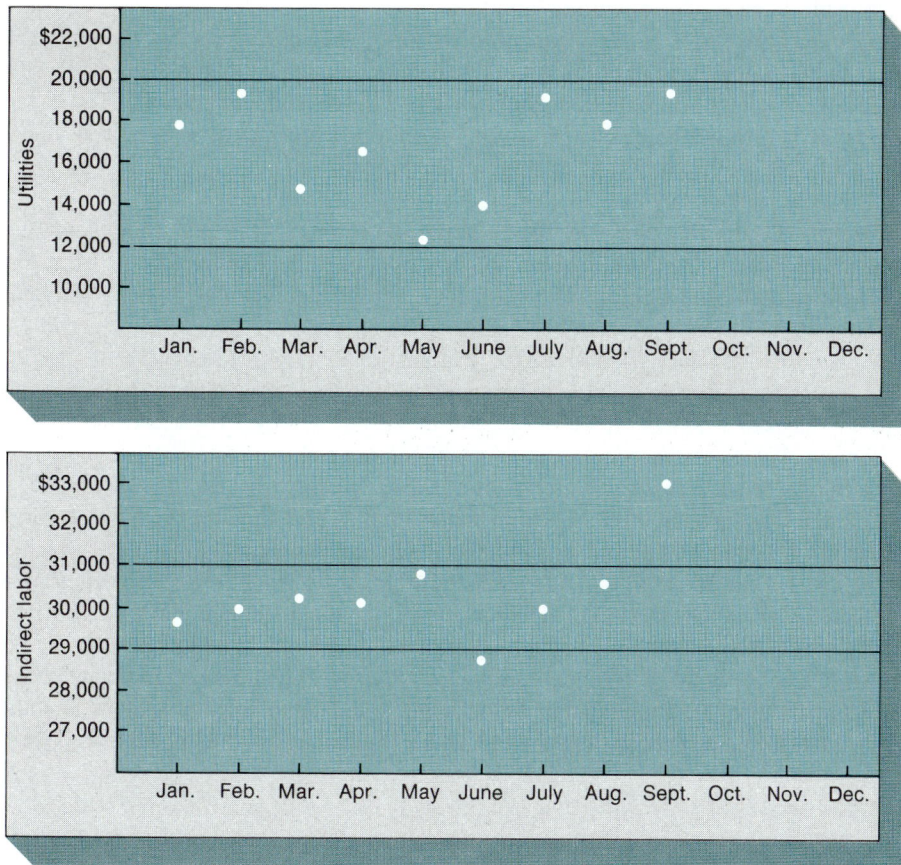

This technique is fairly easy to apply and most people understand it. However, it does not consider normal fluctuation in an item.

Statistical Analysis   A statistical analysis can be used to compare the results of operations this period with prior periods to see if there is a significant deviation. This type of analysis is very useful in identifying deviations that are material but not significant because the fluctuation is within what would be considered normal. Likewise, it is useful in identifying those items that may not be material but are significant because of the abnormal fluctuation.

Example: The charts shown in figure 6.13 are for utilities and indirect labor for Triple A Productions. The plotted points represent the results of operations for the previous nine months. The dotted lines above and below the data points identify an upper and lower limit based on a statistical analysis of the data. Notice that the September point for utilities is within the normal fluctuations for that cost. Management's time will probably be wasted in trying to improve performance in that area in the coming month. Notice also that the September data point for indirect labor lies outside of the normal fluctuation in cost.

Management's attention will be more profitably spent investigating and improving this area because of its abnormal and significant fluctuation from normal operations.

Controllable versus Uncontrollable Costs

No cost is uncontrollable if the organization is viewed in its entirety over a long period of time. But as you look at the organization in the short-run or at separate segments within the organization there are some costs that can be classified as uncontrollable. The concept of control is important because of its significance on performance evaluations and the resulting impact on the form and content of our reports.

Controllable Costs Defined   A **controllable cost** is one that can be influenced by an individual at a particular level of management within a specified period of time. Both parts of this definition are important—(a) the level of management and (b) the length of the time period.

A cost is considered controllable at a particular management level if that level has the power to authorize it. The person who has the most influence over the cost on a day-to-day basis or who has the most decision-making power over the activity in question is in control. For example, a production manager has control over the productivity of direct laborers because he or she assigns job tasks and motivates them to do a good job. However, the same manager may have no control over wages because the hours and rates are fixed by union contracts that are negotiated by top management.

The length of time period has a direct impact on the number of costs that are controllable. Over a long period of time an organization can change almost anything including its advertising and marketing program as well as its production process. New buildings can be constructed and new equipment acquired if the time period is long enough. However, if the time period is short, say three months, it may be very difficult to change even an advertising campaign because of existing contracts with the advertising agency.

Complete versus Partial Control   We generally talk about control as if it were a "yes" or "no" decision. In reality, control varies in degrees from near complete, to partial, to little, or to no control.

Examples: A purchasing agent has complete control over the acquisition of a raw material as long as it meets quality standards. It is complete control because she alone selects the raw materials vendor and negotiates the price.

A production manager has only partial control over equipment repairs and maintenance. He has some control over the care with which the machines are used, which is an important variable in determining the amount of repairs required. He has little or no control over how fast or how well the repairman performs preventive maintenance or repairs the machines.

The amount of property tax paid on the manufacturing facility is uncontrollable for the six production managers who operate within the facility. The amount of property tax is based on the value of the facility as determined by top management several years ago when the facility was constructed, and by a mill levy as determined by the municipality.

Sometimes an individual will have control over acquisition or use but not over both. The purchasing agent described above may have complete control over the acquisition of the raw material but no control over its use. That is under the control of the production manager. This creates some problems in accurately reporting the responsibility of each. A standard cost system and variance analysis (discussed in chap. 15) is used to separate the effectiveness of the purchasing activity from the effectiveness of the using activity.

BEHAVIORAL CONSIDERATIONS IN REPORTING

Chapter 5 discussed some behavioral considerations in preparing and implementing a budget. There are also several behavioral considerations involved in developing reports and providing feedback on performance. Some of the more important conclusions are summarized.

1. The importance of distinguishing between controllable and uncontrollable costs was mentioned earlier. This is important because behavioral implications are involved in using accounting reports to evaluate performance. An individual should not be held responsible for something over which there is no control. Such an evaluation is viewed as unfair because it does not relate to the individual's performance and undesirable behavioral consequences generally result. As a general rule, reports should contain only items for which an individual has partial or complete control. By including partially controllable items, the individual is encouraged to do everything possible to utilize them effectively.

2. Provide rapid feedback on individual and group performance. The value of the report is inversely proportional to the amount of time a person must wait to receive it. Timely reports that are understandable to the workers and supervisors at the department level allow and encourage them to analyze their results and take corrective action where necessary.

3. Feedback is important in determining future levels of aspiration. **Level of aspiration** is a goal that, when barely achieved, has associated with it subjective feelings of success, and when not achieved, subjective feelings of failure. Success generally leads to a rising level of aspiration and failure to a lowering. The stronger the success, the greater the probability of a rise in level of aspiration; the stronger the failure, the greater the probability of a lowering in level of aspiration. Feelings of success are a reward in and of themselves, and the level of aspiration is important in developing the budget for the subsequent period.

4. Reports should focus where possible on positive rewards for achieving the budget. The philosophy of management by exception tends to focus attention on the problem areas of the organization. This is valuable in using management's time effectively, but it should not be used so people are not rewarded when they achieve the budget. Also, management by exception should not lead to "finger pointing." A responsibility accounting system merely identifies who has primary control over an item and where the investigation should begin.

5. Care must be taken to provide reports that are as accurate as possible given the time constraints under which they are developed. There is often a trade-off between timeliness and accuracy. Very accurate reports may take a long time to develop. However, late reports are not as useful. The developer, therefore, must be aware of the user's needs and provide timely information. Users must be informed of estimates and approximations used in developing the report so they will use them appropriately.

Summary

Flexible budgeting is a valuable tool in adjusting the budget for unexpected changes in the volume of business activity. It helps to evaluate the difference between actual and budgeted costs. The variance that is attributable to the change in volume should be separated from the portion that is attributable to the efficiency of the employees. This facilitates accurate performance evaluations and assists in planning future operations.

The flexible budget formula is:

Total cost = Fixed cost + Variable cost per unit of volume × Volume level

Important in developing the formula is the measure of volume or the activity base to be used. Several activity bases are generally studied and the one that is most highly correlated with cost is adopted. The scattergraph method and a least-squares regression and correlation analysis are useful techniques in the selection process.

A responsibility accounting system is a form of segmented reporting in that it structures the organization into segments based on the ability to control. Reports are prepared consistent with the assignment of responsibility and include a comparison of budget and actual data. Significant deviations from the budget are highlighted to assist management in identifying areas of the organization that are out of control or where improvement is most likely. This is consistent with the philosophy of management by exception.

Behavioral considerations are important in developing reports and providing feedback on performance. Timely reports that relate to an individual's area of responsibility and are understandable to the recipient allow and encourage analysis of results and corrective action where necessary. This is an essential part of developing future levels of aspiration. Positive rewards should be provided where possible for achieving the budget. Estimates or approximation should be identified to assist the user in correctly using the information.

Appendix   *Alternate Computations for Coefficient of Correlation and Coefficient of Determination*

There are several formulas that can be used to compute the values of a, b, r, and r^2 in a least-squares regression and correlation analysis. Chapter 6 illustrated the computational formulas frequently used in connection with a statistical analysis. This appendix illustrates the formulas and computation used in a mathematical approach.

The data for Thompson Manufacturing Company that was used throughout chapter 6 will be used to illustrate the alternate computations. Units produced will be used as the activity base for the analysis.

Figure 6.14 summarizes the historical cost data and illustrates the computation of a and b, the y-intercept, and slope of the flexible budget formula respectively. These are the same formulas used in the alternate computation illustrated in the appendix for chapter 3.

The formula to compute r, the coefficient of correlation, is:

$$r = \frac{\sum_{i=1}^{n} (x_i - x)(y_i - y)}{nS_xS_y}$$

Figure 6.14

Thompson Manufacturing Company
Least-Squares Regression Analysis
Units Produced as Activity Base

Month	x Units Produced	y Factory Overhead	$(x_i - \bar{x})$	$(y_i - \bar{y})$	$(x_i - \bar{x})(y_i - \bar{y})$	$(x_i - \bar{x})^2$
May	1,600	$ 4,200	450	$ 900	$ 405,000	202,500
June	1,200	3,500	50	200	10,000	2,500
July	900	3,100	−250	−200	50,000	62,500
August	600	2,200	−550	−1,100	605,000	302,500
September	800	2,600	−350	−700	245,000	122,500
October	1,400	3,900	250	600	150,000	62,500
November	1,550	3,600	400	300	120,000	160,000
Total	8,050	$23,100			$1,585,000	915,000

$$\bar{x} \qquad 1,150$$

$$\bar{y} \qquad\qquad\qquad 3,300$$

$$\text{Slope } (b) = \frac{\Sigma_{i-1}^{n}(x_i - \bar{x})(y_i - \bar{y})}{\Sigma_{i-1}^{n}(x_i - \bar{x})^2} = \frac{1,585,000}{915,000} = 1.73$$

y intercept $(a) = \bar{y} - b(\bar{x}) = 3,300 - 1.73(1,150) = 1,310$

Flexible budget formula:
overhead $= \$1,310 + 1.73(x)$
where $x =$ units produced

---

where $S_x =$ sample standard deviation of the independent variable x (computed as follows):

$$S_x = \sqrt{\frac{\Sigma x_i^2}{n} - (\bar{x})^2}$$

$S_y =$ sample standard deviation of the independent variable y. (Use the equation above for the standard deviation but substitute the observed values of y.)

The standard deviations for x and y must be computed first. The numbers for these computations are taken from figure 6.15.

$$S_x = \sqrt{\frac{10,172,500}{7} - (1,150)^2} = 361.51$$

$$S_y = \sqrt{\frac{79,270,000}{7} - (3,300)^2} = 659$$

The summation of the product of the differences between the observed values of x and y and their means $[\Sigma(x_i - \bar{x})(y_i - \bar{y})]$ was computed in figure 6.14. The value along with the standard deviations computed above are substituted into the equation shown above to compute the value of r.

Coefficient of correlation:

$$r = \frac{1,585,000}{(7)(361.51)(659)} = .95$$

The value of r is squared for the value of r^2.

Coefficient of determination:

$$r^2 = .95^2 = .90$$

Figure 6.15   Computations for sample standard deviations

Month	x Units Produced	x²	y Factory Overhead	y²
May	1,600	2,560,000	$ 4,200	$17,640,000
June	1,200	1,440,000	3,500	12,250,000
July	900	810,000	3,100	9,610,000
August	600	360,000	2,200	4,840,000
September	800	640,000	2,600	6,760,000
October	1,400	1,960,000	3,900	15,210,000
November	1,550	2,402,500	3,600	12,960,000
Total	8,050	10,172,500	$23,100	$79,270,000
Divide by n	÷ 7		÷ 7	
$\bar{x}$	1,150			
$\bar{y}$			$ 3,300	

Self-Study Problem

Hawks Company began operation on July 1, 19X2. The first six months of operations were very disappointing, primarily because their overhead costs were so much higher than they had anticipated. They have asked you to assist them in developing a flexible budget formula and to identify the activity base that is the best predictor of overhead cost.

The accountant for Hawks Company has collected the following information for the first six months of operations:

Month	Overhead Cost	Units Produced	Days Worked
July	$ 4,000	5	120
August	7,000	10	200
September	9,000	15	290
October	8,000	11	170
November	10,000	20	400
December	7,500	8	220

Required

1. Using a least-squares regression analysis, prepare a flexible budget formula for each activity base under consideration.
2. Compute the coefficient of correlation and the coefficient of determination for each activity base.
3. Which activity base do you recommend and why?

Solution to the Self-Study Problem

Requirement 1

Figure 6.16 contains the intermediate computations required to prepare the flexible budget formula. The numbers computed there are substituted in the following equations:

Figure 6.16

Hawks Company
Computations for Correlation and Regression Analysis

Units Produced as the Activity Base:

Month	x Units Produced	y Factory Overhead	xy	x^2	y^2
July	5	$ 4,000	$ 20,000	25	$ 16,000,000
August	10	7,000	70,000	100	49,000,000
September	15	9,000	135,000	225	81,000,000
October	11	8,000	88,000	121	64,000,000
November	20	10,000	200,000	400	100,000,000
December	8	7,500	60,000	64	56,250,000
Total	69	$45,500	$573,000	935	$366,250,000

Days Worked as the Activity Base:

Month	x Employee Days Worked	y Factory Overhead	xy	x^2	y^2
July	120	$ 4,000	$ 480,000	14,400	$ 16,000,000
August	200	7,000	1,400,000	40,000	49,000,000
September	290	9,000	2,610,000	84,100	81,000,000
October	170	8,000	1,360,000	28,900	64,000,000
November	400	10,000	4,000,000	160,000	100,000,000
December	220	7,500	1,650,000	48,400	56,250,000
Total	1,400	$45,500	$11,500,000	375,800	$366,250,000

Units produced as the activity base:

$$a = \frac{(\Sigma y)(\Sigma x^2) - (\Sigma x)(\Sigma xy)}{n(\Sigma x^2) - (\Sigma x)^2}$$

$$= \frac{(45,500)(935) - (69)(573,000)}{(6)(935) - (69)^2} = \$3,540$$

$$b = \frac{n(\Sigma xy) - (\Sigma x)(\Sigma y)}{n(\Sigma x^2) - (\Sigma x)^2}$$

$$= \frac{(6)(573,000) - (69)(45,500)}{(6)(935) - (69)^2} = \$352$$

Flexible budget formula:

Factory overhead = $3,540 + $352(x)

where x = units produced

Days worked as the activity base:

$$a = \frac{(45,500)(375,800) - (1,400)(11,500,000)}{(6)(375,800) - (1,400)^2} = \$3,388$$

$$b = \frac{(6)(11,500,000) - (1,400)(45,500)}{(6)(375,800) - (1,400)^2} = \$18$$

Flexible budget formula:

Factory overhead = $3,388 + $18(x)

where x = days worked

Requirement 2

The values shown in figure 6.16 are also used to compute the coefficients of correlation (r) and determination (r^2).

Units produced as the activity base:

$$r = \frac{n\Sigma xy - (\Sigma x)(\Sigma y)}{\sqrt{[n\Sigma x^2 - (\Sigma x)^2][n\Sigma y^2 - (\Sigma y)^2}}$$

$$r = \frac{(6)(573,000) - (69)(45,500)}{\sqrt{[(6)(935) - (69)^2][(6)(366,250,000) - (45,500)^2]}}$$

$$= \underline{.908}$$

$$r^2 = .908^2 = \underline{.824}$$

Days worked as the activity base:

$$r = \frac{(6)(11,500,000) - (1,400)(45,500)}{\sqrt{[(6)(375,800) - (1,400)^2][(6)(366,250,000) - (45,500)^2]}}$$

$$= \underline{.865}$$

$$r^2 = .872^2 = \underline{.749}$$

Requirement 3

Units produced is the best activity base. It accounts for 82.4% of the variation in factory overhead. Only 74.9% of the variation in factory overhead can be explained by the number of days worked.

Suggested Readings

Cherrington, David J., and Cherrington, J. Owen. "Participation, Performance, and Appraisal." *Business Horizons* 17 (December 1974): 35–45.

———. "The Role of Budgeting in Organizational Improvement." *Michigan Business Review* 27 (July 1975): 12–16.

Goodman, Sam R., and Reece, James S. *Controller's Handbook*. Homewood, Ill.: Dow-Jones Irwin, 1978.

Hays, William L. *Statistics*. New York: Holt, Rinehart, and Winston, 1963.

Sorensen, James E., and Franks, Davis D. "The Relative Contribution of Ability, Self-Esteem and Evaluative Feedback to Performance: Implications for Accounting Systems." *Accounting Review* 47 (October 1972): 735–46.

Weiss, Allen. "The Supervisor and the Budget, Part 3: How the Budget Affects You—How You Affect the Budget." *Supervisory Management* (July 1971): 5–8.

1. Describe what a flexible budget is and explain how it differs from a static budget.
2. Why may it be misleading to compare actual results of operations with budget results when the actual volume of activity was not the same as the budgeted volume?
3. Is the high-low method useful in selecting the best activity base for the flexible budget formula? Explain.
4. Explain how to use the scattergraph method to select the best activity base for the flexible budget formula.
5. What is the range of possible values for the coefficient of correlation and what does it mean?
6. What is the range of possible values of the coefficient of determination and what does it mean?
7. Describe responsibility accounting.
8. Describe the relationship of responsibility accounting to segmented reporting.
9. What is meant by pyramid reporting?
10. What is management by exception and how should reports be structured to facilitate management by exception?
11. Why is a statistical analysis better than a fixed percentage in determining a significant deviation of actual results from the budget?
12. What criteria should be used to determine which costs are controllable?
13. Should partially controllable costs be included in a manager's report under a responsibility accounting system? Explain.
14. What is the relationship between feedback and future levels of aspiration?
15. Why is a rapid feedback important?

Exercises

Exercise 6.1 Fundamentals of Flexible Budgets

A schedule format for a flexible budget is shown below. Determine the amount that should be budgeted for each item for each indicated level of activity by completing the schedule.

Overhead Category	Budget Rate	Levels of Activity (Direct-Labor Hours)			
		45,000	50,000	55,000	60,000
Variable costs (per direct-labor hour):					
Indirect labor	$2.00	$	$	$	$
Indirect materials	1.60				
Repairs	1.20				
Fixed costs (total) Depreciation—					
machinery	$75,000	$	$	$	$
Insurance—factory	25,000				
Total fixed cost	$100,000	$	$	$	$
Total overhead budget		$	$	$	$

Exercise 6.2　Flexible Factory Overhead Budget

Refer to the facts in exercise 5.4. The factory overhead budget prepared was a fixed (or static) budget.

Required

Show a factory overhead cost budget for August adjusted on a flexible basis using intervals of 10% and 20% both up and down from the scheduled production for the month. Your budget will cover five possible production levels for August with the costs broken down into the categories requested in requirement 2 of exercise 5.4.

Exercise 6.3　Selecting from Alternate Volume Bases

Refer to the data in problem 3.8.

Required

1. Using a least-squares regression analysis, prepare a flexible budget formula for repairs and maintenance costs using each of the activity bases under consideration.
2. Compute the coefficient of correlation and the coefficient of determination for each activity base.
3. Which activity base do you recommend and why?

Exercise 6.4　Flexible Budget Concepts

1. A flexible budget is
   a. appropriate for control of factory overhead but *not* for control of direct materials and direct labor.
   b. appropriate for control of direct materials and direct labor but *not* for control of factory overhead.
   c. *not* appropriate when costs and expenses are affected by fluctuations in volume limits.
   d. appropriate for any level of activity.
2. Information needed to prepare a flexible budget includes
   a. total fixed costs, total variable costs, a capacity base, and information about the relevant range.
   b. unit fixed costs and unit variable costs.
   c. total fixed costs, variable costs per unit of capacity, several levels of activity, and an indication of the relevant range.
   d. total fixed costs and total variable costs only.
   e. total costs only.
3. Flexible budgets are useful for
   a. planning purposes only.
   b. planning, performance evaluation, and feedback control reporting.
   c. control of performance only.
   d. nothing at all. They are a waste of time and money because cost behavior is impossible to predict and in any case results never agree with the budget.

4. A recent news report about a bankrupt firm indicates that the chief executive officer of the firm believed that budgetary controls shouldn't be used because they "stifle entrepreneurship" and threaten the "ambience" (pervading atmosphere) of the company. Your position is
   a. total agreement because budgets, including flexible budgets, are known to destroy initiative and motivation.
   b. total disagreement because budgets, including flexible budgets, are the only tool that can give effective guidance to a company in meeting objectives.
   c. total agreement because all budgets are known to be used by top management to manipulate people as well as results.
   d. neither agreement nor disagreement because the procedures used to create and operate a budget can cause the budget to stifle initiative and create a threatening environment in the company.

Exercise 6.5   Flexible Budget Fundamentals

Maxwell Incorporated produces Maxis. The following costs were budgeted for the 95% of normal capacity activity level:

Variable costs (based on the number of Maxis produced):	
Direct labor	$399,000
Direct materials	299,250
Indirect materials	99,750
Indirect labor	49,875
Repairs and maintenance	39,900
Heat, light, and power	19,950
Fixed costs:	
Supervision	$ 18,000
Depreciation on factory equipment	65,000
Rent on special equipment	10,000
Heat, light, and power	32,000
Property taxes	10,000

The total normal production capability is 210,000 Maxis.

Required

1. Prepare a budget of factory overhead costs covering the 90%, 100%, and 110% capacity levels.
2. Determine unit factory overhead costs and total production costs per unit at the three capacity levels in requirement 1.
3. Explain why the unit cost changed from one activity level to another, if there was a change.
4. Identify for Mrs. Maxwell, the company president, the true cost per unit of producing Maxis, which she might use in comparing her firm's cost position with the unit cost of other firms.

Exercise 6.6   Flexible Budget Formulas

The following data reflects the results of analysis recently completed on the cost structure of the Hobart Company.

Item	Amount	Percentage of total which is fixed
Machinery service	$15,000	100
Tools and dies	10,000	60
Production equipment depreciation	5,000	100
Factory heat, light, and power	12,000	40
Factory supervision	11,000	100
Direct labor	35,000	
Marketing salaries	45,000	
Direct materials	30,000	
Indirect materials	12,000	
Indirect labor	4,000	
Office supplies	1,500	
Depreciation on office equipment	5,000	100
Rental of automobiles for sales staff	3,000	100
Other marketing expenses	2,000	35
Other factory overhead	5,000	55

Required

1. Organize the cost information into functional budget form assuming that marketing and administrative expenses were based on net sales of $350,000 and manufacturing costs are based on production of 20,000 units. Show separate sections in each functional budget for variable and fixed costs.
2. Set up budget formulas (with specific dollar amounts) for the following:
   a. Factory overhead
   b. Administrative expenses
   c. Marketing expenses

Exercise 6.7   Flexible Budget—Budget Formula for Different Ranges of Activity

Haymore Incorporated has obtained the following cost data:

Amounts

Item	Fixed	Variable per Labor Hour
Direct labor		$7.80
Direct material		4.50
Indirect labor		2.70
Indirect material		1.80
Rent of special equipment	$ 6,500	
Depreciation	15,000	
Heat, light, and power	1,800	.80
Repairs and maintenance	6,200	.30
Other factory overhead	600	.10

Factory supervision costs are as follows:

Labor Hours	Costs
1–11,999	$1,000
12,000–23,999	2,000
24,000–35,999	3,000

Required

1. Set up flexible factory overhead budgets for 8,000, 14,000 and 26,000 direct-labor hours.
2. Show a *total* production cost formula for each of the three ranges of activity indicated above.

Exercise 6.8 Static and Flexible Budgets and Performance Reports

The Germaine Company prepared a budget for 9,000 units. It included the following costs covering production of its one product Maingers:

Direct labor	$11,070
Direct material	10,710
Indirect labor	6,840
Indirect material	5,040
Factory foreman	2,000
Depreciation	340
Service department allocation	900

The Germaine Company had planned 8,000 units for production during July but, because of unexpected materials supply problems, only 7,500 units were produced. The costs incurred were:

Direct labor	$9,900
Direct material	8,850
Indirect labor	5,700
Indirect material	4,350
Factory foreman	2,000
Depreciation	340
Service department allocation	900

Required

1. Prepare a performance report, including variances from budget, comparing actual costs against a static budget based on July's planned production.
2. Prepare a performance report, including variances from budget, comparing actual costs with a flexible budget covering July's actual production.
3. Comment on the usefulness of the reports in requirements 1 and 2.

Exercise 6.9 Budgeting Concepts (CMA)

1. A continuous budget
   a. drops the current month or quarter and adds a future month or a future quarter as the current month or quarter is completed.
   b. presents a statement of expectations for a period of time but does not present a firm commitment.
   c. presents the plan for only one level of activity and does not adjust to changes in the level of activity.
   d. presents the plan for a range of activity so the plan can be adjusted for changes in activity levels.
   e. classifies budget requests by activity and estimates the benefits arising from each activity.

2. A static budget
    a. drops the current month or quarter and adds a future month or a future quarter as the current month or quarter is completed.
    b. presents a statement of expectations for a period of time but does not present a firm commitment.
    c. presents the plan for only one level of activity and does not adjust to changes in the level of activity.
    d. presents the plan for a range of activity so the plan can be adjusted for changes in activity levels.
    e. divides the activities of individual responsibility centers into a series of packages that are ranked ordinally.
3. A flexible budget
    a. classifies budget requests by activity and estimates the benefits arising from each activity.
    b. presents a statement of expectations for a period of time but does not present a firm commitment.
    c. presents the plan for only one level of activity and does not adjust to changes in the level of activity.
    d. presents the plan for a range of activity so the plan can be adjusted for changes in activity levels.
    e. divides the activities of individual responsibility centers into a series of packages that are ranked ordinally.
4. When an organization prepares a forecast, it
    a. presents a statement of expectations for a period of time but does not present a firm commitment.
    b. consolidates the plans of the separate requests into one overall plan.
    c. presents the plan for a range of activity so the plan can be adjusted for changes in activity levels.
    d. classifies budget requests by activity and estimates the benefits arising from each activity.
    e. divides the activities of individual responsibility centers into a series of packages that are ranked ordinally.

Exercise 6.10 Flexible Budget—Review of the High-Low Points Method

Joplin Jumprope Company has recorded the following overhead amounts for the past six months. Since a causal relationship exists between overhead and direct-labor hours, you have also gathered labor information for the same period:

	Overhead Expenses	Direct-Labor Hours
January	$24,000	21,000
February	16,500	13,000
March	15,000	8,000
April	19,500	15,000
May	21,500	18,000
June	27,000	24,000

Required

1. Determine the flexible budget formula using the high-low method.
2. If direct-labor hours for July were 22,000 hours, what would the budgeted expense for overhead be?

Problem 6.1 Flexible Budgets—Cost Breakdown

Abco is a service company operating in the western United States and Canada. Operations are typically at the 100% capacity level, which involves operating 120,000 hours. During the slack season of the year, capacity utilization is expected to drop to the 70% level. At the 70% capacity level, total budgeted overhead is $240,000. Variable costs are 60% of total costs at the 70% capacity level.

The overhead budget includes the following items at the percentages indicated:

Fixed Costs		Variable Costs	
Item	**% of Total**	**Item**	**% of Total**
Supervision	60%	Supplies	25%
Insurance	5	Clerical wages	40
Taxes	5	Custodial wages	20
Maintenance	15	Mailing and teletype expenses	10
Depreciation	10	Other	5
Other	5	Total	100%
Total	100%		

Required

1. Determine the flexible budget formula of total fixed costs and the variable rate per hour. Show a breakdown of both fixed cost amounts and variable rates per hour for each cost item.
2. Prepare a flexible budget with details of cost items covering the 70% to 110% capacity levels at 10% intervals.

Problem 6.2 Flexible Budget for Factory Overhead Costs

The production and sales managers for C & L, Incorporated have had some uncertainty over the quantity of components to produce. The recent budget of production is for 150,000 components, and the overhead costs related to this budget are:

Factory rent (fixed)	$ 3,000
Factory equipment depreciation (fixed)	5,500
Supervision (fixed)	45,000
Heat, light, and power (40% variable)	18,500
Indirect materials (variable)	225,000
Indirect labor (variable)	150,000
Supplies (variable)	1,500
Repairs (60% fixed)	1,500
Miscellaneous overhead expenses (50% fixed)	12,000

Required

1. Set up a flexible budget covering 100,000, 120,000, 140,000, 160,000, and 180,000 components. Show total variable costs, total fixed costs, and total costs. Also, show unit costs for each variable cost and total unit variable cost.
2. Express the budget data in formula form.
3. How much would be budgeted for 150,000 components in total costs, total variable costs, and total fixed costs?

Problem 6.3   Flexible Budget—Reporting Concepts (CMA)

Pearsons is a successful regional chain of moderate priced restaurants, each with a carryout delicatessen department. Pearsons is planning to expand to a nationwide operation. As the chain gets larger and the territory covered becomes wider, managerial control and reporting techniques become more important.

The company management believes that a budget program for the entire company as well as each restaurant-deli unit is needed. The budget presented below has been prepared for the typical unit in the chain. Once a unit is in operation, it is expected to perform in accordance with the budget.

Typical Pearsons Restaurant-Deli
Budgeted Income
Year Ending December 31
(000 omitted)

	Delicatessen	*Restaurant*	*Total*
Gross sales	$1,000	$2,500	$3,500
Purchases	$ 600	$1,000	$1,600
Hourly wages	50	875	925
Franchise fee	30	75	105
Advertising	100	200	300
Utilities	70	125	195
Depreciation	50	75	125
Lease expense	30	50	80
Salaries	30	50	80
Total	$ 960	$2,450	$3,410
Net income before income taxes	$ 40	$ 50	$ 90

All units are approximately the same size and the amount of space devoted to the carryout delicatessen is similar in each unit. The style of the facilities and the equipment used are all uniform. The unit operators are expected to carry out the advertising program recommended by the corporation. The corporation charges a franchise fee, which is a percentage of gross sales for the use of the company name, the building and facilities design, and the advertising advice.

The unit in Akron, Ohio, was selected to test the budget program. The Akron restaurant-deli performance for the year ending December 31 is shown on page 193 with actual results compared with the typical budgets for Pearsons.

The report was reviewed and discussed by the company management. They concluded that a more meaningful comparison would result if a flexible budget analysis for each of the two lines were performed rather than just the single budget comparison as in the test case.

Required

1. Prepare a schedule that compares a flexible budget for the deli line of the Akron restaurant-deli to its actual performance.
2. Would a complete report, comparing a flexible budget to the performance of each of the two operations, make the problems of the Akron operation easier to identify? Explain by using an example from the problem and your answer to requirement 1.

3. Should a flexible budget comparison to actual performance become part of the regular reporting system for the annual review or for a monthly review? Explain your answer.

Pearsons Restaurant-Deli
Akron, Ohio
Net Income
Year Ending December 31, 19X8
(000 omitted)

	Actual Results				Over (Under) Budget
	Delicatessen	**Restaurant**	**Total**	**Budget**	**Budget**
Gross sales	$1,200	$2,000	$3,200	$3,500	$(300)
Purchases	$ 780	$ 800	$1,580	$1,600	$(20)
Hourly wages	60	700	760	925	(165)
Franchise fee	36	60	96	105	(9)
Advertising	100	200	300	300	—
Utilities	76	100	176	195	(19)
Depreciation	50	75	125	125	—
Lease expense	30	50	80	80	—
Salaries	30	50	80	80	—
Total	$1,162	$2,035	$3,197	$3,410	$(213)
Net income before income taxes	$ 38	$ (35)	$ 3	$ 90	$(87)

Problem 6.4   Flexible Budget—Performance Comparisons (CMA)

The Jason Plant of Cast Corporation has been in operation for fifteen months. Jason employs a standard cost system for its manufacturing operations. The first six months performance was affected by the usual problems associated with a new operation. Since that time the operations have been running smoothly. Unfortunately, the plant has not been able to produce profits on a consistent basis. As the production requirements to meet sales demand have increased, the profit performance has deteriorated.

The plant production manager held a staff meeting in which the plant general manager, the corporate controller, and the corporate budget director were in attendance. He stated that the changing production requirements make it more difficult to control manufacturing expenses. He further noted that the budget for the plant, included in the company's annual profit plan, was not useful for judging the plant's performance because of the changes in the operating levels. The meeting resulted in a decision to prepare a report that would compare the plant's actual manufacturing expense performance with a budget of manufacturing expense based on actual direct-labor hours in the plant.

The plant production manager and the plant accountant studied the cost patterns for recent months, and volume and cost data from other Cast plants. Then they prepared the following flexible budget schedule for a month with 200,000 planned production hours that should result in 50,000 units of output. The corporate controller reviewed and approved the flexible budget.

	Amount	Per Direct-Labor Hour
Manufacturing Expenses		
Variable		
Indirect labor	$160,000	$ .80
Supplies	26,000	.13
Power	14,000	.07
		$1.00
Fixed		
Supervisory labor	64,000	
Heat and light	15,000	
Property taxes	5,000	
	$284,000	

The plant production manager was pleased with the manufacturing expense reports prepared for the first three months after the flexible budget program was approved. The reports showed that manufacturing expenses were in line with the flexible budget allowance. This was also reflected by the report prepared for November, which is presented below, when 50,500 units were manufactured.

Jason Plant
Manufacturing Expenses
Month of November
220,000 Actual Direct-Labor Production Hours

	Actual Costs	Allowed Costs	(Over) Under Budget
Variable			
Indirect labor	$177,000	$176,000	$(1,000)
Supplies	27,400	28,600	1,200
Power	16,000	15,400	(600)
Fixed			
Supervisory labor	65,000	64,000	(1,000)
Heat and light	15,500	15,000	(500)
Property taxes	5,000	5,000	0
	$305,900	$304,000	$(1,900)

Required

1. Explain the advantages of flexible budgeting over fixed budgeting for cost control purposes.
2. Show supporting computations for the allowed costs shown in the expense report for November.
3. Are there other approaches that could be used to show the performance for the month of November? Explain.

Problem 6.5   Flexible Budget—Scattergraph Analysis

Refer to the data given for the Joplin Jumprope Company in exercise 6.10. Using the data given, plot a scattergraph of the overhead expense. Orient the overhead cost on the vertical axis and direct-labor hours on the horizontal axis.

Required

1. Fit a regression line through the points you have plotted by visual inspection.

2. Determine the approximate fixed overhead cost per month. Determine the approximate variable overhead per direct-labor hour.
3. Observe the points on your graph and describe why the high-low method of cost determination would or would not give an accurate flexible budget formula for overhead of the Joplin Jumprope Company.

Problem 6.6 Flexible Budget Completion

An incomplete flexible budget is given below for one month:

Overhead Cost	Cost Formula	Machine-Hours Worked			
		3,000	4,000	5,000	6,000
Variable					
Maintenance			$1,440		
Indirect materials			880		
Indirect labor			640		
Total					
Fixed					
Depreciation			1,440		
Taxes			800		
Supervision			3,500		
Total					

Required

Complete the flexible budget by determining the missing information.

Problem 6.7 Flexible Budget Preparation

The Skinner Scanner Company wants a flexible budget for overhead expense. You have been assigned to assemble data from the past six months. Due to the nature of Skinner's business, machine-hours worked has been adopted as the activity base. Over a relevant range of 3,000 to 6,000 machine hours, you have determined the following flexible budget formula for overhead expenses:

Total overhead costs = $14,500 + ($0.60 × machine-hours worked)

The fixed portion of this formula is broken down as follows:

Fixed Overhead Expense	Percentage
Depreciation	35%
Taxes	25%
Insurance	10%
Supervisory Salaries	30%

The variable portion of the cost formula is broken down as follows:

Variable Overhead Expense	Percentage
Maintenance	30%
Indirect materials	35%
Lubricants	5%
Power	30%

Required

Prepare a flexible budget for the Skinner Scanner Company over the given relevant range in increments of 1,000 machine hours. Include variable as well as fixed overhead expenses broken down into their components.

Problem 6.8   Performance Analysis—Static and Flexible Budgets

The following budget data have been prepared by the We're OK Now Company for the current year:

Selling and administrative expenses:	
Sales salaries (all variable)	$165,000[a]
Advertising (all variable)	22,000
Travel expenses (80% variable)	13,750
Depreciation (straight-line)	4,600
Executive salaries (fixed)	80,000
Taxes (fixed)	108,200
Insurance (fixed)	8,000
General expenses (40% variable)	41,250
Total selling and administrative expenses	$442,800
Manufacturing expenses:	
Direct labor (all variable)	$ 90,000
Direct materials (all variable)	99,000
Factory overhead:	
Indirect labor (all variable)	9,000
Indirect materials (all variable)	1,800
Supervision (fixed)	27,000
Rent (fixed)	2,000
Maintenance (60% variable)	15,000
Utilities (20% variable)	22,500
Total manufacturing expenses	$266,300
Total expenses	$709,100

[a]Selling and administrative expenses are based upon $1,100,000 sales dollars, and manufacturing expenses are based upon direct-labor dollars.

At year end, the records show the following actual results:

Sales salaries	$150,000[b]
Advertising	30,000
Travel expenses	12,000
Depreciation	4,600
Executive salaries	82,000
Taxes	108,000
Insurance	8,000
General expenses	42,000
Direct labor	100,000
Direct materials	99,000
Indirect labor	10,200
Indirect materials	2,000
Supervision	27,000
Rent	2,000
Maintenance	17,200
Utilities	23,500
Total expenses	$717,500

[b]Actual sales were $1,000,000.

Required

1. Prepare a performance report comparing actual costs with the static budget. Include variances and indicate whether each variance is favorable or unfavorable.
2. Prepare a flexible budget covering actual results using the information obtained from the static budget.
3. Prepare a performance report comparing actual costs with the flexible budget. Include variances and indicate whether each variance is favorable or unfavorable.

Problem 6.9   Flexible Budget and the Performance Report

Dan Max has a fleet of snowmobiles. Dan's cost analyst has developed the following budget data for one year:

	Fixed	Variable per Mile Driven
Fuel		$.25
Oil		.10
Chassis and other lubricants	$ 1,000	.05
Repairs	1,200	.06
Parking fees	2,000	
State registration and licenses	600	
Property taxes	1,200	
Comprehensive and liability insurance	1,600	
Depreciation	2,500	
Total	$10,100	$.46

Dan estimates operations of 20,000 miles in a typical year. During the year just ended, Dan's snowmobiles were driven 23,000 miles, and the following expenses were incurred:

Fuel	$6,210
Oil	2,415
Chassis and other lubricants	2,380
Repairs	2,695
Parking fees	2,100
State registration and licenses	650
Property taxes	1,400
Insurance	1,600
Depreciation	2,500

Required

1. Express the budget data in flexible budget formula form ($y = a + bx$).
2. Prepare a performance report for the year comparing actual results with a flexible budget covering the year's actual operations. Include variances and indicate whether each variance is favorable or unfavorable.

Problem 6.10   Flexible Budgets—Performance Reports

The M&A Company has two major departments for which the following budget data have been developed for the month of October:

	Department 1	Department 2
Direct-labor hours	7,000	
Machine hours	3,600	
Costs:		
Direct labor	$35,000	
Direct materials	21,000	
Indirect labor	20,300	
Repair labor wages		$13,320
Supervision	6,000	8,000
Supplies	5,250	5,950
Depreciation	4,000	1,800
Insurance—liability and property	1,000	800

During October the following actual results were obtained:

	Department 1	Department 2
Direct-labor hours	6,500	
Machine hours	3,400	
Costs:		
Direct labor	$34,125	
Direct materials	20,150	
Indirect labor	19,500	
Repair labor wages		$12,920
Supervision	6,200	7,800
Supplies	4,680	5,440
Depreciation	4,000	1,800
Insurance	1,100	900

Depreciation, supervision, and insurance are considered fixed expenses.

Department 1 is a producing department, and variable expenses are based on direct-labor hours. Department 2 is a repairs and maintenance service department, and variable expenses are based on machine hours in the producing department.

Required

1. Prepare a performance report for department 2, comparing actual costs with a flexible budget for October's actual operations. Include variances in your report.
2. Prepare two performance reports for department 1, comparing October's actual expenses against (a) the original budget and (b) a flexible budget for October's actual operations. Include variances from the budget in your report.
3. Comment on the usefulness of your two reports prepared in requirement 2.

Problem 6.11

Luthy Construction Company is considering direct-labor hours and machine hours as activity bases for predicting overhead costs. Data for the last 8 months are shown below:

Month	Overhead Cost	Direct-Labor Hours	Machine Hours
1	$24,800	740	650
2	27,500	1,150	1,100
3	26,900	920	850
4	24,400	960	790
5	29,100	1,350	1,200
6	25,700	840	800
7	21,300	790	750
8	23,600	770	640

Required

1. Prepare a flexible budget formula using (a) the high-low method, and (b) the least-squares method for each activity base.
2. Compute the (a) coefficient of correlation, and (b) coefficient of determination.
3. Which activity base would you recommend and why?

COST–VOLUME–PROFIT ANALYSIS

7

Outline

C ost-volume-profit analysis is a study of the relationships between costs and volume and their impact on profit. Earlier in this text we discussed the relationship between costs and volume and identified various cost patterns including fixed, variable, and semi-variable. These relationships were used in chapter 6 to develop a flexible budget that is used to predict the amount of cost that should be incurred at various levels of output. In this chapter we add revenue to the analysis so conclusions can be made about the profitability of the enterprise at various levels of output.

Cost-volume-profit analysis is primarily a planning tool to assist management in effectively utilizing fixed resources in the short run. Management of a firm, a division, or a department is typically faced with a set of resources that are fixed or can be increased or decreased only slightly in the short run. Cost-volume-profit analysis assists in managing these resources and the fixed costs associated with them by providing answers to the following types of questions: How many units must be produced and sold to break even? What will be the impact on profit if price is changed? How will the breakeven point change if a machine, which adds additional fixed costs, is substituted for direct labor, which is a variable cost?

The analysis of costs, volume, and profit is static in that it is based on a given set of facts. If one or more of the facts are changed, a new analysis must be performed. It is also based on several assumptions that are made to keep the analysis as simple as possible, yet realistic of the real-world environment. If one or more of the assumptions are not correct, the results of the analysis may be incorrect and misleading.

This chapter explains cost-volume-profit analysis, its uses, and its limitations. After completing this chapter, you should be able to:

1. compute the breakeven point in either units of production or sales dollars.
2. prepare a breakeven chart and a profit-volume graph.
3. identify the assumptions inherent in traditional breakeven analysis.
4. identify the revenue required to obtain a desired profit.
5. analyze the effects of a change in price, fixed costs, or variable costs on the breakeven point and on profit.
6. compute the breakeven point for a multiple product entity and analyze the effect on the breakeven point for changes in the product mix.

BREAKEVEN ANALYSIS

A **breakeven analysis** is performed to identify the level of operation at which the entity has covered all costs but has not yet earned any profit. The **breakeven point** identifies the volume of activity at which total revenues equal total costs. This is often an important point to management because it represents a minimum acceptable level of operations. Of course, the desirability of the project or the investment increases as profits increase, but profitable operation can only result when the level of activity exceeds the breakeven point.

The breakeven point is generally computed mathematically and is expressed in either *units of output* or *sales dollars*. Charts and graphs are frequently used to illustrate the breakeven point and to show the effect that changes in volume will have on profits. Our analysis will first consider entities with only a single product, but will later be expanded to include multiple product entities.

Breakeven Analysis in Units

The breakeven point is defined as the level of operations at which total revenues equal total costs. The analysis can be for an entire firm, a division, or a separate department. Breakeven analysis utilizes the contribution margin approach to computing net income, which splits costs into a fixed and variable classification.

Contribution Margin Format

Sales	$ _____
Less: Variable costs	$ _____
Contribution margin	$ _____
Less: Fixed costs	$ _____
Net income	$ _____

Recall that the contribution margin approach first classifies expenses as fixed or variable and groups them together according to their pattern rather than their function. Therefore, both variable and fixed costs in the above format contain selling and administrative costs as well as production costs.

Equation for Breakeven Point in Units   The breakeven point in units can be computed by dividing total fixed costs (F) by the contribution margin provided by each unit.

$$\text{Breakeven in units} = \frac{\text{Total fixed costs}}{\text{Contribution margin per unit}} = \frac{FC}{P-VC}$$

The contribution margin per unit is sales price per unit (P) less variable cost per unit (VC). An example will illustrate the use of this formula:

Example: Packard Incorporated manufactures and sells one type of calculator called Model Q. Model Q sells for $40, and the variable expenses associated with it are $20 for manufacturing and $5 for selling. Fixed costs are $75,000 for manufacturing and $15,000 for selling and administration. How many units must be produced and sold in order to break even?

Solution:

$$\frac{\text{Breakeven}}{\text{point in units}} = \frac{\text{Fixed cost}}{\text{Sale price per unit} - \text{Variable cost per unit}}$$

$$= \frac{\$90,000}{\$40 - \$25} = 6,000 \text{ units}$$

When the price *exceeds* the variable cost, as in the example above, each unit contributes something ($15) toward covering fixed costs and providing a profit. The breakeven point has been reached as soon as the cumulative amount of the contribution margin (6,000 × $15) equals the total fixed costs ($90,000).

If the price is ever *less than* the variable cost, the entity would maximize profits (minimize losses in this case) by producing nothing. In this situation it is not possible to have a breakeven point if there are any fixed costs.

Example: All Grain Company produces home flour mills, which they sell for $120. Variable costs to produce and sell the mills are $125. Annual fixed costs total $75,000. What is the company's breakeven point?

Solution: The company cannot break even under current operating conditions. At zero production the company will lose $75,000. At 10,000 units of production, the company will lose $125,000 [($125 − $120) × 10,000 + $75,000]. Since each additional unit increases the loss by $5, the optimum strategy is to produce nothing.

Breakeven Charts   A **breakeven chart** is a graphical representation of the relationships between costs, revenues, and profits. It is developed by plotting the total cost curve and the total revenue curve on a piece of graph paper. The example above for Packard will be used to illustrate the construction. The revenue and cost curves are:

Revenue = $40 (units)

Cost = $90,000 + $25 (units)

These two lines are plotted on the graph illustrated in figure 7.1.

Figure 7.1　Breakeven charts

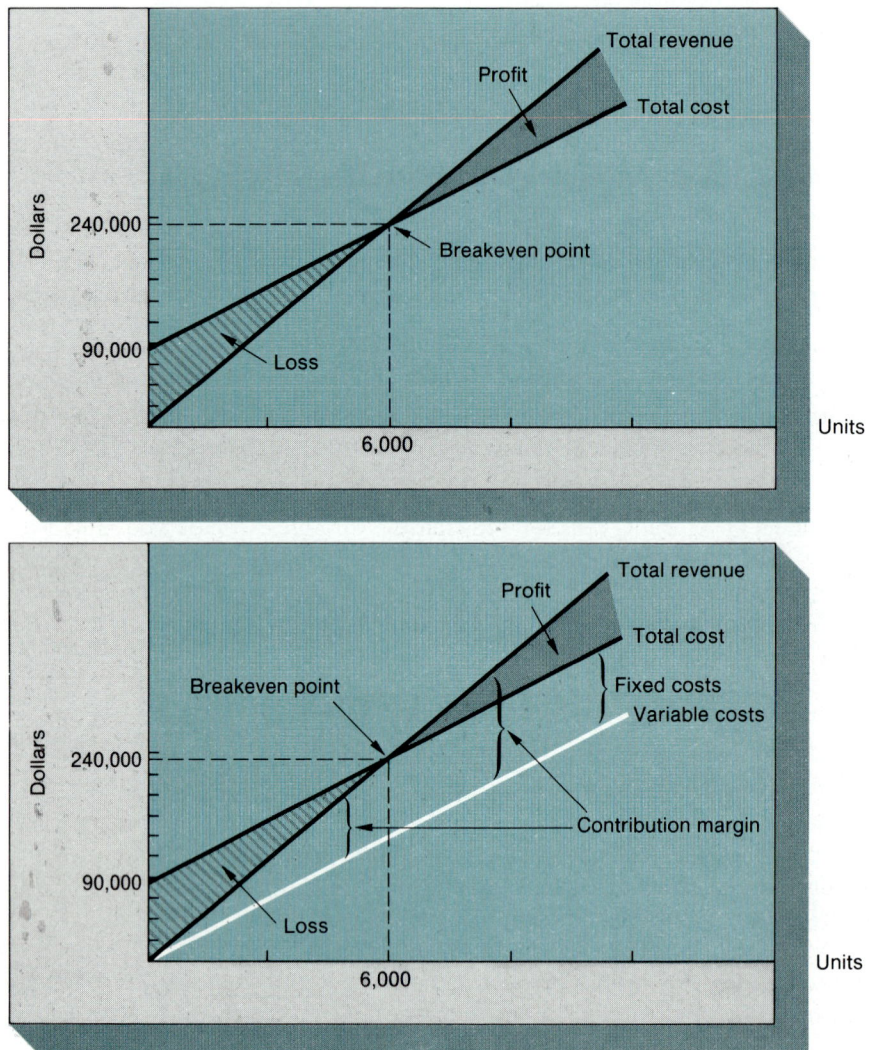

The breakeven point is the point at which the total revenue curve intersects the total cost curve. Sales above this level will provide a profit, while sales below this level will result in a loss. The amount of the profit or loss is shown by the *vertical distance* between the total revenue and total cost curves. These areas have been shaded and labeled on the graph.

Profit-Volume Graph　As the name implies, a **profit-volume** (P/V) **graph** focuses entirely on the relationship between volume and profit. Many people find this graph more useful than the breakeven chart because it shows the amount of profit directly rather than as the difference between the revenue and cost curves.

The profit-volume chart is constructed on a graph in which the vertical axis represents *net income* in dollars. The vertical axis is extended below the origin in order to show a net loss. The horizontal axis represents *volume*. The measure of volume can be in

Figure 7.2   Profit-volume graph

Net income in dollars

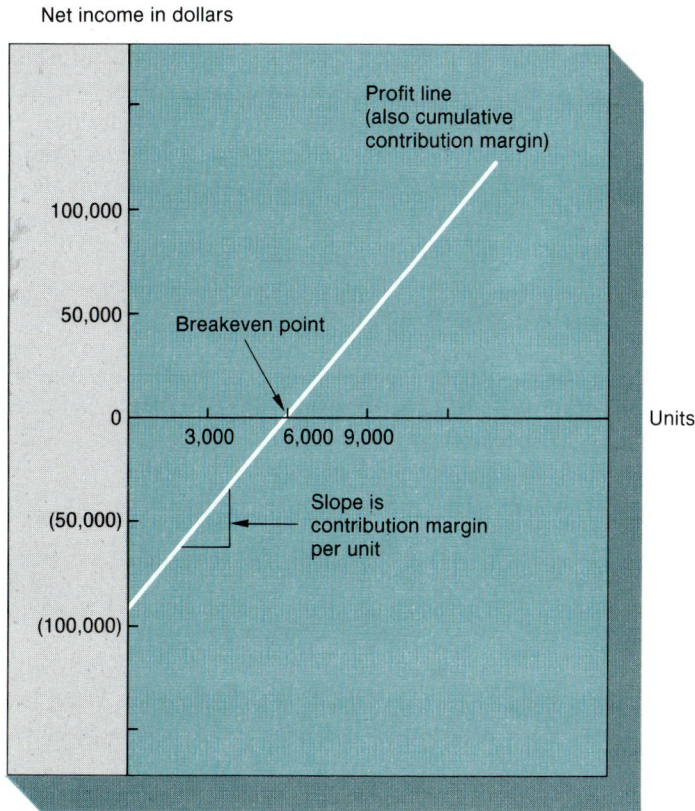

Profit line
(also cumulative
contribution margin)

100,000

50,000

Breakeven point

0

3,000   6,000 9,000   Units

Slope is
contribution margin
per unit

(50,000)

(100,000)

either units or sales dollars, but we will stay with units for now, as shown in figure 7.2. The profit (loss) line is plotted by computing the profit (loss) at several levels of output. These can be taken from the breakeven chart by analyzing the difference between the total revenue and total cost curves. The profit line is straight when both revenue and cost curves are linear and any two points can be used to plot it. The two most commonly used points are (a) the zero production level and (b) the breakeven point. At an output of zero, the loss will be the amount of fixed costs. Using our data for Packard, the coordinates of this point are (0, −90,000). The profit line slopes upward to the right and crosses the horizontal axis at the breakeven point. The coordinates of this point are (6,000, 0).

The formula for the profit line is:

Net income $= -a + bx$

where $a =$ (y-intercept) fixed cost
$b =$ (slope) contribution margin per unit
$x =$ (independent variable) volume in units or sales dollars

Notice that the *slope* of the profit line is equal to the *contribution margin*. Profit increases (loss decreases) by the amount of each unit's contribution margin. Notice also that the profit line represents the *cumulative contribution margin* in dollars at various volume levels. When the profit line crosses the horizontal axis, the cumulative contribution margin is enough to cover fixed costs. Operations above that point provide an income to the company.

Breakeven Analysis in Sales Dollars

The concept of the breakeven point does not change when the analysis is performed in sales dollars. The breakeven point merely identifies the amount of *sales dollars* required to cover all costs but generates no profit.

Equation for Breakeven Point in Sales Dollars   One method of computing breakeven in sales dollars is to compute breakeven in units and multiply the number of units by the sales price per unit. However, sometimes it may not be convenient or efficient because of the way the data is given to first compute the breakeven point in units. The equation for computing the breakeven point in units can be manipulated so it will yield the breakeven point in sales dollars. The breakeven point in sales dollars is equal to fixed costs divided by the contribution margin ratio.

$$\text{Breakeven point in sales dollars} = \frac{\text{Fixed costs}}{\text{Contribution margin ratio}}$$

By definition, the **contribution margin ratio** is the ratio of the contribution margin to sales. The **contribution margin** is the sale price minus variable costs and the ratio is computed by dividing contribution margin by the sales price.

$$\text{Contribution margin ratio} = \frac{\text{Sale price per unit} - \text{Variable costs per unit}}{\text{Sale price per unit}}$$

or

$$= \frac{\text{Total sales} - \text{Total variable costs}}{\text{Total sales}}$$

Example: All Time Company manufactures and sells a watch for $25. Variable costs are $20 per unit and fixed costs total $100,000 per year. What is the required sales revenue for the company to break even? The contribution margin ratio is first computed and then divided into the total fixed costs.

Solution:

$$\text{Contribution margin ratio: } \frac{\$25 - \$20}{\$25} = .20 \text{ or } 20\%$$

$$\text{Breakeven point in sales dollars: } \frac{\$100,000}{.20} = \$500,000$$

Breakeven Charts in Sales Dollars   The breakeven chart does not change when the analysis is performed in sales dollars rather than in units. The breakeven point in sales dollars is obtained by reading the dollar amount on the *vertical axis* that corresponds to the breakeven point. Remember that the number of units is obtained by reading the amount on the *horizontal axis* that corresponds to the breakeven point.

When a profit-volume graph in sales dollars is developed, sales dollars is substituted for units as the volume measure on the horizontal axis. The profit line is the difference between the total revenue and total cost curves for various levels of sales dollars.

Breakeven Analysis for Multiple Products

Our analysis so far has assumed that only one product was being produced and sold, which is not very realistic for most companies. Breakeven analysis can still be performed using either units of production or sales dollars by assuming that the company's sales mix will remain constant.

Sales mix refers to the ratio or relative combination of each product's sales to total sales. It is the composition of total sales broken down among various products or product lines.

Example: Multi Products Incorporated has three products labeled model X, model Y, and model Z. Sales on a monthly basis are expected to be as follows:

	Model X	Model Y	Model Z	Total
Units sold:	1,000	1,500	2,500	5,000
Ratio:	20%	30%	50%	100%

Product mix is usually stated in a ratio, such as (2:3:5) for models X, Y, and Z respectively. This means that for every 2 units of model X that are sold there are 3 units of model Y and 5 units of model Z. Another way of viewing sales mix is to construct in your mind a **market basket** that represents the average expected sales of a company. Within that basket, representing one product mix, Multi Products would have 2 units of model X, 3 units of model Y, and 5 units of model Z, for a total of 10 units.

Breakeven Analysis in Units for Multiple Products   A market basket approach is used to compute a breakeven point in units. A market basket representing the average sales mix is developed. The contribution margin provided by the basket is used to compute the number of baskets that must be sold to break even. The number of individual products required to fill the baskets at the breakeven point is then determined.

Example: Multi Products Incorporated has a sales ratio of 2:3:5 for models X, Y, and Z respectively. Total fixed costs for the year are $200,000. The sale price, variable costs, and contribution margin associated with each product are as follows:

	Model X	Model Y	Model Z
Sale price	$50	$25	$10
Variable costs	30	15	8
Contribution margin	$20	$10	$ 2

Solution: The average market basket is based on the sales ratio and consists of 10 units with a total contribution margin of $80 [(2 × $20) + (3 × $10) + (5 × $2)]. The breakeven point in market baskets is computed using the formula for breakeven point in units.

$$X = \frac{\$200,000}{\$80} = 2,500 \text{ baskets}$$

In order to fill 2,500 baskets it will take the following amounts for each model:

Model X	5,000 units (2,500 × 2)
Model Y	7,500 units (2,500 × 3)
Model Z	12,500 units (2,500 × 5)

This, then, is the breakeven point in units as long as the sales mix stays at (2:3:5).

Breakeven Analysis in Sales Dollars for Multiple Products   The breakeven point in sales dollars for a multiple product entity can be computed by using an average contribution margin ratio. The average contribution margin ratio can be computed on a per unit basis or it can be developed from the income statement. In both cases, the fixed costs are divided by the average contribution margin ratio. The difference is in the level of aggregation in computing the average contribution margin ratio.

When the average contribution margin ratio is computed on a unit basis, the average unit sale price is divided into the average unit contribution margin.

Example: Using the data above for Multi Products Incorporated the average sale price is computed by multiplying the sales ratio by the sale price for individual products and summing the results. The average contribution margin is computed in a similar manner, and the contribution margin ratio is the average contribution margin divided by the average sale price.

Average sale price:

(20% × $50) + (30% × $25) + (50% × $10) = $22.50

Average contribution margin:

(20% × $20) + (30% × $10) + (50% × $2) = $8.00

Average contribution margin ratio:

($8.00 ÷ $22.50) = 35.555%

Breakeven point in sales dollars:

$$\frac{\$200{,}000}{35.555\%} = \$562{,}500 \text{ per year}$$

An average contribution margin ratio can also be developed from an income statement once the fixed and variable costs have been identified. The contribution margin format is most useful for this type of analysis.

Example: C. M. Incorporated has twenty products and the contents of an average market basket are not known. They reported the following net income for January, 19X1. The sales mix and costs for January are expected to continue throughout the coming year. Management was disappointed with the results and wants to know the sales level required to break even.

Sales	$120,000	100%
Variable costs	90,000	75%
Contribution margin	30,000	25%
Fixed costs	40,000	
Net income (loss)	($10,000)	

Solution: The average contribution ratio is 25% ($30,000 ÷ $120,000) and the breakeven point in sales dollars is $160,000 ($40,000 ÷ 25%). Assuming the product mix and costs remain the same as in January, C. M. Incorporated must sell $160,000 per month to break even.

Breakeven analysis in sales dollars is generally easier to compute than breakeven analysis in units for multiple product entities because it does not require a knowledge of the product mix and the average market basket. A contribution margin ratio can be developed from the income statement for use in the breakeven analysis.

Breakeven Charts for Multiple Products   A breakeven chart for a multiple product entity is similar to a single product entity in that it shows dollars on the vertical axis and volume on the horizontal axis. If volume is specified in units, the market basket approach must be followed. One unit is equal to one market basket containing the normal sales mix of the company.

A profit-volume graph is useful in showing the contribution that each product provides to total company profit. A profit-volume chart for Multi Products Incorporated is shown in figure 7.3 with two profit lines—one shows each product's contribution and one shows the average for all products.

Suppose that management of Multi Products expects sales to be $675,000 (3,000 baskets @ $225 each) for the year. The contribution margin provided by each product

Figure 7.3   Profit-volume chart for multiple products

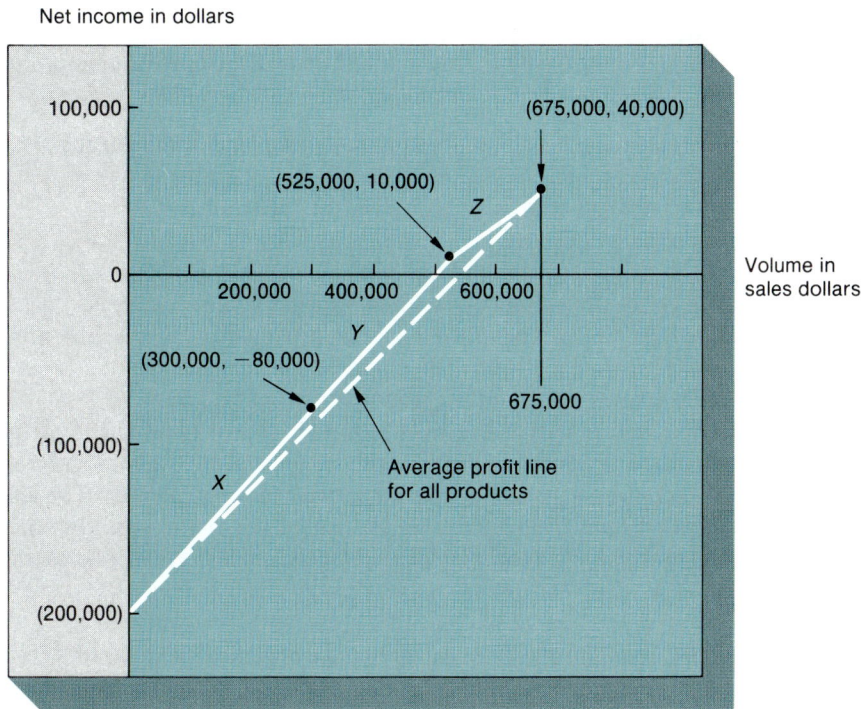

to cover fixed costs and to provide a profit is plotted as a solid line. Segments *X, Y,* and *Z* represent products *X, Y,* and *Z* respectively. The dashed line is the average profit line for all products.

The profit line for individual products is plotted by computing the sales and contribution margin as if only that product was produced and sold. For example, if only model *X* was produced and sold, there would be 6,000 units (3,000 baskets @ 2 each) with total sales of $300,000 (6,000 × $50) and a contribution margin of $120,000 (6,000 × $20). The company's net loss, if only model *X* was sold, would be $80,000. The coordinates of this point are (300,000, −80,000).

Model *Y* is considered next. Sales of model *Y* will be 9,000 units (3,000 baskets @ 3 each) or $225,000 (9,000 × $25) with a contribution margin of $90,000 (9,000 × $10). The cumulative sales for models *X* and *Y* combined are $525,000 and the profit is $10,000. These numbers provide the coordinates of this point.

By adding model *Z* with 15,000 units, $150,000 of sales, and $30,000 of contribution margin, we arrive at a total sales and profit for the year of $675,000 and $40,000 respectively. The products could have been considered in any order. However, a different order will change the shape of the profit line. The beginning and ending points will not change and the average profit line for all products will remain the same.

ASSUMPTIONS UNDERLYING COST-VOLUME-PROFIT ANALYSIS

Although the cost-volume-profit analysis is a valuable tool in making a variety of decisions, the analysis is based on several assumptions and, if the assumptions are not realistic, the analysis will be misleading. Cost-volume-profit analysis is relatively simple to understand and work with and, if the assumptions are not grossly violated, its results will approximate actual results. A more sophisticated analysis is required when the assumptions are violated.

Basic Assumptions

The following list summarizes the basic assumptions underlying cost-volume-profit analysis:

1. Cost data are available for manufacturing, selling, and administrative activities. Costs can be classified as either fixed or variable.
2. Variable costs change at a linear/constant rate per unit.
3. Fixed costs remain constant.
4. Volume is the only factor that affects cost.
5. Unit selling prices do not change as the unit sales volume changes.
6. There is only one product or, if there are multiple products, the sales mix remains constant.
7. There are no constraints on either production or marketing.
8. Productivity remains constant. This is required for cost functions to be linear.
9. All units that are produced are sold in the same period. Or stated differently, there is no significant change in inventory levels between periods. The analysis assumes that all costs incurred during the period are also expensed in the same period. For example, if production exceeds sales, some costs will be carried in inventory rather than expensed.
10. There is a relevant range of validity for these and other underlying assumptions and concepts. The relevant range establishes the limits within which the volume of activity can vary and the sales and cost relationships remain valid.

The relevant range is one of the most important assumptions and is basic to several other assumptions. Within a fairly narrow range of activity the assumptions are generally valid. If the analysis is extended beyond that range, a new chart must be developed with new cost and revenue curves or a more sophisticated analysis using parabolic cost and revenue curves.

Economic Analysis

An economic analysis of cost, volume, and profit avoids many of the above assumptions by using parabolic (nonlinear) cost and revenue curves. Figure 7.4 shows a typical economic analysis.

Notice that the revenue curve comes out of the origin, rises quickly, but levels off, and finally declines. When only a few units are available, a premium price can be charged. However, price must be reduced to sell larger quantities. The point of diminishing returns indicates where total revenue begins to decline. The increase in the number of units sold is not enough to offset the loss due to a reduction in the sales price.

The total cost curve intersects the vertical axis at $1,250, rises initially, then levels off, but rises sharply at higher levels of volume. Some, but not all, fixed costs can be avoided in the short run at very low levels of output. In the example, $1,250 of fixed costs are unavoidable. The initial rise in the cost curve results from discretionary fixed costs that were avoided at zero output and from production inefficiencies associated with low levels of output. As output increases, fixed costs remain relatively constant. However, because of improvements in production efficiency, there is a decline in the rate of increase in the cost curve. Total costs increase rapidly as output approaches plant capacity. Additional fixed costs must be incurred and production inefficiencies result in higher per unit variable costs.

Figure 7.4   Economic breakeven analysis

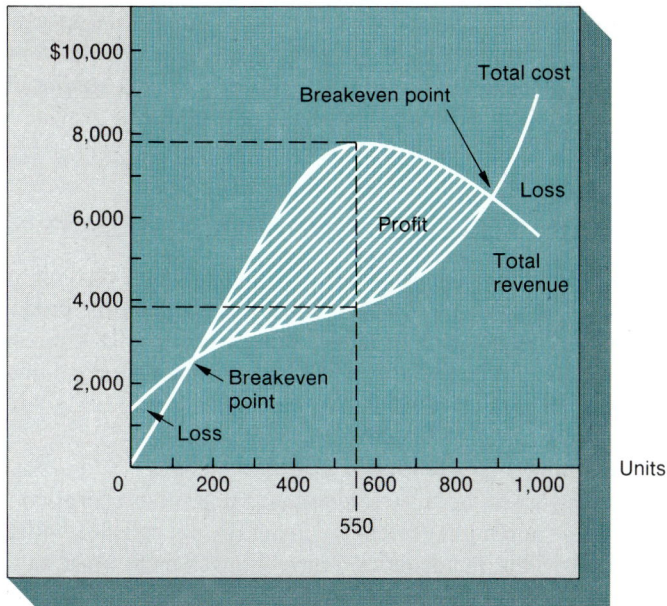

The two points at which total revenues equal total costs are the breakeven points. One is at a relatively low level of output and the other at a relatively high level. A profit will be earned by operating within this range. The areas of profit and loss have been shaded and labeled in figure 7.4.

One of the benefits of this analysis is that it identifies the optimum level of output. Profit will be maximized at the point where there is the maximum vertical distance between the total revenue and total cost curves. This can also be determined by identifying the point at which the slope of the two curves are equal. Output of 550 units in figure 7.4 results in the maximum profit of $4,000 ($7,900 − $3,900).

Sources of Data

Essential data for computing cost-volume-profit analysis include the selling price of the product(s), sales mix for multiple product entities, and costs broken down into a fixed and variable classification. The budget is the best source of this information for companies that have a formal budget. The budget is typically developed by studying historical operating data and adjusting them for expected changes during the coming period. As such, it is directly applicable to current decisions relating to costs, volume, and profit.

The sales portion of the budget contains the selling price of the product(s). The sales mix can be developed from the number of units of each product that are expected to be sold. The flexible budget provides total fixed costs and a variable rate. An adjustment, however, is required if the measure of volume associated with the variable rate is something other than units. Since breakeven analysis is unit based, the variable rate must also be specified in units. For example, if the variable portion of the flexible budget is based on direct-labor hours worked, it would first need to be converted to a variable rate per unit by using the standard for direct-labor hours required to produce each unit.

Companies without a formal budget must go through some of the same analysis as those with a formal budget in collecting the information required for breakeven analysis. Historical cost data can be analyzed using such techniques as the high-low point method, scattergraph method, or least-squares regression analysis to separate fixed and variable costs and to quantify the cost functions. Sales reports can be used to identify sales prices and sales mix. Remember that adjustments may be required to these historical data to make them meaningful for decisions on current and future operations.

Data collection is most difficult for products with which the company has had little or no experience. In these situations, industrial engineering studies are most useful in providing an estimate of the cost data and market studies can provide relevant information on sales price and product mix.

APPLICATIONS OF COST-VOLUME-PROFIT ANALYSIS

The breakeven analysis discussed above is only one application of cost-volume-profit analysis. Cost-volume-profit analysis can provide useful information for product pricing, for analyzing the effect of changes in the product mix or changes in the cost structure by substituting fixed costs for variable costs, and for determining the volume of output required to yield a specified profit.

Level of Volume Required to Achieve a Specified Profit

A breakeven point is important because it identifies the level of operation that will avoid a loss. However, investors and management are generally not satisfied with breaking even. A level of profit that provides an adequate return on investment must be achieved in the long run to make the product or project attractive.

Level of Volume in Units and Sales Dollars   Our equation for computing the breakeven point can be adjusted to compute the volume of sales dollars or units required to provide a specified profit. This is done by adding the desired profit to the fixed costs and dividing by the contribution margin (for units) or the contribution margin ratio (for sales dollars).

$$\text{Volume in units} = \frac{\text{Fixed costs} + \text{Desired profit}}{\text{Contribution margin per unit}}$$

$$\text{Volume in sales dollars} = \frac{\text{Fixed costs} + \text{Desired profit}}{\text{Contribution margin ratio}}$$

Example: Packard Incorporated sells their model Q calculator for $40. Fixed costs are $90,000 per month and variable costs are $25 per unit. How many units must be sold to provide $30,000 net income (before income tax)? What is the sales volume associated with the before-tax net income of $30,000?

Solution:

$$\text{Sales in units} = \frac{\$90,000 + \$30,000}{\$40 - \$25} = 8,000 \text{ units}$$

$$\text{Sales in dollars} = \frac{\$90,000 + \$30,000}{(\$40 - \$25)/\$40} = \frac{\$120,000}{37.5\%} = \$320,000 \text{ sales dollars}$$

Notice that the breakeven point in units multiplied by the sale price (8,000 units × $40) equals $320,000.

After-Tax Profit   In the previous example, the desired profit was specified as a before income tax amount. Income tax is a *tax on income* and income results only after all costs have been covered. Remember that both fixed and variable costs include manufacturing, selling, and administrative costs required to produce and sell the product. No allowance has been made for any income tax on profits.

The income tax problem must be considered with the addition of the profit factor, and the desired profit must be specified as either before or after income tax. When the desired profit is specified as a *before income tax amount,* we ignore the tax and include that amount of profit in the equations as illustrated on page 210. If the profit figure is specified as an *after-tax amount,* it must first be converted to a before-tax amount for inclusion in the equation.

The net income before tax can be computed by working backwards from the desired net income after tax and the tax rate. Remember that net income before tax, multiplied by the tax rate, gives the amount of income tax that is subtracted in deriving the after-tax profit.

Example: Packard Incorporated desired an after-tax net income of $18,000 and they are subject to an average income tax rate of 40%. What is their desired before-tax net income?

Solution: The after-tax net income is divided by one minus the tax rate $(1 - .40)$ to give the before-tax net income. This can be generalized into equation form and used to compute the before-tax net income.

$$\text{Before-tax net income} = \frac{\text{After-tax net income}}{(1 - \text{Tax rate})} = \frac{\$18,000}{(1 - .40)} = \underline{\$30,000}$$

Margin of Safety

The **margin of safety** identifies the amount of reduction in sales that could occur without sustaining a loss. It is the excess of actual or budgeted sales over sales at the breakeven point. The margin of safety may be specified in units of output, sales dollars, or as a percentage of sales. When it is expressed as a percentage of sales, it is called a *margin of safety ratio.*

$$\text{Margin of safety in sales dollars} = \text{Current sales} - \text{Breakeven sales}$$

$$\text{Margin of safety ratio} = \frac{\text{Current sales} - \text{Breakeven sales}}{\text{Current sales}}$$

Example: Marginal Manufacturing Company produces filing cabinets that they sell for $120. Monthly fixed costs are $75,000 and variable costs are $90 per unit. Sales for the past few months have averaged $350,000. Compute the margin of safety in sales dollars and the margin of safety ratio.

Solution:

$$\text{Breakeven point: } \frac{\$75,000}{(\$120 - \$90)/\$120} = \underline{\$300,000}$$

$$\text{Margin of safety: } \$350,000 - \$300,000 = \underline{\$50,000}$$

$$\text{Margin of safety ratio: } \frac{\$350,000 - \$300,000}{\$350,000} = 14.3\%$$

Sales of Marginal Manufacturing Company can be reduced by $50,000 or 14.3% before a loss is sustained.

Sensitivity Analysis

Sensitivity analysis is a "what if" analysis that examines the effect on the outcome for changes in one or more input values. The input values for cost-volume-profit analysis include the sales mix, sale price, units, variable cost per unit, and total fixed cost. A change in any of these items will cause a change in the breakeven point and a change in the amount of profit (loss) at any given level of sales. Remember that the values for these inputs are often only estimates. Also, management may be considering a change in the manufacturing or selling process that would have an impact on one or more of the values. A technique is needed to determine the impact on the breakeven point and on profit for

Figure 7.5   Sensitivity analysis—new product decision

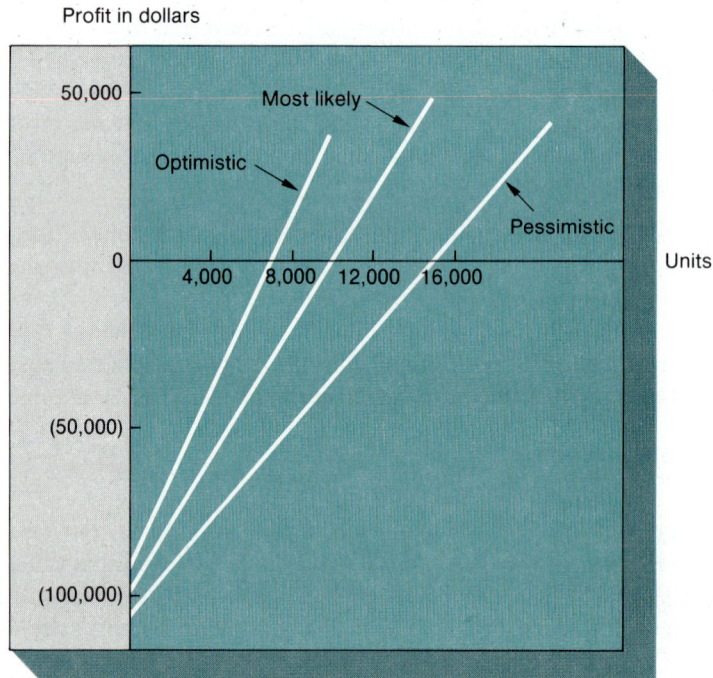

errors in estimating the values, or for changes in the production or selling process. Cost-volume-profit analysis with breakeven charts and profit-volume graphs is often used.

Input Value Errors   Suppose management is considering a new product that must be priced at $40 in order to be competitive in the market. Costs to produce and sell the product are expected to be $30 per unit variable and $100,000 per month fixed. For the first two years, management expects to capture 10% of a total market of 130,000 units. Should management pursue the new product?

If their cost estimates are correct, the answer is probably yes. The breakeven point is 10,000 units [$100,000 ÷ ($40 − $30)], which is less than their expected sales of 13,000 units (10% × 130,000).

Remember, however, that the cost data provided by management are only estimates and that management has had no prior experience with this product. They admit that their cost estimates for both fixed and variable costs could be as much as 10% high or 10% low, but the probability that they would exceed those limits is only remote.

Sensitivity analysis can be used to analyze the impact on the expected breakeven point for the most optimistic and pessimistic estimates.

Optimistic breakeven point: (10% reduction in costs)	$\dfrac{\$90,000}{\$40 - \$27} = 6{,}923$ units
Pessimistic breakeven point: (10% increase in costs)	$\dfrac{\$110,000}{\$40 - \$33} = 15{,}714$ units

The profit-volume graph in figure 7.5 shows the optimistic, most likely, and pessimistic outcomes.

Additional analysis could be performed to determine the amount of increase in cost above the estimate that can be sustained and still break even, assuming they are able to capture 10% of the market or 13,000 units. Management's cost estimates can be as much as 6% low and still break even by capturing only 10% of the market. The computations are shown below with x representing the percentage increase in costs:

$$\frac{\$100,000(x)}{\$40 - \$30(x)} = 13,000 \text{ units}$$

Solving the equation for x:

$x = 1.0612$ or 6.1% increase

There appears to be a reasonable probability that costs will exceed the estimates. If the company only expects to capture 10% of a 130,000 unit market, a loss will be sustained if costs exceed the estimates by more than 6.1%. Management may want to consider additional cost studies or market studies before a final decision is made. Additional cost studies can be used to forecast the actual costs of producing and selling the product more accurately and with more confidence. Market studies can provide information on the total market size and the likelihood of capturing 10% or more of it.

Substituting Fixed and Variable Costs   Costs often change as a result of a decision to change the procedures used to produce or sell a product. An analysis of the change's impact is often desired to assist in the decision-making process. Some changes either increase or decrease fixed or variable costs, or both. Often management is faced with a decision to substitute a fixed cost for a variable cost or vice versa. Sensitivity analysis can be used to study the impact on the breakeven point and profit for these types of changes.

Example: Merge Incorporated is a multiple product entity considering the acquisition of a new machine that would replace two direct-labor workers. Wages for these two individuals currently constitute about 20% of the variable costs. The new machine would initially be used at only 50% capacity but will add about $40,000 per year of fixed costs. The following statement shows the current operating results:

Sales	$350,000	100%
Variable costs	189,000	54%
Contribution margin	161,000	46%
Fixed costs	140,000	
Net income	$ 21,000	

What will be the impact on net income and the breakeven point if the machine is acquired?

Solution: If sales continue at the current level and the machine is acquired, net income will decrease by $2,200.

Additional fixed costs	$40,000
Savings in variable costs	
(20% × $189,000)	37,800
Increase in total costs	$ 2,200

The breakeven point with the new machine is $316,901, which is slightly higher than the existing breakeven point of $304,348.

$$\text{Current breakeven point} = \frac{\$140,000}{46\%} = \$304,348$$

$$\text{New breakeven point} = \frac{\$180,000}{56.8\%^a} = \$316,901$$

$$^a\text{Contribution margin ratio} = \frac{350,000 - 151,200}{350,000} = 56.8\%$$

Figure 7.6   Sensitivity analysis—new machine acquisition

Profit in dollars

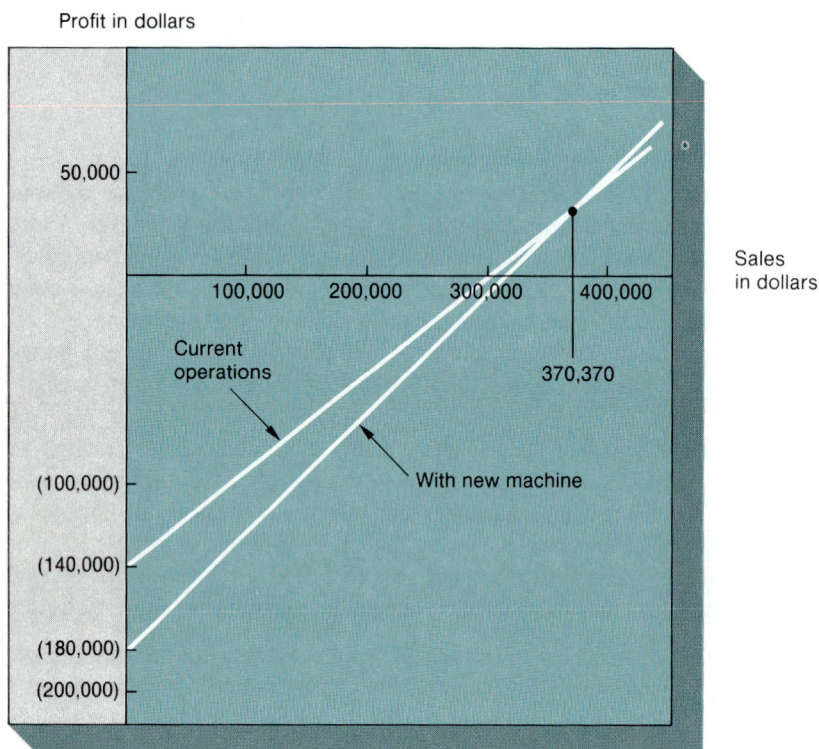

If sales are expected to increase, the new machine may be a very profitable investment. Figure 7.6 shows profit lines under the existing condition and assuming the new piece of equipment is acquired. Notice that the profit line with the new machine has a steeper slope. The new machine will be profitable when sales exceed $370,370 per year. This is determined by computing the point at which the two lines intersect, as follows:

$$-140,000 + .46x = -180,000 + .568x$$
$$.108x = 40,000$$
$$x = \$370,370$$

This type of analysis only considers the impact of the machine during its first year of operations and should not be used as the sole criterion in the acquisition decision. Capital budgeting techniques (discussed in chaps. 22 and 23) consider the contribution of the machine over its entire life and should be used in connection with the above analysis.

Product Pricing   Management does not have much influence over product pricing when the product is sold in a competitive market environment. Market forces of supply and demand dictate to a large extent the price that can be charged for the product. However, the sales price has a significant impact on the breakeven point and on profit. Sensitivity analysis is useful in projecting the effects of price fluctuation on company profitability.

Figure 7.7   Sensitivity analysis—product pricing

Profit in dollars

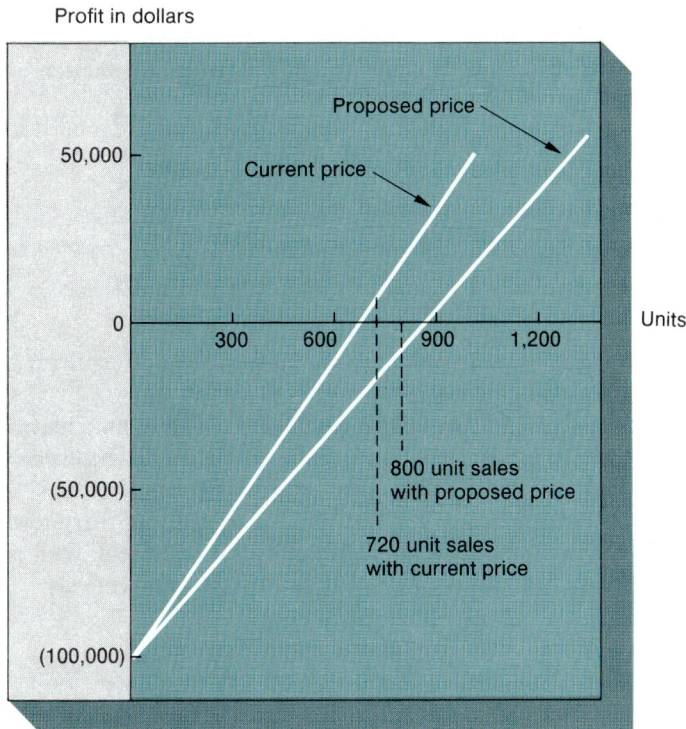

Example: Western Sales Company currently sells their dishwashers for $350. Costs are $100,000 per month fixed and $200 per unit variable. Currently they are selling 800 units per month. However, the economy is in a slight recession and in order to maintain their same sales level they must cut the selling price by 10%. If the current price is maintained, they estimate a 10% loss in sales. What is the breakeven point with each pricing strategy and which strategy would you recommend?

Solution: The breakeven points under the existing price and alternative price are:

$$\text{Existing price} = \frac{\$100,000}{\$350 - \$200} = \underline{667 \text{ units}}$$

$$\text{Alternate price} = \frac{\$100,000}{\$315 - \$200} = \underline{870 \text{ units}}$$

As shown in figure 7.7, maintaining the current price will result in a breakeven point of 667 units. Estimated sales will drop to 720 units (800 × 90%) and profits will be lower than under normal conditions. But at least they can expect to earn a profit.

A 10% cut in price results in a breakeven point of 870 units and estimated sales remain at 800 units. This will result in a loss and is, therefore, an undesirable alternative. The current pricing policy should be continued.

Changes in Product Mix   Sales mix is the composition of total sales broken down among various products or product lines. A change in the product mix generally results in a different breakeven point and level of profitability. Sensitivity analysis can be used to evaluate the effects on sales and profits for alternative sales mixes.

Example: Beckhard Company has three product lines called Regular, Lite, and Draft with annual fixed costs of $280,000. Over the next year they expect a 20% decrease in sales of Regular with those customers switching about half to Lite and half to Draft. You have collected the following information:

	Lite	Regular	Draft
Sale price per case	$4.00	$3.00	$5.00
Variable costs	2.20	1.80	2.50
Contribution margin	$1.80	$1.20	$2.50

Current data:				Total cases
Sales per month (cases)	40,000	100,000	60,000	200,000
Sales ratio	20%	50%	30%	100%

What will be the impact on the breakeven point and on profits if the product mix changes as anticipated?

Solution: Figure 7.8 shows the profit line for the existing and anticipated conditions. Since the shift in product mix is from the product with the lowest contribution margin ratio to products with higher contribution margin ratios, the new breakeven point will be lower. The average contribution margin will be higher and, even though there is no change in the total cases sold, both profits and dollar sales will be higher by $19,978 and $30,000 respectively.

The computations for developing the profit lines follow:
Current Sales Mix:

Average sales price = (20% × $4.00) + (50% × $3.00) + (30% × $5.00) = $3.80

Average contribution margin = (20% × $1.80) + (50% × $1.20) + (30% × $2.50) = $1.71

Average contribution margin ratio = ($1.71 ÷ $3.80) = 45%

Breakeven point = $\dfrac{\$280,000}{45\%}$ = $622,222

Sales = ($4 × 40,000) + ($3 × 100,000) + ($5 × 60,000) = $760,000

Profit = [(45% × $760,000) − $280,000] = $62,000

Anticipated Sales Mix:

	Lite	Regular	Draft	Total
Revised sales (cases)	50,000	80,000	70,000	200,000
Sales ratio	25%	40%	35%	100%

Average sales price = (25% × $4.00) + (40% × $3.00) + (35% × $5.00) = $3.95

Average contribution margin = (25% × $1.80) + (40% × $1.20) + (35% × $2.50) = $1.81

Average contribution margin ratio = ($1.81 ÷ $3.95) = 45.82%

Breakeven point = $\dfrac{\$280,000}{45.82\%}$ = $611,086

Sales = ($4 × 50,000) + ($3 × 80,000) + ($5 × 70,000) = $790,000

Profit = [(45.82% × $790,000) − $280,000] = $81,978

Figure 7.8   Sensitivity analysis—change in product mix

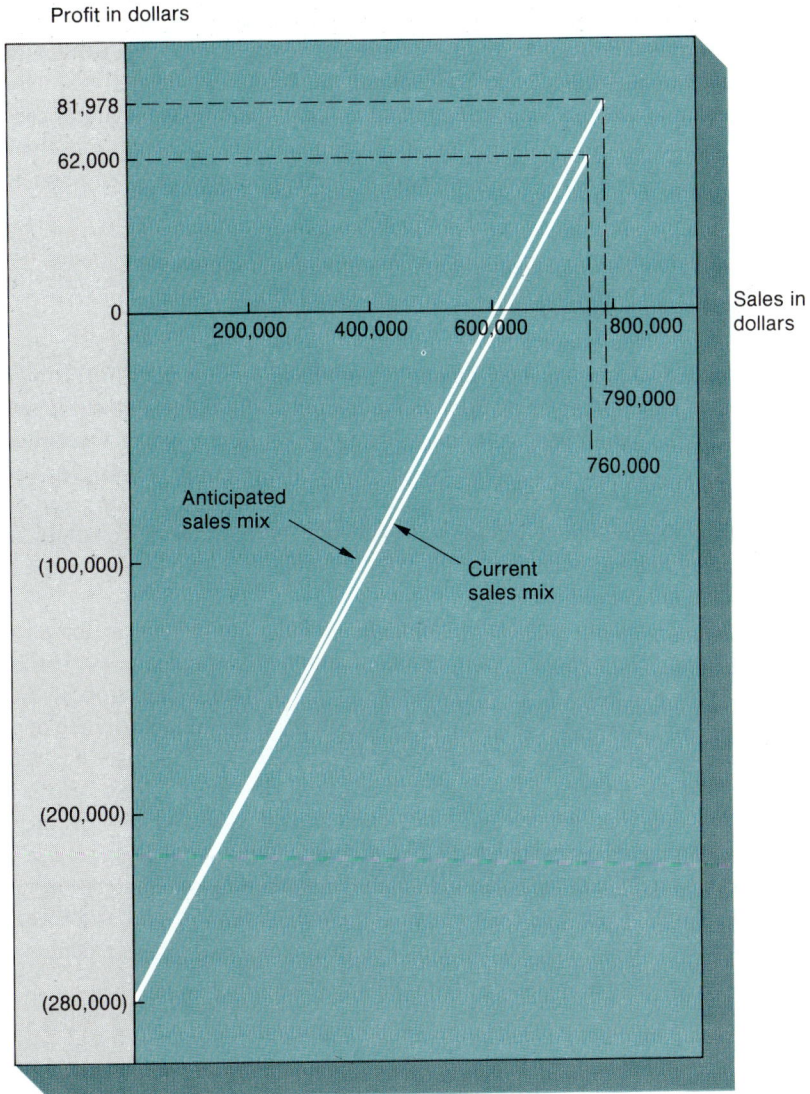

Summary

This chapter focused on cost-volume-profit analysis, its uses, and its limitations. Cost-volume-profit analysis is a study of the relationships between costs and volume and their impact on profit. One of the most common analyses is the breakeven analysis, which identifies the breakeven point. The breakeven point is the level of sales volume, specified in either units or sales dollars, at which total revenues equal total expenses and the business has neither earnings nor a loss. The equations to compute the breakeven point are:

$$\text{Breakeven point in units} = \frac{\text{Fixed costs}}{\text{Sale price per unit} - \text{Variable cost per unit}}$$

$$\text{Breakeven point in sales dollars} = \frac{\text{Fixed costs}}{\text{Contribution margin ratio}}$$

Breakeven and profit-volume charts are useful in graphically illustrating the cost-volume-profit relationships. A breakeven chart contains a total revenue curve and a total cost curve. The point of their intersection identifies the breakeven point. Operations above that point result in a profit; operations below that point result in a loss. The amount of profit or loss is equal to the vertical distance between the total revenue and total cost curves. The profit-volume chart focuses on profit and its relationship to volume. A profit line is developed that is equal to the vertical distance between the total revenue and total cost curves on the breakeven chart.

Cost-volume-profit analysis is useful in providing information for a variety of decisions. Margin of safety identifies the excess of actual or budgeted sales over the breakeven point. It is the amount by which sales could decrease before losses occur. Sensitivity analysis is a "what if" analysis that examines the effect on the outcome when one or more of the input values are changed. Cost-volume-profit analysis can be used to evaluate the impact on the breakeven point or profits for changes in the input values. This is useful in evaluating potential errors in the input data, substituting fixed and/or variable costs, alternate pricing strategies, and changes in the product mix.

There are several assumptions that underlie the breakeven analysis typically used by accountants. Most of the assumptions relate to the linearity of cost and revenue functions within a relevant range of activity. More sophisticated analysis using nonlinear curves is required when the assumptions are not satisfied.

Even Products Company manufactures a product they call MARKY. The following financial projections have been made.

Even Products Company
Financial Projection for Product MARKY
Year Ending December 31, 19X7

Sales (100 units at $200 a unit)		$20,000
Manufacturing cost of goods sold:		
Direct labor	$3,000	
Direct materials used	2,800	
Variable factory overhead	2,000	
Fixed factory overhead	1,000	
Total		8,800
Gross margin		$11,200
Selling expenses:		
Variable	$1,200	
Fixed	2,000	
Administrative expenses:		
Variable	1,000	
Fixed	2,000	
Total		6,200
Operating income		$ 5,000
Income taxes (40%)		2,000
Net income		$ 3,000

Required

1. How many units of MARKY must be sold to break even?
2. What would operating income be if sales increased 25%?
3. Compute sales at the breakeven point if fixed factory overhead increases by $3,400.
4. How many units of MARKY must be sold to realize an after-tax net income of $4,800? Assume fixed costs remain at the level shown in the financial statement above.

Solution to the Self-Study Problem

Requirement 1

Breakeven in units can be computed by the following equation:

$$\text{Breakeven point in units} = \frac{\text{Fixed costs}}{\text{Sale price per unit} - \text{Variable cost per unit}}$$

The fixed costs and variable cost are:

Cost	Fixed	Variable
Manufacturing	$1,000	$ 7,800
Selling	2,000	1,200
Administration	2,000	1,000
Total	$5,000	$10,000

Variable cost per unit is $100 ($10,000 ÷ 100 units).

$$\text{Breakeven point} = \frac{\$5,000}{\$200 - \$100} = 50 \text{ units}$$

Requirement 2

The contribution margin ratio is 50%.

$$\text{Contribution margin ratio} = \frac{\text{Sales price per unit} - \text{Variable costs per unit}}{\text{Sales price per unit}}$$

$$= \frac{\$200 - \$100}{\$200} = 50\%$$

Therefore, the contribution margin will increase at a rate of $.50 for each $1 increase in sales. Fixed costs will not change.

Operating income:	
Current level	$5,000
Increased sales	
($20,000 × 25% × 50%)	2,500
Total	$7,500

Requirement 3

An increase of $3,400 in fixed factory overhead brings the total fixed cost to $8,400 ($3,400 + $5,000). The contribution margin ratio computed in requirement 2 is used in the following equation to compute the breakeven point in sales dollars:

$$\text{Breakeven point in sales dollars} = \frac{\text{Fixed costs}}{\text{Contribution margin ratio}}$$

$$= \frac{\$8,400}{50\%} = \$16,800$$

Requirement 4

In order to realize an after-tax profit of $4,800, operating income must be $8,000.

$$\text{Before-tax net income} = \frac{\text{After-tax net income}}{(1 - \text{Tax rate})} = \frac{\$4,800}{(1 - .40)} = \$8,000$$

This amount is included in the following equation to compute the number of units that must be sold to realize an after-tax net income of $4,800.

$$\frac{\text{Fixed costs} + \text{Desired profit}}{\text{Sales price per unit} - \text{Variable costs}} = \frac{\$5,000 + \$8,000}{\$200 - \$100} = 130 \text{ units}$$

Suggested Readings

Goodman, Sam R., and Reece, James S. *Controllers' Handbook.* Homewood, Ill.: Dow-Jones Irwin, 1978.

Goulet, Peter G. "Attacking Business Decision Problems with Breakeven Analysis." *Management Aids for Small Manufacturers,* no. 234. Washington, D.C.: U.S. Small Business Administration, 1978.

Grossman, Steven, D.; Plum, Charles W.; and Welker, Robert B. "New Dimensions to the Cost-Volume-Profit Technique." *Managerial Planning* 27 (March/April 1979): 35–38.

Hartl, Robert J. "The Linear Total Revenue Curve in Cost-Volume-Profit Analysis." *Management Accounting* (March 1975): 49.

Raun, Donald L. "The Limitations of Profit Graphs, Breakeven Analysis, and Budgets." *The Accounting Review* (October 1964): 930.

Discussion Questions

1. Define cost-volume-profit analysis.
2. What is meant by the breakeven point?
3. What is the relationship between a breakeven chart and a profit-volume chart?
4. Assume a company has no ability to change its sales price, fixed costs, or variable costs. Is the company guaranteed a breakeven point merely by increasing sales? Explain.
5. Describe sales mix. Why is sales mix important in cost-volume-profit analysis?
6. Describe the typical cost-volume-profit graph used in economic analysis.
7. One of the assumptions made by accountants when performing a cost-volume-profit analysis is that productivity remains constant. What will be the effect on the cost and/or revenue curves if this assumption is not valid?
8. One of the assumptions made by accountants when performing cost-volume-profit analysis is that all units produced are sold in the same period. What will be the effect on the analysis if this assumption is not valid?
9. Why is the relevant range an important assumption to the accountant's cost-volume-profit analysis?
10. Where will an accountant generally obtain the data required for a cost-volume-profit analysis?
11. Why is before-tax net income versus after-tax net income relevant when identifying the amount of sales revenue required to achieve a desired profit level?
12. Define margin of safety.
13. How is the margin of safety ratio computed?
14. What is sensitivity analysis? How is it relevant to cost-volume-profit analysis?
15. Assume a change is made in the production process substituting fixed costs for variable costs. Will the breakeven point increase or decrease? Will operating income increase or decrease? Explain.

Exercises

Exercise 7.1 Basic Concepts of Cost-Volume-Profit Analysis

The following statements relate to cost-volume-profit analysis. Indicate whether each statement is true or false and write a brief explanation supporting your answer.

1. Breakeven calculations have little practical value because most managers have to do better than break even.
2. In the breakeven chart in figure 7.1, total fixed costs cannot be identified.
3. If you decided to rent a truck for $3,600 a year for all mileage up to 10,000 and 10 cents for each additional mile, truck rental would be a semivariable cost of the user.
4. If fixed costs are $5,000 a year, variable costs are 15 cents per unit, and the selling price is 20 cents per unit, it will be necessary to sell 1,000,000 units to break even.
5. The breakeven chart in figure 7.1 indicates that there will be a profit if 6,200 units are sold by the firm and a loss if only 5,800 units are sold.
6. The main purpose of cost-volume-profit analysis is to pinpoint the position at which the firm neither makes a profit nor suffers a loss.
7. Data for breakeven analysis can be taken directly from the conventionally prepared (absorption cost) income statement.
8. A successful business manager should set a goal of achieving the breakeven point in each period's operations.

Exercise 7.2 Advanced Concepts of Cost-Volume-Profit Analysis

The following statements relate to several concepts of cost-volume-profit relationships. Indicate whether you agree or disagree with each statement and give a brief explanation supporting your answer.

1. The variable cost ratio is determined by dividing sales revenue by variable costs, and the ratio is the complement of the contribution margin ratio.
2. Breakeven sales in units can be computed by dividing total dollar fixed costs by the contribution margin per unit.
3. The breakeven chart can be regarded as a dynamic analysis in the sense that total fixed costs and the relationship between variable costs and sales revenue will hold true for *any* and *all* levels of sales.
4. In applying cost-volume-profit analysis, managers should understand that an increase in fixed costs will cause both the breakeven point and the contribution margin ratio to increase.
5. The unit profit-volume graph in figure 7.2 shows that, as the number of units sold increases, the fixed costs per unit will also increase.
6. A fundamental concept in cases of multiple products is that changes in the breakeven point are caused by changes in sales prices and are not affected by any changes in the sales mix of the various products.

Exercise 7.3 Concepts of Cost-Volume-Profit Analysis

For each of the following numbered items, identify the item in the right-hand column that best matches the numbered item. No item in the right-hand column should be used more than once.

1. Indicates the point at which the company neither makes a profit nor incurs a loss.
2. A graphic analysis of the relationship of costs and sales revenue to profit.
3. Determined by dividing the dollar contribution margin by dollar sales revenue.
4. Determined by dividing total fixed costs by the contribution margin ratio.
5. Determined by dividing fixed costs by the contribution margin per unit.
6. The amount of total fixed costs and unit variable costs, as well as the slope of the revenue line, are meaningful only within this area.
7. When a shift in this aspect occurs, a change in profit can also be expected unless the same contribution margin ratio is realized on all products.
8. Indicates how much sales may decrease from a particular sales figure before a loss is incurred.
9. The margin of safety expressed as a percentage of sales.
10. This change will not necessarily lead to an increase in volume sufficient to increase profits.
11. A measure of the effect of price changes on volume sold.
12. Products make a favorable contribution as long as the sales revenue exceeds this.

a. Relevant range
b. Unit profit-volume graph
c. Departmentalization
d. Cost-volume-profit analysis
e. Price reduction
f. Variable cost
g. Breakeven chart
h. Breakeven analysis
i. Margin of safety ratio
j. Margin of safety
k. Contribution margin ratio
l. Sales mix
m. Breakeven point in dollars
n. Elasticity of demand
o. Breakeven point in units

Exercise 7.4   Simple Cost-Volume-Profit Analysis Calculations

The following data have been determined for the Rollerberry Company for each month.

Normal plant capacity	1,500 units
Fixed costs	$10,000
Unit sales price	$16
Unit variable costs	7

Required

1. Determine the breakeven point in units. Use the contribution margin (short equation) technique.
2. Determine the breakeven point in dollars, using the contribution technique.
3. Determine the necessary sales volume for the first quarter of the year if the target profit for the quarter is $12,000.

Exercise 7.5   Cost-Volume-Profit Analysis—Margin of Safety Considerations

Data for one month's normal operations for the Gamble Company are as follows:

Sales	$100,000
Variable costs	35,000
Fixed costs	30,000
Normal plant capacity	50,000 units

Required

1. Determine the net income for a normal month.
2. Determine the breakeven point in dollars, units, and percent of capacity.
3. If operations are at normal capacity, determine the margin of safety and the margin of safety ratio.

Exercise 7.6   Cost-Volume-Profit and Sensitivity Analysis

Refer to the data in exercise 7.5.

Required

1. Determine the new breakeven point if the sales price is reduced to $1.80 and the other data remains the same as in the original case.
2. What net profit will be earned at normal capacity if fixed costs increase by $10,000 and the other factors remain as in the original case?
3. If the contribution margin ratio changes to 60%, determine the effects of this change on fixed costs.
4. If the contribution margin per unit changes to $1.20, what must sales be to earn the same net income as determined for the original data in a normal month?

Exercise 7.7   Cost-Volume-Profit Analysis—Effect of Changes in Cost

The income statement for Hansen & Company was as follows for the year:

Sales		$200,000
Less: Expenses		
Variable expenses	150,000	
Fixed expenses	80,000	230,000
Net profit (loss)		$(30,000)

Required

Assume that the variable expenses will always remain the same percentage of sales.

1. What amount of sales will cause Hansen & Company to break even if fixed expenses are increased by $60,000?
2. What amount of sales will cause Hansen & Company to realize a net profit of $25,000, assuming the increase in fixed expenses?

Exercise 7.8   Basic Considerations of Cost-Volume-Profit Analysis

Kevin has recently decided to sell toy planes at a local carnival. He can buy these planes at $1.25 each and retains the option of returning all unsold planes. The cost for leasing the booth is $360. Kevin has decided to sell these planes for $2.00 each.

Required

1. Determine the number of planes Kevin must sell to break even.
2. Kevin wants to earn $150.00 to buy a video game. How many planes must be sold to reach his goal?

Exercise 7.9   Basic Procedures of Cost-Volume-Profit Analysis (CMA)

The following data apply to items 1 through 7.

Siberian Ski Company recently expanded its manufacturing capacity allowing it to produce up to 15,000 pairs of cross-country skis of the mountaineering model or the touring model. The sales department assures management that it can sell between 9,000 and 13,000 of either product this year. Because the models are very similar, Siberian Ski will produce only one of the two models.

The following information was compiled by the accounting department.

	Mountaineering	*Touring*
Selling price per pair	$88.00	$80.00
Variable costs per pair	52.80	52.80

Fixed costs will total $369,600 if the mountaineering model is produced and $316,800 if the touring model is produced. Siberian Ski Company is subject to a 40% income tax rate.

Required

1. The contribution margin ratio of the touring model is
   a. 40.0%.
   b. 66.0%.
   c. 51.5%.
   d. 34.0%.
   e. some amount other than those given above.
2. If Siberian Ski Company desires an after-tax net income of $24,000, how many pairs of touring model skis will the company have to sell?
   a. 13,118
   b. 12,529
   c. 13,853
   d. 4,460
   e. Some amount other than those given above.
3. The total sales revenue at which Siberian Ski Company would make the same profit or loss regardless of the ski model it decided to produce is
   a. $880,000.
   b. $422,400.
   c. $924,000.
   d. $686,400.
   e. some amount other than those given above.
4. If the Siberian Ski Company sales department could guarantee the annual sale of 12,000 skis of either model, Siberian would
   a. produce touring skis because they have a lower fixed cost.
   b. be indifferent about the model sold because each model has the same variable cost per unit.
   c. produce only mountaineering skis because they have a lower breakeven point.
   d. be indifferent about the model sold because both are profitable.
   e. produce mountaineering skis because they are more profitable.
5. How much would the variable cost per unit of the touring model have to change before it had the same breakeven point in units as the mountaineering model?
   a. $2.68/pair increase
   b. $4.53/pair increase
   c. $5.03/pair decrease
   d. $2.97/pair decrease
   e. Some amount other than those given above.
6. If the variable cost per unit of touring skis decreases by 10%, and the total fixed cost of touring skis increases by 10%, the new breakeven point will be
   a. unchanged from 11,648 pairs because the cost changes are equal and offsetting.
   b. 10,730 pairs.
   c. 13,007 pairs.
   d. 12,812 pairs.
   e. some amount other than those given above.

7. Which of the following statements is *not* an assumption made when employing a cost-volume-profit study for decision analysis?
   a. Volume is the only relevant factor affecting costs.
   b. Changes in beginning and ending inventory levels are insignificant in amount.
   c. Sales mix is variable as total volume changes.
   d. Fixed costs are constant over the relevant volume range.
   e. Efficiency and productivity are unchanged.

Exercise 7.10 Cost-Volume-Profit Concepts and Procedures (CMA)

The income statement for Davann Company presented below represents the operating results for the fiscal year just ended. Davann had sales of 1,800 tons of product during the current year. The manufacturing capacity of Davann's facilities is 3,000 tons of product.

Davann Company
Income Statement
Year Ending December 31

Sales		$900,000
Variable costs		
Manufacturing	$315,000	
Selling costs	180,000	
Total variable costs		$495,000
Contribution margin		$405,000
Fixed costs		
Manufacturing	$ 90,000	
Selling	112,500	
Administration	45,000	
Total fixed costs		$247,500
Net income before income taxes		$157,500
Income taxes (40%)		63,000
Net income after income taxes		$ 94,500

Required

1. The breakeven volume in tons of product for the year was
   a. 420 tons.
   b. 1,100 tons.
   c. 495 tons.
   d. 550 tons.
   e. some amount other than those shown above.
2. If the sales volume is estimated to be 2,100 tons in the next year, and if the prices and costs stay at the same levels and amounts next year, the after-tax net income that Davann can expect next year is
   a. $135,000.
   b. $110,250.
   c. $283,500.
   d. $184,500.
   e. some amount other than those shown above.

3. Davann has a potential foreign customer who has offered to buy 1,500 tons at $450 per ton. Assume that all of Davann's costs would be at the same levels and rates as last year. What net income after taxes would Davann make if it took this order and rejected some business from regular customers so as not to exceed capacity?
   a. $297,500
   b. $252,000
   c. $211,500
   d. $256,500
   e. Some amount other than those shown above.

4. Davann plans to market its product in a new territory. Davann estimates that an advertising and promotion program costing $61,500 annually would need to be undertaken for the next two or three years. In addition, a $25 per ton sales commission over and above the current commission to the sales force in the new territory would be required. How many tons would have to be sold in the new territory to maintain Davann's current after-tax income of $94,500?
   a. 307.5 tons
   b. 1,095.0 tons
   c. 273.333 tons
   d. 1,545.0 tons
   e. Some amount other than those shown above.

5. Davann is considering replacing a labor intensive process with an automatic machine. This would result in an increase of $58,500 annually in manufacturing fixed costs. The variable manufacturing costs would decrease $25 per ton. The new breakeven volume in tons would be
   a. 990 tons.
   b. 1,224 tons.
   c. 1,854 tons.
   d. 612 tons.
   e. some amount other than those shown above.

6. Ignore the facts presented in item 5. Now assume that Davann estimates that the per ton selling price would decline 10% next year. Variable costs would increase $40 per ton and the fixed costs would not change. What sales volume in dollars would be required to earn an after-tax net income of $94,500 next year?
   a. $1,140,000
   b. $825,000
   c. $1,500,000
   d. $1,350,000
   e. Some amount other than those shown above.

Problems

Problem 7.1   Basic Cost-Volume-Profit Analysis

Hickman Company produces a single product for which the following data have been determined:

Unit sales price	$24.00
Unit variable cost	18.00
Annual fixed costs	$48,000

Required

Consider each of the following situations independent of each other.

1. Determine the contribution margin for the product, per unit and as a ratio.
2. Using the contribution margin technique (short equation), determine breakeven sales for a year in units and in dollars.
3. Hickman estimates that sales will increase by $40,000 during next year. If other relationships remain the same, by how much should the contribution margin increase? What effect should the sales increase have on net income?

Problem 7.2   Cost-Volume-Profit Analysis and Sensitivity Analysis

Refer to the basic data in problem 7.1.

Required

1. Last year Hickman Company sold 10,500 units. Market research indicates that a 5% cut in selling price accompanied by a $10,000 addition in advertising would result in a 40% increase in unit sales. Should the action suggested by marketing be undertaken? Prepare contribution income statements for last year and for the proposed change to support your conclusion.
2. Assume last year's sales were 10,500 units. An alternative to the price reduction is to leave the price as is and increase sales commissions by $1.00 per unit accompanied by some increase in advertising. Marketing research indicates sales may be increased by 40% by these changes. If profits were maintained at last year's level, by how much could advertising be increased?
3. Assume that sales for this year are running at last year's level. A Canadian customer wants to purchase 2,500 units at a special price. If Hickman wants to double current profits, what price must be quoted to the Canadian customer?

Problem 7.3 Cost-Volume-Profit Analysis—Sales Mix Considerations

The Margets Company sells three products. Budgeted sales by product and in total are shown below for one month:

	Lino	Malo	Nema	Total
Percent of total sales	25%	40%	35%	100%
Sales	$40,000	$64,000	$56,000	$160,000
Less: Variable expense	24,000	41,600	22,400	88,000
Contribution margin	$16,000	$22,400	$33,600	$ 72,000
Contribution margin ratio	40%	35%	60%	45%
Less: Fixed expenses				50,700
Net income				$ 21,300

$$\text{Breakeven sales} = \frac{\$50,700}{.45} = \$112,667$$

Assume that actual sales for July are Lino—$48,000, Malo—$96,000, and Nema—$16,000.

Required

1. Prepare an income statement for July based on actual data. Use the contribution format shown in the budget and assume the individual product variable cost relationship to sales is the same as budgeted and that the fixed costs are as budgeted.
2. Determine breakeven sales based on actual results.
3. Considering Margets met the $160,000 sales budget for July, explain why net income and breakeven sales are different from the budget.

Problem 7.4 Cost-Volume-Profit Analysis—Breakeven and Profit Considerations

You have observed that many of your neighbors have joined the home gardening trend. You have noticed that the soil in your area is very high in clay content and is so compact that many neighbors get very poor plant growth and the resulting yield is poor. The costs of seed, care, fertilizing, and watering is hardly justified.

You get a bright idea that you could assist your neighbors and make some money to help finance your education if you invest in a power soil aerator and do custom soil-conditioning work during the summer. The power aerator costs $450. You estimate that a $25 charge for each garden-conditioning job is reasonable (for a typical size garden spot). You estimate that fuel for the aerator and other supplies will cost $3 for each garden and that you can do six gardens each day.

Required

1. Determine how many gardens you will need to aerate to break even. How many days work will be required?

2. You estimate that if you can clear $5,000 during the summer, you can cover your costs of attending school next year since you have a scholarship to finance part of the costs. If you can earn that much, you wouldn't need support from your father. How many garden jobs will you need to do to clear $5,000? How many days will it take to do this?

3. Suppose your estimate of $25 to do each garden is 10% high (even though professional yard care firms charge $35) for a new operation getting established and that your estimate of fuel and other costs is 25% low. You feel your estimate of the cost of equipment is close since you have estimated a 15% increase in price above that charged for similar equipment last year. What effect will these changes in estimates have on your answers to requirements 1 and 2 above?

4. Identify any factors of cost or revenue that you haven't taken into account above (focus on items not amounts). Describe how you would obtain information about dollar amounts for these factors.

Problem 7.5 Cost-Volume-Profit Analysis and Sensitivity Analysis

Romney Produce Company operates four warehouses in the southwestern part of the United States. They have recently provided you with the following company budget data for next year:

Sales	$25,000,000
Fixed expenses	15,500,000
Variable expenses	8,500,000

Required

Determine the expected profit for each of the following changes from the data presented above, considering each change independently:

1. A 15% increase in fixed costs
2. A 10% increase in total contribution margin (sales remain constant)
3. An 8% increase in total sales
4. An 8% decrease in fixed costs
5. A 10% decrease in total contribution margin (sales remain constant)
6. A 15% decrease in total sales
7. A 5% increase in total sales and 10% increase in fixed costs
8. A 10% decrease in variable costs and 10% increase in fixed costs

Problem 7.6 Cost-Volume-Profit Analysis and Sensitivity Analysis

The Barlow Company operates a chain of women's apparel boutiques. This chain sells for $40 per pack a variety of clothing packs, including blouses, scarves, and jewelry pins. Up to this point, Barlow Company has been relatively successful in this area of sales and is presently evaluating the possibility of opening up another store, that would possess the following revenue and expense relationships:

	Per Pack
Selling price	$40.00
Invoice cost of a pack	$32.00
Sales commissions	2.00
	$34.00

Annual fixed expenses:

Rent	12,400
Salaries	110,000
Utilities	9,500
Other	23,500
	$155,400

Required

Consider each question independently.

1. What is the annual breakeven point in dollars and units?
2. If 30,000 packs were sold, what would be the store's net income (loss)?
3. If sales commissions were increased another 50¢ per pack, what would be the store's breakeven point in dollars and units?
4. If, instead of increasing sales commissions, fixed salaries were increased by $24,000, what would be the annual breakeven point in dollars and units? Is this alternative desirable over the alternative described in requirement 3?
5. Now suppose that in addition to the regular $2.00 commission per pack, the store manager is paid 75¢ for each pack sold in excess of the breakeven point. What would be the store's net income if 40,000 packs were sold?

Problem 7.7 Cost-Volume-Profit Analysis Concepts (CMA)

The SAB Company uses a profit-volume graph similar to the one shown below to represent the cost-volume-profit relationships of its operations. The vertical (y-axis) is the profit in dollars and the horizontal (x-axis) is the volume in units. The diagonal line is the contribution margin line.

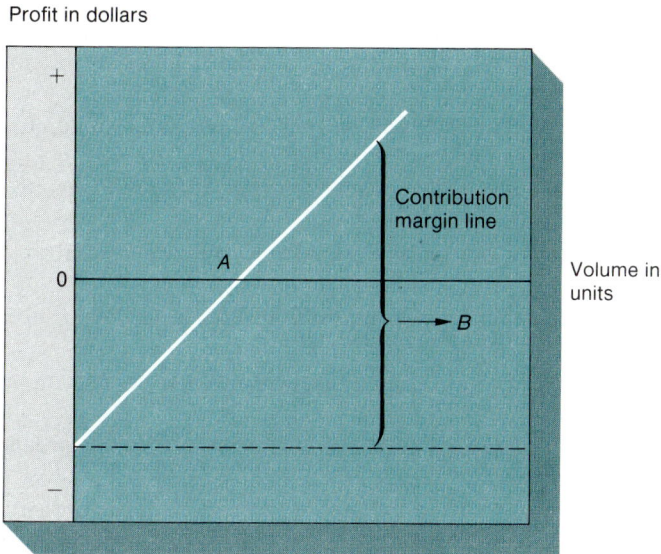

Profit in dollars

Contribution margin line

Volume in units

Required

1. Point A on the profit-volume graph represents
   a. the point at which fixed costs equal sales.
   b. the point at which fixed costs equal variable costs.
   c. a volume level of zero units.
   d. the point at which total costs equal total sales.
   e. the point at which the rate of contribution margin increases.
2. The vertical distance from the dotted line to the contribution margin line denoted as B on the profit-volume graph represents
   a. the total contribution margin.
   b. the contribution margin per unit.
   c. the contribution margin rate.
   d. total sales.
   e. the sum of the variable and fixed costs.
3. If SAB Company's fixed cost were to increase,
   a. the contribution margin line would shift upward parallel to the present line.
   b. the contribution margin line would shift downward parallel to the present line.
   c. the slope of the contribution margin line would be more pronounced (steeper).
   d. the slope of the contribution margin line would be less pronounced (flatter).
   e. the contribution margin line would coincide with the present contribution margin line.

4. If SAB Company's variable costs per unit were to increase but its unit selling price stays constant,
    a. the contribution margin line would shift upward parallel to the present line.
    b. the contribution margin line would shift downward parallel to the present line.
    c. the slope of the contribution margin line would be more pronounced (steeper).
    d. the slope of the contribution margin line would be less pronounced (flatter).
    e. the slope of the contribution margin line probably would change but how it would change is not determinable.
5. If SAB Company decided to increase its unit selling price to offset exactly the increase in the variable cost per unit,
    a. the contribution margin line would shift upward parallel to the present line.
    b. the contribution margin line would shift downward parallel to the present line.
    c. the slope of the contribution margin line would be more pronounced (steeper).
    d. the slope of the contribution margin line would be less pronounced (flatter).
    e. the contribution margin line would coincide with the present contribution margin line.

Problem 7.8   Cost-Volume-Profit and Sensitivity Analysis (CMA)

Pawnee Company's normal operating capacity is 50,000 units of a single product. Sales and production for the current year totaled 40,000 units at an average price of $20 per unit. Variable manufacturing costs were $8 per unit, and variable marketing costs were $4 per unit sold. Fixed costs were incurred uniformly throughout the year and amounted to $188,000 for manufacturing and $64,000 for marketing. There was no year-end work-in-process inventory.

Required

1. Determine Pawnee's breakeven point in sales dollars for the current year.
2. If Pawnee is subject to an income tax rate of 30%, determine the number of units required to be sold in the current year to earn an after-tax net income of $126,000.
3. Pawnee's variable manufacturing costs are expected to increase 10% in the coming year. Determine Pawnee's breakeven point in sales dollars for the coming year.
4. If Pawnee's variable manufacturing costs do increase 10%, determine the selling price that would yield Pawnee the same contribution margin ratio in the coming year.

Problem 7.9 Concepts and Procedures of Cost-Volume-Profit Analysis (CPA)

Each of the following short cases (1–4) are independent of each other. Answer the questions indicated.

1. Pitt Company is considering a proposal to replace existing machinery used for the manufacture of product A. The new machines are expected to cause increased annual fixed costs of $120,000; however, variable costs should decrease by 20% due to a reduction in direct-labor hours and more efficient usage of direct materials. Before this change was under consideration, Pitt had budgeted product A sales and costs for a year as follows:

Sales	$2,000,000
Variable costs	70% of sales
Fixed costs	$400,000

Assuming that Pitt implemented the above proposal by January 1, what would be the increase in budgeted operating profit for product A for the year?

2. Lindsay Company reported the following results from sales of 5,000 units of product A for the month of June:

Sales	$200,000
Variable costs	120,000
Fixed costs	60,000
Operating income	20,000

Assume that Lindsay increases the selling price of product A by 10% on July 1. How many units of product A would have to be sold in July in order to generate an operating income of $20,000?

3. Birney Company is planning its advertising campaign for the year and has prepared the following budget data based on a zero advertising expenditure:

Normal plant capacity	200,000 units
Sales	150,000 units
Selling price	$25.00 per unit
Variable manufacturing costs	$15.00 per unit
Fixed costs:	
Manufacturing	$800,000
Selling and administrative	$700,000

An advertising agency claims that an aggressive advertising campaign would enable Birney to increase its unit sales by 20%. What is the maximum amount that Birney can pay for advertising and obtain an operating profit of $200,000?

4. In planning its operations for the year based on a sales forecast of $6,000,000, Wallace Incorporated prepared the following estimated data:

	Costs and Expenses	
	Variable	Fixed
Direct materials	$1,600,000	
Direct labor	1,400,000	
Factory overhead	600,000	$ 900,000
Selling expenses	240,000	360,000
Administrative expenses	60,000	140,000
	$3,900,000	$1,400,000

What would be the amount of sales dollars at the breakeven point?

Problem 7.10 Cost-Volume-Profit Analysis—Comprehensive Analysis (CMA)

The following data are used in requirements 1 through 3. Refer to those data for each question asked.

Pralina Products Company is a regional firm with three major product lines—cereals, breakfast bars, and dog food. The income statement for the year ending April 30 is shown below. The statement was prepared by product line using absorption (full) costing. Explanatory data related to the items presented in the income statement follow.

Pralina Products Company
Income Statement
Year Ending April 30
(000 omitted)

	Cereals	Breakfast Bars	Dog Food	Total
Sales in pounds	2,000	500	500	3,000
Revenue from sales	$1,000	$400	$200	$1,600
Cost of sales				
Raw materials	$ 330	$160	$100	$ 590
Direct labor	90	40	20	150
Factory overhead	108	48	24	180
Total cost of sales	$ 528	$248	$144	$ 920
Gross margin	$ 472	$152	$ 56	$ 680
Operating expenses				
Selling expenses				
Advertising	$ 50	$ 30	$ 20	$ 100
Commissions	50	40	20	110
Salaries and related benefits	30	20	10	60
Total selling expenses	$ 130	$ 90	$ 50	$ 270
General and administrative expenses				
Licenses	$ 50	$ 20	$ 15	$ 85
Salaries and related benefits	60	25	15	100
Total general and administrative expenses	$ 110	$ 45	$ 30	$ 185
Total operating expenses	$ 240	$135	$ 80	$ 455
Operating income before taxes	$ 232	$ 17	($ 24)	$ 225

1. *Cost of sales.* The company's inventories of raw materials and finished products do not vary significantly from year to year. The inventories at April 30 this year were essentially identical to those at April 30 last year.

   Factory overhead was applied to products at 120% of direct-labor dollars. The factory overhead costs for the fiscal year were as follows:

Variable indirect labor and supplies	$ 15,000
Variable employee benefits on factory labor	30,000
Supervisory salaries and related benefits	35,000
Plant occupancy costs	100,000
	$180,000

   There was no overapplied or underapplied overhead at year-end.

2. *Advertising.* The company has been unable to determine any direct causal relationship between the level of sales volume and the level of advertising expenditures. However, because management believes advertising is necessary, an annual advertising program is implemented for each product line. Each product line is advertised independently of the others.
3. *Commissions.* Sales commissions are paid to the sales force at the rates of 5% on the cereals and 10% on the breakfast bars and dog food.
4. *Licenses.* Various licenses are required for each product line. These are renewed annually for each product line.
5. *Salaries and related benefits.* Sales and general and administrative personnel devote time and effort to all product lines. Their salaries and wages are allocated on the basis of management's estimates of time spent on each product line.

Required

1. The controller of Pralina Products Company has recommended that the company do a cost-volume-profit analysis of its operations. As a first step, the controller has requested that you prepare a revised income statement for Pralina Products Company employing a product contribution margin format that will be useful in cost-volume-profit analysis. The statement should show the profit contribution for each product line and the net income before taxes for the company as a whole.
2. What effect, if any, would there be on net income before taxes determined in requirement 1, if the inventories as of April 30 this year had increased significantly over the inventory levels of April 30 last year? Explain your answer.
3. The controller of Pralina Products Company is going to prepare a report that she will present to the other members of top management explaining cost-volume-profit analysis. Identify and explain the following points that the controller should include in the report.
   a. The advantages that cost-volume profit analysis can provide to a company.
   b. The difficulties Pralina Products Company could experience in the calculations involved in cost-volume-profit analysis.
   c. The dangers that Pralina Products Company should be aware of in using the information derived from the cost-volume-profit analysis.

COST DETERMINATION

A major part of cost accounting is accumulating manufacturing costs and identifying them with the units produced. This process is called cost determination or cost finding and is the topic covered in chapters 8 through 14.

Manufacturing processes can be broadly classified into two types—job order and process costing. Separate accounting procedures are required for each manufacturing process. Special accounting procedures are also required for processes that produce more than one product. These products are called joint products and may be subdivided into main products, by-products, scrap, and waste.

Manufacturing costs can also be broken down into the separate elements of material, labor, and overhead, which provides management with the cost information necessary to effectively control operations.

JOB-ORDER COST SYSTEMS

8

OUTLINE

A primary objective of cost accounting is to provide management with information to assist them in operating a business successfully. The management process includes activities such as setting objectives and formulating a plan of operation, implementing the plan and measuring results to monitor operating activity on a day-to-day basis, and evaluating the results to see if the plan was properly implemented and if the objectives of the organization are being accomplished. Chapters 1 through 7 have dealt primarily with planning business operations. Cost analysis, budgeting, flexible budgeting, and cost-volume-profit analysis are important topics in planning business activity.

This chapter and several that follow focus on the cost accounting aspects of implementing the plan and measuring the results of operations. This is the next phase of the management cycle. These activities are typically referred to as "cost determination" or "cost finding." The primary objectives of cost finding are to account for manufacturing costs and to determine the manufacturing cost per unit of a finished product. A cost per unit is necessary in preparing financial statements for external users. It is also useful in the cost analysis function of the business to evaluate efficiency and to make pricing and budgeting decisions.

Two different accounting systems have been developed to account for two different types of manufacturing processes. One is called a "job-order accounting system" and the other is called a "process cost accounting system." This chapter distinguishes between these two types of accounting systems, identifies the criteria to be used in selecting one of them, and describes the job-order cost accounting system in detail. After completing this chapter you should be able to:

1. explain the flow of costs through the accounts of a manufacturing organization.
2. distinguish between job-order and process cost accounting systems.
3. identify manufacturing processes that are applicable to a job-order cost system.
4. describe the accounting procedures followed in a job-order cost system.
5. distinguish between control accounts and clearing accounts and properly use a subsidiary ledger for the work-in-process account of a job-order cost system.
6. prepare journal entries for the home office and factory under a split-ledger accounting system.

MANUFACTURING ACCOUNTING SYSTEMS

Manufacturing organizations buy raw materials, labor, and other manufacturing components required to convert raw materials into finished products. The manufacturing process complicates the accounting process because of the additional inventories for raw materials and work in process and because of the need to account for the flow of product costs as the units flow through the production process. Financial statements must be adjusted to reflect the results of the manufacturing process and the additional inventories.

Journalizing the flow of costs through the manufacturing process and preparing a cost-of-goods-manufactured statement introduces the cost-finding phase of cost accounting. The chart of accounts used by a manufacturing organization is an integral part of the accounting system.

Chart of Accounts

Every company must have a **chart of accounts** that lists all the accounts used by a company in its accounting system. A coding system is usually developed and each account is given a unique number. Therefore, an account may be referred to by its name (for example, raw materials inventory) or by its number (for example, #115). A common numbering system identifies assets with numbers between 100 and 199, liabilities with numbers

Figure 8.1   Typical chart of accounts for a manufacturing organization

Balance Sheet Accounts (100–299)

Assets (100–199)
Current Assets (100–129)

100	Cash in bank
104	Marketable securities
106	Accounts receivable
107	Allowance for doubtful accounts
110	Notes receivable
115[a]	Raw materials inventory
120[a]	Work-in-process inventory
125[a]	Finished-goods inventory
129	Prepaid expenses

Investments (130–139)

130	Stock investments
135	Bond investments

Property Plant and Equipment (140–159)

140	Land
142	Buildings
143	Accumulated depreciation—buildings
145[a]	Factory equipment
146[a]	Accumulated depreciation—factory equipment
150	Office furniture and fixtures
151	Accumulated depreciation—office furniture and fixtures

Intangible Assets (170–179)

170	Goodwill
175	Patents
178	Franchise and licenses

Other Assets (180–199)

Liabilities and Owners' Equity (200–299)
Current Liabilities (200–239)

200	Accounts payable
205	Notes payable
210	Accrued payroll
215	Other accrued liabilities
220	Payroll taxes payable
225	Current portion of long-term debt
230	Dividends payable

Long-Term Liabilities (240–249)

240	Bonds payable
245	Other long-term debt
248	Deferred income tax payable

Capital (250–299)

250	Common stock
260	Additional paid-in capital
270	Retained earnings
275	Treasury stock

Income Statement Accounts (300–899)

Sales (300–349)

300	Sales revenue
310	Sales returns and allowances
320	Sales discounts

Cost of Goods Sold (350–399)

350	Cost of goods sold

Factory Overhead (400–499)

400[a]	Factory overhead

Marketing Expenses (500–599)

500	Sales supervision salaries
510	Sales employees salaries
520	Freight out
530	Employer payroll taxes on marketing salaries
540	Supplies
550	Utilities
560	Telephone
570	Postage
580	Travel
590	Advertising

Administrative Expenses (600–699)

600	Administrative salaries
605	Administrative clerical salaries
610	Employer payroll taxes on administrative salaries
620	Supplies
630	Light and power
640	Telephone
650	Postage
660	Insurance
670	Legal and accounting
680	Donations
690	Uncollectible accounts receivable

Other Expenses (700–799)

710	Interest
720	Other losses

Other Income (800–899)

800	Investment income
810	Rental income
820	Other gains

[a]Indicates accounts unique to a manufacturing enterprise.

between 200 and 249, and owner's equity with numbers between 250 and 299. Similar groups of numbers are identified for revenues and the different types of expenses.

Figure 8.1 contains a chart of accounts for a manufacturing organization. Accounts that are unique to manufacturing enterprises have a letter *a* by the account number. Notice that the major differences are in the additional inventories shown as current assets, factory machinery and equipment, and overhead accounts.

The number of accounts required to accumulate manufacturing costs and compute a unit cost is really very small. However, external reporting is only one objective of cost accounting. Additional accounts and elaborate coding structures may be developed to accumulate useful information for management decisions. Further refinement and additional sophistication are for the benefit of the users, who should be heavily involved in developing the system.

Control Accounts and Subsidiary Ledgers   All the accounts listed in the chart of accounts are control accounts. A **control account** is a summary account in the general ledger that is supported in detail by individual accounts in a subsidiary ledger. Therefore, a **subsidiary ledger** provides a detailed breakdown of the contents of a control account.

Financial accounting uses control accounts extensively. For example, accounts receivable is a control account used to record the sale of merchandise on account. Any time merchandise is sold on account the debit is to accounts receivable and any collections on account are recorded as a credit to accounts receivable. Balances owed by any individual customer are not reflected in the control account. A subsidiary ledger for accounts receivable is required to keep track of individual customer balances that make up the total accounts receivable balance.

Control accounts and subsidiary ledgers are also used extensively in cost accounting. Raw materials inventory, work-in-process inventory, and finished-goods inventory are all control accounts. A subsidiary ledger is required for each inventory account to keep track of the items in inventory and the costs associated with each item. If the accounting is performed properly, the total cost of the items in the subsidiary ledger will equal the balance in the inventory control account.

The factory overhead account is also a control account. A subsidiary ledger is generally maintained for factory overhead to break down the total overhead cost into subcategories that are meaningful to management for planning and control. Remember that factory overhead includes all manufacturing costs other than direct material and direct labor. This includes several different kinds of costs, some of which will be fixed, some variable, and some semivariable. If overhead costs are unusually high, management is at a loss to know what went wrong without a meaningful cost breakdown.

Figure 8.2 shows the type of detail contained in a subsidiary ledger for a factory overhead account. Notice the coding system for the factory overhead subsidiary ledger. The control account is number 400. The subsidiary ledger accounts are also a 400 number but are differentiated by a decimal number. For example, indirect materials are identified with a .1 decimal number.

Clearing Accounts   A **clearing account** is an account used to facilitate the accounting process. Generally a clearing account is used to hold cost data until it can be transferred or distributed to other accounts. Clearing accounts may or may not be shown in the chart of accounts.

The income summary account used in financial accounting to close revenue and expense accounts into owner's capital or into retained earnings is an example of a clearing account. The net income for the accounting period is recorded in the income summary account as the revenue and expense accounts are closed. It holds the net income until it is distributed to the owner's capital accounts (for a partnership) or transferred to retained earnings (for a corporation).

Figure 8.2   Subsidiary ledger for factory overhead

Factory Overhead

400	Factory-overhead control
400.1	Indirect materials
400.2	Indirect labor
400.3	Freight in
400.4	Overtime premium
400.5	Employer's payroll taxes (factory wages)
400.6	Fuel—factory
400.7	Light and power
400.8	Telephone and telegraph
400.9	Defective work
400.10	Insurance expense
400.11	Depreciation expense—buildings
400.12	Depreciation expense—machinery and equipment
400.13	Repairs and maintenance of building and equipment
400.14	Rent of equipment
400.15	Property tax
400.16	Amortization of patents on company products

Factory overhead is an example of a clearing account for a manufacturing organization. Actual indirect manufacturing costs (manufacturing costs excluding direct costs) are recorded as debits in the factory overhead account. These costs are transferred into work in process by crediting the factory overhead account using the factory overhead rate. Therefore, the factory overhead account holds the indirect manufacturing costs until they are allocated to work in process and distributed to specific units of production.

Occasionally a clearing account is used for payroll costs and costs associated with major pieces of equipment. In both cases the concept is the same—an account is needed to hold costs until a detailed analysis can be performed to determine the amount of direct cost that should be assigned to work in process and the amount of indirect cost that should be assigned to factory overhead.

Flow of Costs through the Manufacturing Accounts

The **cost cycle** refers to the steps taken in tracing the flow of manufacturing costs through the accounts. The objective of the cost cycle is to systematically accumulate the cost of material, labor, and factory overhead incurred in producing a finished product. When the product is sold, the production costs are expensed as cost of goods sold. The sale of the product provides funds for the acquisition of raw materials and other inputs needed for the production process and the cycle is repeated.

Inventory accounts for raw materials, work in process, and finished goods are used to account for the *flow of costs* as the units being produced flow through the production process. The accounts used are descriptive of the activity or process that occurs. Figure 8.3 summarizes the flow of the costs through the production process.

An example for Marko Plastics Company will illustrate the journal entries required to account for the manufacturing process. At the beginning of January 19X2, Marko Plastics Company had a balance in raw materials inventory of $22,000. The work-in-process inventory had a balance of $34,000 and there was $18,000 of finished goods

Figure 8.3   Flow of costs through manufacturing accounts

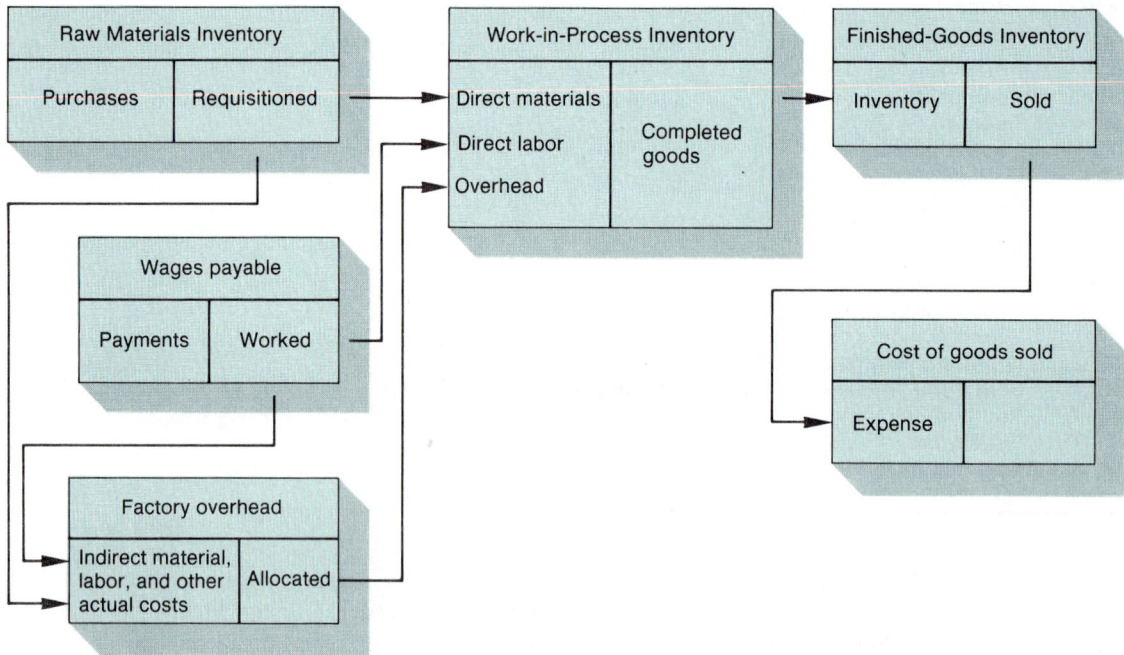

on hand. During January, $57,000 of raw materials were purchased, part paid in cash and part paid on account. The journal entry to record these purchases is:

```
a. Raw materials inventory          57,000
      Cash                                      11,400
      Accounts payable                          45,600
   Record purchases of raw materials.
```

The manufacturing supervisor requested $63,000 of raw materials for use in the production process during January. Of this amount, $7,500 could not be traced to individual products. The journal entry transfers the direct materials into work in process, but the indirect materials go to factory overhead.

```
b. Work-in-process inventory        55,500
   Factory overhead                  7,500
      Raw materials inventory                   63,000
   Record the use of raw materials.
```

Factory payroll for the month totaled $115,000, with $90,000 as direct labor and $25,000 as indirect labor. Once again the direct costs go into work in process and the indirect costs go into factory overhead.

```
c. Work-in-process inventory        90,000
   Factory overhead                  25,000
      Wages payable                             115,000
   Record factory payroll.
```

Other factory overhead costs for the month included equipment rental at $6,300, equipment repairs at $2,200, depreciation on factory building at $4,700, depreciation on factory equipment at $1,200, light and power at $7,800, insurance at $700, and employer's payroll taxes at $12,400. Part of these were paid in cash, part are on account, and others were adjusting entries. However, all of them are debited to factory overhead. The subsidiary ledger for factory overhead would break the total down by type and accumulate each of the amounts with others of the same type.

d.	Factory overhead	35,300	
	Accumulated depreciation—factory equipment		1,200
	Accumulated depreciation—factory building		4,700
	Cash		15,000
	Payroll taxes payable		12,400
	Accounts payable		2,000
	Record other factory overhead.		

Marko Plastics Company uses a predetermined factory overhead rate of 80% of direct-labor cost to allocate factory overhead to work in process. The overhead rate was predetermined at the beginning of the year by estimating (a) the total overhead cost ($480,000) and (b) the total direct-labor cost ($600,000) for the year. The factory overhead rate was then computed as follows:

$$\text{Factory overhead rate} = \frac{\text{Estimated factory overhead}}{\text{Estimated volume}}$$

$$= \frac{\$480,000}{\$600,000} = 80\%$$

This rate is used to allocate the factory overhead into work-in-process inventory.

e.	Work-in-process inventory	72,000	
	Factory overhead		72,000
	Allocate factory overhead to work in process (80% × $90,000).		

Notice from the above journal entries that the actual factory overhead costs total $67,800—indirect material ($7,500) + indirect labor ($25,000) + other overhead ($35,300). The amount allocated into the work-in-process inventory is $72,000, leaving a $4,200 credit balance in the factory overhead account. This means that the factory overhead has been overapplied during the month. However, the $4,200 credit balance is left in the factory overhead account to be offset by underapplied amounts in later months of the year. If operations go as planned for the entire year, the balance in the factory overhead account at the end of the year will be zero.

During January, the manufacturing process was completed on $146,000 of work. Also, merchandise costing $152,000 was sold to customers.

f.	Finished-goods inventory	146,000	
	Work-in-process inventory		146,000
	Transfer completed units to finished-goods inventory.		
g.	Cost of goods sold	152,000	
	Finished-goods inventory		152,000
	Record the cost of units sold.		

Parts of the above journal entries that relate to the manufacturing process are posted in "T" accounts as shown in figure 8.4.

Financial Statements

Financial statements of a manufacturing organization include the additional assets associated with the manufacturing process and a statement of cost of goods manufactured to summarize the results of the production process. Inventories associated with raw materials, work in process, and finished goods are included among the current assets of the business. Building, machinery, and equipment used in the production process are reported as part of property, plant, and equipment.

Figure 8.4   Flow of costs through manufacturing accounts

Marko Plastics Company
January 19X2

		Raw Materials Inventory			
Bal.	$22,000				
a.	57,000		63,000	b.	
Bal.	$16,000				

	Wages Payable		
		115,000	c.

	Factory Overhead			
b.	$ 7,500		72,000	e.
c.	25,000			
d.	35,300			
			$ 4,200	Bal.

		Work-in-Process Inventory			
Bal.	$34,000		146,000	f.	
b.	55,500				
c.	90,000				
e.	72,000				
Bal.	$105,500				

		Finished-Goods Inventory			
Bal.	$ 18,000				
f.	146,000		152,000	g.	
Bal.	$ 12,000				

	Cost of Goods Sold	
g.	$152,000	

Figure 8.5

Marko Plastics Company
Cost-of-Goods-Sold Statement
January 19X2

Finished-goods inventory—January 1, 19X2			$ 18,000
Cost of goods manufactured:			
Work in process—beginning		$ 34,000	
Plus:			
Direct materials	$55,500		
Direct labor	90,000		
Factory overhead	72,000		
Total manufacturing costs		217,500	
Total work in process		251,500	
Less: Ending work in process		105,500	
Cost of goods manufactured			146,000
Goods available for sale			164,000
Less: Ending finished-goods inventory			12,000
Cost of goods sold			$152,000

A cost-of-goods-manufactured statement may be reported separately or included as part of the statement of cost of goods sold. Either way, it summarizes the flow of costs through the work-in-process inventory account for the accounting period. Figure 8.5 contains a cost-of-goods-sold statement for Marko Plastics Company for January 19X2. The cost of goods manufactured is integrated into this statement.

JOB-ORDER VERSUS PROCESS COST SYSTEMS

Job-order and process cost are two types of accounting systems that have been developed to account for two different types of production processes. Job-order costing is used for manufacturing processes that produce products in batches. One or more units of one product are produced in a batch. When that batch is completed, another product is produced in a different batch and the process moves from batch to batch, each batch being a different product.

A **job-order cost system** is commonly used by companies with products that are unique and divisible. Examples of businesses that use job-order costing include construction, furniture manufacturing, printing, repair shops, and service organizations. An automobile repair shop is a good example of a job-order cost system. When you take your car into the garage to be repaired or tuned up, it becomes a batch or a job. Costs associated with the mechanic's time, parts, and overhead are accumulated for your job and are used as a basis for developing the fee for the services rendered. The following are other examples of projects or processes that are applicable to job-order cost systems:

Organization	*Type of Batch*
Construction	Each house is a separate batch because each house has different characteristics.
Furniture manufacturing	Each style of furniture is one batch. For example, several units of one style of chair will be produced in one batch.
Printing	Each item to be printed, whether it is a class handout, book, or advertising flyer is a separate job.
Service organization	A CPA firm is an example of a service organization. Each client is a separate job and time and other resources used to satisfy the client's needs are accumulated as the cost of the job.

Process cost systems are used for manufacturing processes that produce a single product continuously for an extended period of time. Changes in the product are not made or are made only infrequently. Products that lend themselves to a process cost accounting system include cement, petroleum products, flour, beer, glass, steel, textiles, and food processing.

The objective of the job-order and process cost systems is the same—to determine the manufacturing cost per unit of the finished product. This is used to value ending inventory, value cost of goods sold, control costs, develop pricing strategies, and make similar management decisions. The process by which this objective is accomplished, however, is quite different. A job or a batch is the center of a job-order cost system, but the department or cost center is the center of the process cost system. The differences between the two systems is shown in figure 8.6.

The decision to use a job-order cost or a process cost system is determined by the type of product and the production process. Job-order costing is mandatory for most service companies, heavy manufacturing, and construction. Process costing is a must for most homogeneous products. Light manufacturing occasionally provides an option by which either method could be used. It should not be assumed that one company would use only one system throughout the entire organization. For example, a process cost system may be used on the main product and a job-cost system on occasional products or "one-shot" efforts such as a major repair or a capital improvement.

This chapter focuses on the procedures used in a job-order cost system. Chapters 9 and 10 will cover the process cost system.

Figure 8.6   Comparison of job and process cost systems

	Job Cost	Process Cost
Type of product	Diversified product line where products are produced in batches with each batch as a unique product	Homogeneous product produced continuously
Cost accumulation	By job for a specified number of units	By department or cost center for a specified period of time
Cost per unit	Costs accumulated by job divided by units in job; computed when job is complete	Costs accumulated by cost center divided by equivalent unit of production during a period of time
Reporting	By job	By cost center or department

JOB-ORDER COST SYSTEM

A job-order cost system is used to determine the costs associated with a project or a group of units in a production process that is done in separate and distinct batches of product. Other names for a job-order cost system are *specific order cost system,* or simply *job cost system.*

Job-Order Cost Sheet

A critical part of the job-order cost system is the job-order cost sheet. The job-order cost sheet *accumulates* the *manufacturing costs* associated with a particular job or batch of units in a job-order cost system. In a manual accounting system there is a separate sheet of paper for each job. The amount of materials, labor, and overhead required to complete the process are manually posted to the job-order cost sheet. Figure 8.7 shows an example of a job-order cost sheet. The concepts are exactly the same for computerized systems except the job-order cost sheet is a separate file in the computer system and the computer does the posting. Either way, each job is assigned a number and manufacturing costs associated with the job are accumulated on the job-order cost summary.

Flow of Costs in a Job-Order Cost System

Manufacturing costs in a job-order cost system flow through the manufacturing accounts as usual. A separate inventory is maintained for raw materials. Direct materials and direct labor used in producing the finished product are accumulated in the work-in-process account. Overhead costs are accumulated in an overhead account and are allocated to work in process using a predetermined overhead rate. Finished goods are transferred to finished-goods inventory and held there until they are sold. At that time their cost is assigned to the cost-of-goods-sold account.

The unique feature of a job-order cost system is the assignment of a production cost to individual jobs. Each time direct material, direct labor, or factory overhead are assigned to the work-in-process inventory, the costs must also be assigned to a particular job. The job-order cost sheet accumulates the costs associated with that particular job. The job-order cost sheets act as a subsidiary ledger for the work-in-process inventory account. Also, when units are completed and the costs are transferred to the finished-

Figure 8.7   Typical job-order cost sheet

Reynolds Manufacturing
Job-Order Cost Sheet

Customer _____   Job Order # _____
Product _____   Date Started _____
Quantity _____   Date Completed _____

Direct Materials			Direct Labor			Factory Overhead	
Date	Type	Amount	Date	Hours	Amount	Date	Amount

Cost Summary:	Amount	Actual Unit Cost	Budgeted Unit Cost	Variance
Direct material	$	$	$	$
Direct labor				
Factory overhead				
Total job	$	$	$	$
Explanation of variance:				

goods inventory account, the job-order cost sheet for the completed job must be removed from the subsidiary ledger. Therefore, the total of the costs on the job-order cost sheets in the subsidiary ledger of work in process should equal the balance in the work-in-process inventory account.

These accounting procedures will be illustrated using the Marko Plastics Company data summarized earlier for January 19X2. Marko Plastics Company would be classified as a light manufacturing company. They produce a variety of plastic containers and use a job-order cost system. The work-in-process inventory on January 1, 19X2 consisted of one job, number 244, to produce 10,000 five-gallon plastic containers. The job-order cost sheet for Job #244 on January 1, 19X2 is shown in figure 8.8. Three more jobs, numbered 245, 246, and 247, were begun in January and two jobs were completed.

Figure 8.8

Marko Plastics Company
Job-Order Cost Sheet

Customer	Inventory	Job Order #	244
Product	5 gallon containers	Date Started	12/5/X1
Quantity	10,000	Date Completed	

Direct Materials		Direct Labor		Factory Overhead	
Date	Amount	Date	Amount	Date	Amount
12/5/X1	$14,200	12/31/X1	$11,000	12/31/X1	$8,800

Total cost to date $34,000

The journal entries illustrated earlier do not change when the job-order cost system is in use. We merely add the job-order cost sheets as a subsidiary ledger of work in process. Each time there is an entry to work-in-process inventory we update the subsidiary ledger. This is illustrated by reanalyzing the four entries to the work-in-process inventory and by providing additional information on the allocation of costs to each job.

Transferring Raw Materials to Work in Process   Raw materials are transferred from the raw materials inventory into the work-in-process inventory by a materials requisition form that is prepared by a manufacturing supervisor. The raw materials requisition form serves as the source document for entries in the accounting system. Materials that are to be used for a specific job are classified as direct materials and the job-order number is shown on the requisition form. This is used as a basis for posting to the job-order cost sheets. Raw materials that are not used on any one job are classified as indirect materials and transferred to factory overhead.

A total of $63,000 of raw materials were transferred into work in process during January—$7,500 was indirect material and $55,500 was direct material. An analysis of the requisition forms showed the following distribution:

Job Number	Amount
244	$ 2,000
245	15,500
246	18,200
247	19,800

The general journal entry is the same.

Work-in-process inventory	55,500	
Factory overhead	7,500	
Raw materials inventory		63,000
Record the use of raw materials.		

In addition, the debit to the work-in-process inventory is posted to the job-order cost sheets in the subsidiary ledger as illustrated in figure 8.9.

Figure 8.9

Job # 244	Units 10,000				
Direct Materials		Direct Labor		Factory Overhead	
Date	Amount	Date	Amount	Date	Amount
12/5/X1	$14,200	12/31/X1	$11,000	12/31/X1	$8,800
1/31/X2	2,000	1/31/X2	10,000	1/31/X2	8,000
Total	$16,200		$21,000		$16,800

Total cost $54,000
Cost per unit $5.40
($54,000 ÷ 10,000 units)

Job # 245	Units 15,000				
Direct Materials		Direct Labor		Factory Overhead	
Date	Amount	Date	Amount	Date	Amount
1/31/X2	$15,500	1/31/X2	$32,000	1/31/X2	$25,600

Total cost to date $73,100

Job # 246	Units 20,000				
Direct Materials		Direct Labor		Factory Overhead	
Date	Amount	Date	Amount	Date	Amount
1/31/X2	$18,200	1/31/X2	$41,000	1/31/X2	$32,800

Total cost $92,000
Cost per unit $4.60
($92,000 ÷ 20,000 units)

Job # 247	Units 5,000				
Direct Materials		Direct Labor		Factory Overhead	
Date	Amount	Date	Amount	Date	Amount
1/31/X2	$19,800	1/31/X2	$7,000	1/31/X2	$5,600

Total cost to date $32,400

Recording Labor to Work in Process   Individual workers and their supervisors have the responsibility to identify their time as either direct labor or indirect labor. This is accomplished by the use of time cards and a time clock. The employees' time tickets serve as the source documents for entries made in the accounting records, including postings to the job-order cost sheets. Each time workers move from one task to another, they punch their time card into the time clock, which records the time on the card. The employee writes the type of task to which they are going by the side of the time. If they are going to work on a particular job, they would write the job-order number by the time. If the task is part of general factory labor not associated with any particular job, they would write overhead.

The accounting department is responsible for periodically accumulating the labor hours, pricing them, and allocating them to factory overhead and to individual jobs in work in process. This type of analysis for Marko Plastics Company for January 19X2 showed the following results:

Activity/Job	Amount
Overhead	$ 25,000
Work in process:	
244	10,000
245	32,000
246	41,000
247	7,000
Total	$115,000

Once again the general journal entry does not change but the debit to the work-in-process inventory is posted to the job-order cost sheets as shown in figure 8.9. The general journal entry is:

Work-in-process inventory	90,000	
Factory overhead	25,000	
Wages payable		115,000
Record factory payroll.		

Allocating Factory Overhead to Work in Process   The predetermined factory overhead rate is used to allocate overhead to individual jobs in work in process. The basis used to allocate overhead to work in process must be known for each job. For example, if machine hours are used to allocate overhead to work in process then our accounting system must accumulate machine hours by job. When overhead is allocated on the basis of units, direct-labor hours, or direct-labor dollars, the amount for each job is known or developed as a by-product of other computations.

Marko Plastics Company allocates overhead to work in process using an overhead rate of 80% of direct-labor cost. The amount of overhead assigned to each job is 80% of the direct-labor cost identified above. This is computed as follows:

Job	Direct Labor	×	Overhead Rate	=	Overhead Allocation
244	$10,000		80%		$ 8,000
245	32,000		80%		25,600
246	41,000		80%		32,800
247	7,000		80%		5,600
Total					$72,000

The general journal entry is:

Work-in-process inventory	72,000	
Factory overhead		72,000
Allocate factory overhead to work in process.		

The $72,000 debit to the work-in-process inventory recorded in the general journal is posted to the job-order cost sheets in the subsidiary ledger shown in figure 8.9.

Balance Between Subsidiary Ledger and General Ledger   The balance in work in process is $251,500 after the transfer of materials, labor, and overhead.

Beginning balance	$ 34,000
Direct material	55,500
Direct labor	90,000
Factory overhead	72,000
Total	$251,500

A schedule of the subsidiary ledger of work in process is also $251,500 (see fig. 8.10). If we have performed our accounting properly, this balance should always be maintained.

Figure 8.10

Marko Plastics Company
Schedule of Subsidiary Ledger of Work in Process
January 19X2

Job Number	Total Costs to Date
244	$ 54,000
245	73,100
246	92,000
247	32,400
Total	$251,500

Transferring Finished Goods from Work in Process   At the completion of a job, the costs of materials, labor, and overhead are totaled and combined for a total job cost. The cost per unit is computed by dividing the units produced into the total job cost. Actual costs are compared to budgeted costs and the variances are computed. Significant variances should be investigated immediately, and an explanation should be included on the job-order cost sheet. This is very useful in evaluating performance and for future reference when budgeting, bidding for work, and making pricing decisions.

The costs accumulated on the job-order cost sheets for completed jobs are transferred into finished-goods inventory. The unit cost is used to value the units while in inventory and to value cost of goods sold as they are sold. During January 19X2, Marko Plastics Company completed Jobs #244 and #246. The general journal entry debits the finished-goods inventory and credits the work-in-process inventory for $146,000. The job-order cost sheets are removed from the subsidiary ledger at this time.

Jobs #245 and #247 continue in process at the end of January 19X2. Notice that the combined total of these jobs ($73,100 + $32,400 = $105,500) is equal to the balance in the work-in-process inventory account at the end of the month.

COMPLICATIONS TO THE MANUFACTURING ACCOUNTING SYSTEM

There are many items that can complicate the accounting procedures described in this chapter for a manufacturing organization. A split-ledger system, reporting on partially completed jobs, and revenue recognition using percentage completion are three of the more common problems. Each of these will be discussed briefly.

Split-Ledger System

Split ledger describes an accounting system in which the administrative office maintains the general ledger and the factory maintains a factory ledger. Such a system might be required when the administrative offices are physically separated from the factory or when there are several factories and it is not possible for the administrative offices to do all the accounting on one general ledger. When the factory is responsible for business transactions of its own it is often more convenient and information is more timely when it maintains its own limited set of financial records.

The amount of record keeping that is performed at the factory depends upon their autonomy and the type of business transactions over which they have control. Several examples illustrate the relationship between the accounting records and the areas of control.

Factory Responsible For	*Accounts Included in the Factory Ledger*
Sales, billing, and collection of accounts receivable	Sales, accounts receivable, and cash
Sale and billing only	Sales account
Purchase and payment of raw materials	Raw material inventory, accounts payable, and cash
Purchase of raw materials only	Raw materials inventory
Purchase and use of buildings, machinery, and equipment used for manufacturing	Property, plant, and equipment account
Accrual and payment of payroll but not payroll taxes	Payroll account and payroll checking account

The responsibilities of the factory and the administrative office must be specified in advance and the appropriate accounts established. The accounting performed on each set of books must be coordinated for transactions that affect both ledgers. This is accomplished through a factory ledger account on the general ledger of the administrative offices and a general ledger account on the ledger maintained by the factory. Each time the factory enters into a transaction that requires some action by the administrative office, they will debit or credit the general ledger account and send an interoffice memo to the administrative office describing the action to be taken. Likewise, any time the administrative office enters into a transaction that affects the ledger maintained by the factory, it will debit or credit the factory ledger account.

Example: Suppose the factory is responsible for sales but the administrative office is responsible for collections of accounts receivable. When the factory makes a sale they would record:

General ledger	$22,000	
Sales		$22,000

The administrative office will record:

Accounts receivable	$22,000	
Factory ledger		$22,000

The balance in the general ledger account should always equal the balance in the factory ledger account. The general ledger account on the factory ledger is like an owner's equity; it represents the equity of the administrative office in the net assets of the factory. The factory ledger account is like an investment account on the administrative office books; it represents their investment in the factory.

Several transactions for Floss Manufacturing Company will illustrate the split-ledger system. Their administrative offices are some distance from the factory so it was decided to give the factory the responsibility for maintaining the inventory of raw materials, work in process, and finished goods. Furthermore, they are also responsible for all purchases of materials, labor, and overhead and for sales, but all cash receipts and payments are to be made by the administrative office. Figure 8.11 lists the journal entries for both home office and factory for a variety of transactions.

Notice in figure 8.11 that each time the factory ledger account is debited on the general ledger, the general ledger account is credited on the factory ledger, and vice versa. This maintains the equality of the accounts.

Figure 8.11

Floss Manufacturing Company
Split Ledger System

	General Ledger		Factory Ledger	
a.	Purchase of raw materials by factory.			
	Factory ledger	$15,000	Raw materials	$15,000
	Accounts payable	15,000	General ledger	15,000
b.	Transfer raw materials into work in process.			
			Work in process	12,000
	No entry		Factory overhead	2,000
			Raw materials	14,000
c.	Calculate and record payroll by the factory. The factory uses a "payroll" clearing account.			
	Factory ledger	20,000	Payroll	20,000
	Payroll payable	20,000	General ledger	20,000
d.	Allocate payroll to jobs and to factory overhead.			
			Work in process	14,000
	No entry		Factory overhead	6,000
			Payroll	20,000
e.	Employer payroll taxes are computed by the home office, the amount is communicated to the factory, and it is considered as part of factory overhead.			
	Factory ledger	3,000	Factory overhead	3,000
	Payroll taxes payable	3,000	General ledger	3,000
f.	Allocate overhead to individual jobs in work in process.			
			Work in process	13,500
	No entry		Factory overhead	13,500
g.	Transfer jobs that are complete to finished-goods inventory.			
			Finished-goods inventory	40,000
	No entry		Work in process	40,000
h.	Sold $35,000 of finished-goods inventory for $60,000.			
	Accounts receivable	60,000	General ledger	60,000
	Factory lodger	60,000	Cost of goods sold	35,000
			Sales	60,000
			Finished-goods inventory	35,000
i.	Collection of cash by the general office.			
	Cash	60,000		
	Accounts receivable	60,000	No entry	

Reporting for Partially Completed Jobs

Projects accounted for by the job-order cost system frequently extend over several months and even over several years. Management needs periodic reports throughout the project to monitor progress and to take corrective action where necessary. Figure 8.12 illustrates the type of report format that is frequently used to provide progress reports on partially completed jobs.

Cost classifications are listed on the report in meaningful categories. At lower levels of management the cost categories are small and very specific. As summary reports are prepared for middle and upper levels of management, the cost categories are combined in order to keep the length of the report manageable.

The cost categories listed across the report show budgeted data, actual data, and a variance. The budget is broken down into an original or base estimate and a revised estimate. The revised estimate is the original estimate plus or minus change orders from the customer or a redistribution of cost estimates due to a change in the processing method.

Figure 8.12   Report format for partially completed jobs

Cost Classification		Base Estimate	Revised Estimate	Cost This Period	Cumulative Costs To Date	Estimated Costs To Complete	Forecasted Total	Variance
Code	Description							
.10	Direct labor (type)	$500,000	$550,000	$100,000	$300,000	$275,000	$575,000	($25,000)
.50	Direct materials (type)	750,000	750,000	50,000	450,000	290,000	740,000	10,000

Actual costs are broken down by (a) costs incurred this period, (b) cumulative costs to date, and (c) estimated costs to complete this project. The forecasted total cost is the combined total of cumulative costs to date and the estimated costs to complete the project.

The total forecasted costs are compared with the revised estimate to compute a variance. The variance is a key number in identifying to management the areas of the project that are going well and those that are not going so well.

Revenue Recognition for Partially Completed Jobs

Long-term construction contracts, such as buildings, ships, and defense contracts, are generally accounted for by a job-order cost system. There are two generally accepted methods to account for revenues on long-term construction contracts—the completed contract method and the percentage of completion method.

Under the completed contract method of revenue recognition, no income is recognized until the contract is completed. At that time all the costs of the project are known and the income can be computed as the difference between total revenues and total costs. A problem with this method is that it does not recognize income as it is earned. For example, if a project extends over a two-year period, no income would be recognized in the first year because the project is not completed. The entire income would be recognized in the second year. Thus, profits flow to the income statement in an erratic pattern and frequently with substantial fluctuations.

The percentage of completion method recognizes revenue as the contract progresses toward completion. A frequently used method to measure progress toward completion compares the costs incurred to date relative to the total costs required to complete the project. This measure of percentage of completion is used to compute the amount of profits to be recognized.

Example: Magleby Incorporated is a contractor with a contract that will extend over two years. The price of the contract is fixed at $500,000. During the first year, $168,000 of the total estimated cost of $420,000 was incurred. Management feels that the $420,000 original estimate continues to be an accurate estimate of total costs to complete the project. Therefore, the project is 40% complete ($168,000 ÷ $420,000) and Magleby Incorporated should recognize $32,000 (40% × ($500,000 − $420,000)) of profit.

The criteria to be satisfied in order to use the percentage of completion method and the journal entries involved in its application are financial accounting issues covered in most intermediate accounting textbooks. Cost accounting issues include accurate cost estimation and accurate cost accumulation. The budgeting procedures outlined in chapters 5 and 6 and the job-order cost system discussed in this chapter are critical in developing accurate cost data for the percentage of completion method.

Summary

This is the first of several chapters dealing with the cost-finding aspects of cost accounting. The primary objectives of cost finding are to account for manufacturing costs and to determine the cost per unit of a finished product. This information is an integral part of both internal and external reports.

The manufacturing process combines materials, labor, and overhead into a finished product. The journal entries used to acquire these components and transfer them through the accounts as the products move through the production process were explained and illustrated in this chapter.

The job-order and process cost accounting systems have been developed to account for two different types of production processes. A job-order cost system is used in manufacturing processes that produce a variety of products, one product at a time, in batches. The batch is the focus of the accounting system. Both cost accumulation and reporting are batch oriented. A process cost accounting system is used when only one product is produced for an extended period of time. The department or cost center is the focus of a process cost system. Costs are accumulated and reports are prepared for individual departments.

A job-order cost sheet is used in a job-order cost system to accumulate the direct materials, direct labor, and factory overhead used on a job. The job-order cost sheets for jobs in process serve as a subsidiary ledger for the work-in-process inventory account. The jobs in the subsidiary ledger must be updated for each journal entry that has a debit or credit to the work-in-process inventory.

A split-ledger accounting system is frequently used when the general office is physically separated from the factory or when there are several factories. The general ledger is maintained at the administrative offices. A factory ledger is maintained at the factory to account for selected business transactions over which they have primary control. The factory ledger account on the general ledger is a reciprocal account to the general ledger account on the factory ledger. These accounts are used each time there is a transaction on one ledger that needs to be picked up and recorded on the other ledger.

Self-Study Problem

Job-O Company uses job-order costing. Factory overhead is applied to production at a predetermined rate of 200% of the direct-labor cost. Any over- or underapplied overhead is left in the factory overhead account until the end of the year. Additional information follows:

1. Job #100 was the only job in process on February 1, 19X2, with accumulated costs of:

Direct material	$5,000
Direct labor	1,000
Factory overhead	2,000
Total	$8,000

2. Job #101 and #102 were started during February.
3. Material requisitions for February totaled $33,000 ($5,000 for #100, $10,000 for #101, $15,000 for #102, and $3,000 for general factory use.)

4. Labor costs of $25,000 were incurred in February ($4,000 for #100, $7,000 for #101, $9,000 for #102, and $5,000 for general factory work.)
5. Other actual factory overhead costs for February totaled $30,000.
6. The only job still in process on February 28, 19X2, was #102.

Required:

1. Prepare a job-order cost sheet for Job #102.
2. Prepare a statement of cost of goods manufactured for February.
3. Prepare general journal entries for:
   a. Raw materials requisitioned.
   b. Allocation of overhead to work in process.
   c. Transfer of finished goods into the finished-goods inventory.
4. What is the over- or underabsorbed overhead for February?

Solution to the Self-Study Problem

Requirement 1

Job-O Company
Job-Order Cost Sheet   Job #102

Direct Materials	Direct Labor	Factory Overhead
$15,000	$9,000	$18,000

Total cost $42,000

Requirement 2

Job-O Company
Statement of Cost of Goods Manufactured
February, 19X2

Direct materials	$30,000	
Direct labor	20,000	
Factory overhead ($20,000 × 200%)	40,000	$90,000
Plus: Beginning work in process		8,000
Total work in process		$98,000
Less: Ending work in process		42,000
Cost of goods manufactured		$56,000

Requirement 3

a. Raw materials requisitioned:

Work-in-process inventory	30,000	
Factory overhead	3,000	
Raw materials inventory		33,000

b. Allocation of overhead to work in process:

Work-in-process inventory	40,000	
Factory overhead		40,000

c. Transfer of finished goods into the finished-goods inventory:

Finished-goods inventory	56,000	
Work-in-process inventory		56,000

Requirement 4

Actual overhead costs incurred:	
Indirect materials	$ 3,000
Indirect labor	5,000
Other factory overhead	30,000
Total	$38,000
Allocated to work in process	40,000
Overapplied overhead	$ 2,000

Suggested Readings

Clough, Richard H. *Construction Project Management*. New York: John Wiley & Sons, 1972.

Dellinger, Roy E. "Job Cost Reporting for Construction Companies." *Cost and Management* (July–August 1974): 24.

Goodman, Sam R., and Reece, James S. *Controller's Handbook*. Homewood, Ill.: Dow-Jones Irwin, 1978.

Niles, Timothy J., and Dowis, Robert H. "Accounting for New Plant Construction." *Management Accounting* (July 1974): 35.

Wood, T. D., and Sweet, F. H. "Using Job Order Cost in a Small Manufacturing Plant." *Modern Accounting Principles and Practices*. Englewood Cliffs, N.J.: 1978.

Discussion Questions

1. Identify the accounts used to account for the flow of costs associated with the manufacturing process and describe the flow of costs through those accounts.
2. What is a job-order cost sheet and why is it used?
3. Describe the relationship of the job-order cost sheet to the flow of costs through the manufacturing accounts.
4. What is job-order costing and for what types of manufacturing processes is it applicable?
5. What is process costing and for what types of manufacturing processes is it applicable?
6. Under a job-order cost system, are reports prepared by job or by department? Explain.
7. Under a job-order cost system, are costs accumulated by job or by department? Explain.
8. What is a chart of accounts? Which accounts are unique to a manufacturing organization?
9. Identify three accounts that are associated with the manufacturing process and are "control" accounts with a subsidiary ledger.
10. What is the difference between a control account and a clearing account?
11. Why is cost data so important when recognizing revenue on long-term construction contracts on a percentage completion basis?
12. Why does a company use a split-ledger accounting system?

13. Describe the relationship between the factory ledger account and the general ledger account under a split-ledger accounting system.
14. What source documents are used to post direct materials, direct labor, and factory overhead to the job-order cost sheets?
15. What types of errors will cause an inequality between the balance in the work-in-process inventory account and the total costs on the job-order cost sheets in the subsidiary ledger? How would you go about identifying the discrepancy?

Exercises

Exercise 8.1   Job-Order Cost Entries

Stewart Company uses a job-order cost system. Transactions completed during the first month of operations were as follows:

1. Purchased raw materials and supplies, $19,380.
2. Materials and supplies were used as follows:

Direct materials:		
Job 1	$3,200	
Job 2	4,600	
Job 3	800	8,600
Indirect materials		200

3. The factory payroll was as follows:

Direct labor:		
Job 1	$2,800	
Job 2	3,200	
Job 3	500	6,500
Indirect labor		2,500

4. Miscellaneous factory overhead costs totaled $2,800.
5. Factory overhead was applied on a direct-labor cost basis using a rate of 70%.
6. Job 1 (200 units) and Job 2 (300 units) were completed and transferred to finished goods.
7. Shipments to customers were as follows:
   100 units from Job 1
   200 units from Job 2

Required

Set up T accounts for the following accounts and record the transactions for the month in the T accounts.

Factory Ledger	Job Ledger
Materials and supplies	Job 1
Work in process	Job 2
Finished goods	Job 3
Cost of goods sold	
Factory overhead costs applied	
Factory overhead costs control	

Exercise 8.2 Job-Order Cycle Entries—Control and Subsidiary Accounts

Medford Incorporated provided the following data for January.

	Job 1	Job 2	Job 3	
Materials and supplies:				
Inventory, January 1				$10,000
Purchases on account				30,000
Labor:				
Accrued, January 1				$ 3,000
Paid during January (ignore payroll taxes)				25,000
Factory overhead costs:				
Supplies (issued from materials)				$ 1,500
Indirect labor				3,500
Depreciation				1,000
Other factory overhead costs				14,200[a]
Work in process:	*Job 1*	*Job 2*	*Job 3*	*Total*
Work in process, Jan. 1	$1,000	—	—	$ 1,000
Job costs during Jan:				
Direct materials	4,000	$6,000	$5,000	15,000
Direct labor	5,000	8,000	7,000	20,000
Applied factory overhead	5,000	8,000	7,000	20,000

Job 1 started in December, finished during January. Sold to a customer for $21,000 cash in January.
Job 2 started in January, not yet finished.
Job 3 started in January, finished during January, and now in the finished-goods warehouse awaiting sale.
Finished-goods inventory, January 1   —0—

[a]Includes items like utility bills, which are set up for payment.

Required

Record the journal entries, with detail for the respective job orders and factory overhead subsidiary records, for all January events indicated above.

Exercise 8.3 Job-Order Costing—Basic Procedures

Tillman Corporation uses a job-order cost system and has two production departments, M and A. Budgeted manufacturing costs for 19X0 are as follows:

	Department M	Department A
Direct materials	$700,000	$100,000
Direct labor	200,000	800,000
Manufacturing overhead	600,000	400,000

The actual material and labor costs charged to job no. 432 during 19X0 were as follows:

Direct material		$25,000
Direct labor:		
Department M	$ 8,000	
Department A	12,000	20,000

Tillman applies manufacturing overhead to production orders on the basis of direct-labor cost using departmental rates predetermined at the beginning of the year based on the annual budget.

Required

Determine the total manufacturing cost associated with Job no. 432 for 19X0.

Exercise 8.4   Job-Order Costing—Cost Statement

The Rebecca Corporation manufactures special machines made to customer specifications. All production costs are accumulated by means of a job-order costing system. The following information is available at the beginning of the month of October 19X0.

Direct-materials inventory, October 1	$16,200
Work-in-process, October 1	3,600

A review of the job-order cost sheets revealed the composition of the work-in-process inventory on October 1, as follows:

Direct materials	$1,320
Direct labor (300 hours)	1,500
Factory overhead applied	780
	$3,600

Activity during the month of October was as follows:

Direct materials costing $20,000 were purchased.
Direct labor for job orders totaled 3,300 hours at $5 per hour.
Factory overhead was applied to production at the rate of $2.60 per direct-labor hour.

On October 31, inventories consisted of the following components:

Direct-materials inventory	$17,000
Work-in-process inventory:	
Direct materials	$4,320
Direct labor (500 hours)	2,500
Factory overhead applied	1,300
	$8,120

Required

Prepare in good form a detailed statement of the cost of goods manufactured for the month of October.

Exercise 8.5   Journal Entries, Ending Inventory—Job-Order Cost System

The Wonder Manufacturing Corporation uses the job-order cost system. On April 1 the following jobs were in process.

	Job X-61	Job X-62
Materials	$1,200	$ 900
Labor	1,800	3,100
Overhead	1,200	1,600
	$4,200	$5,600

Overhead is applied into process at the rate of 40% of prime costs. During April the following materials requisitions were filled:

Job X-62	$ 600
Job X-63	800
Job X-64	1,400
	$2,800

Also, during the month, job labor tickets were summarized as follows:

Job X-61	$ 500
Job X-62	1,000
Job X-63	600
Job X-64	2,400
	$4,500

Only Jobs X-63 and X-64 are in work in process at the month's end.

Required

1. Prepare summary journal entries for the month's transactions.
2. Determine the April 30 balances for work in process and finished goods. (Assume there is no finished-goods inventory on April 1.)

Exercise 8.6   Journal Entries—Job-Order Cost System with Two Ledgers

The Binderman Manufacturing Company uses a factory ledger and a general ledger to record cost data. Applied factory overhead rates are in use.

The following transactions were recorded for August 19X2.

1. Materials purchased—$35,000 for the factory and $8,000 for the office.
2. Freight incurred and paid on materials received at the factory—$385.
3. Materials put into process—direct, $22,000; factory supplies, $3,000.
4. Purchased factory equipment

List price	$10,000
Trade discount	20%
Cash discount	5%
Transportation costs	$100

5. Payroll for period:

Direct labor (gross pay)	60,000
Indirect labor (gross pay)	15,000
Office payroll (gross pay)	25,000
FICA tax (withholding)	7,000
Federal withholding tax	18,000

6. Employers portion-payroll taxes

FICA tax	7,000
Federal unemployment	4,000

7. Depreciation

Office equipment	7,500
Factory equipment	14,000

8. Overhead applied

50% direct-labor cost

9. Goods finished during period $80,000

10.
Sales	90,000
Cost of goods sold	80,000

Required

Prepare journal entries for the above transactions. Assume the inventories for direct materials, direct labor and the factory overhead accounts are at the factory.

Exercise 8.7   Journal Entries—Job-Order Costing with Two Ledgers

The Carson Company completed the following transactions during the month of October 19X7:

Oct 3:   Materials requisitioned—direct, $2,000; indirect, $1,000.
   4:   Raw materials purchased—$10,000. Terms 2/10, N/30.
   7:   Weekly factory payroll of $1,000 was allocated as follows—direct labor, $940; maintenance, $60. Income taxes were $90; FICA taxes were $45.
   10:   Completed factory job with the following costs—direct labor, $480; materials, $225; factory overhead, 75% of direct labor.
   12:   Shipped completed job to customer per instructions of home office. Billing—$1,150.
   13:   Home office vouchered and paid miscellaneous factory overhead, $400.

Required

Prepare journal entries on the general and factory journals for the above transactions. Assume the inventory and factory overhead accounts are kept at the factory.

Exercise 8.8   Journal Entries—Job-Order Cost System

Sloane Manufacturing Company uses a job-order cost system and compiled the following data for 19X1. (They also use a perpetual inventory system.)

Materials and supplies purchased	$242,000
Direct-material used	190,000
Supplies used	20,000
Direct labor	150,000
Other labor	35,000
Utility costs for the year	65,000
Miscellaneous overhead	40,000
Depreciation, equipment	22,000
Depreciation, buildings	8,000
Applied factory overhead (20% of direct labor)	?
Cost of goods completed	326,000
Material ($170,000)	
Labor ($130,000)	
Sales	500,000
Cost of goods sold	326,000
Selling and administrative expenses	110,000

Required

Prepare the appropriate journal entries covering the above data.

Exercise 8.9   Job Costing, Ledger Summary

Refer to the data in exercise 8.8.

Assume that two jobs were in process during the period, Jobs 208 and 209, one of which was completed (Job 208) and the other (Job 209) is still in process at year end.

Required

1. Set up T accounts covering all transactions indicated and post your journal entries to the T accounts. Include work in process and factory overhead control and subsidiary accounts.
2. Determine end of period balances in the accounts as appropriate.

Exercise 8.10   Job Costing, Statement of Cost of Goods Manufactured and Income Statement

Refer to the data in exercises 8.8 and 8.9.

Required

1. Prepare a statement of cost of goods manufactured in as much detail as the data permits.
2. Prepare an income statement for the year.

Problems

Problem 8.1   Job-Order Costing Entries—Work-in-Process Inventories

The Joy Manufacturing Corporation uses the job-order cost system. The following three jobs were in process on August 1, 19X7.

	75-A	65-B	68-C
Materials	$12,500	$ 7,800	$10,700
Labor	2,800	1,200	5,400
Overhead	4,200	1,800	8,100
	$19,500	$10,800	$24,200

The following costs were incurred during August.

Job	Materials	Labor
75-A		$ 3,200
65-B	$ 3,100	1,800
68-C		1,000
69-B	$ 7,500	6,000
72-A	5,500	1.200
74-C	2,300	200
	$18,400	$13,400

Jobs 72-A and 74-C are still in process on August 31. Overhead is applied at the rate of 150% of direct-labor costs. Actual factory overhead was equal to applied factory overhead.

Required

1. Prepare summary journal entries for the month of August.
2. Prepare a work-in-process subsidiary ledger for each job in process during August.
3. Determine the August 1st and August 31st balances in work in process.
4. Prepare a cost-of-goods-manufactured statement.

Problem 8.2   Job-Order Costing—Work-in-Process Inventory

Brahms Manufacturing Company uses a job-order cost system. Overhead is applied at the rate of 150% of direct-labor costs. Work in process at July 1, 19X0 was:

	C-21	F-15	N-75
Direct materials	$1,200	$1,800	$ 750
Direct labor	1,100	800	600
Applied overhead	1,650	1,200	900
Total	$3,950	$3,800	$2,250

Total work in process: $10,000.

The following materials and labor costs were incurred during July:

Job	Materials	Labor
D-53	$1,500	$ 700
C-21	200	300
F-69	1,000	1,800
F-15		200
Z-83	1,500	500
N-75	500	300
R-48	1,000	400
	$5,700	$4,200

Actual factory overhead costs were $6,300. Jobs Z-83 and R-48 were incomplete at the end of the month.

Required

1. Compute the work in process inventory at July 31, 19X0.
2. Prepare a cost-of-goods-manufactured statement.

Problem 8.3   Job-Order Costing—Complete and Incomplete Job Costs

Jolley Printing Company uses a job-order cost system. The following jobs were in process at the beginning of 19X7:

	65-A	75-B
Material	$ 6,500	$ 7,500
Labor	9,400	8,000
Overhead	4,700	4,000
Total	$20,600	$19,500

Total work in process: $40,100.

The following costs were incurred during 19X7:

	Materials	Labor
65-A	—	$ 2,200
75-B	2,000	1,400
85-C	7,500	8,400
95-D	5,500	6,800
05-E	2,500	3,000
	$17,500	$21,800

Overhead is applied at the rate of 50% of direct-labor cost. Jobs 65-A, 75-B, 85-C, and 95-D were completed and sold. There is no beginning or ending finished-goods inventory. Selling and administrative expenses were $18,500. The jobs were sold for:

65-A	$ 26,000
75-B	31,000
85-C	28,000
95-D	35,000
	$120,000

Required

1. Compute the cost of completed jobs.
2. Compute the ending work in process.
3. Compute the net income for the year.

Problem 8.4   Job-Order Costing—Journal Entries

Lind Manufacturing Company uses a perpetual inventory system and a job-order cost system. The following data was compiled for 19X5 (the current costs of production apply 70% to job 307 and 30% to job 308):

Payroll costs	$150,000
($125,000—direct labor, ignore	
payroll taxes)	
Direct materials purchased	116,000
Direct materials used	85,000
Factory rent	3,000/month
Depreciation, factory building	10,000
Indirect supplies used	15,000
Miscellaneous factory overhead	18,000
Sales	350,000

Factory overhead is applied at the rate of 80% of direct-labor costs. There is no beginning or ending work-in-process inventory. The over- or underapplied factory overhead is not considered material and is charged directly to cost of goods sold at year end. Job 307 was completed and sent to the finished-goods warehouse. On job 307 shipments were made to customers for 95% of the units produced.

Required

Prepare summary journal entries for the above information.

Problem 8.5   Journal Entries of a Split Ledger

Tinker Manufacturing Company records transactions on a general journal and factory journal. Tinker uses a perpetual inventory system. The following transactions occurred during April 19X0:

April payroll data (all unpaid at end of April)	$12,100
FICA taxes (employee)	900
Federal withholding taxes	2,000
FUTA taxes	100
SUTA taxes	500
Direct labor	10,000
Indirect labor	2,000
Office salaries	3,000
Materials purchased	25,000
Freight-in on materials purchased	500
Materials used	21,000
Depreciation	
Office equipment	5,000
Factory equipment	4,000
Rent	
Factory	3,000
Office	5,000
Miscellaneous factory expenses	2,000
(Factory overhead is applied at 60% of direct-labor costs)	
Cost of completed goods	50,000
Cost of goods sold	45,000
Sales	75,000

Required

Prepare summary journal entries for the above transactions on both the factory and general journal. Assume all accounts are maintained in the general ledger except the inventories and the factory overhead account.

Problem 8.6   Job-Order Costing—Split Ledger

The Dearden Manufacturing Company incurred the following costs during July 19X8. The company uses a split ledger with the materials, work-in-process, and finished-goods inventories at the factory. The factory has a factory overhead control and factory payroll account.

Payroll:	
Direct labor	$30,000
Indirect labor	4,000
FICA taxes	600
Federal withholding taxes	2,400
(ignore the employer's share of taxes)	
Materials:	
Purchased	$25,000
Used (5% indirect)	28,000
Factory overhead:	
Factory rent	8,000
Depreciation	4,000
Miscellaneous	2,000
Cost of completed jobs	45,000
Cost of goods sold	55,000
Sales	82,000
Applied factory overhead	50% of direct-labor cost

Required

Prepare summary journal entries for the above transactions on the general journal and the factory journal.

Problem 8.7   Job-Order Cost System—Cost Schedules

Scanlon Printing Company uses a periodic inventory system to account for its printing operations. Since jobs are produced under contract specifications, the cost of completed jobs is immediately included in cost of goods sold. Overhead is applied to each job at a rate of 200% of direct-labor charges. Work in process on November 1, 19X3, consisted of the following job analysis:

Job	Materials	Direct Labor	Overhead Applied	Total Work In Process
B-743	$ 430	$207	$ 414	$1,051
P-418	125	150	300	575
D-017	350	250	500	1,100
A-411	240	175	350	765
	$1,145	$782	$1,564	$3,491

During November, a tabulation of materials requisition forms and labor time tickets showed costs for individual jobs as follows:

Requisition	Job	Material Cost	Time Ticket	Job	Labor Cost
1101	B-743	$ 120	2001	D-017	$ 190
1102	D-017	150	2002	A-411	270
1103	A-411	260	2003	D-017	100
1104	R-218	318	2004	B-743	348
1105	C-100	474	2005	P-418	200
1106	F-041	230	2006	C-100	350
1107	A-415	319	2007	R-218	420
1108	G-200	450	2008	F-041	230
1109	P-504	618	2009	P-504	429
1110	X-219	144	2010	X 219	237
1111	Z-001	275	2011	F-400	820
1112	F-400	760	2012	A-415	910
		$4,118	2013	G-200	560
					$5,064

On November 30, jobs Z-001, A-415, and X-219 were incomplete. All remaining jobs were delivered to customers at cash prices equal to 150% of assigned costs. Actual overhead costs for the month were $11,500.

Required

1. Prepare a schedule to compute the work-in-process inventory balance at November 30.
2. Prepare a schedule to compute cost of goods sold for November, including any amounts of underapplied or overapplied overhead.

Problem 8.8   Job-Order Cost System—Cost Determination

Power Manufacturing Corporation uses a job-order cost system to trace the cost of production. During 19X1, the indicated costs were incurred on the following jobs:

Work in Process Beginning

Job #	Materials	Labor	Factory O/H	Total
L1670	$1,500	$6,000	$8,000	$15,500
J1901	5,000	8,000	4,000	17,000

Direct Materials

Job #	Cost
H702	$16,872
G901	10,980
B168	5,670

Direct Labor

Job #	Hours	Cost
L1670	200	$ 800
J1901	3,000	9,600
. H702	500	1,575
G901	600	1,200
B168	90	180

Factory Overhead

Applied at $2.00
Per direct-labor hour

Jobs completed during the year

#L1670, #J1901, #H702, #G901
Selling and administrative expenses: $25,510

Sales

Job #	Selling Price
L1670	$ 18,000
J1901	45,000
H702	28,000
G901	25,000
	$116,000

Required

1. Compute the ending work in process.
2. Compute the cost of completed jobs.
3. Compute the net operating income for the year.

Problem 8.9   Job-Order Cost Cycle

Refer to the data in problem 8.8.

Required

1. Journalize the cost transactions that occurred in the Power Manufacturing Company during 19X1.
2. Set up the ledger accounts in T account form that are needed to reflect all the cost transactions that occurred. Include accounts for the job subsidiary. Post the transactions to both control and subsidiary accounts.

Problem 8.10 Comprehensive Job-Order Cost Problem (CPA)

The Custer Manufacturing Corporation, which uses a job-order cost system, produces various plastic parts for the aircraft industry. On October 9, 19X2, production was started on job #487 for a hundred front bubbles (windshields) for commercial helicopters.

Production of the bubbles begins in the Fabricating Department in which sheets of plastic (purchased as raw material) are melted down and poured into molds. The molds are then placed in a special temperature and humidity room to harden the plastic. The hardened plastic bubbles are then removed from the molds and hand-worked to remove imperfections.

After fabrication the bubbles are transferred to the Testing Department in which each bubble must meet rigid specifications. Bubbles that fail the tests are scrapped and there is no salvage value.

Bubbles passing the tests are transferred to the Assembly Department in which they are inserted into metal frames. The frames, purchased from vendors, require no work prior to installing the bubbles.

The assembled unit is then transferred to the Shipping Department for crating and shipment. Crating material is relatively expensive and most of the work is done by hand.

The following information concerning job #487 is available as of December 31, 19X2 (the information is correct as stated):

1. Direct materials charged to the job:
   a. The Fabricating Department was charged for 1,000 sq. ft. of plastic at $12.75 per sq. ft. This amount was to meet all plastic material requirements of the job assuming no spoilage.
   b. The Assembly Department was charged for 74 metal frames at $408.52 each.
   c. Packing material for 40 units at $75 per unit was charged to the Shipping Department.

2. Direct-labor charges through December 31, 19X2, were as follows:

	Total	Per Unit
Fabricating Department	$1,424	$16
Testing Department	444	6
Assembly Department	612	12
Shipping Department	256	8
	$2,736	

3. Differences between actual and applied manufacturing overhead for the year ending December 31, 19X2, were immaterial. Manufacturing overhead is charged to the four production departments by various allocation methods, all of which you approve. Manufacturing overhead charged to the Fabricating Department is allocated to jobs based on heat-room hours; the other production departments allocate manufacturing overhead to jobs on the basis of direct-labor dollars charged to each job within the department. The following reflects the manufacturing overhead rates for the year ending December 31, 19X2:

	Rate Per Unit
Fabricating Department	$.45 per hour
Testing Department	.68 per direct-labor dollar
Assembly Department	.38 per direct-labor dollar
Shipping Department	.25 per direct-labor dollar

4. Job #487 used 855 heat-room hours during the year ending December 31, 19X2.

5. Following is the physical inventory for job #487 as of December 31, 19X2:
Fabricating Department:
a. 50 sq. ft. of plastic sheet.
b. 8 hardened bubbles, 1/4 complete as to direct labor.
c. 4 complete bubbles.

Testing Department:
a. 15 bubbles that failed testing when 2/5 of testing was complete. No others failed.
b. 7 bubbles complete as to testing.

Assembly Department:
a. 13 frames with no direct labor.
b. 15 bubbles and frames, 1/3 complete as to direct labor.
c. 3 complete bubbles and frames.

Shipping Department:
a. 9 complete units, 2/3 complete as to packing material, 1/3 complete as to direct labor.
b. 10 complete units; 100% complete as to packing material; 50% complete as to direct labor.
c. 1 unit complete for shipping was dropped off the loading docks. There is no salvage.
d. 23 units have been shipped prior to December 31, 19X2.
e. There was no inventory of packing materials in the shipping department on December 31, 19X2.

6. Following is a schedule of equivalent units in production by department for job #487 as of December 31, 19X2:

Required

Prepare a schedule for job #487 of ending inventory costs for (*a*) raw materials by department, (*b*) work in process by department, and (*c*) cost of goods shipped. All spoilage costs are charged to cost of goods shipped.

Custer Manufacturing Corporation
Schedule of Equivalent Units in Production for Job Number 487
December 31, 19X2

	Plastic (sq. ft.)	*Fabricating Department*		
		Bubbles (units)		
		Materials	*Labor*	*Overhead*
Transferred in from raw materials	1,000			
Production to date	(950)	95	89	95
Transferred out to other departments		(83)	(83)	(83)
Spoilage				
Balance at December 31, 19X2	50	12	6	12

	Testing Department (units)		
	Bubbles		
	Transferred in	*Labor*	*Overhead*
Transferred in from other departments	83		
Production to date		74	74
Transferred out to other departments	(61)	(61)	(61)
Spoilage	(15)	(6)	(6)
Balance at December 31, 19X2	7	7	7

	Assembly Department (units)			
	Transferred in	*Frames*	*Labor*	*Overhead*
Transferred in from raw materials		74		
Transferred in from other departments	61			
Production to date			51	51
Transferred out to other departments	(43)	(43)	(43)	(43)
Balance at December 31, 19X2	18	31	8	8

	Shipping Department (units)			
	Transferred in	*Packing Material*	*Labor*	*Overhead*
Transferred in from raw materials		40		
Transferred in from other departments	43			
Production to date			32	32
Shipped	(23)	(23)	(23)	(23)
Spoilage	(1)	(1)	(1)	(1)
Balance at December 31, 19X2	19	16	8	8

PROCESS COSTING: BASIC PROCEDURES

9

OUTLINE

Process costing is a method used for costing inventories in industries characterized by the continuous mass production of similar finished units. For example, oil, canning, steel, rubber, chemical, textile, glass, cement, paint, mining, shoe, electronic, and food processing industries all use some form of process costing.

Each unit of output in process-costing environments receives essentially the same input of materials, labor, and overhead as any other unit. The large numbers of similar units in a continuous production process make it impractical, if not impossible, to maintain cost accounting records for *each unit* of production. This is unlike the production situation in which the relatively small numbers and dissimilar nature of outputs make it practical and useful to identify production by individual units or batches. For example, the heavy machinery or mobile home industries identify production by individual units.

In manufacturing environments in which each unit receives varying amounts of materials, labor, and overhead, job-order costing (as discussed in chap. 8) is the appropriate accounting procedure. However, in continuous or mass production industries process costing is the appropriate accounting procedure.

This chapter describes the basic process-costing procedures used in these industries. After completing this chapter you should be able to:

1. identify the characteristics of a manufacturing environment in which process costing is appropriate.
2. apply process costing techniques using:
   a. the weighted average method.
   b. the first-in, first-out method.
   c. other modified methods.

CHARACTERISTICS OF PROCESS COSTING

From an accounting viewpoint, one of the most important characteristics to understand about process costing is that it is simply a method for *averaging* costs over a number of homogeneous or similar units. When using job-order costing, manufacturing costs are identified with specific units of production. In a continuous or mass production environment this is not realistic because of the large numbers of units involved. Therefore, the multi-step method or procedure called process costing is used to identify costs with units of production.

In a continuous or mass production environment each product typically passes through a series of production steps called *processes* or *departments*. When using process costing, the first phase of accounting is to assign costs to these processes or departments. Next, the total cost assigned to each process or department is divided by a measure of the total productive effort expended in that process or department during the accounting period. This results in an average per-unit cost of production which is finally applied to inventory quantities to derive total inventory costs.

The major difference between job-order and process costing is that with job-order costing manufacturing costs are identified with one or a few units comprising a "job", but with process costing manufacturing costs are first identified with a process or department and then averaged over the total productive effort of that process or department. Using these averages, costs are then assigned to inventory.

The accounting focus of process costing is centered on departments or processes. Materials, labor, and overhead are accumulated and analyzed by department for product-costing purposes. For planning and control purposes the general cost accounting principles and procedures discussed in other chapters apply equally well to either job-order or process-costing situations.

Due to the departmentalization of costs and different cost flow patterns that are possible in continuous production environments, there are some unique characteristics of product flow and related cost accounting procedures that should be considered. First, a

Figure 9.1   Cost flow diagram

Raw Materials Inventory		Work-in-Process Assembly Department		Work-in-Process Testing Department	
(1)* 80,000	55,340 (2)	12,000	166,920 (5)	22,000	480,000 (6)
		(2) 55,340		(5) 166,920	
		(3) 86,220		(3) 236,400	
		(4) 28,740		(4) 78,800	
		15,380		24,120	

Accrued Payroll	
	322,620 (3)

Finished Goods	
(6) 480,000	450,000 (7)

Applied Factory Overhead	
	107,540 (4)

Cost Of Goods Sold	
(7) 450,000	

*Numbers in parentheses relate to journal entries illustrated in the text.

mass production situation is typically visualized as a **sequential flow** of products from one process or department to the next. For example, in the manufacture of Wedgewood, pieces typically proceed in sequence through mixing, molding, cleaning, glazing, and firing departments. However, there are other possible product flow patterns such as parallel flows and network flows.

Parallel flows relate to situations in which various parts are processed in different departments and then brought together in subsequent processing to form a finished good. For example, in the electronics industry several different circuit boards may be needed as components in one finished unit. These circuit boards may be manufactured simultaneously in different departments operating parallel to one another. Then these various circuit boards are brought together in an assembly department to form the finished product.

Another pattern is **network flows** in which products pass through various departments as needed. For example, in a packing house operation parts of the carcass may flow to different departments in different sequences depending on the desired output. Boxed steaks may flow directly from butchering to packing. However, smoked sausages may go through grinding, smoking, and then to packing. Any number of other combination of flows may exist for other products.

The essential principle is that all product flows must be identified because *inventory cost flows track the product flows*. Therefore, the product flows must be identified to insure proper cost accounting. Once the product flows are identified, the differences between accounting for a complex network flow and a simple sequential flow mainly relate to the amount of detail involved. The reassuring feature of process costing is that regardless of the complexity of the production situation, the basic process-costing principles remain the same.

The following sequence of journal entries illustrates the flow of costs from the acquisition of raw materials through the sale of finished goods in a situation in which products move sequentially through two departments, assembly and testing, to finished-goods inventory. Figure 9.1 diagrams the cost flows implicit in these journal entries.

Close attention should be given to these cost flows and to related journal entries since they portray a basic pattern that underlies even the most complex parallel or network flow. When accounting for complex flows more detail is involved, but the basic principles of process costing remain the same. Once again, cost accounting for planning and control purposes is the same whether using job-order costing or process costing; only the costing aspects are different. However, the departmentalization of costs in a process-costing system does add an additional dimension to the accounting system that aids in planning and control. These additional aspects of departmental accounting are discussed in other chapters.

The first four journal entries outline the cost accounting procedures for materials, labor, and factory overhead. The same accounts are used in process-costing systems as in any other system except for the added detail of using separate departmental accounts for work in process.

1. Purchase of materials:

Raw materials inventory	80,000	
Accounts payable		80,000

2. Issuance of materials:

Work in process—Assembly Department	55,340	
Raw materials inventory		55,340

3. Payroll costs:

Work in process—Assembly Department	86,220	
Work in process—Testing Department	236,400	
Accrued payroll		322,620

4. Overhead costs:

Work in process—Assembly Department	28,740	
Work in process—Testing Department	78,800	
Factory overhead—applied		107,540

Factory overhead is applied to departments on the basis of one-third of payroll costs. For example, the amount of overhead applied to the assembly department is $28,740, which is one-third of $86,220, the amount of payroll cost in the assembly department. Journal entries five and six are unique to departmentalization because they represent cost flows between production departments and between a production department and finished-goods inventory. These journal entries result from the physical transfer of goods. Assigned to these physical units are the material, labor, and overhead costs incurred to that point. The purpose of this chapter is to explain the basis for assigning these costs to physical units of production in a process-costing environment.

5. Transfer of goods—Assembly Department to Testing Department:

Work in process—Testing Department	166,920	
Work in process—Assembly Department		166,920

6. Transfer of goods—Testing Department to Finished Goods:

Finished-goods inventory	480,000	
Work in process—Testing Department		480,000

7. Sales:

Accounts receivable	560,000	
Sales		560,000
Cost of goods sold	450,000	
Finished-goods inventory		450,000

PROCEDURES FOR PROCESS COSTING

The application of process costing has a two-fold objective: (*a*) to value goods manufactured and transferred out either to the next department or to finished-goods inventory during an accounting period and (*b*) to value work-in-process inventory remaining in production at the end of an accounting period. To accomplish this, a five-step procedure is described and a cost of production worksheet and reporting format is illustrated. Remember that in practice these procedures are followed for each department each accounting period.

The five-step process-costing procedure is a logical progression that minimizes errors and provides a self-checking procedure. There are many opportunities for taking shortcuts and several of these will be illustrated. However, care should be taken to thoroughly understand each step before taking shortcuts. The five steps in process costing are:

1. Account for the physical flow of units processed during the period, and determine the percentage completion of work-in-process inventory at the end of the period.
2. Determine the total costs for which an accounting must be made.
3. Compute the work effort of the department for the period in terms of equivalent units of production.
4. Compute costs per equivalent unit of production.
5. Compute total costs for (*a*) work completed and transferred out of the department during the period and (*b*) work-in-process inventory at the end of the period.

The application of these steps is illustrated using the following company situation. An electronics company purchases component parts and assembles and tests them for subsequent resale and ultimate use in larger pieces of equipment. For accounting purposes, the company has two processes—assembly and testing. Raw material is put in process at the beginning of the assembly process with no material added during testing. Labor costs are uniformly utilized throughout both processes, and overhead costs are applied at the rate of one-third of labor costs. The manufacturing process is sequential; after assembly, all goods are transferred to the testing department and finally to finished-goods inventory. Data taken from production records of the assembly department for a typical month of operations is as follows:

Production Statistics—Assembly Department

	Units
Work in process, beginning inventory	6,000
(Materials 100% complete; labor and overhead 75% complete)	
Started in process	80,000
Completed and transferred out	78,000
Work-in-process ending inventory	8,000
(Materials 100% complete; labor and overhead 85% complete)	

Accounting data for both the assembly and testing departments is available in figure 9.1. Also, the journal entries on page 280 are part of this company's records. In actual practice, the only data available at this stage in the accounting process is that generated through journal entry 4; that is, raw materials would have been acquired and materials cost of $55,340 would have been placed in process in the assembly department. Payroll expenses would also have been incurred with $86,220 utilized in the assembly department. Manufacturing overhead would have been incurred with $28,740 being applied to the assembly department. These costs added to the $12,000 of costs previously assigned to work-in-process beginning inventory results in a present balance in the work-in-process account of $182,300.

The next phase in the accounting process is to determine how much of the total costs accumulated in the work-in-process account are associated with (*a*) goods transferred out of the assembly department to the testing department and (*b*) work-in-process inventory remaining in the assembly department. The five steps of process costing are used to make these determinations. There are two basic inventory methods for process costing—the weighted average method and the first-in, first-out method.

Weighted Average Method

The general procedure when using the **weighted average method** is to determine an average cost per unit from the cost of work-in-process beginning inventory plus the cost of current production. This average cost is then used to determine the total cost of work finished during the period and work still in process at the end of the period. The weighted average method is relatively easy to apply and is widely used in actual practice. The steps of process costing using the weighted average method are as follows:

Step 1: *Account for the physical flow of units processed during the period, and determine the percentage completion of work-in-process inventory at the end of the period.* Data concerning the physical flow of units is typically available in the production records of each department. The stage or percentage of completion of work-in-process inventory is usually estimated by engineering or production personnel. These estimates depend on the *proportion* of total effort that has already been applied to the units in process relative to the total effort required to bring these units to completion. Some processes have a relatively uniform flow and consistent content of materials, labor, and overhead in process at any particular time. Typical of this situation are flow industries such as oil refineries. In such instances, the same percentage of completion may be used each period with only periodic investigation to validate their reasonableness.

The practice of using a percentage of completion estimate from period to period is justified because the cost of investigation and estimation to obtain more accurate data each accounting period is usually greater than the benefits of having slightly more accurate percentages. On the other hand, the accuracy of these percentage estimates is a concern when work-in-process inventories fluctuate from period to period. For example, assembly operations may have widely fluctuating materials and labor content at any particular moment in time. Estimating the degree of materials completion is often easier than estimating labor and overhead completion. The physical and visual properties of materials are usually easier to measure than the labor component and certainly easier to measure than virtually invisible overhead.

Production data accounts for the unit flows in the Assembly Department and provides data concerning the degree of completion of work-in-process inventories as indicated below.

Accounting for Units

	Physical Units	Percentage Completion		
		Material	Labor	Overhead
Work in process, beginning	6,000	100%	75%	75%
Transferred in this period	80,000			
Total units to account for	86,000			
Completed and transferred out	78,000			
Work in process, ending	8,000	100%	85%	85%

There are 6,000 units in process at the beginning of the period plus 80,000 units started in process during the period giving a total of 86,000 units to account for. Since there are 8,000 units still in process at the end of the period, 78,000 units (86,000 − 8,000) must have been completed and transferred out of the department during the period. The number of units transferred out is derived in this illustration. In practice, however, units transferred out are physically counted. This could result in a situation in which a number derived as above may be different from a physical count. Reasons for such discrepancies and accounting for lost or spoiled units are covered in subsequent chapters.

Step 2: *Determine the total costs for which an accounting must be made.* This step is accomplished by extracting and summarizing information from departmental work-in-process accounts. At this point in the accounting cycle materials, labor, and overhead costs have been applied to work in process. Data extracted from figure 9.1 and associated journal entries relating to the assembly department indicates that the current balance in the work-in-process account is $182,300 ($12,000 + $55,340 + $86,220 + $28,740). This data is presented as follows:

Total Costs to Account For

	Total	Material	Labor	Overhead
Work in process, beginning	$ 12,000	$ 4,000	$ 6,000	$ 2,000
Costs of the current period	170,300	55,340	86,220	28,740
Total costs to account for	$182,300	$59,340	$92,220	$30,740

The task at hand is to determine how much of the total cost ($182,300) that has been accumulated in the assembly department should be assigned to goods transferred to the testing department and how much should be assigned to the work-in-process ending inventory remaining in the assembly department. This is an averaging procedure implemented through the use of equivalent units of production explained and used in the next process-costing steps.

Step 3: *Compute the work effort of the department for the period in terms of equivalent units of production.* **Equivalent units,** as used in process costing, are a measure of the work effort of a department or a process that expresses partially completed units in terms of whole units. For example, if 5,000 physical units are 60% complete, then 3,000 (.60 × 5,000) equivalent units of production have been expended to bring them to their current state. On the other hand, 40% (100% − 60%) of the total work effort is yet to be expended to actually complete work on these units. Therefore, 2,000 (.40 × 5,000) equivalent units of production will be expended to finish these physical units.

The determination and use of equivalent units of production is probably the most important aspect of process costing because equivalent units are the basis for assigning costs to completed units and to work-in-process ending inventory. For proper calculation of equivalent units, remember that at the end of each accounting period there are probably materials, labor, and overhead costs applied throughout the production process to partially completed units. For appropriate costing of inventories there must be an accurate and efficient accounting of resources currently applied to partially completed goods as well as to work fully completed and transferred out during the period.

The use of equivalent units accomplishes this without the necessity of compiling voluminous statistics dealing with partially completed units in all their stages of production. Instead, equivalent units are based on the percentages generated in step 1, which are applied to the total physical units in process. When using the weighted average method, equivalent units are calculated (*a*) for units that are started and completed during the period and (*b*) for units that are started but not completed at the end of the period. Also, equivalent units of production are typically calculated for each cost category—materials, labor, and overhead—as illustrated for the assembly department in the following schedule.

Equivalent Units of Production

	Physical Units	Equivalent Units					
		Material		Labor		Overhead	
Completed and transferred out	78,000	78,000	(100%)	78,000	(100%)	78,000	(100%)
Work in process, ending	8,000	8,000	(100%)	6,800	(85%)	6,800	(85%)
Total	86,000	86,000		84,800		84,800	

The units that were completed and transferred from the assembly department to the testing department during the period, which included the work-in-process beginning inventory, were 100% complete as to work units expended in all cost categories. Therefore, 78,000 (1.00 × 78,000) equivalent units were generated.

Equivalent units of work-in-process ending inventory is a measure of the number of physical units that could have been brought to completion *if* all attention and effort had been expended to finish as many units as possible. The work-in-process ending inventory of the assembly department consists of 8,000 physical units. They are 100% complete in terms of materials. Therefore, there have been 8,000 (1.00 × 8,000) equivalent units of production in the materials category. However, these same physical units are only 85% complete with regard to labor and overhead. This means that if all labor and overhead *had been* expended to bring as many units as possible to completion, 6,800 (.85 × 8,000) equivalent units would have been produced. This gives a total work effort for the department of 86,000 equivalent units (78,000 + 8,000) for materials and 84,800 equivalent units (78,000 + 6,800) for labor and overhead.

Equivalent units are calculated to provide a rational basis for the assignment of costs to physical units of production. The vehicle used to assign costs is developed in the next step, which relates costs and equivalent units to obtain costs per equivalent unit of production.

Step 4: *Compute costs per equivalent unit of production.* A cost per equivalent unit of production is computed for each cost category by dividing the total costs to account for by the total equivalent units of production as follows:

Cost per Equivalent Unit of Production

	Total	Material	Conversion Costs	
			Labor	Overhead
(1) Total costs to account for		$59,340	$92,220	$30,740
(2) Total equivalent units		86,000	84,800	84,800
Cost per equivalent unit (1) ÷ (2)	$2.140	$ .690	$ 1.088	$ .362

Total conversion costs per unit ($1.088 + $.362) = $1.450

It should be noted that the total cost per equivalent unit of $2.140 is found by adding $.690, $1.088, and $.362 costs per equivalent unit and *not* by dividing the total cost to account for by some total number of equivalent units.

The importance of costs per equivalent unit of production is that they provide a way to assign costs to units completed as well as to work in process on the basis of work effort actually received. Since *totals* are used in the calculation of costs per equivalent unit, this is essentially an averaging process as opposed to specific identification, which is the procedure used in job-costing. The characteristics of a process-costing environment make this the most acceptable method.

Step 5: *Compute total costs for (a) work completed and transferred out of the department during the period and (b) work-in-process inventory at the end of the period.* The actual assignment of costs is accomplished by multiplying equivalent units of production found in step 3 by costs per equivalent unit found in step 4. The following illustration shows these calculations. Costs are first assigned to units completed and transferred out of the department during the period and then to partially completed work remaining in the department at the end of the period. These computations are usually made by cost category as follows.

Accounting for Costs

	Total	Material	Labor	Overhead
Costs transferred out:				
Equivalent units of production		78,000	78,000	78,000
Cost per equivalent unit		× $.690	× $1.088	× $.362
Total	$166,920	$53,820	$84,864	$28,236
Work in process, ending:				
Equivalent units		8,000	6,800	6,800
Cost per equivalent unit		× $.690	× $1.088	× $.362
Total	15,380	$ 5,520	$ 7,398	$ 2,462
Total costs accounted for	$182,300	$59,340	$92,262	$30,698

Several items of interest relate to these calculations. First, process costing is a self-checking procedure as can be seen by comparing the total costs accounted for of $182,300 with the total costs to account for in the prior illustration to verify that they are equal. Another observation is that a shortcut in computing the total cost of goods transferred out is to multiply the equivalent units of goods transferred out by the *total* cost per equivalent unit rather than by the cost per equivalent unit for each cost category. This is a valid shortcut for costing work in process at the end of the period only when equivalent units are identical for each cost category. The self-checking feature and short-cut, when appropriate, are used in all other illustrations of process costing in this chapter.

Now that cost assignments have been made in the final step of process costing, information is available to make the journal entry to transfer costs to the next department in the process. Journal entry number 5 on page 280 accomplishes the task. The debit of $166,920 to "work in process—testing department" transfers the costs associated with the movement of physical units to the testing department. The credit to "work in process—assembly department" results in an ending balance of $15,380 in the account. This amount represents the costs associated with the physical units still in process in the assembly department at the end of the accounting period.

To facilitate learning, the five steps of process costing were presented separately. However, in practice the results of process costing are brought together in departmental cost of production reports as shown in figure 9.2. The cost of production report summarizes the process costs to be accounted for during the period, the units completed and transferred out, the computation of per-unit costs, the costs assigned to work in process at the end of the period, and the costs assigned to units completed and transferred out during the period.

All columns on a typical cost of production report, other than the total column, are necessary to make the computations. However, only a total column is presented on the final report to management.

Now that the accounting and reporting work is complete for the assembly department, attention is shifted to the next department in the production process—the testing department. Production records of the testing department for the current period provide the following data:

Figure 9.2

Assembly Department
Cost of Production Report
(Weighted Average Method)

	Physical Units	Percentage Completion		
		Material	Labor	Overhead
Units accounted for as follows:				
Work in process, beginning	6,000	100%	75%	75%
Transferred in this period	80,000			
Total units to account for	86,000			
Completed and transferred out	78,000			
Work in process, ending	8,000	100%	85%	85%

	Total	Material	Labor	Overhead
Costs to account for:				
Work in process, beginning	$ 12,000	$ 4,000	$ 6,000	$ 2,000
Costs of the current period	170,300	55,340	86,220	28,740
(1) Total costs to account for	$182,300	$ 59,340	$ 92,220	$ 30,740
Equivalent units of production:				
Completed and transferred out		78,000	78,000	78,000
Work in process, ending		8,000	6,800	6,800
(2) Total equivalent units		86,000	84,800	84,800
Cost per equivalent unit (1)÷(2)	$ 2.140	$ .690	$ 1.088	$ .362
Costs accounted for as follows:				
Costs transferred out:				
Equivalent units of production		78,000	78,000	78,000
Cost per equivalent unit		× $ .690	× $1.088	× $.362
Total	$166,920	$ 53,820	$ 84,864	$ 28,236
Work in process, ending:				
Equivalent units		8,000	6,800	6,800
Cost per equivalent unit		× $ .690	× $1.088	× $.362
Total	15,380	$ 5,520	$ 7,398	$ 2,462
Total costs accounted for:	$182,300	$ 59,340	$ 92,262	$ 30,698

Production Statistics—Testing Department

	Units
Work-in-process beginning inventory	7,000
(Materials 100% complete; labor and overhead 60% complete)	
Transferred in from the Assembly Department	78,000
Completed and transferred to finished goods	80,000
Work-in-process ending inventory	5,000
(Materials 100% complete; labor and overhead 70% complete)	

Apart from the quantities involved, the production statistics for the testing department are different from the assembly department in two ways. First, goods are transferred to finished-goods inventory from the testing department rather than to another department for additional processing. This means that the cost at which units are transferred out of the testing department is the cost at which the units are carried in finished-goods inventory.

Figure 9.3

Testing Department
Cost of Production Report
(Weighted Average Method)

	Physical Units	Percentage Completion		
		Transferred In	Material	Labor and Overhead
Units accounted for as follows:				
Work in process, beginning	7,000	100%		60%
Transferred in this period	78,000			
Total units to account for	85,000			
Completed and transferred out	80,000			
Work in process, ending	5,000	100%		70%

	Total	Transferred In	Material	Labor and Overhead
Costs to account for:				
Work in process, beginning	$ 22,000	$ 9,880		$ 12,120
Costs of the current period	482,120	166,920		315,200
(1) Total costs to account for	$504,120	$176,800		$327,320
Equivalent units of production:				
Completed and transferred out		80,000		80,000
Work in process, ending		5,000		3,500
(2) Total equivalent units		85,000		83,500
Cost per equivalent unit (1)÷(2)	$ 6.000	$ 2.080		$ 3.920
Costs accounted for as follows:				
Costs transferred out	$480,000	(80,000 × $6.000)		
Work in process, ending:				
Transferred-in costs	$ 10,400	(5,000 × $2.080)		
Labor and overhead	13,720	(3,500 × $3.920)		
Total	$ 24,120			
Total costs accounted for	$504,120			

Another more significant difference between the departments is that units are started and costs accumulated from a zero basis in the assembly department, but work coming into the testing department already has effort applied and a cost assigned for all of the work previously performed in the assembly department. These costs are called *transferred-in costs* and represent the accumulated cost of materials, labor, and overhead applied in all prior departments. For example, the transferred-in costs for goods received by the testing department during the current period are $166,920; the total amount transferred out to the assembly department as shown in figure 9.2. The important thing about transferred-in costs is that they are handled in the process-costing steps and in the cost of production report *as though they are another cost category like materials, labor, or overhead.* A separate column is added to the cost of production report to handle transferred-in costs.

Rather than discuss each step of process costing for the testing department, the cost of production report for the department is presented in its entirety in figure 9.3. The unique features of process cost accounting for subsequent departments as illustrated by the testing department are then discussed.

Note that figure 9.3 has a separate column to account for transferred-in costs. The amount of $166,920 transferred out of the assembly department as shown in figure 9.2 appears as a transferred-in cost of the testing department in figure 9.3. Notice also that the work-in-process beginning inventory of the testing department contains $9,880 of transferred-in costs. This represents all of the materials, labor, and overhead costs incurred from work performed on these units before they were transferred into this department. Continuing the inspection of the transferred-in column, equivalent units and cost per equivalent unit are computed for transferred-in costs just as for other cost categories.

It should be noted that the cost per equivalent unit of $2.080 for transferred-in costs in the testing department is not the same as the total cost per equivalent unit of $2.140 in the assembly department. Even though it seems like they should be equal, they differ because of the difference in per-unit cost of work-in-process beginning inventory and the per-unit cost of goods transferred in this period. If the cost of production in a prior department remains the same through successive accounting periods then these costs per equivalent unit will be equal.

Finally, examine the assignment of costs to units transferred to finished goods and to work-in-process ending inventory to see that transferred-in costs are also assigned to inventories as though they represented another cost category.

Another important difference between the cost of production reports of the assembly and testing departments is that the materials column is vacant in the report of the testing department. This is because no materials are added in the testing department. All prior materials costs are carried as part of the transferred-in costs accounted for in the testing department. However, materials can be added in processes subsequent to the first process as discussed in chapter 10.

Finally, labor and overhead costs are combined into one column on the cost of production report of the testing department. When overhead is applied as a function of labor, as in this example, it is common practice to combine labor and overhead into a single "conversion cost" category in one column of the report.

Once again, the purpose of the cost of production report is to provide information for costing inventories and transferring costs. Journal entry 6 on page 280 transfers the $480,000 assigned to goods completed and placed in finished-goods inventory. The cost flows shown in figure 9.1 also illustrate how the information generated in the cost of production report of the testing department is utilized in the accounting cycle.

Before proceeding to the next section review the steps of process costing for both the originating and subsequent departments. A clear understanding is important at this point because the remainder of this chapter and chapter 10 will expand on the basics of process costing presented here.

First-in, First-out Method

The **first-in, first-out (FIFO) method** is simply another way of calculating product costs in a continuous or mass production environment. As in the weighted average method, the five process-costing steps apply and the basic format of the cost of production report is the same. The major differences between the two methods are in calculating equivalent units of production, determining costs per equivalent unit, and applying costs per equivalent unit to inventories. To illustrate these differences, the information for the assembly department used to illustrate the weighted average method is recast in figure 9.4 using the FIFO method. All production and cost statistics are the same, only the process-costing method is different.

The calculation of equivalent units using the FIFO method separates the costs associated with work-in-process beginning inventory and costs related to work done in the

Figure 9.4

**Assembly Department
Cost of Production Report
(First-in, First-out Method)**

		Percentage Completion		
	Physical Units	Material	Labor	Overhead
Units accounted for as follows:				
Work in process, beginning	6,000	100%	75%	75%
Transferred in this period	80,000			
Total units to account for	86,000			
Completed and transferred out	78,000			
Work in process, ending	8,000	100%	85%	85%

	Total	Material	Labor	Overhead
Costs to account for:				
Work in process, beginning	$ 12,000	$ 4,000	$ 6,000	$ 2,000
(1) Costs of the current period	170,300	55,340	86,220	28,740
Total costs to account for	$182,300*			
Equivalent units of production:				
Complete work in process, beginning			1,500	1,500
Started and completed		72,000	72,000	72,000
Work in process, ending		8,000	6,800	6,800
(2) Total equivalent units		80,000	80,300	80,300
Cost per equivalent unit (1)÷(2)	$ 2.124	$ .692	$ 1.074	$ .358

Costs accounted for as follows:			
Costs transferred out:			
Work in process, beginning	$ 12,000		
Work completed on work in process, beginning:			
Labor	1,611	(1,500 × $1.074)	
Overhead	537	(1,500 × $ .358)	
Work started and completed	152,928	(72,000 × $2.124)	
Total	$167,076		
Work in process, ending:			
Materials	$ 5,536	(8,000 × $ .692)	
Labor	7,303	(6,800 × $1.074)	
Overhead	2,434	(6,800 × $ .358)	
Total	$ 15,273		
Total costs accounted for	$182,300	(Rounded from $182,349)	

*Totals for material, labor, and overhead are omitted to emphasize the FIFO method.

current period. In contrast, the weighted average method is based on averaging the work done to date, as contained in work-in-process beginning inventory, with work done in the current period. Since the FIFO method distinguishes between work done in the current period and work done in prior periods, it is necessary to calculate equivalent units of production for work effort expended on (*a*) completing work-in-process beginning inventory; (*b*) starting, completing, and transferring out work during the period; and (*c*) bringing work-in-process ending inventory to its current level of completion. For example, the equivalent units of production section of figure 9.4 contains 1,500 equivalent units necessary to complete work-in-process inventory. This number is found by determining that if work-in-process inventory is 75% complete at the beginning of the period then there is 25% of the total effort yet required to complete the units in the current period. Multiplying 6,000 physical units by 25% of the effort required to complete them yields 1,500 equivalent units of production expended during the period on work-in-process beginning inventory.

There were 72,000 (1.00 × 72,000) equivalent units *started,* completed, and transferred out of the department during the current period. The total number of units actually transferred out was 78,000. However, 6,000 of these units were already in process at the beginning of the period and receive a separate accounting. Therefore, only 72,000 units (78,000 − 6,000) were *started* and completed during the period.

The calculation of equivalent units for work-in-process ending inventory is the same for weighted average and FIFO methods.

The calculation of cost per equivalent unit of production also follows the FIFO assumption that costs associated with work-in-process beginning inventory are not mingled with the cost of work done in the current period; that is, to derive costs per equivalent unit of production using the FIFO method, "costs of the *current* period" rather than the "*total* costs to account for" are divided by total equivalent units of production. In this way costs incurred in prior periods are segregated from costs incurred in the current period as assumed by the FIFO method.

The final differences between weighted average and FIFO methods concern the assignment of costs to inventories. First, the prior period costs associated with work-in-process beginning inventory are carried as though they are a "batch" of costs associated with beginning inventory. For example, the $12,000 total cost of work-in-process beginning inventory is a separate cost item in the determination of total costs to transfer out to finished goods. Added to the cost of work-in-process beginning inventory are the current costs necessary to complete these units. For example, 1,500 equivalent units of labor and overhead were required to complete the beginning inventory. Multiplying 1,500 equivalent units by the cost per equivalent unit for labor and overhead, $1.074 and $.358 respectively, gives the productive effort expended this period to complete beginning work in process. Remember that the work-in-process beginning inventory is already complete as to materials. The cost of materials is contained in the $12,000 cost of beginning work in process.

The last portion of the total cost transferred out consists of current costs for materials, labor, and overhead assigned to units started and completed during the current period. This amount is simply computed using the equivalent units for work started and completed this period of 72,000 multiplied by the total costs per equivalent unit of $2.124 as shown in figure 9.4.

The cost of work-in-process ending inventory is also found by multiplying equivalent units of production for materials, labor, and overhead by their respective costs per equivalent unit as shown in figure 9.4. This completes the process-costing procedure for the assembly department using the FIFO method, and the information necessary for recording the transfer of costs to the testing department is now available. The transfer of costs is accomplished with the following journal entry:

Work in process—Testing Department	167,076	
Work in process—Assembly Department		167,076

Tracing costs to the next department, the amount of $167,076 transferred out of the assembly department to the testing department is shown as a "costs of the current period" on the cost of production report of the testing department as shown in figure 9.5.

Figure 9.5

Testing Department
Cost of Production Report
(First-in, First-out Method)

| | | | Percentage Completion | |
	Physical Units	Transferred In	Material	Labor and Overhead
Units accounted for as follows:				
Work in process, beginning	7,000	100%		60%
Transferred in this period	78,000			
Total units to account for	85,000			
Completed and transferred out	80,000			
Work in process, ending	5,000	100%		70%

	Total	Transferred In	Material	Labor and Overhead
Costs to account for:				
Work in process, beginning	$ 22,000	$ 9,880		$ 12,120
(1) Costs of the current period	482,276	167,076		315,200
Total costs to account for	$504,276*			
Equivalent units of production:				
Complete work in process, beginning				2,800
Started and completed		73,000		73,000
Work in process, ending		5,000		3,500
(2) Total equivalent units		78,000		79,300
Cost per equivalent unit (1)÷(2)	$ 6.117	$ 2.142		$ 3.975
Costs accounted for as follows:				
Costs transferred out:				
Work in process, beginning	$ 22,000			
Completed work in process	11,130	(2,800 × $3.975)		
Started and completed	446,541	(73,000 × $6.117)		
Total	$479,671			
Work in process, ending:				
Transferred-in costs	$ 10,710	(5,000 × $2.142)		
Labor and overhead	13,913	(3,500 × $3.975)		
Total	$ 24,623			
Total costs accounted for	$504,276	(Rounded from $504,294)		

*Totals for transferred-in, labor, and overhead costs omitted to emphasize the FIFO method.

Note that a separate column is used to account for transferred-in costs of subsequent departments when using the FIFO method just as when using the weighted average method (see fig. 9.3). Transferred-in costs are handled in the same way as described for the weighted average method. Equivalent units, cost per equivalent unit, and the assignment of costs all treat transferred-in costs as a separate cost category. The calculation of equivalent units for work-in-process beginning inventory and the assignment of costs to complete work-in-process beginning inventory are also similar to the procedures used with the FIFO method in the assembly department. Recording of the transfer of costs from the testing department to finished-goods inventory is as follows:

Finished-goods inventory	479,671	
Work in process—Testing Department		479,671

There is a theoretical question about whether or not the illustration of process costing using the FIFO method is strictly FIFO or a modified FIFO method. The question arises for two reasons. First, each department in a multi-process environment is treated as a separate entity and the FIFO method can be used in any department regardless of the method used in any other department. Variety in inventory costing assumptions among departments makes it doubtful if a strict FIFO costing procedure can be present under such circumstances, unless there is also very careful coordination among departments.

Second, all units transferred into a department during an accounting period are carried at the same unit cost even though there may be several "batches" involved. Thus, the units transferred to the next department carry a weighted average cost. For example, it might be argued that if a strict FIFO method is used the units in process at the beginning and all other "batches" started at various times during the same period should receive a separate accounting. However, such a strict adherence to the FIFO method would quickly become complicated and burdensome except in the very simplest production environment. Therefore, a *modified* or departmental FIFO method as illustrated in this chapter is typically used. Also, the situational factors involved in different production environments lead to other modifications of the basic process-costing system.

Modified Methods

The endless variety of types of industries, products, and processes presents a situation more complex than two inventory costing methods can satisfy. In reality, job-order costing and process costing provide general accounting methods that satisfy requirements at two ends of a continuum of manufacturing types. However, there are many ways to modify these basic methods to satisfy conditions in specific industries, companies, or processes. Two such modifications to process costing are discussed in this section.

The first example relates to the manufacture of products with common processing characteristics but different material requirements. For example, a producer of commemorative medallions uses the same cutting, stamping, finishing, and packaging operations for all products. However, some medallions are made of gold and others of silver. A great difference in material costs but identical processing has led this particular company to account for materials on a job-order basis and to account for labor and overhead on a process-costing basis. Each medallion is identified as a job, batch, or production run, and materials costs are assigned directly to that "job" or medallion. Labor and overhead costs are accounted for using the customary process-costing method with costs being assigned to the medallion "job" based on the costs transferred to finished-goods inventory from the packaging department. Each medallion "job" receives a portion of the total costs transferred to finished goods based on the relative number of medallions processed.

The second example of a modified process costing system is used in the manufacture of items that are essentially alike but have individual characteristics requiring different materials and different processing. For example, shoes are made in different sizes, with different materials, and in different styles. However, the processing operations are essentially the same, differing only in the amount of work effort applied. One particular shoe style may require a lot of decorative sewing but another style may require very little sewing.

In this type of manufacturing situation, products are individually identified by batch or production run when their requirements for materials and/or labor are different enough to warrant separate accounting. Different styles are typically grouped by production run. Even different sizes may justify separate accounting. After production runs are identified, they are accounted for using job-order costing methods and costs are assigned to production runs. However, process-costing methods are used for accounting within the various departments. This means that a cost of production report may be generated for each production run rather than for each accounting period. If this procedure is followed, end-of-the-period reports are a summarization of results from individual production runs.

Another reporting procedure places the results of each production run in a separate section of the cost of production report. Either way, the unique product features are accounted for as in a job-costing environment and the similar mass production features are accounted for as in a process-costing environment.

In each of these examples characteristics of both process costing and job-order costing are present in the manufacturing environment. Where modified methods are used products are typically not homogeneous, but neither are they completely heterogeneous. The variety and degree of differences usually dictate the extent to which the basic methods are modified. However, the fundamental planning and control objectives of cost accounting systems as well as product-costing objectives should always guide the development of modified systems.

Summary

Process costing is a method used to assign costs to inventory in manufacturing operations characterized by the continuous mass production of similar finished units. There are five basic steps in process costing:

1. Account for the physical flow of production and estimate the percentage completion of work-in-process ending inventory.
2. Determine the total costs for which an accounting must be made.
3. Compute equivalent units of production.
4. Determine costs per equivalent unit of production.
5. Assign costs to completed units and to work-in-process ending inventory.

The concept of equivalent units is the key to process costing. Equivalent units are a measure of the work effort expended in a department or process during an accounting period. Costs per equivalent unit are used to assign costs to finished work and work in process.

There are two general methods used to apply process costing—the weighted average method and the first-in, first-out (FIFO) method. The weighted average method is easiest to apply and most widely used. It differs from the FIFO method in that it averages costs of the prior period contained in the work-in-process beginning inventory with costs of the current period. The FIFO method does not mingle costs of the current period with costs incurred in prior periods.

Process-costing procedures are often modified to accommodate unique characteristics of different manufacturing environments. Basic process-costing procedures are used to account for the continuous mass production component of operations while elements of job-order costing are incorporated to account for the unique features in the processing environment.

Self-Study Problem

Wood Products Company uses a fabrication process in the initial construction of its cabinets for mantel clocks. The rough cabinet is then sent to the finishing department for the next phase of processing. Production and accounting statistics summarized from fabrication department records for the current period are as follows:

Production Statistics

	Units
Work-in-process beginning inventory	1,800
(Materials 100% complete; labor 50% complete; and overhead 60% complete)	
Units of wood placed in process	76,000
Work-in-process ending inventory	800
(Materials 100% complete; labor 40% complete; and overhead 50% complete)	

Accounting Statistics

Work-in-process beginning inventory:	
Materials	$ 47,000
Labor	3,600
Overhead	1,000
Total	$ 51,600
Costs of the current period:	
Materials	$1,976,000
Labor	315,200
Overhead	77,000
Total	$2,368,200
Total costs to account for	$2,419,800

Required

Using the first-in, first-out method calculate the following:

1. The cost of work transferred out of the fabrication department during the current period
2. The cost of work-in-process ending inventory

Present your results in the form of a cost of production report suitable for management use.

Solution to the Self-Study Problem

**Fabrication Department
Cost of Production Report
(First-in, First-out Method)**

		Percentage Completion		
	Physical Units	Material	Labor	Overhead
Units accounted for as follows:				
Work in process, beginning	1,800	100%	50%	60%
Transferred in this period	76,000			
Total units to account for	77,800			
Completed and transferred out	77,000			
Work in process, ending	800	100%	40%	50%

	Total	Material	Labor	Overhead
Costs to account for:				
Work in process, beginning	$ 51,600	$ 47,000	$ 3,600	$ 1,000
(1) Costs of the current period	2,368,200	1,976,000	315,200	77,000
Total costs to account for	$2,419,800	$2,023,000	$318,800	$ 78,000
Equivalent units of production:				
Complete work in process, beginning			900	720
Started and completed		75,200	75,200	75,200
Work in process, ending		800	320	400
(2) Total equivalent units		76,000	76,420	76,320
Cost per equivalent unit (1)÷(2)	$ 31.134	$ 26.000	$ 4.125	$ 1.009

Costs accounted for as follows:		
Costs transferred out:		
Work in process, beginning	$ 51,600	
Completed work in process:		
Labor	3,713	(900 × $ 4.125)
Overhead	727	(720 × $ 1.009)
Work started and completed	2,341,277	(75,200 × $31.134)
Total	$2,397,317	
Work in process, ending:		
Materials	$ 20,800	(800 × $26.000)
Labor	1,320	(320 × $ 4.125)
Overhead	404	(400 × $ 1.009)
Total	$ 22,524	
Total costs accounted for	$2,419,800	(Rounded from $2,419,841)

Suggested Readings

American Accounting Association. "Report of the AAA Committee on Cost Concepts and Standards." *Accounting Review* 27 (1952).

Dickey, Robert I., ed. *Accountant's Cost Handbook.* 2d ed. New York: Ronald Press, 1960.

Goodman, S., and Reece, J. *Controller's Handbook.* Homewood, Ill.: Dow-Jones-Irwin, 1978.

Seidler, Lee J., and Carmichael, D. R., eds. *Accountant's Handbook.* 6th ed. New York: Ronald Press, 1981.

Skinner, R. "Process Costing." *Abacus* (December 1978). See also articles of the same title in the June 1979 and June 1980 editions.

Discussion Questions

1. What is process costing and in what types of industries is it used?
2. Discuss characteristics of process costing that differentiate it from job-order processing.
3. Describe three different cost flow patterns that may occur among departments in a process-costing environment.
4. Describe the flow of costs from the acquisition of raw materials through the sale of products in a typical process-costing company. Also, give the typical journal entry(s) made at each phase in the cost flow cycle.
5. What is the two-fold objective of process costing?
6. Discuss the steps of process costing.
7. What is an equivalent unit of production?
8. How are costs assigned to completed work and work-in-process ending inventory using the weighted average method?
9. What are the differences between the weighted average method and the first-in, first-out method?
10. How are costs assigned to completed work and work-in-process ending inventory using the first-in, first-out method?
11. What is the purpose of the cost of production report? Discuss the purpose of each section.
12. What differences, if any, are there between process-costing procedures for initial departments in which products are started in process and accounting procedures for subsequent departments?
13. Why is it a bad idea to shortcut the assignment of costs to work-in-process ending inventory?
14. Describe two modified methods that might be used in a company that does not exactly match either a job-order or process-costing situation.

Exercise 9.1 Process-Costing and Job-Order Concepts (CPA)

1. Which of the following would not be used in job-order costing?
   a. Standards
   b. Averaging of direct-labor and material rates
   c. Direct costing
   d. Factory overhead allocation based on direct-labor hours applied to the job
2. When should process-costing techniques be used in assigning costs to products?
   a. If the product is manufactured on the basis of each order received
   b. When production is only partially completed during the accounting period
   c. If the product is composed of mass-produced homogeneous units
   d. In situations in which standard costing techniques should *not* be used
3. Which of the following production operations would be most likely to employ a job-order system of cost accounting?
   a. Toy manufacturing
   b. Shipbuilding
   c. Crude oil refining
   d. Candy manufacturing
4. A true process-costing system could use each of the following *except*
   a. standards.
   b. individual lots.
   c. variable costing.
   d. responsibility accounting.

Exercise 9.2 Process-Costing Concepts (CPA)

1. Which of the following characteristics applies to process costing but not to job-order costing?
   a. Identifiable batches of production
   b. Equivalent units of production
   c. Averaging process
   d. Use of standard costs
2. In job-order costing, the basic document to accumulate the cost of each order is the
   a. invoice.
   b. purchase order.
   c. requisition sheet.
   d. job cost sheet.
3. Which is the best cost accumulation procedure to use when there is a continuous mass production of like units?
   a. Actual
   b. Standard
   c. Job order
   d. Process

4. Which of the following is a characteristic of a process-costing system?
   a. The work-in-process inventory is restated in terms of completed units.
   b. Costs are accumulated by order.
   c. It is used by a company manufacturing custom machinery.
   d. Standard costs are *not* applicable.
5. An equivalent unit of material or conversion cost is equal to
   a. the amount of material or conversion cost necessary to complete one unit of production.
   b. a unit of work-in-process inventory.
   c. the amount of material or conversion cost necessary to start a unit of production into work in process.
   d. 50% of the material or conversion cost of a unit of finished-goods inventory (assuming a linear production pattern).

Exercise 9.3   Concepts of Cost of Production Reports

1. In a production cost report using process costing, transferred-in costs are similar to
   a. material added at the beginning of the process.
   b. conversion costs added during the process.
   c. costs transferred to the next process.
   d. costs included in beginning inventory.
2. When standard costs are used in a process-costing system, how, if at all, are equivalent units involved or used in the cost report at standard?
   a. Equivalent units are *not* used.
   b. Equivalent units are computed using a "special" approach.
   c. The actual equivalent units are multiplied by the standard cost per unit.
   d. The standard equivalent units are multiplied by the actual cost per unit.
3. An error was made in the computation of the percentage of completion in the current year's work-in-process ending inventory. The error resulted in assigning a *lower* percentage of completion to each component of the inventory than actually was the case. What is the resultant effect of this error upon:
   1. the computation of equivalent units in total?
   2. the computation of costs per equivalent unit?
   3. costs assigned to cost of goods completed for the period?

	1	2	3
a.	understate	overstate	overstate
b.	understate	understate	overstate
c.	overstate	understate	understate
d.	overstate	overstate	understate

4. What are transferred-in costs as used in a process-cost accounting system?
   a. Labor that is transferred from another department within the same plant instead of hiring temporary workers from the outside
   b. Cost of the production of a previous internal process that is subsequently used in a succeeding internal process
   c. Supervisory salaries that are transferred from an overhead cost center to a production cost center
   d. Work-in-process ending inventory of a previous process that will be used in a succeeding process

Exercise 9.4   Equivalent Units—FIFO versus Average Costing

Harrow Company uses a process-costing system. The following information is available for department *A:*

	Units
Work in process, July 1	25,000
Work in process, July 31	20,000
Units started in process	40,000
Units transferred to Department *B*	45,000

	Percentage of Completion	
	July 1	July 31
Materials	80%	70%
Labor	50%	40%
Overhead	30%	20%

Required

1. Determine the equivalent units of production using the weighted average cost method.
2. Determine the equivalent units of production using the FIFO cost method.

Exercise 9.5   Equivalent Units—FIFO versus Average Costing

The following data relate to the activities of the manufacturing department of Hanlock Company during September 19X5:

	Units
Work in process, September 1 (100% complete as to materials; 60% complete as to conversion costs)	25,000
Work in process, September 30 (100% complete as to materials; 40% complete as to conversion costs)	15,000
Units started in process	60,000
Units transferred to the Finishing Department	70,000

Required

1. Compute the equivalent units of production using the weighted average method.
2. Compute the equivalent units of production using the FIFO method.

Exercise 9.6   Average Method, Concepts and Procedures (CPA)

Information for the month of May concerning department *A*, the first stage of Wit Corporation's production cycle, is as follows:

	Materials	Conversion Costs
Work in process, beginning	$ 4,000	$ 3,000
Current costs	20,000	16,000
Total costs	$ 24,000	$19,000
Equivalent units (based on weighted average method)	100,000	95,000
Average unit costs	$ 0.24	$ 0.20
Goods completed		90,000 units
Work in process, ending		10,000 units

Material costs are added at the beginning of the process. The ending work in process is 50% complete as to conversion costs.

Required

Using the weighted average method, determine the cost of completed units and the cost of the units in process at the end of the period.

Exercise 9.7   Materials Cost Determination

Maurice Company adds materials at the beginning of the process in the forming department, which is the first of two stages in its production cycle. Information concerning the materials used in the forming department in April is as follows:

	Units	Materials Costs
Work in process at April 1	12,000	$ 6,000
Units started during April	100,000	$51,120
Units completed and transferred to next department during April	88,000	

Required

Using the weighted average method, determine the materials cost of the work in process at April 30.

Exercise 9.8 Materials Cost Determination

Lucas Company adds materials in the beginning of the process in the forming department, which is the first of two stages in its production cycle. Information concerning the materials used in the forming department in October is as follows:

	Units	Materials Costs
Work in process at October 1	6,000	$ 3,000
Units started during October	50,000	25,560
Units completed and transferred to next department during October	44,000	

Required

Using the weighted average method, determine the following:

1. The materials cost per equivalent unit
2. The materials cost total of units transferred to the next department during October
3. The materials cost total of units in process at October 31

Exercise 9.9 Basic Procedures, Average Method (CPA)

Information concerning department B of the Toby Company is as follows:

	Units	Costs
Beginning work in process	5,000	$ 6,300
Units transferred in	35,000	58,000
	40,000	$64,300
Units completed	37,000	
Ending work in process	3,000	

	Costs			
	Transferred in	Materials	Conversion	Total Costs
Beginning work in process	$ 2,900		$ 3,400	$ 6,300
Units transferred in	17,500	$25,500	15,000	58,000
	$20,400	$25,500	$18,400	$64,300

Conversion costs were 20% complete as to beginning work in process and 40% complete as to ending work in process. All materials are added at the end of the process. Toby uses the weighted average method.

Required

1. Determine the cost per equivalent unit for conversion costs.
2. Determine the portion of the total cost of ending work in process attributable to transferred-in cost.

Exercise 9.10   Equivalent Unit Computations

Gerry Incorporated has four departments—cutting, building, sanding, and finishing. Gerry uses a process-costing system to account for the costs. The following information is available about the work-in-process inventory of Gerry at the end of the fiscal year, August 31, 19X8.

1. Cutting: 2,500, 60% complete as to raw materials
2. Building: 1,200, 70% complete as to conversion costs
3. Sanding: 1,800, 30% complete as to conversion costs
4. Finishing: 3,200, 80% complete as to conversion costs

Required

1. The number of equivalent units of raw materials in all inventories at August 31, 19X8.
2. The number of equivalent units of the building department's conversion costs in all inventories at August 31, 19X8.
3. The number of equivalent units of the finishing department's conversion costs in all inventories at August 31, 19X8.

Problems

Problem 9.1   Essays on Process-Costing Concepts

An important concept in process costing is that of equivalent units.

Required

1. Describe the difference between units placed in process for a period and equivalent units for a period when there is no work-in-process beginning inventory and the work-in-process ending inventory is 50% complete.
2. Describe the difference between units completed for a period and equivalent units for a period when there is no work-in-process beginning inventory and the work-in-process ending inventory is 50% complete.
3. Describe how equivalent units for a period are used to compute the cost of the work-in-process ending inventory.

Problem 9.2   FIFO and Average Costing Procedures (CPA)

1. Information concerning department A of Stover Company for the month of June is as follows:

	Units	Materials Costs
Work in process, beginning	17,000	$12,800
Started in June	82,000	69,700
Units completed	85,000	
Work in process, ending	14,000	

All materials are added at the beginning of the process.

Required

Using the weighted average method, determine the cost per equivalent unit for materials cost.

2. Department one is the first stage of Drucker Company's production cycle. The following information is available for conversion costs for the month of April:

	Units
Work in process, beginning (40% complete)	40,000
Started in April	320,000
Completed in April and transferred to Department two	340,000
Work in process, ending (60% complete)	20,000

Required

Using the FIFO method, determine the equivalent units for conversion cost calculation.

Problem 9.3   Concepts and Procedures of the FIFO Method

1. Material is added at the beginning of a process in a process-costing system. The work-in-process beginning inventory for this process this period was 30% complete as to conversion costs. Using the first-in, first-out method of costing, the total equivalent units for material for this process during this period are equal to the
   a. beginning inventory this period for this process.
   b. units started this period in this process.
   c. units started this period in this process plus the beginning inventory.
   d. units started this period in this process plus 70% of the beginning inventory this period.

2. A company uses a first-in, first-out method of costing in a process-costing system. Material is added at the beginning of the process in department *A,* and conversion costs are incurred uniformly throughout the process. Work-in-process beginning inventory on April 1 in department *A* consisted of 50,000 units estimated to be 30% complete. During April, 150,000 units were started in department *A,* and 160,000 units were completed and transferred to department *B.* Work-in-process ending inventory on April 30 in department *A* was estimated to be 20% complete. What were the total equivalent units in department *A* for April for materials and conversion costs respectively?
   a. 150,000 and 133,000
   b. 150,000 and 153,000
   c. 200,000 and 133,000
   d. 200,000 and 153,000

3. In order to compute equivalent units of production using the FIFO method of process costing, work for the period must be broken down to units
   a. completed during the period and units in ending inventory.
   b. completed from beginning inventory, started and completed during the month, and units in ending inventory.
   c. started during the period and units transferred out during the period.
   d. processed during the period and units completed during the period.

4. Walton Incorporated had 8,000 units of work in process in department *A* on October 1, 19X8. These units were 60% complete as to conversion costs. Materials are added in the beginning of the process. During the month of October, 34,000 units were started and 36,000 units completed. Walton had 6,000 units of work in process on October 31, 19X8. These units were 80% complete as to conversion costs. Using the weighted average method how

much did the equivalent units for the month of October exceed the equivalent units for the month of October using the first-in, first-out method?

	Materials	Conversion Costs
a.	0	3,200
b.	0	3,800
c.	8,000	3,200
d.	8,000	4,800

5. The Ace Company had computed the physical flow (of physical units) for department A, for the month of April 19X9 as follows:

Units completed:

From work in process on April 1, 19X9	10,000
From April production	30,000
	40,000

Materials are added at the beginning of the process. Units of work in process at April 30, 19X9, were 8,000. The work in process at April 1, 19X9, was 80% complete as to conversion costs, and the work in process at April 30, 19X9, was 60% complete as to conversion costs. What are the equivalent units of production for the month of April 19X9 using the FIFO method?

	Materials	Conversion Costs
a.	38,000	36,800
b.	38,000	38,000
c.	48,000	44,800
d.	48,000	48,000

Problem 9.4   Equivalent Unit Computations

The Jorcano Company uses a process-costing system to account for the costs of its only product, product D. Production begins in the fabrication department where units of raw material are molded into various connecting parts. After fabrication is complete, the units are transferred to the assembly department. After assembly is complete, the units are transferred to the packaging department where packing material is placed around the units. The packaging department is considered a production department. After the units are ready for shipping, they are sent to the shipping area.

At year end, the following inventory of the product is on hand:

1. No unused raw material or packing material.
2. Fabrication department—300 units, 1/3 complete as to raw material and 1/2 complete as to direct labor.
3. Assembly department—1,000 units, 2/5 complete as to direct labor.
4. Packaging department—100 units, 3/4 complete as to packing material and 1/4 complete as to direct labor.
5. Shipping area—400 units.

Required

1. Determine the number of equivalent units of raw material in all inventories at year end.
2. Determine the number of equivalent units of fabrication department direct labor in all inventories at year end.
3. Determine the number of equivalent units of packing material in all inventories at year end.

Problem 9.5   Process Costing—Weighted Average Method

On April 1, the Collins Company had 6,000 units of work in process in department B, the second and last stage of their production cycle. The costs attached to these 6,000 units were $12,000 of costs transferred in from department A, $2,500 of materials costs added in department B, and $2,000 of conversion costs added in department B. Materials are added in the beginning of the process in department B. Conversion was 50% complete on April 1. During April, 14,000 units were transferred in from department A at a cost of $27,000, and material costs of $3,500 and conversion costs of $3,000 were added in department B. On April 30, department B had 5,000 units of work in process 60% complete as to conversion costs. Costs attached to these 5,000 units were $9,750 of costs transferred in from department A, $1,500 of material costs added in department B, and $833 of conversion costs added in department B.

Required

1. Using the weighted average method, determine the equivalent units for the month of April for all cost components.
2. Using the weighted average method, determine the cost per equivalent unit for all cost components.
3. Prove that the costs assigned to the 5,000 units of ending work-in-process inventory are correct.

Problem 9.6   Process-Costing Procedures—FIFO and Average (CPA)

Four independent questions are presented below:

1. Sussex Corporation's production cycle starts in the mixing department. The following information is available for the month of April:

	Units
Work in process, April 1 (50% complete)	40,000
Started in April	240,000
Work in process, April 30 (60% complete)	25,000

Materials are added in the beginning of the process in the mixing department.

Required

Using the weighted average method, determine the equivalent units of production for the month of April.

2. The cutting department is the first stage of Mark Company's production cycle. Conversion costs for this department were 80% complete as to the beginning work in process and 50% complete as to the ending work in process. Information as to conversion costs in the cutting department for January is as follows:

	Units	Conversion Costs
Work in process at January 1	25,000	$ 22,000
Units started and costs incurred during January	135,000	$143,000
Units completed and transferred to next department during January	100,000	

Required

Using the FIFO method, determine the conversion cost of the work in process in the cutting department at January 31.

3. The weighted average method of process costing differs from the first-in, first-out method of process costing in that the weighted average method

Required

Select the choice that best completes the statement.

a. requires that work-in-process ending inventory be stated in terms of equivalent units of production.
b. considers the work-in-process ending inventory only partially complete.
c. does *not* consider the degree of completion of work-in-process beginning inventory when computing equivalent units of production.
d. can be used under any cost flow assumption.

4. When using the first-in, first-out method of process costing, total equivalent units of production for a given period of time is equal to the number of units

Required

Select the choice that best completes the description.

a. started into process during the period, plus the number of units in work in process at the beginning of the period.
b. in work in process at the beginning of the period, plus the number of units started during the period, plus the number of units remaining in work in process at the end of the period times the percent of work necessary to complete the items.
c. in work in process at the beginning of the period times the percent of work necessary to complete the items, plus the number of units started during the period, less the number of units remaining in work in process at the end of the period times the percent of work necessary to complete the items.
d. transferred out during the period, plus the number of units remaining in work in process at the end of the period times the percent of work necessary to complete the items.

Problem 9.7   Cost of Production Report—FIFO Method

Crews Company produces a chemical agent for commercial use. The company accounts for production in two cost centers—cooking and mix-pack. In the first cost center, liquid substances are combined in large cookers and boiled; the boiling causes a normal decrease in volume from evaporation. After the "batch" is cooked, it is transferred to second cost center.

Material is added at the beginning of production in each cost center, and labor is added equally during production. Overhead is applied on the basis of 80% of labor cost. The FIFO method is used to cost inventories.

The following information is available for the month of October:

Cost Information	Cooking
Work in process, October 1	
Materials	$ 990
Labor	100
Month of October	
Materials	$39,600
Labor	10,050

Inventory and production records show that cooking had 1,000 gallons 40% processed on October 1 and 800 gallons 50% processed on October 31. Production reports for October show that cooking started 50,000 gallons into production and completed and transferred 40,200 to mix-pack.

Required

Prepare a cost of production report for the cooking department.

Problem 9.8   Cost of Production Report—Weighted Average Method

Prepare a cost of production report for Elko Corporation. All production is done in one department. The following information is available.

	Units
Beginning work in process (100% complete for materials, 75% complete for conversion costs)	10,000
Started in process during the period	70,000
Transferred to finished goods	65,000
Completed and still on hand	2,000
Ending work in process (100% complete for materials, 40% complete for conversion costs)	13,000

		Costs
Opening work in process:		
Materials	$ 2,000	
Labor	3,000	
Factory overhead	1,000	$ 6,000
Added during the period:		
Materials	50,000	
Labor	170,000	
Factory overhead	80,000	$300,000

Required

Prepare a cost of production report using the average costing method.

Problem 9.9   Cost of Production Report—FIFO Method

Refer to the facts and information indicated in problem 9.8.

Required

Prepare a complete cost of production report using the FIFO method.

Problem 9.10   Cost of Production Report—Weighted Average Method

Refer to the facts and information indicated in problem 9.7.

Required

Prepare a complete cost of production report using the weighted average method.

PROCESS COSTING: ADDITIONAL FEATURES

10

OUTLINE

A number of features, in addition to the basic procedures discussed in chapter 9, are necessary for proper implementation of process costing in specific production situations. For example, materials may be added in processes subsequent to the first process. The addition of materials results in either no change or an increase in the number of units in process. In either event there is an effect on product costs for which an accounting must be made.

Another situation requiring special accounting is the loss of units in process due to spoilage or shrinkage. This leaves fewer units to absorb total manufacturing costs. Accounting for the cost of these lost units should be understood. This chapter examines additional process-costing techniques used to account for manufacturing costs in these types of situations. After completing this chapter you should be able to:

1. account for material additions in processes subsequent to the first process when:
   a. there is no change in the number of units in production.
   b. there is an increase in the number of units in production.
2. identify reasons for losing units during production.
3. distinguish between normal and abnormal losses.
4. account for the cost of lost units in a process-costing environment.

This chapter also contains an appendix describing how standard costs may be used in a process-costing environment to enhance management planning and control. Only the mechanics of applying standard costs in a process-costing environment are explained in the appendix; a full discussion of standard costs is provided in chapters 15 and 16.

ADDITION OF MATERIALS IN PROCESSES SUBSEQUENT TO THE FIRST PROCESS

Materials are often added in processes subsequent to the first process. For example, paint, handles, or other trimmings may be added to furniture in a finishing process subsequent to the assembly process. When materials are added in processes subsequent to the first process, it is important to determine if the number of units of production remains the same or if the number of units increases due to the addition.

If the number of units remains the same, accounting for the cost of additional materials is the only additional feature of process costing in subsequent processes. However, if the number of units in production increases due to the addition of materials, additional attention must be given to an accompanying decrease in the per-unit cost of production. A decrease in the per-unit cost of production results from the increase in the number of units over which costs may be spread.

No Change in Units

The number of units will remain the same if the materials simply add to the units already in process. For example, applying decals to plastic toys or placing cabinets on television components represents an addition of materials but not an increase in the number of units of output. On the other hand, adding chemicals during the mixing of paint or blending ingredients during the preparation of fertilizer represents the addition of materials, which results in an increase in the number of units of output.

In both instances there are additional costs for which an accounting must be made. The accounting question is how these additional costs should be spread over the units that are in process, and how prior costs should be reapplied if a larger number of units are now in process? To answer this question, the simplest case is examined first—the addition of materials in processes subsequent to the first process with no increase in the number of units of output.

A manufacturer of cassette tape players uses a number of sequential processes in the production of its consumer models. During the last process the final quality control check is made, good units are placed in plastic cabinets, and finished units are packaged for shipment. Materials are placed in production toward the end of this final process with labor and overhead costs being uniformly applied throughout the process. Data for the current accounting period from production and accounting statistics for this last process are as follows:

Production Statistics

	Units
Work-in-process beginning inventory	1,000
(Materials 40% complete; labor and overhead 60% complete)	
Transferred in	15,000
Work-in-process ending inventory	800
(Materials 50% complete; labor and overhead 50% complete)	

Accounting Data

Work-in-process beginning inventory:		
Transferred-in costs	$	8,480
Materials		400
Labor and overhead		1,792
Total	$	10,672
Costs of the current period:		
Transferred-in costs		$120,000
Materials		15,980
Labor and overhead		50,000
Total		$185,980

The cost of production report in figure 10.1 illustrates the handling of materials costs in this situation. The weighted average method is used in figure 10.1.

In figure 10.1, materials of $15,980 are placed in process during the current period in this final process. Materials costs of $400 were added by this department in the prior period shown in the work-in-process beginning inventory. All materials costs added in prior processes or departments are contained in "transferred-in costs."

Inspection of figure 10.1 shows that accounting for materials placed in process in subsequent departments parallels the accounting for labor and overhead costs. The procedures are basically the same for each cost category, only the amount of detail work is different. The basic procedures also remain the same when using the FIFO method to account for materials added in processes subsequent to the first process.

Increase in Units

Accounting when materials are added in subsequent departments with a resulting increase in the number of units of output is only slightly more involved than accounting when output does not change. Consider the following situation. A manufacturer of industrial cleaners makes a grease-removing solvent in two processes—mixing and blending. Basic ingredients are combined in the mixing department and transferred to the blending department for further processing. Additional materials are added near the beginning of the blending process.

The blending department had 20,000 pounds of product in process at the beginning of the current accounting period. These units were 80% complete as to materials and 60% complete as to labor and overhead. There were 25,000 pounds transferred from mixing to blending during the period, plus there were 15,000 pounds of materials added in the blending department during the period. There were 48,000 pounds of cleaning solvent completed and transferred from blending to finished-goods inventory. Work-in-process

Figure 10.1

Materials Added in Subsequent Departments—No change in Units
Cost of Production Report
(Weighted Average Method)

	Physical Units	Percentage Completion		
		Transferred In	Material	Labor and Overhead
Units accounted for as follows:				
Work in process, beginning	1,000	100%	40%	60%
Transferred in this period	15,000			
Total units to account for	16,000			
Completed and transferred out	15,200			
Work in process, ending	800	100%	50%	50%

	Total	Transferred In	Material	Labor and Overhead
Costs to account for:				
Work in process, beginning	$ 10,672	$ 8,480	$ 400	$ 1,792
Costs of the current period	185,980	120,000	15,980	50,000
(1) Total costs to account for	$196,652	$128,480	$ 16,380	$ 51,792
Equivalent units of production:				
Completed and transferred out		15,200	15,200	15,200
Work in process, ending		800	400	400
(2) Total equivalent units		16,000	15,600	15,600
Cost per equivalent unit (1)÷(2)	$ 12.400	$ 8.030	$ 1.050	$ 3.320
Costs accounted for as follows:				
Costs transferred out	$188,480	(15,200 × $12.400)		
Work in process, ending:				
Transferred-in costs	$ 6,424	(800 × $ 8.030)		
Materials	420	(400 × $ 1.050)		
Labor and overhead	1,328	(400 × $ 3.320)		
Total	$ 8,172			
Total costs accounted for	$196,652			

inventory at the end of the period consisted of 12,000 pounds, which were 90% complete as to materials and 50% complete as to labor and overhead.

Costs recorded by the blending department for the current period are as follows:

Accounting Data

Work-in-process beginning inventory:	
Transferred-in costs	$ 28,000
Materials	10,632
Labor and overhead	6,540
Total	$ 45,172

Costs of the current period:	
Transferred-in costs	$ 56,000
Materials	27,000
Labor and overhead	21,000
Total	$104,000

Figure 10.2

Materials Added in Subsequent Departments—Increase in Units
Cost of Production Report
(Weighted Average Method)

	Physical Units	Percentage Completion		
		Transferred In	Material	Labor and Overhead
Units accounted for as follows:				
Work in process, beginning	20,000	100%	80%	60%
Transferred in this period	25,000			
Placed in process	15,000			
Total units to account for	60,000			
Completed and transferred out	48,000			
Work in process, ending	12,000	100%	90%	50%

	Total	Transferred In	Material	Labor and Overhead
Costs to account for:				
Work in process, beginning	$ 45,172	$ 28,000	$ 10,632	$ 6,540
Costs of the current period	104,000	56,000	27,000	21,000
(1) Total costs to account for	$149,172	$ 84,000	$ 37,632	$ 27,540
Equivalent units of production:				
Completed and transferred out		48,000	48,000	48,000
Work in process, ending		12,000	10,800	6,000
(2) Total equivalent units		60,000	58,800	54,000
Cost per equivalent unit (1) ÷ (2)	$ 2.550	$ 1.400	$ .640	$ .510
Costs accounted for as follows:				
Costs transferred out	$122,400	(48,000 × $2.550)		
Work in process, ending:				
Transferred-in costs	$ 16,800	(12,000 × $1.400)		
Materials	6,912	(10,800 × $ .640)		
Labor and overhead	3,060	(6,000 × $ .510)		
Total	$ 26,772			
Total costs accounted for	$149,172			

  The cost of production report shown in figure 10.2 uses the weighted average method for the blending department.

  When there is an increase in units of output due to the addition of materials in subsequent processes, the only change in the cost of production report is the addition of units "placed in process" in the "units accounted for as follows" section. The addition of 15,000 units of material simply represents a third source of total units for which an accounting must be made. All subsequent process-costing procedures and form of the cost of production report remain as previously discussed.

  Figure 10.3 illustrates process costing using the FIFO method when materials are added in subsequent departments with a resulting increase in units.

  Even though the only procedural change in the cost of production report is the addition of units "placed in process," it is important to recognize a change in unit costs

Figure 10.3

Materials Added in Subsequent Departments—Increase in Units
Cost of Production Report
(First-in, First-out Method)

		Percentage Completion		
	Physical Units	Transferred In	Material	Labor and Overhead
Units accounted for as follows:				
Work in process, beginning	20,000	100%	80%	60%
Transferred in this period	25,000			
Placed in process	15,000			
Total units to account for	60,000			
Completed and transferred out	48,000			
Work in process, ending	12,000	100%	90%	50%

	Total	Transferred In	Material	Labor and Overhead
Costs to account for:				
Work in process, beginning	$ 45,172	$ 28,000	$ 10,632	$ 6,540
(1) Costs of the current period	104,000	56,000	27,000	21,000
Total costs to account for	$149,172	$ 84,000	$ 37,632	$ 27,540
Equivalent units of production:				
Complete work in process, beginning			4,000	8,000
Started and completed		28,000	28,000	28,000
Work in process, ending		12,000	10,800	6,000
(2) Total equivalent units		40,000	42,800	42,000
Cost per equivalent unit (1)÷(2)	$ 2.531	$ 1.400	$ .631	$ .500

Costs accounted for as follows:		
Costs transferred out:		
Work in process, beginning	$45,172	
Work completed on work in process, beginning:		
Material	2,524	(4,000 × $ .631)
Labor and overhead	4,000	(8,000 × $ .500)
Work started and completed	70,868	(28,000 × $2.531)
Total	$122,564	
Work in process, ending:		
Transferred-in costs	$ 16,800	(12,000 × $1.400)
Materials	6,815	(10,800 × $ .631)
Labor and overhead	3,000	(6,000 × $ .500)
Total	$ 26,615	
Total costs accounted for	$149,172	(Rounded from $149,179)

that is not so obvious but nonetheless takes place. The costs transferred into the blending department are assigned to fewer units on entry than on exit simply because more units are generated in blending over which total costs must be spread. For example, there were 25,000 units transferred into the blending department at a total cost of $56,000. Transferred-in costs from prior processes are therefore $2.24 per unit ($56,000 ÷ 25,000 units). Since 15,000 units are added in the blending department, there are now 40,000 units available to absorb manufacturing costs. An increase in the number of units over which the same costs are spread results in a decrease in per-unit transferred-in costs from $2.24 to $1.40 ($56,000 ÷ 40,000 units).

One advantage of using the form of the cost of production report presented in this text is that there is no need to explicitly calculate an adjusted per-unit cost from the preceding department. Rather, the form of the report implicitly recalculates per-unit transferred-in costs, averaging current production costs with work-in-process costs of the prior period.

Some circumstances may cause per-unit costs to be recalculated. First, when a formula for the addition of materials in subsequent processes can be used, an adjusted cost per unit from the preceding department can be calculated, which would benefit management control. In such cases a recalculated transferred-in cost may be a more reliable basis for control than a cost per equivalent unit in the subsequent department. Second, in many processes it is possible to use materials in different proportions or to substitute materials having different costs to produce essentially the same finished product. In such instances management may want detailed departmental reports that make a clear distinction between departments and periods, and it is important that adjusted costs from the preceding department be calculated. The information in chapter 18 concerning mix and yield variances also relates to the preparation, analysis, and use of process-costing reports in these types of manufacturing environments.

ACCOUNTING FOR LOST UNITS

Managerial cost accounting must identify why inputs to a manufacturing process do not always result in good output. Even though the subject has been avoided until now, virtually all manufacturing processes experience waste, scrap, spoilage, shrinkage, or defective units. Whatever the cause, accounting for units lost during production presents a unique challenge when using process-costing techniques. The challenge comes not simply because there are lost units, but because additional differentiation has to be made between abnormal and normal rates of loss. This section focuses on both the management control dimension and the product-costing aspects of normal and abnormal losses that can occur during manufacturing operations.

Reasons for Lost Units

Spoilage, shrinkage, waste, scrap, and defective units all explain why some inputs to manufacturing processes do not end up as good output. However, the primary concern of this section is accounting for lost units in a process-costing environment due to spoilage and shrinkage. Spoilage and shrinkage are the only types of loss that result in lost units. Other conditions such as waste, scrap, and defective units represent lost materials and conversion costs but not lost units. **Defective units** are goods that do not meet quality control standards and are either sold "as is" as second-quality goods or reworked and sold as first-quality goods. **Waste and scrap** are terms for residue such as smoke, dust, or shavings that result from a manufacturing process. In the case of waste and scrap there is no unit identity or cost assignment during the manufacturing process. In the case of defective units, there is a unit identity throughout the manufacturing process and costs are assigned as though they are good units.

In contrast, spoilage and shrinkage represent lost units for which there has been an expenditure of materials, labor, and overhead costs. **Spoilage** is production that does not meet quality control standards and as a result the unit produced is junked or sold for a relatively low disposal value. The cost of spoilage is the net of production costs accumulated to the time of rejection less any disposal or salvage value.

It should be noted that there is a distinction between spoilage and defective units even though there may seem to be a similarity between spoiled units discovered at the end of a production process and defective units. Spoilage is usually not saleable in the same market as firsts or seconds and is typically sold in another type of market often for its intrinsic content. However, defective units are usually sold through regular distribution channels as second-quality items. These factors make a considerable difference between the relative sales value of spoilage and defective units. The salvage value of spoilage is significantly lower than the selling price of seconds.

Shrinkage represents lost units resulting from a reduction in volume of output due to such things as evaporation, temperature variations, or chemical reaction. Shrinkage may result in the production of waste, but the important difference between the two is that shrinkage typically results in lost units, but waste does not. For example, waste in the form of dust or shavings does not result in lost units. Waste only results in a loss of materials but not a loss of units of production. However, shrinkage results in a reduction in the total units to account for.

These differences in terminology are important because the procedural steps of process costing are adjusted to handle lost units through spoilage and shrinkage while other accounting techniques apply in the case of waste, scrap, or defective units. The process-costing aspects of spoilage and shrinkage are discussed in this chapter. Accounting for waste, scrap, defective units and the job-order costing aspects of spoilage and shrinkage are discussed in chapter 12.

Normal and Abnormal Rates of Loss

A **normal rate of loss** is the rate of loss that is expected to occur under efficient operating conditions. Most production processes will generate bad units along with good ones. It may be technologically possible to reduce the probability of generating bad units to very low levels. However, as loss rates are reduced, costs of production usually increase. Production is efficient when the cost of lowering loss rates is greater than the benefit derived from having additional good output.

Manufacturing operations are considered to be efficient at this point even though some bad units are being produced along with the good. In reality this point is rarely calculated, but limits are set within which losses are expected to be controlled with acceptable costs. For example, between 5% and 7% of the nails produced may be expected to be bent or between 3% and 4% of the glass bottles produced may break. Reducing losses with new machinery or more intensive supervision may be possible, but if the cost of doing so is more than the value of the additional good nails or bottles then the loss rate is considered to be normal. Therefore, the normal rate of loss is synonymous with planned or expected loss that will occur even under efficient operating conditions. The accounting significance of normal loss is that since it is an ordinary and expected cost of obtaining good output it is *inventoried as part of the cost of good production.*

On the other hand, an **abnormal rate of loss** is the rate of loss that is not expected to occur under efficient operating conditions. It is that part of total loss that falls outside normal or expected limits. Abnormal loss may result from a bad batch of materials, machine malfunction, carelessness, or accidents. For example, the cost of bent nails in excess of a 7% loss limit or broken bottles in excess of a 4% breakage limit is considered abnormal loss. The accounting significance of abnormal loss is that since it is not an ordinary and necessary cost of obtaining good output it is considered a period cost and is immediately *charged as a loss* in the period incurred.

The implications for management between normal and abnormal losses are that losses within normal limits are indicative of a controlled situation, but the presence of abnormal losses suggests that the process is not adequately controlled. Since normal losses are inherent in the manufacturing process, no amount of remedial action aside from changing the process will eliminate them. However, management's attention and influence over preventive maintenance, proper materials, or similar aspects of production can usually alter abnormal losses. Therefore, it is important that (a) losses due to spoilage or shrinkage be measured and reported, (b) costs of normal versus abnormal losses be segregated, and (c) costs of normal losses be inventoried and costs of abnormal losses be charged as a loss in the current period.

COST FLOWS AND PROCESS-COSTING PROCEDURES

The practical application in accounting records of the concept of normal versus abnormal losses results in the following cost flows. These cost flows are based on the typical situation in which inspection or discovery of spoilage and shrinkage occurs at the end of a process immediately before goods being transferred to the next process or, if completed, to finished-goods inventory. Accounting for losses that occur at other points in the production process is discussed later in this chapter.

Lost Units at the End of a Process

Costs incurred for the production of both good and bad output are charged to departmental work-in-process accounts. The cost of normal losses combined with the cost of good production then flows from process to process until work is completed and total accumulated costs are charged to finished-goods inventory. When finished products are sold, cost of goods sold is charged with the combined costs of good production plus the accumulated cost of normal losses.

The cost of abnormal losses, rather than being carried in either work-in-process accounts of subsequent departments or in finished-goods inventory, is charged directly to a separate "cost of abnormal losses" account in the period in which it is incurred. This account is normally closed each period to cost of goods sold. However, it may be shown on the income statement as a separate item. These cost flows are illustrated in figure 10.4.

The following journal entries also illustrate these cost flows. Assume that a total of $410,850 has been charged to a department that performs the final processing on a particular product. Assume also that the total costs are assigned to good production, lost units, and work-in-process ending inventory as follows:

Good production transferred out	$315,000
Cost of normal losses	31,500
Cost of abnormal losses	15,750
Work in process, ending	48,600
Total	$410,850

1. To establish total costs to account for in the final process:

Work in process—final department	410,850	
Various accounts		410,850

2. Transfer of goods; final department to finished goods:

Finished-goods inventory	346,500	
Work in process—final department		346,500

$315,000 (cost of good production transferred out) + $31,500 (cost of normal losses) = $346,500

3. Abnormal losses charged to a loss account:

Loss from abnormal spoilage and shrinkage	15,750	
Work in process—final department		15,750

Figure 10.4   Cost flow of normal versus abnormal losses

Normal Losses

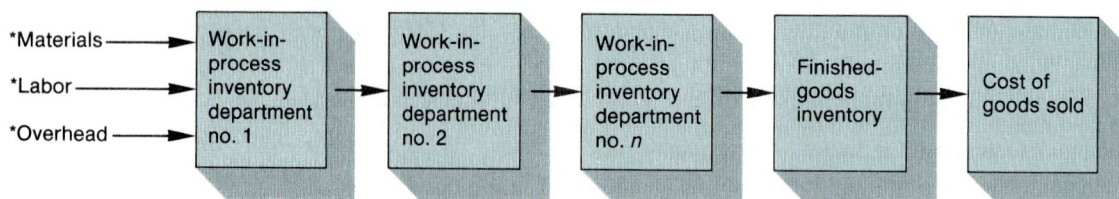

Abnormal Losses

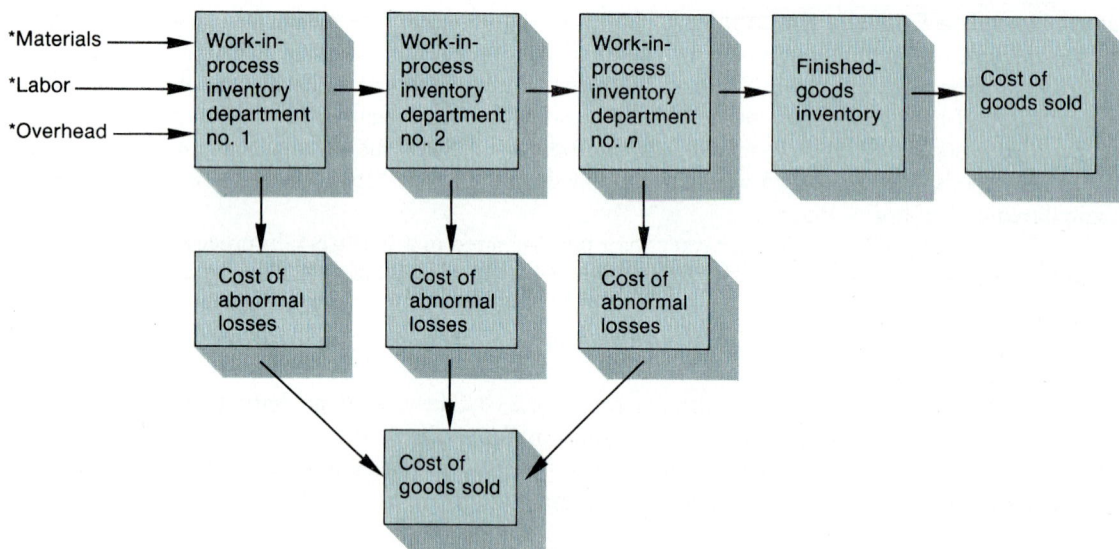

*Materials, labor, and overhead may be added in any department—not just the first department.

---

4. Sales of $500,000 with a cost of goods sold of $300,000:

Accounts receivable	500,000	
Sales		500,000
Cost of goods sold	300,000	
Finished-goods inventory		300,000

Besides this approach, there is an alternative and more conceptually based approach that can be used. This alternative approach has the following features. First, the total cost of lost units is segregated from the cost of good production. This is accomplished, using the data above, by debiting a separate "cost of lost units" account for $47,250 ($31,500 + $15,750), the sum of normal and abnormal losses. This treatment highlights the total problem of lost units and provides a monitoring vehicle for management. Second, the part of the total cost of lost units that is abnormal, $15,750 in this case, is transferred to a "cost of abnormal spoilage" account and the cost of normal spoilage, $31,500 in this case, is transferred to finished-goods inventory along with the cost of good units finished and transferred of $315,000.

The emphasis of the more practical approach first illustrated is on product costing while the emphasis of the more conceptually oriented approach is on planning and control. Regardless of the accounting techniques used, a well-designed cost of production report can present information in a form that will meet the needs of both product costing and management control. To illustrate this point and to show how lost units are handled in a cost of production report, consider the following situation.

Pottery Company accumulates the cost of glazing one of its products using process-costing techniques. The major portion of materials costs are placed in production at the beginning of processing in the glazing department with a minor amount of materials being added at various times through the first half of the process. There is no change in units due to the addition of materials. Labor and overhead costs are incurred evenly throughout the process. Some of the pottery pieces are spoiled as a result of misapplication of glaze or improper machine handling. Due to the nature of the process these losses are not discovered until inspection of the finished units just before being transferred to finished goods. Production records show that about 10% of the units are spoiled in the glazing process.

At the beginning of the accounting period, work-in-process inventory for this product was $106,550, representing 8,000 pieces with $48,000 of transferred-in costs, $50,000 of materials costs (85% completed), and $8,550 of labor and overhead costs (50% completed).

During the period, 19,000 pieces were transferred in from the prior process. Materials costing $143,500 were placed in process during the current period, and direct labor of $26,000 was charged to the glazing department. Manufacturing overhead of $20,800 was applied to production at the rate of 80% of direct-labor cost. Therefore, total labor and overhead costs of $46,800 ($26,000 + $20,800) were charged to the glazing department during the period.

The work-in-process ending inventory consisted of 4,000 units, 70% complete as to materials and 40% complete as to labor and overhead. There were 20,000 good units transferred to finished goods after final inspection. Lost units totaled 3,000 units. Normal spoilage of 10% of good output or 2,000 units was expected, which means that there were 1,000 units of abnormal spoilage.

The cost of production report for the glazing department using the weighted average method of process costing is shown in figure 10.5.

Several features of figure 10.5 are important to review. First, the format of the first section accounting for physical units is slightly modified due to the added detail required to report lost units. This account format could have been used in all previous cost of production report illustrations and is preferred by many accountants and managers. Second, to eliminate ambiguity and to provide information for management control purposes differentiation is made throughout the report between normal and abnormal losses. Third, equivalent units of production must be calculated for bad as well as good units to enable appropriate cost assignments. Since bad units are not discovered in this situation until final inspection after all processing is complete, 100% of transferred-in materials, labor, and overhead costs are included in the equivalent unit computation.

For convenience in making journal entries, costs allocated to good production of $315,000 are added to the cost of normal losses of $31,500 to obtain a total cost of $346,500, which is transferred to finished-goods inventory. The cost of abnormal losses of $15,750 is transferred to a loss account and shown on the income statement of the current period. The journal entries presented at the beginning of this section relate to the operations of the glazing department and should be reviewed in the context of the cost flows shown in figure 10.4 and the cost of production report in figure 10.5.

Figure 10.5

Glazing Department
Cost of Production Report
(Weighted Average Method—With Lost Units)

	Physical Units	Percentage Completion		
		Transferred In	Material	Labor and Overhead
Units to account for:				
Work in process, beginning	8,000	100%	85%	50%
Transferred in this period	19,000			
Total units to account for	27,000			
Units accounted for as follows:				
Completed and transferred out	20,000			
Normal loss	2,000			
Abnormal loss	1,000			
Work in process, ending	4,000	100%	70%	40%
Total units accounted for	27,000			

	Total	Transferred In	Material	Labor and Overhead
Costs to account for:				
Work in process, beginning	$106,550	$ 48,000	$ 50,000	$ 8,550
Costs of the current period	304,300	114,000	143,500	46,800
(1) Total costs to account for	$410,850	$162,000	$193,500	$ 55,350
Equivalent units of production:				
Completed and transferred out		20,000	20,000	20,000
Normal loss		2,000	2,000	2,000
Abnormal loss		1,000	1,000	1,000
Work in process, ending		4,000	2,800	1,600
(2) Total equivalent units		27,000	25,800	24,600
Cost per equivalent unit (1)÷(2)	$ 15.750	$ 6.000	$ 7.500	$ 2.250

Costs accounted for as follows:		
Costs transferred out:		
Good production	$315,000	(20,000 × $15.750)
Normal loss	31,500	(2,000 × $15.750)
To finished goods	$346,500*	
Abnormal loss	15,750	(1,000 × $15.750)
Total costs transferred out	$362,250	
Work in process, ending:		
Transferred-in costs	$ 24,000	(4,000 × $ 6.000)
Materials	21,000	(2,800 × $ 7.500)
Labor and overhead	3,600	(1,600 × $ 2.250)
Total	$ 48,600	
Total costs accounted for	$410,850	

*The cost per unit of goods transferred to Finished-Goods Inventory is $17.325 ($346,500 ÷ 20,000 units).

Care should be taken to reflect the proper per-unit cost of items transferred to finished-goods inventory. The per-unit cost of goods transferred to finished-goods inventory is found by dividing the *total* cost of goods transferred to finished goods by the number of *good* units transferred. In this case, the cost per unit of items completed and transferred is $17.325 per unit ($346,500 ÷ 20,000 units).

When using the FIFO method, proper handling of the cost of normal losses is conceptually more difficult. Usually two "batches" of units are completed during an accounting period (one from beginning work in process and one from units started and completed during the period). The cost of normal losses should be split between them. However, normal spoilage or shrinkage is a cost of the current period. Therefore, attaching any of these costs to beginning work in process, as though these units had been started and completed in the current period, is a contradiction of the FIFO assumption. Therefore, the usual procedure, and one that is easy to apply in practice, is to allocate the cost of normal losses to goods completed and transferred out during the period. Figure 10.6 shows the treatment of losses using the FIFO method.

Care should be taken to use a proper base for the calculation of normal losses. This base is usually determined as part of a budgetary or planning process before actual operations begin for the accounting period. There are two acceptable bases—good output and normal input for good output actually produced. Actual input should not be used as a base for computing *normal* losses because actual input may contain abnormal as well as normal losses. To illustrate, assume that under normal conditions 11,000 units of input result in 10,000 units of good output or a normal loss of 1,000 units. This represents a normal loss rate of approximately 9.1% based on normal input or a 10% loss rate based on good output. Figure 10.7 illustrates these relationships.

The difficulty with using total input as a base can be illustrated by assuming that during a particular period it actually took 11,500 units to produce 10,000 units of good output. Because the numbers have been kept quite simple it is apparent that there are 500 units of abnormal loss in this situation—1,500 units of total loss less 1,000 units of normal loss. However, applying a loss rate of either 9.1% or 10% to total input does not result in an accurate finding of 500 units of abnormal loss. In fact, since the relationship among normal input, good output, and normal loss is predetermined, the only unknown quantity is abnormal loss. This means that it is not possible to develop a loss rate (before actual results are available) that can be applied to total input to accurately uncover abnormal loss. Without an expected or predetermined loss rate it is not possible to differentiate between normal and abnormal loss.

It is most convenient to apply a single loss rate when calculating normal loss. However, because of random influences in virtually all production processes, actual loss rates typically fluctuate around some average value. This should be kept in mind as abnormal losses are analyzed and loss rates revised. For example, assume that a given loss rate is used throughout a year when, from an engineering perspective, there have been no abnormal losses. In comparing actual losses with expected normal losses small differences will probably still occur. Sometimes actual losses will be less than expected normal losses and sometimes they will be greater. The net difference over a number of periods is expected to be zero if the normal loss rate accurately represents the manufacturing process.

Since losses in excess of expected normal losses are defined as abnormal, small abnormal losses will occasionally occur even though the process is not out of control and there is no need to stop or adjust operations. If this is the case, how persistent and how large must abnormal losses be before they indicate a process that is truly out of control and where investigation is warranted? Chapter 16 answers this and other questions about how to determine when indicators such as abnormal losses actually signal an out-of-control condition that requires management intervention.

Figure 10.6

Glazing Department
Cost of Production Report
(First-in, First-out Method—With Lost Units)

	Physical Units	Percentage Completion Transferred In	Material	Labor and Overhead
Units to account for:				
Work in process, beginning	8,000	100%	85%	50%
Transferred in this period	19,000			
Total units to account for	27,000			
Units accounted for as follows:				
Completed and transferred out	20,000			
Normal loss	2,000			
Abnormal loss	1,000			
Work in process, ending	4,000	100%	70%	40%
Total units accounted for	27,000			

	Total	Transferred In	Material	Labor and Overhead
Costs to account for:				
Work in process, beginning	$106,550	$ 48,000	$ 50,000	$ 8,550
(1) Costs of the current period	304,300	114,000	143,500	46,800
Total costs to account for	$410,850	$162,000	$193,500	$ 55,350
Equivalent units of production:				
Complete work in process, beginning			1,200	4,000
Started and completed		12,000	12,000	12,000
Normal loss		2,000	2,000	2,000
Abnormal loss		1,000	1,000	1,000
Work in process, ending		4,000	2,800	1,600
(2) Total equivalent units		19,000	19,000	20,600
Cost per equivalent unit (1)÷(2)	$ 15.825	$ 6.000	$ 7.553	$ 2.272

Costs accounted for as follows:		
Costs transferred out:		
Work in process, beginning	$106,550	
Work completed on work in process, beginning:		
Material	9,064	(1,200 × $ 7.553)
Labor and overhead	9,088	(4,000 × $ 2.272)
Good units started and completed	189,900	(12,000 × $15.825)
Normal loss	31,650	(2,000 × $15.825)
To finished goods	$346,252*	
Abnormal loss	15,825	(1,000 × $15.825)
Total costs transferred out	$362,077	
Work in process, ending:		
Transferred-in costs	$ 24,000	(4,000 × $ 6.000)
Materials	21,148	(2,800 × $ 7.553)
Labor and overhead	3,635	(1,600 × $ 2.272)
Total	$ 48,783	
Total costs accounted for	$410,850	(Rounded from $408,860.)

*The cost per unit of goods transferred to Finished-Goods Inventory is $17.313 ($346,252 ÷ 20,000 units).

Figure 10.7   Bases for calculating expected normal losses

| | Units | Bases for Calculating Normal Losses | |
		Good Output	Normal Input
Normal input	11,000	90.0%	100.0%
Good output	10,000	100.0	90.9
Normal loss	1,000	10.0%	9.1%

Another consideration in accounting for lost units because of spoilage or shrinkage concerns the point in the process at which losses are discovered. Typically an inspection or quality control check is made at the end of a process immediately before goods are transferred to the next process or to finished goods. However, in some processes spoilage or shrinkage may be detected at intermediate stages in the process.

Lost Units at the Beginning and at Other Points During a Process

Normal losses occuring at the beginning of a process result in a reduction of the number of units over which total costs can be spread. Therefore, by simply reducing the number of units to be accounted for by the number of units of normal loss at the beginning of a process effectively spreads their cost over all other good units. For abnormal losses at the beginning of a process, the number of units to account for is reduced just as with normal losses. In addition, however, any costs associated with abnormal losses, such as transferred-in costs, are immediately charged to a loss account, which also reduces the total costs to account for in the department.

Often normal and abnormal losses are discovered simultaneously. However, in some instances abnormal losses may be detected at a different point in processing than normal losses. Whatever the circumstances, the cost of abnormal losses should be charged to a loss account and reported in the current period.

For normal losses discovered at other points during a process, the general rule is to *allocate the cost of normal losses to units that have passed the point in a process where the losses are discovered.* For example, if losses are discovered at the midpoint of processing then all units passing this point during operations of the current period are allocated a portion of the cost of normal losses. This means that beginning work in process that is less than 50% complete at the beginning of the period probably passes the midpoint during current operations as do any items that are started and completed during the period. Also, ending work in process that is at least 50% complete also passes the midpoint of operations during the current period. Therefore, all of these units should be allocated a portion of the cost of normal losses. For example, if 15,000 good units from beginning work in process, 75,000 good units from work started and completed, and 10,000 good units from ending work in process passes the midpoint of processing then the cost of normal losses would be allocated on the basis of $15/100_{ths}$ plus $75/100_{ths}$ to units transferred out and $10/100_{ths}$ to work-in-process ending inventory.

This general rule can be applied for inspection and discovery of losses at any point during processing. To illustrate, assume the same situation as shown in figures 10.5 and 10.6 except that inspection occurs at a point where materials, labor, and overhead costs are 80% complete. Results adjusted for this assumption are shown in figure 10.8 using the weighted average method.

An important point to observe concerning the allocation of normal losses in figure 10.8 is that percentage completion figures are shown for both normal and abnormal losses because the discovery of losses occurred at a point in processing other than at the beginning or at final inspection. These percentages guide the proper calculation of equivalent

Figure 10.8

Glazing Department
Cost of Production Report
Lost Units Are Discovered at 80% of Processing
(Weighted Average Method)

		Percentage Completion		
	Physical Units	Transferred In	Material	Labor and Overhead
Units to account for:				
Work in process, beginning	8,000	100%	85%	50%
Transferred in this period	19,000			
Total units to account for	27,000			
Units accounted for as follows:				
Completed and transferred out	20,000			
Normal loss	2,000	100%	80%	80%
Abnormal loss	1,000	100%	80%	80%
Work in process, ending	4,000	100%	70%	40%
Total units accounted for	27,000			

	Total	Transferred In	Material	Labor and Overhead
Costs to account for:				
Work in process, beginning	$106,550	$ 48,000	$ 50,000	$ 8,550
Costs of the current period	304,300	114,000	143,500	46,800
(1) Total costs to account for	$410,850	$162,000	$193,500	$ 55,350
Equivalent units of production:				
Completed and transferred out		20,000	20,000	20,000
Normal loss		2,000	1,600	1,600
Abnormal loss		1,000	800	800
Work in process, ending		4,000	2,800	1,600
(2) Total equivalent units		27,000	25,200	24,000
Cost per equivalent unit (1)÷(2)	$ 15.985	$ 6.000	$ 7.679	$ 2.306

Costs accounted for as follows:		
Costs transferred out:		
Good production	$319,700	(20,000 × $15.985)
Normal loss	27,976[2]	
To finished goods	$347,676[1]	
Abnormal loss	13,988[3]	
Total costs transferred out	$361,664	
Work in process, ending:		
Transferred-in costs	$ 24,000	(4,000 × $ 6.000)
Materials	21,501	(2,800 × $ 7.679)
Labor and overhead	3,690	(1,600 × $ 2.306)
Total	49,191	
Total costs accounted for	$410,850	(Rounded from $410,855.)

Figure 10.8   *Continued*

1. The cost per unit of goods transferred to finished-goods inventory is $17.384 ($347,676 ÷ 20,000 units).

2. Cost of Normal Loss:

Transferred-in costs	$ 12,000	(2,000 × $ 6.000)
Materials	12,286	(1,600 × $ 7.679)
Labor and overhead	3,690	(1,600 × $ 2.306)
Total	$ 27,976	

3. Cost of abnormal loss:

Transferred-in costs	$ 6,000	(1,000 × $ 6.000)
Materials	6,143	(800 × $ 7.679)
Labor and overhead	1,845	(800 × $ 2.306)
	$ 13,988	

units of production for lost units. For example, 1,000 units of abnormal loss discovered where units are 80% complete result in 800 (1,000 × .8) equivalent units of production for material, labor, and overhead and 1,000 equivalent units for transferred-in costs.

Another important point to observe is that the cost of normal loss is allocated completely to the 20,000 completed units transferred out because these are the only units that are assumed to have passed the point in the process where losses are discovered. If work in process was all 90% complete then it would be assumed that an additional 4,000 units would have been inspected and passed the 80% completion point where losses are discovered. Using this later assumption, the cost of normal losses would be allocated on the basis of 24,000 units (20,000 + 4,000) instead of 20,000 units. This means that there would be 20,000/24,000$_{ths}$ of the cost of normal losses allocated to units transferred out and 4,000/24,000$_{ths}$ allocated to work-in-process ending inventory.

Since there is such a diversity of production processes and inspection procedures, it is important that accountants understand the basic principles of accounting for lost units so they can be appropriately applied in each individual circumstance.

Summary

A number of unique accounting problems arise when using process-costing procedures. When materials are added in processes subsequent to the first process, there might be no change in the number of units in process or there might be an increase in the number of units. When there is no change in the number of units, accounting procedures remain the same except for the addition of materials cost as another cost category in that process. When the number of units increase, the additional units are added to the number of units for which an accounting must be made. In so doing, the cost per equivalent unit for transferred-in costs and all other cost categories are automatically adjusted when using the form of the cost and production report illustrated in this chapter. Otherwise, revised per-unit transferred-in costs must be calculated. With adjusted unit costs, process-costing procedures relating to the assignment of costs remain the same.

Spoilage and shrinkage may result in a decrease in the number of units in process. Nearly every manufacturing process operates with some level of lost units; preventing all losses is usually impossible except at a very high cost. How the cost of lost units is handled depends on whether losses are considered to be normal or abnormal. The cost of normal losses is assigned to inventory and eventually charged to cost of goods sold in the period of sale. The cost of abnormal losses is charged to a separate loss account and reported on the income statement in the period in which the abnormal loss is incurred.

The cost of normal losses are allocated to those good units having passed the point in processing where losses are discovered.

Some special points to remember:

1. When materials are added in processes subsequent to the first process and the number of units:
   a. remains the same, treat materials cost just as any other cost category.
   b. increases, add the increase in the number of units to the total for which an accounting must be made and follow the usual process-costing procedures.
2. Track the flow of bad as well as good units.
3. Distinguish between normal and abnormal losses.
4. Charge the cost of abnormal losses to a loss account and report on the income statement of the current period.
5. Charge the cost of normal losses to inventories at the point in the process where losses are discovered.
   a. At final inspection, assign costs to good units transferred out during the period.
   b. At some intermediate point during processing, assign costs to good units that have passed the point of discovery during the period. Under this condition some cost of lost units may be assigned to work-in-process ending inventory.

Appendix   *Process Costing and Standard Costs*

This appendix shows how to accomplish the *mechanics* of using standard costs in a process-costing environment. To fully understand the usefulness of combining standard costs and process costing you should review this appendix after studying chapters 15 and 16, which are devoted to standard costing.

Standard costs are predetermined or budgeted costs that are expected to be attained during actual production. When using standard costs, accountants, engineers, production managers, and others involved in company planning typically cooperate in developing a budget containing anticipated results of operations. As part of the budget, standard or expected costs of production are developed. Part of a hypothetical budget containing expected or standard costs follows:

Standard Costs

	Per Unit
Materials	$ .70
Labor	.80
Overhead	.60
Total	$2.10

Standard costs take the place of costs per equivalent unit of production when using process-costing methods. To illustrate, figure 10.9 contains a cost of production re-

Figure 10.9

Assembly Department
Cost of Production Report
(Using Standard Costs)

	Physical Units	Percentage Completion		
		Material	Labor	Overhead
Units accounted for as follows:				
Work in process, beginning	6,000	100%	75%	75%
Transferred in this period	80,000			
Total units to account for	86,000			
Completed and transferred out	78,000			
Work in process, ending	8,000	100%	85%	85%

	Total	Material	Labor	Overhead
Costs to account for:				
Work in process, beginning	$ 10,500	$ 4,200	$ 3,600	$ 2,700
Costs of the current period	170,300	55,340	65,760	49,200
Total costs to account for	$180,800	$ 59,540	$ 69,360	$ 51,900
Equivalent units of production:				
Complete work in process, beginning			1,500	1,500
Completed and transferred out		72,000	72,000	72,000
Work in process, ending		8,000	6,800	6,800
Total equivalent units		80,000	80,300	80,300
Cost per equivalent unit	$ 2.100	$ .700	$ .800	$ .600

	Total	Material	Labor	Overhead
Costs accounted for as follows:				
Costs transferred out:				
Work in process, beginning	$ 10,500	$ 4,200	$ 3,600	$2,700
Work completed on work in process: beginning	2,100		1,200[1]	900[2]
Work started and completed	151,200	50,400[3]	57,600[4]	43,200[5]
Total	$163,800	$ 54,600	$ 62,400	$ 46,800
Work in process, ending	15,120	5,600[6]	5,440[7]	4,080[8]
Total standard costs	$178,920	$ 60,200	$ 67,840	$ 50,880
Total costs to account for	180,800	59,540	69,360	51,900
Cost variances	$ 1,880 U	$ 660 F	$ 1,520 U	$ 1,020 U

1. $1,500 \times \$ .80 = \$ 1,200$
2. $1,500 \times \$ .60 = \$ 900$
3. $72,000 \times \$ .70 = \$50,400$
4. $72,000 \times \$ .80 = \$57,600$
5. $72,000 \times \$ .60 = \$43,200$
6. $8,000 \times \$ .70 = \$ 5,600$
7. $6,800 \times \$ .80 = \$ 5,440$
8. $6,800 \times \$ .60 = \$ 4,080$

port using standard costs. The following data are also needed to develop the cost of production report.

Production Statistics

	Units
Work-in-process beginning inventory	6,000
(Materials 100% complete; labor and overhead 75% complete)	
Started in process	80,000
Completed and transferred out	78,000
Work-in-process ending inventory	8,000
(Materials 100% complete; labor and overhead 85% complete)	

Accounting Statistics

Work-in-process beginning inventory:	
Materials	$ 4,200
Labor	3,600
Overhead	2,700
Total	$ 10,500
Costs of the current period:	
Materials	$ 55,340
Labor	65,760
Overhead	49,200
Total	$170,300
Total costs to account for	$180,800

The most important thing to observe in figure 10.9 is that costs per equivalent unit are not calculated as they are when using either weighted average or FIFO methods. Standard per-unit costs are used in place of costs per equivalent unit. This results in goods transferred out and work-in-process ending inventory being costed at standard rather than at actual costs. This facilitates the comparison of actual with budgeted results. For example, actual costs incurred by the department contained in "total costs to account for" and budgeted amounts contained in "total standard costs" are compared to determine what, if any, differences occurred. This is done by subtracting the "total standard costs" from the "total costs to account for" resulting in "cost variances" as shown on the report. A "U" after a variance amount indicates an unfavorable outcome, and an "F" after a variance amount indicates a favorable outcome. For example, there is a total variance of $1,880 U, which indicates that total *actual* costs exceeded budgeted or *standard* costs by $1,880. In contrast, total actual materials costs were less than standard costs resulting in a $660 favorable variance.

A final observation concerning the mechanics of constructing a cost of production report with standard costs is that costs are assigned to inventories as with the FIFO method. This emphasizes the results of current-period operations and facilitates the analysis of variances because costs of two periods are not mingled.

The use of standard costs is a completely general procedure relative to job-order, process, or hybrid costing systems; that is, the use of standard costs represents a modification of each of these basic systems rather than being a separate or different type of costing system. Comparing the usefulness of standard costs to the various basic costing systems makes it apparent that standard costs and process costing make the best partnership. The continuous flow, mass production environment of process costing lends itself best to the use of budgets as a tool for management control. Variances provide useful information for analyzing and adjusting mass production processes.

The use of standard costs also overcomes many of the conflicts between weighted average and FIFO methods. This is especially true in manufacturing situations where there are various ways that inputs can be combined to produce a variety of similar products. For example, a Wedgewood manufacturer uses various clays, finishing processes, and glazes on product pieces with varying finishes, shapes, and sizes. When many such combinations are possible, the averaging inherent in process costing may not provide sufficient detail for product costing or control purposes. However, it may not be practical to modify process-costing procedures due to the great number of possible alternatives that may arise. In such situations standard costs provide a more reasonable approach to providing useful cost information.

Self-Study Problem

Chemco Incorporated manufactures a single product that passes through four sequential processes. Accounting and production data for the current accounting period for department 3 of the operation are as follows:

Production Statistics

	Units
Work-in-process beginning inventory	2,000
(Materials 100% complete; labor and overhead 40% complete)	
Received from Department 2	50,000
Started in process due to the addition of materials	20,000
Transferred to Department 4	64,000
Work-in-process ending inventory	6,000
(Materials 100% complete; labor and overhead 30% complete)	

Accounting Data

Work-in-process beginning inventory:		
Transferred-in costs	$ 5,600	
Materials	2,500	
Labor and overhead	500	
Total	$ 8,600	
Costs of the current period:		
Transferred-in costs	$206,500	
Materials	91,000	
Labor and overhead	244,550	
Total	$542,050	

Materials are added at the beginning of the process. All losses are discovered at final inspection just before units are transferred to department 4. Department 3 has a normal loss rate of 2.5% of good units produced.

Required

Prepare a cost of production report for department 3 using the FIFO method of process costing. Prepare journal entries to record the cost of abnormal losses and to transfer costs to department 4.

Solution to the Self-Study Problem

The following journal entries are derived from given information and the accompanying cost of production report.

1. To establish total costs to account for in department 3:

Work in process—Department 3	550,650	
Various accounts		550,650

2. Transfer of goods; department 3 to department 4:

Work in process—Department 4	346,500	
Work in process—Department 3		346,500

3. Abnormal losses charged to a loss account:

Loss from abnormal spoilage and shrinkage	3,160	
Work in process—final department		3,160

Department 3
Cost of Production Report
Lost Units Are Discovered at Final Inspection
(First-in, First-out Method)

		Percentage Completion		
	Physical Units	Transferred In	Material	Labor and Overhead
Units to account for:				
Work in process, beginning	2,000	100%	100%	40%
Transferred in this period	50,000			
Placed in process	20,000			
Total units to account for	72,000			
Units accounted for as follows:				
Completed and transferred out	64,000			
Normal loss	1,600	(.025 × 64,000 units)		
Abnormal loss	400	(by subtraction)		
Work in process, ending	6,000	100%	100%	30%
Total units accounted for	72,000			

	Total	Transferred In	Material	Labor and Overhead
Costs to account for:				
Work in process, beginning	$ 8,600	$ 5,600	$ 2,500	$ 500
(1) Costs of the current period	542,050	206,500	91,000	244,550
Total costs to account for	$550,650	$212,100	$ 93,500	$245,050
Equivalent units of production:				
Completed work in process, beginning				1,200
Started and completed		62,000	62,000	62,000
Normal loss		1,600	1,600	1,600
Abnormal loss		400	400	400
Work in process, ending		6,000	6,000	1,800
(2) Total equivalent units		70,000	70,000	67,000
Cost per equivalent unit (1) ÷ (2)	$ 7.900	$ 2.950	$ 1.300	$ 3.650

Costs accounted for as follows:		
Costs transferred out:		
Work in process, beginning	$ 8,600	
Work completed on work in process, beginning	4,380	(1,200 × $ 3.650)
Work started and completed	489,800	(62,000 × $ 7.900)
Normal loss	12,640	(1,600 × $ 7.900)
To finished goods	$515,420	
Abnormal loss	3,160	(400 × $ 7.900)
Total costs transferred out	$518,580	
Work in process, ending:		
Transferred-in costs	$ 17,700	(6,000 × $ 2.950)
Materials	7,800	(6,000 × $ 1.300)
Labor and overhead	6,570	(1,800 × $ 3.650)
Total	$ 32,070	
Total costs accounted for	$550,650	

Suggested Readings

Belkaoui, Ahmed. *Cost Accounting.* New York: The Dryden Press, 1983.

Bower, James B.; Schlosser, Robert E.; and Zlatkovich, Charles T. *Financial Information Systems: Theory and Practice* (chapters 18 and 19). Boston: Allyn & Bacon, 1972.

Kaplan, Robert S. *Advanced Management Accounting.* Englewood Cliffs, N.J.: Prentice-Hall, 1982.

National Association of Accountants. "Accounting for Labor Costs and Labor-Related Costs." *Research Series No. 32.* New York, 1957.

———. "Cost Control of Spoiled Work." *Accounting Practice Report No. 12.* New York, 1971.

Discussion Questions

1. When materials are added in processes subsequent to the first process, what are the possible outcomes with respect to the number of units in process?
2. What is the effect on the per-unit cost of production when the number of units in process increases as a result of adding materials in processes subsequent to the first process?
3. Explain how materials costs are handled in a cost of production report when they are added in processes subsequent to the first process and there is no increase in the number of units.
4. What change is necessary in the cost of production report when there is an increase in the number of units in process due to materials being added in processes subsequent to the first process?
5. Why is it usually not necessary to specifically calculate a revised per-unit cost for transferred-in costs when using the form of cost of production report illustrated in this chapter?
6. Under what circumstances should a revised per-unit cost for transferred-in costs be calculated?
7. Define spoilage and shrinkage. How are they different? How are they the same?
8. How do waste, scrap, and defective units differ from spoilage and shrinkage?
9. Explain the difference between normal and abnormal rates of loss.
10. Are normal and abnormal losses controllable by management? Explain.
11. Discuss the cost flows for normal versus abnormal losses, and give journal entries to illustrate these cost flows.
12. What are two acceptable bases for the calculation of normal losses? Why is actual output not an acceptable base?
13. What is the general rule for deciding whether the cost of normal losses should be allocated only to units transferred out or to work-in-process ending inventory *and* units transferred out?
14. List some of the special points to remember about process costing when losses occur.
15. What are standard costs and how are they incorporated on a cost of production report?
16. Describe some of the advantages of using standard costs in process costing.

Exercises

Exercise 10.1   Definitions of Job-Order and Process Costing

Presented below are four independent questions concerning a typical manufacturing company that uses a process-cost accounting system. Your response to each question should be complete, including simple examples or illustrations where appropriate.

Required

1. What is the rationale supporting the use of process costing instead of job-order costing for production costing purposes? Explain.
2. Define equivalent production (equivalent units produced). Explain the significance and use of equivalent production for product-costing purposes.
3. Define normal spoilage and abnormal spoilage. Explain how normal spoilage costs and abnormal spoilage costs should be reported for management purposes.
4. How does the first-in, first-out (FIFO) method of process costing differ from the weighted average method of process costing? Explain.

Exercise 10.2   Lost and Spoiled Unit Concepts (CPA)

Determine the best answer for each of the following items:

1. Normal spoilage and abnormal spoilage should be classified as:

	Normal	Abnormal
a.	Period cost	Period cost
b.	Product cost	Period cost
c.	Period cost	Product cost
d.	Product cost	Product cost

2. Materials are added at the start of the process in the blending department, the first stage of the production cycle. The following information is available for the month of July:

	Units
Work in process, July 1	60,000
(60% complete as to conversion costs)	
Started in July	150,000
Transferred to the next department	110,000
Lost in production	30,000
Work in process, July 31	70,000
(50% complete as to conversion costs)	

   Under the system used by the company, the costs incurred on lost units are absorbed by the remaining good units. Inspection occurs at the 80% stage of production. Using the weighted average method, what are the equivalent units for the materials unit cost calculation?
   a. 120,000
   b. 145,000
   c. 180,000
   d. 210,000

3. Which of the following is an inventoriable cost?

	Abnormal Spoilage	Normal Spoilage
a.	No	No
b.	No	Yes
c.	Yes	No
d.	Yes	Yes

4. Purchased materials are added in the second department of a three-department operation. This addition increases the number of units produced in the second department and would always
   a. change the direct-labor cost percentage in the work-in-process ending inventory.
   b. increase to the unit cost transferred in from the first department.
   c. increase total unit costs.
   d. decrease total work-in-process ending inventory.

5. Purchased materials are added in the second department of a three-department operation. The addition does not increase the number of units produced in the second department and would
   a. not change the dollar amount transferred to the next department.
   b. decrease total work-in-process inventory.
   c. increase the factory overhead portion of the work-in-process ending inventory.
   d. increase total unit cost.

Exercise 10.3   Equivalent Units—FIFO versus Average Costing

Blakely Incorporated uses a process-costing system to account for the costs of its two departments, manufacturing and packing. The following information is available for the month of March 19X2:

	Units	
	Manufacturing	Packing
In process at beginning	3,000	5,000
Started in process	25,000	
Received from preceding dept.		20,000
Transferred to next dept.	20,000	
Transferred to finished goods		17,000
Completed and on hand	2,000	
Still in process	5,000	7,000
Lost in process	1,000	1,000

	% Completion of Work in Process	
	Manufacturing	Packing
Beginning inventory		
Materials	80%	
Conversion costs	20%	50%
Ending inventory		
Materials	100%	
Conversion costs	30%	70%

Required

1. Determine the equivalent units of production for the manufacturing department's materials and conversion costs using:
   a. the FIFO method
   b. the weighted average method
2. Determine the equivalent units of production for the packing department's material and conversion costs, using:
   a. the FIFO method
   b. the weighted average method

Exercise 10.4 Concepts of Lost Units

1. Normal spoilage is properly classified as
   a. an extraordinary item.
   b. a period cost.
   c. a product cost.
   d. a deferred charge.
2. If the amount of spoilage in a manufacturing process is abnormal, it should be classified as a
   a. deferred charge.
   b. joint cost.
   c. period cost.
   d. product cost.
3. Cargain Company has noticed that more spoiled units seem to occur in their manufacturing process on Monday than on any other day of the week. The plant is closed on Saturday and Sunday. If appropriate data to determine the relationship between spoiled units and the day of the week are collected, the resultant number should
   a. provide a measure of the extent to which the day of the week accounts for the variability in the spoiled units.
   b. provide a measure of the extent to which the spoiled units account for the variability in the day of the week.
   c. establish that one variable is the cause of another variable.
   d. establish that the day of the week is the cause of the spoiled units.
4. In a process-costing system that assumes that normal spoilage occurs at the end of a process, the cost attributable to normal spoilage should be assigned to
   a. work-in-process ending inventory.
   b. cost of goods manufactured and work-in-process ending inventory in the ratio of units worked on during the period to units remaining in work-in-process inventory.
   c. cost of goods manufactured (transferred out).
   d. a separate loss account in order to highlight production inefficiencies.
5. Milton Incorporated had 8,000 units of work in process in its department M on March 1, which were 50% complete as to conversion costs. Materials are introduced at the beginning of the process. During March, 17,000 units were started, 18,000 units were completed, and there were 2,000 units of normal spoilage. Milton had 5,000 units of work in process at March 31, which were 60% complete as to conversion costs. Under Milton's cost accounting system, spoiled units reduce the number of units over which total cost can be spread.

Using the weighted average method, the equivalent units for March for conversion costs were

a. 17,000.
b. 19,000.
c. 21,000.
d. 23,000.

6. Spoilage occurring during a manufacturing process can be considered normal or abnormal. The proper accounting for each of these costs is as follows:

	Normal	Abnormal
a.	Product	Period
b.	Product	Product
c.	Period	Product
d.	Period	Period

7. The type of spoilage that should not affect the recorded cost of inventories is

a. abnormal spoilage.
b. normal spoilage.
c. seasonal spoilage.
d. standard spoilage.

Exercise 10.5   Weighted Average Cost Procedures (CMA)

JC Company employs a process-costing system. A unit of product passes through three departments—molding, assembly, and finishing—before it is completed.

The following activity took place in the finishing department during May:

	Units
Work-in-process inventory—May 1	1,400
Units transferred in from the Assembly Department	14,000
Units spoiled	700
Units transferred out to finished-goods inventory	11,200

Raw material is added at the beginning of the process in the finishing department without changing the number of units being processed. The work-in-process inventory was 70% complete as to conversion on May 1 and 40% complete as to conversion on May 31. All spoilage was discovered at final inspection before the units were transferred to finished goods; 560 of the units spoiled were within the limit considered normal.

JC Company employs the weighted average costing method. The equivalent units and the current costs per equivalent unit of production for each cost factor are as follows:

	Equivalent Units	Current Costs per Equivalent Unit
Cost of prior departments	15,400	$5.00
Raw materials	15,400	1.00
Conversion cost	13,300	3.00
		$9.00

Required

1. Determine the cost of production transferred to the finished-goods inventory.
2. Determine the cost assigned to the work-in-process inventory on May 31.

3. If the total costs of prior departments included in the work-in-process inventory of the finishing department on May 1 amounted to $6,300, determine the total cost transferred in from the assembly department to the finishing department during May.
4. Determine the cost associated with the abnormal spoilage.
5. Determine how the cost associated with abnormal spoilage ordinarily would be treated.

Exercise 10.6   Cost of Production Report—Normal and Abnormal Spoilage

The Zigler Company uses process costing. In department C, conversion costs are incurred uniformly during the process. Materials are added at the end of the process after an inspection is made. Normal spoilage is expected to be 5% of good output.

The following information is evident for department C for January:

	Units	$ Amount
Received from Department B	24,000	168,000
Transferred to finished goods	18,000	
Ending inventory (75% complete)	4,000	
Department C materials costs		36,000
Department C conversion costs		91,200

Required

Prepare a complete cost of production report for department C, including a quantity schedule (i.e., a schedule accounting for units) and an equivalent unit schedule.

Exercise 10.7   Equivalent Units—FIFO Method

Alpha Company uses a process-costing system. On September 1, 19X2, the manufacturing department had 8,000 units in process, which were 80% complete as to materials costs and 40% complete as to conversion costs. During September, 25,000 units are started in process and 28,000 units are transferred to the next department. There are no lost units. On September 30, 19X2, work in process is 70% complete as to materials costs and 60% complete as to conversion costs.

Required

1. Would the amount the equivalent units for materials costs differ if the first-in, first-out method were used instead of the weighted average method?
2. Would the amount the equivalent units for conversion costs differ if the first-in, first-out method were used instead of the weighted average method?

Exercise 10.8   Equivalent Units—Normal Spoilage

Kopper Incorporated began business on April 1, 19X9. Kopper has two departments, *A* and *B,* and uses a process-costing system. During April, Kopper incurred $80,000 of materials costs and $45,000 of conversion costs. Of the 45,000 units started in process, 5,000 were lost in process, 30,000 were transferred to department *B,* and 10,000 were still in process. The ending work-in-process units were 100% complete as to materials costs and 60% complete as to conversion costs. All losses are considered normal. Inspection occurs at the end of the process.

Required

1. Determine the equivalent units of production.
2. Determine the cost per equivalent unit for materials and conversion costs.
3. Determine the total costs transferred to department *B*.

Exercise 10.9   Quantity Schedule—Equivalent Units

Poole Incorporated produces a chemical compound by a unique chemical process that Poole has divided into two departments, *A* and *B,* for accounting purposes. The process functions as follows:

1. The formula for the chemical compound requires one pound of chemical *X* and one pound of chemical *Y.* In the simplest sense, one pound of chemical *X* is processed in department *A* and transferred to department *B* for further processing. In department *B* one pound of chemical *Y* is added when the process is 50% complete. When the processing is complete, the finished chemical compound is transferred to finished goods. The process is continuous, operating twenty-four hours a day.
2. Normal spoilage occurs in department *A.* During the first few seconds of processing 5% of chemical *X* is lost.
3. No spoilage occurs in department *B.*
4. In department *A* conversion costs are incurred uniformly throughout the process and are allocated to good pounds produced because spoilage is normal.
5. In department *B* conversion costs are allocated equally to each equivalent pound of output.
6. The following data are available for the month of October:

	Department A	Department B
Work in process, October 1	8,000 pounds	10,000 pounds
Stage of completion of beginning inventory (one batch per department)	3/4	3/10
Started or transferred in	50,000 pounds	?
Transferred out	46,500 good pounds	?
Work in process, October 31	?	12,000
Stage of completion of ending inventory (one batch per department)	1/3	1/5
Total equivalent pounds of material added in department *B*	—	44,500 pounds

Required

1. Prepare a quantity schedule (schedule accounting for units) for both departments.
2. Determine the equivalent units of production for material and conversion costs.

Exercise 10.10   Normal and Abnormal Spoilage

The Klammer Company uses process costing in accounting for production. Two materials are used. Material *A* is added at the beginning of the process. Inspection is at the 90% stage; material *B* is then added to the good units. Normal spoilage units amount to 5% of good output.

Company records contain the following information for January:

Started during the period	20,000 units
Material *A*	$26,740
Material *B*	$ 9,000
Direct-labor cost	$75,160
Factory overhead	$93,950
Transferred to finished goods	14,000 units
Ending inventory (95% complete)	4,000 units

Required

Prepare a cost of production report, complete with schedules "accounting for units" and "equivalent units," using the weighted average method.

Problems

Problem 10.1   Cost of Production Report—Normal Spoilage

Orson Incorporated began a new process on July 1, 19X2. The process manufactures a single product, which is manufactured in two departments. The finishing department is the last department before the product is transferred to finished goods. The accounting department has gathered the following information regarding the finishing department.

Units received from preceding dept.	75,000 units
Units transferred to finished goods	60,000 units
Units completed and on hand	5,000 units
Units still in process (50% complete as to conversion costs)	8,000 units
Units lost in process	2,000 units
Transferred from preceding dept.	$61,050
Costs added by department:	
Labor	$20,925
Factory overhead	$27,900

Normal spoilage is 5% of units completed during the month. Approximately one half of the losses occur at the 25% stage and one half occurs at the 75% stage. No additional work is done on lost units. Lost units are scrapped.

Required

Prepare a cost of production report for the finishing department for July 19X2, using the weighted average method.

Problem 10.2   Cost of Production Report—Materials Added in Second Department

Kofford Chemical Incorporated manufactures chemical products in three departments—mixing, refining, and packaging. Kofford uses a process-costing system to account for its costs. Most of the chemicals are added in the mixing department. One additional chemical, chemical E, is added in the refining department. The following data are available for the refining department for October 19X7:

Units received from Mixing Department	25,000 units
Cost transferred from Mixing Department	$62,000
Cost added by department	
Material	$15,500
Labor	$11,376
Factory overhead	$ 7,110
Units transferred to the Packaging Department	23,000 units
Units still in process	8,000 units

The chemical increased the units in process by 6,000 units. The ending inventory is 100% complete as to materials. As to conversion costs, 40% are 60% complete, 40% are 70% complete, and 20% are 80% complete. There is no beginning work in process.

Required

Prepare a cost of production report for the refining department for October 19X7, using the weighted average method.

Problem 10.3   Cost of Production Report—Weighted Average Method

Lakeview Corporation is a manufacturer that uses the weighted average process-costing method to account for costs of production. Lakeview manufactures a product that is produced in three separate departments—molding, assembling, and finishing. The following information was obtained for the assembling department for the month of June.

Work in process, June 1—2,000 units composed of the following.

	Amount	Degree of Completion
Transferred in from the Molding Department	$32,000	100%
Costs added by the Assembling Department		
Direct materials	$20,000	100%
Direct labor	7,200	60%
Factory overhead applied	5,500	50%
	32,700	
Work in process, June 1	$64,700	

The following activity occurred during the month of June:

10,000 units were transferred in from the Molding Department at a cost of $160,000.
$150,000 of costs were added by the Assembling Department:

Direct materials	$ 96,000
Direct labor	36,000
Factory overhead applied	18,000
	$150,000

8,000 units were completed and transferred to the finishing department.

On June 30, there were still 4,000 units in work in process. The degree of completion of work in process on June 30 was as follows:

Direct materials	90%
Direct labor	70%
Factory overhead applied	35%

Required

Prepare in good form a cost of production report for the assembling department for the month of June. Show supporting computations in good form. The report should include the following:

1. equivalent units of production
2. total manufacturing costs
3. cost per equivalent unit
4. dollar amount of ending work in process
5. dollar amount of inventory cost transferred out

Problem 10.4 Materials Added in Subsequent Department—Weighted Average Method

Roy Company manufactures product X in a two-stage production cycle in departments A and B. Materials are added at the beginning of the process in department B. Roy uses the weighted average method. Conversion costs for department B were 50% complete as to the 6,000 units in the beginning work in process and 75% complete as to the 8,000 units in the ending work in process. There were 12,000 units completed and transferred out of department B during February. An analysis of the costs relating to work in process and production activity in department B for February is as follows:

	Transferred In	Materials Costs	Conversion
Work in process, February 1:			
Costs attached	$12,000	$2,500	$1,000
February activity:			
Costs added	29,000	5,500	5,000

1. The total cost per equivalent unit transferred out for February for product X, rounded to the nearest penny, was
   a. $2.75.
   b. $2.78.
   c. $2.82.
   d. $2.85.
2. In a process-costing system how is the unit cost affected in a cost of production report when materials are added in a department subsequent to the first department and the added materials result in additional units?
   a. It causes an increase in the preceding department's unit cost, which necessitates an adjustment of the transferred-in unit cost.
   b. It causes a decrease in the preceding department's unit cost, which necessitates an adjustment of the transferred-in unit cost.
   c. It causes an increase in the preceding department's unit cost but does *not* necessitate an adjustment of the transferred-in unit cost.
   d. It causes a decrease in the preceding department's unit cost but does not necessitate an adjustment of the transferred-in unit cost.

Problem 10.5   Cost of Production Report—FIFO Method, Lost Units

Carman Incorporated has developed a process that produces widgets. The widgets are assembled in the assembly department and packaged for sale in the packaging department. Packaged widgets are moved to the finished-goods storeroom until they are sold. The accounting department has gathered the following cost and production data for the month of March 19X3:

	Assembly	*Packaging*
Work-in-process beginning inventory		
Cost from preceding dept.		17,500
Materials (100% complete)	13,750	5,450
Labor (50% complete, assembly; 60% complete, packaging)	7,500	6,900
Factory overhead (50% complete, assembly; 50% complete, packaging)	5,450	7,700
Costs added during the month		
Materials	75,680	24,800
Labor	43,008	39,650
Factory overhead	36,864	42,700
Work-in-process ending inventory % of completion		
Materials	100%	100%
Conversion costs	30%	70%
Units in process at beginning	6,500 widgets	4,300 widgets
Units started in process	35,400	
Units transferred to next dept.	31,000	27,900
Units still in process	9,900	7,400
Units lost in process	1,000	—

The units lost in the assembly department are lost near the beginning of the assembly process. None of the lost units are from the beginning work in process and all losses are normal.

Required

Prepare a cost of production report for all departments for March 19X3 using the FIFO method.

Problem 10.6   Equivalent Units and Unit Costs—Weighted Average Method

Lyman Company uses a process-costing system. The following information is available for the finishing department, the second and last department in Lyman's system:

Beginning work in process, November 1, 19X4:	
Transferred in from the Manufacturing Dept.	$20,000
Materials	8,400
Labor	4,000
Factory overhead	2,000
Cost added during November	
Transferred in	$43,000
Labor	7,040
Factory overhead	6,280

Percentage of completion of work in process:	*November 1*	*November 30*
Materials	100%	100%
Conversion costs	50%	40%

Production statistics:	
Units in process, Nov. 1	10,000
Units in process, Nov. 30	4,000
Units transferred in	20,000
Units shipped	26,000

Lyman accounts for the costs by the weighted average method.

Required

1. Determine the equivalent units of production for materials and conversion costs for the month of November.
2. Determine the cost per equivalent unit for materials, labor, and factory overhead costs.

Problem 10.7   Cost of Production Report—FIFO Method

Melody Corporation is a manufacturing company that produces a single product known as Jupiter. Melody uses the first-in, first-out (FIFO) process-costing method for both financial statement and internal management reporting.

Data for the month of April are presented below:

1. The beginning inventory consisted of 2,500 units, which were 100% complete as to raw material and 40% complete as to direct labor and factory overhead.
2. An additional 10,000 units were started during the month.
3. The ending inventory consisted of 2,000 units, which were 100% complete as to raw material and 40% complete as to direct labor and factory overhead.
4. There were 10,500 units completed and transferred to finished goods.
5. There is $55,200 in the work in process account on April 1.
6. Costs applicable to April production are as follows:

	Actual Cost
Raw material used	$121,000
Direct labor	105,575
Factory overhead	31,930

Required

1. For each element of production for April (raw material, direct labor, and factory overhead), compute the following:
   a. equivalent units of production
   b. cost per equivalent unit of production
2. Prepare a cost of production report.

Show supporting computations in good form.

Problem 10.8   Cost of Production Report—Weighted Average Method

You are engaged in the audit of the January 31 financial statement of Spirit Corporation, a manufacturer of a digital watch. You are attempting to verify the costing of the ending inventory of work in process and finished goods, which were recorded on Spirit's books as follows:

	Units	Costs
Work in process (50% complete as to labor and overhead)	300,000	$ 660,960
Finished goods	200,000	$1,009,800

Materials are added to production at the beginning of the manufacturing process, and overhead is applied to each product at the rate of 60% of direct-labor costs. There was no finished-goods inventory on January 1.

A review of Spirit's inventory cost records disclosed the following information:

| | | Costs | |
	Units	Materials	Labor
Work in process, January 1			
(80% complete as to labor and overhead)	200,000	$ 200,000	$ 315,000
Units started in production	1,000,000		
Material costs		1,300,000	
Labor costs			1,995,000
Units completed	900,000		

Required

Prepare a cost of production report for Spirit Corporation for January using the weighted average method.

Problem 10.9   Cost of Production Report—FIFO and Weighted Average Methods—Spoilage with Recovery Value (CPA)

The Minsky Processing Company manufactures one product through two processes. For each unit of Process no. 1 output, two units of material A are put in at the start of processing. For each unit of Process no. 2 output, three cans of material B are put in at the end of processing. Two pounds of Process no. 1 output are placed in at the start of Process no. 2 for each unit of finished goods started.

Spoilage generally occurs in Process no. 2 when processing is approximately 50% complete. The company uses FIFO costing for Process no. 1 and weighted average costing for Process no. 2.

Data for March:

1. Units transferred:

From Process no. 1 to Process no. 2	2,200 pounds
From Process no. 2 to finished goods	900 gallons
From finished goods to cost of goods sold	600 gallons

2. Units spoiled in Process no. 2: 100 gallons.
3. Materials unit costs: A, $1.51 per unit; B, $2 per can
4. Conversion costs: Process no. 1, $3,334; Process no. 2, $4,010
5. Spoilage recovery: $100 (treated in Process no. 2 as a reduction in the cost that came from Process no. 1)
6. Inventory data:

| | Process no. 1 | | Process no. 2 | |
	Beginning	Ending	Beginning	Ending
Units	200	300	200	300
Fraction complete, conversion cost	1/2	1/3	1/2	2/3
Costs:				
Materials	$560			
Conversion cost	108		$ 390	
Prior department cost			2,200	

Required

Prepare a cost of production report with a quantity schedule for March for both processes.

Problem 10.10 Cost of Production Reports—Multiple Departments

The Mintz Corporation manufactures seven-inch rulers in three departments—mixing, shaping, and finishing. A process-costing system is used to account for the goods manufactured. The following information is available:

| | Departments | | |
Units	Mixing	Shaping	Finishing
Opening work in process			
Mixing (all materials, 30% conversion)	10,000		
Shaping (all materials, 60% conversion)		18,000	
Finishing (all materials, 45% conversion)			5,000
Started in process during the period	90,000		
Transferred out	—	—	—
Completed and still on hand	4,000	2,000	6,000
Closing work in process			
Mixing (all materials, 75% conversion)	7,000		
Shaping (all materials, 35% conversion)		8,000	
Finishing (all materials, 75% conversion)			9,000
Costs			
Opening work in process			
Materials	15,000		
From preceding department		9,620	11,630
Labor	8,075	13,954	6,531
Overhead	10,215	9,792	4,650
Total	33,290	33,366	22,811
Added during the period			
Materials	195,000		
Labor	100,000	40,000	60,000
Overhead	40,000	35,000	45,000
Total	335,000	75,000	105,000

Required

1. Prepare a cost of production report for all three departments using the weighted average costing method.
2. Prepare a cost of production report for all three departments using the FIFO costing method.

Problem 10.11 Cost of Production Reports—Spoiled Units

Dartmouth Manufacturing began business July 1, 19X5. Dartmouth uses a process-costing system for the company's two departments—department A and department B. The following information is available for department B:

Cost of units transferred:	$105,000
Cost added by department:	
Labor	$ 35,200
Factory overhead	26,400
Transferred from department A	20,000 units
Transferred to finished goods	12,000 units
Ending inventory (60% complete as to conversion costs)	6,000 units

The units are inspected at the 75% stage. Normal spoilage is considered to be 8% of good units inspected. Spoiled units are not processed further.

Required

1. Prepare a cost of production report for department B, using the weighted average method.
2. Prepare a cost of production report for department B, assuming that ending inventory is 90% complete, using the weighted average method.

JOINT PRODUCTS AND BY-PRODUCTS: COST ALLOCATIONS AND DECISIONS

11

OUTLINE

J oint products and by-products are a part of many manufacturing operations in which one product cannot be produced without the simultaneous production of one or more other products. For example, copper mining, oil refining, cheese making, lumber milling, and vegetable canning all produce joint products and/or by-products. The equitable assignment of total manufacturing costs to various joint products and by-products is often a difficult and complicated accounting problem. However, the assignment of joint costs is important for inventory costing, income determination, and financial reporting purposes. Also, appropriate costing of joint products and by-products provides management with data for evaluating profit performance and for planning and control purposes. This chapter explains how to account for joint product costs and how joint product costs are used in management decisions. After completing this chapter you should be able to:

1. identify joint product costs.
2. differentiate between joint products and by-products.
3. allocate joint product costs using either physical measures or market measures as an allocation base.
4. account for the cost of by-products.
5. use joint product and by-product costs in management decisions.

THE JOINT PRODUCT ENVIRONMENT

Joint products are produced whenever a resource or input results in more than one useful output. For example, hogs represent a single input to a meat packing operation in which pork chops, roasts, bacon, ham, and any number of other useful items are produced. A distinguishing characteristic of joint product operations is that no single group of joint products may be produced without the production of other joint products. For example, it is not reasonable to expect the only output from the slaughter of cattle will be steaks; a hide, hamburger, and various other cuts of meat are also supplied. Joint products may be produced in various proportions (for example, steaks can be ground into hamburger) but the economic and physical characteristics inherent in such operations naturally result in the production of joint products.

A **by-product** is basically a joint product with a relatively minor sales value when compared with other joint products. Examples of by-products include remnants from the manufacture of textiles, cotton seed from the processing of cotton, and sawdust from the milling of lumber. It is not always clear what constitutes a joint product and what constitutes a by-product because judgment must be exercised in determining what constitutes a "relatively minor sales value." Also, shifts in the relative sales values of products may result in the need to reclassify by-products. For example, there are products that result from the manufacture of cheese and photographic film that once were considered by-products. However, these by-products are now classified as joint products because of newly discovered uses and their increased relative importance in the joint product group.

Various terminology is used in accounting practice for joint products, by-products, scrap, and waste. Usage varies depending on the business environment and management viewpoint. For example, some sewage plants consider their output as waste, while others have developed recycling programs and account for their output as by-products. Some metal fabrication plants treat saleable trimmings as scrap, while others account for trimmings as by-products. The distinction between waste and by-products is that waste usually does not have a sales value. The distinction between scrap and by-products is that by-products have a relatively higher sales value than scrap. Also, by-products may require additional processing to be marketable. These differences are not merely a matter of semantics for accountants. An accountant who makes the proper distinction between joint products, by-products, scrap, and waste overcomes potential cost allocation problems and develops appropriate inventory values and related information for financial statement users and company managers.

Figure 11.1   Joint product and by-product processing and cost flows

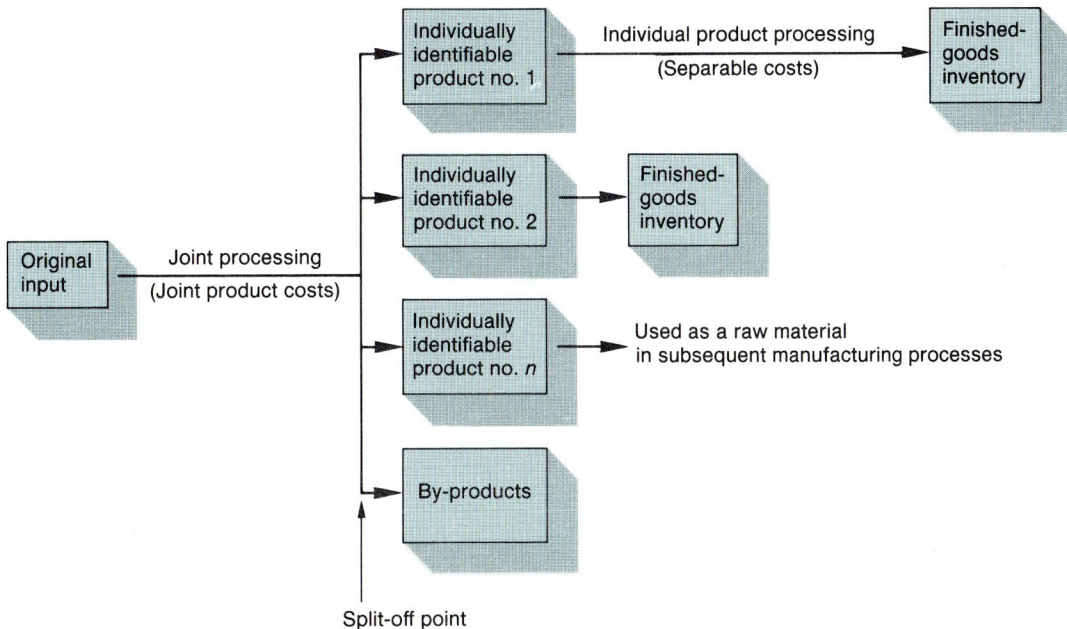

Joint product costs, also called joint costs, are those manufacturing costs incurred during the processing of original inputs before the point where joint products become individually identifiable. For example, all material, labor, and overhead costs incurred to process the carcass of a hog to the point where it is divided into its various categories of dressed meat are considered joint or common costs. At the point of division, which is called the **split-off point,** joint product categories such as sides for bacon and shoulders for roasts become individually identifiable.

Costs incurred after the split-off point are assigned to individual products and are classified as **separable** or **direct product costs.** For example, the cost of trimming, slicing, and packaging bacon are separable costs assigned solely to bacon, because it is an individually identifiable joint product in the processing cycle. The *total* cost of bacon consists of an allocated portion of joint costs plus the separable costs of processing bacon beyond the split-off point. Figure 11.1 illustrates the difference between joint costs and separable costs in a joint product manufacturing environment.

As shown in figure 11.1 there are several different possibilities for production and cost flows. For example, substitute the production of bacon for individually identifiable product no. 1. This product undergoes individual processing beyond the split-off point before it is inventoried and sold. However, perhaps the joint product is not processed further, as shown with product no. 2. In this case a joint product is simply inventoried and sold with no additional manufacturing costs being applied. For example, whole sides of bacon are sold as soon as they are divided from the main carcus without additional trimming, slicing, or packaging. These represent a joint product that is sold without subsequent processing.

Another possibility for joint product cost and production flow is the situation in which a joint product is reintroduced into the manufacturing process as a raw material. For example, coal and gas are the major raw material inputs in the manufacture of coke.

Gas is used to heat the coal, which results in the production of many joint products including coke, benzol, tar, and coke oven gas. The gas recovered from the coking process is then typically reintroduced into the coking process to heat subsequent batches of coal.

Figure 11.1 indicates that by-products can be generated at the split-off point or at any stage of the manufacturing process. For example, hides and entrails occur rather early in a packing house operation, while trimmings usually result from final dressing operations. These various production and cost flow possibilities in joint product and by-product environments present unique cost allocation problems.

There are two main reasons why joint product cost allocations are important. First, all product costs must be assigned to inventory to meet requirements for financial reporting, regulatory accounting, and income tax purposes. The assignment of costs to inventories provides for the proper identification of manufacturing costs with cost-of-goods-sold, work-in-process, and finished-goods inventories. Second, for some industries production costs are assigned to goods and services sold in order to derive a selling price. For example, the prices charged by regulated utilities are usually related to the cost of supplying the services. Therefore, accountants should understand the joint product manufacturing environment and know (*a*) what methods are available for allocating joint product costs, (*b*) how to account for by-products, and (*c*) what impact joint product cost allocations have on management decisions.

JOINT PRODUCT COST ALLOCATION METHODS

There are several ways to allocate joint costs to products. These cost allocations are made for purposes of inventory valuation and subsequent income determination. Inventory values are important because they affect (*a*) financial position through the amount of inventory shown on the balance sheet and (*b*) net income through a company's cost of goods sold shown on the income statement.

The following situation illustrates the various accounting methods available for allocating joint product costs. In one of its operations, Chemical Company uses Alpha as primary input and produces two products, Beta and Gamma. Alpha is refined in a common process that produces unfinished Beta and Gamma. Unfinished Beta can be sold for $.34 per pound or further refined in a separate process to yield finished Beta, which is saleable at $1.60 per pound. Unfinished Gamma can also be sold at a price of $.26 per pound or receive additional work in a separate process yielding finished Gamma, which has a sales price of $1.80 per pound.

Approximately 400,000 pounds of Alpha are processed each accounting period with Beta and Gamma being produced in the following proportions:

Product	Quantity (lbs)
Beta	250,000
Gamma	150,000
Total	400,000

At a normal level of processing the following manufacturing costs are typical when both unfinished Beta and Gamma are further refined. The costs incurred beyond the split-off point that are identifiable with specific joint products are called separable costs or direct product costs.

	Joint Product Costs	Separable Costs	
		Beta	Gamma
Materials	$ 60,000	$ 64,700	$ 14,600
Labor	25,000	139,300	146,000
Overhead	15,000	42,000	29,400
	$100,000	$246,000	$190,000

The basic assumptions in the previous situation are modified as required to illustrate various cost allocation alternatives. However, the question is how should the $100,000 joint product cost of processing Alpha be allocated to the resulting joint products Beta and Gamma?

Physical Measures

Physical measures such as units, weight, or volume may be used as a basis for allocating joint costs. For example, assume that the Chemical Company uses pounds of output as the basis for allocating joint costs. Since the company produces 400,000 total pounds of Beta and Gamma, $250/400_{ths}$ and $150/400_{ths}$ of the total joint cost of $100,000 is allocated respectively to Beta and Gamma. By expressing the allocation formula as an average unit cost, common costs are allocated to the joint products at the rate of $.25 per pound ($100,000 ÷ 400,000 pounds). The following general formula can be used to make this computation:

$$\text{Cost per unit of physical measure} = \frac{\text{Total joint product cost}}{\text{Units of physical measure}}$$
$$\text{(i.e., weight, volume, etc.)}$$

The amount of joint product cost allocated to each joint product is then calculated by multiplying the cost per unit of physical measure by the total units of physical measure for each product as follows:

Joint Product	Pounds Produced	Cost per Pound	Joint Costs Allocated
Beta	250,000	$.25	$ 62,500
Gamma	150,000	.25	37,500
			$100,000

Care should be exercised to insure that the same unit of measure is used for the allocation of costs to joint products. For example, joint products for export may be measured in liters or kilograms, while other joint products may be measured in pounds or cubic feet. In those instances where joint products are measured using different units of measure, it is necessary to convert them to a common term before cost allocation. For example, in the manufacture of coke, gas measured in cubic feet and liquids measured in gallons are converted to pounds per ton of coal processed before joint costs are allocated.

A variation in the use of physical measures as an allocation base is to assign relative weights to each joint product. These weights are intended to reflect significant factors in the production process that relate to the amount of joint cost that should be allocated to each product. The amount of time consumed, the type of labor utilized, the difficulty of the process, the size of the product, or the amount of material consumed may all be relevant weighting factors. To implement this technique, relative weights in the form of "points" are assigned to each product and then used as multiplication factors in the joint cost allocation process. For example, assume that Beta and Gamma are assigned weights of 8 and 20 because of the relative difficulty of handling each product. Using weighted pounds produced as the allocation base, joint costs are allocated as follows:

Joint Product	Pounds Produced	Weight (Points)	Weighted Units	Joint Costs Allocated
Beta	250,000	8	2,000,000	$ 40,000[a]
Gamma	150,000	20	3,000,000	60,000[b]
			5,000,000	$100,000

[a] (2,000,000 ÷ 5,000,000) × $100,000 = $40,000
[b] (3,000,000 ÷ 5,000,000) × $100,000 = $60,000

The use of a physical measure as an allocation base adequately accomplishes the task of spreading the cost of production in proportion to physical units produced. Also, the use of a physical measure is easy to understand and apply. However, these cost allocations typically have no relationship with the revenue-producing potential of individual joint products. Therefore, managers and accountants are cautioned that analysis of product profitability should not be based on data containing joint cost allocations. The allocation process is inherently arbitrary and may produce results that give a distorted view of the relative profitability of different products. Such distortions may lead to improper management decisions. For example, if weight is used to allocate the joint costs of slaughtering cattle, then steak would have the same per-pound cost as tongue, tail, or hamburger. Because of this, some cuts may consistently be very profitable, while other cuts may consistently show losses inconsistent with economic reality.

Market Measures

Market measures are the most popular basis for allocating joint product costs. Two market measures commonly used are relative sales value and expected realizable value. The popularity of these measures arises from the belief that costs should be allocated on a basis related to the revenue-generating power of the joint products. The assumption is that the greatest proportion of joint product costs should be assigned to the joint product with the highest revenue-generating power. The least joint product cost should be assigned to the joint products with the lowest revenue-generating power.

Underlying the use of market measures is the notion that market prices reflect the actual costs incurred to produce each joint product. If this view is taken, then joint costs should be allocated based on relative market values. Even if the opposite view is taken, the use of market measures is still useful because gross profit statistics remain the same for all products when using market measures; that is, gross profit statistics do not become biased by joint cost allocations when using market measures. This feature is very important for proper appraisal of profit performance.

Relative Sales Value   A common market measure used to allocate joint costs is the predicted **relative sales value** of joint products in the ordinary course of business. A product's relative sales value is its estimated sales price at the split-off point. For example, Chemical Company sells both Beta and Gamma as unfinished products and uses their relative sales value as the basis for allocating joint costs. The predicted market value for Beta is $85,000 (250,000 units $\times$ $.34 per unit) and $39,000 (150,000 units $\times$ $.26 per unit) for Gamma. This gives a total predicted market value of $124,000 ($85,000 + $39,000) of which Beta represents 68.5% ($85,000 ÷ $124,000) and Gamma represents 31.5% ($39,000 ÷ $124,000). Based on these percentages, the joint product cost of $100,000 incurred in the common process is allocated as follows:

Joint Product	Pounds Produced	Market Price (per pound)	Total Market Value	Percentage Weighting	Joint Costs Allocated
Beta	250,000	$.34	$ 85,000	68.5%	$ 68,500
Gamma	150,000	.26	39,000	31.5%	31,500
			$124,000	100.0%	$100,000

In summary, the amount of joint product cost allocated to each product is determined as follows. First, total expected sales value is found by multiplying the predicted sales price of each joint product by total expected unit sales. Joint costs are then allocated to joint products based on each joint product's proportionate share of the predicted total sales value.

When products are not processed beyond the split-off point, as in the previous example, each joint product has the same gross profit rate when using relative sales values as the allocation base. As indicated, it is quite unlikely that joint products will have the same gross profit rate when using physical measures. This can be shown by comparing results in partial income statements for Chemical Company prepared first by using a market measure to allocate joint costs and then by using a physical measure to allocate joint costs. For simplicity, assume that there are no beginning inventories held by Chemical Company and that all production is sold during the current period.

The joint cost allocations of $68,500 for Beta and $31,500 for Gamma calculated in the previous example using a market measure are used in the following partial income statement:

Partial Income Statement
(Joint Product Costs Allocated Using a Market Measure)

	Total	Beta	Gamma
Sales	$124,000	$85,000	$39,000
Cost of goods sold	100,000	68,500	31,500
Gross profit	$ 24,000	$16,500	$ 7,500
Gross profit rate	19%	19%	19%

The gross profit rate is the same for each joint product when using a market measure. These results are contrasted with gross profit rates obtained when joint costs are allocated using a physical measure. The following partial income statement uses joint cost allocations of $62,500 for Beta and $37,500 for Gamma, which were calculated in the previous section using pounds of output as the allocation base.

Partial Income Statement
(Joint Product Costs Allocated Using a Physical Measure)

	Total	Beta	Gamma
Sales	$124,000	$85,000	$39,000
Cost of goods sold	100,000	62,500	37,500
Gross profit	$ 24,000	$22,500	$ 1,500
Gross profit rate	19%	26%	4%

Management needs to be aware that when physical measures are used to allocate joint product costs gross profit statistics can be significantly different than when using a market measure. If management is not aware of this phenomenon, the effects of joint cost allocations may be mistakenly attributed to some other factor or management decision.

Expected Realizable Value   Assume that Beta and Gamma are sold immediately after split-off. However, there may *not* be a market for joint products at the split-off point and management may have no choice but to process beyond the split-off point. On the other hand, management may decide to process products beyond the split-off point for economic reasons even though there may be a market for these joint products. When joint products are processed beyond the split-off point, the relative market values of the joint products *at the split-off point* should still be used as the market measure for allocating joint costs. However, when price quotations are not available for joint products at the split-off point, the best alternative basis for allocating joint costs is the expected realizable value of the joint products at the split-off point.

Expected realizable value is defined, for purposes of joint cost allocations, as the ultimate predicted selling price of a joint product less anticipated costs of completion and sales. Expected realizable values are found by first calculating the ultimate expected market value of joint products and then working backwards to obtain expected realizable values at the split-off point. Joint product costs are then allocated based on expected realizable values *as though* they are actual market values at the split-off point. Thus, the expected realizable value actually represents a hypothetical market value at the split-off point.

Assume that there is no market for either unfinished Beta or unfinished Gamma. This indicates that both products require additional processing to place them in a marketable condition. The expected costs of separate processing beyond the split-off point, also referred to as separable costs, are $246,000 for Beta and $190,000 for Gamma at the normal production volume of 250,000 pounds of Beta and 150,000 pounds of Gamma. The ultimate selling price for Beta is $1.60 per pound and for Gamma is $1.80 per pound. From this data it is possible to calculate the net sales value of Beta and Gamma as follows:

Joint Product	Pounds Produced	Ultimate Market Price (per pound)	Ultimate Market Value	Less: Costs Beyond Split-off Point	Expected Realizable Value
Beta	250,000	$1.60	$400,000	$246,000	$154,000
Gamma	150,000	1.80	270,000	190,000	80,000
					$234,000

If there are marketing or administrative costs incurred after the split-off point that are associated with individual joint products, such costs are handled the same as manufacturing costs beyond the split-off point and should also be subtracted to arrive at a product's expected realizable value.

After calculation, the net sales values of joint products are used on a percentage basis to allocate joint costs in the same fashion as when using actual market values. To illustrate, the joint cost of $100,000 to process Alpha into Beta and Gamma is allocated as follows when using expected realizable value as an allocation base:

Joint Product	Expected Realizable Value	Percentage Weighting	Joint Costs Allocated
Beta	$154,000	65.8%	$ 65,800
Gamma	80,000	34.2	34,200
	$234,000	100.0%	$100,000

Remember that expected realizable values are actually hypothetical or artificial market values and only represent a next best alternative to using actual market values at the split-off point. This means that whenever a market exists for intermediate products at the split-off point, relative sales values should be used. This guide should be followed even though some joint products may have a market at the split-off point, while others must be processed further before a market is available. Therefore, actual market values may be used along with hypothetical market values (expected realizable values) as the basis for allocating joint costs.

The following partial income statement presents the results of joint cost allocations when there is processing beyond the split-off point. Once again it is assumed for simplicity that there are no beginning inventories and that all production is sold in the current period.

Partial Income Statement

	Total	Beta	Gamma
Sales	$670,000	$400,000	$270,000
Cost of goods sold:			
Joint costs	$100,000	65,800	34,200
Costs beyond split-off	436,000	246,000	190,000
Total cost of goods sold	$536,000	$311,800	$224,200
Gross profit	$134,000	$ 88,200	$ 45,800
Gross profit rate	20%	22%	17%

Note that in the previous illustration gross profit rates for joint products are different even though a market measure is used as an allocation base. Gross profit rates remain the same only when there is no processing beyond the split-off point. If management does not want joint cost allocations to bias gross profit statistics then the following modification can be made to the joint cost allocation process. First, the overall gross profit rate is calculated to determine what gross profit rate should be assigned to each joint product. Then, joint cost allocations are determined by subtracting from the ultimate market value of joint products (a) the amount of gross profit using the overall gross profit rate and (b) costs beyond the split-off point. The following schedule illustrates this calculation using information and the overall gross profit rate of 20% from the previous example:

	Total	Beta	Gamma
Ultimate market value	$670,000	$400,000	$270,000
Less: Gross profit of 20%	134,000	80,000	54,000
Total cost	$536,000	$320,000	$216,000
Less: Costs beyond split-off	436,000	246,000	190,000
Joint cost allocation	$100,000	$ 74,000	$ 26,000

The joint product cost allocation of $74,000 for Beta and $26,000 for Gamma derived in the illustration above is used in the following partial income statement to show that this revised allocation process results in the same gross profit rate for each joint product. Sales amounts and assumptions are the same as in previous partial income statements.

Partial Income Statement

	Total	Beta	Gamma
Sales	$670,000	$400,000	$270,000
Cost of goods sold:			
Joint costs	$100,000	74,000	26,000
Costs beyond split-off	436,000	246,000	190,000
Total cost of goods sold	$536,000	$320,000	$216,000
Gross profit	$134,000	$ 80,000	$ 54,000
Gross profit rate	20%	20%	20%

ALTERNATIVES TO MAKING JOINT PRODUCT COST ALLOCATIONS

Even though there are difficulties with each of the joint cost allocation methods, firms subject to the external reporting requirements of the Securities and Exchange Commission, Financial Accounting Standards Board, Cost Accounting Standards Board, Federal Trade Commission, Internal Revenue Service, and other such bodies must make cost allocations where appropriate to value inventories. Although there are a number of acceptable ways to allocate joint costs, the choice of methods affects the reported results of operations as demonstrated in this chapter. Due to the arbitrary nature of cost allocations, information about a company can be improperly interpreted resulting in improper decisions. For these reasons the management of some companies avoids making joint cost allocations whenever possible.

The main purpose for making joint cost allocations is to determine inventory values. Therefore, if cost allocations are to be avoided, other methods for valuing inventories that do not rely on joint cost allocations must be found. Several alternatives are available for making such inventory valuations. The first alternative is to simply carry inventories at their sales value at the split-off point or, if price quotations are unavailable, at their net sales value. As separable costs are incurred, they are added to this initial inventory value to obtain the total inventory value at any point during processing. Remember that the net sales value is a joint product's ultimate sales value less anticipated costs to complete and sell the product. The use of sales values has some merit in situations where products experience a rapid turnover or where profit margins are very small. Where there is rapid turnover and the time between products being inventoried and sold is very short, the probability that products will be sold at prevailing prices is quite high. This rationale gives some justification to carrying products at sales value. For example, perishable goods may be valued at their sales value.

A major difficulty with carrying inventories at sales value is that by doing so income is recognized before there is a sales transaction. To avoid the difficulty of recognizing profits before they are realized, another alternative to making joint cost allocations is to subtract a normal profit from a product's net sales value. For example, assume that Chemical Company has 10,000 pounds of Beta in inventory at the end of the period and uses its sales less a normal gross profit of 20% of sales to value its inventory. The following schedule shows how the Beta inventory would be valued assuming a market price of $.34 per pound for Beta:

Sales value of Beta (10,000 units × $.34 per pound)	$3,400
Less: Normal gross profit (.20 × $3,400)	680
Inventory carrying value	$2,720

Actual samples of this alternative can be found in the meat packing, mining, and canning industries.

ACCOUNTING FOR BY-PRODUCTS

Even though by-products are simply joint products with a relatively minor sales value, there are significant differences between accounting for joint products and accounting for by-products. The major difference revolves around the question of whether or not any inventory cost should be assigned to by-products before they are sold. Some feel that by-products should be assigned part of the joint manufacturing costs and accounted for as any other joint product. However, others feel that since, by definition, by-products have a minor value no costs should be assigned to them at the time of production. Rather, at the time by-products are sold the net amount realized should be shown on the income statement either as revenue or as a reduction in manufacturing costs. These differing views, the accounting procedures necessary to implement them, and some practical and theoretical considerations for deciding which approach to adopt are discussed in the following sections.

Assigning a Cost to By-products at the Time of Production

Assigning a cost to by-products at the time of production most nearly resembles the accounting methods used to allocate joint costs. The inventory cost assigned to by-products using this method is the net sales value of by-products *produced*. Net sales value is estimated by subtracting from the expected market value of the by-products produced (*a*) any anticipated separable manufacturing costs of further processing and (*b*) any marketing or administrative costs necessary to complete and dispose of the by-products. The accounting procedure used to recognize the value of by-products is to debit a by-product inventory account and credit work in process for the amount of the net sales value assigned to the by-products produced. (Note that this journal entry reduces the amount of joint product costs to be allocated among joint products. The remaining joint product costs are allocated to joint products using one of the methods previously discussed in this chapter.)

To illustrate the accounting procedure used for by-products consider the following situation. Chemical Company uses Alpha as a primary input to produce two joint products, Beta and Gamma, and a by-product, Sigma. After some additional processing subsequent to split-off, Sigma can be sold for $.50 per pound. Assume for simplicity that Beta and Gamma are sold at the split-off point for $.34 and $.26 per pound. Assume that production is in the following proportions:

Product	Quantity (pounds)
Beta	250,000
Gamma	150,000
	400,000
Sigma	50,000
Total	450,000

The joint manufacturing costs incurred in the common process to produce these quantities of Beta, Gamma, and Sigma total $100,000. Separable costs required to further process Sigma to place it in a saleable condition are as follows:

	Cost (per pound)
Material	$.04
Labor	.03
Overhead	.02
Marketing and administrative	.01
	$.10

Using the net sales value of Sigma as a basis, the task at hand is to assign a cost to the 50,000 pounds of Sigma produced in the common process. The net sales value of Sigma at the time of production is $20,000 [50,000 pounds *produced* × $.40 ($.50 − $.10) per pound]. Therefore, $20,000 of work in process is reclassified as by-product inventory, the cost associated with the by-product produced during the current period.

Also assume that 48,000 pounds of Sigma are sold during the period. If there is no beginning by-product inventory, 2,000 pounds of Sigma will remain in inventory at the end of the period. The ending balance in the inventory account is then $800 (2,000 pounds × $.40 per pound). The following journal entries illustrate the accounting process:

1. At the time of production the by-product inventory account is charged with the expected net sales value of the by-products produced.

| By-product inventory | 20,000 | |
| Work in process | | 20,000 |

2. As subsequent processing costs are incurred to place the by-products in a marketable condition, actual manufacturing costs are charged to the by-product inventory account. It is assumed that 48,000 pounds of Sigma have been processed and sold.

By-product inventory	4,320	
Material (48,000 × .04)		1,920
Payroll (48,000 × .03)		1,440
Overhead applied (48,000 × .02)		960

Figure 11.2   Income statement—cost assigned at the time of production

Sales, joint products	$117,800[a]
Cost of goods sold:	
Gross production costs	$100,000
Less: net sales value of by-products produced	20,000
Net production costs	$ 80,000
Less: ending inventory of joint products	4,000[b]
Cost of goods sold	$ 76,000
Gross margin	$ 41,800
Less: marketing/administrative expenses	10,000
Income from operations	$ 31,800

[a]Sales: Beta—250,000 × .95 × $.34 = $ 80,750
        Gamma—150,000 × .95 × $.26 =   37,050
                                                              $117,800

[b].05 × $80,000 = $4,000.

3. Marketing and administrative costs are also charged to the by-product inventory account as they are incurred.

By-product inventory   480
    Marketing/administrative expense (48,000 × .01 = 480)   480

4. There are 48,000 pounds of Sigma sold for cash at $.50 per pound.

Cash   24,000
    By-product inventory (48,000 × .50 = 24,000)   24,000

The following ledger account summarizes the above transactions and verifies that the ending balance in the by-product inventory account is $800 as previously calculated.

By-product Inventory

(1)	20,000	24,000	(4)
(2)	4,320		
(3)	480		
	24,800	24,000	
Bal.	800		

For simplicity, the above illustration assumes that the 2,000 pounds of Sigma on hand at the end of the period have not been processed beyond the split-off point. If these units had received additional processing or if marketing or administrative costs had been incurred on their behalf then the by-product inventory account would include the net sales value of the by-products *plus* any other separable manufacturing, marketing, or administrative costs incurred *beyond* the split-off point.

An income statement using this method of accounting for by-products is shown in figure 11.2. To clearly illustrate how using this method of accounting for by-products affects the amount of production costs being inventoried, it is assumed that 95% of each joint product produced during the period is sold at the split-off point.

Note in figure 11.2 that the net sales value of by-products is deducted from the total cost of joint products produced resulting in a reduced amount to allocate between Beta and Gamma, the joint products in this situation. As a result, $80,000 is allocated to the joint products Beta and Gamma rather than $100,000 that would have been al-located if by-products were not assigned an inventory value. This results in a reduced per-unit cost for joint products. Even though a balance sheet is not illustrated, the by-product inventory is treated in the same way on the balance sheet as finished-goods inventory.

Recognizing the Cost of By-products at the Time of Sale

Another approach to by-product accounting is to maintain memorandum records of the physical amount of by-products produced and on hand without assigning any monetary cost to by-products produced. Then, when by-products are sold, the amount of net revenue actually realized is reported on the income statement either as revenue or as a reduction of total manufacturing costs of joint products.

This method avoids time consuming and often complicated cost allocations and is justified with the rationale that the production of by-products is simply a coincidental and unavoidable result of manufacturing the main joint products. The rationale is that since no manufacturing costs are directly incurred for the purpose of producing by-products no part of the joint costs incurred should be allocated to by-products. Rather, net revenue received from the sale of by-products is handled on the income statement as either (a) additional sales revenue, (b) a reduction in the cost of production, (c) a reduction in the cost of sales, or (d) other income.

The amount of net revenue from by-products *sold* is the amount of gross revenue received less (a) any separable costs incurred beyond the split-off point to place the by-products in a salable condition and (b) any marketing or administrative costs incurred to dispose of the by-products.

To illustrate, assume the same facts regarding Sigma as contained in the preceding illustration. As previously calculated, gross revenue from the sale of Sigma is $24,000 (48,000 pounds $\times$ $.50 per pound). Separable manufacturing, marketing, and administrative costs applicable to by-products sold is $4,800 (48,000 pounds $\times$ $.10 per pound). Therefore, the net revenue realized from the sale of by-products is $19,200 ($24,000 − $4,800). Figure 11.3 shows how the net revenue of $19,200 is presented on an income statement using each of the four alternative methods of accounting.

There is no balance sheet illustrated. Even though there are 2,000 pounds of Sigma on hand at the end of the period there is no financial disclosure required when using this method because no manufacturing costs are assigned to by-products. The manufacturing costs that would have been assigned to by-products when using the previous method are instead part of the costs associated with the joint products either sold during the period or in ending inventory. However, note in figure 11.3 that when by-product costs are shown as a reduction of the cost of production the joint product ending inventory is less than under other accounting treatments resulting in slightly lower net income.

Comparison of the Two Methods

There are practical as well as theoretical considerations in selecting which method to use to account for by-products. Theoretically, assigning a net sales value to by-products at the time of production has the most appeal because it results in a better matching of costs and revenues. However, the additional effort involved in making cost allocations and maintaining financial inventory records may encourage the recognition of by-product values at the time of sale rather than at the time of production. Another drawback when assigning an inventory value to by-products is that there is no assurance that the by-products can be sold at the same market price that prevailed when the inventory value was established. Therefore, as a practical matter, the stability of the market for by-products and the reliability of estimates of future market prices favor recognizing the value of by-products at the time of sale.

Timing effects related to the recognition of revenues and expenses represent the major difference between the accounting results when using these methods. For example,

Figure 11.3   Income statement—cost assigned at the time of sale

	As Sales Revenue	As a Reduction of the Cost of Production	As a Reduction of the Cost of Sales	As Other Income
Sales, joint products	$117,800	$117,800	$117,800	$117,800
Sales, by-products	19,200			•
Total	$137,000	$117,800	$117,800	$117,800
Cost of goods sold:				
Gross production costs	$100,000	$100,000	$100,000	$100,000
Less: sales of by-products		19,200		
Net production costs	$100,000	$ 80,800	$100,000	$100,000
Less: ending inventory of joint products	5,000[a]	4,040[b]	5,000	5,000
Cost of goods sold (gross)	$ 95,000	$ 76,760	$ 95,000	$ 95,000
Less: sales of by-products			19,200	
Cost of goods sold (net)	$ 95,000	$ 76,760	$ 75,800	$ 95,000
Gross margin	$ 42,000	$ 41,040	$ 42,000	$ 22,800
Less: marketing/ administrative expenses	10,000	10,000	10,000	10,000
Income from operations	$ 32,000	$ 31,040	$ 32,000	$ 12,800
Revenue from sale of by-products				19,200
Income before taxes	$ 32,000	$ 31,040	$ 32,000	$ 32,000

[a] .05 × 100,000 = 5,000
[b] .05 × 80,800 = 4,040

if by-product inventories are sold within two accounting periods, net income will be the same using either method when the two periods are taken together. Since the basic difference between the two methods is timing some feel that by-product value should be recognized at the time of sale in business situations where by-product quantities are relatively constant from period to period and where by-product prices are relatively stable.

JOINT COSTS AND MANAGEMENT DECISIONS

There are a number of manufacturing situations in which management must decide whether joint products should be processed beyond the split-off point or simply sold at the split-off point. For example, meat packers must decide whether to sell meat as cut or to continue the curing and packing process. Petroleum refiners must decide what combination of processes and final products will yield the most profit.

The decision to sell or process further hinges on expected future costs and revenues and *not* on how joint costs are allocated or on the method used to account for by-products. Joint cost allocations are simply not relevant to the decision to sell or process further. Relevant costs and revenues (or, in economic terms, incremental costs and incremental revenues) are expected future costs that differ among decision alternatives (see chap. 20). The key to making appropriate management decisions is to compare expected future costs (incremental costs) with expected future revenues (incremental revenues).

Figure 11.4   Comparison of incremental costs and revenue

Incremental Price from Selling Finished Versus Unfinished Products

Product	Price for Unfinished Product	Price for Finished Product	Incremental Price
Beta	$.34	$1.60	$1.26
Gamma	.26	1.80	1.54

Incremental Revenue

Product	Incremental Price	Units of Production	Incremental Revenue
Beta	$1.26	250,000	$315,000
Gamma	1.54	150,000	231,000

Comparison of Incremental Costs with Incremental Revenue

Product	Incremental Revenue	Incremental Costs[a]	Profit (Loss)
Beta	$315,000	$246,000	$ 69,000
Gamma	231,000	190,000	41,000
Total	$546,000	$436,000	$110,000

[a]Amounts are developed in a prior illustration.

The focus is on the *future* and incremental costs and revenues. Since joint costs are *past* costs at the split-off point they are not relevant to the decision to sell or process further.

Although it is true that joint manufacturing costs are relevant for the decision by Chemical Company to engage in the business of processing Alpha, once that decision has been made, the decision to process Beta and Gamma beyond the split-off point does not depend on joint costs but rather on expected future costs and expected future revenues. To illustrate, let's examine the situation presented earlier and determine if it is in fact an appropriate decision to process Beta and Gamma beyond the split-off point. Expected future costs are assumed to consist only of separable manufacturing costs relating to Beta and Gamma of $246,000 and $190,000 respectively. Figure 11.4 contains an analysis of expected future costs and revenues that differ between the decision alternatives to sell or process further.

From the analysis in figure 11.4 it is clear that the company should process both Beta and Gamma beyond the split-off point. By doing so, net income will increase by a total of $110,000 over what it would be if the joint products are sold at the split-off point. The analysis also indicates that neither joint costs nor the method used to allocate joint costs is relevant since they are not future or incremental costs. These results can be verified by preparing (*a*) an income statement assuming sale at the split-off point and (*b*) an income statement assuming sale after further processing and comparing net income under each assumption. The incremental approach provides a more efficient vehicle for making such decisions.

The difficulty encountered if joint costs are considered in such decisions is illustrated by assuming that *finished* Gamma has a selling price of $1.65 rather than $1.80, a reduction of $.15 per unit in incremental revenues. Repeating the analysis indicates

---

Figure 11.5   Comparison of incremental costs and revenue

Incremental Price from Selling Finished Versus Unfinished Products

Product	Price for Unfinished Product	Price for Finished Product	Incremental Price
Beta	$.34	$1.60	$1.26
Gamma	.26	1.65	1.39

Incremental Revenue

Product	Incremental Price	Units of Production	Incremental Revenue
Beta	$1.26	250,000	$315,000
Gamma	1.39	150,000	208,500

Comparison of Incremental Costs with Incremental Revenue

Product	Incremental Revenue	Incremental Costs[a]	Profit (Loss)
Beta	$315,000	$246,000	$ 69,000
Gamma	208,500	190,000	18,500
Total	$523,500	$436,000	$ 87,500

[a]Amounts are developed in a prior illustration.

---

that even at this lower price it is profitable to process Beta beyond the split-off point. See figure 11.5 for this analysis.

However, if the analysis is made on a total cost basis (which includes joint costs) rather than on an incremental cost basis (which excludes joint costs), there are conflicting results depending on which joint cost allocation method is used. For example, assume that the physical measure using relative weights is used to allocate joint costs. As illustrated earlier the amount of allocated joint costs is $60,000 and the amount of separable costs of processing beyond the split-off point is $190,000. Using this data, an analysis on a total cost basis indicates that processing Gamma beyond split-off is unprofitable as indicated below:

Total market value of Gamma ($1.65 × 150,000 units)		$247,500
Total cost to produce Gamma:		
Allocated joint costs	$60,000	
Separable costs of further processing	190,000	250,000
Loss from processing Gamma		$ (2,500)

If the physical measure of units of production is used to allocate joint costs, the amount of allocated joint costs is $31,500, as illustrated earlier, rather than $60,000. The separable costs of processing beyond the split-off point remain at $190,000 using either assumption. However, due to different allocated joint costs the results on a total cost basis indicate that it is profitable to process Gamma as indicated below:

Total market value of Gamma ($1.65 × 150,000 units)		$247,500
Total cost to produce Gamma:		
Allocated joint costs	$ 31,500	
Separable costs of further processing	190,000	221,500
Gain from processing Gamma		$ 26,000

This inconsistency shows how reliance on irrelevant information such as joint cost allocations may interfere with the decision process. In this situation management could become confused and decide not to process Gamma beyond the split-off point when in reality not doing so would cause net income to decline. Therefore, joint cost allocations should not be used for deciding whether a product should be sold at the split-off point or processed further. Neither should joint costs be used in an analysis of the profitability of different product lines.

Summary

Joint products, and therefore joint product costs, are part of a large variety of manufacturing environments. Accounting for joint product costs focuses on three general questions. First, how should joint costs be allocated to joint products and by-products? Second, what are the available methods of accounting for by-products? Finally, what impact, if any, do joint product costs have on deciding whether a product should be sold at the split-off point or processed further?

There are two general bases used to allocate joint product costs—physical measures and market measures. Physical measures use units, weight, or volume as the basis for allocating joint product costs. A variation in the use of physical measures is to assign relative weights to each joint product in addition to using units, weight, or volume as the allocation base. Market measures use the expected realizable value of the joint products at the split-off point as the allocation base. If there is no available market for the joint product at the split-off point, then hypothetical sales values may be used as an allocation base. Since joint product cost allocations are inherently arbitrary some firms avoid making cost allocations wherever possible. In such instances, inventory carrying values for joint products are usually set equal to their expected sales values less a normal gross profit.

There are two general methods of accounting for by-products. First, by-products may be assigned a value at the time of production equal to their estimated net sales value. Second, no inventoriable costs are assigned to by-products; rather, net revenue realized from the sale of by-products is recognized on the income statement of the period of sale. There are many practical and theoretical questions to consider when deciding which method of accounting is appropriate for a given business situation.

Joint product cost allocations are made for purposes of product costing and income determination. Joint product costs are not relevant in the decision to process beyond the split-off point. Such decisions should be based on expected future costs, which differ between the decision to process further or to sell at the split-off point.

Self-Study Problem

Lester Company processes Wizon in Department 1 where it is split off into products X, Y, and Z. Product X is sold at the split-off point with no further processing. Products Y and Z require further processing to finish them before they can be sold. Product Y is finished in Department 2 and product Z is finished in Department 3. The following is a summary of costs and other related data for the year ending December 31, 19X2.

	Department		
	1	2	3
Direct labor	$28,000	$ 90,000	$130,000
Manufacturing overhead	20,000	42,000	98,000
	$48,000	$132,000	$228,000

	Product		
	X	Y	Z
Gallons processed	60,000	60,000	120,000
Gallons on hand at December 31, 19X2	20,000	-0-	30,000
Sales (in dollars)	$60,000	$192,000	$283,500

The cost of Wizon purchased during the year was $192,000. There were no inventories on hand on January 1, 19X2, and there was no Wizon on hand on December 31, 19X2. All products on hand at year end were complete as to processing, and there were no cost variances.

Required

1. Calculate the total amount of joint costs to allocate among products X, Y, and Z at December 31, 19X2.
2. Allocate total joint costs to products X, Y, and Z using market measures as an allocation base.
3. What is the total cost of product Y sold during the year?
4. Product X could have been processed in Department 4 at a total separable cost of $1.20 per unit. The market price for finished product X is $2.50 per unit. Did management make the appropriate decision to sell product X at the split-off point?

Solution to the Self-Study Problem

Requirement 1

The total joint costs to be allocated:

	Department 1
Materials (cost of Wizon)	$192,000
Direct labor	28,000
Manufacturing overhead	20,000
Total	$240,000

Requirement 2

The allocation of joint costs based on market measures:

Product	Units Produced	Ultimate Market Price (per unit)	Ultimate Market Value	Less: Costs Beyond Split-off Point	Expected Realizable Value
X	60,000	$1.50[a]	$ 90,000	$ -0-	$ 90,000
Y	60,000	3.20[b]	192,000	132,000	60,000
Z	120,000	3.15[c]	378,000	228,000	150,000
					$300,000

[a] $60,000 ÷ (60,000 − 20,000 = 40,000 units) = $1.50 per unit
[b] $192,000 ÷ 60,000 units = $3.20 per unit
[c] $283,500 ÷ (120,000 − 30,000 = 90,000 units) = $3.15 per unit

Product	Expected Realizable Value	Percentage	Joint Costs Allocated
X	$ 90,000	30%	$ 72,000
Y	60,000	20%	48,000
Z	150,000	50%	120,000
	$300,000	100%	$240,000

Requirement 3

Total cost of product Y sold for the year:

	Costs
Joint costs allocated	$ 48,000
Costs beyond split-off	132,000
Total	$180,000

Requirement 4

Decision to sell product X at the split-off point:

	Product X (per unit)
Ultimate selling price	$2.50
Selling price at split-off	1.50
Incremental price	$1.00
Less: Incremental cost	1.20
Difference	$ (.20)

Yes, management made the correct decision to sell product X at the split-off point since incremental costs exceed the incremental price for further processing.

Suggested Readings

Feller, R. E. "Accounting for Joint Products in the Petroleum Industry." *Management Accounting* (September 1977): 41–44, 48.

Jensen, Daniel L. "A Class of Mutually Satisfactory Allocations." *Accounting Review* (October 1977): 842–56.

Louderback, J. G. "Another Approach to Allocating Joint Costs: A Comment." *Accounting Review* (July 1976): 683–85.

Moriarity, Shane. "Another Approach to Allocating Joint Costs." *Accounting Review* (October 1975): 791–95.

Nurnberg, H. "Joint and By-product Costs." In *Handbook of Cost Accounting,* edited by S. Davidson and R. L. Weil. New York: McGraw-Hill, 1978.

Plet, E. J. "Extra Bonus from Technology: Silver, Film and Other Salvage." *Newspaper Controller* (August 1981): 1 and 10.

Discussion Questions

1. Define and contrast joint product, by-product, and scrap. Give examples of each.
2. Describe the impact changing market values might have on the classification and accounting for joint products and by-products.
3. Define and contrast joint cost and separable cost and tell at what stage in the manufacture of joint products each typically occurs.
4. Define the relationship of the split-off point to joint costs and separable costs.
5. Discuss the general methods available for the allocation of joint costs and describe the strengths and weaknesses of each.
6. When weights are used in connection with a physical measure to allocate joint costs, what do these weights represent?
7. If management feels that the allocation of joint costs should have no effect on the firm's gross profit rate, what allocation method should be used? Why?
8. Define expected realizable value and describe the market condition that would lead to its use in the allocation of joint costs.
9. Describe how costs that are incurred beyond the split-off point are incorporated in the calculation of net sales values.
10. Discuss the alternatives available for costing inventories if joint cost allocations are not made.
11. Describe how sales prices might be adjusted when they are used as the basis for assigning a cost to joint product inventories.
12. Describe the two general methods for accounting for by-products. Which method is most closely related to accounting for joint costs?
13. Discuss the various income statement presentations that would be made when using either method of accounting for by-products.
14. Describe some theoretical and practical considerations in deciding which method of accounting for by-products should be adopted in a particular business situation.
15. Why do joint cost allocations have limited usefulness for planning and control decisions? What type of costs are relevant for planning and control decisions?

16. Describe the method of cost analysis that yields valid results when management needs to decide if a joint product should be processed beyond the split-off point.

Exercise 11.1 Joint Product Concepts (CPA)

1. When two products are produced during a common process, what is the factor that determines whether the products are joint products or one principal product and a by-product?
   a. Potential marketability for each product
   b. Amount of work expended in the production of each product
   c. Relative total sales value
   d. Management policy
2. If a company obtains two saleable products from the refining of one ore, the refining process must be accounted for as
   a. a mixed cost process.
   b. a joint process.
   c. an extractive process.
   d. a reduction process.
3. If two or more products share a common process before they are separated, the joint cost should be allocated so that
   a. a proportionate amount of the total cost is assigned to each product by means of a quantitative basis.
   b. it maximizes total earnings.
   c. it minimizes variations in a units of production cost.
   d. it does *not* introduce an element of estimation into the process of accumulating costs for each product.
4. Aronson Chemical Company produces three products from one initial material mix. After the products acquire separate identities, each requires additional processing. The costs of the initial processing, which will be allocated among the products in proportion to their relative market values, are known as
   a. imputed costs.
   b. original costs.
   c. prime costs.
   d. joint costs.

Exercise 11.2 Joint Cost Allocation Methods (CPA)

1. Each of the following is a method by which to allocate joint costs *except*
   a. relative sales value.
   b. relative profitability.
   c. relative weight, volume, or linear measure.
   d. average unit cost.
2. Which of the following components of production are allocable as joint costs when a single manufacturing process produces several saleable products?
   a. Materials, labor, and overhead
   b. Materials and labor only
   c. Labor and overhead only
   d. Overhead and materials only

3. Joint costs are most frequently allocated based upon relative
   a. profitability.
   b. conversion costs.
   c. sales value.
   d. prime costs.
4. One of the accepted methods of accounting for a by-product is to recognize the value of the by-product as it is produced. Under this method, inventory costs for the by-product would be based on
   a. an allocation of some portion of joint costs but not any subsequent processing costs.
   b. neither an allocation of some portion of joint costs nor any subsequent processing costs.
   c. subsequent processing costs less an allocation of some portion of joint costs.
   d. an allocation of some portion of joint costs plus any subsequent processing costs.
5. Joint product costs generally are allocated using
   a. relative sales value at split-off.
   b. additional costs after split-off.
   c. relative profitability.
   d. direct-labor hours.

Exercise 11.3 Joint Cost Allocations (CPA)

Forward Incorporated manufactures products P, Q, and R from a joint process. Additional information is as follows:

	Product			
	P	Q	R	Total
Units produced	4,000	2,000	1,000	7,000
Joint costs	$36,000	?	?	$ 60,000
Sales value at split-off	?	?	$15,000	$100,000
Additional costs if processed further	$ 7,000	$ 5,000	$ 3,000	$ 15,000
Sales value if processed further	$70,000	$30,000	$20,000	$120,000

Required

1. Assuming that joint costs are allocated using the relative sales value at split-off approach, what were the joint costs allocated to products Q and R?
2. Assuming that joint costs are allocated using the relative sales value at split-off approach, what was the sales value at split-off for product P?

Exercise 11.4   Joint Cost Allocations

Gilbert Manufacturing Company manufactures two products, Alt and Bat. Initially, they are processed from the same raw material and then, after split-off, they are further processed separately. Additional information is as follows:

	Alt	Bat	Total
Final sales value	$9,000	$6,000	$15,000
Joint costs prior to split-off point	?	?	6,600
Costs beyond split-off point	3,000	3,000	6,000

Required

Using the relative sales value approach, what are the assigned joint costs of Alt and Bat respectively?

Exercise 11.5   Joint Cost Allocations—Alternative Methods (CPA)

Vreeland Incorporated manufactures products X, Y, and Z from a joint process. Joint product costs were $60,000. Additional information is as follows:

Product	Units Produced	Sales Value at Split-off	Sales Values and Additional Costs If Processed Further	
			Sales Values	Additional Costs
X	6,000	$40,000	$55,000	$9,000
Y	4,000	35,000	45,000	7,000
Z	2,000	25,000	30,000	5,000

Required

1. Assuming that joint product costs are allocated using the physical measures (units produced) approach, what were the total costs allocated to product X?
2. Assuming that joint product costs are allocated using the relative sales value at split-off approach, what were the total costs allocated to product Y?

Exercise 11.6   Joint Cost Allocation by Relative Sales Value Method (CPA)

Miller Manufacturing Company buys zeon for $.80 a gallon. At the end of processing in Department 1, zeon splits off into products A, B, and C. Product A is sold at the split-off point with no further processing. Products B and C require further processing before they can be sold; product B is processed in Department 2 and product C is processed in Department 3. The following is a summary of costs and other related data for the year ending June 30.

	Department		
	1	2	3
Cost of zeon	$96,000	—	—
Direct labor	$14,000	$45,000	$65,000
Factory overhead	$10,000	$21,000	$49,000

	Products		
	A	B	C
Gallons sold	20,000	30,000	45,000
Gallons on hand at June 30	10,000	—	15,000
Sales in dollars	$30,000	$96,000	$141,750

There were no inventories on hand at the beginning of the year, and there was no zeon on hand at June 30. All gallons on hand at June 30 were complete as to processing. There were no factory overhead variances. Miller uses the relative sales value method of allocating joint costs.

Required

1. For allocating joint costs, determine the relative sales value of product A for the year ending June 30.
2. Determine the joint costs to be allocated for the year ending June 30.
3. Determine the cost of product B sold for the year ending June 30.
4. Determine the value of the ending inventory for product A.

Exercise 11.7   Joint Cost Allocation—Relative Sales Value Method

Sideways Company manufactures products A, B, and C from a joint process. Additional information is as follows:

	Product			
	A	B	C	Total
Units produced	8,000	4,000	2,000	14,000
Joint costs	$ 72,000	?	?	$120,000
Sales value at split-off	?	?	$30,000	$200,000
Additional costs if processed further	$ 14,000	$10,000	$ 6,000	$ 30,000
Sales value if processed further	$140,000	$60,000	$40,000	$240,000

Required

Assuming that joint costs are allocated using the relative sales value at split-off approach, determine the sales value at split-off for product A.

Exercise 11.8 Joint Cost Procedures—Sales Value Determination (CPA)

Stellar Corporation manufactures products R and S from a joint process. Additional information is as follows:

	Product		
	R	S	Total
Units produced	4,000	6,000	10,000
Joint costs	$36,000	$ 54,000	$ 90,000
Sales value at split-off	?	?	?
Additional costs if processed further	$ 3,000	$ 26,000	$ 29,000
Sales value if processed further	$63,000	$126,000	$189,000
Additional margin if processed further	$12,000	?	$ 40,000

Required

Assuming that joint costs are allocated on the basis of relative sales value at split-off, determine the sales value at the split-off point for product S.

Exercise 11.9 Joint Cost Allocation (CPA)

Superior Company manufactures products A and B from a joint process, which also yields the by-product X. Superior accounts for the revenues from its by-product sales as miscellaneous revenue. Additional information is as follows:

	Product			
	A	B	X	Total
Units produced	15,000	9,000	6,000	30,000
Joint costs	?	?	?	$270,000
Sales value at split-off	$290,000	$150,000	$10,000	$450,000

Required

Assuming that joint product costs are allocated using the relative sales value at split-off approach, determine the joint cost allocated to each product produced.

Exercise 11.10 Joint Cost Allocation (CPA)

The Rote Company manufactures products C and R from a joint process. The total joint costs are $60,000. The sales value at the split-off point was $75,000 for 8,000 units of product C and $25,000 for 2,000 units of product R. Assuming that total joint costs are allocated using the relative sales value at split-off approach, what were the joint costs allocated to product C?

Problems

Problem 11.1   Joint Cost Allocation—Sales Value at Split-off Point

Barker Electric Incorporated manufactures products *G, H,* and *I.* Additional information is given below:

	G	H	I	Total
Units produced	?	5,000	8,000	16,000
Joint cost	?	$25,000	?	$ 80,000
Sales value at split-off	?	?	$72,000	$120,000

Required

Fill in the missing blanks, assuming Barker used the sales value at split-off point for allocating joint costs.

Problem 11.2   Joint Cost Allocation—Relative Sales Value Method

The Harrison Corporation produces three products—Alpha, Beta, and Gamma. Alpha and Gamma are joint products while Beta is a by-product of Alpha. No joint cost is to be allocated to the by-product. The production processes for a given year are as follows:

In Department One, 110,000 pounds of raw material, Rho, are processed at a total cost of $120,000. After processing in Department One, 60% of the units are transferred to Department Two and 40% of the units (now Gamma) are transferred to Department Three.

In Department Two, the material is further processed at a total additional cost of $38,000. Then 70% of the units (now Alpha) are transferred to Department Four, and 30% emerge as Beta, the by-product, to be sold at $1.20 per pound. Selling expenses related to disposing of Beta are $8,100.

In Department Four, Alpha is processed at a total additional cost of $23,660. After this processing, Alpha is ready for sale at $5 per pound.

In Department Three, Gamma is processed at a total additional cost of $165,000. In this department, a normal loss of units of Gamma occurs that equals 10% of the good output of Gamma. The remaining good output of Gamma is then sold for $12 per pound.

Required

Prepare a schedule showing the allocation of the $120,000 joint cost between Alpha and Gamma using the relative sales value approach. The net realizable value of Beta should be treated as an addition to the sales value of Alpha.

Problem 11.3   Joint Cost Allocation (CPA)

Two independent situations are given below:

1. Andy Company manufactures products N, P, and R from a joint process. The
   following information is available:

| | Product | | | |
	N	P	R	Total
Units produced	12,000	?	?	24,000
Sales value at split-off	?	?	$50,000	$200,000
Joint costs	$ 48,000	?	?	$120,000
Sales value if processed further	$110,000	$90,000	$60,000	$260,000
Additional costs if processed further	$ 18,000	$14,000	$10,000	$ 42,000

Required

Assuming that joint product costs are allocated using the relative sales value at split-off
approach, determine the sales value at split-off for products N and P.

2. Kyle Company manufactures products S and T from a joint process. The sales
   value at split-off was $50,000 for 6,000 units of product S and $25,000 for
   2,000 units of product T.

Required

Assuming that the portion of the total joint costs properly allocated to product S using
the relative sales value at split-off approach was $30,000, what were the total joint costs?

Problem 11.4   Joint Products and Decision Analysis (CPA)

From a particular joint process, Watkins Company produces three products—X, Y, and
Z. Each product may be sold at the split-off point or processed further. Additional processing requires no special facilities, and production costs of further processing are entirely variable and traceable to the products involved. In 19X3, all three products were
processed beyond split-off. Joint production costs for the year were $60,000. Sales values
and costs needed to evaluate Watkins' 19X3 production policy follow:

| | | | Additional Costs and Sales Values If Processed Further | |
Product	Units Produced	Sales Value at Split-off	Sales Values	Added Costs
X	6,000	$25,000	$42,000	$9,000
Y	4,000	41,000	45,000	7,000
Z	2,000	24,000	32,000	8,000

Joint costs are allocated to the products in proportion to the relative physical volume of
output.

Required

1. For units of Z, determine the unit production cost most relevant to a sell or
   process further decision.
2. To maximize profits, determine which products Watkins should subject to
   additional processing.

Problem 11.5   Joint Cost Allocation—Alternative Methods

Johnson Electronic Corporation manufactures two products—A and B. The following information is available:

	A	B	Both
Joint manufacturing costs			$250,000
Direct costs	$75,000	$100,000	
Per-unit sales value at split-off point	$8	$8	
Per-unit sales value after further processing	$10	$15	
Unit production	15,000	10,000	

The same number of units were sold as produced during 19X2. The products are considered to be joint products.

Required

Determine the total cost and unit cost of product A and product B under the following assumptions:

1. Joint costs are allocated using sales value at the split-off point.
2. Joint costs are allocated using the average units produced method.

Problem 11.6   Joint Cost Allocations—Alternative Methods

Jefferson, Incorporated manufactures products X, Y, and Z from a joint process. Joint product costs were $120,000. The products are processed further. Additional information is as follows:

Product	Units Produced	Sales Value at Split-off	Sales Values	Additional Costs
			Sales Values and Additional Costs If Processed Further	
X	9,000	$90,000	$120,000	$15,000
Y	4,500	60,000	80,000	10,000
Z	4,500	50,000	65,000	5,000

Required

1. Determine the total costs assigned to products X, Y, and Z using the relative sales value at split-off approach.
2. Determine the total costs assigned to products X, Y, and Z using the units produced approach.

Problem 11.7   Joint Product Costing—Determining Total and Unit Costs

Doolittle Company produces two products from a single process. Product X, a liquid, can be sold for $2.35 per gallon at the split-off point and for $5 per gallon as a finished product. Product Y, a solid, can be sold for $3.25 per pound at the split-off point and for $4 per pound as a finished product.

During last year 400,000 gallons of X and 100,000 pounds of Y were produced. Joint costs were $1,200,000. Separate, or direct processing costs for the year were $600,000 for X and $120,000 for Y.

Required

Assume that X and Y are treated as joint products. Determine the total and unit costs for X and Y using the following methods:

1. Relative ultimate sales value
2. Sales value at the split-off point

Problem 11.8   Analysis on Further Processing Decisions—Joint Products (CMA)

The Cum-Clean Corporation produces a variety of cleaning compounds and solutions for both industrial and household use. While most of its products are processed independently, a few are related.

Grit 337 is a coarse cleaning powder with many industrial uses. It costs $1.60 a pound to make and has a selling price of $2.00 a pound.

A small portion of the annual production of this product is retained for further processing in the Mixing Department where it is combined with several other ingredients to form a paste, which is marketed as a silver polish selling for $4.00 per jar. This further processing requires 1/4 pound of Grit 337 per jar. Other ingredients, labor, and variable overhead associated with this further processing cost $2.50 per jar. Variable selling costs amount to $.30 per jar. If the decision were made to cease production of the silver polish, $5,600 of fixed Mixing Department costs could be avoided. Assume that the demand for Grit 337 is very poor and the company is considering alternative uses.

Required

Determine the minimum number of jars of silver polish that would have to be sold to justify further processing of Grit 337.

Problem 11.9   Sell at Split-off or Process Further Considerations

The following two situations are independent of each other.

1. Yardley Corporation uses a joint process to produce products *A, B,* and *C.* Each product may be sold at its split-off point or processed further. Additional processing costs are entirely variable and are traceable to the respective products produced. Joint production costs for 19X5 were $50,000 and are allocated by Yardley using the relative sales value at split-off approach. Relevant data follow:

			Sales Values and Additional Costs If Processed Further	
		Sales		
	Units	Value at	Sales	Additional
Product	Produced	Split-off	Values	Costs
A	20,000	$ 45,000	$60,000	$20,000
B	15,000	75,000	98,000	20,000
C	15,000	30,000	62,000	18,000
		$150,000		

Required

Determine which products Yardley should subject to further processing to maximize profits.

2. A company manufactures two joint products at a joint cost of $1,000. These products can be sold at the split-off point or when they have been further processed at an additional cost and sold as higher-quality items at a higher price.

Required

Describe the criteria a company like this one should use in deciding whether to sell each product at the split-off point or to process each product further. Include in your discussion reference to the role of the joint costs.

Problem 11.10   Joint Costs—Evaluation of Costing Results (CMA)

Doe Corporation grows, processes, cans, and sells three main pineapple products—sliced pineapple, crushed pineapple, and pineapple juice. The outside skin is cut off in the cutting department and processed as animal feed. The skin is treated as a by-product. Doe's production process is as follows:

1. Pineapples first are processed in the cutting department. The pineapples are washed and the outside skin is cut away. Then the pineapples are cored and trimmed for slicing. The three main products (sliced, crushed, juice) and the by-product (animal feed) are recognizable after processing in the cutting department. Each product is then transferred to a separate department for final processing.
2. The trimmed pineapples are forwarded to the slicing department in which the pineapples are sliced and canned. Any juice generated during the slicing operation is packed in the cans with the slices.

3. The pieces of pineapple trimmed from the fruit are diced and canned in the crushing department. Again, the juice generated during this operation is packed in the can with the crushed pineapple.
4. The core and surplus pineapple generated from the cutting department are pulverized into a liquid in the juicing department. There is an evaporation loss equal to 8% of the weight of the good output produced in this department. This loss occurs as the juices are heated.
5. The outside skin is chopped into animal feed in the feed department.

The Doe Corporation uses the net realizable value method (relative sales value method) to assign costs of the joint process to its main products. The by-product is inventoried at its market value.

A total of 270,000 pounds was entered into the cutting department during May. The schedule presented below shows the costs incurred in each department, the proportion by weight transferred to the four final processing departments, and the selling price of each end product.

Processing Data and Costs
May 1981

Department	Costs Incurred	Proportion of Product by Weight Transferred to Departments	Selling Price per Pound of Final Product
Cutting	$60,000	—	none
Slicing	4,700	35%	$.60
Crushing	10,580	28	.55
Juicing	3,250	27	.30
Animal feed	700	10	.10
Total	$79,230	100%	

Required

1. The Doe Corporation uses the net realizable value method to determine inventory values for its main products and by-products. Calculate the following:
   a. The pounds of pineapple that result as output for pineapple slices, crushed pineapple, pineapple juice, and animal feed
   b. The net realizable value at the split-off point of the three main products
   c. The amount of the cost of the cutting department assigned to each of the three main products and to the by-product in accordance with corporate policy
   d. The gross margins for each of the three main products
2. Comment on the significance to management of the gross margin information by main product.
3. In the production of joint products either a by-product or scrap could be generated.
   a. Distinguish between a by-product and scrap.
   b. Would the proper accounting treatment for scrap differ from that for by-products? Explain your answer.

MATERIALS AND LABOR: COSTING AND CONTROL

12

OUTLINE

A major objective of cost accounting is to accumulate and assign costs to cost objects such as units of production, departments, or other activities for which management desires a separate measurement or evaluation. This accounting effort is referred to as **costing. Control** is the ongoing process of implementing management's plans and providing feedback of actual results so that managers can evaluate performance and make any needed adjustments to keep operations in line with plans and objectives. Costing and control are interrelated because costing provides a fundamental component of feedback needed for management control. Together they provide the basis for an effective cost accounting system.

Chapters 12, 13, and 14 contain an in-depth examination of costing and control aspects of each manufacturing cost element—materials, labor, and overhead. The objective of these chapters is to explain how a cost accounting system can be designed to provide management with appropriate cost information necessary for the effective control of operations. After completing this chapter you should be able to:

1. handle purchase discounts, freight, and other materials acquisition costs.
2. distinguish between scrap, spoiled materials, and defective units and be able to apply the appropriate accounting treatment for each of these depending on the particular business situation.
3. develop a system of controls for materials handling.
4. use economic order quantity (EOQ) models in controlling the size of investment in inventories.
5. develop a system for costing and control of labor.
6. use learning curve and budgetary concepts in controlling labor costs.

MATERIALS COSTING

The cost of materials received is typically not the amount shown on a vendor invoice. For example, cash discounts and materials handling costs represent possible modifications to the invoice price. Also, the cost of materials received may not be the same as the cost of materials issued because of adjustments made for scrap, shortages, or defective units. Therefore, it is important to understand how materials costs are accumulated and assigned so accounting records reflect the actual cost of operations.

Materials Received

The vendor's invoice provides the basis for determining the cost of materials entered on the inventory records. It provides a description of each item, the quantity shipped, individual prices, freight charges, and the terms of sale. Trade and quantity discounts may also appear on the vendor's invoice. The effect of such discounts is to reduce the total price of materials purchased, and there is normally not an explicit accounting for either trade or quantity discounts.

Purchase Discounts   The terms of sale typically include any available **purchase discounts** also referred to as cash discounts. For example, a vendor may specify terms such as 2/15, n/30, which means that the buyer may deduct 2% from the total invoice price if payment is made within the discount period—in this example, 15 days after the invoice date. Otherwise, the total invoice amount is due within the payment period—in this example, 30 days. It is usually profitable to pay the invoice within the discount period, since purchase discounts are designed to make prompt payment an attractive alternative for the buyer. For example, with terms 2/10, n/30 on a $100 purchase the discount or cash price is $98 ($100 − $2 discount). Not taking the discount results in borrowing $98 for 20 (30 − 10) days and paying $2 for the privilege. Since there are approximately eighteen

20-day periods in a year, the effective interest rate is 36% (2/100 × 18). Therefore, the company should take the cash discount if it has the cash or can borrow money at an interest rate less than 36%.

The decision whether or not to take purchase discounts is a financing decision, and materials should be recorded at the invoice price less the amount of purchase discounts permitted, whether they are taken or not. This procedure is known as recording purchases net of discounts. Lost discounts are not considered an inventoriable cost. Rather, they should be treated as a separate item and shown on the income statement as a financing expense. For example, if a $1,000 purchase containing the terms 2/10, n/30 is paid after the discount period the following journal entry would be made if the payable had been recorded net of discounts:

Accounts payable	980	
Purchase discounts lost	20	
Cash		1,000

This procedure is designed to provide proper disclosure for management review of the total financing activity. Some firms elect to record purchases at the gross invoice amount and then record the amount of purchase discounts taken. However, this procedure does not automatically provide exception type information, which is usually preferred for management control.

Freight   Accounting theory recognizes that freight is an ordinary and necessary cost of materials. However, there are many different ways to handle freight charges depending on the business situation. For example, if the number of items received is relatively small or individually identifiable, such as when new automobiles are received at a dealership, it may be appropriate to calculate the transportation cost applicable to each item. However, when there are different items received representing various commodity classes and transportation rates, such as when lawn care equipment is shipped with garden chemicals, it may be very difficult to trace freight charges to specific items. In such instances it may be necessary to compute the relationship between the number of pounds in the shipment and then allocate freight charges on a per-pound basis. For example, if the freight charge on a shipment is $250 and the total weight of the items is 625 pounds, the average freight cost is $.40 per pound (625 pounds ÷ $250). Therefore, if a specific item weighed 130 pounds, it would be assigned a $52 freight charge.

If the number of items received is very large, procedures that are sound in theory do not always work in practice because of the volume of clerical operations that might be involved. A common practice in accounting for freight charges is to accumulate all freight cost in a single freight-in account and, as materials are issued and charged to work-in-process inventory, a portion of freight-in is also charged to the work-in-process inventory. The amount of freight going to work in process is based on previously estimated amounts of freight-in and total materials cost for an accounting period. For example, if total freight-in is estimated to be $8,000 and the total materials cost is estimated to be $160,000 during the next year, then freight-in would be applied to the work-in-process inventory at the rate of 5% of materials cost as follows:

$$\frac{\$8{,}000 \text{ estimated freight-in}}{\$160{,}000 \text{ estimated materials cost}} = 5\% \text{ application rate}$$

As materials are issued, the work-in-process inventory is debited with the cost of materials plus 5% for transportation costs. Freight-in is credited for 5% of the cost of materials issued. Assuming the freight-in application rate is 5%, the following journal entries are made when (*a*) $5,000 of materials are received with terms 2/10, n/30 and a freight charge of $275 and (*b*) $1,000 of materials are issued to production:

1. Receipt of incoming materials recorded net of discounts.

Freight-in	275	
Materials inventory (.98 × 5,000)	4,900	
Accounts payable		5,175

2. Issue of materials to production.

Work-in-process inventory	1,050	
Materials inventory		1,000
Freight-in (.05 × 1,000)		50

This same principle applies for indirect materials except that the factory overhead is debited rather than the work-in-process inventory. At the end of the accounting period, any balance remaining in the freight-in account is usually allocated between inventories and cost of goods sold or is simply closed to cost of goods sold.

Another method of accounting for freight is to estimate the total freight costs for the period and include this amount in the calculation of the factory overhead application rate. Using this method, the freight-in account is a subsidiary account under control of the factory overhead account as explained in chapters 13 and 14.

Other Acquisition Costs   Accounting theory also recognizes that other acquisition costs such as receiving, inspection, storage, insurance, and issuance costs that are ordinary and necessary to acquire, maintain, and position materials are proper additions to the cost of materials purchased. However, there are often practical limitations on the extent to which such costs are assigned to individual items received. The costs involved may not justify the clerical expense required to make cost allocations with a high degree of accuracy.

A procedure used to assign other acquisition costs to materials whenever it is not practical to charge individual units with their exact share of costs is to compute an application rate similar to the overhead application rate, and use it to assign costs in an approximate fashion. A rate is calculated for each materials-related function, such as purchasing, receiving, and warehousing. These rates are then used to apply other acquisition costs to the materials account.

Depending on which function is involved, there are a number of allocation bases that might be used to allocate other acquisition costs. For example, the cost of operating the purchasing department might be allocated to materials based on the estimated number of purchase orders processed or the estimated dollar volume of purchases. Receiving department costs might be allocated on the basis of the number of items or the tonage of materials received. Warehousing costs might be allocated on the basis of the dollar value of items or the number of square footage occupied. The selection of an appropriate base should be made on the strength of the relationship between each possible base and the actual utilization of materials related costs.

To illustrate the use of this method, data for a materials handling situation are presented below. The cost application rates for each department are found by dividing the estimated costs for the period by the estimated application base.

Department	Estimated Cost for the Period	Estimated Application Base	Application Rate
Purchasing	$100,000	5,000 purchase orders	$20 per purchase order
Receiving	50,000	$1,400,000 value received	$.04 per dollar value received
Warehousing	160,000	100,000 square feet	$1.60 per square foot

Assume that during the current month there were 420 purchase orders processed, $110,000 worth of materials received, and 8,500 square feet occupied. Under these conditions, the following journal entry would be made to record the application of other materials costs to the materials inventory:

Materials inventory	26,400	
Applied Purchasing Department expenses		8,400
(420 × $20 = $8,400)		
Applied Receiving Department expenses		4,400
($110,000 × $.04 = $4,400)		
Applied Warehouse Department expenses		13,600
(8,500 × $1.60 = $13,600)		

Actually distributing the $26,400 among different items or purchases could be very involved and time-consuming. Typically materials acquisition costs are applied to each product or to each invoice as it is processed. Therefore, the journal entry above may actually represent a summary of individual cost applications made for each invoice that was processed during the period.

The actual expenditures made to operate each of the materials related departments are accumulated in an "actual" departmental expense account. Due to forecast error or unexpected operating results the debit balance in the "actual" account may not equal the credit balance in the "applied" account. These differences are called overapplied materials acquisition costs if the applied amount is greater than actual costs or underapplied materials acquisition costs if the reverse is the case. Insignificant over- or underapplied amounts may not require management attention. However, significant amounts should trigger management review and analysis.

Over- or underapplied materials acquisition costs are closed at the end of an accounting period to either the cost-of-goods-sold account or directly to the income summary account. To illustrate, assume that the total actual cost of operating the purchasing department is $98,000 and that 5,100 purchase orders were processed during the period resulting in an applied amount of $102,000 (5,100 × $20). Assuming that the overapplied amount of $4,000 ($102,000 − $98,000) is closed to the cost-of-goods-sold account, the following journal entry is made for the purchasing department:

Applied Purchasing Department expenses	102,000	
Actual Purchasing Department expenses		98,000
Cost of goods sold		4,000

Rather than using two accounts, an applied and an actual account, many firms simply use a departmental expense control account with debits to the account representing actual expenditures and credits to the account representing applied amounts. Any balance in the account at the end of an accounting period represents over- or underapplied acquisition costs, which is closed to cost of goods sold or the income summary account. The end results are the same regardless of the account structure used.

Materials Issued

Accounting for materials issued is quite simple. For example, if materials requisitioned during the week total $8,000 for direct materials and $2,000 for indirect materials, the following journal entry is made:

Work-in-process inventory	8,000	
Factory overhead	2,000	
Materials inventory		10,000

Difficulties in accounting for materials issued arise when materials are purchased at different times at different prices. This results in different costs for essentially the same materials. When this occurs an assumption must be made about the flow of costs through the materials account. An intuitive approach would be to have the flow of costs coincide with the physical flow of units, but this is not a requirement. For example, one cost flow assumption may be used for internal management accounting while another may be used for financial statements and income tax purposes. The assumption used should give an accurate reflection of periodic income when costs are subtracted from revenues. There are three facets underlying this notion: first, the proper matching of costs and revenues; second, the costing of materials inventories transferred from period to period; and third, providing relevant information for evaluating company policies relating to the purchase, manufacture, and sale of materials.

There are three generally accepted cost flow assumptions or methods that may be applied to inventories whether they are materials, work in process, or finished goods. However, the method selected must be consistently applied for similar categories of materials. The three basic cost flow assumptions are first-in, first-out (FIFO), last-in, first-out (LIFO), and average cost.

The **FIFO** method assumes that the cost flow of materials resembles a cafeteria line—the first in are the first out. The cost of the first materials received is assumed to be the cost of the first materials issued. The assumption is that the oldest materials in stock are issued first.

The **last-in, first-out (LIFO) method** assumes that the cost flow of materials resembles a situation in which materials are figuratively placed in a barrel when they are received. As materials are requisitioned they are withdrawn from the top of the barrel with the last items received being the first items out. Therefore, the cost of the last materials received is assumed to be the cost of the first materials issued. The assumption is that the newest materials in stock are issued first.

The **average cost method,** as the name implies, uses the average cost of materials purchased to determine the cost of materials issued. The average cost of materials purchased can be calculated in several ways depending on how often the cost figure is to be revised. For example, a moving average can be calculated after each purchase of materials by dividing the total cost of materials available by the number of units on hand. Issues of materials are then recorded at that cost until the next purchase when a new moving average is calculated. Or, an average purchase cost for materials could be calculated monthly or quarterly and applied to materials issued during the corresponding future period.

Scrap Recovery

Scrap consists of material residues that occur in many manufacturing operations. Examples of scrap include shavings from the manufacture of furniture, flashing from the production of steel, and remnants from the manufacture of clothing. Scrap has a relatively minor recovery value and may be either reused or sold. For control purposes, scrap should be weighed, counted, or quantified by some expedient means and returned to the storeroom as soon as it is practical in order to prevent manipulation or theft. Maintaining records of scrap recovery is important because the production of excessive scrap may indicate inefficient operations. Actual amounts of scrap should be compared with standard or expected amounts and corrective action taken if there are unacceptable deviations from expectations.

There are many different methods used to account for scrap. The major difference between these methods relates to (*a*) whether the value of scrap is recorded at the time it occurs or (*b*) whether the value of scrap is recorded at the time it is sold. Deciding on the appropriate time to record the value of scrap depends on such factors as whether or not the sales value of the scrap is known, the materiality of the total value of scrap, the availability and stability of a market for scrap, and the expected time lag between the occurrence and sale of scrap. Scrap is typically recorded at the time it occurs if the following general conditions apply—the value of scrap is known, the total value of scrap is significant, there is a reasonably stable market for scrap, and there are frequent or regular sales of scrap.

Another element in deciding which method to use in accounting for scrap is whether scrap is considered to be (*a*) linked to a particular job or product, (*b*) an inevitable part of general manufacturing operations, or (*c*) a source of other income.

Accounting theory indicates that linking scrap to particular jobs or products is the most appropriate treatment. However, implementing such a procedure may present some problems. For example, associating scrap with each individual job or production run may not be feasible. The amount involved may not justify the additional accounting necessary to identify costs with jobs. However, if a significantly different amount of scrap is expected to occur because of individual job characteristics or if customers expect "scrap credits" on their individual jobs, then identifying scrap with individual jobs is the most appropriate accounting treatment.

When a normal, uniform amount of scrap results from manufacturing operations, it may be accurate enough, even in theory, to include scrap as part of the cost of general manufacturing operations included in factory overhead. This treatment does not link scrap with particular jobs. Rather, all production bears part of the cost of scrap by incorporating expected scrap recovery as part of the predetermined factory overhead application rate. This procedure eliminates the clerical burden of assigning scrap value to particular jobs. The actual result of incorporating a credit for scrap sales is to reduce the predetermined overhead application rate by the amount of the expected sales. This treatment is widely used in practice.

Scrap is also accounted for as a source of income because of the ease of applying this method. However, there are several theoretical difficulties with this treatment. For example, if the value of scrap is recorded at the time scrap occurs, then income from scrap sales may be recognized before the actual transaction to sell scrap takes place. However, as long as income from scrap sales is not significant, neither product costs nor periodic income will be materially misstated. Therefore, treating scrap as a source of other income represents an expedient accounting procedure when the amount of scrap is not significant and remains relatively constant from period to period.

The two methods of either recording scrap value when it occurs or when the scrap is sold when combined with the three costing treatments of either linking scrap to particular jobs or products, treating scrap as a part of general manufacturing operations, or considering scrap a source of other income results in six possible ways to account for scrap. Figure 12.1 contains an outline of the journal entries that would be made under each alternative method.

Spoiled Materials

Spoiled materials consist of production that contains significant imperfections or production that does not meet quality control standards. Spoiled materials are junked and usually sold for some disposal value. The distinction between spoiled materials and defective units is that the additional expenditure in materials, labor, and overhead needed to remedy the defects in spoiled units is greater than the additional revenue expected from the sale of the corrected units. Therefore, imperfect production can be treated as either spoiled materials or as defective units depending on whether imperfections can be economically remedied.

Accounting for spoilage in a process-costing environment was discussed in chapters 9 and 10. This chapter explains accounting for spoilage in a job-order costing environment. The accounting treatment used for the cost of spoiled materials depends on the nature of the spoilage. The cost of spoilage that results when machines and labor are operating at desired levels of precision should be allocated to all units produced during the period. This treatment recognizes that eliminating all spoilage is a very costly production in most manufacturing operations. Therefore, the cost of a normal level of spoilage is considered part of the overall cost of production. However, if spoilage is the result of unusual or unexpected conditions, such as very exacting specifications on a particular job, the cost of spoilage should be charged directly to particular jobs or production runs.

Figure 12.1   Journal entries for methods of accounting for scrap

Costing Treatment	Method 1 (Value assigned when scrap occurs)	Method 2 (Value assigned when scrap sold)

1. Scrap is linked to particular jobs or products	Scrap is returned to storeroom:
	 Scrap Material Inventory
	    Work-in-Process Inventory
	 Scrap is sold:
	 Cash or Accounts Receivable
	    Scrap Material Inventory
		Scrap is returned to storeroom:
		 No entry made
		
		 Scrap is sold:
		 Cash or Accounts Receivable
		    Work-in-Process Inventory

2. Scrap is part of general manufacturing operations	Scrap is returned to storeroom:
	 Scrap Materials Inventory
	    Factory Overhead
	 Scrap is sold:
	 Cash or Accounts Receivable
	    Scrap Materials Inventory
		Scrap is returned to storeroom:
		 Memorandum entry only
		
		 Scrap is sold:
		 Cash or Accounts Receivable
		    Factory Overhead

3. Scrap is a source of other income	Scrap is returned to storeroom:
	 Scrap Materials Inventory
	    Income from Sale of Scrap
	 Scrap is sold:
	 Cash or Accounts Receivable
	    Scrap Materials Inventory
		Scrap is returned to storeroom:
		 Memorandum entry only
		
		 Scrap is sold:
		 Cash or Accounts Receivable
		    Income from Sale of Scrap

Normal Spoilage   If spoilage is an inherent part of the manufacturing process, the cost of spoiled units is included as part of factory overhead. This is done by including an estimate of total spoilage costs in the predetermined overhead application rate, which subsequently applies to all units of production. To illustrate, assume that a company plans to produce 100,000 units of a particular product, 5% of which are expected to be defective and accounted for as spoilage. Spoiled units can be sold for $.80 each. Costs of production are expected to be:

	Per Unit
Materials	$ .50
Labor	.60
Overhead (200% of direct labor)	1.20
Total	$2.30

Incorporated in the overhead application rate is an $.08 per unit expected loss from spoiled materials. Given the above costs, the following summary journal entry would be made to account for the total costs of placing 100,000 units into production during the period:

Work-in-process inventory	230,000	
Materials (100,000 × $.50)		50,000
Labor (100,000 × $.60)		60,000
Overhead (100,000 × $1.20)		120,000

There were 5,000 units spoiled during the period. Their sale at $.80 each will result in a cost recovery of $4,000 ($.80 × 5,000). The journal entry to record the cost of spoiled units less cost recovery from their expected sale is as follows:

Spoiled materials inventory	4,000	
Actual factory overhead	7,500	
Work-in-process inventory		11,500
(5,000 × $2.30 per unit)		

As indicated above, the total cost of spoiled units was $7,500 ($2,500 materials + $3,000 labor + $6,000 overhead − $4,000 cost recovery = $7,500 cost of spoilage). However, each good unit of production was charged $.08 for spoilage as part of the overhead application rate for a total of $7,600 (95,000 good units × $.08 per unit) for a difference of $100 ($7,600 applied − $7,500 actual). This difference is the result of having slightly less spoilage during the period than had been expected. Such differences are accounted for as part of total over- or underapplied overhead.

To complete the accounting cycle, the following journal entry transfers the cost of the remaining 95,000 good units to the finished-goods inventory. It is assumed that all units started during the period were completed.

Finished-goods inventory	218,500	
Work-in-process inventory		218,500
(95,000 × $2.30 per unit)		

Abnormal Spoilage   Spoilage that is caused by unusual or unexpected factors such as exacting specifications or difficult processing requirements is called **abnormal spoilage.** The cost of these spoiled units should be charged to particular jobs. However, if the spoilage is due to an oversight or error on the part of the manufacturer, then the cost of abnormal spoilage should not be charged to the individual job but should receive a separate accounting.

To illustrate accounting for abnormal spoilage caused by adherence to exacting specifications, assume the same basic cost data as in the illustration above, except that a special order for 2,000 units was processed with special specifications. Production records indicate that the normal spoilage rate triples when attempting to meet such specifications. As a result, 2,300 units are actually placed in production to obtain the required 2,000 good units of output. The proper accounting procedure under these circumstances is to charge the cost of spoiled units directly to the job rather than spreading the cost of spoiled units over all units produced. Therefore, to properly assign the cost of lost units to this job, the number of units charged to this job is not the 2,000 good units delivered but the 2,300 total units produced to obtain the 2,000 good units.

The following summary journal entry is made to record the total costs placed into production for this particular job. Assume that spoiled units are not discovered until the end of the manufacturing process.

Work-in-process inventory	5,290	
Materials (2,300 × $.50)		1,150
Labor (2,300 × $.60)		1,380
Applied overhead (2,300 × $1.20)		2,760

Just as before, these spoiled units can be sold for $.80 each. Given this information, the following journal entry would be made:

Spoiled materials inventory (300 × $.80)	240	
Work-in-process inventory		240

Finally, the cost of the 2,000 good units relating to this job would be transferred to the finished-goods inventory with the following journal entry:

Finished-goods inventory ($5,290 − $240)	5,050	
Work-in-process inventory		5,050

The amount transferred to the finished-goods inventory is the total manufacturing cost for this order (including the cost of spoiled units) less the expected sales value of spoiled goods. The total cost for this order is $2.53 per unit ($5,050 ÷ 2,000 units) compared with $2.30 per unit for regular production when a normal rate of spoilage is applied as part of factory overhead. Therefore, abnormal spoilage will typically result in different per-unit costs for each job depending on the spoilage rate.

Finally any difference between the expected value recorded for spoiled materials inventory and the actual amount realized can be handled in one of two ways. Any difference can be allocated among work in process, finished goods, or costs of goods sold depending on the completion status of production during the period. Or, as an expedient, the difference can be simply closed to factory overhead.

Defective Units

Defective units contain imperfections that can be economically reworked so they can be subsequently sold at or near regular prices. Accounting for defective units parallels accounting for spoiled materials. If defective units are a random occurrence during normal manufacturing operations, then the additional reworking costs required to correct defects are charged to overhead and allocated to all units produced. To accomplish this, an estimate of rework costs is made at the beginning of the period and included as part of the predetermined overhead application rate. However, if defective units are the result of unusual specifications or job-related requirements, the cost of reworking defective units is charged directly to those particular jobs.

To illustrate, consider a situation in which the following summary entry is made to accumulate manufacturing costs incurred during the current period. Overhead is applied at 200% of direct-labor cost.

Work-in-process inventory	90,000	
Materials		30,000
Labor		20,000
Applied overhead		40,000

Additional costs were incurred because several units were found to be defective. These units were subsequently reworked and transferred to finished goods as first-quality units. Rework costs consisted of $2,000 for materials and $3,000 for labor. Overhead is applied as a cost of rework at the regular overhead application rate. Assuming that these defective units occurred as a normal, expected part of manufacturing operations, then the following journal entries would be made to first record the cost of rework and then transfer the cost of all completed units to the finished-goods inventory. It is assumed that there are no work-in-process inventories at the beginning or end of the period.

1. To record the cost of reworking defective units:

Actual factory overhead	11,000	
Materials		2,000
Labor		3,000
Applied factory overhead		6,000

2. To transfer completed units to finished-goods inventory:

| Finished-goods inventory | 90,000 | |
| Work-in-process inventory | | 90,000 |

An estimate of total rework costs would have been included in the calculation of the overhead application rate at the beginning of the period. Through this mechanism the cost of reworking defective units is spread over all units of production as a normal cost of operations. As a result, overhead applications are higher than if rework costs are identified with specific jobs. Any difference between the estimated rework costs and actual rework costs is handled as part of over- or underapplied overhead.

Assuming that in the illustration above defective units resulted from specific job requirements, the cost of reworking defective units is charged to particular jobs. The following journal entries would be made to first record the cost of rework and then transfer the cost of completed units to the finished-goods inventory:

1. To record the cost of reworking defective units:

Work-in-process inventory	11,000	
Materials		2,000
Labor		3,000
Applied factory overhead		6,000
Posting to work-in-process Subsidiary Ledger:		
Job no. 13–967	5,000	
Job no. 14–878	4,000	
Job no. 18–347	2,000	

2. To transfer completed units to finished-goods inventory:

Finished-goods inventory	101,000	
Work-in-process inventory		101,000

The journal entries above identify the cost of correcting defective units with each specific job responsible for their occurrence.

MATERIALS CONTROL

Materials control has many important aspects. Materials of the desired quality must be on hand at the appropriate time and in the right location to support manufacturing operations. The procedures for handling materials should guard against waste, misuse, spoilage, and obsolescence. There are also several important ways in which the size of investment in inventory can be controlled.

Purchasing Materials

Procedures for acquiring materials should be established with the following objectives in mind. First, materials should be purchased only when a need exists. Second, materials of the desired quality should be purchased at the most favorable price. Third, payment for materials should be approved only on materials received and in good condition. Finally, someone should be responsible for physically safeguarding materials from the time of receipt. To accomplish these objectives, the organization should provide a clear description of responsibilities and an accounting system with built-in checks and balances. Typically, four organizational functions are involved in the materials acquisition cycle—stores, purchasing, receiving, and accounting. Figure 12.2 outlines the relationships and functions of these organizational areas.

The purchasing cycle typically begins with a *purchase requisition,* which is usually initiated in the stores department. The need to order materials usually results from a physical check or a computer system that senses that the quantity of materials on hand is at the reordering minimum. Other purchase requests may come from engineering, research, or other departments when there are special needs for materials. Also, requests may come from job managers and supervisors who foresee unusual quantity demands. In any event, all acquisition requests should be processed through one department such as the stores department with approved purchase requisitions providing initial authorization for purchases.

The materials requisition contains descriptions, quantities, stock numbers, and other necessary purchasing information. It is sent to the purchasing department where

Figure 12.2   Materials purchasing procedures

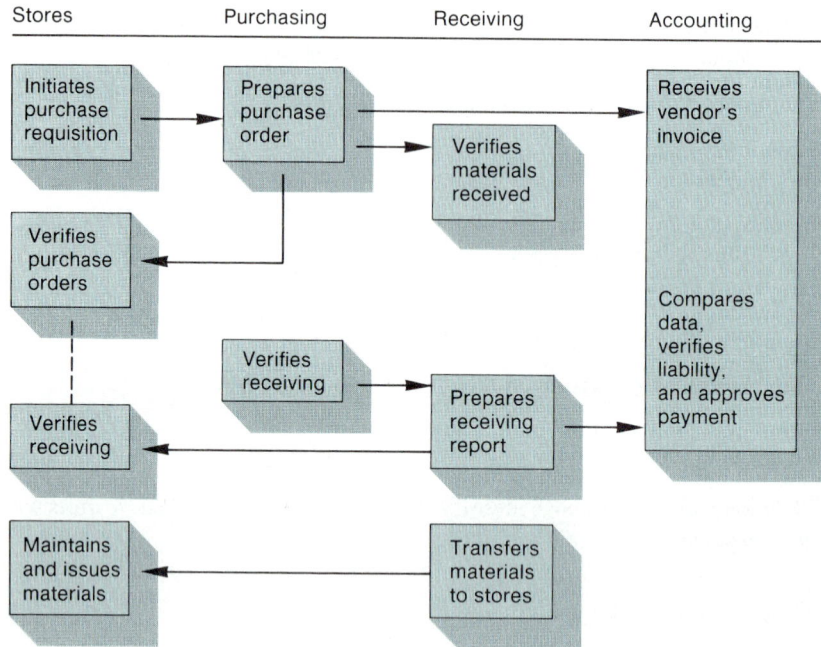

Stores	Purchasing	Receiving	Accounting
Initiates purchase requisition	Prepares purchase order	Verifies materials received	Receives vendor's invoice
Verifies purchase orders			
Verifies receiving	Verifies receiving	Prepares receiving report	Compares data, verifies liability, and approves payment
Maintains and issues materials		Transfers materials to stores	

the actual ordering takes place. The stores department keeps a copy of the purchase requisition to verify, at a later date, that all purchase requests have been processed and that materials have been received. The purchasing department then prepares a *purchase order,* which is a written authorization to a vendor to supply materials. A purchase order should be issued for every materials acquisition even if the order is placed by telephone or with a sales representative. The purchase order contains a complete description of items ordered, prices, terms, shipping instructions, required delivery dates, and other information needed to identify materials of the desired specifications and quality.

The original purchase order is sent to the vendor. Additional copies are generated and distributed internally for control purposes. For example, a copy is usually supplied to the originator of the purchase requisition as evidence that a purchase order has been processed and as a cross-check on the accuracy of information. The receiving and accounting department also receive copies in anticipation of their role when materials are received and payment is made. Finally, the purchasing department keeps a copy to verify, at a later date, that all items ordered have been received.

Upon receipt of materials, the receiving department prepares a *receiving report,* which details what items were actually received and indicates if any damage occurred in transit. Bills of lading, packing lists, and a copy of the original purchase order are attached to the receiving report to be used for cross-checking and as support for transportation or other acquisition costs to be paid.

The receiving department keeps a copy of the receiving report and sends all primary documents to the accounting department where they are matched with the vendor's invoice. A copy of the receiving report is also sent to the purchasing department to verify that materials ordered have been received. If all items on a purchase order are not received, follow-up should determine if the purchase order should be kept "open" anticipating that the remainder of the order will be received or if it should be cancelled. If cancelled, a new purchase order may need to be executed with the same or another vendor who can and will supply the needed materials. A copy of the receiving information is also sent with the materials to the stores department. The receiving information is used to update inventory records.

The accounting department assembles a copy of the purchase order, the receiving report, and the vendor's invoice and compares prices, terms, and quantities, and checks for arithmetical accuracy. If materials have been received as ordered, the invoice is approved for payment and the finance department issues a check.

The size of the company or the type of business may result in more extensive or modified purchasing procedures. For example, some hardware wholesalers perform only cursory counts in the receiving department because the cost of detailed counts, such as counting each nut and bolt, would be unreasonably expensive. Occasional check counts of significant items and reliance on the basic integrity of vendors and their own accounting systems is usually the most cost effective approach.

Maintaining and Issuing Materials

The stores department is responsible for receiving, safeguarding, handling, issuing, and maintaining appropriate accounting records for materials. Materials are typically safeguarded by designating individuals who are responsible, by using secured areas for storage, and by issuing materials only for authorized purposes. The primary accounting concern relates to the record keeping that should accompany the physical movement of materials. As materials are delivered to the stores department, inventory records should be updated with the quantity of items and the date received. Records in the form of bin cards, ledger sheets, or computer files are typically maintained for each individual item. Materials are issued based on a *materials requisition,* which is an authorized order to issue or deliver materials for a particular purpose or job. The completed materials requisition has two purposes. First, it is the basis for accumulating the cost of materials charged to the work-in-process inventory account. When materials are issued for maintenance or other general factory usage, the materials requisition is the basis for charges to the actual factory overhead account. A copy of the materials requisition is sent to the accounting department for recording of costs. Second, the materials requisition, as well as the receiving report, is the basis for maintaining physical accountability for materials in inventory.

Economic Order Quantity (EOQ) Models

Materials control is a vital concern for management because there is typically a relatively large investment carried in inventories. Depending on the type of industry and the characteristics of individual firms, a manufacturing company has approximately one third of its total investment in inventories. No wonder managers are concerned with minimizing the cost of acquiring, handling, and maintaining inventories. However, management is also concerned with having sufficient inventories available to cushion the effects of uneven flows in the receipt, production, and sale of goods. These and other factors influence the cost benefit tradeoffs that make inventory control especially challenging. For example, consider the cost of carrying sufficient inventory to facilitate production and sales. Management must include the following costs in their decision making:

1. Investment of working capital or interest on borrowed capital
2. Storage or warehousing
3. Handling
4. Deterioration, shrinkage, or obsolescence
5. Property taxes and insurance

However, the cost of *not* carrying sufficient inventories includes:

1. Idle time, overtime, extra setup time because of disruptions in production due to stockouts
2. Higher prices, extra purchasing, transportation, and handling costs because of frequent small orders
3. Lost sales and loss of customer goodwill
4. Extra managerial and clerical burden to handle stockout and back order situations

Materials management requires a trade off between the conflicting costs of carrying sufficient inventories and the costs of *not* carrying sufficient inventories. To make management's task even more difficult, some of these costs such as the cost of lost sales and the loss of customer goodwill are difficult to quantify. Materials management is so important that many techniques for planning and controlling inventories have been developed. These techniques typically focus on fundamental questions regarding *when* and *how much* inventory to order. Some techniques used for low-volume, low-cost inventories are very simple and easily implemented, and require little cost to operate. Others used for high-volume, high-cost inventories are rather complex and rely on computer technology to implement.

A simple but effective technique used to manage low-value, noncritical items is called a two-bin system. Using this method, inventory is separated by some means into two bins—a main bin and a reserve bin. To begin the cycle, both bins are full and materials are issued from the main bin. The reserve bin contains enough inventory to satisfy requirements from the time an order is placed for more inventory until the time when goods are received. When the main bin becomes empty, a purchase requisition is initiated and the reserve bin is tapped until the order arrives. When the materials arrive both bins are replenished and another inventory cycle begins.

Another more sophisticated approach involves calculating an economic order quantity (EOQ) to determine *how much* should be purchased at a time. Then, production and sales schedules are used to determine *when* orders of this size should be placed.

EOQ is the order quantity that minimizes the *total* of (*a*) the cost of ordering plus (*b*) the cost of carrying inventory. Finding the point at which the total of these costs is at a minimum requires knowledge of how these costs behave. The cost of ordering and the cost of carrying inventory have an inverse relationship. As order size is increased, the average amount of inventory on hand also increases and the cost of handling and carrying inventory increases. However, as order size is increased, fewer orders are needed to satisfy total requirements and the cost of placing and receiving orders decreases. With one cost increasing and the other cost decreasing as a function of order size, there is an ideal order size at which the cost of ordering plus the cost of carrying inventory is at a minimum. The order size where this occurs is called the **economic order quantity (EOQ)**. These cost relationships and a graphical determination of EOQ are presented in figure 12.3.

In addition to a graphical approach, EOQs can be calculated by using either a tabular approach for approximate results or a formula for exact results. The following EOQ calculations illustrate both of these approaches.

The data items required to calculate the EOQ for a particular inventory item are:

1. A forecast of the total quantity of units required during an accounting period
2. The cost of placing an order
3. The cost of carrying one unit of inventory in stock for one accounting period

Figure 12.3   Economic order quantity (EOQ)

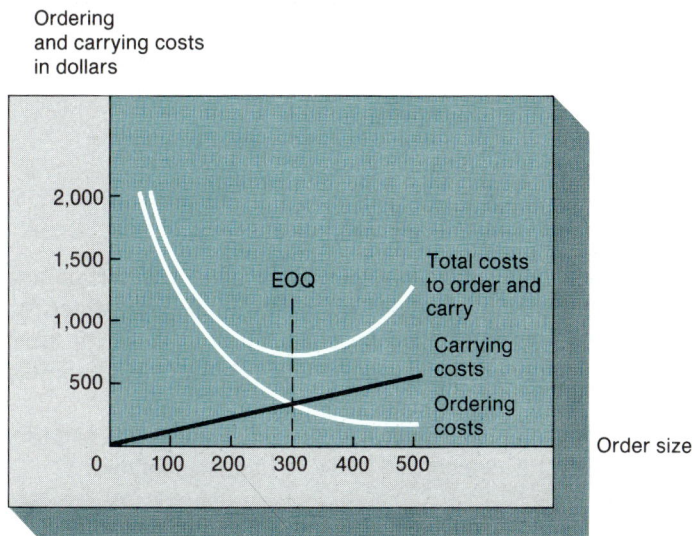

Figure 12.4   Tabular calculation of economic order quantity (EOQ)

Annual Requirement	5,000	5,000	5,000	5,000	5,000
Order size	100	200	300	400	500
Number of orders (annual requirement ÷ order size)	50	25	17	13	10
Total ordering costs (number of orders × $18 per order)	$ 900	$ 450	$ 306	$ 234	$ 180
Average inventory (order size ÷ 2)	50	100	150	200	250
Total carrying costs (average inventory × $2 per unit)	$ 100	$ 200	$ 300	$ 400	$ 500
Total ordering and carrying costs	$1,000	$ 650	$ 606	$ 634	$ 680

For example, a company uses a particular item for which the following statistics have been gathered:

Annual materials requirements	5,000 units
Cost of placing an order	$18 per order
Carrying costs	$2 per unit per year

When using the tabular approach, the first step is to arbitrarily select a number of order sizes near what is thought to be the EOQ. Then, the number of orders that are required to satisfy total requirements is calculated by dividing total requirements by each respective order size. The total costs of ordering and carrying inventories are then calculated using the procedures outlined in figure 12.4.

The final step is to select the order size with the minimum total cost. The order size with the minimum total cost is the EOQ. The minimum in this case is $606 at an EOQ of approximately 300 units. Note that the graphical solution in figure 12.3 and the tabular solution in figure 12.4 relate to the same inventory situation.

A formula that can be used to calculate precise EOQ results is as follows:

$$EOQ = \sqrt{\frac{2RO}{C}}$$

where
R = Total materials requirements for one period
O = Cost of placing an order
C = Cost of carrying one unit of inventory for one period

The mathematical determination of this formula and certain assumptions underlying its use are explained in the appendix at the end of this chapter. When using the EOQ formula use the same time period for both R and C. Also, for firms that express carrying cost as a percentage of unit cost, C can be replaced with "unit cost × carrying cost percentage."

Using the data presented earlier with R = 5,000 units, O = $18 per order, and C = $2 per unit, the EOQ is determined to be 300 units as follows:

$$\sqrt{\frac{2 \times 5,000 \times 18}{2}} = 300$$

The EOQ of 300 units found using both methods is simply the result of a chance selection of the right order size when using the tabular method.

The EOQ model presented has a major shortcoming in that it does not contain all relevant costs that affect the order size decision. For example, neither the total purchase price nor a provision for quantity discounts are included in this model. Such items are important if, for example, a firm does not have adequate financing or if for other reasons it may need to purchase in quantities less than the EOQ. Also, the availability of quantity discounts may shift the EOQ to a larger order size. To illustrate, assume that the following discount schedule is available for the EOQ situation shown in figure 12.4:

Order Size (Units)	Quantity Discount
0–99	0%
100–199	4
200–299	5
300–399	6
400 +	8

Incorporating these quantity discounts results in the EOQ being shifted from 300 to approximately 400 units as illustrated by the order size with the minimum total annual cost in figure 12.5. There are advanced models that are used when such factors are considered, but they are not presented in this text.

EOQ answers the question *how much* to order. Several other factors must be considered before answering the question *when* to order. Typically, what happens is that a **reorder point** is established so that as the number of units on hand declines, a purchase requisition is triggered when the reorder point is reached. The order point is set depending on (*a*) **lead time,** the time between placing an order and having the materials delivered, (*b*) **safety stock,** an added cushion of inventory maintained to protect against stockouts, and (*c*) the average rate of inventory usage. To illustrate how the order point is set, consider the previous situation with annual usage equal to 5,000 units and an EOQ of 300 units. Assuming that there are 50 productive weeks in a year, the weekly usage of this item is 100 units per week (5,000 units ÷ 50 weeks). By examining records of prior purchases, it is determined that there is an average lead time of two weeks for the delivery of this item. Therefore, if there is no requirement for safety stock the order point is set

Figure 12.5   Calculation of economic order quantity (EOQ) with quantity discount

Order size	100	200	300	400	500
Total ordering and carrying costs[a]	$ 1,000	$ 650	$ 606	$ 634	$ 680
Total cost of materials (5,000 units × $3 per unit)	$15,000	$15,000	$15,000	$15,000	$15,000
Less: applicable discount	600	750	900	1,200	1,200
Net cost of materials	$14,400	$14,250	$14,100	$13,800	$13,800
Total annual cost	$15,400	$14,900	$14,706	$14,434	$14,480

[a]From figure 12.4.

Figure 12.6   Rate of usage, lead time, and order point

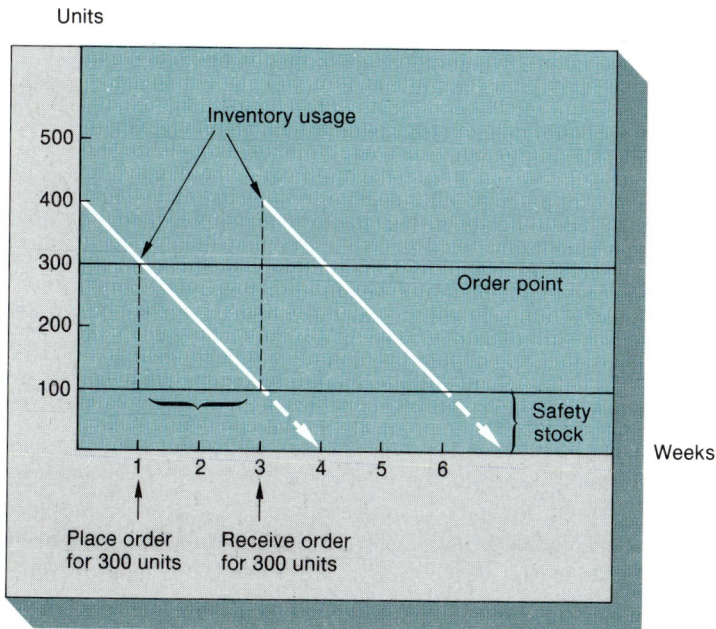

at 200 units (2 weeks × 100 units per week). As inventory declines a purchase requisition is initiated when the quantity on hand reaches 200 units. Inventory continues to decline for the next two weeks while the order is processed and goods are in transit. The inventory level finally reaches zero just as the new order is received. However, if the order is delayed for some reason or if there is an unexpectedly high usage for this item, a stockout situation will exist until the order is received. Therefore, management decides that a one week supply of this item should be maintained as *safety stock* to protect against stockouts. This would increase the order point to 300 units (1 + 2 = 3 weeks × 100 units per week). The relationships among lead time, safety stock, and inventory usage are illustrated in figure 12.6.

Figure 12.6 assumes that 400 units are on hand at the beginning of the inventory cycle. Inventory declines from that point to the order point, 300 units, by the end of the first week of operations and an order is placed. The order is received in two weeks as expected, and the total inventory quantity is restored to its beginning level and the cycle starts over. The layer of safety stock provides a one-week cushion for delayed orders or other unexpected usage of this item.

Several observations should be noted about EOQ. First, with only slight modification, the EOQ formula and procedures are equally appropriate in computing the optimum size of a production run. The formula used to obtain an EOQ for production runs is as follows:

$$EOQ = \sqrt{\frac{2RS}{C}}$$

where
R = Total production requirements for one period
S = Setup costs for a production run (adjust machines, etc.)
C = Cost of carrying one unit of inventory for one period

Second, EOQ is based on the assumption that usage or demand for materials or products is uniform through time as shown by the straight lines in figure 12.6. However, seasonal factors or lumpy demand are common in many product situations and require materials management to go beyond EOQ calculations to answer the questions when and how much to purchase. This is when materials management becomes even more complex and when computer technology is required for proper control.

LABOR COSTING

The cost of labor includes more than the amounts computed for each employee on an hourly or piece-work basis. There are a number of additional labor-related costs including payroll taxes, pension contributions, hospitalization insurance, bonuses, and vacation pay, just to mention a few. Since payments to employees take many forms, it is important that these costs be properly accumulated and matched with the appropriate period and production of that period. There are three general categories of labor costs—labor benefits, fringe benefits, and employer taxes.

Labor benefits include wages, salaries, and compensation from incentive plans. Wages represent payments based on hourly or piece rates. Salaries are fixed periodic payments made to employees. Incentive compensation is based on employee performance exceeding predetermined goals or standards. These types of labor costs are distinguished from fringe benefit costs in that fringe benefits are generally paid indirectly to employees. However, the cost of fringe benefits is a component of total labor costs and represents a significant cost of doing business. Examples of fringe benefits include holiday pay for certain days during the year, vacation pay for a specific number of days off each year based on the employee's tenure, and retirement pay set aside for future pension payments. Also included as fringe benefit costs are the cost of a host of stock and thrift plans by which employees are allowed to buy company stock at favorable prices or borrow company funds at favorable interest rates.

Employer payroll taxes include social security (FICA) and unemployment taxes. The employer must pay an amount equal to the FICA taxes withheld from employees. In addition, unemployment taxes are levied by state and federal governments to provide unemployment compensation to workers who are laid off.

Since our purpose here is to present the unique cost accounting aspects of labor costs in manufacturing operations, the financial accounting aspects of payroll accounting are greatly simplified.

There are two general sets of journal entries required to account for labor costs. The first set of journal entries records the cost and payment of labor benefits including salaries, wages, and incentive plans. The debit side of the journal entry, which is most important for cost accounting purposes, contains the distribution of labor costs among various cost categories representing the purposes for which labor costs were incurred. These categories and accounts include work in process for the cost of direct labor, factory overhead for the cost of indirect labor, marketing expense for the cost of marketing labor, and administrative expense for the cost of administrative labor. The credit side of the journal entry to record labor costs contains the liability to employees for net earnings plus all other liabilities related to payroll withholding. For example, the first set of journal entries records the cost and payment of payroll as follows:

Work-in-process inventory	4,600	
Factory overhead	1,400	
Marketing expense	800	
Administrative expense	1,000	
FICA tax payable		470
Federal income tax payable		1,800
State income tax payable		400
Union dues payable		250
Medical insurance payable		360
Payroll payable		4,520
Payroll payable	4,520	
Cash		4,520

The second set of journal entries records the cost and payment of the employer's payroll expenses arising from FICA and federal and state unemployment taxes. Payroll expenses applicable to direct labor should be assigned to work in process and payroll expenses applicable to indirect labor should be assigned to factory overhead. Payroll expenses applicable to selling and administrative labor should be assigned to their respective expense accounts as follows:

Work-in-process inventory	432	
Factory overhead	134	
Marketing expense	76	
Administrative expense	94	
FICA tax payable		470
State unemployment tax payable		234
Federal unemployment tax payable		32

This is generally recognized as the correct approach. However, because of the extra effort involved to distinguish between payroll expenses for direct versus indirect labor, some employers accumulate payroll taxes for *all* factory personnel in the factory overhead account. When this procedure is followed, an estimate of total payroll expenses is included in the overhead application rate.

For simplicity, the basic payroll journal entries illustrated above do not contain provisions for vacation, overtime, or other similar types of pay. Accounting for vacation pay is illustrative of benefits that are earned throughout the year but are usually paid only once during the year. To insure that vacation pay, for example, is spread over the entire year and not recognized in total in the period when it is paid, special accrual procedures must be followed. The procedure most widely used is to include an estimate of vacation pay as part of the factory overhead application rate and charge the actual cost of vacation pay to the factory overhead account as part of the regular payment of payroll.

To illustrate, assume that a factory employee earns $50 a day and in addition receives 10 working days of paid vacation as part of the employment agreement. As indicated, the $500 cost of vacation pay (10 days × $50 per day) should be spread over the whole year and not totally recognized in the payroll period when it is actually paid.

To accomplish this, a portion of the total cost is recognized in each pay period. For simplicity, it is assumed that there are 50 pay periods in a year with 5 working days in each period. The following journal entry is made each pay period for this employee:

Work-in-process inventory (5 days × $50 per day)	250	
Factory overhead ($500 ÷ 50 pay periods)	10	
Accrued vacation pay		10
Payroll and withholdings payable		250

The debit to the factory overhead account recognizes that part of total vacation pay is applicable to the current period. Similar entries made for all employees each pay period result in total vacation pay being recognized in the appropriate periods during the year.

When an employee actually takes the vacation and vacation pay is made, the following journal entries are prepared:

Accrued vacation pay	500	
Withholdings payable		205
Payroll payable		295
Payroll payable	295	
Cash		295

Notice that rather than debiting an expense account when vacation pay is paid the accrued vacation pay account is debited. The debit in the previous journal entry to factory overhead records the actual cost of vacation pay.

Overtime pay is required for most workers engaged in interstate commerce who work more than 40 hours per week. When overtime is paid, gross earnings are divided into two parts—regular earnings and an overtime premium. The overtime premium is found by multiplying the overtime hours by the overtime rate. If the overtime premium occurred because of specific job requirements, the overtime cost should be assigned to specific jobs. However, when overtime cannot be attributed to specific jobs because of general factory conditions, it should be charged to the factory overhead account. This means that an estimate of the overtime premium should be included in the factory overhead application rate.

LABOR CONTROL

Effective control over labor and labor-related costs is achieved through (a) planning production requirements, (b) use of labor time and wage standards, (c) labor performance reports, and (d) appropriate payment for labor. Accountants share responsibility for all aspects of labor control. However, of particular concern to the cost accountant are the payroll procedures used to account for labor costs and to provide information for management on how labor has performed by comparing actual results with expected performances. Also, control of labor costs through incentive plans is important for accountants to understand.

Payroll Procedures

Payroll procedures for controlling labor costs should insure that (a) persons employed are authorized, (b) persons receiving wages have performed services, and (c) persons employed have worked efficiently. Just as for materials, the organization should provide a clear description of payroll responsibilities and an accounting system with built-in checks and balances. Typically, five organizational functions are involved in payroll accounting—personnel, timekeeping, production, payroll, and cost accounting. Figure 12.7 outlines the relationships and functions of these organizational areas.

In situations where employees work on an hourly or piece-work basis, payroll procedures typically begin in the personnel department with the hiring of workers and

Figure 12.7 Payroll procedures

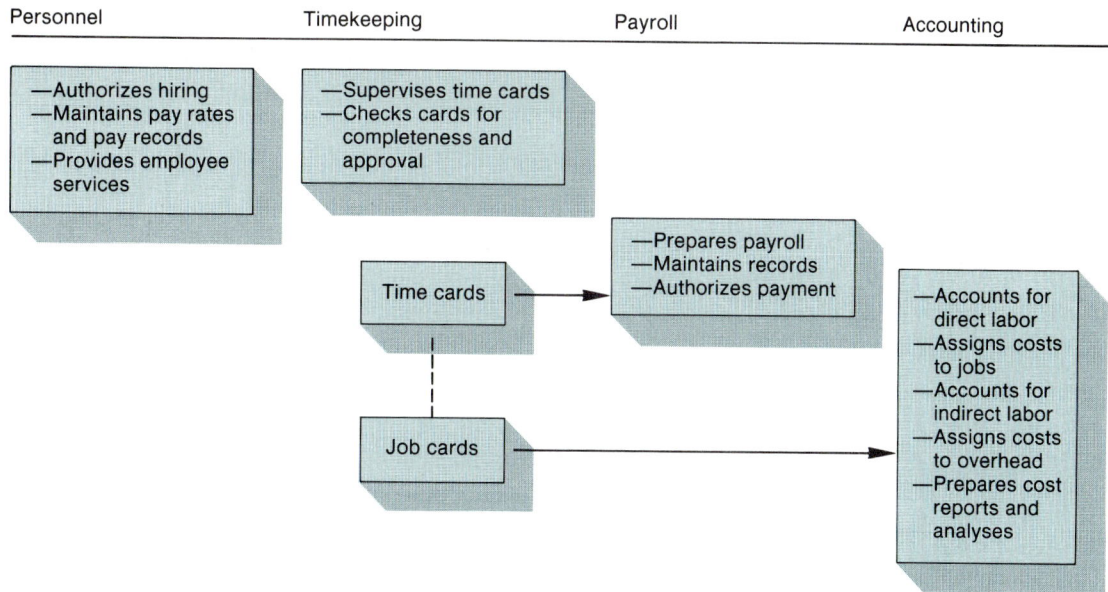

Personnel	Timekeeping	Payroll	Accounting

—Authorizes hiring
—Maintains pay rates and pay records
—Provides employee services

—Supervises time cards
—Checks cards for completeness and approval

Time cards

Job cards

—Prepares payroll
—Maintains records
—Authorizes payment

—Accounts for direct labor
—Assigns costs to jobs
—Accounts for indirect labor
—Assigns costs to overhead
—Prepares cost reports and analyses

the establishment of pay rates. The personnel department acts in close cooperation with the production departments in providing a number of employee services. From an accounting control viewpoint the personnel department also acts as a check on the authorization and the granting of appropriate pay rates. Direct supervision and timekeeping are the responsibility of individual production departments. The payroll cycle actually begins in the production department with the preparation of a *time* or *clock card*. The time card provides for the identification of each individual employee, the amount of time worked each payroll period, and an indication of time off and/or overtime. Time cards should be reviewed and authorized by production department supervisors before they are sent to the timekeeping department for subsequent processing. Also, either as part of the time card or on a separate *job ticket,* work performed on specific jobs or production runs is normally recorded by each employee.

Authorized time cards are sent to the timekeeping department, which typically performs two main functions. First, using the time card as its data source, total hours worked by each employee are accumulated so that earnings can be calculated by the payroll department. Second, timekeeping usually accumulates labor hours by job to facilitate distribution of costs to individual jobs (direct labor) or to factory overhead (indirect labor) by the cost accounting department. In large operations the timekeeping function is best handled by specially trained personnel in a separate organizational function. However, in some cases the employee performs the timekeeping function.

Time card data are periodically transmitted to the payroll department in which the detailed work of payroll and check preparation takes place. The payroll department computes gross and net pay for each worker, computes the total payroll, and maintains individual earnings records. Payroll payments are usually made by check.

The results of payroll computations are then transmitted in the form of a payroll distribution report to the cost accounting department where individual jobs, products, processes, or departments are charged with labor costs. Cost accounting is also responsible for reconciling job cost data with payroll data as a check on the integrity of the payroll system.

Figure 12.8   Learning curve

Average hours

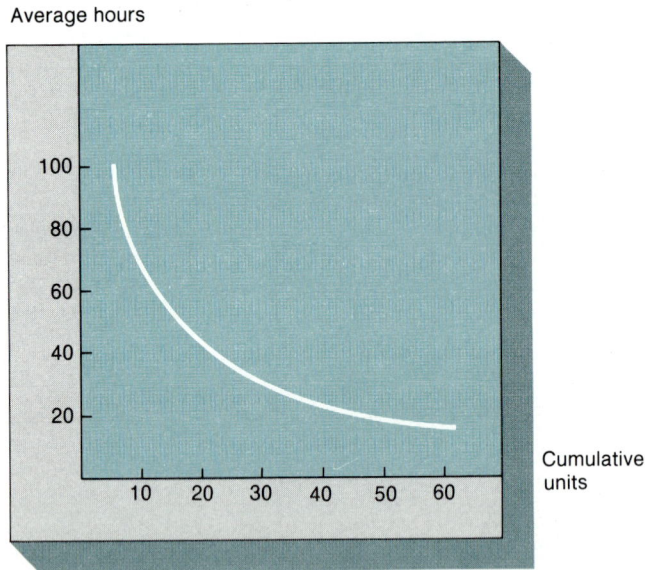

Cumulative units

Learning Curves

Learning curves are important for planning and controlling labor costs because they provide a mechanism for predicting the labor time required to perform repetitive production work. Learning curves are based on the observed fact that as workers gain experience in performing tasks they become more proficient and take less time to complete the same task. Case studies have found a very predictable relationship between the number of times repetitive work is performed and the rate of learning that takes place.

The rate of learning and the related improvement in job performance is so regular that labor requirements, budget allowances, performance standards, and cost estimates can be made with a high degree of accuracy. A **learning curve** is actually the graphical (mathematical) representation of the relationship between labor time and production quantity. It shows that when new products or processes are begun, learning also begins. Thereafter, efficiency improves in a nonlinear manner until learning is essentially complete and a "steady state" prevails. Figure 12.8 illustrates a learning curve, sometimes called an experience or improvement curve.

In more precise terms, a learning curve illustrates a time and cost relationship by which as *cumulative* production increases the *average* time and cost per unit systematically declines. Case studies reveal that each time the *cumulative quantity* of production is *doubled* the *cumulative average* hours per unit are reduced by a constant percentage. The mathematics of a learning curve are given in the appendix at the end of this chapter.

Learning curve percentages typically range from 60% to 90%. For example, an 80% learning curve indicates that doubling output will result in the cumulative average per-unit time of production to be 80% of the previous cumulative average time.

To illustrate the learning curve, assume that it takes 50 labor hours to produce the first 2 units of a particular product. This results in a cumulative average of 25 hours per unit produced (50 cumulative hours ÷ 2 units of production). If another batch of 2 units is produced, a doubling of production, then it is expected that the cumulative average hours of production for the 4 units will be 80% of 25 hours or 20 hours. Therefore, total production time for the total of 4 units is expected to be 80 hours (20 hours average per unit × 4 units). The following schedule shows the relationship between the number of items produced, the cumulative average hours, and the total hours using an 80% learning curve:

Cumulative Number of Units	Cumulative Average Hours	Total Hours
1	31.25	31.25
2	25 (.8 × 31.25)	50 (2 × 25)
4	20 (.8 × 25)	80 (4 × 20)
8	16 (.8 × 20)	128 (8 × 16)

The value in the learning curve theory is that, if still another batch of 4 units (another doubling of output to a total of 8 units) is contemplated, it is possible to accurately predict the additional labor requirement with suprising accuracy. For example, if the company is submitting a competitive bid for the manufacture of these items, it may be very important to predict the learning curve effects so that an appropriately low bid can be submitted. This can be done quite easily. If output is doubled, then the cumulative average hours required should be 80% of the prior cumulative average. In this instance, 16 hours (.80 × 20 hours) are the cumulative average hours expected to produce the total of 8 units. Therefore, total production time for the 8 units is estimated to be 128 hours (16 hours cumulative average × 8 units). Since total production time for the first 4 units is 80 hours and the total time for 8 units is expected to be 128 hours then the time required on the last 4 units is 48 hours (128 hours for 8 units − 80 hours for 4 units). If the effect of learning had been ignored, then the predicted labor requirement would probably have been much higher and the company may have lost the bid.

Learning curves can be applied to labor-related costs as well as to labor hours. Costs such as overhead, waste, and spoilage may vary in proportion to labor hours and can be predicted with learning curves. However, costs such as taxes, insurance, and management salaries may not be predictable with learning curves. To illustrate, assume that a company produced a prototype aircraft costing $1.8 million. A total of $1.0 million is considered labor-related costs. The company receives an order for 16 of these aircraft including the prototype. What is the total expected labor-related costs for this order, assuming a 90% learning curve?

Number of Aircraft	Cumulative Average Costs
1	$1,000,000
2	900,000 (.9 × $1,000,000)
4	810,000 (.9 × $ 900,000)
8	729,000 (.9 × $ 810,000)
16	656,100 (.9 × $ 729,000)

The total labor-related cost for 16 aircraft is $10,497,600 (16 aircraft × $656,100 average cost per aircraft). This is almost $6 million less than if no learning is assumed in building the aircraft. Note that the learning curve does not continue indefinitely, but it still provides an invaluable tool in manufacturing situations where learning is involved.

Summary

Materials typically represent a substantial investment of capital and make up a large percentage of the cost of production. Therefore, it is important that they be properly costed and rigidly controlled. There are a number of departments that accomplish this objective—stores, purchasing, receiving, and accounting. The accounting department serves as a check on the system of internal controls, which links the activities of all of these departments. Also, the accounting department has primary responsibility for cost determination including (a) assigning costs to materials purchased, (b) maintaining records of the internal flow of materials related costs, and (c) assigning costs to materials used.

Primarily two questions relate to the costing of materials—what costs should be included as part of the cost of materials received and what costs should be assigned to materials issued? Answers to both questions require a great deal of judgment and many cost-benefit trade-offs. For example, it is usually clear that the purchase price is included as a cost of materials, but that purchase discounts are not included as a cost of materials purchased. In addition, the cost of freight, receiving, inspection, storage, insurance, and similar acquisition costs should also be included as a cost of materials. The difficulty in accounting for materials acquisition costs is finding an economical method for assigning them to individual items purchased. Usually, acquisition and handling costs are allocated to materials inventory using some predetermined application rate rather than by following some tedious procedure of direct assignment to individual items.

The question of what costs to assign to materials issued is answered in the selection of an inventory cost flow assumption. Three basic assumptions are available—first-in, first-out (FIFO), last-in, first-out (LIFO), and average cost.

Additional costing and control problems arise from the need to account for scrap, spoiled materials, and defective units. Depending on the business environment there are two general methods of accounting for scrap and three costing considerations for how costs should be treated. The choice of methods hinges on whether the value of scrap is recorded when scrap occurs or when it is sold. Costing considerations depend on whether scrap is linked to particular jobs or products, is considered a part of general manufacturing operations, or is treated as a source of other income.

The accounting treatment given the cost of spoiled materials and defective units depends on whether the causes are considered to be a normal part of operations or are identifiable with specific jobs or processes. If causes are a normal part of operations, then the cost is generally included as part of factory overhead. If causes are identifiable with specific jobs or processes, then the cost is charged directly to specific jobs or production runs.

The economic order quantity (EOQ) model is a powerful tool for planning and control of materials. An EOQ model assists in controlling the size of the investment in inventory and helps to minimize ordering and handling costs. EOQ models help to answer the questions when and how much to order.

Labor costs also represent a substantial portion of the cost of production. Labor costs include not only wages and salaries but also a host of other payroll and fringe benefit costs. The accounting department cooperates with personnel, timekeeping, and production departments to insure that labor is properly authorized, paid, assigned to production, and reported for management review. The details of payroll accounting are primarily a financial accounting function. However, the costing and control of the labor component of production is a major concern of the cost accountant.

Finally, learning curves have been developed from results of numerous case studies to explain the relationship between the number of times repetitive work is performed and the rate with which learning takes place. The rate of learning and improvement are so predictable that labor budgets, standards, and cost estimates can be made with a high degree of accuracy using learning curves.

Appendix   *The Mathematics of Economic Order Quantity and Learning Curve*

ECONOMIC ORDER QUANTITY

The determination of economic order quantity is based on ordering, carrying, and total costs expressed as follows:

$$\text{Ordering costs} = O\,\frac{R}{Q}$$

$$\text{Carrying costs} = C\,\frac{Q}{2}$$

$$\text{Total costs} = O\,\frac{R}{Q} + C\,\frac{Q}{2}$$

where
R = Total materials requirements for one period
O = Cost of placing an order
C = Cost of carrying one unit of inventory for one period
Q = Order size (in units)

Using calculus to find the minimum total, the total costs function is differentiated with respect to Q and set equal to zero as follows:

$$\frac{dTC}{dQ} = \frac{-OR}{Q^2} + \frac{C}{2} = 0$$

Solving for Q yields:

$$Q = \sqrt{\frac{2RO}{C}} = \text{Economic order quantity (EOQ)}$$

The EOQ formula is based on the following assumptions:

1. Demand is known with certainty.
2. Demand is continuous over time rather than being discrete.
3. Lead time is known with certainty.
4. Lead time is constant.
5. Ordering costs and carrying costs are constant.
6. The system is never out of stock (stockout costs are infinite).

LEARNING CURVE

A learning curve is expressed mathematically as:

$$Y = lX^b$$

where
X = Cumulative total units produced
l = Input quantity required to produce the first unit of output
r = Learning rate
b = Index of learning, $b = \dfrac{\text{Log } r}{\text{Log } 2}$

Self-Study Problems

ECONOMIC ORDER QUANTITY (EOQ)

Lakewood Hardware Company has provided the following information concerning one of its products. Sales statistics indicate that usage is quite uniform so average inventory is assumed to equal one-half of the order quantity.

Usage	400 units per month
Ordering costs	$18 per order
Inventory carrying costs	$.50 per unit per month
Safety stock	150 units
Lead time	2 weeks

Required

Calculate the following:

1. Economic order quantity
2. Reorder point

Solution to the Self-Study Problem

Requirement 1

$$EOQ = \sqrt{\frac{2 \times 400 \times 18}{.50}} = 170$$

Requirement 2

	Units
Usage during lead time	200
(400 units per month ÷ 2 weeks)	
Safety stock	150
Reorder point	350

LEARNING CURVE

Alpha-Macro Company, specialists in machine manufacture and design, received an order for a unique type of materials handling machine. The customer presented blueprints and specifications and requested Alpha-Macro to prepare a bid for the manufacture of four machines. Alpha-Macro suggested that the total contract price be postponed until after the first machine was built and that the final price include (a) the cost of materials, (b) labor and labor-related overhead costs based on an 80% learning curve, and (c) a 40% markup on materials and labor costs.

The customer agreed and the first machine was built with the following costs:

Materials	$10,000
Direct labor (500 hours × $12)	6,000
Labor-related overhead (500 × $8)	4,000
Total	$20,000

Required

Prepare a price quotation for the four machines based on the experience of making the first machine.

Solution to the Self-Study Problem

Number of Machines Produced	Cumulative Average Hours	Total Hours Worked
1	500	500
2	400 (.8 × 500)	800 (2 × 400)
4	320 (.8 × 400)	1,280 (4 × 320)

Therefore, the total hours required to manufacture four machines is predicted to be 1,280 (4 machines × 320 average hours per machine).

Price Quotation

Materials (4 × $10,000)	$40,000
Direct labor (1,280 hours × $12)	15,360
Labor-related overhead (1,280 hours × $8)	10,240
Total	$65,600
Markup (.4 × $65,600)	26,240
Bid	$91,840

Suggested Readings

Abernathy, William J., and Wayne, Kenneth. "Limits of the Learning Curve." *Harvard Business Review* (September–October 1974): 109–19.

American Institute of Certified Public Accountants. "Practical Techniques and Policies for Inventory Control." *Management Services Technical Study No. 6.* New York, 1968.

Backes, Robert W. "Cycle Counting: A Better Method for Achieving Accurate Inventory Records." *Management Accounting* (January 1980): 42–46.

Gillespie, Jackson F. "An Application of Learning Curves to Standard Costing." *Management Accounting* (September 1981): 63–65.

Imhoff, E. A., Jr. "The Learning Curve and Its Applications." *Management Accounting* (February 1978): 44–46.

Morse, W., and Scheiner, J. "Cost Minimization, Return on Investment, Residual Income: Alternative Criteria for Inventory Models." *Accounting and Business Research* (Autumn 1979): 320–24.

National Association of Accountants. "Techniques in Inventory Management." *N.A.A. Research Report No. 40.* New York, 1962.

Discussion Questions

1. Define costing and control. Explain the role of the accounting department in the costing and control of materials and labor.
2. What expenditure items should be included in the cost of materials purchased? What items are excluded from the cost of materials purchased?
3. Describe two major functions that each of the following departments serves in the purchasing process—stores, purchasing, receiving, and accounting.
4. What are the three basic cost flow assumptions used when costing materials are issued? Describe the cost flows each assumes for costing purposes.
5. What is the major problem with assigning materials acquisition costs to units received? What accounting procedure is typically used to overcome this difficulty?

6. Define scrap, defective units, and spoiled units.
7. What are the methods and considerations for deciding which method is appropriate for accounting for scrap?
8. Describe the general procedures used to account for the cost of defective and spoiled units if these costs are not attributable to any particular job. How do these procedures differ if defective and spoiled units are the result of exacting specifications on specific jobs?
9. What is an EOQ model and how does it help answer the questions when and how much to buy?
10. Define lead time, reorder point, and safety stock.
11. What are some of the costs of carrying inventory? What are some of the costs of not carrying enough inventory?
12. Describe the basic function of each major document used to account for labor and material costs.
13. What expenditures are properly recorded as part of labor costs?
14. What special accounting treatment is given holiday and vacation pay? Why?
15. Some feel that payroll expenses on direct labor should be charged to work in process while others charge payroll expenses to factory overhead. Give the theoretical and practical reasons why this difference exists.
16. What is the difference between the journal entry to record the payroll and the journal entry to record payroll expenses?
17. What is the basic theory behind the learning curve?
18. Describe how the learning curve might be used in (a) budgeting labor costs, (b) establishing standards for labor performance, or (c) bidding on specific jobs.

Exercises

Exercise 12.1   Basic Payroll Procedures

The Mills Manufacturing Company has a weekly payroll. The following summary covers the company payroll for the week ending February 18:

Employee	Hours or Function Worked in	Hourly or Weekly Rate
Harold Zapel	Factory: 36 direct, 4 indirect	$8 per hour
John Yazzie	Factory: 40 direct	$10 per hour
Kenneth Walch	Factory: 38 indirect	$7 per hour
Lewis Vincent	Sales	$400 per week
Monte Uhlman	Sales	5% of sales $
Nona Tresnak	Administrative	$350 per week

Monte Uhlman took firm sales orders of $6,000.
FICA taxes are 6.7% and federal income taxes average 12% of gross wages.

Required

1. Determine each employee's gross earnings, withholdings, and net pay for the week.
2. Prepare a payroll analysis showing the amount of gross pay and employer FICA that should be classified as direct labor, indirect labor, marketing and administrative costs respectively.
3. Prepare the journal entry to record employee's salaries and wages and the distribution of labor costs.
4. Prepare the journal entry to record the employer's payroll expenses.

Exercise 12.2 Basic EOQ Analysis

The Nashville Company manufactures small electric power tools. It has assembled data that indicates a typical annual usage of 4,000 six-inch circular saw blades. Inventory carrying costs are estimated at 10% of average inventory cost. Each saw blade costs $2. The cost to place a purchase order is $6.

Required

1. Using the formula method, determine the EOQ for saw blades.
2. How many orders will Nashville need to place each year using the most economic quantity determined in requirement 1?

Exercise 12.3 Basic Learning Curve Analysis

The Champion Chip Company has developed a new computer chip. It took 3 direct-labor hours to produce the first chip. The labor rate is $6 per hour. The steady state is expected to occur when 16 chips have been produced. The firm has determined a 90% learning curve is applicable in the production of chips.

Required

1. Compute the cumulative average labor time needed and the output of chips per hour up to the steady state point.
2. Determine the average labor cost per chip at the steady state.

Exercise 12.4 Payroll Entries

The Aster Company has completed the computation of wages earned during the payroll period ending May 31. Summary information follows:

Factory wages	$52,500[a]
Administrative salaries	28,000
Marketing salaries	16,000
FICA tax rate	6.7%
Federal income taxes	9,650
State unemployment tax rate	2.2%
Federal unemployment tax rate	.7%
Credit union savings	1,200

[a]$40,000 direct labor

Required

1. Prepare journal entries to set up, pay, and distribute the payroll.
2. Assume no employee has earned over $6,000 since January 1. Make the entry to record the employer's payroll tax liability.

Exercise 12.5   EOQ Concepts and Procedures

The Fan-tas-tic Company produces a household cleanser. The principal chemical material used in the cleanser is purchased in gallon containers from the Pon Do Company. Fan-tas-tic has gathered the following data regarding the chemical material:

Annual requirement	4,000 gallons
Costs per gallon	$1.50
Administrative clerical costs	$1.30 for each purchase order
Stationery, postage, etc.	$1.00 for each purchase order
Insurance and inventory property taxes	$ .15 per gallon per year
Minimum desired return on inventory investment	10%

Required

1. Identify the total cost of placing each order and the total cost, in dollars, of carrying a gallon in inventory for the year.
2. Determine the economic order quantity using the formula method.

Exercise 12.6   Learning Curve

The Signal-Sell Company produces a special part used in satellite tracking devices. Recently they have been asked to submit a bid on a contract for 900 units of this special part. The first production of 300 parts with the specifications required for the potential contract involved the following costs for labor and factory overhead:

Direct labor—12,000 hours @ $10/hr $120,000
Factory overhead—applied @ 100% of direct-labor cost[a]

[a]Factory overhead is 60% variable. The fixed portion of overhead is primarily depreciation on equipment and other capacity costs.

The Signal-Sell Company has analyzed operations and has identified an 80% learning curve is applicable.

Required

Determine an estimate of the labor and overhead costs that could be used in submitting a minimum bid on the contract for 900 units of the special part.

Exercise 12.7   Basic Materials Ordering Procedures

Watson Company's production plans specify the following needs for material 29–N:

July	3,200 units
August	2,900 units
September	3,500 units

On July 1, the inventory of 29–N was 2,800 units. Materials on order show contracted delivery in July of 3,200 units and contracted delivery in August of 2,900 units. A minimum reserve of 70% of the July 1 inventory is required to be maintained throughout the year.

Required

1. How many units of material 29–N should Watson order for delivery in September?
2. Estimate the quantity of material 29–N on hand at September 1 and at September 30.

Exercise 12.8   Spoiled Units

Garrison Components makes stereo products. Production lot number 85–38 calls for the manufacture of 2,800 cabinet speakers. These speakers have the following unit costs:

Direct materials	$ 39.20
Direct labor	34.40
Factory overhead (includes $2 allowance for spoiled work)	29.60
	$103.20

After completion of the lot, 140 did not pass inspection (a normal amount). These speakers were sold for $31.20. Each cost element of the production phase has a separate work-in-process account.

Required

1. Make the entries necessary if the loss is charged to all production.
2. Make the entries necessary if the loss is charged specifically to lot number 85–38.

Exercise 12.9   Defective Units

Biddie Company has received a special order for 50 custom water pumps. Because of the customization, spoilage is expected to exceed normal rates. The materials costs for the pumps are $66 per unit; labor cost is $72 per unit; and factory overhead is applied at 100% of labor cost. During production, 7 units were found to be defective. These units were reworked with the following additional per-unit costs—materials, $5; labor, $9; and overhead was applied again at the 100% of labor rate. Of the 50 units reaching completion, 3 were classified as not meeting the specifications of the client. These were sold separately for $175 each, which was credited to the special order. The client accepted the order as being complete with the delivery of 47 pumps.

Required

Determine the correct unit cost of the delivered pumps.

Exercise 12.10   Labor Cost Planning

Quinn Sprinkler Systems produces irrigation control equipment. Big City Parks & Recreation Department has placed an order for 500 electronic control devices. The order requires work in plastics, electronics, and assembly. You have drawn up the following daily budget to meet the order in the time allotted:

	Devices Scheduled	Hours Budgeted
Electronics	20	50
Plastics	20	30
Assembly	20	25

After two days of production, you receive the following feedback:

	Devices Produced	Hours Expended
Day 1:		
Electronics	22	48
Plastics	16	30
Assembly	15	22
Day 2:		
Electronics	24	49
Plastics	19	30
Assembly	19	23

Required

1. What action should you take based on the report of day 1 production?
2. What action should you take based on the report of day 2 production?

Problems

Problem 12.1 Concepts and Procedures for Materials

The following two situations are independent of each other.

1. The following information is available for Digby Company's material Y:

Annual usage in units	10,000
Working days per year	250
Normal lead time in working days	30
Maximum lead time in working days	70

Required

Assuming that the units of material Y will be required evenly throughout the year, determine the reorder point.

2. Several key estimates are necessary to compute the economic order quantity.

Required

List and describe these key estimates.

Problem 12.2 Journal Entries for Scrap, Spoiled, and Defective Units

The following transactions (unless specified) have not yet been recorded. All took place during the current period.

1. Materials for production were erroneously recorded as a $480 charge to supplies.
2. Goods with a cost of $750 were returned by a customer and erroneously recorded as a debit to materials and a credit to accounts receivable at the cost amount. The sales price for the units was $1,100.

3. Scrap materials were returned to the storeroom. They were valued at an estimated sales price—$70 from supplies and indirect materials, and $135 from direct materials.
4. A job order of 800 units required additional work to be done on 20 units. Costs per unit applied in the reworking were materials, $5; labor, $3; and $4 for factory overhead, which includes a $.50 allowance for rework of defective units. The company uses one of the two following assumptions in recording such costs:
   a. Reworking cost is charged to the specific job.
   b. Reworking cost is allocated to all production.
5. Normal spoilage of 150 units occurred in the finishing department. The 150 units have a total estimated sales value of $900. These units had been charged with $1,000 of materials, $600 of labor, and $400 of factory overhead. The following assumptions must be looked at alternatively:
   a. Spoilage cost is charged to the specific job.
   b. Spoilage cost is allocated to all production.

Required

Make the journal entries to correctly record each of the transactions listed. Where alternatives exist, make the entries under each alternative separately. Assume that perpetual inventory records are kept and that there is only one work-in-process account.

Problem 12.3 Labor Costs and the Learning Curve (CMA)

The Kelly Company plans to manufacture a product called Electrocal, which requires a substantial amount of direct labor on each unit. Based on the company's experience with other products that required similar amounts of direct labor, management believes that there is a learning factor in the production process used to manufacture Electrocal.

Each unit of Electrocal requires 50 square feet of raw material at a cost of $30 per square foot for a total material cost of $1,500. The standard direct-labor rate is $25 per direct-labor hour. Variable manufacturing overhead is assigned to products at a rate of $40 per direct-labor hour. The company adds a markup of 30% on variable manufacturing cost in determining an initial bid price for all products.

Data on the production of the first two lots (16 units) of Electrocal is as follows:

1. The first lot of 8 units required a total of 3,200 direct-labor hours.
2. The second lot of 8 units required a total of 2,240 direct-labor hours.

Based on prior production experience, Kelly anticipates that there will be no significant improvement in production time after the first 32 units. Therefore, a standard for direct-labor hours will be established based on the average hours per unit for the rest of the units.

Required

1. What is the basic premise of the learning curve?
2. Based upon the data presented for the first 16 units, what learning rate appears to be applicable to the direct labor required to produce Electrocal? Support your answer with appropriate calculations.

3. Calculate the standard for direct-labor hours that Kelly Company should establish for each unit of Electrocal.
4. After the first 32 units have been manufactured, Kelly Company was asked to submit a bid on an additional 96 units. What price should Kelly bid on this order of 96 units? Explain your answer.
5. Knowledge of the learning curve phenomenon can be a valuable management tool. Explain how management can apply the learning curve in the planning and controlling of business operations.

Problem 12.4   Concepts of Inventory Models (CMA)

ROAT Company is a regional manufacturing company that operates with a typical manufacturing plant utilizing a raw material, work-in-process, and finished-goods inventory system. Raw materials are purchased and stored until their introduction into the manufacturing process. Upon completion the finished product is stored in the company's warehouse until their final sale.

ROAT's controller recently read an article, which stated that the annual cost of carrying inventory from the raw material phase through the finished-goods phase can cost between 15 and 30% of the average value of the total inventory. As a consequence of the article, the controller asked the company's cost accounting department to prepare an analysis and estimate of ROAT's inventory carrying cost. The analysis indicated that ROAT's carrying costs were greater than 25% of the average inventory value. The study confirmed the controller's belief that inventory carrying costs might be an excellent area to implement cost reductions.

At a management meeting, the production manager suggested that the inventory carrying costs be shifted to suppliers and customers. This could be accomplished by not requesting raw materials from suppliers until needed in the manufacturing process and by transferring the finished goods to customers immediately following completion.

Required

1. Identify three types of inventory carrying costs and give specific examples of each type of cost.
2. The production manager of ROAT Company has suggested that inventory carrying costs be shifted to suppliers and customers. Identify and discuss the circumstances that would have to exist to make such a proposal feasible with respect to:
   a. raw materials inventories.
   b. finished-goods inventories.
3. Suppose ROAT Company is successful in shifting a portion of all of its inventory carrying costs to suppliers and customers.
   a. Identify the inventory carrying costs ROAT might be able to reduce by shifting the inventory burden.
   b. Identify possible areas of increased costs that could offset, in whole or part, the reduction of inventory carrying costs.

Problem 12.5 Economic Order Quantity and Safety Stock (CMA)

SaPane Company is a regional distributor of windshields. With the introduction of the new subcompact car models and the expected high level of consumer demand, management recognizes a need to determine the total inventory cost associated with maintaining an optimal supply of replacement windshields for the new subcompact cars introduced by each of the three major manufacturers. SaPane is expecting a daily demand for 36 windshields. The purchase price of each windshield is $50.

Other costs associated with ordering and maintaining an inventory of these windshields are as follows:

1. The historical ordering costs incurred in the purchase order department for placing and processing orders is shown below:

Year	Orders Placed and Processed	Total Ordering Costs
1978	20	$12,300
1979	55	12,475
1980	100	12,700

Management expects the order costs to increase 16% over the amounts and rates experienced during the last three years.

2. A clerk in the receiving department receives, inspects, and secures the windshields as they arrive from the manufacturer. This activity requires 8 hours per order received. This clerk has no other responsibilities and is paid at the rate of $9 per hour. Related variable overhead costs in this department are applied at the rate of $2.50 per hour.

3. Additional warehouse space will have to be rented to store the new windshields. Space can be rented as needed in a public warehouse at an estimated cost of $2,500 per year plus $5.35 per windshield.

4. Breakage cost is estimated to be 6% of the unit cost.

5. Taxes and fire insurance on the inventory are $1.15 per windshield.

6. The desired rate of return on the investment in inventory is 21% of the purchase price.

Six working days are required from the time the order is placed with the manufacturer until it is received. SaPane uses a 300-day work year when making economic order quantity computations. The economic order quantity formula is:

$$EOQ = \sqrt{\frac{2 \,(\text{Annual demand}) \,(\text{Ordering cost})}{\text{Storage cost}}}$$

Required

Calculate the following values for SaPane Company.

1. The value for ordering cost that should be used in the EOQ formula
2. The value for storage cost that should be used in the EOQ formula
3. The economic order quantity
4. The minimum annual relevant cost at the economic order quantity point
5. The reorder point in units

Problem 12.6   Economic Order Quantity Concepts (CMA)

H. P. Maxim Company uses a simple economic order quantity (EOQ) model that assumes instantaneous replenishment and known constant demand to minimize the sum of ordering costs and carrying costs for a raw material used in the manufacture of toys.

1. An analytical technique useful in finding the order quantity that minimizes the sum of these costs is
   a. line of balance.
   b. integral calculus.
   c. probability theory.
   d. linear algebra.
   e. differential calculus.
2. If the annual total of ordering and carrying cost is given by the equation $y = 200,000/x + .05x$, in which x is the number of units in each order, the quantity ordered that minimizes this total is
   a. 633 units.
   b. 2,000 units.
   c. 6,325 units.
   d. 4,000 units.
   e. some amount other than those shown above.
3. If Maxim's purchasing department orders raw materials in quantities larger than the optimum quantity obtained using the simple economic order quantity model in order to obtain a quantity discount, the company will experience
   a. carrying costs lower than if the optimum quantity were ordered.
   b. ordering costs higher than if the optimum quantity were ordered.
   c. ordering costs the same as if the optimum quantity were ordered.
   d. carrying costs higher than ordering costs.
   e. ordering costs higher than carrying costs.

Problem 12.7   EOQ—Setup and Carrying Costs (CMA)

Pointer Furniture Company manufactures and sells office furniture. In order to compete effectively in different quality and price markets, it produces several brands of office furniture. The manufacturing operation is organized by the item produced rather than by the furniture line. Thus, the desks for all brands are manufactured on the same production line. For efficiency and quality control reasons, the desks are manufactured in batches. For example, 10 high-quality desks might be manufactured during the first two weeks in October and 50 units of a lower-quality desk during the last two weeks. Because each model has its own unique manufacturing requirement, the change from one model to another requires the factory's equipment to be adjusted.

Pointer's management wants to determine the most economical production run for each item in its product lines. The manager of the cost accounting department is going to adapt the economic order quantity (EOQ) inventory model for this analysis.

One of the cost parameters that must be determined before the model can be employed is the setup cost incurred when there is a change to a different furniture model. The cost accounting department has been asked to determine the setup cost for the desk (model JE 40) in its junior executive line as an example.

The equipment maintenance department is responsible for all changeover adjustments on production lines in addition to the preventive and regular maintenance of all the production equipment. The equipment maintenance staff has a 40-hour workweek; the size of the staff is changed only if there is a change in the workload that is expected to persist for an extended period of time. The equipment maintenance department had 10 employees last year, and each employee averaged 2,000 hours for the year. They are paid $9.00 an hour and employee benefits average 20% of wage costs. The other departmental costs, which include such items as supervision, depreciation, insurance, etc., total $50,000 per year.

Two workers from the equipment maintenance department are required to make the change on the desk line for model JE 40. They spend an estimated 5 hours in setting up the equipment as follows:

Machinery changes	3 hours
Testing	1 hour
Machinery readjustments	1 hour
Total	5 hours

The desk production line on which model JE 40 is manufactured is operated by 5 workers. During the changeover these workers assist the maintenance workers when needed and operate the line during the test run. However, they are idle for approximately 40% of the time required for the changeover.

The production workers are paid a basic wage rate of $7.50 an hour. Two overhead bases are used to apply the indirect costs of this production line because some of the costs vary in proportion to direct-labor hours while others vary with machine hours. The overhead rates applicable for the current year are as follows:

	Based on Direct-Labor Hours	Based on Machine Hours
Variable	$2.75	$ 5.00
Fixed	2.25	15.00
	$5.00	$20.00

These department overhead rates are based upon an expected activity of 10,000 direct-labor hours and 1,500 machine hours for the current year. This department is not scheduled to operate at full capacity because production capability currently exceeds sales potential at this time.

The estimated cost of the direct materials used in the test run totals $200. Salvage material from the test run should total $50.

Required

1. Prepare an estimate of Pointer Furniture Company's setup cost for desk model JE 40 for use in the economic production run model. For each cost item identified in the problem, justify the amount and the reason for including the cost item in your estimate. Explain the reason for excluding any cost item from your estimate.
2. Identify the cost items that would be included in an estimate of Pointer Furniture Company's cost of carrying the desks in inventory.

Problem 12.8   EOQ Analysis—Different Methods

Refer to the basic information in exercise 12.2

Required

1. Determine EOQ using the tabular (trial-and-error) method. Set up your order sizes in intervals of 500 units.
2. Determine EOQ by setting up a graph. Plot ordering and carrying costs on the vertical axis and order quantity on the horizontal axis of your graph.
3. Compare and discuss your results obtained by the three different methods of analysis—formula, tabular, and graphic.

Problem 12.9   Journal Entries for Spoiled Units

The Proctor Company manufactures product *C* at a per-unit cost of $6 that consists of $1 for materials, $2 for labor, and $3 for factory overhead. During May, 1,000 units were spoiled that can be sold for $.60 each. The accountant said that the entry for these 1,000 spoiled units could be one of these four:

1. Spoiled goods		600	
Work in process—materials			100
Work in process—labor			200
Work in process—factory overhead			300
2. Spoiled goods		600	
Factory overhead control		5,400	
Work in process—materials			1,000
Work in process—labor			2,000
Work in process—factory overhead			3,000
3. Spoiled goods		600	
Loss on spoiled goods		5,400	
Work in process—materials			1,000
Work in process—labor			2,000
Work in process—factory overhead			3,000
4. Spoiled goods		600	
Accounts receivable		5,400	
Work in process—materials			1,000
Work in process—labor			2,000
Work in process—factory overhead			3,000

Required

List the circumstances under which each of the above entries would be appropriate.

Problem 12.10   Spoiled Goods—Revision of Contract Billing

The Space Magic Company just completed a contract with NASA covering the production of 250 special components used in space rocket boosters.

Materials costs for each component were $47.50. There were 5,260 direct-labor hours used on the contract at a cost of $8 per labor hour. The direct-labor time on the contract included 10 hours required to correct defects in one component. Factory overhead is applied at the rate of $4 per direct-labor hour.

During final inspection 11 components were discovered to have been spoiled or defective during production. Of these units 10 could not be corrected and had to be sold as scrap for $50 each. Additional materials costing $15 were used to correct the defects in the one component. NASA agreed to accept 240 components as completion of the contract.

Space Magic submitted the following billing to NASA:

Materials	$11,810.75
Labor	41,799.45
Factory overhead	20,899.80
Total manufacturing costs	$74,510.00
5% to cover administrative overhead and profit	3,725.50
Total billing (240 components)	$78,235.50

NASA submitted the billing to the disbursement audit division for review and payment. Audit has challenged the billing from Space Magic on the grounds that the cost of the spoiled components (reduced by the scrap recovery value) as well as the costs of correcting defects on the one component have been charged to the contract. Audit claims that contract regulations require costs of spoilage and correcting defects to be spread over all products produced by a company.

Required

1. Compute a corrected billing to submit to NASA.
2. Reconstruct all journal entries the Space Magic Company has made that relate to the data shown in the original billing.
3. Make the journal entries needed to bring the records into agreement with the corrected billing.

FACTORY OVERHEAD: COSTING AND CONTROL I

13

OUTLINE

F actory overhead costs are given special consideration in this chapter and chapter 14. Accounting for factory overhead differs from accounting for direct material and direct labor because factory overhead costs have some unique characteristics. First, the total amount of factory overhead that should be assigned to goods produced during an accounting period may not be known until the end of an accounting period, long after some goods are finished and sold. In contrast, the cost of direct materials and direct labor is typically known at the time of production. Also, factory overhead may fluctuate considerably from month to month due to factors other than the volume of production. However, the cost of direct materials and direct labor usually fluctuates with the volume of production. Finally, factory overhead typically consists of both fixed and variable costs, unlike direct-materials and direct-labor costs, which are strictly variable.

This chapter explains how to account for these unique aspects of factory overhead costs. This chapter reviews and refines some cost concepts discussed in previous chapters, examines methods for recording and applying overhead costs, discusses the handling of over- and underapplied overhead, and illustrates management reporting of overhead costs. After completing this chapter you should be able to:

1. define factory overhead costs.
2. differentiate between variable and fixed factory overhead.
3. apply factory overhead costs to units of production.
4. select an activity base appropriate for the application of factory overhead in particular manufacturing situations.
5. account for factory overhead costs in the general ledger.
6. prepare meaningful factory overhead cost reports for management use.

FACTORY OVERHEAD COST CONCEPTS

A complete understanding of two cost concepts is necessary before the development of additional principles of factory overhead costing and control. These cost concepts include a definition of factory overhead costs and an analysis of the various cost behavior patterns that factory overhead costs may exhibit.

Factory Overhead Costs

Although the origin of the term **overhead** is not clear, it has become a common brief expression for indirect manufacturing costs. *Indirect manufacturing costs, factory overhead costs,* or simply *overhead* are defined as all manufacturing costs other than direct materials and direct labor. The cost of materials that physically become part of work in process represents a direct-materials cost. However, the cost of indirect materials such as the cost of lubricating oil that does not become an identifiable part of work in process but is necessary for factory operations represents an indirect manufacturing cost. The wages of a machine operator whose work is directly associated with the production of finished goods is considered a direct-labor cost. However, the labor cost of a repair and maintenance person is only indirectly related to the cost of finished goods and is considered an indirect manufacturing cost.

Other terms such as factory burden and manufacturing expense are also used to refer to overhead costs. However, the use of such terms is discouraged because they tend to be ambiguous and misleading. For brevity, the term factory overhead or simply overhead is used throughout this text to refer to indirect manufacturing costs.

Variable, Fixed, and Mixed Overhead Costs

In order to provide managers with appropriate information for purposes of product costing, planning, and control, it is essential that overhead costs be differentiated by how they behave when there are changes in the level of production. There are three general cate-

Figure 13.1   Examples of cost behavior patterns

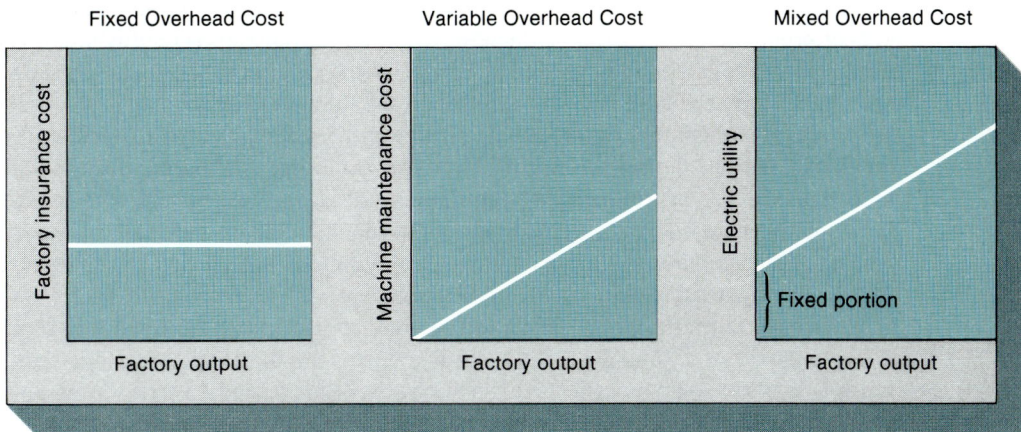

gories used to classify overhead cost behavior—variable overhead costs, fixed overhead costs, and mixed overhead costs.

Variable overhead costs are factory overhead costs that vary in proportion to the level of manufacturing activity. Examples of variable overhead could include manufacturing supplies or repair and maintenance labor.

Fixed overhead costs are factory overhead costs that remain constant or fixed as the volume of manufacturing activity changes. Examples of fixed overhead could include factory depreciation and factory supervisory salaries.

Mixed overhead costs are indirect manufacturing costs that have both a fixed cost component and a variable cost component. For example, a certain utility cost may include a fixed "connect fee" plus a per-unit charge for services. This type of rate structure results in the total utility bill being a mixed cost. Mixed costs are usually separated into variable and fixed components and reported in these respective cost categories on budgets and management reports. Figure 13.1 illustrates different types of costs and their behavior patterns.

The determination of whether specific costs are actually variable, fixed, or mixed depends on an examination of the cost behavior of each type of expenditure in relation to the volume of manufacturing output. Chapter 5 discussed specific techniques for categorizing overhead costs into behavior categories. A number of benefits are derived from a behavioral analysis of overhead costs. The principle benefit, discussed later in this chapter, is that a cost analysis according to cost behavior develops more useful information for management control than would otherwise be available.

OVERHEAD APPLICATION FOR PRODUCT COSTING

One role of overhead accounting is to give managers reasonably accurate and timely information concerning the total actual costs incurred to manufacture a product. Total per-unit manufacturing costs are then used to assign costs to inventory, calculate the cost of goods sold, and determine the amount of income from operations. Generally accepted accounting principles require that actual costs incurred, including overhead, be assigned to goods manufactured.

Product costs are also used in many types of management decisions. For example, product costs may be used to determine an appropriate selling price for a product. Because product costs are used for so many purposes it is important that they be as accurate and timely as possible.

Obtaining accurate and timely product cost information for direct materials and direct labor is relatively easy. By their very nature, direct costs can be traced to specific units of production. For example, the cost of a kitchen appliance is readily identified with the cost of manufacturing a particular mobile home. Also, the labor cost of the worker who installs the appliance is easily identified with the cost of producing a particular mobile home. However, unlike direct-materials and direct-labor costs, it is difficult, if not impossible, to trace indirect or overhead costs to specific units of production. To illustrate, maintenance expenditures on factory equipment are recognized manufacturing costs, but it is difficult to identify the specific units of production that are benefited by a particular maintenance expenditure. Rather, it is more representative of the actual situation to view such costs as *benefiting all units of production over a given period of time.*

Selecting an appropriate period of time to use as the basis for budgeting and applying overhead is sometimes difficult. The most common time period is a year, but it is also possible to use a monthly, quarterly, or other time period for calculating and using overhead application rates. The selection of an appropriate time period is discussed later. For now, an annual time period is assumed.

Overhead Application

Total overhead costs may not be known with certainty until the end of an accounting period. This would be the case if property taxes are assessed and paid near the end of a company's fiscal year. However, managers typically cannot wait until the end of an accounting period to make a number of decisions dependent on full cost information.

Also, overhead costs may fluctuate considerably from month to month during an accounting period. For example, machine repair costs may fluctuate from month to month, but the benefits from repair costs accrue to units produced over a much longer period of time. It would be unrealistic and result in improperly fluctuating product costs to charge the cost of such items as machine repair incurred in a given month to that month's production rather than to all the units benefited.

To deal with these unique characteristics of overhead costs and to provide management with timely, reasonably accurate, and consistent product cost information, accountants have developed a procedure referred to as **overhead application** for determining what overhead to assign to units of production.

Overhead application is accomplished with the following steps:

1. Overhead costs are identified and categorized as being either variable or fixed, and a forecast of total overhead cost is made. Methods of forecasting or budgeting total overhead costs were discussed in chapters 6 and 7. Figure 13.2 illustrates a manufacturing overhead budget developed using flexible budget concepts.

   Note that in figure 13.2 the variable costs per unit are determined and then multiplied by the anticipated volume of production (70,000 units in this case) to calculate total budgeted variable costs. Fixed costs are then added as a lump sum to variable costs to arrive at the total budgeted overhead.

2. An activity base is selected to be used as the basis for assigning overhead costs to units of production. An *activity base* is a measure of productive activity that most nearly explains the variation in amount of actual overhead absorbed by units of production.

   Typically, an activity base is chosen about which data is readily available and routinely recorded during the manufacturing process. For example, direct-labor hours, direct-labor cost, machine hours, direct-materials cost, and units of production are common activity bases.

Figure 13.2   Manufacturing overhead budget

(Based on 70,000 units of production at 1 hour of direct labor per unit.)
For the year ending December 31, 19X8

	Amount per Unit	Total Amount
Budgeted overhead:		
Variable items:		
Indirect labor	$1.00	$ 70,000
Repair and maintenance	.30	21,000
Utilities (variable portion)	.20	14,000
Idle time	.05	3,500
Other variable overhead	.05	3,500
	$1.60	$112,000
Fixed items:		
Supervisory salaries		$ 50,000
Depreciation		28,000
Insurance		10,000
Utilities (fixed portion)		4,000
Other fixed overhead		6,000
		$ 98,000
Total budgeted overhead		$210,000

3. A forecast or budget is made to show the *total expected volume* of the activity base for the coming period. For example, if direct-labor hours are chosen as the activity base, then the total number of direct-labor hours expected to be employed are forecasted or budgeted for the next year.

When budgeting an activity base, direct-labor hours in this instance, it is important to understand what is being assumed concerning plant capacity. For example, it should be clear whether the activity level being forecasted assumes a plant operating at peak engineering efficiency or if the capacity assumption takes into consideration such realities as maintenance, down time, and holidays. Budgets based on different assumptions of plant capacity have important implications for analyzing end-of-the-period results. Plant capacity concepts will be discussed later.

4. An overhead application rate is calculated by dividing total budgeted overhead by the total budgeted activity level. This overhead application rate is then used to apply overhead costs to units of production.

To illustrate the calculation and use of an overhead rate, figure 13.2 indicates a situation in which total expected overhead is budgeted to be $210,000. The activity base chosen in this situation is direct-labor hours. Each unit of product requires one hour of direct labor for a total budget of 70,000 hours for the year. Given this information, the overhead application rate is calculated as follows:

$$\frac{\text{Total budgeted overhead}}{\text{Total budgeted activity base}} = \frac{\$210,000}{70,000} = \$3.00 \text{ per direct-labor hour}$$

This rate is a **predetermined overhead application rate** because it is *pre*determined as part of the budgetary process rather than determined from the results of actual operations after they occur.

Figure 13.3   Job cost summary

Job No. A136-4   **Date Started: 5/15/19X8**

Cost Category	Hours	Rate	Cost
Materials	—	—	$4,500.00
Direct labor	200	$6.50	1,300.00
Overhead applied	200	3.00	600.00
Total Cost			$6,400.00

---

5. Overhead costs are applied to production using the overhead rate that was determined using steps 1 through 4. For example, consider the job cost information summarized in figure 13.3.

   Materials and labor costs are determined as the job moves through the production process. However, unlike direct costs, overhead is applied to jobs using the predetermined overhead rate—$3.00 per direct-labor hour in this example. This particular job required 200 direct-labor hours resulting in $600 (200 hours × $3.00 per hour) of overhead being assigned. The total cost for the job of $6,400 represents the full cost of production.

Before proceeding to refine these concepts it should be noted that the $3.00 application rate is actually the total of a variable overhead application rate of $1.60 ($112,000 ÷ 70,000) plus a fixed overhead application rate of $1.40 ($98,000 ÷ 70,000). The full significance of a variable plus a fixed rate is discussed later in this chapter and in chapter 14.

In the above illustration, direct-labor hours are used as the activity base, but machine hours could have been used instead. For example, assume that the total budgeted machine hours are 50,000 and that 140 machine hours are used on the job shown in figure 13.3. The new overhead rate based on machine hours is:

$$\frac{\text{Total budgeted overhead}}{\text{Total budgeted activity base}} = \frac{\$210,000}{50,000} = \$4.20 \text{ per machine hour}$$

Using this different overhead rate to apply overhead costs would result in $588.00 (140 machine hours × $4.20 per machine hour) being applied to the job in figure 13.3 rather than applying $600.00 when direct-labor hours are used. This difference is expected due to the very nature of the overhead application process when using different activity bases. This shows that the selection of an appropriate activity base is an important matter, because an inappropriate base could result in the improper assignment of costs to jobs. It also emphasizes the fact that an activity base is intended to provide a common denominator for productive activity among units produced.

Concepts Underlying the Overhead Application Process

Several concepts that underlie the overhead application process include the selection of an activity base, time period considerations, and capacity concepts.

Selection of an Activity Base   An activity base has two major functions. First, it provides the foundation for the development of a flexible budget. Second, it provides the basis for applying overhead costs to work in process. For these reasons it is important that the activity base provide a high correlation between actual production costs and the amount of overhead incurred by each unit of production. For example, if overhead costs relate mainly to machine operation, then machine hours are a more appropriate activity base than materials cost.

The cost of measuring and administering an activity base is another factor that should be considered in its selection. Recent developments in automated data acquisition and processing technology have greatly diminished the clerical costs of budgetary and overhead accounting. However, when several different activity bases provide essentially the same results, then the most cost effective base should be chosen.

There are any number of measures that could be used as an activity base. However, the following five represent those most commonly used.

1. *Units of Production.* This base is easy to use because units of production are routinely part of the information in a cost accounting system. The units of production basis is typically used when there is only one product produced or when the different products manufactured are quite homogeneous. Otherwise, the application of overhead may result in unrealistic product costs. For example, in a job costing environment a major job that produces only a few units receives less applied overhead than a minor job that produces many units.

   Using the units of production basis, overhead is applied using a rate per unit of production. For example, if total budgeted overhead is $360,000 and the total budgeted units of production are 180,000 units, then overhead is applied to each unit of production at the rate of $2.00 ($360,000 ÷ 180,000 units) per unit produced.

2. *Materials Cost.* This base is appropriate when there is a high correlation between the cost of materials and the amount of overhead used in production. This situation typically occurs when a single product is produced or when all products are homogeneous in terms of materials used. However, if one product uses relatively higher priced materials than another but the amount of overhead used is approximately the same, then the use of materials cost would result in an inappropriate amount of overhead being applied to work in process.

   When using materials cost as a basis, overhead is applied using a rate per dollar of materials cost. For example, if total budgeted overhead is $360,000 and total budgeted cost of direct materials is $1,400,000, then overhead is applied to each unit of production at the rate of $.25 ($360,000 ÷ $1,440,000) per dollar of direct-materials cost. If a particular job has $2,000 of direct-materials cost, then $500 ($2,000 × $.25) is applied to work in process.

3. *Direct-Labor Cost.* This is another base that is easy to use because necessary information is readily available in payroll records. Direct-labor cost is an appropriate activity base when there is a close relationship between the cost of labor and the amount of overhead used in manufacturing a product. However, when jobs that use essentially the same amount of overhead require labor having different skill levels resulting in different labor costs for each job, then direct-labor cost may be inappropriate as an activity base.

   Using direct-labor cost, overhead is applied using a rate per dollar of labor cost. For example, if the total budgeted overhead is $360,000 and the total budgeted direct-labor cost is $1,000,000, then overhead is applied to each unit of production at the rate of $.36 ($360,000 ÷ $1,000,000) per dollar of direct-labor cost. If a particular job has $900 of direct-labor cost, then $324 ($900 × $.36) is applied to work in process.

4. *Direct-Labor Hours.* Direct-labor hours is a very popular activity base. Like direct-labor cost, the use of direct-labor hours is also appropriate when labor operations are a major factor in the manufacturing process. One reason for the popularity of direct-labor hours is that information for its use is routinely accumulated for purposes other than overhead application. Therefore, the use of direct-labor hours as an overhead base adds little in incremental costs to the operation of the cost accounting system.

Direct-labor hours is usually preferred over direct-labor cost when workers are paid different rates for the same type of work. For example, a person with seniority may be paid more than another even though they perform the same task. In this situation, the use of direct-labor cost would result in a disproportionate share of overhead applied to the units of production.

Using the direct-labor hour base, overhead is applied using a rate per direct-labor hour. For example, if total budgeted overhead is $360,000 and the total budgeted direct-labor hours is 200,000 hours, then overhead is applied to each unit of production at the rate of $1.80 ($360,000 ÷ 200,000 hours) per direct-labor hour.

5. *Machine Hours.* This method is appropriate when machine operation is an important part of the manufacturing process and when there is a direct relationship between machine activity and overhead used. However, this method typically requires additional record keeping to accumulate the information needed to apply overhead to work in process.

Using machine hours, overhead is applied using a rate per machine hour. For example, if total budgeted overhead is $360,000 and the total budgeted machine hours are 400,000 hours then overhead is applied to each unit of production at the rate of $.90 ($360,000 ÷ 400,000 hours) per machine hour.

Time Period Considerations   Instead of using an annual time period, it is also possible to use a monthly, quarterly, or other time period for calculating and using overhead application rates. When deciding what time period to use for an overhead rate, two major considerations are fluctuations in the volume of activity and the uniformity of overhead expenditures through time.

Fluctuations in the volume of activity have little effect on unit production costs for materials, labor, and variable overhead. However, the unit cost of fixed overhead will change with the level of production. For example, if fixed overhead costs are expected to be $10,000 per month and the volume of production in January is 10,000 units, then the fixed cost portion of the overhead rate is $1.00 per unit. However, if the production forecast for February is set at 8,000 units, then the fixed cost portion of the overhead rate is computed to be $1.25. Thus, overhead rates may differ from month to month due *only* to monthly changes in the volume of production. Therefore, the selection of an annual, monthly, or other period of time for applying the activity base should depend on how well the derived overhead rate represents the actual, typical, or normal per-unit production costs.

The second major consideration in selecting a base period is the uniformity of overhead expenditures through time. Expenditures for overhead items range from being highly uniform through time to being highly erratic. For example, monthly rent on the factory building is very stable from month to month. However, other expenditures may range from being seasonal in the case of air-conditioning costs to once-per-year in the case of property taxes. For example, it seems unrealistic under these circumstances to have the cost of production of units made in March be more or less than those made in July simply because property taxes are paid in March rather than in July. This type of monthly fluctuation in overhead costs is the major reason for computing overhead rates on a time period longer than a week or month.

In most situations it is felt that a rate based on the *operating cycle of a business* (which is usually an annual cycle) provides an average of activity that is most representative of the actual or normal costs of production.

Capacity Concepts   When budgeting the expected level of an activity base, it is important to understand the meaning of plant capacity. The discussion to this point in the chapter has been based on an "expected level of activity" as a measure of plant capacity. However, the term "expected level of activity" is ambiguous because it is not clear if it refers to the activity level attainable if the plant is operating at peak engineering efficiency or if it takes into consideration such realities as unavoidable delays or even expected idle time.

When a factory is first built it has some basic level of productive capacity. Determining initial plant size is essentially a capital budgeting decision (see chaps. 22 and 23). Once the basic productive capacity is in place and ready to operate, another notion of capacity becomes the prime consideration; that is, to what extent is the available capacity expected to be utilized? In this connection, four capacity concepts to consider are theoretical capacity, practical capacity, normal capacity, and expected capacity.

1. **Theoretical capacity** refers to the upper limit of production capabilities from an engineering and economic viewpoint. Theoretical capacity includes operating the plant at full potential with 100% efficiency. No interruptions are contemplated for such things as breakdowns or maintenance. Theoretical capacity could also include additional levels of output achievable by using overtime or subcontracting to augment production if they are economically feasible. Since theoretical capacity does not allow for normal interruptions and unavoidable delays, it is typically not used as a basis for measuring capacity.

2. **Practical capacity** refers to the more realistic production level at which machine breakdowns, machine maintenance, and other idle time events are considered to be a normal part of operations. This capacity level is often used to apply overhead costs.

    Note that theoretical capacity and practical capacity relate to production capabilities of a firm. However, normal capacity and expected capacity are concepts that relate to consumer demand.

3. **Normal capacity** is the level of production volume that is expected to meet average consumer demand over some specified period of time—often three to five years. Normal capacity is essentially a long-run measure of expected average sales activity, which takes into consideration seasonal and cyclical fluctuations in demand.

    Since normal capacity is long-run in nature, overhead could be overapplied in some years and underapplied in other years. The net effect of overapplied and underapplied amounts of overhead for a period of years is expected to be equal and offsetting. The use of normal capacity is beneficial when the desire of management is to have long-run criteria for product costing and control. However, when normal capacity is used, caution should be exercised to insure that all concerned fully understand and are able to evaluate the potential impact of using a long-run concept in the short run. For example, over- or underapplied overhead should be evaluated realizing that on a year-by-year basis it may have resulted simply because a long-run capacity concept was used to make short-run cost application.

4. **Expected capacity** is the level of plant activity that is expected to meet consumer demand for the next planning period—usually one year. Expected capacity is usually the basis of the annual master budget for a company. Under this concept, overhead costs are budgeted on a year-by-year basis taking into consideration cyclical and trend patterns anticipated to affect only

the upcoming year. The use of an expected capacity concept tends to place unit production costs at more realistic levels in the short run, makes the cost accounting more responsive to the current business environment, and provides information with less ambiguity for management control of overhead costs. Therefore, expected capacity is the common capacity concept for both product costing and management control purposes.

GENERAL LEDGER ACCOUNTING

As indicated, accounting for overhead costs has two major objectives. First, overhead costs are accumulated and applied for the purpose of estimating how much it actually costs to produce each unit of output. This is referred to as the product-costing objective. In addition, overhead costs are accumulated and reported for the purpose of helping management to make planning and control decisions. *Both* of these objectives should be kept in mind as the general ledger accounting for overhead is examined.

The reason for reemphasizing this matter is that the traditional orientation of general ledger accounting for overhead costs tends to focus on the product-costing objective. However, the importance of planning and control cannot be overemphasized. A well-founded information system centered on the general ledger and supplemented with other procedures and reports can provide meaningful information for planning and control as well as for product-costing purposes.

The Accounting Process

The calculation of the overhead rate is part of the budgetary process that takes place before any actual overhead costs are incurred or recorded. Due to the factors of timing and uneven expenditure patterns, the overhead rate is used to apply overhead to units of production independent of the incurrence of actual overhead costs. This peculiarity in overhead accounting gives rise to the following typical account structure. A **factory overhead control account** is used to accumulate the *actual* overhead costs incurred. A **factory overhead applied account** is used to record the amount of overhead *applied* to work in process by using the predetermined overhead application rate. Sometimes, only a *factory overhead account* is used with the debit side representing actual overhead costs and the credit side representing applied overhead costs.

The factory overhead control account serves management as a control vehicle for overhead costs incurred and also serves as the control account over the *factory overhead subsidiary ledger*. Just as the accounts receivable control account has a subsidiary ledger of individual customer accounts, the factory overhead control account has a subsidiary ledger that consists of accounts representing individual categories of actual overhead expenditure. Figure 13.4 lists typical overhead cost categories that could be used as subsidiary account classifications or subsidiary account titles.

As actual overhead costs are incurred during the period, the factory overhead control account is debited. The offsetting credit is made to either a liability account, the cash account, or some other appropriate asset account. Also, the amount of actual expenditure is posted to the appropriate account in the factory overhead subsidiary ledger. For example, a cash expenditure of $250.00 for factory supplies would result in the following journal entry and subsidiary posting:

General Ledger:

Factory overhead control   250.00
    Cash   250.00
To record expenditure for factory supplies.

Factory Overhead Subsidiary Ledger:

Factory supplies   250.00
To post to subsidiary ledger.

Figure 13.4   Factory overhead subsidiary accounts

Typical Overhead Cost Categories

Supervisor/foreman salaries	Repairs and maintenance
Other indirect labor	Factory supplies
Overtime premium	Oil and gas
Idle time	Electric
Vacation/holiday expense	Water
FICA taxes	Depreciation-factory building
Unemployment taxes	Depreciation-machinery
Group/hospitalization insurance	Property taxes
Pension plan expense	Fire and casualty insurance

The recording of actual overhead costs continues throughout the accounting period as costs are incurred and takes place independently of the application of overhead costs to work in process. Only at the end of a specified accounting period are differences between actual costs and applied costs compared and analyzed.

The application of overhead costs to work in process is based on the use of a predetermined overhead application rate. The overhead rate is used to determine the amount of overhead costs to apply to work in process. To illustrate, refer to the job statistics in figure 13.3. During the production process, 200 direct-labor hours were expended on the job. Using the predetermined overhead rate of $3.00 per direct-labor hour, total overhead applied to work in process for this job is $600.00. The journal entry to record the application of overhead for this job is:

General Ledger:

Work-in-process control	600.00	
Factory overhead applied		600.00

To record the application of overhead to work in process for job number A136–4.

Analysis of Budgeted versus Actual Overhead

Since the recording of actual overhead and applied overhead are carried on as separate accounting functions, the probability is remote that the balance in the factory overhead control account will ever be the same as the balance in the factory overhead applied account. In fact, the difference at various times during the accounting period may be quite large. However, at the end of an accounting period (usually a year) the balances in the two accounts should be nearly equal.

Any difference between balances in the factory overhead applied account and the factory overhead control account at the end of an accounting period represents the amount by which budgeted (applied) amounts differed from actual expenditures. For example, unexpected changes in the cost of maintenance supplies or the unexpected use of more labor to perform maintenance functions could result in over- or underapplied overhead. An analysis of any differences between applied and actual overhead provides important information for management planning and control.

An analysis of differences between these accounts begins with the computation of under- or overapplied overhead. **Underapplied overhead** occurs when the balance in the factory overhead applied account is less than (under) the balance in the factory overhead control account. **Overapplied overhead** occurs when the balance in the factory overhead applied account is greater than (over) the balance in the factory overhead control account. To illustrate, figure 13.5 part *a* shows account balances assuming that actual overhead expenditures made during the period amounted to $212,000 in comparison with overhead

Figure 13.5   Recording of under- or overapplied overhead

Part A: Overapplied Overhead

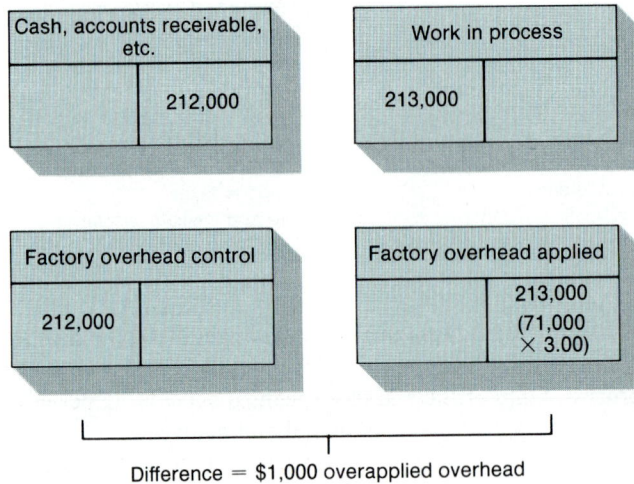

Cash, accounts receivable, etc.	
	212,000

Work in process	
213,000	

Factory overhead control	
212,000	

Factory overhead applied	
	213,000
	(71,000 × 3.00)

Difference = $1,000 overapplied overhead

Part B: Underapplied Overhead

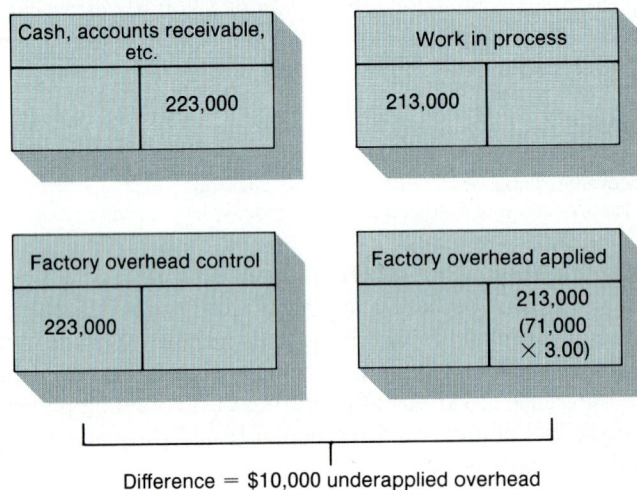

Cash, accounts receivable, etc.	
	223,000

Work in process	
213,000	

Factory overhead control	
223,000	

Factory overhead applied	
	213,000
	(71,000 × 3.00)

Difference = $10,000 underapplied overhead

applied to work in process during the period of $213,000. The application of overhead resulted from an assumed activity level of 71,000 direct-labor hours with an overhead application rate of $3.00 per direct-labor hour. The difference of $1,000 between actual and applied overhead represents overapplied overhead.

If instead of 71,000 direct-labor hours only 70,000 direct-labor hours had been expended, then only $210,000 (70,000 hours × $3.00 per hour) would have been applied to work in process. In this case there would have been a difference of $2,000 between the accounts, which would be *underapplied* overhead.

Disposition of Under- or Overapplied Overhead

The size of any under- or overapplied overhead largely depends on the forecasting skill of those preparing the overhead budget. No matter how skilled the budget manager, it is almost inevitable that there will be some amount of under- or overapplied overhead. In addition, unexpected changes in business conditions may result in very large amounts of under- or overapplied overhead.

The relative magnitude of any under- or overapplied overhead influences how the overhead accounts are closed at the end of an accounting period and what disposition is made of any under- or overapplied amount. If, by some chance, the ending balances in the factory overhead control and factory overhead applied accounts are equal at the end of the period, then these accounts can be closed against each other with an equal credit and debit respectively and no additional accounting is necessary. However, more likely a difference in account balances will exist. If the amount of under- or overapplied overhead is immaterial, a widely accepted practice at year end is to simply close the overhead accounts against each other with the difference going as an adjustment to cost of goods sold. Using this approach, the following journal entry closes the overhead accounts illustrated in figure 13.5 part *a:*

Factory overhead applied	213,000	
Factory overhead control		212,000
Cost of goods sold		1,000

To close overhead accounts and charge overapplied overhead to cost of goods sold.

If overhead had been underapplied during the period, the closing entry would have resulted in a debit (increase) to the cost-of-goods-sold account.

This procedure is a simple way to handle insignificant or immaterial amounts of under- or overapplied overhead. However, when amounts are large, as would be the case when there is an unexpected and large change in prices for overhead items, it is best to use a more accurate procedure in handling under- or overapplied overhead. Theoretically, if there is under- or overapplied overhead at the end of an accounting period, the amount of overhead charged to individual jobs during the period is in error. With actual cost data available at year end, the accountant can recompute an "actual" overhead rate and adjust the amount of overhead costs assigned to each job during the year. Accordingly, adjustments would be made to all affected account balances and accounting records.

This procedure results in a precise, after-the-fact application of overhead. However, most firms do not go to this much corrective detail even for significant amounts of over- or underapplied overhead. Rather, the typical procedure is to prorate under- or overapplied overhead to work in process, finished goods, and cost of goods sold. The proration often is made in proportion to the allocated overhead in each of these accounts.

To illustrate this procedure, assume that in figure 13.5 part *b* actual overhead amounted to $223,000 because of unexpected increases in overhead costs. With the amount of overhead applied remaining at $213,000, the result is $10,000 of underapplied overhead rather than $1,000 of overapplied overhead as previously illustrated.

Figure 13.6 shows assumed amounts of overhead in work in process, finished goods, and cost of goods sold accounts at the end of the year. Relative proportions are also calculated in figure 13.6.

The adjustment amounts shown in figure 13.6 are found by multiplying the relative proportions times the $10,000 underapplied overhead to obtain the adjustment amount applicable to each account. The journal entry to close the overhead accounts under these circumstances and using this allocation procedure is as follows. The amounts debited to work in process and finished goods are typically posted to individual job cost sheets for proper job costing.

Work in process	300	
Finished goods	2,200	
Cost of goods sold	7,500	
Factory overhead applied	213,000	
Factory overhead control		223,000

To close overhead accounts and charge underapplied overhead to work in process, finished goods, and cost of goods sold.

Figure 13.6   Allocation of underapplied overhead

Account	Amount of Overhead in Account	Proportion of Total	Adjustment Amount
Work in Process	$ 72,000	.03	$ 300
Finished goods	528,000	.22	2,200
Cost of goods sold	1,800,000	.75	7,500
Total	$2,400,000	100%	$10,000

Allocating under- or overapplied overhead using this procedure assumes that the proportion of direct-materials, direct-labor, and overhead costs are relatively uniform among jobs or products produced. In most situations this is a valid assumption. However, if this assumption is not warranted, then the procedure illustrated will result in an improper allocation of under- or overapplied overhead. In such situations, it may be necessary to resort to the detail of job-by-job cost adjustments previously discussed.

Under- or overapplied overhead may also be handled using a total cost approach. Using this method any under- or overapplied overhead is closed to work in process, finished goods, and cost of goods sold based upon the balance of total costs in each account. This method is not as precise, but it is easier to apply since only ending balances are required for its use.

MANAGEMENT REPORTING OF OVERHEAD FOR PLANNING AND CONTROL

A principle benefit of the budgetary and accounting procedures discussed in this chapter is that information is made available for management to assess the quality of past performance as a basis for future planning and control. Whether examining the firm as a whole or each individual department, analysis of past performance begins with a detailed examination of the causes for any under- or overapplied overhead.

The difference between actual overhead incurred and the amount of overhead applied to work in process is the result of two possible conditions. First, under- or overapplied overhead results if more or less overhead costs are incurred for the number of units produced than originally budgeted. This may happen because unexpected fluctuations occur in the price of overhead items or because unexpected changes occur in overhead used. A second condition resulting in under- or overapplied overhead is the production of more or less units than originally budgeted.

Either of these general causes of under- or overapplied overhead can be identified with a category of overhead costs. The first cause is identified with both variable and fixed overhead. The second cause is identified with fixed overhead only. This situation makes it appropriate to provide management with overhead analysis reports that separately analyze variable and fixed overhead costs. The combined analysis explains why total overhead is under- or overapplied. Such reports are typically developed showing company-wide results with detail reports developed for each individual production or service department.

Variable Overhead Reporting

The variable overhead portion of a performance report consists of a detailed listing of overhead items or accounts. For each overhead item, amounts are given for (*a*) the budgeted cost, (*b*) the actual costs incurred, (*c*) the difference between budgeted and actual

---

Figure 13.7   Comparison of budgeted and actual overhead

(Flexible budget based on 71,000 direct-labor hours.)

	Variable Rate per Direct-Labor Hour	Budgeted Amount	Actual Amount	Variance from Budget
Variable items:				
Indirect labor	$1.00	$ 71,000	$ 71,700	$ 700 U[a]
Repair and maintenance	.30	21,300	20,900	400 F
Utilities (variable portion)	.20	14,200	14,250	50 U
Idle time	.05	3,550	3,450	100 F
Other variables	.05	3,550	3,700	150 U
Total	$1.60	$113,600	$114,000	$ 400 U
Fixed overhead		$ 98,000	$ 98,000	–0–
Total		$211,600	$212,000	$ 400 U
Volume variance [(71,000 − 70,000) × $1.40[b]]				1,400 F
Overapplied overhead				$1,000 F

[a]F = Favorable

U = Unfavorable

[b]Fixed overhead application rate: $3.00 total − $1.60 variable = $1.40 fixed

   Variable items:
      Favorable = Actual amount is less than budgeted amount
      Unfavorable = Actual amount is greater than budgeted amount
Volume variance = Fixed overhead rate × (Budgeted hours − Actual hours)
   Favorable = Actual activity base used is greater than the budgeted activity base
   Unfavorable = Actual activity base used is less than the budgeted activity base
   Overapplied overhead = Favorable
   Underapplied overhead = Unfavorable

---

costs incurred, and (*d*) an indication whether actual expenditures are greater than or less than the budgeted amount. Figure 13.7 shows such a report. The information contained in the report is extracted from the illustrations in this chapter. The variable overhead items and rates are those given in figure 13.2. The budgeted cost is calculated using flexible budget procedures with the *actual level of production* of 71,000 direct-labor hours for 71,000 units produced as illustrated in figure 13.5.

   This type of report makes it possible to quickly pinpoint how well specific variable overhead items are being utilized in the production process. This information provides the point of departure for investigation into the causes of deviations from budget and the formulation of remedies or rewards for poor or good performance as appropriate. For example, the unfavorable variance for indirect labor may have been the result of an unexpected machine breakdown that required more maintenance labor than had been expected.

   Even though this type of report is a valuable tool for planning and control, it does not provide sufficient information to determine specific causes for the over- or under budget amounts. Specifically, the report in figure 13.7 does not indicate if the over- or under budget amounts are caused by unexpected prices paid for overhead items or by the efficiency with which overhead items are utilized. For example, is the $50 over budget for utilities due to the utilities increasing their rates or because utilities are inefficiently used? Or is the $50 over budget caused by a combination of such factors? Even though this report is very useful, a more comprehensive comparison of budgeted and actual variable overhead would be helpful. Such a report is developed in chapters 15 and 16 in connection with the use of standard costs.

Fixed Overhead Reporting

The fixed overhead portion of the performance report shown in figure 13.7 is oversimplified. Total budgeted and total actual fixed costs are shown to be equal. This is consistent with the notion that fixed costs remain fixed. In reality, however, there may be small differences between budgeted and actual fixed costs. For example, the cost of insurance, a fixed cost, may unexpectedly increase. The self-study problem at the end of the chapter illustrates a situation in which fixed costs change. Remember, the only restriction that classifies a cost as fixed is that any change is unrelated to changes in the volume of production. Accounting and reporting for fixed costs that change is fully discussed in chapter 14.

An interesting outcome of overhead accounting is that the total amount of fixed overhead *applied* to work in process *fluctuates* with the level of production. The use of a predetermined overhead application rate results in fixed overhead being applied along with variable overhead to work in process *as though* fixed costs are variable. Accounting for overhead in this way is in accordance with generally accepted accounting principles and has many advantages because of the unique characteristics of overhead costs. However, a consequence of accounting for fixed costs in this way is that the amount of fixed costs applied to work in process equals budgeted fixed costs *only* at the budgeted level of activity.

This phenomenon is accounted for by calculating a **volume variance,** which shows the difference between the budgeted amount of fixed overhead and the amount of fixed overhead applied to work in process. To illustrate, fixed overhead is applied in the example above at the rate of $1.40 per direct-labor hour, whereas the variable overhead rate is $1.60 per hour. Therefore, the amount of fixed overhead applied will equal budgeted overhead only at the activity level of 70,000 hours, which was used to calculate the predetermined overhead application rate. Figure 13.8 graphically indicates this point. Note that the level of production is measured in terms of the activity base used to calculate the overhead rate. In figure 13.8, direct-labor hours was used. However, any other activity base such as machine hours or units of production could have been used.

By examining figure 13.8 it can be seen that budgeted fixed overhead remains the same for various levels of production. However, fixed overhead applied to production on a per-unit basis makes applied fixed overhead behave as though it is a variable cost. If actual production equals budgeted production of 70,000 direct-labor hours, then the amount of fixed overhead applied to work in process is also equal to budgeted fixed costs of $98,000. However, if 71,000 direct-labor hours were actually utilized as in the example above, the results are $99,400 (71,000 hours × $1.40 per hour) of fixed overhead being applied to work in process. The difference of $1,400 is the amount of the *volume variance.* A volume variance will occur whenever the actual level of activity is different from the budgeted or estimated activity level used to calculate the overhead application rate. The formula for calculating the volume variance is:

$$\text{Volume variance} = \left[\begin{array}{c} \text{Budgeted level} \\ \text{of production} \end{array} - \begin{array}{c} \text{Actual level} \\ \text{of production} \end{array} \right] \times \begin{array}{c} \text{Fixed part of} \\ \text{overhead rate} \end{array}$$

The volume variance has nothing to do with the price paid or the efficiency of usage of fixed overhead. Also, since the volume variance is simply the result of the actual level of activity being different from the budgeted level of activity, it can only be controlled at higher levels of management where production volume is controlled. For these reasons, the volume variance is shown on managerial reports as a balancing number only to indicate that all over- or underapplied overhead has been accounted for.

Figure 13.8   Volume variance

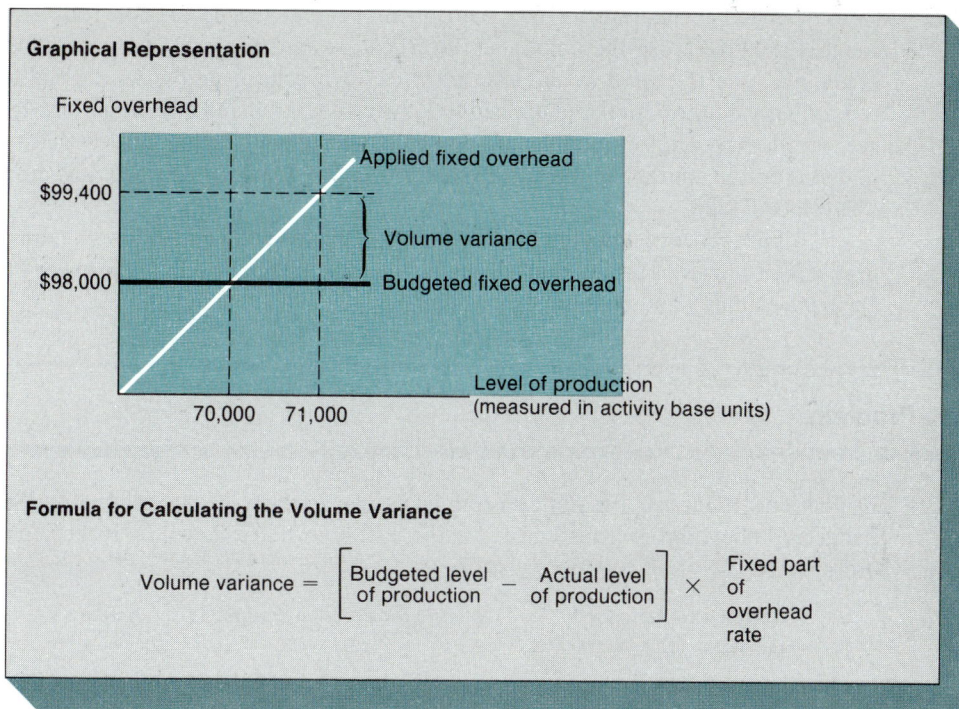

Graphical Representation

Fixed overhead

Applied fixed overhead

$99,400

Volume variance

$98,000 — Budgeted fixed overhead

Level of production
(measured in activity base units)

70,000   71,000

Formula for Calculating the Volume Variance

$$\text{Volume variance} = \left[\begin{array}{c} \text{Budgeted level} \\ \text{of production} \end{array} - \begin{array}{c} \text{Actual level} \\ \text{of production} \end{array} \right] \times \begin{array}{c} \text{Fixed part} \\ \text{of} \\ \text{overhead} \\ \text{rate} \end{array}$$

Further discussion about the volume variance and the analysis of fixed overhead costs requires a more refined analysis, which depends on the use of standard costs as discussed in chapters 15 and 16.

Summary

Accounting for factory overhead has a number of unique features that require accounting procedures different from those for direct materials and direct labor. Since the amount of actual overhead is not known with certainty until the end of an accounting period, overhead costs are assigned to work in process by using a predetermined overhead application rate. This rate is found by dividing total budgeted overhead by a total budgeted activity base.

An activity base is a measure of productive activity that represents the relationship between units of production and the amount of overhead costs absorbed by units of production. There are a number of activity bases that may be used depending on the manufacturing situation. For example, direct-labor hours and machine hours are common activity bases. The activity base chosen should accurately represent the amount of overhead costs absorbed by units of production.

The development of an overhead application rate is part of the budgetary process. Two aspects of this process relate especially to overhead costs. First, total overhead typically consists of fixed as well as variable costs. Proper identification and classification of fixed and variable costs is vital for proper overhead accounting and management reporting. Second, a proper understanding of plant capacity and the consequences of using theoretical, practical, normal, or expected capacity assumptions are important for proper reporting and control of overhead costs.

When accounting for overhead in the general ledger, an overhead *applied* account is used to record the amounts of overhead assigned to work in process. An *actual* account is used to record actual expenditures for overhead items. At the end of an accounting period the actual and applied totals are compared and any under- or overapplied overhead is reported. Any under- or overapplied overhead is either closed to cost of goods sold or prorated among the work-in-process inventory, the finished-goods inventory, or the cost of goods sold.

The procedures outlined in this chapter provide a meaningful way to assign overhead costs to units of production as well as a way to provide useful information for management planning and control of operations.

Self-Study Problem

Bridgerland Products, a manufacturing company, recently began operations. The firm's budgeted and actual overhead costs for the past month are shown by its accounting records:

Overhead Account	Variable Rate	Budget	Actual
Variable overhead:			
Indirect materials	$1.20	$ 3,600	$ 3,200
Indirect labor	1.30	3,900	4,200
Payroll-related costs	.90	2,700	3,000
Utilities	.40	1,200	1,400
Miscellaneous	.20	600	400
	$4.00	$12,000	$12,200
Fixed:			
Supervisor's salary		2,000	2,000
Depreciation		3,500	3,600
Property tax		300	300
Insurance		200	200
		$ 6,000	$ 6,100
Total		$18,000	$18,300

The company uses direct-labor hours to calculate a predetermined rate to apply manufacturing overhead. Budgeted direct-labor hours are 3,000, but 3,100 hours of direct labor were actually worked. Since the company has been in business for only a short period of time, it uses a monthly rate to apply overhead to work in process.

During the past month, Bridgerland worked on a number of different jobs. Statistics for two of these jobs are as follows:

	Job 12	Job 15
Materials cost	$6,000	$8,000
Direct-labor cost	$9,000	$12,000
Direct-labor hours	1,000	800

Required

1. Calculate the predetermined overhead application rate using direct-labor hours as the base.

2. Give the journal entries to record (*a*) overhead applied to work in process and (*b*) actual overhead expenditures. In the explanation of the first journal entry, indicate how much overhead is applied to Jobs 12 and 15 this month.
3. How much over- or underapplied overhead resulted from this month's operations?
4. Prepare a flexible budget for variable overhead at the 3,100-hour level of activity.
5. Calculate the portion of the predetermined overhead application rate that is applicable to fixed costs.
6. Calculate the volume variance. Tell if it is favorable or unfavorable, and explain its significance to management.
7. Prepare a management report comparing budgeted and actual overhead.

Solution to the Self-Study Problem

1. Predetermined overhead application rate:

$$\frac{\$18,000 \text{ total budgeted overhead}}{3,000 \text{ total direct-labor hours}} = \$6.00 \text{ per hour}$$

2. (*a*) Entry to record overhead applied to work in process:

Work-in-process control	18,600	
Factory overhead applied		18,600

To record the application of overhead based on 3,100 direct-labor hours at $6.00 per hour.

Job 12: 1,000 hrs. × $6 per hr. = $6,000

Job 15: 800 hrs. × $6 per hr. = $4,800

(*b*) Entry to record actual overhead:

Factory overhead control	18,300	
Cash, etc.		18,300

To record actual expenditures for manufacturing overhead.

3. Over- or underapplied overhead:

Overhead applied to work in process	$18,600
Actual overhead expenditures	18,300
Overapplied overhead	$ 300

4. Flexible budget for manufacturing overhead:

	Variable Rate	Budgeted Amount (3,000 hrs.)	Budgeted Amount (3,100 hrs.)
Variable items:			
Indirect materials	$1.20	$3,600	$3,720
Indirect labor	1.30	3,900	4,030
Payroll-related costs	.90	2,700	2,790
Utilities	.40	1,200	1,240
Miscellaneous	.20	600	620
	$4.00	$12,000	$12,400
Fixed items	2.00	6,000	6,000
Total	$6.00	$18,000	$18,400

5. Fixed overhead application rate:

$$\frac{\$6,000}{3,000} = \$2.00 \text{ per hour}$$

6. Volume variance:

Actual direct-labor hours	3,100
Budgeted direct-labor hours	3,000
Difference	100
Fixed overhead application rate	× $2
Volume variance	$ 200 Favorable

The volume variance indicates the amount of difference between actual overhead and applied overhead caused by working more or less hours than budgeted.

7. Comparison of budgeted and actual overhead:

	Variable Rate	Budgeted Amount	Actual Amount	Variance from Budget
Variable items:				
Indirect materials	$1.20	$3,720	$3,200	$520 F
Indirect labor	1.30	4,030	4,200	170 U
Payroll-related costs	.90	2,790	3,000	210 U
Utilities	.40	1,240	1,400	160 U
Miscellaneous	.20	620	400	220 F
Total	$4.00	$12,400	$12,200	$200 F
Fixed overhead		$6,000	$6,100	$100 U
Total		$18,400	$18,300	$100 F
Volume variance				200 F
Overapplied overhead				$300 F

Suggested Readings

Beresford, Dennis R., and Neary, Robert D. "Allocation of Direct and Indirect Costs." *Financial Executive* (August 1980): 10.

Fremgen, James M., and Liao, Shu S. "The Allocation of Corporate Indirect Costs." *Management Accounting* (September 1981): 66–67.

Goodman, S., and Reece, J., eds. *Controller's Handbook,* chapter 11. Homewood, Ill.: Dow-Jones Irwin, 1978.

Murray, Daniel R. "How Management Accountants Can Make a Manufacturing Control System More Effective." *Management Accounting* (July 1981): 25–31.

National Association of Accountants (N.A.A.). "Accounting for Costs of Capacity." *N.A.A. Research Series Report No. 39.* New York: National Association of Accountants, 1961.

Discussion Questions

1. Define overhead and explain the difference between fixed, variable, and mixed overhead.
2. Describe three types of wages that are usually considered to be indirect manufacturing costs.
3. What are some difficulties encountered in obtaining timely overhead costs?

4. Describe the processes of overhead accumulation and overhead application.
5. What is the function of an activity base? What are the major criteria for selecting an appropriate activity base?
6. Name the five most common activity bases. Describe a situation in which each would be the most appropriate activity base to use.
7. What is the purpose of a predetermined overhead application rate? What is the formula for its calculation?
8. When choosing a base period for allocating overhead, why do managers often prefer an annual rate to a monthly or quarterly rate?
9. What purposes are served by keeping departmental subsidiary ledgers for overhead?
10. Why might there be differences between the factory overhead control account and the factory overhead applied account? At what point in the accounting cycle should such differences be "smoothed"?
11. What are the terms used to describe the net differences that might occur between budgeted versus actual overhead?
12. Explain why fixed overhead rates might fluctuate from period to period even though fixed costs remain unchanged.
13. Define volume variance. What significance does it have for the management and control of overhead costs?
14. When associated with overhead variances, the terms favorable and unfavorable have unique meanings. What are their meanings when associated with variable overhead variances? What are their meanings when associated with the volume variance?

Exercises

Exercise 13.1   Basics of Factory Overhead and the Uses of Predetermined Rates

Capital Company uses a flexible budget system and prepared the following information for last year:

	Percent of Capacity	
	80%	90%
Direct-labor hours	48,000	54,000
Variable factory overhead	$ 48,000	$ 54,000
Fixed factory overhead	$108,000	$108,000
Total factory overhead rate per direct-labor hour	$ 3.25	$ 3.00

Capital Company operated at 80% of capacity during last year. They applied factory overhead based on the 90% capacity level.

Required

Assuming that actual factory overhead was equal to the budgeted amount for the attained capacity, determine the amount of over- or underapplied overhead for the year.

Exercise 13.2   Factory Overhead Rates and Application of Overhead to Jobs

The cost department of the Park Company made the following estimates for the year:

Factory overhead	$212,500
Materials cost	$425,000
Labor cost	$125,000
Production in cases	22,000
Labor hours	110,000

Required

1. Determine the factory overhead rate based on (*a*) labor cost, (*b*) labor hours, and (*c*) materials cost.
2. Determine the amount of overhead to be charged to Job 829 by each rate in requirement 1, given the following information about Job 829:

	Job 829
Materials cost	$10,500
Labor cost	$ 7,400
Labor hours	$ 3,700

Exercise 13.3   Factory Overhead Costing Results—Over- or Underapplied

Peters Company uses a flexible budget system and prepared the following information for the year:

	Percent of Capacity	
	80%	90%
Direct-labor hours	24,000	27,000
Variable factory overhead	$ 48,000	$ 54,000
Fixed factory overhead	$108,000	$108,000
Total factory overhead rate per direct-labor hour	$6.50	$6.00

Peters operated at 80% of capacity last year but applied factory overhead was based on the 90% capacity level. Actual factory overhead was $158,000 for the year.

Required

1. Determine the amount of overhead applied for the year.
2. Determine the amount of under- or overapplied overhead for the year.

Exercise 13.4   Factory Overhead Concepts—Review of Cost Behavior Determination

Handy Company has estimated overhead of $96,000 for 6,000 labor hours per month and $144,000 for 14,000 labor hours per month. Handy is preparing to handle factory overhead using predetermined overhead rates in place of the practice that has been used—waiting until year end and assigning actual overhead to production.

Handy estimates that 12,000 labor hours represents normal capacity operation.

Required

1. Determine the variable overhead rates per labor hour in the overhead estimates. Use the high and low points method for this requirement and for requirement 2.

2. Determine the fixed cost overhead total in the overhead estimates.
3. Determine a predetermined overhead rate for normal capacity.

Exercise 13.5 Factory Overhead and Job Costing

Baehr Company is a manufacturing company with a fiscal year that runs from July 1 to June 30. Baehr uses a job-order accounting system for its production costs.

A predetermined overhead rate based upon direct-labor hours is used to apply overhead to individual jobs. A flexible budget of overhead costs was prepared for the fiscal year as shown below:

Direct-labor hours	100,000	120,000	140,000
Variable overhead costs	$325,000	$390,000	$455,000
Fixed overhead costs	216,000	216,000	216,000
Total overhead	$541,000	$606,000	$671,000

Although the annual ideal capacity is 150,000 direct-labor hours, Baehr's officials have determined 120,000 direct-labor hours as normal capacity for the year.

The information presented below is for November, during which Jobs 77–50 and 77–51 were completed.

Inventories November 1	
Raw materials and supplies	$ 10,500
Work in process (Job 77–50)	54,000
Finished goods	112,500
Purchases of raw materials and supplies	
Raw materials	$135,000
Supplies	15,000
Materials and supplies requisitioned for production	
Job 77–50	$ 45,000
Job 77–51	37,500
Job 77–52	25,500
Supplies	12,000
	$120,000
Factory direct-labor hours (Incurred this month)	
Job 77–50	3,500 hours
Job 77–51	3,000 hours
Job 77–52	2,000 hours
Labor costs	
Direct-labor wages	$ 51,000
Indirect-labor wages (4,000 hours)	15,000
Supervisory salaries	6,000
Building occupancy costs	
(heat, light, depreciation, etc.)	
Factory facilities	$6,500
Sales offices	1,500
Administrative offices	1,000
	$9,000
Factory equipment costs	
Power	$4,000
Repairs and maintenance	1,500
Depreciation	1,500
Other	1,000
	$8,000

Required

1. Determine the predetermined overhead rate to be used to apply overhead to individual jobs during the fiscal year.
2. Determine the amount of overhead applied to all jobs during November using the rate you obtained in requirement 1.

Exercise 13.6 Factory Overhead and Job Costing

Refer to the data in exercise 13.5. Without prejudice to your answer in exercise 13.5, assume the predetermined overhead rate is $4.50 per direct-labor hour.

Required

1. Determine the *total cost* of Job 77–50.
2. Determine the factory overhead costs applied to Job 77–52 during November.
3. Determine the actual factory overhead incurred during November.

Exercise 13.7 Factory Overhead and Year-End Disposition of Overhead Balances

At the end of the last fiscal year, Bailey Company had the following account balances:

Factory overhead control	$ 1,000	(credit balance)
Cost of goods sold	980,000	
Work-in-process inventory	38,000	
Finished-goods inventory	82,000	

Required

1. List and briefly describe the various possible methods of disposing over- or underapplied overhead.
2. Determine the disposition of the $1,000 overapplied overhead for Bailey Company if the amount is prorated (allocated) to the work-in-process and finished-goods inventories and to cost of goods sold.
3. Show the disposition you obtained in requirement 2 in general journal form.
4. Which method of disposition of the year-end overapplied overhead would you recommend for the Bailey Company? Explain your recommendation.

Exercise 13.8 Factory Overhead Concepts and Variance Analysis

GYPCO Company has set a factory overhead rate of $9.00 per hour. Budgeted overhead for 3,000 hours per month is $48,000 and at 7,000 hours is $72,000. Actual factory overhead for the month of July was $54,000 and the actual volume was 5,000 hours.

Required

Determine the following:

1. Variable overhead in the overhead rate, using the high-low method
2. Budgeted fixed overhead
3. Normal volume or normal capacity hours
4. Applied factory overhead
5. Over- or underapplied factory overhead
6. Variance from budget
7. Volume variance

Exercise 13.9 Factory Overhead

A summary of accounts has been prepared for the LHC Company at the end of June. The work-in-process and factory overhead accounts are shown below:

Work in Process

June 1 balance	3,580	64,480	Cost of goods manufactured
Direct materials	21,600		
Direct labor	25,000		
Factory overhead	27,500		

Factory Overhead Control

Indirect material	5,160	27,500	charged to production at a
Indirect labor	12,500		predetermined % of direct-
Supervision	2,000		labor cost
Repairs and maintenance	1,540		
Utilities	1,200		
Other	5,700		

Required

1. Determine the work-in-process ending inventory in total and broken down into individual amounts of materials, labor, and factory overhead. Materials costs in the inventory amount to $3,960.
2. Determine the total factory overhead incurred during June and the amount of under- or overapplied overhead.

Exercise 13.10 Factory Overhead and Journal Entries

Wonder Company produces and sells Wundra software materials for personal computers. Wonder uses a predetermined overhead rate in all departments. Direct-labor hours are used in the final assembly department to apply overhead to production.

The following transactions occurred during May in the final assembly department:

1. The payroll was recorded and distributed. The total for the department was $15,000 of which $3,000 was indirect. The FICA rate is 7%, and federal income taxes average 10% of gross earnings. All workers earn $10 per hour.
2. Supplies for specific use in the department were purchased on account for $3,500. These supplies are accounted for in the department's own inventory account.
3. Materials used in production included $8,000 direct and $1,800 indirect materials and supplies. The indirect materials and supplies came from the department's own inventory account.
4. The employer's payroll taxes were recorded. The rates are FICA 7%, state unemployment 2.7%, and federal unemployment 1.4%.
5. The following costs were recorded during May to be paid: repairs, $125; equipment rental $325; and utilities $350.
6. Adjusting entries were recorded. They included depreciation on equipment at $750 and expired insurance of $125.
7. Overhead was applied to work in process. The rate used in the department is $5.50 per direct-labor hour.

Required

1. Set up journal entries to record the transactions indicated for the final assembly department for the month of May.
2. Summarize the total overhead incurred during May and determine the amount of under- or overapplied overhead.

Problems

Problem 13.1 Factory Overhead and Job Costs Using Different Bases

During the past month, the Bigelow Company had the following costs:

Materials used	39,000
Direct labor	48,000
Indirect materials	6,000
Indirect labor	8,000
Supervisor's salary (factory operations)	6,000
Labor fringe cost (factory labor)	5,600
Depreciation on factory building	2,000
Factory machinery depreciation	4,000
Property tax on factory facilities	600
Selling and administrative expense	7,000
Insurance on factory facilities and inventory	400
Miscellaneous factory overhead	2,400
Power and light (factory operations)	1,000
Advertising	3,000

During the past month, Bigelow worked on three orders. Costs and other pertinent data in connection with these orders are:

	Job 221	Job 222	Job 223
Materials cost	$12,000	$16,000	$11,000
Direct-labor hours	1,950	2,700	975
Machine hours	1,600	1,800	600
Direct-labor cost	$16,000	$24,000	$8,000

Required

1. Determine the total factory overhead to be assigned to production.
2. Determine the total cost of each job, using each of the following as the basis for charging factory overhead:
   a. Direct-labor costs
   b. Direct-labor hours
   c. Machine hours

Problem 13.2 Factory Overhead—Analysis of Over- or Underapplied Overhead

Factory overhead for a company has been estimated as follows for the month of March:

Fixed factory overhead	$ 50,000
Variable factory overhead	$150,000
Estimated direct-labor hours	100,000

Production for March reached 80% of the estimated level and actual factory overhead totaled $174,000.

Required

1. Determine the overhead rate for March and the overhead applied during March.
2. Determine the over- or underapplied factory overhead.
3. Determine the budget and volume variances.

Problem 13.3 Factory Overhead Application and Analysis of Variances

The Duncan Company's factory overhead for April is summarized below. Normal capacity is used as the activity level for computing the predetermined factory overhead rate. Normal capacity is 1,600 hours. During April actual activity was 80% of normal.

Expense	Estimated Factory Overhead at 100% of Normal	Estimated Factory Overhead at 80% of Normal	Actual Factory Overhead
Superintendence	$1,100	$1,100	$1,100
Depreciation	650	650	650
Property tax	720	720	720
Rent	900	900	900
Power	600	480	530
Maintenance labor	840	672	790
Insurance	350	350	350
Factory supplies	480	384	425
Indirect labor	960	768	710
Payroll taxes	280	224	234
Total	$6,880	$6,248	$6,409

Required

1. Determine the predetermined overhead rate and the overhead applied during April.
2. Determine the over- or underapplied factory overhead.
3. Determine the volume variance.
4. Prepare a report showing the variance from budget for each variable overhead item, the volume variance and the amount of over- or underapplied overhead.

Problem 13.4 Determination and Use of Overhead Rates Using Different Bases

The Mann Company's budget data for March are shown below:

Estimated factory overhead	$360,000
Production scheduled	40,000 units
Direct-labor hours scheduled	100,000 hours
Estimated direct-labor cost	$500,000
Machine hours scheduled	120,000 hours

Required

1. Compute the overhead rate using the various bases indicated.
2. Assume that the total overhead estimate is composed of a variable estimate of $240,000 and a fixed estimate of $120,000. Compute variable and fixed overhead rates using machine hours.
3. Prepare the journal entry that would be required to charge the overhead to production using the labor hour rate determined in requirement 1 assuming 99,000 labor hours are used during the period.

4. Complete the following journal entry for overhead incurred:

?	359,200
Stores control (factory supplies)	65,000
Accumulated depreciation—machinery	80,000
Prepaid insurance—factory inventory and equipment	20,000
Payroll (indirect labor)	156,200
Accounts payable (overhead from current period disbursements)	38,000

Problem 13.5   Factory Overhead and the End of Period Evaluation of Results

Refer to the data in problem 13.4.

Required

1. Was the factory overhead over- or underapplied during March and by how much?
2. Assume that the $359,200 overhead incurred consisted of $120,500 of fixed costs and $238,700 of variable costs. Determine the over- or underapplied variable and fixed overhead for the period.

Problem 13.6   Determining Overhead Rates and Evaluating Overhead Information

Tastee-Treat Company prepares, packages, and distributes six frozen vegetables in two different size containers. The different vegetables and different sizes are prepared in large batches. Tastee-Treat employs an actual job-order costing system with factory overhead assigned to batches by a predetermined rate on the basis of direct-labor hours. The factory overhead costs incurred by Tastee-Treat during two recent years (adjusted for changes using current prices and wage rates) are presented below:

	Year 1	Year 2
Direct-labor hours worked	2,760,000	2,160,000
Factory overhead costs incurred		
Indirect labor	$11,040,000	$ 8,640,000
Employee benefits	4,140,000	3,240,000
Supplies	2,760,000	2,160,000
Power	2,208,000	1,728,000
Heat and light	552,000	552,000
Supervision	2,865,000	2,625,000
Depreciation	7,930,000	7,930,000
Property taxes and insurance	3,005,000	3,005,000
Total overhead costs	$34,500,000	$29,880,000

Required

Tastee-Treat Company expects to operate at a 2,300,000 direct-labor hour level of activity next year. Using the data above, calculate the rate Tastee-Treat should employ to assign manufacturing overhead to its products. State any assumptions you make regarding cost behavior and back up your answer with a schedule showing your estimation of overhead costs, by overhead item, for the 2,300,000 direct-labor hour level of activity.

Problem 13.7 Factory Overhead—Variances and Job Cost Results (CMA)

The following data apply to the operations of Mack Incorporated:

Department 203—Work in Process—Beginning of Period

Job No.	Material	Labor	Overhead	Total
1376	$17,500	$22,000	$33,000	$72,500

Department 203 costs for the year:

Incurred by Jobs	Material	Labor	Other	Total
1376	$ 1,000	$ 7,000	—	$ 8,000
1377	26,000	53,000	—	79,000
1378	12,000	9,000	—	21,000
1379	4,000	1,000	—	5,000
Not Incurred by Jobs				
Indirect materials and supplies	15,000	—	—	15,000
Indirect labor	—	53,000	—	53,000
Employee benefits	—	—	$23,000	23,000
Depreciation	—	—	12,000	12,000
Supervision	—	20,000	—	20,000
Total	$58,000	$143,000	$35,000	$236,000

Department 203 overhead rate for the year:

Budgeted overhead		
Variable—Indirect materials		$ 16,000
Indirect labor		56,000
Employee benefits		24,000
Fixed— Supervision		20,000
Depreciation		12,000
Total		$128,000
Budgeted direct-labor dollars		$80,000
Rate per direct-labor dollar ($128,000 ÷ 80,000)		160%

Required

1. Determine the actual overhead for Department 203 for the year.
2. Determine for Department 203 the overhead applied to each job, the total applied, and the amount of over- or underapplied overhead.

Problem 13.8 Factory Overhead and the End of Year Summary

Refer to the data in problem 13.7.

Required

1. Analyze the over- or underapplied overhead into budget and volume variances.
2. Job No. 1376 was the only job completed and sold during the year. Determine the amount included in cost of goods sold for this job.
3. Determine the cost of work-in-process inventory at the end of the year.
4. If underapplied overhead was distributed between cost of goods sold and work-in-process inventory, how much of the underapplied overhead was charged to the year-end work-in-process inventory?

Problem 13.9 Factory Overhead Comprehensive Evaluation of Procedures (CMA)

The Herbert Manufacturing Company manufactures custom-designed restaurant and kitchen furniture. Herbert Manufacturing uses a job-order cost accounting system. Actual overhead costs incurred during the month are applied to the products on the basis of actual direct-labor hours required to produce the products. The overhead costs consist primarily of supervision, employee benefits, maintenance costs, property taxes, and depreciation.

Herbert Manufacturing recently won a contract to manufacture the furniture for a new fast-food chain that is expanding rapidly in the area. In general, this furniture is durable but of a lower quality than Herbert Manufacturing normally manufactures. To produce this new line, Herbert Manufacturing must purchase more molded plastic parts for the furniture than for its current line. Through innovative industrial engineering, an efficient manufacturing process for this new furniture has been developed that requires only minimum capital investment. Management is very optimistic about the profit improvement the new product line will bring.

At the end of October, the start-up month for the new line, the controller has prepared a separate income statement for the new product line. On a consolidated basis the gross profit percentage was normal; however, the profitability for the new line was less than expected.

At the end of November the results were somewhat improved. Consolidated profits were good, but the reported profitability for the new product line was less than expected. John Herbert, president of the company, is concerned that knowledgeable stockholders will criticize his decision to add this lower-quality product line at a time when profitability appeared to be increasing with their standard product line.

The results presented on page 449 are for the first nine months of the current year and for October and November. Additional data regarding operations for October and November are presented on page 449.

Herbert Manufacturing Company
(000 omitted)

	Fast-Food Furniture	Custom Furniture	Consolidated
Nine months year-to-date			
Gross sales	—	$8,100	$8,100
Direct material	—	$2,025	$2,025
Direct labor			
Forming	—	758	758
Finishing	—	1,314	1,314
Assembly	—	558	558
Overhead	—	1,779	1,779
Cost of sales	—	$6,434	$6,434
Gross profit	—	$1,666	$1,666
Gross Profit			
Percentage	—	20.6%	20.6%
October, 1978			
Gross sales	$400	$ 900	$1,300
Direct material	$200	$ 225	$ 425
Direct labor			
Forming	17	82	99
Finishing	40	142	182
Assembly	33	60	93
Overhead	60	180	240
Cost of sales	$350	$ 689	$1,039
Gross profit	$ 50	$ 211	$ 261
Gross profit			
Percentage	12.5%	23.4%	20.1%
November, 1978			
Gross sales	$800	$ 800	$1,600
Direct material	$400	$ 200	$ 600
Direct labor			
Forming	31	72	103
Finishing	70	125	195
Assembly	58	53	111
Overhead	98	147	245
Cost of sales	$657	$ 597	$1,254
Gross profit	$143	$ 203	$ 346
Gross profit			
Percentage	17.9%	25.4%	21.6%

Mrs. Jameson, cost accounting manager, has stated that the overhead allocation based only on direct-labor hours is no longer appropriate. On the basis of a recently completed study of the overhead accounts, Jameson feels that only the supervision and employee benefits should be allocated on the basis of direct-labor hours and the balance of the overhead should be allocated on a machine-hour basis. In her judgment the increase in the profitability of the custom design furniture is due to a misallocation of overhead in the present system.

The actual direct-labor hours and machine hours for the past two months are shown below:

	Fast-Food Furniture	Custom Furniture
Machine Hours		
October		
Forming	660	10,700
Finishing	660	7,780
Assembly	—	—
	1.320	18,480
November		
Forming	1,280	9,640
Finishing	1,280	7,400
Assembly	—	—
	2,560	17,040
Direct-Labor Hours		
October		
Forming	1,900	9,300
Finishing	3,350	12,000
Assembly	4,750	8,700
	10,000	30,000
November		
Forming	3,400	8,250
Finishing	5,800	10,400
Assembly	8,300	7,600
	17,500	26,250

The actual overhead costs for the past two months were:

	October	November
Supervision	$ 13,000	$ 13,000
Employee benefits	95,000	109,500
Maintenance	50,000	48,000
Depreciation	42,000	42,000
Property taxes	8,000	8,000
All other	32,000	24,500
Total	$240,000	$245,000

Required

1. Based on Mrs. Jameson's recommendation, reallocate the overhead for October and November using direct-labor hours as the allocation base for supervision and employee benefits. Use machine hours as the base for the remaining overhead costs.
2. Determine a revised statement of operating results for October and November incorporating the revised overhead amounts you determined in requirement 1.

Problem 13.10   Factory Overhead and Evaluation of Operating Results

Refer to the data in problem 13.9.

Required

1. Support or criticize Mrs. Jameson's conclusion that the increase in custom design profitability is due to a misallocation of overhead. Use the answers you developed in problem 13.9 to support your analysis.
2. Mrs. Jameson has also recommended that consideration be given to using predetermined overhead application rates calculated on an annual basis rather than allocating actual cost over actual volume each month. She stated that this is particularly applicable now that the company has two distinct product lines. Discuss the advantages of predetermined overhead rates prepared on an annual basis.

FACTORY OVERHEAD: COSTING AND CONTROL II

14

OUTLINE

In chapter 13 principles of factory overhead accounting were discussed using a factory-wide perspective in which (*a*) one factory-wide predetermined overhead application rate is calculated, (*b*) one set of accounts is used to record applied and actual overhead, and (*c*) one set of reports is used to analyze under- or overapplied overhead. This chapter develops additional aspects of overhead accounting using a departmental rather than factory-wide perspective. From a departmental viewpoint *separate departmental* overhead application rates, accounts, and reports are used rather than just one factory-wide rate, set of accounts, and reports.

The additional detail of departmental accounting has several advantages. For example, departmentalization usually provides more meaningful cost allocations to jobs and products than factory-wide accounting. Also, the potential usefulness of information for planning and control is enhanced by having costs accumulated and reported at a department level rather than at a factory level.

This chapter explains overhead accounting principles that relate to departmentalization in manufacturing companies. After completing this chapter you should be able to:

1. explain the meaning of departmentalization and give advantages and disadvantages of departmentalization for (*a*) product costing and (*b*) management control.
2. define production and service departments and explain how they are related.
3. apply various methods of allocating service department costs.
4. determine the number and configuration of service and production departments in a particular factory operation.
5. apply departmental overhead costs by behavior.

DEPARTMENTALIZATION OF OVERHEAD COSTS

The principles related to departmental accounting for overhead costs are simply an extension of the overhead accounting principles discussed in chapter 13. The processes of budgeting, computing a predetermined overhead application rate, and applying overhead to work in process are the same whether using factory-wide or departmental accounting. Only the added detail of departmental accounting and certain cost allocation concepts are different.

A **department,** for cost accounting purposes, is a subunit of a manufacturing firm for which a separate measurement of costs is made. The objective of subdividing operations into departments is to facilitate more accurate product costing and more effective cost control. Terms other than department that might be used when referring to the same subunit concept are cost object, cost center, cost pool, and factory segment.

Production and Service Departments

Departments within a factory operation can be classified as being either production departments or service departments. **Production departments** include those departments that are directly engaged in the manufacturing activity and contribute to the content and form of the finished product. Examples of typical production departments include cutting, assembly, and finishing departments. Other examples of production departments are given in figure 14.1.

Service departments, as their name suggests, provide services or assistance to other departments. Service departments contribute to the production process in an indirect manner and do not directly shape or form the finished product. Examples of service departments include personnel, cafeteria, and maintenance departments. Figure 14.1 lists typical service departments in manufacturing firms.

Service department costs are used in an organization to provide information in greater detail for more accurate product costing and more effective cost control than would

Figure 14.1   Typical production and service departments

Production Departments

Assembly	Milling
Cutting	Mixing
Finishing	Packing
Knitting	Refining
Machining	

Service Departments

Accounting	Personnel
Administration	Planning
Cafeteria	Purchasing
Custodial/Grounds	Receiving
First Aid/Medical	Scheduling
General Factory	Security
Internal Auditing	Shipping
Production Control	Stores
Quality Control	Utilities
Maintenance	

otherwise be available. The costs incurred in service departments, although not directly expended in the production process, are generally felt to be as much a cost of production as are direct materials, direct labor, and factory overhead that is incurred as a direct cost of a production department. In fact, service department costs are simply overhead costs that are accumulated in separately designated service departments rather than in production departments.

Service Department Cost Allocation

From a product-costing viewpoint, costs incurred in service departments should be included as a component of total production costs. This is accomplished by allocating the costs incurred in each service department to benefiting production departments. Amounts allocated to each production department are usually based on the relative quantity of services received by each production department from the various service departments.

Allocated service department costs are then added to the overhead costs directly incurred by each production department. Finally, total overhead accumulated in each production department is allocated to units of production as a component of each production department's predetermined overhead application rate. Figure 14.2 illustrates potential overhead cost flows among three service departments and two production departments.

Note in figure 14.2 that service departments may provide assistance to other service departments as well as to production departments. Note also that figure 14.2 does not include all costs incurred by a manufacturing company. Costs incurred for purposes far removed from the production process or that do not have a direct connection with the production process may be charged as a corporate office expense rather than charged to factory departments and then to units of production. Such costs are treated as period expenses on the income statement and are included in accounts other than cost of goods manufactured or cost of goods sold.

The process of allocating service department costs to production departments generally takes place twice during an accounting period. Budgeted service department costs are allocated to production departments when departmental manufacturing budgets are prepared before the start of the accounting period. Then, actual service department

Figure 14.2   Allocation of service department costs to units of production

Service Departments   Production Departments   Units of Production

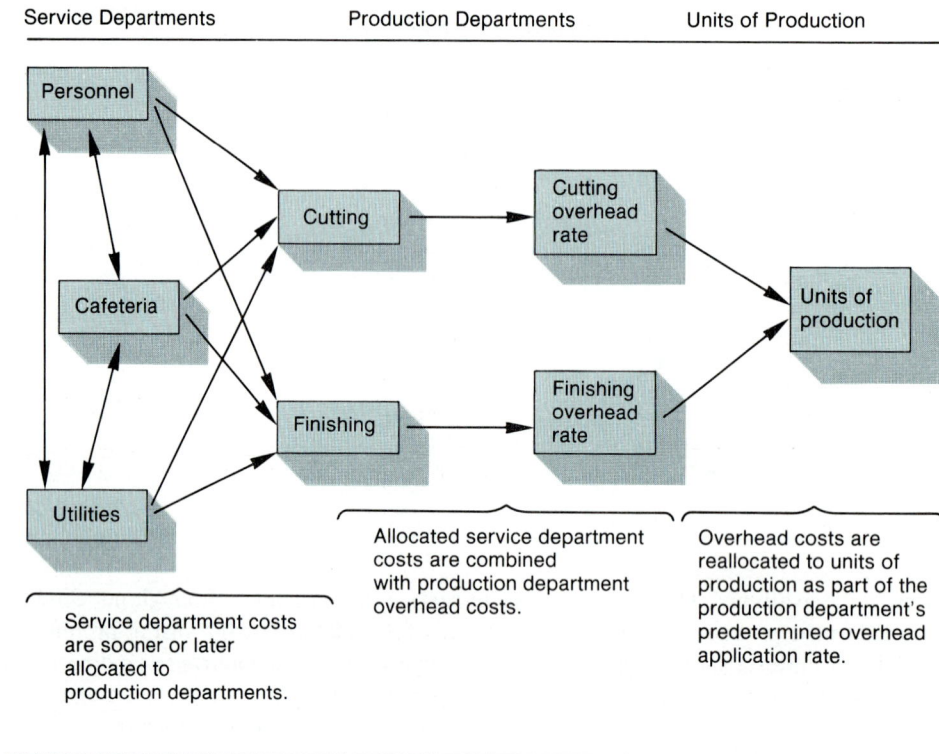

Service department costs are sooner or later allocated to production departments.

Allocated service department costs are combined with production department overhead costs.

Overhead costs are reallocated to units of production as part of the production department's predetermined overhead application rate.

costs are allocated to production departments when end-of-the-period results are accounted for. However, the process is essentially the same whether done at the beginning of an accounting period using budget data, or done at the end of an accounting period using actual data. Although the illustrations that follow could relate to either time, they deal primarily with the budgetary process due to its fundamental importance in developing predetermined overhead application rates.

Before costs can be properly accumulated and allocations made, departments must be identified. Each activity for which an accounting is to be made must be identified with a particular department. Otherwise, there would not be a clear basis for either product costing or cost control. Principles relating to the definition of departments and assignment of activities are discussed later in this chapter. For now, assume that various production and service departments are in place and focus on the proper accumulation of overhead costs in departments.

Accumulating Overhead Costs by Department

The concept of *traceability of costs* is important when deciding which costs should be assigned to what departments. Usually, this decision is not very complicated. For example, if a custodial department is selected as a service department, then the costs associated with the custodial function are identified with and accumulated in the custodial department accounts. Custodial salaries, fringe benefits, supplies, and depreciation on custodial equipment that originate within the custodial function should become part of the costs associated with that department.

In other instances, however, cost accumulation may be more complicated. For example, the cost of utilities like electricity may directly benefit some departments while

Figure 14.3   Cutting department factory overhead budget

(Based on 70,000 units of production at 1 hour of direct-labor per unit.)
For the year ending December 31, 19X8

	Amount per Unit	Total Amount
Budgeted overhead:		
Variable items:		
Indirect labor	$1.00	$ 70,000
Repair and maintenance	.30	21,000
Utilities (variable portion)	.20	14,000
Idle time	.05	3,500
Other variable overhead	.05	3,500
	$1.60	$112,000
Fixed items:		
Supervisory salaries		$ 50,000
Depreciation		28,000
Insurance		10,000
Utilities (fixed portion)		4,000
Other fixed overhead		6,000
		$ 98,000
Total budgeted overhead before allocated amounts		$210,000
Total allocated from service departments		$ 39,500
Total budgeted overhead		$249,500
Predetermined overhead application rate (Based on 70,000 direct-labor hours)		$3.56/hr

indirectly benefiting all departments. In such situations, a company may use meters or some other device to measure departmental consumption. Under these conditions, each department is assigned its direct share of the cost of the electrical bill. However, the plant probably also incurs electrical costs that are not directly traceable to any specific department. For example, the cost of lighting the outside of the plant building is usually not traceable to specific departments. This type of overhead cost is typically accumulated in a service department, probably a utilities department in this example. Then, a portion of the total cost is allocated to each benefiting department on some rational basis such as the proportion of total space lighted.

As used in the above illustration, the terms direct and indirect are associated with overhead in terms of its traceability to departments. Direct overhead refers to those overhead costs that are traceable directly to specific departments. Indirect overhead refers to those overhead costs that are first accumulated in service departments and then assigned to other departments through an allocation process. Therefore, the use of service departments results in part of the overhead costs of a production department being direct overhead and part being indirect overhead, for example, allocated service department costs. Figure 14.3 contains the factory overhead budget for the cutting department of a textile company.

Figure 14.3 shows that the total budgeted overhead of $210,000 is the total direct overhead cost of the cutting department before the allocation of any indirect or service department costs. Adding the service department cost allocations results in an addition to the overhead budget by the amount of allocated service department costs.

Figure 14.4   Commonly used service department allocation bases

Basis	Potential Department Users
Number of employees	Administration, Cafeteria, First Aid/Medical, Personnel
Square or cubic footage of space occupied	Administration, Custodial/Grounds, General Factory, Security, Utilities
Hours of service rendered	Accounting, First Aid/Medical, Internal Auditing, Maintenance, Personnel, Planning
Volume handled	Accounting, Cafeteria, Purchasing, Receiving, Shipping, Stores
Metered usage	Production Control, Utilities, Quality Control

Once departments have been identified and total costs have been accumulated in each department, the basis used to allocate service department costs to production departments should be determined.

Selection of an Activity Base

Service department costs are allocated to production departments by using an activity base in much the same way that overhead costs in production departments are allocated to work in process by using a predetermined overhead application rate. One difference is that the activity base suggested for allocating overhead is sometimes not appropriate for allocating service department costs. For example, direct-labor hours may be an appropriate base for allocating overhead to units of production but may be a poor base for allocating service department costs to production departments.

The activity base selected for allocating service department costs should reflect as accurately as possible the correlation between the quantity of services provided by service departments and the benefits received by the various production departments. Since costs allocated to production departments will ultimately affect product costs and since product costs, in turn, influence many aspects of firm operations (such as pricing decisions), it is important that a cause-and-effect or benefit linkage be present. It may be tempting to allocate costs on an "ability-to-bear" basis such as sales dollars or gross margin. This should be avoided whenever there is a basis available that exhibits a cause-and-effect linkage. Such bases typically result in a more equitable allocation of service department costs. Whenever an activity base is used that reflects a cause-and-effect relationship more meaningful information results for management decision making.

In order to provide a high correlation between cause and effect, each service department may use a different base according to the nature of the services rendered. For example, the base used to allocate personnel department costs may be the number of employees in each department served. However, the base used to allocate custodial costs may be the square footage of space occupied by each department served. Figure 14.4 gives examples of common allocation bases with examples of service departments for which they may be appropriate.

Note that figure 14.4 does not contain activity bases that are used in chapter 13 to allocate production department overhead. They are excluded from figure 14.4 simply to distinguish between the process of allocating service department costs to production departments versus the use of predetermined overhead application rates to assign total overhead costs accumulated in production departments to work in process. Activity bases such as direct-labor hours or machine hours may, in fact, be appropriate. However, care should be exercised in their use when allocating service department costs.

When a service department's costs are fixed, the use of a variable allocation base, as determined by production department activity, should be avoided because of the potential for inaccurate allocations. For example, the number of machine hours worked may have little correlation with the cost of services received from the personnel department. The use of machine hours, in this example, may result in an inequitable allocation of personnel department costs. Instead, fixed costs may be allocated as a lump sum to producing departments.

Another consideration in the selection of an allocation base is the availability of data and the ease with which allocations are made. Elaborate measurement systems and complex allocation computations may result in costs that exceed the benefits from such systems. An accountant should try to use a base for which data are already available or are easily gathered and maintained. Allocation schemes should be well understood and acceptable to the department managers who must rely on them for decision-making information.

Activity Bases Recommended by the Cost Accounting Standards Board

The Cost Accounting Standards Board (CASB) has specified a hierarchy of preferable activity bases for companies working on certain government contracts. It should be noted that for companies not engaged in government contracting that the selection of an allocation base is entirely up to the company. Any rational and systematic allocation method can be used for both internal and external reporting. However, the hierarchy specified by the CASB may be useful to any firm concerned with the use of an appropriate allocation base.

The first category of activity bases, specified by the CASB, represent a measure of the activity (input) of the providing department. For example, square footage or hours of service rendered constitute measures of service department activity. Activity measures provide an appropriate activity base when there is a direct and definitive relationship between the inputs to the providing department and the benefits flowing to the receiving department.

The second category of bases in the CASB hierarchy represents measures of output of the providing department. These measures are preferred when activity (input) measures do not provide a direct and definitive linkage or when such measures are unavailable or impractical to obtain. Output is generally measured in terms of units of product (services) rendered by the service department. Examples of output measures include the number of hires processed by the personnel department and the number of items handled by the stores department.

When there is no practical measure of either activity (input) or output then the third category preferred by the CASB is the use of surrogate measures. A surrogate measure is any quantifiable measure of activity in the *receiving* department that is representative of the amount of services received. Such measures typically vary with the level of services received. For example, suppose that the services provided by a personnel department cannot be adequately measured on either an activity or output basis. As a surrogate measure, the number of personnel in receiving departments may be representative of the benefits received and might be an appropriate allocation base.

The final category of preferred activity bases is the measure of overall plant activity. Examples of overall plant activity include total materials cost, machine hours, or labor hours. Resorting to an overall activity measure is justified when there is no other base to provide a clear cause-benefit relationship among departments. For example, the plant manager's salary or the cost of property taxes may not have a direct or definitive relationship to benefiting departments. In such instances, the CASB prefers the selection of a base that is representative of overall management or plant activity.

Other CASB guidelines for the allocation of overhead costs are discussed in the appendix at the end of this chapter.

Figure 14.5   Factory statistics for service department cost allocation

Department	Personnel Transactions Processed	Number of Employees	Space Occupied (Square Feet)
Production:			
Cutting	150	400	60,000
Finishing	250	600	60,000
Total	400	1,000	120,000
Service:			
Personnel	20	15	4,000
Cafeteria	40	20	10,000
Utilities	60	120	—
Total	120	155	14,000
Grand total	520	1,155	134,000

Allocation Methods

Several methods could be used to allocate service department costs—the *direct method,* the *step method* (sometimes called multi-step or step-down method), and the *reciprocal method* (sometimes called the algebraic or linear algebra method). To illustrate the use of each of these methods, assume a plant situation in which there are two production departments (cutting and finishing) and three service departments (personnel, cafeteria, and utility). Assumed departmental statistics are given in figure 14.5.

Direct Method   The **direct method** is used to allocate service department costs directly to production departments with no allocation of service department costs to any other service department. Although this method is the easiest to apply, its use should be restricted to situations in which service departments do not, in fact, render service to other service departments or in which such service is considered immaterial in its effect on final product costs. For example, if the direct method is used to allocate service department costs in the situation illustrated in figure 14.5, then the potential service of the custodial department to the cafeteria is assumed to be either nonexistent or immaterial in its effect on product costs.

Each service department illustrated in this example uses a different base to allocate costs. The base used to allocate personnel department costs is the number of personnel transactions processed for each production department. The base used to allocate cafeteria costs is the number of employees in each production department. The base used to allocate utilities costs is the amount of floor space occupied by each production department.

Using the direct method, service department costs are allocated to production departments based on the relative proportion or percentage of the activity base associated with each production department. Figure 14.6 shows the calculation of these percentages for the cutting and finishing departments.

Using the relative percentages calculated in figure 14.6, service department costs are allocated directly to production departments as illustrated in figure 14.7.

Remember, the reason for making these computations is to provide the information needed to develop manufacturing overhead budgets and to make an ultimate assignment of actual overhead to work in process.

Figure 14.6   Direct method of allocation: Factory statistics and percentages

Department	Personnel Transactions Processed		Number of Employees		Space Occupied (Square Feet)	
	Number	Percent	Number	Percent	Number	Percent
Cutting	150	37.5%	400	40.0%	60,000	50.0%
Finishing	250	62.5	600	60.0	60,000	50.0
	400	100.0%	1,000	100.0%	120,000	100.0%

Figure 14.7   Direct method of allocation: Allocation procedure

	Service Departments			Production Departments	
	Personnel	Cafeteria	Utilities	Cutting	Finishing
Overhead costs					
Before allocation	$20,000	$30,000	$40,000	$210,000	$300,000
Allocation:					
Personnel	(20,000)			7,500	12,500
{Percent}	{100.0%}			{37.5%}	{62.5%}
Cafeteria		(30,000)		12,000	18,000
{Percent}		{100.0%}		{40.0%}	{60.0%}
Utilities			(40,000)	20,000	20,000
{Percent}			{100.0%}	{50.0%}	{50.0%}
Total production department overhead after allocation				$249,500	$350,500
Predetermined overhead application rates:					
Cutting ($249,500 ÷ 70,000 direct-labor hours)				$3.56/hr	
Finishing ($350,500 ÷ 90,000 direct-labor hours)					$3.89/hr

Step Method   The **step method** is used to allocate service department costs in situations where service departments provide services to *other service departments* as well as to production departments. Ultimately all service department costs find their way to production departments. The step method simply recognizes the cost of services provided by one service department to another service department and provides for a more precise ultimate application of overhead costs.

To apply the step method, a sequence for allocating service department costs must first be chosen. This sequence is usually determined by applying some rational or systematic criteria. For example, the first service department chosen might be the one that provides the most service to others, the second provides the next amount of services, and so forth. Such a ranking gives guidance as to which service department's costs are to be allocated first, second, third, and so forth. Assume that after applying some criteria it is determined that the personnel, cafeteria, and utilities departments are to be ranked in that order for purposes of allocating service department costs.

Figure 14.8   Step method of allocation: Factory statistics and percentages

Department	Personnel Transactions Processed		Number of Employees		Space Occupied (Square Feet)	
	Number	Percent	Number	Percent	Number	Percent
Production:						
Cutting	150	30%	400	36%	60,000	50%
Finishing	250	50	600	53	60,000	50
Service:						
Personnel	na	0	na	0	na	0
Cafeteria	40	8	na	0	na	0
Utilities	60	12	120	11	na	0
	500	100%	1,120	100%	120,000	100%

na = not applicable (Costs of service departments are not allocated to themselves when using the step method.)

Using this sequence, the allocation of service department costs begins with the allocation of personnel department costs to the other service and production departments. The process continues in a step-by-step fashion with the allocation of total cafeteria costs to utilities and production departments. Finally, the utilities department's costs are allocated to production departments.

Before actual cost allocations are made, it is necessary to determine the percentage of each service department's cost that is to be allocated to a certain service and production department. Percentages are calculated using overhead application bases in generally the same way as when using the direct method. However, the step-wise process must be taken into consideration when calculating these percentages. To illustrate, assume that personnel department costs are allocated on the basis of the number of personnel transactions processed, that cafeteria department costs are allocated on the basis of the number of employees in each department, and that utilities department costs are allocated on the basis of space occupied. Figure 14.8 gives factory statistics for each of these bases and illustrates the calculation of percentages for each production and service department.

Note that, since personnel department costs are allocated first, zero personnel department costs are allocated to itself. Therefore, no factory statistics and 0% are shown for the personnel department in figure 14.8. Also note that this same general principle applies to subsequent departmental allocations consistent with the step method.

Now that percentage allocation numbers have been developed, actual cost allocations can be made as shown in figure 14.9.

Personnel department costs are first allocated to all other service departments *and* to production departments. Cafeteria costs plus allocated personnel department costs are allocated next to the utilities department and to production departments. Finally, utilities costs plus previously allocated costs are allocated to production departments. Through this process all service department costs are eventually assigned to production departments.

When using the step method compared with the direct method, there could be a significant difference in the amount of costs that ultimately reach production departments. Such differences have a direct effect on the amount of costs assigned to each unit of production and could consequently have a significant impact on firm operations when costs of production are used in management decisions. Therefore, it is vital that the allocation method chosen be representative of the actual cost of producing each product.

Figure 14.9   Step method of allocation: Allocation procedure

	Service Departments			Production Departments	
	Personnel	Cafeteria	Utilities	Cutting	Finishing
Overhead costs					
Before allocation	$20,000	$30,000	$40,000	$210,000	$300,000
Allocation:					
Personnel	(20,000)	1,600	2,400	6,000	10,000
{Percent}	{100%}	{8%}	{12%}	{30%}	{50%}
Cafeteria		(31,600)	3,476	11,376	16,748
{Percent}		{100%}	{11%}	{36%}	{53%}
Utilities			(45,876)	22,938	22,938
{Percent}			{100%}	{50%}	{50%}
Total production Department overhead After allocation				$250,314	$349,686

Predetermined overhead application rates:
Cutting ($250,314 ÷ 70,000 direct-labor hours) $3.58/hr

Finishing ($349,686 ÷ 90,000 direct labor hours) $3.89/hr

Reciprocal Method   The **reciprocal method** is used to allocate service department costs in situations where service departments render service to one another in a mutual or complementary relationship. This situation is typical of most service department relationships and represents the most theoretically accurate method. It is a rare manufacturing situation in which all service departments serve only production departments and do not simultaneously serve other service departments. The step method goes part way in recognizing these reciprocal relationships, but the results of the step method only approximate a theoretical solution when reciprocal relationships are present. Such approximations may be adequate in many specific company situations, but in other situations more precision may be desirable.

The application of the reciprocal method relies on the use of simultaneous equations. To illustrate the procedure, let's begin with a simple situation. Assume that a firm has only two service departments (department A and department B) and two production departments (department 1 and department 2). Department A provides services to department B as well as to both production departments based on the percentage of space occupied by each department. Department B provides services to department A and to both production departments based on the number of employees in each of these departments.

These relationships and associated percentages are outlined in figure 14.10 along with the respective departmental costs before allocation. Remember that the objective of this procedure is to allocate total service department costs of $20,000 ($8,000 for department A plus $12,000 for department B) to the production departments.

Once the relationships illustrated in figure 14.10 are determined, the next step in applying the reciprocal method is to formulate total cost functions for the service departments *taking into consideration their reciprocal relationships*. For example, the total cost to be allocated by department A is $8,000 plus 10% of department B's costs. On the

Figure 14.10   Reciprocal method of allocation: Factory statistics and percentages

Department	Personnel Transactions Processed Number	Percent	Number of Employees Number	Percent	Overhead Costs Before Allocation
Production:					
Department 1	30	20%	15,000	30%	$ 40,000
Department 2	105	70	25,000	50	60,000
					$100,000
Service:					
Department A	15	10	na	0	8,000
Department B	na	0	10,000	20	12,000
					$ 20,000
	150	100%	50,000	100%	$120,000

Note: The objective is to allocate total service department costs of $20,000 to the production departments.

other hand, the total cost to be allocated by department B is $12,000 plus 20% of department A's costs. Stated algebraically this reciprocal relationship is shown as follows:

Let A = total costs of department A

B = total costs of department B

(1) $A = \$8,000 + .1B$

(2) $B = \$12,000 + .2A$

The next step in the reciprocal method is to solve the above equations simultaneously for either A or B. This can be done by substituting the value of B in equation (2) for B in equation (1) and solving for A. Then the value of A can be substituted for A in equation (2) and solved for B as follows:

Substituting in (1): $A = \$8,000 + .1(\$12,000 + .2A)$

$A = \$8,000 + \$1,200 + .02A$

$.98A = \$9,200$

$A = \$9,388$

Substituting in (2): $B = \$12,000 + .2(\$9,388)$

$B = \$13,878$

The final step using the reciprocal method is to allocate the total cost for each service department calculated in the above process to other service departments and to the production departments based on the percentage of services provided by each service department. Figure 14.11 illustrates this final step.

The mathematical technique shown above can be used to allocate service department costs in simple situations. However, in more involved situations it may be necessary to use matrix algebra to find the solution. The appendix at the end of this chapter discusses the use of matrix algebra to make reciprocal allocations.

Accountants and managers should carefully consider using the reciprocal method because of its theoretical accuracy. It clearly outperforms the other methods when there is a heavy interdependence among service departments. Even when the other methods are used, their results should be periodically tested against results using the reciprocal method to determine if cost allocations using the other methods continue to be adequate.

Figure 14.11   Reciprocal method of allocation: Allocation procedure

	Service Departments		Production Departments	
	A	B	1	2
Overhead costs before allocation	$8,000	$12,000	$40,000	$60,000
Allocation of reciprocal costs				
Department A	(9,388)	1,878	2,816	4,694
(Percent)	(100%)	(20%)	(30%)	(50%)
Department B	1,388	(13,878)	2,776	9,714
(Percent)	(10%)	(100%)	(20%)	(70%)
Total	–0–	–0–	$45,592	$74,408

Predetermined overhead application rates:				
Department 1: Based on 9,000 direct-labor hours			$5.07/hr	
Department 2: Based on 11,000 direct-labor hours				$6.76/hr

ADVANTAGES OF DEPARTMENTALIZATION

The segregation of factory overhead costs by department has several advantages over factory-wide overhead accounting. The first advantage is that the costs assigned to each job or unit of production may be more representative of actual or true costs of production when departmental accounting is used. This is especially true when various departments have different cost characteristics and provide different levels of input to each job. For example, consider a plant with two production departments. If one department is capital intensive and the other department is labor intensive, and if each job that passes through the plant spends a different amount of time in each department, a factory-wide overhead application rate will probably give inaccurate cost allocations.

The use of several department overhead application rates in such situations will probably result in more accurate product costs than if a single factory-wide rate had been used. A factory-wide rate may obscure the unique contribution made by each department to various types of products.

The second advantage of departmentalized accounting is that overhead expenditures can be more easily identified with the specific managers or supervisors who control such costs. Identifying overhead expenditures that originate within a department with the manager responsible typically results in more efficient and effective use of overhead than when accounting takes place at a factory-wide level. Also, a comparison at the department level of actual expenditures with budgeted amounts provides management with an important tool for monitoring and controlling overhead expenditures.

A major disadvantage of departmentalization is that it requires an expanded accounting system to accumulate, allocate, and report departmental detail. However, management may find that the added benefits derived from the more detailed information more than offset the additional costs of operating an expanded accounting system.

THE NUMBER AND CONFIGURATION OF DEPARTMENTS

The extent to which manufacturing operations should be subdivided into departmental categories is a common dilemma for company executives. For example, a plant manager may ask if it is adequate to have one factory-wide department for indirect overhead accumulation or if there should be a number of service departments created for this purpose.

In a small plant where all units of production pass uniformly through all departments, a single factory-wide rate or pool may be an appropriate and accurate way to allocate overhead costs. On the other hand, if the processing of each job or unit of production is unique, individual overhead costs should be allocated using individual overhead rates. In practice, most manufacturing operations are not so involved as to require allocations using individual-cost rates. However, most are sufficiently involved to require more detailed allocations than provided by factory-wide rates. The question is where on this continuum from individual-cost to factory-wide allocations is the appropriate place for an allocation scheme to operate? Stated another way, how many departments should be created in an individual situation to give adequate information for product costing and cost control?

A comprehensive overhead cost pool is a factory-wide pool that results in the use of a factory-wide overhead application rate. The major disadvantage of using a factory-wide pool is that any pooling of overhead costs results in the *averaging* of costs before they are allocated. Such averaging inevitably yields less accurate product-costing information than if costs had been individually allocated. The question is how many (if any) cost pools should be created beyond a factory-wide pool to optimize the cost-benefit relationship that exists in each factory situation?

The application of economic theory to this question tells us that the creation of more detailed cost pools (that is, moving along the continuum from factory-wide to individual-cost allocations) should continue until the expected increase in costs resulting from more detailed allocations is greater than the expected benefits derived from these more exacting allocations. Although measurement of these cost-benefit relationships is possible, such measurements are often very difficult to make. In these situations it may be necessary to develop additional guidelines for determining the appropriate extent of departmentalization. Several considerations in formulating such guidelines follow.

Homogeneity of Costs

A pervasive concept affecting the degree of departmentalization is the homogeneity of overhead costs. In factory overhead accounting, **homogeneity of overhead costs** refers to the similarity of costs that permits grouping of costs for accumulation and allocation without compromising the accuracy of product costing.

One of the best ways to determine whether overhead costs are homogeneous is to compare the actual cost allocations made to units of production when costs are applied using a factory-wide rate or applied using multiple departmental rates. If the amount of overhead costs assigned to each unit of production using factory-wide rates is equivalent to the amount of overhead costs assigned to each unit of production using multiple departmental rates, then the individual costs are considered to be homogeneous, and there is no justification for the extra accounting involved in the use of departmental rates. If the use of departmental rates results in different costs being assigned to units of production, this indicates that individual costs are heterogeneous and are appropriate candidates for departmentalization.

For example, consider two overhead cost pools—pool *A* and pool *B*. The question is should the pools be kept separate and make individual allocations for each pool or should the two pools be combined into a larger pool and make one cost allocation? Assume that each product or job is routed through or receives benefits from each pool. Assume also that pool *A* consists of very costly automatic equipment and the process relies on intensive use of machinery. On the other hand, that pool *B* is labor intensive and requires a great deal of skilled workmanship in its processes. As a result, simply due to the differences in the amount of depreciation expense in each pool, it can be expected that overhead costs would be relatively large in pool *A* and relatively small in pool *B*. Assume that the overhead costs of the pools are allocated based on direct-labor hours. Figure 14.12 depicts the numeric details of this situation.

Figure 14.12   Homogeneity of cost pools

	Separate Cost Pools		Combined Cost Pool
	Pool A	Pool B	(Pool A/B)
Budgeted overhead amount	$105,000	$15,000	$120,000
Direct-labor hours	15,000	15,000	30,000
Overhead application rate per direct-labor hour	$7.00	$1.00	$4.00

Overhead application to jobs:	
Job #1:	
Pool A: 10 hrs. @ $7.00/hr.	$70.00
Pool B: 2 hrs. @ $1.00/hr.	2.00
Total	$72.00
Combined cost pool: 12 hrs. @ $4.00/hr.	$48.00
Job #2:	
Pool A: 4 hrs. @ $7.00/hr.	$28.00
Pool B: 8 hrs. @ $1.00/hr.	8.00
Total	$36.00
Combined cost pool: 12 hrs. @ $4.00/hr.	$48.00

Now consider the overhead costs that would be allocated to two different jobs routed through pools *A* and *B*. Job 1 requires 10 hours of pool *A* time and 2 hours of pool *B* time. Job 2 requires 4 hours of pool *A* time and 8 hours of pool *B* time. If separate cost pools are used to make the allocation, then job 1 is allocated $72.00 of overhead while job 2 is allocated only $36.00 of overhead—a significant difference. However, if cost pools *A* and *B* are combined, then both jobs would be allocated $48.00 of overhead—no difference. The disparity between allocated costs using an aggregated cost pool and separate cost pools indicates that the costs in pools *A* and *B* are heterogeneous and should not be combined for product costing.

In summary, the extent of factory-wide versus departmental accounting depends mostly on the homogeneity of the costs involved. When costs are homogeneous they may be combined into a factory-wide rate with little loss in the accuracy of product-costing information. However, using a factory-wide rate when costs are heterogeneous results in less accurate cost allocations. Reliance on such data may also result in less reliable management decisions.

Production Departments

The number and configuration of production departments in a given plant depends mainly on the physical characteristics of the manufacturing process and the emphasis management places on cost control. Physical characteristics of the manufacturing process that should be considered include the type of processes or operations involved, the amount and type of machinery used, the physical location of each operation relative to other operations, and the product-flow relationships of processes. Generally speaking, departmental boundaries should be made at points that logically separate functional operations, at points that recognize natural breaks in the production flow, and at points where the physical control of production units is important.

The relative emphasis that management places on cost control also influences the number and configuration of production departments. For example, a desire for tighter cost control usually leads to a larger number of production departments, which in turn makes for more explicit cost control assignments. It is not uncommon in such situations to find departments organized around the operation of a single machine. A full discussion of cost centers and responsibility accounting is contained in chapter 19.

Service Departments

Since all service department costs are considered indirect production costs, the·focus for determining the number and configuration of service departments should be cost control considerations rather than product costing considerations. Therefore, the selection of an organizational structure that facilitates effective cost control should be the foremost consideration. Usually service departments are selected on the basis of functional supervisory responsibility. This provides a desirable coordination of functional and cost responsibility necessary for effective cost control.

Other important considerations include the type of services involved, the number of employees in each service function, the total cost of providing each service, and the physical location of each service function. Based on these considerations, management concepts rather than accounting concepts should guide the organization of service departments. In some situations management philosophy and homogeneity of costs may dictate one department to be called "general factory," representing a cost pool of all service functions.

ALLOCATION OF COSTS BY BEHAVIOR

Often it may be advisable to separate service department costs into their fixed and variable components and then make a separate allocation of each component. This approach avoids inequitable allocations that might result from allocating heterogeneous cost pools. From a managerial viewpoint, the analysis of overhead costs into their fixed and variable components is also useful for more effective planning and control of departmental operations.

Variable Costs

Variable service department costs are costs that fluctuate in proportion to the level of services provided. For example, paper supplies in a data-processing department could be considered a variable cost, since such a cost would vary in proportion to the extent of services rendered. Such variable service department costs should be allocated to production departments in proportion to the actual level of usage by each production department. For example, if the costs of preparing management reports varies in proportion to the machine hours used to prepare them, then the variable costs of data processing could be allocated on the basis of machine hours spent preparing reports for other departments.

This type of allocation system actually represents a "charge for services" concept rather than a traditional cost allocation concept. Charging for services rendered, when departments have the choice of consuming as much or as little as they want, also tends to encourage more efficient utilization of such services as well as provide more accurate cost allocations. However, if departments do not have the choice of consuming as much or as little as they want, as is usually the case with fixed service department costs, then a different method of allocation is appropriate.

Fixed Costs

Fixed service department costs are costs that do not fluctuate in proportion to the level of services provided. For example, depreciation on computer equipment is usually considered a fixed cost, since it is expected to remain virtually constant regardless of the level of services rendered. As a general rule, fixed costs should be allocated based on predetermined activity levels. To illustrate, consider the example of a data-processing department. Before purchasing its machinery a study was conducted to determine the capacity that should be built into the equipment to handle the expected current demand for data-processing services as well as accommodate anticipated future increases in demand over the useful life of the equipment.

Based on the information from its study, the proportion of total capacity built into the equipment was identified with each department. This made it possible to allocate the fixed data-processing costs to departments based on the percentage of total capacity identified with each department. Since in the long run both the costs and capacity relationships are fixed in such situations, the allocation takes the form of a lump-sum amount that remains constant through time until there are changes in the capacity or service relationships of the departments.

Summary

This chapter expands on the principles of overhead accounting discussed in chapter 13. The added detail of departmental accounting is presented in this chapter. Manufacturing operations are typically subdivided into various departments to provide more detail for purposes of product costing and management control. Production departments are departments that are directly engaged in the actual manufacturing process. Service departments provide assistance to other departments. For example, cutting and assembly are typical production departments and personnel and maintenance are typical service departments.

Service department costs represent overhead costs accumulated in departments other than production departments. Since service department costs represent an indirect manufacturing cost, it is important that they be assigned in some equitable way to units produced. This assignment is accomplished by using a procedure in which service department costs are first allocated to production departments and then reallocated to units of production along with other production department costs.

Service department costs are allocated using an activity base in much the same way as overhead costs are allocated to units of production using an activity base. However, different activity bases are usually used to allocate service department costs than are used to allocate overhead of production departments. Typical activity bases for allocating service department costs include the number of reports processed, floor space occupied, or the number of employees hired.

Methods that might be used to allocate service department costs include the direct method, step method, and reciprocal method. The direct method is used to allocate service department costs directly to production departments with no allocation of service department costs to any other service department. The step method is used to allocate service department costs to other service departments when service departments render services to each other as well as to production departments. The reciprocal method is used to allocate service department costs when service departments provide services to one another in a mutual or complementary relationship.

Service department costs may be allocated as one amount or they can be subdivided into fixed and variable components and then allocated in two amounts by cost behavior. Allocation by cost behavior is primarily done to provide more detailed information for management control.

The extent to which manufacturing operations are departmentalized depends on a number of factors. First, from a conceptual viewpoint, similar (homogeneous) costs should be grouped together. Second, from a situational viewpoint, production departments should be selected based on the physical characteristics of the manufacturing process. The emphasis is on both product costing and cost control when organizing production departments. When organizing service departments, cost control should be the major consideration.

Service department costs may be allocated as one amount or they may be subdivided into their fixed and variable components and then allocated in two amounts by cost behavior. Allocation by cost behavior requires more detailed computations and is primarily done to provide more detailed information for management control. Many firms find that the added benefits of allocating costs by behavior exceed the additional computational costs.

Appendix *Applicable Standards of the Cost Accounting Standards Board*

Several *cost accounting standards* of the Cost Accounting Standards Board (CASB) are directly related to the problems of overhead accounting. Even though these standards are only required of firms engaged in certain types of government contracts, there are several theoretical and practical principles associated with their use that all cost accountants should understand.

The overall objective of cost accounting standards is to provide for an equitable assignment of costs to work performed. The general principle is that all costs of performing work under a particular contract should be assigned to that contract. This includes the assignment of all direct and indirect materials and labor *plus* an equitable portion of all period costs such as executive salaries. Such costs are considered an ordinary and necessary cost of a contract.

The allocation of period costs, as well as inventoriable costs, to government contracts means that the contractor typically performs additional accounting to allocate some types of costs to contracts that may not be allocated to products under other circumstances. For example, general and administrative expenses are not typically allocated to products but are shown on the income statement as a period expense. However, a firm working on government contracts allocates a portion of general and administrative costs to each contract. These types of allocations may be made by memorandum only and not recorded by journal entry because their main purpose is simply to establish the "full cost" of a government contract.

STANDARD 402: Consistency in Allocating Costs Incurred for the Same Purpose

This standard insures that each cost be assigned *only once* to products or services acquired by the government. This standard guards against double counting some types of costs. The standard specifies that all costs incurred for the same general purpose must be treated as either direct costs or as indirect costs when such costs are assigned to products or services acquired by government contract; that is, if some costs are treated as indirect costs, then other costs incurred for the *same general purpose* cannot be treated as direct costs.

For example, consider a contractor who places all travel costs into an indirect cost pool and then allocates this pool to government contracts using direct-labor hours as an allocation base. This standard requires that the travel costs incurred by personnel whose salaries are considered direct-labor costs of a government contract be placed in the travel cost pool and allocated with other travel costs rather than charged directly to the contract. All costs incurred for the *same purpose* must be either allocated or directly assigned. Therefore, the possible combination of directly assigning some travel costs to contracts and allocating other travel costs via an indirect cost pool is not allowed. Requiring consistency in how costs incurred for the same purpose are assigned to government contracts is expected to reduce the possibility of some travel costs being assigned to a contract twice.

STANDARD 403: Allocation of Home Office Expenses to Segments

A **home office** is a function or office that is responsible for managing or directing other parts of the business. Home offices may perform supervisory, managerial, or administrative functions. They may also perform service functions similar in character to the service department functions previously discussed in this chapter.

A **segment** is a subdivision of a business that typically has a service or reporting relationship to the home office. Subsidiaries, product lines, and plants could all be considered segments of a business. Segments usually produce a product or service and are responsible for profits.

This standard specifies that home office expenses are to be allocated to segments based on a beneficial or causal relationship existing between them. In addition, the standard states that home office costs should be *directly assigned* to segments to the maximum extent possible. Other costs, not amenable to direct assignment, are to be placed in homogeneous cost pools and allocated to segments in the same way that service department costs are allocated to production departments. The standard specifies what some of these cost pools might contain and what bases might be appropriate for their allocation. Figure 14.13 lists the pools and bases suggested by the standard.

After examining the home office cost pools and associated allocation bases in figure 14.13, it is quite evident that the concepts and procedures for allocating home office expenses are virtually the same as those already examined with regard to the allocation of service department costs. Only the level in the organization hierarchy is different. For example, home office expenses may be allocated to a plant, which also has a number of service and production departments. At the plant level, allocated home office expenses are reallocated to units of production in much the same way as service department costs incurred at the plant level are allocated to units of production. Thus, the full cost of a government contract using this procedure includes direct materials, direct labor, allocated service department costs, and allocated home office expenses.

STANDARD 410: Allocation of Business Unit General and Administrative Expenses to Final Cost Objectives

This standard specifies the criteria for allocating general and administrative (G&A) expenses and home office expenses to **final cost objectives,** which is defined to be an object of final cost accumulation. A final cost objective is typically a contract, but it could also be the cost of services rendered or the cost of units produced.

The first general provision of this standard specifies that allocations of home office expenses be included in the G&A expense pool of the receiving organizational unit. For example, consider a firm that consists of a home office and three manufacturing plants. The home office expenses are first allocated to each plant as outlined in Standard 403. Then, allocated home office expenses are placed in the G&A expense pool of each plant. Finally, the G&A expense pool in each plant is allocated to final cost objectives as outlined in this standard.

The second general provision of this standard specifies that G&A expense pools will be allocated *only* to final cost objectives. This allocation is to be based on a measure of total cost inputs such as direct-labor or direct-materials cost. For example, a G&A expense pool, which includes allocated home office expenses, is appropriately allocated directly to units of production using total direct-labor cost as the basis for the allocation.

Only the general provisions of these standards are outlined here. Before application, the actual standards and CASB literature should be consulted for specific provisions and application guidelines.

Figure 14.13   Home office expenses and allocation bases

Home Office Expense/Function	Illustrative Allocation Bases
Centralized Service Functions:	
1. Personnel administration	1. Number of personnel, labor hours, payroll, number of hires
2. Data-processing services	2. Machine time, number of reports
3. Centralized purchasing and subcontracting	3. Number of purchase orders, value of purchases, number of items
4. Centralized warehousing	4. Square footage, value of material, volume
5. Company aircraft service	5. Actual or standard rate per hour, mile, passenger mile, or similar unit
6. Central telephone service	6. Usage costs, number of instruments
Staff Management and Specific Activities:	
1. Personnel management	1. Number of personnel, labor hours, payroll, number of hires
2. Manufacturing policies (quality control, industrial engineering, production scheduling, tooling, inspection and testing, etc.)	2. Manufacturing cost input, manufacturing direct labor
3. Engineering policies	3. Total engineering costs, engineering direct labor, number of drawings
4. Material/purchasing policies	4. Number of purchase orders, value of purchases
5. Marketing policies	5. Sales, segment marketing costs
Central Payments or Accruals:	
1. Pension expenses	1. Payroll or other factor on which total payment is based
2. Group insurance expenses	2. Payroll or other factor on which total payment is based
3. State and local income taxes and franchise taxes	3. Any base or method that results in an allocation equal or approximate to a segment's proportionate share of the tax imposed by the jurisdiction in which the segment does business, as measured by the same factors used to determine taxable income for that jurisdiction

Source: *Cost Accounting Standards Board Standards, Rules and Regulations,* U.S. Government Printing Office, Washington, D.C. 20402.

Appendix *Reciprocal Allocations Using Matrix Algebra*

To demonstrate the use of matrix algebra techniques, figure 14.14 illustrates a situation involving three service departments providing reciprocal services. This is actually the same data used to demonstrate the direct and step methods shown in the chapter.

To apply the reciprocal method in this situation, it is necessary to develop three simultaneous equations as follows:

Let A = total costs of *Personnel* service department

B = total costs of *Cafeteria* service department

C = total costs of *Utilities* service department

(1) $A = \$20,000 + 0P + .07C + .04U$

(2) $B = \$30,000 + .08P + 0C + .16U$

(3) $C = \$40,000 + .12P + .10C + 0U$

These equations have been formulated by reading across the rows of percentages for service departments in figure 14.14. This figure assumes that none of the service departments has a reciprocal relationship with itself. This explains why each equation has a zero as the coefficient in its own department's cost function. For example, equation (1) has a zero as the coefficient of P indicating that the personnel department renders no services to itself. If a service department has a reciprocal relationship with itself (as would actually be expected with the personnel department, processing transactions for its own employees) then the zero in equation (1) would be replaced with the appropriate percentage of services rendered to itself.

The next step when using matrix algebra techniques is to simplify the service department equations and put them in a form amenable to matrix manipulations as follows:

(1) $P - .07C - .04U = 20,000$

(2) $-.08P + C - .16U = 30,000$

(3) $-.12P - .10C + U = 40,000$

Figure 14.14   Reciprocal method of allocation: Factory statistics and percentages

Department	Personnel Transactions Processed		Number of Employees		Space Occupied (Square Feet)	
	Number	Percent	Number	Percent	Number	Percent
Production:						
Cutting	150	30%	400	33%	60,000	40%
Finishing	250	50	600	50	60,000	40
Service:						
Personnel (P)	na	0	80	7	6,000	4
Cafeteria (C)	40	8	na	0	24,000	16
Utilities (U)	60	12	120	11	na	0
	500	100%	1,200	100%	150,000	100%

na = not applicable

Proceeding to matrices:

Let: A = the matrix of coefficients

B = the vector of service department costs before allocation

X = the vector of reciprocal service department costs (the unknown amounts in this situation)

$$\begin{array}{ccc} A & X & = & B \end{array}$$

$$\begin{bmatrix} 1 - .07 & - & .04 \\ -.08 & 1 & - 1.16 \\ -.12 & - .10 & 1 \end{bmatrix} \begin{bmatrix} A \\ B \\ C \end{bmatrix} = \begin{bmatrix} 20,000 \\ 30,000 \\ 40,000 \end{bmatrix}$$

To solve for X, the matrix A must be inverted and multiplied by vector B:

$$X = A^{-1} B$$

The next four steps are used to invert A. The adjoint determinant method for inverting matrices is illustrated here, however, there are other methods available for inverting matrices.

Step 1: Obtain the *minor* for each element in A. This is done by calculating the determinant of each submatrix of A, obtained by deleting the i_{th} row and j_{th} column. For example, the submatrix found after deleting the first row and first column of A is:

$$\begin{bmatrix} 1 - .16 \\ -.10 & 1 \end{bmatrix}$$

The *determinant* of this submatrix can be calculated by subtracting the product of the *cross-diagonal* elements from the product of the *main diagonal* elements as follows:

$$|(1 \times 1) - (-.10 \times -.16)| = .984$$

Repeating this process for all elements of A results in the following:

$$\begin{bmatrix} \begin{bmatrix} 1 & -.16 \\ -.10 & 1 \end{bmatrix} & \begin{bmatrix} -.08 & -.16 \\ -.12 & 1 \end{bmatrix} & \begin{bmatrix} -.08 & 1 \\ -.12 & -.10 \end{bmatrix} \\ \begin{bmatrix} -.07 & -.04 \\ -.10 & 1 \end{bmatrix} & \begin{bmatrix} 1 & -.04 \\ -.12 & 1 \end{bmatrix} & \begin{bmatrix} 1 & -.07 \\ -.12 & -.10 \end{bmatrix} \\ \begin{bmatrix} -.07 & -.04 \\ 1 & -.16 \end{bmatrix} & \begin{bmatrix} 1 & -.04 \\ -.08 & -.16 \end{bmatrix} & \begin{bmatrix} 1 & -.07 \\ -.08 & 1 \end{bmatrix} \end{bmatrix} =$$

$$\begin{bmatrix} .9840 & -.0992 & .1280 \\ -.0740 & .9952 & -.1084 \\ .0512 & -.1632 & .9944 \end{bmatrix} = \text{the matrix of minors for each element of } A$$

Step 2: Convert the minors for each element in A into *cofactors* by multiplying each element by $(-1)^{i+j}$, where i and j are the subscripts of each element. This step yields the following matrix:

$$\begin{bmatrix} .9840 & .0992 & .1280 \\ .0740 & .9952 & .1084 \\ .0512 & .1632 & .9944 \end{bmatrix}$$

Figure 14.15   Reciprocal method of allocation: Allocation procedure

	Service Departments			Production Departments	
	Personnel	*Cafeteria*	*Utilities*	*Cutting*	*Finishing*
Overhead costs					
Before allocation	$20,000	$30,000	$40,000	$210,000	$300,000
Allocation:					
Personnel	(24,639)	1,971	2,956	7,392	12,320
{Percent}	{100%}	{8%}	{12%}	{30%}	{50%}
Cafeteria	2,763	(39,475)	3,947	13,027	19,738
{Percent}	{7%}	{100%}	{10%}	{33%}	{50%}
Utilities	1,876	7,504	(46,903)	18,761	18,762
{Percent}	{4%}	{16%}	{100%}	{40%}	{40%}
	–0–	–0–	–0–	$249,180	$350,820

Predetermined overhead application rates:

Cutting ($249,180 ÷ 70,000 direct-labor hours) $3.56/hr

Finishing ($350,820 ÷ 90,000 direct-labor hours) $3.90/hr

Step 3: Calculate the *determinant* of A by (*a*) multiplying the elements in *any* column (or *any* row) of the original matrix A by their corresponding cofactors computed in step 2 and (*b*) summing their products. Any row or column will yield the same result. For example, the determinant of A (that is $|A|$) using:

Column 1: $(1)(.9840) + (-.08)(.0740) + (-.12)(.0512) = .97194$

Row 3: $(-.12)(.0512) + (0.10)(.1632) + (1)(.9944) = .97194$

Step 4: *Transpose* the A matrix of cofactors by making its rows into columns. This yields the *adjoint matrix,* which is then divided by the determinant of A to obtain the inverse matrix A^{-1}.

$$\frac{\begin{bmatrix} .9840 & .0740 & .0512 \\ .0992 & .9952 & .1632 \\ .1280 & .1084 & .9944 \end{bmatrix}}{.97194} = \begin{bmatrix} 1.0124 & .0761 & .0527 \\ .1021 & 1.0239 & .1679 \\ .1317 & .1115 & 1.0231 \end{bmatrix} = A^{-1}$$

Having inverted matrix A, all that remains to the solution of the equation $X = A^{-1}B$ is to multiply A^{-1} by B to obtain X as follows:

$$X = \begin{bmatrix} 1.0124 & .0761 & .0527 \\ .1021 & 1.0239 & .1679 \\ .1317 & .1115 & 1.0231 \end{bmatrix} \times \begin{bmatrix} 20,000 \\ 30,000 \\ 40,000 \end{bmatrix} = \begin{bmatrix} 24,639 \\ 39,475 \\ 46,903 \end{bmatrix} = \begin{bmatrix} P \\ C \\ U \end{bmatrix}$$

The above results indicate that the reciprocal costs for allocation by the personnel, cafeteria, and utilities departments are respectively $24,639, $39,475, and $46,903. The allocation procedure in figure 14.15 shows the final results using the reciprocal service department costs calculated in the above procedure.

As the above illustration demonstrates, the computations using the reciprocal method can become quite tedious when there are a number of service departments involved in providing reciprocal services. Therefore, it is suggested that computations involving more than three service departments be left to a computer due to the time involved and the probability of error using manual methods.

Self-Study Problem

Perpotkin Corporation is trying to decide whether to use the direct, step, or reciprocal method to allocate service department costs to production departments. The corporation has three service and three production departments with reciprocal service arrangements. The balances in the departmental accounts before distribution of service department costs are given in the following schedule. Also, contained in the following schedule are statistics for each service department's allocation base:

		Allocation Base and Statistics		
Department	Balance in Department Overhead Accounts	Personnel Department: Personnel Transactions	Maintenance Department: Maintenance Hours	General Department: General Hours
Producing:				
Layout	$125,000	2,500	3,500	2,500
Assembly	90,000	2,500	3,000	2,000
Finishing	105,000	2,000	2,000	2,000
Service:				
Personnel	16,000	0	1,000	2,000
Maintenance	29,500	1,000	0	1,500
General	42,000	2,000	500	0

Production departments assign costs to work in process using direct-labor hours as the allocation base. Direct-labor hours worked for the layout, assembly, and finishing departments for the current period are, respectively, 90,000, 65,000, and 70,000 hours.

Required

Prepare schedules allocating service department costs using the direct, step, and reciprocal methods. Which method do you suggest management use to allocate service department costs? Why?

Solution to the Self-Study Problem

Direct Method of Allocation: Factory Statistics and Percentages

Department	Transactions Processed Number	Transactions Processed Percent	Maintenance Hours Number	Maintenance Hours Percent	General Hours Number	General Hours Percent
Layout	2,500	36%	3,500	41%	2,500	38%
Assembly	2,500	36	3,000	35	2,000	31
Finishing	2,000	28	2,000	24	2,000	31
	7,000	100%	8,500	100%	6,500	100%

Allocation Procedure Using Direct Method

	Service Departments			Production Departments		
	Personnel	*Maintenance*	*General*	*Layout*	*Assembly*	*Finishing*
Overhead costs						
before allocation	$16,000	$29,500	$42,000	$125,000	$90,000	$105,000
Allocation:						
Personnel	(16,000)			5,760	5,760	4,480
{Percent}	{100%}			{36%}	{36%}	{28%}
Maintenance		(29,500)		12,095	10,325	7,080
{Percent}		{100%}		{41%}	{35%}	{24%}
General			(42,000)	15,960	13,020	13,020
{Percent}			{100%}	{38%}	{31%}	{31%}
Total production department overhead after allocation				$158,815	$119,105	$129,580

Predetermined overhead application rates:

Layout ($158,815 ÷ 90,000 direct-labor hours) $1.76/hr

Assembly ($119,105 ÷ 65,000 direct-labor hours) $1.83/hr

General ($129,580 ÷ 70,000 direct-labor hours) $1.85/hr

Step Method of Allocation: Factory Statistics and Percentages

	Transactions Processed		Maintenance Hours		General Hours	
Department	*Number*	*Percent*	*Number*	*Percent*	*Number*	*Percent*
Production:						
Layout	2,500	25%	3,500	39%	2,500	38%
Assembly	2,500	25	3,000	33	2,000	31
Finishing	2,000	20	2,000	22	2,000	31
Service:						
Personnel	na	0	na	0	na	0
Maintenance	1,000	10	na	0	na	0
General	2,000	20	500	6	na	0
	10,000	100%	9,000	100%	6,500	100%

Allocation Procedure Using Step Method

	Service Departments			Production Departments		
	Personnel	*Maintenance*	*General*	*Layout*	*Assembly*	*Finishing*
Overhead costs						
before allocation	$16,000	$29,500	$42,000	$125,000	$90,000	$105,000
Allocation:						
Personnel	(16,000)	1,600	3,200	4,000	4,000	3,200
{Percent}	{100%}	{10%}	{20%}	{25%}	{25%}	{20%}
Maintenance		(31,100)	1,866	12,129	10,263	6,842
{Percent}		{100%}	{6%}	{39%}	{33%}	{22%}
General			(47,066)	17,885	14,590	14,591
{Percent}			{100%}	{38%}	{31%}	{31%}
Total production department overhead after allocation				$159,014	$118,853	$129,633

Predetermined overhead application rates:

Layout ($159,014 ÷ 90,000 direct-labor hours) $1.77/hr

Assembly ($118,853 ÷ 65,000 direct-labor hours) $1.83/hr

General ($129,633 ÷ 70,000 direct-labor hours) $1.85/hr

Allocation Procedure Using Reciprocal Method

Let: P = personnel; M = maintenance; G = general
(1) $P = 16,000 + .10M + .20G$
(2) $M = 29,500 + .10P + .15G$
(3) $G = 42,000 + .20P + .05M$

Rewriting equations (1) through (3):
(1) $P - .10M - .20G = 16,000$
(2) $-.10P + M - .15G = 29,500$
(3) $-.20P - .05M + G = 42,000$

Multiplying equation (2) by 10 and adding to equation (1):
$$P - .10M - .20G = 16,000$$
$$-P + 10.00M - 1.50G = 295,000$$
$$9.90M - 1.70G = 311,000$$

Multiplying equation (3) by 5 and adding to equation (1):
$$P - .10M - .20G = 16,000$$
$$-P - .25M + 5.00G = 210,000$$
$$-.35M + 4.80G = 226,000$$

Eliminating M between the resulting equations:
$$9.90M - 1.70G = 311,000$$
$$-.35M + 4.80G = 226,000$$
$$(.35)(9.90M) - (.35)(1.70G) = (.35)(311,000)$$
$$(9.90)(-.35M) + (9.90)(4.80G) = (9.90)(226,000)$$
$$3.465M - .595G = 108,850$$
$$-3.465M - 47.520G = 2,237,400$$
$$46.925G = 2,346,250$$
$$G = 50,000$$

Substituting $G = 50,000$ into a previous equation:
$$9.90M - 1.70G = 311,000$$
$$9.90M - 1.70(50,000) = 311,000$$
$$9.90M = 396,000$$
$$M = 40,000$$

Substituting $M = 40,000$ and $G = 50,000$ into a previous equation:
$$P - .10M - .20G = 16,000$$
$$P - .10(40,000) - .20(50,000) = 16,000$$
$$P = 30,000$$

Reciprocal Method of Allocation: Factory Statistics and Percentages

Department	Transactions Processed Number	Percent	Maintenance Hours Number	Percent	General Hours Number	Percent
Production:						
Layout	2,500	25%	3,500	35%	2,500	25%
Assembly	2,500	25	3,000	30	2,000	20
Finishing	2,000	20	2,000	20	2,000	20
Service:						
Personnel	na	0	1,000	10	2,000	20
Maintenance	1,000	10	na	0	1,500	15
General	2,000	20	500	5	na	0
	10,000	100%	10,000	100%	10,000	100%

Solution

The direct method is recommended for allocating service department costs because it gives essentially the same results in this case as the other methods but it is easier to calculate.

Allocation Procedure Using Reciprocal Method

	Service Departments			Production Departments		
	Personnel	Maintenance	General	Layout	Assembly	Finishing
Overhead costs before allocation	$16,000	$29,500	$42,000	$125,000	$ 90,000	$105,000
Allocation:						
Personnel	(30,000)	3,000	6,000	7,500	7,500	6,000
{Percent}	{100%}	{10%}	{20%}	{25%}	{25%}	{20%}
Maintenance	4,000	(40,000)	2,000	14,000	12,000	8,000
{Percent}	{10%}	{100%}	{5%}	{35%}	{30%}	{20%}
General	10,000	7,500	(50,000)	12,500	10,000	10,000
{Percent}	{20%}	{15%}	{100%}	{25%}	{20%}	{20%}
Total production department overhead after allocation	–0–	–0–	–0–	$159,000	$119,500	$129,000

Predetermined overhead application rates:

Layout ($159,000 ÷ 90,000 direct-labor hours) $1.77/hr

Assembly ($119,500 ÷ 65,000 direct-labor hours) $1.84/hr

General ($129,000 ÷ 70,000 direct-labor hours) $1.84/hr

Suggested Readings

Belkaoui, Ahmed. *Cost Accounting: A Multidimensional Emphasis*. Chicago: The Dryden Press, 1983.

Kaplan, R. "Variable and Self Service Costs in Reciprocal Allocation Models." *The Accounting Review* (October 1973): 738–48.

Livingston, J. L. "Matrix Algebra and Cost Allocation." *The Accounting Review* (July 1968). 503–8.

Mayotte, Russell J. "How One Utility Allocates Steam Service Costs." *Management Accounting* (March 1980): 26–36.

Seidler, Lee J., and Carmichael, D. R., eds. *Accountants' Handbook*. 6th ed. New York: John Wiley & Sons, 1981.

Discussion Questions

1. What is a department? What are some of the advantages of departmentalization?
2. Describe the difference between production and service departments and give examples of each.
3. Describe the allocation process through which service department costs become part of the cost of units of production.
4. What is the purpose of an allocation base? Give several examples of allocation bases. For each example, tell which type of service department is the likely user.
5. Describe the Cost Accounting Standards Board's hierarchy of preferred allocation bases.
6. Name three methods used to allocate service department costs.

7. Describe the direct method of allocation and give some of its advantages and disadvantages.
8. Describe the step method of allocation and give some of its advantages and disadvantages.
9. Describe the reciprocal method of allocation and give some of its advantages and disadvantages.
10. What difference is there between using factory-wide versus departmental rates for allocating service department costs?
11. What are the advantages and disadvantages of using factory-wide versus departmental rates?
12. What is a homogeneous cost pool? How is the allocation of service department costs connected with the homogeneity of cost pools?
13. Describe any differences that exist between cost allocations when fixed versus variable costs are involved.
14. Define theoretical capacity, normal capacity, and expected capacity.
15. What are the general provisions of cost accounting Standard 402?
16. Define the terms home office and segment.
17. According to cost accounting Standard 403, what are the preferred methods of allocating home office expenses?
18. Define final cost objective.
19. According to cost accounting Standard 410, how should general and administrative expenses be allocated to final cost objectives?

Exercises

Exercise 14.1 Basic Concepts for Production and Service Departments

For each description listed below, put a check in the blank indicating whether the description is or is not a proper inference.

	Proper	Not Proper
1. Production departments render a service that relates directly to the production of a product.	_____	_____
2. Examples of production departments include production control, machinery repairs, and shipping.	_____	_____
3. A departmentalized factory is usually divided along lines of identifiable responsibility centers.	_____	_____
4. When relatively few employees are involved, service activities are frequently combined in order to gain more effective cost control.	_____	_____
5. Direct departmental expenses do not originate with any specific departments, but rather are incurred for all departments.	_____	_____
6. The overtime premium portion of overtime paid to direct-labor employees should always be charged to work in process.	_____	_____
7. Indirect departmental expenses include factory costs such as power, light, and maintenance.	_____	_____
8. Factory expenses such as depreciation, property tax, and insurance should be allocated by using the number of factory employees as a distribution base.	_____	_____

9. It is not unusual to use different distribution bases for allocating the overhead of the different service departments to other service and production departments.   _____ _____

10. A factory survey produces the underlying data for allocating indirect departmental expenses to production departments.   _____ _____

11. The expenses of production departments must be allocated to service departments to establish predetermined factory overhead rates.   _____ _____

12. Service department costs may be allocated only to production departments if no material differences in final production department costs result.   _____ _____

13. The expenses of the service department with the largest factory overhead costs should always be distributed first when using the step method.   _____ _____

14. Once costs for a service department are allocated, that department is usually considered closed and no further distributions are made to it when using the direct or the step methods.   _____ _____

15. Departmental expense analysis sheets are not needed as long as specific expense accounts are kept in the ledger.   _____ _____

Exercise 14.2   Allocation of Service Department Costs—Step Method

The factory overhead worksheet for Brandon Incorporated had the following columnar totals after the direct and indirect departmental expense assignments had been made:

Service departments:	A—$36,000
	B—$28,000
	C $20,000
Production departments:	D—$80,000
	E—$75,000

Required

Complete a schedule showing the allocation of overhead to the production departments if the service department costs are allocated to the production and other service departments as follows:

Department A costs: 20% to B, 15% to C and E, 50% to D

Department B costs: 35% to C, 35% to D, 30% to E

Department C costs: 40% to D, 60% to E

Exercise 14.3   Service Department Allocation—Direct Method (CMA)

Barrylou Corporation is developing departmental overhead rates based upon direct-labor hours for its two production departments—molding and assembly. The molding department employs 20 people and the assembly department employs 80 people. Each person in these two departments works 2,000 hours per year. The production-related overhead costs for the molding department are budgeted at $200,000 and the assembly department costs are budgeted at $320,000. Two service departments—repair and power—directly support the two production departments and have budgeted costs of $48,000 and $250,000 respectively. The production departments' overhead rates cannot be determined until the service departments' costs are properly allocated. The following schedule reflects the use of the repair department's and power department's output by the various departments.

	Department			
	Repair	Power	Molding	Assembly
Repair hours	0	1,000	1,000	8,000
KWH	240,000	0	840,000	120,000

Required

Calculate the overhead rates per direct-labor hour for the molding department and the assembly department using the direct allocation method to charge the production departments for service department costs.

Exercise 14.4 Service Department Allocation—Reciprocal Method

Refer to the data in exercise 14.3.

Required

1. Allocate the service department overhead to each other and to the production departments using the reciprocal method (sometimes referred to as the algebraic method) of distribution.
2. Calculate overhead rates per direct-labor hour for the two production departments using your results from requirement 1.
3. Compare the results obtained in this exercise with the results in exercise 14.3. Discuss the arguments that are made in support of the reciprocal method.

Exercise 14.5 Step Method Allocation of Service Department Costs

The following information is available for the Edwardian Company regarding departmental direct overhead for the production and service departments:

Direct Factory Overhead

Service Departments			Production Departments	
G	H	I	A	B
$24,960	$28,000	$22,000	$38,000	$56,000

An analysis of service rendered indicates the following proportions of service rendered by each service department:

Department G: 30% to H, 20% to I, 20% to A, and 30% to B
Department H: 30% to I, 35% to A, and 35% to B
Department I: 50% to each A and B

Required

1. Set up a schedule showing service department overhead allocations using the step method. (Round to the nearest dollar.)
2. Determine overhead rates for departments A and B assuming direct-labor hours are used as a base and that 20,000 and 35,000 hours are estimated for A and B respectively. (Carry rates to 5 decimals.)

Exercise 14.6   Direct Method of Service Department Cost Allocation

Refer to the data in exercise 14.5.

Required

1. Set up a schedule showing allocation of service department costs to production departments using the direct method.
2. Determine overhead rates for departments *A* and *B* assuming the direct-labor hours indicated in requirement 2 of exercise 14.5.

Exercise 14.7   Job Cost Results from Using Alternative Allocation Methods

Refer to the data in exercise 14.5 and exercise 14.6. Without prejudice to your answers to those two exercises, assume the overhead rates for departments A and B are as follows:

	Rate	
Department	Using Step Method	Using Direct Method
A	$3.72	$3.65
B	$2.70	$2.75

During May, jobs 108 and 109 were produced. Job 108 required 600 labor hours in department *A* and 800 labor hours in department *B*. Job 109 required 1,000 and 1,500 labor hours in departments *A* and *B* respectively.

Required

1. Determine the overhead costs applied to jobs 108 and 109 using overhead rates obtained from the step method.
2. Determine the overhead costs applied to jobs 108 and 109 using the rates obtained from the direct method.
3. Comment on the results you obtained in requirements 1 and 2.

Exercise 14.8   Overhead Cost Allocation—Dispute over Allocation Base

The AT Company has seven production departments. The plant custodial department provides clean-up services for all departments. Custodial department costs have been allocated equally to each department in the past.

   Some production department supervisors have been complaining about the custodial cost allocations that are currently being made. They point out that the departments vary in size (in terms of space occupied) and that because there are different production processes in some departments more cleanup has to be done. They contend that equal allocation of custodial costs isn't equitable under the circumstances.

   The controller and the production manager claim that the equal allocation procedure being used is justifiable because it saves the extra costs of making the allocations by other possible methods. In any case, they point out, the allocation procedures don't really affect operation results since custodial costs are within the company.

Required

What do you suggest the AT Company should do to allocate custodial costs? Explain.

Exercise 14.9 Evaluation of the Proper Basis for Allocating Service Department Costs

Maxwell Company has four production and two service departments. Each production department produces an individual product through all steps from design implementation and materials preparation to final finishing. The service departments—design support and repairs and maintenance—have had their costs allocated for years to the production departments on the basis of sales revenue produced.

Recently, a new university accounting graduate was hired in cost accounting. Her assignment is to allocate service department costs to the four production departments. After the first month on the job she suggested to the production manager and the controller that sales revenue is not a good basis for service department cost allocation. The following information, which might be useful in evaluating an alternative allocation approach, was presented:

	Service Departments		Production Departments			
	Design Support	Repairs and Maintenance	1	2	3	4
Direct overhead	$26,000	8,000	$40,000	$35,000	$52,000	$45,000
Design hours	—	300	600	450	700	500
Repairs and maintenance hours	200	—	600	250	350	500

Required

1. Do you agree with the new cost accountant's criticism of using sales revenue as a base for service department cost allocation? Explain. Are there possible circumstances that justify the use of sales revenue as an allocation base for service department costs? Explain.
2. What basis would you recommend the Maxwell Company use for service department cost allocation? Explain.

Exercise 14.10 Service Department Overhead Allocation—Step Method

Belli-Pitt Manufacturing Company has two operating departments—A and B—and three service departments—X, Y, and Z. The controller for Belli-Pitt has prepared the following projection of operations for the coming year:

Department	Direct Materials	Direct Labor	Factory Overhead	Total
A	$241,000	$1,401,000	$498,000	$2,140,000
B	285,000	898,000	802,000	1,985,000
X	-0-	48,000	49,000	97,000
Y	25,000	72,000	41,000	138,000
Z	-0-	54,000	36,000	90,000

Using various allocation bases, the controller developed the following estimates of percentages of effort devoted to other departments by service departments.

	% of Effort				
Service to	X	Y	Z	A	B
Service by					
X	0%	10%	8%	48%	34%
Y	5	0	11	36	48
Z	2	8	0	40	50

Required

1. Prepare a schedule showing the allocation of service department costs using the step method. Begin with the department that performs the largest percentage of service for other *service* departments.
2. Determine the total overhead rates as a percentage of labor cost for each operating department.
3. If at the end of the year the *total* factory overhead amounts to $1,650,000 and if departments A and B had direct-labor costs of $1,420,000 and $913,000 respectively, what can you say about the company's over- or underapplied factory overhead *in total?*

Problems

Problem 14.1   Departmental Overhead Distribution—Direct Method

Marshall Incorporated applies factory overhead on the following bases:

In department F, 45% of F's material cost
In department G, $4.70 per direct-labor hour in G

The following accounts and their balances at month's end are as follows:

Work in process—materials	$50,000
Work in process—direct labor	28,000
Work in process—applied factory overhead	26,000
Indirect labor	15,000
Factory office	4,000
Depreciation and insurance on building	5,000
Power plant expenses	3,000

	Production Departments		
Other information	F	G	Power Plant
Direct materials	$28,000	$22,000	
Direct labor	11,000	16,500	
Direct-labor hours	2,600	3,200	
Power used	56%	44%	
Floor space occupied	1100 sq. ft.	500 sq. ft.	400 sq. ft.

Indirect labor and factory office are apportioned in the ratio of direct-labor cost. No service department costs are allocated to other service departments except for the appropriate portion of depreciation and insurance that is applicable to the power plant.

Required

1. Prepare a distribution sheet showing the distribution of service department factory overhead costs to production departments.
2. Determine the over- or underapplied factory overhead in total and for each production department after all overhead has been allocated to the production departments.

Problem 14.2   Factory Overhead Distribution Schedule and Rate Calculation

Cassel Chemical Company consists of three production departments and four service departments. For the purpose of creating factory overhead rates, the accountant prepared the cost distribution sheet shown below. It contains operational data gathered by the accountant.

Data	Total	Preparation	Mixing	Packaging	Utilities	Maintenance	Materials Handling	Factory Office
Operational Data:								
Floor space (sq. ft.)	53,000	10,000	12,000	16,000	3,000	3,000	5,000	4,000
Maintenance hours	6,820	1,860	2,480	930	620		620	310
Metered hours (in hundreds)	4,000	1,400	1,600	320		200	320	160
Expenses:								
Indirect labor	$22,000	$3,800	$2,600	$2,400	$3,500	$4,000	$3,300	$2,400
Payroll taxes	2,522	440	532	420	230	355	320	225
Indirect materials	5,703	700	938	2,300	920	150	150	545
Depreciation	850	100	150	50	100	200	200	50
Total	$31,075	$5,040	$4,220	$5,170	$4,750	$4,705	$3,970	$3,220

For the distribution of expenses of the service departments, the following procedures had been decided upon:

1. Utilities: 80% on metered hours of power
   20% on floor square footage
2. Maintenance: maintenance hours excluding utilities
3. Materials
   Handling: 48% to preparation, 32% to mixing, and 20% to packaging—
   pounds handled is 395,300 in preparation and 262,850 in mixing
4. Factory
   Office: preparation, 40%; mixing, 30%; packaging, 30%

Required

1. Complete a cost distribution sheet using the step method. No reciprocal charging should take place. (Round off all amounts to the nearest dollar.)
2. Determine the factory overhead rates based on pounds handled in preparation and mixing and on the direct-labor cost of $86,000 in packaging. (Round off to the nearest cent.)

Problem 14.3   Allocation of Service Department Costs—Step Method

The Wing Company has three production departments and three service departments. The following information was given for August:

Department	Direct Departmental Expenses	Square Feet	Employees	Equipment in $
Cutting	$17,000	1200	25	$ 60,000
Forming	34,000	2000	30	100,000
Finishing	20,000	800	15	80,000
Building service	8,000	400	10	10,000
Health service	5,000	300	10	2,000
Repairs service	12,000	300	10	30,000
Total	$96,000	5000	100	$282,000

The bases for distributing expenses of the service departments are:

Building service = area occupied
Health service = number of employees
Repairs service = investment in equipment

Wing Company assigns service department expenses to other service departments. However, after a department's expenses are allocated, no expenses are allocated back to it.

Required

Distribute the expenses of the service departments, beginning with the building service, then the health service, then the repairs service. (Round to the nearest dollar.)

Problem 14.4 Factory Overhead—Service Department Allocations (CPA)

The Marker Manufacturing Company has two production departments—fabrication and assembly—and three service departments—general factory administration, factory maintenance, and factory cafeteria. The following summarizes the costs and other data for each department before allocation of service department costs for the year ending June 30:

	Fabrication	Assembly	General Factory Administration	Factory Maintenance	Factory Cafeteria
Direct-labor costs	$1,950,000	$2,050,000	$90,000	$82,100	$87,000
Direct-material costs	$3,130,000	$950,000	—	$65,000	$91,000
Factory overhead costs	$1,650,000	$1,850,000	$70,000	$56,100	$62,000
Direct-labor hours	562,500	437,500	31,000	27,000	42,000
Number of employees	280	200	12	8	20
Square footage occupied	88,000	72,000	1,750	2,000	4,800

The costs of the general factory administration department, factory maintenance department, and factory cafeteria are allocated on the basis of direct-labor hours, square footage occupied, and number of employees respectively. Round all final calculations to the nearest dollar.

Required

1. Assuming that Marker elects to distribute service department costs directly to production departments without interservice department cost allocation, determine the amount of factory maintenance department costs that would be allocated to the fabrication department.
2. Assuming the same method of allocation as in requirement 1, determine the amount of general factory administration department costs that would be allocated to the assembly department.
3. Assuming that Marker elects to distribute service department costs to other service departments (starting with the service department with the greatest total costs) as well as the production departments, determine the amount of factory cafeteria department costs that would be allocated to the factory maintenance department. (Note: Once a service department's costs have been allocated, no subsequent service department costs are recirculated back to it.)
4. Assuming the same method of allocation as in requirement 3, determine the amount of factory maintenance department costs that would be allocated to the factory cafeteria.

Problem 14.5 Reciprocal Distribution of Factory Overhead

The estimated departmental factory overhead for production departments A and B and service departments L, M, and N (before any service department allocations) are:

Production Departments		Service Departments	
A	$120,000	L	$40,000
B	$180,000	M	$40,000
		N	$20,000

The reciprocal services performed by each department for other departments are as follows:

	Services Provided		
Departments	L	M	N
Production—A	—	30%	40%
Production—B	50%	40	30
Service—L	—	20	—
Service—M	20	—	—
Service—N	30	10	—
Sales	—	—	20
General Administration	—	—	10
	100%	100%	100%

Required

1. Determine the final amount of estimated overhead for each service department after reciprocal transfer costs have been calculated using the reciprocal method.
2. Determine the total factory overhead for each production department and the amount of department N cost assigned to the sales department and to the general administration.

Problem 14.6 Reciprocal Distribution of Factory Overhead

The financial vice-president of the Manville Company has instructed the cost department to use an algebraic procedure for allocating service department costs to production departments. The firm's three production departments are served by three service departments, each of which consumes part of the services of the other two. After the direct departmental costs have been determined, the account balances of the service departments and interdependence of the departments were indicated as follows:

Department	Departmental Overhead Before Distribution of Service Departments	Service Provided		
		Powerhouse	Cafeteria	Custodial
Smelting	$250,000	25%	35%	25%
Concentrating	180,000	25	30	20
Refining	210,000	20	20	20
Powerhouse	32,000	—	10	20
Cafeteria	59,000	10	—	15
Custodial	84,000	20	5	—
	$815,000	100%	100%	100%

Required

Set up a schedule showing the analysis to determine the following:

1. The final amount of overhead for each service department after reciprocal transfer costs have been calculated using the reciprocal method
2. The total factory overhead for each production department after all allocations are completed

---

Problem 14.7 Cost Allocation—Evaluation of Allocation Bases (CMA)

Columbia Company is a regional office supply chain with twenty-six independent stores. Each store has been responsible for its own credit and collections. The assistant manager in each store is responsible for credit activities including the collection of delinquent accounts because the stores do not need a full-time employee assigned to credit activities. The company has experienced a sharp rise in uncollectibles during the last two years. Corporate management has decided to establish a collections department in the home office to be responsible for the collection function company-wide. The home office of Columbia Company will hire the necessary full-time personnel. The size of this department will be based upon the historical credit activity for the stores.

The new centralized collections department was discussed at a recent management meeting. A method to assign the costs of the new department to the stores has been difficult to determine because this type of home office service is somewhat unique. Alternative methods are being reviewed by top management.

The controller favored using a predetermined or standard rate for charging the costs to the stores. The predetermined rate would be based on budgeted costs. The vice-president of sales preferred an actual cost charging system.

In addition, the basis for the collection charges to the stores was also discussed. The controller identified the following four measures of services (allocation bases) that could be used:

1. Total dollar sales
2. Average number of past-due accounts
3. Number of uncollectible accounts written off
4. The cost equally divided between all of the stores

The executive vice-president stated that he would like the accounting department to prepare a detailed analysis of the two charging methods and the four service measures (allocation bases).

Required

1. Evaluate the two methods identified—predetermined (standard) rate versus actual cost—that could be used to charge the individual stores the costs of Columbia Company's new collections department in terms of the following:
   a. Practicality of application and ease of use
   b. Cost control
   Also indicate whether a centralized or decentralized type of organizational structure would be more conducive for each charging method.
2. For each measure of service (allocation base) identified by the controller of Columbia Company do the following:
   a. Discuss whether the service measure (allocation base) is appropriate to use in this situation.
   b. Identify the behavioral problems, if any, that could arise as a result of adopting the service measure (allocation base).

Problem 14.8   Cost Allocation—Government Requirements (CMA)

The Anderson Company, a moderate-sized manufacturing firm, was awarded a negotiated defense contract of $4,000,000 on May 1. Anderson has never been subject to cost accounting standards which cover defense contracts because it had no defense contracts prior to the $4,000,000 award. Management wants to continue with the company's present cost accounting practices but is not sure that these practices are in compliance with defense contract requirements. The accounting department has been asked to review its cost accounting practices for compliance with government standards for defense contracts.

The Huron Division, which will perform the contract, is one of four segments of the Anderson Company. The review disclosed that the Huron Division includes selling costs as part of its general and administrative expenses. In negotiating the contract the division had used cost of sales as a base for allocating general and administrative expenses to the contract to arrive at the final contract amount.

The applicable defense contract cost standard to which Anderson Company must comply in this situation is Cost Accounting Standard 410, "Allocation of Business Unit General and Administrative Expenses to Final Cost Objectives." This standard defines general and administrative expenses as any management, financial, and other expense that is incurred by or allocated to a business unit and is for the general management and administration of the business unit as a whole.

Cost Standard 410 requires the use of a cost input base for allocation of general and administrative expenses to a cost objective (such as a defense contract). Cost input was defined as the cost that for contract costing purposes is allocable to the production of goods and/or services during a cost accounting period.

Required

1. Did the Huron Division of Anderson Company comply with the provisions of Cost Accounting Standard 410 as discussed above when it used a cost of sales base for allocating general and administrative expenses? Explain why or why not.
2. According to the provisions of the standard, is the classification of selling costs used by Huron Division appropriate? Explain.

Problem 14.9   Factory Overhead and Journal Entries

Backman Foundry produces manhole and sewer covers. Three production operations are needed. There are no service departments. Support activities needed by production departments such as custodial and maintenance are either provided directly to production departments or else contracted for with outside providers. Thus, all overhead costs are charged directly to production department overhead control accounts.

Before the current year began, management initiated the use of predetermined overhead rates for the first time. These rates were to be used for the first six months of the year. At the end of June a thorough review of results was to be made. Revisions in rates were to be affected as indicated by the review of results.

The production departments and the overhead rates set for the first six months are as follows:

Casting	$5 per machine hour
Stamping	$3 per direct-labor hour
Finishing	60% of direct-labor cost

During the first six months the summary operating data are as follows:

Department	Actual Operating Statistics	Factory Overhead Incurred
Casting	3,200 machine hours	$22,000
Stamping	9,600 direct-labor hours	30,000
Finishing	$75,000 of direct-labor costs	40,000

The June 30 review indicates that the operations and the overhead incurred during the first six months can be expected to be typical for the remainder of the year under expected conditions.

Required

1. Determine the overhead applied to production during the first six months in each department and indicate the over- or underapplied overhead.
2. Make summary journal entries to record the overhead incurred and overhead applied to production for the first six months of the year.
3. Determine revised overhead rates for each department based on the operating data for the first six months of the year.

Problem 14.10 Cost Allocation—Evaluation of Assertions Made in a Dialogue

The following discussion was printed in the Lybrand Journal in 1960 as well as in the numerous other sources. The original source is unknown.

In discussing the cost incident to various types of operation, the following analogy was drawn. A restaurant adds a rack of peanuts for the counter, intending to pick up a little additional profit in the usual course of business. Consider the actual problem faced by the restauranteur (Joe) as revealed by his accountant-efficiency-expert.

Eff Ex: Joe, you said you put in these peanuts because some people ask for them, but do you realize what this rack of peanuts is costing you?

Joe: It ain't gonna cost. It's gonna be a profit. Sure, I had to pay $25 for a fancy rack to hold bags, but the peanuts cost 6¢ a bag and I sell 'em for 10¢. Figger I sell 50 bags a week to start. It'll take 12½ weeks to cover the cost of the rack. After that I gotta clear profit of 4¢ a bag. The more I sell the more I'll make.

Eff Ex: This is an antiquated and completely unrealistic approach, Joe. Fortunately, modern accounting procedures permit a more accurate picture that reveals the complexities involved.

Joe: Huh?

Eff Ex: To be precise, those peanuts must be integrated into your entire operation and be allocated their appropriate share of business overhead. They must share a proportionate part of your expenditures for rent, heat, light, equipment depreciation, decoration, salaries for your waitresses, cook, . . .

Joe: The cook? What's he gotta do with peanuts? He don't even know I got 'em!

Eff Ex: Look, Joe, the cook is in the kitchen. The kitchen prepares the food. The food is what brings people in here, and the people ask to buy peanuts. That's why you must charge a portion of the cook's wages, as well as a part of your own salary to peanut sales. This carefully calculated cost analysis sheet indicates the peanut operation should pay exactly $1,278 per year toward these general overhead costs.

Joe: The peanuts? $1,278 a year for overhead? The nuts?

Eff Ex: It's really a little more than that. You also spend money each week to have the windows washed and to have the place swept out in the mornings. Keep soap in the washroom and provide free cokes to the police. That raises the total to $1,313 per year.

Joe: (thoughtfully) But the peanut salesman said I'd make money. Put 'em on the end of the counter, he said, and get 4¢ a bag profit.

Eff Ex: (with a sniff) He's not an accountant. Do you actually know what the portion of the counter occupied by the peanut rack is worth to you?

Joe: Ain't worth nothing. No stool there, just a dead spot at the end.

Eff Ex: The modern cost picture permits no dead spots. Your counter contains 60 square feet and the counter grosses $15,000/year, so the square foot of space occupied by the peanut rack is worth $250 per year. Since you have taken area away from general counter use, you must charge the value of the space of the occupant.

Joe: You mean I gotta pay $250 a year more to the peanuts?

Eff Ex: Right. That raises their share of the general operation costs to a grand total of $1,563 per year. Now then, if you sell 50 bags of peanuts per week, these allocated costs will amount to 60¢ per bag.

Joe: What?

Eff Ex: Obviously, to that must be added your purchase price of 6¢ per bag, which brings the total to 66¢. So you see, by selling peanuts at 10¢ per bag you are losing 56¢ on every sale.

Joe: Somethin's crazy?

Eff Ex: Not at all! Here are the figures. They prove your peanut operation cannot stand on its own feet.

Joe: (brightening) Suppose I sell lotsa peanuts, thousand bags a week 'stead of fifty?

Eff Ex: (tolerantly) Joe, you don't understand the problem. If the volume of peanut sales increases, your operating costs will go up. You'll have to handle more bags, with more time, more depreciation, more everything. The basic principle of accounting is firm on that subject—the bigger the operation the more general overhead costs that must be allocated. No, increasing the volume of sales won't help.

Joe: Okay. You are so smart. You tell me what I gotta do.

Eff Ex: (condescendingly) Well, you could first reduce operating expenses.

Joe: How?

Eff Ex: Move to a building with cheaper rent. Cut salaries. Wash the windows biweekly. Have the floor swept only on Thursday. Remove the soap from the washrooms. Decrease the square foot value of your counter. For example, if you can cut your expenses 50%, you will reduce the amount allocated to peanuts from $1,563 down to $781.50 per year, reducing the cost to 36¢ per bag.

Joe: (slowly) That's better?

Eff Ex: Much, much better. However, even then you would lose 26¢ per bag if you charge only 10¢. Therefore, you must also raise your selling price. If you want a net profit of 4¢ per bag, you would have to charge 40¢.

Joe: (flabbergasted) You mean after I cut operating costs 50% I still gotta charge 40¢ for a 10¢ bag of peanuts? Nobody's that nuts about nuts! Who's gonna buy 'em?

Eff Ex: That's a secondary consideration. The point is at 40¢ you'd be selling at a price based upon a true and proper evaluation of your then reduced costs.

Joe: (eagerly) Look! I gotta better idea. Why don't I just throw the nuts out. Put 'em in a trash can?

Eff Ex: Can you afford it?

Joe: Sure. All I got is about 50 bags of peanuts. It cost about three bucks, so I lose $25 on the rack. But I'm out of this nutsy business and no more grief.

Eff Ex: (shaking head) Joe, it isn't quite that simple. You are in the peanut business! The minute you throw those peanuts out, you are adding $1,563 of annual overhead to the rest of your operations. Joe, be realistic. Can you afford to do that?

Joe: (completely crushed) It's unbelievable! Last week I made money. Now I'm in trouble, just because I think peanuts on a counter is a gonna bring me some extra profit, just because I believe 50 bags of peanuts a week is easy.

Eff Ex: (with raised eyebrow) That is the object of modern cost studies, Joe, to dispel those false illusions.

Required

1. What is Joe's operating result on the "peanut" business? Is he losing 56¢ on the sale of every bag of peanuts? Explain.

2. Has the efficiency expert identified some relevant issues in his discussion with Joe? Explain.

3. If the volume of peanut sales is increased, does more cost have to be assigned to that aspect of operations? Explain.

4. Should Joe get out of the peanut business? Why or why not?

COST CONTROL

PART

IV

C ost control is critical in order to achieve the desired profit outlined in the budget. The various techniques used to control costs are outlined in chapters 15 through 19.

A standard cost system is a cost control technique that identifies the costs that should be incurred during normal operations. At the end of a time period, actual costs are compared with the standard costs and any differences are called variances. Variance analysis highlights areas of the operation in which corrective action is needed.

The development of a good cost accounting system is critical for effective cost control. The advent of the computer has had a significant impact on cost accounting systems. A variety of reports can be provided by the system to assist management in controlling costs. Some of the most frequently used reports include gross margin analysis, segment performance reports, and reports based on variable costing.

STANDARD COSTS FOR MATERIALS AND LABOR

15

OUTLINE

Budgets provide a formal mechanism for comparing actual results with plans and goals. Flexible budgets, as discussed in chapter 7, provide a key element of responsibility accounting by which plans and actions of responsible persons are coordinated and monitored by higher levels of management. Flexible budgets provide both a planning tool and a criterion against which actual performance can be evaluated. Standard or predetermined costs greatly enhance the effectiveness of flexible budgets and are widely used as the basis for their development and for providing feedback to management.

This chapter explains how standard costs are used in cost accounting systems. After completing this chapter you should be able to:

1. define standard costs and explain their role in providing feedback for cost control.
2. use materials and labor standards in the development of budgets.
3. record materials and labor costs using a standard cost system.
4. calculate materials and labor variances.
5. explain who is responsible for materials and labor variances.
6. develop appropriate standards for materials and labor.
7. determine when it is appropriate to investigate variances.

COST CONTROL SYSTEMS

Just as manufacturing enterprises grow and mature, their managerial control systems seem to evolve with the volume and complexity of operations. A system of control often begins with a set of historical records that compares the results of operations for two succeeding periods. Financial results of the current period are compared with results of the prior period, differences are noted, and causes of differences are investigated. Following such an analysis, managerial action can be taken to correct unfavorable situations or to promote favorable results.

The usefulness of a historical comparison is limited; it is often difficult to precisely identify specific causes of differences. For example, assume that the volume of sales for a particular company remained the same from one period to the next. However, the cost of goods sold increased from one period to the next resulting in a decrease in operating income. Management may want to know what caused the increase in the cost of goods sold and discovers that the cost of materials and labor increased. However, without more specific information management may not be able to determine the real significance of each increase. For example, it is not possible using historical comparisons to determine the relative impact of changes in materials or labor prices compared with changes in the efficiency with which materials or labor were used.

More information can be developed to monitor and control operations with the use of budgets. Flexible budgets are the most effective budget in a manufacturing environment. However, flexible budgets are made even more effective when they are based on standard costs. A fully mature cost control system uses the combination of standard costs and flexible budgets to provide complete and meaningful performance appraisal and feedback to management.

The comparison of flexible budgets based on standard costs with actual results of operations provides information to answer questions concerning the impact of (*a*) changes in prices paid for materials, (*b*) changes in rates paid for labor, (*c*) the efficiency with which materials were utilized, and (*d*) the efficiency with which labor was utilized. With this feedback management is equipped with information necessary to make meaningful decisions about the future conduct of operations.

Note that standard costs are used in conjunction with either job-order or process-costing systems and the use of standard costs does not constitute another accounting system. Rather, standard costs are applicable to both job-order and process-costing systems in the same way that budgets are applicable to both systems. As indicated, standard costs

Figure 15.1   Standard costs for bronze bookends

Materials

Quantity standard	×	Price standard	=	Standard cost
3 pounds per bookend	×	$4.00 per pound	=	$12.00 per bookend

Labor

Efficiency standard	×	Rate standard	=	Standard cost
1 hour per unit	×	$7.00 per hour	=	$7.00 per bookend

Combined Standard Costs per Unit

Materials	$12.00
Labor	7.00
Total	$19.00

are simply used as the basis for developing manufacturing budgets whichever basic system is used. These budgets are then used as a criteria against which to judge the quality of actual performance.

STANDARD COSTS DEFINED

A **standard** is a criterion for measurement. Standards in cost accounting refer to a norm or normal amount of quantities or prices to be paid for the materials and labor required to make some product or provide some service. Standards are expressed in terms of specific items of input—the units of materials, the hours of labor, the price of materials, the rate for labor, and the percent of plant capacity required to manufacture one unit of output. A **cost,** as related to standard costs, is the outlay or sacrifice that is incurred for each unit of output.

The combination of the terms standard and cost into **standard cost** refers to the expected cost of production under normal operating conditions. Typically, a standard cost is a unit cost concept. It is a cost per unit that the firm should try to achieve if the results of operations are to be as desired. It is a target, expected or forecast cost. The underlying philosophy of management dictates what should be targeted or expected costs. For example, management may expect the least costs possible under ideal manufacturing conditions or management may consider the consequences of such factors as lost time for maintenance as part of what is expected. Different philosophies and the development of standards will be discussed later in this chapter.

Standard costs are used in responsibility accounting in the following general way. As actual production takes place, standard or expected costs are compared with actual costs incurred and any differences or variances are recorded. The variance between actual costs incurred compared with projected standard costs can then be used as feedback to management for control purposes.

Standard costs are developed for each manufacturing cost component—materials, labor, and overhead. Standard costs for materials and labor are discussed in this chapter. Standard costs for factory overhead will be discussed in chapter 16.

Standard costs consist of two components—a quantity standard and a price standard. Multiplying the quantity standard times the price standard gives a standard cost. To illustrate, figure 15.1 contains the standard cost calculations for the manufacture of one type of bronze bookend. The use of these standards is discussed throughout this chapter.

Materials Standards

As shown in figure 15.1, materials standards consist of two components—a *materials quantity standard* and a *materials price standard*. Multiplying the price standard times the quantity standard gives the standard materials cost per unit. For example, to manufacture one bookend, it is expected to require three pounds of materials per bookend (the material quantity standard) at an expected cost of $4.00 per pound (the material price standard), giving a materials standard cost per unit of $12.00.

The materials quantity standard is developed from a combination of engineering design studies and prior manufacturing experience. Materials quantity standards should take into consideration acceptable levels of spoilage, waste, shrinkage, and evaporation. After the product has been through a developmental stage, current production experience may be the best guide for adjusting quantity standards to accurately reflect expected materials usage.

The materials price standard should reflect the market prices that are expected to prevail during the budgeted accounting period. Determination of an appropriate price standard is complicated because prices are largely controlled by factors external to the firm and are subject to unexpected change. Suppliers' price lists and the judgment of the firm's purchasing agents can provide the basis for setting cost standards. A suggested rule is to review price standards at the beginning of each budgetary period and make adjustments as appropriate.

Labor Standards

Just like materials standards, labor standards consist of two components—a labor efficiency (quantity) standard and a labor rate (price) standard. Although the underlying concept is the same, the accepted terminology for labor differs slightly from that used for materials. As illustrated in figure 15.1, a *labor efficiency standard* is used instead of a quantity standard to indicate how efficiently the available hours of labor are utilized. Instead of a cost standard, a *labor rate standard* is used to indicate the cost of labor based on a per hour rate.

Multiplying the rate standard times the efficiency standard gives the standard labor cost per unit. For example, one bookend requires one hour of labor (the labor efficiency standard) at an expected rate of $7.00 per hour (the labor rate standard) giving a labor standard cost per unit of $7.00.

The labor efficiency standard is usually determined through the use of time and motion studies of actual worker performance. Taking into consideration personal needs, fatigue, and production factors outside the control of the individual worker, the average effort of workers with average skills is used to develop efficiency standards.

The labor rate standard is based on employment agreements. Labor rates may be determined by individual employee agreements with the firm's personnel department or by collective bargaining agreements with which a number of employees are covered by union contract. In either event, the agreed hourly or piece rates and bonus agreements provide the basis for labor rate standards.

Note that standard costs for labor may be developed using average wage rates and average quantities. This is usually the case when there are several workers who work on the same project but are paid different rates. It may be too costly to itemize and account for each person's labor component. Therefore, averages are used in the development of standards.

STANDARDS AS BUDGETARY GOALS
AND PERFORMANCE BENCHMARKS

Standard costs relate to one unit of production and can be referred to as a unit concept. On the other hand, budgets portray an aggregate concept in that the budget is derived by multiplying standard costs by the planned level of output. Therefore, standard costs are literally a basic building block of manufacturing budgets.

Standard costs must be visualized as a *unit* concept and budgets must be visualized as an *aggregate* concept; otherwise, the more detailed aspects of standard cost systems will seem confusing. Figure 15.2 illustrates this relationship and provides a materials and labor budget for a manufacturer of bronze bookends.

Figure 15.2 shows that the total standard cost for materials and labor for each bookend is $19.00. If the level of activity is 5,000 bookends, the total budgeted standard cost of materials and labor is $95,000. The term *total standard costs allowed* is alternate terminology for *total budgeted costs*.

As indicated, standard costs provide the foundation of a feedback and control system in manufacturing operations. Figure 15.3 shows data from accounting records concerning the production of bookends for one period.

Actual results of operations can be compared with budgeted results to provide feedback to management concerning the attainment of goals and to serve as a benchmark

---

**Figure 15.2   Materials and labor budget for bronze bookends
(for 5,000 units of production)**

	Standard Costs	Budgeted Costs
Standard costs:		
Materials	$12.00	$60,000
Labor	7.00	35,000
Total	$19.00	$95,000

Alternative computations:
Materials: 5,000 units $\times$ 3 pounds per unit $\times$ $4.00 per pound = $60,000
Labor: 5,000 units $\times$ 1 hour per unit $\times$ $7.00 per hour = $35,000

Figure 15.3   Production results

Units produced	5,000	
Materials:		
Pounds of materials purchased	15,000	
Pounds of materials used	14,740	
Price per pound of materials	$\times$ $4.05	
Total materials cost		$59,697
Labor:		
Hours of labor used	5,060	
Rate per hour paid labor	$\times$ $7.00	
Total labor cost		$35,420
Total materials and labor costs		$95,117

Figure 15.4   Budget variances

	Budgeted[a] Costs	Actual[b] Costs	Budget Variance
Direct materials	$60,000	$59,697	$ 303 F
Direct labor	35,000	35,420	420 U
Total	$95,000	$95,117	$ 117 U

F = Favorable
U = Unfavorable

[a]See figure 15.2.
[b]See figure 15.3.

against which to evaluate performance. This can be done in successive levels of detail. As shown in figure 15.4, an overall or total budget variance can be calculated to show how much total actual results differed from total budgeted results.

Budget variances indicate the total deviation of actual costs from expected costs. In the example above, total actual costs exceeded budgeted costs resulting in an unfavorable total budget variance. However, the total actual cost of materials was less than expected resulting in a favorable budget variance for materials. Total labor costs exceeded the budget and resulted in an unfavorable budget variance for labor. The combination of the favorable budget variance for materials and the unfavorable budget variance for labor resulted in the unfavorable total budget variance.

MATERIALS AND LABOR VARIANCES

Budget variances do not give the complete story about deviations between budgeted and actual results. For example, it is not yet clear in figure 15.4 what contributed to the favorable materials variance. Some additional information can be gleaned by visually comparing production results in figure 15.3 with the standards in figure 15.1.

The firm paid more for raw materials than expected, which would have contributed to an unfavorable materials variance. Fewer raw materials were used in production than expected, which would have contributed to a favorable materials variance. However, the relative impact of these price and quantity differences is not clear without further investigation. This same type of ambiguity also exists in the analysis of the budget variance for labor.

To completely and meaningfully analyze the total budget variance, each component of standard costs must be analyzed; that is, materials variances are analyzed in terms of the materials price standard and the materials quantity standard. The labor variances are analyzed in terms of the labor rate standard and the labor efficiency standard. This level of analysis results in (a) a *materials price variance* that identifies the effect of differences in prices paid for materials, (b) a *materials quantity (usage) variance* that identifies the effect of differences in the quantities of materials used, (c) a *labor rate variance* that identifies the effect of differences in the rates paid workers, and (d) a *labor efficiency (usage) variance* that identifies the effect of differences in the quantities of labor used. Figure 15.5 shows formulas that are used to calculate these variances.

The rationale underlying the variance formulas is that by holding one of the cost components constant it is possible to isolate the effect of differences on the other component. For example, if the quantity of materials is held constant at the level of actual usage and it is multiplied by the difference between the standard price and the actual price of materials, it is possible to isolate the effect of changes in prices. Also, if the price of materials is held constant at the standard price and it is multiplied by the difference

Figure 15.5   Formulas for computing materials and labor variances

Materials

Price variance:

$$\left[\begin{array}{c}\text{Standard price of materials} \\ \text{(per unit)}\end{array} - \begin{array}{c}\text{Actual price of materials} \\ \text{(per unit)}\end{array}\right] \times \begin{array}{c}\text{Actual quantity of materials} \\ \text{purchased or used}^1\end{array}$$

Quantity (usage) variance:

$$\left[\begin{array}{c}\text{Standard quantity of materials} \\ \text{for units produced}\end{array} - \begin{array}{c}\text{Actual quantity of materials} \\ \text{used}\end{array}\right] \times \begin{array}{c}\text{Standard price of materials} \\ \text{(per unit)}\end{array}$$

Labor

Rate variance:

$$\left[\begin{array}{c}\text{Standard rate for labor} \\ \text{(per hour)}\end{array} - \begin{array}{c}\text{Actual rate paid for labor} \\ \text{(per hour)}\end{array}\right] \times \begin{array}{c}\text{Actual hours of labor} \\ \text{used}\end{array}$$

Efficiency (usage) variance:

$$\left[\begin{array}{c}\text{Standard hours of labor} \\ \text{for units produced}\end{array} - \begin{array}{c}\text{Actual hours of labor} \\ \text{used}\end{array}\right] \times \begin{array}{c}\text{Standard rate for labor} \\ \text{(per hour)}\end{array}$$

Formulas	where	and
$PV = (SP - AP) \times AQ$	PV = Price variance	AH = Actual hours of labor used
$QV = (SQ - AQ) \times SP$	QV = Quantity variance	AP = Actual price (per unit) of materials
$RV = (SR - AR) \times AH$	RV = Rate variance	AQ = Actual quantity of materials (purchased or used)
$EV = (SH - AH) \times SR$	EV = Efficiency variance	AR = Actual rate paid (per hour) for labor
		SH = Standard hours of labor for units produced
		SP = Standard price (per unit) of materials
		SQ = Standard quantity of materials for units produced
		SR = Standard rate for labor

[1]Materials price variances are typically recognized at the time of purchase. However, they may be recognized at the time of issue as illustrated in Figure 15.7 and discussed on page 507.

between the budgeted and actual usage of materials, it is possible to isolate the effect of changes in quantities. This underlying principle is also used to calculate labor variances.

Figure 15.6 shows an application of the variance formulas. The data used in figure 15.6 are the standard costs for bronze bookends given in figure 15.1 and the results of operations given in figure 15.3.

An alternative to the use of formulas is a tabular approach to the calculation of variances. The tabular approach is actually based on an expansion and comparison of the variance formulas in figure 15.5. For example, expanding the materials variance formulas by multiplication results in the following (see fig. 15.5 for an explanation of the formula's abbreviations):

Price variance $= [(AQ)(SP)-(AQ)(AP)]$
Quantity variance $= [(SQ)(SP)-(AQ)(SP)]$

Both variance formulas contain a common expression—$(AQ)(SP)$. This feature, which also occurs with labor variances, makes it possible to use the framework in figure 15.7 to calculate materials and labor variances.

You may prefer to use the tabular approach to calculate variances. However, in doing so remember that the tabular approach is simply a convenient way to apply the basic variance formulas and not a different calculation.

Figure 15.6   Materials and labor variances for bronze bookends

---

Materials

Price variance: (purchased)	$ 750 U
Price variance: (Issued) ($4.00 − $4.05) × 14,740 pounds =	$ 737 U
Quantity variance: (15,000 pounds − 14,740 pounds) × $4.00 =	1,040 F
Budget variance	$ 303 F

Labor

Rate variance: ($7.00 − $7.00) × 5,060 hours =	$ -0-
Efficiency variance: (5,000 hours − 5,060 hours) × $7.00 =	420 U
Budget variance	$ 420 U

Figure 15.7   Framework for analysis of variances

Direct Materials

Actual price × Actual quantity (Issued)	Standard price × Actual quantity (Issued)	Standard price × Standard quantity (Issued)
$4.05 × 14,740 = $59,697	$4.00 × 14,740 = $58,960	$4.00 × 15,000 = $60,000

Price variance $737 U

Quantity variance $1,040 F

Actual price × Actual quantity (Purchased)	Standard price × Actual quantity (Purchased)
$4.05 × 15,000 = $60,750	$4.00 × 15,000 = $60,000

Price variance $750 U

Direct Labor

Actual rate × Actual hours	Standard rate × Actual hours	Standard rate × Standard hours
$7.00 × 5,060 = $35,420	$7.00 × 5,060 = $35,420	$7.00 × 5,000 = $35,000

Rate variance $-0-

Efficiency variance $420 U

RESPONSIBILITY FOR VARIANCES

The objective of a standard cost system and the calculation of variances is to provide feedback for planning and cost control. To achieve *effective* cost control each reported variance must be associated with a responsible person. The person given the responsibility must also have the authority to control that item of material or labor in the production process. If a definite linkage does not exist between reported variances and a manager who is responsible and able to exercise control, the effectiveness of a standard cost system will be compromised.

Variance reports must be prepared on a timely basis. Depending on the production environment, variance reports may be needed on an hourly, daily, weekly, or monthly basis. For example, control over material usage for a fast-moving, continuous process such as generating instant cake mixes may require hourly monitoring, but control over material usage for ship building may require only weekly or monthly reporting.

The reporting of major variances may trigger an investigation by responsible personnel in an attempt to identify causes and implement improvements in operations. The question of when variances are significant enough to warrant investigation is treated in a later section of this chapter.

Materials

The head of the purchasing department is responsible for materials price variances. Production supervisors are responsible for materials quantity variances. However, there may be times when part of a materials price variance is the responsibility of a production supervisor. For example, price variances may result because a supervisor specifies that certain materials should be purchased from a specific vendor. Price variances in such situations should be attributed to the requesting person.

It is generally accepted that purchasing officers are responsible for *all* materials price variances. However, in some instances price variances should be a shared responsibility. For example, consider the situation in which additional materials must be purchased at an unfavorable price because a production supervisor is inefficient. It could be reasoned that the production supervisor is not only responsible for the resulting unfavorable quantity variance but also responsible for part of any associated price variance. However, general practice, as reflected in the variance formulas, indicates that in such instances the purchasing officer shoulders full responsibility for all price variances.

Sometimes an unfavorable variance may be tolerated in order to obtain an even larger favorable variance. For example, the opportunity may arise to acquire a batch of raw materials having exceptionally high quality but at a price that is above standard. It may be reasoned that even though an unfavorable price variance will result, the materials can be used very efficiently resulting in an even larger favorable quantity variance.

There are any number of reasons why materials variances occur. For example, price variances may occur because of unexpected vendor price changes, because of the availability of quantity discounts, or simply because of changes in the bargaining power of the purchasing agent. Quantity variances may result from faulty workmanship, careless handling, or the purchase of inferior materials.

Labor

Department supervisors are responsible for both labor rate and labor efficiency variances. However, labor rates are usually not subject to the same degree of control as labor efficiency variances. Labor rates are typically the result of union contract negotiations or come from individual employment agreements. Because of this, standard rates may simply be a function of actual labor rates. Therefore, if standard rates for labor reflect actual labor rates, then labor rate variances should be relatively small and are the responsibility of individual supervisors.

When standard rates for labor are not kept current with actual labor rates, labor rate variances may be relatively large. In such instances, it may be difficult to determine what part of the rate variance is the responsibility of individual supervisors and what part is the responsibility of contract negotiators. Therefore, to maintain the accountability of supervisors for rate variances, it is recommended that labor rate standards be adjusted as employment agreements change—usually on an annual basis.

Labor variances could occur for a number of reasons. For example, labor rate variances could result from a supervisor's use of workers with different rates than originally specified for particular jobs. Labor efficiency variances could also result from such factors as unexpected changes in the quality of materials, unexpected differences in the technological level of machinery, or unexpected rates of spoilage and rework.

RECORDING MATERIALS, LABOR, AND RELATED VARIANCES

Two general methods are used to record materials and labor costs when standard costing is used. The first method recognizes materials price variances when materials are purchased. The second method recognizes materials price variances when materials are placed in production. Using either method, materials usage variances are recognized when materials are placed in process. The following data concerning materials for bronze bookends is used to illustrate recording materials costs and their related variances using each of these methods:

Standard cost	$4.00/pound
Purchase price	$4.05/pound
Amount purchased	20,000 pounds
Amount placed in production	14,740 pounds
Budgeted usage	15,000 pounds

Note that the journal entries used in this section represent the total activity of an accounting period. Conceptually, individual journal entries are made when materials are received and then again when materials are placed in production. In actual practice, journal entries are usually made to record the materials price variance when materials are received. However, journal entries that record the materials being placed in production and the incurrence of labor costs may not be made until each job or production run is complete. This happens because all of the data necessary to make these entries cannot be accumulated until jobs are completed.

Materials

There are three important concepts to remember about materials when using a standard cost system. First, materials are placed in the work-in-process inventory at standard cost and the work-in-process inventory is carried at standard cost. Second, the materials quantity variance is recognized when materials are issued and placed in production. Third, the materials price variance can be recognized either when materials are purchased or when materials are issued. Therefore, depending on when the materials price variance is recognized, the materials inventory will be carried at either actual cost or standard cost. The following illustrates each method of recognizing the materials price variance and the related effect each has on the carrying cost of materials inventory.

Recognize Price Variance at Time of Purchase   When the materials price variance is recognized at the time of purchase the following journal entries are made. The first journal entry records the receipt of materials, the incurrence of a liability, and the recognition of any price variance.

Materials inventory ($4.00/lb. × 20,000 lbs.)	$80,000	
Materials price variance ([$4.00−$4.05] × 20,000 lbs.)	1,000	
Accounts payable ($4.05 × 20,000 lbs.)		$81,000

The second journal entry is made when materials are issued and placed in production with the recognition of any materials quantity variance.

Work in process ($4.00 × 15,000 lbs.)	$60,000	
Materials quantity variance ([15,000 lbs. − 14,740 lbs.] × $4.00)		1,040
Materials inventory ($4.00 × 14,740 lbs.)		58,960

Recognize Price Variance at Time of Issue   When the materials price variance is recognized at the time materials are placed in production, the following journal entry is made at the time of purchase.

Materials inventory ($4.05 × 20,000 lbs.)	$81,000	
Accounts payable		$81,000

The following journal entry is made when materials are issued and placed in production.

Work in process ($4.00 × 15,000 lbs.)	$60,000	
Materials price variance ([$4.00−$4.05] × 14,740 lbs.)	737	
Materials quantity variance ([15,000 lbs.−14,740] × $4.00)		1,040
Materials inventory ($4.05 × 14,740 lbs.)		59,697

Note that materials costs are added to the work-in-process inventory at the standard rate for the actual number of units produced. Therefore, the work-in-process inventory is carried at standard cost when using either system.

Recognizing materials price variances at the time of purchase rather than at the time of issue has several advantages. One advantage is that price variances are reported on a more timely basis, which permits faster response by management to unfavorable situations. If price variances are not revealed until materials are placed in production, the time may have passed when the most effective corrective action could have been taken.

Another advantage of recording price variances at the time of purchase is that the materials inventory is maintained at standard cost. This means that the inventory records can be maintained by recording only quantities, and that could result in some clerical savings. However, if it is important to carry inventories at actual cost rather than at standard cost, then recognition of price variances may be delayed until materials are placed in production.

It is important to note that the work-in-process inventory is always carried at standard cost whether or not the materials inventory is maintained at standard cost. Therefore, to provide consistency in carrying inventories at standard cost, recognizing price variances at the time of purchase is preferred.

Finally, if price variances are recognized when materials are placed in production, an additional difficulty arises in deciding which purchase price to use when materials have been purchased at more than one price. The choice of a cost flow assumption such as LIFO, FIFO, or average cost to value the raw materials inventory may have an impact on the usefulness of materials price variances. For example, if the FIFO method is used, then the inventory items that are issued may carry relatively old prices. Using old prices against current standards may result in variances that are difficult to interpret in terms of current business conditions.

A third method that can be used to record materials and recognize materials variances is a hybrid of the two general methods already described. When using this third method a *purchase price variance* is recorded when materials are purchased and a *usage price variance* is recorded when materials are placed in production. To avoid confusion with the methods already described, this third method is illustrated in the appendix at the end of this chapter.

Labor

Information furnished by the payroll department provides the basis for recording labor costs and related rate and efficiency variances. The hours and rates previously used in the bronze bookend example illustrate the recording of labor.

Actual hours used	5,060
Budgeted hours allowed	5,000
Actual rate paid	$7.00
Standard rate	$7.00

The following journal entry is made to record labor costs and recognize the labor efficiency variance.

Work in process (5,000 hrs. × $7/hr.)	$35,000	
Labor efficiency variance		
([1 hr/unit × 5,000 units] − 5,060 hrs.) × $7	420	
Wages payable (5,060 hrs. × $7.00)		$35,420

If the actual rate paid had been $7.10 per hour instead of $7.00 per hour, then an unfavorable labor rate variance would have resulted. The following journal entry would be used to record labor costs and related rate and efficiency variances under this new assumption.

Work in process (5,000 hrs. × $7/hr.)	$35,000	
Labor efficiency variance	420	
Labor rate variance ([$7.00/hr. − $7.10/hr.] × 5,060 hrs.)	506	
Wages payable ($7.10/hr. × 5,060 hrs.)		$35,926

Just as for materials, labor costs are added to the work-in-process inventory at the standard rate for the actual number of units produced. Labor rate and efficiency variances comprise the difference between standard (budgeted) labor costs and the actual payroll liability.

Disposition of Variances

Two methods are available for handling the balances in variance accounts at the end of an accounting period. Although each method is briefly discussed and illustrated here in order to complete the accounting cycle for materials and labor, a more comprehensive discussion including overhead cost variances is contained in chapter 16.

Standard cost variances may be written off immediately to cost of goods sold. This method is used when variances are considered insignificant or immaterial and when standard costs are felt to be representative of "actual" costs of production. The following journal entry illustrates the disposition of variances when this method is used.

Cost of goods sold (income summary)	623	
Materials quantity variance	1,040	
Materials price variance		737
Labor rate variance		506
Labor efficiency variance		420

Standard cost variances may also be prorated among inventories and cost of goods sold. This method is used when variances are significant or when standard costs are not considered representative of "actual" manufacturing costs. The basis for proration is usually the proportion of total manufacturing costs in each cost category. To illustrate, the following schedule contains assumed quantities and percentages of materials and labor costs in work in process, finished goods, and cost of goods sold:

	Materials and Labor	
Account	Amount	Percent
Work in process	$ 40,000	25%
Finished goods	16,000	10
Cost of goods sold	104,000	65
Total	$160,000	100%

Based on the above proportions, the following schedule indicates how the variances are to be prorated:

	Total Amount (100%)	Work in Process (25%)	Finished Goods (10%)	Cost of Goods Sold (65%)
Materials price variance	$ 737.00	$ 184.25	$ 73.70	$ 479.05
Materials quantity variance	(1,040.00)	(260.00)	(104.00)	(676.00)
Labor rate variance	506.00	126.50	50.60	328.90
Labor efficiency variance	420.00	105.00	42.00	273.00
Total	$ 623.00	$ 155.75	$ 62.30	$ 404.95

Using the amounts in this schedule, the following journal entry is made to allocate standard cost variances:

Work in process	155.75	
Finished goods	62.30	
Cost of goods sold	404.95	
Materials quantity variance	1,040.00	
Materials price variance		737.00
Labor rate variance		506.00
Labor efficiency variance		420.00

Any number of proration schemes are more detailed than the procedure just illustrated. For example, it may be desirable to allocate variances in a step-wise fashion by first allocating the materials price variance to the materials efficiency variance and raw materials inventory as well as to work in process, finished goods, and cost of goods sold. Then, the remaining variances are allocated to work in process, finished goods, and cost of goods sold. Whether using a simple allocation as illustrated or a complex allocation scheme the basic principles remain the same.

INVESTIGATION OF VARIANCES

How does a manager know whether a specific variance is large enough to warrant investigation? This question arises in standard cost systems because, by intuition, one would expect that some variances will occur even though the production process is performing within satisfactory limits. One would expect random favorable and unfavorable variances to occur under normal conditions simply as a result of chance variations in the production environment.

If the above is true, then a more fundamental question concerns the magnitude of the range or tolerance limits within which variances may be allowed to fluctuate without investigation. Once such tolerance limits are established, management can proceed on an exception basis to investigate variances. For some classes of materials or labor, small variances may require investigation where relatively large variances may be required to justify investigation for other items. Therefore, variance analysis and the decision to investigate should be subjected to a cost-benefit analysis in the same way that other elements of a management reporting system are evaluated. Two of the most common ways to set tolerance limits for variance control are to develop rules of thumb or to use statistical techniques.

Rules of thumb arise from past experience or intuition. They take the form of "investigate all materials variances in excess of $1,000" or "investigate all labor variances exceeding 20% of total standard costs." From such rules of thumb a range of acceptable variances can be calculated. For example, using the rule of thumb for materials suggested above, a materials quantity variance falling within a plus or minus $1,000 region will be assumed to have arisen because there are random variations in the production process, and the added costs of investigation and corrective action are not warranted.

Statistical techniques utilize probability theory and past performance to establish acceptable ranges within which variances are allowed to fluctuate without investigation. When using statistical techniques the boundaries of the acceptable region for fluctuations are referred to as *control limits*. For example, if the statistical method employed indicates that the control limits for a labor efficiency variance should be plus or minus $1,500, then a variance of $1,600 would indicate that the production process is "out of control" and should be investigated. However, variances within the $1,500 limit would indicate the production process is operating "in control" and no investigation is required.

DEVELOPMENT OF STANDARDS

Standard setting is primarily the responsibility of supervisors, department managers, and other line personnel directly involved with operations. Standard setting is usually an integral part of an organization's budgetary process. Accountants, industrial engineers, market researchers, and other technical advisers extend advice and assist in the development of both standards and the budget. However, line personnel are ultimately responsible for departmental performance and should make the primary decisions concerning standards.

Higher management must provide the basic guidelines for the development of standards and then review standards for reasonableness and adherence to established guidelines. Typically, the standard-setting process involves a great amount of discussion, bargaining, and even arbitration among those involved. Central to the process, however, are some basic concepts and guidelines.

Standard-Setting Philosophies

Standard setting is based upon basic philosophies concerning how demanding the standards should be. One philosophy holds that **ideal standards** should be set with perfect manufacturing conditions in mind. Standards based upon this philosophy relate to the least possible costs that can be expected under the best conceivable manufacturing conditions. Existing equipment and specifications are considered from an ideal perspective.

If the philosophy of management is that standards set for maximum efficiency provide the best goals for motivation, then ideal standards are appropriate. However, remember that all variances will probably be unfavorable when using such a philosophy. This is because ideal or perfect manufacturing conditions rarely occur in practice. Therefore, operating personnel may become frustrated by not being able to achieve perfect standards if they are not aware that ideal standards have been formulated.

An alternative philosophy holds that **currently attainable standards** should be set under efficient operating conditions. Currently attainable standards are less demanding than ideal standards. They allow for ordinary equipment failure, normal lost time, and normal spoilage. However, currently attainable standards are usually set tightly enough so that they are difficult to achieve. Variances using currently attainable standards are as likely to be favorable or unfavorable depending on the effort expended to attain them. With good effort standards may be achieved resulting in favorable variances. In this way operating personnel feel a sense of accomplishment when currently attainable standards are achieved.

Currently attainable standards seem to provide better motivation for operating personnel than other possible philosophies. If line managers feel (*a*) that the standard is indeed attainable, (*b*) that they are in control of the variables the standard measures, and (*c*) that data is accurately reported, then the standard is usually accepted as a norm for behavior. The ability to generate favorable variances with somewhat more than expected efficiency may motivate operating personnel, especially if bonuses are contingent on achieving attainable standards.

A final point about standard-setting philosophies is that standards are not answers to questions. Standards are attention directors for management. Rather than answering questions, standards are intended to raise questions and draw attention to situations that should be examined. In the examination process, the variances generated from applying standards provide clues for pinpointing causal relationships. From this viewpoint, considering the magnitude and complexity of interrelationships in most organizations, management should not jump to conclusions concerning "favorable" or "unfavorable" variances. Conclusions about a situation being either favorable or unfavorable should follow proper investigation. Variances provide feedback and clues, not answers.

Physical Standards

Physical standards are also an integral part of a standard cost system. Physical standards come from physical estimates based on engineering standards. For example, physical standards for materials are usually expressed in terms of pounds, gallons, or units of input for each unit of output produced. For labor, physical standards are typically expressed in terms of hours or minutes of labor per unit of output produced. Multiplying the physical standard by the price expected to be paid for materials and labor results in standard costs. The importance of this process should not be overlooked because the result in *dollars* is the common denominator and measuring stick in a standard cost system instead of pounds or hours. This provides for uniformity and consistency in planning and controlling manufacturing operations.

Physical standards for materials are derived from product specifications usually contained in blueprints. Along with product specifications, consideration is given to the production method, normal waste, and unavoidable spoilage. In addition to product specifications, physical standards are often refined using test production runs under controlled conditions. Test runs should be conducted under conditions that are as close to normal as possible. This will avoid standards being set on artificially inefficient or super-efficient results. There will also probably be a refinement period in which the results of actual operations will be used to adjust physical standards.

Physical standards for labor are developed using time and motion studies. Predicting the human element in a production environment is a difficult task. The human element increases the likelihood of disputes about establishing physical standards for labor. Therefore, to be an effective base for standards, the conditions under which labor performance is measured are critical. Both the manufacturing operation itself and the manufacturing environment must be considered. Instructions and training for the worker, materials availability, materials handling requirements, equipment, and organization of the work space are factors that must be considered.

Allowances are usually made in labor standards for learning, rest time, and fatigue. Because there is a potential for disagreement and disputes, a delicate balance usually exists regarding labor standards that are too loose, attainable, or unattainable. For example, if a bonus system is based on the attainment of standard performance, then the time standard should be set at a level that is fair to the firm in terms of value received as well as fair to the worker in terms of rewarding above average performance. After taking into consideration all of these factors through study and observation, time and motion engineers set labor efficiency standards.

Physical standards for materials and labor along with their cost components are usually represented on a *standard cost card* as shown in figure 15.8. Standard cost cards are usually maintained for each product and show the quantities and prices for all productive inputs including overhead.

Figure 15.8   Standard cost card

Standard Cost Card			
Product: XYZ Fitting		Date: Jan. 1, 19X8	

Materials			
Inventory number	*Standard quantity*	*Standard unit cost*	*Total*
C1351	2	$6.70	$13.40
B4962	1	1.20	1.20
2853	4	2.35	9.40
		Total	$24.00

Labor			
Department number	*Standard hours*	*Standard hourly rate*	*Total*
1	2	$4.00	$ 8.00
3	3	4.10	12.30
4	1	4.65	4.65
		Total	$24.95
		Total materials and labor	$48.95

Summary

Manufacturing costs are affected by factors over which management can exercise control. An important role of cost accounting is to facilitate management's efforts by providing information for effective control decisions. A widely accepted procedure is to use flexible budgets based on standard costs as the criterion against which actual results are compared. Standard costs are the dollar outlays expected to be incurred to manufacture a particular product in a given manufacturing environment. Differences between standard and actual costs, referred to as variances, can be used to isolate why results differed from plans. Significant variances can be investigated so that either corrective action can be taken or beneficial results can be rewarded.

Variances can isolate the effect of differences between planned and actual (a) prices paid for materials (materials price variance), (b) usage of materials (materials quantity variance), (c) rates paid for labor (labor rate variance), and (d) usage of labor (labor efficiency variance). Formulas as well as a tabular approach are available for calculating each of these variances.

The effectiveness of a standard cost system depends on the assignment of responsibility to company managers and supervisors. Responsibility for each variance should be assigned to the person who has the authority to control that item of material or labor in the production process. The purchasing agent is responsible for the materials price variance. Supervisors are responsible for the materials and labor usage variances and may also be responsible for labor rate variances. However, labor rates are often set through contract negotiations or by agreement with the personnel department.

Variances are recorded in the general ledger using appropriately titled accounts. The materials price variance is usually recorded at the time materials are purchased even though they could be recorded when materials are placed in production. The materials quantity variance is recorded when materials are placed in production. Labor variances are recorded when the payroll liability is recorded. Variance accounts are closed at the end of the accounting period in one of two ways. If variances are insignificant, they are closed directly to cost of goods sold or to income summary. If variances are significant, they are prorated among inventories and cost of goods sold.

Management must determine when a variance is significant enough to warrant further investigation. Rules of thumb and statistical techniques are used to establish control limits within which variances are allowed to fluctuate without further investigation. However, a variance falling outside of control limits indicates that the process is out of control and investigation is warranted.

There are several philosophies underlying the development of standards. Currently attainable standards are felt to be most effective for management control. Ideal standards based on perfect conditions are often frustrating because they may not be attainable. Loose standards do not provide motivation for quality behavior.

In conclusion, standard costs provide a valuable planning and control tool for management. However, the standard cost system is not complete until standard costs for overhead are included.

Appendix   *A Hybrid Method for Recognizing Materials Price Variances*

This method provides for the recognition of a materials *purchase price variance* and a materials *usage price variance*. This method also provides for the disclosure of materials inventory at cost and standard cost. This is accomplished by having two materials price variance accounts. A materials *purchase price variance* account is used to record price variances when materials are received. It also serves as an inventory at both cost and standard cost. A materials *usage price variance* account is used to record the price variance associated with materials placed into production. The journal entry to record materials received using data from the chapter illustration is as follows:

Materials inventory ($4.00 × 20,000 lbs.)	$80,000	
Materials purchase price variance ([$4.00 − $4.05] × 20,000 lbs.)	1,000	
Accounts payable ($4.05 × 20,000 lbs.)		$81,000

This journal entry is identical to the first journal entry when recognizing the materials price variance at the time of purchase except for the title of the price variance account. Debits to the materials purchase price variance account provide recognition of variances at the time of purchase and the balance in the account at any moment in time provides a valuation amount to reflect the cost of materials inventory. For example, a partial balance sheet immediately after the above purchase would take the following form:

Materials inventory at standard cost	$80,000
Plus: Unfavorable purchase price variance	1,000
Materials inventory at cost	$81,000

When using this method, there are two journal entries made when materials are issued and placed in production. These journal entries are:

Work in process ($4.00 × 15,000 lbs.)	$60,000	
Materials quantity variance ([15,000 lbs. − 14,740 lbs.] × $4.00)		1,040
Materials inventory ($4.00 × 14,740 lbs.)		58,960

and

Materials usage price variance	$ 737	
Materials purchase price variance ([$4.00−$4.05] × 14,740 lbs.)		737

The first journal entry is identical to the journal entry when placing materials into production and recognizing materials price variances at the time of purchase. The second journal entry is used to indicate the amount of price variance related to materials placed into production and to properly value the amount of purchase price variance relating to materials still in the materials inventory. For example, a partial balance sheet immediately following the above issuance of materials would be:

Materials inventory at standard cost	$21,040[a]
Plus: Unfavorable purchase price variance	263
Materials inventory at cost	$21,303[b]

[a]20,000 lbs. − 14,740 lbs. issued = 5,260 lbs. at $4.00 = $21,040.
[b]5,260 lbs. at $4.05 = $21,303.

This combination of methods provides for both the immediate recognition of price variances when materials are received and the valuation of materials inventory at cost and standard cost. The advantages of this method should be balanced with the extended amount of record keeping necessary to support it.

Karen Company uses flexible budgets and a standard cost system to control materials and labor costs. Information from the standard cost card for one of its products, ABC Fasteners, is given below:

Materials

Inventory Number	Standard Quantity	Standard Unit Cost	Total
AA1	4	$2.00	$ 8.00
BB2	6	5.00	30.00
	Total materials		$38.00

Labor

Department Number	Standard Hours	Standard Hourly Rate	Total
1	2	$7.50	$15.00
2	1	9.00	9.00
	Total labor		$24.00
	Total materials and labor		$62.00

Two materials are used in the production of ABC Fasteners—AA1 and BB2. Production takes place in two departments with different standard labor rates. Production for the past week resulted in 6,000 good fasteners being produced.

Materials purchased during the past week were:

AA1: 26,000 units at $2.04 per unit = $ 53,040
BB2: 37,000 units at $4.98 per unit = $184,260
$237,300

Actual materials used to produce the 6,000 good units were:

AA1: 23,500 units
BB2: 36,100 units

Actual labor costs for the past week were:

Department 1: 12,100 hrs. at $7.50/hr. = $ 90,750
Department 2: 5,990 hrs. at $9.10/hr. = $ 54,509
$145,259

Assume that Karen Company recognizes materials price variances at the time of purchase and that the purchasing department is responsible for materials price variances. Individual department managers are responsible for the materials quantity variance as well as the labor rate and efficiency variances. Material AA1 is placed in production in department 1 and material BB2 is placed in production in department 2.

Required

1. Prepare a schedule showing the budget variances resulting from the past week's operations.
2. Compute the materials price variance, the materials quantity variance, the labor rate variance, and the labor efficiency variance.
3. Show the journal entries to record the above variances.
4. Prepare a responsibility report for the managers of departments 1 and 2 and give a brief analysis of each department's performance.

Solution to the Self-Study Problem

Requirement 1

	Budgeted Costs	Actual Costs	Budget Variances
Direct materials	$228,000(1)	$227,500(3)	$ 500 F
Direct labor	144,000(2)	145,259(4)	1,259 U
Total	$372,000	$372,759	$ 759 U

(1) 6,000 good units × $38.00 standard materials cost per unit

(2) 6,000 good units × $24.00 standard labor cost per unit

(3)   Standard price × Actual hours
 AA1: $2.00/unit × 23,500 units used = $ 47,000
 BB2: $5.00/unit × 36,100 units used = $180,500
  Total materials budget $227,500

(4)   Actual rate × Actual hours
 Dept. 1: $7.50/hr. × 12,100 hrs. = $ 90,750
 Dept. 2: $9.10/hr. × 5,990 hrs. = $ 54,509
  Total labor budget $145,259

Note that the materials budget uses standard prices rather than actual prices. This is because the firm recognizes the materials price variance when materials are purchased. This results in the materials budget variance being synonymous with the materials quantity variance.

Requirement 2

Materials price variance:

 AA1: ($2.00 − $2.04) × 26,000 = $1,040 U
 BB2: ($5.00 − $4.98) × 37,000 =   740 F
       $ 300 U

Materials quantity variance:

 AA1: (24,000 − 23,500) × $2.00 = $1,000 F
 BB2: (36,000 − 36,100) × $5.00 =   500 U
      $ 500 F

Labor rate variance:

 Dept. 1: ($7.50 − $7.50) × 12,100 =   –0–
 Dept. 2: ($9.00 − $9.10) × 5,990 = $599 U
        $599 U

Labor efficiency variance:

 Dept. 1: (12,000 − 12,100) × $7.50 = $750 U
 Dept. 2: (6,000 − 5,990) × $9.00 =   90 F
       $660 U

Requirement 3

(a) To record materials acquisition

Materials inventory	237,000[a]	
Materials price variance	300	
Accounts payable		237,300

[a](26,000 × $2.00) + (37,000 × $5.00)

(*b*) To record materials placed in production

Work in process	228,000[a]	
Materials quantity variance		500
Materials inventory		227,500[b]

[a](24,000 × $2.00) + (36,000 × $5.00)
[b](23,500 × $2.00) + (36,100 × $5.00)

(*c*) To record labor costs

Work in process	144,000[c]	
Labor rate variance	599	
Labor efficiency variance	660	
Wages payable		145,259

[c](12,000 × $7.50) + (6,000 × $9.00)

Requirement 4

Department 1	Direct Materials	Direct Labor	Total
Budgeted costs	$180,000	$ 54,000	$234,000
Controllable variances:			
Materials quantity	1,000 F		1,000 F
Labor rate		–0–	–0–
Labor efficiency		750 U	750 U
Total controllable costs	$179,000	$ 54,750	$233,750
Department 2			
Budgeted costs	$ 48,000	$ 90,000	$138,000
Controllable variances:			
Materials quantity	500 U		500 U
Labor rate		599 U	599 U
Labor efficiency		90 F	90 F
Total controllable costs	$ 48,500	$ 90,509	$139,009
Grand total	$227,500	$145,259	$372,759

Note that the responsibility report contains only those costs that are controllable by each department manager. Remember that the materials price variance is the responsibility of the purchasing manager. Therefore, the materials price variance does not appear on this report.

Department 1 experienced a favorable materials quantity variance and an unfavorable labor efficiency variance. Workers could have exercised extra caution during the week in the handling materials in an effort to reduce waste, which could have resulted in the favorable materials quantity variance. However, additional caution may have also required more total time in the production process resulting in an unfavorable labor efficiency variance.

Department 2 experienced an unfavorable materials quantity variance, an unfavorable labor rate variance, and a favorable labor efficiency variance. This could have resulted from adding more skilled labor to the production process than previously planned. Using more skilled labor could have resulted in both the unfavorable labor rate variance and the favorable labor efficiency variance. An improperly adjusted machine could have been responsible for the unfavorable materials quantity variance.

Taken as a whole, the production process seems to be within acceptable control limits. For example, the largest unfavorable variance is the materials quantity variance of $1,000, which is less than one half of 1% of total materials cost.

Suggested Readings

Coe, Teddy L. "Cost Accumulation and Analysis." *Accountants' Handbook,* edited by Lee J. Seidler. 6th ed. New York: Ronald Press, 1981.

Inman, Mark Lee. "Doing Without Standard Costing and Budgetary Control." *Management Accounting* (England: Institute of Cost and Management Accountants) (April 1981): 36–37.

Morse, Wayne J. *Cost Accounting: Processing, Evaluating and Using Cost Data.* 2d ed. Reading, Mass.: Addison-Wesley Publishing Co., 1981.

Ross, Timothy, and Bullock, R. J. "Integrating Measurement of Productivity Into a Standard Cost System." *Financial Executive* (October 1980): 34–36.

Wood, T. D., and Sweet, F. H. "Practical Approach to Standard Costing." *Modern Accounting Principles and Practices.* Englewood Cliffs, N.J.: Prentice-Hall, 1978, pp. 355–74.

Discussion Questions

1. Define standard cost and explain how standard costs are used in connection with flexible budgets and responsibility accounting.
2. Is the use of standard costs equally applicable to job-order and process-costing systems?
3. Explain the components of a materials or labor standard.
4. What is a variance?
5. List each materials and labor variance, give the formula for its calculation, and explain the meaning of each variance.
6. Outline the tabular approach to calculating materials and labor variances and explain the basis for its use.
7. Explain why responsibility for particular variances should be assigned to individual managers.
8. List the managers who are typically responsible for each materials and labor variance.
9. Explain why the materials price variance may be recognized at different points in the accounting cycle.
10. Outline the journal entries for recording variances assuming that (*a*) the materials price variance is recognized at the time of purchase and (*b*) the materials price variance is recognized at the time of issue.
11. List the alternative accounting procedures that could be used to close the variance accounts at the end of an accounting period. Under what conditions should each be used?
12. Does every variance indicate that the production process is "out of control"? Explain.
13. What are two common methods used to determine when a variance should be investigated?
14. What are two philosophies that management could use when setting standards?
15. Explain how physical standards are established for (*a*) materials and (*b*) labor.
16. Sketch a "standard cost card" and explain its contents and use.

Exercise 15.1 Standard Cost Concepts

1. A standard cost system may be used in
   - a. either job-order costing or process costing.
   - b. job-order costing but *not* process costing.
   - c. process costing but *not* job-order costing.
   - d. neither process costing nor job-order costing.
2. The absolute minimum cost that would be possible under the best conceivable operating conditions is a description of which type of standard cost?
   - a. Currently attainable (expected)
   - b. Ideal
   - c. Normal
   - d. Practical
3. If the actual hours worked exceed the standard hours allowed, what type of variance will occur?
   - a. Favorable labor usage (efficiency) variance
   - b. Favorable labor rate variance
   - c. Unfavorable labor usage (efficiency) variance
   - d. Unfavorable labor rate variance
4. An unfavorable materials price variance occurs because of
   - a. price increases on raw materials.
   - b. price decreases on raw materials.
   - c. less than anticipated levels of waste in the manufacturing process.
   - d. more than anticipated levels of waste in the manufacturing process.

Exercise 15.2 Standard Cost Concepts and Procedures for Labor Costs

Sullivan Corporation's direct-labor costs for the month of March were as follows:

Standard direct-labor hours	42,000
Actual direct-labor hours	40,000
Direct-labor rate variance—favorable	$ 8,400
Standard direct-labor rate per hour	$ 6.30

Required

1. Determine Sullivan's total direct-labor payroll for the month of March.
2. Determine Sullivan's direct-labor efficiency variance for March.

Exercise 15.3 Standard Cost Concepts and Procedures for Material Costs

Durable Company installs shingle roofs on residential houses. The standard material cost for a type *R* house is $1,250 based on 1,000 units at a cost of $1.25 each. During April Durable installed roofs on 20 type *R* houses, using 22,000 units of material at a cost of $1.20 per unit and a total cost of $26,400.

Required

1. Determine the materials price variance for Durable Company for April.
2. Determine the materials quantity variance for Durable Company for April.

Exercise 15.4   Standard Costs and Variances for Materials

During March, Younger Company's direct-materials costs for the manufacture of product *T* were as follows:

Actual unit purchase price	$ 6.50
Standard quantity allowed for actual production	2,100
Quantity purchased and used for actual production	2,300
Standard unit price	$ 6.25

Required

1. Determine Younger's materials price and usage variances for March.
2. Identify the department that is customarily held responsible for materials usage variances. Explain why.

Exercise 15.5   Materials Standards and Variances

Throop Company had budgeted 50,000 units of output using 50,000 units of raw materials at a total material cost of $100,000. Actual output was 50,000 units of product requiring 45,000 units of raw materials at a cost of $2.10 per unit. Calculate the direct-material price variance and usage variance.

Exercise 15.6   Labor Standards and Variances—Journal Entries

Information on Barber Company's direct-labor costs for the month of January is as follows:

Actual direct-labor hours	34,500
Standard direct-labor hours	35,000
Total direct-labor payroll	$241,500
Direct-labor efficiency variance—favorable	$ 3,200

Required

1. Determine Barber Company's labor rate variance.
2. Explain what a direct-labor efficiency variance means.
3. Make journal entries to record the direct-labor payroll and to charge labor costs to production assuming standard labor costs are charged to inventory.

Exercise 15.7   Determination of Materials Standards and Cost (CMA)

Danson Company is a chemical manufacturer that supplies industrial users. Danson plans to introduce a new chemical solution and needs to develop a standard product cost for this new solution.

The new chemical solution is made by combining a chemical compound (nyclyn) and a solution (salex), boiling the mixture, adding a second compound (protet), and bottling the resulting solution in 10-liter containers. The initial mix, which is 10 liters in volume, consists of 12 kilograms of nyclyn and 9.6 liters of salex. A 20% reduction in volume occurs during the boiling process. The solution is then cooled slightly before 5 kilograms of protet are added; the addition of protet does not affect the total liquid volume.

The purchase prices of the raw materials used in the manufacture of this new chemical solution are as follows:

Nyclyn	$1.30 per kilogram
Salex	1.80 per liter
Protet	2.40 per kilogram

Required

Determine the standard quantity for each raw material needed to produce a 10-liter container of Danson Company's new chemical solution and the standard materials cost of a 10-liter container of the new product.

Exercise 15.8 Materials and Labor Variances—Standard Cost System (CMA)

The Lonn Manufacturing Company produces two primary chemical products to be used as base ingredients for a variety of products. The 19X8 budget (000s omitted) for the two products was:

	X-4	Z-8	Total
Production output in gallons	600	600	1,200
Direct material	$1,500	$1,875	$3,375
Direct labor	900	900	1,800
Total prime manufacturing cost	$2,400	$2,775	$5,175

The following planning assumptions were used for the budget:

Direct-material yield of 96%.
Direct-labor rate of $6 per hour.

The actual direct production cost (000s omitted) for 1978 was:

	X-4	Z-8	Total
Production output in gallons	570.0	658.0	1,228.0
Direct material	$1,368.0	$2,138.5	$3,506.5
Direct labor	936.0	1,092.0	2,028.0
Total prime manufacturing cost	$2,304.0	$3,230.5	$5,534.5

The actual production yield was 95% for X-4 and 94% for Z-8. The direct-labor cost per hour for both products was $6.50.

Required

1. Calculate the following for product X-4:
   a. The direct-material price variance
   b. The direct-material efficiency variance
2. Calculate the following for product Z-8:
   a. The direct-labor rate variance
   b. The direct-labor efficiency variance

Exercise 15.9   Entries for Direct Materials and Direct Labor

The Krazy Kradle Company produces unique baby cradles. During June, 11,200 standard cradles were produced. Five units of materials at a cost of $1.80 per unit are required for each cradle produced. During June, 57,500 units of materials were used in production. During June, 60,000 units of materials were purchased at a cost of $1.78 each.

The payroll for direct labor during June was $138,000. The average wage rate was $6 per hour. In order to produce one cradle 2 hours of labor are required at a standard rate of $5.80 per hour.

Assume there were no beginning inventories of direct materials or work in process and that all production of cradles during June was completely finished.

Required

1. Determine the number of units and the cost assigned to the ending direct-materials inventory assuming that
   a. materials inventory is kept at actual cost.
   b. materials inventory is kept at standard cost.
2. Prepare journal entries for the purchase and use of direct materials assuming that
   a. the materials account is kept at actual cost.
   b. the materials account is kept at standard cost.
3. Prepare all journal entries for recording and distributing the payroll. Ignore payroll taxes.

Exercise 15.10   Standard Cost Variance Disposition

Nanron Company has a process standard cost system for all its products. All inventories are carried at standard cost during the year. The inventories and cost of goods sold are adjusted for all variances considered significant at the end of the fiscal year for financial statement purposes. All products are considered to flow through the manufacturing process to finished goods and ultimate sale in a FIFO pattern.

The standard cost of one of Nanron's products manufactured in the Dixon Plant, unchanged from the prior year, is shown below:

Raw materials	$2.00
Direct labor (.5 direct-labor hour @ $8.00)	4.00
Manufacturing overhead	3.00
Total standard cost	$9.00

There is no work-in-process inventory of this product due to the nature of the product and the manufacturing process.

The schedule below reports the manufacturing and sales activity measured at standard cost for the current fiscal year:

	Units	Dollars
Product manufactured	95,000	$855,000
Beginning finished-goods inventory	15,000	135,000
Goods available for sale	110,000	$990,000
Ending finished-goods inventory	19,000	171,000
Cost of goods sold	91,000	$819,000

The manufacturing performance relative to standard costs both this year and last year were not good. The balance of the finished-goods inventory—$140,800—reported on the balance sheet at the beginning of the year included a $5,800 adjustment for variances from standard cost. The unfavorable standard cost variances for labor for the current fiscal year consisted of a wage rate variance of $32,000 and a labor efficiency variance of $20,000 (2,500 hours @ $8.00). There were no other variances from standard cost for this year.

Required

Assume that the unfavorable labor variances totalling $52,000 are considered significant by management and are to be allocated to the finished-goods inventory and to cost of goods sold. Determine the amount that will be shown on the year-end balance sheet for the finished-goods inventory, and the amount that will be shown for the cost of goods sold on the income statement prepared for the fiscal year.

Problems

Problem 15.1   Standard Costs—Materials and Labor (CMA)

Dash Company adopted a standard cost system several years ago. The standard costs for its single product are as follows:

| Material | 8 kilograms @ $5.00 per kilogram | $40.00 |
| Labor | 6 hours @ $8.20 per hour | $49.20 |

The following operating data was taken from the records for November:

1. In process beginning inventory—none
2. In process ending inventory—800 units, 75% complete as to labor; material issued at the beginning of processing
3. Units completed—5,600 units
4. Budgeted output—6,000 units
5. Purchases of materials—50,000 kilograms
6. Total actual labor costs—$300,760
7. Actual hours of labor—36,500 hours
8. Material usage variance—$1,500 unfavorable
9. Total material variance—$750 unfavorable

Required

1. Determine the labor rate variance for November.
2. Determine the labor efficiency variance for November.
3. Determine the actual kilograms of material used in the production process during November.
4. Determine the actual price paid per kilogram of material during November.

Problem 15.2 Standard Costs, Inventory Amounts, and Journal Entries

Refer to the data in problem 15.1.

Required

1. Determine the total amount of material and labor cost transferred to the finished-goods account for November.
2. Determine the total amount of material and labor cost in the work-in-process inventory at the end of November.
3. Show journal entries to record the purchase of materials and payroll and the charging of materials and labor costs to production.

Problem 15.3 Standard Costs, Materials and Labor, and Variances

Fashions Unlimited manufactures ladies blouses of one quality, produced in lots to fill each special order from its customers, comprised of department stores located in various cities. Fashions sews the particular store's labels on the blouses. The standard costs for a dozen blouses are:

Direct materials	24 yards @ $1.10	$26.40
Direct labor	3 hours @ $4.90	14.70
Manufacturing overhead	3 hours @ $4.00	12.00
Standard cost per dozen		$53.10

During June, Fashions worked on three orders, for which the month's job cost records disclose the following:

Lot No.	Units in Lot (Dozens)	Material Used (Yards)	Hours Worked
22	1,000	24,100	2,980
23	1,700	40,440	5,130
24	1,200	28,825	2,890

The following information is also available:

1. Fashions purchased 95,000 yards of material during June at a cost of $106,400. The materials price variance is recorded when goods are purchased. All inventories are carried at standard cost.
2. Direct labor during June amounted to $55,000. According to payroll records, production employees were paid $5.00 per hour.
3. Manufacturing overhead during June amounted to $45,600.
4. A total of $576,000 was budgeted for manufacturing overhead for the year based on estimated production at the plant's normal capacity of 48,000 dozen blouses annually. Manufacturing overhead at this level of production is 40% fixed and 60% variable. Manufacturing overhead is applied on the basis of direct-labor hours.
5. There was no work in process on June 1. During June, lots 22 and 23 were completed. All material was issued for lot 24, which was 80% completed as to direct labor.

Required

1. Prepare a schedule of lots 22, 23, and 24 for June showing the computation of total material, labor, and overhead at standard cost.
2. Prepare a schedule showing the computation of the materials price variance for June. Indicate whether the variance is favorable or unfavorable.
3. Prepare a schedule showing, for each lot produced during June, the computations of the
   a. materials quantity variance in yards.
   b. labor efficiency variance in hours.
   c. labor rate variance in dollars.
   Indicate whether each variance is favorable or unfavorable.

Problem 15.4 Standard Costs and Control Reports (CMA)

The Ashley Company manufactures and sells a household product marketed through direct mail and advertisements in home improvement and gardening magazines. Although similar products are available in hardware and department stores, none is as effective as Ashley's model.

Ashley uses a standard cost system in its manufacturing accounting. The standards have not undergone a thorough review in the past 18 months. The general manager has seen no need for such a review due to the following reasons.

1. The material quality and unit costs were fixed by a three-year purchase commitment signed in July 19X9.
2. A three-year labor contract had been signed in July 19X9.
3. There have been no significant variations from standard costs for the past three quarters.

The standard cost for the product, as established in July 19X9, is presented below:

Material	.75 lb. @ $1.00 per lb.	$0.75
Direct labor	.3 hrs. @ $4.00 per hour	1.20
Overhead	.3 hrs. @ $7.00 per hour	2.10
Standard manufacturing cost per unit		$4.05

The standard for overhead costs was developed from the following budgeted costs based upon an activity level of 1.0 million units (300,000 direct-labor hours).

Variable manufacturing overhead	$ 600,000
Fixed manufacturing overhead	1,500,000
Total manufacturing overhead	$2,100,000

The earnings statement and the factory costs for the first quarter are shown on the next page. The first quarter results indicate that Ashley probably will achieve its sales goal of 1.2 million units for the current year. A total of 320,000 units were manufactured during the first quarter in order to increase inventory levels needed to support the growing sales volume.

ACTION Hardware, a national chain, recently asked Ashley to manufacture and sell a slightly modified version of the product, which ACTION would distribute through its stores. ACTION has offered to buy a minimum quantity of 200,000 units each year over the next three years and has offered to pay $4.10 for each unit, f.o.b. shipping point.

Ashley Company
First Quarter Earnings
Period Ending March 31, 1981

Sales (300,000 units)		$2,700,000
Cost of goods sold		
Standard cost of goods	$1,215,000	
Variation from standard costs	12,000	1,227,000
Gross profit		$1,473,000
Operating expenses		
Selling		
Advertising	$ 200,000	
Mailing list costs	175,000	
Postage	225,000	
Salaries	60,000	
Administrative		
Salaries	120,000	
Office rent	45,000	
Total operating expenses		825,000
Income before taxes		$ 648,000
Income taxes (45%)		291,600
Net income		$ 356,400

Ashley Company
Factory Costs
For the Quarter Ending March 31, 1981

Materials	$ 266,000
Direct labor	452,000
Variable manufacturing overhead	211,000
Fixed manufacturing overhead	379,000
Total manufacturing costs	$1,308,000
Less: Standard cost of goods manufactured	1,296,000
Unfavorable variation from standard cost	$ 12,000

Ashley's management is interested in the proposal because it represents a new market. Ashley has the capacity to meet the production requirements. However, in addition to the possible financial results of taking the order, Ashley must consider carefully the other consequences of this departure from its normal practices. The president asked the assistant general manager to estimate the financial aspects of the proposal for the first twelve months.

The assistant recommended that the order not be accepted and presented the following analysis to support the recommendation.

Sales Proposal of ACTION Hardware
First Twelve Months Results

Proposed sales (200,000 @ $4.10)	$820,000
Estimated costs and expenses	
Manufacturing (200,000 @ $4.05)	$810,000
Sales salaries	10,000
Administrative salaries	20,000
Total estimated costs	$840,000
Net loss	$(20,000)

Note: None of our regular selling costs are included because this is a new market. However, a 16.6% increase in sales and administrative salaries has been incorporated because sales volume will increase by that amount.

Required

1. Review the financial analysis of the ACTION hardware proposal prepared by the assistant general manager.
   a. Criticize the first year's financial analysis.
   b. Using only the data given, present a more suitable analysis for the first year of the order.
2. Identify the additional financial data Ashley Company would need to prepare for a more comprehensive financial analysis of the ACTION proposal for the three-year period.
3. Discuss the nonfinancial issues Ashley's management should address in considering the ACTION proposal.

Problem 15.5   Standard Costs and Performance Reports (CMA)

The Kalman Company, a subsidiary of the Camper Corporation, submits interim financial statements. Camper combines these statements with similar statements from other subsidiaries to prepare its quarterly statements. The following data are taken from the records and accounts of the Kalman Company.

1. Sales forecasts for the year are:

Quarter	Stove Units	Percent
First	450,000	30%
Second	600,000	40
Third	150,000	10
Fourth	300,000	20
	1,500,000	100%

   Sales have been achieved as forecasted in the first and second quarters of the current year.

2. Management is considering increasing the selling price of a stove from $30 to $34. However, management is concerned that this increase may reduce the already low sales volume forecasts for the third and fourth quarters.

3. The production schedule calls for 1,500,000 stoves this year. The manufacturing facilities can produce 1,720,000 units per year or 430,000 units per quarter during regular hours. The quarterly production schedule shown below was developed to meet the seasonal sales demand and is being followed as planned.

Quarter	Scheduled Production (in Units)	Percent
1	465,000	31%
2	450,000	30
3	225,000	15
4	360,000	24
	1,500,000	100%

4. The standard manufacturing cost of a stove unit, as established at the beginning of the current year, is shown below. This standard cost does not incorporate any charges for overtime.

Material	$ 4.00
Labor	9.00
Variable overhead	2.00
Fixed overhead	3.00
Standard cost per stove	$18.00

5. A significant and permanent price increase in the cost of raw material resulted in a material price variance of $270,000 for the materials used in the second quarter.

6. There was a $120,000 unfavorable direct-labor variance in the second quarter due in part to overtime pay to meet the heavy production schedule. An overtime premium equal to .5 times the standard labor rate is paid whenever production requires working beyond regular hours. The remaining amount of the labor variance during the quarter occurred as a result of unexpected inefficiencies.

7. The second quarter unfavorable overhead variance of $36,000 was entirely related to the excess direct-labor costs.

8. Total fixed overhead expected to be incurred and budgeted for the year is $4,500,000. Through the first two quarters, $2,745,000 of fixed overhead has been absorbed into the production process. Of this amount, $1,350,000 was absorbed in the second quarter. The high production activity resulted in a total fixed overhead volume variance of $495,000 for the first two quarters.

9. Selling expenses are 10% of sales and are expected to total $4,500,000 for the year.

10. Administrative expenses are $6,000,000 annually and are incurred uniformly throughout the period.

11. Inventory balances as of the end of the second quarter are as follows:

Raw material—at actual cost	$400,000
Work in process 50% complete—at standard cost	72,000
Finished goods—at standard cost	900,000

12. The stove product line is expected to earn $7,500,000 before taxes this year. The estimated state and federal income tax expenses for the year are $4,500,000.

13. Any unplanned variances that are significant and permanent in nature are prorated to the applicable accounts during the quarter in which they are incurred.

Required

Prepare the second quarter interim income statement for the Kalman subsidiary of Camper Corporation.

Problem 15.6   Standard Costs and Motivation (CMA)

The Kristy Company has grown from a small operation of 50 people to 200 employees during a ten-year period. Kristy designs, manufactures, and sells environmental support equipment. In the early years each item of equipment had to be designed and manufactured to meet each customer's requirements. The work was challenging and interesting for the employees since innovative techniques were often needed in the production process to complete an order according to a customer's requirements. In recent years Kristy has been able to develop several components and a few complete units that can be used to meet the requirements of several customers.

The early special design and manufacture work has given the Kristy Company a leadership position in its segment of the pollution control market. Kristy takes great pride in the superior quality of its products and this quality has contributed to its dominant role in this market segment. To help ensure high-quality performance, Kristy hires the most highly skilled personnel available and pays them above the industry average. This policy has resulted in a labor force that is very efficient, stable, and positively motivated toward company objectives.

The recent increase in government regulations requiring private companies to comply with specific environmental standards has made this market very profitable. Consequently, several competitors have entered the market segment once controlled by Kristy. Although Kristy still maintains a dominant position in its market, it has lost several contracts to competitors who offer similar equipment to customers at a lower price.

The Kristy manufacturing process is very labor intensive. The production employees played an important role in the early success of the company. As a result, management gave employees a great deal of freedom to schedule and manufacture customers' orders. For example, when the company increased the number of orders accepted, more employees were hired rather than pressuring current employees to produce at a faster rate. In management's view, the intricacy of work involved required ample time to ensure the work was done right.

Management introduced a standard cost system they believed would be beneficial to the company. They thought it would identify the most economical way to manufacture much of the equipment, would give management a more accurate picture of the costs of the equipment, and would be used in evaluating actual costs for cost control. Consequently, the company should become more price competitive. Although the introduction of standards would probably lead to some employee discontent, management thought that the overall result would be beneficial. The standards were introduced on June 1 of this year.

During December, the production manager reported to the president that the new standards were creating problems in the plant. The employees had developed bad attitudes, absenteeism and turnover rates had increased, and standards were not being met. In the production manager's judgment, employee dissatisfaction has outweighed any benefits management thought would be achieved by the standard cost system. The production manager supported this contention with the data presented below during which monthly production was at normal volume levels.

Required

1. Explain the general features and characteristics associated with the introduction and operation of a standard cost system that make it an effective cost control tool.
2. Discuss the apparent impact of Kristy Company's cost system on the following:
   a. Cost control
   b. Employee motivation
3. Discuss the probable causes for employee dissatisfaction with the new cost system.

Exhibit A
Kristy Company
Labor and Materials Operating Data

	J	F	M	A	M	J	J	A	S	O	N
Absenteeism rates:	1%	1%	1%	1%	.5%	1%	2%	4%	6%	8%	11%
Turnover rate:	.2%	.5%	.5%	.5%	.3%	.8%	.7%	1.4%	1.9%	2.5%	2.9%
Direct labor Efficiency Variance: (Unfavorable)	—	—	—	—	—	$(10,000)	$(11,500)	$(14,000)	$(17,000)	$(20,500)	$(25,000)
Direct materials Usage variance: (Unfavorable)	—	—	—	—	—	$(4,000)	$(5,000)	$(6,500)	$(8,200)	$(11,000)	$(14,000)

Problem 15.7   Materials and Labor Standards

The Lenco Company employs a standard cost system as part of its cost control program. The standard cost per unit is established at the beginning of each year. Standards are not revised during the year for any changes in material or labor inputs or in the manufacturing processes. Any revisions in standards are deferred until the beginning of the next fiscal year. However, in order to recognize such changes in the current year, Lenco includes planned variances in the monthly budgets prepared after such changes have been introduced.

The following labor standard was set for one of Lenco's products effective July 1, the beginning of the fiscal year.

Class I labor	4 hrs.	@ $ 6.00	$24.00
Class II labor	3 hrs.	@ 7.50	22.50
Class V labor	1 hr.	@ 11.50	11.50
Standard labor cost per 100 units		$58.00	

The standard was based upon the quality of material that had been used in previous years and what was expected to be available for the current fiscal year. The labor activity is performed by a team consisting of four persons with class I skills, three persons with class II skills, and one person with class V skills. This is the most economical combination for the company's processing system.

The manufacturing operations occurred as expected during the first five months of the year. The standard costs contributed to effective cost control during this period. However, there were indications that changes in the operations would be required in the last half of the year. Lenco had received a significant increase in orders for delivery in the spring. There were an inadequate number of skilled workers available to meet the increased production. As a result, the production teams, beginning in January, would be made up of more class I labor and less class II labor than the standard required. The teams would consist of six class I persons, two class II persons, and one class V person. This labor team would be less efficient than the normal team. The reorganized teams work more slowly so that only 90 units are produced in the same time period that 100 units would normally be produced. No raw materials will be lost as a result of the change in the labor mix. Completed units have never been rejected in the final inspection process as a consequence of faulty work; this is expected to continue.

In addition, Lenco was notified by its material supplier that a lower quality material would be supplied after January 1. One unit of raw material is required normally for each good unit produced. Lenco and its supplier estimated that 5% of the units manufactured would be rejected upon final inspection due to defective material. Normally, no units are lost due to defective material.

Required

1. How much of the lower quality material must be entered into production in order to produce 42,750 units of good production in January with the new labor teams? Show your calculations.
2. How many hours of each class of labor will be needed to produce 42,750 good units from the material input? Show your calculations.
3. What amount should be included in the January budget for the planned labor variance due to the labor team and material changes? What amount of this planned labor variance can be associated with (a) the material change and (b) the team change? Show your calculations.

Problem 15.8   Labor Variances and Job-Order Costing (CMA)

Mary's Pie Company produces pies in quantity for various fast-food restaurants. The labor standard for each pie calls for 1/4 hour at $4 per hour.

During May, the following job orders (among others) were put into production:

Job Order #	# of Pies
206	500
207	350
208	300 (2/3 complete on May 31)

The actual payroll for May by job was as follows:

Job Order #	Actual Hours	Actual Cost
206	128	$524.80
207	85	344.25
208	27	106.50

Required

1. Determine the labor rate and efficiency variances for each job order and in total for the month.
2. Make journal entries for the total payroll to show the setup and distribution of labor costs.

Problem 15.9   Standard Costs and Labor Variances

Landeau Manufacturing Company has a process cost accounting system. An analysis that compares the actual results with both a monthly plan and a flexible budget is prepared monthly. The standard direct-labor rates used in the flexible budget are established each year when the annual plan is formulated and is held constant for the entire year.

The standard direct labor rates in effect for the fiscal year ending June 30 and the standard hours allowed for the output for the month of April are shown in the schedule below:

	Standard Direct-Labor Rate Per Hour	Standard Direct-Labor Hours Allowed for Output
Labor class III	$8.00	500
Labor class II	$7.00	500
Labor class I	$5.00	500

The wage rates for each labor class increased on January 1, under the terms of a new union contract negotiated in December. The standard wage rates were not revised to reflect the new contract.

The actual direct-labor hours worked and the actual direct-labor rates per hour experienced for the month of April were as follows:

	Actual Direct-Labor Rate Per Hour	Actual Direct-Labor Hours
Labor class III	$8.50	550
Labor class II	$7.50	650
Labor class I	$5.40	375

Required

1. Calculate the dollar amount of the total direct-labor variance for the month of April for the Landeau Manufacturing Company. Analyze the total variance into the following components:
   a. Direct-labor rate variance
   b. Direct-labor efficiency variance
2. Discuss the advantages and disadvantages of a standard cost system in which the standard direct-labor rates per hour are not changed during the year to reflect such events as a new labor contract.

STANDARD COSTS FOR FACTORY OVERHEAD

16

OUTLINE

T his chapter continues the discussion of standard costs begun in chapter 15. Just as for direct materials and direct labor, standard costs for factory overhead help to plan, coordinate, and monitor manufacturing operations. Standard costs for factory overhead provide the third and final cost element in a responsibility accounting system in which flexible budgets are used for planning and control. Standard costs for factory overhead are also used with standard costs for direct materials and direct labor for product costing.

Separate attention is given to standard costs for factory overhead because they possess two unique characteristics. First, unlike direct materials and direct labor overhead costs cannot be traced to individual units of production. Second, unlike direct materials and direct labor, which are strictly variable, total factory overhead includes *both* variable and fixed costs. Therefore, the budgetary and variance analysis procedures when using standard costs for factory overhead differ from those used for direct materials and direct labor.

This chapter reviews selected flexible budget and factory overhead topics and then explains how to account for factory overhead when using standard costs for factory overhead. After completing this chapter you should be able to:

1. develop a flexible budget for factory overhead.
2. calculate standard overhead application rates.
3. calculate standard costs for factory overhead.
4. perform general ledger accounting for factory overhead when using standard overhead application rates.
5. analyze factory overhead variances using several alternative analysis techniques.
6. account for the disposition of factory overhead variances.

STANDARD COSTS FOR FACTORY OVERHEAD

As defined in chapter 13, *factory overhead* consists of all costs incurred in a manufacturing operation other than direct materials and direct labor. The traceability of costs determines whether they are classified as direct materials and direct labor or as factory overhead. Direct materials and direct labor can be traced to specific units of production. However, factory overhead cannot be traced to specific units of production and includes such items as insurance, taxes, supplies, maintenance, repairs, idle time, and factory depreciation. Even though overhead costs cannot be traced to specific units of production, overhead is still a manufacturing cost and needs to be assigned as part of the cost of each unit produced. In a standard cost system, the mechanism for making this assignment is a predetermined or standard overhead application rate.

The term *standard cost,* as defined in chapter 15, has the same meaning when applied to overhead as it does when applied to materials or labor; that is, *standard costs for overhead* are expressed as the per-unit amount of factory costs (other than direct materials and direct labor) that are expected to be incurred under normal operating conditions to produce one unit of output. As actual production takes place, total standard costs are compared with actual costs incurred during the period. Differences or variances between actual costs and standard costs are then analyzed and used as feedback to management for planning and control. Standard costs are also used during the period to assign costs to units of production.

The following lists the accounting process when using standard costs for factory overhead:

1. Develop a factory overhead flexible budget based on standard costs.
2. Calculate standard overhead application rates for fixed and variable overhead costs.

3. Calculate standard costs using standard overhead application rates.
4. Assign costs to units of production.
5. Compare total actual overhead with the flexible budget (standard costs).
6. Analyze any differences or variances between actual costs and standard costs.

This process is designed to provide feedback to management for planning and control that would not be available without the use of standard costs.

THE OVERHEAD BUDGET

As discussed in chapter 15, a flexible budget for direct materials and direct labor typically begins with the development of per-unit standard costs for materials and labor. These per-unit costs are then multiplied by the expected volume of production to determine total budgeted standard costs for the period. However, because overhead costs have unique characteristics the budgetary procedure for overhead is different; that is, *total* factory overhead is estimated first. Then standard overhead application rates are calculated by dividing total budgeted costs by the total expected volume of activity. Activity is measured using some base such as direct-labor hours or machine hours as discussed in chapters 13 and 14. Finally, standard costs are calculated by multiplying the standard overhead application rate by the standard amount of the activity base allowed to produce each unit of output.

The budgetary procedure is reversed for factory overhead because overhead costs are not traceable to specific units of production. For example, it is relatively easy to determine how much metal should be used in the production of a bronze bookend. However, it is not readily apparent how much factory depreciation should be assigned to each bookend. Therefore, the budgetary procedure for overhead costs is to first compile total expected costs and then derive per-unit standard costs.

Another important feature of overhead budgets using standard costs is that they clearly distinguish between fixed factory overhead and variable factory overhead. Variable overhead costs fluctuate with the level of production in the same way as direct materials and direct labor. Fixed overhead costs remain constant for different levels of activity within a relevant range of total expected activity.

The distinction between fixed and variable overhead is maintained in the budgetary process so that standard costs are calculated for *both* variable overhead and fixed overhead. The distinction between fixed and variable overhead is also carried through the remainder of the accounting process so that information is provided about why actual overhead costs may have deviated from budgeted amounts.

A *flexible budget for factory overhead* is illustrated for a hypothetical factory department in figure 16.1. Note that the overhead budget is compiled at several different levels of expected output, which is consistent with the concept of flexible budgeting. Also, note that a clear distinction is made between fixed and variable overhead costs.

The expected level or volume of production for the coming accounting period is referred to as the **standard activity level.** The choice of a standard activity level results from a process best described as "judgmental forecasting," which requires consideration of such factors as expected sales, inventory levels, and plant capacity. The activity level of 10,000 direct-labor hours in figure 16.1 is used as the standard activity level in the rest of the illustrations in this chapter.

Although direct-labor hours is the activity base used in this chapter to illustrate the standard activity level, other measures such as machine hours or units of output could also be used as an activity base.

Figure 16.1   Flexible budget for factory overhead

Department 1

Standard direct-labor hours	10,000	12,000	14,000
Variable factory overhead:			
Indirect labor	$10,000	$12,000	$14,000
Supplies	2,200	2,640	3,080
Repairs	800	960	1,120
Total	$13,000	$15,600	$18,200
Fixed factory overhead:			
Supervision	$ 5,000	$ 5,000	$ 5,000
Insurance	1,300	1,300	1,300
Depreciation	500	500	500
Taxes	200	200	200
Total	$ 7,000	$ 7,000	$ 7,000
Total factory overhead	$20,000	$22,600	$25,200

OVERHEAD APPLICATION AND GENERAL LEDGER ACCOUNTING

The next step in the budgetary process is to calculate standard overhead application rates for (a) variable overhead, (b) fixed overhead, and (c) total overhead costs. This is done by dividing budgeted overhead by the standard activity level as indicated by the following general formula:

$$\frac{\text{Factory overhead}}{\text{(Variable, fixed, or total)}} \div \text{Standard activity level} = \text{Standard overhead application rate}$$

Figure 16.2 contains overhead application rates based on the flexible budget shown in figure 16.1. Remember that the standard activity level is 10,000 direct-labor hours.

The final step in the budgetary process is to calculate the standard cost of overhead using the standard overhead application rates. In general, this is accomplished by multiplying the standard overhead application rates for variable and fixed overhead by the standard amount of the activity base allowed for each unit of production. For example, the standard variable overhead application rate of $1.30 per direct-labor hour is multiplied by 2 standard hours allowed for each unit giving a standard cost for variable overhead of $2.60 per unit. The standard fixed overhead application rate of $.70 per direct-labor hour is multiplied by 2 standard hours allowed for each unit giving a standard cost for fixed overhead of $1.40 per unit.

From a total cost perspective, the standard costs for overhead are combined with standard costs for materials and labor to give the total standard cost for a particular product. Figure 16.3 shows a simplified standard cost card for ABC Fasteners that contains all standard cost elements.

Now that standard costs for overhead have been calculated, we can show their use in accounting for overhead.

Variable Overhead

To illustrate the accounting for variable overhead in a standard cost system, consider the following information for ABC Fasteners during the current accounting period. Budget and standard cost data from figures 16.1 and 16.3 are also repeated below for convenient reference:

Figure 16.2   Calculation of standard overhead application rates

Standard variable overhead application rate:
    $13,000 variable overhead ÷ 10,000 hours = $1.30 per direct-labor hour

Standard fixed overhead application rate:
    $7,000 fixed overhead ÷ 10,000 hours   = $ .70 per direct-labor hour

Total standard overhead application rate:
    $20,000 total overhead ÷ 10,000 hours   = $2.00 per direct-labor hour

Figure 16.3   Simplified standard cost card

ABC Fasteners

Direct materials (6 pounds at $4.00 per pound)	$24.00
Direct labor (2 hours at $4.00 per hour)	8.00
Variable overhead (2 hours at $1.30 per hour)	2.60
Fixed overhead (2 hours at $.70 per hour)	1.40
Total	$36.00

Data Concerning Actual Costs and Production Volume

Actual variable overhead incurred	$15,000
Actual direct-labor hours used	12,100 hours
Fasteners produced this period	6,000 units

Budget and Standard Cost Data

Budgeted variable overhead	$13,000
Standard variable overhead application rate	$ 1.30 per hour
Standard cost for variable overhead	$ 2.60 per unit

Before proceeding with the actual journal entries, there are several items to note. First, for simplicity a single variable factory overhead control account is used to illustrate the accounting process for variable overhead and a single control account is used to illustrate accounting for fixed overhead. Second, the journal entries used to illustrate the accounting process represent an aggregation of many individual journal entries and many individual postings to subsidiary ledgers that are typically made during an entire accounting period.

The following journal entries record (*a*) actual expenditures made during the period for variable overhead items and (*b*) variable overhead applied to work in process during the period using the standard cost for fixed overhead.

The amount of actual expenditures for variable factory overhead is given at $15,000. The following journal entry is made to record this actual variable overhead incurred.

Variable factory overhead control	15,000	
Cash, accounts payable, etc.		15,000

The total standard variable overhead applied to work in process is calculated by multiplying the units of good output by the standard cost per unit for variable overhead as shown below:

Formula for Application of Standard Variable Factory Overhead

Units of good output	×	Standard cost for variable overhead	=	Standard *variable* overhead to apply to work in process
6,000 units	×	$2.60	=	$15,600

The following journal entry is made to record the application of variable factory overhead to work in process.

Work in process	15,600	
Variable factory overhead control		15,600

An alternative method of computation is to multiply the units of good output (6,000 units) by the number of standard direct-labor hours allowed per unit (2 hours), which gives the number of *standard hours allowed* for the good output (12,000 hours). Then the total standard hours allowed (12,000 hours) is multiplied by the standard variable overhead application rate ($1.30 per hour) to give the total standard variable overhead to apply to work in process.

Any balance in the variable factory overhead control account at the end of an accounting period represents over- or underapplied overhead. In the illustration above there is $600 of overapplied factory overhead. The analysis and disposition of over- or underapplied overhead will be discussed after examining the accounting entries for fixed factory overhead.

Fixed Overhead

To illustrate the accounting for fixed overhead in a standard cost system, consider the following information for ABC Fasteners during the current accounting period. Budget and standard cost data from figures 16.1 and 16.3 are repeated below for convenient reference:

Data Concerning Actual Costs and Production Volume

Actual fixed overhead incurred	$7,900
Actual direct-labor hours used	12,100 hours
Fasteners produced this period	6,000 units

Budget and Standard Cost Data

Budgeted fixed overhead	$7,000
Standard fixed overhead application rate	$ .70 per hour
Standard cost for fixed overhead	$ 1.40 per unit

The following journal entries record (*a*) actual expenditures made during the period for fixed overhead items and (*b*) fixed overhead applied to work in process during the period using the standard cost for fixed overhead.

Actual expenditures for fixed factory overhead items are given at $7,900. The journal entry to record these expenditures is as follows:

Fixed factory overhead control	7,900	
Cash, accounts payable, etc.		7,900

The amount of standard fixed overhead to apply to work in process is calculated by multiplying the units of good output by the standard cost per unit for fixed overhead as follows:

Formula for Application of Standard Fixed Factory Overhead

Units of good output	×	Standard cost for fixed overhead	=	Standard fixed overhead to apply to work in process
6,000 units	×	$1.40	=	$8,400

The following journal entry illustrates the application of fixed factory overhead to work in process at standard cost.

Work in process	8,400	
Fixed factory overhead control		8,400

An alternative method of computation could be to multiply the units of good output (6,000 units) by the number of standard direct-labor hours allowed per unit (2 hours), which gives the number of *standard hours allowed* for the good output (12,000 hours). Then the total standard hours allowed (12,000 hours) is multiplied by the standard fixed overhead application rate ($.70 per hour) to give the total standard fixed overhead to apply to work in process.

Any balance in the fixed factory overhead control account at the end of an accounting period represents under- or overapplied overhead. In the illustration above there is $500 of overapplied overhead. The analysis and disposition of under- or overapplied overhead will be discussed later in this chapter.

The general ledger accounting for overhead illustrated above used separate control accounts for fixed and variable overhead. However, there are any number of different bookkeeping procedures and account configurations that could be used. For example, one control account could be used for both fixed and variable overhead. Or the number of accounts could be increased by having an "actual" overhead account and an "applied" overhead account for both fixed and variable overhead. The number and type of accounts used in an accounting system for overhead depend on the detail, timing, and type of overhead reporting desired by management.

SPECIAL CONSIDERATIONS IN FIXED OVERHEAD ACCOUNTING

By definition, budgeted fixed factory overhead remains constant for all levels of output over the relevant range of productive activity. However, as illustrated, the accepted practice is to treat fixed overhead as though it is a variable cost. This is done by assigning fixed overhead to units of production using a fixed overhead application rate.

Using a per-unit rate to apply fixed overhead in the same way that variable factory overhead is applied creates a situation that deserves special consideration because the results of operations could be misinterpreted. The reason for concern is immediately apparent when comparing the behavior of budgeted fixed and variable overhead costs with the behavior of applied overhead costs. Figure 16.4 contains graphs of budgeted and applied variable and fixed overhead costs. These graphs are derived from the data presented in previous illustrations.

Note in figure 16.4 that the graph for budgeted variable overhead is identical to the graph of applied variable overhead; that is, applied variable overhead is equal to budgeted variable overhead at each level of output. All truly variable costs will exhibit these same cost behavior patterns. For example, graphs for direct materials and direct labor would show this same general relationship between budgeted and applied costs.

However, it is a different situation with fixed costs. The graph for budgeted fixed costs is horizontal indicating that fixed overhead is expected to be the same for each level of output within the relevant range. However, if fixed overhead is assigned to work in process on a per-unit basis, then the graph of applied fixed overhead resembles the be-

Figure 16.4   Comparison of variable and fixed overhead

Variable Overhead:

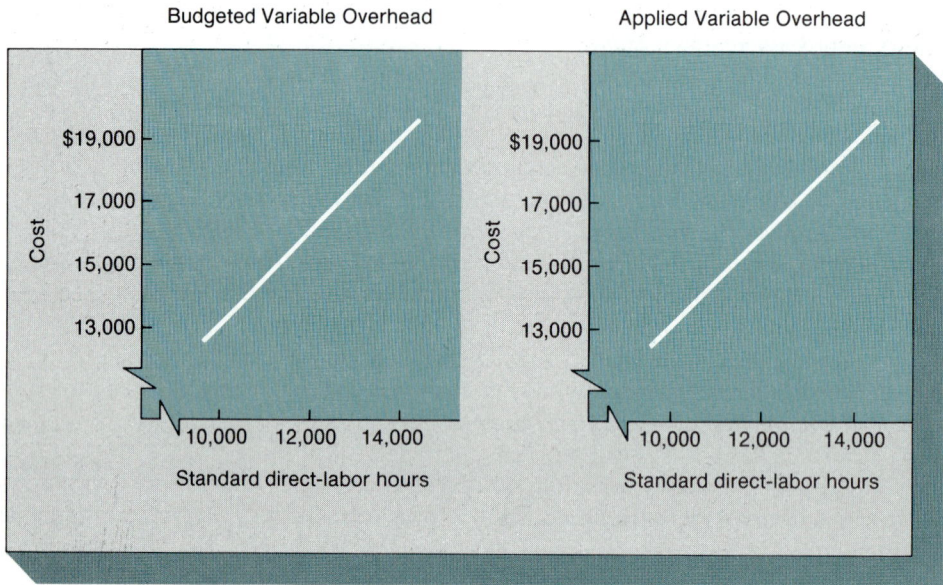

Budgeted Variable Overhead

Applied Variable Overhead

Fixed Overhead:

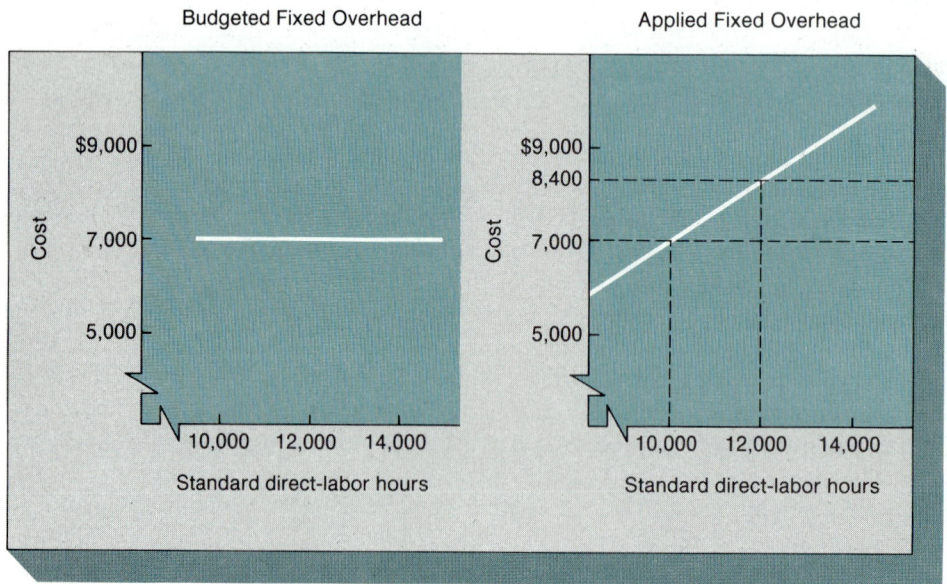

Budgeted Fixed Overhead

Applied Fixed Overhead

havior of a variable cost. As a result, budgeted fixed overhead is equal to applied fixed overhead only at one level of output—the *standard activity level.*

To illustrate, when the actual volume of activity for the period turns out to be 10,000 direct-labor hours, then $7,000 (10,000 hours × $.70 per hour = $7,000) of fixed overhead will be applied to work in process, which, as expected, is the amount of budgeted fixed costs. However, if the actual volume of activity turns out to be 12,000 rather than 10,000 direct-labor hours, then $8,400 (12,000 hours × $.70 per hour = $8,400) of fixed overhead will be applied to work in process—a difference of $1,400 ($8,400 − $7,000) between budgeted fixed overhead and applied fixed overhead. This means that fixed overhead will be either under- or overapplied to work in process simply because the level of actual activity is not equal to the standard level of activity. In this case, fixed overhead is overapplied by $1,400.

To emphasize this concept, figure 16.4 shows that applied fixed overhead is equal to budgeted fixed overhead *only* at the standard activity level. Also, compare the variable overhead graphs with the fixed overhead graphs to see that this phenomenon is unique to fixed overhead.

The difference between budgeted fixed factory overhead and applied fixed factory overhead is called the production volume variance or simply the **volume variance.** Mathematically the volume variance is found in the following way:

$$\left[\begin{array}{c}\text{Predetermined standard} \\ \text{activity level}\end{array} - \begin{array}{c}\text{Standard hours allowed} \\ \text{for good output}\end{array}\right] \times \begin{array}{c}\text{Standard fixed costs} \\ \text{per unit}\end{array} = \text{Volume variance}$$

$$[10{,}000 \text{ hours} \quad - \quad 12{,}000 \text{ hours}] \quad \times \quad \$.70 \text{ per hour} \quad = \quad \$1{,}400$$

The volume variance is designated favorable (F) if actual activity exceeds the budgeted or standard activity level. The volume variance is designated unfavorable (U) if the opposite occurs. The terms favorable and unfavorable when applied to the volume variance are not intended to render a qualitative judgment. Rather, a favorable variance simply indicates that more plant capacity was utilized than originally budgeted and an unfavorable variance indicates that less plant capacity was utilized than originally budgeted. Whether either variance is judged good or bad depends on top management's assessment relative to overall company goals. The volume variance is the responsibility of top management since it is a measure of overall utilization of plant capacity.

In reality, the probability is very low that the actual activity level will be equal to the budgeted or standard activity level. Therefore, it is almost certain that firms using a standard cost system will experience a volume variance. Given this situation, several questions arise: Is a volume variance good or bad? Can the volume variance be controlled? If it can be controlled, by whom? Finally, what are the reasons why actual overhead is different from applied overhead?

ANALYSIS OF OVERHEAD VARIANCES

Overhead accounting in a standard cost system has two general purposes—to provide data for product costing and to provide information for planning and control decisions. Overhead application emphasizes product costing. This section emphasizes the planning and control aspects of overhead accounting by which standard costs provide a budgetary benchmark against which actual performance can be compared. Actual costs incurred are compared with standard or expected costs and differences are analyzed to provide guidance for management.

The analysis of overhead variances begins with the *total overhead variance,* which is the difference between total actual overhead incurred and total overhead applied to work in process. In the ABC Fastener example, there is $600 of overapplied variable overhead and $500 of overapplied fixed overhead for a total overhead variance of

Figure 16.5   General framework for overhead variance analysis

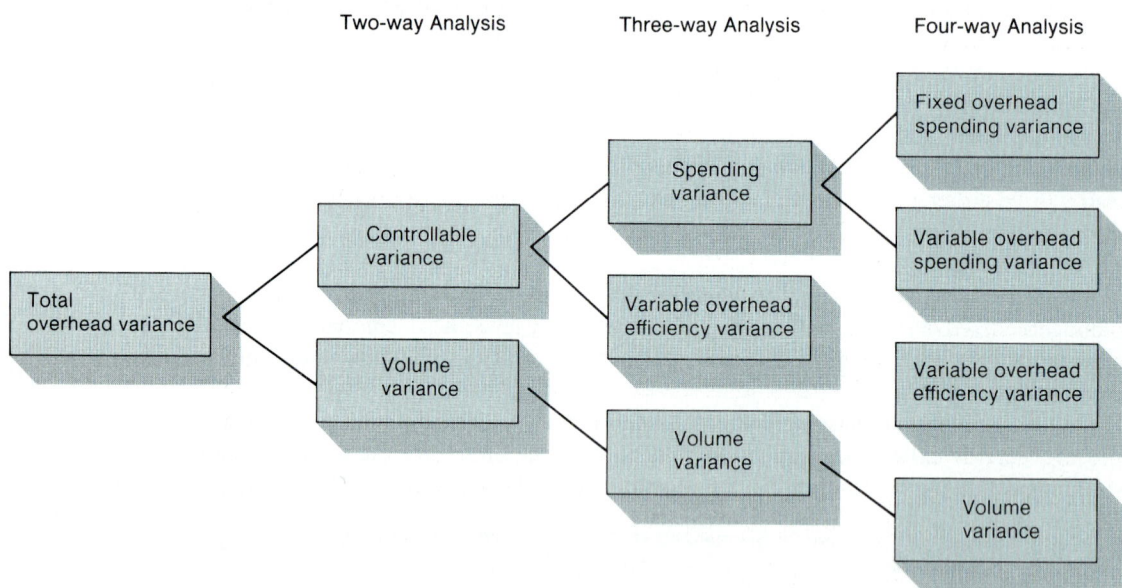

$1,100 F. Overapplied overhead is designated a favorable variance and underapplied overhead is designated an unfavorable variance.

Simply reporting an overhead variance of $1,100 F provides very little information to management. Management needs some indication why this deviation from the budget occurred, whether this deviation is good or bad, and who, if anyone, can control its causes. There are several common methods for analyzing the total overhead variance and breaking it down into its causal components.

Framework for Overhead Variance Analysis

Depending on the level of detail desired by management, there are three general ways to analyze the total overhead variance. Minor differences in terminology and computational techniques exist among different firms and authors. However, the following framework incorporates the most widely used methods and uses what seems to be the most widely accepted terminology.

Analysis of an overhead variance can be done using a two-way analysis, a three-way analysis, or a four-way analysis as shown in figure 16.5.

Each way to analyze the total overhead variance simply represents more detail as one progresses from the two-way to the four-way analysis. The more detailed the analysis, the more apparent the opportunities for fine-tuning the operations.

A quick scan of the variances and their descriptions indicates the cost area involved and the type of information provided by each. The most thorough analysis is obtained with the four-way analysis. However, the two-way or three-way methods may suffice in many factory situations. In any event, the discussion that follows begins with the $1,100 F total overhead variance and progressively analyzes it using each level of detail. Do not jump ahead to the four-way analysis because there are conceptual and computational foundations built along the way that will help you to understand and interpret four-way analysis of variances.

Two-Way Analysis

The two-way analysis of overhead variances separates what is called a controllable variance and the volume variance. Calling one variance controllable may give the impression that the volume variance is uncontrollable. However, both variances are controllable, but at different levels in the organization. Since the volume variance relates to *total* manufacturing activity, the factors affecting it are probably only controlled at higher levels of management.

On the other hand, the **controllable variance** relates to factors such as the price paid for overhead items, such as custodial supplies and insurance, and the efficiency with which overhead items are utilized. These factors are typically controlled at lower levels in an organization—usually at the department level. Therefore, the segregation between the controllable variance and the volume variance simply makes it possible to place responsibility for the controllable variance with lower-level supervisors who control daily operations and to place the responsibility for the volume variance with higher-level management who control overall plant activity.

A two-way analysis can be performed quite simply by calculating the volume variance as previously illustrated and then finding the controllable variance by taking the difference between the volume variance and the total overhead variance. For example, the volume variance calculated in the previous illustrations is $1,400 F. The difference between a $1,400 F volume variance and a $1,100 F total overhead variance is a $300 U controllable variance.

For conceptual reasons and to lay the foundation for the three-way and four-way analysis techniques, let's look at a tabular approach to performing a two-way analysis. Figure 16.6 contains an outline for calculating the controllable and volume variances. Formulas that underly this analysis are also given in figure 16.6.

The calculations for both the controllable and the volume variance utilize the flexible budget for factory overhead. For this reason figure 16.6 contains a formula for computing the flexible budget for factory overhead based on an actual activity level equal to the standard hours allowed for actual good output.

A formula is useful at this time because the flexible budget calculated before operations began probably did not contain calculations at the actual level of activity. For example, figure 16.1 contains the factory overhead flexible budget for the 10,000, 12,000, and 14,000-hour levels of activity. If the actual standard hours allowed for good output turns out to be one of these levels of activity, then the total overhead budget can be read directly from the previously computed budget in figure 16.1. However, most likely the standard hours allowed will not coincide exactly with one of the levels of activity included in the flexible budget. For example, if 5,500 good ABC Fasteners had been produced, the number of standard hours allowed would have been 11,000 hours (5,500 units $\times$ 2 hours per unit = 11,000 hours). The 11,000-hour level of activity is not included in the budget in figure 16.1. Therefore, the formula in figure 16.6 represents a convenient computational tool to derive the total overhead budget at the end of the period when variances are analyzed.

The unfavorable controllable variance indicates that there may be ways to improve the efficiency and effectiveness of some overhead items. To be able to specifically pinpoint areas for corrective action, a more detailed analysis of the controllable variance is needed.

Three-Way Analysis

The three-way analysis of overhead variances provides an additional level of detail for the controllable variance. The volume variance is the same for the two-way analysis and three-way analysis and is not repeated as part of this discussion.

The controllable variance can be further analyzed in terms of a spending variance and a variable overhead efficiency variance. The **variable overhead efficiency variance** helps

Figure 16.6   Controllable and volume variances—two-way analysis

Framework

	Actual Overhead Incurred	Flexible Budget for Factory Overhead	Total Overhead Applied to Work in Process
Variable:	$15,000	$15,600[a]	$15,600
Fixed:	7,900	7,000	8,400
Total:	$22,900	$22,600	$24,000

$300 U
Controllable variance

$1,400 F
Volume variance

$1,100 F
Total overhead variance

Formulas and Calculations

Flexible Budget for Factory Overhead

Total standard hours allowed for good output (6,000 units × 2 hours per unit)	12,000	hours
× Standard variable overhead application rate	× $1.30	per hour
Budgeted variable overhead	$15,600	
+ Budgeted fixed costs	+ 7,000	
Flexible budget for factory overhead	$22,600	

Controllable Variance

Actual overhead incurred	$22,900	
− Flexible budget for factory overhead	22,600	
Controllable variance	$ 300	U

Volume Variance

Flexible budget for factory overhead	$22,600	
− Total overhead applied to work in process	24,000[b]	
Volume variance	$ 1,400	F

[a]See formula computation for budgeted variable overhead.
[b]Variable overhead cost per hour $1.30
Fixed overhead cost per hour .... + .70
Total overhead cost per hour $2.00
Actual hours worked .... × 12,000
Total overhead applied to work in process $24,000

to evaluate the efficiency with which the activity base is utilized. If direct-labor hours is used as the activity base, then the variable overhead efficiency variance will vary in the same direction as the labor efficiency variance. On the other hand, if machine hours is used as the activity base, the variable overhead efficiency variance helps to evaluate the efficiency with which machine hours were utilized. The **spending variance** is an indicator of how well actual overhead expenditures were kept within the budget independent of the efficiency with which the activity base was utilized. A complete explanation of the spending variance is developed with the four-way analysis.

A three-way analysis requires that a flexible budget for factory overhead be calculated based on the total actual hours used. Comparing a flexible budget based on the *total actual hours* used with a flexible budget based on the total *standard hours allowed* for good output helps to isolate the amount of total overhead variance relating to the efficiency with which labor was utilized. If machine hours had been used as the activity base, then the variable overhead efficiency variance would be calculated using flexible budgets based on the total actual machine hours and standard machine hours allowed. Therefore, the variable overhead efficiency variance is generally calculated using flexible budgets based on whatever activity base is in use.

Figure 16.7 contains the framework and related formulas for computing the spending and variable overhead efficiency variances.

Figure 16.7   Spending and variable overhead efficiency variances—three-way analysis

Framework

	Actual Overhead Incurred	Flexible Budget for Factory Overhead (Based on Actual Hours Used)	Flexible Budget for Factory Overhead (Based on Standard Hours Allowed)
Variable:	$15,000	$15,730[a]	$15,600[b]
Fixed:	7,900	7,000	7,000
Total:	$22,900	$22,730	$22,600

$170 U
Spending variance

$130 U
Variable overhead efficiency variance

$300 U
Controllable variance

Formulas and Calculations

Flexible Budget for Factory Overhead (Based on Actual Hours)

Total actual hours used	12,100	hours
× Standard variable overhead application rate	× $1.30	per hour
Budgeted variable overhead	$15,730	
+ Budgeted fixed costs	+ 7,000	
Flexible budget for factory overhead	$22,730	

Spending Variance

Actual overhead incurred	$22,900
− Flexible budget for factory overhead (based on actual hours)	− 22,730
Spending variance	$ 170 U

Variable Overhead Efficiency Variance

Flexible budget for factory overhead (based on actual hours)	$22,730
− Flexible budget for factory overhead (based on standard hours allowed)	− 22,600[c]
Variable overhead efficiency variance	$ 130 U

[a]See formula computation for budgeted variable overhead.
[b]See figure 16.6.
[c]See figure 16.6.

Supervisors and other line personnel have the responsibility for the variable overhead efficiency variance because they are usually the ones responsible for activity bases such as direct labor or machine hours.

Four-Way Analysis

The four-way analysis of overhead variances produces an additional level of detail and understanding for the spending variance. The volume variance and the variable overhead efficiency variance remain the same for the three-way analysis and four-way analysis.

As indicated, the spending variance can be further analyzed in terms of a fixed overhead budget variance and a variable overhead spending variance. The *variable overhead spending variance* gives any difference between actual expenditures for variable overhead and budgeted expenditures due to differences in prices. The variable overhead spending variance is somewhat like the materials price variance or the labor rate variance.

The **fixed overhead spending variance** gives any difference between actual fixed overhead incurred and budgeted fixed overhead.

The framework for calculating these variances is essentially the same as that used to determine the spending variance in the three-way analysis. The only difference between the three-way analysis and the four-way analysis is that calculations are made separately for variable overhead costs and fixed overhead costs; that is, the variable overhead spending variance relates only to variable costs and the fixed overhead spending variance relates only to fixed costs. Figure 16.8 contains the framework and related formulas for computing the variable overhead spending variance and the fixed overhead spending variance. Figure 16.8 also contains the calculation of the variable overhead efficiency variance and the controllable variances so that the framework can be easily related to the three-way analysis.

The unfavorable fixed overhead spending variance indicates that more was expended for fixed cost items than was expected. The fact that there may be cost differences in the fixed cost items appears irregular unless it is remembered that fixed costs may change even though they are expected to remain the same within the relevant range of activity. However, fixed costs do not change in proportion to the volume of output. For example, property tax assessments may change, insurance coverage may be altered, and depreciation charges may be increased leading to a change in costs that otherwise are properly classified as fixed.

To conclude this section on the calculation of overhead variances, figure 16.9 contains a total framework for calculating all of the variances using either two-way, three-way, or four-way analysis methods. Figure 16.9 combines figures 16.6, 16.7, and 16.8.

Finally, figure 16.10 places the analysis of overhead variances into their conceptual relationship by giving the general framework for overhead variances contained in figure 16.5 along with the dollar amounts for all of the variances illustrated in this chapter. Note that the total of the variances using any analysis always equals the total overhead variance.

Reporting Variances

It is important that reports be prepared detailing individual overhead items. Such reports give management the item-by-item information necessary to effectively control future overhead costs. Figure 16.11 contains an overhead report relating the example of this chapter.

The overhead report in figure 16.11 contains both variable and fixed costs. In reality, the fixed cost portion may be omitted depending on whether fixed costs are controllable at the department level. The responsibility for fixed overhead budget variances and the volume variance usually resides at higher levels of management. However, lower-level managers may be able to control fixed overhead expenditures to the extent that they

Figure 16.8   Fixed overhead budget and variable overhead spending variances—four-way analysis

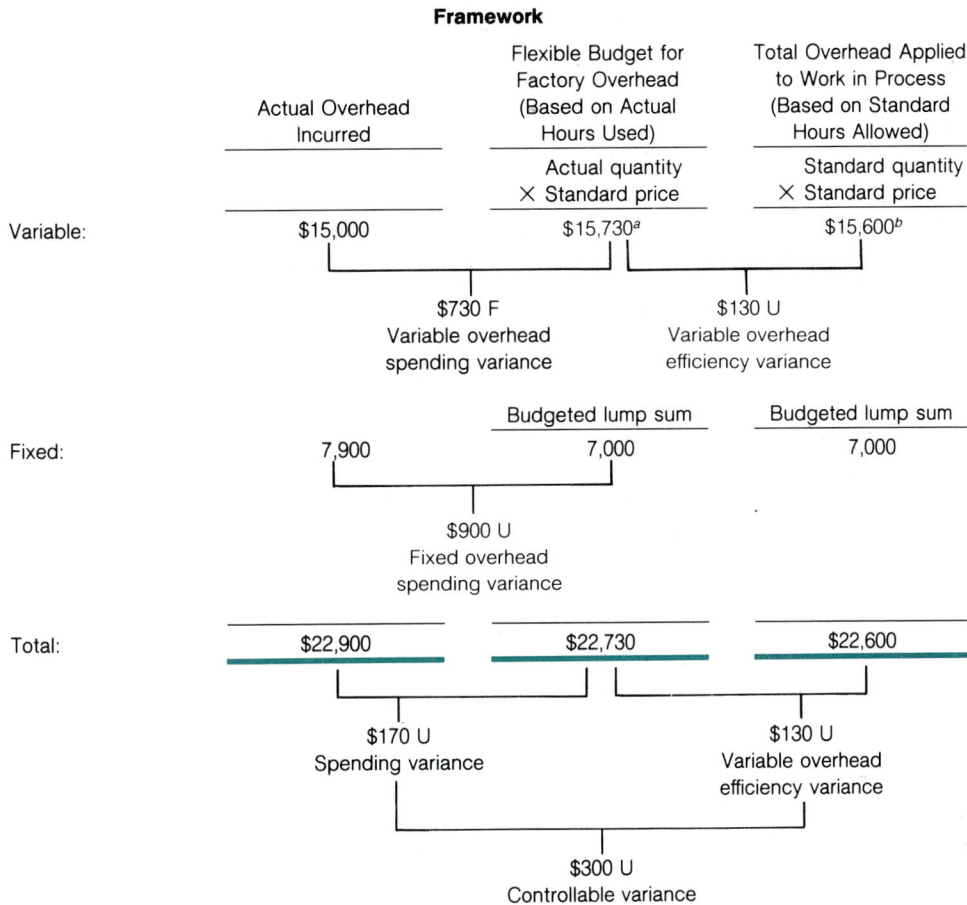

Framework

	Actual Overhead Incurred	Flexible Budget for Factory Overhead (Based on Actual Hours Used)	Total Overhead Applied to Work in Process (Based on Standard Hours Allowed)
		Actual quantity × Standard price	Standard quantity × Standard price
Variable:	$15,000	$15,730[a]	$15,600[b]

$730 F
Variable overhead spending variance

$130 U
Variable overhead efficiency variance

		Budgeted lump sum	Budgeted lump sum
Fixed:	7,900	7,000	7,000

$900 U
Fixed overhead spending variance

Total:	$22,900	$22,730	$22,600

$170 U
Spending variance

$130 U
Variable overhead efficiency variance

$300 U
Controllable variance

Formulas and Calculations

Flexible Budget for Variable Factory Overhead (Based on Actual Hours)

Total actual hours used	12,100	hours
× Standard variable overhead application rate	× $1.30	per hour
Budgeted variable overhead	$15,730	

Variable Overhead Spending Variance

Actual variable overhead incurred	$15,000	
− Flexible budget for variable factory overhead (Based on actual hours)	− 15,730	
Variable overhead spending variance	$ 730	F

Fixed Overhead Spending Variance

Actual fixed overhead incurred	$ 7,900	
−Budgeted fixed overhead	− 7,000	
Fixed overhead spending variance	$ 900	U

[a]See formula computation for budgeted variable overhead.
[b]See figure 16.6.

Figure 16.9   Analysis of total overhead variance

	Actual Overhead Incurred	Flexible Budget for Factory Overhead (Based on Actual Hours Used)	Total Overhead Applied to Work in Process (Based on Standard Hours Allowed)	Total Overhead Applied to Work in Process
		Actual quantity × Standard price	Standard quantity × Standard price	Standard quantity × Standard price
Variable:	$15,000	$15,730	$15,600	$15,600

$730 F
Variable overhead spending variance

$130 U
Variable overhead efficiency variance

		Budgeted lump sum	Budgeted lump sum	Standard quantity × Fixed overhead application rate
Fixed:	7,900	7,000	7,000	8,400

$900 U
Fixed overhead spending variance

$1,400 F
Volume variance

| Total: | $22,900 | $22,730 | $22,600 | $24,000 |

3-way analysis

$170 U
Spending variance

$130 U
Variable overhead efficiency variance

$1,400 F
Volume variance

2-way analysis

$300 U
Controllable variance

$1,400 F
Volume variance

$1,100 F
Total overhead variance

4-way analysis (brackets Variable and Fixed rows)

---

are discretionary fixed costs. Therefore, lower-level managers should be held responsible for all costs that are controllable at the department level.

DISPOSITION OF STANDARD COST VARIANCES

There are two general ways to handle standard cost variances at the end of an accounting period. Depending on the situation and the conceptual viewpoint of management, either of these two methods could be used. First, standard cost variances may be *treated as a period expense* with the variance accounts being closed directly to cost of goods sold or to income summary. Second, standard cost variances could be *treated as inventoriable costs* with the variance accounts being allocated among inventories and cost of goods sold. The accounting procedures using each of these methods are illustrated on the following pages. Figure 16.12 contains a schedule of standard cost variances used in these illustrations. Remember that favorable variances are represented in general ledger accounts by credit balances and unfavorable variances by debit balances.

Figure 16.10   General framework for overhead variance analysis

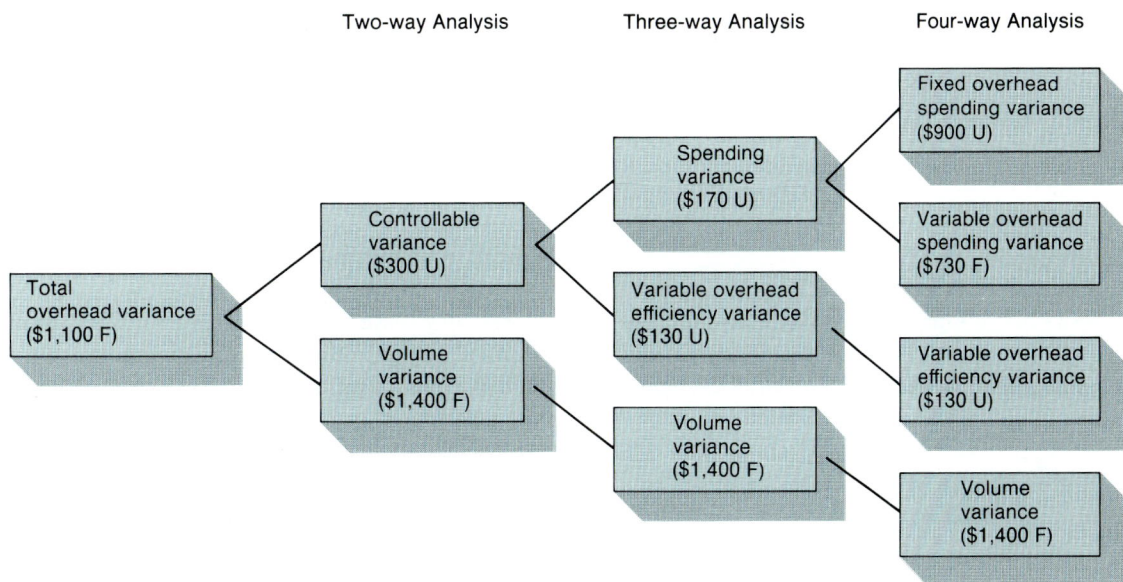

Figure 16.11   Overhead report

Department 1

Variable Overhead Spending Variance

Item	Actual Expenditure	Flexible Budget for Variable Overhead (Based on Actual Hours Used)	Variance
Indirect labor	$11,500	$12,050	$550 F
Supplies	2,460	2,680	220 F
Repairs	1,040	1,000	40 U
Total	$15,000	$15,730	$730 F

Fixed Overhead Spending Variance

Item	Actual Expenditure	Budgeted Amount	
Supervision	$ 5,700	$ 5,000	700 U
Insurance	1,500	1,300	200 U
Depreciation	500	500	–0–
Taxes	200	200	–0–
Total	$ 7,900	$ 7,000	$900 U
Variable overhead efficiency variance			$ 130 U
Volume variance			1,400 F
Total overhead variance			$1,100 F

Figure 16.12   Schedule of variances

Materials price variance	$ 500 U
Materials usage variance	700 F
Labor rate variance	1,000 U
Labor efficiency variance	400 F
Total overhead variance	1,100 F
Total	$ 700 F

Treated as a Period Expense

One viewpoint is that standard costs represent a close approximation to the actual or "true" cost of inventories and cost of goods sold. It is almost impossible to determine the "true" cost of inventories, but carefully developed standard costs may be the best estimate that management has of the actual cost of production. If this is the case, then deviations from standard or expected costs may be considered to be period expenses rather than inventoriable costs and variance accounts are closed directly to cost of goods sold or to income summary. In reality, whatever view is taken, insignificant or immaterial variances are usually treated as a period expense because of the simplicity in this method of accounting.

As indicated, when cost variances are considered to be period expenses, all variance accounts are closed to either cost of goods sold or to an income summary account. For example, the entry to close the variance accounts given in figure 16.12 using this method is as follows:

Materials usage variance	700	
Labor efficiency variance	400	
Total overhead variance	1,100	
Cost of goods sold (income summary)		700
Materials price variance		500
Labor rate variance		1,000

Figure 16.13 illustrates the financial statement presentation when cost variances are closed to income summary. Note that all inventories are carried on the balance sheet at standard cost.

A refinement of this procedure is to recognize that part of the materials price variance relates to materials still in the materials inventory at the end of the accounting period. This refinement is actually a partial allocation of overhead variances. For example, part of the $500 materials price variance in the example above relates to materials that are still in the materials inventory. The above accounting procedure may be modified by prorating the materials price variance between the materials inventory and the income summary. To illustrate, assume that the balance of the materials inventory account at the end of the period represents 10% of the purchases made during the period. In order to prorate the materials price variance and close variance accounts the following journal entry could be made:

Materials inventory (10% of $500)	50	
Materials usage variance	700	
Labor efficiency variance	400	
Total overhead variance	1,100	
Cost of goods sold (income summary)		750
Materials price variance		500
Labor rate variance		1,000

Figure 16.13   Financial statement presentation when variances are closed to income summary

Partial Income Statement
For the Period Ending December 31, 19X8

Sales		$580,000
Cost of goods sold (at standard)		360,000
Gross profit (at standard)		$220,000
Plus: Net standard cost variances		700
Gross profit (adjusted)		$220,700
Less: Distribution expenses	$110,000	
General and administrative expenses	50,000	160,000
Income from operations		$ 60,700

Partial Balance Sheet
December 31, 19X8

Inventories (at standard):		
Finished goods	$ 40,000	
Work in process	34,000	
Materials	20,000	
Total	$ 94,000	

Treated as an Inventoriable Cost

The alternative to treating standard cost variances as period expenses is to treat them as inventoriable costs. The purpose of prorating variances as inventoriable costs is to adjust the standard cost to an actual cost. This is the theoretically most correct method. This method is used when variances are significant or material in size. This method is also used when standard costs are thought to be artificial and do not represent the actual cost of production and cost of goods sold.

When using this method, cost variances are allocated among inventories (materials, work in process, and finished goods) and cost of goods sold. Then, the cost of goods sold at standard cost plus a prorated share of standard cost variances is closed to income summary. Inventories, using this method, appear on the balance sheet at the standard cost plus a prorated share of standard cost variances.

A variety of methods can be used to allocate overhead variances. One of these methods, which is illustrated on page 553, adopts the rationale that cost variances should be prorated in proportion to the standard-cost balances in the related inventory and cost-of-goods-sold accounts. For example, the materials price variance is allocated to the materials inventory, materials usage variance, work in process, finished goods, and cost of goods sold in proportion to the amount of standard materials cost in each account. The materials price variance is allocated to the materials quantity variance since the materials quantity variance is costed at standard cost instead of at actual cost.

The materials quantity variance plus the allocated portion of the materials price variance is allocated to work in process, finished goods, and cost of goods sold in proportion to the amount of standard materials cost in these accounts.

The rationale for not allocating any materials quantity variance to materials inventory is that the quantity variance relates to the *usage* of materials and not to the *acquisition* of materials. Therefore, the allocation of materials quantity variance to materials inventory is not appropriate.

Figure 16.14   Percentages of costs in inventories and cost of goods sold

Percentages of Costs in Inventories and Cost of Goods Sold

Item		Materials Inventory	Materials Quantity Variance	Work in Process	Finished Goods	Cost of Goods Sold	Total/ Percent
Materials: (Including materials inventory)	Amount:	$20,000	$700	$10,200	$12,000	$108,000	$150,900
	Percent:	{13.2%}	{.5%}	{6.8%}	{8.0%}	{71.5%}	{100.0%}
(Excluding materials inventory)	Amount:			$10,200	$12,000	$108,000	$130,200
	Percent:			{7.8%}	{9.2%}	{83.0%}	{100.0%}
Labor:	Amount:			$14,200	$16,800	$151,000	$182,000
	Percent:			{7.8%}	{9.2%}	{83.0%}	{100.0%}
Overhead:	Amount:			$ 9,600	$11,200	$101,000	$121,800
	Percent			{7.8%}	{9.2%}	{83.0%}	{100.0%}
Total Amount		$20,000	$700	$34,000	$40,000	$360,000	

Proration of Variances Based on Above Percentages

			Allocated to:			
Variance	Amount	Materials Inventory	Materials Quantity Variance	Work in Process	Finished Goods	Cost of Goods Sold
Materials price	$500 U	$66	$3[a]	$34	$ 40	$357
Materials quantity	700 F					
	3 U[a]					
	697 F			(54)[b]	(64)	(579)
Labor rate	1,000 U			78	92	830
Labor efficiency	400 F			(32)	(36)	(332)
Overhead	1,100 F			(86)	(101)	(913)
Total	$ 700 F	$66		$(60)	$(69)	$(637)

[a]Same number
[b]Amounts in parentheses indicate credit items necessary to close favorable variance account balances.

Labor and overhead variances are allocated to work in process, finished goods, and cost of goods sold in proportion to the amount of the respective labor and overhead standard costs in each of these accounts.

The procedure, percentage computations, and variance allocations using this method are shown in figure 16.14. Account balances and variance amounts are taken from the example in this chapter.

Figure 16.15   Financial statement presentation when variances are allocated to inventories and cost of goods sold

Partial Income Statement
For the Period Ending December 31, 19X8

Sales		$580,000
Cost of goods sold		359,363
Gross profit		$220,637
Less: Distribution expenses	$110,000	
General and administrative expenses	50,000	160,000
Income from operations		$ 60,637

Partial Balance Sheet
December 31, 19X8

Inventories:		
	Finished goods	$ 39,931
	Work in process	33,940
	Materials	20,066
	Total	$ 93,937

The journal entry to record the disposition of standard cost variances in accordance with the allocations in figure 16.14 is as follows:

Materials	66	
Materials usage variance	700	
Labor efficiency variance	400	
Total overhead variance	1,100	
Work in process		60
Finished goods		69
Cost of goods sold		637
Materials price variance		500
Labor rate variance		1,000

The financial statement presentation that would result when allocating standard cost variances in this fashion is shown in figure 16.15.

A comparison of the "income from operations" obtained when variances are treated as period expenses (fig. 16.13) and when variances are treated as inventoriable costs (fig. 16.15) shows a difference of $63 ($60,700 − $60,637) greater income when variances are allocated. This difference can be reconciled by computing the difference between inventory balances in the examples. This illustrates the potential impact on financial statements of closing cost variances to the income summary versus allocating cost variances to inventories and cost of goods sold. The difference in this illustration is immaterial in amount, however, in other situations the difference could be quite substantial.

As a final note, budgeted fixed factory overhead, by definition, remains constant at all levels of output over the relevant range of productive activity. Therefore, it would seem reasonable to treat fixed factory overhead as a lump sum period expense rather than as an inventoriable cost like direct materials, direct labor, and variable factory overhead. In fact, there is an accounting method known as direct costing that does treat fixed overhead as a period expense. However, chapter 18 will explain that direct costing is only used for internal management purposes.

Generally accepted accounting for external reporting requires that all factory overhead be assigned to units of production. The method of accounting that is used to assign all overhead to units of production is called full or absorption costing. The name of full or absorption costing is used because inventory is assigned the "full" cost of production, including the cost of fixed overhead as in this example. Because direct costing is not acceptable for external reporting, it should be assumed that any discussion of cost accounting systems assumes the use of full costing principles unless stated otherwise.

Summary

Standard costs for factory overhead are used in the same general way that standard costs for materials and labor are used. When developing a flexible budget for factory overhead, however, the process is slightly different. Because of the indirect nature of overhead costs, total overhead is first compiled and then standard overhead application rates are calculated. Finally, these standard overhead application rates are used as the basis for developing standard costs for factory overhead.

The use of standard costs for factory overhead makes it possible to analyze why actual expenditures for factory overhead may have been different from budgeted or expected amounts. The total difference, called the total overhead variance, can be analyzed with various levels of detail.

The first level of detail, called a two-way analysis, analyzes the total overhead variance into a controllable variance and a volume variance. The volume variance gives the difference between budgeted fixed factory overhead and applied fixed factory overhead. A volume variance results simply because the actual level of activity is different from the budgeted level of activity. The controllable variance relates to factors such as the price paid for overhead items and the efficiency with which overhead items are utilized.

The next level of detail, called a three-way analysis, analyzes the controllable variance into a spending variance and a variable overhead efficiency variance. The variable overhead efficiency variance helps to evaluate the efficiency with which the activity base, such as direct labor, is utilized. The spending variance is an indicator of how well actual overhead expenditures were kept within the budget independent of the efficiency with which the activity base was utilized.

The final level of detail, called a four-way analysis, analyzes the spending variance into a variable overhead spending variance and a fixed overhead spending variance. The variable overhead spending variance gives the difference between actual expenditures for variable overhead and budgeted expenditures due to differences in prices. This variance is somewhat like the materials price variance or the labor rate variance. The fixed overhead budget variance gives any difference between actual fixed overhead incurred and budgeted fixed costs.

There are two general ways to account for standard cost variances at the end of an accounting period. First, standard cost variances may be treated as a period expense. When using this treatment variance accounts are simply closed to either the cost of goods sold or to the income summary account.

The second method of handling standard cost variances is to treat them as inventoriable costs. When using this treatment the balances in the various variance accounts are allocated among inventories (materials, work in process, and finished goods) and cost of goods sold.

These principles of accounting for standard costs for factory overhead are intended to accomplish the dual objectives of providing information for product costing and to provide feedback to management for planning and control.

Bloomington Products specializes in the production of a single major component used in automobile transmissions. Engineering estimates and financial forecasts have yielded the following standard costs per unit:

Materials (10 pounds @ $3 per pound)	$30
Labor (2 hours @ $12 per hour)	24
Variable overhead (2 hours @ $2 per hour)	4
Fixed overhead (2 hours @ $4 per hour)	8
Total standard cost per unit	$66

The total flexible budget for factory overhead indicates that the company expects total overhead to be $120,000 at a standard activity level of 20,000 direct-labor hours.

Actual expenditures for the period are listed below. There were no beginning or ending inventories of materials.

Materials	$450,000
Labor	332,000
Variable overhead	48,000
Fixed overhead	82,000
Total costs	$912,000
Actual units produced	12,000
Actual cost per unit	$ 76

When he saw that the actual cost of production was $76 per unit, the shop foreman explained that his operation had performed beyond expectations and that others in the organization were responsible for the large cost overrun. For example, he pointed out that (a) purchasing had paid $3.60 for materials that were expected to cost only $3.00 per pound and (b) personnel had conceded to a wage increase resulting in the average wage rate being $13.28 rather than $12.00. The shop foreman remarked, "I am responsible for all quantity and efficiency variances, but it is clear that we have done our job or else the cost overrun would be even larger than it is!"

Required

You have been asked to analyze the situation and prepare a brief report indicating how much, if any, of the responsibility for the large cost overrun rests with the shop foreman.

Solution to the Self-Study Problem

Direct Materials

Actual price × Actual quantity	Standard price × Actual quantity	Standard price × Standard quantity
	$3.00 × 125,000[a] = $375,000	$3.00 × 120,000[b] = $360,000
$450,000		

Price variance
$75,000 U

Quantity variance
$15,000 U

[a]Actual materials purchased and used = $450,000 ÷ $3.60 per pound = 125,000 pounds.
[b]Standard materials allowed for 12,000 units of output = 12,000 units × 10 pounds allowed per unit = 120,000 total pounds allowed.

Direct Labor

Actual rate × Actual hours	Standard rate × Actual hours	Standard rate × Standard hours
	$12.00 × 25,000[a] =	$12.00 × 24,000[b] =
$332,000	$300,000	$288,000

Rate variance
$32,000 U

Efficiency variance
$12,000 U

[a]Actual labor hours used = $332,000 ÷ $13.28 per hour = 25,000 hours.
[b]Standard hours allowed for 12,000 units = 12,000 units × 2 hours per unit = 24,000 hours.

Factory Overhead

	Actual Overhead Incurred	Flexible Budget for Factory Overhead (Based on Actual Hours Used)	Total Overhead Applied to Work in Process (Based on Standard Hours Allowed)	Total Overhead Applied to Work in Process
		(25,000 × $2.00)	(24,000 × $2.00)	(24,000 × $2.00)
Variable:	$48,000	$50,000	48,000	48,000

$2,000 F
Variable overhead
spending variance

$2,000 U
Variable overhead
efficiency variance

		Budgeted lump sum	Budgeted lump sum	(24,000 × $4.00)
Fixed:	82,000	80,000	80,000	96,000

$2,000 U
Fixed overhead
budget variance

$16,000 F
Volume variance

Total:	$130,000	$130,000	$128,000	$144,000

–0–
Spending variance

$2,000 U
Variable overhead
efficiency variance

$16,000 F
Volume variance

$2,000 U
Controllable variance

$16,000 F
Volume variance

$14,000 F
Total overhead variance

Summary of Variances Controllable by Department Managers

Controllable by Shop Foreman

Materials quantity variance	$15,000 U	
Labor efficiency variance	12,000 U	
Variable overhead efficiency variance	2,000 U	
Total controllable by shop foreman	$29,000 U	21%

Controllable by Other Department Managers

Materials price variance	$75,000 U	
Labor rate variance	32,000 U	
Variable overhead spending variance	2,000 F	
Total	$109,000 U	79%
Total controllable by department managers	$138,000 U	100%

Suggested Readings

Elikai, Fara, and Moriarity, Shane. "Variance Analysis with PERT/COST." *Accounting Review* (January 1982): 161–70.

Ericson, Joseph H., Jr. "Standard Costs in Action." *Management Accounting* (August 1978): 25–32.

Gillespie, Jackson F. "An Application of Learning Curves to Standard Costing." *Management Accounting* (September 1981): 63–65.

Hicks, James O., Jr. "The Application of Exponential Smoothing to Standard Cost Systems." *Management Accounting* (September 1978): 28–32.

Mullett, Matthew J. "Benefits from Standard Costing in the Restaurant Industry." *Management Accounting* (September 1978): 47–54.

Discussion Questions

1. Give the meaning of standard costs for overhead and explain how they relate to standard costs for materials and labor.
2. Outline the accounting process for using standard costs for overhead.
3. What is a standard activity level and how is it used?
4. Explain the general procedure used to develop a flexible budget for factory overhead.
5. What are standard overhead application rates and how are they used?
6. What is the relationship between standard overhead application rates and standard costs?
7. Give journal entries with hypothetical numbers to record actual and applied (*a*) variable overhead and (*b*) fixed overhead.
8. "Fixed overhead is applied to work in process as though it is a variable cost." Explain this concept and provide graphs of budgeted and applied fixed costs to support your explanation.
9. What are the consequences of applying fixed overhead to work in process using a fixed overhead application rate as though it is a variable cost?
10. Define the volume variance and explain what is responsible for its incurrence.
11. What is the meaning of a favorable volume variance and an unfavorable volume variance?

12. Define the total overhead variance and sketch the general framework for its analysis.
13. Give the framework and related formulas for analyzing the total overhead variance using (a) a two-way analysis, (b) a three-way analysis, and (c) a four-way analysis.
14. Give the outline of an overhead variance report suitable for management reporting. How might this report be different if fixed overhead variances are controllable only at higher levels of management?
15. Explain two methods of accounting for standard cost variances at the end of an accounting period.
16. What is the difference between full costing and direct costing?

Exercises

Exercise 16.1   Overhead Spending and Efficiency Variances

The following information has been obtained for the Barkley Company:

	Budget per Standard Direct-Labor Hour	Actual Costs
Direct labor	$1.55	$37,200
Direct materials	1.40	32,400
Controllable overhead costs:		
Indirect materials	.90	21,360
Indirect labor	.75	18,240
Supplies	.20	4,800
Lubricants	.16	4,800
Maintenance	.14	3,120
Repairs	.21	4,800
Other	.09	2,160

Normal capacity: 25,750 direct-labor hours
Standard direct-labor hours: 25,000
Actual direct-labor hours: 24,000

Required

Determine the efficiency and spending variances for overhead. Indicate whether the variances are favorable or unfavorable.

Exercise 16.2   Standards and Variable Factory Overhead Variances

King Company estimates that it will operate its manufacturing facilities at 800,000 direct-labor hours for the year. The estimate for total budgeted overhead is $2,000,000. The standard variable overhead rate is estimated to be $2 per direct-labor hour or $6 per unit. The actual data for the year are presented below:

Actual finished units	250,000
Actual direct-labor hours	764,000
Actual variable overhead	$1,610,000
Actual fixed overhead	$ 392,000

Required

1. Determine the variable overhead spending variance for the year.
2. Determine the variable overhead efficiency variance for the year.

Exercise 16.3   Standards and Fixed Factory Overhead Variances

Refer to the data in exercise 16.2

Required

1. Determine the fixed overhead spending variance for the year.
2. Determine the overhead volume variance for the year.

Exercise 16.4   Standards and Variable Factory Overhead Variances (CMA)

Standard Company has developed standard overhead costs based on a capacity of 180,000 direct-labor hours as follows:

Standard costs per unit:

Variable portion	2 hours @ $3 = $ 6
Fixed portion	2 hours @ $5 = 10
	$16

During April, 85,000 units were scheduled for production, but only 80,000 units were actually produced. The following data relate to April:

1. The actual direct-labor cost incurred was $644,000 for 165,000 actual hours of work.
2. The actual overhead incurred totaled $1,378,000—$518,000 variable and $860,000 fixed.
3. All inventories are carried at standard cost.

Required

1. Determine the variable overhead spending variance for April.
2. Determine the variable factory overhead efficiency variance for April.

Exercise 16.5   Standards and Fixed Factory Overhead Variances

Refer to the data in exercise 16.4.

Required

1. Determine the fixed overhead spending variance for April.
2. Determine the overhead volume variance for April.

Exercise 16.6   Standard Cost Concepts and Procedures

Owl-Wobber Manufacturing Company uses a standard cost system for accounting for the cost of production of its only product—product A. The standards for the production of one unit of product A are as follows:

Direct materials: 10 feet of item 1 at $.75 per foot and 3 feet of item 2 at $1 per foot.
Direct labor: 4 hours at $15 per hour.
Factory overhead is applied at 150% of standard direct-labor costs.

There was no inventory on hand at May 1, 19X2. The following is a summary of cost-related data for the production of product *A* during the year ended April 30, 19X3:

> 100,000 feet of item 1 were purchased at $.78 per foot.
> 30,000 feet of item 2 were purchased at $.90 per foot.
> 8,000 units of product *A* were produced, which required 78,000 feet of item 1, 26,000 feet of item 2, and 31,000 hours of direct labor at $16 per hour.
> 6,000 units of product *A* were sold.

At April 30, 19X3, there are 22,000 feet of item 1, 4,000 feet of item 2, and 2,000 completed units of product *A* on hand. All purchases and transfers are "charged in" at standard cost.

Required

1. Determine for the year ending April 30, 19X3, the total debits to the raw materials account for the purchase of item 1.
2. Determine for the year ending April 30, 19X3, the total debits to the work-in-process account for direct labor.
3. Determine for the year ending April 30, 19X3, the total debits to the work-in-process account for factory overhead.

Exercise 16.7   Standard Costs and End of Period Variance Disposition

Refer to the data in exercise 16.6.

Required

1. Determine the balance in the materials efficiency variance account for item 2.
2. If all standard variances were prorated to inventories and cost of goods sold, determine the amount of materials efficiency variance for item 2 to be prorated to the raw materials inventory.
3. If all standard variances were prorated to inventories and cost of goods sold, determine the amount of materials price variance for item 1 to be prorated to the raw materials inventory.

Exercise 16.8   Standard Costs and Overhead Variances—Two-Way Analysis

McQueen Furniture Creations uses a standard cost approach in their accounting system. For the month of April, the following information has been collected:

Normal capacity (in direct-labor hours)	4,000 hours
Total overhead at normal capacity	
Fixed	$ 6,400
Variable	9,600
Total	$16,000
Overhead rate per direct-labor hour	
Fixed	$ 1.60
Variable	2.40
Total	$ 4.00
Actual overhead	$15,200
Actual direct-labor hours	3,475 hours
Standard hours allowed for actual production	3,400 hours

Required

1. Determine the manufacturing overhead variances for McQueen Furniture Creations using the two-way analysis.
2. Prepare journal entries for the overhead expense in April using the two-way variance analysis.

Exercise 16.9 Standards for Factory Overhead—Three-Way Analysis

Refer to the data in exercise 16.8.

Required

1. Determine the manufacturing overhead variances for McQueen Furniture Creations using the three-way analysis.
2. Prepare journal entries for the overhead expense in April using the three-way variance analysis.

Exercise 16.10 Standards for Factory Overhead—Four-Way Analysis

Refer to the data in exercise 16.8. Also assume that actual fixed overhead is $6,600 of the $15,200 total actual overhead.

Required

1. Determine the manufacturing overhead variances for McQueen Furniture Creations using the four-way analysis.
2. Prepare journal entries for the overhead expense in April with the four-way variance analysis.

Problems

Problem 16.1 Materials, Labor, and Factory Overhead Standards and Variances

Armando Corporation manufactures a product with the following standard costs:

Direct materials—20 yards @ $1.35 per yard	$27
Direct labor—4 hours @ $9.00 per hour	36
Factory overhead—applied at 5/6 of direct labor	
Ratio of variable costs to fixed costs: 2 to 1	30
Total standard cost per unit of output	$93

Standards are based on normal monthly production involving 2,400 direct-labor hours (600 units of output).

The following information pertains to the month of July:

Direct materials purchased—18,000 yards @ $1.38 per yard	$24,840
Direct materials used—9,500 yards	
Direct labor—2,100 hours @ $9.15 per hour	19,215
Actual factory overhead	16,650

In July, 500 units of the product were actually produced.

Required

1. Prepare schedules computing the following:
   a. Variable factory overhead rate per direct-labor hour
   b. Total fixed factory overhead based on normal activity
2. Prepare the following schedules for the month of July, indicating whether each variance is favorable or unfavorable:
   a. Materials price variance (based on purchases)
   b. Materials usage variance
   c. Labor rate variance
   d. Labor efficiency variance
   e. Controllable factory overhead variance
   f. Factory overhead volume variance

Problem 16.2 Standard Costs, Materials, Labor, and Factory Overhead

Eastern Company manufactures special electrical equipment and parts. Eastern employs a standard cost accounting system with separate standards established for each product.

A special transformer is manufactured in the transformer department. Production volume is measured by direct-labor hours in this department, and a flexible budget system is used to plan and control department overhead.

Standard costs for the special transformer are determined annually in September for the coming year. The standard cost of a transformer was computed at $67 as shown below:

Direct materials		
Iron	5 sheets @ $2.00	$10.00
Copper	3 spools @ $3.00	9.00
Direct labor	4 hours @ $7.00	28.00
Variable overhead	4 hours @ $3.00	12.00
Fixed overhead	4 hours @ $2.00	8.00
Total		$67.00

Overhead rates were based upon normal monthly capacity of 4,000 direct-labor hours. Practical capacity for this department is 5,000 direct-labor hours per month. Variable overhead costs are expected to vary with the number of direct-labor hours actually used.

During October, 800 transformers were produced. This was below expectations because a work stoppage occurred during contract negotiations with the labor force. Once the contract was settled, the department scheduled overtime in an attempt to catch up to expected production levels.

The following costs were incurred in October:

Direct Material	Direct-Materials Purchased	Materials Used
Iron	5,000 sheets @ $2.00 per sheet	3,900 sheets
Copper	2,200 spools @ $3.10 per spool	2,600 spools
Direct labor		
Regular time:	2,000 hours @ $7.00	
	1,400 hours @ $7.20	
Overtime:	600 of the 1,400 hours were subject to overtime premium. The total overtime premium of $2,160 is included in variable overhead in accordance with company accounting practices.	
Variable overhead:	$10,000	
Fixed overhead:	$ 8,800	

Required

1. Indicate and explain the most appropriate time to record any variation of actual material prices from standard.
2. Determine the total material quantity variance for October.
3. Determine the labor rate (price) variance for October.
4. Determine the variable overhead spending variance for October.
5. Determine the efficiency variance for variable overhead for October.
6. Determine the spending variance for fixed overhead for October.
7. Determine the fixed overhead volume variance for October.
8. Explain the most usual cause of an unfavorable fixed overhead volume variance.

Problem 16.3 Standard Costs and Variances—Extending from the Flexible Budget Reports

Refer to problem 6.4 for the basic data needed in this problem.

Required

1. Calculate the excess amount over the standard cost spent on manufacturing expense items during November. Analyze this excess amount into those variances due to the following:
    a. Efficiency
    b. Spending
2. Explain what the management of the company should do to reduce the following:
    a. The spending variance
    b. The efficiency variance

Problem 16.4 Standard Cost Concepts and Procedures—Two Variances

Information on Ripley Company's overhead costs for January production activity is as follows:

Budgeted fixed overhead	$ 75,000
Standard fixed overhead rate per direct-labor hour	$ 3
Standard variable overhead rate per direct-labor hour	$ 6
Standard direct-labor allowed for actual production	24,000
Actual total overhead incurred	$220,000

Ripley has a standard cost and flexible budgeting system and uses the two-variance method (two-way analysis) for overhead variances.

Required

Determine the overhead controllable and volume variances for January.

Problem 16.5   Standard Cost Variance for Overhead

Union Company uses a standard cost accounting system. The following overhead costs and production data are available for August:

Standard fixed overhead rate per direct-labor hour	$ 1.00
Standard variable overhead rate per direct-labor hour	$ 4.00
Normal monthly direct-labor hours	40,000
Actual direct-labor hours worked	39,500
Standard direct-labor hours allowed for actual production	39,000
Overall overhead variance—favorable	$ 2,000

Required

1. Determine the amount of overhead applied for August.
2. Determine the amount of actual overhead incurred during August.
3. Assume the Union Company uses the three-way variance method. Determine the overhead spending, efficiency, and volume variances.

Problem 16.6   Standard Cost Concepts—Two Variances

Dickey Company had total underapplied overhead of $15,000 during March. Additional information is as follows:

Variable Overhead

Applied based on standard direct-labor hours allowed	$42,000
Budgeted based on standard direct-labor hours	42,000

Fixed Overhead

Applied based on standard direct-labor hours allowed	30,000
Budgeted based on standard direct-labor hours	27,000

Required

1. Determine the actual total overhead incurred during March.
2. Assume the Dickey Company uses the two-variance method. Determine the overhead controllable and volume variances.

Problem 16.7   Standard Costs and Flexible Budgets

Owen Huffy, production manager for C. H. L. Incorporated evaluates the performance of the production departments by comparing budget and standard costs with actual costs. The following data was collected for department 88 during last year:

Factory Overhead	Budget Data		Actual Data	
	Variable	Fixed	Variable	Fixed
Indirect labor	$31,500		$33,000	
Indirect materials	22,400		25,300	
Supplies	1,910		2,200	
Maintenance	2,020	800	2,200	800
Repairs	1,740	1,200	1,980	1,200
Depreciation		4,800		4,800
Supervision		19,800		19,800
Rent		1,510		1,510
Miscellaneous	430	890	440	890
Total	$60,000	$29,000	$65,120	$29,000

The overhead rate, used to apply the above overhead budget to work in process, is computed by using a normal capacity base equivalent to 80% of theoretical capacity.

Theoretical capacity (100%) for department 88 is 25,000 direct-labor hours, and the standard number of direct-labor hours allowed is 21,000. Department 88 actually incurred 22,000 direct-labor hours during the year.

Required

1. Develop a flexible budget for the following capacity levels: 70, 80, 90, and 100%. Include unit costs for variable overhead, fixed overhead, and total overhead.
2. Assuming that the fixed costs are not controllable, prepare a performance report comparing the flexible budget with actual results for department 88. Include variances and indicate whether they are favorable or unfavorable.
3. Since the company maintains a standard cost system, determine the following variance *only* for total overhead costs (not for each overhead item):
   a. Spending variance
   b. Volume variance
   c. Variable efficiency variance

Problem 16.8 Standard Cost Concepts and Motivation Issues

The Kelly Company, founded twenty years ago, has achieved a moderate degree of success. Kelly manufactures and sells pottery items. All manufacturing takes place in one plant with four departments. Each manufacturing department produces only one product. The four products of Kelly Company are plaques, cups, vases, and plates. Sam Kelly, the president and founder, credits the company's success to the well-designed quality products and to an effective cost control system. The system was installed early in the firm's existence to improve cost control and to serve as a basis for planning.

Kelly Company establishes standard costs for material and labor with the participation of plant management. Each year the plant manager, the department heads, and the time-study engineers are invited by top management to recommend changes in the standards for the next year. Top management reviews these recommendations and the records of actual performance for the current year before setting the new standards. As a general rule, tight standards representing very efficient performance are established. Top management does this so that no inefficiency or slack will be included in cost goals. The plant manager and department heads are charged with cost control responsibility and the variances from standard costs are used to measure their performance in carrying out this charge.

No standards are set for factory overhead because the management believes it is too difficult to predict and relate overhead to output. The actual factory overhead for the departments and the plant is accumulated in one "pool." The actual overhead is then allocated to the departments on the basis of departmental output. The following schedule is a three-year summary of overhead allocation among the departments.

	19X5		19X6		19X7	
Department	Units Produced	Allocated[a] Overhead	Units Produced	Allocated[a] Overhead	Units Produced	Allocated[a] Overhead
Plaques	300,000	$120,000	330,000	$126,000	180,000	$ 60,000
Cups	250,000	100,000	270,000	103,091	360,000	120,000
Vases	200,000	80,000	220,000	84,000	300,000	100,000
Plates	250,000	100,000	280,000	106,909	360,000	120,000
Totals	1,000,000	$400,000	1,100,000	$420,000	1,200,000	$400,000

[a]Dollar amounts are rounded to the nearest dollar.

Kelly's executives are convinced that more effective cost control can be obtained than is currently being realized from the standard cost system. A review of cost performance for recent years disclosed several factors that led them to this conclusion. The following factors were disclosed:

1. Unfavorable variances were the norm rather than the exception, although the size of the variances was quite uniform.
2. Department managers took steps that, while benefiting their own departments, were detrimental to overall company performance.
3. Employee motivation, especially among firstline supervisors, appeared to be low.

Required

1. What are the probable effects, if any, on the motivation of the plant managers and department heads from (*a*) the participative standard cost system and (*b*) the use of "tight" standards? Explain the reasons for your conclusions.
2. What effect, if any, will the practice of applying actual overhead costs on the basis of the actual units produced have on the motivation of department heads to control overhead costs? Explain your answer.

Problem 16.9   Standard Costs—Reconstructing Data from Given Variances

The Sherman Company has the following budget and standard data for its single product:

> Materials—3 gallons at $3 per gallon
> Variable factory overhead budget of $160,000 for 80,000 direct-labor hours
> Fixed overhead budget of $240,000
> Budgeted direct-labor cost for 80,000 hours—$640,000
> Labor—2 hours per unit

During May, production was below budget and the following variances from standard were noted:

1.	Labor efficiency variance	$16,000 U
2.	Materials quantity variance	6,000 U
3.	Materials price variance based on purchases (.05 per gallon)	5,500 U
4.	Labor rate variance	7,200 U
5.	Variable overhead spending variance	1,000 U
6.	Variable overhead efficiency variance	9,000 U
7.	Fixed overhead spending variance	2,000 F
8.	Fixed overhead volume variance	30,000 U

Required

1. Determine how many units were produced during May.
2. Determine the actual quantity of materials purchased.
3. Determine the actual labor hours and actual payroll cost.
4. Determine the actual variable and actual fixed overhead incurred.
5. Determine the fixed overhead applied to production.
6. Determine the number of excess gallons and excess labor hours used during May above standard.

Problem 16.10 Overhead Variances, Process Costing, and Variance Disposition

Lundberg Company used a process-costing system tied to standard costs. The finishing department adds labor and overhead costs to the products received from the blending department.

The standard costs per unit in finishing are as follows:

Labor (one hour)	$6.00
Factory overhead	
Variable	2.50
Fixed	1.25

The standard capacity is 10,000 units.

During March, the finishing department completed and sent to finished goods 9,500 units. They received 9,600 units from blending during March and had 500 units in process on March 1—1/4 complete, and 600 units in process on March 31—2/3 complete.

There were 300 units of finished product in stock on March 31 and none on March 1.

During March, 9,850 labor hours were used; $25,000 of variable overhead was incurred; and $12,400 of fixed overhead was incurred. The actual labor rate was at standard.

Required

1. Determine the variances for labor and factory overhead for March. Use the three-way method of analysis for overhead. Clearly identify the equivalent units produced.
2. Prepare journal entries to record actual labor and overhead costs charged to production including the variances incurred.
3. Determine the ending inventory standard cost for work in process, finished goods, and cost of goods sold.
4. Assume that Lundberg adjusts all accounts to actual cost for financial statement purposes at the end of each month. Determine the disposition of the labor efficiency variance at March 31 and show the disposition in journal entry form.

ACCOUNTING SYSTEMS FOR MANAGEMENT PLANNING AND CONTROL

17

OUTLINE

T he procedures and practices discussed in this text must be integrated into a cost accounting system. This chapter explains what the cost accounting system should consist of and how it is developed. After completing this chapter you should be able to:

1. identify the role of the cost accounting system within a fully integrated management information system.
2. describe the flow of costs through a computerized cost accounting system and its relationship to other divisions of the company.
3. describe the procedures followed in developing or acquiring computer software for a cost accounting system.
4. explain the controls that a cost accountant uses to insure accurate processing within the cost accounting system.

COST ACCOUNTING SYSTEMS

Recent developments in mini- and microcomputer technology have made computers available to both medium- and smaller-sized organizations. They have also resulted in decentralization of much of the data processing in larger organizations. The computer has now become an integral part of many people's jobs. Few manual cost accounting systems will remain in existence because of the new technology, reduced processing costs, additional computational power, and added capacity provided by the computer. Also, many of the applications that assist management in the decision functions of the organization are now computerized.

Anyone working in cost accounting must understand the cost accounting system as it fits into the entire information system of the organization.

Cost Accounting as a Subsystem of the Management Information System

A **management information system** may be defined as a computer-based information processing system that supports the operation, management, and decision function of an organization. The management information system must be able to support all the functional areas within the organization including marketing, manufacturing, personnel, and finance.

Within the management information system there is a subsystem commonly called the accounting information system. The accounting information system includes all activities involved with recording, classifying, summarizing, and reporting business transactions. It includes both external reporting to stockholders, creditors, and governmental agencies as well as internal reporting to management.

Examples of systems included in a management information system but not included as part of the accounting information system are the personnel information system and the marketing information system. A personnel information system might include information on educational training, medical history, prior job experience, fluency in foreign languages, results on performance evaluations, and character references. Typically these things are of no interest to the accounting information system. However, some information such as marital status and number of exemptions are relevant to both accounting and personnel information systems.

Cost accounting is a subsystem of the accounting information system, which is designed to assist management in operating the business smoothly and profitably. The cost accounting system can be split into two functions—cost determination and cost analysis. Cost determination seeks to identify the cost of manufacturing individual products or product components. This information is used to evaluate the manufacturing process, value ending inventories, and determine the cost of goods sold. Cost analysis uses the cost data described above along with other data that are collected or developed as needed to help management make decisions that relate to current and future operations.

Figure 17.1   The management information system relative to the management cycle

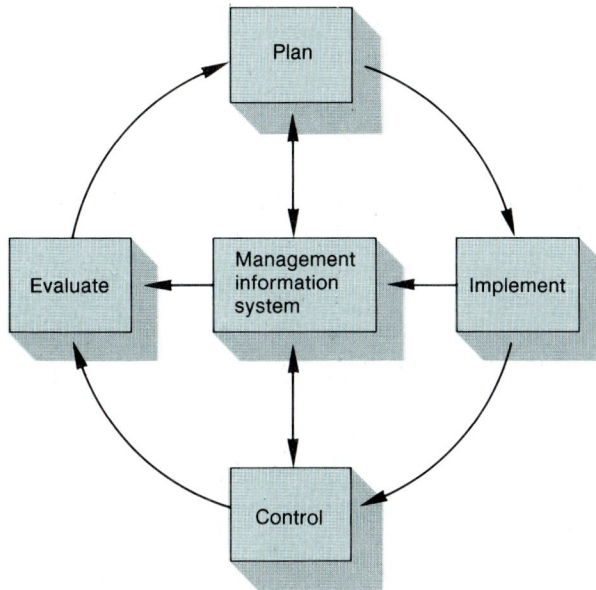

Figure 17.1 shows the relationship of the management information system to the management cycle. The management cycle may be defined as the activities performed by management from one planning period to the next. An operating plan is developed at the beginning of the period. Throughout the period, management attempts to implement the plan. Corrective action is taken to control the activity whenever actual operations differ significantly from planned operations. A final evaluation is performed at the end of the period and is used as a basis for developing a new plan for the coming period.

Note that the management information system is central to all activities. It provides management with the data required to develop the plan or budget for the coming period. As the plan is executed, data are collected on the results of operations. These are compared to the budget to compute the variances that help management to identify areas of the business in which corrective action is required. The information system provides the final results for the period that are used to evaluate performance and serve as a basis for developing the plan for the next operating cycle.

Fully Integrated Management Information System

A management information system is referred to as fully integrated when the informational needs of each subsystem are coordinated and each draws information from a common source. The common source of information is called the **data base.** A fully integrated management information system enters data into the system only once. Information that is collected in any area of the business is immediately made available to all other areas of the business through the common data base. All records and files are updated for the new information regardless of where it is captured.

The subsystems of a management information system usually correspond with the functional areas of the organization. Figure 17.2 shows several functional areas and their relationship to the fully integrated system. Each functional area has special informational needs at each level of management. Top management is concerned primarily

---

Figure 17.2   Components of a management information system

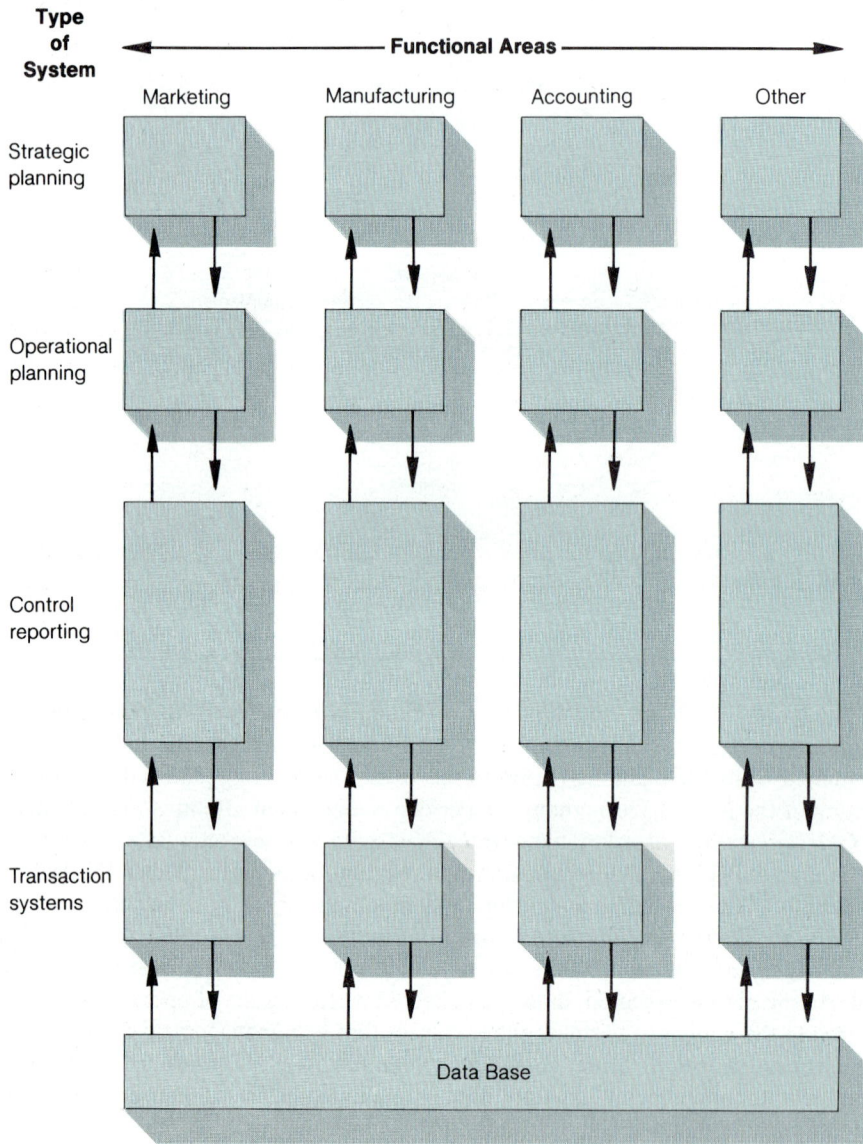

with strategic planning while middle and lower management is responsible for operational planning and control reporting. Each functional area is supported by the common data base.

Most of the benefits from a fully integrated system stem from the data entering into the system only once and sharing it. Benefits generally include reduced personnel for data processing, reduced rate of operator error, and less time devoted to error correction. Information is more timely, more accurate, and consistent across functional areas. There is also less redundancy of information in the files of the enterprise.

The process of hiring a new employee illustrates the operation of a fully integrated information system and some of its benefits. Suppose a new employee is hired by the personnel division of a company according to a job description developed by the manufacturing supervisor. At the time of employment the personnel department collects the information required for the employee's file. Among other things this includes the pay rate, marital status, and number of dependents. The employee's record becomes part of the company's data base that is available to authorized users in other functional areas. This information is subsequently accessed by the cost accounting function when posting direct labor to individual job tickets and when preparing the employee's paycheck. By sharing this data, cost accounting did not have to contact the employee and collect the same data again. They also avoided having to develop and maintain their own personnel file.

The major problem with a fully integrated information system is in designing a data base that is flexible to the changing needs of the organization and yet satisfies the needs of all users at each level of management and for each functional area. The controller or a representative from the cost accounting function plays a key role in the development of the data base and in the development of the entire information system. Accounting for financial transactions is a requirement for all functional areas. Therefore, the cost accountant must not only be knowledgeable about accounting but must also be knowledgeable about computer processing and the development and implementation of computerized information systems.

HOW MUCH INFORMATION?

The objective of an accounting information system is to provide information that is useful to both internal and external parties who have an interest in the organization. Some information provided by the cost accounting system is required by law or by generally accepted accounting principles. However, much of the information provided for management decisions is not required, but is given with the hope that it will assist management in operating the business more profitably. Questions that must constantly be asked when providing nonrequired information include: "How much information should be provided?" "Is the benefit of additional information worth its cost?"

Let's first identify some of the information that must be provided by the cost accounting system to be in compliance with the law and with generally accepted accounting principles. Then we will consider the cost/benefit analysis of additional information.

Required Information

Public Law Number 95–213, titled the Foreign Corrupt Practices Act, was passed by the United States Congress in December 1977. There are three major sections of the act, two of which identify what constitutes foreign corrupt practices and penalties associated with them. The other section identifies accounting standards that must be met by every company, domestic or foreign, that is subject to the Securities Act of 1934.

This act requires that a company must (a) make and keep books, records, and accounts that, in reasonable detail, accurately and fairly reflect the transactions and dispositions of the assets of the issuer and (b) devise and maintain a system of internal accounting controls that will provide reasonable assurance of the following:

1. Transactions are executed in accordance with management's general or specific authorization.
2. Transactions are recorded as necessary (a) to permit preparation of financial statements in conformity with generally accepted accounting principles or any other criteria applicable to such statements and (b) to maintain accountability for assets.
3. Access to assets is permitted only in accordance with management's general or specific authorizations.
4. The recorded accountability for assets is compared with the existing assets at reasonable intervals and appropriate action is taken with respect to any differences.

The implementation of controls required by this act for a cost accounting system will be discussed later in this chapter. First we will focus on the information that must be provided by the system to prepare financial statements in accordance with generally accepted accounting principles and with Internal Revenue Service (IRS) requirements.

The major objective of generally accepted accounting principles in accounting for inventory is to obtain an appropriate matching of costs against revenues in order to properly determine realized income. The inventory at any given date is the balance of costs applicable to goods on hand remaining after the matching of absorbed costs with concurrent revenues. This balance is carried forward to future periods.

Generally accepted accounting principles identify cost as the primary basis of accounting for inventory, which has been defined generally as the price paid or consideration given to acquire an asset. As applied to inventories, cost means the sum of the applicable expenditures and charges *directly* or *indirectly* incurred to bring an article to its existing condition and location. This has special significance for a manufacturing organization because of their indirect manufacturing costs that we call overhead. The exclusion of overhead from an inventory cost does not constitute an acceptable accounting procedure.

The Internal Revenue Code also specifies the full cost method (sometimes called the absorption method) of inventory costing:

> In order to conform as nearly as may be possible to the best accounting practices and to clearly reflect income, both direct and indirect production costs must be taken into account in the computation of inventoriable costs in accordance with the "full absorption" method of inventory costing.

In order to provide financial statements that are in accordance with generally accepted accounting principles and to satisfy reporting requirements with the IRS, the cost accounting system must be based on the full cost method of inventory valuation.

Under the full cost method of inventory costing production costs must be allocated to goods produced during the period, whether sold during that period or in inventory at the close of the period. Thus, inventoriable costs include all direct production costs (direct material and direct labor) as well as the indirect production costs (manufacturing overhead). A manufacturing overhead rate or a standard cost method is generally used to allocate manufacturing overhead to the units produced.

Cost-Benefit Analysis of Additional Information

Additional information should be provided as long as the marginal value of the new information exceeds its marginal cost. The value of additional information is often very difficult to measure, but conceptually it is described as the improvement in the decision made by management as a result of the new information. The cost of information is the amount paid to capture, store, process, and report it to management.

Value of information = Benefit from improved decisions − Cost of providing information

An example will illustrate the type of analysis that is required to evaluate the costs and benefits of additional information. Suppose Nebeker Incorporated manufactures two products, malt and silt, from a common raw material. Somewhere during the production process, each product becomes separately identifiable. However, no separate accounting has been made of production costs by product after the split-off point because both products have only been saleable in a finished state.

An offer has just been received from a foreign company to purchase 100,000 pounds of malt at the split-off point for $4.00 per pound over the next year. Malt currently sells for $5.00 per pound, and selling and administrative expenses will not be affected by this decision. Figure 17.3 shows the results of operations for the year just ended. Operations for the coming year are anticipated to be about the same, assuming the foreign offer is rejected.

Figure 17.3

Nebeker, Inc.
Projected Income Statement
Assuming all Sales to United States Customers

Sales revenue			
Malt (200,000 lbs. @ $5.00/lb.)			$1,000,000
Silt (50,000 lbs. @ $7.50/lb.)			375,000
Total			$1,375,000
Manufacturing costs:			
Material	$400,000		
Labor	600,000		
Overhead	200,000		
Total		$1,200,000	
Selling and administrative expenses		100,000	
Total			1,300,000
Net income			$ 75,000

Management felt they had inadequate information on which to make a decision, but their intuition suggested they should reject the offer. After all, $4.00 was rather low and a "gut feel" said that their profit would be greater if the malt was processed to a finished state and sold through normal market channels within the United States. One young executive, however, disagreed and suggested that they hire a consulting firm to analyze their costs to determine the amount of processing costs that were incurred on malt after the split-off point. "If it costs more than $1 to process the malt after the split-off point," she argued, "we would be further ahead to sell the malt to the foreign company." The management team reluctantly agreed to contact a consulting firm for an estimate of their consulting fee for such a study.

A reputable consulting firm was contacted and a proposal was obtained from them. The proposal identified two phases to the study:

Phase	Cost	Scope
I	$5,000	Analyze direct material and direct labor to identify the cost to process malt after the split-off point.
II	$5,000	Analyze manufacturing overhead to identify the amount that could be avoided if 100,000 pounds of malt were not processed after the split-off point.

The young executive was successful in convincing other members of management to commit themselves to the project one phase at a time. The results of phase I could be obtained and analyzed before they committed themselves to phase II.

After a few days the consulting firm submitted the phase I report. The report indicated that $.70 of direct material and $.50 of direct labor per pound are incurred in processing malt after the split-off point. Based on this information, the young executive argued that the foreign offer should be accepted and that phase II of the study should be eliminated. The added $1.00 ($5.00 − $4.00) from processing the product and selling it in its finished state was less than the $1.20 ($.70 + $.50) of direct costs required to process the malt to a finished state. The elimination of any overhead costs would simply make it more desirable to sell the malt in its raw state to the foreign company. Once again management adopted the young executive's suggestion and accepted the foreign offer.

For illustration purposes note that if phase II of the consulting firm's proposal had been pursued they would have found that $10,000 of overhead would be eliminated

Figure 17.4

Nebeker, Inc.
Projected Income Statement
Assuming Foreign Offer Is Accepted

Sales revenue			
Malt (100,000 lbs. @ $5.00/lb.)			$ 500,000
Silt (50,000 lbs. @ $7.50/lb.)			375,000
Foreign sales—Malt (100,000 lbs. @ $4.00/lb.)			400,000
Total			$1,275,000
Manufacturing costs:			
Material		$330,000	
Labor		550,000	
Overhead		190,000[a]	
Total		$1,070,000	
Selling and administrative expenses		100,000	
Total			1,170,000
Net income			$ 105,000

[a]The overhead amount recorded here is net of the saving achieved by selling malt in its raw state. If phase II of the consultant's project is not pursued, this would not be known until the end of the year. However, let's assume that he knows it now in order to compute the value of the information.

by not processing 100,000 pounds of malt to a finished state. This $10,000 savings will be achieved during the year when the company sells the malt in its raw state. The point is that the $10,000 savings is a result of this decision even though they don't know the amount at the time they made the decision. Let's assume we know this amount in order to compute the value of the information provided by the consultants.

The young executive felt a personal victory had been achieved, but she was concerned that the consultant's fee had used up a major portion of the additional earning from the foreign sale. In the quiet of her office she prepared a revised forecast for the coming year, which is shown in figure 17.4. From this she computed the value of the information provided by the consulting firm. Without the additional information they would have rejected the foreign offer and earned $75,000 of net income. With the additional information they accepted the offer and will have $105,000 of net income. The benefit of the improved decision is the $30,000 increase in net income.

$$\text{Benefit of an improved decision} = \$105,000 - 75,000$$
$$= \$30,000$$

The cost to capture, store, analyze, and report the information to management was all contained in the $5,000 consulting fee.

$$\text{Cost of the information} = \$5,000$$

The organization is $25,000 better off by having the information provided by the consulting firm. The young executive felt satisfied that her contribution to the company was greater than her salary for the week.

$$\text{Value of information} = \text{Benefit of improved decisions} - \text{Cost of the information}$$
$$\text{Value of the information} = \$30,000 - \$5,000$$
$$= \$25,000$$

There are two questions that should be considered at this point: Would the company have been better off by having the consultants complete phase II of the study? What would the value of the information be if the additional processing costs for malt after the split-off point had been $.80 per pound ($.40 per pound for direct material, $.30 per pound for direct labor, and $10,000 of overhead for 100,000 pounds)?

The company would have been $5,000 worse off by having the consultants complete phase II of the study. The decision would have still been to sell the malt to the foreign company, but the cost of the information would have been $10,000. The net benefit to the firm would be only $20,000 rather than $25,000 as computed above.

$$\text{Value of information} = \$30,000 - \$10,000$$
$$= \underline{\$20,000}$$

If the results of the study had shown additional processing costs of only $.80 per pound, then the company should reject the foreign offer. The additional processing costs of $.80 per pound provide $1.00 of additional revenue when the product is processed to its finished state and sold through normal market channels. Since operations do not change and net income remains at $75,000, the improvement or benefit from this decision alternative is zero. However, they still must pay the consulting firm $10,000 for both phases of the study. The net result to the company would be a $10,000 loss.

$$\text{Value of information} = 0 - \$10,000$$
$$= \underline{(\$10,000)}$$

In summary, the value of information is equal to the benefit provided by the improvement in the decision-making process less the cost of providing it. If the decision is not changed, then there is no benefit to having it, other than the comfort it provides management to know that they have made a good decision. Additional information should be provided as long as management is able to use it to make better decisions and as long as the improvement exceeds the cost associated with providing it.

DEVELOPING A COST ACCOUNTING SYSTEM

The development of the cost accounting system must be integrated with the entire information system of an organization. The structure of the information system and how it is to be developed is planned and documented in a master plan. Standard procedures are then followed in developing individual applications identified in the master plan. This set of standard procedures is typically referred to as the "systems analysis and design life cycle." In this section we will identify the contents of the master plan and how it is developed, as well as the individual steps included in the systems analysis and design life cycle. By understanding this process the cost accountant will be able to provide valuable input into the development and operation of the system.

Master Plan

The objectives of the information system and the order by which it is developed is laid out in an information systems master plan. The **master plan** contains a summary of current capabilities of the information system as well as a projection of future requirements for labor, hardware, software, and financial resources. It generally covers a two-to-five year time period, but places greatest emphasis on the planned activities of the coming year. Development activities as well as activities and requirements associated with operating the system are included in the master plan.

The development of the information system is broken into subsystems called "applications." Examples of individual applications include (a) the accounts receivable and billing system, (b) the fixed asset accounting system, (c) the cost accounting system, and (d) the personnel information system. The development portion of the master plan includes new applications that have been requested by various user departments and sig-

Figure 17.5   Master plan contents

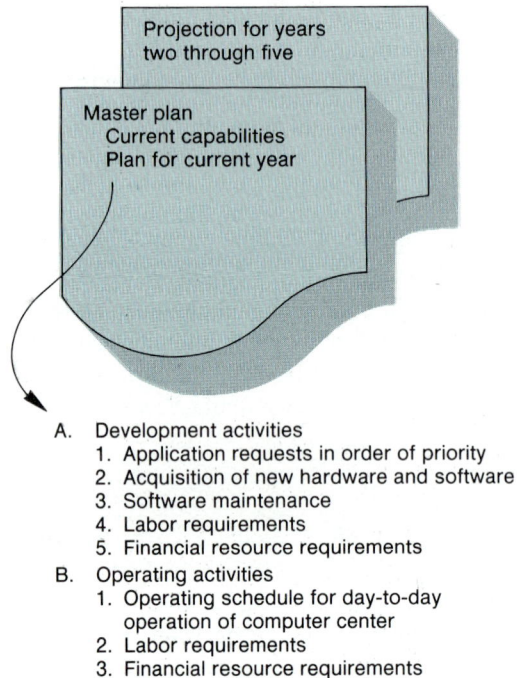

A. Development activities
    1. Application requests in order of priority
    2. Acquisition of new hardware and software
    3. Software maintenance
    4. Labor requirements
    5. Financial resource requirements
B. Operating activities
    1. Operating schedule for day-to-day
       operation of computer center
    2. Labor requirements
    3. Financial resource requirements

nificant modifications to existing applications. Once an application has been developed and is operational, it comes within the operating section of the master plan. Figure 17.5 shows the master plan and its contents.

The first step in developing a computerized cost accounting system or in modifying an existing system is to get an approved project included in the organization's master plan. The controller, or a responsible individual from that division, works with the director of information systems to develop a "proposal for application development." This is included along with other application modification and development requests in the annual update to the master plan prepared by the information systems division of the company. The revised master plan is then reviewed by a standing steering committee composed of a variety of information system users at middle and upper levels of management. This group reviews each application being requested with special emphasis on the priority by which they are to be developed. Top management ultimately reviews, modifies, and approves the master plan.

The criteria used to rank the applications in the master plan are generally based heavily on a quantitative analysis of the expected cost and benefits. Since the life of most applications extends beyond one year, the cost-benefit analysis is a capital budgeting problem, which will be discussed in detail in chapters 22 and 23. Qualitative factors, however, must also be considered. Factors such as an orderly development of the information system and effective utilization of data-processing personnel may also be relevant criteria.

Once the cost accounting application moves to the top of the priority list of applications for development, the information systems division organizes a project team to develop and implement the application. The project team is headed by a project director with one or more analysts and/or programmers, depending on the nature of the project. Also, a special steering committee is appointed from other user departments that may be

Figure 17.6   Systems development project team

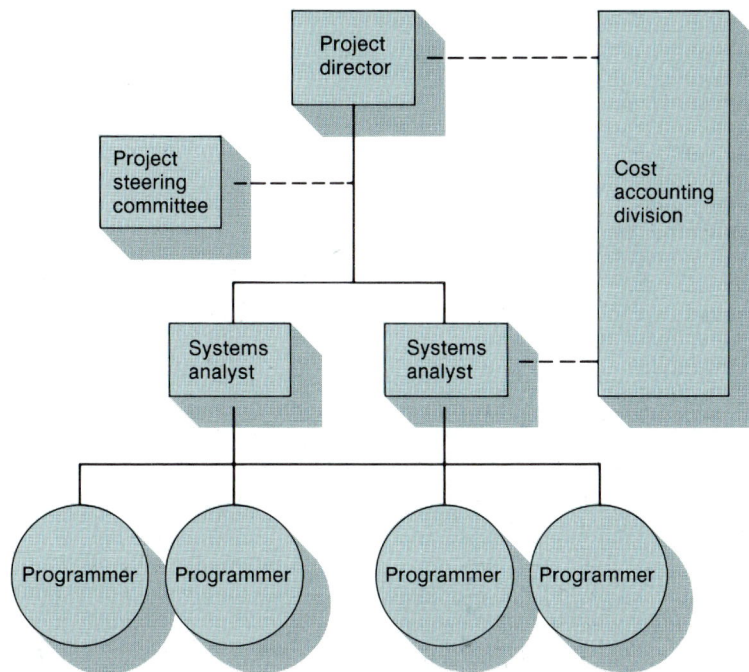

affected by the application. The objective of the committee is to provide broad-based input into the development of the application and to keep all interested departments informed of the development and implementation activities. For example, if a change is being made in the process-costing system to account for direct materials, a representative would probably be appointed to the steering committee from the financial reporting division, manufacturing division, raw materials storeroom, and perhaps from the finished-goods warehouse.

Figure 17.6 shows that the project director has supervisory responsibility over the project. Much of the preliminary investigation of the problem and the development of the application proposal may have been done by the person ultimately appointed as project director. The systems analysts develop a system to satisfy the information needs of the users. They are responsible for working with the user to identify the information desired, the decision rules that are used, and the source of input data. Flowcharts, report layouts, and input forms are some techniques used to document their work. These are used as a basis to design a system to process the inputs and provide the necessary information. Programmers receive program specifications from the systems analysts and develop instructions in the form of code to control the operation of the computer.

The primary responsibility of the cost accountant is to provide information to the systems analysts and to critically review their work. The systems analysts frequently provide the cost accountant with a copy of their flowcharts to see if they accurately reflect the existing system. They are also asked to review report layouts and input forms to see if they contain all the necessary information and if they are in a convenient format. The cost accountants can do these things if they know something about the systems analysis and design life cycle.

Figure 17.7   Systems analysis and design life cycle

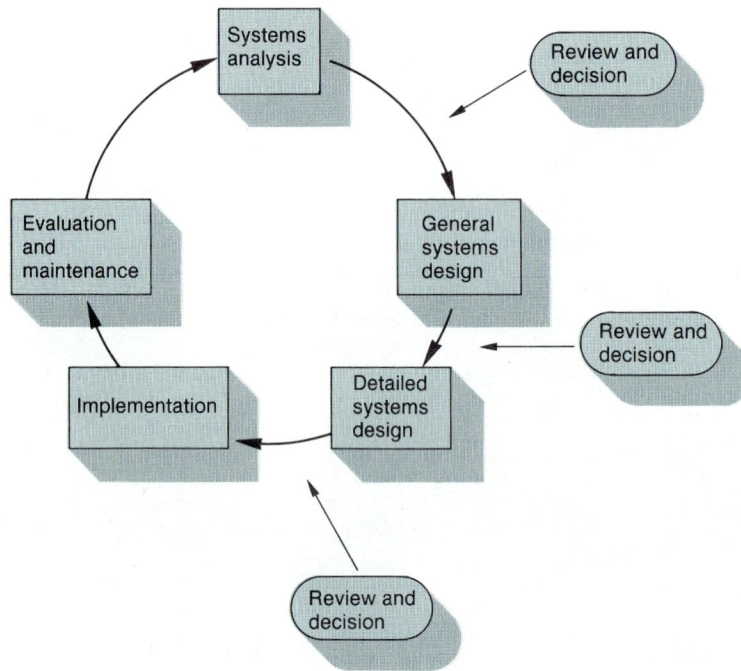

Systems Analysis and Design Life Cycle

The systems analysis and design life cycle is used to describe the activities followed in the development of an approved application. This is a multistep process that contains several review and decision points. The reviews are intended to verify that adequate progress is being made toward the desired result and that the planned system will meet the needs of the user. The steps included in the cycle are shown in figure 17.7.

Systems Analysis Phase   Generally a problem or a perceived opportunity initiates the application request. During this phase the project team must obtain a clear understanding of the problem or the opportunity and identify how the system operates. Generally this is a fact-finding process in the form of interviews, group meetings, and document analysis. The results of these activities are documented in the form of interview notes, copies of documents in use, and flowcharts.

Flowcharting is commonly used to summarize the flow of documents and information during this phase of the analysis and design life cycle. Once developed, flowcharts are useful in analyzing the strengths and weaknesses of the existing system and in structuring the new system and programs during the systems design phase.

The following are the three major types of flowcharts:

1. *Document/procedural flowcharts* show the flow and control of documents through a system and the major activities performed on them. This is the most general of all flowcharts and can be applied to both manual and computer operations.
2. *System flowcharts* show the relationship of the inputs to the various computer files and computer programs to process the data, update the files, and provide output reports. These apply only to computer processing.

3. *Program flowcharts* provide the detailed logic of individual computer programs. They illustrate the sequence followed in reading transactions, opening and closing files, mathematical computations, decisions, and loops within a program.

Flowcharting is a means of communication that uses configurations and symbols to communicate the way a system operates. Figure 17.8 shows the standard flowcharting symbols and gives a brief explanation of each one. Like other forms of communication there are some rules that must be followed. However, the form of the layout and the amount of detail included are left up to the developer. Some of the more important rules include the following:

1. The assumed flow is top-to-bottom and left-to-right. If you go contrary to the assumed flow, you *must* use directional arrows.
2. All writing except for the alternatives of a decision symbol should be contained within the symbol or in a legend at the bottom of the flowchart.
3. Multipart documents are shown by either of the following:
   a. Overlapping document symbols could be used with the total number of parts underlined in the upper left-hand corner of the top symbol. Example: A cash receipt with an original and two copies could be shown as:

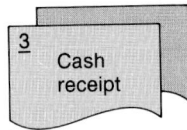

   b. Overlapping symbols, one for each copy, could be used with a sequential part number in the upper right-hand corner of each symbol. Example: The cash receipt with an original and two copies could be shown as:

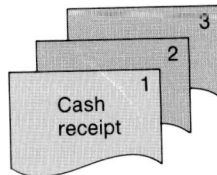

4. Multiple attached documents are shown overlapping with their identifiers on their face. Example: A packet containing the purchase requisition, purchase order, and receiving report would be shown as:

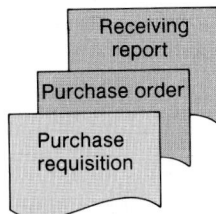

5. Each copy of every document must flow to a permanent file, a terminal symbol, or a connector symbol to another flowchart.
6. A permanent file is distinguished from a temporary file by a horizontal line across the file symbol. The order of the file contents is indicated by a letter— "A" for alphabetic, "N" for numerical, and "D" by date.

Document/procedure flowcharts are frequently developed during the systems analysis phase to help obtain a clear picture of how the current system operates. The

Figure 17.8   Standard flowcharting symbols

Process:

Represents an operation or a group of operations (for example, compute payroll taxes).

Input/Output:

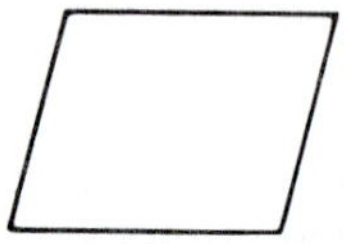

Represents the input of information into a process or the output of information from a process.

Document:

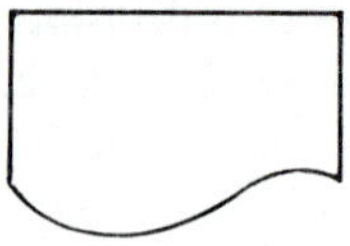

Input, output, or the transfer of information on a formal document.

Manual Operation:

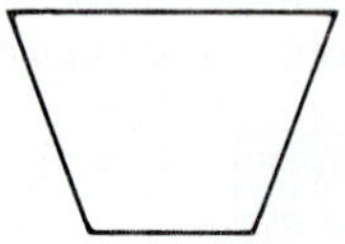

A manual process (for example, inspect invoice) or a process using equipment that operates at the speed of a human processor (for example, keypunching).

Communication Link:

Automatic transfer of information on-line from one location to another.

Flowlines:

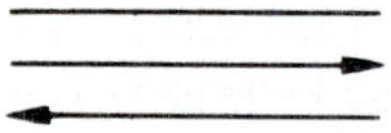

The assumed flow is top to bottom and left to right. Arrows must be included if the flow is not normal.

Annotation:

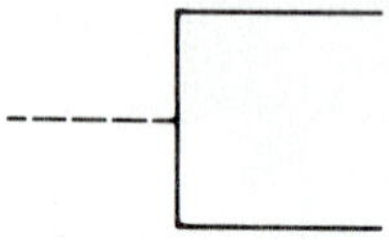

Connected to another flowchart symbol to provide additional comments for documentation.

Off-Line Storage:

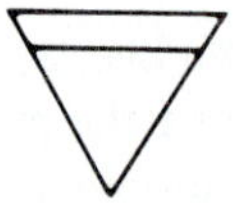

Any off-line storage not directly accessible by the computer. The type of organization is indicated by "N" for numerical, "D" for date, and "A" for alphabetic. The horizontal line through the symbol identifies it as a permanent rather than a temporary file.

Punched Tape:

Input/output using punched tape.

Magnetic Tape:

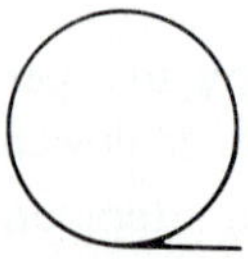

Input/output using magnetic tape.

Punched Card:

Input/output using punched cards.

Figure 17.8   *Continued*

Display:

To output information during processing on a CRT or typewriter.

On-Line Storage:

On-line storage such as disk, drum, or magnetic strip that is directly accessible by the computer.

Auxiliary Operation:

Represents a process using off-line equipment that is not limited by operator speed (for example, tape to disk converter).

Manual Input:

For input entered manually through a keyboard or console switch at the time of processing.

Decision:

Represents a decision point in a program. Depending on the relationship of the values compared, the flow of processing may go to the right, to the left, or down to the bottom.

On-Page Connector:

The flow continues on the same page where a similar symbol with the same letter is located, for example,

Off-Page Connector:

The flow continues on another page of the flowchart where a similar symbol with the same letter is located, for example,

The number 4 in the symbol on the left indicates the flow continues on page 4 of the flowchart. The symbol on the right is on page 4 and the number 2 indicates that the flow came from page 2.

Terminal:

Represents an entry or exit point for the system.

Predefined Process:

Represents a subroutine specified elsewhere.

Figure 17.9   Document/procedure flowchart for receiving report

Area of Control:

| Warehouse— Receiving Agent | Accounting—Clerk #1 | Accounting—Clerk #2 |

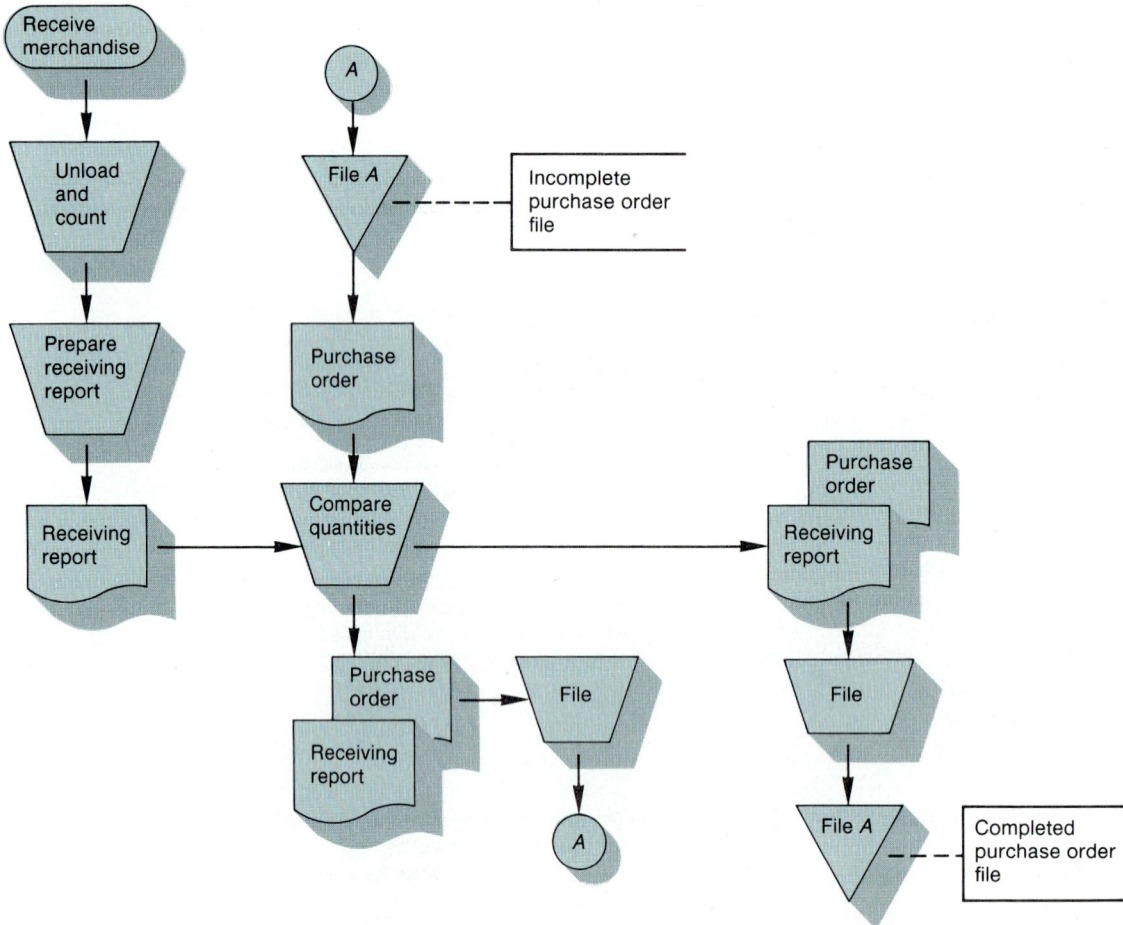

flowchart shows by functional area the flow of documents and major activities performed on them. After it has been developed the cost accountant is frequently asked to review it for accuracy and completeness. It is then used in assessing the strengths and weaknesses of the system.

Example   A receiving agent is assigned to be at the warehouse when a shipment of merchandise is scheduled to arrive. He unloads the truck, counts the merchandise, and prepares a receiving report that is sent to the accounting department. An accounting clerk pulls the purchase order and compares the quantity received with the quantity ordered. If the order is incomplete, both the receiving report and the purchase order are filed alphabetically in the purchase order file. If the order is complete, both reports are sent to a second accounting clerk where they are filed alphabetically pending receipt of the vendor's invoice. Figure 17.9 contains a document/procedure flowchart.

Figure 17.10   Systems flowchart—raw material transfers

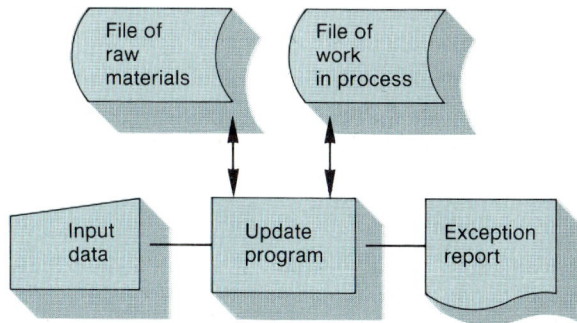

Accurately documenting the existing system is a major activity of the systems analysis phase of the project.

At the end of this phase, the facts obtained are related to the problem at hand and some tentative conclusions are reached concerning the quality of the existing system and some alternative system approaches. These activities and results are summarized in a report to the user and to the steering committee.

General Systems Design Phase   Systems design can be defined as the drawing, planning, sketching, or arranging of many separate elements into a viable, unified whole. This stage focuses on determining the most desirable alternative or problem solution identified in the last stage and on how the system is designed to meet the user's requirements. Decisions at this phase include. Should the system be centralized or decentralized? Where will the inputs originate and how will they be converted into machine readable form for processing by the computer? Where will output be made available and in what form will it be provided? Remember that the general systems design phase provides only a conceptual model of the system, much like a blueprint is a conceptual model of a house. The actual construction begins during the detailed systems design phase.

Some results of the general systems design phase are documented in the form of revised document/procedure flowcharts and the development of systems flowcharts. The development of the new system frequently results in a proposed change in the flow of documents through the system and the activities performed on them. Revised document flowcharts illustrate these changes.

Systems flowcharts are frequently used to document the computerized portion of the proposed system. They show the relationship of the inputs to the computer process that updates the files and prepares the reports or other outputs from the system.

Example   Transfers of raw materials into work in process are entered into a computer terminal by the raw materials storeroom clerk. The computer updates two on-line files—perpetual inventory of raw materials and work in process on a job-order cost system. When the balance on hand for any item in raw materials inventory falls below the reorder point, the program automatically generates an exception report identifying the need to purchase additional items and the suggested quantity. Figure 17.10 illustrates the systems flowchart.

Detailed Systems Design Phase   The development of the system takes place during the detailed systems design phase. This includes acquisition of required hardware, ac-

Figure 17.11   Purchasing hardware/software externally

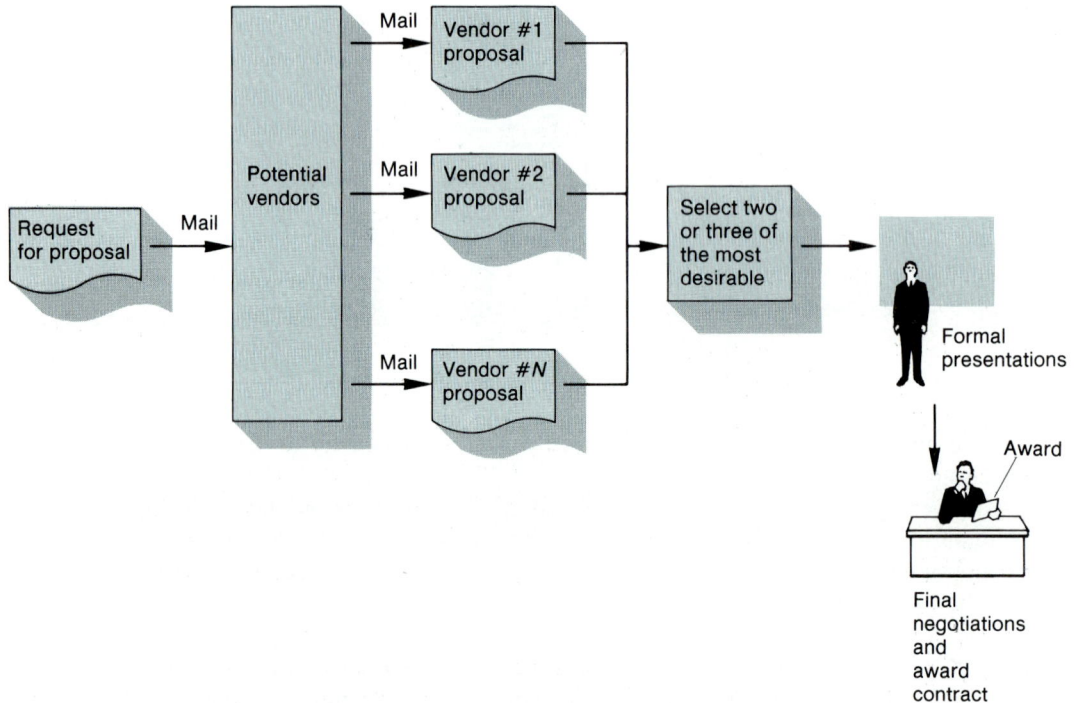

quisition or development of software, and development of support materials such as operating procedure manuals.

The decision to acquire packaged software externally or to develop it internally is a critical one. Generally, both time and cost are reduced when packaged software are purchased externally. However, in many cases, packaged software cannot be located to fit the exact needs of the organization. In these situations you must decide whether it is easier and cheaper to buy a package that comes close to fitting the organization's needs and modify it as required or to start over from scratch and develop an entirely new package. Regardless of the decision, it never hurts to shop the market to identify what is available.

Different approaches can be taken to acquire hardware and software, but the best approach is to develop a "request for proposal" (RFP) and send it to several potential vendors. Vendors who think they can satisfy the needs identified in the RFP respond in the form of a "proposal." The proposals are reviewed and analyzed to select two or three that seem to be the most attractive. These vendors are invited to make a formal presentation of their hardware and/or software as shown in figure 17.11. The most desirable vendor is selected and final negotiations are completed for the purchase.

Software that is developed internally starts with a report layout. The cost accountant should provide a great deal of input at this point to identify both the form and content of the desired information. It is critical that this be well thought out and reviewed carefully. This is so important that frequently the systems analyst will ask you to sign a document stating that you have reviewed the report layouts and that they are satisfactory for your needs. The content of the input in the system, the files, and the processing all depend upon the output desired. A subsequent change in the report layout, as minor as it may seem, may require substantial rework in the design of input forms, file layouts, and program code.

Occasionally the accountant is asked to review portions of the program logic to verify that the programmer has the correct concept in mind. A program flowchart shows the detailed logic to be followed within the program. Program flowcharts tie into the system flowcharts by identifying the logic followed by the computer in the process symbol of the system flowchart.

Example Suppose in the previous example we wanted to build a control in the computer update program to print out a message to the raw materials storeroom clerk when the quantity requisitioned for any job exceeds the standard. Figure 17.12 shows this part of the program flowchart.

Operating procedures manuals must also be developed during the detailed systems design phase. The operating procedures manuals describe in detail the procedures that must be followed in order to input data into the system and to get reports from it. These manuals are extremely important for training employees during the implementation phase and for training new employees during the on-going operation of the system. Access to the operating procedures manual should be controlled and only authorized personnel should have access to them. Otherwise, unauthorized personnel could get access to sensitive information and manipulate the accounting records to defraud the company merely by a careful reading of an uncontrolled operating procedures manual.

Review and Decision Points The users and the steering committees can review the results of each of the three development stages discussed above before proceeding to the next phase. The type of review is essentially the same. However, each succeeding review can be more detailed than the one before as more information is gathered about the requirements of the system and the expected benefits.

The reviews provide a checkpoint on documentation and on the feasibility of the system. Documentation consists of forms, records, worksheets, flowcharts, and other documents that describe the procedures followed in developing the system and the procedures to be followed in operating the system. Documenting the system should occur throughout the analysis and design life cycle. Systems analysts and programmers should provide complete documentation of the work that is performed, the results accomplished, and the systems that are developed. Documentation provides some assurance that the system has been carefully designed.

It is extremely important to have good documentation when attempting to modify an existing system. Without good documentation, a simple modification can be almost as costly as developing an entirely new system. A user should follow up on documentation to make sure it is complete and accurate.

A feasibility analysis is performed to verify that the new system will measure up to expectations. The measures of feasibility and the type of analysis performed are summarized below:

1. Economic Feasibility. Are the expected benefits from the new system worth the costs required to design, implement, and operate it? This is a cost-benefit analysis that involves the use of capital budgeting techniques that will be discussed in chapters 22 and 23.
2. Technical Feasibility. Do we have the technical capability (hardware and personnel) to carry out the project? If not, can we obtain the required technical capability within the cost constraints outlined above?
3. Operational Feasibility. Will the system be used by the people for whom it is intended?

Figure 17.12   Program flowchart—inventory update

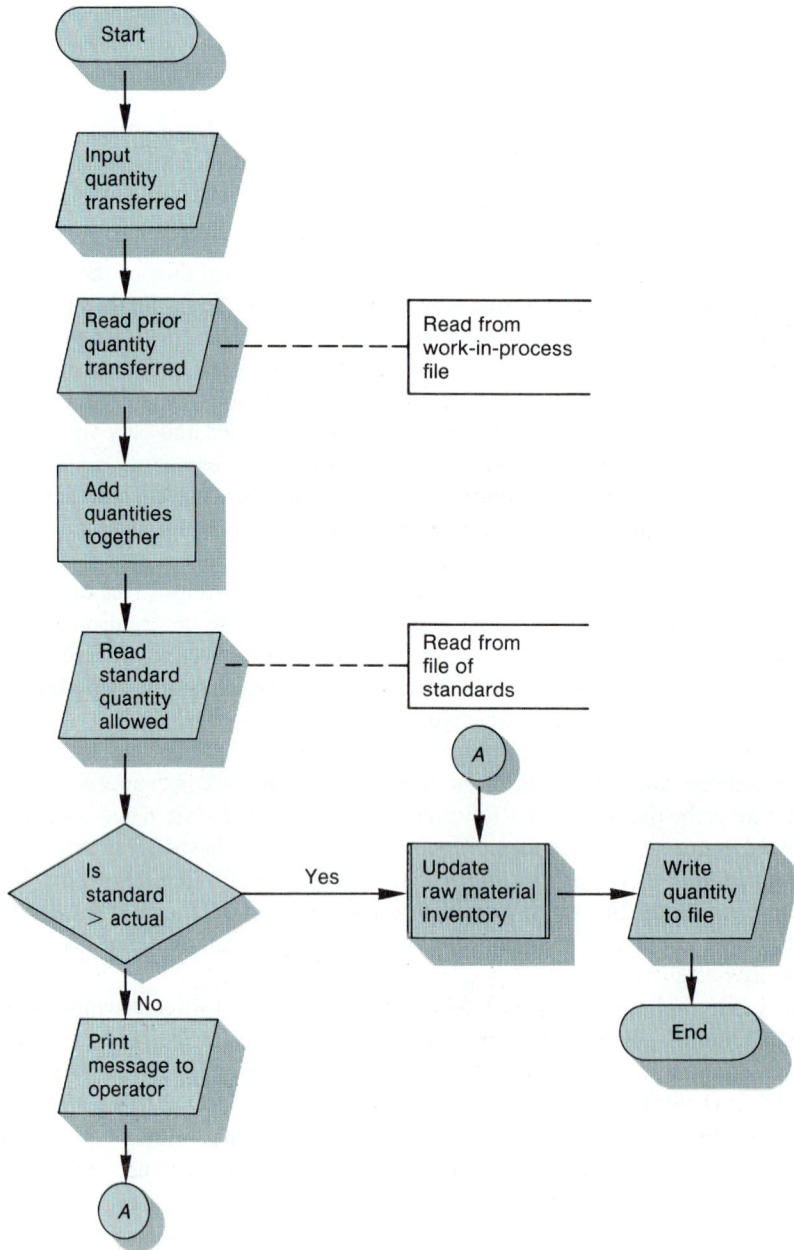

```
                    ┌──────────┐
                    (  Start   )
                    └────┬─────┘
                         ↓
                  ╱─────────────╱
                 ╱  Input       ╱
                 ╱  quantity    ╱
                 ╱  transferred ╱
                ╱──────┬───────╱
                       ↓
              ╱─────────────╱          ┌──────────────┐
             ╱  Read prior  ╱ ─ ─ ─ ─  │ Read from    │
             ╱  quantity    ╱          │ work-in-     │
             ╱  transferred ╱          │ process file │
            ╱──────┬───────╱           └──────────────┘
                   ↓
            ┌─────────────┐
            │  Add        │
            │  quantities │
            │  together   │
            └──────┬──────┘
                   ↓
            ╱─────────────╱            ┌──────────────┐
           ╱  Read        ╱ ─ ─ ─ ─ ─  │ Read from    │
           ╱  standard    ╱            │ file of      │
           ╱  quantity    ╱            │ standards    │
           ╱  allowed     ╱            └──────────────┘
          ╱──────┬───────╱
                 ↓                              ( A )
            ◇──────────◇    Yes                   ↓
           ◇  Is        ◇ ─────────→  ┌──────────────┐   ╱─────────╱
           ◇  standard   ◇            │ Update       │  ╱  Write   ╱
           ◇  > actual   ◇            │ raw material │─╱  quantity ╱
            ◇──────────◇             │ inventory    │ ╱  to file  ╱
                 │ No                └──────────────┘╱─────┬─────╱
                 ↓                                         ↓
          ╱─────────────╱                            ┌─────────┐
         ╱  Print       ╱                            (   End   )
         ╱  message to  ╱                            └─────────┘
         ╱  operator    ╱
        ╱──────┬───────╱
               ↓
             ( A )
```

4. Legal Feasibility. Are there conflicts between the proposed system and the organization's legal obligations?

5. Scheduling Feasibility. Can the project be implemented by the required date?

A negative response to any of these measures at any of the review and decision points can terminate the project. The most detailed feasibility analysis is done just before implementation. The decision to implement is the final decision and once implementation begins it is very difficult to turn back without significant disruption to organizational stability.

Implementation   Implementation of the new system involves conversion from the existing system to the new system. The people whose jobs will be affected by the new system must be retrained. New hardware and software are installed and existing files are converted to the format required by the new system. A system test is generally performed just before formally adopting the new system. The system test requires the newly trained people who will be using the system to enter and process fictitious data (called test data) through the system. Accurate results and smooth processing of the system test indicates that the system is ready for formal implementation. Frequently, both the old system and the new system are operated for a short period of time in what is called *parallel processing*. Parallel processing provides a check on the accuracy of the new system and provides a back-up system in case the new system fails. At some point, however, the use of the old system must be discontinued.

Evaluation and Maintenance   After the system has been implemented and allowed to operate for a short period of time, it should be evaluated to see if the anticipated benefits have in fact been achieved. This includes not only a check on the realization of cost savings or increased revenue, but also a check on the adequacy of the information for the user's needs.

Program maintenance refers to the program modifications required to keep the system current. Some values, such as the manufacturing overhead rate, may have been included in the computer programs as a constant. As the overhead rate changes from year to year, the programs must be modified for that change. Changes in input and file content are other factors that require program modifications.

Behavioral Considerations

Behavioral problems frequently occur during the analysis, design, and implementation of a computerized cost accounting system. The primary cause for the behavioral problems is resistance to change. Occasionally someone will lose their job when a new system is implemented. But most people who desire to remain with the company can do so as long as they are willing to be retrained for employment within the new system or in some other part of the organization. Aggression, avoidance, and projection are behavioral problems commonly encountered.

Aggression is defined as an attack intended to beat or destroy the system. This type of behavior is commonly exhibited by manufacturing personnel who are required to enter input data into the system. For example, direct laborers may be required by the new system to input the job number and the time they start and stop working on the job into a computer terminal located on the manufacturing floor. Aggressive behavior is exhibited when the terminal is mysteriously run over by a forklift truck or when honey is poured between the keys on the keyboard.

Projection is blaming the new system for causing difficulties that are in fact caused by something else. This type of behavior is commonly exhibited by people who work with the system. A comment like, "The system doesn't give me the information I need when I need it," may be a problem with the system. But more likely the problem is that the individual has not learned where to look on the report to get the information needed.

Avoidance is when a person withdraws from the system development activities or does not use the new system. People who have had little or no experience with the computer generally avoid becoming involved. This frequently happens to accountants and management at middle and upper levels. For example, a controller who does not understand computer processing might say to the director of information system, "You go ahead and computerize our accounting records but don't bother me. Just make sure the data is 100% accurate and the reports look about like the ones we have now." Or a vice-president with a terminal on his desk that can help him in a dozen ways to do his job better might say, "I'm not going to use this thing because typing is a waste of my time." What he is really saying is, "I don't know how to use this thing and if I try and make a mistake, I'll be embarrassed."

These behavioral problems are occasionally exhibited during the analysis and design phases, but most frequently they are exhibited during the implementation phase. By this time, however, it is generally too late to avoid them. Most activities that eliminate or reduce behavioral problems must be taken during the analysis and design phases. These include participation, planning, communication, retraining, and system testing.

Participation is one of the most effective techniques to avoid behavioral problems. Those who will be affected by the system should be allowed to participate in its development. There are several benefits that participation provides to the design and implementation of a system. Many of these are the same benefits that result from allowing people to participate in developing the budget.

1. Participation is ego-enhancing and builds self-esteem, which results in more favorable attitudes.
2. Participation can be challenging and intrinsically satisfying, leading to positive attitudes.
3. Users who participate in developing the system are more knowledgeable about the technical aspects of the change and are better trained to use it.
4. Participation usually results in more commitment to the change, which insures that the new system will be used.
5. The new system is usually better because user participants know more about the old system and the needs of the new system than the information systems personnel.

The steering committee that was discussed earlier is important in making sure that the system is well planned and well communicated to those affected by it. Open communication establishes a feeling of trust between the users and designers of the system.

Retraining and system testing are part of the activities performed during implementation of the system. It is extremely important that employees are well trained and that the system is well tested before implementation. If the system is implemented without these things being accomplished, the system will probably fail, and it will be much more difficult to get people to use the system a second time. Even if the new system is completely free of errors and the people know exactly how to use it, they will still resist using it because of the bad experience they had earlier.

Most behavioral problems associated with system changes can be either minimized or avoided. Proper planning, good communication, participation, and following the other steps outlined in the analysis and design life cycle avoid most of the behavioral problems.

COST ACCOUNTING SYSTEM CONTROLS

Federal law requires companies that are subject to the Securities Act of 1934 to have an adequate system of controls. They are required to execute transactions in accordance with management's instructions, maintain accountability for assets, allow access to assets by only authorized personnel, and compare actual assets with recorded assets at reasonable intervals and take appropriate action with respect to any differences.

The concept of controls is the same regardless of the method used to process the data. In general, an internal control system is a series of checks and balances to verify that things are as they should be. This includes a variety of activities such as the following:

1. There should be separation of duties and responsibilities so that the work of one individual is checked by the work of another individual.

2. Production and work standards should identify the amount of expected output. Standard output is compared to actual output and management follows up on significant variances.
3. Physical counts of inventories at periodic intervals identify actual quantities on hand that can be compared with recorded quantities.
4. Responsibility accounting systems identify the individual with the greatest ability to control an item. Accounting records and reports are developed to show each individual's area of responsibility and the results of their activities.

The types of checks and balances that are built into a computerized accounting system are different than some of those used in a manual accounting system. For example, one small computer can do the work of several individuals. Therefore, there is not as much separation of duties and responsibilities in a computerized system as in a manual system. Also, people can be relied upon to ask questions or get clarification on transactions that do not look reasonable. The computer does not have that capability unless it has been specifically included as an input, output, or program control.

Our objective in this section is to identify the controls that are relevant to a computerized cost accounting system. These are administrative controls, input controls, processing controls, and output controls. The purpose of having these controls is to reduce unidentified errors and to reduce the probability of fraud.

Administrative Controls

Administrative controls are concerned with getting the right people into the right jobs initially and with managing them effectively during their employment with the firm.

When hiring an employee for a cost accounting position, it is extremely important that the individual is honest and ethical and is technically qualified for the job. Individuals who have access to the company's assets or to the accounting records are in the best position to defraud the company. A high standard of personal integrity is a major factor in determining honesty. Significant progress has been made recently in developing test instruments that can be used as part of the employment screening process to measure personal integrity. Feedback on past job performance and character references should also be obtained to evaluate personal integrity. There is always the chance, however, that if financial pressures become so great or if the opportunity to defraud the company seems so easy an otherwise honest individual will perform a dishonest act. For these reasons it is always wise to bond employees who are in sensitive accounting positions.

Formal training programs should be a normal part of an employee's work. It is extremely important that new employees are properly trained in their job responsibilities. During an in-house training program the new employee is taught the company's way of doing things. Over time, significant changes continue to occur in generally accepted accounting principles and new techniques are constantly being developed to assist management in the decision functions of the business. The cost accountant must keep current with these changes in order to continue to be a valuable contributor to the organization.

Technical capability is usually assessed by college degrees and by obtaining feedback on performance from previous jobs. Qualifying oneself to receive a Certificate in Management Accounting (CMA) or as a Certified Public Accountant (CPA) is also evidence of technical capability. To date, companies have not typically required a CMA or CPA as minimum qualifications for a cost accounting position. However, it is expected that the CMA will become as important to cost/managerial accounting as the CPA is to public accounting. Any individual who is seriously considering cost accounting as a career path should pursue the CMA.

Personnel administration deals with effectively managing an individual once employed with the firm. This includes adequate separation of duties and responsibilities, rotation of personnel, mandatory vacations, standard operating procedures, performance evaluations, and termination and exit interviews.

Separation of Duties and Responsibilities   The cost accountant must make sure that people who have access to the assets of the company do not also have access to the accounting records. If they do, there needs to be some system to verify that all assets have been used for legitimate company purposes.

Example   Under the old manual accounting system Short Company had a group of cost accountants maintain a perpetual inventory of the raw materials storeroom. Materials were issued only upon a written requisition from the production supervisor. The requisition was prepared in triplicate. The production supervisor kept one copy, sent another copy to the cost accountants, and the original went to the raw materials storeroom clerk. After the requisition was filled, the clerk sent the original copy to the cost accountants. They matched the original with the copy received from the production supervisor and made the entry to update the accounting records.

When Short Company computerized the cost accounting system, it was decided to eliminate several cost accountants by having the raw material storeroom clerk enter the items issued into a computer terminal, which automatically updated the inventory records. The clerk soon found that he could take inventory for personal use (and sell it on the black market). To cover up the theft he made an entry into the system to reduce inventory and charge indirect material. That way his stock of raw materials was always in balance with the perpetual inventory. The result of the fraud did not show up until the end of the year. Then it showed up as an unabsorbed overhead item that no one could easily trace back to the storeroom clerk. No investigation was initiated the first year because it was considered abnormal. After two years and a time-consuming investigation the problem was identified. Before the investigation was complete, however, the clerk had quit his job and left the country.

The problem was resolved by not allowing the new storeroom clerk to input changes to the inventory records. His terminal was changed so that it would only provide output in the form of inventory balances on hand. All input was keyed into the system by a keypunch clerk in the data-processing division. Requisition forms prepared by the manufacturing supervisor and filled by the storeroom clerk were used as a basis for the input.

Rotation of Personnel   Most computer frauds require an individual to be in a partic-ular position for an extended period of time in order to take advantage of the system. First the employee must learn the system and all the controls thoroughly in order to identify a weakness in it. The person then uses his/her position to take advantage of the system's weakness and defraud the company.

Many frauds are like an invisible window into the system that no one can see except the person who built it. The system may pass large amounts of assets through the window over an extended period of time. Rotation of personnel at periodic intervals will discourage fraudulent schemes from being developed initially and will terminate most of those that have been developed.

Note that this control, as with most controls, is not without a cost to administer. Employees must be retrained each time they are moved to a new job and they will be less productive initially because they are at the low point of their learning curve.

Mandatory Vacations   Since most computer frauds require the person to perform a specific activity at a regular time interval, most frauds can be uncovered if the person is absent for an extended period of time, such as two weeks. It is important that the indi-vidual be physically absent from work for the entire vacation period and that problems associated with his/her job are handled by someone else. Most computer frauds are discovered by someone else investigating a problem situation. If the problems are accumulated until the individual returns from vacation, then the fraud can be perpetuated by the way the problem is handled.

Example   A $21.3 million dollar bank fraud against Wells Fargo Bank was perpetuated by an operations officer for more than two years, even though the bank had a mandatory two-week vacation requirement. Each Friday afternoon of the vacation period the officer would slip into the office under some guise and in ten minutes would complete the necessary paperwork to perpetuate the fraud. If he had not been allowed into the office, the fraud would have been detected the following week.

Standard Operating Procedures   Standard operating procedures outline in detail the steps to be followed in performing a job. Standardization of jobs helps to insure that every job is performed completely and accurately and that the work of many people is coordinated. It provides a standard that others can rely on and that can be used as a basis for performance evaluations.

Performance Evaluations   The primary objective of a performance evaluation is to provide feedback and reward incentives to help individuals perform their jobs well and accomplish the goals of the organization.

The performance of each individual on the cost accounting staff should be evaluated periodically. The evaluation should be based, as much as possible, on quantitative data, such as timeliness and accuracy of reports, quantity of output, and the amount of money and time required to complete a task. Subjective evaluations should be given to other areas that are important to the job, such as the ability to delegate and supervise, the ability to cope with unexpected obstacles, the effectiveness of oral and written communications, poise, appearance, and maturity.

Terminations and Exit Interviews   Terminating an individual is never a pleasant task, but the procedures followed in terminating someone who has access to accounting records maintained on the computer is very important. Occasionally, individuals will feel that they have received the short end of the deal and will do something drastic to "get even" with the company.

Example   A computer operator was informed that her services would not be needed any longer and that the company was giving her the two-week notice required by their employment contract. During her last two weeks on the job she systematically erased all the accounting files of the company, including back-up copies. The company had to spend much time and money to reconstruct their files.

Generally, an individual should not have access to the computer, accounting programs, or files after they have been given their termination notice. They should clean out their desk in the presence of a security guard and be asked to leave the premises. The company should not expect any benefit from the required severance pay.

Exit interviews should be held with anyone who voluntarily terminates employment with the company. It creates goodwill with the individual, verifies that all manuals and other materials belonging to the company are left with the company and frequently uncovers problems with the job or company in general.

Input Controls

Input controls are designed to verify that the input into the computer process is complete and accurate. We want to verify that all the required input is present, that no additional data has been added, and that the data has been accurately converted into machine-readable form for processing by the computer.

As a general rule, all data should originate outside the data-processing center. For example, a computer operator should never be able to originate and input a transaction into the system. Cost accounting personnel in the various operating departments should identify the data to be processed, accumulate it, and submit it to the data-processing division to be processed. The form of submission may be batch or on-line, depending on the processing mode used by the company.

Input controls are among the most important because subsequent controls generally cannot detect inaccurate input.

Example   Bill was a very conscientious employee in the manufacturing division of a company. As a reward for his efforts he was promoted to the cost accounting staff and changed from a waged employee to a salaried employee. One of Bill's responsibilities as a salaried employee was to prepare the payroll summary for all waged employees in that division. The summary showed each employee's name, number, and hours worked.

Each pay period Bill prepared the payroll list and gave it to the manufacturing supervisor for his review and signature on the bottom of the last page. Bill's job then required him to take the form to the data-processing department in which the data was entered into the computer. Before Bill submitted it, however, he added his name and a normal number of hours on the bottom of the list of waged employees.

The computer performed all the extensions, maintained the files, prepared the checks, and mailed them directly to the employees. Thus Bill was paid twice—once as a waged employee and once as a salaried employee. The computer programs were not designed to compare salaried and waged employees to verify that an individual was not being paid as both. Adequate input controls should have prevented this.

Some of the most important input controls include control totals, capturing data in machine-readable form, and approval of input data in the originating department.

Control Totals   A control total identifies the total amount of input to be processed. The control total may be one of several types:

1. Financial control total is the total dollar amount of the input, such as the total payroll for the period.
2. Hash control total is the total of some numbers that are not a normal part of the processing. A total of the employees' numbers is an example.
3. Record count control total is the total number of input transactions or records to be processed. If a record count on the number of employees to be paid in the example above had been developed and checked by the supervisor, Bill would not have been able to insert his fraudulent data.

The control totals are used frequently during the processing of the data to verify that all data is present and processed. For example, as the computer prepares checks in a payroll run, the number of checks prepared can be counted as a control total and compared with the number of employees authorized to be paid by the department supervisor. A control clerk who receives the output from the computer can compare the control totals before sending the checks to the employees.

Capture Data in Machine-Readable Form   Data should be collected in machine-readable form whenever possible to reduce processing errors. Each human process increases the probability of error and allows fraudulent data to be inserted. Turnaround documents capture the output of one process in machine-readable form that can be used as input for a subsequent process. Turnaround documents should be used whenever possible.

Originating Department Approval   The originating department should code, review, and approve all input transactions. Also, sensitive documents such as checks, purchase orders, and requisition forms should be prenumbered and controlled.

Processing Controls

Processing controls is a broad category that includes all controls connected with the processing of data by the computer. It includes built-in hardware controls, operating system controls, file reconstruction capability, and controls to prevent or detect computer operator errors. In addition, it includes programmed controls to check the reasonableness of the data and the accuracy of the processing in much the same way as a person would do when processing the data manually. Based on previous experience and a knowledge of the process, a person can look at the amount of a transaction and see if it is within normal limits. They also develop techniques to check out the computations for accuracy, and they can look at the results to see if they are reasonable.

Checkpoints, called edit checks, need to be built into the computer programs so the computer can perform the same kinds of tests that a person would perform. It is primarily the responsibility of the cost accountant to identify the computer tests that should be included in the programs and see that they are included by the systems analysts and programmers. Remember that the analysts and programmers know a lot about computers, data processing, and programming, but they are not cost accountants and do not understand cost accounting systems. Major problems generally occur when the cost accountant does not work closely with the analysts and programmers in developing their system.

Example   A relatively new manufacturing company was rather pleased with their pre-audit net income of $1 million. Their joy turned to disappointment, however, when the auditors required a physical count of their raw materials inventory and a $2 million shortage was identified. The $1 million profit went to a $1 million loss with one adjusting entry. The cause of the discrepancy was an error in the program to account for the raw materials inventory. The inventory was increased for items shown on the purchase orders rather than for items shown on the receiving reports. Items that were ordered but never received and items on back order were never taken out of the inventory balance. This error had also caused numerous disruptions to the manufacturing process due to out-of-stock items, but they never could identify the cause until the audit and a thorough investigation. The perpetual inventory system showed an item in stock, but it could not be located when requisitioned for a production run. The production run would have to be delayed while the item was ordered from the supplier.

Some of the most common program controls include limit and reasonableness test, crossfooting, and control totals.

Limit and Reasonableness Test   A computer program can be written to compare the input amounts with predefined limits. As long as the input amount is within the limits it is processed normally. Input that exceeds the defined limits must be processed on an exception basis. Tests can also be performed on the output to see if it is reasonable in relation to the process or activity being performed. Output that is not reasonable is highlighted for further investigation.

Example   Young Company is a manufacturing organization that uses a job-order cost system. Experience shows that 95% of the jobs take between 50 and 90 direct-labor hours to complete. These amounts could be used as a limit test on the amount of direct labor charged to the job. Experience also shows that the total cost of the job is between 300% and 350% of the total direct-labor cost. These amounts could be used as reasonableness checks on the total job cost.

Crossfooting   Footing is the process of totaling a column of numbers. Crossfooting is the process of comparing several column totals to verify that they are in balance. For example, several material and labor charges are typically posted to each job in a job-order cost system. Totaling the material charges, direct-labor charges, and overhead charges is footing. Combining these amounts and comparing the total to a running balance of the total job cost is a process of crossfooting. As long as these amounts are equal the computer does nothing. The computer should be instructed to print out an error message whenever the crossfooting does not balance so that the mistake can be identified and corrected.

Control Totals   The same type of control totals that are developed by the department preparing the input should also be prepared by the computer programs. Output from the computer process should include the control totals developed by the computer program. For example, if the computer is preparing the payroll checks for the manufacturing division of a company, the computer could count the number of checks prepared as a record count control total and the total amount of all checks prepared as a financial control total.

Output Controls

Output controls are designed to assure that the output is complete, that no errors were identified by the computer during processing. The person who has the responsibility of output controls is the control clerk or a member of the control group because he or she usually receives the output. As a general rule, the output should not be given back to the person who prepared the input. That would allow the individual to cover up mistakes or hide fraudulent entries before the output is distributed to other users.

The control clerk or control group reconciles the control totals prepared by the inputting department with those prepared by the computer. They must follow up on any discrepancies between the control totals. They also have the responsibility to follow up on errors identified by the computer in processing the data. Each computer run should have an error report listing the transactions it was unable to process. The control clerk must identify the source and cause of the error and get a correcting entry into the computer system.

The output from the computer system frequently contains sensitive information. The control clerk should control the dissemination of documents and information to only authorized personnel.

Summary

Changes in computer technology have made the cost of data processing so cheap that most companies are computerizing their information systems. An integrated information system provides many benefits to the organization including less redundancy in the data files and more accurate, uniform, and timely information in all functional areas. The cost accounting portion of the system supports other functional areas and draws from the data that they collect.

The cost accountant plays a key role during the analysis and design of the information system. Systems analysts and programmers frequently look to the controller when identifying the types of decisions that are made, the information needed to make those decisions, and the operation of the existing systems. The controller also provides valuable input in identifying the types of controls that need to be built into the system.

Behavioral considerations are important in determining the long-term success of a systems project. Regardless of how good the information system is, it will fail if it does not have the support of those whom it is intended to serve. Participation in the development of the system is one of the most effective techniques to avoid behavioral problems. Effective communication between the designers and potential users during the development process is also very important.

Self-Study Problem (CMA)

Business organizations are required to modify or replace a portion or all of their financial information system in order to keep pace with their growth and to take advantage of improved information technology. The process involved in modifying or replacing an information system, especially if computer equipment is involved, requires a substantial commitment of time and resources. When an organization undertakes a change in its information system, a series of steps or phases is taken. The steps or phases included in a systems study include the following:

1. Survey of the existing system
2. Analysis of information collected in the survey and development of recommendations for corrective action
3. Design of a new or modified system
4. Equipment study and acquisition
5. Implementation of a new or modified system

These steps or phases tend to overlap rather than being separate and distinct. In addition, the effort required in each step or phase varies from one system to another depending upon such factors as the extent of the changes or the need for different equipment.

Required

1. Explain the purpose and reasons for surveying an organization's existing system during a systems study.
2. Identify and explain the general activities and techniques that are commonly used during the systems survey and analysis phases of a systems study conducted for a financial information system.
3. The systems survey and analysis phases of a financial information systems study are often carried out by a project team composed of a systems analyst, a management accountant, and other persons in the company who would be knowledgeable and helpful in the systems study. What would be the role of the management accountant in these phases of a financial information systems study?

Solution to the Self-Study Problem

1. The *purposes* for surveying an organization's existing system during a systems study include the following:
   a. To determine how the existing system functions and how the work is accomplished
   b. To determine the feasibility of redesigning and converting the existing system to new hardware
   c. To determine the constraints of the current system

   The *reasons* for surveying an organization's existing system during a systems study include the following:
   a. To assess the effectiveness and weaknesses of the existing system
   b. To gain an understanding of the existing system that provides benefits later during any revision or redesign
   c. To provide a source for design ideas and identify the resources that are available

2. The general activities and techniques that are commonly used during the systems survey and analysis phases of a systems study include the following:
   a. Study and review the existing organization structure to determine how it functions
   b. Review and collect internal documents and reports to determine design, content, use, frequency of preparation, and so forth
   c. Develop and use questionnaire forms to determine processing frequencies, input/output volumes, and other information useful to the systems study
   d. Conduct personal interviews with operating personnel to confirm and expand upon data gathered from the questionnaire
   e. Develop flowcharts for both the system and documents

3. The systems survey and analysis phases of a financial information systems study would probably be dominated by the systems people. However, the management accountant would be of assistance in assessing management's needs for required reports and their format. The management accountant could also provide information about the following aspects of the system:
   a. The source documents in use
   b. The relevance, reliability, and timeliness of input/output data
   c. The internal controls that exist and that should be incorporated into any new or redesigned system

Suggested Readings

Cushing, Barry E. *Accounting Information Systems and Business Organizations*. Reading, Mass.: Addison-Wesley Publishing Company, 1982.

Moscove, Stephen A., and Simkin, Mark G. *Accounting Information Systems*. New York: John Wiley & Sons, 1981.

Page, John, and Hooper, Paul. *Accounting and Information Systems*. Reston, Va.: Reston Publishing Company, 1982.

Sollenberger, Harold M. "Major Changes Caused by the Implementation of a Management Information System." NAA Research Monograph #5. New York: National Association of Accountants, 1969.

Wilkinson, Joseph W. *Accounting and Information Systems*. New York: John Wiley & Sons, 1982.

Discussion Questions

1. What is the difference between a management information system and an accounting information system?
2. What is meant by a fully integrated management information system?
3. Identify the major benefits and problems associated with a fully integrated information system.
4. What impact does the Foreign Corrupt Practices Act have on the development of a cost accounting system?
5. Describe the value of additional information. If the additional information does not change the decision, does it have any value?
6. What is the information system master plan? Why is the master plan important when developing an accounting information system?
7. What is the primary objective of the systems analysis phase of the systems analysis and design life cycle?
8. Distinguish between program flowcharts, systems flowcharts, and document/procedure flowcharts.
9. In which phase of the systems analysis and design life cycle is the conceptual model of the system developed?
10. What does RFP stand for and why is it used?
11. Why are the output reports the first items to be developed for any particular application?
12. What is meant by feasibility analysis and why is it used? What are the most common measures of feasibility?
13. What is parallel processing and in which phase of the systems analysis and design life cycle is it used?
14. What are the most common behavioral problems encountered during the computerization of a cost accounting system?
15. Why is it important for the controller to be involved in identifying the controls that should be built into the cost accounting system?
16. What types of control totals can be developed? Are control totals an input control, output control, or processing control? Explain.
17. What is a limit and reasonableness test? Is it used as an input control, output control, or processing control? Explain.

Exercises

Exercise 17.1   General Concepts of Information Systems (CMA)

Select the best answer for each of the multiple choice questions that follow.

1. Which of the following is *not* a general objective of all information systems?
   a. A system should provide information that is timely and relevant for decision making by management and operating personnel.
   b. The output of a system should be highly accurate.
   c. A system should have sufficient capacity to accommodate levels of normal activity; any additional capacity proves too costly in the long run.
   d. A system should be as simple as permitted so that its structure and operation can be easily understood and its procedures easily accomplished.
   e. A system should be flexible to accommodate changes of reasonable magnitude when required.

2. When designing a computer-based information system, the initial step in the systems design process is to determine the
   a. required output.
   b. source documents that serve as the basis for input.
   c. processing required.
   d. decisions for which data will be required.
   e. file information required during processing.

3. The most important factor in planning for a major change in a computer-based system is
   a. the organization of the systems department.
   b. the ability of the systems programmers to write appropriate software.
   c. the selection of the most advanced computer equipment.
   d. giving the systems people a free hand in all changes.
   e. the participation of top management in the planning process.

4. A systems survey is the process of obtaining an accurate perspective on the existing system in order to identify weaknesses that can be corrected in the new system. Which one of the following steps is *not* considered part of this system survey?
   a. Interviews are conducted with operating people and managers.
   b. The complete documentation of the system is obtained and reviewed.
   c. Measures of processing volume are obtained for each operation.
   d. Equipment sold by various computer manufacturers is reviewed in terms of capability, cost, and availability.
   e. Work measurement studies are conducted to determine the time required to complete various tasks or jobs.

5. In conducting a feasibility study, technical feasibility refers to whether
   a. a proposed system is attainable, given the existing technology.
   b. the systems' manager can coordinate and control the activities of the systems department.
   c. an adequate computer site exists for the proposed system.
   d. the proposed system will produce economic benefits that will exceed its costs.
   e. the system will be effectively used within the operating environment of an organization.

6. In conducting a feasibility study, operational feasibility refers to whether
   a. a proposed system is attainable, given the existing technology.
   b. a system's manager can coordinate and control the activities of the systems department.
   c. an adequate computer site exists for the proposed system.
   d. the proposed system will produce economic benefits that will exceed its costs.
   e. the system will be used effectively within the operating environment of an organization.

7. Complete documentation is important for efficient operation and control of an electronic data-processing system. Which of the following is *not* a benefit of good documentation?
   a. Documentation provides various types of batch or control totals that are used to indicate a loss of records or an error in processing.
   b. Documentation simplifies the program maintenance function.
   c. Documentation facilitates communication among system users, analysts, and programmers during systems development.

    d. Documentation facilitates regular progress reviews of systems development work.

    e. Documentation provides a referral and training tool for system users, operators, and new systems employees.

8. In the life cycle of systems development and implementation, the optimal timing for completing the documentation of a computer-based system would be

    a. after the entire systems project is completed but before the post audit is conducted.

    b. after the post-audit phase of the systems project is completed.

    c. in time for the go or no-go decision phase of the systems planning committee.

    d. before starting the programming phase.

    e. as each phase of the systems life cycle is completed.

9. Which one of the following is the most widely used device for documenting electronic data-processing systems?

    a. Decision tables

    b. Systems flowcharts

    c. Automated flowcharts generated from software

    d. Hierarchy charts

    e. Gantt charts

10. A document flowchart represents

    a. the sequence of logical operations performed during the execution of a computer program.

    b. the possible combinations of alternative logic conditions and corresponding courses of action for each condition in a computer program.

    c. the flow of data through a series of operations in an automated data-processing system.

    d. the flow of forms relating to a particular transaction through an organization.

    e. the manual of all program flowcharts for an entire systems application.

Exercise 17.2 Data-Processing Controls (CMA)

Select the best answer for each of the multiple choice questions that follow.

1. Management has requested that a questionable computer report item be traced to its original source document. What kind of electronic data-processing systems documentation would be most useful?

    a. Program manual

    b. Operating manual

    c. Systems testing procedure

    d. System audit report

    e. System audit trail

2. Which of the following policies or practices is most likely to represent a weakness in internal controls pertaining to an electronic data-processing system?

    a. Computer operators are denied access to the system/program documentation library.

    b. Employees in the data-processing department are prohibited from initiating requests for changes to master files.

    c. Computer programmers are permitted to operate the computer for regular processing runs involving programs that they have written.

    d. Computer operators who run the programs pertaining to inventory are prohibited from making test counts of goods on hand in order to check the accuracy of the computer inventory files.

    e. All corrections of errors in the master file are reviewed and approved by a supervisory-level employee who is independent of the data-processing department.

3. A source document with an invalid number of hours worked for one week, such as 93 hours instead of 39, would be best detected by
    a. keypunching controls.
    b. a limit test in an edit run.
    c. a hash total of hours worked.
    d. a record count total.
    e. a key verifying control.

4. Transactions that were erroneous and had been previously rejected by the computer system apparently were not being reentered and reprocessed once they had been corrected. This erroneous condition is best controlled by
    a. comparing a record count of transactions input into the system.
    b. a comparison of the batch control totals.
    c. scanning the error control log.
    d. scanning the console log.
    e. desk checking.

5. Which one of the following control functions normally would *not* be the responsibility of the input/output control group of the data-processing department?
    a. Review of the efficiency and effectiveness of systems design
    b. Scanning of the console log
    c. Review and distribution of computer output
    d. Maintenance of an error log
    e. Resolution of control totals

6. For a routine management report produced on the computer, which of the following control duties is most likely to be the sole responsibility of the user department?
    a. Scanning the report for garbled output
    b. Checking input totals against report totals
    c. Determining that figures in the report are reasonable
    d. Verifying record count totals
    e. Checking the console listing for improper operator procedures

7. Which of the following best describes business and scientific computing needs for input/output and computing speed?
    a. Business needs both and scientific needs neither.
    b. Business needs both and scientific only needs input/output.
    c. Business needs computing speed and scientific needs input/output.
    d. Business needs neither and scientific needs computing.
    e. Business needs input/output and scientific needs computing.

8. Which of the following academic backgrounds and personal characteristics is least needed to be a systems analyst?
    a. An understanding of human behavior
    b. A knowledge of accounting fundamentals
    c. Experience as a programmer
    d. Ability to work with people
    e. A knowledge of the firm

9. Which of the following methods of control is *not* applicable to computer systems?
   a. Crossfooting
   b. Check digits
   c. Limit checks
   d. Labels written on magnetic tape by the computer
   e. None of the above

10. Which of the following applications would be least likely to be done on a real-time basis?
    a. Airline reservations
    b. Preparation of payroll checks
    c. A "dial a computer" stock market quotation system
    d. A computerized traffic light control system
    e. Computer monitoring of coronary care patients in a hospital

Exercise 17.3   Input, Output, and Process Controls (CMA)

A well-designed management information system using electronic data-processing equipment will include methods of assuring that the data are appropriate to the situation and are accurate.

Required

1. Describe procedures that should exist in order to assure that the input data are accurate and appropriate.
2. Describe procedures that would assure that all data were processed and processed properly.
3. Describe procedures that would assure that the output data are accurate and appropriate.

Exercise 17.4   An Example of Inadequate Controls[1]

The following correspondence (battle) was reported to have taken place between an accounts receivable computer in a department store and one of the store's customers.

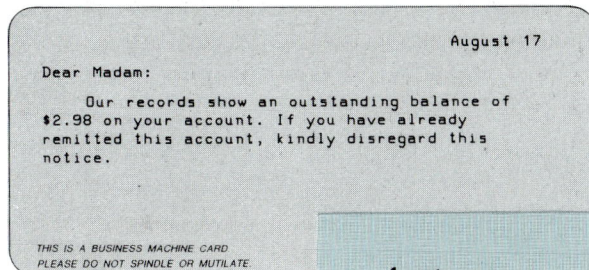

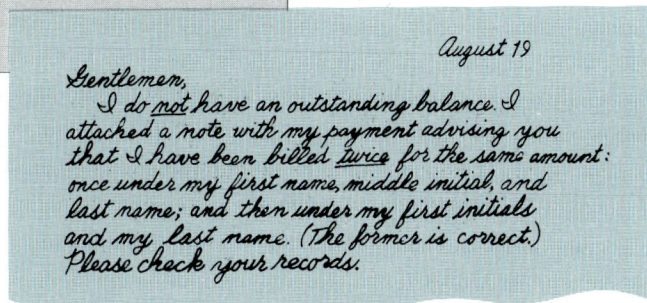

> August 17
>
> Dear Madam:
>
> Our records show an outstanding balance of $2.98 on your account. If you have already remitted this account, kindly disregard this notice.
>
> THIS IS A BUSINESS MACHINE CARD
> PLEASE DO NOT SPINDLE OR MUTILATE.

> August 19
>
> Gentlemen,
> I do *not* have an outstanding balance. I attached a note with my payment advising you that I have been billed *twice* for the same amount: once under my first name, middle initial, and last name; and then under my first initials and my last name. (The former is correct.) Please check your records.

[1] Adapted from *Saturday Review*, August 13, 1965.

September 17

Dear Madam:

Our records show a delinquent balance of
$2.98 on your account. Please remit $3.40. This
includes a handling charge.

THIS IS A BUSINESS MACHINE CARD.
PLEASE DO NOT SPINDLE OR MUTILATE.

September 19

Dear Machine,
You're not paying attention! I am NOT
delinquent. I do not owe this money. I was
billed TWICE for the same purchase.
Please look into this.

October 17

Dear Madam:

Our records show you to be delinquent for
three months. Please remit the new charges of
$13.46, plus $4.10. (This includes a handling
charge.) May we have your immediate attention to
this matter.

THIS IS A BUSINESS MACHINE CARD.
PLEASE DO NOT SPINDLE OR MUTILATE.

October 19

Dear Machine,
My attention! You want MY attention!
Listen here, YOU ARE WRONG!!! I don't owe
you $4.10. CAN YOU UNDERSTAND THAT? I also
DON'T owe you the new charge of $13.46.
You billed ME for my MOTHER'S purchase.
Please correct this statement at once!

November 17

Dear Madam:

Our records now show you to be delinquent for
four months in the total amount of $17.56, plus
$1.87 handling charges.

Please remit in full in ten days or your
account will be turned over to our Auditing
Department for collection.

THIS IS A BUSINESS MACHINE CARD.
PLEASE DO NOT SPINDLE OR MUTILATE.

November 19

Dear Human Machine Programer,
DEAR ANYONE HUMAN.
WILL YOU PLEASE TAKE YOUR HEAD OUT OF THE
COMPUTER LONG ENOUGH TO READ THIS? I DON'T OWE
YOU THIS MONEY!!! I DON'T OWE YOU ANY MONEY. NONE.

December 17

Dear Madam:

Is there some question about your statement?
Our records show no payments on your account
since August. Please call DI7-9601 and ask for
Miss Gilbert at your earliest convenience.

THIS IS A BUSINESS MACHINE CARD.
PLEASE DO NOT SPINDLE OR MUTILATE.

December 18

. . . deck the halls with boughs of holly . . . "Good afternoon. Carver's hopes you have enjoyed its recorded program of carols. May I help you?"

"Hello. Yes . . . My bill is . . . should I wait for a 'beep' before I talk?"

"About your bill?"

"Yes. Yes, it's my bill. There's a mistake . . ."

"One moment, please. I'll connect you with Adjustments!"

"Good afternoon and Merry Christmas. This is a recorded message. All our lines are in service now. If you will please be patient, one of our adjusters will be with you as soon as the line is free. Meanwhile, Carver's hopes you will enjoy its program of Christmas carols" . . . deck the halls with boughs of holly . . .

December 26

Dear Machine,
I tried to call you on December 18. Also on the 19th, 20th, 21st. and the 23rd and the 24th. But all I got was a recorded message and those Christmas carols. Please, oh, please, won't you turn me over to a human? Any human?

January 17

Dear Madam:

Our Credit Department has turned your delinquent account over to us for collection. Won't you please remit this amount now? We wish to cooperate with you in every way possible, but this is considerably past due. May we have your check at this time?

Very truly yours,
Henry J. Hooper, Auditor

January 19

Dear Mr. Hooper,
You doll! You gorgeous HUMAN doll! I refer you to letters I sent to your department dated the 19th of August, September, October, and November, which should clarify the fact that I owe you nothing.

February 17

Dear Madam:

According to our microfilm records, our billing was in error. Your account is clear; you have no balance.
We hope there will be no further inconvenience to you. This was our fault.

Very truly yours,
Henry J. Hooper, Auditor

February 19

Dear Mr. Hooper,
Thank you! Oh, thank you, thank you, thank you!

March 17

Dear Madam:

Our records show you to be delinquent in the amount of $2.98, erroneously posted last August to a nonexistent account. May we have your remittance at this time?

THIS IS A BUSINESS MACHINE CARD.
PLEASE DO NOT SPINDLE OR MUTILATE

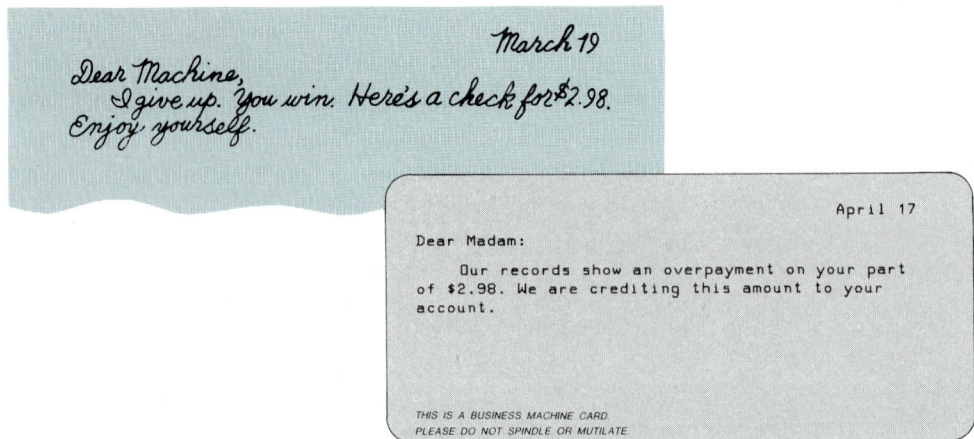

Dear Machine,
I give up. You win. Here's a check for $2.98.
Enjoy yourself.

March 19

April 17

Dear Madam:

Our records show an overpayment on your part
of $2.98. We are crediting this amount to your
account.

THIS IS A BUSINESS MACHINE CARD.
PLEASE DO NOT SPINDLE OR MUTILATE.

Required

Discuss the issues, evident in the narrative, that relate to automated accounting systems and recommend the design changes you believe would enable avoidance of the problems that occurred.

Exercise 17.5 Systems Design—Feasibility Analysis

A request has been made to design a corporate distribution system to be used in both long-range planning and daily management of operations. Cost data on the present distribution system are scanty and out of date. Significant cost savings are expected, but they are not included in the proposal. Responsibility for distribution lay with the marketing vice-president, a man who has made no major changes in distribution policy or practices for 15 years and has a well-earned reputation for being hostile to innovation. Perhaps understandably, he has not been consulted on the proposal, yet his support would obviously be indispensable to its success.

Required

1. Without reference to the above situation, identify what feasibility analysis is and the factors that should be considered.
2. With reference to the above situation, which areas of feasibility analysis would you study most? Why?

Exercise 17.6 General Concepts of Computer Data Processing (CMA)

Select the best answer for each of the multiple choice questions that follow.

1. Software refers to
   a. the peripheral equipment in a data-processing installation.
   b. pliable media, such as cards and magnetic tape.
   c. the central processing unit and its components.
   d. the programming support of a computer system.
   e. none of the above.
2. A company is considering installing a management information system (MIS). One of the basic requirements for an MIS would be
   a. punched cards.

    b. desk calculators.

    c. magnetic tape storage.

    d. remote terminals.

    e. a data base.

3. The primary justification for installation of a computer system is that
   a. the benefits of the system are greater than the costs.
   b. the information provided by the system is useful.
   c. the work force can be cut back in size.
   d. the communication provided by a system is improved.
   e. the system coordinates the parts of a business.

4. In preparing flowcharts for a new data-processing system, one normally would
   a. develop one system flowchart and then allow each programmer to develop his or her own program flowchart.
   b. begin developing the program flowcharts and work toward the system flowcharts.
   c. develop the system charts first, followed by a coordinated series of program charts.
   d. develop one flowchart that included both systems and program attributes.
   e. not spend much effort on them, because flowcharts are rarely used once the charts are prepared.

5. The underlying concept of control in a management information system is the concept of
   a. standard operating procedures.
   b. organizational structure.
   c. behavioral attitudes.
   d. feedback.
   e. systems boundaries.

6. In order to maintain good internal control within the computer department,
   a. computer operators need to be good programmers.
   b. programmers should have control over day-to-day production runs.
   c. computer operators should be allowed to make changes in programs as needed in order to keep the computer running.
   d. programmers and computer operators should be in separate sections of the computer department.
   e. the tape librarian should be able to operate the computer.

7. Ander and Company has designed an electronic data-processing system utilizing the data-base systems concept. In this system, transactions are entered into the system only once. In order to accomplish this, Ander's files
   a. must utilize magnetic tape.
   b. must be separated by function (such as marketing has a set of files, production has a set, and so forth).
   c. must be located in an integrated file located in on-line storage.
   d. must be updated in a real-time environment.
   e. must be handled in some other manner than described above.

8. Doncor Producing Company has completed the design of a new purchase order system. As a part of this work, a diagram was prepared that emphasizes the inputs and outputs and shows the flow of data through the entire system. This diagram is known as
   a. a program flowchart.
   b. a documentation table.
   c. an organization chart.
   d. a systems flowchart.
   e. a decision table.

9. In preparing a detailed program flowchart of the input edit run for batched inventory transactions, which flowchart symbol adopted by the American National Standards Institute (ANSI) would you use to represent the accessing of transactions?

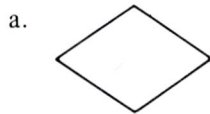

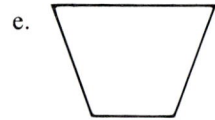

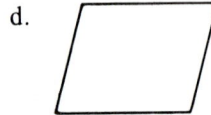

a. (diamond)   c. (circle)   e. (trapezoid)

b. ⟶   d. (parallelogram)

10. One primary purpose of a data-base information system is to
    a. eliminate multiple access to a particular piece of stored data.
    b. eliminate redundancy in the data base of a company.
    c. lessen the integration of information-producing activities so a given department may easily ascertain its current status.
    d. provide each application program with its own fixed data file.
    e. make it possible to have data compatible with a variety of computer hardware.

11. Flowcharts generally do *not* show
    a. manual operations.
    b. computer-based operations.
    c. flow of forms.
    d. peak volumes of data.
    e. manual controls.

12. When contrasting the design for a routine computer-based report for low levels of management with that for high levels of management, the report design for the low-level managers should be
    a. more timely and more detailed.
    b. less timely and less detailed.
    c. more timely and less detailed.
    d. of a longer time horizon.
    e. less quantitative.

Exercise 17.7 Documenting Data-Processing Applications

The documentation of data-processing applications is an important step in the design and implementation of any computer-based system. Documentation provides a complete record of data-processing applications. However, documentation is a phase of systems development that often is neglected. While documentation can be tedious and time consuming, the lack of proper documentation can be very costly for an organization.

Required

1. Identify and explain briefly the purposes proper documentation can serve.
2. Discuss briefly the basic types of information that should be included in the documentation of a data-processing application.

3. What policies should be established to regulate access to documentation data for purposes of information or modification for the following four groups of company employees?
   a. Computer operators
   b. Internal auditors
   c. Production planning analysts
   d. Systems analysts

Exercise 17.8   Systems Analysis and Design Life Cycle (CMA)

Curtis Company operates in a five-county industrial area. The company employs a manual system for all of its record keeping except payroll; the payroll is processed by a local service bureau. Other applications have not been computerized because they could not be cost justified previously.

The company's sales have grown substantially over the past five years. With this growth rate, a computer-based system seemed more practical. Consequently, Curtis Company engaged the management consulting department of their public accounting firm to conduct a feasibility study for converting their record-keeping systems to a computer-based system. The accounting firm reported that a computer-based system would improve the company's record-keeping system and still provide material cost savings.

Therefore, Curtis Company decided to develop a computer-based system for their records. Curtis wants to hire a person with experience in systems development as manager of systems and data processing. This person's responsibilities will be to oversee the entire systems operation with special emphasis on the development of the new system.

Management knows you are familiar with the analysis and design of information systems and has asked you to prepare a brief memo to inform them of what they should expect.

Required

Describe the major steps that will be undertaken to develop and implement Curtis Company's new computer-based system.

Exercise 17.9   Systems Design—Identifying Documents and Document Flow (CMA)

Wooster Company is a beauty and barber supplies and equipment distributorship servicing a five-state area. Management generally has been pleased with overall operations of the company until now. However, the present purchasing system has evolved through practice rather than having been formally designed. Consequently, it is inadequate and needs to be redesigned.

A description of the present purchasing system is as follows. Whenever the quantity of an item is low, the inventory supervisor phones the purchasing department with the item description and quantity to be ordered. A purchase order is then prepared in duplicate in the purchasing department. The original is sent to the vendor, and the copy is retained in the purchasing department filed in numerical order. When the shipment arrives, the inventory supervisor sees that each item received is checked off on the packing slip accompanying the shipment. The packing slip is then forwarded to the accounts payable department. When the invoice arrives, the packing slip is compared with the invoice in the accounts payable department. Once any differences between the packing slip and the invoice are reconciled, a check is drawn for the appropriate amount and is mailed to the vendor with a copy of the invoice. The packing slip is attached to the invoice and filed alphabetically in the paid invoice file.

Wooster Company intends to redesign its purchasing system from the time when an item needs to be ordered until payment is made. The system should be designed to ensure that all of the proper controls are incorporated into the system.

Required

1. Identify the internally and externally generated documents that would be required to satisfy the minimum requirements of a basic system and indicate the number of copies of each document that would be needed.
2. Explain how all of these documents should interrelate and flow among Wooster's various departments including the final destination or file for each copy.

Exercise 17.10   Data Processing—Flowchart Symbols and General Concepts (CMA)

Select the best answer for each of the multiple choice questions that follow.

Slayton Company is designing a new payroll system. System and program flowcharts will be prepared in the process of designing and developing the new system. Standard flowcharting symbols will be used in preparing the system and program flowcharts.

1. The symbol that would be used to determine if an employee's wages are above or below the maximum limit for FICA taxes is

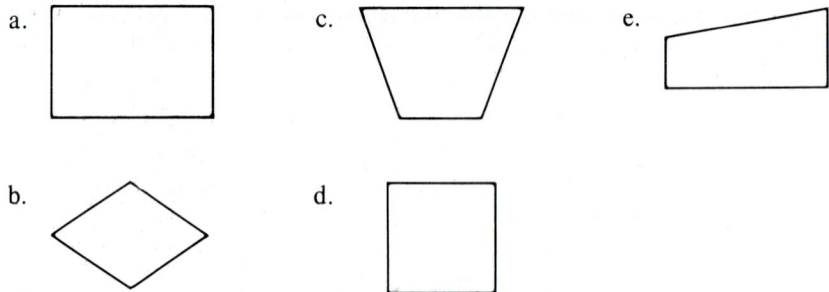

2. The symbol that would be used to represent the printing of the employees' paychecks by the computer is

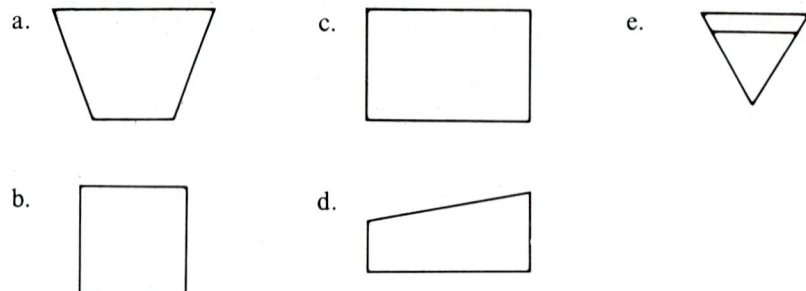

3. The symbol that would be used to represent the employees' checks that have been printed by the computer is

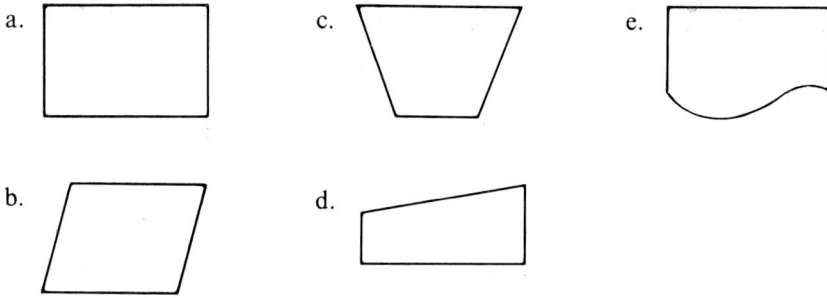

a. [square]   c. [trapezoid]   e. [document symbol]

b. [parallelogram]   d. [slanted quadrilateral]

4. The symbol that would be used to represent the physical act of collecting employees' time cards for processing is

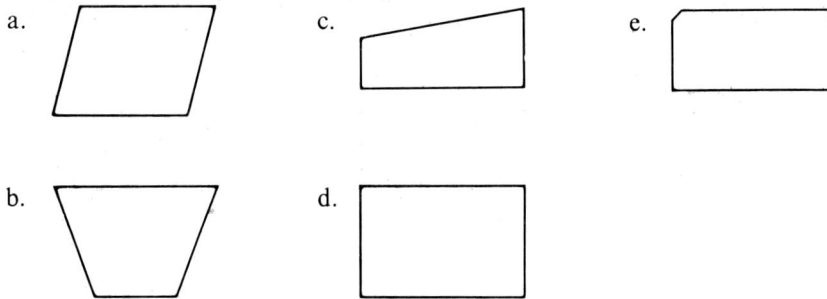

a. [parallelogram]   c. [slanted quadrilateral]   e. [rounded rectangle]

b. [inverted trapezoid]   d. [rectangle]

5. The symbol that would be used to represent the employees' payroll records that are stored on magnetic tape is

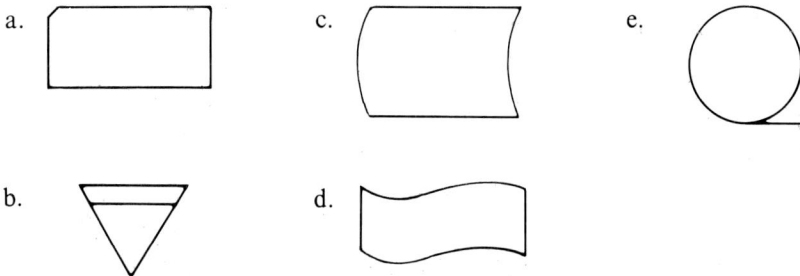

a. [rounded rectangle]   c. [magnetic tape symbol]   e. [circle]

b. [inverted triangle]   d. [document symbol]

6. The symbol that would be used to represent the weekly payroll register that is generated by the computer is

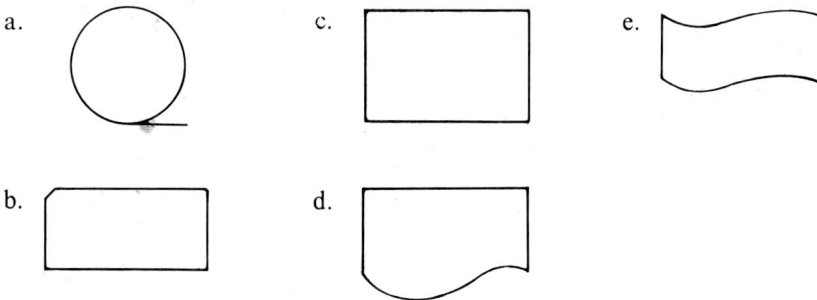

a. [circle]   c. [rectangle]   e. [document symbol]

b. [rounded rectangle]   d. [document symbol]

7. The symbol that would be used to represent the file of hard-copy, computer-generated payroll reports for future reference is

a. 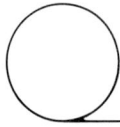   c. 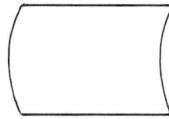   e.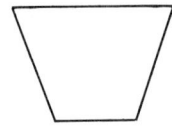

b. (inverted triangle)   d.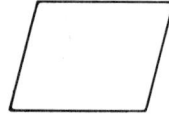

8. In recent years many businesses have formed a common information source within their business organization called a data base. One advantage of building data bases is the simultaneous updating of files with common data elements. Another major advantage of the data-base concept is that
   a. data-base systems can be used as efficiently with microprocessors as with large computers.
   b. data-base systems are simple to install and maintain.
   c. data-base systems are generally less expensive than separate file maintenance systems.
   d. less duplication of data occurs with a data-base system.
   e. fewer skilled people are required to run a data-base system than any other system.

9. Jones Auto Parts Company, a small sole proprietorship, has decided to change from manual to computerized inventory management. Frequently, in implementing a new system, both the old and new systems are maintained during a shakedown period. This changeover technique is called
   a. parallel running conversion.
   b. pilot testing.
   c. back-up system conversion.
   d. debugging.
   e. systems conversion management.

10. Many customers, managers, employees, and suppliers have blamed the computer for making errors. In reality, computers make very few mechanical errors. The most likely source of errors in a fully operational computer-based system is due to errors in
    a. programming.
    b. operator actions.
    c. systems analysis.
    d. processing.
    e. input.

Problem 17.1 Flowchart, File, and Output Design (CMA)

Huron Company manufactures and sells eight major product lines with fifteen to twenty-five items in each product line. All sales are on credit, and orders are received by mail or telephone. Huron Company has a computer-based system that employs magnetic disks as a file medium.

All sales orders received during regular working hours are typed into an intelligent terminal that performs two functions—(a) prepares a sales order immediately and (b) stores the relevant data on a disk for shipment or back order, billing and update of accounts receivable, and update of inventory. However, the activities are done on an after-hour basis on the mainframe computer. After closing, the information is transferred to the mainframe computer by communication lines. Processing is completed during the night to update the files for the current day's activities and to facilitate the shipment of goods the following day. In summary, an order received one day is processed that night and shipped the next day.

The daily processing that has to be accomplished at night includes the following activities:

1. Preparing the invoice to be sent to the customer at the time of shipment
2. Updating accounts receivable file
3. Updating finished-goods inventory
4. Listing of all items back-ordered and short

Each month the sales department would like to have a sales summary and analysis. At the end of each month the monthly statements should be prepared and mailed to customers. Management also wants an aging of accounts receivable each month.

Required

1. Identify the master files that Huron Company should maintain in this system to provide for the daily processing. Indicate the data content that should be included in each file and the order in which each file should be maintained.
2. Using standard flowcharting symbols, prepare the following two systems flowcharts:
   a. Daily processing required to update the accounts receivable and finished-goods inventory and to prepare the required daily reports
   b. Monthly reports requested by the sales department and other required monthly reports and statements
3. Describe (a) the items that should appear in the monthly sales analysis report(s) the sales department should have and (b) the input data and master files that would have to be maintained to prepare these reports.

Problem 17.2 Data-Processing Controls (CMA)

The Vane Corporation is a manufacturer that has been in business for the past eighteen years. During this period, the company has grown from a very small family-owned operation to a medium-sized manufacturer with several departments. Despite the growth, a substantial number of the procedures employed by Vane Corporation have been in effect since the business was started. Just recently Vane Corporation has computerized its payroll function.

The payroll function operates in the following manner. Each worker picks up a weekly time card on Monday morning and writes in his name and identification number. These blank cards are kept near the factory entrance. The workers write on the time card their daily arrival and departure times. On the following Monday the factory supervisors collect the completed time cards for the previous week and send them to data processing.

In data processing the time cards are used to prepare the weekly time file. This file is processed with the master payroll file, which is maintained on magnetic tape according to worker identification number. The checks are written by the computer on the regular checking account and imprinted with the treasurer's signature. After the payroll file is updated and the checks are prepared, the checks are sent to the factory supervisors who distribute them to the workers or hold them for the workers to pick up later if they are absent.

The supervisors notify data processing of new employees and terminations. Any changes in hourly pay rate or any other changes affecting payroll are usually communicated to data processing by the supervisors.

The workers also complete a job time ticket for each individual job they work on each day. The job time tickets are collected daily and sent to cost accounting where they are used to prepare a cost distribution analysis.

Further analysis of the payroll function reveals the following:

1. A worker's gross wages never exceed $300 per week.
2. Raises never exceed $0.55 per hour for the factory workers.
3. No more than 20 hours of overtime is allowed each week.
4. The factory employs 150 workers in ten departments.

The payroll function has not been operating smoothly for some time, but even more problems have surfaced since the payroll was computerized. The supervisors have indicated that they would like a weekly report indicating worker tardiness, absenteeism, and idle time, so they can determine the amount of productive time lost and the reason for the lost time. The following errors and inconsistencies have been encountered in the past few pay periods:

1. A worker's paycheck was not processed properly, because he had transposed two numbers in his identification number when he filled out his time card.
2. A worker was issued a check for $1,531.80 when it should have been $153.18.
3. One worker's paycheck was not written, and this error was not detected until the paychecks for that department were distributed by the supervisor.
4. Part of the master payroll file was destroyed when the tape reel was inadvertently mounted on the wrong tape drive and used as a scratch tape. Data processing attempted to reestablish the destroyed portion from original source documents and other records.
5. One worker received a paycheck for an amount considerably larger than he should have. Further investigation revealed that 84 had been punched instead of 48 for hours worked.
6. Several records on the master payroll file were skipped and not included on the updated master payroll file. This was not detected for several pay periods.
7. In processing nonroutine changes a computer operator included a pay rate increase for one of his friends in the factory. This was discovered by chance by another employee.

Required

Identify the control weaknesses in the payroll procedure and in the computer processing as it is now conducted by the Vane Corporation. Recommend the changes necessary to correct the system. Arrange your answer in the following columnar format:

Control Weaknesses   *Recommendations*

Problem 17.3 Computer Data Processing—Behavioral Problems (CMA)

Audio Visual Corporation manufactures and sells visual display equipment. The company is headquartered near Boston. The majority of sales are made through seven geographical sales offices located in Los Angeles, Seattle, Minneapolis, Cleveland, Dallas, Boston, and Atlanta. Each sales office has a warehouse located nearby to carry an inventory of new equipment and replacement parts. The remainder of the sales are made through manufacturers' representatives.

Audio Visual's manufacturing operations are conducted in a single plant that is highly departmentalized. In addition to the assembly department, there are several departments responsible for various components used in the visual display equipment. The plant also has maintenance, engineering, scheduling, and cost accounting departments.

Early in 19X5, management decided that its management information system (MIS) needed upgrading. As a result, the company ordered an advanced computer in 19X5, which was installed in July 19X6. The main processing equipment is still located at corporate headquarters, and each of the seven sales offices is connected with the main processing unit by remote terminals.

The integration of the new computer into the Audio Visual information system was carried out by the MIS staff. The MIS manager and the four systems analysts who had the major responsibility for the integration were hired in the spring of 19X6. The department's other employees—programmers, machine operators and key-punch operators—have been with the company for several years.

During its early years, Audio Visual had a centralized decision-making organization. Top management formulated all plans and directed all operations. As the company expanded, some of the decision making was decentralized although the information processing was still highly centralized. Departments had to coordinate their plans with the corporate office but they had more freedom in developing their sales programs. However, as the company expanded, information problems developed. As a consequence, the MIS department was given the responsibility to improve the company's information processing system when the new equipment was installed.

The MIS analysts reviewed the information system in existence before the acquisition of the new computer and identified weaknesses. They then redesigned old applications and designed new applications in developing the new system to overcome the weaknesses. During the 18 months since the acquisition of the new equipment, the following applications have been redesigned or developed and are now operational—payroll, production scheduling, financial statement preparation, customer billing, raw material usage in production, and finished-goods inventory by warehouse. The operating departments of Audio Visual affected by the systems changes were rarely consulted or contacted until the system was operational and the new reports were distributed to the operating departments.

The president of Audio Visual is very pleased with the work of the MIS department. During a recent conversation the president stated, "The MIS people are doing a good job and I have full confidence in their work. I touch base with the MIS people frequently, and they have encountered no difficulties in doing their work. We paid a lot of money for the new equipment and the MIS people certainly cost enough, but the combination of the new equipment and new MIS staff should solve all of our problems."

Recently, two other conversations regarding the computer and information system have taken place. One was between Jerry Adams, plant manager, and Bill Taylor, the MIS manager; the other was between Adams and Terry Williams, the new personnel manager.

Taylor-Adams Conversation

Adams: "Bill, you're trying to run my plant for me. I'm supposed to be the manager, yet you keep interfering. I wish you would mind your own business."

Taylor: "You've got a job to do but so does my department. When we analyzed the information needed for production scheduling and by top management, we saw where improvements could be made in the work flow. Now that the system is operational, you can't reroute work and change procedures because that would destroy the value of the information we're processing. And while I'm on that subject, it's getting to the point where we can't trust the information we're getting from production. The mark sense cards we receive from production contain a lot of errors."

Adams: "I'm responsible for the efficient operation of production. Quite frankly, I think I'm the best judge of production efficiency. The system you installed has reduced my work force and increased the work load of the remaining employees, but I don't see that this has improved anything. In fact, it might explain the high error rate in the cards."

Taylor: "This new computer costs a lot of money and I'm trying to be sure that the company gets its money's worth."

Adams-Williams Conversation

Adams: "My best production assistant, the one I'm grooming to be a supervisor when the next opening occurs, came to me today and said he was thinking of quitting. When I asked him why, he said he didn't enjoy the work anymore. He's not the only one who is unhappy. The supervisors and department heads no longer have a voice in establishing production schedules. This new computer system has taken away the contribution we used to make to company planning and direction. We seem to be going way back to the days when top management made all the decisions. I have more production problems now than I used to. I think it boils down to a lack of interest on the part of my management team. I know the problem is within my area but I thought you might be able to help me."

Williams: "I have no recommendations for you now but I've had similar complaints from purchasing and shipping. I think we should get your concerns on the agenda for our next plant management meeting."

Required

1. Apparently the development of and transition to the new computer-based system has created problems among the personnel of Audio Visual Corporation. Identify and briefly discuss the apparent causes of these problems.

2. How could the company have avoided the problems? What steps should be taken to avoid such problems in the future?

Problem 17.4   Data Processing—Report Design (CMA)

Denny Daniels is production manager of the Alumalloy Division of WRT Incorporated. Alumalloy has limited contact with outside customers and has no sales staff. Most of its customers are other divisions of WRT. All sales and purchases with outside customers are handled by other corporate divisions. Therefore, Alumalloy is treated as a cost center for reporting and evaluation purposes rather than as a revenue or profit center.

   Daniels perceives the accounting department as a historical number generating process that provides little useful information for conducting his job. Consequently, the entire accounting process is perceived as a negative motivational device that does not reflect how hard or how effectively he works as a production manager. Daniels tried to discuss these perceptions and concerns with June Scott, the controller for the Alumalloy Division. Daniels told Scott, "I think the cost report is misleading. I know I've had better production over a number of operating periods, but the cost report still says I have excessive costs. Look, I'm not an accountant, I'm a production manager. I know how to get a good quality product out. Over a number of years, I've even cut the raw materials used to do it. But the cost report doesn't show any of this. Basically, it's always negative, no matter what I do. There's no way you can win with accounting or the people at corporate who use those reports."

   Scott gave Daniels little consolation. Scott stated that the accounting system and the cost reports generated by headquarters are just part of the corporate game and almost impossible for an individual to change. "Although these accounting reports are pretty much the basis for evaluating the efficiency of your division and the means corporate uses to determine whether you have done the job they want, you shouldn't worry too much. You haven't been fired yet! Besides, these cost reports have been used by WRT for the last 25 years."

   Daniels perceived from talking to the production manager of the Zinc Division that most of what Scott said was probably true. However, some minor cost reporting changes of Zinc had been agreed to by corporate headquarters. He also knew from the trade grapevine that the turnover of production managers was considered high at WRT, even though relatively few were fired. Most seemed to end up quitting, usually in disgust, because of beliefs that they were not being evaluated fairly. The following are typical comments of production managers who have left WRT:

1. "Corporate headquarters doesn't really listen to us. All they consider are those misleading cost reports. They don't want them changed and they don't want any supplemental information."
2. "The accountants may be quick with numbers but they don't know anything about production. As it was, I either had to ignore the cost reports entirely or pretend they are important even though they didn't tell how good a job I had done. No matter what they say about not firing people, negative reports mean negative evaluations. I'm better off working for another company."

   A recent copy of the cost report prepared by corporate headquarters for the Alumalloy Division is shown below. Daniels does not like this report because he believes it fails to reflect the division's operations properly, thereby resulting in an unfair evaluation of performance.

Allumalloy Division
Cost Report
for the Month of April, 19X0
(000 omitted)

	Master Budget	Actual Cost	Excess Cost
Aluminum	$ 400	$ 437	$ 37
Labor	560	540	(20)
Overhead	100	134	34
Total	$1,060	$1,111	$ 51

Required

1. Comment on Denny Daniel's perception of the following:
   a. June Scott, the controller
   b. corporate headquarters
   c. the cost report
   d. himself as a production manager
   Discuss how his perception affects his behavior and probable performance as a production manager and employee of WRT.
2. Identify and explain three changes that could be made in the cost information presented to the production managers that would make the information more meaningful and less threatening to them.

Problem 17.5   Spreadsheet Application for Budgeted Income Statement

J. K. Bit Machines is in the process of developing their budget for the next four quarters. The following data has been collected to assist in the budgeting process:

Sales are expected to be $45,000 for the first quarter and increase by 2% each quarter through the end of the year.
Cost of goods sold is expected to remain constant at 40% of sales.
Variable costs include:
Selling at 20% of sales
Administrative at 15% of sales
Fixed costs include:
Depreciation at $3,000 per quarter
Interest at $2,500 per quarter
Other at $1,500 per quarter

Required

1. Prepare a budgeted income statement for the next four quarters using the data provided above. Use a computerized spread sheet, such as LOTUS or VISI CALC. Set up the worksheet so that sales for the second through fourth quarter are a percentage of the prior quarter's sales and so that cost of goods sold and the variable expenses for each quarter are computed from that quarter's sales. Also, set up the fixed expenses so that the second, third, and fourth quarters are computed from the amount entered for the first quarter.

Include formulas to automatically compute gross margin and net income. Also, include a total column to show the total for the year of each account in the income statement. Print a copy of your statement.

2. Perform a sensitivity analysis by making the following changes:
   a. Change the expected growth rate of sales to 1% per quarter.
   b. Change the cost-of-goods sold percentage to 42% of sales.
   c. Change the Other fixed expenses to $2,500 per quarter.

Print out a copy of the statement after each change above. Make the changes cumulative; that is, after changing an item, leave it at the changed amount rather than going back to the original data.

Problem 17.6   Spreadsheet Application for Cost/Volume Profit Analysis

Hicks Incorporated produces a single product for which the following data have been determined:

Unit sales price	$24.00
Unit variable cost	18.00
Annual fixed costs	$48,000

Required

1. Use a computerized spreadsheet application such as LOTUS or VISI CALC to prepare a cost-volume-profit analysis. The worksheet should be set up so that by entering the unit sales price, unit variable cost, and annual fixed cost the program automatically computes (a) breakeven points in units and (b) breakeven point in sales dollars. Enter the above data and print out the result.

2. Hicks Incorporated in considering a 5% cut in selling price and a $10,000 addition to the advertising budget. What is the impact on the breakeven point if these changes are made? Print out the modified results.

3. Hicks Incorporated is also considering a change in the production process that would replace workers classified as direct labor with a new machine. Referring back to the original data, if this change is made, variable costs will decrease by $3.00 per unit and fixed costs will increase by $8,000 per year. What is the impact on the breakeven point if these changes are made? Once again, print out the result.

Problem 17.7   Spreadsheet Application for Least-Squares Regression and Correlation Analysis

High-overhead, Incorporated began operation on January 1, 19X1. The first year of operations were very disappointing, primarily because their overhead costs were so much higher than they had anticipated. They have asked you to assist them in developing a flexible budget formula and to identify the activity base that is the best predictor of overhead cost.

The accountant for High-overhead has collected the following information for the first year of operations:

Month	Overhead Cost	Units Produced	Hours
January	$ 4,000	50	400
February	7,000	60	800
March	9,000	65	550
April	6,500	55	500
May	9,600	70	650
June	10,000	80	750
July	7,500	75	900
August	12,000	65	680
September	14,000	45	700
October	13,500	85	900
November	12,500	75	540
December	15,000	95	840

Required

1. Using a computerized spreadsheet application, prepare a worksheet to perform a least-squares regression and correlation analysis. Compute the values of a, fixed factory overhead, b, variable factory overhead, r, coefficient of correlation, and r^2, the coefficient of determination using (a) units produced as the activity base, and (b) hours worked as the activity base. Note: To compute the coefficient of correlation use the following formula: $r = (Sx/SY)*b$ where: Sx is the sample standard deviation of the independent variable x, Sy is the sample standard deviation of the dependent variable y, and b is the slope of the regression line.
2. Which activity base do you recommend and why?

Problem 17.8   Spreadsheet Application for Flexible Budgeting

Workmore Company has obtained the following cost data:

Item	Fixed	Variable per Labor Hour
Direct labor		$7.80
Direct material		4.50
Indirect labor		2.70
Indirect material		1.80
Equipment rental	$ 6,500	
Depreciation	15,000	
Heat, light, and power	1,800	.80
Repairs and maintenance	6,200	.30
Other factory overhead	600	.10

Factory supervision costs are as follows:

Labor hours	Costs
1–11,999	$1,000
12,000–23,999	2,000
24,000–35,999	3,000

Required

1. Using a computerized spreadsheet such as LOTUS or VISI CALC, set up a flexible budget statement. Develop the formulas in the worksheet so that the computer automatically computes the amount of cost that should have been incurred for each item once the actual level of production has been entered. Include a column for actual cost data and a column for variances between actual costs and budgeted costs. The computer should compute the variances automatically. The following column headings are suggested:

	Flexible Budget				
	---	---	---	---	---
Item	Variable	Fixed	Budgeted Cost	Actual Cost	Variance

2. Enter the following actual data into the worksheet:

Actual volume: 14,000 direct-labor hours

Direct labor	$110,000
Direct material	62,000
Indirect labor	38,000
Indirect material	25,000
Equipment rental	6,500
Depreciation	15,500
Heat, light, and power	13,500
Repair and maintenance	10,500
Other factory overhead	2,000
Factory supervision	2,200

Print out a copy of the results.

Problem 17.9   Spreadsheet Application for Capital Budgeting

ITC, Incorporated is considering the acquisition of a piece of capital equipment that will cost $200,000. It has a useful life of 5 years and the ACRS will be used for both tax and book accounting. The equipment will result in the following before-tax cash flows:

Reduction in direct-labor cost	$50,000
Increased revenues	20,000
Increased operating costs	5,000

ITC has not decided whether it is to their best advantage to take the full investment credit and reduce the basis of the asset for ACRS, or to reduce the investment credit by the required 2% and recover the full cost of the asset. They would like you to provide them with the information to make the decision by preparing a computerized spreadsheet that will compute net present value and the internal rate of return for each alternative. They would like it in a generalized form so that they can inset the same type of data for any asset that has a 5-year useful life.

Assume ITC is subject to a 35% tax rate and that their minimum desired rate of return is 10%.

Required

1. Use an electronic spreadsheet application such as LOTUS or VISI CALC to prepare a generalized spreadsheet as described above. Print out the results.
2. Enter the data given above for the new equipment acquisition assuming they take the full investment credit and adjust the basis of the equipment for ACRS. Print out the result.
3. Enter the data given above for the new equipment acquisition assuming they reduce the investment credit and recover the full cost of the asset. Print out the result.
4. Should the company use the full investment credit with the adjusted basis for cost recovery, or should they reduce the investment credit and take the full cost recovery? Explain!

VARIABLE COSTING AND GROSS MARGIN ANALYSIS

18

OUTLINE

T here are two significant ways in which cost accounting systems can be augmented to provide additional useful information for management decisions. First, *variable costing,* also called direct costing, can be used as an alternative method of product costing and income determination. Second, *gross margin analysis* can be used to analyze differences between budgeted and actual results. Both tools are widely used in cost accounting systems. This chapter explains how to apply variable costing and gross margin analysis and how to interpret their results. After you have completed this chapter you should be able to:

1. define variable or direct costing and tell how it relates to the traditional cost accounting system known as absorption or full costing.
2. apply variable costing to provide useful information for management decisions.
3. explain why variable costing is not used for reporting to users of financial statements who are external to the company.
4. define gross margin analysis.
5. apply gross margin analysis to help explain why deviations occurred between budgeted and actual gross margin.
6. apply gross margin analysis to help explain why deviations occurred between gross margins of succeeding years.

VARIABLE COSTING

Variable costing, also called direct costing, is an alternative approach to product costing and income determination. It is similar to the traditional product costing method discussed elsewhere in this text, (known as absorption, full, or conventional costing), with one important exception. The one exception is that when variable costing is used, fixed manufacturing overhead is *not* included as an inventoriable cost. Instead, fixed manufacturing overhead is charged off as a period expense. Because of the effect of this change on operating income and inventory values and for other philosophical reasons, accounting standard setting and regulatory bodies such as the Securities and Exchange Commission deny the use of variable costing for *external* reporting purposes. However, it has widespread acceptance by management for *internal* reporting as a powerful tool for management decision making.

It is important to understand what happens when fixed manufacturing overhead is charged as an expense in the income statement in the period when the cost is incurred rather than becoming an expense as a cost of goods sold in a subsequent period of sale. Figure 18.1 contrasts the cost flows of absorption costing versus variable costing.

When using variable costing the assumption is that only those manufacturing costs that fluctuate directly with the volume of production should be inventoried. All other costs, which are fixed costs and are a function of time, are assumed to be more closely related to the capacity to produce each year than to the production of specific units of output in a year. Therefore, it is argued that such costs should be charged as a current period cost rather than being inventoried, carried forward in time, and finally charged as a cost in future periods when the inventory is ultimately sold. On the other hand, the assumption with **absorption costing** is that all manufacturing costs, whether variable or fixed, are necessary to produce goods and should be inventoried. Under this assumption all manufacturing costs are charged as a cost of goods sold in the period of sale.

Comparison of Variable Costing and Absorption Costing

The concept of variable costing is deceptively simple and at face appears to be redundant to a discussion on the contribution approach. However, the use of variable costing has a subtle but important impact on product costing and income determination that accountants and managers should fully understand. Figure 18.2 shows a comparison of variable

Figure 18.1   Comparison of cost flows—variable costing versus absorption costing

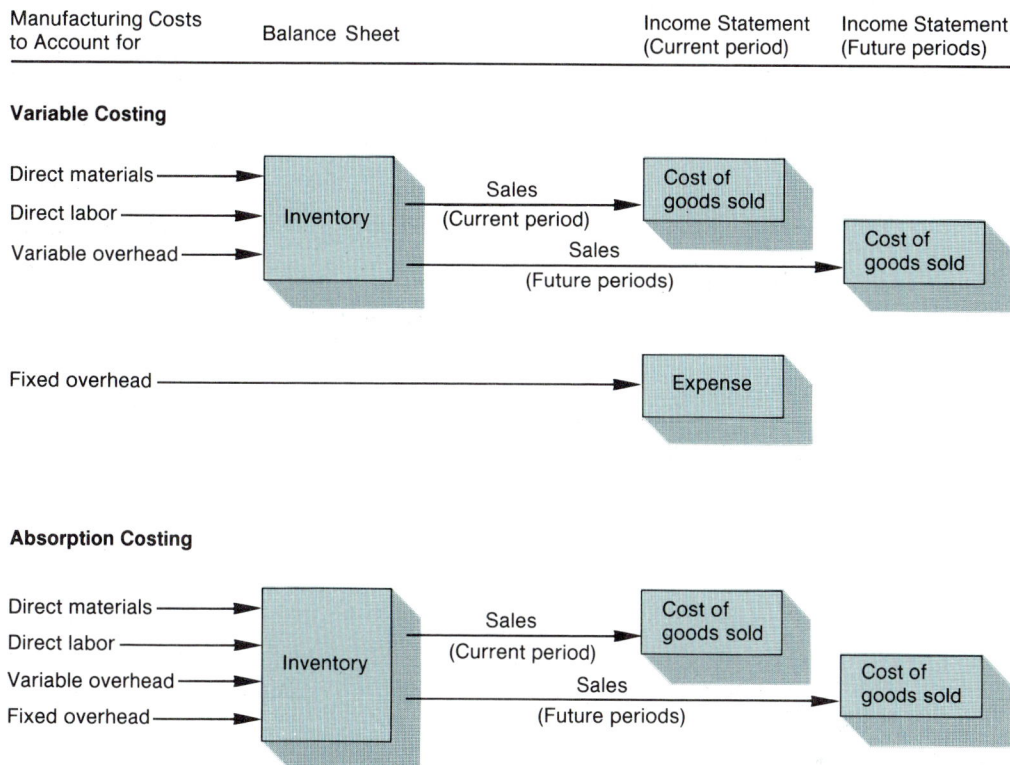

cost and absorption cost income statements for a manufacturing company during its first four years of operation. Assume that the company uses a standard cost system and that the following production and sales statistics are identical to budgeted amounts except for the volume of production. Fixed manufacturing overhead is applied to work in process based on a long-run average production level of 2,200 units per year.

Standard Manufacturing Costs

	Unit Cost
Direct materials	$ 5.00
Direct labor	4.00
Variable manufacturing overhead	3.00
Total variable manufacturing costs	$12.00
Fixed manufacturing overhead	2.00
Total manufacturing costs	$14.00

Manufacturing, Sales, and Inventory Quantity Statistics

Units	Year 1	Year 2	Year 3	Year 4
Beginning inventory	–0–	200	600	100
Manufactured	2,200	2,500	1,700	2,900
Available for sale	2,200	2,700	2,300	3,000
Sold	2,000	2,100	2,200	2,150
Ending inventory	200	600	100	850

Figure 18.2   Comparison of variable and absorption costing income statements

Variable Costing

	Year 1	Year 2	Year 3	Year 4
Sales @ $20	$40,000	$42,000	$44,000	$43,000
Variable manufacturing cost of goods sold:				
Direct materials @ $5	$11,000	$12,500	$ 8,500	$14,500
Direct labor @ $4	8,800	10,000	6,800	11,600
Variable manufacturing overhead @ $3	6,600	7,500	5,100	8,700
Total variable manufacturing costs	$26,400	$30,000	$20,400	$34,800
Plus: Beginning inventory	–0–	2,400	7,200	1,200
Variable manufacturing cost of goods available for sale	$26,400	$32,400	$27,600	$36,000
Less: Ending inventory	2,400	7,200	1,200	10,200
Variable manufacturing cost of goods sold	$24,000	$25,200	$26,400	$25,800
Variable selling and administrative expenses @ $1	2,200	2,500	1,700	2,900
Total variable costs	$26,200	$27,700	$28,100	$28,700
Contribution margin	$13,800	$14,300	$15,900	$14,300
Less: Fixed costs:				
Fixed manufacturing costs	$ 4,400	$ 4,400	$ 4,400	$ 4,400
Fixed selling and administrative costs	1,000	1,000	1,000	1,000
Total fixed costs	$ 5,400	$ 5,400	$ 5,400	$ 5,400
Operating income	$ 8,400	$ 8,900	$10,500	$ 8,900

Absorption Costing

	Year 1	Year 2	Year 3	Year 4
Sales @ $20	$40,000	$42,000	$44,000	$43,000
Cost of goods sold:				
Cost of goods manufactured:				
Direct materials @ $5	$11,000	$12,500	$ 8,500	$14,500
Direct labor @ $4	8,800	10,000	6,800	11,600
Variable manufacturing overhead @ $3	6,600	7,500	5,100	8,700
Fixed manufacturing overhead @ $2	4,400	5,000	3,400	5,800
Total cost of goods manufactured	$30,800	$35,000	$23,800	$40,600
Beginning inventory	–0–	2,800	8,400	1,400
Cost of goods available for sale	$30,800	$37,800	$32,200	$42,000
Less: Ending inventory	2,800	8,400	1,400	11,900
Cost of goods sold	$28,000	$29,400	$30,800	$30,100
Gross margin	$12,000	$12,600	$13,200	$12,900
Selling and administrative expenses:				
Variable @ $1	$ 2,200	$ 2,500	$ 1,700	$ 2,900
Fixed	1,000	1,000	1,000	1,000
Total selling and administrative expenses	$ 3,200	$ 3,500	$ 2,700	$ 3,900
Operating income before volume variance	$ 8,800	$ 9,100	$10,500	$ 9,000
Volume variance	–0–	$ 600	$ (1,000)	$ 1,400
Operating income	$ 8,800	$ 9,700	$ 9,500	$10,400

Volume variance:
  Formula: (Actual volume—Budgeted volume) × Fixed overhead per unit
    Year 1: (2,200 - 2,200) × $2.00 = –0–
    Year 2: (2,500 - 2,200) × $2.00 = $600 favorable
    Year 3: (1,700 - 2,200) × $2.00 = $1,000 unfavorable
    Year 4: (2,900 - 2,200) × $2.00 = $1,400 favorable

Comparing the results for these two methods for the first year of operations indicates a difference of $400 ($8,800 − $8,400 = $400) in operating income when using variable costing versus absorption costing. This difference is due to fixed costs of $400 (200 units @ $2.00 = $400) being carried in inventory at the end of the period when using absorption costing rather than being charged off as an expense when using variable costing.

This can be verified by observing that ending inventories are different by $400 ($2,800 − $2,400 = $400) when using these two methods. It is also important to recognize that *if* all units produced had been sold in the first year of operations, there would be no difference between these methods in either ending inventory or operating income. Differences arise between these two methods only when inventories are maintained from one period to the next.

The significance of all this for income determination can be further illustrated by comparing the results of operations for the subsequent three years as shown in figure 18.2. Inventory amounts that affect both the balance sheet and income statement are different for each year.

Inventory Amounts

	Year 1	Year 2	Year 3	Year 4
Absorption costing	$2,800	$8,400	$1,400	$11,900
Variable costing	2,400	7,200	1,200	10,200
Difference	$ 400	$1,200	$ 200	$ 1,700

These differences are the result of excluding fixed manufacturing overhead from inventories when using variable costing. This is why inventory values are always lower when using variable costing than when using absorption costing. When using absorption costing, fixed costs are applied to inventory as part of the predetermined overhead application rate. When using variable costing, the only component of the predetermined overhead application rate is variable overhead. Although the above inventory differences relate only to the finished-goods inventory, the results would be the same if work-in-process inventories had been included.

Work-in-process inventories have not been included in this chapter's examples in order to keep the illustrations as uncluttered as possible. These examples also contain no materials, labor, or variable overhead variances. The presence of any such variances would not affect the results when comparing variable costing with absorption costing. The volume variance is included to illustrate how standard cost variances are handled in this type of situation. Note that there is no volume variance using variable costing because fixed costs are treated as a lump sum cost in the period incurred. Also note that variable costing is not dependent on standard costs or budgetary methods. A standard cost environment is used to illustrate variable costing because it represents a comprehensive and highly probable situation.

Another important observation when comparing variable costing with absorption costing is that the contribution margin, which is computed when using variable costing, is consistently greater than the gross margin, which is computed when using absorption costing as shown in figure 18.2.

Some argue that a greater contribution margin may lead to different and probably inappropriate management decisions than when gross margin is the reference number. For example, marketing management may lower prices or ask for higher bonuses when using the contribution margin rather than the lower gross margin. The impact of variable costing on management decisions will be discussed later in this chapter.

The main point is that the difference between variable costing and absorption costing is simply a timing difference; that is, fixed manufacturing overhead will ultimately be charged as an expense using both accounting methods and the differences that are apparent in the short run will not be differences in the long run.

Figure 18.3   Reconciliation of income from operations

Calculation of Differences in Income from Operations

	Year 1	Year 2	Year 3	Year 4
Absorption costing	$ 8,800	$ 9,700	$ 9,500	$10,400
Variable costing	8,400	8,900	10,500	8,900
Difference	$ 400	$ 800	(1,000)	$ 1,500

**Reconciliation of Differences
(Inventory Change—Dollar Method)**

	Year 1	Year 2	Year 3	Year 4
Absorption costing:				
Ending inventory	$ 2,800	$ 8,400	$ 1,400	$11,900
Less: Beginning				
inventory	–0–	2,800	8,400	$ 1,400
Change	$ 2,800	$ 5,600	(7,000)	$10,500
Variable costing:				
Ending inventory	$ 2,400	$ 7,200	$ 1,200	$10,200
Less: Beginning				
inventory	–0–	2,400	7,200	1,200
Change	$ 2,400	$ 4,800	$ (6,000)	$ 9,000
Difference in operating				
income	$ 400	$ 800	$ (1,000)	$ 1,500

(Inventory Change—Units Method)

	Year 1	Year 2	Year 3	Year 4
Ending inventory	200	600	100	850
Less: Beginning				
inventory	–0–	200	600	100
Change—Increase				
(decrease)	200	400	(500)	750
Fixed costs per unit	× $2	× $2	× $2	× $2
Difference in operating				
income	$400	$800	$(1,000)	$1,500

Another observation about the differences between variable costing and absorption costing concerns the difference in the operating income of each method. This difference is simply the amount of fixed manufacturing costs that are charged to inventory using the absorption costing method versus no fixed manufacturing costs that are applied to inventory when using the variable costing method. Therefore, it is relatively easy to reconcile the operating incomes calculated using each method. Figure 18.3 shows two ways to perform this reconciliation.

A final observation is that the operating income fluctuates directly with sales when using variable costing. However, when using absorption costing, operating income does not necessarily fluctuate directly with sales depending on the relationship of sales to production. For example, in a period when inventories increase, as is the case when production exceeds sales, absorption costing will typically result in a higher operating income than the variable costing method. In a period when sales exceed production, variable costing will typically result in higher operating income.

This can be verified by inspecting the comparison of income from operations in figure 18.3. Production volume exceeds sales and operating income is higher under absorption costing in years 1, 2, and 4 as expected. Also as expected, operating income using variable costing is higher in year 3 when sales exceed the volume of production. These relationships hold when using standard costing and LIFO inventory costing methods. When FIFO and average costing inventory valuation methods are used, care should be exercised in generalizing the above relationships.

The reason why the relationship among sales, production, and operating income illustrated in figure 18.3 holds true can be further explained as follows. If there is a difference between the volume of sales and the volume of production during an accounting period, there will be a change in the number of units carried in ending inventory. Remember that fixed costs are carried in inventory when using absorption costing but are not carried in inventory when using variable costing. Therefore, the *amount of change* in the cost of ending inventory *will be different* between these two methods.

To illustrate, consider an inventory of 1,200 units with a full cost per unit of $8 and a variable cost per unit of $7. The difference of $1 represents the amount of fixed costs per unit inventoried when using absorption costing. If sales exceed production by 200 units during the next accounting period, then there will be a decrease in inventory by 200 units to 1,000 units (1,200 units − 200 units). Therefore, the cost of ending inventory when using absorption costing will decline from $9,600 (1,200 units × $8 per unit) to $8,000 (1,000 units × $8 per unit)—a change of $1,600. However, when using variable costing the cost of ending inventory will decline from $8,400 (1,200 units × $7 per unit) to $7,000 (1,000 units × $7)—a change of $1,400. The amount of inventory cost change is different by $200 ($1,600 − $1,400) between the two methods. This change can also be found by multiplying the fixed cost component, which is inventoried using absorption costing but not inventoried using variable costing, by the number of units of inventory change ($1 × 200 units = $200).

Finally, the value of ending inventory shown on the balance sheet will be different between methods. A lower inventory cost will be shown for variable costing versus absorption costing because of the fixed cost element.

Variable Costing as a Management Tool

Executives and managers generally agree that variable costing represents a powerful analytical tool. This is true primarily because in a variable costing system the per-unit direct costs and the contribution margin remain constant for various levels of production and sales. When using absorption costing, the relationship among costs, volume, and prices may be obscured because of the way fixed costs are handled. Fixed costs are applied to production in an absorption costing system on a per-unit basis as though they were a function of volume when, in reality, they are not (as discussed in chaps. 13 and 14).

A prerequisite to the installation and use of a variable costing system is the identification and classification of costs into their fixed and variable components (see chap. 5). Once costs are properly classified and the system is in operation, there are a number of ways in which variable costing is particularly advantageous and useful as a management tool.

Variable costs are typically the only costs relevant to short-run, routine decisions. Because variable costs are reliable in forecasting as well as reporting results of operations, variable costing systems are used to develop budgets and profit plans.

Another practical advantage of variable costing is that net income tends to fluctuate directly with sales volume. This feature enables management to identify changes in sales with their effect on net income.

Nonroutine management decisions are also facilitated by variable costing. Whether or not to expand into new markets, engage in special promotional activities, or produce new product lines are examples of such decisions. The concept of variable costing goes hand-in-hand with the techniques related to nonroutine decision making (see chap. 20) and facilitates the use of cost-volume-profit analysis (as discussed in chap. 8).

The format of a variable costing income statement enhances management decision making. The contribution margin helps to project changes in net income that accompany changes in sales. Also, fixed costs are reported as a definable group on the variable costing income statement rather than as a component in a number of other cost categories reported on an absorption costing statement. This makes the effect of fixed costs on profits more readily understood.

Results of operations are also more clearly defined under variable costing than under absorption costing. Top management is typically responsible for the level of manufacturing operations relating to both long-run capacity and short-run production volumes. Thus, any variances that arise relating to fixed costs, which are essentially the responsibility of top management, should not be included as though they are the responsibility of lower-level managers. Variable costing implicitly recognizes this principle by charging fixed costs against revenue in the accounting period when incurred rather than being charged to inventory. Many feel that this makes it possible for management reports to be more representative of controllable cost flows than if fixed costs are included in inventory. Production managers should receive reports showing responsibility for only those cost factors controllable in production departments. For example, reports for production managers should exclude lump-sum fixed costs and fixed cost variances over which production managers have no control. However, it should be noted that department managers may be responsible for some fixed costs. When this is so, controllable fixed costs should be included on management reports. The main point is that variable does not mean controllable and fixed does not mean uncontrollable.

External Reporting Considerations

For internal management, delineating between fixed and variable costs and the use of variable costing in connection with the contribution approach has widespread acceptance. However, neither the Internal Revenue Service, the Securities and Exchange Commission, nor generally accepted accounting principles approve of variable costing for *external* reporting. Therefore, many firms maintain information relating to fixed and variable costs within their cost accounting systems in sufficient detail to enable the generation of either variable cost or absorption cost financial statements as needed.

The typical procedure is to expand the chart of accounts so that both fixed and variable cost classifications are accommodated. Overhead control accounts are also expanded so there is a "manufacturing overhead control—variable account" as well as a "manufacturing overhead control—fixed account." This makes it possible to exclude fixed overhead from being inventoried. When overhead is applied to work in process, it is only the variable portion that is applied using a "variable manufacturing overhead applied account." Differences between actual and applied variable overhead are calculated and reported as discussed in chapters 15 and 16. The "manufacturing overhead control—fixed account" is closed to income summary like any other period expense account.

When a company sets up its cost accounting system using the variable costing concept, it is necessary for external reporting purposes to convert the financial statements to absorption costing at the end of each reporting period. This requires a few calculations that are neither expensive nor time consuming. The conversion procedure involves adjusting the inventory values and operating income for the period by the amount of fixed costs excluded from the determination of inventory values when using a variable costing system. The items of information necessary to make the conversion calculations for each accounting period under a FIFO inventory system are as follows:

1. The number of units (*a*) manufactured and (*b*) sold
2. The standard (budgeted or denominator) level of activity
3. The quantities carried in beginning and ending inventories
4. The amount of budgeted fixed costs
5. The changes, if any, in other cost elements

The steps in the actual conversion process are as follows:

1. Calculate the predetermined fixed manufacturing overhead application rate that would have been used under the absorption costing concept.
2. Convert the inventory values under variable costing to absorption costing by adding an amount equal to the number of units in each inventory multiplied by the fixed overhead application rate.
3. Calculate the volume variance by multiplying the difference between budgeted and actual production volume by the fixed overhead application rate.
4. Construct the absorption costing financial statements using information available in the variable costing statements plus the converted inventory values and the volume variance.

The conversion process's validity can be verified by performing the following:

1. Calculate the increase or decrease in units of inventory.
2. Multiply the increase or decrease in inventory units by the predetermined fixed manufacturing overhead application rate to get the difference in operating income between the variable costing and absorption costing methods.

Assuming that there have been no other changes in costs, this difference in operating income can be used to verify the validity of the conversion process. For example, the following operation traces the conversion and validation process using data contained in figures 18.2 and 18.3 for the first year of operations.

1. The predetermined fixed manufacturing overhead application rate is given as $2.00 per unit.
2. Beginning inventory—converted: $2,400 + (200 \times $2) = $2,800.
   Ending inventory—converted: $7,200 + (600 \times $2) = $8,400.
3. The volume variance is a favorable $600 as calculated in figure 18.2.
4. Figure 18.2 contains the actual construction of the absorption costing income statement using the above data.

A balance sheet is not shown because all relevant information for the conversion is contained in the income statement. Figure 18.3 contains the validation calculations for the above procedure. You should now refer to years 2 and 3 in figures 18.2 and 18.3 and perform the conversion and validation calculations.

Conversion of financial statements from absorption costing to variable costing is essentially the opposite of the above except that there is no need to consider the volume variance because fixed costs are subtracted as a period expense on the variable cost income statement.

Conversion from variable costing to absorption costing becomes necessary because of the position taken by the American Institute of Certified Public Accountants (AICPA), the Securities and Exchange Commission (SEC), and the Internal Revenue Service (IRS). Companies seem to be using variable costing in ever-increasing numbers for internal management purposes. However, the AICPA, SEC, and IRS believe that variable costing is inappropriate for reporting results of operations externally.

The basis for the AICPA's position is its Accounting Research Bulletin no. 43, which states that "as applied to inventories, cost means in principle the sum of the applicable expenditures and charges directly or *indirectly* incurred in bringing an article to its existing condition and location" (emphasis added). In other words, inventory costs should contain both variable and fixed cost elements. The AICPA does recognize that some overhead items such as excessive spoilage and rehandling costs may be charged as period expenses rather than being inventoried. However, the basic position on variable or direct costing remains as stated in Bulletin no. 43. The Financial Accounting Standards Board (FASB), the current standard-setting body, has not yet taken a position contrary to the AICPA position.

The SEC does not accept financial reports based on the variable costing approach unless inventories and income numbers are adjusted to reflect an absorption costing basis. This position is based primarily on the attitude that variable costing is not a generally accepted accounting procedure. The SEC also has a policy regarding consistency in reporting among regulated companies, and acceptance of variable costing would probably lead to more inconsistency in reporting.

The IRS specifically states that variable or direct costing is "not in accordance with the regulations." The regulations define inventory costs to include "indirect expenses incident to and necessary for production of the particular article, including in such indirect production costs an appropriate portion of management expenses."

GROSS MARGIN ANALYSIS

Gross margin analysis, also known as gross profit analysis, is a technique for performing a detailed analysis of changes in gross margin between budgeted and actual results or between actual gross margin of succeeding years. Gross margin analysis provides information helpful for answering such questions as—Why did gross margin for the period decrease? Was the decrease due to reduced sales, increased costs or a combination of factors?

Gross margin analysis is especially useful when a company markets several products because it provides information concerning how changes in the relative mix of different products sold affect deviations in gross margin. The affect on gross margin of changes in the sales volume for different products can also be analyzed.

Management should understand why actual gross margin deviated from the budget when a standard cost system is being used. When a standard cost system is not being used, management should understand why the gross margin of one period differed from the gross margin of the prior period. However, it often is not a simple task to identify specific causal relationships because gross margin is a composite of a number of sales and cost elements. Without the proper analytical tools management must guess whether a given change in gross margin is the result of changes in the volume of sales, changes in one or more cost elements, or changes in the selling prices of one or more products.

Isolating the Components of Variance

The procedures used to analyze changes in gross margin parallels the procedures used to analyze variances in a standard cost system. However, gross margin analysis is not dependent on either the use of a standard cost system or a budget. When a cost accounting system other than a standard cost system is used, the results of operations for the previous accounting period are used as the "standard" in gross margin analysis. A standard cost system is assumed for the illustration in this chapter because it is the most common system. The self-study problem at the end of this chapter illustrates gross margin analysis when a standard cost system is not in use.

Gross margin analysis begins by identifying the difference between actual gross margin and budgeted gross margin. This difference is called the **gross margin variance.** The gross margin variance is then further analyzed into its component parts—(a) a sales price variance, (b) a sales mix variance, (c) a sales volume variance, and (d) a cost price variance. By studying each of these variances, management is provided with the information to effectively investigate and correct undesirable results or promote desirable outcomes.

The **sales price variance** represents the effect on gross margin of differences in sales prices between budgeted and actual results. For example, if actual sales prices are not equal to budgeted prices, the amount of the total difference in gross margin that is attributable to the difference in prices must be determined.

The **sales mix variance** represents the effect on gross margin of differences in sales mix between budgeted and actual results. The sales mix of a company relates to the relative proportion of each product sold. For example, a company that plans to sell a total of 100,000 units or 50,000, 40,000, and 10,000 units of products *A, B,* and *C* respectively has a sales mix, or relative sales proportion, of 50:40:10. If actual sales result in a total of 100,000 units sold but at a mix of 55,000, 30,000, and 15,000 units of products *A, B,* and *C* respectively, then the actual sales mix of 55:30:15 is different from the planned sales mix. The amount of the total difference in gross margin that is attributable to the change in relative sales volume must be determined.

The **sales volume variance** represents the effect on gross margin of differences in the quantities of units sold between budgeted and actual results. For example, if the volume of actual sales is not equal to the budgeted sales volume, the amount of the total difference in gross margin that is attributable to the difference in volume must be determined.

The **cost price variance** represents the effect on gross margin of differences in manufacturing costs between budgeted and actual results. When using a standard cost system, the cost price variance can be further analyzed into variances for materials, labor, and manufacturing overhead (as explained in chaps. 15 and 16).

Calculating the Variances

The computational procedures of gross margin analysis are illustrated using the income statement information contained in figure 18.3. A multi-product company is assumed for this illustration because this is the environment in which gross margin analysis is most beneficial.

The difference in the gross margin of $20,100 between budgeted and actual results in figure 18.4 represents the gross margin variance. The challenge is to analyze this

---

Figure 18.4   Income statement

	Budgeted			Actual			Difference
	Units	Price/ Cost	Amount	Units	Price/ Cost	Amount	Amount
Sales:							
Product M	12,000	$30.00	$360,000	10,200	$32.00	$326,400	$ (33,600)
Product N	7,000	25.00	175,000	8,400	25.00	210,000	35,000
Product Z	2,000	20.15	40,300	3,000	19.50	58,500	18,200
Total	21,000		$575,300	21,600	(1)	$594,900	$ 19,600
Cost of goods sold:							
Product M	12,000	$24.00	$288,000	10,200	$24.50	$249,900	$ (38,100)
Product N	7,000	20.00	140,000	8,400	19.00	159,600	19,600
Product Z	2,000	18.00	36,000	3,000	18.00	54,000	18,000
Total	21,000		$464,000	21,600	(2)	$463,500	$ (500)
Gross margin		(3)	$111,300			$131,400	$ 20,100

(1) Actual average price per unit = ($594,900 ÷ 21,600) = $27.5416.
(2) Actual average cost per unit = ($463,500 ÷ 21,600) = $21.4583.
(3) Budgeted average gross margin per unit = ($111,300 ÷ 21,000) = $5.30.
Budgeted gross margin per unit:
  Product M: ($30.00 - $24.00) = $6.00
  Product N: ($25.00 - $20.00) = $5.00
  Product Z: ($20.15 - $18.00) = $2.15

Figure 18.5   Formulas for gross margin analysis

For Standard Cost Systems

Gross margin variance = Budgeted gross margin − Actual gross margin

Sales price variance = [Actual prices − Budgeted prices] × Actual sales

Sales mix variance = [Budgeted gross margin per unit − Budgeted weighted average gross margin] × Actual sales

Budgeted sales mix variance[a] = [Budgeted gross margin per unit − Budgeted weighted average gross margin] × Budgeted sales

Sales volume variance = [Actual sales − Budgeted sales] × Weighted average gross margin

Cost price variance = [Budgeted costs − Actual costs] × Actual sales

For Other Cost Accounting Systems

The above formulas can be adjusted for use with actual or nonstandard types of cost accounting systems by substituting "current year" for "actual" items and "prior year" for "budgeted" items in the formulas.

Note: All prices and costs in these formulas are per-unit amounts. Sales are in units.

[a]This variance and formula are used in the detail analysis of the sales mix variance.

variance to determine what portions are the result of (*a*) differences in selling price, (*b*) differences in sales mix, (*c*) differences in sales volume, or (*d*) differences in the costs of production.

A fundamental principle in such an analysis is that in order to isolate the effect of one factor, all other factors must be held constant. To facilitate the application of this principle relative to the sales mix and volume variances, it is necessary to calculate the "budgeted average gross margin per unit." Figure 18.4 shows this computation.

Note that the computation of the "budgeted average gross margin per unit" relates to the *total* expected results. In contrast, the "budgeted gross margin per unit" relates to the expected results for each *individual* product. The final procedure is to calculate the effect of price and cost changes by holding the volume factor constant. Then the effect of sales mix and volume changes is calculated by holding the price and cost factors constant. Formulas for calculating the variances are given in figure 18.5.

The computations necessary to analyze the gross margin variance of $20,100 shown in figure 18.4 are as follows. Unless otherwise noted, all prices, costs, and quantities relate to the units of production and sales.

Sales Price Variance

	Actual Prices	−	Budgeted Prices	×	Actual Sales	=	Sales Price Variance
Product *M*:	$32.00	−	$30.00 = $2.00	×	10,200	=	$20,400 F
Product *N*:	25.00	−	25.00 = −0−	×	8,400	=	−0−
Product *Z*:	19.50	−	20.15 = −0.65	×	3,000	=	1,950 U
Total sales price variance							$18,450 F

The favorable sales price variance of $18,450 indicates that the bulk of the gross margin variance is due to differences in sales prices for the various products sold by the firm. The above product analysis indicates that the price change for product *M* had a significant positive effect on the increase in gross margin. Product *N* did not affect the increase because there was no price change. There was a small negative effect from the decline in the price of product Z.

Sales Mix Variance

	Budgeted Gross Margin	−	Budgeted Average Gross Margin	×	Actual Sales	=	Sales Mix Variance
Product M:	$6.00	−	$5.30 = $.70	×	10,200	=	$7,140 F
Product N:	5.00	−	5.30 = −.30	×	8,400	=	2,520 U
Product Z:	2.15	−	5.30 = −3.15	×	3,000	=	9,450 U
Total sales mix variance							$4,830 U

The total unfavorable sales mix variance indicates that the relative proportion of product sales shifted toward those products with lower gross margins per unit. For example, because there was a large increase in the relative sales of product Z and because product Z has the lowest gross margin per unit the result is a large unfavorable variance.

The sales mix variance should be interpreted carefully to avoid unwarranted conclusions. Confusion can arise because the *total* sales mix variance and the individual product variances should be interpreted separately. For example, the total sales mix variance of $4,830 in the illustration above is a valid indicator of the total effect on the gross margin of the shift in sales mix. However, examination of the impact by individual product should be made relative to budgeted or anticipated variances, which are actually part of the budget. The following is a calculation of the sales mix variance using budgeted results:

Budgeted Sales Mix Variance

	Budgeted Gross Margin	−	Budgeted Average Gross Margin	×	Budgeted Sales	=	Budgeted Sales Mix Variance
Product M:	$6.00	−	$5.30 = $.70	×	12,000	=	$8,400 F
Product N:	5.00	−	5.30 = −.30	×	7,000	=	2,100 U
Product Z:	2.15	−	5.30 = −3.15	×	2,000	=	6,300 U
Total sales mix variance							$ −0−

As anticipated, the total sales mix variance is zero on a budgeted basis. Because there is a "budgeted sales mix variance" for each product it is necessary to compare actual individual product variances with budgeted results to obtain a clearer picture of the impact of each product on the change in total mix. Such a comparison might be as follows:

Final Sales Mix Variance

	Actual Sales Mix Variance	Budgeted Sales Mix Variance	Difference
Product M:	$7,140 F	$8,400 F	$1,260 U
Product N:	2,520 U	2,100 U	420 U
Product Z:	9,450 U	6,300 U	3,150 U
Total	$4,830 U	−0−	$4,830 U

Note that an increase in an unfavorable variance when comparing budgeted with actual results represents an unfavorable outcome. Comparing budgeted versus actual variances, as above, gives a clearer indication of the actual impact, by product, of the change in the relative sales mix.

Sales Volume Variance

	Actual Sales	−	Budgeted Sales	=		×	Average Gross Margin	=	Sales Volume Variance
Product M:	10,200	−	12,000	=	−1,800	×	5.30	=	$9,540 U
Product N:	8,400	−	7,000	=	1,400	×	5.30	=	7,420 F
Product Z:	3,000	−	2,000	=	1,000	×	5.30	=	5,300 F
Total sales volume variance									$3,180 F

Figure 18.6   Report of gross margin analysis

	Product M	Product N	Product Z	Total
Sales price variance	$20,400 F	$ -0-	$ 1,950 U	$18,450 F
Sales mix variance	1,260 U	420 U	3,150 U	4,830 U
Sales volume variance	9,540 U	7,420 F	5,300 F	3,180 F
Cost price variance	5,100 U	8,400 F	-0-	3,300 F
	$4,500 F	$15,400 F	$ 200 F	$20,100 F

Figure 18.7   Income statement using actual sales and budgeted prices and costs

	Income Statement		
	Units	Price/Cost	Amount
Sales:			
Product M	10,200	$30.00	$306,000
Product N	8,400	25.00	210,000
Product Z	3,000	20.15	60,450
Total	21,600	(1)	$576,450
Cost of goods sold:			
Product M	10,200	24.00	$244,800
Product N	8,400	20.00	168,000
Product Z	3,000	18.00	54,000
Total	21,600	(2)	$466,800
Gross margin		(3)	$109,650

(1) Average price per unit using actual sales at budgeted prices = ($576,450 ÷ 21,600) = $26.6875.
(2) Average cost per unit using actual sales at budgeted costs = ($466,800 ÷ 21,600) = $21.6111.
(3) Average gross margin per unit using actual sales at budgeted prices and costs = ($109,650 ÷ 21,600) = $5.0764.

The sales volume variance isolates the impact on gross margin of changes in sales volume. It is quite clear how much the decreased sales volume of product M and the increased sales volume of products N and Z affected gross margin.

It is also worthwhile to compare the sales volume variances with the sales mix variances relative to other factors, such as price changes, that occurred during the period. For example, if products M and N are substitute goods for product Z, product Z's price decline from $20.00 to $19.50 per unit may have contributed to the change in sales mix as well as to the increased sales of product Z. If such cause-and-effect relationships can be identified, gross margin analysis can be helpful in making any number of production and marketing decisions.

Cost Price Variance

	Budgeted Costs	Actual Costs		Actual Sales		Cost Price Variance
Product M:	$24.00	− $24.50 = $−.50	×	10,200	=	$5,100 U
Product N:	20.00	− 19.00 = 1.00	×	8,400	=	8,400 F
Product Z:	18.00	− 18.00 = -0-	×	3,000	=	-0-
Total cost price variance						$3,300 F

The favorable cost price variance of $3,300 would be further analyzed in a standard cost system by calculating the materials, labor, and manufacturing overhead variances to gauge the relative impact of and responsibility for each cost element.

The results of gross margin analysis can be summarized in a management report that shows each variance component by product and in total. This report can also be used to prove the results of the variance calculations by comparing the grand total of variances with the original gross margin variance analyzed. Figure 18.6 shows such a report.

As a final note, an aggregate approach to gross margin analysis can be used to calculate total variances directly without the detail of individual product variances. When individual product detail is not required, the aggregate approach provides a shortcut to gross margin analysis.

The first step when using the aggregate approach is to calculate an income statement using the actual sales volume at budgeted prices and costs. Such an income statement is presented in figure 18.7 using the data from figure 18.4.

Using the data from figures 18.4 and 18.7 the gross margin analysis is repeated below on an aggregate basis. Variances can be verified with those previously calculated.

Sales Price Variance

Average price using actual sales at budgeted prices (fig. 18.7)	$26.6875
Actual average price (fig. 18.4)	− 27.5416
	$ .8541
Actual quantity sold	× 21,600
Sales price variance	$ 18,450 F

Sales Mix Variance

Budgeted average gross margin (fig. 18.4)	$ 5.3000
Average gross margin using actual sales at budgeted prices and costs	− 5.0764
	$ .2236
Actual quantity sold	× 21,600
Sales mix variance	$ 4,830 U

Sales Volume Variance

Budgeted total sales	$ 21,000
Actual total sales	− 21,600
	$ 600
Budgeted average gross margin (fig. 18.4)	× 5.30
Sales volume variance	$ 3,180 F

Cost Variance

Actual average cost (fig. 18.4)	$21.4583
Average cost using actual sales at budgeted costs (fig. 18.7)	− 21.6111
	$ .1528
Actual total sales	× 21,600
Cost variance	$ 3,300 F

Summary

There is almost universal agreement that variable or direct costing is a desirable alternative to the traditional absorption costing system. The separation of variable and fixed costs and treating fixed overhead costs as a period cost rather than as an inventoriable cost has definite advantages for management use. Variable costing systems are better adapted to management decisions ranging from profit planning to the analysis of departmental operations. However, variable costing is not acceptable for external reporting. Therefore, as a practical matter, a variable costing system is maintained and adjustments are made to financial statements at the end of accounting periods to reflect results on an absorption costing basis.

Gross margin, or gross profit analysis, provides a way to isolate reasons why actual gross margin deviated from budgeted gross margin. If a standard cost system is not in use, gross margin analysis helps to isolate reasons why gross margin changed between two accounting periods. The difference between actual gross margin and budgeted gross margin can be analyzed into the following component parts:

1. A sales price variance representing the effect of differences in sales prices
2. A sales mix variance representing the effect of shifts in relative sales volumes
3. A sales volume variance representing the effect of differences in actual sales volume
4. A cost price variance representing the effect of differences in production costs

Gross margin analysis is especially useful in multi-product environments because results can be expressed in total or by product class. Information from gross margin analysis can also be correlated with other operating results to provide information useful in a variety of management decisions.

Appendix   *Analysis of Contribution Margin*

Changes in contribution margin can be analyzed in the same way that changes in gross margin are analyzed. The procedures are generally the same and the same types of questions are answered. However, remember that gross margin analysis is a tool used to analyze changes in gross margin when an absorption costing system is used, but contribution margin analysis is a tool used to analyze changes in contribution margin when a direct costing system is used.

The variances used to perform contribution margin analysis are briefly explained below and then an example analysis is shown. Figure 18.8 contains budgeted and actual variable cost income statements.

Only an aggregate analysis of contribution margin is illustrated in this appendix. A detailed product analysis can be performed by adjusting the formulas in figure 18.5 to reflect the change from "gross margin" to "contribution margin." Figure 18.9 contains a variable cost income statement with the actual sales volume at budgeted prices and costs. This information is necessary when performing an analysis on an aggregate basis.

Contribution Margin Variance
The contribution margin variance is the difference between actual contribution margin and the budgeted contribution. The objective of the contribution margin analysis is to separate the contribution margin variance into its component parts—(a) sales price variance, (b) sales mix variance, (c) sales volume variance, and (d) cost price variance.

Budgeted contribution margin	$ 1,200
Actual contribution margin	− 1,600
Contribution margin variance	$ 400 F

Figure 18.8   Income statement

	Budgeted			Actual			Differ-ence
	Units	Price/Cost	Amount	Units	Price/Cost	Amount	Amount
Sales:							
Product X	20	$20.00	$ 400	40	$30.00	$1,200	$ 800
Product Y	20	40.00	800	40	40.00	1,600	800
Product Z	20	60.00	1,200	20	60.00	1,200	–0–
Total	60		$2,400	100	(1)	$4,000	$1,600
Variable cost of goods sold:							
Product X	20	$10.00	$ 200	40	$20.00	$ 800	$ 600
Product Y	20	20.00	400	40	20.00	800	400
Product Z	20	30.00	600	20	40.00	800	200
Total	60		$1,200	100	(2)	$2,400	$1,200
Contribution margin		(3)	$1,200			$1,600	$ 400

(1) Actual average price per unit = ($4,000 ÷ 100) = $40.
(2) Actual average cost per unit = ($2,400 ÷ 100) = $24.
(3) Budgeted average contribution margin per unit = ($1,200 ÷ 60) = $20.

Figure 18.9   Income statement using actual sales and budgeted prices and costs

	Income Statement		
	Units	Price/Cost	Amount
Sales:			
Product X	40	$20.00	$ 800
Product Y	40	40.00	1,600
Product Z	20	60.00	1,200
Total	100	(1)	$ 3,600
Variable cost of goods sold:			
Product X	40	$10.00	$ 400
Product Y	40	20.00	800
Product Z	20	30.00	600
Total	100	(2)	$ 1,800
Contribution margin		(3)	$ 1,800

(1) Average price per unit using actual sales at budgeted prices = ($3,600 ÷ 100) = $36.
(2) Average cost per unit using actual sales at budgeted costs = ($1,800 ÷ 100) = $18.
(3) Average contribution margin per unit using actual sales at budgeted prices and costs = ($1,800 ÷ 100)
= $18.

Sales Price Variance

The sales price variance shows the effect on contribution margin of having the actual selling prices being more or less than the budgeted amount.

Average price using actual sales at budgeted prices (fig. 18.9)	$	36
Actual average price (fig. 18.8)	−	40
	$	4
Actual quantity sold	×	100
Sales price variance	$	400 F

Sales Mix Variance

The sales mix variance shows the effect on contribution margin of selling more or less high-profit items than the proportions indicated in the original budget.

Budgeted average contribution margin (fig. 18.8)	$	20
Average gross margin using actual sales at budgeted prices and costs	−	18
	$	2
Actual quantity sold	×	100
Sales mix variance	$	200 U

Sales Volume Variance

The sales volume variance, also called the quantity variance, shows the effect on contribution margin of the difference between the actual total unit sales and the budgeted total unit sales computed under the assumption that actual sales are in the same unit proportions as budgeted sales.

Budgeted total sales	$	60
Actual total sales	−	100
	$	40
Budgeted average contribution margin (fig. 18.8)	×	20
Sales volume variance	$	800 F

Cost Price Variance

The cost price variance shows the effect on contribution margin of *variable expenses* being more or less than the level budgeted.

Actual average cost (fig. 18.8)	$	24
Average cost using actual sales at budgeted costs (fig. 18.9)	−	18
	$	6
Actual total sales	×	100
Cost variance	$	600 F

Summary of variances:

Sales price variance	$400 F
Sales mix variance	200 U
Sales volume variance	800 F
Cost price variance	600 U
Contribution margin variance	$400 F

VARIABLE COSTING

The following information concerns the first two years of operation for a newly created division of a manufacturing company.

Standard Manufacturing Costs

	Unit Cost
Direct materials	$ 4.00
Direct labor	4.00
Variable manufacturing overhead	2.00
Total variable manufacturing costs	$10.00
Fixed manufacturing overhead	4.00
Total manufacturing costs	$14.00

Standard capacity—200,000 units
Selling price—$25.00 per unit
Selling and administrative expenses: Variable—$2.00 per unit of sales
                                      Fixed   —$300,000

Production and Sales Statistics

	Year 1	Year 2
Units produced	220,000	170,000
Units sold	180,000	200,000
Inventory change	+40,000	−30,000

Required

Prepare partial comparative income statements for the first two years of operations using both absorption costing and variable costing methods. Also, prepare a schedule reconciling the differences, if any, in net income between the two methods.

Solution to the Self-Study Problem

Comparative Income Statements

Variable Costing (in 000's)

	Year 1	Year 2
Sales @ $25	$4,500	$5,000
Variable manufacturing cost of goods sold:		
Direct materials @ $4	$ 880	$ 680
Direct labor @ $4	880	680
Variable manufacturing overhead @ $2	440	340
Total variable manufacturing costs	$2,200	$1,700
Plus: Beginning inventory	–0–	400
Variable manufacturing cost of goods available for sale	$2,200	$2,100
Less: Ending inventory	400	100
Variable manufacturing cost of goods sold	$1,800	$2,000
Variable selling and administrative expenses @ $2	360	400
Total variable costs	$2,160	$2,400
Contribution margin	$2,340	$2,600
Less: Fixed costs:		
Fixed manufacturing costs	$ 800	$ 800
Fixed selling and administrative costs	300	300
Total fixed costs	$1,100	$1,100
Operating income	$1,240	$1,500

Absorption Costing (in 000's)

	Year 1	Year 2
Sales @ $25	$4,500	$5,000
Cost of goods sold:		
Cost of goods manufactured:		
Direct materials @ $4	$ 880	$ 680
Direct labor @ $4	880	680
Variable manufacturing overhead @ $2	440	340
Fixed manufacturing overhead @ $4	880	680
Total cost of goods manufactured	$3,080	$2,380
Beginning inventory	–0–	560
Cost of goods available for sale	$3,080	$2,940
Less: Ending inventory	560	140
Cost of goods sold	$2,520	$2,800
Gross margin	$1,980	$2,200
Selling and administrative expenses:		
Variable @ $2	$ 360	$ 400
Fixed	300	300
Total selling and administrative expenses	$ 660	$ 700
Operating income before volume variance	$1,320	$1,500
Volume variance	80	$ (120)
Operating income	$1,400	$1,380

Volume variance:

Formula: (Actual volume − Budgeted volume) × Fixed overhead per unit
Year 1: (220,000 − 200,000) × $4.00 = $ 80,000 Favorable
Year 2: (170,000 − 200,000) × $4.00 = $120,000 Unfavorable

Reconciliation of Differences in Income from Operations
Differences in Income from Operations (In 000's)

	Year 1	Year 2
Absorption costing	$1,400	$1,380
Variable costing	1,240	1,500
Difference	$ 160	$ (120)

Reconciliation

	Year 1	Year 2
Change in inventory	$ 40	$ (30)
Fixed costs per unit	× 4	× 4
Difference	$160	$ (120)

GROSS MARGIN ANALYSIS

The following information concerns two years of operations of a company that does not use a standard cost system. Its management wants to analyze why gross margin increased so dramatically in the second year of operations. Data from company records concerning sales, cost of goods sold, and gross margin is as follows:

Income Statement

	Year 1			Year 2		
	Units	Price/Cost	Amount	Units	Price/Cost	Amount
Sales:						
Product A	40,000	$ 5.23	$209,200	40,000	$ 6.00	$240,000
Product B	16,000	10.00	160,000	20,000	13.20	264,000
Product C	14,000	8.00	112,000	8,000	7.00	56,000
Total	70,000		$481,200	68,000		$560,000
Cost of goods sold:						
Product A	40,000	4.35	$174,000	40,000	$ 5.60	$224,000
Product B	16,000	8.00	128,000	20,000	8.00	160,000
Product C	14,000	7.00	98,000	8,000	7.00	56,000
Total	70,000		$400,000	68,000		$440,000
Gross margin			$ 81,200			$120,000

Budgeted weighted average gross margin per unit (year 1):

($81,200/70,000) = $1.16.

Budgeted gross margin per unit (year 1):

Product A: ($ 5.23 − $4.35) = $ .88
Product B: ($10.00 − $8.00) = $2.00
Product C: ($ 8.00 − $7.00) = $1.00

Required

Analyze the gross margin increase of $38,300 ($120,000 − $81,200) by calculating sales price, cost price, sales mix, and sales volume variances. Also prepare a report for management detailing your gross margin analysis.

Solution to the Self-Study Problem

The computation of the variances related to gross margin analysis using the above data is given as follows:

Sales Price Variance

	Year 2 Prices	−	Year 1 Prices	×	Year 2 Sales	=	Sales Price Variances
Product A:	$ 6.00	−	$ 5.23 = $ .77	×	40,000	=	$30,800 F
Product B:	13.20	−	10.00 = 3.20	×	20,000	=	64,000 F
Product C:	7.00	−	8.00 = 1.00	×	8,000	=	8,000 U
Total sales price variance							$86,800 F

Sales Mix Variance

	Year 1 Gross Margin	−	Year 1 Weighted Average Gross Margin	×	Year 1 Sales	=	Sales Mix Variance
Product A:	$ .88	−	$1.16 = $−.28	×	40,000	=	$11,200 U
Product B:	2.00	−	1.16 = .84	×	20,000	=	16,800 F
Product C:	1.00	−	1.16 = −.16	×	8,000	=	1,280 U
Total sales mix variance							$ 4,320 U

Budgeted Sales Mix Variance

	Year 1 Gross Margin	−	Year 1 Weighted Average Gross Margin	×	Year 2 Sales	=	Sales Mix Variance
Product A	$ .88	−	$1.16 = $−.28	×	40,000	=	$11,200 U
Product B	2.00	−	1.16 = .84	×	16,000	=	13,440 F
Product C	1.00	−	1.16 = −.16	×	14,000	=	2,240 U
Total sales mix variance							$ −0−

Comparison of Actual and Budgeted Sales Mix Variance

	Actual Sales Mix Variance	Budgeted Sales Mix Variance	Difference
Product A	$11,200 U	$11,200 U	$ −0−
Product B	16,800 F	13,440 F	3,360 F
Product C	1,280 U	2,240 U	960 F
Total	$ 4,320 F	−0−	$4,320 F

Sales Volume Variance

	Year 2 Sales	−	Year 1 Sales	×	Year 1 Weighted Average Gross Margin	=	Sales Volume Variance
Product A	40,000	−	40,000 = −0−	×	$1.16	=	$ −0−
Product B	20,000	−	16,000 = 4,000	×	1.16	=	4,640 F
Product C	8,000	−	14,000 = −6,000	×	1.16	=	6,960 U
Total sales volume variance							$2,320 U

Cost Price Variance

	Year 1 Costs	−	Year 2 Costs	×	Year 2 Sales	=	Cost Price Variance
Product A	$4.35	−	$5.60 = $−1.25	×	40,000	=	$50,000 U
Product B	8.00	−	8.00 = −0−	×	20,000	=	−0−
Product C	7.00	−	7.00 = −0−	×	8,000	=	−0−
Total cost price variance							$50,000 U

Report of Gross Margin Analysis

	Product A	Product B	Product C	Total
Sales price variance	$30,800 F	$64,000 F	$ 8,000 U	$86,800 F
Sales mix variance	−0−	3,360 F	960 F	4,320 F
Sales volume variance	−0−	4,640 F	6,960 U	2,320 U
Cost price variance	50,000 U	−0−	−0−	50,000 U
	$19,200 U	$72,000 F	$14,000 U	$38,300 F

Suggested Readings

Baiman, Stanley, and Demski, Joel S. "Variance Analysis Procedures as Motivational Devices." *Management Science* (August 1980): 840–48.

Earnest, Kenneth R. "Applying Motivational Theory in Management Accounting." *Management Accounting* (December 1979): 41–44.

Jablonsky, Stephen F., and Dirsmith, Mark W. "Is Financial Reporting Influencing Internal Decision Making?" *Management Accounting* (July 1979): 40–45.

LaTour, Stephen A. "Variance Explained: It Measures Neither Importance nor Effect Size." *Decision Sciences* (January 1981): 150–60.

Morse, Wayne J. *Cost Accounting: Processing, Evaluating and Using Cost Data.* 2d ed. Reading, Mass.: Addison-Wesley Publishing Co., 1981.

Discussion Questions

1. What is the principal difference between variable costing and absorption costing?
2. Why is variable costing considered unacceptable for external reporting?
3. What costing system is acceptable for external reporting? Why?
4. Why does management often keep both variable costing and absorption costing systems?
5. What are three advantages of management having an income statement in the variable costing format?
6. Why is the chart of accounts expanded when direct costing is used?
7. When will operating income using variable costing exceed operating income computed using absorption costing?
8. Even though variable costing has many merits, explain any hidden dangers that are present in its use.
9. Define gross margin and explain why its use is significant for management.
10. What causes changes in gross margin?
11. Define "mix" and explain how it relates to gross margin analysis.
12. Name four variances that can be computed to help explain differences in gross margin. Explain what information each variance supplies management about sales or costs.
13. What are the formulas for calculating each variance of the gross margin analysis?
14. Explain how the analysis and interpretation differs between the total sales mix variance and individual product sales mix variances.
15. What differences are there between gross profit analysis when a standard cost system is used compared to when a standard cost system is not used?
16. Explain the aggregate procedure for calculating gross margin variances when detail product information is not required.

Exercises

Exercise 18.1   Absorption and Variable Costing Procedures

Current manufacturing and sales information for the Joplin Juice Company are given below:

Units produced	20,000
Units sold	18,000
Units in beginning inventory	–0–
Direct material used	$40,000
Direct labor	44,000
Selling and administrative expenses:	
Variable	$24,000
Fixed	46,000
Factory overhead:	
Variable	$35,000
Fixed	52,000

Required

1. Under the absorption costing method, give the value of the finished-goods ending inventory.
2. Under the variable costing approach, give the value of the finished-goods ending inventory.
3. Which method would show a higher net income for Joplin in the current year? How much higher?

Exercise 18.2   Identification of Income Reporting Method

Well Water Incorporated began production of a product called Suvi Sunshine in 19X1. Operating information relating to production of Suvi Sunshine in 19X1 is given below:

Variable costs per unit:	
Direct materials	$8
Direct labor	3
Factory overhead	1
Selling and administrative expenses	2
Fixed costs for the year:	
Factory overhead	140,000
Selling and administrative expenses	180,000

During 19X1, Well Water produced 80,000 units and sold 72,000 units. The finished-goods ending inventory was valued at $96,000 for the unsold units.

Required

1. Is Well Water using absorption costing or variable costing to value the finished-goods ending inventory? Show calculations.
2. Assume that Well Water will be preparing financial statements for its stockholders.
   a. Is $96,000 the correct value for the finished-goods ending inventory on the statements?
   b. If $96,000 is incorrect, what figure should be assigned to the finished-goods ending inventory?

Exercise 18.3 Basic Absorption and Variable Costing Procedures

Martino Company produces and sells one product line. Costs recorded in the first year of production are as follows:

Variable costs per unit:	
Direct material	$10
Direct labor	4
Factory overhead	5
Selling and administrative expenses	3
Fixed costs per year:	
Factory overhead	42,000
Selling and administrative expenses	30,000

During the first year, Martino manufactured 10,000 units but sold only 6,000. The selling price is $39 per unit.

Required

1. Compute the cost per unit of product under the absorption costing method.
2. Compute the cost per unit of product under the variable costing method.
3. Prepare a simple absorption costing income statement for the current year.
4. Prepare a simple variable costing income statement for the current year.

Exercise 18.4 Converting from an Absorption to a Variable Costing Income Report

The Bird Company began operations during the past year. The financial results of this first year are as follows (absorption costing method):

Bird Company
Income Statement

Sales		$825,000
Less cost of goods sold:		
Opening inventory	–0–	
Cost of goods produced (36,000 × $17)	612,000	
Goods available for sale	612,000	
Less ending inventory (3,000 × $17)	51,000	561,000
Gross margin		$264,000
Less selling and administrative expenses		99,000
Net income		$165,000

The selling and administrative expenses for the year were all fixed. The product's $17 unit cost is made up of the following:

Direct materials	$ 6
Direct labor	4
Variable factory overhead	3
Fixed factory overhead (144,000 ÷ 36,000)	4
Total unit cost	$17

Required

1. Prepare an income statement for the Bird Company using the variable costing method.
2. Explain any differences in net income between your variable costing results and the absorption costing results shown above.

Exercise 18.5   Absorption Costing Income Statement

Hanson's Hoses Incorporated began production of a terrific new product in 19X5. Selected operating results are given below:

Production:	
Units produced	25,000
Units sold	22,000
Variable costs:	
Direct material	$62,500
Direct labor	45,000
Factory overhead	30,000
Sales and Administrative expenses	22,000
Fixed costs:	
Factory overhead	$50,000
Sales and administrative expenses	35,000
Sales price per unit	$ 11

Required

Prepare, in good form, an income statement for Hanson's Hoses during 19X5 using the absorption costing method.

Exercise 18.6   Variable Costing Income Statement

Use the information given in exercise 18.5 for Hanson's Hoses Incorporated during 19X5.

Required

Prepare, in good form, an income statement for the year 19X5 using the variable costing method.

Exercise 18.7   Variable Costing Income Statements for Multiple Years

Sandberg Mills began production January 1, 19X3. Using the absorption costing method, Sandberg has reported income as follows for the first two years:

	19X3	*19X4*
Sales	$798,000	$945,000
Less cost of goods sold:		
Beginning inventory	–0–	56,000
Cost of goods manufactured	588,000	588,000
Goods available for sale	588,000	644,000
Less ending inventory	56,000	14,000
Cost of goods sold	532,000	630,000
Gross margin	266,000	315,000
Less selling and administrative expenses (fixed $114,000)	190,000	204,000
Net income	$ 76,000	$111,000

Production took place as follows:

	19X3	*19X4*
Units produced	42,000	42,000
Units sold	38,000	45,000

No work in process inventories existed at the end of either year.

Variable cost per unit is computed:

Direct material	$ 3.50
Direct labor	6.00
Factory overhead	2.00
Fixed factory overhead (105,000 ÷ 42,000)	2.50
Total cost per unit	$14.00

Required

1. Prepare, in good form, an income statement for years 19X3 and 19X4 under the variable costing method.
2. Reconcile the net income for each year from the variable costing income statement to the net incomes of the absorption costing method.

Exercise 18.8   Absorption and Variable Costing Comparative Statements (CMA)

The vice-president for sales of Huber Corporation has received the following income statement for November 19X5. The statement has been prepared on the direct-cost basis and is reproduced below. The firm has just adopted a direct costing system for internal reporting.

Huber Corporation
Income Statement
For the Month of November 19X5
(000 omitted)

Sales		$2,400
Less: Variable standard cost of goods sold		1,200
Manufacturing margin		$1,200
Less: Fixed manufacturing costs at budget	$600	
Fixed manufacturing cost spending variance	0	600
Gross margin		$ 600
Less: Fixed selling and administrative costs		400
Net income before taxes		$ 200

The controller attached the following notes to the statement:

1. The unit sales price for November averaged $24.
2. The standard unit manufacturing costs for the month were:

Variable cost	$12
Fixed cost	4
Total cost	$16

The unit rate for fixed manufacturing costs is a predetermined rate based upon a normal monthly production of 150,000 units.
3. Production for November was 45,000 units in excess of sales.
4. The inventory at November 30 consisted of 80,000 units.

Required

1. The vice-president for sales is not comfortable with the direct cost basis and wonders what the net income would have been under the absorption cost basis.
   a. Present the November income statement on an absorption cost basis.
   b. Reconcile and explain the difference between the direct costing and the absorption costing net income figures.
2. Explain the features associated with a direct cost income measurement that should be attractive to the vice-president for sales.

Exercise 18.9   Absorption Costing Statement and Procedures

Cooper's Hoops 'n Barrels manufactures a barrel that has become popular recently. The operating results for Cooper's first month of production are given below:

Units produced	1,000
Units sold	850
Selling price per unit	$ 45
Production costs:	
Variable per unit	
Direct materials	$ 10
Direct labor	15
Overhead	2
Fixed overhead	7,200
Selling and administrative costs:	
Variable	10% of sales
Fixed	$4,200

Required

Prepare, in good form, an income statement under the absorption costing method. Calculate the cost to produce a single barrel.

Exercise 18.10   Variable Costing Statement and a Comparison of Results

Refer to the information in exercise 18.9.

Required

1. Prepare, in good form, an income statement under the variable costing method. Calculate the cost to produce a single barrel.
2. Which income statement would you be most likely to use in a presentation made to Cooper's creditors? Assume you are in Cooper's management.
3. Reconcile the difference between the net income figures computed in exercise 18.9 and in requirement 1 above.

Problems

Problem 18.1   Absorption and Variable Costing Concepts and Procedures

Just Frames began production in 19X5. It is now the beginning of 19X8 and the president of the company knows about both the absorption and variable costing methods. He would like a summary of the first three years of operations presented.

Just Frames uses a FIFO inventory method. The yearly operations information is as follows:

Production costs

Direct materials per unit	$ 2.00
Direct labor per unit	1.50
Factory overhead	
Variable per unit	.50
Fixed	$144,000
Selling and administrative costs	
Variable	30% of sales
Fixed	$32,000
Sales price (per unit)	$12.50

Sales and production units

	19X5	19X6	19X7
Sales	45,000	36,000	45,000
Production	45,000	54,000	36,000

Required

1. Prepare a three-year comparative income statement using the absorption costing approach.
2. Prepare a three-year comparative income statement using the variable costing approach.
3. Reconcile the absorption costing and variable costing net income figures for each year.
4. Using the absorption method income statements prepared in requirement one, prepare a chart comparing sales volume to absorption net income. Explain to the president of Just Frames why the absorption net income does not vary directly proportionate to the sales figures. Compare 19X5 to 19X6 and then 19X5 to 19X7.

Problem 18.2   Absorption and Variable Costing and Their Tie to Standard Costing

Rogers Company uses a standard absorption costing approach, which shows the following account balances as of December 31, 19X5.

Total costs using standard unit prices:

Raw materials	87,500
Work in process	50,000
Finished goods	150,000
Cost of goods sold	300,000
Total	587,500

Variances (unfavorable)

Direct-material quantity	25,000
Direct-material price	30,000
Direct-labor rate	8,000
Direct-labor efficiency	25,000
Underapplied overhead	12,000
Total	100,000
Sales	800,000

There are no beginning inventories.

Assume that all variances not prorated are considered adjustments to cost of goods sold. Assume that the data given are all that are available and that prorations are therefore made directly to raw materials, work in process, finished goods, and cost of goods sold.

Required

1. Compute the gross margin using the absorption costing method in each of the following specific situations.
    a. A standard costing system is used without any variance proration.
    b. A standard costing system is used with proration of all variances.
    c. A normal absorption costing system is used without proration of underapplied overhead.
    d. A normal absorption costing system is used with proration of underapplied overhead.
    e. A system of historical rather than predetermined costs is used.
2. Analyze the gross margin results found in requirement 1. Does one system write off costs to expense quicker than the others? What other observations can you make in comparing the five systems? Would you say that the current standards are reasonable? Why or why not?
3. Assume more data are available to you now. How would you prorate the variances to make the system more accurate?

Problem 18.3 Alternative Income Results Using Absorption and Variable Costing with Variances from Standard Costs

Hannaphase Incorporated is in its first year of production. They use the standard absorption costing approach, which shows the following unadjusted account balances at year end:

Raw materials ending inventory	20,000
Work-in-process ending inventory	15,000
Finished-goods ending inventory	25,000
Cost of goods sold	60,000
Direct-materials price variance	8,000
Direct-materials quantity variance	2,000
Direct-labor rate variance	600
Direct-labor efficiency variance	2,000
Factory overhead actually incurred (fixed = 8,000)	20,000
Factory overhead applied at standard rate	16,000
Underapplied factory overhead	4,000
Selling and administrative expenses	24,000
Sales	100,000

All variances are unfavorable for the period described. The materials price variances are measured at purchase and not when materials are used. Assume that the proportion of direct materials, direct labor, and factory overhead remains constant in work in process, finished goods, and cost of goods sold. The direct-material component represents 60% of the ending inventory of work in process, finished goods, and cost of goods sold.

Required

1. Prepare comparative income statements using absorption costing and variable costing methods for each of the following situations:
    a. A standard costing system is used without any variance allocation.
    b. A standard costing system is used with allocation of all variances.
    c. A normal (historical) costing system is used without allocation of underapplied overhead.
    d. A normal costing system is used with allocation of underapplied overhead.
    e. A system of historical rather than predetermined costs is used.
2. Analyze your findings in requirement 1. What differences do you see and why do they exist?

Problem 18.4 Absorption Costing Review of Variance Allocations (CMA)

Packless Incorporated has a standard process-costing system for all products. All inventories are carried at standard during the year. The inventories *and* cost of goods sold are adjusted at fiscal year end for the financial statement. All products are considered to flow through the manufacturing process to finished goods and ultimate sales in a first-in, first-out fashion.

The standard cost of one of Packless's products manufactured in the Mason plant, unchanged from the previous year, is as follows:

Raw materials	$2.00
Direct labor (.25 hour @ 16.00)	4.00
Manufacturing overhead	3.00
Total standard cost	$9.00

There is no work-in-process inventory of this product due to the nature of the manufacturing process. The following schedule reports the manufacturing and sales activity measured at standard cost for the current fiscal year:

	Units	Dollars
Product manufactured	95,000	$855,000
Finished-goods beginning inventory	15,000	135,000
Goods available for sale	110,000	$990,000
Finished-goods ending inventory	19,000	171,000
Cost of goods sold	91,000	$819,000

The manufacturing performance relative to standard costs both this year and last year was not good. The balance of the finished-goods inventory ($140,800) reported on the balance sheet at the beginning of the year included a $5,800 adjustment for variances from standard cost. The unfavorable standard cost variances for labor for the current fiscal year consisted of a wage-price variance of $32,000 and a labor-efficiency variance of $20,000 (1,250 hours @ $16.00). There were no other variances from standard cost for this year.

Required

Assume that the unfavorable labor variances totaling $52,000 are considered material in amount by management and are to be prorated to finished-goods inventory and to cost of goods sold. Determine the amount that will be shown on the year-end balance sheet for finished-goods inventory, and the amount that will be shown for cost of goods sold on the income statement prepared for the fiscal year.

Problem 18.5 Multiple Year Comparison Absorption and Variable Costing

The sales department at Jaeger Mix Company is in a tizzy. Mrs. Michaels, the sales director, just received the comparative income statements for the last three months and she feels something is afoul with the projections. In spite of steady increases in sales, the income has been dropping just as steadily. Mrs. Michaels has approached you and your colleagues in the accounting department and voiced her concerns: "If sales increases hurt us this bad, we might as well cut back." Below is the report Mrs. Michaels just received:

Jaeger Mix Company
Monthly Income Statements

	January	February	March
Sales	$250,000	$275,000	$300,000
Less cost of goods sold:			
Opening inventory	12,500	50,000	62,500
Cost of current production			
Variable costs	65,000	60,000	40,000
Fixed costs	97,500	90,000	60,000
Goods available for sale	175,000	200,000	162,500
Less ending inventory	50,000	62,500	12,500
Cost of goods sold	125,000	137,500	150,000
Underapplied or (overapplied) fixed overhead costs	(7,500)	—	30,000
Cost of goods sold at actual	117,500	137,500	180,000
Gross margin	132,500	137,500	120,000
Less selling and administrative expenses	122,500	132,500	142,500
Net income	$ 10,000	$ 5,000	$ (22,500)

The March loss has Mrs. Michaels especially confused. She is sure there is a better way of reporting income so she can encourage her sales force.

Operations data for the first quarter are as follows:

	January	February	March
Sales in units	25,000	27,500	30,000
Production in units	32,500	30,000	20,000

The January opening inventory consisted of 2,500 units. Your department uses a budgeted production volume of 30,000 units for applying fixed overhead.

Required

1. Prepare an income statement for the same three months, using the variable costing approach.
2. Compute the breakeven points under absorption costing and variable costing.
3. Reconcile the variable costing income statements to the absorption costing income statements month by month.
4. Explain to Mrs. Michaels the incongruities she expressed to you and why there seems to be no correlation of profit to sales.

Problem 18.6   Analysis of Variances in Contribution Margin (CMA)

The Markley Division of Rosette Industries manufactures and sells patio chairs. The chairs are manufactured in two versions—a metal model and a plastic model of a lesser quality. The company uses its own sales force to sell the chairs to retail stores and to catalog outlets. Generally, customers purchase both metal and plastic versions.

The chairs are manufactured on two different assembly lines located in adjoining buildings. The division management and sales department occupy the third building on the property. The division management includes a division controller responsible for the divisional financial activities and the preparation of reports explaining the differences between actual and budgeted performance. The controller structures these reports so that the sales activities are distinguished from cost factors and so each can be analyzed separately.

The operating results for the first three months of the fiscal year as compared to the budget are presented in the third column. The budget for the current year was based upon the assumption that Markley Division would maintain its present market share of the estimated total patio chair market (plastic and metal combined). A status report had been sent to corporate management toward the end of the second month indicating that divisional operating income for the first quarter would probably be about 45% below budget; this estimate was just about on target. The division's operating income was below budget even though industry volume for patio chairs increased by 10% more than was expected at the time the budget was developed.

Markley Division
Operating Results for the First Quarter

	Actual	Budget	Favorable (unfavorable) relative to the budget
Sale in units			
Plastic model	60,000	50,000	10,000
Metal model	20,000	25,000	(5,000)
Sales revenue			
Plastic model	$630,000	$500,000	$130,000
Metal model	300,000	375,000	(75,000)
Total sales	$930,000	$875,000	$ 55,000
Less variable costs			
Manufacturing (at standard)			
Plastic model	$480,000	$400,000	$(80,000)
Metal model	200,000	250,000	50,000
Selling			
Commissions	46,500	43,750	(2,750)
Bad debt allowance	9,300	8,750	(550)
Total variable costs (except variable manufacturing variances)	$735,800	$702,500	$(33,300)
Contribution margin (except variable manufacturing variances)	$194,200	$172,500	$ 21,700
Less other costs			
Variable manufacturing costs variances from standards	$ 49,600	$ —	$(49,600)
Fixed manufacturing costs	49,200	48,000	(1,200)
Fixed selling and administrative costs	38,500	36,000	(2,500)
Corporation offices allocation	18,500	17,500	(1,000)
Total other costs	$155,800	$101,500	$(54,300)
Divisional operating income	$ 38,400	$ 71,000	$(32,600)

The manufacturing activities for the quarter resulted in the production of 55,000 plastic chairs and 22,500 metal chairs. The costs incurred by each manufacturing unit are presented below:

			Plastic Model	Metal Model
Raw materials (stated in equivalent finished chairs)				
	Quantity	Price		
Purchases				
Plastic	60,000	$5.65	$339,000	
Metal	30,000	$6.00		$180,000
Usage				
Plastic	56,000	$5.00	280,000	
Metal	23,000	$6.00		138,000
Direct labor				
9,300 hours @ $6.00 per hour			55,800	
5,600 hours @ $8.00 per hour				44,800
Manufacturing overhead				
Variable				
Supplies			43,000	18,000
Power			50,000	15,000
Employee benefits			19,000	12,000
Fixed				
Supervision			14,000	11,000
Depreciation			12,000	9,000
Property taxes and other items			1,900	1,300

The standard variable manufacturing costs per unit and the budgeted monthly fixed manufacturing costs established for the current year are presented below:

	Plastic Model	Metal Model
Raw material	$ 5.00	$ 6.00
Direct labor		
1/6 hour @ $6.00 per DLH	1.00	
1/4 hour @ $8.00 per DLH		2.00
Variable overhead		
1/6 hour @ $12.00 per DLH	2.00	
1/4 hour @ $8.00 per DLH		2.00
Standard variable manufacturing cost per unit	$ 8.00	$10.00
Budgeted fixed costs per month		
Supervision	$4,500	$3,500
Depreciation	4,000	3,000
Property taxes and other items	600	400
Total budgeted fixed costs for month	$9,100	$6,900

Required

1. Explain the variance in Markley Division's contribution margin attributable to sales activities by calculating the following:
   a. Sales price variance
   b. Sales mix variance
   c. Sales volume variance
2. What portion of the sales volume variance, if any, can be attributed to a change in Markley Division's market share?
3. Analyze the variance in Markley Division's variable manufacturing costs ($49,600) in as much detail as the data permit.

4. Based upon your analyses prepared for requirements 1, 2, and 3 answer the following:
   a. Identify the major cause of Markley Division's unfavorable profit performance.
   b. Did Markley's management attempt to correct this problem? Explain your answer.
   c. What other steps, if any, could Markley's management have taken to improve the division's operating income? Explain your answer.

Problem 18.7   Absorption and Variable Costing and the Analysis of Comparative Results (CMA)

CLK Company is a manufacturer of electrical components. The company maintains a significant inventory of a broad range of finished goods because it has built its business upon prompt shipments of any stock item.

CLK manufactured all items it sold until recently when it discontinued the manufacturing of five items. The items were dropped from the manufacturing process because the unit costs computed by CLK's full cost system did not provide a sufficient margin to cover shipping and selling costs. The five items are now purchased from other manufacturers at a price that allows CLK to make a very small profit after shipping and selling costs. CLK keeps these items in its product line in order to offer a complete line of electrical components.

The president is disappointed at recent profitability performance. He thought that the switch from manufacture to purchase for the five items would improve profit performance. However, the reverse has occurred. All other factors affecting profits—sales volume, sales prices, and incurred selling and manufacturing costs—were as expected so the profit problem can be traced to this decision. The president has asked the controller's department to reevaluate the financial effects of the decision.

The task was assigned to a recently hired assistant controller. She has reviewed the data used to reach the decision to purchase rather than manufacture. Her conclusion is that the company should have continued to manufacture the item. In her opinion the incorrect decision was made because full (absorption) cost data rather than direct (variable) cost data was used to make the decision.

Required

1. List the features of direct (variable) costing as compared to full (absorption) costing that make it possible for her conclusion to be correct.
2. For internal measurement, compare the income, return on investment, and inventory values under full (absorption) costing and direct (variable) costing for periods in which
   a. inventory quantities are rising.
   b. inventory quantities are declining.
   c. inventory quantities are stable.
3. What advantages are said to accrue to decision making if direct (variable) costing is used?

Problem 18.8   Analysis of Variance between Budget and Actual Results

JK Enterprises sold 550,000 units during the first quarter ending March 31, 19X1. These sales represented a 10% increase over the number of units budgeted for the quarter. In spite of the sales increase, profits were below budget as shown in the following condensed income statement:

JK Enterprises
Income Statement
For the First Quarter Ending March 31, 1981
(000 omitted)

	Budget	Actual
Sales	$2,500	$2,530
Variable expenses		
Cost of goods sold	$1,475	$1,540
Selling	400	440
Total variable expenses	$1,875	$1,980
Contribution margin	$ 625	$ 550
Fixed expenses		
Selling	$ 125	$ 150
Administration	275	300
Total fixed expenses	$ 400	$ 450
Income before taxes	$ 225	$ 100
Income taxes (40%)	90	40
Net income	$ 135	$ 60

The accounting department always prepares a brief analysis explaining the difference between the budgeted net income and the actual net income. This analysis, which has not been completed for the first quarter, is submitted to top management with the income statement.

Required

Prepare an explanation of the $125,000 unfavorable variance between the first quarter budgeted and actual before-tax income for JK Enterprises by calculating a single amount for each of the following variations:

1. Sales price difference
2. Variable unit cost difference
3. Volume difference
4. Fixed cost difference

Problem 18.9 Analysis of Actual Versus Budget Operating Results (CPA)

The income statement of Duo Incorporated is presented below. These data relate to the calculation of variances that explain the differences between the actual profit and budgeted profit in terms of sales price, cost, sales mix, and sales volume.

Duo Inc.
Income Statement for
the Year Ending
December 31, 1977
(000 omitted)

	Product AR-10		Product ZR-7		Total	
	Budget	**Actual**	**Budget**	**Actual**	**Budget**	**Actual**
Unit sales	2,000	2,800	6,000	5,600	8,000	8,400
Sales	$6,000	$7,560	$12,000	$11,760	$18,000	$19,320
Cost of goods sold	$2,400	$2,800	$ 6,000	$ 5,880	$ 8,400	$ 8,680
Fixed costs	1,800	1,900	2,400	2,400	4,200	4,300
Total costs	$4,200	$4,700	$ 8,400	$ 8,280	$12,600	$12,980
Net profit	$1,800	$2,860	$ 3,600	$ 3,480	$ 5,400	$ 6,340

Required

1. Determine the net effect on profit of the unit sales volume variance of product AR-10.
2. Determine the net effect on profit of the sales price variance for product ZR-7.
3. Determine the net effect on profit from the change in the unit cost of goods sold of product ZR-7.
4. If products AR-10 and ZR-7 are substitutes for each other, a sales mix and sales volume variation for the combined products can be calculated. If this combination is calculated, determine the net effect on profit of the change in the unit sales mix.
5. Determine the sales volume variation calculation that would complement the variance calculated in requirement 4.

Problem 18.10 Absorption and Variable Costing and Gross Margin Analysis (CMA)

Part 1

Indiana Corporation began its operations on January 1. They produce a single product that sells for $9 per unit. Indiana uses an actual (historical) cost system. In the first year, 100,000 units were produced and 90,000 units were sold. There was no work-in-process inventory at December 31.

Manufacturing costs and selling and administrative expenses for the year were as follows:

	Fixed Costs	**Variable Costs**
Raw materials	—	$1.75 per unit produced
Direct labor	—	1.25 per unit produced
Factory overhead	$100,000	.50 per unit produced
Selling and administrative	70,000	.60 per unit sold

Required

1. Determine Indiana's operating income for the year using the direct costing method.
2. Describe the information that must be known about a production process in order to institute a direct costing system.

Part 2

During January Gable Incorporated produced 10,000 units of product *F* with costs as follows:

Direct materials	$40,000
Direct labor	22,000
Variable overhead	13,000
Fixed overhead	10,000
	$85,000

Required

1. Determine Gable's unit cost of product *F* for January 19X1 calculated on the direct costing basis.
2. Describe and discuss the major factor, related to manufacturing costs, that causes the difference in net earnings computed using absorption costing and net earnings computed using direct costing.

Part 3

Garfield Company, which sells a single product, provided the following data from its income statements for the calendar years 19X1 and 19X0.

	19X1
Sales (150,000 units)	$750,000
Cost of goods sold	525,000
Gross profit	$225,000

	19X0 *(Base Year)*
Sales (180,000 units)	$720,000
Cost of goods sold	575,000
Gross profit	$145,000

Required

Prepare an analysis of the variation in gross profit between the two years to determine the effects of changes in sales price and sales volume.

SEGMENT PERFORMANCE

19

OUTLINE

The natural growth and development of business organizations usually results in the delegation of authority to an expanding group of management personnel and the development of well-defined management subdivisions such as departments and branches. These subunits can be specified by product line, geographical area, customer class, or any other criteria appropriate for management reporting and control. In a generic sense, the term segment could be used to refer to any type of business subdivision. However, the term *segment* in accounting literature generally refers to a business subdivision that is given responsibility for the profitable utilization of the invested capital in its domain.

This chapter explains how a cost accounting system can be designed to help top management evaluate the performance of business segments. After you have completed this chapter you should be able to:

1. explain the concepts of centralization and decentralization and describe their implications for the evaluation of segment performance.
2. explain the role of a responsibility center and the difference between cost centers, profit centers, and investment centers.
3. use return on investment, residual income, and contribution margin analysis to evaluate segment performance.
4. handle difficulties that might be encountered in implementing the various approaches to evaluating segment performance.

CENTRALIZATION AND DECENTRALIZATION

Centralization and decentralization are the terms used to describe the degree of management delegation within an organization. These are end points forming a continuum of delegated responsibility. **Decentralization** implies that many job activities and related decision-making functions and a great amount of authority are delegated to subordinates by higher levels of management. **Centralization** implies that little responsibility for decision making has been delegated to lower levels of management. Typically, business organizations are neither completely centralized nor completely decentralized. Most businesses have some degree of decentralization or delegation of authority.

The extent to which authority is delegated depends on a number of factors including management philosophy and the general business environment. The question is not should an organization be centralized or decentralized, but rather, to what degree is decentralization or delegation appropriate to maintain management control and how should the activities and responsibilities within the firm be divided, coordinated, and controlled?

Firms that exhibit a high degree of decentralization possess some or all of the following characteristics:

1. An organizational structure that is *large, complex,* or *geographically dispersed*
2. A mix of *diversified products*
3. A number of *dispersed customers or suppliers*
4. A need for *timely decisions* in remote parts of the organization
5. A desire for *freedom to make decisions* at lower levels of the organization

The extent to which an organization is decentralized depends on the costs and benefits involved. Some of the claimed benefits of decentralization include the following:

1. *Better decisions* because of segment management's greater familiarity with local conditions
2. *More freedom for top management* to pursue strategic planning since many decisions are made at lower levels in the organization
3. *Increased incentive for segment managers* to perform well because of greater responsibility for operations

4. *More on-the-job training* for lower level management
5. *Potential for greater job satisfaction* due to more people being involved in the management process

Potential costs of decentralization should be considered when making decisions to delegate authority. Some of these costs of decentralization include the following:

1. *Inferior decisions* due to a lack of similar goals between individual segment managers and top management
2. *Duplication of administrative talent and services* in segments
3. *More costly* management reporting and feedback systems due to more levels of administration and more detail
4. *More difficulty in coordinating* interdependent operations

Decentralization usually does not occur instantly; it evolves through growth, experience, trial, and error. The role of an accountant during this process is that of information system designer and manager. The accounting system must be sensitive to organizational changes to provide an effective reporting and feedback system for management control.

The primary accounting challenge in decentralized organizations is finding the best ways to measure and evaluate the performance of each segment of the business and each manager responsible for segment operations. *Both* a segment and the manager of a segment need to be evaluated. However, the decisions that need to be made for each one, the corresponding basis for evaluation and the information used to base the evaluation will be different. The primary decision *for a segment* of a firm is whether to expand, contract, maintain, or sell the segment. However, *for the manager* the decision is whether the resources available to the manager have been effectively used as they were intended.

Responsibility accounting, introduced in chapters 4 and 6, provides the basic concepts underlying segment reporting and performance evaluation. All company units need to have their performance evaluated whether in centralized or decentralized organizations. However, the degree of decentralization effects the scope of management responsibility, which in turn effects the manner in which segments are evaluated. This chapter augments the basic concepts of responsibility accounting with an emphasis on decentralized organizations.

RESPONSIBILITY CENTERS

Decentralization results in an organization being divided into a number of distinct responsibility centers. A **responsibility center** is a subdivision of a business over which control of operations is found. Responsibility centers may include the entire company, a division, a department, an operation, or even an individual. As businesses become more decentralized, several distinct types of responsibility centers evolve with unique accounting and control requirements. These different types of responsibility centers include cost centers, profit centers, and investment centers.

Cost centers are subdivisions of a business assigned responsibility for only the incurrence and proper utilization of costs. For example, a custodial department is typically a cost center because it incurs only costs in the performance of custodial services, and there is no expectation or responsibility to generate revenues.

On the other hand, **profit centers** are subdivisions of a business assigned responsibility for both costs and revenues. For example, a producer of instant cake mixes may consider each type of cake mix to be a profit center because segment management may be assigned responsibility for both the costs incurred and the revenues generated by each mix.

Finally, **investment centers** are assigned responsibility for costs, revenues, and the profitable utilization of invested capital. For example, an appliance division of a large company may be considered an investment center if its management is assigned responsibility for costs incurred, revenues generated, and the profitable utilization of capital invested in the division. The important distinction between profit and investment centers is that profit centers are responsible for profits, but investment centers are responsible for both generating profits *and* efficiently using the capital created by those profits.

Distinctly different methods are used to evaluate the performance of these various types of responsibility centers. Cost centers are usually evaluated on the basis of costs incurred in relation to budgeted and standard costs. Profit centers are typically evaluated on the relationship of sales and costs to budgeted amounts. In addition, contribution margin, ratio measures, and other indicators of profitable performance may be applied to profit center evaluation. Investment centers are usually evaluated using measures that relate profits to invested capital in terms of the rate of return earned by invested funds. The remainder of this chapter focuses on approaches that can be used to measure and evaluate the performance of investment centers as segments of a business. The terms segment and investment center are considered interchangeable throughout the rest of this chapter.

APPROACHES FOR EVALUATING PERFORMANCE

The accounting approaches for evaluating segment performance examined in this section are return on investment, residual income, and segment margin analysis. These methods are used when managers are delegated almost complete authority over their own segments. Where such autonomy exists, managers have almost as much control over operations as if they were running their own business.

One advantage of investment centers is that they are virtually independent operations with little ambiguity about who is responsible for their success or failure. Accordingly, management compensation packages, bonus plans, and funds for expansion of operations are often allocated to segments based on an analysis of how well each segment is doing with currently invested funds. As a result, there may be keen competition among segment managers to do well in these measures. In order to properly use performance measures as effective management tools it is important to recognize the power inherent in them. A brief analysis of the questions that arise when considering the desired behavioral outcomes of segment evaluation indicate the importance of an appropriate accounting system being implemented to evaluate segment performance.

First, consider the implications associated with maintaining segment independence. The accounting system should promote autonomy yet insure that segments are behaving in a way that also promotes overall company goals. Even though a segment is independent, some questions arise. Should segment managers be allowed to engage in transactions that enhance segment performance measures but are detrimental to company profits taken as a whole? Is there some way to preserve the independence of segment managers and yet insure that their decisions will be congruent with overall company goals?

Second, the accounting system should provide an equitable and comparable measure of performance for its managers. This is not always easy in complex organizations. Consider the situation in which a manager with an excellent record of success is asked by top management to take over an ailing segment. To nurse the segment back to good health may take years or may not even be possible. In such situations questions arise concerning what performance measures should be used to evaluate a manager who accepts such a task. What compensation scheme should be used? Is it possible for a manager to be equitably treated in such situations?

Finally, the accounting system should provide information identifying the most economically profitable segments in the firm. It should identify which segments are using the funds already entrusted to them in the most profitable way. It should also provide information for the analysis of potential investment opportunities and give management a reasonable assurance of investing in the most profitable activities.

These items give rise to analytical and behavioral requirements that make the choice of an appropriate accounting system vital to the profitable operation of decentralized organizations. The methods discussed in this section have gained widespread acceptance largely because they provide help in answering these questions. Generally, these methods foster segment independence, provide an equitable basis for evaluation of segment managers, and supply an equitable criteria for channeling investment funds into the most profitable alternatives.

Return on Investment

Return on investment (ROI) is a widely used measure of business profitability that focuses attention on the optimum use of invested capital. The basic components of the ROI equation are net income from the income statement and invested capital from the balance sheet.

$$\text{Return on investment} = \frac{\text{Net income}}{\text{Invested capital}}$$

To illustrate the calculation of ROI, consider a business segment with net income of $50,000 and invested capital of $275,000. The ROI for this segment is 18%.

$$18\% = \frac{\$50,000}{\$275,000}$$

ROI has gained widespread usage as a measure of business performance for several reasons. First, ROI is easy to calculate from data that are readily available in a traditional accounting system and can be applied equally well to individual segments or to a company as a whole. Second, ROI incorporates into one measure a number of important factors that contribute to profitability. Further expansion would show that virtually all elements of the income statement and balance sheet are synthesized in the ROI statistic.

Another reason for the widespread usage of ROI is that it focuses the attention of management on how well assets are employed in the process of earning profits. Evaluating segment performance on a measure such as net income or sales without regard to the amount of invested capital may be misleading. For example, consider a situation in which two segments of a business have equal net income; however, one segment has a larger asset base with which to generate the same level of income. If management considers only the absolute amount of net income, a more efficient use of assets by one of the segments may be overlooked. The most critical test of profitability is not the absolute amount of sales or profits, but the relationship of profits to the amount of invested capital used to generate them.

A final reason for the popularity of ROI is that it may be used to compare investment opportunities. Projected ROI statistics can be used to guide initial investment dollars. Actual ROI calculations can provide management with an indicator of how well invested capital is currently being employed and whether funds should be shifted from one segment to another. Actual ROI statistics can also be used to verify expected ROI numbers in validating the budgetary process. Finally, comparative ROI statistics for segments can also play a key role by simply drawing management's attention to areas where help might be needed or to areas where additional investment might be warranted.

The ROI formula can be expanded using the following relationships:

$$\text{Profit margin} = \frac{\text{Net income}}{\text{Sales}}$$

$$\text{Capital turnover} = \frac{\text{Sales}}{\text{Invested capital}}$$

Combining these relationships we obtain the following ROI formula:

$$\text{Return on investment} = \frac{\text{Net income}}{\text{Sales}} \times \frac{\text{Sales}}{\text{Invested capital}}$$

or

$$\text{Return on Investment} = \text{Profit margin} \times \text{Capital turnover}$$

To illustrate, a company with a net income of $50,000, sales of $625,000, and invested capital of $312,500 has a profit margin of 8%, capital turnover of 2 times, and ROI of 16%.

The basic ROI formula and its expanded version recognize the basic ingredients of profit making—sales, costs, and invested capital. Generally, ROI is increased by increasing sales, by decreasing costs, or by reducing the amount of invested capital if funds can be used more profitably elsewhere. The expanded ROI equation also recognizes the importance and interrelationship of profit margin and capital turnover ratios. Capital turnover is the ratio of sales to invested capital. Capital turnover is a rough approximation of the number of times assets circulate through the business from cash to inventory, through sales to accounts receivable, and back to cash again.

Profit margin is the ratio of net income to sales and represents the additional amount customers are willing to pay above the cost of goods sold and all other expenses. Overall profitability depends on the interaction of capital turnover and profit margin, that is, each time a dollar of invested capital circulates through the company it is increased by the amount of the profit margin with total profits being dependent on how many times each investment dollar circulates through the system in an accounting period.

Since the number of times investment dollars circulate through the system is indicated by the capital turnover ratio, increasing either the profit margin or the capital turnover ratio will increase ROI. For example, a company with a profit margin of 10% earns 10 cents on each dollar as it circulates through the company. With a capital turnover ratio of 6 times, the company's total return on investment is 60 cents for each dollar of invested capital. Increasing either the 10% profit margin or the 6 times capital turnover will increase ROI.

Examining the components and interrelationships in the calculation of ROI makes it clear that there are a number of alternative ways to improve performance. However, remember that even though ROI is simple to calculate and points to seemingly easy ways to improve ROI performance, the basic economic theory underlying the operation of a firm cannot be ignored. Decision makers and accountants should guard against a naive approach to using ROI. For example, increasing prices in anticipation of increasing sales, net income, and ROI may be a poor decision if the demand curve for the product is elastic. If demand is elastic, increasing prices may actually result in less sales, lower net income, and reduced ROI.

Another favorite target for increasing net income and ROI is cutting operating costs. In some business situations cutting costs may increase net income without adversely affecting other components of ROI. However, in other situations, cutting costs may result in short-run increases in net income but have detrimental long-run effects. For example, reduced repair and maintenance activities may reduce costs in the short run but may have adverse effects on the ability of the firm to produce efficiently in the long run.

Traditionally, the management of net income has been the focus for improving profitability. As indicated, the ROI equation also emphasizes the importance of proper asset management. ROI can be increased by keeping cash, inventory, accounts receivable, and other assets at a minimum. This means that idle cash should be invested, inventories should be kept at proper levels, credit should be judiciously managed, and acquisition of plant assets should be based on an expected level of economic benefit.

Figure 19.1   Effects on return on investment of various management decisions

	$\dfrac{\text{Net income}}{\text{Sales}}$	$\times$	$\dfrac{\text{Sales}}{\text{Invested capital}}$	$=$ ROI
		or		
	Profit margin	$\times$	Capital turnover	$=$ ROI
Present situation (in thousands of dollars):	$\dfrac{80}{1,600}$	$\times$	$\dfrac{1,600}{400}$	$=$ 20%
Management decision and result:				
A. Reducing operating expenses by $5,000 results in increased net income, a larger profit margin, and higher ROI.	$\dfrac{85}{1,600}$	$\times$	$\dfrac{1,600}{400}$	$=$ 21%
B. Reducing assets by $40,000 with no change in net income results in more frequent capital turnover and higher ROI.	$\dfrac{80}{1,600}$	$\times$	$\dfrac{1,600}{360}$	$=$ 22%
C. Reduced prices result in a $50,000 increase in sales and a $5,000 increase in net income. The combined effect is a larger profit margin, more frequent capital turnover and higher ROI.	$\dfrac{85}{1,650}$	$\times$	$\dfrac{1,650}{400}$	$=$ 21%
D. Increased advertising expenditures result in a $100,000 increase in sales but no change in net income. The combined effect is a smaller profit margin, a more frequent capital turnover, but no change in ROI.	$\dfrac{80}{1,700}$	$\times$	$\dfrac{1,700}{400}$	$=$ 20%

The management of invested capital is just as important as the management of net income. However, the components of net income can be affected more dramatically in the short run than the components of invested capital. Therefore, net income typically receives the most attention in the ROI equation. This indicates the importance of long-range and strategic planning so that invested capital can receive the same degree of control as net income. Attention to all parts of the equation increases the prospect of optimizing the profitability of business operations.

Figure 19.1 gives a few examples from the vast array of possible management options regarding the management of ROI and shows the effect of various business decisions on ROI. Each example in figure 19.1 is independent of the others.

Residual Income

Residual income (RI) is another measure of business profitability that focuses attention on the optimum use of invested capital. RI is the amount of net income that is earned during a period beyond that needed to provide a minimum desired rate of return on invested capital. The first step in calculating RI is to multiply the amount of invested capital in a segment by the segment's minimum desired rate of return. This calculation results in **imputed interest** on invested capital. Imputed interest represents a hypothetical or opportunity cost of using the capital invested in the segment.

RI is then calculated by subtracting the amount of imputed interest on invested capital from the segment's after-tax net income. A positive RI indicates that the segment is earning net income in excess of that required to provide a minimum desired rate of return. If RI is zero, then the segment's net income is exactly equal to that amount required to earn the desired minimum rate of return. If RI is negative, the segment is earning less net income than is necessary to earn a minimum rate of return. The dollar amount

Figure 19.2   Calculation of residual income and return on investment

Residual Income

Net income (after taxes)	$100,000
Imputed interest (.2 $\times$ 400,000)	80,000
Residual income	$ 20,000

Return on Investment

$$\text{Return on investment} = \frac{\$100,000}{\$400,000} = 25\%$$

of a negative RI indicates the increase in net income needed to earn the minimum desired rate of return.

Since RI is a dollar measure rather than a percentage measure, it is most widely used when management wants to emphasize the maximization of the *number of dollars* of income rather than *a percentage* return on investment. Figure 19.2 contains the ROI and RI calculations for a segment with invested capital of $400,000 and a minimum desired rate of return of 20%.

Accountants and managers should realize that even though ROI and RI seem to be related measures with similar results, using or emphasizing one over the other may lead to different segment evaluations. For example, consider a company with an overall ROI objective of 20% with a very profitable segment earning a ROI of 25%. This very profitable segment accepts an investment opportunity requiring invested capital of $100,000, which is predicted to earn $21,000 in net income—a ROI of 21%. From a top management point of view, the acceptance of this opportunity is appropriate because it is expected to earn a ROI in excess of the company's objective. However, the use of ROI for evaluation in this case will make it appear that accepting the investment opportunity was a poor decision because the segment ROI will decline as a result. The segment's ROI will decline because the expected ROI of the project is less than the segment's current ROI.

If the situation is not understood by top management, the decrease could result in a lower segment evaluation than might be justified. This could also lead to reduced pay or a smaller bonus for the segment manager when compensation is based on segment performance. However, if RI is used for segment evaluation, then segment performance will show an improvement consistent with economic reality. This situation is illustrated in figure 19.3.

The situation shown in figure 19.3 makes several important points. First, there are situations that could arise in which segment managers may be inclined to behave in a way that is not preferred from a top management viewpoint. Therefore, segment performance measures should be designed to discourage such suboptimal decisions due to a lack of goal congruence between individual segment managers and top management.

Second, figure 19.3 shows a subtle but important difference between the objectives of ROI and RI. When using ROI the objective is to maximize ROI. When using RI the objective is to maximize the amount of net income in excess of a minimum desired ROI. The choice of methods depends on many factors including management's philosophy about a compensation scheme for segment managers and whether to place emphasis on percentages or dollars. Since the calculations are not difficult, the presentation of both ROI and RI numbers as shown in figure 19.3 would provide a clear picture of segment performance.

Figure 19.3   Comparison of return on investment (ROI) and residual income (RI)

	Investment Opportunity	Current Situation	Projected Total
Invested capital	$100,000	$400,000	$500,000
Net income (after tax)	$ 21,000	$100,000	$121,000
Imputed interest at 20%			
(.2 × $100,000)	(20,000)		(20,000)
(.2 × $400,000)		(80,000)	(80,000)
Residual income	$ 1,000	$ 20,000	$ 21,000
Return on investment:	21%[a]	25%[b]	24%[c]

[a]($21,000 ÷ $100,000)
[b]($100,000 ÷ $400,000)
[c]($121,000 ÷ $500,000)

Figure 19.4   Calculation of weighted average cost of capital

	Percent of Total Equity	Current Cost	Weighted Cost
Debt	.30	20%	6.0
Equity	.70	15%	10.5
			16.5%

The calculation of RI is subject to a number of other top management objectives or preferences. First, instead of using the minimum desired rate of return, the company's average cost of capital might be used to calculate the amount of imputed interest. The average cost of capital incorporates the cost of equity capital and the cost of debt capital weighted by their respective proportions in the total capital structure. Figure 19.4 shows the computation of an average cost of capital using the percentage of debt and equity capital as weights.

The weighted average cost of capital of 16.5% can be used in the RI calculation to compute the amount of imputed interest. The management philosophy inherent in using the average cost of capital is that as long as a segment earns a rate of return in excess of the average cost of capital the segment should expand.

Another set of related management preferences regarding the computation of residual income concerns the use of segment contribution margin instead of after-tax net income and the use of controllable investment instead of invested capital. It can be argued that in the short run segment managers cannot control expenses related to fixed costs. Therefore, it may be felt that segments should be evaluated on variable costs and revenues as incorporated in a segment's contribution margin rather than on numbers that include fixed costs. In addition, investment in working capital may be felt to constitute the controllable portion, in the short run, of invested capital. Thus, some believe that the measure of residual income may be made more sensitive in evaluating segment performance by using segment contribution margin and investment in working capital as alternative measures.

Figure 19.5   Segment margin analysis for divisions

(000 omitted)

	Company Total	Division A	Division B
Sales	$550,000	$250,000	$300,000
Less: Variable expenses	300,000	100,000	200,000
Contribution margin	$250,000	$150,000	$100,000
Less: Direct fixed costs	25,000	10,000	15,000
Segment margin	$225,000	$140,000	$ 85,000
Less: Indirect fixed costs	20,000		
Net income	$205,000		

A final management preference concerns what rate of return to use in calculating imputed interest when various segments are experiencing different rates of return. Generally in such instances each segment should use a different rate of return selected by top management in consultation with each segment manager. This makes it possible for top management to recognize the unique identity and role of each segment in the overall company plan. Segments that do not achieve ROI objectives may be considered for sale and segments that exceed ROI objectives may be expanded. Such factors as the maturity of the segment, its market position, or other situational factors can be more clearly evaluated when individual segment rates of return are used rather than when all segments are tied to a common rate of return.

Segment Margin Analysis

Another common measure of segment performance is segment margin analysis. The *segment margin* is the contribution margin of a segment less all other direct fixed costs of the segment. Contribution margin analysis differentiates between fixed and variable costs, as discussed in chapter 4, in the calculation of net income. However, where segments are involved, it is not only advisable to differentiate between fixed and variable costs, but also between **avoidable fixed costs,** those fixed costs that would be avoided if the segment is discontinued, and **unavoidable fixed costs,** those fixed costs that would continue even though a segment is discontinued.

Segment margin analysis is simply contribution margin analysis with the additional differentiation between avoidable and unavoidable fixed costs. For example, consider a company that uses segment margin analysis to evaluate the performance of its two divisions. Figure 19.5 shows the numeric components of such an evaluation.

Figure 19.5 shows how segment margin represents income after all costs directly attributable to segment operations are subtracted from segment revenue. Segment margin represents the amount a segment contributes toward net income and toward covering those fixed costs that are incurred for the benefit of the company as a whole.

Depending on the detail of segment analysis desired by top management, figure 19.5 may represent only the first level of analysis. For example, suppose that division *B* handles two significant product lines, each of which is in turn considered a segment by top management. Segment margin analysis can be used to evaluate these product lines as shown in figure 19.6.

The information in figure 19.6 indicates that $14,000 of direct fixed costs can be avoided depending on the elimination or continuance of either one or both of the product lines—$8,000 related to product 1 and $6,000 related to product 2. However, $1,000 of fixed costs are common or shared by both products and cannot be eliminated unless the

Figure 19.6   Segment margin analysis for products

(000 omitted)

	Division B	Product 1	Product 2
Sales	$300,000	$250,000	$ 50,000
Less: Variable expenses	200,000	155,000	45,000
Contribution margin	$100,000	$ 95,000	$ 5,000
Less: Avoidable fixed costs (products)	14,000	8,000	6,000
Segment margin (products)	$ 86,000	$ 87,000	$ (1,000)
Less: Unavoidable fixed costs (division)	1,000		
Segment margin (division)	$ 85,000		

whole division is eliminated. If division *B* is discontinued, a total of $15,000 of fixed costs would be avoided. The individual product segment margins calculated in figure 19.6 represent the amount of the total net income of the company that would change if that particular product line is discontinued. Remember that avoidable fixed costs are those that would be eliminated if a segment is discontinued.

The comparison of product segment margins in figure 19.6 provides some additional insights into segment margin analysis. Product 1 clearly contributes the most to divisional net income. Product 2 not only contributes less, but a negative segment margin raises questions concerning the viability of the product line. This points out that segment analysis not only provides information for relative performance evaluation, but also provides information for decisions concerning whether or not operations should be continued.

A positive segment margin justifies continuing segment operations. A negative segment margin indicates that there may not be justification for continuance of the segment. In such instances, an analysis of segment contribution margin may be helpful in making a final decision. For example, continuation of a segment with a negative segment margin and a negative contribution margin should be seriously questioned. However, when considering discontinuance other factors need to be considered. For example, is the situation expected to continue for a short or long period of time? Also, what effect will discontinuance have on other products of the firm?

In situations where the segment margin is negative and the contribution margin is positive, management may also consider discontinuing segment operations. A positive contribution margin indicates that variable costs are being covered, and a negative segment margin indicates that avoidable fixed costs are not being covered. Not only is the viability of the segment in serious question, but because some fixed costs can be avoided net income will increase if the segment is discontinued. However, because fixed costs are involved, how soon discontinuance can occur may depend on the time frame within which the firm's commitments to the segment's direct fixed costs can be avoided. This points out that when direct fixed costs are considered avoidable, it is important that the time required for avoidance be a criterion for classification.

CONSIDERATIONS FOR IMPLEMENTATION

Return on investment, residual income, and segment margin analysis are all quite flexible and easily adapted to evaluate segment performance in various types of business situations. As a result, the basic approaches to segment evaluation are implemented in a great variety of ways. A number of management options have already been mentioned. Other important concepts relating specifically to the implementation of ROI and RI are examined in this section.

The budgetary process has important ramifications for the effectiveness of ROI or RI as management tools. What is included as invested capital and how invested capital is valued may affect management decisions when using ROI or RI. Therefore, this section focuses on considerations for implementing ROI and RI that are helpful for their effective use in particular business and management environments. Limitations inherent in ROI and RI are also discussed and suggestions are made on how to overcome them.

The Role of Budgets

Because major differences exist between decisions regarding managers of segments and decisions regarding the segments themselves, it is important to differentiate between the performance of a segment as a business activity and the performance of a segment manager as a planner, organizer, and controller. Evaluating managers based only on controllable elements of a segment performance is an important principle in manager evaluation.

One of the most effective tools for differentiating between manager performance and segment performance is the budget. Actual results compared against separate budgeted criteria for both manager and segment performance avoid any unfortunate evaluation of managers based on uncontrollable items. In addition, it may be more appropriate to judge manager performance against budgeted goals rather than against the performance of other managers or other segments. Also, the budgetary process makes it possible to treat each segment in its unique business situation and tends to avoid inappropriate comparisons among segments where situational factors make such comparisons invalid.

Use of a budget typically contributes to goal congruence between top management and segment management. The communication channels that open and the dialogue that accompanies a constructive budgetary process foster goal congruence. In situations where top management simply compiles budgets generated at lower levels or where budgets are used as punitive tools, the communication necessary to establish goal congruence is usually lacking. Where preparation of the budget provides an opportunity for several levels of management to communicate concerning strategic planning as well as operational matters, there usually emerges a commonality of purpose and commitment to specific goals unattainable without such communication.

The use of budgets to attain goal congruence guards against segment managers making decisions that tend to improve segment evaluation measures, but are detrimental to the company as a whole.

The Investment Base

Segment evaluation focuses on the efficiency with which invested capital is utilized. The assets that are actually included as invested capital (the investment base) may differ among companies because there is no theoretically correct investment base. The selection of an investment base depends on individual situational factors and management philosophy. For example, one segment may include all assets in the investment base while another segment may only include working capital.

Another dimension of the investment base concerns the method used to determine the value of assets included in the investment base. For example, historical cost may be used by one company while another company uses replacement cost to value its assets. Both the composition and the valuation of the investment base have important implications for proper segment evaluation.

Composition   There are a variety of alternative criteria that could be used to determine what should be included in the investment base. For example, total assets available, total assets employed, and total assets employed less current liabilities are all possible ways to define invested capital. They are not the only ways to define the composition of the investment base, but they are representative of those in popular usage and provide points of departure for the development of other bases more appropriate for a given business situation.

The *total assets available* to the segment manager is probably the most widely used investment base because it assumes that the segment manager is responsible for the most profitable use of all assets included in the segment. However, some situations may dictate that top management give oversight or custodial responsibility to a segment manager for currently unproductive assets. For example, when construction in process or idle land is involved, only *total assets employed* may be included in the investment base. The manager's stewardship over unemployed assets is typically evaluated on some nonfinancial basis.

The composition of the investment base may be determined by the degree of control that can be exercised over the assets in question. For example, when the segment manager has control over the amount of short-term credit that is utilized by the segment, there may be an opportunity for manipulation of the amount of assets employed. In such instances, it may be appropriate to exclude from the investment base the amount of assets that are supplied by short-term creditors. In such instances, the investment base could be defined as *total assets employed less current liabilities.*

In some instances, it may be appropriate to include company assets in the investment base of a segment even though they are not explicitly part of the segment. Just as costs of service facilities and home office functions are allocated to benefiting departments as discussed in chapter 14, it may be appropriate to include *allocated assets* in the investment base for purposes of segment evaluation. For example, if accounts receivable are handled at corporate headquarters and if segment managers are considered responsible for all assets resulting from business conducted by the segment, then it may be appropriate to allocate accounts receivable to segments. On the other hand, if there is a question concerning the controllability of centralized accounts receivable by segment managers, then it may not be appropriate to allocate the accounts receivable to segments.

An investment base with some appeal for stockholders but one that should be used with caution in segment evaluation is *stockholders' equity.* The rate of return on stockholders' equity is very useful in assessing the outcome of financing decisions from the stockholder's viewpoint. However, return on stockholders' equity has limited usefulness in assessing individual segment performance from a management viewpoint. For example, consider division A of a company that has \$2 million of employed assets financed with \$1,750,000 of common stock. The net income of division A is \$400,000. Division A's ROI, using either total assets employed or stockholder's equity as an investment base, is 20%. However, consider division B of a company that also has \$2 million of employed assets but has financed its assets with \$1,000,000 of common stock and \$750,000 of long-term debt at 15% interest. In terms of ROI comparison, division B presents an entirely different picture. Division B also earns \$400,000 of net income before interest on the long-term debt, but net income after deducting interest expense is \$287,500 [\$400,000 − (.15 × \$750,000) = \$287,500]. Figure 19.7 presents comparative numbers for the two divisions and shows ROI calculations based on the total assets and on stockholder's equity. Income taxes are ignored in this analysis because the results would not be different if taxes were included.

ROI percentages using total assets as the investment base are the same except when interest expense on a long-term debt is included in the calculation. Since the incurrence of interest expense is usually considered a corporate financing decision, net income before interest expense is typically used to calculate ROI.

The result of using net income before interest expense is that ROI is a consistent 20% between segments. This is intuitively correct because both managers seem to be doing equally well managing segment assets. However, when stockholders' equity is used as the investment base, even if interest expense is added back to net income, there is a large

Figure 19.7   Stockholder's equity as an investment base

	Division A	Division B
(1) Total assets	$2,000,000	$2,000,000
Current liabilities	$ 250,000	$ 250,000
Long-term debt @ 15%		750,000
(2) Common stockholders' equity	1,750,000	1,000,000
Total liabilities and equity	$2,000,000	$2,000,000
(3) Income before interest expense	$ 400,000	$ 400,000
Interest on long-term debt		112,500
(4) Net income (ignoring taxes)	$ 400,000	$ 287,500
ROI based on total assets and:		
Income before interest on long-term debt (Row 3 ÷ Row 1)	20.0%	20.0%
Income after interest on long-term debt (Row 4 ÷ Row 1)	20.0%	14.0%
ROI based on stockholders' equity and:		
Income before interest on long-term debt (Row 3 ÷ Row 2)	22.9%	40.0%
Income after interest on long-term debt (Row 4 ÷ Row 2)	22.9%	28.8%

divergence between ROI of the two subsidiaries—22.9% for division *A* versus 40.0% for division *B*.

This illustrates that calculations using stockholders' equity are very helpful in evaluating financing decisions when money can be borrowed at rates below a segment's internal rate of return. However, the divergence of rates of return between the two divisions due only to the method of financing illustrates the potential for unwarranted conclusions about the quality of individual segment performance. Also, when segments are compared against each other and when assets in any of the segments are financed with borrowed money, it is suggested that ROI be calculated on net income adjusted for interest expense.

Valuation   Assets included in the investment base may be valued in a number of different ways. The major reason for being concerned about the valuation of the assets in the investment base is illustrated as follows. Divisions *A* and *B* each earn identical amounts of net income producing and selling similar products with assets having the same productive capacity. However, the ROI for division *A* is substantially greater than the ROI for division *B*. The reason for the disparity in division ROI is that the assets of division *A* were acquired several years before those of division *B* and in the interim there was a substantial increase in the general level of prices for identical goods and services.

This means that the assets of division *A* are carried in historical cost records at a much lower value than those of division *B* resulting in higher ROI for division A, even though the investment base is essentially the same and the two divisions are experiencing the same results from operations. The measuring unit (the dollar) for determining the value of the investment base has changed through time resulting in distortions when making segment evaluations. A way to value assets is needed that will represent each investment base so its productive capacity is measured with a constant unit of measure. There are two generally accepted approaches to valuing assets included in the investment base—constant dollar accounting and current value accounting.

Figure 19.8   Return on investment calculated with constant dollar accounting adjustments to the investment base

	Division A	Division B
(1) Investment base in historical dollars	$1,048,951	$1,442,300
(2) Index of current prices	140	140
(3) Index of prices at date of acquisition	98	135
(4) Translation factor (Row 2 ÷ Row 3)	1.43	1.04
(5) Cost of assets in terms of current dollars (Row 4 × Row 1)	$1,500,000	$1,500,000
(6) Net income	$ 150,000	$ 150,000
(7) ROI before constant dollar adjustment (Row 6 ÷ Row 1)	14.3%	10.4%
(8) ROI after constant dollar adjustment (Row 6 ÷ Row 5)	10.0%	10.0%

Constant dollar accounting adjusts asset values contained in historical cost financial records for changes in the purchasing power of the dollar. The purchasing power of the dollar is determined by the amount of goods and services that can be acquired in exchange. Due to inflation (rising prices) or deflation (falling prices) the purchasing power of the dollar may change through time. Due to the problem of changes in the purchasing power of the dollar, the United States and many foreign governments routinely publish *indexes* designed to measure the relative amounts of these changes.

A **price index** is a weighted average of a "basket" of goods and services at a specific time. Assets in the investment base that have been measured in dollars with varying purchasing power (as contained in historical cost records) can be restated in terms of the current purchasing power of the dollar by using price indexes. The restatement is accomplished by multiplying the amount of the investment in historical dollars by the following fraction referred to as the **translation factor.**

$$\frac{\text{Index of current prices}}{\text{Index of prices prevailing when asset acquired}}$$

To illustrate the translation process, consider an asset that cost $1,000 last year when the price index was 80. To restate the value of the asset in terms of current prices when the index is 120, the following calculation is made:

$$\frac{120}{80} = 1.50 \times \$1,000 = \$1,500$$

To further illustrate the usefulness of price level adjustments to the investment base, consider the situation of division *A* and division *B* with identical net income and productive capacities. The expectation is that making the adjustments suggested by constant dollar accounting should result in the same ROI for both divisions. Figure 19.8 verifies this intuitive reasoning.

Note that in periods of rising prices, as shown in figure 19.8, ROI calculations also become inflated in real economic terms when using historical cost accounting. This happens because the current productive capacity is replaced with more costly plant assets.

Constant dollar accounting has advantages—it is simple to compute, easy to understand, and objective in nature. However, the major disadvantage is that by using general price indexes, the adjustment of the investment base may only approximate actual current values. An approach that may give a more accurate value to the investment base is called current value accounting.

Current value accounting abandons historical costs as a basis for valuation and turns to other methods of obtaining current asset values. When using current value ac-

Figure 19.9   Depreciation and return on investment (ROI)

	Year			
	1	*2*	*3*	*4*
Operating income	$10,000	$10,000	$10,000	$10,000
Depreciation expense[a]	7,500	7,500	7,500	7,500
Net income	$ 2,500	$ 2,500	$ 2,500	$ 2,500
Investment base (Cost less accumulated deprecia-tion at beginning of the year)	$30,000	$22,500	$15,000	$ 7,500
Return on investment	8.3%	11.1%	16.7%	33.3%

[a]Assuming assets that cost $30,000 with no residual value depreciated over four years using the straight-line method.

counting, management is primarily interested in what the investment base is currently worth independent of what costs were incurred to obtain the asset. What is desired is a measure of the true economic value of an asset. From economic theory, this measure is the present value of the future net cash flows from the assets in the investment base.

As a practical matter, however, replacement cost is often used as a measure of the current value of an asset. *Replacement cost* represents what it would cost to obtain similar assets to replace the productive capacity of the current investment base in terms of future net cash flows. The key to measuring replacement cost is expected net cash flows, not technological or physical features of the assets in question.

Determining the replacement cost of some types of assets for which active markets exist may not be very difficult. For example, determining the replacement cost of a delivery truck may be relatively easy because of existing markets for such assets. However, as assets become more specialized or where no active markets exist, determining the replacement cost becomes more difficult and more subjective. A special-purpose computer may not have a counterpart for which replacement costs are available. In such instances, appraisals may be used to approximate current values. However, appraisals are inherently subjective and should be used with caution.

Specific price indexes for particular categories of assets may also be used to obtain a better approximation of current values than would otherwise be available when using general price indexes. For example, if a specific price index for computing equipment is available, it might be used to approximate the current value of a special-purpose computer.

Still another dilemma concerning the valuation of assets in the investment base is whether depreciable assets should be included at their undepreciated cost or at net book value. The advantage of using net book value is that net income on the income statement and total assets on the balance sheet can be used without adjustment when calculating RI or ROI. However, a difficulty in using net book value is that a decreasing net book value due to depreciation will result in an increasing rate of return on the same assets as they grow older. Figure 19.9 shows this phenomenon.

The results in figure 19.9 would be even more dramatic if an accelerated method of depreciation had been used. To overcome this difficulty, the use of undepreciated cost in the investment base will provide stable rates of return through time. The use of undepreciated cost also facilitates comparisons among segments. However, using undepreciated cost ignores the reality of an asset's declining value in use.

Summary

Return on investment (ROI), residual income (RI), and segment margin analysis are methods used by top management to evaluate the performance of relatively autonomous business subdivisions known as segments. These methods can be used to evaluate both the performance of segments as economic entities and the performance of segment managers as planners, organizers, and controllers. The primary focus of segment evaluation is the profitable utilization of invested capital.

Segment evaluation methods are deceptively simple to apply because they are easy to calculate. However, a number of economic and behavioral considerations should be factored into their use to avoid unexpected results or incongruent management behavior. The use of budgets as a communicative tool is especially important. Other considerations for implementation include what rates of return are appropriate, what should be included as invested capital, and how should invested capital be valued.

A primary objective of segment evaluation is to provide an equitable basis for comparisons. Therefore, it is usually desirable to compare actual results against budgeted amounts rather than to evaluate one segment against another. Also, there should be a clear differentiation between segment and manager performance in both budgeted and actual results.

Minimum desired rates of return should be tailored to the specific economic and business circumstances of each segment. The weighted average cost of capital is an interest rate commonly used in segment evaluation. However, judgment should be exercised so that rates are set at levels that promote goal congruence between top management and segment management.

There are a number of different ways to determine what constitutes a segment's invested capital. Total assets, assets employed, total assets less current liabilities, and stockholder's equity represent possible measures of invested capital. The measure that represents controllable assets, as viewed by the segment manager, is usually the most appropriate measure of invested capital for segment evaluation.

Invested capital can be valued by using historical costs, as found in traditional financial records, or by using some form of current value accounting. The use of current values provides a more realistic measure of the actual economic state of affairs. However, current values are less objective than historical costs and should be used with caution.

Appendix   *Compound Interest Method of Depreciation*

To provide a stable rate of return as assets grow older and at the same time incorporate depreciation charges in the investment base, the compound interest method of depreciation can be used. The compound interest method of depreciation views depreciation as though it represents cost recovery on investments. The rate of cost recovery is found by using compound interest techniques. For example, consider assets purchased for $30,000 with an estimated useful life of four years having no salvage value. Budget estimates indicate that the assets are predicted to generate net cash operating income of $10,508 each year for four years. This can be viewed as receiving an ordinary annuity of four rents in the amount of $10,508 whose present value is $30,000—the purchase price of the assets.

The interest rate (in this case, the internal rate of return for these assets) that equates the rents and present value must be calculated or found by referring to a present

Figure 19.10   Depreciation and return on investment (ROI)

Calculation of Depreciation Expense Using Compound Interest Method

Year	Investment Base Beginning of Year	Predicted Net Cash Operating Income	Return of Investment @ 15% per Year	Depreciation Expense	Investment Base End of Year
1	$30,000	$10,508	$4,500	$6,008	$23,992
2	23,992	10,508	3,599	6,909	17,083
3	17,083	10,508	2,562	7,946	9,137
4	9,137	10,508	1,371	9,137	–0–

Return of investment @ 15% = .15 × Investment base beginning of year
Depreciation = Predicted net cash operating income − Return of investment @ 15% per year
Investment base end of year (Investment base beginning of next year) = Investment base beginning of year − Depreciation

Calculation of Return on Investment

	Year			
	1	2	3	4
Operating income	$10,508	$10,508	$10,508	$10,508
Depreciation expense	6,008	6,909	7,946	9,137
Net income	$ 4,500	$ 3,599	$ 2,562	$ 1,371
Investment base (Cost less accumulated depreciation at beginning of the year)	$30,000	$23,992	$17,083	$ 9,137
Return on investment	15%	15%	15%	15%

value table. Referring to the tables for the present value of an ordinary annuity indicates that the internal rate of return for this piece of equipment is 15%. This rate of return is used to calculate the amount of depreciation (investment recovery) using the compound interest method as shown in figure 19.10.

As shown in figure 19.10, the use of compound interest depreciation results in a stable rate of return through time. This can also be very useful in evaluating investment performance in comparison with specific ROI target percentages because any other type of evaluation will be flawed because it does not provide for a constant rate of return over time.

This method of depreciation is useful for segment evaluation. However, the compound interest method is not acceptable for external financial reporting due to the subjective considerations in determining the appropriate internal rate of return.

The following are selected financial and operating statistics for the toy products division of a major corporation that routinely evaluates segment performance using methods discussed in this chapter.

Invested capital	$2,000,000
Sales	$3,000,000
Variable cost of sales	1,300,000
Contribution margin	$1,700,000
Fixed costs	800,000
Net income	$ 900,000

Requirements

1. What is the division's capital turnover ratio?
2. What is the division's profit margin?
3. What is the division's ROI?
4. Assuming that the division imputes interest at 25%, what is the division's RI?
5. Assuming that $200,000 of fixed costs are avoidable, what is the division's segment margin?
6. Presented with an investment opportunity that is expected to earn a return of 35%, what manager behavior can be expected if the firm uses ROI for segment evaluation? RI?
7. What alternative measures are available to define the investment base other than total assets?
8. What alternative ways are available to value the investment base other than historical cost?

Solution to the Self-Study Problem

1. Capital turnover ratio $= \dfrac{\$3,000,000}{\$2,000,000} = 1.5$ times

2. Profit margin $= \dfrac{\$900,000}{\$3,000,000} = 30\%$

3. ROI $= \dfrac{\$900,000}{\$2,000,000} = 45\%$ or   ROI $= 1.5 \times .30 = 45\%$

4. RI:

Net income	$900,000
Imputed interest ($2,000,000 × .25)	500,000
Residual income	$400,000

5. Segment margin:

Sales	$3,000,000
Variable cost of sales	1,300,000
Contribution margin	$1,700,000
Avoidable fixed costs	200,000
Segment margin	$1,500,000

6. If ROI is used to evaluate segment performance, investment opportunities with an expected ROI less than 45% will be rejected because segment ROI will decline if accepted. If RI is used, the opportunities with an expected ROI equal to or greater than a minimum desired rate of return will be accepted.

Assuming a minimum desired rate of return of 25%, the opportunity will be accepted because it will add to RI.

7. Alternative measures available to define invested capital include total assets available, total assets employed, total assets employed less current liabilities, and stockholder's equity. The choice of the measure depends on the control that is exercised over the investment base by the segment manager.

8. Alternative ways to value the investment base in addition to historical cost include constant dollar accounting using price level adjustments and current value accounting using such indicators of current value as replacement cost.

Suggested Readings

Brown, Russell S. "Measuring Manufacturing Performance: A Targeting Approach." *Management Accounting* (June 1980): 25–29.

Chow, Chee W., and Waller, William S. "Management Accounting and Organizational Control." *Management Accounting* (April 1982): 36–41.

Largay, James A., III, and Levy, Ferdinand K. "Using Segment Reporting and Input-Output Analysis for Management Planning." *Management Accounting* (November 1978): 46–50.

Louderback, Joseph G., and Manners, George E., Jr. "Integrating ROI and CVP." *Management Accounting* (April 1981): 33–39.

Mays, Robert L., Jr. "Divisional Performance Measurement and Transfer Prices." *Management Accounting* (April 1982): 20–28.

Discussion Questions

1. Define centralization and decentralization. Why are these management concepts important for cost accounting?
2. Name some characteristics of firms that are relatively decentralized.
3. What are some of the claimed benefits and potential costs of decentralization?
4. Define the concept of "responsibility center" and describe the difference between cost, profit, and investment centers.
5. What is the generic meaning of the term "segment" in terms of business organization? Define how "segment" is used in cost accounting literature with regard to responsibility centers.
6. Describe several behavioral implications of evaluating segments of a business.
7. What is the general equation for calculating return on investment (ROI)?
8. How does ROI relate to profit margin and capital turnover ratios?
9. What are some of the reasons why ROI has gained such widespread usage?
10. "ROI is a broad, long-run measure while net income is a narrow, short-run measure." Explain.
11. How is residual income (RI) measured?
12. Define the meaning of an imputed cost and describe what role imputed interest has in the calculation of RI.
13. What is the basic difference between ROI and RI in terms of management philosophy and use?
14. Describe a circumstance in which a management decision might differ depending on whether ROI or RI is utilized as an evaluation method.

15. What management preferences are available for the calculation of RI?
16. Describe how segment margin analysis is an extension of contribution margin analysis.
17. Describe the role budgets play in segment evaluation.
18. What are several alternative ways to define invested capital for segment evaluation purposes?
19. Describe two alternative methods (other than historical cost) that could be used to value assets used to measure invested capital.

Exercises

Exercise 19.1   Concepts of Segment Analysis

1. In financial reporting for segments of a business enterprise, which of the following assets should be included as an identifiable asset of industry segment *A*?
   a. An intangible asset used by industry segment *A*
   b. An advance from nonfinancial industry segment *A* to another industry segment
   c. An allocation of a tangible asset used for general corporate purposes and *not* used in the operations of any particular industry segment
   d. An allocation of a tangible asset used by another industry segment that transfers products to industry segment *A*.
2. For measuring the performance of division managers, which investment base is inferior? Why?
   a. Total assets available
   b. Total assets employed
   c. Net working capital plus other assets
   d. Stockholders' equity

Exercise 19.2   Basic Procedures of Segment Analysis

The following information is for the period just ending for the Maximum Company:

	Total	%	X	%	Y	%
Sales	$700,000	100	$	100	$	100
Less variable expenses	_____		260,000	65		
Contribution margin	$350,000		$		$	70
Less direct fixed expenses	_____			20		
Segment margin	$	20	$ 60,000		$	
Less common fixed expenses	105,000					
Net income	$					

Required

Reconstruct the income statement by filling in the blanks.

Exercise 19.3 Segment Analysis—ROI and RI

A division has assets of $400,000 and net income of $90,000.

Required

1. What is the division's ROI?
2. If interest is imputed at 16%, what is the residual income?
3. What effect on management behavior can be expected if ROI is used to gauge performance?
4. What effects on management behavior can be expected if RI is used to gauge performance?

Exercise 19.4 Segment Performance and Contribution Analysis

Mike Lacey, president of Bintub Company, made the following statement. "We're slowly doing better. The latest monthly income statement loss of $21,250 is the smallest yet. If we can just build up segments A and C. . . ." Presented below is the latest monthly income statement:

	Total	Segment A	Segment B	Segment C
Sales	$500,000	$200,000	$125,000	$175,000
Cost of goods sold	371,250	150,000	90,000	131,250
Gross margin	$128,750	$ 50,000	$ 35,000	$ 43,750
Less operating expenses:				
Selling	$ 75,000	$ 30,000	$ 11,250	$ 33,750
Administrative	75,000	30,000	18,750	26,250
Total	$150,000	$ 60,000	$ 30,000	$ 60,000
Net income (loss)	$ (21,250)	$ (10,000)	$ 5,000	$ (16,250)

Leigh Buff, Lacey's new financial consultant, has recommended that he isolate direct and common costs and has come up with the following:

	Segment A	Segment B	Segment C
Variable costs (as a % of sales):			
Production (materials, labor, variable overhead)	20%	30%	25%
Selling	5%	5%	5%
Direct fixed costs:			
Production	$50,000	$15,000	$35,000
Selling (salaries and advertising)	$20,000	$ 5,000	$25,000

In addition:

1. All administrative costs are common to the three segments.
2. All fixed production costs over the $50,000, $15,000, and $35,000 amounts shown above should be considered common to the three segments.
3. Work-in-process and finished-goods inventories can be ignored.

However, Lacey was not totally confident in Buff's recommendations and did nothing about it. Later that week, Lacey was informed that due to supply shortages out of Bintub's control, production in either segment A or segment B would have to be cut back. Lacey took a look at the segmented income statement previously presented and declared, "From this income statement, our course of action is obvious. Cut back on segment A!"

Required

1. Prepare a new segmented monthly income statement using the contribution approach. Show both amount and percentage columns for each segment.
2. Do you agree with Lacey's decision to cut back on segment *A?* Why?
3. Assume that Lacey is also considering elimination of segment *C,* due to its $16,250 loss. What points should Buff raise for or against elimination?

Exercise 19.5 Segment Reporting and Analysis

Eric Smith is the president of DJ Company that manufactures products *P, Q,* and *R* in two different areas, *A* and *B.* For the year ending December 31, the following information was presented to Smith:

	Total Company	Area A	Area B
Sales	$180,000	$105,000	$ 75,000
Cost of goods sold	130,000	75,000	55,000
Gross margin	$ 50,000	$ 30,000	$ 20,000
Selling and administrative expenses	30,000	21,500	8,500
Net income	$ 20,000	$ 8,500	$ 11,500
Ratio of net income to sales	11.1%	8.1%	15.3%

Smith was not satisfied after looking at the above results and requested additional information on area *A* because of the lower ratio of net income to sales. Smith has even suggested recently that DJ Company terminate activity in area *A.* The additional information per Smith's request is as follows:

	Product P	Product Q	Product R
[a]Sales	$ 50,000	$50,000	$80,000
Variable manufacturing expenses as a % of sales	40%	70%	50%
Variable selling expenses	$ 1,000	$ 1,500	$ 1,600
Variable selling expenses as a % of sales	2%	3%	2%

Product Sales	Area A	Area B	Total
[b]P	$ 35,000	$15,000	$ 50,000
Q	40,000	10,000	50,000
R	30,000	50,000	80,000
	$105,000	75,000	$180,000

[a]Fixed administrative expenses total $8,700 per year. These expenses are common to the two sales areas, but were allocated in the income statement to the two sales areas on a basis of sales dollars. This allocation resulted in $5,075 being allocated to area *A* and $3,625 being allocated to area *B.*
[b]Fixed selling expenses total $17,200 per year. $10,000 of this amount is a result of sales activity in area *A,* and the remainder is incurred in area *B.*

Fixed manufacturing overhead is common to the two areas.

Required

1. Prepare a contribution-type income statement by area and in total for DJ Company for the year (detail sales, variable manufacturing expenses, and variable selling expenses by product).
2. Based on the available data, would you recommend elimination of area *A?* Why?

Exercise 19.6   Segment Reporting

Cooper Incorporated sells footballs and basketballs. During the past year, Cooper's income statement was as follows:

	Total Sales	Footballs	%	Basketballs	%
Sales	$10,000	$4,000	100	$6,000	100
Less variable expenses	4,800	2,200	55	2,600	43-1/3
Contribution margin	$ 5,200	$1,800	45	$3,400	56-2/3
Less direct fixed expenses	3,000	600		2,400	
Segment margin	$ 2,200	$1,200		$1,000	
Less common fixed expenses	1,800				
Net income	$ 400				

The footballs and basketballs are sold in an American market and a Canadian market as follows:

	American	Canadian
Football sales	$2,400	$1,600
Basketball sales	3,800	2,200
Total sales	$6,200	$3,800

The common fixed expenses above are partly traceable to the American market, Canadian market, and general administration as follows:

American market fixed expenses	$ 500
Canadian market fixed expenses	700
General administration fixed expenses	600
Total common fixed expenses	$1,800

Required

Prepare a segmented income statement, as above, but this time with the segments defined as the American and Canadian markets. (It is *not* necessary to state segment sales or variable expenses in percentages.) The direct fixed expenses of the product lines should not be allocated to the markets; treat these as common fixed expenses on this segmented statement.

Exercise 19.7   Segment Concepts

Multipro Incorporated manufactures a variety of pharmaceuticals, medical instruments, and other related medical supplies. Eighteen months ago Multipro developed and began to market a new product line of antihistamine drugs under various trade names. Sales and profitability of this product line during the current fiscal year greatly exceeded management's expectations. The new product line will account for 10% of Multipro's total sales and 12% of its operating income for the fiscal year ending June 30, 19X0. Management believes sales and profits will be significant for several years.

Multipro is concerned about its market position relative to its competitors should disclosure be made about the volume and profitability of its new product line in its annual financial statements. Management is not sure how the Financial Accounting Standard Board's Statement of Financial Accounting Standards No. 14, "Financial Reporting for Segments of a Business Enterprise," applies in this case.

Required

1. What is the purpose of requiring that segment information be disclosed in financial statements?
2. Identify and explain the factors to consider when attempting to decide how products should be grouped to determine a single business segment.
3. What options, if any, does Multipro have regarding the disclosure of its new antihistamine product line? Explain your answer.

Exercise 19.8 Segment Reporting and Analysis

Texland Company has just published their financial statement. Their income statement appeared as follows:

Texland Company
Income Statement

Sales	$260,000
Less variable expenses	140,000
Contribution margin	$120,000
Less fixed expenses	115,000
Net income	$ 5,000

Jo Ann Landers, president of Texland, is concerned about the low-income figure and is determined to improve it. The following additional information is also available:

Texland is divided into two sales regions, Alpha and Beta. Reports show that 40% of sales come from Alpha and $51,000 of variable expenses are traceable to Alpha. This region is also responsible for $35,000 of fixed expenses, compared to $37,000 for Beta.

Required

Landers has determined that a segmented financial statement would be helpful as well as a recommendation about what to do. She has asked you to do both.

Exercise 19.9 Segment Analysis with a Product Line Emphasis

Anderson Golf Club Company sells two different sets of golf clubs—set *A* and set *B*. The following is the income statement for the quarter just ended:

	Total Company	Set A	Set B
Sales	$140,000	$95,000	$45,000
Less variable expenses	80,000	60,000	20,000
Contribution margin	$ 60,000	$35,000	$25,000
Less direct fixed expenses	45,000	22,000	23,000
Product line segment margin	$ 15,000	$13,000	$ 2,000
Less common fixed expenses	11,000		
Net income	$ 4,000		

Anderson will allocate $2,500 to direct advertising, which it plans on using for promoting either set *A* or set *B*. If spent on set *A*, sales of this set will increase by $12,000. If spent on set *B*, sales of this set will increase by $7,500.

Required

On which set should Anderson Golf Club Company spend the advertising funds? Why?

Exercise 19.10   Segment Reporting on Departmental Performance

Bogart Company makes overcoats that are sold by two different departments—*A* and *B*. Below are operating data for the last year:

	Total Company	Department A	Department B
Sales	$420,000	$180,000	$240,000
Less variable expenses	315,000	120,000	195,000
Contribution margin	$105,000	$ 60,000	$ 45,000
Less direct fixed expenses	80,000	50,000	30,000
Department segment margin	$ 25,000	$ 10,000	$ 15,000
Less common fixed expenses	18,000		
Net income	$ 7,000		

Required

1. How much would total net income increase if sales in department *A* increased by $42,000?
2. How much would total net income increase if sales in department *B* increased by $42,000?
3. As president of Bogart Company, in which department would you be most interested in increasing sales? Why?

Problems

Problem 19.1   Segment Analysis—A Review of Concepts (CMA)

1. The basic objective of the RI approach of performance measurement and evaluation is to have a division maximize its
   a. ROI rate.
   b. imputed interest rate charge.
   c. cash flows.
   d. cash flows in excess of a desired minimum amount.
   e. income in excess of a desired minimum return.
2. The imputed interest rate used in the RI approach for performance measurement and evaluation can best be characterized as the
   a. historical weighted average cost of capital for the company.
   b. marginal after-tax cost of new equity capital.
   c. average return on investment that has been earned by the company over a particular time period.
   d. target ROI set by management.
   e. average prime lending rate for the year being evaluated.
3. Which of the following items would most likely *not* be incorporated into the calculation of a division's investment base when using the RI approach for performance measurement and evaluation?
   a. Fixed assets employed in divisional operations
   b. Vacant land being held by the division as a potential site for a new plant
   c. Divisional inventories when division management exercises control over the inventory levels

d. Divisional accounts payable when division management exercises control over the amount of short-term credit utilized

e. Divisional accounts receivable when division management exercises control over credit policy and credit terms

4. A segment of an organization is referred to as a profit center if it has the

   a. authority to make decisions affecting the major determinants of profit including the power to choose its markets and sources of supply.

   b. authority to make decisions affecting the major determinants of profit including the power to choose its market and sources of supply and significant control over the amount of invested capital.

   c. authority to make decisions over the most significant cost of operations including the power to choose the sources of supply.

   d. authority to provide specialized support to other units within the organization.

   e. responsibility for combining the raw materials, direct labor, and other factors of production into a final output.

5. A segment of an organization is referred to as an investment center if it has the

   a. authority to make decisions affecting the major determinants of profit including the power to choose its markets and sources of supply.

   b. authority to make decisions affecting the major determinants of profit including the power to choose its market and sources of supply and significant control over the amount of invested capital.

   c. authority to make decisions over the most significant costs of operations including the power to choose the sources of supply.

   d. authority to provide specialized support to other units within the organization.

   e. responsibility for developing markets for and selling of the output of the organization.

6. A segment of an organization is referred to as a service center if it has the

   a. responsibility for developing markets for and selling of the output of the organization.

   b. responsibility for combining the raw materials, direct labor, and other factors of production into a final output.

   c. authority to make decisions affecting the major determinants of profit including the power to choose its markets and sources of supply.

   d. authority to provide specialized support to other units within the organization.

   e. authority to make decisions over the most significant costs of operations including the power to choose the sources of supply.

7. A segment of an organization is referred to as an expense center if it has the

   a. responsibility for developing markets for and selling of the output of the organization.

   b. authority to make decisions affecting the major determinants of profit including the power to choose its markets and sources of supply.

   c. authority to make decisions over the most significant costs of operations including the power to choose the sources of supply.

   d. authority to provide specialized support to other units within the organization.

   e. responsibility for combining the raw materials, direct labor, and other factors of production into a final output.

Problem 19.2   Segment Analysis—A Division Emphasis

Bodine Corporation began operations on January 1. Operating data for their first year of operations is as follows for their two divisions—Y and Z.

	Total Company	Division Y	Division Z
Sales	$40,000	$26,000	$14,000
Less variable expenses	28,000	19,000	9,000
Contribution margin	$12,000	$ 7,000	$ 5,000
Less direct fixed expenses	6,000	3,500	2,500
Division segment margin	$ 6,000	$ 3,500	$ 2,500
Less common fixed expenses	4,000		
Net income	$ 2,000		

Required

1. How much will division Y's segment margin increase if sales increase by $6,000?
2. How much will division Z's segment margin increase if sales increase by $6,000?
3. If, as sales manager, your salary was based upon Bodine's net income, in which division would you be most interested in increasing sales? Why?

Problem 19.3   Segment Analysis—A Division Emphasis

CUTCO has two different divisions—a brick division and a door division. The following information is available concerning operations for the year ending December 31.

	Total Company	Brick Division	Door Division
Sales	$90,000	$55,000	$35,000
Less variable expenses	60,000	38,000	22,000
Contribution margin	$30,000	$17,000	$13,000
Less direct fixed expenses	20,000	15,000	5,000
Divisional segment margin	$10,000	$ 2,000	$ 8,000
Less common fixed expenses	4,000		
Net income	$ 6,000		

Required

1. How much would the brick division's net income increase if sales increased by $8,000?
2. How much would the door division's net income increase if sales increased by $8,000?
3. What would be the brick division's segment margin if sales increased by $8,000 due to a $1,000 direct advertising expense spent exclusively on the brick division?
4. What would be the door division's segment margin if sales increased by $12,000 due to a $1,000 direct advertising expense spent exclusively on the door division?

Problem 19.4 Segment Performance by ROI Analysis

The following data are for Dee Company's division *A:*

Average available assets:

Receivables	$ 600,000
Inventories	400,000
Fixed assets, net	1,000,000
	$2,000,000
Fixed costs	$ 500,000
Variable costs	$10 per unit
Desired rate of return on average available assets	25%
Expected volume	400,000 units

Required

1. What average unit sales price does division *A* need in order to obtain the desired rate of return on average available assets?
2. What would be the expected turnover of assets?
3. What would be the net income percentage of dollar sales?
4. What rate of return would be earned on assets available if sales volume is 500,000 units, assuming no changes in price or variable costs per unit?

Problem 19.5 Segment Performance Analysis (CMA)

The Jackson Corporation is a large, divisionalized manufacturer. Each division is viewed as an investment center and has virtually complete autonomy for product development, marketing, and production.

Performance of division managers is evaluated periodically by senior corporate management. Divisional ROI is the sole criterion used in performance evaluation under current corporate policy. Corporate management believes ROI is an adequate measure because it incorporates quantitative information from the divisional income statement and balance sheet in the analysis.

Some division managers complained that a single criterion for performance evaluation is insufficient and ineffective. These managers have compiled a list of criteria they believe should be used in evaluating division managers' performance. The criteria include profitability, market position, productivity, product leadership, personnel development, employee attitudes, public responsibility, and balance between short-range and long-range goals.

Required

1. Jackson's management believes that ROI is an adequate criterion to evaluate division management performance. Discuss the shortcomings or possible inconsistencies of using ROI as the sole criterion to evaluate divisional management performance.
2. Discuss the advantages of using multiple criteria versus a single criterion to evaluate divisional management performance.
3. Describe the problems or disadvantages that can be associated with the implementation of the multiple performance criteria measurement system suggested to Jackson Corporation by its division managers.

Problem 19.6 Performance Analysis Alternatives (CMA)

Divisional managers of SIU Incorporated have been expressing growing dissatisfaction with the current methods used to measure divisional performance. Divisional operations are evaluated every quarter by comparison with the static budget prepared during the previous year. Divisional managers claim that many factors are completely out of their control but are included in this comparison. This results in an unfair and misleading performance evaluation.

The managers have been particularly critical of the process used to establish standards and budgets. The annual budget, stated by quarters, is prepared six months before the beginning of the operating year. Pressure by top management to reflect increased earnings has often caused divisional managers to overstate revenues and/or understate expenses. In addition, once the budget had been established, divisions were required to "live with the budget." Frequently, external factors such as the state of the economy, changes in consumer preferences, and actions of competitors have not been adequately recognized in the budget parameters that top management supplied to the divisions. The credibility of the performance review is curtailed when the budget cannot be adjusted to incorporate these changes. Top management, recognizing the current problems, has agreed to establish a committee to review the situation and to make recommendations for a new performance evaluation system. The committee consists of each division manager, the corporate controller, and the executive vice-president who chairs the committee. At the first meeting, one division manager outlined an Achievement of Objectives System (AOS). In this performance evaluation system, divisional managers would be evaluated according to three criteria:

1. Doing better than last year. Various measures would be compared to the same measures of the previous year.
2. Planning realistically. Actual performance for the current year would be compared to realistic plans and/or goals.
3. Managing current assets. Various measures would be used to evaluate the divisional management's achievements and reactions to changing business and economic conditions.

One division manager believed this system would overcome many inconsistencies of the current system because divisions could be evaluated from three different viewpoints. In addition, divisional managers would be able to show how they would react and account for changes in uncontrollable external factors.

A second division manager was also in favor of the proposed AOS. However, she cautioned that the success of a new performance evaluation system would be limited unless it had the complete support of top management. Further, this support should be visible within all divisions. She believed that the committee should recommend some procedures that would enhance the motivational and competitive spirit of the divisions.

Required

1. Explain whether or not the proposed AOS would be an improvement over the measure of divisional performance now used by SIU Incorporated.
2. Develop specific performance measures for each of the three criteria in the proposed AOS that could be used to evaluate divisional managers.
3. Discuss the motivational and behavioral aspects of the proposed performance system. Also, recommend specific programs that could be instituted to promote morale and give incentives to divisional management.

Problem 19.7   ROI Analysis (CMA)

The Notewon Corporation is a highly diversified company that grants its divisional executives a significant amount of authority in operating the divisions. Each division is responsible for its own sales, pricing, production, costs of operations, and the management of accounts receivable, inventories, accounts payable, and use of existing facilities. Cash is managed by corporate headquarters; all cash in excess of normal operating needs of the divisions is transferred periodically to corporate headquarters for redistribution or investment.

The divisional executives are responsible for presenting requests to corporate management for investment projects. The proposals are analyzed and documented at corporate headquarters. The final decision to commit funds to acquire equipment, to expand existing facilities, or to invest rests with corporate management. This procedure for investment projects is necessitated by Notewon's capital allocation policy.

The corporation evaluates the performance of division executives by the ROI measure. The asset base is composed of the fixed assets employed plus working capital exclusive of cash.

The ROI performance of a divisional executive is the most important appraisal factor for salary changes. In addition, the annual performance bonus is based on the ROI results with increases in ROI having a significant impact on the amount of the bonus.

The Notewon Corporation adopted the ROI performance measure and related compensation procedures about ten years ago. Notewon did this to increase the awareness of divisional management to the importance of the profit/asset relationship and to provide additional incentive to the divisional executives to seek investment opportunities.

Notewon seems to have benefited from the program. The ROI for the corporation as a whole increased during the first years of the program. Although the ROI has continued to grow in each division, the corporate ROI has declined in recent years. The corporation has accumulated a sizeable amount of cash and short-term marketable securities in the past three years.

Notewon's management is concerned about the increase in the short-term marketable securities. A recent article in a financial publication suggested that the use of ROI was overemphasized by some companies with results similar to those experienced by Notewon.

Required

1. Describe the specific actions division managers might have taken to cause the ROI to grow in each division but decline for the corporation. Illustrate your explanation with appropriate examples.
2. Explain, using the concepts of goal congruence and motivation of divisional executives, how Notewon Corporation's overemphasis on the use of the ROI measure might result in the recent decline in the corporation's ROI and the increase in cash and short-term marketable securities.
3. What changes could be made in Notewon Corporation's compensation policy to avoid this problem? Explain your answer.

Problem 19.8   ROI Analysis (CMA)

The Riverside Corporation is a major regional retailer. The chief executive officer (CEO) is concerned with the slow growth of both sales and net income, and the subsequent effect on the trading price of the common stock. Selected financial data for the past three years are presented:

Riverside Corporation (In millions of dollars)

	19X1	19X2	19X3
1. Sales	$187.0	$192.5	$200.0
2. Net income	5.6	5.8	6.0
3. Dividends declared and paid	2.5	2.5	2.5
December 31 balances			
4. Owners' equity	63.2	66.5	70.0
5. Debt	30.3	29.8	30.0
Selected year-end financial ratios:			
Net income to sales	3.0%	3.0%	3.0%
Investment turnover	2×	2×	2×
6. Return on equity	8.9%	8.7%	8.6%
7. Debt to total capital	32.4%	30.9%	30.0%

The CEO believes that the price of the stock has been adversely affected by the downward trend of the return on equity, the relatively low dividend payout ratio, and the lack of dividend increases. In order to improve the price of the stock, he wants to improve the return on equity and dividends.

He believes that Riverside should be able to meet these objectives by:

1. Increase sales and net income at an annual rate of 10% a year.
2. Establish a new dividend policy calling for a dividend payout of 50% of earnings or $3,000,000, whichever is greater.

The 10% annual sales increase will be accomplished through a new promotional program. He believes the present net income to sales ratio of 3% will be unchanged by the cost of this new program and any interest paid on new debt. He expects that Riverside can accomplish this sales and income growth while maintaining the current relationship of total investment to sales. Any capital needed to maintain this relationship that is not generated internally would be acquired through long-term debt financing. The CEO hopes that debt would not exceed 35% of total capital.

Required

1. Using the CEO's program, prepare a schedule showing the appropriate data for the years 19X4, 19X5, and 19X6 for the items numbered 1 through 7 on the schedule presented above.
2. Can the CEO meet all his requirements if a 10% per year growth in income and sales is achieved? Explain your answer.
3. What alternative actions should the CEO consider in order to improve the return on equity and support increased dividend payments?
4. Explain the reasons the CEO might have for wanting to limit debt to 35% of total capital.

Problem 19.9   ROI and Residual Income

Bio-grade Products is a multi-product company manufacturing animal feeds and feed supplements. The need for a widely based manufacturing and distribution system has led to a highly decentralized management structure. Each divisional manager is responsible for production and distribution in corporate products in one of eight geographical areas of the country.

Residual income is used to evaluate divisional managers. The residual income for each division equals each division's contribution to corporate profits before taxes less a 20% investment charge on a division's investment base. The investment base for each division is the sum of its year-end balances of accounts receivable, inventories, and net plant fixed assets (cost less accumulated depreciation). Corporate policies dictate that divisions minimize their investments in receivables and inventories. Investments in plant fixed assets are a joint division/corporate decision based on proposals made by divisional plant managers, available corporate funds, and general corporate policy.

Alex Williams, divisional manager for the southeastern sector, prepared the 19X1 and preliminary 19X2 budgets in late 19X0 for his division. Final approval of the 19X2 budget took place in late 19X1 after adjustments for trends and other information developed during 19X1. Preliminary work on the 19X3 budget also took place at that time. In early October of 19X2, Williams asked the divisional controller to prepare a report presenting performance for the first nine months of 19X2. The report is shown below.

Required

1. Evaluate the performance of Alex Williams for the nine months ending September 19X2. Support your evaluation with pertinent facts from the problem.
2. Identify the features of Bio-grade Products divisional performance measurement reporting and evaluating system that need to be revised if it is to reflect effectively the responsibilities of the divisional managers.

Bio-grade Products—Southeastern Sector
(000 omitted)

	19X2			19X1	
	Annual Budget	*Nine-Month Budget[a]*	*Nine-Month Actual*	*Annual Budget*	*Actual Results*
Sales	$2,800	$2,100	$2,200	$2,500	$2,430
Divisional costs and expenses					
Direct materials and labor	$1,064	$ 798	$ 995	$ 900	$ 890
Supplies	44	33	35	35	43
Maintenance and repairs	200	150	60	175	160
Plant depreciation	120	90	90	110	110
Administration	120	90	90	90	100
Total divisional costs and expenses	$1,548	$1,161	$1,270	$1,310	$1,303
Divisional margin	$1,252	$ 939	$ 930	$1,190	$1,127
Allocated corporate fixed costs	360	270	240	340	320
Divisional contribution to corporate profits	$ 892	$ 669	$ 690	$ 850	$ 807
Imputed interest on divisional investment (20%)	420	321[b]	300[b]	370	365
Divisional residual income	$ 472	$ 348	$ 390	$ 480	$ 442

	Budgeted Balance 12/31/X2	Budgeted Balance 9/30/X2	Actual Balance 9/30/X2	Budgeted Balance 12/31/X1	Actual Balance 12/31/X1
Division investment:					
Accounts receivable	$ 280	$ 290	$ 250	$ 250	$ 250
Inventories	500	500	650	450	475
Plant fixed assets (net)	1,320	1,350	1,100	1,150	1,100
Total	$2,100	$2,140	$2,000	$1,850	$1,825
Imputed interest (20%)	$ 420	$ 321[b]	$ 300[b]	$ 370	$ 365

[a]Bio-grade's sales occur uniformly throughout the year.
[b]Imputed interest is calculated at only 15% to reflect that only nine months or three fourths of the fiscal year has passed.

Problem 19.10   Segment Analysis (CMA)

Valmar Products is a plumbing supply distributing company that carries the products of several manufacturers. Valmar sells its products to retail plumbing stores and to contractors over the counter. In addition, Valmar places orders for plumbing supplies and related materials for specific building and plumbing contractors directly with the manufacturers' factories. These special orders are sent directly to the contractors from the factories. Valmar bills the contractors for the direct orders and pays the manufacturer after the contractor has paid for the order. All customer orders except the direct-shipment orders are filled from Valmar's inventories in its warehouse.

The income statement shown below presents the operating results for the past two fiscal years. In addition, the operating results by product line for the most recent fiscal year are presented on page 695. For internal reporting purposes, the selling expenses, warehouse costs, and other operating expenses are allocated to the product lines on the basis of sales.

Valmar Products
Income Statement
For the Fiscal Years Ending May 31
(000 omitted)

	19X0	19X1
Revenue from sales	$12,000	$10,000
Cost of goods sold	9,810	8,300
Gross margin	$ 2,190	$ 1,700
Operating expenses		
Selling expenses	$ 250	$ 200
Warehouse costs	150	150
Other operating expenses	100	100
Total operating expenses	$ 500	$ 450
Net income from operations	$ 1,690	$ 1,250
Interest expense	250	300
Income before taxes	$ 1,440	$ 950
Income taxes (40%)	576	380
Net income	$ 864	$ 570

Jeremy Lypor, president of Valmar, is concerned because the current year's operating results are not up to expectations and have deteriorated from last year's results. The operating results by product line indicate that the cash counter sales are marginally profitable and the direct-shipment business may not be worth the effort. However, Lypor does not have adequate information with which to make decisions concerning the separate product lines, nor does he have enough information to enable him to decide which lines should be promoted in order to improve the total results.

Statistics regarding the number of orders handled and the average book value of inventory carried in the warehouse were developed at the request of Lypor and are presented in the schedule on page 695. In addition, the following information has been developed regarding Valmar's operations.

1. Commissions amounting to 50% of the selling expenses are paid to salespersons on the basis of a flat percentage of sales billed; this same percentage is also paid on all cash counter sales.
2. The other operating expenses and the balance of the selling expenses are related directly to the number of orders handled.
3. Warehouse expenses are related to the value of inventory in the warehouse.
4. Money is borrowed to carry inventory in the warehouse.

Valmar Products
Product-Line Operating Results
For the Fiscal Year Ending May 31, 19X1
(000 omitted)

	Trims and Accessories	Valve and Pipe Fittings	Fixtures	Cash Counter Sales	Direct Shipments	Total
Sales	$2,000	$3,000	$1,000	$1,000	$3,000	$10,000
Cost of sales	1,480	2,445	705	865	2,805	8,300
Gross margin	$ 520	$ 555	$ 295	$ 135	$ 195	$ 1,700
Allocated operating expenses	90	135	45	45	135	450
Operating income	$ 430	$ 420	$ 250	$ 90	$ 60	$ 1,250
Return on sales	21.5%	14.0%	25.0%	9.0%	2.0%	12.5%

	Number of Orders Handled		Average Value of Inventory	
	Quantity	Percent	Amount (000 omitted)	Percent
Trims and accessories	1,008	12%	$ 160	10%
Valve and pipe fittings	6,048	72	1,248	78
Fixtures	756	9	160	10
Cash counter sales	—	—	32	2
Direct shipments	588	7	—	
Totals	8,400	100%	$1,600	100%

Required

1. Lypor has requested that the present product line statement be reviewed to determine if it can be revised to make it more useful in managing Valmar's business. Prepare a revised product line statement for Valmar Products and explain all changes that were made in the revised statement.

2. Based upon your revised product line statement for Valmar Products and the other facts presented in the problem, what advice would you give to Lypor regarding the following:

   a. The direct-shipment business
   b. The cash counter sales business
   c. The other three product lines

   Explain your response in each case.

DECISION ANALYSIS

PART

V

Techniques for identifying and evaluating relevant costs in decision analysis are outlined in chapters 20 through 24. Cost data is a major input into the decision-making process and it is imperative that the costs be relevant to the decision. Product pricing is another major input into the decision. Establishing product prices for both intercompany sales as well as external sales is an important decision in itself.

The decision to buy capital equipment is very important because of the size of the investment and because of the length of the investment's life. Capital budgeting assists in making this type of decision.

An important decision that you must make is which, if any, professional certification to achieve. Cost and managerial accounting topics are a significant part of the examinations that must be passed in order to be a certified public accountant (CPA) or to receive a Certificate in Management Accounting (CMA).

RELEVANT COSTS FOR DECISIONS

20

OUTLINE

Accountants, engineers, economists, and others are frequently called upon to pool their expertise to provide information for making a large variety of business decisions. Because cost accounting information is an essential component in nearly every business decision, it is important that accountants understand both the decision-making process itself and the proper use of cost accounting information in that process. However, understanding how to properly use cost accounting information in decisions may be challenging because different types of costs are useful for making different types of decisions. It is not always clear what types of costs are relevant for which types of decisions.

Improper accumulation or analysis of cost information may lead to poor decisions with unfortunate consequences. This chapter explains the appropriate use of cost accounting information in business decisions. After completing this chapter you should be able to:

1. describe the role of cost accounting information in decisions.
2. differentiate between routine and nonroutine decisions.
3. apply criteria for identifying costs relevant in nonroutine decisions.
4. analyze cost accounting information in nonroutine decisions.
5. determine the effect on nonroutine decisions of short-run versus long-run considerations, taxes, the time value of money, and qualitative factors.

THE ROLE OF COST INFORMATION IN DECISIONS

The types of decisions emphasized in this chapter are often referred to as **nonroutine decisions** because they are not directly related to the ordinary, repetitive production cycle of a firm. For example, discontinuing a product line, replacing present equipment with new machinery, making a component rather than buying one from outside vendors, and accepting a special order below customary prices are all examples of nonroutine decisions.

Accounting for **routine decisions,** on the other hand, relates to the accumulation and reporting of information for everyday control of operations and for ordinary product-costing purposes. This chapter focuses on the development of concepts and procedures for handling decisions that arise only periodically in a firm's life and are, therefore, called nonroutine decisions.

The primary function of information, including cost accounting information, in the process of making nonroutine decisions is to increase the knowledge level of the decision maker. **Knowledge** refers to one's understanding of reality or the true state of nature, and concerns what is, what was, or what may be. Knowledge is vital in making all types of decisions. However, because nonroutine decisions are infrequently made most firms do not have the mechanisms for formulating all of the necessary information for these decisions built into their accounting systems. Therefore, the process for acquiring knowledge for nonroutine decisions is somewhat different from routine decisions.

Knowledge is vital in making nonroutine business decisions because it helps the decision maker to do the following:

1. Describe the problem or decision situation at hand.
2. Formulate alternative courses of action.
3. Reduce the number of all possible courses of action to those that are actually viable alternatives.
4. Reduce the uncertainty related to the success or failure of each viable alternative.
5. Choose the course of action that appears most likely to accomplish organizational goals.

To illustrate how information facilitates the decision-making process, consider the following situation. The management of a firm is trying to decide whether or not to add a new product line or continue to operate with existing lines. In the process of considering this decision, management collects as much information as possible about other product lines and their potential impact on company operations. Cost accounting information is essential for such decisions. Also, information concerning the probable acceptance of each product in the marketplace, the forecasted sales of each new line, and the probable impact of new product lines on the sales of existing lines are examples of additional items that might be considered.

After accumulation, this information is analyzed by product line to provide a forecast of the expected contribution to earnings and the probability of success or failure for each product line. At this point, after the accumulation and analysis of information, management has increased knowledge with which to make a decision; that is, (*a*) the problem or decision situation has been described, (*b*) alternative courses of action have been formulated, and (*c*) the probable returns and uncertainty associated with each viable alternative are apparent. Cost accounting information has fulfilled its function in helping the decision maker acquire the knowledge necessary to make an appropriate decision.

The decision process then proceeds with management comparing the expected contribution from each project and making a decision. This is an abbreviated view of the actual decision process, but it illustrates that the role of cost accounting information in the decision-making process is to help the decision maker to (*a*) acquire some of the knowledge necessary for understanding the decision situation, (*b*) formulate the problem in a way that highlights the current state of knowledge, (*c*) analyze possible decision alternatives, and (*d*) increase the probability of selecting the best course of action.

RELEVANT COSTS

There are a great variety of nonroutine decision situations and a great many different types of cost accounting information. Variable costs, historical costs, standard costs, conversion costs, marginal costs, and opportunity costs are just some of the types of costs discussed in this text. Determining which type of cost accounting information is actually relevant in a given business decision is one of the most important aspects of the decision-making process. Adding irrelevant information may confuse the decision maker or may draw the attention of the decision maker away from other relevant information. In addition, there is always the danger that irrelevant information will be improperly used in analyzing decision alternatives. Inappropriate use of irrelevant cost accounting information may lead to the selection of a suboptimal course of action.

Relevant costs are simply the types of costs that are useful in a particular decision situation. Relevant costs can be identified by determining if they satisfy two necessary criteria—if they are *expected future costs* and if they are *different among decision alternatives*.

Costs That Are Expected Future Costs

Costs that satisfy the criteria of being *expected future costs* are costs that are expected to be incurred in the future as a result of choosing a particular decision alternative. Management decisions are made and actions are taken in order to achieve specific goals. Because goals are achieved in the future, decisions must be made based on expected future circumstances that include expected future costs and revenues.

The "future" refers to the time period affected by the decision. For example, a manager evaluating whether to take or refuse a special order would consider the materials, labor, and overhead costs expected to be incurred as a result of taking the order. Historical or past costs incurred in making similar orders may be useful information for predicting what *might be* the cost of the special order. However, historical costs do not satisfy the criterion of expected future costs and are almost never relevant in decisions. Historical costs that are expected to continue at the same level into the future are actually expected future costs, not historical costs, and are, therefore, relevant in decisions.

Costs That Are Different among Decision Alternatives

Only costs that differ among decision alternatives are relevant to a decision. For example, assume that the alternatives in a given decision situation are to purchase either machine X or machine Y. If the machines cost $10,000 and $12,000 respectively, then their costs are relevant to the decision at hand because the prices differ between machines. Actually, the $2,000 difference between the cost of the machines is the relevant component of information. However, if both machines cost the same, then their cost has no relevance for the decision.

Other information components such as the disposal value of the machines or the future cost savings from purchasing the machines might differ between machines and, as a result, constitute the relevant costs for this decision. When there are no cost (or revenue) differences among different alternatives, then the decision maker may be neutral or indifferent about the choice of alternatives from an economic viewpoint. In such circumstances the final decision may be based on nonquantifiable factors.

ANALYSIS OF COST INFORMATION FOR NONROUTINE DECISIONS

For a more detailed illustration of the application of the criteria for determining relevance, consider the following situation. A company is trying to decide if it should replace an old machine with a new, more efficient machine. Information about the old and new machines is given below:

Old Machine

Original cost	$100,000
Book value	80,000
Current disposal value	30,000
Remaining life	5 years

New Machine

Current cost	$120,000
Disposal value in 5 years	–0–
Expected life	5 years

The new machine is expected to reduce annual variable operating costs from $1,075,000 to $775,000. Annual revenue from sales is expected to remain at $2,500,000 regardless of the machinery used.

At first management might consider the immediate impact on net income of replacing the old machine. With a book value of $80,000 and a current disposal value of only $30,000, an immediate effect would be the recognition of a $50,000 ($80,000 − $30,000) "loss on disposal" of the old machine. Management may be more inclined to continue with the old machine and show $16,000 depreciation expense on the income statement for the next five years rather than show such a large "loss on disposal" in the current year.

However, such a hasty and incomplete analysis rarely results in making the best decision from a cost viewpoint. A more complete analysis, as shown in figure 20.1, reveals that the most cost effective decision is to purchase the new machine. In this example, the book value of the old machine is a historical cost and does not meet the criterion of a cost that is different between alternatives. The use of historical costs, book values, or any other irrelevant information may cloud the decision analysis and may contribute toward poor decisions. To avoid the pitfalls of using incomplete or irrelevant information, it is suggested that a thorough and systematic approach be adopted for making nonroutine decisions.

Figure 20.1   Five-year analysis of net income for decision to keep old machine or purchase new machine

(000 omitted)

	Keep Old Machine	Purchase New Machine	Difference
Sales	$2,500	$2,500	$-0-
Variable operating expenses	(1,075)	(775)	300
Old machine:			
Book value written off by:			
Periodic depreciation	(80)		
or			-0-
Lump-sum sale		(80)	
Current disposal value		30	30
New machine:			
Current cost written off by:			
Periodic depreciation		(120)	(120)
Net income	$1,345	$1,555	$210
Calculation of loss on disposal of old machine:			
Book value of old machine		$80,000	
Current disposal value of old machine		30,000	
Loss on disposal of old machine		$50,000	

Total Cost Approach

A suggested set of procedures to follow in making nonroutine decisions is given below. This is referred to as the total cost approach to nonroutine decisions.

1. Accumulate all potentially relevant information about each alternative under consideration.
2. Eliminate those costs (revenues) that are *not expected future costs* (revenues).
3. Eliminate those costs (revenues) that are *not different among alternatives*.
4. Evaluate alternatives based on the remaining relevant and differential information.

To illustrate the use of this approach, refer to the situation concerning the possible replacement of an old machine. Figure 20.1 follows step 1 above and gives a summary of potentially relevant information for the five-year period affected by the decision to replace the old machine.

Having accumulated the potentially relevant information, the next step is to identify and eliminate costs and revenues that are not expected future costs. Forecasted sales and the current disposal value of the old machine are both expected future revenues, depending on which alternative is chosen. Variable operating expenses and the cost of the new machine are both expected future costs. The only cost that is not an expected future cost is the book value of the old machine. Therefore, the book value of the old machine should be eliminated from further consideration based on the future cost criterion of relevance.

The next step in the analysis is to eliminate those costs and revenues that are not different between decision alternatives. Sales do not differ between alternatives; neither does the book value of the old machine. Book value is handled in a different way in the accounting records depending on which alternative is chosen. For example, if the old machine is retained, book value is written off by periodic depreciation charges over the machine's remaining useful life. If the new machine is acquired, book value of the old machine

Figure 20.2   Report to management—five-year analysis of net income for decision to keep old machine or purchase new machine

(000 omitted)

	Differential Revenues and Expenses
Decrease in variable operating expenses	$300
Disposal value of old machine	30
Cost of new machine	(120)
Increase in net income over the life of the new machine	$210

is written off as part of a sales transaction. However, this difference in accounting procedure does not alter the fact that the net result is that book value does not differ between alternatives over the period of time affected by the decision. Thus, the book value of old equipment fails to meet both criteria of relevance.

The final step in the analysis is to evaluate alternative courses of action based on the remaining differential information. The relevant items of information and the net effect on income are shown in the "difference" column of figure 20.1. Assuming that each alternative course of action has an equal probability of success or failure, the results indicate that the firm would be better off by $210,000 over the next five years by choosing to purchase the new machine.

Figure 20.1 illustrates a format that is useful for gathering and analyzing available information. It emphasizes the *differences* among alternatives so that only those factors that should influence the final decision are highlighted. Yet, all information related to the decision situation is openly and clearly presented so there is no ambiguity about what information has been considered, how the analysis was made, and what information is actually relevant to the decision at hand.

The final report to management might contain only information that is relevant to the decision at hand. For example, using the data from figure 20.1 as supporting information, figure 20.2 illustrates a final report to management.

When more than two decision alternatives are being considered, it is usually not helpful to calculate and show a number of "difference" columns. Rather, the relevant information for each alternative is reported, and the decision is based on a ranking of final total results.

Note that capital budgeting principles that will be presented in chapters 22 and 23 apply to the calculation of costs and revenues that are "given" in this chapter. These are additional procedures such as the calculation of present values of future cash flows that may be necessary to determine the appropriate numbers to use in a decision analysis. However, the principles discussed in this chapter remain the same regardless of the detail involved in generating the basic information items.

Contribution Approach

The use of contribution margin analysis, discussed in chapters 4 and 18, can be very useful in making nonroutine decisions. A major feature of the contribution approach is that variable and fixed costs are clearly identified at the outset, which greatly simplifies the information analysis. This is especially useful in situations where all variable costs are relevant and all fixed costs are irrelevant. However, it should be emphasized that variable costs may or may not be relevant and fixed costs may or may not be irrelevant. In each case it will depend on whether the cost/revenue is a future item that is expected to differ among alternatives. Variable costs should not be presumed to be relevant and fixed costs should not be presumed to be irrelevant.

Figure 20.3   Cost and revenue information for competing products

	Product A	Product B
Sales (per unit)	$20	$30
Variable costs (per unit)	15	21
Contribution margin	$ 5	$ 9

Figure 20.4   Scarce resource information for competing products

	Product A	Product B
Contribution margin per unit (fig. 20.3)	$5.00	$9.00
Pounds of alloy required to produce one unit	÷ 2	÷ 4
Contribution margin per pound of alloy	$2.50	$2.25
Total available pounds of alloy	× 5,000	× 5,000
Total contribution	$12,500	$11,250

In situations where relevancy does not follow cost behavior patterns, the contribution approach is still a useful starting point. The contribution approach also assists in analyzing the short-run versus long-run effects of decisions.

Where possible, the total cost approach and the contribution approach should be used simultaneously to verify the accuracy and validity of the information analysis. A characteristic of many nonroutine decisions is that the "obvious" is not always the best course of action. Comparing results using both approaches may be useful in uncovering oversights and invalid reasoning. However, in some nonroutine decisions the contribution approach is a superior method of analysis because an optimal solution using the total cost approach might require the use of extended computations or even trial-and-error methods.

To illustrate the use of the contribution approach in making nonroutine decisions, consider the following situation. A company that manufactures two products wanted to emphasize one product in their production and marketing efforts. The dilemma arises because both products use a particular metal alloy that is in scarce supply. Because a limited quantity of the metal alloy is available, management would like to promote the product that will contribute the most to company profits. Cost and revenue information for the two products is given in figure 20.3.

Product *B* seems to be the logical choice for promotion because it has the larger contribution margin per unit. However, the supplier of the alloy indicates that only 5,000 pounds of the alloy will be available to the company during each accounting period for the foreseeable future. Therefore, the availability of the metal alloy, a *scarce resource,* is a *constraining factor* in this situation.

Scarce resources may include raw materials availability (as in this example), floor space, machine hours, labor hours, or budget constraints. When constraining factors are involved, emphasis shifts for maximizing profits from contribution margin *per unit* to contribution margin *per unit of scarce resource*. For example, it takes 4 pounds of the alloy to produce one unit of *B,* and it takes 2 pounds of the alloy to produce one unit of *A.* Figure 20.4 shows the results of considering the contribution margin per unit of metal alloy.

Figure 20.5   Analysis of information under constrained conditions

Possible Production (in units) of Each Product

	Product A	Product B
Pounds of alloy available	5,000	5,000
Pounds of alloy required per unit	÷ 2	÷ 4
Potential production in units	2,500	1,250

Projected Income Statements for the Production of Each Product

	Product A		Product B		Dollar
	Per Unit	Amount	Per Unit	Amount	Difference
Sales	$20	$50,000	$30	$37,500	$12,500
Variable costs	15	37,500	21	26,250	11,250
Contribution margin		$12,500		$11,250	$ 1,250

This example shows how the contribution approach can provide important input into the solution of nonroutine decisions. A suggested procedure is to verify results found using one approach with the other approach. Figure 20.5 shows how the results using the contribution approach can be verified by using the total cost approach.

The above example shows how to deal with a situation in which there is only one constraint—the limited availability of one scarce resource. However, a typical situation involves multiple constraints caused by the availability of a number of different resources. In such situations, an analytical tool called linear programming is necessary to make appropriate profit maximizing decisions. The use of linear programming is illustrated in the appendix at the end of this chapter.

SOME EXAMPLES OF NONROUTINE DECISIONS

The following are examples of nonroutine decisions that commonly occur in manufacturing operations. The decision types selected for illustration are intended to provide sufficient background to enable the application of solution principles in a wide variety of decision situations.

Make or Buy

A decision faced by many manufacturing firms is whether to make their own subassemblies and parts or to buy them from outside suppliers. For example, consider a company that produces a number of different subassemblies that eventually become part of a final product. The company has accumulated the following cost information concerning its annual production of one of these subassemblies.

	Cost per Unit	Total Cost for 5,000 Units
Direct materials	$ 4	$ 20,000
Direct labor	12	60,000
Variable overhead	8	40,000
Fixed overhead	6	30,000
Total	$30	$150,000

An external supplier has offered to provide the firm with their annual needs of this particular subassembly at a price of $29 per unit—an apparent savings of $1 per

Figure 20.6   Analysis of information for make or buy decision

5,000 Units of a Certain Subassembly

	Make Internally	Buy Externally	Difference
Cost to buy externally @ $29		$145,000	$(145,000)
Cost to make internally:			
Direct materials @ $4	$20,000		20,000
Direct labor @ $12	60,000		60,000
Variable overhead @ $8	40,000		40,000
Fixed overhead[a]	30,000	20,000	10,000
Total	$150,000	$165,000	$(15,000)

[a]$10,000 of fixed costs can be avoided if the subassemblies are purchased externally.

unit. Without the benefit of additional analysis, this $1 difference between the cost of making the subassembly and the price of buying the subassembly from the outside supplier might influence management to buy the subassemblies with the expectation of saving $5,000 each year. However, as previously illustrated, the best course of action in nonroutine decisions is rarely so obvious, and it is wise to develop a formal analysis rather than jump to a premature conclusion based on incomplete information.

Applying the concepts developed in this chapter, figure 20.6 presents an analysis of information using the total cost approach to making nonroutine decisions.

All of the costs in figure 20.6 are expected future costs and satisfy the first criterion of relevance. The cost to buy externally and the variable manufacturing costs of making the subassembly are all different between decision alternatives and satisfy the second criteria of relevance.

However, not all fixed overhead such as insurance, depreciation, executive salaries, and property taxes can be avoided if the decision is made to buy from the external supplier; that is, $20,000 of fixed overhead does not differ between decision alternatives. The difference of $10,000 is the only part of fixed overhead that satisfies both criteria of relevance and is, therefore, included in the difference column. The results of the analysis indicate that if the company purchases the subassemblies from the outside supplier, net income would not increase by $5,000 but decrease by $15,000. Therefore, based on quantitative factors, the appropriate decision is to continue to manufacture the subassemblies.

Opportunity costs should also be considered in such circumstances. *Opportunity costs* represent the measurable advantage of a foregone alternative. Opportunity costs are essentially expected future costs that will probably differ among decision alternatives. For example, a decision to satisfy needs internally rather than externally may also depend on whether the space and productive capacity now used to manufacture the subassemblies can be put to some alternative use. The *opportunity cost* of the capacity idled by discontinuing production of the subassemblies must be determined. If there are no alternative uses for the idled capacity, then the opportunity cost is zero. If there is no opportunity cost, the decision to continue to manufacture the subassemblies is based on an analysis similar to the above illustration.

However, if the idle capacity could be used for some other purpose, then the contribution to net income generated by the alternative use should be considered in the analysis of the make or buy decision. For example, assume that the capacity used to produce the subassemblies illustrated in figure 20.6 could be used to produce a different product that would generate a contribution margin of $18,000 per year, as shown in figure

---

Figure 20.7   Analysis of information for make or buy decision

---

5,000 Units of a Certain Subassembly

	Make Internally	Buy Externally	Difference
Cost to buy externally @ $29		$145,000	$(145,000)
Cost to make internally:			
Direct materials @ $4	$ 20,000		20,000
Direct labor @ $12	60,000		60,000
Variable overhead @ $8	40,000		40,000
Fixed overhead[a]	30,000	20,000	10,000
Opportunity cost of idle capacity	18,000		18,000
Total	$168,000	$165,000	$ 3,000

[a]$10,000 of fixed costs can be avoided if the subassemblies are purchased externally.

20.7. Note that the amount of avoidable fixed overhead may change under these conditions. However, for purposes of this example avoidable fixed overhead is assumed to remain the same.

The $18,000 added contribution would result in an increase in net income of $3,000. Therefore, the appropriate decision is to purchase the subassemblies from an outside supplier and use the idle capacity to produce the new product.

Special Orders

Management frequently faces the decision of accepting or rejecting special orders for their product at a price below the usual selling price. For example, consider the following situation in which a company produces a single product. The company's budgeted income statement is given in figure 20.8.

The company has received a special order from a foreign corporation for 15,000 units. The company has been offered a price of $4.50 per unit even though the customary selling price for this item is $6.00. The decision to accept or reject a special order such as this depends on several factors. The first consideration should be whether there is sufficient plant capacity available so the special order can be produced without affecting production for regular sales. If the plant is operating at full capacity, the special order should be viewed as an alternative use of plant capacity. It is quite clear that accepting the special order at a price of $4.50 with the plant operating at full capacity would result in an unacceptable decline in gross profit of $22,500—the difference in selling price of $1.50 ($6.00 − $4.50) times 15,000 units.

If the plant is not operating at full capacity, the decision to accept or reject the special order should consider the opportunity cost of the idle capacity. Idle capacity usually has an opportunity cost greater than zero because management is continuously searching for the most profitable ways to utilize available capacity. Therefore, there may be several alternatives under consideration at any one time. A special order may be simply one of many alternative uses of excess plant capacity.

In light of the availability of alternative choices, remember that the decision to accept a special order is typically a short-run decision made on the expectation of increasing the current contribution margin rather than on the expectation of sustaining long-run profits. As a result, management may be reluctant to accept a special order when there are other long-run opportunities for excess capacity even though a special order may be more profitable in the short run. For example, a special order expected to contribute $10,000 to profits in the next year may be rejected in favor of a three-year contract

Figure 20.8   Budgeted income statement

Based on Planned Production and Sales of 250,000 Units

	Per Unit	Amount
Sales	$6.00	$1,500,000
Cost of goods sold	4.80	1,200,000
Gross profit	$1.20	$ 300,000
Selling expenses	.40	100,000
Operating income	$ .80	$ 200,000

Figure 20.9   Standard cost of production

Based on a Relevant Range of Production of 250,000 to 300,000 Units

	Per Unit
Direct material	$2.00
Direct labor	1.60
Variable manufacturing overhead	.50
Total variable costs	$4.10
Fixed manufacturing overhead	$175,000.00

that is expected to yield only $7,000 in the next year. This may be appropriate if the total expected contribution over the next three years is greater under the contract than with alternative short-run special orders.

Management in the previous illustration may be reluctant to accept the special order under any circumstances because the offered price of $4.50 does not cover the per-unit cost of production of $4.80. Management realizes that the long-run survival of the firm is jeopardized unless the company can continue to cover *all* costs and provide a normal rate of return on employed capital.

However, under appropriate circumstances, accepting the special order may benefit the firm in the short run without sacrificing long-run objectives. For example, assume that the company described in figure 20.8 has current excess plant capacity and that the excess capacity has no alternative uses. Additional information concerning the standard cost of producing each unit of this company's product is given in figure 20.9.

By examining the variable and fixed cost components of these operations, it becomes clear that if the special order is accepted even at a selling price of $4.50 a contribution will be made to cover fixed costs and gross profit. The amount of the contribution is $.40 per unit ($4.50 selling price — $4.10 variable manufacturing costs). The total increase in gross profit from accepting this special order will be $6,000 ($.40 per unit × 15,000 units). The analysis of information in figure 20.10 verifies this calculation.

When there is excess plant capacity, the relevant costs in a special order decision include *sales* and *variable manufacturing costs*. For example, under the circumstances just illustrated, a comparison of the gross margin and the proposed selling price may lead to an inappropriate decision. This could happen because, unlike contribution margin, gross margin contains irrelevant information—fixed manufacturing costs.

Note in the above example that net income did not increase by the same amount as gross profit. Because selling expenses have a fixed as well as a variable component,

Figure 20.10   Analysis of information for a special order decision

	Order Not Accepted		Order Accepted		
	Per Unit	Total	Per Unit	Total	Total Difference
Sales:					
Regular (250,000)	$6.00	$1,500,000	$6.00	$1,500,000	
Special (15,000)			4.50	67,500	$ 67,500
Total	$6.00	$1,500,000		$1,567,500	$ 67,500
Cost of goods sold:					
Variable:					
Regular	4.10	1,025,000	4.10	1,025,000	
Special			4.10	61,500	61,500
Fixed:	.70	175,000		175,000	
Total	$4.80	$1,200,000		$1,261,500	$ 61,500
Gross profit	$1.20	$ 300,000		$ 306,000	$ 6,000
Selling expenses:					
Variable:					
Regular	$ .30	$ 75,000	.30	$ 75,000	
Special			.30	4,500	$ 4,500
Fixed	.10	25,000		25,000	
Total	$ .40	$ 100,000		$ 104,500	$ 4,500
Net income	$ .80	$ 200,000		$ 201,500	$ 1,500

part of selling expense is relevant information and must be included in the decision analysis. This illustrates the importance of collecting and analyzing *all* potentially relevant items of information so the total effect on net income is known. For example, if variable selling expenses had been $.40 per unit, then the increase in gross margin from accepting the special order would have been offset by an increase in variable selling expense ($.40 per unit $\times$ 15,000 units = $6,000). Net income would remain the same whether or not the special order is accepted. This points out that costs other than manufacturing costs may be relevant in the special order decision.

The above situation also illustrates the wisdom of comparing *total* amounts rather than *unit* amounts. For example, comparing the offered price of $4.50 against the cost of production of $4.80 might have resulted in the special order being unwisely rejected. The allocation of fixed costs to units of production is a necessary process for income determination and for other purposes. However, in situations where total fixed costs are unaffected, they are irrelevant and their inclusion in the unit cost may lead to inappropriate decisions.

Operate or Shut Down

One of the most significant nonroutine decisions managers must make is when to add new product lines and whether or not to continue to operate or shut down existing product lines. These decisions are typically very critical because they involve large amounts of capital and a number of employees in various departments of the company. A multitude of factors should be considered, ranging from the costs and revenues involved to the impact of losing trained employees and established markets. Reentering a market, hiring and training of new employees, morale of other employees, and loss of community goodwill are some factors that should be considered even though such factors are not easily quantified.

Figure 20.11   Sales and cost information by product line

	Total	Product A	Product B	Product C
Sales @ $1.00	$290,000	$130,000	$100,000	$ 60,000
Variable costs @ $.50	145,000	65,000	50,000	30,000
Contribution margin @ $.50	$145,000	$ 65,000	$ 50,000	$ 30,000
Fixed costs:				
Avoidable	$ 85,000	$ 20,000	$ 30,000	$ 35,000
Unavoidable	20,000	5,000	10,000	5,000
Total fixed costs	$105,000	$ 25,000	$ 40,000	$ 40,000
Net income (loss)	$ 40,000	$ 40,000	$ 10,000	$ (10,000)

The decision to shut down a segment of a business is made primarily on the effect the decision will have on net income. However, great care should be exercised to avoid premature decisions. For example, consider the situation in which a company carries three major product lines, one of which is clearly unprofitable from a traditional accounting viewpoint. Cost and sales information for this company are given in figure 20.11. Amounts are given for each product line and for the company in total. Also, fixed costs are segregated into those that are avoidable and those that are unavoidable if that particular product line is discontinued.

It appears that the company's overall performance can be improved by dropping product C due to its net loss of $10,000. However, this is another case in which the best course of action is not so obvious. First, if product C is dropped, the company will lose $30,000 of contribution margin that helps to cover fixed costs. Second, not all fixed costs can be avoided by a shutdown of product C plant. Key management employees cannot be discharged, maintenance costs of buildings and equipment will continue, and taxes and insurance must be paid.

A fundamental principle in the decision to continue operations or to shut down is the comparison of lost contribution margin with the amount of fixed costs that can be avoided. If the lost contribution exceeds avoided fixed costs, the decision should be to continue to operate the product line. If lost contribution is less than avoided fixed costs, the decision should be to shut down the product line. For example, figure 20.11 shows a lost contribution of $30,000, which is less than the avoided fixed costs of $35,000 by $5,000. Therefore, the appropriate decision is to shut down so there will be an increase in net income of $5,000. This result is verified in figure 20.12, which contains an analysis of relevant information.

If the amount of avoidable fixed costs in the above example had been $25,000 instead of $35,000, then lost contribution would have been greater than the avoided fixed costs. Therefore, the appropriate decision would be to continue to operate to avoid an increase in net loss (decrease in net income) of $5,000. This situation is shown in figure 20.13.

As shown in figure 20.13, the company is attempting to minimize losses rather than maximize net income. In such situations it is helpful to determine at what volume of production and sales the loss will be greater or less than the level of unavoidable fixed costs. Because unavoidable fixed costs represent a cost of being shut down, management should know the sales volume that must be maintained to justify the decision to continue to operate. In the above situation, the question is at what sales volume will the loss be greater than the cost of being shut down?

The answer to this question can be derived in two ways. Comparative income statements can be prepared at different levels of sales and production as shown in figure

Figure 20.12   Analysis of information for operate or shut-down decision

	Operate Product C	Shut Down Product C	Difference
Sales	$60,000		$(60,000)
Less variable costs	30,000		(30,000)
Contribution margin	$30,000		$(30,000)
Less fixed costs:			
Avoidable	$35,000		$(35,000)
Unavoidable	5,000	$ 5,000	
Total fixed costs	$40,000	$ 5,000	$(35,000)
Net income (loss)	$(10,000)	$ (5,000)	$ (5,000)

Figure 20.13   Analysis of information for operate or shut-down decision

	Operate Product C	Shut Down Product C	Difference
Sales	$60,000		$(60,000)
Less variable costs	30,000		(30,000)
Contribution margin	$30,000		$(30,000)
Less fixed costs:			
Avoidable	$25,000		$(25,000)
Unavoidable	15,000	$ 15,000	
Total fixed costs	$40,000	$ 15,000	$(25,000)
Net income (loss)	$(10,000)	$ (15,000)	$ 5,000

Figure 20.14   Comparative income statement for product C

Units of production/sales	Shut Down	25,000	50,000	75,000	80,000
Sales @ $1.00	0	$25,000	$50,000	$75,000	$80,000
Variable costs @ $.50	0	12,500	25,000	37,500	40,000
Contribution margin @ $.50	0	$12,500	$25,000	$37,500	$40,000
Less fixed costs:					
Avoidable	0	$25,000	$25,000	$25,000	$25,000
Unavoidable	$15,000	$15,000	$15,000	$15,000	$15,000
Total fixed costs	$15,000	$40,000	$40,000	$40,000	$40,000
Net loss	$15,000	$27,500	$15,000	$ 2,500	0

20.14. Then the level of production and sales at which the net loss exceeds the cost of being shut down can be observed. In this example, the question to ask is at what level of production does the cost of being shut down of $15,000 (the amount of unavoidable fixed costs) equal or exceed the operating loss? The **shut-down point** represents the level of production and sales at which the operating loss equals the cost of being shut down. In this situation, the minimum volume of sales and production that is necessary for the company to continue to operate a product line is 50,000 units. If production and sales drop below 50,000 units, then it would be desirable to shut down operations.

These results can also be found with logic and computations that parallel a breakeven analysis. For example, it is advisable to continue to operate as long as the contribution to fixed costs is at least equal to the amount of avoidable fixed costs—$25,000 in the previous situation. As shown in figure 20.11 each unit of product C contributes $.50 to recovering avoidable fixed costs. Therefore, in order to recover $25,000 of the avoidable fixed costs, 50,000 units of product C must be sold.

$$\frac{\text{Avoidable fixed costs}}{\text{Contribution per unit}} = \text{Shut-down point}$$

$$\frac{\$25,000}{\$.50} = 50,000 \text{ units}$$

The shut-down point is directly related to the breakeven point (see chapter 7). For example, the breakeven point represents the minimum volume of sales and production that is necessary for the company to cover total (avoidable and unavoidable) fixed costs. For product C, the breakeven point is 80,000 units. The *breakeven point* in figure 20.14 is the level of production at which the net income (loss) is zero.

$$\frac{\text{Total fixed costs}}{\text{Contribution per unit}} = \text{Breakeven point}$$

$$\frac{\$40,000}{\$.50} = 80,000 \text{ units}$$

It should be pointed out that an organization may decide to operate below the shut-down point in the short run for a variety of rational economic and noneconomic reasons. For example, the costs of reopening need to be considered before shutting down as well as the effect that shutting down has on other products.

OTHER CONSIDERATIONS IN NONROUTINE DECISIONS

Other topics affecting nonroutine decisions include the short-run versus the long-run aspects of decisions, the effect of the time value of money, and the role of qualitative factors in decisions.

Short-run versus Long-run Considerations

Many nonroutine decisions are long-run rather than short-run decisions. Therefore, it is important for several reasons that the analysis of decision alternatives cover the total time period affected and not just the immediate future. Considering the total time period helps the decision maker to avoid the trap of maximizing short-run results to the detriment of long-run income. For example, the alternative in the first illustration in the chapter of keeping the old machine is attractive in the short run because it avoids a large loss on disposal. However, the short-run impact of keeping the old machine clearly conflicts with the long-run objective of maximizing net income. This highlights the importance of providing information for the total time period affected.

This illustration also shows the importance of having the reward structure and other motivational factors affecting decision makers incorporate long-run as well as short-run performance measures. Otherwise, decision makers might be tempted to choose an alternative that is to their personal advantage but suboptimizes company profits.

Another advantage of considering the long-run impact of nonroutine decisions is that it avoids the unwarranted assumption that all fixed costs are irrelevant and that all variable costs are relevant. Some types of costs if considered in the short run appear fixed when they are actually incremental or semivariable in the long run. The implication is that if only the short run is considered, a cost that is incremental and satisfies the criteria of relevance may be mistakenly considered to be irrelevant. For example, if production increases under a particular alternative, then additional equipment, supervision, or other fixed cost items may have to be added resulting in an incremental increase in what is normally considered fixed costs.

An assumption that variable costs are always relevant may lead to an inappropriate analysis because the variable costs may not differ among alternatives. For example, a newly purchased delivery truck with a higher per-mile cost than the old truck may actually have the same total variable costs because it has more capacity and is driven fewer total miles. In this situation, the variable costs do not differ between alternatives and are irrelevant. Remember that variable costs may remain unchanged and that fixed costs may change if the time period under consideration is long enough or if fixed cost items are affected by the decision.

Taxes and the Time Value of Money

Income tax payments are an expected future cost that will probably differ among decision alternatives. In most nonroutine decisions, income tax considerations are relevant. To preserve the simplicity of the previous examples, income tax considerations were not included. However, income tax information is readily incorporated in the decision analysis by applying the criteria of relevance and following the analysis steps as outlined earlier in this chapter.

For example, if a new machine is acquired and a loss on the disposal of the old machine is anticipated, there will probably be a future tax saving. The amount of the tax saving depends on such factors as the similarity of the assets affected, the organization's effective tax rate, and the presence of any recapture provisions. Assuming a $50,000 loss on the disposal of an old machine when the effective tax rate is 50% and no other tax provisions apply, an income tax saving of $25,000 (.5 × $50,000) will result. This is relevant information and should be considered in the analysis.

Note that when tax effects are considered, the book value of an old asset is still irrelevant information. Even though book value is a component in the calculation determining the amount of future tax effects, book value itself is irrelevant information.

Another item of relevant information not included in the examples of this chapter is the time value of money. Cash received today is worth more than the same amount of cash received at some future date. Because nonroutine decisions typically affect cash flows over a number of years, the present value of the cash flows should be used, not their future gross amounts.

For example, assume that the $25,000 tax saving in the above situation is expected to be realized one year from now. Using an interest rate of 10%, the amount that should be considered in the decision analysis is $22,727.27 ($25,000 ÷ 1.10)—the present value of $25,000 one year, hence discounted at 10% interest. The amount of $22,727.27 can be verified by reversing the above calculation; that is, if the company had received a cash benefit of $22,727.27 today instead of a year from today, the cash could have been invested and earned a 10% return giving the company $25,000 ($22,727.7 × 1.10) of cash one year from now.

Therefore, the time value of money should be considered when making nonroutine decisions. The present values of future cash flows should be calculated and used in the decision analysis rather than simply using future gross amounts.

The Role of Qualitative Factors

Accountants, like mathematicians and statisticians, deal with numbers and tend to emphasize the quantitative aspects of decisions over the qualitative aspects. **Quantitative considerations** are those aspects of a decision situation that may be expressed in terms of numbers such as dollars of cost, units of output, or years of life. **Qualitative considerations** are those aspects of a decision situation that are difficult to express in terms of numbers or other types of mathematical expression. For example, a proposed acquisition of a new machine may necessitate the relocation of several workers who are members of a local labor union. The union's reaction to the proposed acquisition may have a profound impact on management's final decision even though the union's impact may not be easily quantified.

There are several other classical examples of decision situations with important qualitative factors. The decision to continue to purchase certain components even though the part could be produced internally at a reduced cost might be made based on qualitative considerations even though qualitative and economic considerations are not separate issues. For example, maintaining a long-run source of supply may be an overriding consideration when compared with temporary cost savings. Second, the decision to reject a one-time order that would add to net income but at a price below that normally charged to regular customers could result from qualitative rather than quantitative factors. Even though accepting the special order might increase income, the impact on their regular customers of selling below customary prices may influence management's decision to reject the order even though the total impact is not quantifiable.

Summary

Relevant costs are those expected future costs that differ in amount among the decision alternatives being considered. When using cost accounting information in a decision analysis it is not always clear which of the many different types of costs are relevant in a given decision situation. Also, many types of costs are not explicitly maintained in accounting records and must be quantified or must be predicted from available historical data. Memorized techniques must give way to the application of cost accounting and decision principles.

Successful accountants and decision makers exercise considerable judgment in gathering and analyzing cost information. Providing relevant costs for decisions is one of the accountant's most critical roles as a member of the firm's management team. To avoid confusion and poor decisions, accountants and decision makers should have a mutual understanding of what each cost concept means and how each relates to making nonroutine decisions. The following is a list of common cost terms, their meanings, and a brief discussion on their relationship to the criteria of relevance.

Cost Term	Relationship to Decisions
1. Avoidable costs	Costs that can be reduced or eliminated by reducing the level of operations or by discontinuing some element of operations. Expected future costs that may differ among decision alternatives. Also called *escapable* costs.
2. Differential costs	a. The difference between the cost of separate decision alternatives. An expected future cost that represents the amount of difference among decision alternatives. Also called *incremental* costs.

	b. Changes in total historical costs that result from changes in operations. May be used as predictor of expected future costs.
3. Discretionary costs	Costs that are not essential but may be desirable to the accomplishment of a particular objective. If management intends to incur discretionary costs, they are future costs that may differ among decision alternatives. Otherwise, they are not a future cost.
4. Fixed costs	Costs that do not change in proportion to output. They are expected future costs (unless avoidable) that typically do not differ among alternatives. Fixed costs may be incremental costs in the long run.
5. Imputed costs	Costs that represent the value in use of company resources. Imputed costs are hypothetical costs in that they do not require cash outlays nor do they appear in traditional accounting records. Examples include salaries of owner-operators, interest on invested capital, rental value of company properties, and the interest differential on loans made at rates below the current market rate. They are expected future costs that will probably differ among decision alternatives.
6. Opportunity costs	Costs that represent the measurable advantage of a foregone alternative. They are expected future costs that will probably differ among decision alternatives.
7. Out-of-pocket costs	Costs that result in short-run cash expenditures due to making a particular decision. They are expected future costs that will probably differ among alternatives.
8. Outlay costs	Costs that result in cash expenditures. They are expected future costs that will probably differ among alternatives.
9. Postponable costs	Costs that may be shifted to the future with little or no effect on the efficiency of current operations. They constitute a deferral of costs rather than an avoidance. If management intends to incur a postponable cost within the period affected by the decision, they are future costs that may differ among alternatives. Otherwise, they are not future costs.
10. Sunk costs	Costs that are historical, irrevocable, and not recoverable. They are not a future cost.
11. Unavoidable costs	Costs that cannot be reduced or eliminated by reducing the level of operations or by discontinuing some element of operations. They are future costs that do not differ among alternatives.
12. Variable costs	Costs that change in proportion to output. They are expected future costs that will probably differ among alternatives.

Appendix *Linear Programming*

Linear programming is a mathematical tool used for making decisions in situations where constraining or limiting factors are present. For example, a scarcity of raw materials, limited machine hours, or a shortage of skilled labor may be constraining factors in a production environment. Linear programming is one of the most effective tools for deciding what mix of products to produce under constrained circumstances.

Accountants and managers should know enough about linear programming to be able to (*a*) identify problem areas that could be solved using linear programming, (*b*) help formulate the objective, variables, and constraints in a particular problem situation, and (*c*) understand the solution process sufficiently well to facilitate communication with technical personnel or the computer to obtain a solution. This appendix simply provides an introduction to linear programming using a graphical approach.

For example, consider the following cost accounting situation in which linear programming can be applied. A firm produces two products—*X* and *Y*. The contribution margin per unit for *X* is $26 and the contribution margin per unit for *Y* is $30. It takes 6 hours of skilled labor to produce one unit of *X* and 9 hours of skilled labor to produce one unit of *Y*. However, the firm has only 54 hours of skilled labor available each day. The firm also has a limited supply of a certain material that is required to produce both *X* and *Y*. Product *X* requires 8 pounds per unit and product *Y* requires 4 pounds per unit. The average supply of this raw material is 32 pounds per day.

Management estimates that average daily sales of *X* will not exceed 3 units. All other productive inputs are in plentiful supply, and as many units of *Y* as can be produced can be sold.

The firm wants to maximize the contribution margin and wants to know how many units of each product should be produced each day to accomplish this objective. The steps to answering this question using linear programming are as follows:

1. Determine the objective function—a mathematical expression that describes what the firm wants to accomplish.
2. Determine the basic relationships or constraints that specify the available feasible alternatives.
3. Determine which of the feasible alternatives provides the optimum solution.

Each of these steps is applied to the above data as follows:

1. *Determine the objective function.* A profit objective might be expressed in terms of minimizing costs or maximizing profits. In this situation the objective is to maximize the total contribution margin. This can be expressed mathematically as:

   Total contribution margin = 26X$ + 30Y$

   where *X* equals the number of *X* units per day and *Y* equals the number of *Y* units per day. Each is multiplied by their respective contribution margins per unit. The goal is to determine the number of *X* and *Y* units that should be produced and sold to yield the maximum total contribution margin.
2. *Determine the basic relationships or constraints that specify the available feasible alternatives.* From the data in our example there are three types of relationships that represent constraints on the production of *X* and *Y*. First, a *labor constraint* requires 6 hours of skilled labor for each unit of *X* and 9 hours for each unit of *Y*. Because only 54 total hours are available in a day, this constraint can be expressed in mathematical form as:

   $6X + 9Y \leq 54$

Figure 20.15   Linear programming—graphical solution

Production of y (units)

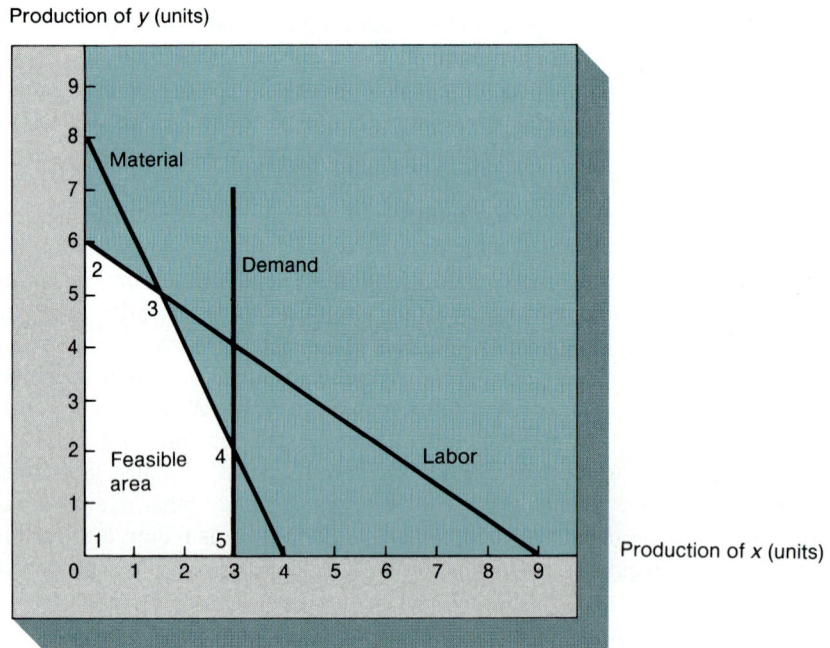

The inequality sign ($\leq$) indicates that total production cannot exceed 54 hours. It may be that the optimum level requires less than 54 hours, but it may not exceed 54 hours.

A *material constraint* indicates that the requirement for a particular raw material is 8 pounds per unit of X and 4 pounds per unit of Y. Because there are only 32 pounds per day of this particular raw material available, this constraint is expressed as:

$$8X + 4Y \leq 32$$

Finally, a *demand constraint* indicates that an average of only 3 units of X can be sold per day. This constraint is expressed as:

$$X \leq 3$$

These constraints taken together define the feasible alternative solutions from which the optimum solution is selected. The above constraints can be combined graphically to give an area of feasible production output (see fig. 20.15).

The area of feasible productive output is defined by the lines representing each constraint. For example, the labor constraint indicates that if all labor is used to produce Y ($X = 0$), then 9 units of Y per day can be produced. On the other hand, if all labor is used to produce X ($Y = 0$), then 6 units of X per day can be produced.

Combining all of the constraints, the optimal solution falls somewhere on the line that defines the extreme boundary of the area of feasible production output. Actually, because of the mathematical properties involved, the optimal solution is at one of the corners of the boundary of the area of feasible production output.

3. *Determine which of the feasible alternative solutions provides the optimum solution.* To determine which alternative provides the optimum solution, the objective function is calculated using the product mix found at each corner of the boundary of feasible production output. The product mix is found by reading values for X and Y from the graph. There are five corners in the situation above.

	Product Mix (Units)	
Corner	X	Y
1	0	0
2	0	6
3	1.5	5
4	3	2
5	3	0

Using the above values for X and Y in the objective function results in the following total contribution margins.

X		Y		Total Contribution Margin
26(0)	+	30(0)	=	0
26(0)	+	30(6)	=	180
26(1.5)	+	30(5)	=	189
26(3)	+	30(2)	=	138
26(3)	+	30(0)	=	78

The firm should produce an average of 1.5 units of X and 5 units of Y each day to obtain a maximum contribution margin of $189 per day.

Self-Study Problems

Note

The problems presented in this section are intended to review the process of analyzing information for nonroutine decisions in decision situations not previously illustrated.

CHOICE OF ORDER TO ACCEPT

Logan Company has excess capacity built into its current plant in anticipation of an expected increase in sales of its regular product line. To use this excess capacity in the most profitable way, Logan has solicited one-time orders for products from other companies. Two large orders have been received and they appear to be profitable. However, only one of the orders can be accepted.

One of the orders is for 330,000 J-fittings at a price of $1.20 per unit. The other order is for 400,000 K-fittings at $1.40 per unit. The standard costs for these products are as follows:

	J-Fittings	K-Fittings
Materials	$ .50	$ .70
Direct labor	.20	.24
Factory overhead	.40	.36
	$1.10	$1.30

Factory overhead is applied to work in process on a machine-hour basis at $8.50 per hour. Factory overhead is estimated to be 25% variable and 75% fixed. There are no marketing costs associated with either of these orders, and the administrative costs are the same for each order.

Required

Which order should the Logan Company accept?

Solution to the Self-Study Problem

Logan Company should accept the order for K-fittings because it will provide the greater contribution margin.

	J-Fittings		K-Fittings	
Sales price per unit		$1.20		$1.40
Variable production costs per unit:				
Materials	$.50		$.70	
Direct labor	.20		.24	
Factory overhead (25% of standard)	.10		.09	
		.80		1.03
Contribution margin per unit		$ .40		$ .37
Total contribution margin:				
J-Fittings (330,000 units × $.40)		$132,000		
K-Fittings (400,000 units × $.37)				$148,000

SELL OR PROCESS FURTHER

Mendon Company, when it produces Zodium, also generates a by-product Bodium, and sells it for $40 per barrel. Mendon is considering adding additional chemicals to Bodium to produce an industrial cleaning compound called Dirtium to be sold to wholesalers at $24 per 100 pounds. The chemical additives to make Dirtium must be added at the rate of 40 pounds per 100 pounds of Bodium. Additional costs would be:

Chemicals	$14.00 per 100 pounds of input
Direct labor	6.00 per 100 pounds of output
Variable factory overhead	3.00 per 100 pounds of output

An additional $80,000 of promotion and advertising costs will be incurred each year if Dirtium is produced. The current volume of Bodium is 5,000,000 pounds, or 2,500 barrels. Facilities are adequate to produce Dirtium.

Required

Prepare an analysis to help the management of Mendon Company decide if they should produce Dirtium or sell Bodium without further processing.

Solution to the Self-Study Problem

Mendon Company should continue to process Bodium and produce Dirtium because it will increase the net income by $170,000. The contribution analysis is as follows:

Sales (70,000[a] × $18)		$1,260,000
Costs:		
Chemicals (20,000[b] × $14)	$280,000	
Direct labor (70,000[a] × $6)	420,000	
Variable overhead (70,000[a] × $3)	210,000	
Promotion and advertising	80,000	
		990,000
Contribution from Dirtium		$ 270,000
Contribution foregone by not selling		
Bodium (2,500 × $40)		100,000
Increase in operating income from processing		
Bodium into Dirtium		$ 170,000

$$a \quad \frac{5,000,000 \times 1.4}{100} = 70,000$$

$$b \quad \frac{5,000,000 \times .4}{100} = 20,000$$

Suggested Readings

Bartenstein, Edwin. "Different Costs for Different Purposes." *Management Accounting* (August 1978): 42–47.

Ford, Jerry L. "How to Communicate with Management." *Management Accounting* (March 1979): 12–17.

Gambino, Anthony J. "The Make-or-Buy Decision." *Management Accounting* (December 1980): 55–59.

Hale, Jack A., and Ryan, Lanny J. "Decision Science and the Management Accountant." *Management Accounting* (January 1979): 42–45.

Kim, Suk H. "Making the Long-term Investment Decision." *Management Accounting* (March 1979): 41–49.

Discussion Questions

1. Describe the difference between routine and nonroutine decisions.
2. Define knowledge and explain the role of knowledge in the decision-making process.
3. Define what constitutes a relevant cost for decisions. Explain the criteria for identifying relevant costs.
4. What are the steps involved in the total cost approach to decisions?
5. What are key elements of the contribution approach to decisions?
6. What constitutes a constraining factor in a decision analysis?
7. Define opportunity cost and tell when it is appropriate to include opportunity costs in a decision analysis.
8. What is a special order? Under what conditions should special orders be accepted?
9. Describe the role of fixed costs in the operate or shut-down decision.

10. Explain the difference between avoidable and unavoidable fixed costs and tell how each affects nonroutine decisions.
11. What is a shut-down point? How does a shut-down point differ from a breakeven point?
12. How might a long-run view versus a short-run view affect the outcome of a decision?
13. Describe how the time value of money should be incorporated into the analysis of nonroutine decisions.
14. What are the differences between quantitative and qualitative considerations in decision making? Are accountants concerned with qualitative considerations or only with quantitative considerations? Why?

Exercises

Exercise 20.1   Basic Concepts of Relevant Costs and Decisions

The Blade Division of Dana Company produces hardened steel blades. One third of the Blade Division's output is sold to the Lawn Products Division of Dana; the remainder is sold to outside customers. The Blade Division's estimated sales and standard cost data for the fiscal year ending June 30 are as follows:

	Lawn Products	Outsiders
Sales	$15,000	$40,000
Variable costs	(10,000)	(20,000)
Fixed costs	(3,000)	(6,000)
Gross margin	$ 2,000	$14,000
Unit sales	10,000	20,000

The Lawn Products Division has an opportunity to purchase 10,000 identical quality blades from an outside supplier at a cost of $1.25 per unit on a continuing basis. Assume that the Blade Division cannot sell any additional products to outside customers.

Required

Should Dana allow its Lawn Products Division to purchase the blades from the outside supplier? Show support for your answer.

Exercise 20.2   Constraining Factors of Contribution Analysis

Johnson Incorporated manufactures product X and product Y, which are processed as follows:

	Type A Machine	Type B Machine
Product X	6 hours	4 hours
Product Y	9 hours	5 hours

The contribution margin is $12 for product X and $7 for product Y. The available time daily for processing the two products is 120 hours for machine type A and 80 hours for machine type B.

Required

Do an analysis showing the contribution per machine hour generated by the two products.

Exercise 20.3 Relevant Costs for a Special Order

Argus Company, a manufacturer of lamps, budgeted sales of 400,000 lamps at $20 per unit for 19X1. Variable manufacturing costs were budgeted at $8 per unit and fixed manufacturing costs at $5 per unit. A special order offering to buy 40,000 lamps for $11.50 each was received by Argus in April 19X1. Argus has sufficient plant capacity to manufacture the additional quantity of lamps; however, the production would have to be done by the present work force on an overtime basis at an estimated additional cost of $1.50 per lamp. Argus will not incur any selling expenses as a result of the special order.

Required

Determine the effect on operating income if the special order could be accepted without affecting normal sales.

Exercise 20.4 Relevant Costs—Make or Buy Decisions

Plainfield Company manufactures part *G* for use in its production cycle. The costs per unit for 10,000 units of part *G* are as follows:

Direct materials	$ 3
Direct labor	15
Variable overhead	6
Fixed overhead	8
	$32

Verona Company has offered to sell Plainfield 10,000 units of part *G* for $30 per unit. If Plainfield accepts Verona's offer, the released facilities could be used to save $45,000 in relevant costs in the manufacture of part *H*. In addition, $5 per unit of the fixed overhead applied to part *G* would be totally eliminated.

Required

Determine which alternative is more desirable and by what amount it is more desirable.

Exercise 20.5 Relevant Costs—Special Order

Lincoln Company, a glove manufacturer, has enough idle capacity available to accept a special order of 20,000 pairs of gloves at $12 a pair. The normal selling price is $20 a pair. Variable manufacturing costs are $9 a pair, and fixed manufacturing costs are $3 a pair. Lincoln will not incur any selling expenses as a result of the special order.

Required

Determine the effect on operating income if the special order could be accepted without affecting normal sales.

Exercise 20.6 Relevant Cost Concepts

1. The type of costs presented to management for a special-order decision should be limited to
   a. relevant costs.
   b. standard costs.
   c. controllable costs.
   d. conversion costs.

2. In a make-or-buy decision,
   a. only variable costs are relevant.
   b. fixed costs that can be avoided in the future are relevant.
   c. fixed costs that will continue regardless of the decision are relevant.
   d. only conversion costs are relevant.

3. Argus Company, a manufacturer of lamps, budgeted sales of 400,000 lamps at $20.00 per unit. Variable manufacturing costs are $8.00 per unit, and fixed manufacturing costs are $5.00 per unit. A special order offering to buy 40,000 lamps for $11.50 each was received by Argus in April 19X0. Argus has sufficient plant capacity to manufacture the additional quantity of lamps; however, the production would have to be done by the present work force on an overtime basis at an estimated additional cost of $1.50 per lamp. Argus will not incur any selling expenses as a result of the special order. What would be the effect on operating income if the special order could be accepted without affecting normal sales?
   a. $ 60,000 decrease
   b. $ 80,000 increase
   c. $120,000 decrease
   d. $140,000 increase

4. The Reno Company manufactures part no. 498 for use in its production cycle. The cost data per unit for 20,000 units of part no. 498 are as follows:

Direct materials	$ 6
Direct labor	30
Variable overhead	12
Fixed overhead applied	16
	$64

The Tray Company has offered to sell 20,000 units of part no. 498 to Reno for $60 per unit. Reno will make the decision to buy the part from Tray if there is a savings of $25,000 for Reno. If Reno accepts Tray's offer, $9 per unit of the fixed overhead applied would be totally eliminated. Furthermore, Reno has determined that the released facilities could be used to save relevant costs in the manufacture of part no. 575. In order to have a savings of $25,000, the amount of relevant costs that would be saved by using the released facilities in the manufacture of part no. 575 would have to be
   a. $ 80,000.
   b. $ 85,000.
   c. $125,000.
   d. $140,000.

5. In deciding whether to manufacture a part or buy it from an outside vendor, a cost that is irrelevant to the short-run decision is
   a. direct labor.
   b. variable overhead.
   c. fixed overhead that will be avoided if the part is bought from an outside vendor.
   d. fixed overhead that will continue even if the part is bought from an outside vendor.

Exercise 20.7 Make or Buy Decision Analysis

Motor Company manufactures 10,000 units of part M–1 for use in its production annually. The following costs are reported:

Direct materials	$ 20,000
Direct labor	55,000
Variable overhead	45,000
Fixed overhead	70,000
	$190,000

Valve Company has offered to sell Motor 10,000 units of part M–1 for $18 per unit. If Motor accepts the offer, some facilities presently used to manufacture part M–1 could be rented to a third party at an annual rental of $15,000. Additionally, $4 per unit of the fixed overhead applied to part M–1 would be totally eliminated.

Required

Should Motor accept Valve's offer, and why?

Exercise 20.8 Joint Products—Sell or Process Further

The Trevina Company produces products X, Y, and Z in a joint process. Joint costs for a typical month are $50,000. Product Y is sold as is at the split-off point. Products X and Z can be sold at the split-off point or processed further. The operating statistics for a typical month are as follows:

Product	Weight	Sales Value at Split-Off	Final Sales Value	Separate Processing Costs
X	150,000 pints	$37,500	$112,500	$80,000
Y	50,000 pints	17,500	—	none
Z	50,000 pints	35,000	90,000	45,000

Assume that all costs incurred after the split-off point are variable and that there are no inventories of work in process or finished goods.

Required

1. Determine operating income in *total* (do not make a joint cost allocation) assuming all products are sold at the split-off point.
2. Determine the operating income in total assuming further processing of products X and Z.
3. Determine, with complete support, which products should be sold at the split-off point and which should be processed further.

Exercise 20.9 Investment Decision Using Relevant Costs

Marshall Redding recently sold off some investments that had been producing only mediocre returns. He has been investigating several possible firms that might be purchased outright with the possibility of rehabilitation. Marshall thinks he might enjoy the challenge of turning a firm with marginal returns into a real winner. The problem he has had with his recently liquidated investments is that he has not been in a controlling position.

One firm Marshall might acquire outright is a manufacturer of felt novelty items, which are sold both through wholesalers and retailers. The present owners are asking $700,000 for the firm. Included in the $700,000 is $200,000 of work-in-process and finished-goods inventories. The $200,000 inventory cost was determined by normal absorption cost procedures. The amount includes $90,000 of variable production costs, $100,000 of direct fixed production costs, and $10,000 of allocated general factory overhead.

Required

Determine and explain how much you think the minimum amount is that Marshall should pay for the inventory if he decides to negotiate a purchase of the felt novelty firm.

Exercise 20.10 Relevant Costs of Operating a Copying Machine

The costs of operating one office copier that makes 100,000 copies per year have been estimated as follows:

Inking materials	$ 500
Paper	500
Cleaning supplies	100
Feed rollers[a]	200
Maintenance contract	200
Depreciation (5,000 ÷ 5 yr life)	1,000
Total	$2,500

[a]Parts that have to be replaced after about 20,000 copies to maintain consistent paper feed.

The cost per copy is 2 1/2¢ (2,500 ÷ 100,000).

Required

1. If only 80,000 copies are made instead of 100,000, what would be the cost per copy? Show support for your answer. What would be the cost per copy if 110,000 copies were made?
2. The office manager would like to have the convenience of having a copier in his home. Home use would probably involve about 25,000 copies. What would be your estimate of the cost per copy if the manager purchases one for home use? Show support for your answer.
3. Identify alternatives that the office manager might look at for personal (home) copy needs. Describe the costs that are relevant to the alternatives.

Problems

Problem 20.1 Relevant Costs and Decisions (CPA)

Auer Company had received an order for a piece of special machinery from Jay Company. Just as Auer Company completed the machine, Jay Company declared bankruptcy, defaulted on the order, and forfeited the 10% deposit paid on the selling price of $72,500.

Auer's manufacturing manager identified the costs already incurred in the production of the special machinery for Jay as follows:

Direct materials used		$16,600
Direct labor incurred		21,400
Overhead applied:		
Manufacturing:		
Variable	$10,700	
Fixed	5,350	16,050
Fixed selling and administrative		5,405
Total cost		$59,455

Another company, Kaytell Corporation, would be interested in buying the special machinery if it is reworked to Kaytell's specifications. Auer offered to sell the reworked special machinery to Kaytell as a special order for a net price of $68,400. Kaytell has agreed to pay the net price when it takes delivery in two months. The additional identifiable costs to rework the machinery to the specifications of Kaytell are as follows:

Direct materials	$ 6,200
Direct labor	4,200
	$10,400

A second alternative available to Auer is to convert the special machinery to the standard model. The standard model lists for $62,500. The additional identifiable costs to convert the special machinery to the standard model are:

Direct materials	$ 2,850
Direct labor	3,300
	$ 6,150

A third alternative for the Auer Company is to sell, as a special order, the machine as is for a net price of $52,000. However, the potential buyer of the unmodified machine does not want it for 60 days. The buyer is offering a $7,000 down-payment with final payment upon delivery.

The following additional information is available regarding Auer's operations:

1. The sales commission rate on standard models is 2% and the sales commission rate on special orders is 3%. All sales commissions are calculated on the net sales price (the list price less cash discount, if any).
2. Normal credit terms for sales of standard models are 2/10, net/30. Credit terms for special orders are negotiated with the customer.
3. The application rates for manufacturing overhead and the fixed selling and administrative costs are as follows:

Manufacturing	
Variable	50% of direct-labor cost
Fixed	25% of direct-labor cost
Selling and administrative	
Fixed	10% of the total direct-material, direct-labor, and manufacturing overhead costs

4. Normal time required for rework is one month.
5. A surcharge of 5% of the sales price is placed on all customer requests for minor modifications of standard models.
6. Auer normally sells a sufficient number of standard models for the company to operate at a volume in excess of the breakeven point.

Auer does not consider the time value of money in analyses of special orders and projects whenever the time period is less than one year because the effect is not significant.

Required

1. Determine the dollar contribution of each alternative. How much will it add to the Auer Company's before-tax profits?
2. If Kaytell makes Auer a counter offer, what is the lowest price Auer should accept for the reworked machinery from Kaytell? Explain your answer.
3. Discuss the influence fixed factory overhead costs should have on the sales prices quoted by Auer Company for special orders.

Problem 20.2   Decision Analysis of a Charitable Organization Mailing Campaign

Janice Watson recently was appointed executive director of a charitable foundation. The foundation raises money for its activities in a variety of ways but the most important source of funds is an annual mail campaign.

The campaign takes place in the spring of each year. The foundation's staff makes every effort to secure newspaper, radio, and television coverage of the foundation's activities for several weeks before the mail campaign. In previous years, the foundation has mailed brochures that describe its charitable activities and requested contributions from the recipients of the brochures. The addresses for the mailing are generated from the foundation's own file of past contributors and from mailing lists purchased from brokers.

The foundation's staff is considering three alternative brochures for use in the upcoming campaign. All three will be 8½″ × 11″ in size. The simplest and most readily available for bulk mailing is a sheet of white paper with a printed explanation of the foundation's program and a request for funds. A more expensive brochure on colored stock will contain pictures as well as printed copy. However, this brochure may not be ready in time to take advantage of bulk postage rates, but there is no doubt that it can be ready in time for mailing at first-class postal rates. The third alternative would be an elegant, multicolored brochure printed on glossy paper with photographs as well as printed copy. The printer assures the staff that it will be ready on time to meet the first-class mailing schedule but asks for a delivery date one week later just in case there are production problems.

The foundation's staff has assembled cost and revenue information for mailing the three alternative brochures to 2,000,000 potential contributors (see below). The postal rates are $0.02 per item for bulk mail and $0.13 per item for presorted first-class mail. First-class mail is more likely to be delivered on time than bulk mail. The charge by outside companies who will be hired to handle the mailing is $0.01 per unit for the plain and colored paper brochures and $0.02 per unit for the glossy paper brochure.

Required

1. Calculate the net revenue contribution for each brochure for each mailing alternative.
2. The foundation must choose one of the three brochures for this year's campaign. The criteria established by the foundation's board of directors—net revenue raised, image as a well-run organization, and image as a fiscally responsible organization—must be considered when making the choice. Evaluate the three alternative brochures in terms of the three criteria.

Type of Brochure	Brochure Costs				Revenue Potential (000 omitted)		
	Design	Type Setting	Unit Paper Cost	Unit Printing Cost	Bulk Mail	First Class	Late First Class
Plain paper	$ 300	$ 100	$.005	$.003	$1,200	—	—
Colored paper	$1,000	$ 800	$.008	$.010	$2,000	$2,200	—
Glossy paper	$3,000	$2,000	$.018	$.040	—	$2,500	$2,200

Problem 20.3   Relevant Cost Information for Decision Analysis—One Time Bid (CMA)

Jenco Incorporated manufactures a combination fertilizer/weedkiller under the name Fertikil. This is the only product Jenco produces at this time. Fertikil is sold nationwide through normal marketing channels to retail nurseries and garden stores.

Taylor Nursery plans to sell a similar fertilizer/weedkiller compound through its regional nursery chain under its own private label. Taylor has asked Jenco to submit a bid for a 25,000 pound order of the private brand compound. Although the chemical composition of the Taylor compound differs from Fertikil, the manufacturing process is very similar.

The Taylor compound would be produced in 1,000 pound lots. Each lot would require 60 direct-labor hours and the following chemicals:

Chemicals	Quantity in Pounds
CW–3	400
JX–6	300
MZ–8	200
BE–7	100

The first three chemicals (CW–3, JX–6, MZ–8) are all used in the production of Fertikil. BE–7 was used in a compound that Jenco has discontinued. This chemical was not sold or discarded because it does not deteriorate and there have been adequate storage facilities. Jenco could sell BE–7 at the prevailing market price less $.10 per pound selling/handling expenses.

Jenco also has on hand a chemical called CN–5, which was manufactured for use in another product that is no longer produced. CN–5, which cannot be used in Fertikil, can be substituted for CW–3 on a one-for-one basis without affecting the quality of the Taylor compound. The quantity of CN–5 in inventory has a salvage value of $500.

Inventory and cost data for the chemicals that can be used to produce the Taylor compound are as shown below:

Raw Material	Pounds in Inventory	Actual Price per Pound When Purchased	Current Market Price per Pound
CW–3	22,000	$ .80	$ .90
JX–6	5,000	$ .55	$ .60
MZ–8	8,000	$1.40	$1.60
BE–7	4,000	$ .60	$ .65
CN–5	5,500	$ .75	(salvage)

The current direct-labor rate is $7.00 per hour. The manufacturing overhead rate is established at the beginning of the year and is applied consistently throughout the year using direct-labor hours as the base. The predetermined overhead rate for the current year, based on a two-shift capacity of 400,000 total direct-labor hours with no overtime, is as follows:

	Per Direct-Labor Hour
Variable manufacturing overhead	$2.25
Fixed manufacturing overhead	3.75
Combined rate	$6.00

Jenco's production manager reports that the present equipment and facilities are adequate to manufacture the Taylor compound. However, Jenco is within 800 hours of its two-shift capacity this month before it must schedule overtime. If need be, the Taylor compound could be produced on regular time by shifting a portion of Fertikil production to overtime. Jenco's rate for overtime hours is 1½ times the regular pay rate or $10.50 per hour. There is no allowance for any overtime premium in the manufacturing overhead rate.

Jenco's standard markup policy for new products is 25% of full manufacturing cost.

Required

Assume Jenco has decided to submit a bid for a 25,000-pound order of Taylor's new compound. The order must be delivered by the end of this month. Taylor has indicated that this is a one-time order. Determine the minimum bid amount for the Taylor order.

Problem 20.4   Relevant Cost Information for Repeat Orders

Refer to the facts in problem 20.3. Assume that Taylor Nursery plans to place regular orders for 25,000-pound lots of the new compound during the coming year. Jenco expects the demand for Fertikil to remain strong again in the coming year. Therefore, the recurring orders from Taylor will put Jenco over its two-shift capacity. However, production can be scheduled so that 60% of each Taylor order can be completed during regular hours or Fertikil production could be shifted temporarily to overtime so that the Taylor orders could be produced on regular time. Jenco's production manager has estimated that the prices of all chemicals will stabilize at the current market rates for the coming year and that all other manufacturing costs are expected to be maintained at the same rates or amounts.

Required

Calculate the price Jenco should quote Taylor Nursery for each 25,000-pound lot of the new compound assuming that there will be recurring orders during the coming year.

Problem 20.5   Decision Analysis with Probability Considerations (CMA)

Jackston Incorporated manufactures and distributes a line of Christmas toys. Jackston had neglected to keep its dollhouse line current. As a result, sales have decreased to approximately 10,000 units per year from a previous high of 50,000 units. The dollhouse has been redesigned recently and is considered by company officials to be comparable to its competitors' models. Jackston plans to redesign the dollhouse each year in order to compete efficiently. Joan Blocke, the sales manager, is not sure how many units can be sold next year, but she is willing to place probabilities on her estimates. Blocke's estimates on the number of units that can be sold during the next year and the related probabilities are as follows:

Estimated Sales in Units	Probability
20,000	.10
30,000	.40
40,000	.30
50,000	.20

The units would be sold for $20 each.

The inability to estimate the sales more precisely is a problem for Jackston. The number of units of this product is small enough to schedule the entire year's sales in one production run. If the demand is greater than the number of units manufactured, then sales will be lost. If demand is below supply, the extra units cannot be carried over to the next season and would be given away to various charitable organizations. The production and distribution cost estimates are as follows:

	Units Manufactured			
	20,000	*30,000*	*40,000*	*50,000*
Variable costs	$180,000	$270,000	$360,000	$450,000
Fixed costs	140,000	140,000	160,000	160,000
Total costs	$320,000	$410,000	$520,000	$610,000

Jackston intends to analyze the data to facilitate making a decision as to the proper size of the production run.

Required

1. Prepare a payoff table for the different sizes of production runs required to meet the four sales estimates prepared by Joan Blocke for Jackston. If Jackston relied solely on the expected monetary value approach to make decisions, what size of production run would be selected?
2. Identify the basic steps that are taken in any decision process. Explain each step by reference to the situation presented in this problem and your answer for each requirement.

Problem 20.6   Relevant Costs and Product Line Decisions (CMA)

The Scio Division of Georgetown Incorporated manufactures and sells four related product lines. Each product is produced at one or more of the three manufacturing plants of the division. A product line profitability statement (see below) for the year ending December 31, 19X7 shows a loss for the baseball equipment line. A similar loss is projected for 19X8.

The baseball equipment is manufactured in the Evanston Plant. Some football equipment and all miscellaneous sports items also are processed through this plant. A few miscellaneous items are manufactured, and the remainder are purchased for resale. The item purchased for resale is recorded as materials in the records. A separate production line is used to produce the products of each product line.

A schedule on page 736 presents the costs incurred at the Evanston Plant in 19X7. Inventories at the end of the year were substantially identical to those at the beginning of the year.

Product-Line Profitability—19X7
(000s omitted)

	Football Equipment	Baseball Equipment	Hockey Equipment	Miscellaneous Sports Items	Total
Sales	$2,200	$1,000	$1,500	$500	$5,200
Cost of goods sold:1					
Material	$ 400	$ 175	$ 300	$ 90	$ 965
Labor and variable overhead	800	400	600	60	1,860
Fixed overhead	350	275	100	50	775
Total	$1,550	$ 850	$1,000	$200	$3,600
Gross profit	$ 650	$ 150	$ 500	$300	$1,600
Selling expense:1					
Variable	$ 440	$ 200	$ 300	$100	$1,040
Fixed	100	50	100	50	300
Corporate administration expenses	48	24	36	12	120
Total	$ 588	$ 274	$ 436	$162	$1,460
Contribution to corporation	$ 62	$ (124)	$ 64	$138	$ 140

**Evanston Plant Costs—19X7
(000s omitted)**

	Football Equipment	Baseball Equipment	Miscellaneous Sports Items	Total
Material	$100	$175	$ 90	$ 365
Labor	$100	$200	$ 30	$ 330
Variable overhead:1				
Supplies	$ 85	$ 60	$ 12	$ 157
Power	50	110	7	167
Other	15	30	11	56
Subtotal	$150	$200	$ 30	$ 380
Fixed overhead:1				
Supervision[a]	$ 25	$ 30	$ 21	$ 76
Depreciation[b]	40	115	14	169
Plant rentals[c]	35	105	10	150
Other[d]	20	25	5	50
Subtotal	$120	$275	$ 50	$ 445
Total costs	$470	$850	$200	$1,520

[a]The supervision costs represent salary and benefit costs of the supervisors in charge of each product line.
[b]Depreciation cost for machinery and equipment is charged to the product line on which the machinery is used.
[c]The plant is leased. The lease rentals are charged to the product lines on the basis of square feet occupied.
[d]Other fixed overhead costs are the cost of plant administration and are allocated arbitrarily by management decision.

The management of Georgetown has requested a profitability study of the baseball equipment line to determine if the line should be discontinued. The marketing department of the Scio Division and the accounting department at the plant have developed the following additional data to be used in the study:

1. If the baseball equipment line is discontinued, the company will lose approximately 10% of its sales in each of the other lines.
2. The equipment now used in the manufacture of baseball equipment is quite specialized. It has a current salvage value of $105,000 and a remaining useful life of five years. This equipment cannot be used elsewhere in the company.
3. The plant space now occupied by the baseball equipment line could be closed off from the rest of the plant and rented for $175,000 per year.
4. If the line is discontinued, the supervisor of the baseball equipment line will be released. In keeping with company policy he would receive severance pay of $5,000.
5. The company has been able to invest excess funds at 10% per annum.

Required

1. Should Georgetown discontinue the baseball equipment line? Support your answer with appropriate calculations and qualitative arguments.
2. A member of the Board of Directors of Georgetown Incorporated has inquired whether the information regarding the discontinuance of product lines should be included in the financial statements on a regular monthly basis for all product lines. Draft a memorandum in response to the board member's inquiry. Your memorandum should (a) state why or why not this information should be included in the regular monthly financial statements distributed to the board and (b) detail the reasons for your response.

Problem 20.7   Make or Buy Decision Analysis with Learning Curve Considerations (CMA)

The Xyon Company has purchased 80,000 pumps annually from Kobec Incorporated. The price has increased each year and reached $68.00 per unit last year. Because the purchase price has increased significantly, Xyon management has asked that an estimate be made of the cost to manufacture pumps in its own facilities. Xyon's products consist of stamping and castings. Xyon has little experience with products requiring assembly.

The engineering, manufacturing, and accounting departments have prepared a report for management that included an estimate for an assembly run of 10,000 units. Additional production employees would be hired to manufacture the subassembly. However, no additional equipment, space, or supervision would be needed.

The report states that total costs for 10,000 units are estimated at $957,000 or $95.70 a unit. The current purchase price is $68.00 a unit so the report recommends a continued purchase of the product.

Components (outside purchases)	$120,000
Assembly labor[a]	300,000
Factory overhead[b]	450,000
General and administrative overhead[c]	87,000
Total costs	$957,000

[a]Assembly labor consists of hourly production workers.

[b]Factory overhead is applied to products on a direct-labor dollar basis. Variable overhead costs vary closely with direct-labor dollars.

	Percent of Direct-Labor Dollars
Fixed overhead	50%
Variable overhead	100%
Factory overhead rate	150%

[c]General and administrative overhead is applied at 10% of the total cost of material (or components), assembly labor, and factory overhead.

Required

1. Was the analysis prepared by the engineering, manufacturing, and accounting departments of Xyon Company and the recommendation to continue purchasing the pumps that followed from the analysis correct? Explain your answer and include any supportive calculations you consider necessary.
2. Assume Xyon Company could experience labor cost improvements on the pump assembly consistent with an 80% learning curve. An assembly run of 10,000 units represents the initial lot or batch for measurement. Should Xyon produce the 80,000 pumps in this situation? Explain your answer.

Problem 20.8   Relevant Costs and Decisions—Tie to Cost-Volume-Profit Analysis

BE&H Manufacturing is considering dropping a product line. It currently produces a multipurpose woodworking clamp in a simple manufacturing process that utilizes special equipment. Variable costs amount to $6.00 per unit. Fixed overhead costs, exclusive of depreciation, have been allocated to this product at a rate of $3.50 a unit and will continue whether or not production ceases. Depreciation on the special equipment amounts to $20,000 a year.

If production of the clamp is stopped, the special equipment can be sold for $18,000. If production continues, the equipment will be useless for further production at the end of one year and will have no salvage value. The clamp has a selling price of $10 a unit.

Required

Ignoring tax effects, determine the minimum number of units that would have to be sold in the current year to break even.

Problem 20.9 Relevant Costs and Decisions—An Evaluation of Cost Data

The promotion department of the Doxolby Company is responsible for the design and development of all promotional materials for the corporation. This includes all promotional campaigns and related literature, pamphlets, and brochures. Top management is reviewing the effectiveness of the promotion department to determine if the department's activities could be managed better and more economically by an outside promotion agency. As a part of this review, top management has asked for a summary of the promotion department's costs for the most recent year. The following cost summary was supplied:

Promotion Department Costs for the year ending November 30

Direct department costs	$257,500
Charges from other departments	44,700
Allocated share of general administrative overhead	22,250
Total costs	$324,450

The direct department costs consist of those costs that can be traced directly to the activities of the promotion department, such as staff and clerical salaries including related employee benefits and supplies. The charges from other departments represent the costs of services that are provided by other departments at Doxolby at the request of the promotion department. Doxolby has developed a charging system for such interdepartmental uses of services. For instance, the "in-house" printing department charges the promotion department for the promotional literature printed. All such services provided to the promotion department by other departments of Doxolby are included in the "Charges from Other Departments." General administrative overhead is comprised of such costs as top management salaries and benefits, depreciation, heat, insurance, and property taxes. These costs are allocated to all departments in proportion to the number of employees in each department.

Required

Discuss the usefulness of the cost figures as presented for the promotion department of Doxolby Incorporated as a basis for a comparison with a bid from an outside agency to provide the same type of activities as Doxolby's own promotion department.

Problem 20.10 Relevant Costs and Special Orders (CMA)

Framar Incorporated manufactures automation machinery according to customer specifications. Framar is relatively new and has grown each year. Framar operated at about 75% of practical capacity during the past fiscal year. The operating results for the most recent fiscal year are presented below:

Framar Inc.
Income Statement
For the Year Ending September 30
(000s omitted)

Sales		$25,000
Less: Sales commissions		2,500
Net sales		$22,500
Expenses:		
Direct material		$ 6,000
Direct labor		7,500
Manufacturing overhead—variable:		
Supplies	$ 625	
Indirect labor	1,500	
Power	125	2,250
Manufacturing overhead—fixed:		
Supervision	$ 500	
Depreciation	1,000	1,500
Corporate administration		750
Total expenses		$18,000
Net income before taxes		$ 4,500
Income taxes (40%)		1,800
Net income		$ 2,700

Most of the management personnel had worked for firms in this type of business before joining Framar, but none of the top management had been responsible for overall corporate operations or for final decisions on prices. Nevertheless, Framar has been successful.

The top management of Framar wants to have a more organized and formal pricing system to prepare quotes for potential customers. Therefore, it has developed the pricing formula shown below. The formula is based upon the company's operating results achieved during the past fiscal year. The relationships used in the formula are expected to continue during the next year. Framar expects to operate at 75% of practical capacity during the next fiscal year.

APA Incorporated has asked Framar to submit a bid on some custom-designed machinery. Framar used the new formula to develop a price and submitted a bid of $165,000 to APA. The calculations to arrive at the bid price are given next to the pricing formula shown below:

Pricing Formula

Details of Formula		APA Bid Calculations
Estimated direct-materials cost	$XX	$ 29,200
Estimated direct-labor cost	XX	56,000
Estimated manufacturing overhead calculated at 50% of direct labor	XX	28,000
Estimated corporate overhead calculated at 10% of direct labor	XX	5,600
Estimated total costs excluding sales commissions	$XX	$118,800
Add 25% for profits and taxes	XX	29,700
Suggested price (with profits) before sales commissions	$XX	$148,500
Suggested total price equals suggested price divided by .9 to adjust from 10% sales commissions	$XX	$165,000

Required

1. Calculate the impact the order from APA Incorporated would have on Framar Incorporated's net income after taxes if Framar's bid of $165,000 were accepted by APA.
2. Assume APA has rejected Framar's price but has stated that it is willing to pay $127,000 for the machinery. Should Framar manufacture the machinery for the counter-offer of $127,000? Explain your answer.
3. Calculate the lowest price Framar can quote on this machinery without reducing its net income after taxes if it should manufacture the machinery.
4. Explain how the profit performance next year would be affected if Framar accepted all of its work at prices similar to the $127,000 counter-offer of APA described in requirement 2.

TRANSFER AND PRODUCT PRICING

21

OUTLINE

Pricing, in any of its forms, is a complex subject that requires consideration of a number of interrelated factors. Economic theory, statistical analysis, market research, engineering estimates, accounting information, and management judgment are all part of the pricing decision. Cost accounting information is especially important in pricing decisions because a firm's profitability and long-run viability depend on an appropriate relationship between revenues and costs. Because cost accounting information can range from objective historical costs to estimates of future costs that defy objective measurement, accountants and managers should understand how various types of cost accounting information relate to the pricing decision.

This chapter explains two general areas of pricing—pricing for intracompany transfers and pricing for product sales. After you have completed this chapter you should be able to:

1. define the role of cost accounting information in pricing goods and services for (*a*) intracompany transfers and (*b*) external sales.
2. implement various approaches to establishing transfer prices.
3. account for intracompany transfers.
4. implement various approaches to setting prices for sales to external parties.
5. apply certain principles that might lead to modifications in cost-based prices.

DEFINITION AND COMPARISON OF TRANSFER AND PRODUCT PRICING

There are two general categories of pricing decisions—pricing for intracompany transfers, which is called transfer pricing, and pricing for sales to parties outside the company, which is called product pricing. **Transfer pricing** refers to the assignment of monetary values to goods and services exchanged among subdivisions of an organization. Transfer pricing becomes a relevant consideration when a company is decentralized and divided into relatively autonomous subunits that are usually free to transact business outside as well as inside the company. For example, consider a company that is made up of a number of product divisions, two of which are the refrigeration and electronics divisions. The refrigeration division may acquire needed components either from the electronics division of the company or from outside suppliers. If acquired from the electronics division, the monetary values assigned to the components in such intracompany transfers are termed transfer prices.

On the other hand, **product pricing** refers to the assignment of monetary values to goods and services exchanged with parties external to an organization. For example, if the electronics division in the situation above also sells components to others outside the company, the monetary values assigned to components in such transactions are called product prices.

The reason for differentiating between transfer and product pricing is that different management, economic, and cost accounting principles apply in each situation. For example, transfer pricing is only relevant when goods and services are transferred from one subunit of a company to another. However, product pricing is relevant whenever goods and services are sold to external parties.

PRICING FOR INTRACOMPANY TRANSFERS

As indicated, transfer pricing is important when relatively independent operating units of a company engage in intracompany transfers of goods and services. However, transfer pricing is especially important when a company uses segment performance measures, as discussed in chapter 19, to evaluate the functions of the operating units engaging in intracompany transfers. Transfer pricing is important because when intracompany transfers occur, the finished output of one or more subunits becomes the input or raw material of one or more other subunits. This means that the *revenue* of one subunit becomes a *cost* of another subunit. Therefore, the prices used to value intracompany transfers influence the income and/or costs reported by each subunit. Because there is such a direct linkage between segment performance measures and transfer prices, it is important that transfer prices be set at values that provide appropriate incentives to division managers, encourage goal congruence in management decisions, and foster the desired level of autonomy among segments.

A primary consideration for determining what might be an appropriate transfer price is the degree to which authority and responsibility is delegated to subunit managers. In cost center situations, where subunit managers are only responsible for costs and not revenues, transfers of goods and services from one cost center to another might be made at a transfer price equal to the total costs accumulated to date. However, in profit center and investment center environments, where subunit managers are given responsibility for *revenues* as well as costs, a cost-based transfer price may not be satisfactory.

This is especially true in situations where subunit managers have the freedom to buy and/or sell goods and services to parties external as well as internal to the firm. In such situations a cost-based transfer price may provide a poor guide to performance evaluation and may even result in suboptimization of company operations. For example, consider a large computer manufacturer that operates a number of component divisions and several assembly divisions. The component divisions make various subassemblies that can either be sold to other computer manufacturers or transferred to one of the company's assembly divisions. Assume that the company is not operating at full capacity.

The assembly divisions acquire needed subassemblies from either outside suppliers or from one or more of the company's component divisions. The following information relates to one subassembly made by a component division that is used in at least one of the company's assembly divisions.

	Cost per Subassembly
Materials	$ 400
Labor	100
Overhead (70% variable)	1,000
Total	$1,500

Management of the component division may feel that an appropriate transfer price should be one that at least covers the full cost of production of subassemblies. Accordingly, the component division may set its transfer price at $1,500 per unit. However, the outside purchase price available to the assembly division for an identical subassembly is $1,400—$100 less than it would cost if acquired from the company's component division. Given a transfer price of $1,500, the assembly division manager is inclined to purchase from the outside supplier because of the apparent cost saving. From a total company viewpoint, the subassembly should be acquired from the component division because the purchase price is greater than the variable or differential costs incurred in the component division, as illustrated below:

Total cost to the company to purchase externally		$1,400
Costs to the company to transfer internally:		
Materials	$400	
Labor	100	
Variable overhead	700	
Total		1,200
Difference (extra cost to purchase externally)		$ 200

If the assembly division purchases these particular subassemblies from an outside supplier, the entire company's net income will be $200 less for each unit purchased. This situation illustrates a typical dilemma in decentralized organizations and also points out the importance of appropriate transfer pricing policies. Should the assembly division be allowed to purchase the subassemblies from outside suppliers? On the one hand, top management may want to preserve the autonomy of division managers by not interfering in such situations. However, completely decentralized decision making when such suboptimization could occur is usually not acceptable to top management.

What is needed is a transfer policy that simultaneously accomplishes a number of objectives. First, a transfer pricing policy should motivate subunit managers to fulfill overall company goals and objectives. Second, transfer prices should provide a fair, equitable, and objective basis for evaluation when profit performance is involved. Finally, transfer pricing policies should foster a desired level of autonomy among subunits of the business.

With intracompany transfers, the interests of both the buyer and the seller as well as top management should be considered. An advantage given to any one of these parties may result in a disadvantage to another. The behavioral aspects of this problem become even more apparent when one considers the position of a division manager who is paid a bonus based on the division's profit performance or return on investment. Under these circumstances division managers are motivated to keep prices high for what is transferred out and to pay the lowest price for what is transferred in. As illustrated in the previous example, division managers motivated in this way may make decisions that are good for the division but detrimental to the company as a whole. The assembly division manager is motivated to purchase the component from an outside supplier because it will increase the division's net income and, in turn, will increase any bonus based on profitability. However, suboptimization will occur if this course of action is allowed. Perhaps a transfer price based on something other than the full cost of production would be more appropriate in this situation. For example, a transfer price of $1,400, the outside purchase price, may solve the dilemma. First, a transfer price of $1,400 makes the assembly division management indifferent about the price for the subassemblies. Therefore, the likelihood of keeping the subassembly business within the company accomplishes the first objective of goal congruence.

Second, the component division is unlikely to sell any subassemblies to external buyers at a price higher than $1,400 because of the external competition. Therefore, the second objective of transfer pricing is accomplished. However, to recognize the interdependence of the two divisions, the $200 contribution to fixed costs earned by the component division with a transfer price of $1,400 might be allocated between the component and assembly divisions. This procedure would result in an ultimate transfer price of $1,300 as calculated below:

Transfer Price as Viewed by the Assembly Division

Transfer price based on external market price	$1,400
Less: Shared portion of contribution to fixed costs (one-half of $200)	(100)
Transfer price to internal divisions	$1,300

Transfer Price as Viewed by the Component Division

Total variable costs to internal divisions	$1,200
Add: Shared portion of contribution to fixed costs (one-half of $200)	100
Transfer price to internal divisions	$1,300

The third objective of autonomy is accomplished through top management formulating a transfer pricing policy that allows division managers to exercise their own decision prerogative and, at the same time, foster overall company goals.

The transfer pricing policies implicit in the above example illustrate a possible solution in one situation for one firm. However, there are diverse types of situations and a number of alternative approaches to establishing appropriate transfer prices. Several commonly used approaches are discussed in the following section to provide you with a basis for formulating transfer pricing policies in any number of different situations.

Alternative Approaches to Establishing Transfer Prices

There is no all-pervasive rule for establishing appropriate transfer prices. Accounting policies, objectives of transfer pricing, and the diverse nature of business operations make it unlikely that a single approach will satisfy all prerequisites in every situation. Therefore, a number of possible approaches to setting transfer prices have been developed and are used in various business situations. Armed with this background and a repertoire of possible transfer pricing methods, accountants should be well equipped to advise top management on transfer pricing policies.

Market Price   The **market price** approach to setting transfer prices uses the prevailing price in external markets at the time the transfer is made. A discount off the market price is usually given to recognize any economies from making intracompany transfers. When a number of alternative transfer prices are being considered, the market price establishes a ceiling for all possible transfer prices. Lower prices may be justified, but prices higher than those available in a competitive market are rarely justified. The following are the advantages of using market prices:

1. Arm's-length transactions in the open market are approximated.
2. Subunit autonomy is fostered.
3. Equity is promoted in the evaluation of profit performance.
4. Better control is provided for the source of supply and the quality of products.

The following are the disadvantages of using market prices:

1. Quoted prices may not apply due to differences in quality, quantity, credit, and delivery terms.
2. Dumping or distress prices may cause artificially low market prices.
3. Accounting for transfers is more complex due to the profit or loss element, which is introduced into the system.
4. The actual cost of finished goods is more difficult to determine.

When there is a perfectly competitive external market for the goods or services being transferred, most decentralized companies that use profit performance as an evaluation criteria find that market prices provide an optimal transfer price. Under conditions of perfect competition and profit performance evaluation, all transfer pricing objectives are met when using market prices.

First, the autonomy of subunits is fostered because market prices approximate an arm's-length transaction as if external parties are dealing with both subunits.

Second, because there is usually a profit component in market prices, market prices provide an appropriate measure when subunits are either profit or investment centers.

Finally, overall company goals are usually met when using market prices because there is little chance of suboptimization. This is so because when suboptimization occurs, someone in the external market is selling at a price below differential manufacturing costs. In perfectly competitive markets there is no incentive for a firm to engage in such a pricing activity because it can sell all of its product at a price that usually covers differential manufacturing costs plus a profit component.

Full Cost   Full cost transfer pricing is probably the oldest and most widely used method when organizations are relatively centralized. **Full cost** includes actual fixed and variable manufacturing costs. A portion of selling and administrative costs may also be added to manufacturing costs for transfer pricing purposes. The following are the advantages of using full cost transfer prices:

1. Data are readily available in existing accounting records.
2. The method is easy to understand and apply because there are no intracompany profits involved.
3. The costing of finished goods is simplified.
4. Transferred costs may be used to measure production efficiency when compared with budgeted costs.

The following are the disadvantages of using full cost transfer pricing:

1. Measuring profit performance of relatively autonomous subunits is not possible because profits are not included as part of intracompany transfers.
2. The producing subunit may not be motivated to control costs that are to be transferred to other subunits.
3. The objectivity required in segment performance evaluation is lacking because there is no attempt to simulate an arm's-length transaction.
4. Suboptimization may occur if the transferring subunit is not operating at full capacity.

The disadvantages of the full cost approach are such that full cost is not an appropriate transfer pricing method in decentralized organizations. In relatively centralized organizations, full cost transfer pricing may promote management objectives. However, all approaches based on full cost suffer from the following shortcoming. Full costs do not offer a sound basis for management to delegate authority to relatively autonomous subunits of a business and do not provide an accurate guide for decision making under conditions of decentralization. Although the use of cost accounting information as the only basis for setting transfer prices may provide an acceptable short-run measure, it does not incorporate long-range profitability objectives of a firm.

To overcome some difficulties of using full cost, *standard full cost* and *full cost plus a markup* are possible alternative transfer pricing methods. If appropriate care is exercised in setting standards, standard full costs will eliminate the problem of production inefficiencies being passed on by transferring subunits. Standard full costs also promote planning and timely decision making because any uncertainty about the prices of goods or services transferred during the budgetary period is removed.

Full cost plus a markup used as a transfer price is intended to provide a synthetic market price for making transfers. When it is believed that incorporating actual market prices is too costly or when prevailing market prices are perceived to be unrealistic, full cost plus a markup may provide a good practical substitute to using market prices.

Variable Cost   A variable cost approach to transfer pricing uses actual variable manufacturing costs as the transfer price. In some situations a portion of variable selling and administrative costs may also be included in the transfer price. When considering a range of possible transfer prices, variable cost usually provides the floor or lowest price at which intracompany transfers should be made.

Variable cost transfer pricing has the major advantage of promoting the best utilization of facilities in the short run because contribution margin becomes the focus of attention. As discussed more fully in chapter 4, contribution margin is especially useful for making management decisions because total fixed costs remain the same in the short run. However, fixed costs cannot be ignored in the long run because all costs must be covered to yield a profit. Therefore, transfer prices based on variable costs should be used with caution if there is danger that they may indicate a profitable situation in the short run but in the long run encourage unprofitable operations.

The major disadvantage of variable cost transfer pricing is that it is a cost-based transfer pricing approach and inherits many of the same weaknesses as full cost transfer pricing. To help overcome some of these weaknesses, several refinements to the basic approach might be considered. For example, *standard variable costs* may deal with the problem of cost inefficiencies being passed on to receiving subunits. Also, *variable cost plus a lump sum* based on monthly or annual activity may be used to approximate covering full costs plus a profit. Other objections concerning the lack of a profitability measure may be overcome by allocating profit received by the selling subunit back to transferring subunits based on some equitable measure of subunit activity.

Variable Cost Plus Opportunity Cost   In most business situations, variable costs plus opportunity costs can provide guidance for establishing a close approximation to the theoretically correct minimum transfer price. The theoretical minimum transfer price is found by adding variable costs incurred to the point of transfer plus the opportunity costs to the firm as a whole, which result from making the internal transfer. Variable costs are used in this situation as an approximation for the more theoretically correct outlay or differential costs.

    Outlay costs refer to cash outflows incurred to the point of transfer as a result of producing transferred goods and services. **Differential costs** refer to the increase in total company costs incurred to the point of transfer as a result of producing transferred goods and services. Outlay or differential costs represent two views of the same economic concept.

    Economic theory indicates that outlay or differential costs plus opportunity costs is the theoretically sound measure for the appropriate minimum transfer price. However, to implement economic theory in a particular business situation, variable costs usually represent an available and acceptable accounting measure that closely approximates outlay or differential costs.

    Opportunity costs represent the maximum contribution to profits lost by the firm as a whole if goods or services are transferred internally rather than being sold externally. For example, an electronic subassembly produced by division A of a company has a total variable per-unit cost of $56. Assuming that the subassembly could be sold to external buyers at a price of $60, a $4 per-unit contribution margin would result. If division A transfers the subassemblies to division B rather than selling them externally, the opportunity cost to the firm as a whole would be $4 per unit—the contribution to profits foregone by not selling externally. In this situation, the appropriate minimum transfer price should be $60 per unit—variable costs of $56 per unit plus opportunity costs of $4 per unit. However, if there is no external market for the subassembly, the opportunity cost to the firm as a whole is zero because there is no foregone opportunity. In this situation, the variable cost of $56 per unit is the theoretical minimum transfer price.

    The use of variable plus opportunity cost to establish a theoretical minimum transfer price has some practical weaknesses. First, opportunity costs are not ordinarily recorded in accounting records because they are usually difficult and costly to measure on a routine basis. Also, a reliable indication of actual opportunity costs depends on the availability of a perfectly competitive market for the transferred good or service. More often than not, markets for intermediate products are either nonexistent or imperfect. This means that one buyer or one seller, acting alone, can influence the market price for goods or services. This results in intricate cost and price interdependencies that make the determination of opportunity cost and an appropriate transfer price very difficult.

    The absence of a perfectly competitive market in such situations presents a very difficult analytical environment for decision makers, which leads to several important general observations concerning transfer prices. First, in many business situations there is not one correct transfer price but rather a schedule of possible transfer prices based on the various parameters of company operations. In some situations, various transfer prices may be possible depending on the quantities of the intermediate product or finished goods bought or sold in the marketplace. Second, the capacity level at which transferring subunits are operating may have an impact on what is an appropriate transfer price. For example, if the transferring division is operating at full capacity, then it need not lower its price below the external market price because of the opportunity cost involved. Finally, transfer pricing policies in organizations where many interdependencies exist should be established and monitored on a firmwide basis.

These observations lead to the consideration of two additional approaches to setting transfer prices—dual transfer prices and negotiation.

Dual Transfer Prices   There may be business situations in which one transfer price does not fulfill all the needs of management. It may be that one method results in transfer prices that are more useful for evaluating performance and another method gives prices that are more appropriate for making economic decisions. For example, market prices may be more useful for evaluating segment performance, while variable costs may be more useful in determining if a transfer should be made. In such situations, management may find it beneficial to use **dual transfer prices**—one price for the transferring division and another price for the receiving division.

Dual transfer prices typically enhance the reported results of each subunit and generally encourage appropriate economic decisions from the viewpoint of the organization as a whole. For example, consider the situation in which a chemical company with a mining division produces material that can be sold externally or transferred to a milling division for additional processing and subsequent sale. Business and economic conditions are such that it is advantageous to have the mining and milling divisions cooperate by making internal transfers. However, the mining division manager may be unwilling to transfer internally at a price less than that available for similar material in the marketplace.

On the other hand, the milling division manager may feel that such a transfer price is unfair because it allows the mining division a profit at the expense of the milling division. One solution in such a situation would be for top management to determine that the transfer should be made and then allocate total contribution to the firm between the two cooperating divisions. Such an approach may be equitable from the viewpoint of top management but can be damaging in decentralized organizations where subunits are intended to have a great deal of autonomy.

When profit or investment centers are involved, it may be more appropriate to use a dual transfer pricing approach; that is, the mining division may be allowed to use a market-based transfer price to encourage it to make the internal transfer, and the milling division may be allowed to use a variable cost transfer price to overcome the objections of the milling division manager. The results of such an arrangement are illustrated below. Assume the transfer of 10,000 tons of material with a variable cost to the mining division of $40 per ton. The external market price for the intermediate product is assumed to be $96 per ton.

Mining Division

Sales to milling division @ $96	$960,000
Variable costs @ $40	400,000
Contribution	$560,000

Milling Division

Sales of finished product @ $220		$2,200,000
Variable costs:		
From mining division @ $40	$ 400,000	
Milling division @ $120	1,200,000	
	$1,600,000	
Contribution		$ 600,000

Dual transfer pricing seems to be an acceptable approach in this situation because the mining division manager is receiving the market price and the milling division manager is paying only variable costs. This encourages the division managers to act in accordance with overall company goals.

There is a major weakness in such an approach because situations may arise in which each division manager may appear to benefit but the company as a whole may lose. This could happen for two reasons. First, the relative looseness inherent in dual pricing methods tends to reduce the incentive on the part of subunit managers to control costs. Second, adopting dual pricing methods without an analysis of the effect on the total company's operations may result in transfers being made with an overall effect of reducing the total company's contribution.

To illustrate, if the milling division in the previous example had received $200 per ton rather than $220 per ton for its finished product, making the transfer would not be appropriate. The difference in price alters the overall company contribution, which would decline by $160,000 as shown below.

Mining Division

Sales to milling division @ $96	$960,000	
Variable costs @ $40	400,000	
Contribution if sold externally		$560,000

Milling Division

Sales of finished product @ $200	$2,000,000	
Variable costs:		
From mining division @ $40	$ 400,000	
Milling division @ $120	1,200,000	
	$1,600,000	
Contribution if transferred internally		400,000
Lost contribution from transferring internally		$160,000

This shows the consequences of using dual transfer prices and making the transfer when the mining division should have sold the material in the external market. Extra care should be exercised under a dual pricing scheme because the performance of each division is enhanced, which possibly masks detrimental effects to the company as a whole. It is also observed that additional bookkeeping is involved when dual transfer prices are used because profit in transferring subunits needs to be eliminated when company-wide financial statements are prepared for the use of external parties. Even though dual pricing seems to be a viable alternative, it has not gained widespread usage.

Negotiation   Because there are difficulties inherent in other approaches, top management may resort to setting transfer prices by **negotiation.** The objective of negotiated transfer prices is to give a fair return to the supplying subunit and a fair cost to the receiving subunit. A negotiated transfer price is an attempt at simulating conditions under which arm's length or market prices are set. The philosophy when using negotiation is that relatively autonomous subunit managers, bargaining in good faith, will arrive at prices equivalent to prices based on actual marketplace negotiations between independent buyers and sellers.

Negotiation may be especially appropriate in situations where there are large volumes of transferred goods or services. Quoted market prices usually apply to normal order sizes. Prices for larger volumes are typically set by negotiation in the marketplace as well. Therefore, market prices may not be that much more objective than prices set by relatively independent division managers negotiating a mutually agreeable price.

When negotiation is used to set transfer prices, situations may arise in which subunit managers cannot agree and top management may be required to intervene and arbitrate a transfer price. For example, if the good or service is unique so a reference market for similar goods or services does not exist and managers cannot reach an agreement, then top management may need to intervene. In any event, there needs to be sufficient top management review of purchasing and transfer price decisions to avoid suboptimization. However, frequent intervention by top management may nullify the purposes of decentralization. There must be a balance between taking full control or allowing full autonomy over purchase decisions.

Negotiation is usually very time consuming and quite costly to the firm. Negotiation typically involves the participation of more management personnel than if market prices, for example, are used. Frequent management involvement is also required to re-examine and update transfer prices as business conditions change.

The advantages and disadvantages of the various approaches to establishing transfer prices indicate that factors in the business environment determine which of several possible approaches is most appropriate in a specific business situation. Management must recognize the tradeoffs of each approach in fulfilling overall company objectives, fostering a desired level of autonomy among subunits, and providing a fair, equitable, and objective basis for evaluating performance.

Accounting Entries for Intracompany Transfers

Transfer prices are usually governed by managerial objectives and not by generally accepted accounting principles for external reporting. Therefore, intracompany transfers are typically made at prices other than at inventoriable cost. This means that when financial statements are prepared for external reporting, inventory balances usually must be adjusted to reflect appropriate cost values, and related intracompany sales and profit must be eliminated. To accomplish this, the accounting system should be designed so there is a clear distinction between external and internal transactions and at the same time management is provided with summary information concerning the relative importance of intracompany transfers.

To illustrate, assume that division *A*, the supplying division, transfers goods to division *B*, the purchasing division, at a negotiated transfer price of cost plus a 25% markup on cost. Summary entries to record transfers made between the two divisions are as follows:

Supplying Division's Books

Accounts receivable—division *B*	20,000	
Sales—intracompany		20,000
Cost of goods sold—intracompany	16,000	
Inventory		16,000

Purchasing Division's Books

Inventory (purchases)—intracompany	20,000	
Accounts payable—division *A*		20,000

Assume that inventoriable costs of $6,000 are added by division *B* to the materials transferred from division *A*. The total inventory value for division *B* is $26,000. Assume also that division *B* then sells three-fourths of the inventory, $19,500, to external purchasers for $27,500. Entries summarizing this latter event are as follows:

Supplying Division's Books

No entries required

Purchasing Division's Books

Accounts receivable—trade	27,500	
Sales		27,500
Cost of goods sold—trade	19,500	
Inventory—intracompany		19,500

This procedure indicates that the two divisions operate like two different companies when handling intracompany transfers. However, when the financial statements of all divisions are consolidated for external reporting, entries are necessary (*a*) to adjust the value of ending inventory in the purchasing division and (*b*) to eliminate intracompany sales, receivables, and profit. The following entries are typically made by the company controller:

Company's Books

Accounts payable—division *A*	20,000	
Accounts receivable—division *B*		20,000
Sales—intracompany	20,000	
Cost of goods sold—intracompany		16,000
Cost of goods sold—trade (.75 × 4,000)		3,000
Inventory—intracompany (.25 × 4,000)		1,000

The above journal entry shows how the intracompany profit of $4,000 ($20,000 − $16,000 = $4,000) "earned" by division *A* in making intracompany transfers is eliminated from company records. Intracompany profit is passed on to receiving subunits, division *B* in this example, in the form of increased inventory cost. Because transferred inventory is either sold or still on hand at the end of the period, intracompany profit is eliminated in two steps. First, three-fourths of the transferred inventory was sold to external parties. Therefore, three-fourths of the intracompany profit associated with the inventory sold is eliminated from the "cost of goods sold—trade" account. The remaining one-fourth of intracompany profit still resides in ending inventory of division *B* and is eliminated by reducing the "inventory—intracompany" account balance.

PRICING FOR PRODUCT SALES

Cost accounting information is a vital component in pricing goods and services for sales to external customers. A firm's profitability and long-run viability depend on an appropriate relationship between costs and revenues. Even though this essential relationship exists between costs and revenues, costs are only one of a myriad of considerations in the pricing decision. Because of this, it is important that accountants have a balanced view of how costs are used in pricing decisions.

In addition to cost accounting information, the pricing decision is affected by many factors both inside and outside the company. Influences outside the company might include the expected or actual reaction of customers and competitors to particular pricing decisions. Customers usually have the option of turning to competitors' products, substituting other similar products, or even manufacturing the needed products themselves. Also, competitors may influence a pricing decision because they usually have the option of either meeting or undercutting prices.

Influences inside the company that affect pricing policies include management's philosophy about a "fair return" or charging "what the market will bear." In addition, the relationship of costs and the volume of production is an important pricing consideration. Finally, the selection of a long-run or a short-run view affects how management approaches the pricing decision.

Even without an exhaustive discussion on all of the influences on prices, it can be seen that cost accounting information is just one of a number of considerations in setting prices. However, costs generally provide a starting point for the pricing decision even if the price ultimately chosen may have little or no relationship to underlying costs. Also, cost information is a basic tool for evaluating specific pricing policies because it provides the vehicle for examining the expected impact on profitability of specific price decisions.

Several approaches to using cost information in establishing pricing policies are explained in the following section. Also, some complicating factors that might necessitate modifications to these basic approaches are explored.

Alternative Cost-Based Approaches to Product Pricing

The major advantages of cost-based pricing are that they are understandable, predictable, explainable, and justifiable on objective criteria. Experience has shown that they are generally profitable and seem to be more socially acceptable than other pricing techniques. As a result, cost-based pricing methods are in widespread use. The major shortcomings of cost-based pricing formulas are that they generally do not take into account such factors as market conditions, product life cycles, or general economic conditions.

The challenge of management is to benefit from the advantages of cost-based pricing approaches and yet develop pricing policies that are responsive to these other important considerations. The following are ways cost accounting information can be incorporated in pricing policies *in combination with other factors.*

Rate of Markup or Gross Margin   One of the most common ways to use costs as a basis for pricing is to apply a target rate of markup or gross margin. A **rate of markup** is a target rate applied against the cost of a product or service to establish a selling price in external markets. This target rate is usually applied to either the purchase cost of a product or to total manufacturing costs. A firm that wants to receive a particular target markup on cost would use the following formula:

$$\text{Selling price} = \text{Cost} + [\text{Target markup} \times \text{Cost}]$$

For example, if the cost of a particular product is $.80 per unit and the company's target markup on cost is 20%, then the selling price would be $.96 per unit.

$$\text{Selling price} = .80 + (.20 \times .80) = .96$$

If a company wants to receive a desired gross margin on sales, the pricing formula is:

$$\text{Selling price} = \text{Cost} \times \frac{1}{1 - \text{Target gross margin}}$$

Thus, if the cost of a particular product is $.80 per unit and the company's pricing formula is based on a desired gross margin of 20%, then the selling price would be $1.00 per unit.

$$\text{Selling price} = .80 \times \frac{1}{1 - .20} = 1.00$$

This price, based on the desired gross margin, can be verified with the following calculation:

	Dollars	*Percent*
Sales	$1.00	100%
Cost of goods sold	.80	80
Gross profit (margin)	$ .20	20%

The target rates used in such formulas are often traditional industry rates that have withstood the test of time. Even though these pricing methods are simple to apply and easily understood, their weakness is that they explicitly incorporate few of the many factors affecting the pricing decision. For example, such pricing formulas are not inherently sensitive to market conditions and may result in prices that lose business in weak markets or that fail to take advantage of strong markets. For example, being out of stock or holding clearance sales results from using target rates insensitive to the marketplace. Perhaps a better approach would be to correlate target rates with market indicators. For example, an indicator of market strength is thought to be the percent of plant capacity being utilized in the industry. Excess capacity in an industry usually brings downward pressure on prices and lower target rates would be more appropriate under such conditions.

A historical relationship between plant capacity (operating rate) and target markups, derived with the use of regression analysis, may provide a basis for systematically adjusting target rates. In addition, other market factors such as the product life cycle and market growth rate may also provide useful criteria for adjusting target rates. For example, in the growth phase of a product, higher margins are typically needed to finance new facilities. However, later in the life cycle, lower margins may be appropriate to meet competitive pressures.

Variations on the rate of markup method include markup on conversion cost and markup on variable cost. Markup on variable costs emphasizes the contribution approach to pricing. Sales less variable costs indicate the amount of contribution made to recovering fixed costs and providing for a profit on operations. One great advantage of paying attention to the contribution margin is that in doing so variable and fixed costs are identified. As a result, cost-volume-profit relationships are more easily discernible and make the evaluation of a range of possible prices and their consequences possible.

Probably the next major advantage of emphasizing the contribution approach is that it offers more insight into the long-run versus short-run effects of various prices. For example, to preserve a skilled labor force, prices may be allowed to drop in the short run to levels that just cannot be sustained in the long run. The proposition facing management in such situations is whether the expected long-run benefits of preserving a skilled labor force equal or exceed the short-run sacrifice of lost contribution. Information is immediately available to answer such questions if variable costs are routinely part of the pricing decision.

Some companies fear that, when using a variable-cost approach, prices will be consistently under the price necessary to cover *all* costs, both variable and fixed. This could happen, but survey results indicate that a variable cost approach to pricing generally does not result in unprofitable operations (NAA Research Report no. 37). One reason why this is true is because a target pricing formula can be developed using variable costs that will result in a selling price similar to one that might be arrived at if markup on full cost had been used. To illustrate, consider a product with total per-unit costs amounting to $60 with $50 of the total being variable. In this situation, a 20% markup on the full cost of $60 per unit results in a selling price of $72, which is essentially the same result as using a 44% markup on variable cost.

Markup on full cost: [$60 + (.20 × $60)] = $72
Markup on variable cost: [$50 + (.44 × $50)] = $72

The purpose of this illustration is not to indicate that markup on variable cost is the same as markup on full cost. Rather, the point is that markup on variable cost is not inherently unprofitable. Decision makers should simply realize that to obtain equivalent profitability levels, rates of markup based on variable cost must usually be set higher than rates of markup on full cost. It is generally felt that when the emphasis is on contribution margin rather than on the underlying costs, better pricing decisions will result.

Markup on conversion cost is appropriate when direct-labor and factory overhead costs are the primary cost elements of a good or service, such as when factory capacity is limited by labor constraints or when a customer furnishes materials for the manufacture of a product. For example, consider a production situation in which the amount of available labor is a constraining factor and in which several products require about the same amount of materials but varying amounts of labor and overhead. To generate the same amount of profit per unit of scarce labor resource, management may decide to set selling prices based on a percentage markup on conversion cost as follows:

		Example Product
Materials		$34.00
Conversion costs:		
Labor	$16.00	
Overhead	12.00	
Total		$28.00
Full cost		$62.00
Markup on conversion cost (30% of $28.00)		8.40
Selling price		$70.40

A valid concern when using any of the markup-on-cost methods is that all costs may not be considered in the pricing decision. For example, when prices are set to yield a specific rate of gross margin, selling and administrative expenses are not an explicit part of the computation of gross margin. However, the overall cost situation should be considered in the pricing decision. A distinct advantage of differentiating between variable and fixed costs when the contribution approach is used is that *total* variable costs, including variable selling and administrative expenses, are explicitly incorporated in the markup formula. Also, total fixed costs can be incorporated in the decision when using the contribution approach by using cost-volume-profit analysis.

Related to a target rate of markup on cost is a pricing method known as *cost-plus pricing*. This method prevails in situations where it is difficult or impossible to predict the total cost of producing a product or service. For example, the government may want to contract for the production of a new weapons system. Because of the probable lack of experience producing this product and the attendant risk involved in such situations, rather than set a specific price before proceeding to let a contract, a contract is let on a cost-plus basis. The price in such situations is usually the full cost of production plus a percentage markup on the cost, which constitutes profit.

Cost-plus pricing focuses attention on the proper determination of costs. If a company devotes all of its resources to one product or to one service, there is little difficulty with cost-plus pricing. However, a more typical situation is one in which a cost-plus contract is just one of many activities in a given company. Determining which costs apply to which activity can be very confusing and even subject to manipulation. The Cost Accounting Standards Board (CASB) was created by Congress for this and other reasons. CASB standards are intended to provide guidance concerning which costs may be applicable to a particular contract so misunderstandings and inequities are avoided when using the cost-plus pricing approach.

Rate of Return on Assets Employed   Another common way to incorporate cost information in the pricing decision is to base selling prices on a desired rate of return on assets employed. A **rate of return on assets employed** is a target rate of return applied against total assets employed. There are a number of techniques for implementing this approach, two of which are illustrated below. A per-unit selling price can be directly calculated by using the following formula:

$$\text{Selling price} = \frac{\text{Total cost} + (\text{Desired rate of return} \times \text{Assets employed})}{\text{Unit sales volume}}$$

For example, a firm that has a desired rate of return on assets employed of 22% with total assets of $6,000,000, total annual costs of $2,400,000, and an anticipated sales volume of 10,000 units would use a selling price of $37.20 per unit.

$$\text{Selling price} = \frac{\$2,400,000 + (.22 \times \$6,000,000)}{100,000} = \$37.20$$

This pricing method is appropriate when only one product or a number of very similar products are sold by a company. When a company has a diversified product mix, a pricing method that can be applied on an individual product basis is needed. One way to accomplish this is to calculate a percentage markup on cost that is subsequently applied on an individual product basis. This percentage markup on cost can be derived by using the following formula:

$$\text{Markup on cost} = \text{Desired rate of return} \times \frac{\text{Assets employed}}{\text{Annual costs}}$$

For example, a firm that has a desired return on assets employed of 22% with total assets of $6,000,000 and total annual costs of $2,400,000 would use a percentage markup on cost of 55%.

$$\text{Markup on cost} = .22 \times \frac{\$6,000,000}{\$2,400,000} = .55$$

This method is especially useful in firms that sell numerous types of products with varying costs and selling prices. However, this general method also fails to incorporate a number of influences on the pricing decision from sources both inside and outside the firm. For example, the amount of assets employed is an internal factor that influences prices using this method. The amount of assets employed typically varies in proportion to sales because more assets in the form of cash, accounts receivable, and inventories are needed to support increased sales volume. The previous formula used to directly calculate a selling price could be adjusted in the following way to incorporate such factors:

$$\text{Selling price} = \frac{\dfrac{\text{Total cost} + (\text{Desired rate of return} \times \text{Fixed assets})}{\text{Unit sales volume}}}{1 - \left(\text{Desired rate of return} \times \dfrac{\text{Current assets}}{\text{Sales}} \right)}$$

Influences on the pricing decision from sources outside the firm can also be incorporated in the above formulas in several ways. For example, the target rate of return on employed capital can be based on the current cost of capital after adjustment for such external factors as the risk that the product may not pay off. Or, the total cost number may be adjusted to reflect the estimated costs that a competitor (or would-be competitor) would most likely incur to enter the market. In this way a ceiling below which prices should be set can be established so surplus capacity is not attracted into the industry.

Considerations for Modification of Cost-Based Prices

Having developed the general numeric techniques for rate of markup on gross margin and rate of return on assets employed, it is important to discuss a number of considerations that could lead decision makers to modify the prices obtained using these basic techniques.

This information will help to reinforce the notion that pricing in any of its forms is a complex matter and should be approached with much judgment. Lack of understanding on the part of the decision maker of all aspects of the decision environment may lead to improper pricing regardless of the quality and availability of cost accounting information.

Past versus Future Orientation   The relevant costs to consider in making pricing decisions are anticipated future costs, not past costs. Historical cost information may provide a valuable basis for predicting future costs, but should not be confused with anticipated future costs, which are the only relevant costs in the pricing decision. Often the availability, precision, or objectivity of historical costs may entice management to assume that they are the relevant costs for pricing decisions.

Any number of factors, both inside and outside the company, can make historical costs useless even as predictors of future costs. More efficient methods of production, changes in plant facilities, changes in product specifications, labor unrest, and inflation are just a few examples of factors affecting the predictive usefulness of historical costs. Therefore, historical costs must be adjusted for changes in the business environment to make product prices sensitive to actual market conditions.

Another future-oriented consideration concerns the almost inevitable fact that once put on the market a product will receive almost continuous price revisions. Therefore, it is important that the same degree of attention given to establishing an optimum price at the outset also be given any subsequent changes in prices. Management should constantly monitor the changing market environment and analyze potential price changes in terms of their profitability due to anticipated changes in costs and revenues.

Standard Costs   The use of standard costs in product pricing decisions has several advantages. First, standard costs are quickly available with little added clerical cost. Second, standard costs are usually based on the best estimate of future costs that will be incurred in an efficiently operating plant at actual capacity.

If prices are based on standard costs it is essential that the standards be current, attainable standards. If standards are based on theoretical conditions, then standards used for pricing should be adjusted by the ratio of standard costs to actual costs as indicated by normal balances in variance accounts. This type of adjustment converts theoretical standards to currently attainable standards. It is also important that standards be closely monitored and that the standards receive timely revisions as manufacturing conditions change. Finally, significant deviations between standard and actual costs should be promptly reported to determine if price adjustments should be made.

One way to make standard costs more responsive to current market conditions is to use current market prices for materials and labor. Current costs for these items combined with standard costs for other standard cost elements provide cost information that is very sensitive to current market conditions yet attuned to the prevailing conditions in the firm.

Volume Changes   One of the most perplexing questions facing decision makers is how a price change may affect volume, which in turn affects costs and profits. Basic microeconomic theory is useful in this situation. However, some rather fundamental measures can be very helpful in correlating volume and price changes. Many firms find it useful to consider relative price rather than absolute price. This means expressing the company's price as a ratio of the average industry price or as a ratio of the price leader in the industry. It is also useful to express the volume of production in terms of the company's market share of the total volume in the marketplace. This tends to remove the influences of general economic changes when using volume measures in pricing decisions. Using these two measures it may be possible to discover a correlation between market share and relative prices that have prevailed in the past. If there is such a correlation in the pattern of change, it could be used to predict what may happen in the future. However, care should be taken to screen out of such correlation data price and volume changes arising from abnormal conditions. For example, volume increases from a surge of hedge buying immediately following the announcement of a price increase should be excluded from correlation calculations.

Summary

Pricing includes so many interacting factors that there are usually no easy answers. Pricing decisions require a great deal of judgment, information, and skill. Cost accounting information is one key consideration in both pricing for intracompany transfers and pricing for product sales.

Transfer prices are used in companies that exchange goods and services among operating subunits. When company subdivisions are relatively autonomous, transfer prices become especially important because the revenue of one division becomes a cost of another division. In such situations the interests of both the receiving and the transferring subunits should be considered. The interests of top management should also be considered to avoid suboptimization.

There is no all-pervasive rule for establishing appropriate transfer prices. Common bases for establishing transfer prices include using the prevailing price in the marketplace, actual production costs, standard costs, and opportunity costs. Transfer prices should be chosen on the basis of how well they accomplish overall company objectives, foster division autonomy, and provide an incentive for division management. Because of the complexity of the problem, it may be necessary to resort to negotiated transfer prices or even setting dual transfer prices, which is one price for the transferring subunit and another price for the receiving subunit.

Pricing for product sales is even more complex than transfer pricing because of the many external market considerations. Cost accounting information generally provides a starting point for the product pricing decision. Other considerations such as market conditions or the anticipated response of competitors are factors that may influence or modify cost-based prices. There are a number of cost-based approaches to product pricing that fall into two general categories—rate of markup or gross margin and rate of return on assets employed.

It is imperative that decision makers remember that historical costs are relevant in decisions only to the extent that they are valid predictors of future costs. Predictions based on historical costs should be modified appropriately for anticipated economic and business conditions so appropriate pricing decisions are made.

Self-Study Problems

TRANSFER PRICING

The Northern Refrigeration Company is a multidivisional company that has delegated full profit responsibility to division managers. The compressor division produces a major subassembly that can be incorporated in the final product of other divisions or can be sold to other companies in a competitive market. This subassembly is currently used by the refrigerator division in one of its product lines. Division managers have complete autonomy to accept or reject transfers of goods or services from other divisions.

The following information is available to each division manager concerning expected costs and selling prices of subassemblies:

Compressor Division

Variable manufacturing costs	$240
Fixed manufacturing costs	120
Total	$360
Expected selling price	$400

Refrigerator Division

Variable costs for completion	$300
Expected selling price	$800

Requirements

1. Prepare an analysis of the effect of using the market price, full cost, variable cost, and variable plus opportunity approaches to establishing transfer prices.
2. What transfer price do you recommend in this situation? Why?
3. What is your recommendation if the market price for the final product declines to $600?

Solution to the Self-Study Problem

1. Analysis of various approaches to setting transfer prices:

Market Price

	Compressor Division	Refrigerator Division	Northern Company
Prices:			
Transfer price—subassembly	$400		
Selling price—final product		$800	$800
Costs:			
Variable costs—compressor division	$240		$240
Transferred costs—subassembly		$400	
Variable costs—refrigerator division		300	300
Total	$240	$700	$540
Contribution margin	$160	$100	$260

Full Cost

	Compressor Division	Refrigerator Division	Northern Company
Prices:			
Transfer price—subassembly	$360		
Selling price—final product		$800	$800
Costs:			
Variable costs—compressor division	$240		$240
Transferred costs—subassembly		$360	
Variable costs—refrigerator division		300	300
Total	$240	$660	$540
Contribution margin	$120	$140	$260

Variable Cost

	Compressor Division	Refrigerator Division	Northern Company
Prices:			
Transfer price—subassembly	$240		
Selling price—final product		$800	$800
Costs:			
Variable costs—compressor division	$240		$240
Transferred costs—subassembly		$240	
Variable costs—refrigerator division		300	300
Total	$240	$540	$540
Contribution margin	$-0-	$260	$260

Variable Plus Opportunity Cost

Variable cost		$240
Opportunity cost:		
Market price	$400	
Less: Variable cost	240	
Opportunity cost		160
Total		$400

2. The market price of $400, which is also the transfer price that results when using the variable cost plus opportunity cost approach, is the appropriate transfer price in this situation. When competitive markets are available, the market price usually represents the maximum transfer price that should be considered. In this situation it is also the theoretical minimum transfer price. The compressor division manager is indifferent about whether subassemblies are sold internally or externally at a transfer price of $400. The manager of the compressor division will be unwilling to transfer subassemblies at a price below $400 because of the ready market for subassemblies at $400. Any price below $400 will reduce the division's contribution margin. The refrigerator division manager should be satisfied with a transfer price of $400 because it is the best price available from any supplier of subassemblies.

3. If the market price for the final product is $600 rather than $800, then the refrigerator division either needs to reduce costs or look for some other final product(s) to produce. Otherwise every subassembly used in the refrigerator division of Northern Company loses $100 in contribution. Compare the contribution margins in the following analysis with those in the previous analyses.

	Compressor Division	Refrigerator Division	Northern Company
Prices:			
Transfer price—subassembly	$400		
Selling price—final product		$600	$600
Costs:			
Variable costs—compressor division	$240		$240
Transferred costs—subassembly		$400	
Variable costs—refrigerator division		300	300
Total	$240	$700	$540
Contribution margin	$160	$(100)	$ 60

PRODUCT PRICING

Toyland Products, a newly created toy division of a major conglomerate, will soon begin marketing its first product. The following information is available concerning the division and its new product:

	New Product (per unit)
Variable costs	$6.00
Fixed costs	2.00
Total	$8.00

Assets employed in the division = $1,500,000
Desired rate of return on assets employed = 24%
Expected level of production and sales = 100,000 units
Average industry markup on cost = 45%

Requirements

1. What would be the selling price for the new product if the average industry markup on cost is used as the pricing method?
2. What rate of gross profit will result if the price derived in requirement 1 is actually used?
3. Calculate the selling price of the new product if the desired rate of return on assets employed is used as the pricing method.
4. What percentage markup on variable cost will yield the same selling price as a 45% markup on full cost?

Solution to the Self-Study Problem

1. The selling price based on 45% markup on cost:

   Selling price = $8.00 + (.45 × $8.00) = 1.45 × $8.00 = $11.60

2. The rate of gross profit with a selling price of $11.60:

	Dollars	Percent
Sales	$11.60	100%
Cost of goods sold	8.00	79
Gross profit	$ 3.60	31%

3. The selling price based on 24% return on assets employed:

$$\text{Selling price} = \frac{\$800,000 + (.24 \times 1,500,000)}{100,000} = \$11.60$$

4. The markup rate on variable cost to yield approximately the same price as a 45% markup on total cost:

   Basic formula:

   Selling price = Variable cost + (Markup rate × Variable cost)

   Basic formula rewritten to solve for the markup rate:

   $$\text{Markup rate} = \frac{\text{Selling price}}{\text{Variable cost}} - 1$$

   $$\text{Markup rate} = \frac{\$11.60}{\$6.00} - 1 = 93\%$$

Suggested Readings

Bailey, Earl L., ed. *Pricing Practices and Strategies.* Conference Board Report no. 751. New York: The Conference Board, 1978.

Benke, Ralph L., Jr., and Edwards, James Don. "Transfer Pricing: Techniques and Uses." *Management Accounting* (June 1980): 44–47.

Berry, Leonard Eugene. "Advising Clients on Pricing." *Journal of Accountancy* 149 (March 1980): 34–38.

Gordon, Lawrence A.; Cooper, Robert; Falk, Haim; and Miller, Danny. "The Pricing Decision." *Management Accounting* (March 1981): 59–60.

Hernandez, William H. "Pricing Policies Under Inflation." *Management Accounting* (January 1982): 51–55.

Stern, Roy D. "Accounting for Intracompany Inventory Transfers." *Management Accounting* (September 1980): 41–44.

Discussion Questions

1. Why is cost accounting information important in pricing decisions?
2. What are the meanings of transfer pricing and product pricing?
3. Why is transfer pricing so important in relatively decentralized organizations?
4. What are the objectives of transfer pricing?
5. What are the advantages and disadvantages of using market prices for intracompany transfers?
6. What are the advantages and disadvantages of using cost-related transfer prices?
7. Which transfer pricing methods establish the ceiling and theoretical minimum transfer prices?
8. What cost concept is a practical alternative to using outlay or differential costs?
9. When would it be appropriate to use dual transfer prices?
10. What is the basic philosophy underlying the use of negotiation to set transfer prices?
11. Explain what series of journal entries are necessary to account for intracompany transfers.
12. Explain the role of cost accounting information in setting prices for product sales.
13. What are the major advantages of a cost-based pricing method?
14. Give the basic pricing formulas when using rate of markup, gross margin, and rate of return on assets employed.
15. Explain two common variations on the rate of markup methods for setting product prices.
16. Explain how the reaction of customers and competitors can affect product prices.
17. Why is a future versus a past orientation important when setting product prices?
18. Explain how the effect of volume changes can be incorporated in the pricing decision.
19. Under what conditions are standard costs useful when making pricing decisions?

Exercises

Exercise 21.1   Transfer Pricing Concepts

For each of the transfer pricing policies listed below, describe the individual components of the final transfer price.

1. Market price
2. Full cost
3. Variable cost
4. Variable plus opportunity cost
5. Dual transfer prices
6. Negotiated market price

Exercise 21.2   Transfer Pricing Concepts

No standard has been pronounced defining the proper method of setting intracompany transfer prices. An accountant must therefore be prepared to suggest an appropriate pricing technique for each circumstance. Using the list in exercise 21.1, describe a set of circumstances for which each transfer pricing approach proves advantageous.

Exercise 21.3   Choosing a Transfer Price

The Timeworks Division of Electrosond Company makes a timer device used in the production of a variety of appliances. The timing device is sold on the open market at $18 per unit. Electrosond has recently acquired a promising microwave oven company that now operates as the Heatwave Division. The oven manufacturer requires a timing device similar to that produced by the Timeworks Division and has been purchasing these from an external source at $18 less a 5% quantity discount. The Timeworks Division has capacity to produce 15,000 timing devices per month and currently sells only 12,000. Electrosond management would like the new Heatwave Division to purchase their required 2,000 timers internally.

Timeworks per unit cost is calculated below:

Materials	$ 6
Labor	5
Overhead: Variable	3
Fixed (based on 12,000 production)	1
	$15

Required

1. Assuming that each division is a profit center, choose a transfer price that you would recommend. Explain the advantages of this price.
2. Assume now that the Timeworks Division is selling all 15,000 units externally at the time of the Heatwave acquisition. What do you recommend under these circumstances?

Exercise 21.4 Markup Pricing—Full and Variable Costing

Consider the following per-unit costs of Wilson Company's new product line.

Variable costs:		
Materials	$12.00	
Labor	7.00	
Manufacturing overhead	3.00	
Fixed costs:		
Manufacturing overhead		
(based on expected production		
and sales of 20,000 units)	5.00	
Total	$27.00	

The average rate of markup on full costs is 21% in the industry.

Required

1. Calculate the outside selling price Wilson should set if the markup on full cost method is applied using the industry average rate.
2. What markup percentage would be required to arrive at the same price using the markup on variable cost method?
3. Using the price you found in requirements 1 and 2, find the gross profit percentage (round to the nearest tenth of a percent).

Exercise 21.5 Gross Margin Pricing

Refer to the cost information of the Wilson Company in exercise 21.4.

Rather than setting the price according to the industry average markup on cost, Wilson wants to achieve a gross margin of 21%.

Required

Calculate the selling price Wilson will use to reach their goal of 21% gross margin on the new product line.

Exercise 21.6 Markup on Conversion Costs

Refer to the cost information on the Wilson Company in exercise 21.4.

Plant capacity and labor restrict the total output of all product lines. Management has therefore adopted a policy of setting the selling price based on a 30% markup on conversion costs.

Required

Calculate the selling price Wilson will use under their conversion cost policy.

Exercise 21.7   Pricing and Return on Investment

Oden Freezers is new in a competitive industry. Their production of a top-of-the-line freezer employs assets of $45,600,000. Oden hopes to achieve a return on assets employed of 24%. Manufacturing and sales cost information is as follows:

	Oden Freezer (per unit)
Total variable costs:	$265
Total fixed costs:	115
Total cost per unit	$380
Unit sales and production volume	60,000 units

Required

Calculate the minimum sales price Oden should use to achieve the desired rate of return on assets employed at the given sales volume.

Exercise 21.8   Pricing

Assume that the freezers produced in exercise 21.7 by Oden Freezers are just one of many product lines. Oden still desires a 24% rate of return on assets employed. Use all information as it was given in exercise 21.7.

Required

1. Calculate the markup percentage on cost with the given facts.
2. What price would Oden set for the freezer if the markup on cost calculated in requirement 1 is used?

Exercise 21.9   Contribution Approach to Pricing

Adams Incorporated produces and sells small motors. Recently Adams was asked to submit a bid on the sale of 100 units for a local manufacturer. Per-unit costs were accumulated and estimates are shown below based on 100 additional units produced.

	Per Unit
Direct materials	$ 37
Shipping materials	3
Direct labor	45
Receiving and handling (60% fixed)	6
Factory overhead:	
Fixed	12
Variable	19
General and administrative costs	15
Total	$137

Just as the president was about to submit his bid, he learned that a bid of $120 was already submitted as the lowest bid.

Required

Can Adams bid lower than the $120 already submitted? What price could Adams submit? Show your computations.

Exercise 21.10   Markup Pricing

MacAlbert Products has begun production of a new sprinkler unit. Management has been concerned with setting an appropriate selling price for the new unit. The following unit costs are to be assigned:

Variable Costs:	
Materials	$3.50
Labor	2.00
Manufacturing overhead	.50
Fixed Costs:	
Manufacturing overhead	
(based on 100,000 unit expected	
production and sales)	1.50
Total cost per unit	$7.50

The industry has recorded near full capacity output in the last two years. Due to the market strength of sprinkler products, the price has steadily risen. The rise has settled recently with the industry average markup of 55% of full costs.

Required

1. If MacAlbert chooses to set prices by the markup on full cost approach, what will be the unit sales price of the new product (use the industry average rate)?
2. What will be the gross profit percentage if the price determined in requirement 1 is used?
3. If MacAlbert sets prices using 100% markup of conversion costs, what selling price would they use?
4. What would you expect to happen to prices if the firms in the industry began reporting excess capacity?
5. Explain the problems that can arise in using strictly a markup on cost method in pricing.

Problems

Problem 21.1   Pricing Special Order (CPA)

Woody Company, a manufacturer of sneakers, has enough idle capacity to accept a special order of 20,000 pairs of sneakers at $6 a pair. The normal selling price is $10 a pair. Variable manufacturing costs are $4.50 a pair, and fixed manufacturing costs are $1.50 a pair. Woody will not incur any selling expenses as a result of the special order.

Required

What would be the effect on operating income if the special order could be accepted without affecting normal sales?

Problem 21.2   The Contribution Approach on the Pricing Decision

The Newhouse Company has established a pricing formula for its single product, using the following absorption cost estimates:

Sales	$200,000
Cost of goods sold	120,000[a]
Gross margin	$ 80,000
Selling and administrative expenses	60,000[b]
Estimated net income	$ 20,000

[a]Including $40,000 of fixed costs.
[b]Including $40,000 of fixed costs.

The sales price would be determined by adding two-thirds (80,000 ÷ 120,000) of the cost of production to the cost of production.

Required

1. Prepare an estimated income statement based on the contribution margin concept.
2. Determine the markup percentage based on variable costs that would be used in pricing if the contribution approach were used.
3. Compare and contrast the absorption costing and contribution approaches to pricing. Indicate the advantages and disadvantages of each.

Problem 21.3   Negotiated Transfer Pricing (CMA)

National Industries is a diversified corporation with separate and distinct operating divisions. Each division's performance is evaluated on the basis of total dollar profits and return on division investment.

The Windair Division manufactures and sells air-conditioner units. The coming year's budgeted income statement, based upon a sales volume of 15,000 units, is shown below.

Windair Division
Budgeted Income Statement
For the Coming Fiscal Year

	Per Unit	Total (000)
Sales revenue	$400	$6,000
Manufacturing costs:		
Compressor	70	1,050
Other raw materials	37	555
Direct labor	30	450
Variable overhead	45	675
Fixed overhead	32	480
Total manufacturing costs	214	3,210
Gross margin	186	2,790
Operating expenses:		
Variable selling	18	270
Fixed selling	19	285
Fixed administrative	38	570
Total operating expenses	75	1,125
Net income before taxes	$111	$1,665

Windair Division's manager believes sales can be increased if the unit selling price of the air conditioners is reduced. A market research study conducted by an independent firm at the request of the manager indicates that a 5% reduction in the selling price ($20) would increase sales volume 16% or 2,400 units. Windair has sufficient production capacity to manage this increased volume with no increase in fixed costs.

At the present, Windair uses a compressor in its units, which it purchases from an outside supplier at a cost of $70 per compressor. The division manager of Windair has approached the manager of the Compressor Division regarding the sale of compressor units to Windair. The Compressor Division currently manufactures and sells a unit exclusively to outside firms that is similar to the unit used by Windair. The specifications of the Windair compressor are slightly different. This would reduce the Compressor Division's raw material cost by $1.50 per unit. In addition, the Compressor Division would not incur any variable selling costs in the units sold to Windair. The manager wants all of the compressors it uses to come from one supplier and has offered to pay $50 for each compressor unit.

The Compressor Division has the capacity to produce 75,000 units. The coming year's budgeted income statement for the Compressor Division is shown below and is based upon a sales volume of 64,000 units without considering Windair's proposal.

Compressor Division
Budgeted Income Statement
For the Coming Fiscal Year

	Per Unit	Total (000)
Sales revenue	$100	$6,400
Manufacturing costs:		
Raw materials	12	768
Direct labor	8	512
Variable overhead	10	640
Fixed overhead	11	704
Total manufacturing costs	41	2,624
Gross margin	59	3,776
Operating expenses:		
Variable selling	6	384
Fixed selling	4	256
Fixed administrative	7	448
Total operating expenses	17	1,088
Net income before taxes	$ 42	$2,688

Required

1. Should Windair Division institute the 5% price reduction on its air-conditioner units even if it cannot acquire the compressors internally for $50 each? Support your conclusion with appropriate calculations.
2. Without prejudice to your answer to requirement 1, assume Windair needs 17,400 units. Should the Compressor Division be willing to supply the compressor units for $50 each? Support your conclusion with appropriate calculations.
3. As the manager of the Compressor Division, what is the minimum transfer price you could charge for the new compressor? Show computations.
4. Without prejudice to your answer to requirement 1, assume Windair needs 17,400 units. Would it be in the best interest of National Industries for the Compressor Division to supply the compressor units at $50 each to the Windair Division? Support your conclusion with appropriate calculations.

Problem 21.4   Pricing Methods

Merriweather Patio Division will soon be marketing its first line of patio umbrellas. The outside selling price is now being sought. The following information has been collected concerning this division:

	Umbrellas (per unit)
Variable costs:	$12.50
Fixed costs:	4.50
Total per unit	$17.00

Assets employed in the division:	$890,000
Desired rate of return on assets employed:	21%
Expected level of first-year sales and production:	180,000 units
Average industry markup on cost:	55%

Required

1. Give the outside selling price Merriweather will set if the average industry markup on full cost is used as the pricing method.
2. What rate of gross profit will result if Merriweather uses the price calculated in requirement 1? (Round to three decimals.)
3. What markup percentage on variable costs would be used to calculate the same price as a 55% markup on full cost?
4. What would be the selling price of the umbrella if the desired rate of return on assets employed method is used for pricing?

Problem 21.5   Pricing and Rate of Return on Assets Employed

Hollis Hampers is a new manufacturing firm. They are gearing up for production of clothes hampers. Assets used for these clothes hampers have a value of $350,000. Hollis has a desired rate of return of 20% on assets employed. The following total costs of manufacturing and sales have been estimated:

	Hollis Hamper (per unit)
Variable costs:	$7.50
Fixed costs (based on production and sales of 20,000 units):	2.30
Total costs	$9.80

Required

1. Calculate the minimum sales price Hollis Hampers must use to reach their desired rate of return on assets employed.
2. Assume that Hollis sells numerous products of which the hamper is just one. Assume also that the assets employed have not changed and the per-unit costs given now represent all units of production. Calculate the percentage markup on cost Hollis might use to calculate sales prices if the desired rate of return on assets employed is raised to 22%. (Round to three figures.)

Problem 21.6 Pricing Evaluation of a Special Order

Ganzell Electronics produces a component part used in the manufacture of microcomputers. They are located in California and have primarily catered to the hi-tech industry in the Silicone Valley. Their manufacturing plant produces 300,000 components annually, which is 60% of capacity. Cost data for the component are as follows:

	Per unit
Direct materials	$20
Direct labor	14
Manufacturing overhead (60% fixed, based	
on manufacture of 300,000 units)	10
Shipping expense	2
Sales commission	1
	$47

Other costs of Ganzell Electronics are annual and fixed:

Selling	200,000
Administrative	100,000
Total	300,000

The component is currently being sold for $52 per unit in the Valley. Because excess capacity exists, Ganzell would like to expand sales. The president of Ganzell has just received an offer from a midwestern firm to purchase 100,000 components at a price of $48 per unit. Because the offer is from a different region, some costs will be altered. The variable shipping expense would be increased by 50%, but there would be no sales commission on this order. The fixed selling costs would also be increased by 25%.

Required

1. Using a contribution approach to pricing, determine if Ganzell should accept or reject the offer. Make your computation presentable to the president.
2. What noncost matters should also be considered before the offer is accepted or rejected?

Problem 21.7 Contribution Approach to Pricing (CMA)

E. Berg and Sons build custom-made pleasure boats that range in price from $10,000 to $250,000. For the past 30 years, Mr. Berg, Sr., has determined the selling price of each boat by estimating the costs of material, labor, a prorated portion of the overhead, and adding 20% to these estimated costs.

For example, a recent price quotation was determined as follows:

Direct materials	$ 5,000
Direct labor	8,000
Overhead	2,000
	15,000
Plus 20%	3,000
Selling price	$18,000

The overhead figure was determined by estimating total overhead costs for the year and allocating them at 25% of direct labor.

If a customer rejected the price and business was slack, Mr. Berg, Sr., would often be willing to reduce his markup to as little as 5% over estimated costs. Thus, average markup for the year is estimated at 15%.

Mr. Ed Berg, Jr., has just completed a course on pricing and believes the firm could use some of the techniques discussed in the course. The course emphasized the contribution approach to pricing, and Mr. Berg, Jr., feels that such an approach would be helpful in determining the selling prices of their custom-made pleasure boats.

Total overhead, which includes selling and administrative expenses for the year, has been estimated at $150,000, of which $90,000 is fixed and the remainder is variable in direct proportion to direct labor.

Required

1. Assume the customer in the example rejected the $18,000 quotation and also rejected a $15,750 quotation (5% markup) during a slack period. The customer countered with a $15,000 offer.
   a. What is the difference in net income for the year between accepting or rejecting the customer's offer?
   b. What is the minimum selling price Mr. Berg, Jr., could have quoted without reducing or increasing company net income?
2. What advantages does the contribution approach to pricing have over the approach used by Mr. Berg, Sr.?
3. What possible dangers are there, if any, to the contribution approach in pricing?

Problem 21.8   Transfer Pricing

For several years the Yardbird Company has operated a washing machine division. The division uses 40,000 pumps annually in its production. They have been purchasing the pumps from an independent supplier for $20. This year Yardbird acquired a pump division.

The new pump division produces a pump that fits the specifications of the washing machine division. In the past these pumps have been sold on the market for $22 apiece. The costs of producing the pump are:

Direct materials	$ 7
Direct labor	6
Variable overhead	3
Fixed overhead[a]	2
Total cost per unit	$18

[a]Based on total capacity of 120,000 units.

The pump division is presently selling 80,000 units per year. Sales discussions have begun between the two divisions, which are treated as separate profit centers.

Required

1. If you were the manager of the pump division, would you be willing to meet the washing machine division's price of $20 per unit? What would be the minimum price you would accept to supply the washing machine division's need and not hurt your division's results?
2. Should the pump division be required to accept the $20 per-unit price from the washing machine division for the good of Yardbird as a whole? Explain.

3. Suppose the pump division agrees to supply all the internal pump needs, but requires a price be set at $22 apiece. How will accepting this price affect the following?
   a. The pump division
   b. The washing machine division
   c. Yardbird Company as a whole
4. Suggest a transfer pricing policy other than described in requirements 2 and 3 that would be equitable for both divisions. Show your computations.
5. Assume instead that the pump division is already selling 120,000 units externally. If the pump division is required by Yardbird management to sell 40,000 units to the washing machine division, how would the operating income of Yardbird Company be affected?

Problem 21.9 Transfer Pricing

Consider the following independent situations:

1. Division S manufactures product D. Costs and revenue data for product D are as follows:

External sales price per unit	$50
Variable costs per unit	38
Fixed costs per unit (based on capacity)	6
Division S capacity in units	30,000

   Division S is currently producing and selling all 30,000 units of product D annually. The home office has approached the division S manager and requested that they supply division T with 5,000 units of product E. To make room for production of product E, division S must cut back by a third production of D to 20,000. Division S has estimated the following costs of product E:

Variable costs per unit	$66
Fixed costs per unit	12

   Division S will use the same equipment and personnel for both products. What transfer price should division S charge division T for each unit of product E?

2. Division M has only one product. Its cost and revenue data are as follows:

External sales price per unit	$60
Variable costs per unit	40
Fixed costs per unit (based on capacity)	10
Capacity in units	18,000

   At present, division M produces and sells at capacity to outside customers. If they were to sell instead to division O, $3 can be trimmed off the variable unit cost. Division O currently is supplied by an outside producer at a unit cost of $56. What price should be used for any sales to division O of M's product from an overall company point of view?

3. Refer to part 2 above. Would you expect the proposed transaction to take place? Explain your reasoning. What circumstances would reverse your expectations?

Problem 21.10   Transfer Pricing

The yellow division of Laboratory Products Incorporated completes the final steps in the company's process. The yellow division has as its sole supplier of an intermediate product the red division of Laboratory Products. Due to the highly technical nature of the product, red division's costs are essentially fixed. Production and costs are as follows:

Units per Day	Total Costs per Day
1,000	$250
2,000	300
3,000	350
4,000	400

(The minimum cost per day is $250 and each increment of 1,000 units beyond the first 1,000 units costs an additional $50.)

The red division has set its price at $.20 per unit. This price is found to be the optimal price.

The yellow division adds its own costs in completing production. Their divisional costs are as follows:

Units of Output	Total Cost of Output
1,000	$ 625
2,000	750
3,000	875
4,000	1,000

(Any output up to 1,000 units costs $625 in the yellow division. For each additional 1,000 units output, the cost increases $125.)

The final product is sold by the yellow division to external customers. Because sales volume increases only if price is decreased or more is spent on sales promotion, the marginal revenue decreases as sales increase. Estimates of sales show:

Sales in Units	Net Revenue at Sales Level
1,000	$ 875
2,000	1,325
3,000	1,650
4,000 ·	1,850
5,000	2,000
6,000	2,000

Required

1. Prepare a schedule of revenues, costs (including transfer costs), and net income at varying levels of output for the yellow division.
2. From your answer to requirement 1, locate yellow division's maximum net income. What are red division's and Laboratory Products' net incomes at this level?
3. If you were to combine the two divisions into one investment and profit center, the results may differ. Repeat requirement 1 after combining the red and yellow divisions into one profit center. What is the maximum net income now?
4. Compare the overall net income results for Laboratory Products found in requirements 2 and 3. Why do they differ? Which transfer pricing policy would assist in maximizing overall company profits when red and yellow are to be maintained as separate investment and profit centers?

CAPITAL BUDGETING: PART I

OUTLINE

Acquisitions of property, plant, and equipment are among the most important decisions made by management because of their long-term impact on the company. Equipment may last as long as fifteen to twenty years and buildings commonly last thirty to fifty years. An error in the acquisition of one of these assets affects not only the current year but the ensuing years as well. Occasionally, a company is not able to recover from a bad decision in acquiring one of these capital assets. Buildings and equipment are often specialized, and the only way the original investment can be recovered is through normal use in business operations.

The analytical techniques and tools available to help make these capital investment decisions is the topic of this chapter. This chapter also identifies what capital budgeting is and explains the alternative capital budgeting procedures commonly used, with greater emphasis on those techniques that help management choose the best alternative. After completing this chapter you should be able to:

1. define capital budgeting.
2. use each of the following techniques in making capital budgeting decisions:
   a. Net present value
   b. Internal rate of return
   c. Payback
   d. Accounting rate of return
3. describe the strengths and weaknesses of each of the above methods.

INTRODUCTION TO CAPITAL BUDGETING

Capital budgeting is the process used to identify whether or not a capital investment will be profitable or to select from a variety of capital investment alternatives those that will be the most profitable. **Capital assets,** more commonly referred to as fixed assets, are generally the larger or more prominent assets of the entity. They are long-term assets, such as buildings, machinery, or a tract of land, that are relatively durable and can be used repeatedly in the production of goods and services. Budgeting, you will recall, is a plan of operations based on estimates of the future. The master budget includes an itemized allotment of funds for the future period, including an allocation for capital assets. Therefore, *capital budgeting refers to the allocation of money for the acquisition or maintenance of a company's fixed assets.*

There are many types of capital budgeting decisions. Among the most common are the following:

1. Acquisition of new equipment to reduce operating costs through increased mechanization
2. Construction of a new factory or warehouse to increase capacity or reduce dependence on an outside supplier
3. Replacement of an old machine with a new machine to do the same job (which is complicated somewhat by the fact that the new machine may have more capacity, cost less to operate, and improve quality)

Cash Flow Orientation

The philosophy behind investments in capital assets is no different from any other investment. For example, a primary objective of an investment in stock is to increase wealth. An investment is considered to be a good investment when the cash received through dividends and final sale of the stock returns the original investment *and* provides a return on the investment.

The objective of investing in capital assets is to obtain cash by providing goods and services to customers or by saving cash that is currently being paid to provide those same goods and services. A good investment is also made when the cash earned or saved

Figure 22.1   Investment characteristics of capital assets

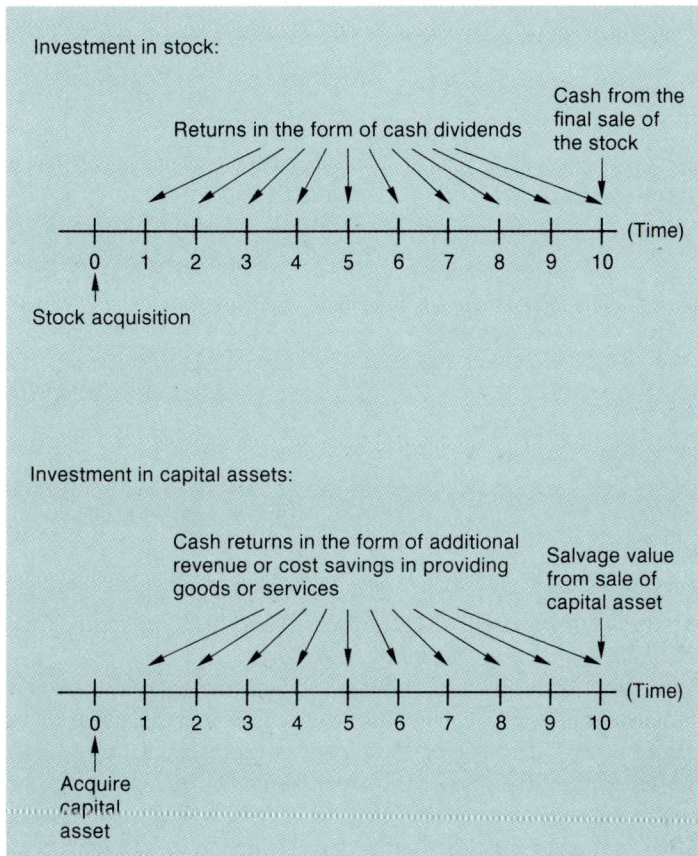

is enough to return the original investment and provide a competitive return on the investment. Figure 22.1 shows a comparison of the cash flows associated with investments in stock and capital assets.

The same type of analysis is relevant for all investment proposals. The important assumptions and criteria of the analysis include the following:

1. Each investment alternative is considered as a separate project.
2. The cash that is paid for the investment is compared with the cash that it returns to evaluate its desirability.
3. The entire life of the investment must be considered.
4. Each investment alternative should be able to return its original investment in cash and provide an adequate return on the money invested.

Note that the cash flow orientation of capital budgeting is different from the accrual concept followed in financial accounting. The concept of revenue recognition under the accrual basis of accounting requires concentrating on the earning process rather than the timing of cash receipts. Therefore, revenue is recognized when it is earned and expenses, including depreciation, are matched with the revenues they generate. Capital budgeting ignores revenue recognition and matching concepts and considers the cash receipts

---

Figure 22.2   Capital budgeting versus accrual accounting

Organizational life

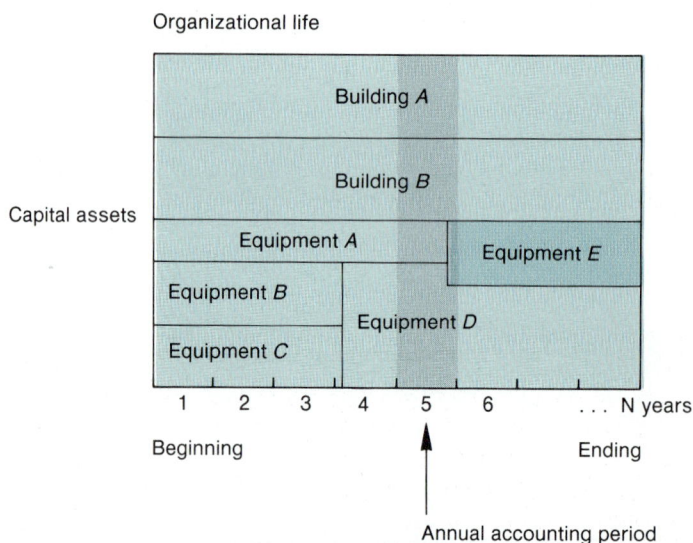

and cash disbursements associated with a project. Therefore, *the entire focus of capital budgeting is on the amounts and timing of cash flows.*

The differences between capital budgeting and the accrual concepts of financial accounting are shown in figure 22.2, which shows the life of an organization and the assets that the organization uses. The life of each asset is represented on the horizontal axis. Suppose that we are in the fifth year of the organization's life. For financial reporting we attempt to measure net income by identifying the revenues that these assets provide during the year and by matching the expenses incurred in generating those revenues. Because the fixed assets are used to generate revenues, a portion of the original cost is charged to expense through an acceptable depreciation method. The relevant time period and data for this analysis is identified by the shaded portion of figure 22.2 representing the annual accounting period for year 5.

Notice that equipment *E* was acquired during year 5. The decision to acquire it was a capital budgeting decision. The shaded portion of equipment *E* shows the relevant time period and data for the capital budgeting decision to consider the desirability of purchasing that piece of equipment. The purchase price of the equipment was compared to the cash flows it is expected to provide over its useful life, which may be 20 to 30 years long, to see if there was an adequate return on the investment. The difference in focus of the capital budgeting decision from the annual accounting report is shown by the two shaded areas in figure 22.2. The procedures used to determine the adequacy of the return will be explained later, but first we need to review the concept of cash flows.

Charting Cash Inflows and Outflows

Cash that a company receives or saves as a result of a capital investment are called *cash inflows,* whereas the money that is spent in acquiring, maintaining, or operating the asset is a *cash outflow.* Cash inflows and outflows are generally identified as one of the following three types:

1. Cash outflow associated with the initial investment. The initial investment is made at the start of the project life. If the life of an investment is represented

on a time line, time period zero generally represents the beginning of the capital investment project. Suppose that equipment E in the previous example costs $100,000. The cash outflow associated with the initial investment can be charted on our time line as follows:

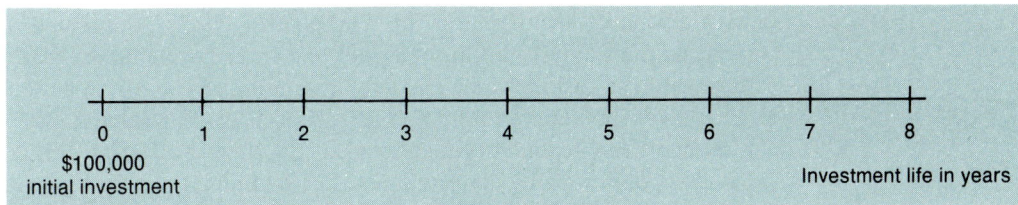

2. Net cash flows from operating the asset over its useful life. The operation of a capital asset generally results in both cash inflows and outflows. The term "cash inflows" is used in a broad sense to include both *cash revenues* as well as *cash savings*. Cash outflows refer to the actual costs of operating and maintaining the asset. The *cash inflows and outflows from operating the asset are generally netted together to provide an annual net cash inflow or outflow from operating a project.*

Equipment E will be used to produce one of the existing products and a new product. The new product will provide $16,000 of additional sales each year. Direct material and labor for the product will cost $10,000 annually. In addition, there will be a net reduction of one direct laborer on the existing product, thus saving $8,500 in cash that would have to be paid to the worker if the equipment is not acquired. The cash outlay for electricity, repairs, maintenance, and other overhead are expected to be $2,000 per year. The net cash flows resulting from the operation of equipment E are $12,500.

Revenue	$16,000
Direct costs	(10,000)
Direct labor	8,500
Overhead	(2,000)
Net cash inflow	$12,500

These are added to the time line as follows:

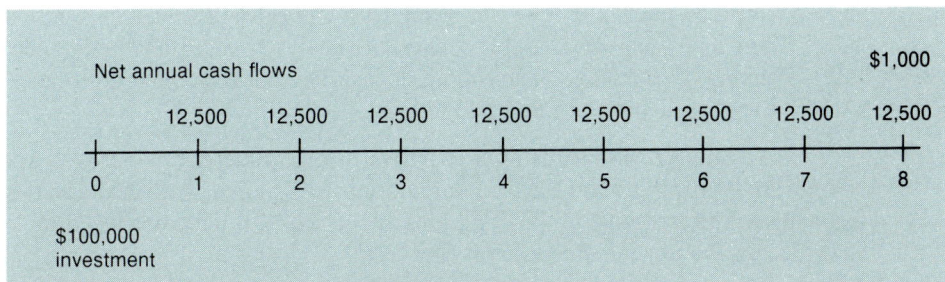

Notice in the example above that depreciation is not included. Recall that depreciation is the allocation of the original investment over its useful life in an attempt to correctly match expenses with revenues. Because capital budgeting is cash-flow oriented, the entire initial investment is considered as an outflow at time period zero. Ignoring income taxes, there is no cash flow associated with depreciation, so it is excluded from our analysis. Chapter 23 explains the effect income tax has on capital budgeting decisions and how depreciation affects the payment of income taxes.

Technically it could be argued that because the cash flows are expected to occur evenly throughout the year they should be shown on the time line at a mid-year point rather than at a year-end point. However, this would complicate our analysis, because present and future value tables commonly assume that the cash flow occurs at the beginning or end of the period. Using a mid-year point would require a different set of present value tables for capital budgeting techniques that consider the time value of money. Also, expected cash flows are only estimates. The additional precision provided by using a mid-year timing of cash flow is not felt to be justified given the lack of precision involved in estimating cash flows. Therefore, all capital budgeting techniques assume that cash flows occur at the end of each year.

3. Salvage value of the capital asset at the end of its useful life. Most capital assets can be sold for a nominal amount at the end of their useful life. The cash provided is an inflow and should be considered in the analysis.

Suppose that equipment E can be sold for $1,000 at the end of eight years. The time line and the related cash flows from equipment E will look as follows:

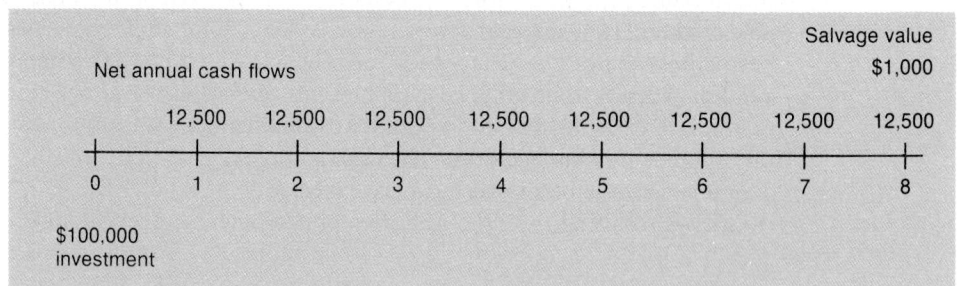

									Salvage value
	Net annual cash flows								$1,000
	12,500	12,500	12,500	12,500	12,500	12,500	12,500	12,500
0	1	2	3	4	5	6	7	8

$100,000 investment

Charting the cash flows for equipment E as shown above can be most useful in setting up the relevant information for a capital budgeting decision. It is customary to put cash outflows *below* the line representing the years of useful life of the investment. The annual net cash inflows from operations are recorded *above* the time line along with any salvage value. This type of cash flow analysis is most useful because it shows not only the amounts, but also the timing of cash flows. The timing of cash flows is very important in several of the approaches to capital budgeting.

A "tabular format" is an alternative to the "time line" approach and is more convenient in making many of the computations associated with the capital budgeting techniques. The amounts, timing, and identity of the cash flows are listed in columns as shown below for the equipment E proposal:

Cash Flow for Equipment *E* Proposal

Type	Timing	Amount
Initial investment	Now	$100,000
Net cash inflows	Years 1–8	12,500 per year
Salvage value	Year 8	1,000

The tabular approach will be used throughout this chapter.

CAPITAL BUDGETING TECHNIQUES

There are many techniques used in capital budgeting decisions. The various techniques can be broadly classified into the following four categories:

1. Net present value
2. Internal rate of return
3. Payback period
4. Accounting rate of return

Capital budgeting decisions usually take one of two forms—**screening decisions** in which one investment alternative is being considered and the objective is to know if it is a desirable investment or **preference decisions** in which several alternatives are being considered and the objective is to select from the competing alternatives the ones that are most profitable.

Net Present Value

The **net present value** method is generally considered to be the most accurate technique for capital budgeting decisions because it considers the time value of money, allows for an adjustment for risk, and provides a measure of the investment's profitability. Both amount and timing of cash flows is important because of the time value of money. Money received today is more valuable than money that will be received several years in the future. Money on hand today can be invested to earn a return that compounds with time. Hence, *an investment opportunity that promises early returns is more desirable than one that provides late returns.*[1]

The information that must be collected to use the net present value method are the *cash outflow* associated with the *acquisition,* the net *cash inflows* associated with annual operations, and the *estimated salvage value.* In addition, a minimum desired rate of return or a **cut-off rate** must be selected. Other names for the cut-off rate include "cost of capital" or "hurdle rate." This rate of return is generally specified by management and identifies a *minimum level of profitability that must be achieved by the investment.* The process by which it is selected and its computation are discussed in chapter 23.

Analysis of a Single Investment Alternative   The net present value of a proposed investment is computed by subtracting the present value of the cash outflows from the present value of the cash inflows. The investment proposal is desirable at the specified rate of return when the *net present value is greater than or equal to zero.* A positive net present value means that the investment rate of return is greater than the minimum desired rate of return. A net present value of zero means that the investment rate of return equals the minimum desired rate of return. A negative net present value indicates that the rate of return on the capital investment is less than management's cut-off rate. Therefore, it is an undesirable investment at the specified rate of return.

Example: Chapman Incorporated is considering the expansion of its product line. This expansion will require the acquisition of new and rather expensive equipment, called TR1. The equipment costs $250,000 and will have a useful life of seven years with $20,000 salvage value. It is expected that the annual net cash inflows from operations will be $70,000. Will the proposed expansion be profitable if Chapman has a minimum desired rate of return of 20% for this type of capital investment?

---

[1]It is assumed that you have had experience in working with present and future value concepts. You should understand the difference between present value and future value and be able to compute the present value or future value of a dollar amount or of an annuity from present and future value tables. The appendix at the end of this chapter reviews each of these concepts. A quick review may be helpful at this point.

Solution: The cash flows are summarized below:

Type	Timing	Amount
Investment	Now	$250,000
Net cash inflows	Years 1–7	70,000 per year
Salvage value	Year 7	20,000
Desired rate of return		20%

The net present value is computed as follows:

Present Value of Cash Inflows

Net cash from operations		
($70,000 × 3.605)	$252,350	
Salvage value		
($20,000 × .279)	5,580	
Total		$257,930

Present Value of Cash Outflows

Initial investment		
($250,000 × 1.0)		250,000
Net present value		$ 7,930

Decision: The investment proposal is desirable at a 20% minimum rate of return.

Notice in the solution above that the present values of the cash inflows and outflows are computed by multiplying the dollar amounts by the present value factors obtained from the present value tables in the appendix at the end of this chapter. The present value of the cash outflows is subtracted from the present value of the cash inflows for the project's net present value. The positive net present value of $7,930 indicates that its rate of return exceeds 20% and that it is a desirable investment.

The minimum desired rate of return is very important in determining the desirability of the investment. A slightly different rate of return may change the results.

Example: Suppose that Chapman Incorporated in the example above specified a 22% desired minimum rate of return. Is the investment desirable at this rate?

Solution: The net present value is computed using a 22% interest rate.

Present Value of Cash Inflows

Net cash from operations		
($70,000 × 3.416)	$239,120	
Salvage value		
(20,000 × .249)	4,980	
Total		$244,100

Present value of cash outflows:

Initial investment		
($250,000 × 1.0)		250,000
Net present value		($ 5,900)

Decision: Reject the proposal at a 22% cut-off rate.

The above analysis has considered only one investment alternative and the investment is considered desirable if the net present value is positive at the desired minimum rate of return.

Analysis of Multiple Investment Alternatives   When two or more investment alternatives are being considered it is a preference decision. The net present value of each investment is computed using the minimum rate of return. The one with the highest net present value is most profitable as long as their cost and life are equal. When their cost is not equal, a *profitability index* is computed by dividing the present value of the cash flows by the initial investment.

$$\text{Profitability index} = \frac{\text{Present value of cash flows}}{\text{Initial investment}}$$

The alternative with the highest profitability index is generally the most desirable, because it provides the *highest return per dollar of investment*. The profitability index does not identify profitability in an absolute sense, but profitability relative to the amount invested.

Example: Suppose Chapman Incorporated, referred to in the previous example, is content with a 20% minimum rate of return and that they have two other alternatives—equipment TR2 and TR3—for producing the new product. TR2 also costs $250,000, is slightly cheaper to operate, but has no salvage value. Annual net cash flows from operations are expected to be $71,000 per year. Cash flows are shown below:

Cash Flows for TR2

Type	Timing	Amount
Investment	Now	$250,000
Net cash inflows	Years 1–7	71,000 per year
Desired rate of return		20%

TR3 costs only $221,500, has no salvage value, but repair and maintenance costs are expected to increase each year over the life of the asset. The expected net cash flows are shown below:

Cash Flows for TR3

Type	Timing	Amount
Investment	Now	$221,500
Not cash inflows	Year 1	75,000
	Year 2	70,000
	Year 3	65,000
	Year 4	60,000
	Year 5	55,000
	Year 6	50,000
	Year 7	45,000
Desired rate of return		20%

Which of the three equipment proposals is most profitable?

Solution: The computation of the net present values is shown in figure 22.3. The net present value and profitability index are shown below for each alternative.

Equipment	Net Present Value	Profitability Index	
TR1	$7,930	1.032	($257,930 ÷ $250,000)
TR2	5,955	1.024	($255,955 ÷ $250,000)
TR3	7,525	1.034	($229,025 ÷ $221,500)

The net present value can be used to compare TR1 and TR2 because they both require the same initial investment. The higher net present value for TR1 indicates that it is more profitable than TR2. However, it is not valid to compare the net present values of TR1 and TR3 because their initial investments are different. As the profitability index shows, TR3 is a better investment than TR1. Even though the net present value is lower, it provides a greater return on the dollars invested than TR1.

Figure 22.3   Computation of net present values for investment alternatives of Chapman, Inc.

TR2: Present value of cash inflows:
    Net cash from operations
        ($71,000 × 3.605) $255,955
    Present value of cash outflows:
      Initial investment
        ($250,000 × 1.0)   250,000
    Net present value $ 5,955

TR3: Present value of cash inflows:
    Net cash from operations

Year 1 ($75,000 × .833)	$62,475	
Year 2 ($70,000 × .694)	48,580	
Year 3 ($65,000 × .579)	37,635	
Year 4 ($60,000 × .482)	28,920	
Year 5 ($55,000 × .402)	22,110	
Year 6 ($50,000 × .335)	16,750	
Year 7 ($45,000 × .279)	12,555	
Total		$229,025

    Present value of cash outflows:
      Initial investment
        ($221,500 × 1.0)   221,500
    Net present value $ 7,525

Incremental versus Total Cost Approach   An incremental approach or a total cost approach can be used to chart cash flows when only two competing proposals are being considered. The *total cost approach* has been used in the examples above. It *considers each proposal separately and charts the relevant cash flows for each*. The net present value is computed using the cut-off rate.

Under the *incremental approach* the *added cost of investing* in the most expensive proposal is charted as the initial investment, and the *additional revenues* and *salvage value* that it provides are charted as the annual net cash inflow. The net present value of these cash flows should equal the difference between the net present value of the competing alternatives under the total cost approach.

To illustrate the two approaches let's assume that Midway Company is trying to decide between purchasing or leasing a warehouse. Either way they will have use of it for its entire remaining life of five years. The relevant cash flows on a total cost approach are shown below.

Cash Flows for Purchase and Lease

Type	Timing	Purchase Amounts	Lease Amounts
Initial investment	Now	$60,000	$11,000
Net cash inflows	Years 1–5	23,000 per year	5,000 per year
Salvage value	5	10,000	–0–
Desired rate of return		20%	20%

The net present value for each proposal is computed and the difference between them is $8,858.

Present Value of Cash Inflows

	Lease	*Purchase*
($5,000 × 2.991)	$14,955	
($23,000 × 2.991)		$68,793
($10,000 × .402)		4,020
Total	14,955	72,813
Initial investment	11,000	60,000
Net present value	$ 3,955	$12,813
Difference		$8,858

The cash flows can be restructured as follows for an incremental approach. The cash flows for the lease option are subtracted from the purchase option—$49,000 initial investment is $60,000–$11,000, $18,000 annual cash flow is $23,000–$5,000, and $10,000 salvage value is $10,000–$0.

Incremental Cash Flows for Purchase Rather Than Lease

Type	*Timing*	*Amount*
Initial investment	Now	$49,000
Net cash inflows	Years 1–5	18,000 per year
Salvage value	Year 5	10,000
Desired rate of return		20%

The net present value is computed using the same cut-off rate with the same $8,858 difference.

Present Value of Cash Inflows

($18,000 × 2.991)	$53,838
($10,000 × .402)	4,020
Total	57,858
Initial investment	49,000
Net present value	$ 8,858

The difficulty in using the incremental approach is in knowing whether the additional net present value is worth the additional investment. In this case Midway Company is investing an additional $49,000 for an increased net present value of $8,858. Because the net present value is positive, we can conclude that the return on the additional investment is greater than the 20% cut-off rate, but we need to go back to the total cost approach to identify which proposal is most profitable. The profitability index shows that the lease option is most profitable.

Profitability Index

Purchase	
($72,813 ÷ $60,000)	1.21
Lease	
($14,955 ÷ $11,000)	1.36

The incremental approach is most useful when comparing two investment proposals with equal investments but unequal and uneven cash flows over their useful lives.

Figure 22.4 summarizes the objective, informational requirements, computation format, and decision rules for the net present value method.

Figure 22.4   Net present value

Objective: Determine whether the present value of future cash flows at a desired rate of return will be greater than or less than the cost of the proposed investment.

Informational requirements:
1. Initial investment
2. Annual cash inflows
3. Minimum desired rate of return

Computation format:
Present value of cash inflows:
(Cash flow) × (Present value factor) $ _____

Present value of cash outflows:
(Initial investment) $ _____

Net present value $ _____

Decision rules:
Single investment alternative: Accept the investment proposal when the net present value is greater than or equal to zero.

Multiple investment alternatives: The alternative with the highest profitability index is the most profitable.

$$\text{Profitability index} = \frac{\text{Present value of cash inflows}}{\text{Initial investment}}$$

Strengths and Weaknesses of Net Present Value   The major strength of the net present value method is that it considers both the amount and timing of all cash flows in measuring an investment's rate of return against the minimum rate of return specified by management. A positive net present value indicates that it is profitable. Even though it does not identify an exact rate of profitability, it does measure profitability compared to the cut-off rate.

Another advantage of the net present value method is the minimum amount of computation required to identify investment profitability. Given a desired cut-off rate, only one series of calculations is required to compute the net present value or the profitability index. This is much more efficient than the trial-and-error method often required under the internal rate of return method.

For a person unfamiliar with present value concepts this method may be difficult to work with and the concept of positive versus negative net present values may not make much sense. Instruction in present value and future value computations is relatively recent in formal business education. People who have not had a college education or who received their education several years ago may be unfamiliar with present value concepts. Even those managers who have had some education in present value concepts seem to have difficulty understanding net present values and interpreting their meaning in capital investment decisions. An internal rate of return seems to be more meaningful to them.

Internal Rate of Return

Several names are used to describe this technique including internal rate of return, discount yield, time adjusted rate of return, and compound return on investment. We will use the title internal rate of return because it is fairly descriptive of the results and because it is a common title.

The *initial cash investment* and the *estimated net cash inflows, including salvage value,* over the life of the investment are the items of information required for this method.

The **internal rate of return** is the interest rate that equates the present value of future cash inflows with the initial cash investment. Under this method the *net present value is specified as zero* and the *objective* of the computation *is to identify the interest rate that results in a zero net present value.* A minimum desired rate of return is not required for the computation; nevertheless, management must have some minimum rate in mind to compare with the internal rate to determine the desirability of the investment. The project is *desirable* as long as the *internal rate of return equals or exceeds the cut-off rate.* From a profitability standpoint, any project whose internal rate of return is below the desired minimum should be rejected.

Single Investment Alternative with Equal Annual Cash Flows   The internal rate of return method is easiest to apply when the investment alternative has equal annual cash flows and no salvage value. An equal annual cash flow is an annuity, the present value of which can be computed by multiplying the amount of the annuity by the present value factor. When the net present value is specified as zero, the relationship between the present value of the cash flows and the initial investment can be manipulated as follows:

(Annual cash flow) × (Annuity factor) − Initial investment = 0

Present value of annual cash flows

Net present value specified as zero

(Annual cash flow) × (Annuity factor) = Initial investment

$$\text{Annuity factor} = \frac{\text{Initial investment}}{\text{Annual cash flows}}$$

Given the initial investment and annual cash flows, the annuity factor can be computed using the above equation. If the annuity factor and the years of useful life are known, the internal rate of return can be determined from the table of present values of an annuity.

Example: Dean Incorporated is considering the acquisition of equipment that will cost $100,000 and have a useful life of 5 years with zero salvage value. The equipment will be used to manufacture a subassembly that has been purchased from an outside supplier. Annual net cash inflows (savings) from manufacturing this part internally are expected to be $33,400. Management feels that investment proposals of this type should provide at least a 23% rate of return in order to enhance the overall profitability of the company. What is the internal rate of return on this project and should the equipment be acquired?

Solution: The annuity factor that will equate the present value of the cash inflows with the investment is 2.994.

$$\text{Annuity factor} = \frac{\$100,000}{\$33,400} = 2.994$$

The interest rate associated with this factor is obtained from the table of present values of an annuity by locating the row of annuity factors corresponding with the useful life of the project. Because the equipment has a useful life of 5 years, go down the column of periods to 5 and across the table until an annuity factor is located that is equal to 2.994. The desired factor of

2.994 lies between 3.127 at 18% and 2.991 at 20%. Because the annuity factor of 2.991 is so close to the desired factor, we can say that the internal rate of return is slightly under 20%. Management should therefore reject the equipment proposal because it does not meet their minimum expectation of 23%.

Present and future value tables can be purchased which have periods from 1 to 10,000 and interest rates that vary by each 1/8% from 1/8% to 99 7/8%. The internal rate of return can always be obtained from these tables without any interpolation. Interpolation, however, may be required when using summary tables as presented in the appendix and when the annuity factors in the table are not close to the specified annuity factor. Even then, the answer may be obvious and interpolation may not be necessary. For example, if the cut-off rate is 16% and the internal rate of return is between 20% and 22%, interpolation will not improve the decision-making process.

Interpolation is a process of estimating an intermediate interest rate among those listed on the table. The relative position of the desired annuity factor to those listed on the table is used to estimate the interest rate.

Example:　Suppose that Dean Incorporated in the example above estimates that annual cash flows will be $26,000. What is the internal rate of return associated with this investment proposal?

Solution:　The desired annuity factor of 3.846 ($100,000 ÷ $26,000) lies between 3.993 at 8% and 3.791 at 10%. The following computation illustrates the interpolation process.

Interest Rates	Annuity Factor	Difference
8%	3.993 ⎱	
?	3.846 ⎰	.147
10%	3.791 ⎰	.055
Total　　2%		.202

The interpolated interest rate is:

$$8\% + [(.147 \div .202) \times 2\%] = 8\% + 1.46\% = 9.46\%$$

Notice that the desired annuity factor of 3.846 is 72.7% (.147 ÷ .202) of the way between 3.993 and 3.791. Therefore, 72.7% of the difference between 8% and 10% is added to the 8% rate to estimate the internal rate of return.

Single Investment Alternative with Unequal Annual Cash Flows　A trial-and-error approach must be used to determine the internal rate of return when the annual cash flows are not equal. The process involves selecting an estimated internal rate of return and using it to compute the net present value. If the net present value is *positive*, a *higher rate is selected*. When the net present value is *negative*, a *lower rate is selected*. The net present value is again computed under the newly selected interest rate and the process continues until the net present value is zero. Interpolation may be required when the actual internal rate of return is not equal to one of the interest rates for which present value factors are listed on the table.

Example:　Dean Incorporated is also considering the acquisition of a semi-truck and trailer to be used to haul their raw materials from the supplier and their finished product to the retail outlets. The combined cost of the rig is $90,000 and the expected cash inflows (savings) over its useful life along with the salvage value are shown:

Figure 22.5   Trial-and-error calculation for internal rate of return

Present value of cash inflows:

Year	Amount	Present Value at 24%		Present Value at 20%		Present Value at 22%	
1	$40,000	(.806)	$32,240	(.833)	$33,320	(.820)	$32,800
2	30,000	(.650)	19,500	(.694)	20,820	(.672)	20,160
3	30,000	(.524)	15,720	(.579)	17,370	(.551)	16,530
4	20,000	(.423)	8,460	(.482)	9,640	(.451)	9,020
5	30,000	(.341)	10,230	(.402)	12,060	(.370)	11,100
Total			$86,150		$93,210		$89,610

Present value of cash outflows:

($90,000 × 1.0)	$90,000	$90,000	$90,000
Net present value	($ 3,850)	$ 3,210	($ 390)

	Interest Rate	Net Present Value	Difference
Interpolation:	20%	$3,210	
			$3,210
	?	–0–	
			390
	22%	($ 390)	
Difference	2%		$3,600

Internal rate of return = 20% + [(3,212 ÷ 3,600) × 2%] = 21.78%

Cash Flows for Semi-Truck and Trailer

Type	Timing	Amount
Initial investment	Now	$90,000
Net annual savings	Year 1	40,000
	Year 2	30,000
	Year 3	30,000
	Year 4	20,000
	Year 5	15,000
Salvage value	Year 5	15,000

What is the internal rate of return on this proposal and is it a desirable investment alternative?

Solution: First pick an estimated internal rate of return and compute the net present value. Suppose we first picked 24%. We would compute the net present value of ($3,850) as shown in figure 22.5. A negative net present value indicates that the rate selected is too high, so a lower rate is selected, say 20%. At this rate a positive net present value of $3,210 is computed, so we know that the actual rate lies between 20% and 24%. A third rate of 22% is used and the net present value is ($390). The negative amount indicates that the internal rate of return lies between 20% and 22%.

Without interpolation we would say that it is slightly below 22%. Interpolation indicates that it is 21.78%.

Multiple Investment Alternatives   The internal rate of return is a measure of profitability and it can be used to select from among alternative investment proposals. Other

---

Figure 22.6   Internal rate of return

Objective: Compute an interest rate that equates the present value of the projected future net cash flows with the initial investment.

Informational requirements:

    1. Initial investment
    2. Annual cash flows

Computation format:

    1. Equal annual cash flows: Compute the annuity factor by dividing the initial investment by the annual cash flows and locate the internal rate of return from the present value tables that correspond with the computed annuity factor and the years of useful life of the proposal.
    2. Unequal annual cash flows: Through trial and error using various interest rates, identify the interest rate that provides a net present value of zero.

        Present value of cash flows:

(Cash flow) × (Present value factor)	$ _____
Initial investment	$ _____
Net present value	$ –0–

    3. Use interpolation where necessary.

Decision rules:

    Single investment alternative: Accept the investment proposal if the internal rate of return exceeds a minimum rate specified by management.

    Multiple investment alternatives: Select the investment alternative(s) with the highest internal rate of return as long as it (they) exceeds the minimum rate specified by management.

---

things being equal, *an investment alternative with the highest internal rate of return will be the most profitable* and should be selected. Let's continue to use Dean Incorporated as an example. Suppose that management feels that any investment alternatives over 18% will enhance company profitability.

    Assume the two proposals outlined above are the only ones being considered. The relevant data are summarized below. If Dean Incorporated only has enough cash to finance one project, which should it be?

Proposal	Cost	Internal Rate of Return
Manufacturing equipment	$100,000	20.0%
Truck and trailer	90,000	21.78%

    The truck and trailer will probably be selected.

    The $90,000 invested in the truck and trailer will yield 21.78%, which is higher than the 20% return on the manufacturing equipment.

    Figure 22.6 summarizes the objective, informational requirements, computation format, and decision rules for the internal rate of return method.

Strengths and Weaknesses of Internal Rate of Return   The internal rate of return method, like the net present value method, considers both the amount and timing of all cash flows over the life of the investment and adjusts them for the time value of money. A benefit of this method over the net present value method is that it computes the exact rate of the investment's profitability in the form of a percentage rate of return. Interest rates are often more meaningful to work with than net present values. This seems to be particularly true for users who have not been trained in the use of positive and negative net present values.

Weaknesses of the internal rate of return method include the following: (*a*) no consideration is given to the relative dollar size of alternative investments and (*b*) additional computations are required when using the trial-and-error approach. Needless to say, the trial-and-error approach can be tedious and time consuming when you only have a small calculator and an old set of present value tables. The advent of the computer with package software has eliminated much of the tedious computation. Mini- and microcomputers have made computer processing available to even the medium- and smaller-sized organizations.

Payback

The payback method computes a *payback period* that *is the length of time required to recover the initial investment*. This method continues to be one of the most widely used yardsticks for appraising capital investment proposals. Frequently it is used in connection with the net present value method or the internal rate of return method because of the different type of information that it provides.

The *information required* to compute payback are the *initial investment* and the *annual cash flows* from earnings or savings. Management must also have in mind a *desired payback period* they can use to determine the acceptability of the proposal. However, that is part of the decision analysis and not part of the computation.

Payback stresses risk reduction by identifying projects that have the shortest length of time during which the initial investment is outstanding. The emphasis is on cost recovery rather than profitability.

Payback Period   **Payback period** is the length of time required for the initial investment to be recovered from earnings or savings. Generally, the time value of money is not considered.

For investments with equal annual cash flows, the payback period is computed by dividing the initial investment by the annual cash inflow.

$$\text{Payback period} = \frac{\text{Initial investment}}{\text{Annual cash inflows}}$$

Example: MOC Incorporated is considering the construction of a new warehouse at a cost of $300,000. The expected useful life is 20 years with $60,000 salvage value. The new facility will provide storage space for finished products that are currently being stored at a leased facility. In addition, MOC will be able to produce the finished product at a more even rate throughout the year rather than constantly adjusting the production level to meet short-term fluctuations in demand. The expected annual cost savings from these benefits are $50,000 per year. Compute the payback period.

Solution: The initial investment will be recovered in 6.0 years, computed as follows:

$$\text{Payback period} = \frac{\$300,000}{\$50,000} = \underline{6.0 \text{ years}}$$

If the annual cash flows are not equal, they are accumulated until the cumulative amount of cash flows equals the initial investment. Just remember that the payback period is the length of time required to recover the initial investment. Interpolation may be required to determine the portion of the payback year required to recover the balance of the investment. When making the interpolation it is assumed that cash flows occur evenly throughout the year.

Example: MOC Incorporated is also considering the purchase of a $40,000 computer with an estimated useful life of 5 years and no salvage value. The computer will be used for internal accounting with any excess time being sold on a time share basis. The annual cash flows are:

Year 1	$ 9,000
Year 2	12,000
Year 3	15,000
Year 4	12,000
Year 5	5,000

What is the payback period?

Solution: The cash flows are accumulated until the initial investment is recovered. Notice that only part of the cash flows in year 4 are required for the cumulative cash flows to equal $40,000. The column "years of payback" shows the portion of the year included in the payback period. The payback period is 3.33 years.

Year	Annual Cash Flows	Cumulative Cash Flows	Years of Payback
1	$ 9,000	$ 9,000	1.00
2	12,000	21,000	1.00
3	15,000	36,000	1.00
4	12,000	40,000	.33[a]
Payback period			3.33 years

[a]Straight-line interpolation indicates that one third of year 4 is required to recover the last $4,000 ($40,000–$36,000) of the initial investment.

$$\frac{\$4,000}{\$12,000} \times 1 \text{ year} = .33 \text{ year}$$

Decision Analysis Using Payback Period When only one investment proposal is being considered, management must identify an acceptable payback period to be used as a benchmark for accepting or rejecting the proposal. *The proposal is rejected unless its payback period is within the desired length of time specified by management.*

Example: Assuming MOC Incorporated is only considering the warehouse construction project previously described and that they have a maximum payback period of 6 years for capital investment projects, should the warehouse be constructed?

Solution: The warehouse construction project would be accepted because the expected payback period of 6 years is within the maximum allowable.

When several investment proposals are being considered, the payback periods are ranked from low to high. The proposals with the *shortest payback periods are the most desirable* but only as long as they are within management's desired payback period.

Example: Assume that MOC Incorporated is considering both the warehouse and the computer projects outlined above but they only have the resources to do one of them this year. Which should they select?

Solution: Comparing their payback periods indicates that the initial investment in the computer is recovered over two years faster than the investment in the warehouse. Under the payback method the computer would probably be accepted.

Project	Payback Period
Warehouse	6 years
Computer	3⅓ years

Evaluation of the Payback Period   The objective of the payback method is not to measure profitability but to measure the amount of time necessary to generate an amount of cash inflows equal to the original cost of the asset. There is always some risk associated with future cash flows but the payback method seeks to reduce this risk as much as possible by selecting projects that return the initial investment in the shortest period of time.

This type of analysis can be useful for companies that have a poor cash position. Timely cash flows are often more critical than profit maximization for newly established or developing companies. Therefore, projects that return the initial investment quickly may be more desirable than a more profitable project that ties up money for an extended period of time.

A major weakness of the payback method is that it does not measure profitability. Remember that measuring profitability is not one of the objectives of this method. Nevertheless, decisions based on the payback period often result in minimizing profits. This can be shown by using the warehouse and computer proposals for MOC Incorporated.

The cash flows for both proposals are summarized below:

Cash Flows for Warehouse and Computer

Type	Timing	Warehouse Amount	Computer Amount
Initial investment	Now	$300,000	$40,000
Net cash flows	Years 1–20	50,000	
	Year 1		9,000
	Year 2		12,000
	Year 3		15,000
	Year 4		12,000
	Year 5		5,000
Salvage value	Year 20	60,000	
	Year 5		–0–

In order for an investment to be profitable it must return an amount greater than the initial investment. The more an investment returns after investment recovery and the quicker it is received, the more profitable the investment. However, the payback period does not consider any cash flows after recovery of the initial investment. For example, it ignores the fact that the warehouse will continue in operation 14 years after investment recovery and also ignores the $60,000 salvage value. In comparing the projects it does not recognize that the computer only provides 1⅔ years of service after investment recovery and that it has no salvage value.

The net present value method or the internal rate of return method can be used to compare the profitability of the two investments. The detail of these computations is shown in figure 22.7 and the final answers are summarized below.

Net Present Value Method @ 16%

Project	Net Present Value	Profitability Index	Internal Rate of Return
Warehouse	($490)	.998	15.97%
Computer	($4,707)	.882	10.73%

As shown by the profitability index and the internal rate of return, the warehouse is a more profitable investment than the computer, even though its payback period is almost twice as long.

Figure 22.7   Computation of net present value and internal rate of return for MOC Incorporated investment alternatives

Warehouse

Present value of cash flows at 16%:		Present value of cash flows at 14%:	
Annual ($50,000 × 5.929)	$296,450	Annual ($50,000 × 6.623)	$331,150
Salvage ($60,000 × .051)	3,060	Salvage ($60,000 × .073)	4,380
Total	$299,510	Total	$335,530
Initial investment	300,000	Initial investment	300,000
Net present value	($ 490)	Net present value	$ 35,530
Profitability index	.998	Internal rate of return	15.97%
($299,510 ÷ $300,000)		[14% + (35,530 ÷ 36,020 × 2%)]	

Computer

Present value of cash flows at 16%:			Present value of cash flows at 10%		
Year			**Year**		
1	($ 9,000 × .862)	$ 7,758	1	($ 9,000 × .909)	$ 8,181
2	($12,000 × .743)	8,916	2	($12,000 × .826)	9,912
3	($15,000 × .641)	9,615	3	($15,000 × .751)	11,265
4	($12,000 × .552)	6,624	4	($12,000 × .683)	8,196
5	($ 5,000 × .476)	2,380	5	($ 5,000 × .621)	3,105
Total		$ 35,293	Total		$ 40,659
Initial investment		40,000	Initial investment		40,000
Net present value		($ 4,707)	Net present value		$ 659
Profitability index		.882	Internal rate of return		10.73%
($35,293 ÷ $40,000)			[10% + ($659 ÷ 5,366 × 6%)]		

Another major weakness of the payback method is that it does not consider the time value of money. This can be illustrated by assuming two investment alternatives that cost $12,000 each and provide the following cash flows.

Cash Flows for Proposals A and B

Type	Timing	Proposal A Amount	Proposal B Amount
Initial investment	Now	$12,000	$12,000
Net cash flows	Year 1	–0–	4,000
	Year 2	–0–	4,000
	Year 3	12,000	4,000
	Year 4	4,000	12,000
	Year 5	4,000	–0–
	Year 6	4,000	–0–
Desired rate of return		10%	10%

Notice that both proposals have a payback period of 3 years, which would indicate an indifference in their relative desirability. If, however, we consider the time value of money, it is obvious that proposal B is much more desirable. Using the net present value method and a 10% interest rate, figure 22.8 shows that the present value of our return on proposal B is worth $4,392 ($8,876 − $4,484) more than proposal A.

Figure 22.8   Comparison of proposals with equal payback periods using net present value method

Proposal A

Present value of cash flows at 10%:

Year		
3	($12,000 × .751)	$ 9,012
4–6	[$ 4,000 × (4.355 - 2.487)]	7,472
	Total	$16,484
Initial investment		12,000
	Net present value	$ 4,484

Proposal B

Present value of cash flows at 10%:

Year		
1–3	($ 4,000 × 3.170)	$12,680
4	($12,000 × .683)	8,196
	Total	$20,876
Initial investment		12,000
	Net present value	$ 8,876

Modifications of Payback   Modifications of the payback method have been developed in an attempt to minimize the deficiencies. The modifications include payback reciprocal and present value payback.

The **payback reciprocal** method is intended to provide a measure of an investment's profitability. It is computed by dividing the annual cash flows by the initial investment.

$$\text{Payback reciprocal} = \frac{\text{Annual cash flows}}{\text{Initial investment}}$$

As long as the *useful life* of the project is *at least twice as long* as *the payback period,* the payback reciprocal will provide a reasonable estimate of the internal rate of return. However, the payback reciprocal method can only be used to evaluate investment proposals that have *equal annual cash flows.*

Let's continue to use the example of the warehouse proposal for MOC Incorporated. It has equal annual cash flows of $50,000 per year and the useful life of 20 years is more than twice the payback period of 6 years. The payback reciprocal is 16.6%.

$$\text{Payback reciprocal} = \frac{\$\ 50,000}{\$300,000} = 16.6\%$$

Notice that this is a reasonable approximation of the internal rate of return of 15.97% that we computed earlier (see fig. 22.7).

The constraints under which the payback reciprocal will provide valid results can be summarized as follows:

1. Annual cash flows must be equal in amount.
2. The useful life of the project must be at least twice as long as the payback period in order for the payback reciprocal to provide a reasonable approximation of the internal rate of return.

Figure 22.9   Warehouse proposal—MOC Inc.

Year	Annual Cash Flow	Present Value Factor	Present Value Amount	Cumulative Present Value	Years of Payback
1	$50,000	.909	$45,450	$ 45,450	1.00
2	50,000	.826	41,300	86,750	1.00
3	50,000	.751	37,550	124,300	1.00
4	50,000	.683	34,150	158,450	1.00
5	50,000	.621	31,050	189,500	1.00
6	50,000	.564	28,200	217,700	1.00
7	50,000	.513	25,650	243,350	1.00
8	50,000	.467	23,350	266,700	1.00
9	50,000	.424	21,200	287,900	1.00
10	50,000	.386	19,300	300,000	.63[a]
Present value payback					9.63 years

[a](12,100 ÷ 19,300) × 1 year = .63 or 63% of year 10 to recover the balance of the $300,000 investment.

These constraints significantly limit its usefulness. This method simply cannot be used to evaluate many proposals because they do not satisfy one or both of these constraints. Also, the payback reciprocal only approximates the internal rate of return. Remember that the internal rate of return can be easily computed when the annual cash flows are equal. Therefore, most people who understand the time value of money and know how to use the present value tables compute the internal rate of return directly rather than approximate it by the payback reciprocal method.

The **present value payback** method utilizes the time value of money concepts to compute the payback period. The present value payback period is the length of time required for the present value of the cash flows to equal the initial investment. In addition to knowing the initial investment and annual cash flows, a minimum desired rate of return must be identified. The present value of the annual cash flows is computed and accumulated until the cumulative amount is equal to the initial investment.

The present value payback period for the warehouse proposal of MOC Incorporated is computed in figure 22.9 using a minimum desired rate of return of 10%. The present value payback period is 9.63 years.

The procedure shown in figure 22.9 must be used when the annual cash flows are not equal. However, if the annual cash flows are equal, the present value payback period can be obtained from the present value of an annuity table. We want to determine the number of periods that will equate the present value of the annuity to the original investment. This can be represented in the following equation form:

Initial investment = (Annual cash flows) × (Present value factor)

Manipulating it we get:

$$\text{Present value factor} = \frac{\text{Initial investment}}{\text{Annual cash flows}}$$

The present value factor can be computed and used with the minimum desired rate of return to locate the years required to recover the initial investment. The number of years associated with the specified interest rate and computed annuity factor is the present value payback period.

Figure 22.10   Payback

Objective: Identify the period of time required for cash flows from earnings or savings to recover the initial investment.

Informational requirements:

    1. Initial investment
    2. Annual cash flows from earnings or savings

Computation format:

    1. When annual cash flows are equal:

$$\text{Payback period} = \frac{\text{Investment}}{\text{Annual cash flows}}$$

    2. When annual cash flows are not equal:
       Accumulate the annual cash flows until the cumulative amount equals the initial investment.

Decision rules:

    Single investment alternative: Accept an investment proposal if the payback period is within a limit specified by management.

    Multiple investment alternatives: Rank the payback periods from low to high and accept the proposals with the shortest payback periods as long as they are within the limit specified by management.

Modification of payback:

    1. Payback reciprocal $= \dfrac{\text{Annual cash flows}}{\text{Initial investment}}$

    2. Present value payback: The length of time for the present value of cash flows at the desired rate of return to recover the initial investment.

The present value factor for the warehouse proposal is 6.0 ($300,000 ÷ $50,000). Using the present value of an annuity table, go down the minimum desired rate of return column, which is specified by MOC Incorporated as 10%, until you come to an annuity factor of 6.0. It lies between 5.759 at 9 years and 6.145 at 10 years. Interpolation would be used to compute 9.63 years as the present value payback period.

The present value payback method utilizes present value techniques to compute the minimum life necessary for the proposal to recover the initial investment and still earn the minimum rate of return specified by management. It is related to the net present value method in that the cash flows are discounted at the desired rate of return. If the present value of all cash flows does not recover the initial investment, it is similar to a negative net present value and the project should be rejected. A present value payback period indicates a positive net present value and a profitable investment. However, this method falls short because it does not consider the amount or timing of cash flows after the present value payback period.

Figure 22.10 summarizes the objectives, computations, and major decision rules for the payback method and related modifications.

Accounting Rate of Return

The **accounting rate of return method** is also called the unadjusted rate of return, approximate rate of return, book-value rate of return, and financial statement method. Each of these titles has some merit because they describe the method. For example, this method does not adjust for the time value of money and is occasionally used to estimate the internal rate of return. Thus the titles "unadjusted" and "approximate" are descriptive of these characteristics. Also, this method is designed to provide a rate of return that is consistent with the rate of return on total assets that would be computed under the accrual basis of accounting. Hence, we have the titles "book value," "financial statement," and simply "accounting" to provide descriptions of these characteristics.

The objective of the accounting rate of return is to compute *a rate of return* on the proposed capital investment that is *consistent with the rate of return on total assets computed under the accrual basis of accounting*. The rate of return on total assets is generally computed by dividing the total assets into the net income. Under the accrual basis of accounting, the net income is net of the depreciation expense and the total assets include the book values of depreciable fixed assets.

The formula for the accounting rate of return divides the average annual net income by either the initial investment or the average investment.

$$\text{Accounting rate of return} = \frac{\text{Average annual net income}}{\text{Initial investment}}$$

or

$$\text{Accounting rate of return} = \frac{\text{Average annual net income}}{\text{Average investment}}$$

where   Average annual net income is the average annual cash flow less depreciation expense. Average investment (also called "average book value") is the initial investment plus salvage value divided by two.

In order to be consistent with the accrual concept of net income, the annual cash flows are adjusted for depreciation expense. When annual cash flows are not equal, an annual average is computed. Straight-line depreciation is used because it gives an annual average of depreciation expense for any of the depreciation methods.

No consensus has been reached among accountants about the correct denominator value for the equation. The initial investment is perhaps the most commonly used and is justified because it provides a rate of return on the incremental dollars invested in the project. The average investment method, however, is more consistent with the rate of return on total assets computed under the accrual basis of accounting. The book values of fixed assets decrease each year by the depreciation expense. An on-going business will have assets at all stages—some new, some ready for salvage, and some at mid-life. Therefore, an average investment is more consistent with the average book values of all fixed assets within an organization. Unless specified otherwise, we will use the initial investment to compute the accounting rate of return.

For capital budgeting, the denominator amount will not make any difference in the relative ranking of investment alternatives under the accounting rate of return method as long as the salvage value is zero on all projects. The rate of return on average investment will be twice the rate on the initial investment, but the relative ranking should be the same. However, if there is a salvage value on some projects, their rate of return will not double. The result may be a different ranking of investment alternatives.

Example: Kelly's Flour Mill is considering the following two investment proposals.

Mill *X*—This new mill utilizes the latest technology in mill design to cool the grinding stones. Cooling the stones keeps the flour cool and allows continuous production at a higher rate of output. The new mill will cost $60,000, will provide increased cash flow of $10,000 per year, and will last for 15 years with zero salvage value. The existing mill will be kept for back-up purposes.

Bagger—The flour is currently weighed and packaged by hand. The new bagger has the capability of weighing the flour, bagging it, and sealing the bag. It will cost $30,000 and is expected to last 10 years with $5,000 salvage value. Annual cash flows are expected to be:

Years	Amount
1–3	$4,000 per year
4–6	5,000 per year
7–10	6,000 per year

The cash flows for this investment will increase over time as production increases. The new bagger will be able to handle the increase, thus avoiding the hiring of additional manual labor.

Compute the accounting rate of return for each proposal using both (*a*) initial investment and (*b*) average investment as the denominator amount.

Solution: Using the initial investment as the denominator for our equation the following rates are computed.

Mill X

$$\text{Rate} = \frac{\$10,000 - \$4,000^a}{\$60,000} = 10\%$$

^{a}Depreciation expense: $\dfrac{\$60,000}{15 \text{ years}} = \$4,000 \text{ per year}$

Bagger

$$\text{Rate} = \frac{\$5,600^b - \$2,500^c}{\$30,000} = 10.3\%$$

^{b}Average annual cash flows:

Years		
1–3	(3 × $4,000)	$12,000
4–6	(3 × $5,000)	15,000
7–10	(4 × $6,000)	24,000
Salvage value		5,000
Total		$56,000
Divide by years of useful life		÷ 10
Average annual cash flow		$ 5,600 per year

^{c}Depreciation expense: $\dfrac{\$30,000 - \$5,000}{10 \text{ years}} = \$2,500 \text{ per year}$

Using the average investment as the denominator for our equation, the following rates are computed.

Mill X

$$\text{Rate} = \frac{\$10,000 - \$4,000}{\$30,000^d} = 20\%$$

^{d}Average investment: $\dfrac{\$60,000 + 0}{2} = \$30,000$

Bagger

$$\text{Rate} = \frac{\$5,600 - \$2,500}{\$17,500^e} = 17.7\%$$

^{e}Average investment: $\dfrac{\$30,000 + \$5,000}{2} = \$17,500$

Decision Making Using Accounting Rate of Return   Management must identify a *minimum acceptable rate of return* that can be used as a benchmark to determine the desirability of an investment proposal. One argument in favor of using an accounting rate of return is that management can look to existing financial statements to compute a rate of return that is being earned on existing assets. If the proposed investments provide a rate of return higher than the existing rate, the profitability of the company would be enhanced by the new investment.

When *one investment alternative* is being considered, it is a desirable investment if the *accounting rate of return equals or exceeds the minimum rate* specified by management. When *several alternatives* are being considered, their accounting rates of return are ranked from high to low. Those with the *highest rates are most desirable* as long as they equal or exceed the minimum rate specified by management.

Management of Kelly's Flour Mill has specified a 10% minimum rate of return on capital investment decisions using the initial investment as the denominator amount. Assuming that mill *X* is the only proposal being considered, it would be acceptable because its rate of return equals the minimum rate specified by management.

If both the bagger and mill X proposals are being considered and only one proposal could be funded, the Bagger proposal would be considered more desirable because of its slightly higher rate of return. Notice, however, that mill X is more desirable when an average investment is used as the denominator amount.

| | Accounting Rate of Return | |
Project	Initial Investment	Average Investment
Mill X	10%	20%
Bagger	10.3%	17.7%

Strengths and Weaknesses of the Accounting Rate of Return   The accounting rate of return is a measure of profitability that is consistent with profitability measures normally computed from accrual basis financial statements. It not only provides a measure that can be used to evaluate investment proposals, but similar computations can be made on the actual results of operations over the life of the asset using the accounting numbers generated by normal accounting procedures to compare actual results with the planned results. Thus, it is useful for both decision analysis and for subsequent evaluation and follow-up.

The primary weakness of the accounting rate of return is that it is an averaging technique that does not consider the time value of money. Many people view this weakness as being so important that it completely eliminates the usefulness of this method. These problems are most significant for proposals with uneven cash flows. Kelly's Flour Mill can be used to illustrate the danger in basing investment decisions on the accounting rate of return. When both the mill and the bagger were being considered using the initial investment as the denominator amount, the bagger was identified as the most profitable. Considering the time value of money by either the net present value or the internal rate of return (as shown in fig. 22.11), the bagger is far less profitable than the mill.

Project	Profitability Index at 14% Rate	Internal Rate of Return
Mill X	1.024	14.5%
Bagger	.881	11.6%

Notice also that the accounting rate of return was not a very good predictor of the internal rate of return.

Figure 22.12 summarizes the objectives, computation, and major decision rules for the accounting rate of return method.

SELECTING THE EVALUATION TECHNIQUE

There is a wide variety of techniques available for capital budgeting. The computation and analysis of the strengths and weaknesses of each technique provide useful information in selecting a technique that is best for the analysis. Our objective here is to summarize the selection criteria and to compare the net present value method with the internal rate of return method to identify their differences and the additional factors that should be considered when selecting one of them.

Selection Criteria
The technique selected for capital budgeting decision analysis should satisfy the following criteria:

1. It should accurately summarize the merits of the investment proposal preferably into a single number.
2. It should be understandable to those who use it.

Figure 22.11   Computation of net present value and internal rate of return for investment proposals of Kelly's flour mill

Mill X

Present value of cash flows at 14%:			Present value of cash flows at 16%:	
(10,000 × 6.142)	$61,420		($10,000 × 5.575)	$55,750
Initial investment	60,000		Initial investment	60,000
Net present value	$ 1,420		Net present value	($ 4,250)
Profitability index	1.024		Internal rate of return	14.5%
($61,420 ÷ $60,000)			[14% + (1,420 ÷ 5,670 × 2%)]	

Bagger

Present value of cash flows at 14%:

Years		
1–3 ($4,000 × 2.322)	$ 9,288
4–6 ($5,000 × 3.889 − 2.322)	7,835
7–10 ($6,000 × 5.216 − 3.889)	7,962
Salvage value ($5,000 × .270)	1,350
Total	26,435
Initial investment	30,000
Net present value	($ 3,565)
Profitability Index	.881
($26,435 ÷ $30,000)	

Present value of cash flows at 8%:

Years		
1–3 ($4,000 × 2.577)	$10,308
4–6 ($5,000 × 4.623 − 2.577)	10,230
7–10 ($6,000 × 6.710 − 4.623)	12,522
Salvage value ($5,000 × .463)	2,315
Total	35,375
Initial investment	30,000
Net present value	$ 5,375
Internal rate of return:	11.6%
[8% + ($5,375 ÷ $8,940 × 6%)]	

Figure 22.12   Accounting rate of return

Objective: Compute a rate of return that is consistent with the rate normally computed under the accrual basis of accounting.

Informational requirements:

1. Initial investment
2. Annual cash flows
3. Annual depreciation (straight-line method)

Computation format:

$$\text{Rate} = \frac{\text{Annual cash flow} - \text{Depreciation}}{\text{Initial investment}}$$

Decision rule:

Single investment proposal: Accept an investment proposal if the accounting rate of return exceeds a minimum rate specified by management.

Multiple investment proposals: Rank the investments from high to low according to their rate of return. Those exceeding the minimum specified by management are desirable.

Modification:

Use of average investment as the denominator in the above equation with an adjustment in the minimum acceptable rate specified by management.

3. It should facilitate comparisons between projects.
4. It should provide an accurate measure that is consistent with the long-term objectives of the company in terms of liquidity or profitability.

The last criterion is probably the most valid in selecting one technique over another. The evaluation technique selected for a capital budgeting decision should be consistent with the objective to be achieved. If the primary objective is cash flow and liquidity, then the payback method is appropriate. It indicates how long money is at risk and how soon it will be recovered. This may be most important when instability, uncertainty, and technological change make it difficult to predict cash flows beyond the first few years of investment life. If profitability is the primary objective of the investment, then the net present value or internal rate of return should be used. Both of these methods are superior to payback reciprocal, present value payback, and accounting rate of return because they consider the time value of money and all cash flows over the entire life of the investment. Our objective in this section is to compare the net present value method with the internal rate of return method to identify their differences and the factors that should be considered when selecting one of them.

The net present value method and the internal rate of return method will give the same answer in capital budgeting decisions that compare investment alternatives of equal lives and equal dollar investments. This can be illustrated with proposals Y and Z. Each proposal costs $40,000 and has a useful life of 10 years. The annual cash flows and salvage values are shown below.

Proposal	Y	Z
Cost	$40,000	$40,000
Annual cash flow	6,000	8,000
Salvage value	20,000	–0–
Useful life	10 years	10 years

Analysis

Net present value at 14%:	($3,304)	$1,728
Internal rate of return:	12.2%	15.1%

The net present values are ($3,304) and $1,728 for proposal Y and Z respectively, using a 14% cut-off rate. Because of the negative net present value at this rate, proposal Y would be considered unprofitable and would be rejected. Proposal Z's positive net present value means that it is profitable and would probably be accepted.

The same results are obtained using the internal rate of return. Because the 12.2% return on proposal X is less than 14%, it would be rejected. The 15.1% return on proposal Y is over the cut-off rate and is, therefore, a profitable project.

The net present value method and the internal rate of return method may not give the same results when the lives of the investment alternatives are not equal or when they require a different initial investment. Also, the two methods are not equally easy to work with when allocating limited money to competing investment alternatives. The investment proposals for TLC Incorporated, shown in figure 22.13, will be used to investigate these differences.

TLC Incorporated has $12,000 available for investment in capital equipment. Any money not invested in equipment will be put into a savings certificate at 14%, which is also the company's minimum desired rate of return. Three investment proposals labeled A, B, and C have been developed. The net present value and internal rate of return have also been developed for each proposal. Which proposal or set of proposals would you recommend to TLC Incorporated? No doubt your decision will be confused by the differences in useful lives and initial investments. Let's consider each separately.

Figure 22.13   Investment alternatives with unequal lives and unequal investments

| | Capital Equipment Proposals | | | Savings Certificate |
	A	B	C	
Cost	$10,000	$10,000	$12,000	$2,000
Useful life	2 years	5 years	5 years	Variable
Cash flows:				
Year 1	$6,545	$3,200	$3,795	$ 280
2	6,545	3,200	3,795	280
3	—	3,200	3,795	280
4	—	3,200	3,795	280
5	—	3,200	3,795	280
Salvage	–0–	–0–	–0–	2,000
Analysis:				
Net present value at 14%:	$780	$986	$1,029	–0–
Internal rate of return:	20%	18%	17.5%	14%

Unequal Investment Lives   Proposals *A* and *B* each cost $10,000, but proposal *A* has a useful life of only 2 years and proposal *B* lasts for 5 years. If the internal rate of return is used as the decision criteria, proposal *A* seems to be the most profitable at 20%. If the net present value is used, proposal *B* at $986 seems more profitable than proposal *A* at only $780.

The difference between these results is caused by the difference in the rate at which dollars are assumed to be reinvested during the remaining life of the shortest project. Notice that there are no cash flows shown for proposal *A* for years 3 through 5. The internal rate of return method assumes that proposal *A* will be repeated or that another project will be available to provide a rate of return equal to the 20% earned on proposal *A*. Therefore, it assumes that money will be reinvested at the internal rate of return of the project under consideration.

The net present value method assumes that money will be reinvested at the discount rate. The net present value of money invested at the discount rate is zero. Therefore, the $780 net present value for proposal *A* is based entirely on year 1 and year 2 cash flows. This accounts for the lower net present value for proposal *A* than for proposal *B*.

The problem of unequal lives can best be resolved by making an assumption about the reinvestment of money from the project with the shortest life. If money will be reinvested at the minimum desired rate of return, then the net present value most accurately reflects investment profitability. If the project can be repeated or if equally profitable projects will be available, then the internal rate of return accurately reflects investment profitability. The net present value method can still be used under the second assumption, but the cash flows from the reinvestment would need to be charted, discounted, and included in the net present value. When this is done, the two methods will give the same answer.

Assume that any money TLC Incorporated receives from proposal *A* will be reinvested at the cut-off rate and that proposal *B* is determined to be more profitable than proposal *A*. Proposals *B* and *C* must now be evaluated because of the difference in initial investment.

Unequal Initial Investments   Proposals *B* and *C* each have a useful life of 5 years but *B* costs only $10,000 and *C* costs $12,000. Once again, the results from net present value seem to contradict those of internal rate of return. Proposal *B* has the highest internal rate of return (18% versus 17.5%) and proposal *C* has the highest net present value ($1,029 versus $986).

A further complication is the amount of money available for investment. TLC Incorporated has $12,000 available for investment. If proposal *B* is adopted, the remaining $2,000 would be invested in a savings certificate at 14%, which would provide a zero net present value and an internal rate of return of 14%. The investment choice is between proposal *C* and a combination of proposal *B* and the savings certificate.

In situations such as this, the net present value method provides the easiest answer. The *most profitable combination of projects will be those with the highest combined net present values.* Proposal *B* and the savings certificate have a combined net present value of $986 ($986 + 0), which is less than the $1,029 from proposal *C*. Therefore, proposal *C* is more profitable.

If we try to use the internal rates of return, we can't combine 18% and 14% to compare with the 17.5% without additional computation. Proposal *C* costs $2,000 more than *B* but yields $595 ($3,795 − $3,200) per year more cash flow. The internal rate of return on the additional money invested in proposal *C* must be computed to compare with the 14% alternative provided by the savings certificate.

$$\text{Annuity factor} = \frac{\$2,000}{\$595} = 3.3613$$

Percent	Annuity Factor	Difference
14%	3.433 ⎫	.072
?	3.361 ⎬	
16%	3.274 ⎭	.087
Total		.159
Internal rate of return		14.91%

[14% + (.072 ÷ .159 × 2%)]

A 14.91% return on the additional money invested in proposal *C* is more than the savings certificate provides and is the most profitable project.

In summary, the net present value method is generally easier to work with than the internal rate of return method. It only requires one set of computations. Net present values can be combined when allocating money to competing investment alternatives to identify the most profitable combination of projects. When dealing with projects of unequal lives, some assumption must be made concerning reinvestment of money from the shorter-lived project. The net present value method is consistent with the assumption that money is reinvested at the minimum desired rate of return.

Planning and Control Over Capital Expenditures

Development of the capital budget is part of the normal budgeting process described in detail in chapter 6. One section of the master budget is called the capital budget. It identifies the capital assets to be acquired or constructed and the amount of money to be allocated to each. The procedures discussed in this chapter deal with identifying the projects that are most profitable and allocating money to them.

The capital budget can only be as good as the projects included in it. Every attempt must be made to identify the most profitable projects available to the company. This requires input from all segments of the organization and a fairly exhaustive search of alternatives to existing processes. So often we become used to the status quo that we stop looking for alternatives or reject some very desirable alternatives without adequate consideration.

The accountant's role in developing the capital budget is primarily data gathering and quantifying the impact of a proposed change on revenues and operating costs. Assistance is also provided to management in quantifying and selecting a cut-off rate and in evaluating the profitability of alternative proposals. Many people at the top management level are involved in the final decision, but the computations, analysis, and manner of presentation provided by the accountant have a significant impact on the outcome.

After the capital budget is approved and implemented, there needs to be a reconciliation of actual results with the anticipated results. It is important that the follow-up evaluation be consistent with the technique used to evaluate the desirability of the proposal in the first place. For example, an accounting rate of return on the actual results is not comparable to an internal rate of return on expected results. An accurately performed post-implementation review may reveal one of several things, including the following:

1. The expected benefits are being achieved and the capital investment project is profitable as anticipated.
2. The expected benefits are not being achieved because conversion to the new process or equipment has not been complete. Some people continue to use the old methods, which result in duplicate processing costs.
3. The project is not as profitable as anticipated because the estimates of projected benefits were overstated, or estimated costs were understated. This type of information can be very useful in refining the estimation techniques used for future capital budgeting decisions.

Once again the accountant plays a significant role in this post-implementation review. In order for the analysis to be meaningful, accrual accounting numbers must be adjusted and special reports must be prepared.

Complications to Capital Budgeting

Capital budgeting is complicated somewhat by three factors.

1. Income tax considerations. Almost every cash flow has a related impact on income taxes that must be paid to the state and federal governments. Some items, such as depreciation, do not by themselves affect cash flows but, when income taxes are considered, there is a related cash flow.
2. Selecting a minimum desired rate of return. The two most useful capital budgeting techniques both require a cut-off rate. The net present value method uses it as part of the computation, and the internal rate of return method uses it as a benchmark to accept or reject a proposal. The development of an acceptable cut-off rate for a particular organization is a complex and controversial problem.
3. Projecting future cash flows. Future cash flows have been provided in the examples in this chapter as if we had a crystal ball that can be used to predict the future with 100% certainty. This is rarely the case and small errors in predicting cash flows may have a significant impact on the outcome of our decision. Sensitivity analysis is useful in evaluating the effect of estimation errors on the outcome of the decision.

Chapter 23 covers each of these complications in some detail.

Summary

Capital budgeting is a process used to determine investment profitability or to select from a variety of investment alternatives those that will be most profitable. The results of this analysis constitute the capital budget section of the master budget.

The profitability of a proposed investment is based on expected cash flows over the life of the project. Cash flows may be analyzed using (*a*) net present value, (*b*) internal rate of return, (*c*) payback period, or (*d*) accounting rate of return. The net present value or the internal rate of return are considered superior to the other methods because they consider both the amount and timing of cash flows over the entire life of the investment. The net present value method is generally easier to work with than the internal rate of return because it requires less computation. The payback period method measures liquidity rather than profitability. Its use is often justified in situations where cash flow is more critical than maximizing profits.

Care must be exercised in selecting and using a capital budgeting technique. The objective of the analysis should first be identified and a technique should be selected that meets the objective. Also, the assumptions upon which the technique operates should be kept in mind when the results are used in a decision-making process.

Appendix *Time Value of Money*

Money at different points in time is not comparable because of the time value of money. Inflation and the opportunity cost associated with idle cash make comparisons inaccurate. This complicates capital budgeting decisions because they have a relatively long life. Present value or future value computations are made to adjust for time and interest so all cash flows are at a common point in time.

Future Value of $1 Sum   A sum of money ($P$) invested today at a given interest rate (i) will increase in value over time (n). The future value can be computed as:

$$F = P(1 + i)^n$$

Factors have been computed for various combinations of i and n $[F_{in} = (1 + i)^n]$ and are shown in the future value tables. A portion of a future value table is shown below. The equation $F = P(F_{in})$ is relevant when using factors from the table. The sum of money (P) is multiplied by the factor obtained from the table for the given interest rate and number of periods to obtain the future value (F).

The Future Amount of $1: $F_{in} = (1 + i)^n$

Period	8%	10%	12%
1	1.0800	1.1000	1.1200
2	1.1664	1.2100	1.2544
3	1.2597	1.3310	1.4049
4	1.3605	1.4641	1.5735
5	1.4693	1.6105	1.7623

A more complete table of future amounts of $1 are shown in table 1 on page 804.

Example: How much will $10,000 be worth in 4 years if money is worth 10%?

Formula Solution:

$F = \$10,000 (1 + .10)^4$
$= 10,000 (1.4641)$
$= \$14,641$

Table Solution:

$F = \$10,000 (1.4641)$
$= \$14,641$

Notice that the factor of 1.4641 is obtained from the table above using 4 as the number of periods and 10% as the interest rate. You should be familiar with the above equations and be able to use the table factors to compute the future value of a sum of money when the number of periods and interest rate are given.

Present Value of $1 Sum   The present value or discounted value of a $1 sum is just the opposite of a future value. The question is what amount (P) must be invested today at a given interest rate (i) to be worth a specified amount (F) in a given number of years (n)? The future value equation can be solved for P to obtain:

$$P = F \frac{1}{(1+i)^n}$$

The interest factor can be specified as follows. Notice that this is the reciprocal of F_{in} computed above.

$$P_{in} = \frac{1}{(1+i)^n}$$

Various combinations of i and n have been computed and are included in the following present value table.

The Present Amount of $1: $P_{in} = \left[\dfrac{1}{(1+i)^n}\right]$

Period	8%	10%	12%
1	0.9259	0.9091	0.8929
2	0.8573	0.8264	0.7972
3	0.7938	0.7513	0.7118
4	0.7350	0.6830	0.6355
5	0.6806	0.6209	0.5674

A more complete table of present values of $1 is shown in table 2 on page 804.
The present value amount is computed by multiplying the present value factor obtained from the table by the future dollar amount.

Example: An investment will pay $14,641 in 4 years. What is the present value of the payout if money is worth 10%?

Table solution: $P = \$14,641 (.6830)$
$= \$10,000$

The present value factor of .6830 is obtained from the present value table using 4 as the number of periods and 10% as the interest rate.

Annuity An "ordinary annuity" is a series of equal cash flows at the *end* of equal intervals of time. An "annuity due" is a series of equal cash flows at the beginning of equal intervals of time.

Example of a 3-Year Ordinary Annuity of $100

	$100	$100	$100	Time in years
0	1	2	3	

Example of a 3-Year Annuity Due of $100

$100	$100	$100		Time in years
0	1	2	3	

Future Value of an Annuity The future value of an annuity can be computed by moving each of the annuity amounts to the end of the annuity's life using the factors from table 1 on page 804.

Example: What is the future value of a $100 *ordinary annuity* for 3 years when money is worth 10%?

$$F = \$100(1.2100) + \$100(1.100) + 100(1.000)$$
$$= \$100(3.3100)$$
$$= \underline{\$331}$$

The direct formula for computing the future value of an ordinary annuity is:

$$F = A\frac{(1+i)^n - 1}{i}$$

Values of the interest factor have been computed and are shown in the following table.

Amount of Ordinary Annuity of $1: $FA_{in} = \left[\dfrac{(1+i)^n - 1}{i}\right]$

Period	8%	10%	12%
1	1.0000	1.0000	1.0000
2	2.0800	2.1000	2.1200
3	3.2464	3.3100	3.3744
4	4.5061	4.6410	4.7793
5	5.8666	6.1051	6.3528

A more complete table of future values of ordinary annuities is shown in table 3 on page 805.

Notice that the factor for 10% and 3 periods in the table above is 3.3100, which is the same as the factor computed in the previous example when the annual factors obtained from table 1 were totaled. The computation in the example above is simplified by obtaining the annuity factor directly from the annuity table. The future value of the annuity is then computed by multiplying the annuity factor by the annuity amount.

Ordinary annuity factors in the table above can be converted to annuity due factors by adding 1 to the number of periods and subtracting 1.0000 from the factor.

Example: What is the future value of a $100 *annuity due* for 3 years when money is worth 10%?

$$F = \$100(3.641)$$
$$= \underline{\$364.10}$$

The factor 3.641 is computed by obtaining the table factor for 4 periods (3 + 1) at 10% (4.641) and subtracting 1.0000 from the factor.

Present Value of an Annuity   The present value of an annuity can be computed by moving each of the annuity amounts to the present time period using the factors from table 2 on page 804. However, it is more efficient to compute the present value using the annuity formula or by using a factor from the table of present values of an annuity of $1.

The formula for computing the present value of an ordinary annuity is:

$$P = A\frac{1 - (1+i)^{-n}}{i}$$

Interest factors have been computed and are included in the table entitled present value of an ordinary annuity of $1. A portion of this table is shown below. A more complete table is shown in table 4 on page 805.

Present Value of an Ordinary Annuity of $1: $PA_{in} = \left[\dfrac{1 - (1+i)^{-n}}{i}\right]$

Period	8%	10%	12%
1	0.9259	0.9091	0.8929
2	1.7833	1.7355	1.6901
3	2.5771	2.4869	2.4018
4	3.3121	3.1699	3.0373
5	3.9927	3.7908	3.6048

To find the present value of an ordinary annuity you multiply the annuity amount by the annuity factor obtained from the table for the given number of periods and interest rate.

Example: What is the present value of an *ordinary annuity* of $100 for 3 years when interest is 10%?

$P = \$100\,(2.4869)$
$\quad = \$248.69$

The ordinary annuity factors in the table above can be changed to annuity due factors by subtracting 1 from the number of periods and adding 1.0000 to that factor.

Example: What is the present value of a $100 *annuity due* for 3 years and a 10% interest rate?

$P = \$100\,(2.7355)$
$\quad = \$273.55$

The factor 2.7355 used above is computed by obtaining the factor from the table for 2 periods (1.7355) and adding 1.0000 to it.

Compound Interest   Unless stated otherwise, it is assumed that interest is compounded annually. Frequently, however, interest will be stated as an annual amount but compounded semiannually, quarterly, or even monthly. In these cases you must adjust the interest rate and number of periods. The following rules are useful when making these adjustments.

1. Adjust the interest rate according to the compounding period. For example, if the interest rate is 16% compounded semiannually, you would use an 8% (16% ÷ 2) interest rate per period.
2. Adjust n from the number of years to the number of compounding periods. For example, if the note is for 5 years with interest compounded semiannually, then you would use 10(5 × 2) periods.

The revised interest rate and number of periods would then be used in any of the above formulas or tables.

Table 1 Future Amount of $1 in n Periods $F = P(1 + i)^n$

n	2%	8%	10%	12%	14%	16%	18%	20%	22%	24%	30%
1	1.0200	1.0800	1.100	1.120	1.140	1.160	1.180	1.200	1.22	1.24	1.30
2	1.0404	1.1664	1.210	1.254	1.300	1.346	1.392	1.440	1.49	1.54	1.69
3	1.0612	1.2597	1.331	1.405	1.482	1.561	1.643	1.728	1.82	1.91	2.20
4	1.0824	1.3605	1.464	1.574	1.689	1.811	1.939	2.074	2.22	2.36	2.86
5	1.1041	1.4693	1.611	1.762	1.925	2.100	2.288	2.488	2.70	2.93	3.71
6	1.1262	1.5869	1.772	1.974	2.195	2.436	2.700	2.986	3.30	3.64	4.83
7	1.1487	1.7138	1.949	2.211	2.502	2.826	3.185	3.583	4.02	4.51	6.27
8	1.1717	1.8509	2.144	2.476	2.853	3.278	3.759	4.300	4.91	5.59	8.16
9	1.1951	1.9990	2.358	2.773	3.252	3.803	4.435	5.160	5.99	6.93	10.60
10	1.2190	2.1589	2.594	3.106	3.707	4.411	5.234	6.192	7.30	8.59	13.79
11	1.2434	2.3316	2.853	3.479	4.226	5.117	6.176	7.430	8.91	10.66	17.92
12	1.2682	2.5182	3.138	3.896	4.818	5.936	7.288	8.916	10.87	13.21	23.30
13	1.2936	2.7196	3.452	4.363	5.492	6.886	8.599	10.699	13.26	16.39	30.29
14	1.3195	2.9372	3.797	4.887	6.261	7.988	10.147	12.839	16.18	20.32	39.37
15	1.3459	3.1722	4.177	5.474	7.138	9.266	11.974	15.407	19.74	25.20	51.19
16	1.3728	3.4259	4.595	6.130	8.137	10.748	14.129	18.488	24.09	31.24	66.54
17	1.4002	3.7000	5.054	6.866	9.276	12.468	16.672	22.186	29.38	38.74	86.50
18	1.4282	3.9960	5.560	7.690	10.575	14.463	19.673	26.623	35.85	48.04	112.46
19	1.4568	4.3157	6.116	8.613	12.056	16.777	23.214	31.948	43.74	59.57	146.19
20	1.4859	4.6610	6.728	9.646	13.743	19.461	27.393	38.338	53.36	73.86	190.05
21	1.5157	5.0338	7.400	10.804	15.668	22.574	32.324	46.005	65.10	91.59	247.06
22	1.5460	5.4365	8.140	12.100	17.861	26.186	38.142	55.206	79.42	113.57	321.18
23	1.5769	5.8715	8.954	13.552	20.362	30.376	45.008	66.247	96.89	140.83	417.54
24	1.6084	6.3412	9.850	15.179	23.212	35.236	53.109	79.497	118.21	174.63	542.80
25	1.6406	6.8485	10.835	17.000	26.462	40.874	62.669	95.396	144.21	216.54	705.64

Table 2 Present Value of $1 in n Periods $P = F\left[\dfrac{1}{(1 + i)^n}\right]$

n	2%	8%	10%	12%	14%	16%	18%	20%	22%	24%	30%
1	0.9804	0.9259	0.9091	0.8929	0.8772	0.8621	0.8475	0.8333	0.8197	0.8065	0.7692
2	0.9612	0.8573	0.8264	0.7972	0.7695	0.7432	0.7182	0.6944	0.6719	0.6504	0.5917
3	0.9423	0.7938	0.7513	0.7118	0.6750	0.6407	0.6086	0.5787	0.5507	0.5245	0.4552
4	0.9238	0.7350	0.6830	0.6355	0.5921	0.5523	0.5158	0.4823	0.4514	0.4230	0.3501
5	0.9057	0.6806	0.6209	0.5674	0.5194	0.4761	0.4371	0.4019	0.3700	0.3411	0.2693
6	0.8880	0.6302	0.5645	0.5066	0.4556	0.4104	0.3704	0.3349	0.3033	0.2751	0.2072
7	0.8706	0.5835	0.5132	0.4523	0.3996	0.3538	0.3139	0.2791	0.2486	0.2218	0.1594
8	0.8535	0.5403	0.4665	0.4039	0.3506	0.3050	0.2660	0.2326	0.2038	0.1789	0.1226
9	0.8368	0.5002	0.4241	0.3606	0.3075	0.2630	0.2255	0.1938	0.1670	0.1443	0.0943
10	0.8203	0.4632	0.3855	0.3220	0.2697	0.2267	0.1911	0.1615	0.1369	0.1164	0.0725
11	0.8043	0.4289	0.3505	0.2875	0.2366	0.1954	0.1619	0.1346	0.1122	0.0938	0.0558
12	0.7885	0.3971	0.3186	0.2567	0.2076	0.1685	0.1372	0.1122	0.0920	0.0757	0.0429
13	0.7730	0.3677	0.2897	0.2292	0.1821	0.1452	0.1163	0.0935	0.0754	0.0610	0.0330
14	0.7579	0.3405	0.2633	0.2046	0.1597	0.1252	0.0985	0.0779	0.0618	0.0492	0.0254
15	0.7430	0.3152	0.2394	0.1827	0.1401	0.1079	0.0835	0.0649	0.0507	0.0397	0.0195
16	0.7284	0.2919	0.2176	0.1631	0.1229	0.0930	0.0708	0.0541	0.0415	0.0320	0.0150
17	0.7142	0.2703	0.1978	0.1456	0.1078	0.0802	0.0600	0.0451	0.0340	0.0258	0.0116
18	0.7002	0.2502	0.1799	0.1300	0.0946	0.0691	0.0508	0.0376	0.0279	0.0208	0.0089
19	0.6864	0.2317	0.1635	0.1161	0.0829	0.0596	0.0431	0.0313	0.0229	0.0168	0.0068
20	0.6730	0.2145	0.1486	0.1037	0.0728	0.0514	0.0365	0.0261	0.0187	0.0135	0.0053
21	0.6598	0.1987	0.1351	0.0926	0.0638	0.0443	0.0309	0.0217	0.0154	0.0109	0.0040
22	0.6468	0.1839	0.1228	0.0826	0.0560	0.0382	0.0262	0.0181	0.0126	0.0088	0.0031
23	0.6342	0.1703	0.1117	0.0738	0.0491	0.0329	0.0222	0.0151	0.0103	0.0071	0.0024
24	0.6217	0.1577	0.1015	0.0659	0.0431	0.0284	0.0188	0.0126	0.0085	0.0057	0.0018
25	0.6095	0.1460	0.0923	0.0588	0.0378	0.0245	0.0160	0.0105	0.0069	0.0046	0.0014

Table 3 Future Amount of an Annuity of \$1 per Period $F = A\left[\dfrac{(1+i)^n - 1}{i}\right]$

n	2%	8%	10%	12%	14%	16%	18%	20%	22%	24%	30%
1	1.000	1.000	1.000	1.00	1.00	1.00	1.00	1.00	1.00	1.00	1.0
2	2.020	2.080	2.100	2.12	2.14	2.16	2.18	2.20	2.22	2.24	2.3
3	3.060	3.246	3.310	3.37	3.44	3.51	3.57	3.64	3.71	3.78	4.0
4	4.122	4.506	4.641	4.78	4.92	5.07	5.22	5.37	5.52	5.68	6.2
5	5.204	5.867	6.105	6.35	6.61	6.88	7.15	7.44	7.74	8.05	9.0
6	6.308	7.336	7.716	8.12	8.54	8.98	9.44	9.93	10.44	10.98	12.8
7	7.434	8.923	9.487	10.09	10.73	11.41	12.14	12.92	13.74	14.62	17.6
8	8.583	10.637	11.436	12.30	13.23	14.24	15.33	16.50	17.76	19.12	23.9
9	9.755	12.488	13.579	14.78	16.09	17.52	19.09	20.80	22.67	24.71	32.0
10	10.950	14.487	15.937	17.55	19.34	21.32	23.52	25.96	28.66	31.64	42.6
11	12.169	16.645	18.531	20.65	23.04	25.73	28.76	32.15	35.96	40.24	56.4
12	13.412	18.977	21.384	24.13	27.27	30.85	34.93	39.58	44.87	50.89	74.3
13	14.680	21.495	24.523	28.03	32.09	36.79	42.22	48.50	55.75	64.11	97.6
14	15.974	24.215	27.975	32.39	37.58	43.67	50.82	59.20	69.01	80.50	127.9
15	17.293	27.152	31.772	37.28	43.84	51.66	60.97	72.04	85.19	100.82	167.3
16	18.639	30.324	35.950	42.75	50.98	60.92	72.94	87.44	104.93	126.01	218.5
17	20.012	33.750	40.545	48.88	59.12	71.67	87.07	105.93	129.02	157.25	285.0
18	21.412	37.450	45.599	55.75	68.39	84.14	103.74	128.12	158.40	195.99	371.5
19	22.840	41.446	51.159	63.44	78.97	98.60	123.41	154.74	194.25	244.03	484.0
20	24.297	45.762	57.275	72.05	91.02	115.38	146.63	186.69	237.99	303.60	630.2
21	25.783	50.423	64.003	81.70	104.77	134.84	174.02	225.03	291.35	377.46	820.2
22	27.299	55.457	71.403	92.50	120.44	157.41	206.35	271.03	356.44	469.06	1067.3
23	28.845	60.893	79.543	104.60	138.30	183.60	244.49	326.24	435.86	582.63	1388.5
24	30.422	66.765	88.497	118.16	158.66	213.98	289.49	392.48	532.75	723.46	1806.0
25	32.030	73.106	98.347	133.33	181.87	249.21	342.60	471.98	650.96	898.09	2348.8

Table 4 Present Value of an Annuity of \$1 per Period $P = A\left[\dfrac{1-(1+i)^{-n}}{i}\right]$

n	2%	8%	10%	12%	14%	16%	18%	20%	22%	24%	30%
1	0.980	0.926	0.909	0.8929	0.8772	0.8621	0.8475	0.8333	0.8197	0.8065	0.7692
2	1.942	1.783	1.736	1.6901	1.6467	1.6052	1.5656	1.5278	1.4915	1.4568	1.3609
3	2.884	2.577	2.487	2.4018	2.3216	2.2459	2.1743	2.1065	2.0422	1.9813	1.8161
4	3.808	3.312	3.170	3.0373	2.9137	2.7982	2.6901	2.5887	2.4936	2.4043	2.1662
5	4.713	3.993	3.791	3.6048	3.4331	3.2743	3.1272	2.9906	2.8636	2.7454	2.4356
6	5.601	4.623	4.355	4.1114	3.8887	3.6847	3.4976	3.3255	3.1669	3.0205	2.6427
7	6.472	5.206	4.868	4.5638	4.2883	4.0386	3.8115	3.6046	3.4155	3.2423	2.8021
8	7.325	5.747	5.335	4.9676	4.6389	4.3436	4.0776	3.8372	3.6193	3.4212	2.9247
9	8.162	6.247	5.759	5.3283	4.9464	4.6065	4.3030	4.0310	3.7863	3.5655	3.0190
10	8.983	6.710	6.145	5.6502	5.2161	4.8332	4.4941	4.1925	3.9232	3.6819	3.0915
11	9.787	7.139	6.495	5.9377	5.4527	5.0286	4.6560	4.3271	4.0354	3.7757	3.1473
12	10.575	7.536	6.814	6.1944	5.6603	5.1971	4.7932	4.4392	4.1274	3.8514	3.1903
13	11.348	7.904	7.103	6.4235	5.8424	5.3423	4.9095	4.5327	4.2028	3.9124	3.2233
14	12.106	8.244	7.367	6.6282	6.0021	5.4675	5.0081	4.6106	4.2646	3.9616	3.2487
15	12.849	8.559	7.606	6.8109	6.1422	5.5755	5.0916	4.6755	4.3152	4.0013	3.2682
16	13.578	8.851	7.824	6.9740	6.2651	5.6685	5.1624	4.7296	4.3567	4.0333	3.2832
17	14.292	9.122	8.022	7.1196	6.3729	5.7487	5.2223	4.7746	4.3908	4.0591	3.2948
18	14.992	9.372	8.201	7.2497	6.4674	5.8178	5.2732	4.8122	4.4187	4.0799	3.3037
19	15.678	9.604	8.365	7.3658	6.5504	5.8775	5.3162	4.8435	4.4415	4.0967	3.3105
20	16.351	9.818	8.514	7.4694	6.6231	5.9288	5.3527	4.8696	4.4603	4.1103	3.3158
21	17.011	10.017	8.649	7.5620	6.6870	5.9731	5.3837	4.8913	4.4756	4.1212	3.3198
22	17.658	10.201	8.772	7.6446	6.7429	6.0113	5.4099	4.9094	4.4882	4.1300	3.3230
23	18.292	10.371	8.883	7.7184	6.7921	6.0442	5.4321	4.9245	4.4985	4.1371	3.3253
24	18.914	10.529	8.985	7.7843	6.8351	6.0726	5.4509	4.9371	4.5070	4.1428	3.3272
25	19.523	10.675	9.077	7.8431	6.8729	6.0971	5.4669	4.9476	4.5139	4.1474	3.3286

Self-Study Problem

The Elder Company is planning to purchase a new machine at a cost of $300,000. It will be depreciated by the straight-line method over a 10-year useful life with no salvage value, and a full year's depreciation will be taken in the year of acquisition. The new machine is expected to produce a cash flow from operations of $66,000 a year in each of the next 10 years. A 16% rate of return and a 4-year payback is desired on all capital investments.

Required

1. Compute the net present value.
2. Compute the internal rate of return.
3. Compute the payback period.
4. Compute the accounting rate of return.
5. How would you advise management on the proposed acquisition?

Solution to the Self-Study Problem

Requirement 1

The net present value is computed by subtracting the initial investment from the present value of the cash flows at a 15% interest rate.

Present Value of Cash Flows

($66,000 × 4.8332)	$318,991.20
Initial investment	300,000.00
Net present value	$ 18,991.20

Requirement 2

The internal rate of return is the interest rate that equates the present value of the cash flows with the initial investment. The present value factor that equates these is computed by dividing the initial investment by the annual cash flows. (This can only be done when annual cash flows are equal.) The interest rate is then obtained from the present value table.

Present Value Factor

($300,000 ÷ $66,000)   4.5455

From the present value table we can see that the interest rate is between 16% and 20%. Through interpolation we find the interest rate to be approximately 17.8%.

Interest Rates	Annuity Factor	Difference
16%	4.8332	
		.2877
?	4.5455	
		.3530
20%	4.1925	
4%		.6407

16% + [(.2877 ÷ .6407) × 4%] = 17.8%

Requirement 3

When annual cash flows are equal, the payback period can be computed by dividing the initial investment by the annual cash flows.

Payback Period

($300,000 ÷ $66,000)   4.5 years

Requirement 4

The accounting rate of return is computed by dividing the average net income (annual cash flow less depreciation expense) by the initial investment or average book value. Using the initial investment as the denominator, the accounting rate of return is 12%.

Accounting Rate of Return

$$\frac{\$66,000 - \$30,000^a}{\$300,000} = 12\%$$

[a]Depreciation Expense
($300,000 ÷ 10 years) = $30,000

Requirement 5

The proposed investment satisfies the 16% minimum desired rate of return but falls slightly short of a 4-year payback. Management must decide whether cash flow or profitability is most important. With the major emphasis on profitability, the proposal should be accepted.

Suggested Readings

Hertz, David B. "Incorporating Risk in Capital Expenditure Analysis." In *Controller's Handbook,* edited by Sam R. Goodman and James S. Reece. Homewood, ILL.: Dow Jones-Irwin, 1978.

House, William C., Jr. "Sensitivity Analysis in Making Capital Investment Decisions." *NAA Research Monograph #3.* New York: National Association of Accountants, 1968.

Kempster, John H. "Financial Analysis to Guide Capital Expenditure Decisions." *NAA Research Report #43.* New York: National Association of Accountants, 1967.

Murdy, J. L. "Analyzing Capital Expenditure Proposals." In *Controller's Handbook,* edited by Sam R. Goodman and James S. Reece. Homewood, ILL.: Dow Jones-Irwin, 1978.

National Association of Accountants. "Financial Analysis Techniques for Equipment Replacement Decisions." *NAA Research Monograph #1.* New York: National Association of Accountants, 1965.

Discussion Questions

1. What are capital assets? Why is capital budgeting analysis required when purchasing capital assets?
2. Depreciation expenses must be treated separately from other revenues and expenses in capital budgeting decisions. Why is this so and how should it be treated?
3. Distinguish between a "screening decision" and a "preference decision" in capital budgeting.
4. Describe how to compute a net present value. If the net present value is a negative number, should the proposal be rejected? Explain.
5. Explain what the controller meant by the following. "We are rejecting many capital investment proposals in today's economy that would have been acceptable only a few years ago." How could this be true when the cost of the investment and its net cash flows have not changed?
6. Why is the minimum desired rate of return so important in capital budgeting decisions?
7. How is the profitability index computed and what does it mean?
8. Describe how to compute an internal rate of return. Given an internal rate of return of 12%, should the proposal be accepted or rejected?
9. Describe how to compute the payback period. Given a payback period of 5 years, should the proposal be accepted or rejected?
10. Why is present value payback an improvement over the regular payback analysis? What does it mean when the present value payback period is longer than the life of the capital asset?
11. Does the net present value method stress profitability or cash flow? Explain.
12. Comparing net present value, internal rate of return, payback, and accounting rate of return, which method(s) is(are) the "best"? Explain.
13. Describe how to compute the accounting rate of return.
14. Net present value and internal rate of return may not provide the same answer when comparing two investment proposals with *different investment lives.* Why is this so and which method provides the best answer?
15. Net present value and internal rate of return may not provide the same answer when comparing two investment proposals with *different initial investments.* Why is this so and which method provides the best answer?

Exercises

Exercise 22.1   Basic Capital Budgeting Analysis

Clark Company has equipment that is expected to produce $48,000 in operating cash inflows during each of the next 5 years. It has also been estimated that the equipment can be sold for $176,000 today but will be worthless in 5 years.

Required

Should Clark Company dispose of the equipment now or continue to use it for the next 5 years assuming cost of capital is 10%?

Exercise 22.2   Internal Rate of Return Analysis

G & A Corporation has just acquired a 3-year contract with a government agency to produce 1,000 computer chips per year to use with a new computer hardware system. The sales price will be $130 per chip. Total variable costs, including overhead but exclusive of the machinery required, are estimated at $50 per chip. The president of the corporation is evaluating several alternatives to meet this demand.

One alternative is the purchase of a new chip assembler machine at a cost of $160,000. Maintenance requirements would be about $800 per year. This new machine is expected to have a salvage value that is negligible at the end of 3 years due to obsolescence of the product.

Depreciation of all equipment is done on a straight-line basis, and 20% is the minimum desired rate of return on new investments.

Required

Compute the internal rate of return on the initial investment and give your recommendations to the president of G & A Corporation.

Exercise 22.3   Investment Analysis

Clark Company can obtain additional equipment at a cost of $90,000. This equipment will produce an expected annual operating cash flow of $23,500 for the next 5 years.

Required

Assuming a 10% cost of capital, should the equipment acquisition be made?

Exercise 22.4   Capital Budgeting Concepts

Choose the best answer for each of the following questions.

1. In capital budgeting analysis the "payback reciprocal" may provide a quick and useful estimate of the internal rate of return only when
   a. cash inflows do not extend beyond the length of the payback period.
   b. cash inflow amounts vary erratically during the life of the investment.
   c. most of the cash inflows from an investment precede the investment outlay.
   d. cash inflows are uniform throughout the life of an investment that is long relative to its payback period.
   e. the investment outlays are made uniformly throughout the life of the investment.
2. Depreciation is incorporated explicitly in the discounted cash flow analysis of an investment proposal because it
   a. is a cost of operations that cannot be avoided.
   b. results in an annual cash outflow.
   c. is a cash inflow.
   d. reduces the cash outlay for income taxes.
   e. represents the initial cash outflow spread over the life of the investment.

3. Making the common assumption in capital budgeting analysis that cash inflows occur in lump sums at the end of individual time periods during the life of an investment project, when in fact they flow more or less continuously through that life,
   a. results in increasingly overstated estimates of net present value as the life of the investment project increases.
   b. results in understated estimates of net present value.
   c. results in a higher estimate for the internal rate of return of the investment.
   d. will result in inconsistent errors being made in estimating net present values so that projects cannot be evaluated reliably.
   e. is done because present value tables for continuous flows cannot be constructed.
4. The net present value of a proposed project represents the
   a. cash flows less the present value of the cash flows.
   b. cash flows less the original investment.
   c. present value of the cash flows plus the present value of the original investment less the original investment.
   d. present value of the cash flows less the original investment.
5. Which of the following is necessary in order to calculate the payback period for a project?
   a. Useful life
   b. Minimum desired rate of return
   c. Net present value
   d. Annual cash flow

Exercise 22.5   Capital Budgeting—A Potpourri of Concepts (CPA)

Choose the best answer for each of the following questions.

1. In order for a project to be acceptable to a company using the present value method of analysis, the return on invested capital must
   a. at least equal the amount of cash to cover interest and principal payments for any debt obtained to finance the project.
   b. generate sufficient capital to pay for itself within the economic life of the assets committed to the project.
   c. at least equal the return on invested capital currently being generated by the company.
   d. generate sufficient capital resources to justify any additional capital expenditures and reduce idle capacity within the company.
2. What technique is used to deal with a range of possibilities in a capital budgeting model?
   a. Present value concepts
   b. Sensitivity analysis
   c. Markov analysis
   d. Discounted cash flow
3. The net present value and time-adjusted rate of return methods of decision making in capital budgeting are superior to the payback method in that they
   a. are easier to implement.
   b. consider the time value of money.
   c. require less input.
   d. reflect the effects of depreciation and income taxes.

4. What capital budgeting method assumes that funds are reinvested at the company's cost of capital?
    a. Payback
    b. Accounting rate of return
    c. Net present value
    d. Time-adjusted rate of return

Exercise 22.6 Basic Procedures of Capital Budgeting

As the new manager of division X of the Stinger Corporation, you have just been given the following information. For $60,000, you can buy a newly developed machine that will save $12,000 in cash operating costs for the next 8 years, after which the machine will have no value. Stinger has recently set their minimum desired rate of return at 12%.

Required

Calculate the following:
    1. Payback period
    2. Net present value
    3. Internal rate of return
    4. Net present value or profitability index

Exercise 22.7 Budgeting Analysis

Dave McBrodie, a recent graduate from State U, has just been handed the following information concerning two options available to Jamrock Corporation:

Option	Required Investment	Net Cash Inflows Year 1	Year 2	Year 3	Year 4
1	$105,000	$45,000	$40,000	$30,000	$20,000
2	$160,000	$60,000	$50,000	$50,000	$50,000

Dave knows that Jamrock has been previously able to earn 8% on similar options.

Required

Advise the management of Jamrock Corporation about which option should be selected by submitting computations of net present values. Your job depends on it! Compute a profitability index for each option.

Exercise 22.8 Present Value Procedures of Capital Budgeting

Tracy Corporation is planning to invest $80,000 in a 3-year project. Tracy's expected rate of return is 10%. The present value of $1 at 10% for one year is .909, for two years is .826, and for three years is .751. The expected cash flow will be $30,000 for the first year (present value of $27,270) and $36,000 for the second year (present value of $29,736).

Required

Assuming the rate of return is exactly 10%, determine the cash flow for the third year.

Exercise 22.9   Compound Interest Concepts of Capital Budgeting

Cooper plans to invest $2,000 at the end of each of the next 10 years. Assume that Cooper will earn interest at an annual rate of 6% compounded annually. The future amount of an ordinary annuity of $1 for 10 periods at 6% is 13.181. The present value of $1 for 10 periods at 6% is 0.558. The present value of an ordinary annuity for $1 for 10 periods at 6% is 7.360.

Required

Determine the amount of the investment after the end of 10 years.

Exercise 22.10   Present Value Procedures of Capital Budgeting

Gene Incorporated invested in a machine with a useful life of 6 years and no salvage value. The machine was expected to produce annual cash inflow of $2,000. The present value of an ordinary annuity of $1 for 6 periods at 10% is 4.355. The present value of $1 for 6 periods at 10% is 0.564.

Required

Assuming that Gene used a time-adjusted rate of return of 10%, what was the amount of the original investment?

Problems

Problem 22.1   Capital Budgeting Analysis

The manager of division B is considering two different projects, each of which will require the same initial investment. Below are the schedules of prospective operating income for both projects 1 and 2.

	Cash Inflows	
Year	Project 1	Project 2
1	$20,000	$10,000
2	5,000	10,000
3	5,000	10,000
4	10,000	10,000
Total	$40,000	$40,000

Required

Which project should the manager decide upon? Why? Assume the company considers a 10% return as minimum.

Problem 22.2   Capital Budgeting Analysis

Jill Horn, management consultant for a successful corporation in west Texas, has been asked to evaluate three different projects, each of which will produce a yearly cash flow of $35,000. Initial investment in each of the three projects is $140,000. Project 1 has a useful life of 4 years, project 2 has a useful life of 6 years, and project 3 has a useful life of 5 years. The company requires a minimum return of 12% on capital projects.

Required

1. Assuming that payback time is the sole criterion for her decision, which project should Jill Horn select? Why?
2. Which project will yield the highest rate of return?

Problem 22.3 Basic Analysis of Capital Budgeting

Disco Dippo Incorporated is faced with the decision of continuing with their old equipment or purchasing new equipment at a cost of $23,000. This new equipment is expected to have a useful life of 9 years and is expected to save them $5,000 each of the first 3 years, $4,000 for the next 3 years, and $2,000 for the final 3 years. Disco's minimum rate of return is 10%.

Required

Compute the following:

1. Payback time
2. Internal rate of return
3. Net present value
4. Profitability index

Problem 22.4 Net Present Value Analysis

You have recently been approached by a friend concerning a go-cart racetrack investment. This go-cart racetrack would cost $80,000 in cash. This price allows you to use an existing track, subject to an annual lease payment of $16,700 (these payments are made at the end of each year) for the remaining life of the lease. The price also includes go-carts that have an expected salvage value of $9,000 at the end of 8 years, which is when the lease will expire. The leased property originally cost $45,000. Yearly income is expected to be $70,000, and yearly operating costs will be $38,000.

Required

Using the net present value criterion, would the go-cart racetrack be a wise investment? Assume a 12% interest rate.

Problem 22.5 Various Procedures of Capital Budgeting

Stallcab Incorporated has been in the manufacturing business for 10 years. Although their machinery is still functioning satisfactorily, it has been suggested that new, more efficient machinery would be cost-beneficial.

Last week, a salesman stopped by and displayed a whole new equipment line that would reduce cash operating costs by $11,000 per year. The cost of the machinery is $96,000 and has an estimated useful life of 18 years.

Required

Assuming the salesman's estimations are correct, compute the following:

1. Payback period
2. Internal rate of return

You are unsure of the salesman's integrity. Therefore, compute the internal rate of return if the following are true:

1. The useful life is 10 years instead of 18.
2. The useful life is 25 years instead of 18.
3. The cash operating costs reduction is $7,000 per year instead of $11,000 (18-year useful life).

Problem 22.6   Various Procedures of Capital Budgeting

The Criddle Company has been operating a small food counter for the convenience of their employees. The counter, which uses space not feasibly used for any other purpose, has been managed by a senior citizen whose annual salary is $3,000. Yearly operations have consistently shown a loss as follows:

Sales		$20,000
Food and supplies cash expenses	$19,000	
Salary	3,000	22,000
Net loss		$(2,000)

An equipment company has offered to sell Criddle automatic vending machines for a total cost of $13,000 cash. Old equipment not used in the food counter operation is carried at zero book value; it could be sold now for $1,000. Sales terms are COD (cash on delivery). The old equipment will be worth nothing 10 years from now.

The predicted useful life of the equipment is 10 years, with zero scrap value. The new vending machines will easily serve the same volume that the food counter handled. A catering company will completely service and supply the machines. Prices and variety of food and drink will be the same as those that prevailed at the food counter. The catering company will pay 5% of gross receipts to the Criddle Company and will pay all costs of foods and repairs. The senior citizen will be discharged but other opportunities will be available to him. Criddle's only cost will be the initial outlay for the new machines.

Required

1. Prepare a prospective annual income statement under the new plan. What is the annual income difference between the alternatives? (Assume straight-line depreciation.)
2. Compute the payback period.
3. Compute the following:
   a. The present value under the discounted cash flow method if relevant cost of company capital is 20%. Compute the profitability index.
   b. The rate of return under discounted cash flow methods.
4. Compute the payback reciprocal.
5. Management is very uncertain about the prospective revenue from the vending equipment. Suppose that the gross receipts amounted to $14,000 instead of $20,000. Repeat the computation in requirement 3a.
6. What would be the minimum amount of annual gross receipts from the vending equipment that would justify making the investment? Show your computations.

Problem 22.7   Evaluation of the Procedures for Capital Budgeting (CMA)

Peterdonn Corporation made a capital investment of $100,000 in new equipment 2 years ago. The analysis made at that time indicated the equipment would save $36,400 in operating expenses per year over a 5-year period, or a 24% return on capital before taxes per year based upon the internal rate of return analysis.

The department manager believed that the equipment had "lived up" to its expectations. However, the departmental report showing the overall return on investment (ROI) rate for the first year in which this equipment was used did not reflect as much improvement as had been expected. The department manager asked the accounting section to "break out" the figures related to this investment to find out why it did not contribute more to the department's ROI.

The accounting section was able to identify the equipment and its contribution to the department's operations. The report presented to the department manager at the end of the first year is shown below.

Reduced operating expenses due to new equipment	$ 36,400
Less: Depreciation—20% of cost	20,000
Contribution before taxes	$ 16,400
Investment—beginning of year	$100,000
Investment—end of year	$ 80,000
Average investment for the year	$ 90,000

$$\text{ROI} = \frac{16,400}{90,000} = 18.2\%$$

The department manager was surprised that the ROI was less than 24% because the new equipment performed as expected. The staff analyst in the accounting section replied that the company ROI for performance evaluation differed from that used for capital investment analysis. The analyst commented that the discrepancy could be solved if the company used a different method of depreciation for its performance evaluation reports.

Required

1. Explain why the return on investment of 18.2% for the new equipment as calculated in the department's report by the accounting section differs from the 24% internal rate of return calculated at the time the machine was approved for purchase.
2. Will the use of a different method of depreciation solve the discrepancy as the analyst claims? Explain your answer.
3. Explain how Peterdonn Corporation might restructure the data from the discounted cash flow analysis so the expected performance of the new equipment is consistent with the operating reports received by the department manager.

Problem 22.8   Capital Budgeting—Post Audit (CMA)

Dickson Incorporated has formal policies and procedures to screen and ultimately approve capital projects. Proposed capital projects are classified as one of the following types:

1. Expansion requiring new plant and equipment
2. Expansion by replacement of present equipment with more productive equipment
3. Replacement of old equipment with new equipment of similar quality

All expansion projects and replacement projects costing more than $50,000 must be submitted to the top management capital investment committee for approval. The investment committee evaluates proposed projects considering the costs and benefits outlined in the supporting proposal and the long-range effects on the company. The projected revenue and/or expense effects of the projects, once operational, are included in the proposal. Once a project is accepted, the committee approves an expenditure budget for the project from its inception until it becomes operational. The expenditures required each year for the expansions or replacements are also incorporated into Dickson's annual budget procedure. The budgeted revenue and/or cost effects of the projects, for the period in which they become operational, are incorporated into the 5-year forecast.

Dickson Incorporated does not have a procedure for evaluating projects once they have been implemented and become operational. The vice-president of finance has recommended that Dickson establish a post-completion audit program to evaluate its capital expenditure projects.

Required

1. What are the benefits a company could derive from a post-completion audit program for capital expenditure projects?
2. What are the practical difficulties in collecting and accumulating information that would be used to evaluate a capital project once it becomes operational?

Problem 22.9   Various Methods of Capital Budgeting for Uneven Cash Flows

The Meiga Drilling Company is considering the purchase of a new hydralift machine. The cost of the machine is $56,000. Useful economic life is estimated to be 7 years and disposal costs are expected to equal salvage value. Estimates of cash-operating cost savings have been made by the special projects group as follows:

Year	Amount
1	$20,000
2	16,000
3	12,000
4	8,000
5	7,000
6	6,000
7	5,000
	$74,000

Required

1. Determine the payback period.
2. Determine the net present value. Assume a minimum required return of 14%. Compute the profitability index.
3. Determine the internal rate of return.
4. Determine the accounting rate of return.

Problem 22.10 Capital Budgeting and Sensitivity Analysis

Salem Community Hospital is considering replacement of some hospital kitchen equipment with new more efficient items. The new equipment will cost $40,000 and is estimated to save $10,000 in cash-operating costs per year.

The old equipment was purchased 12 years ago at a cost of $15,000 and is fully depreciated. There is no evident salvage or trade-in value for the old equipment. The old equipment could be used indefinitely.

The new equipment is expected to have a useful life of 10 years and will have no salvage value at the end of the 10 years.

Required

1. Determine the payback period.
2. Determine the net present value. Assume a cut-off rate of return of 12%.
3. The project analysis team is uncertain about the reliability of the life estimate and the amount of the operating savings. You have been asked to compute the net present value under each of the following *changes* in the original conditions:
   a. Useful life of 8 years instead of 10 years
   b. Useful life of 12 years instead of 10 years
   c. Operating savings of $7,000 instead of $10,000
   d. Operating savings of $14,000 instead of $10,000
   e. Operating savings of $8,000 instead of $10,000 and a useful life of 6 years instead of 10 years

CAPITAL BUDGETING: PART II

23

OUTLINE

C apital budgeting is the process of allocating money for the purchase or construction of capital assets. Chapter 22 outlined four techniques that are commonly used in capital budgeting decisions. The application of these techniques is complicated somewhat by income taxes, which we have ignored, and the determination of a minimum desired rate of return, which we assumed has been given. In addition, one of the questions often asked in capital budgeting is how the decision would change if actual operating results are slightly different from the estimates. Sensitivity analysis can be used to evaluate the effect of changes in the input values.

This chapter investigates these complications to the capital budgeting process. After completing the chapter you should be able to:

1. explain the impact of income taxes on capital budgeting decisions and adjust cash flows for the effects of income taxes.
2. define cost of capital and explain its relationship to the minimum desired rate of return for capital budgeting decisions.
3. compute cost of capital using a weighted average of both debt and equity capital.
4. apply sensitivity analysis to determine the potential impact on the decision for variations in the input data.

INCOME TAX EFFECTS ON CAPITAL BUDGETING

Chapter 22 introduced capital budgeting but ignored the impact of income taxes on cash flows resulting from a capital investment project. Many organizations such as universities, hospitals, and governmental units do not pay any income taxes so the cash flows require no tax adjustment. The analysis presented in chapter 22 is applicable to these entities.

Most profit-oriented entities are subject to income taxes and the expected cash flows must be adjusted for the income tax effect. The major effects of income taxes can be broadly classified into three areas—effects on normal cash flows, depreciation, and investment credit. Each of these areas will be explored in detail and then integrated with a comprehensive illustration.[1]

Income Tax Effect on Normal Cash Flows

Cash flows have been classified as (a) net cash flows from operations, (b) an initial investment, and (c) salvage (terminal) value. Let's first consider the net cash flows from operations and the related income taxes.

Net cash flows from operations result from cash inflows in the form of additional revenues and from cash savings in the form of expense reductions. Either way the organization is not able to retain the entire benefit. *A cash inflow in the form of revenue increases net income and income taxes payable to the government. Cash savings in the form of an expense reduction takes away from deductible items on the tax return. This also increases both taxable income and taxes payable.*

The following example will be used to show the net of tax computation for normal cash flows from operations. Brown Incorporated is a consulting organization owned and operated by Ed Brown. Mr. Brown is a consultant for top management of several large corporations around the country. Brown Incorporated is considering the acquisition of a private plane that can be used in traveling from one company to another. It is expected to result in additional revenue of $13,000 per year by eliminating the travel delays com-

---

[1]Our objective here is not to provide a comprehensive review of the effects of income taxes on capital budgeting. Only the highlights will be reviewed in an attempt to illustrate the process that must be followed to compute the net of tax cash flows and how they are used in each capital budgeting technique. You are referred to the income tax regulations for a more comprehensive review of income taxes.

monly experienced on commercial flights. Additional operating costs associated with the plane, excluding depreciation, will be $6,000 per year. Brown Incorporated is subject to a 40% marginal income tax rate.

The comparative income statements below show the income tax effect on the annual cash flows from operations.

Brown, Inc.
Projected Income Statements
(Excluding Depreciation)

	Without Proposed Airplane	With Proposed Airplane	Difference
Revenue	$80,000	$93,000	$13,000
Less expenses:			
Wages	20,000	20,000	–0–
Travel	40,000	46,000	6,000
Net taxable income	20,000	27,000	7,000
Tax payable (40%)	8,000	10,800	2,800
Net income	$12,000	$16,200	$ 4,200

The difference in net income can be summarized as follows:

Additional revenue	$13,000	
Less increase in tax payable (40%)	5,200	
Net of tax		7,800
Additional expense	$ 6,000	
Less decrease in tax payable (40%)	2,400	
Net of tax		$3,600
Combined net of tax increase in cash flows		$4,200

Notice in the example above that the net of tax cash flow for both taxable cash receipts and tax deductible cash expenditures can be computed by multiplying one minus the tax rate by the before-tax cash flow amount [$13,000 × (1 − .40) = $7,800].

Two formulas can be developed from this to compute the net of tax cash flows from operations:

Taxable Cash Receipts in the Form of Additional Revenue

(1 − Tax rate) × Cash receipt = Net of tax cash inflow

Tax Deductible Cash Expenditure

(1 − Tax rate) × Cash expenditure = Net of tax cash outflow

As long as both cash inflows and outflows are subject to income taxes they can be offset against each other before adjusting for the income tax effect.

No adjustment is required for cash flows not subject to income taxes. For example, a cash flow associated with an increase in working capital is not deductible for tax purposes. The amount of the increase in working capital is the cash flow included in the investment analysis.

Accelerated Cost Recovery System—Depreciation

Depreciation is the allocation of the cost of an asset to accounting periods over its useful life. For financial reporting the objective of depreciation is to match the cost of the asset to the benefits it provides. A depreciation method that is systematic and rational and relates costs to benefits should be selected for financial reports.

Capital budgeting is cash flow oriented and the cost of an asset is a cash outflow when payment is made. The entry to record depreciation has been ignored until now because, by itself, it does not affect cash flow (a debit to depreciation expense and a credit to accumulated depreciation).

However, depreciation has an effect upon cash flows for companies that are required to pay income taxes. Depreciation is a deductible item on the income tax return. It reduces taxable income and taxes payable. The reduction in taxes payable is a cash savings that must be included in the investment analysis.

The Economic Recovery Tax Act of 1981 made significant changes in the income tax deduction allowed for depreciation. Congress was convinced that the asset lives using existing depreciation methods were not providing the stimuli essential for economic expansion. Thus, the Accelerated Cost Recovery System (ACRS) was developed. *Depreciable property* is called "recovery property," and depreciation is referred to as **cost recovery.** Under ACRS the cost of recovery property is *recovered* (expensed), using accelerated methods of recovery, over periods of time that are much *shorter than their useful lives.*

Recovery property is divided into one of four groups depending on the type of asset and its use. The following summarizes each group and the type of assets that are included.

1. Eligible 3-year property
   a. Personal property such as autos, light-duty trucks, machinery, and equipment used in research and experimentation
   b. All other property, such as special tools, that has a useful life of four years or less under the class life asset depreciation range (ADR) system
2. Eligible 5-year property
   a. All personal property not included in the above group, such as heavy-duty trucks, lathes, machines, equipment, ships, aircraft, and office furniture
   b. Public utility property with a previous class life of 18 years or less, such as nuclear fuel assemblies and natural gas production plants
3. Eligible 10-year property
   a. Depreciable real property with a useful life of 12.5 years or less, including manufactured residential houses and theme park structures
   b. Public utility property with a class life between 18 and 25 years, such as railroad tank cars
4. Eligible 15-year property
   a. Depreciable real property with a useful life over 12.5 years
   b. Public utility property with a useful life over 25 years

The amount of cost recovery to be taken in any year is determined by multiplying the cost or adjusted basis of the asset by the applicable percentage from the table shown in figure 23.1.[2] The table shown in figure 23.1 is based on an accelerated depreciation method using 150% declining balance in the early years and switching to a straight-line rate for the remainder of the recovery period. Also built into the table is a **half-year convention**—a half year of depreciation is taken in the year of purchase regardless of when the asset was purchased. *Salvage value* under ACRS *is ignored* in computing the annual cost recovery.

The airplane purchase that Brown Incorporated is considering can be used to illustrate the computation of cost recovery and its effect on income taxes. The airplane will be purchased in 19X4 for $40,000. It is expected to have a useful life of 12 years with $5,000 salvage value. The airplane is eligible for a 5-year cost recovery even though the useful life is over twice that long. The following computations are used for annual

[2]The Economic Recovery Tax Act of 1981 had additional tables that allowed faster cost recovery for assets placed in service in 1985 and subsequent years. However, the Tax Equity and Fiscal Responsibility Act (TEFRA) of 1982 repealed the scheduled increases.

Figure 23.1   Cost recovery percentages

If the recovery year is:	The applicable percentage for the class of property is:			
	3-year	*5-year*	*10-year*	*15-year*
1	25	15	8	5
2	38	22	14	10
3	37	21	12	9
4		21	10	8
5		21	10	7
6			10	7
7			9	6
8			9	6
9			9	6
10			9	6
11				6
12				6
13				6
14				6
15				6

This table uses 150% declining-balance method in the early years and switches to the straight-line method for the remainder of the recovery period. Also included is the "half-year convention" in the year of purchase.

cost recovery and the net of tax cash flows. Notice that salvage value is excluded from the computations.

Year	Computation	Recovery Amount	Tax Rate	Net of Tax Cash Flow
1	15% × $40,000	$6,000	40%	$2,400
2	22% × $40,000	$8,800	40%	$3,520
3	21% × $40,000	$8,400	40%	$3,360
4	21% × $40,000	$8,400	40%	$3,360
5	21% × $40,000	$8,400	40%	$3,360

By having additional depreciation expense on the tax return, income taxes payable are reduced by the income tax rate times the additional depreciation expense. The cash flow associated with depreciation is computed as follows:

(Depreciation) × (Tax rate) = Net of tax cash inflow

The following financial statements with and without the aircraft depreciation in the first year of operation illustrate the net of tax cash inflow (savings) associated with the depreciation.

Brown, Inc.
Projected Income Statement—First Year

	Without Aircraft Depreciation	With Aircraft Depreciation
Revenue	$93,000	$93,000
Less expenses:		
Wages	20,000	20,000
Travel	46,000	46,000
Depreciation	–0–	6,000
Net taxable income	$27,000	$21,000
Taxes payable (40%)	10,800	8,400
Net income	$16,200	$12,600

Note that the reduction in taxes payable of $2,400 ($10,800 − $8,400) is equal to the first year depreciation multiplied by the tax rate ($6,000 × 40% = $2,400).

The Impact of Accelerated Cost Recovery on Capital Investment

The Economic Recovery Tax Act of 1981 allows a taxpayer not to elect the accelerated write-off method described above. For one or more classes of property placed in service during the year, the straight-line depreciation method may be used and the recovery period may be extended according to the table below. However, the half-year convention must still be used in the year of purchase and salvage value is ignored.

Type of Property	The Taxpayer May Elect a Recovery Period of:
3–year	3, 5, or 12 years
5–year	5, 12, or 25 years
10–year	10, 25, or 35 years
15–year	15, 35, or 45 years

When is it rational for a taxpayer to select the straight-line method over the same or an extended period of recovery? The proposed airplane purchase by Brown Incorporated illustrates the impact of the new cost recovery method on capital investment. The net of tax cash inflows associated with cost recovery are shown in figure 23.2 using (a) 5-year recovery and the accelerated method and (b) 12-year (useful life) recovery and the straight-line method. The present value of the tax savings by using the shorter period and the accelerated method is $3,567 ($11,382 − $7,815). In present value dollars, Brown Incorporated is $3,567 better off by using the faster cost recovery.

As long as the taxpayer has taxable income that depreciation can be offset against, the taxpayer will be better off to use the accelerated cost recovery method. This includes current year income as well as prior years income that a net operating loss could be carried back and offset against to receive an immediate income tax refund.[3] Money received now or in the immediate future is worth more than money received over an extended period of time because of the time value of money. As a general rule, the accelerated cost recovery method over the shortest possible time period should be selected as long as the company is operating at a profit.

This example also shows why ACRS stimulates capital investment. The ACRS allows greater depreciation in the early years of the asset that results in less income taxes. By paying less income tax during the early years of the project, the company has more money for operations or other investments. Thus, projects that are only marginally profitable when depreciated over their useful life become very profitable when depreciated over the lives specified by ACRS.

Investment Tax Credit (ITC)

Investment tax credit is a credit against income taxes for depreciable personal property (excluding buildings and their structural components) that is purchased and placed in service during the year. Unlike depreciation that is a deduction in computing taxable income, *investment tax credit is subtracted from income taxes that are computed on taxable income.* Therefore, there is a dollar-for-dollar cash flow associated with the investment credit. The investment credit can only be taken in the year of purchase. The immediacy of the return makes the investment credit very valuable.

---

[3]Income tax laws require a net operating loss to be carried back against income of the previous three years. If income tax has been paid during those years, an immediate refund may be received. When the loss is greater than the income for the previous three years, the remaining loss is carried forward to be offset against income of subsequent years.

Figure 23.2   Impact of accelerated cost recovery on capital investment

Accelerated, 5-year Cost Recovery

Cash Flows

Type	Timing	Amount
Reduction in taxes payable	Year 1	$2,400
	Year 2	3,520
	Years 3–5	3,360 per year
Desired rate of return		12%

Net of tax cash inflows and present value computation:

Year	Cost Recovery	Tax Rate	Net of Tax Cash Flow	Present Value Factor @ 12%	Present Value
1	$6,000	40%	$2,400	.893	$ 2,143
2	8,800	40	3,520	.797	2,805
3–5	8,400	40	3,360	1.915[a]	6,434
Total					$11,382

Straight-line, 12-year Cost Recovery

Type	Timing	Amount
Reduction in taxes payable	Year 1	$ 667
	Years 2–12	1,333 per year
	Year 13	667
Desired rate of return		12%

Net of tax cash inflows and present value computation:

Year	Cost Recovery	Tax Rate	Net of Tax Cash Flow	Present Value Factor @ 12%	Present Value
1	$1,667	40%	$ 667	.893	$ 595
2–12	3,333	40	1,333	5.301[b]	7,067
13	1,667	40	667	.229	153
Total					$ 7,815

[a](3.605 − 1.690 = 1.915)
[b](6.194 − .893 = 5.301)

The amount of investment tax credit is based on the recovery period of the property used in determining the deduction for cost recovery. The credit is currently 10% of the cost of the asset. For eligible 5-year and 10-year personal property and for 15-year public utility property, 100% of the cost qualifies for the 10% credit. For eligible 3-year property, only 60% of the cost of the property qualifies for investment credit, which is equivalent to a 6% credit.

Example: Streuling Company purchased a car for $12,000 and some manufacturing equipment for $30,000 at various times during 19X3. The investment credit is computed as follows:

Asset	Recovery Period	Cost	Applicable Credit	Investment Credit
Car	3-years	$12,000	6%	$ 720
Manufacturing equipment	5-years	$30,000	10%	$3,000
Total				$3,720

The Tax Equity and Financial Responsibility Act of 1982 (TEFRA) required changes in computing investment tax credit and cost recovery for assets placed in service after December 31, 1982. You can select from two options:

1. Use the normal investment credit percentages as outlined above and reduce the basis of the property by one half of the investment credit. Cost recovery percentages are applied to the adjusted basis of the property.
2. Reduce the investment credit by 2% and use the full cost of the property in computing annual cost recovery.

Example: Let's assume a delivery truck (heavy-duty) was purchased on January 1, 19X3 for $16,000. This qualifies as 5-year recovery property. The ITC and ACR under the options outlined above are computed as follows:

Option 1

ITC: 10% × $16,000 = $1,600

ACR:

Cost	$16,000
Half of ITC (1/2 × $1,600)	800
Adjusted basis	$15,200

Year	Adjusted Basis	×	ACR %	=	ACR
1	$15,200		15%		$2,280
2	15,200		22%		3,344
3	15,200		21%		3,192
4	15,200		21%		3,192
5	15,200		21%		3,192

Option 2

ITC: 8% × $16,000 = $1,280

ACR:

Year	Basis	×	ACR %	=	ACR
1	$16,000		15%		$2,400
2	16,000		22%		3,520
3	16,000		21%		3,360
4	16,000		21%		3,360
5	16,000		21%		3,360

The option that is most profitable will be dependent upon the marginal tax rate and cost of capital for each individual taxpayer.

Any investment tax credit is generally deducted from the cost of the investment to compute the net cash outflow required for the acquisition. An immediate deduction is justified because of the quarterly tax deposits required for the payment of estimated income taxes. The purchase of a qualifying asset with its related investment credit provides an immediate reduction in the current quarter's federal income tax deposits.

The airplane that Brown Incorporated is considering is personal depreciable property with a cost recovery period of 5 years. The full $40,000 cost qualifies for the 10% investment credit. The cash outflow associated with the acquisition is $36,000 computed as follows:

Acquisition price	$40,000
Less investment credit ($40,000 × 10%)	$ 4,000
Net of tax cash outflow	$36,000

Salvage Value

Salvage value is not considered in computing annual cost recovery under ACRS. Therefore, the entire cost of the asset will be written off during the recovery period, which in most cases will be much shorter than the useful life of the asset.

When the asset is sold or retired, there is a potential gain or loss based on the difference between the sale price and book value. As a general rule, the gain (loss) is taxed as ordinary income (loss).[4]

The cash flow associated with salvage value must be computed net of tax. The following equation can be used to compute the net of tax cash flow for an asset sold at a gain or loss, with or without any salvage value.

$$\text{Cash proceeds from sale} - \left[\left(\text{Cash proceeds from sale} - \text{Book value}\right) \times (\text{Tax rate})\right] = \text{Net of tax cash flow}$$

The center portion of the equation computes the gain or loss by subtracting the book value from the sale price. The income tax effect is computed by multiplying the gain (loss) by the tax rate. In the case of a gain, this amount is then subtracted from the cash proceeds from the sale; a loss is added to the cash proceeds for the net of tax cash flow.

The expected salvage value from the airplane that Brown Incorporated is considering is $5,000. Because the airplane will be fully depreciated at the end of year 5, a book value of zero is used in the computation. The after-tax cash flow expected in year 12 from the sale of the airplane is $3,000.

$$\$5,000 - [(\$5,000 - 0) \times 40\%] = \underline{\$3,000}$$

Generally in capital budgeting proposals the asset is expected to be held beyond the recovery period so the asset will be fully depreciated at the time the salvage value is received. In this case the entire proceeds will be ordinary income and the net of tax cash flow can be computed as other revenue. Be sure to note that *this is only applicable to fully depreciated assets.*

$$\text{Cash proceeds from sale of fully depreciated asset} \times (1 - \text{Tax rate}) = \text{Net of tax cash flow}$$

For Brown Incorporated the computation is:

$$(\$5,000) \times (1 - .40) = \$3,000$$

Comprehensive Illustration

The proposed airplane acquisition by Brown Incorporated will be used to illustrate the various capital budgeting techniques when income tax is included. The relevant facts are summarized below:

Proposal: Brown Incorporated is considering the acquisition of an airplane at a cost of $40,000. It is expected to have a useful life of 12 years with $5,000 salvage value. As a result of having the airplane, revenues are expected to increase by $13,000 and annual cash outlays for operating the airplane are expected to be $6,000 more than current travel costs. Management has elected to use the ACRS over 5 years and has identified a 12% minimum desired rate of return.

Compute the (*a*) net present value, (*b*) internal rate of return, (*c*) payback period, and (*d*) accounting rate of return.

---

[4]Technically, part of the gain could be taxed at a capital gain rate but only after ordinary income has been recognized to the extent of prior recovery deductions. Further, when one asset from a group of assets is sold, the entire cash proceeds is ordinary income. The book value of the asset remains in the group account and is expensed through normal recovery charges over the remaining life of the group.

Figure 23.3   Brown Inc.—expected cash flows for airplane acquisition

---

Type	Timing	Amount
Initial investment	Now	$36,000
Tax savings from cost recovery	Year 1	2,280
	Year 2	3,344
	Years 3–5	3,192 per year
Annual inflow from other operations	Years 1–12	4,200 per year
Salvage value	Year 12	3,000

The procedures followed in analyzing the investment proposal are the same as those discussed in chapter 22. The cash flows associated with the investment, annual operations, and salvage value are charted and applied to one or more of the capital budgeting techniques. The only difference is that each of the cash flows (initial investment, operations, and salvage value) must be taken net of any related income tax. The computations for each of these items has been illustrated above. However, the net of tax cash flows from cost recovery (depreciation) must be modified for the adjustment to the basis (cost) for one half of the investment tax credit. The adjusted basis is:

Cost	$40,000
Half of ITC (1/2 × $4,000)	2,000
Adjusted basis	$38,000

The annual tax savings from cost recovery is:

Year	ACR Computation	Recovery Amount	×	Tax Rate	=	Net of Tax Cash Flow
1	15% × $38,000	$5,700		40%		$2,280
2	22% × $38,000	8,360		40%		3,344
3	21% × $38,000	7,980		40%		3,192
4	21% × $38,000	7,980		40%		3,192
5	21% × $38,000	7,980		40%		3,192

The resulting cash flows are shown in figure 23.3.

Net Present Value   Net present value is computed by subtracting the initial investment from the present value of expected cash flows at the minimum desired rate of return. If the net present value is positive, it is a desirable investment at the cut-off rate.
Present value of cash flows at a 12% cut-off rate:

Cost Recovery

Year			
1	($2,280 × .893)	$2,036	
2	($3,344 × .797)	2,665	
3–5	($3,192 × 1.915)	$6,113	$10,814

Other Annual Inflows from Operations

1–12	($4,200 × 6.194)	$26,015

Salvage Value

12	($3,000 × .257)	771
Total		$37,600
Initial investment		$36,000
Net present value		$ 1,600

Internal Rate of Return   The internal rate of return is the interest rate that equates the present value of future cash flows with the initial investment. The investment is desirable when the interest rate exceeds a minimum rate specified by management.

Because the net present value is positive with a 12% rate, a slightly higher rate, say 14%, is used and the net present value is computed again.

Present value of cash flows at 14%:

Cost Recovery

Year			
1	($2,280 × .877)	$2,000	
2	($3,344 × .769)	$2,572	
3–5	($3,192 × 1.786)	$5,701	$10,273

Other Annual Inflows from Operations

1–12	($4,200 × 5.660)	$23,772

Salvage Value

12	($3,000 × .208)	624
Total		$34,669
Initial investment		$36,000
Net present value		($ 1,331)

The net present values for 12% and 14% can be used to interpolate the internal rate of return.

Rate	Net Present Value
12%	$1,600
14%	1,331
Total	$2,931
Internal rate of return	13.1%

12% + [(1,600 ÷ 2,931) × 2%]

Payback Period   Payback period is the length of time required to accumulate cash flows equal to the initial investment. The proposal is desirable if the period of time is less than a maximum time specified by management. The payback period for Brown Incorporated is 4.97 years.

Year	Annual Cash Flows	Cumulative Cash Flows	Payback Years
1	$6,480	$ 6,480	1.00
2	$7,544	$14,024	1.00
3	$7,392	$21,416	1.00
4	$7,392	$28,808	1.00
5	$7,192	$36,000	.97[a]
Total			4.97 years

[a]($7,192 ÷ 7,392 × 1.0)

Accounting Rate of Return   The accounting rate of return is computed by dividing the average annual cash flows net of tax less annual depreciation by the initial investment.

$$\frac{\text{Annual cash flow} - \text{Depreciation}}{\text{Initial investment}} = \text{Accounting rate of return}$$

The investment is desirable if the rate of return exceeds the minimum rate specified by management.

The average annual cash flows are computed by adding all the cash flows net of tax ($68,600) and dividing by the life of the asset (12 years). The average annual cash flow for Brown Incorporated is $5,717 ($68,600 ÷ 12 years). For financial reporting purposes, Brown Incorporated has elected to use straight-line depreciation with a useful life of 12 years and zero salvage value. Annual depreciation is $3,333 ($40,000 ÷ 12 years). The accounting rate of return is 6.6%.

$$\frac{\$5,717 - \$3,333}{\$36,000} = \underline{6.6\%}$$

In summary, income tax is a significant item in capital budgeting decisions. Almost every item must be adjusted for the effect it has on income taxes paid to the government. The capital budgeting techniques do not change, only the computation of the cash flows used in the analysis. Depreciation, with the option to use ACRS, has a significant impact on cash flows when income taxes are considered.

COST OF CAPITAL

In applying the capital budgeting techniques we have had a cut-off rate given. Cost of capital is generally used as a basis for developing the minimum desired rate of return. Remember that the computation of cost of capital is a controversial issue with diverging points of view. A detailed study of the cost of capital is reserved for a finance course. Our objective here is to identify what cost of capital is, how it relates to cost accounting and capital budgeting, and review some of the basic concepts involved in its computation.

Cost of Capital Defined

Cost of capital is the rate of return that must be earned on invested capital in order to leave the market price of the firm's common stock unchanged. It identifies the breakeven point for the organization. If the firm earns more than (less than) this rate, the value of the firm and the market price of the common stock will increase (decrease). Therefore, it is an appropriate rate to be used as the minimum desired rate of return for investment decisions.

Capital (financial) **components** include liabilities, preferred stock, and common stock. All assets, including the acquisition of property, plant, and equipment, must be financed by one or more of these capital components.

Each capital component has a cost which is called the **component cost.** For example, the cost of bonds is the after-tax cost of interest. For preferred stock it is the annual dividend that is expected to be paid. The cost of common stock is based on expected dividends plus appreciation in the value of the stock. All these component costs must be combined in a meaningful way into an average cost of capital that can be used in investment decisions. A weighted average is commonly used.

To illustrate the computation of the weighted average, assume that we begin Capital Corporation by selling ourselves and others 100 shares of common stock at $40 per share ($4,000). In pricing the common stock we evaluated the expected business activity and the risk associated with it. We also looked at the alternative uses of our money. After careful consideration a 15% rate of return was considered to be a fair return on our money. Bonds are also issued for $2,000. The bonds carry a 10% interest rate and are sold at their face value. The balance sheet of the newly organized Capital Corporation is as follows:

Capital Corporation
Balance Sheet

Assets		_Liabilities & Owner's Equity_	
Cash	$6,000	Bonds payable	$2,000
		Common stock	$4,000
		Total	$6,000

The critical question is how much must Capital Corporation earn during its first year of operations to leave the price of its common stock at $40 per share? Assuming that the corporate tax rate is 40% and the 15% estimate of the return required by the common stockholders is accurate and remains constant during the year, the weighted average cost of capital can be computed. The after-tax cost of each capital component is weighted by the proportion of the total capital that it provides.

Capital Component	Proportion of Total Capital	×	Component Cost	=	Weighted Average Cost of Capital
Bonds	1/3	×	.06[a]	=	.02
Common stock	2/3	×	.15	=	.10
Total					.12

[a]The after-tax cost is obtained by multiplying the interest rate by one minus the tax rate [.10 × (1 − .40)].

Capital Corporation must earn 12% after tax on its investments or 20% [12% ÷ (1 − 40%)] before interest and taxes in order to satisfy the expectations of the common stockholders. This can be illustrated by a simplified version of the income statement.

Capital Corporation
Income Statement
Year 1

Earnings before interest and taxes (20% × $6,000)	$1,200
Interest (10% × $2,000)	200
Net income before taxes	$1,000
Income taxes (40% × $1,000)	400
Net income	$ 600
Return required by common stockholders	15%
Total market value ($600 ÷ 15%)	$4,000
Market price per share ($4,000 ÷ 100 shares)	$ 40

By earning $1,200 (20% × $6,000) before interest and taxes, Capital Corporation is able to pay the interest on the bonds and the taxes to the government and leave $600 for the common stockholders. This is equal to 15% of their investment, which satisfies their expected return. Thus, the value of their common stock will remain at $40 per share.

Had the earnings been more, the return would have exceeded the stockholders' expectations. If the higher rate of return is expected to continue, potential investors would be attracted and the price of the stock would be bid up. On the other hand, if net income had been lower, say $400, common shareholders would have been disappointed. Because they can invest their money in other corporations of less risk and earn 10%, or in corporations of equal risk and earn 15%, they will want to sell their stock in Capital Corporation and the price of the stock will be driven down. Only by earning a rate of return that is equal to the weighted average cost of capital will the value of the firm remain the same.

Marginal Cost of Capital (MCC)

The **marginal cost of capital** (MCC) is the rate of return that must be earned on *additional* capital in order to leave the market value of the common stock unchanged. Many capital budgeting projects are financed out of new capital to the organization. The marginal cost of capital should be used as a cut-off rate in evaluating these proposals.

To illustrate, assume that Capital Corporation invested the $6,000 at the beginning of year 1 in a long-term project that yields 12% after tax. Also assume that the net income of $600 was paid to the common shareholders in the form of a dividend at the end of year 1. At the beginning of year 2, Capital Corporation is considering another investment proposal that will cost $2,000. Management has decided to raise the needed capital by issuing additional bonds carrying a 10% interest charge. However, this additional debt financing will increase the debt to equity ratio to 50:50. The threat of bankruptcy and the costs associated with it increases substantially as the amount of debt increases to 50% or more of total capital. As a result of the increased risk, common shareholders will require a 20% rate of return on their investment in Capital Corporation. What is the new weighted average cost of capital? What is the marginal cost of capital associated with the new debt financing? How much must Capital Corporation earn on the new investment to leave the price of the common stock unchanged?

The weighted average cost of capital is changed by two factors—First, a higher proportion of total capital is now being financed by debt with a lower after-tax cost of capital. Second, the component cost for common stock has increased because of higher risk associated with the debt financing. The new weighted average cost of capital is computed as follows:

Capital Component	Proportion of Total Capital	×	Component Cost	=	Weighted Average Cost of Capital
Bonds	1/2	×	.06	=	.03
Common stock	1/2	×	.20	=	.10
Total					.13

Capital Corporation must now earn 13% after taxes or 21.67% $[13\% \div (1 - 40\%)]$ before interest and taxes in order for the price of common stock to remain the same. Notice on the partial income statement that follows and the analysis that follows that the price of the common stock stays at $40 per share as long as the new expectations are met.

Capital Corporation
Income Statement
Year 2

Earnings before interest and taxes (21.67% × $8,000)	$1,734
Interest (10% × $4,000)	400
Net income before taxes	$1,334
Income taxes (40% × $1,334)	534
Net Income	$ 800
Return required by common stockholders	20%
Total market value ($800 ÷ 20%)	$4,000
Market price per share ($4,000 ÷ 100 shares)	$ 40

The key concept from this analysis is that the *marginal cost of the new capital* ($2,000 of new debt) *may not be equal to the cost of that capital component* (10% before tax or 6% after tax). This can be seen by comparing the income statements for years 1 and 2. In order for the value of the firm to remain the same, earnings before interest and taxes must increase $534 ($1,734 − $1,200). However, the $6,000 of original capital was invested on a long-term basis to yield only $1,200 before interest and taxes. The $534 of additional earnings must come entirely from the new investment. Thus, the before interest and income tax rate of return must be 26.7% ($534 ÷ $2,000) and the after-tax rate of return must be 16% [26.7% × (1 − 40%)].

A standard equation can be used to compute the marginal cost of capital. In order to apply the equation, first compute the weighted average cost of capital under the old and new capital structures, and then compute the increase (decrease) in the weighted average cost of capital. The equation is:

$$MCC = \begin{array}{c} \text{New} \\ \text{weighted} \\ \text{average cost} \\ \text{of capital} \end{array} \pm \left[\begin{array}{c} \text{Increase (decrease)} \\ \text{in weighted average} \\ \text{cost of capital} \end{array} \times \left(\frac{\text{Capital before the increase}}{\text{Increase in capital}} \right) \right]$$

Applying the equation to Capital Corporation we have:

$$\text{MCC} = 13\% + 1\% \left[\left(\frac{\$6,000}{\$2,000}\right)\right] = \underline{16\%}$$

A 16% minimum desired rate of return should be used in evaluating the new investment proposal of Capital Corporation. If the investment provides anything less than this amount, the expectations of the common shareholders will not be met and the price of the common stock will be driven down. Of course, a return greater than 16% would exceed their expectation and the value of the firm will increase.

In summary, a project financed by new debt should not be evaluated using the interest cost of the debt. The interest rate charged is only the explicit cost of the debt. The total cost of the new debt is equal to the explicit cost of the debt plus the effect that the use of additional debt financing has on the cost and availability of existing debt and equity capital. *The marginal cost of capital is the rate that must be earned on additional capital to leave the value of the firm unchanged and it is the rate that should be used as the cut-off rate for capital investment decisions.*

Thus far in our analysis we have assumed that the after-tax cost of capital for each capital component is known. We will now consider how each of these are computed.

Cost of Debt

A debt that has no interest charge, such as accounts payable, has no explicit cost associated with it. When we talk about the cost of debt we are generally talking about notes payable, mortgages, or bonds, which all bear interest.

Without any income taxes, the cost of debt would be equal to the *effective interest rate* paid on the debt. The effective interest rate, also called the yield to maturity, is the interest rate that equates the present value of future payments to the amount of money received. The effective interest rate should not be confused with the face rate or coupon rate of the bond. The *face rate* of the bond identifies the amount of interest to be paid. If that amount is more than (less than) expected by potential investors, then the amount they will be willing to pay for the bond will be more than (less than) the face value of the bond. The effective interest rate is the rate that equates the present value of interest and principal payments to the amount received from investors.

Because interest expense is deductible in computing taxable income, companies subject to income taxes must adjust the effective interest rate for the income tax savings that the interest provides. The after-tax cost of debt can be computed as follows:

After-tax cost of debt = Effective interest rate $\times$ (1 − Tax rate)

To illustrate the after-tax cost of debt, assume that Super Sales Incorporated issues $5,000 of 11% face value bonds to yield 10%. They are 10-year bonds that pay interest of $275 semiannually. The amount of cash received upon issuance is $5,312 (the present value of 20 annuity payments of $275 and $5,000 in 20 periods at 5%). With an income tax rate of 45%, the after-tax cost of the debt is:

After-tax cost of debt = 10% (1 − 45%) = $\underline{5.5\%}$

Notice that the yield rate, not the face interest rate, is used to compute the cost of debt. The yield rate is an accurate before-tax cost of debt because it is based on the amount that must be paid for principal and interest over the life of the bond, relative to the sale price of the bond.

Cost of Preferred Stock

The cost of preferred stock is based on the dividend that must be paid annually. Preferred stock may have a variety of dividend policies, including noncumulative or participating, but the most common dividend policy is a cumulative dividend specified as a percentage of the par value of the stock. A 9% cumulative preferred stock with a $100 par value will pay an annual dividend of $9.

Income taxes are not relevant in computing the cost of preferred stock because preferred dividends are not deductible in computing taxable income. Also, there is no maturity date for preferred stock.[5] It is assumed that the annual dividend will be paid forever. The present value of an annuity that lasts forever is computed as follows:

$$\text{Present value of a perpetual annuity} = \frac{\text{Annuity amount}}{\text{Interest rate}}$$

The present value of the perpetual dividend is the amount an investor will be willing to pay for the preferred stock. The price of the stock is determined in the market as an average of the yield rates acceptable to potential investors. The actual price may be higher or lower than the par value depending on the market rate as compared to the dividend rate. Potential investors will use a market rate that reflects their attitude toward the risk of the investment as well as the opportunity cost of their money. The price they pay is known, but the interest rate they use is unknown, which is the item of information that is needed to compute the weighted average cost of capital. The above equation can be manipulated as follows to compute the interest rate, given the price of the preferred stock and the annual dividend:

$$\frac{\text{Interest rate}}{\text{(cost of preferred stock)}} = \frac{\text{Annuity (dividend) amount}}{\text{Purchase price of the stock}}$$

Example: What is the component cost of capital for a $100 par value, 9% cumulative preferred stock that is sold for $90?

Solution:

$$\frac{\text{Interest rate}}{\text{(cost of preferred stock)}} = \frac{\$9}{\$90} = \underline{10\%}$$

The component cost of capital in the example above is 10%. This is the yield rate used by investors to compute the purchase price of the stock. It is also the component cost that should be used in computing the weighted average cost of capital.

Cost of Common Stock and Retained Earnings

The capital provided by common shareholders is contained in several accounts including common stock, paid-in capital in excess of par, and retained earnings. The amounts in each of these accounts must be combined to compute the proportion of total capital provided by common shareholders.

Common shareholders have the right to receive dividends declared by the board of directors and to share in the growth of the firm from earnings retained and reinvested in the business. They generally share in growth by (*a*) selling their stock at an appreciated value at some time in the future or by (*b*) receiving larger dividends with the passage of time.

The procedures for computing the cost of common stock and retained earnings can be viewed as an extension of those used in computing the cost of preferred stock. In addition to the expected dividend and price of the stock, a growth factor must be added

---

[5]Convertible preferred stock provides an added complexity that will not be considered here.

to the equation. The following equation is generally used to compute the cost of common stock and retained earnings.

Cost of common stock[6] and retained earnings $= \dfrac{D}{MPPS} + G$

Where: D = Cash dividend at the end of the first year
$MPPS$ = Current market price per share
G = Constant growth rate

The market price per share is the only factor in the above equation that is known with any degree of certainty. The expected dividend to be paid at the end of the year can be estimated by management with some degree of accuracy, but it is clearly not as precise as the interest rate on bonds or the dividends on preferred stock. The expected growth rate is the most difficult to predict. Techniques for estimating the expected growth rate are based on (a) dividend policy and (b) appreciation in the market value of the stock.

Growth in the annual dividend can be used for companies that have a stable dividend history and pay out most of their earnings as dividends.

Example: Company X has common stock outstanding with a current market price of $20 per share. Their dividend record over the past 4 years has been as follows:

19X3	$2.00
19X4	2.20
19X5	2.42
19X6	2.66

Analysis of the dividend record shows a compound annual rate of increase of 10%. However, changes in the economic environment cause management to question their ability to maintain this growth rate. An 8% rate seems more likely and the dividend for 19X7 is projected at $2.87. Cost of common stock and retained earnings is computed at 22.35%.

$\text{Cost} = \dfrac{\$2.87}{\$20.00} + 8\% = \underline{22.35\%}$

Some companies either do not pay dividends or have an erratic dividend history. For these companies it is more useful to look at the appreciation in the value of their common stock.

Example: Company Y has paid $3 per share annually on their common stock outstanding and has reinvested all additional earnings within the business. As a result, the company has grown and the market price has increased. Year-end market prices and the annual growth percentages are shown below:

	Year-End Market Price	Annual Growth Percentage
19X1	$33.25	
19X2	36.50	9.8%[a]
19X3	39.12	7.2
19X4	42.75	9.3

[a][($36.50 − $33.25) ÷ 33.25]

An average of the annual growth percentages indicate that company Y will probably grow at 8.8% [(9.8% + 7.2% + 9.3%) ÷ 3] during the year. Their cost of common stock and retained earnings is computed at 15.8%.

$\text{Cost} = \dfrac{\$3.00}{\$42.75} + 8.8\% = \underline{15.8\%}$

[6]If it is a new issue of common stock, the full market price is generally not received. A portion of the sale price is usually paid as an underwriter's fee. For such issues, the net amount received per share should be substituted in the equation for the market price per share.

Figure 23.4   Blaylock Inc.—capital structure

Liabilities

Current liabilities		$ 26,300	12.5%
Bonds payable	$50,000		
Less: Discount	1,550	48,450	23.0%

Owner's Equity

Preferred stock (400 shares of 8%, $100 par value)	$38,400		18.3%
Common stock ($1 par)	25,000		46.2%
Retained earnings	71,850		
Total		135,250	
Total liabilities and owner's equity		$210,000	100%

Notes to the financial statement:
1. The bonds that carry a 13.5% interest rate and mature in 15 years were sold to yield 14%.
2. Preferred stock is 8% cumulative on a par value of $100. It was sold for $96 per share.
3. Annual dividend on common stock is expected to be $2.50 per share, based on an annual growth rate of 8%. The current market price per share is $15.
4. Blaylock Incorporated is subject to a 40% income tax rate.

Comprehensive Illustration

The capital structure of Blaylock Incorporated will be used to illustrate the computation of each component cost and the weighted average cost of capital. Figure 23.4 summarizes the capital components of Blaylock Incorporated. To keep our example as simple as possible we will assume that the book values and market values of the debt and stock are equal. Therefore, the weighting would not change if we used market values rather than book values. The notes to the financial statement contain important information for the computations that follow.

The component cost of each capital component must first be computed as follows:

Current liabilities: The current liabilities are non-interest bearing so their component cost is zero.[7]

Bonds payable: The yield rate is used, not the bond interest rate.

$$\text{Component cost} = 14\% \times (1 - 40\%) = \underline{8.4\%}$$

Preferred stock: The yield rate is computed as follows:

$$\text{Component cost} = \frac{\$8}{\$96} = \underline{8.33\%}$$

Common stock and retained earnings:

$$\text{Component cost} = \frac{\$2.50}{\$15.00} + 8\% = \underline{24.67\%}$$

[7]There is no common agreement on how to handle current liabilities. Even though there is no explicit cost associated with accounts payable, there may be an implicit cost due to loss of cash discounts, higher prices for goods purchased on account by slow paying customers, and similar items. Some people recommend estimating these costs and associating them with current liabilities. Some people suggest that cost of capital should be based only on long term financing so they exclude any current liabilities in the computation. In order to keep our example both simple and complete, we will include current liabilities but will assume that their component cost is zero.

Each component cost is combined to compute the weighted average cost of capital.

Capital Component	Proportion of Total Capital	×	Component Cost	=	Weighted Average Cost of Capital
Current liabilities	12.5%	×	.00%	=	.00%
Bonds payable	23.0	×	8.40	=	1.93
Preferred stock	18.3	×	8.33	=	1.52
Common stock	46.2	×	24.67	=	11.40
					14.85%

The weighted average cost of capital for Blaylock Incorporated is 14.85%. Blaylock's operations and investments must earn 14.85% after tax in order for the common stock to continue to sell for $15 per share. A 14.85% cut-off rate is appropriate for capital budgeting decisions using money that is reinvested in the company. Projects that earn exactly 14.85% will leave the value of the firm unchanged. Those that earn over 14.85% will enhance the value of the firm and will have a positive impact on the market price of their common stock.

SENSITIVITY ANALYSIS IN CAPITAL BUDGETING

Sensitivity analysis can be used to measure the effect of a change in one or more of the input values in a capital budgeting decision. Sensitivity analysis cannot eliminate estimation errors nor can it eliminate the risks associated with the selection of any given project. It provides *a means for evaluating the effect of errors on the outcome to show where the greatest risks lie.* Based on this information, management can elect to (*a*) investigate certain estimates more thoroughly before making a final decision, (*b*) accept the proposal as it is, or (*c*) reject the proposal without further analysis. A decision to investigate certain areas more intensively may lead to improved estimates and thereby reduce the risk of making a wrong choice.

Our discussion of sensitivity analysis will use the net present value technique. This technique is easy to use and provides a good measure of investment profitability. A similar analysis could be performed using other capital investment techniques.

The basic inputs to a capital budgeting decision using net present value are (*a*) minimum desired rate of return, (*b*) initial investment, (*c*) net cash flows from operations, and (*d*) salvage value. Sensitivity analysis can be used to measure the impact on net present value when one or more of these input values are changed. Small changes in input values that have a large impact on net present value are of most interest. These are the areas in which further analysis will be most useful.

Selecting a Minimum Desired Rate of Return

Cost of capital has been recommended as the most appropriate cut-off rate for capital investment decisions because it is the rate of return that must be earned on invested capital in order to leave the market price of the firm's common stock unchanged. The value of the firm and the market value of the common stock will increase if the firm is able to earn more than this rate. Because this rate is so important in sensitivity analysis, we should evaluate the basis upon which it is developed and compute the effect of changes in those basic assumptions. Also, there may be some cases in which the discount rate should be different than the cost of capital because of the risk associated with the investment being analyzed. Let's consider several possibilities.

Errors in Estimating the Component Cost of Capital Stock   Recall from our discussion on cost of capital the importance of the component cost of each capital component in computing the weighted average cost of capital. The information used in computing

Figure 23.5   Cutt-off Inc.—weighted average cost of capital

Capital Component	Proportion of Total Capital	×	After-Tax Cost L	O	P	=	Weighted Average Cost of Capital L	O	P
Current debt	10%	×	0%			=	0%	0%	0%
Long-term debt	30	×	6			=	1.8	1.8	1.8
Common stock	60	×	20			=	12.0		
				24.5%				14.7	
					9%				5.4
Total	100%						13.8%	16.5%	7.2%

L—Most likely estimate
O—Optimistic estimate
P—Pessimistic estimate

the component cost of long-term debt and preferred stock is fairly accurate, but subjective estimates are often required with common stock. The expected dividend and growth rate are very tentative. Sensitivity analysis can be used to measure the impact of an error in these estimates on the cut-off rate.

To illustrate, assume that Cutt-off Incorporated is a fairly new company without an established dividend history or stock price pattern. Their capital structure consists of non-interest-bearing current liabilities, bonds with a 6% after-tax cost, and common stock. The proportion of total capital provided by each is shown in figure 23.5. Common stock currently sells for $10 per share. In estimating the component cost of common stock, a dividend of $1.00 is most likely, although it could be as high as $1.25 or as low as $.30 per share. Also, a growth rate of 10% is felt to be most likely, but it could be as high as 12% or as low as 6%. The component cost of common stock is first computed using these most likely, optimistic, and pessimistic estimates. The results are then used in computing the weighted average cost of capital. Figure 23.5 shows the computation of the weighted average cost of capital.

Most Likely (L)

$$\text{Cost} = \frac{\$1.00}{\$10.00} + 10\% = \underline{20\%}$$

Optimistic (O)

$$\text{Cost} = \frac{\$1.25}{\$10.00} + 12\% = \underline{24.5\%}$$

Pessimistic (P)

$$\text{Cost} = \frac{\$.30}{\$10.00} + 6\% = \underline{9\%}$$

The weighted average cost of capital for Cutt-off Incorporated may be as high as 16.5% or as low as 7.2%, but the most likely estimate is 13.8%. This is a rather wide range and perhaps some additional analysis should be required.

Rate Adjustment for Nonproductive Projects   By using the weighted average or marginal cost of capital as the cut-off rate in capital budgeting decisions we are assuming that all capital investment projects have a productive rate of return. Projects for pollution control, OSHA, or sanitation may be required by government regulation or by a sense of moral obligation to employees or the community, but they do not generally provide a direct cash flow. Therefore, *the rate of return on productive projects must be set higher than the cost of capital in order for the average return on all projects to equal or exceed the breakeven point.*

To illustrate, assume that Cutt-off Incorporated has determined that their after-tax cost of capital is 14%. If the balance between productive and nonproductive projects is 75–25, the productive projects must earn 18.67% after tax in order for the average rate of return to be 14%. This can be illustrated as follows:

Type	Proportion	Amount Invested	Rate of Return	After-Tax Return
Productive	75%	$ 75,000	18.67%	$14,000
Nonproductive	25	25,000	.00	–0–
Total	100%	$100,000		$14,000

$$\text{Average return} = \frac{\$14,000}{\$100,000} = 14\%$$

The rate of return required on productive projects can be computed by dividing the desired average return by the percentage of productive projects ($14\% \div 75\% = 18.67\%$).

Variable Rate Among Projects   The weighted average cost of capital represents the average risk associated with investments in the capital securities of a company. Investors of each security assess both the risk and opportunity cost associated with the investment in determining the price they are willing to pay. The weighted average cost of capital is computed from the prices of the various securities.

Each individual capital investment project has some risk associated with the amount and time of cash flows. If the project risk is higher than the average firm risk and the project is adopted, then the average firm risk will increase and the cost of capital will increase. In order to adjust for this, *a higher cut-off rate may be selected for higher risk projects.* Likewise, *a lower cut-off rate could be selected for projects that are less risky than the firm average.*

Cutt-off Incorporated uses their weighted average cost of capital of 14% on projects with an average amount of risk. The rate may be adjusted upward (or downward) in proportion to the increased (decreased) risk associated with the project. The following rates have been selected for the current proposals.

Proposal	Amount	Risk Rating	Cut-off Rate
ZOL–1	$50,000	Average	14%
ZOL–2	25,000	Risky	16%
BL–10	25,000	Very risky	20%

Variable Rate per Year for an Individual Project   Cash flows in the immediate future can be predicted with more accuracy and are less risky than cash flows in the distant future. One benefit of the net present value method is that a variable rate can be used for different cash flows each year to reflect the difference in risk associated with each.

To illustrate, assume we are a service bureau considering the acquisition of a computer that costs $52,000 net of investment credit. Contracts for work during the next 5 years will provide $12,000 cash flow net of tax. Cash flows in the following 5 years are expected to be $6,000, but they are heavily dependent on technological advances. Salvage value is expected to be $5,000, but only if there are no significant changes in technology. The firm's 14% cost of capital is used to discount the cash flows for the first 5 years, but an 18% discount rate is felt to more accurately assess the risk associated with cash flows, including salvage value, in the last 5 years. The net present value is computed as follows:

Present Value of Cash Flows

Years	Rate		
1–5	14%	($12,000 × 3.433)	$41,196
6–10	18%	($ 6,000 × 1.367)	8,202
Salvage	18%	($ 5,000 × .191)	955
		Total	$50,353
Investment			$52,000
Net present value			($ 1,647)

Had the 14% cost of capital been used on all cash flows the project would have had a positive net present value of $1,244 ($53,244 − $52,000). At this rate it appears to be a desirable investment. However, when the discount rate is adjusted to more accurately reflect the risk associated with the individual cash flows, it is not as desirable. The $1,647 negative net present value indicates that the proposal should not be accepted.

Predicting and Evaluating Cash Flows

Of the cash flows associated with capital budgeting, only the initial investment can be known with any degree of accuracy. Even that may not be fixed when it involves the construction or development of an asset with a risk of budget overruns that the company must absorb. Cash inflows from operations are among the most difficult to predict, yet they are the most important in determining the desirability of the project. Salvage value is generally not too critical because it is a one-time receipt and because it is received so far in the future that its present value is generally not significant.

Expected Value   Expected value is one technique for estimating the expected cash flow when there is a range of possible cash flows with probabilities associated with various points within that range. The *probabilities are multiplied by the dollar amounts and totaled* to compute the expected value.

To illustrate, we will use the purchase of a new kidney machine being considered by Cache Valley Hospital. As shown below, the annual range of possible cash flows varies from a high of $46,000 to a low of $13,000. Estimated probabilities for those points and various points in between are also shown. The expected value is $27,800.

Possible Annual Cash Flows	×	Probability	=	Expected Value
$13,000	×	20%	=	$ 2,600
26,000	×	50	=	13,000
38,000	×	20	=	7,600
46,000	×	10	=	4,600
Total		100%	=	$27,800

We know the actual cash flows will vary from year to year based upon machine usage. But the expected value is the best estimate of the annual cash flows. If the range and probabilities are accurate, and if we operated the machine for several years, the average cash flow over time would be $27,800. Expected value is very useful in reducing the range of possible values to the one most likely value that can be used by one of the capital budgeting techniques.

Multiple Computations of Net Present Value   Net present value can be computed several times using different assumptions about possible cash flows to measure the impact on the outcome of the decision. The results may be charted on a graph to show how the net present value or profitability index changes with the different cash flows.

Figure 23.6   X-ray machine of Cache Valley Hospital

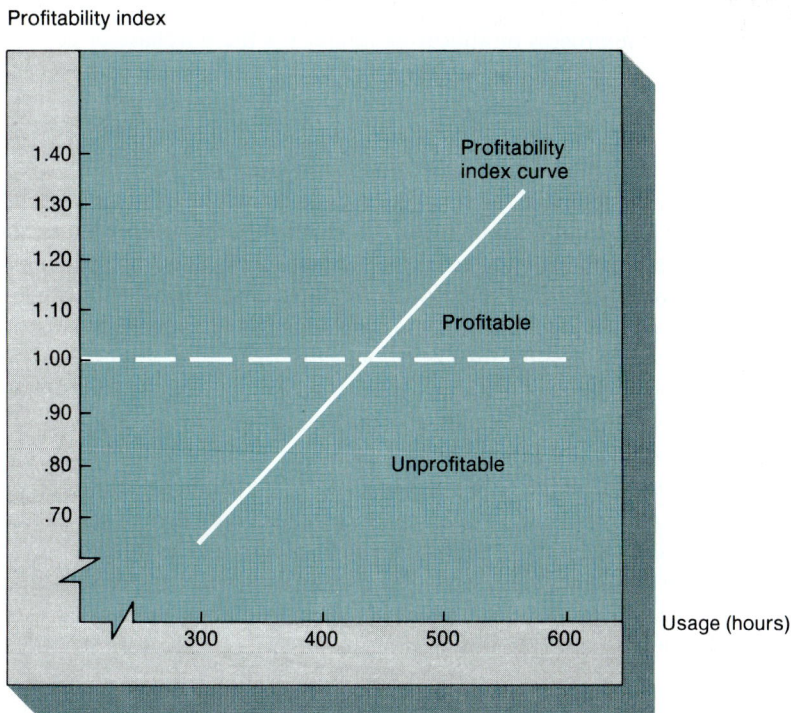

Cache Valley Hospital frequently has overcrowding in the emergency room due to a bottleneck around the X-ray machine. Patients are frequently sent to the Children's Hospital for X rays and returned to Cache Valley Hospital for treatment. A new X-ray machine will cost $200,000 installed and will have a useful life of 15 years with a zero salvage value. A 10% cut-off rate is used for investment decisions. The new X-ray machine will generate $60 of revenue per hour when it is being used. Is it a desirable investment if it is used for 600 hours per year? Will it be profitable at only 500 or 400 hours per year?

The net present value and profitability index is computed for each level of output. Figure 23.6 summarizes the results.

Present Value of Cash Flows

Revenue:	600 hours	500 hours	400 hours
[($60 × 600) × 7.606]	$273,816		
[($60 × 500) × 7.606]		$228,180	
[($60 × 400) × 7.606]			$182,544
Initial investment	$200,000	$200,000	$200,000
Net present value	$ 73,816	$ 28,180	($ 17,456)
Profitability index	1.37	1.14	.91

The indifference point for Cache Valley Hospital lies in between 400 and 500 hours of usage per year. If management feels that the usage will exceed this amount, the investment should be pursued. A study might be commissioned by management to log the number of patients that are sent to Children's Hospital and the type of X ray needed. These results could be used to estimate more precisely how much usage the new machine would have and put management in a better position to make an informed decision.

Summary

Capital budgeting is the process of allocating money for the purchase or construction of fixed assets. The process involves the estimation of cash flows associated with each project and comparing them with the initial investment to see whether or not the project is desirable.

Income tax laws have a significant impact on estimated cash flows for profit oriented businesses. Cash inflows in the form of revenue cannot be fully realized because of the additional income tax that must be paid. On the other hand, cash outflows in the form of operating expenses don't really cost the full amount because of the reduction in taxes payable. Depreciation (cost recovery) also has a related cash flow when income taxes are included in the analysis. The investment must be adjusted for investment credit and the salvage value must be adjusted for the tax on the gain. In general, almost every cash flow has a related income tax effect. All items must be computed net of the related income tax effects before applying one of the capital budgeting techniques.

Cost of capital is the rate of return that must be earned on invested capital in order for the market price of the firm's common stock to remain unchanged. A weighted average cost of capital can be computed using the after-tax cost of each capital component and proportion of total capital that each component provides. The weighted average cost of capital is the rate that should be used as the minimum desired rate of return for capital investment decisions when internally generated funds are being used. When new funds are being raised to finance the investment projects, the marginal cost of capital should be used.

Sensitivity analysis is useful in measuring the effect of small changes in one or more of the input values on the results of a capital investment decision. The cut-off rate may be adjusted for potential errors in computing the weighted average cost of capital. Also, the rate may be adjusted for unproductive projects or for projects with a risk factor that is different than the average risk associated with the firm. Different rates can even be applied each year to cash flows within the same project to reflect the different risk associated with each cash flow.

Expected value is useful in developing the estimated cash flows when the potential cash flows are a range with probabilities associated with points throughout the range. As an alternative, the net present value can be computed several times using different estimates of cash flows to test the impact on the decision.

Self-Study Problem

Josephinski Incorporated has had a problem with stock-outs of major inventory items for several years. Preliminary analysis indicates that this results because poor information is provided on quantities in inventory due to slow processing of sales and purchases of items with high turnover. A proposal has been made to buy a small computer facility at a total cost of $200,000. There is expected to be a net reduction of 3 bookkeeping employees at an average salary of $10,800 per year. A special study was just completed showing that an average of 30 days sales were lost (based on current sales and a 360-day year) as a result of stock-outs. Total sales during the preceding year were $720,000 with a gross profit margin of 40%. It is estimated that 80% of the lost sales could have been avoided with a computerized information system. Annual operating costs of the computer facility, other than employee wages, are expected to be $5,000 per year. The expected useful life of the facility is 10 years with an estimated salvage value of zero. The effective tax rate is 40% and Accelerated Cost Recovery System (ACRS) using a 5-year life is being used for both book and tax purposes. Management wants to take the full 10% investment credit and adjust the basis as required by tax law for computing annual cost recovery. Analyze the desirability of the above proposal using the net present value method. Assume that money is worth 10% and that all cash flows are at the end of the year, except the investment tax credit, which will occur at the beginning of year 1.

Solution to the Self-Study Problem

The net of tax cash flows must first be computed for each item. Present value factors are then applied to these amounts.

Reduction in Bookkeeping Employees

Annual cash savings	
(3 employees at $10,800 per year)	$32,400
Net of tax [$32,400 × (1 − .40)]	19,440
Present value of savings ($19,440 × 6.1446)	$119,451

Increase in Gross Profits by Reducing Lost Sales

Annual loss in sales per year	
($720,000 ÷ 360 days = $2,000/day × 30 days)	$ 60,000
Reduction by new computer ($60,000 × 80%)	48,000
Increased gross profit ($48,000 × 40%)	19,200
Net of tax [$19,200 × (1 − .40)]	11,520
Present value of increase ($11,520 × 6.1446)	$ 70,786

Reduction in Income Tax for Cost Recovery (Depreciation)

Cost	$200,000
Half of ITC (1/2 × $20,000)	10,000
Adjusted basis	$190,000

Year	ACR Computation	ACR	×	Tax Rate	=	Cash Flow	×	Present Value Factor	=	Present Value
1	$190,000 × 15%	$28,500		40%		$11,400		.9091		$10,364
2	$190,000 × 22%	41,800		40%		16,720		.8264		13,817
3	$190,000 × 21%	39,900		40%		15,960		.7513		11,991
4	$190,000 × 21%	39,900		40%		15,960		.6830		10,901
5	$190,000 × 21%	39,900		40%		15,960		.6209		9,910
								Total		$56,983

Computer Operating Costs

Annual cash outflow	$ 5,000
Net of tax [$5,000 × (1 − .40)]	3,000
Present value of cost ($3,000 × 6.1445)	$18,434

Net Cost of Investment

Investment cost	$200,000
Investment tax credit (10%)	20,000
Net cost	$180,000

All of the above items are combined as follows to compute the net present value.

Present Value of Cash Inflows

Bookkeeping	$119,451
Gross profit	70,786
Cost recovery	56,983
Operating costs	(18,434)
Total	228,786
Initial investment (net)	180,000
Net present value	$ 48,786

Suggested Readings

Edwards, James W. "Effects of Federal Income Taxes on Capital Budgeting." *NAA Research Monograph #5*. New York: National Association of Accountants, 1969.

Hertz, David B. "Incorporating Risk in Capital Expenditure Analysis." In *Controller's Handbook,* edited by Sam R. Goodman and James S. Reece. Homewood, Ill.: Dow Jones-Irwin, 1978.

House, William C., Jr. "Sensitivity Analysis in Making Capital Investment Decisions." *NAA Research Monograph #3*. New York: National Association of Accountants, 1968.

Kempster, John H. "Financial Analysis to Guide Capital Expenditure Decisions." *NAA Research Report #43*. New York: National Association of Accountants, 1967.

Murdy, J. L. "Analyzing Capital Expenditure Proposals." In *Controller's Handbook,* edited by Sam R. Goodman and James S. Reece. Homewood, Ill.: Dow Jones-Irwin, 1978.

National Association of Accountants. "Financial Analysis Techniques for Equipment Replacement Decisions." *NAA Research Monograph #1*. New York: National Association of Accountants, 1965.

Discussion Questions

1. When computing the net of tax cash flows associated with cost recovery (depreciation), do you take the reduction in taxes payable or the increase (decrease) in net income associated with the cost recovery? Explain.
2. Why must both cash revenues as well as cash expenditures be adjusted for income taxes in making capital budgeting decisions?
3. What is the formula to compute the net of tax cash flows from taxable receipts? What is the formula to compute the net of tax cash flows for cost recovery? Why are the formulas different?
4. Why do we generally deduct any investment credit from the cost of the initial investment rather than include it as a cash flow at the end of year 1?
5. Why should enterprises that are operating at a profit always use ACRS over the shortest period of time?
6. How does the computation of the internal rate of return differ when income taxes are included in the analysis?
7. Explain how salvage value is adjusted for income taxes for a net cash flow.
8. Define cost of capital.
9. Why is cost of capital an appropriate measure for the minimum desired rate of return?
10. Differentiate between "weighted average cost of capital" and "component cost of capital."
11. Differentiate between "weighted average cost of capital" and "marginal cost of capital."
12. Explain how to compute the component cost of capital for a bond payable.
13. Explain how to compute the component cost of capital for preferred stock. Why is income tax ignored in this computation?

14. Explain how to compute the component cost of capital for common shareholders.
15. Describe expected value and identify where it is most effectively used in capital budgeting decisions.

Exercises

Exercise 23.1 Capital Budgeting Tax Effects (CMA)

1. Ander Company can invest $4,980 in a piece of equipment with a three-year life. If the minimum desired rate of return is 10% after taxes and the annual expected cash savings net of taxes is $2,500, the amount (rounded to the nearest dollar) by which the annual cash flows could change before the company would be indifferent to acquiring the equipment is a
   a. decrease of $415.
   b. decrease of $2,480.
   c. decrease of $1,245.
   d. decrease of $500.
   e. decrease of $2,000.
2. Carco Incorporated wants to use discounted cash flow techniques when analyzing its capital investment projects. Carco is aware of the uncertainty involved in estimating future cash flows. A simple method some companies employ to adjust for the uncertainty inherent in their estimates is
   a. to prepare a direct analysis of the probability of outcomes.
   b. to use accelerated depreciation.
   c. to adjust the minimum desired rate of return.
   d. to increase the estimates of the cash flows.
   e. to ignore salvage values.
3. The accountants for OEM Incorporated have proposed that sensitivity analysis be incorporated into the company's capital budgeting program. This proposal is based on the fact that the major contribution of sensitivity analysis will be the determination of
   a. a measure of the probability distribution of cash outflows.
   b. a financial measure of the new investment from alternative values for the parameters.
   c. a financial measure of the value of the new investment.
   d. a measure of the probability of the calculated outcome.
   e. a measure of the probable maximum rate of return.
4. The accountant from Ronier Incorporated has prepared an analysis of a proposed capital project using discounted cash flow techniques. One manager has questioned the accuracy of the results because the discount factors employed in the analysis assumed that the cash flows occurred at the end of the year when actually the cash flows occurred uniformly throughout each year. The net present value calculated by the accountant
   a. will not be in error.
   b. will be slightly overstated.
   c. will be unusable for actual decision making.
   d. will be slightly understated but usable.
   e. will produce an error the direction of which is undeterminable.

5. Budcon Incorporated has a small capital budget. When faced with indivisible projects each of which is estimated to generate a return that exceeds the company's cost of capital, Budcon should select the combination of projects that will fully utilize the budget and
    a. maximize the sum of the net present values.
    b. maximize the sum of the internal rates of return.
    c. minimize the sum of the payback periods.
    d. have the highest present value indexes.
    e. are ranked the highest by their net present values.

6. Future Incorporated is in the enviable situation of having unlimited capital funds. The best decision rule, in an economic sense, would be for the company to invest in all projects in which
    a. the payback was less than 4 years.
    b. the accounting rate of return was greater than the earnings as a percent of sales.
    c. the payback reciprocal is greater than the internal rate of return.
    d. the internal rate of return is greater than zero.
    e. the net present value is greater than zero.

Exercise 23.2 Capital Budgeting and Net Present Value Analysis

On January 1, Jenkins Incorporated purchased for $520,000 a new machine with a useful life of 8 years and no salvage value. The machine will be depreciated using the straight-line method and is expected to produce annual cash flow from operations, net of income taxes, of $120,000. The net present value of an ordinary annuity of $1 for 8 periods at 14% is 4.639. The present value of $1 for 8 periods at 14% is 0.351. The machine does not qualify for investment credit.

Required

Assuming that Jenkins uses a rate of return of 14%, determine the net present value for the project.

Exercise 23.3 Capital Budgeting and Cash Flow from Operations

Jarvis Incorporated, a calendar year company, purchased a new machine for $28,000 on January 1. The machine has an estimated useful life of 8 years with no salvage value and is being depreciated on the straight-line basis. The accounting (book value) rate of return is expected to be 15% after tax on the initial increase in required investment, and using a full year of depreciation in the year of purchase.

Required

Assuming a uniform cash inflow, determine the amount of the cash flow from operations, net of taxes, that this investment is expected to provide.

Exercise 23.4 Capital Budgeting and Net Present Value Analysis

Roberts Incorporated contemplates the purchase of a machine for $240,000. The machine has a useful life of 5 years with no salvage value. Straight-line depreciation will be used under the half-year average in the year of purchase. The machine is expected to generate $80,000 of cash flow from operations before income taxes in each of the 5 years. Roberts' expected rate of return is 12% after tax. Roberts is subject to a 40% tax rate. Assume the machine qualifies for investment credit and Roberts has elected to take the full investment credit and adjust the basis of the property as required by tax law.

Required

Prepare a net present value analysis on the machine.

Exercise 23.5 Capital Budgeting and Payback Analysis

The Polar Company is planning to purchase a new machine for $30,000. The payback period is expected to be 5 years. The new machine is expected to produce cash flow from operations, net of income taxes, of $7,000 a year in each of the next 3 years and $5,500 in the following year. Depreciation of $5,000 a year will be charged to income for each of the 5 years of the payback period.

Required

Determine the amount of cash flow from operations, net of taxes, that the new machine is expected to produce in the last (fifth) year of the payback period.

Exercise 23.6 Capital Budgeting and Payback Period

Energy Company is planning to spend $84,000 for a new machine with a 12-year useful life that will be depreciated using the accelerated cost recovery system over 5 years. The related cash flow from operations, before income taxes, is expected to be $10,000 a year for each of the first 5 years and $12,000 for each of the next 7 years. The machine qualifies for investment credit and the company has elected to take the 2% reduction and recover the full cost. The company is subject to a 30% tax rate.

Required

Determine the payback period.

Exercise 23.7 Capital Budgeting—Determining the Original Cost

Virginia Company invested in a 4-year project. Virginia's expected rate of return is 10%. Additional information on the project is as follows:

Year	Cash Inflow from Operations, Net of Income Taxes	Present Value of $1 at 10%
1	$4,000	.909
2	4,400	.826
3	4,800	.751
4	5,200	.683

Required

Assuming a positive net present value of $1,000, determine the amount of the original investment.

Exercise 23.8 Capital Budgeting and the Accounting Rate of Return

The Fudge Company is planning to purchase a new machine, which it will depreciate on a straight-line basis over a 10-year period with no salvage value and a full year's depreciation taken in the year of acquisition. The new machine is expected to produce cash flow from operations, net of income taxes, of $66,000 a year in each of the next 10 years. The accounting (book value) rate of return on the initial investment is expected to be 12%.

Required

Determine the cost of the new machine.

Exercise 23.9 Capital Budgeting (Including Tax Effect) and Net Present Value Analysis

Juan Carlos, president of Beto's Tortilla Company, is presently considering an investment of $69,000 to purchase a tortilla-making machine that will last 12 years, at which point the machine will have no residual value. Cash operating savings of $12,000 before income tax will result annually if the new machine is purchased. The tortilla company's minimum desired rate of return is 12% after taxes.

Required

1. Compute the net present value of the new machine, disregarding income tax effects.
2. Compute the net present value of the new machine, assuming a 40% tax rate and use of accelerated cost recovery depreciation with the equipment qualifying for 5-year recovery.
3. Compute the net present value of the new machine, assuming the same facts in requirement 2 and, in addition, an investment tax credit of 10%. Assume the company elects to adjust the amount of investment credit and recover the full cost of the machine.

Exercise 23.10 Capital Budgeting (Including Tax Effect) and Various Evaluation Methods

If June Corporation acquires the new equipment currently being considered, cash savings of $6,000 a year before income tax for the next 9 years will result. The new equipment will cost $27,000 and will have a $1,000 residual value at the end of its 9-year useful life. June Corporation's minimum desired after-tax rate of return is 10%. The tax rate is estimated to be 45% of taxable income.

Required

Assume that June Corporation will elect to use 5-year accelerated cost recovery for depreciation and take full investment credit with an adjusted basis.

1. Compute the payback period.
2. Compute the internal rate of return.
3. Compute the net present value.
4. Compute the net present value or profitability index.

Problem 23.1   Capital Budgeting—Payback and Accounting Rate of Return

Plastics Incorporated is considering the purchase of a $40,000 machine, which will be depreciated on a straight-line basis over an 8-year period with no salvage value and with a full year of depreciation in the year of purchase. The machine is expected to generate net cash income before income taxes of $12,000 a year. Assume that the income tax rate is 50%.

Required

1. Determine the payback period.
2. Determine the accounting (book value) rate of return on the initial increase in required investment.

Problem 23.2   Capital Budgeting (Including Tax Effect) and Project Analysis

A small manufacturing company is contemplating the purchase of a small computer in order to reduce the cost of its data-processing operations.

Presently the manual bookkeeping system involves the following direct-cash expenses per month:

Salaries	$7,500
Payroll taxes	1,700
Supplies	600
	$9,800

Existing furniture and equipment are fully depreciated in the accounts and have no salvage value. The cost of the computer, including installation and accessory equipment, is $100,000. This entire amount is depreciable for income tax purposes using the accelerated cost recovery system over 3 years. Assume they elect to take full investment credit and adjust the recovery basis of the computer.

Estimated annual costs of computerized data processing are as follows:

Supervisory salaries	$15,000
Other salaries	24,000
Payroll taxes	7,400
Supplies	7,200
	$53,600

The computer is expected to be obsolete in 3 years, at which time its salvage value is expected to be $20,000. The company follows the practice of treating salvage value as inflow at the time that it is likely to be received.

Required

1. Compute the savings in annual cash outflow after taxes. Assume a 50% tax rate.
2. Decide whether or not to purchase the computer, using the present value method of discounted cash flow analysis. Assume a minimum rate of return of 10% after taxes.

Problem 23.3   Various Methods of Capital Budgeting and After-Tax Analysis (CMA)

Hazman Company plans to replace an old piece of equipment that is obsolete and is expected to be unreliable under the stress of daily operations. The equipment is fully depreciated, and no salvage value can be realized upon its disposal.

One piece of equipment being considered would provide annual cash savings of $7,000 before income taxes. The equipment would cost $18,000 and have an estimated useful life of 5 years. No salvage value would be used for depreciation because the equipment is expected to have no value at the end of 5 years.

Hazman will use the accelerated cost recovery system for 5-year property on all equipment for both book and tax purposes. Hazman is subject to a 40% tax rate and has an after-tax cost of capital of 14%. Assume they elect to reduce the investment credit by 2% and use the full cost of the property in computing annual cost recovery.

Required

Assume all operating revenues and expenses occur at the end of the year.

1. Calculate for Hazman Company's proposed investment in new equipment the after-tax
   a. payback period.
   b. accounting rate of return.
   c. net present value.
   d. profitability (present value) index.
   e. internal rate of return.
2. Identify and discuss the issues Hazman Company should consider when deciding which of the five decision models identified in requirement 1 it should employ to compare and evaluate alternative capital investment projects.

Problem 23.4   Capital Budgeting and After-Tax Effects— Selective Analysis (CMA)

Rockyford Company must replace some machinery. This machinery has zero book value but its current market value is $1,800. One possible alternative is to invest in new machinery that has a cost of $40,000. This new machinery would produce estimated annual pre-tax operating cash savings of $12,500. The estimated useful life of the machinery is 4 years. Rockyford uses straight-line depreciation with half-year depreciation in the year of purchase. The new machinery would have an estimated salvage value of $2,000 at the end of 4 years; however, the salvage value can be ignored for the purpose of depreciation because it does not represent at least 10% of the cost of the asset. The investment in this machinery would require an additional investment in working capital of $3,000.

If Rockyford accepts this investment proposal, the disposal of the old machinery and the investment in the new equipment will take place on December 31, 19X1. The cash flows from the investment will occur during the calendar years 19X1–19X5.

Rockyford is subject to a 40% income tax rate for all ordinary income and capital gains and has a 10% after-tax cost of capital. All operating and tax cash flows are assumed to occur at year end.

Required

1. Determine the present value of the after-tax cash flow arising from the disposal of the old machinery in 19X1.
2. Determine the present value of the after-tax cash flows for all 4 years attributable to the operating cash savings.
3. Determine the present value of the tax shield effect of remaining depreciation at the end of year 1, December 31, 19X2.
4. Determine the present value of the after-tax cash flows arising from the disposal of the new machinery at its salvage value at the end of year 4, December 31, 19X5.
5. Determine the present value of the net effect on the income tax payments related to the project in year 2.
6. Describe how Rockyford's additional investment in working capital of $3,000 required in year 1 should be handled in evaluating the replacement project.

Problem 23.5   Capital Budgeting and the Cost of Capital (CMA)

The income statement shown below and the bar graph shown on page 852 were among the financial information presented at the November meeting of the board of directors of the Martin Company. The meeting was to be devoted to an analysis of the past year's results (a record year for sales and earnings) and to the consideration of major asset acquisitions.

The bar graph was intended to display the relationship of various expense categories to revenues. The interest, preferred stock dividends, and earnings available to common stockholders were combined into one figure entitled "cost of capital" because an estimate of the cost of capital would be an important part of the discussions regarding the asset acquisitions.

Martin Company
Income Statement
For the year ended September 30, 19X1
(in millions)

	Amount	Percent
Revenues:		
Sales	$225	90%
Other	25	10
Total revenue	$250	100%
Expenses:		
Wages and salaries	$ 50	20%
Merchandise and supplies	105	42
Depreciation	20	8
Interest	25	10
Income taxes	25	10
Total expense	$225	90%
Net income	$ 25	10%
Less: Cash dividends to preferred stockholders	5	2
Earnings available to common stockholders	$ 20	8%

Required

1. Evaluate the cost of capital percentage (20%) displayed in the bar graph. Is this cost of capital suitable for use in the asset acquisition? Why or why not?
2. If you reject the use of the 20% cost of capital, describe how Martin Company should develop a cost of capital figure for the board meeting that is suitable for use in asset acquisition analysis.

Bar graph showing the percentage distribution of the total revenues

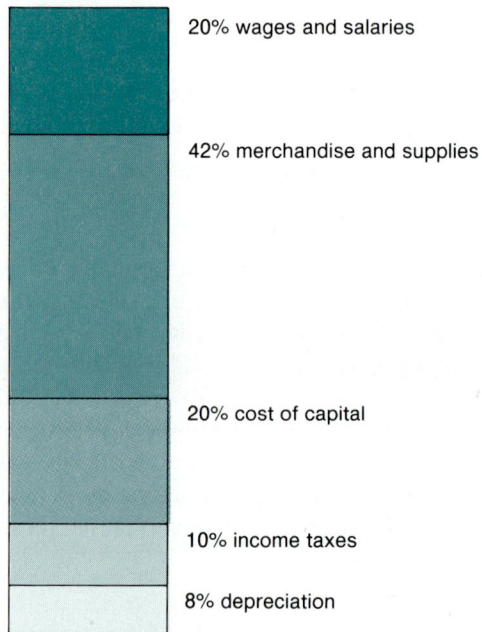

20% wages and salaries

42% merchandise and supplies

20% cost of capital

10% income taxes

8% depreciation

Problem 23.6   Net Present Value Analysis

Wyle Company is considering a proposal to acquire new manufacturing equipment. The new equipment has the same capacity as the current equipment but will provide operating efficiencies in direct and indirect labor, direct-material usage, indirect supplies, and power. Consequently, the savings in operating costs are estimated at $150,000 annually.

The new equipment will cost $300,000 and will be purchased at the beginning of the year when the project is started. The equipment dealer is certain that the equipment will be operational during the second quarter of the year in which it is installed. Therefore, 60% of the estimated annual savings can be obtained in the first year. Wyle will incur a one-time expense of $30,000 to transfer the production activities from the old equipment to the new equipment. No loss of sales will occur, however, because the plant is large enough to install the new equipment without interfering with the operations of the current equipment. The equipment dealer states that most companies use a 3-year life when depreciating this equipment using the accelerated cost recovery system.

The current equipment has been fully depreciated and is carried in the accounts at zero book value. Management has reviewed the condition of the current equipment and has concluded that it can be used an additional 5 years. Wyle Company would receive $5,000 net of removal costs if it elected to buy the new equipment and dispose of its current equipment at this time.

Wyle currently leases its manufacturing plant. The annual lease payments are $60,000. The lease, which will have 4 years remaining when the equipment installation would begin, is not renewable. Wyle Company would be required to remove any equipment in the plant at the end of the lease. The cost of equipment removal is expected to equal the salvage value of either the old or new equipment at the time of removal.

Wyle Company is subject to a 40% income tax rate and requires an after-tax return of at least 12% on any investment. Wyle elects to take full advantage of any investment credit and adjust the recovery basis as required by tax law.

Required

1. Calculate the annual incremental after-tax cash flows for Wyle Company's proposal to acquire the new manufacturing equipment.
2. Calculate the net present value of Wyle Company's proposal to acquire the new manufacturing equipment using the cash flows calculated in requirement 1 and indicate what action its management should take. For ease in calculation, assume all recurring cash flows take place at the end of the year.

Problem 23.7 Capital Budgeting Analysis (CMA)

Wisconsin Products Company manufactures several different products. One of the firm's principal products sells for $20 per unit. The sales manager of Wisconsin Products has stated repeatedly that she could sell more units of this product if they were available. In an attempt to substantiate her claim the sales manager conducted a market research study last year at a cost of $44,000 to determine potential demand for this product. The study indicated that Wisconsin Products could sell 18,000 units of this product annually for the next 5 years.

The equipment currently in use has the capacity to produce 11,000 units annually. The variable production costs are $9 per unit. The equipment has a book value of $60,000 and a remaining useful life of 5 years with straight-line depreciation in use. The salvage value of the equipment is negligible now and will be zero in 5 years.

A maximum of 20,000 units could be produced annually on the new machinery that can be purchased. The new equipment costs $300,000 and has an estimated useful life of 5 years with no salvage value at the end of 5 years. Wisconsin Product's production manager has estimated that the new equipment would provide increased production efficiencies that would reduce the variable production costs to $7 per unit.

Wisconsin Products Company would use the accelerated cost recovery system for 5-year property for tax purposes. The firm is subject to a 40% tax rate, and its after-tax cost of capital is 16%. The company elects to reduce the investment credit and recover the full cost of the investment.

The sales manager felt so strongly about the need for additional capacity that she attempted to prepare an economic justification for the equipment although this was not one of her responsibilities. Her analysis, presented below, disappointed her because it did not justify acquiring the equipment.

Required Investment

Purchase price of new equipment		$300,000
Disposal of existing equipment:		
Loss of disposal	$60,000	
Less tax benefit (40%)	24,000	36,000
Cost of market research study		44,000
Total investment		$380,000

Annual Returns

Contribution margin from product:	
Using the new equipment [18,000 × ($20 − 7)]	$234,000
Using the existing equipment [11,000 × ($20 − 9)]	121,000
Increase in contribution margin	$113,000
Less depreciation	60,000
Increase in before-tax income	$ 53,000
Income tax (40%)	21,200
Increase in income	$ 31,800
Less 16% cost of capital on the additional investment required	
(.16 × $380,000)	60,800
Net annual return of proposed investment in new equipment	$(29,000)

Required

1. The controller of Wisconsin Products Company plans to prepare a discounted cash flow analysis for this investment proposal. The controller has asked you to prepare corrected calculations of the required investment in the new equipment and the recurring annual cash flows. Explain the treatment of each item of your corrected calculations that is treated differently from the original analysis prepared by the sales manager.
2. Calculate the net present value of the proposed investment in the new equipment.

Problem 23.8   Net Present Value Analysis (CMA)

The WRL Company makes cookies for its chain of snack food stores. On January 2, 19X1, WRL Company purchased a special cookie cutting machine; this machine has been utilized for three years. WRL Company is considering the purchase of a newer, more efficient machine. If purchased, the new machine would be acquired on January 2, 19X4. WRL Company expects to sell 300,000 dozen cookies in each of the next four years. The selling price of the cookies is expected to average $.50 per dozen.

WRL Company has two options—(*a*) to continue to operate the old machine or (*b*) to sell the old machine and purchase the new machine. No trade-in was offered by the seller of the new machine. The following information has been assembled to help decide which option is more desirable.

	Old Machine	New Machine
Original cost of machine at acquisition	$80,000	$120,000
Salvage value at the end of useful life for depreciation purposes	10,000	20,000
Useful life from date of acquisition	7 years	4 years
Expected annual cash operating expenses:		
Variable cost per dozen	$.20	$.14
Total fixed costs	$15,000	$ 14,000
Depreciation method used for tax purposes:	Straight-line	Accelerated cost recovery three-year
Estimated cash value of machines:		
January 2, 19X4	$40,000	$120,000
December 31, 19X7	$ 7,000	$ 20,000

WRL Company is subject to an overall income tax rate of 40%. They elect to take full investment credit and adjust the basis of the asset as required by tax law. Assume that all operating revenues and expenses occur at the end of the year. Assume that any gain or loss on the sale of machinery is treated as an ordinary tax item.

Required

1. Use the net present value method to determine whether WRL Company should retain the old machine or acquire the new machine. WRL requires an after-tax return of 16%.

2. Without prejudice to your answer to requirement 1, assume that the quantitative differences are so slight between the two alternatives that WRL Company is indifferent to the two proposals. Identify and discuss the nonquantitative factors that are important to this decision that WRL Company should consider.

3. Identify and discuss the advantages and disadvantages of using discounted cash flow techniques (for example, the net present value method) for capital investment decisions.

Problem 23.9   Capital Budgeting—Net Present Value Analysis and Inflation Considerations (CMA)

Catix Corporation is a divisionalized company. Each division has the authority to make capital expenditures up to $200,000 without approval from the corporate headquarters. The corporate controller has determined that the cost of capital for Catix Corporation is 12%. This rate does not include an allowance for inflation, which is expected to occur at an average rate of 8% over the next 5 years. Catix pays income taxes at a rate of 40%.

The Electronics Division of Catix is considering the purchase of an automated assembly and soldering machine for use in the manufacture of its printed circuit boards. The machine would be placed in service in early 19X1. The divisional controller estimates that if the machine is purchased, two positions will be eliminated yielding a cost savings for wages and employee benefits. However, the machine would require additional supplies and more power to operate the machine. The cost savings and additional costs in current 19X1 prices are as follows:

Wages and employee benefits of the two positions eliminated ($25,000 each)	$50,000
Cost of additional supplies	$ 3,000
Cost of additional power	$10,000

The new machine would be purchased and installed at the end of 19X0 at a net cost of $80,000. If purchased, the machine would be depreciated on a straight-line basis for both book and tax purposes with a full year of depreciation in the year of purchase. The machine will become technologically obsolete in 4 years and will have no salvage value at that time.

The Electronics Division compensates for inflation in capital expenditure analyses by adjusting the expected cash flows by an estimated price level index. The adjusted after-tax cash flows are then discounted using the appropriate discount rate. The estimated year-end index values for each of the next 5 years are presented below:

Year	Year-End Price Index
19X0	1.00
19X1	1.08
19X2	1.17
19X3	1.26
19X4	1.36
19X5	1.47

The Plastics Division of Catix compensates for inflation in capital expenditure analyses by adding the anticipated inflation rate to the cost of capital and then using the inflation adjusted cost of capital to discount the project cash flows. The Plastics Division recently rejected a project with cash flows and economic life similar to those associated with the machine under consideration by the Electronics Division. The Plastics Division's analysis of the rejected project was as follows:

Net pre-tax cost savings	$37,000
Less incremental depreciation expenses	20,000
Increase in taxable income	$17,000
Increase in income taxes (40%)	6,800
Increase in after-tax income	$10,200
Add back non-cash expense (depreciation)	20,000
Net after-tax annual cash inflow (unadjusted for inflation)	$30,200
Present value of net cash inflows using the sum of the cost of capital (12%) and the inflation rate (8%) or a minimum required return of 20%	$77,916
Investment required	(80,000)
Net present value	$(2,084)

All operating revenues and expenditures occur at the end of the year.

Required

1. Using the price index provided, prepare a schedule showing the net after-tax annual cash flows adjusted for inflation for the automated assembly and soldering machine under consideration by the Electronics Division.
2. Without prejudice to your answer to requirement 1, assume that the net after-tax annual cash flows adjusted for inflation for the project being considered by the Electronics Division are as follows:

	19X1	19X2	19X3	19X4
Net after-tax annual cash flow adjusted for inflation	$30,000	$35,000	$37,000	$40,000

Calculate the net present value for Electronic Division's project that will be meaningful to management.
3. Evaluate the methods used by the Plastics Division and the Electronics Division to compensate for expected inflation in capital expenditure analyses.

Problem 23.10 Capital Budgeting—Lease versus Purchase (CMA Adapted)

LeToy Company produces a wide variety of children's toys, most of which are manufactured from stamped parts. The production department recommended that a new stamping machine be acquired. The production department further recommended that the company only consider using the new stamping machine for 5 years. Top management has concurred with the recommendation and has assigned Ann Mitchum of the budget and planning department to supervise the acquisition and to analyze the alternative financing available.

After careful analysis and review, Mitchum has narrowed the financing of the project to two alternatives. The first alternative is a lease agreement with the manufacturer of the stamping machine. The manufacturer is willing to lease the equipment to LeToy for 5 years even though it has an economic useful life of 10 years. The lease agreement requires LeToy to make annual payments of $62,000 at the beginning of each year. The manufacturer (lessor) retains the title to the machine and there is no purchase option at the end of 5 years. Investment credit is claimed by the lessor and does not flow through to LeToy (lessee). This agreement would be considered a lease by the Internal Revenue Service.

The second alternative would be for LeToy to purchase the equipment outright from the manufacturer for $240,000. LeToy can claim an investment tax credit of $19,200 if it purchases the equipment without adjusting the recovery basis. Preliminary discussions with LeToy's bank indicate that the firm would be able to finance the asset acquisition with a 15% term loan.

LeToy would depreciate the equipment over 5 years using the accelerated cost recovery method. The market value of the equipment at the end of 5 years would be $45,000. However, LeToy would use zero salvage value for depreciation purposes.

All maintenance, taxes, and insurance are the same under both alternatives and are paid by LeToy. LeToy requires an after-tax cut-off return of 18% for investment decisions and is subject to a 40% corporate income tax rate on both operating income and capital gains and losses.

Required

1. Calculate the relevant present value cost of the leasing alternative for LeToy Company.
2. Calculate the relevant present value cost of the purchase alternative for LeToy Company.

PROFESSIONAL EXAMINATIONS

24

OUTLINE

C ongratulations on completing the technical material included in the study of cost accounting. By completing chapters 1 through 23 of this text and working a representative sample of questions at the end of each chapter, you have learned what cost accounting is and the basic concepts and procedures included in it. It's nice to know the material and feel the satisfaction of a personal achievement. For many people, however, knowing is not enough. A professional certification is desired as evidence that they know the material at a level that qualifies them to be among an elite group of professional accountants.

Obtaining a professional certification is a major objective of most accountants. Two of accounting's most recognized professional certifications are the Certified Public Accountant (CPA) and the Certificate in Management Accounting (CMA). This chapter introduces you to each of these certifications and identifies the role of cost accounting in obtaining them.

After completing this chapter you should be able to:

1. distinguish between the CPA certificate and the CMA and identify what each certification allows you to do.
2. describe the cost accounting concepts generally tested in the CPA and CMA examinations.

CERTIFIED PUBLIC ACCOUNTANT

To be licensed as a CPA you must pass the Uniform CPA Examination and satisfy other state requirements with respect to residency, continuing education, and experience in the practice of public accounting under the direction of a licensed CPA. The license allows you to offer and perform accounting services to others. In most states it is a class B misdemeanor to offer accounting services to others without a license to practice. A common penalty is six months in the county jail, a $299 fine, or both for each offense.

Many states have recently adopted the policy of providing a CPA Certificate upon successful completion of the Uniform CPA Examination. Holders of a CPA Certificate can identify themselves as a CPA but they are not allowed by themselves to offer accounting services. They must work under the direction of someone else who has a license to practice.

Passing the Uniform CPA Examination and being able to identify yourself as a CPA is a major accomplishment. Our objective is to identify the content of the Uniform CPA Examination with special emphasis on the cost and managerial accounting concepts that are frequently tested.

Content of the Uniform CPA Examination

The Uniform CPA Examination is prepared by the Board of Examiners of the American Institute of Certified Public Accountants (AICPA). All states use the same examination and offer it at the same time. It is given twice each year—early November and early May.

Questions for the examination come from several sources. A substantial portion of the examination is prepared by the staff of the AICPA examination division. Consultants, who are usually educators, are frequently asked to develop questions in specified areas or on designated topics. However, anyone can submit questions for use in the examination and many people do. Contributions not used in the current examination are stockpiled for use in future examinations.

The examination is broken into five parts. The title of each part, the day on which it is offered, and the time allocation is shown in figure 24.1. Notice that the entire exam is given in 2½ days for a total of 19½ hours. In addition, most states have an ethics examination that takes 2 to 2½ hours on Wednesday morning. So it is a long and grueling examination.

Figure 24.1   Parts of the Uniform CPA Examination

Part	Day	Time	Total Hours
Accounting Practice			
Part I	Wednesday	1:30 P.M. – 6:00 P.M.	4½
Auditing	Thursday	8:30 A.M. – 12:00 noon	3½
Accounting Practice			
Part II	Thursday	1:30 P.M. – 6:00 P.M.	4½
Business Law	Friday	8:30 A.M. – 12:00 noon	3½
Accounting Theory	Friday	1:30 P.M. – 5:00 P.M.	3½
			19½

Figure 24.2   Content specification outline for the Uniform CPA Examination

Accounting Practice

    I.   Presentation of financial statements or worksheets (15%).
    II.   Measurement, valuation, realization, and presentation of assets in conformity with generally accepted accounting principles (10%).
    III.   Valuation, recognition, and presentation of liabilities in conformity with generally accepted accounting principles (5%).
    IV.   Ownership structure, presentation, and valuation of equity accounts in conformity with generally accepted accounting principles (5%).
    V.   Measurement and presentation of income and expense items, their relationship to matching and periodicity, and their relationship to generally accepted accounting principles (15%).
    VI.   Other financial topics (5%).
    VII.   *Cost accumulation, planning, and control (15%).*
    VIII.   Not-for-profit and governmental accounting (10%).
    IX.   Federal taxation—individuals (10%).
    X.   Federal taxation—corporations and partnerships (10%).

The accounting practice portion of the examination has two parts that are combined for grading and reporting purposes, making a total of four parts on the uniform examination. Each part is worth 100 points and 75 points are required for a passing score. Cost accounting is covered in the accounting practice and accounting theory sections of the examination. Accounting practice parts I and II both have a significant portion devoted to cost accounting.

On August 31, 1981, the Board of Examiners of the AICPA adopted "Content Specification Outlines for the Uniform Certified Public Accountant Examination," to be effective in November 1983. Figures 24.2 and 24.3 show the content specifications for the practice and theory portions of the examination. Included with each outline is a percentage breakdown by topic area of the 100 points available for each part. Notice that 15% of each part is devoted to cost accounting topics, namely "Cost Accumulation, Planning, and Control."

Figure 24.4 shows the detailed topics listed under the "Cost Accumulation, Planning, and Control" section. The detailed topics are the same for both accounting practice and accounting theory sections of the examination. In fact, most topics under accounting practice and accounting theory are the same except for federal income taxes, which are omitted from accounting theory. Therefore, study for the theory and practice sections

---

Figure 24.3   Content specification outline for the Uniform CPA Examination

---

Accounting Theory

I.	General concepts, principles, terminology, environment, and other professional standards (15%).
II.	Measurement, valuation, realization, and presentation of assets in conformity with generally accepted accounting principles (15%).
III.	Valuation, recognition, and presentation of liabilities in conformity with generally accepted accounting principles (10%).
IV.	Ownership structure, presentation, and valuation of equity accounts in conformity with generally accepted accounting principles (5%).
V.	Measurement and presentation of income and expense items, their relationship to matching and periodicity, and their relationship to generally accepted accounting principles (20%).
VI.	Other financial topics (10%).
VII.	*Cost accumulation, planning, and control (15%).*
VIII.	Not-for-profit and governmental accounting (10%).

Figure 24.4   Detailed content of cost accumulation, planning, and control topics on the Uniform CPA Examination

---

A. Nature of cost elements
  1. Direct material
  2. Direct labor
  3. Overhead (actual, applied, and allocation methods)

B. Job-order costing

C. Process costing

D. Standard costing and variance analysis

E. Joint costing

F. By-product costing

G. Spoilage, waste, and scrap

H. Absorption and direct costing

I. Transfer pricing

J. Product pricing

K. Budgeting and flexible budgeting

L. Breakeven and cost-volume-profit analysis

M. Gross profit analysis

N. Differential cost analysis
  1. Activity levels
  2. Sunk costs
  3. Contribution to profit
  4. Uncertainty
  5. Time periods

O. Capital budgeting techniques
  1. Net present value
  2. Internal rate of return
  3. Payback period
  4. Accounting rate of return

P. Performance analysis
  1. Return on investment
  2. Residual income
  3. Controllable revenue and costs

Q. Quantitative techniques for planning and control
  1. Regression and correlation analysis
  2. Learning curves
  3. Economic order quantity
  4. PERT/cost
  5. Sensitivity analysis
  6. Probability analysis
  7. Linear programming

---

should be done simultaneously. An adequate study of the theory behind a concept as well as the application of the concept to accounting problems should prepare you for both sections of the examination.

Examination Questions

There are a variety of questions on the CPA Examination including accounting problems, multiple choice questions, and essay questions. Accounting practice parts I and II have

Figure 24.5   Cost accounting—topic frequency on CPA examination

Cost Accumulation, Planning, and Control Topic Areas	Percentage of Cost Accounting Exam Time Allocated To Each Topic Area[a]
Nature of cost elements	7
Job-order costing	3
Process costing	22
Standard costing and variance analysis	19
Joint costing	6
By-product costing	1
Spoilage, waste, and scrap	1
Absorption and direct costing	3
Transfer pricing	1
Product pricing	1
Budgeting and flexible budgeting	6
Breakeven and cost-volume-profit analysis	5
Gross profit analysis	2
Differential cost analysis	3
Capital budgeting techniques	9
Performance analysis	1
Quantitative techniques for planning and control	10
Total	100%

[a]These percentages are based on examinations for the period May 1978 through May 1982. Practice parts I and II, and Theory were combined for the computation. The amount of time devoted to individual topics was determined by counting the number of multiple choice questions, problems, and essay questions on each topic and the estimated time allocated for them.

problems and multiple choice questions. The theory portion has multiple choice questions and essay problems. Usually each section of the examination is approximately 40% objective questions and 60% problems or essay questions.

By studying previous examinations, you can get a pretty good idea of the type of questions that will be asked and the topics that are most frequently tested. Cost accounting topics are generally as follows:

Accounting Practice I—A set of 20 objective questions covering both managerial accounting and quantitative methods. The estimated time is between 45 to 55 minutes.

Accounting Practice II—A major problem on a cost accounting topic. The estimated time is between 45 to 55 minutes.

Accounting Theory—Several objective questions that may be grouped separately as a small problem or combined with other topics to form a large problem. Regardless of the way it is packaged, about 30 to 40 minutes is allocated to objective questions on managerial accounting and quantitative methods.

In addition, there may be one essay question on a cost accounting topic. Historically, one such question has been included about half the time with 15 to 30 minutes allocated for it.

Figure 24.5 shows the topic frequency within the cost accounting portions of the examination. As you can see, some topics are given rather heavy emphasis. Process costing, standard costing, and variance analysis are tested the most—a combined total of approximately 41% in these areas. The nature of cost elements, joint costing, budgeting, cost-volume-profit analysis, capital budgeting, and quantitative techniques also receive heavy emphasis with a combined total of 43% in these areas. Candidates would be well advised to spend a significant amount of their cost accounting study time on these topics.

CERTIFICATE IN MANAGEMENT ACCOUNTING

The Certificate in Management Accounting provides the professional designation for persons who follow careers in management accounting and financial management. There is no legal requirement to have a CMA in order to perform services as a management or cost accountant. However, employers prefer and some are beginning to require a CMA for those employed as managerial accountants. Academic institutions also recognize it as a professional designation.

Like the CPA Examination, the CMA Examination is academically oriented; that is, the material tested on the CMA Examination is best learned in an academic program and performance on the exam does not improve with an extended period of time in practice. Therefore, an individual would be well advised to take the CMA Examination as soon as possible after completing college. Many people fail to take it at that time because they intend to pursue a career in public accounting. However, that is a very short term approach to developing a career. A majority of the people who begin their careers in public accounting eventually find themselves working in management, management accounting, or financial management. Passing the CMA Examination early in your career provides increased flexibility in selecting a career path.

In order to obtain a Certificate in Management Accounting you must (*a*) pass all five parts of the examination within a consecutive three-year period and (*b*) complete two years of professional experience in management accounting within seven years after passing the examination. Full-time continuous experience at a level where judgments are regularly made that employ the principles of management accounting satisfy the professional experience requirement.

Content of the CMA Examination

The National Association of Accountants (NAA) organized the Institute of Management Accounting (IMA) in 1972. The institute's sole function is to administer the CMA designation, which includes the preparation and grading of the CMA Examination. You must be a member of the IMA to sit for the CMA Examination and to hold a Certificate in Management Accounting. Admission as a member of the institute requires the applicant to have a good moral character, to be employed or expect to be employed in management accounting, and satisfy one of the following conditions:

1. Hold a baccalaureate degree from an accredited college or university. Application for membership can be made in the last term or semester and permission will be granted to sit for the CMA Examination pending receipt of the degree.
2. Obtain a satisfactory score on the Graduate Record Examination (GRE) or the Graduate Management Admission Test (GMAT). The Credentials Committee of the Institute makes the determination of what constitutes a satisfactory score.
3. Be a Certified Public Accountant or hold a comparable professional certification in a foreign country.

The examination is given semiannually in June and December in several major cities throughout the United States. You select from among the announced locations the city in which you want to sit for the examination.

The examination consists of the following five parts:

1. Economic and business finance
2. Organization and behavior, including ethical considerations
3. Public reporting standards, auditing, and taxes
4. Period reporting for internal and external purposes
5. Decision analysis, including modeling and information systems

Figure 24.6   Content of individual parts of the CMA examination

Part 1:   Economics and Business Finance
     A.   Enterprise Economics—Microeconomics
     B.   Institutional Environment of Business
     C.   National and International Economics
     D.   Working and Capital Management
     E.   Long-term Finance and Capital Structure

Part 2:   Organization and Behavior, Including Ethical Considerations
     A.   Organization Theory and Decision Making
     B.   Motivation and Perception
     C.   Communication
     D.   Behavioral Science Application in Accounting
     E.   Ethical Consideration

Part 3:   Public Reporting Standards, Auditing, and Taxes
     A.   Reporting Requirements
     B.   Audit Protection
     C.   Tax Accounting

Part 4:   Periodic Reporting for Internal and External Purposes
     A.   Concepts of Information
     B.   Basic Financial Statements
     C.   Profit Planning and Budgetary Controls
     D.   Standard Costs for Manufacturing
     E.   Analysis of Accounts and Statements

Part 5:   Decision Analysis, Including Modeling and Information Systems
     A.   Fundamentals of the Decision Process
     B.   Decision Analysis
     C.   Nature and Techniques of Model Building
     D.   Information Systems and Data Processing

The exam parts are scheduled consecutively over a 2½ day period and each part is 3½ hours in length. Figure 24.6 lists some subtitles for each part of the exam to provide some flavor for the concepts tested.

Parts may be taken in any combination and in any order as long as at least two parts are taken each time you sit for the examination until only one part remains. However, all parts must be passed within a consecutive 3-year period. A minimum successful passing grade is 70%.

Examination Questions

The type of questions included on the exam are objective questions, essay questions, and accounting problems. Between 10 and 15% of each part are multiple choice questions, except part II, which is all essay. One difference between CMA exam questions and CPA exam questions is that they are more analysis oriented. Essay questions and accounting problems are generally combined. As a result they frequently require mathematical computations, but they almost always require an analysis and interpretation of the results.

An analysis of previous examinations can provide a good indication of topics covered and the amount of time allocated to them. Individual parts of the exam will be reviewed with respect to the cost accounting topics covered in each.

Part I—Economics and Business Finance. Between 25 and 35% of this part of the exam is devoted to cost accounting topics. Topics that are most frequently tested include budgeting, cost-volume-profit analysis, differential cost analysis, cost of capital, and capital budgeting. Individual problems are typically 30 minutes in length and focus on the impact of an event or decision alternative on a business organization.

Part II—Organization and Behavior. The cost accounting topics included in this section of the examination are performance analysis and behavioral considerations associated with budgeting, standard costing, cost allocation, and report content. These topics constitute about 30 to 35% of this part of the examination. Most are essay questions with an estimated time of 30 minutes each.

Part III—Public Reporting Standards. Generally there are no cost accounting topics covered on this part of the examination.

Part IV—Periodic Reporting for Internal and External Purposes. Approximately 50% of this portion of the exam is on cost accounting topics. Recent examinations have had a set of multiple choice questions as the first problem. The time allotted to this problem varies (as does the number of multiple choice questions) but it ranges between 20 to 40 minutes and generally about half of them are on cost accounting topics.

The remainder of the questions are accounting problems and essay questions. They vary in length between 20 to 60 minutes. Frequently tested topics include budgeting, standard costing and variance analysis, performance analysis, and overhead allocation. Other topics included in this part in recent years include transfer pricing, direct costing versus absorption costing, process costing, capital budgeting, gross-profit analysis, and accounting for by-products and scrap.

Part V—Decision Analysis. Depending on your definition of cost accounting, this part of the exam may contain either a rather high or a low percentage of cost accounting topics. If cost accounting is defined rather broadly to include most quantitative techniques as well as the analysis and design of cost accounting systems, then 70 to 80% of the exam relates to cost accounting. If you exclude the systems and quantitative techniques, then only 30 to 40% is cost accounting.

Most of the questions are problem oriented with some essay analysis of the results. Frequently the first problem is a set of multiple choice questions. Estimated time for all problems generally varies between 20 and 40 minutes.

Cost accounting topics that are most frequently tested include capital budgeting, differential cost analysis, and product pricing. Each exam usually has one and sometimes two problems on systems analysis and design or computer data processing. Quantitative techniques that have been tested recently include linear programming, learning curves, economic order quantity, PERT/cost, probability analysis, simulation analysis, and regression analysis.

As you will notice from the preceding analysis, there are a few cost accounting topics that are tested in several parts of the examination. Within individual parts there are some that are tested so frequently, that even though they only appear in one part of the exam, they should be a major part of the candidate's preparation time. These more important topics are summarized below.

1. Budgeting including behavioral problems associated with budgets
2. Differential cost analysis
3. Standard costing and variance analysis
4. Performance analysis
5. Capital budgeting
6. Quantitative techniques
7. Systems design and report content

Summary

Passing the Uniform CPA Examination is a necessary step to become certified as a CPA. However, to be qualified to offer accounting services as an independent consultant, you must also be licensed by the state.

A significant portion of the CPA examination is on cost accounting topics. About 15% of the practice and theory portions of the examination cover cost accumulation, planning, and control. Topics receiving the most emphasis are process costing, standard costing, variance analysis, joint costing, budgeting, cost-volume-profit analysis, capital budgeting, and quantitative techniques.

In recent years the CMA has achieved recognition as a quality professional designation. Because it has not been around for a long time, the general public is not aware of it and many students fail to sit for the examination when they are most qualified to pass it. Even though a career in public accounting is desired initially, great flexibility is provided by passing the CMA exam early.

A substantial part of the entire CMA exam comes from cost and managerial accounting topics. Some topics receive more attention on the exam than others, and you would be well advised to spend a major portion of your study time on them.

Suggested Readings

American Institute of Certified Public Accountants. *Information for CPA Candidates*. New York, N.Y.: AICPA, 1975.

Gleim, Irvin N. *CMA Examination Review*. Gainesville, Fl.: Accounting Publications, 1981.

Gleim, Irvin N., and Delaney, Patrick R. *CPA Examination Review*. Somerset, N.J.: John Wiley & Sons, annually.

Institute of Management Accountants. *CMA: A Professional Designation for Management Accountants and Financial Managers*. Ann Arbor, Mich.: Institute of Management Accountants, 1982.

Needles, Belverd E., Jr., and Williams, Doyle Z. *The CPA Examination: A Complete Review*. Boston, MA.: Houghton Mifflin Company, annually.

Discussion Questions

1. Is a professional certification important to you? Why?
2. What does passing the CPA Examination qualify you to do?
3. What does passing the CMA Examination qualify you to do?
4. What is wrong with the following attitude? "Since I want to go into public accounting first, I will wait to sit for the CMA Examination until I am ready to leave public accounting."
5. Which cost accounting topics are most frequently tested on the CPA Examination?
6. Which cost accounting topics are most frequently tested on the CMA Examination?

7. Compare the topics listed in questions 6 and 7 above. Which topics are common to both lists?
8. Which parts of the CPA Examination have questions on cost accounting topics? How much of each part is on cost accounting?
9. Which parts of the CMA Examination have questions on cost accounting topics? How much of each part is on cost accounting?
10. What organizations have responsibility for the CMA Examination and the CPA Examination?

GLOSSARY

abnormal rate of loss The rate of loss that is not expected to occur under efficient operating conditions.

abnormal spoilage Spoilage that is caused by unusual or unexpected factors occurring in production.

absorption costing An approach to product costing and income determination that charges all manufacturing costs to inventory. Manufacturing costs become an expense in the period in which inventory is sold. Absorption costing is also known as full costing or traditional costing.

accounting The process of recording, classifying, summarizing, and reporting the economic activities of an organization.

accounting rate of return A measure of investment profitability computed by dividing the average annual cash inflows less depreciation by the initial investment. Average book value of the investment is frequently used in the denominator in place of the initial investment.

activity base A measure of volume of business activity that is highly correlated with the amount of cost incurred.

administrative controls Controls concerned with getting the right people into the right jobs initially and with managing them effectively during their employment with the firm.

administrative cost Expenses incurred in carrying out the administrative or general management functions of a firm. Expenses are charged to the period; that is, they are matched against revenue in the period in which they are incurred.

average cost method An inventory cost flow assumption that uses the average cost of materials purchased to determine the cost of materials issued.

avoidable fixed costs Costs that can be reduced or eliminated by reducing the level of operations or by discontinuing some element of operations.

breakeven analysis A study of the relationships between costs, revenues, and profits to identify a breakeven point.

breakeven chart A graph that contains a total revenue curve and a total cost curve. The point of their intersection identifies the breakeven point.

breakeven point The level of sales volume, specified in either units of output or sales dollars, at which total revenues equal total costs and the business has neither earnings nor losses.

budget An itemized estimate of the operating results of an enterprise for a future time period. A formal quantitative expression of an enterprise's plans.

budgeted costs Costs that are expected to be incurred in a future period.

by-product A joint product with a relatively minor sales value when compared with other joint products.

capital asset Larger, more prominent assets of an entity that are relatively durable and can be used repeatedly in the production of goods and services.

capital budgeting Determining the desirability of investing in fixed assets.

capital components Items on the right-hand side of the balance sheet, including liabilities, preferred stock, and common stock. These items provide money for the purchase of assets.

capital cost A term used to describe the cost of plant and equipment.

capitalized cost (*See* unexpired cost.)

centralization A management term which implies that little responsibility for decision making has been delegated to lower levels of management. (*See* decentralization.)

chart of accounts A listing of all accounts used by a company in its accounting system.

clearing account An account used to facilitate the accounting process. Sometimes used to hold cost data until it can be transferred or distributed to other accounts.

coefficient of correlation A value *(r)* that measures the association or correlation between two variables. In flexible budgeting, the variables are manufacturing costs and an activity base.

coefficient of determination A value *(r²)* that measures the amount of variation of the dependent variable *y* that is explained by the independent variable *x*.

committed cost A cost that is the inevitable consequence of a previous commitment.

common fixed costs Those fixed costs that are common to segments.

component cost The after-tax cost associated with each capital component.

continuous budgeting A method that requires the budget for the next fiscal year (four quarters) to be revised and updated at the end of each quarter.

contribution margin The sale price per unit minus variable cost per unit, or the amount that each unit contributes to cover fixed costs and provide a profit.

contribution margin ratio The sales price less variable costs divided by sales price, or the ratio of contribution margin to sales.

contribution report An income statement format that focuses first on cost behavior and then on management function. The report follows a format of revenue less variable costs equals contribution margin less fixed costs equals net income.

control The ongoing process of implementing management's plans and providing feedback of actual results so managers can evaluate performance and make any needed adjustments to keep operations in line with plans and objectives.

control account A summary account in the general ledger that is supported in detail by individual accounts in a subsidiary ledger.

controllable cost A cost that is subject to significant influence by a particular manager within the time period under consideration.

controllable variance The sum of the spending and variable overhead efficiency variance.

controller The person responsible for all accounting activities within the organization.

conversion costs Costs that are required to convert raw materials into a finished product.

cost A measurement, in monetary terms, of the amount of resources used to acquire goods or services. As related to standards, it is the outlay or sacrifice that is incurred for each unit of output.

cost accounting The process of accumulating the costs of a manufacturing process and identifying them with the units produced.

cost center A subdivision of a business assigned responsibility for only the incurrence and proper utilization of costs.

cost cycle The steps taken in tracing the flow of manufacturing costs through the accounts.

costing The accumulation and assignment of costs to cost objectives such as units of production, departments, or other activities for which management desires a separate measurement or evaluation.

cost objective The purpose for which a cost is measured, assigned, or classified.

cost of capital The rate of return that must be earned on invested capital in order to leave the market price of the firm's common stock unchanged.

cost price variance The effect on gross margin of differences in manufacturing costs between budgeted and actual results.

cost recovery Terminology used in the Economic Recovery Tax Act of 1981 to describe depreciation.

cost-volume-profit analysis A study of the relationships between costs and volume and their impact on profit.

currently attainable standards A level of standard that allows for ordinary equipment failure, normal lost time, and normal spoilage.

cut-off rate   An interest rate that identifies the minimum rate of return acceptable to management. Also called a hurdle-rate.

data bank   A data base that contains all information relating to a particular organization.

data base   A common source of information.

decentralization   A management term that implies that many job activities and related decision-making functions have been delegated to subordinates by higher levels of management. (*See* centralization.)

defective units   Goods that do not meet quality control standards and are either sold "as is" as second-quality goods or reworked and sold as first-quality goods.

department   A subunit of a manufacturing firm created to facilitate product costing and cost control.

dependent variable   The variable *y* that is under investigation and is described by another variable.

differential costs   The increase in total company costs incurred as a result of an alternate decision. (*See* relevant costs.)

direct cost   A cost that can be economically traced to a single cost object.

direct fixed costs   Those fixed costs that can be directly identified with a segment.

direct labor   The cost of employees who work directly on the product and whose efforts can be economically traced to a particular unit of finished product.

direct material   Raw material components that can be physically identified with or traced to the finished product.

direct method   A method for allocating service department costs directly to production departments with no allocation of service department costs to any other service department.

direct product cost   (*See* separable cost.)

discretionary cost   A cost for which the size or the time of incurrence is a matter of choice.

dual transfer prices   One transfer price for the transferring subunit and another transfer price for the receiving subunit.

economic order quantity (EOQ)   The order size for purchases that minimizes the total cost of ordering plus the cost of carrying inventory.

equivalent units   As used in process costing, a measure of the work effort of a department, process, or operation.

expected capacity   The level of productive activity for the accounting period that is expected to meet consumer demand for the upcoming year; a short-run measure.

expected realizable value   The ultimate predicted selling price of a joint product less anticipated costs of completion and sales.

expired cost   A cost with an immediate benefit that is recorded as an expense.

factory overhead   (*See* indirect manufacturing costs.)

factory overhead applied account   The account used to record the amount of overhead applied to work in process by using the predetermined overhead application rate.

factory overhead control account   The account used to accumulate actual overhead costs incurred.

final cost objective   An object of final cost accumulation such as a job, a unit of production, or a government contract. A term used by the Cost Accounting Standards Board.

financial accounting   Accounting that specializes in satisfying the information needs of external users, such as stockholders, potential investors, creditors, and governmental agencies.

first-in, first-out (FIFO) method   An inventory cost flow assumption that differentiates between costs of the previous period, costs that are contained in a work-in-process beginning Inventory, and costs incurred during the current period.

fixed costs   Costs that remain constant in dollar amount as the volume of production or sales changes.

fixed overhead   Manufacturing costs that remain constant or fixed as the volume of manufacturing activity changes.

fixed overhead budget variance   The difference between actual fixed overhead incurred and budgeted fixed overhead.

flexible budget   A formula used to adjust budgeted cost at various levels of business activity.

flexible budgeting   A technique used to adjust the budget for various levels of business activity.

flowcharting   An approach used to summarize the flow of documents and information through the use of symbols which depict the system's characteristics.

full cost   Actual fixed and variable costs of producing a good or service. For pricing purposes, the full cost may also include an allocated portion of selling and administrative expenses.

gross margin   The margin obtained from subtracting the cost of goods sold from sales revenue.

gross margin analysis   A technique for performing a detailed analysis of changes in gross margin between budgeted and actual results or between actual gross margin of succeeding years. Also known as gross profit analysis.

gross margin variance   The difference between actual gross margin and budgeted gross margin.

half-year convention   A half year of depreciation is taken in the year of purchase regardless of when the asset was purchased.

high-low method   A method of developing a cost equation by analyzing the change in cost that corresponds to the change in volume between the high and low points of activity.

historical costs   Costs that were incurred in a past period.

home office   A function or office that is responsible for managing or directing other parts of the business. A term used by the Cost Accounting Standards Board.

homogeneity of overhead costs   Costs that are similar so they can be grouped for accounting and allocation without compromising the accuracy of final product costs.

ideal standards   These standards are sometimes referred to as perfect or theoretical standards. Standards under this philosophy relate to the least possible costs that can be expected under the best conceivable manufacturing conditions.

imputed interest   A hypothetical or opportunity cost of using the capital invested in the segment. A cost that is not entered into the accounting records but is useful for cost analysis.

incremental costs   (*See* marginal costs.)

independent variable   The variable x that is used to describe another dependent variable.

indirect cost   A cost that is not directly traceable to the manufactured product, is associated with the manufacture of two or more units of finished product, or is an immaterial cost that cannot be economically traced to a single unit of finished product.

indirect manufacturing costs   All manufacturing costs other than direct materials and direct labor. Also referred to as overhead.

input controls   Controls designed to verify that the input into the computer process is complete and accurate.

internal rate of return   The interest rate that equates the present value of future cash inflows with the initial investment.

interpolation   A process of selecting an intermediate point based on the relative distance of the desired point to those that are listed.

investment center   A subdivision of a business assigned responsibility for costs, revenues, and the profitable utilization of invested capital.

irrelevant costs   Costs that do not relate to any of the decision alternatives, are historical in nature, or are the same under all decision alternatives.

job-order costing   A method for costing inventories in industries characterized by dissimilar jobs or orders that receive varying amounts of work effort.

job-order cost system   A system of accounting used for manufacturing processes that produce products in batches or by unique divisible orders.

joint product   Products produced whenever a single resource or input results in more than one useful output.

joint product cost   Those manufacturing costs incurred during the processing of original inputs before the point where joint products become individually identifiable.

knowledge   One's understanding of reality or the true state of nature. Knowledge concerns what is, what was, and what may be.

last-in, first-out (LIFO) method   An inventory cost flow assumption by which the cost of the last materials received is assumed to be the cost of the first materials issued.

lead time   The time between placing an order and having the materials delivered.

learning curve   A graphical (mathematical) representation of the relationship between labor time and production quantity when learning exists in a repetitive production environment.

least-squares method   A method of developing a cost equation for an observed set of data by mathematically computing a regression line that minimizes the sum of the squares to the lengths of the vertical-line segments from the observed data points to the regression line.

level of aspiration A goal that, when barely achieved, has associated with it subjective feelings of success, and when not achieved, subjective feelings of failure.

managed cost (*See* discretionary cost.)

management by exception The philosophy that managers should focus their attention on areas of the business in which current operations are significantly different from previous operations or from the budget.

management information system A computer-based information-processing system that supports the operation, management, and decision-making functions of organization.

managerial accounting An internal accounting process designed to provide management with the necessary information to operate a business successfully.

manufacturer A type of firm that performs the manufacturing function, and that converts raw materials into units of finished product.

manufacturing costs All costs from the acquisition of raw materials, through production, until the product can be turned over to the marketing division to be sold.

marginal cost of capital The rate of return that must be earned on additional capital in order to leave the market value of common stock unchanged.

marginal costs The costs associated with the next unit or the next project.

margin of safety Actual or budgeted sales over sales at the breakeven point; the amount of reduction in sales that could occur without sustaining a loss.

market basket An assumed basket containing the average sales mix of an entity.

market price The prevailing monetary value of goods and services in markets external to an organization.

master budget A budget that contains a complete set of pro forma financial statements with detailed supporting schedules. Also called comprehensive budgeting.

master plan A plan that contains a summary of current capabilities of the information system as well as a projection of future requirements for labor, hardware, software, and financial resources.

matching concept The criterion used to determine when a cost (asset) becomes an expense.

mixed costs (*See* semivariable costs.)

mixed overhead Indirect manufacturing costs that have both a fixed cost component and a variable cost component.

negotiation The process of setting transfer prices by discussion or bargaining between subunit managers.

net present value The present value of future cash inflows less the present value of future cash outflows, discounted at a minimum desired rate of return.

network flow The manufacture and movement of products through various processes or departments as needed.

nonroutine decisions All management decisions not directly related to the ordinary, repetitive production cycle of the business.

normal capacity The level of productive activity that is expected to meet consumer demand for three to five years; a long-run measure.

normal rate of loss The rate of loss that is expected to occur under efficient operating conditions.

opportunity cost In a transfer pricing context, the maximum contribution to profits that are lost by the firm as a whole if goods and services are transferred internally rather than being sold externally. The cost or value of an opportunity foregone when one course of action is chosen over another.

outlay cost Cash outflows incurred to the point of transfer as a result of producing transferred goods and services.

out-of-pocket costs Costs that must be met with a current expenditure.

output controls Controls designed to assure that the output is complete, that no errors were identified by the computer during processing, and that the output is safeguarded and used by those who are authorized to examine it.

overapplied overhead The amount by which applied overhead exceeds actual overhead.

overhead A brief expression for indirect manufacturing costs.

overhead application The assignment of overhead costs to units of production.

parallel flow The simultaneous manufacture of component parts that are subsequently assembled to form a finished product.

payback period The number of years required for the cumulative cash flows to equal the initial investment.

payback reciprocal An estimate of the internal rate of return that is computed by dividing annual cash flows by the initial investment.

performance reporting Technique used to report the results of operations. Operating results are organized and presented according to an individual's ability to control an item and in such a way as to compare budgeted results with actual results.

period costs Costs assigned to a time period or the costs matched against revenue in the period of incurrence.

practical capacity The level of expected production at which machine breakdowns, machine maintenance, and other idle time events are considered to be a normal part of operations.

predetermined overhead application rate A rate per unit of activity base used to apply overhead costs to work in process. The predetermined overhead application rate is calculated by dividing total budgeted overhead by the total budgeted units of the chosen activity base.

preference decision Analysis involving several investment proposals where the objective is to identify the proposals that are most profitable.

present value payback The number of years required for the present value of future cash flows, discounted at a minimum desired rate of return, to equal the initial investment.

price index A measure of relative prices used to adjust historical costs for changes in the general price level.

prime costs The most important or significant costs traceable to units of finished product.

process costing A method used for costing inventories in industries characterized by the continuous mass production of similar finished units.

process cost system A system of accounting used for manufacturing processes that produce a single product continuously for an extended period of time.

processing controls All controls connected with data processing by the computer, including hardware controls, program controls, operating system controls, and file reconstruction capability.

product costs Cost assigned or charged to a product. These costs "flow" through the stages of initial recognition of costs and subsequent regroupings of costs where they are recorded in inventory accounts. These costs are matched against revenue or become period costs when a unit of product is sold.

production department A department that is directly engaged in a manufacturing activity and contributes directly to the content and form of the finished product.

product pricing Assigning monetary values to goods and services exchanged with parties external to an organization.

profit center A subdivision of a business assigned responsibility for both costs and revenues.

profit-volume graph A graph that contains a profit line showing the amount of profit (loss) or different levels of volume.

pro forma statement Budgeted financial statement.

programmed cost (*See* discretionary cost.)

purchase discounts A percentage the buyer may deduct from the total invoice price if payment is made within the discount period. Also referred to as cash discounts.

pyramid reporting A reporting structure used in responsibility accounting that shows detailed information on individual items that are controllable at that level of management and summary information on items that are controllable at lower levels of management.

qualitative considerations Those aspects of a decision situation that are difficult to express in terms of numbers or other types of mathematical expression.

quantitative considerations Those aspects of a decision situation that may be expressed in terms of numbers.

rate of markup A target rate applied against the cost of a product or service to establish a selling price in external markets.

rate of return on assets employed A target rate applied against total assets employed to establish a selling price for goods and services in external markets.

reciprocal method A method of allocating service department costs when service departments render services to one another in a mutual or complementary relationship.

relative sales value A product's estimated selling price less estimated costs of completion and sale.

relevant costs   Future costs that are different under one decision alternative than under another decision alternative.

relevant range of production   A range of operating volume within which the cost relationships will be reliable.

reorder point   The point at which a purchase requisition is triggered when the number of units on hand declines.

residual income (RI)   A measure of business profitability that focuses attention on the optimum use of invested capital. RI is the amount of net income that is earned during a period beyond that needed to provide a minimum desired rate of return on invested capital. RI is a dollar measure.

responsibility accounting   A form of internal reporting that is based on the ability to control. Each individual's report contains the items they have the ability to control.

responsibility center   A subdivision of a business over which control of operations is found.

return on investment (ROI)   A widely used measure of business profitability that focuses attention on the optimum use of invested capital. ROI is calculated by dividing net income by invested capital. ROI is a ratio measure.

routine decisions   Decisions relating to the accumulation and reporting of information for everyday control of operations and for ordinary product-costing purposes.

safety stock   Inventory supply that protects against stockouts.

sales mix   The ratio or relative combination of each product's sales to total sales. The composition of total sales broken down by products, product mix, or product lines.

sales mix variance   The effect on gross margin of differences in sales mix between budgeted and actual results.

sales price variance   The effect on gross margin of differences in sales prices between budgeted and actual results.

sales volume variance   The effect on gross margin of differences in the quantities of units sold between budgeted and actual results.

scatter diagram   A graph with the values of observed data plotted on it.

scattergraph method   A method of developing a cost equation by visually fitting a regression line to observed data points plotted on a graph.

screening decision   Analysis involving only one investment proposal. The objective of this analysis is to determine if it meets minimum standards for acceptance.

segment   A segment is a separable part or activity of a company about which cost data may be prepared for analysis. A subdivision of a business that typically has a service or reporting relationship to a home office. A term used by the Cost Accounting Standards Board.

segment margin   Contribution margin of a segment less direct fixed costs.

segment reporting   The process of breaking an enterprise into reportable segments and preparing financial information by segments.

selling costs   All costs associated with the marketing and selling of a product.

semivariable costs   Costs that have both a fixed and a variable cost element.

sensitivity analysis   A "what if" analysis that examines the effect on the outcome for changes in one or more input values.

separable costs   Costs that are incurred after the split-off point and can be identified with individual joint products. Also referred to as direct product costs.

sequential flow   The manufacture and movement of products from one process or department to the next in a serial fashion.

service department   A department that provides services or assistance to production departments.

shrinkage   Lost units resulting from a reduction in volume of output due to such things as evaporation, temperature variations, or chemical reaction.

shut-down point   The minimum volume of production and sales that is necessary to justify operation of a product line or a segment of a business.

slope   The amount of change in y for each unit change in x.

spending variance   This variance is an indicator of how well actual overhead expenditures are kept within the budget independent of the efficiency with which the activity base was utilized.

split ledger   An accounting system in which the administrative office maintains the general ledger and the factory maintains a factory ledger.

split-off point   The point in the manufacturing process where joint products become individually identifiable.

spoilage   Production that does not meet quality control standards and as a result is junked or sold for a relatively low disposal value.

standard A criterion for measurement. Standards in cost accounting refer to a norm or normal amount of quantities or prices to be paid for the materials and labor required to make a product or provide some service.

standard activity level The expected level or volume of production for the coming accounting period.

standard cost The expected cost of production under normal operating conditions. A standard cost is typically a unit cost concept.

static budget A budget that is relevant to only one level of business activity and is not easily adjustable for changes in the level of operation.

step method A method of allocating service department costs to production departments and to other service departments when service departments render services to each other.

step-variable cost A variable cost that increases or decreases in ''chunks'' of cost with small changes in volume.

subsidiary ledger A ledger that provides a detailed breakdown of the contents of the control account to which it relates.

sunk costs Past costs that have already been incurred.

theoretical capacity The upper limit of production capabilities.

total cost All costs associated with a particular activity or limited to a specific category.

total manufacturing cost The combined cost of direct material, direct labor, and factory overhead.

transfer pricing Assigning monetary values to goods and services exchanged among subunits of an organization.

transferred-in costs The accumulated cost of materials, labor, and overhead applied in all previous processes or departments.

translation factor The ratio of a current price index to a historical price index used to adjust historical costs for changes in the general price level.

treasurer The financial executive responsible for all functions classified under money management.

unavoidable fixed costs Costs that cannot be reduced or eliminated by reducing the level of operations or by discontinuing some element of operations.

uncontrollable costs Costs over which a given manager does not have a significant influence.

underapplied overhead The amount by which actual overhead exceeds applied overhead.

unexpired cost A cost with a future benefit that is recorded as an asset.

unit cost The cost associated with a single unit of product or limited to a specific category.

variable costing An alternative approach to product costing and income determination that charges fixed manufacturing overhead as an expense in the period incurred rather than fixed manufacturing overhead becoming a cost of inventory and charged to expense in the period in which the inventory is sold. Variable costing is also known as direct costing.

variable costs Costs that vary in total as the volume of production or sales changes.

variable overhead Manufacturing costs that vary in proportion to the level of manufacturing activity.

variable overhead efficiency variance This variance evaluates the efficiency with which the activity base is utilized.

variable overhead spending variance The difference between actual expenditures for variable overhead and budgeted expenditures due to differences in prices.

volume variance The difference between budgeted fixed factory overhead and applied fixed factory overhead.

waste and scrap Terms for residue such as smoke, dust, or shavings that result from a manufacturing process.

weighted average method An inventory cost flow assumption that averages costs of the previous period, that are contained in a work-in-process beginning inventory, and costs incurred during the current period.

y intercept Identifies the amount of y when x is zero.

INDEX